GROLIER

ENCYCLOPEDIA
OF KNOWLEDGE

Grolier Incorporated
Danbury, Connecticut

ISBN 0-7172-5300-7 (complete set)
ISBN 0-7172-5314-7 (volume 14)

Printed and manufactured in the United States of America.

This publication is an abridged version of the *Academic American Encyclopedia*.

1 0 9 8 7 6 5 4 3

Nuevo León [nway'-voh lay-ohn'] Nuevo León is a state in northeastern Mexico, bordering the United States. Traversed by the Sierra Madre Oriental, Nuevo León has an area of 64,924 km² (25,067 mi²) and a population of 3,066,466 (1990). Its capital is MONTERREY. Cotton, wheat, and sugarcane are the most important crops, and iron, steel, and textiles are the main industrial products. Silver and gold are mined. During the Spanish colonial period and the 19th century, Nuevo León experienced many Indian incursions from the north. It became a state of Mexico in 1824.

Nuffield Radio Astronomy Laboratories The Nuffield Radio Astronomy Laboratories of the University of Manchester in England house what was once the world's largest fully steerable radio telescope, the 250-ft-diameter (76-m) Mark I (later IA) paraboloid, or dish, reflector. The laboratories were established as the Jodrell Bank Experimental Station in 1945. Bernard LOVELL proposed construction of the Mark I telescope, which was built (1953–57) with support principally from the Nuffield Foundation and the British government.

nuisance In law, a nuisance is an unreasonable interference by a person with the personal or property rights of another. A public nuisance is one that affects a substantial portion of the community, such as a case of water and air pollution or the use of explosives. A public nuisance can constitute a possible criminal offense. A private nuisance is one that affects an individual or a small number of people, such as when someone gives a noisy party. When an action is brought for damages or to obtain an injunction against an alleged nuisance, a court will weigh the harm done by the activity against its value to society.

Nujoma, Sam [nuh-joh'-muh] Sam Nujoma, b. May 12, 1929, founded the South West Africa People's Organization (SWAPO) in Namibia in 1959. Nujoma, a former clerk, went into exile in 1960 as leader of the external wing of SWAPO controlling the People's Liberation Army of Namibia, which from the mid-1960s to 1989 conducted a guerrilla war against South Africa from bases in Angola, Tanzania, and Zambia. In 1973 the United Nations recognized SWAPO as the "authentic representative" of the Namibian people. In 1988, Nujoma agreed to abide by a UN-sponsored peace accord signed by Angola, South Africa, and Cuba that would lead to independence for Namibia. He returned to Namibia in September 1989 and became Namibia's first president when it gained full independence on Mar. 21, 1990.

null set see SET THEORY

nullification In U.S. history, nullification was a political doctrine holding that a state might reject, or nullify, any federal law that it considered unconstitutional. The position was first advanced in the KENTUCKY AND VIRGINIA RESOLUTIONS of 1798, which declared that the ALIEN AND SEDITION ACTS violated the Bill of Rights. These acts were allowed to expire, though, and no test of the right of a state to nullify a federal law occurred until 1832.

In 1828 the U.S. Congress passed a protective tariff law that became known in the antiprotectionist South as the Tariff of Abominations (see TARIFF ACTS). Southerners charged that the act was not only discriminatory in economic terms but also unconstitutional; John C. CALHOUN argued that the federal tariff could be declared null and void and its enforcement prohibited by individual states.

The issue was temporarily defused by the election (1828) to the presidency of Andrew JACKSON, who promised tariff revision. The Tariff Act of 1832, however, was only slightly milder than its predecessor, and South Carolina called a convention that passed an Ordinance of Nullification forbidding collection of tariff duties in the state. Jackson responded with a declaration that upheld the constitutionality of the tariff, denied the power of an individual state to block enforcement of a federal law, and threatened armed intervention to collect duties. At his request Congress passed both a Force Act and a compromise tariff in 1833. South Carolina nullified the Force Act, but by accepting the tariff, averted conflict with the federal government. The theory of nullification profoundly influenced Southern political thought about STATE RIGHTS and helped pave the way for secession and the U.S. Civil War.

numbat An inhabitant of Australian forests and deserts, the numbat, or marsupial anteater, *Myrmecobius fasciatus*, is the sole living species in the family Myrmecobiidae. It grows up to 27.5 cm (11 in) long, plus a 17-cm (7-in) tail, and weighs up to 450 g (1 lb). The grayish brown or brick red back is crossed by 6 or 7 white stripes. The animal has 52 small, weak teeth and a long, extendable tongue used to feed on termites and ants. The female lacks a pouch, and only long hairs around her nipples protect her young.

The numbat, or marsupial anteater, uses its long, sticky tongue to capture and eat termites, the staple of its diet.

number Numbers are a human invention brought about by the need to measure and count things. Early peoples had only a primitive concept of number, so the development of an abstract number sequence was a major advance. Mathematical growth has led to ever-broadening ideas of what numbers are.

Counting began with 1, 2, many; it slowly evolved until the numbers consisted of 1, 2, 3, 4, . . . , or what are called the counting numbers or positive integers. Such numbers describe how many elements there are in a collection of objects and are called cardinal numbers. A related sequence of numbers describes how elements in a collection are ordered, or positioned; such numbers are called ordinal numbers—for example, first (1st), second (2d), third (3d), and fourth (4th).

As civilizations became more advanced, it became necessary to measure parts of things. Initially the concept of a FRACTION was avoided by subdividing existing units into smaller ones, like the division of an hour into 60 minutes. By 1500 BC, however, the Egyptians (and perhaps the Babylonians before them) had developed the use of fractions, or positive RATIONAL NUMBERS.

Mathematics progressed, and a systematic study of geometry was undertaken. The Greeks discovered—by means of the theorem of Pythagoras (see PYTHAGORAS, THEOREM OF)—that in a square with sides of length one, the length of its diagonal d is a number whose square is two ($d^2 = 2$). At first, they attempted to find a rational number whose square was 2, but finally they proved (about 460 BC) that $d = \sqrt{2}$ was not rational. The concept of a number, therefore, had to be expanded to include these IRRATIONAL NUMBERS, or surds. Another mysterious number arose naturally: namely, π (pi), the ratio of the circumference of a circle to its diameter. By the 18th century it was shown that π was irrational.

Meanwhile the idea of a negative number began to emerge (around 200 BC in China and later in the West), but the concept of a number was not actually broadened to include negative numbers until about the 16th century. The concept of ZERO made its appearance in about the 9th century in India (and independently in the Maya culture). It was initially used as a place holder in numerical notation and was basic to the development of the system of Hindu–Arabic NUMERALS.

With the invention of the "infinite processes" used in CALCULUS and the use of DECIMALS, the concept of a number could be broadened to include all infinite decimals. It was found that the roots of polynomial equations (algebraic numbers) were not the only possible numbers; in 1851, Joseph Liouville demonstrated that other numbers do exist, and in 1873, Georg CANTOR showed that in a certain sense almost all numbers are TRANSCENDENTAL NUMBERS, that is, they are not algebraic. Moreover, it was proved that π was a transcendental number.

The concept of a number is still broadening. Fairly early it was realized that $\sqrt{-1}$ was not a number in the accepted sense. This eventually led to pure imaginary numbers, COMPLEX NUMBERS, and quaternions. In modern mathematics new numbers are still being invented.

number theory   Number theory is a branch of mathematics that deals with properties of the integers: . . . ,
–3, –2, –1, 0, 1, 2, 3, ... Number theorists are interested in properties such as whether a number is an even number, a PRIME NUMBER, or the sum of two primes. The roots of the subject were laid down by the followers of PYTHAGORAS OF SAMOS in ancient Greece, by DIOPHANTUS of Alexandria, and by Hindu writers such as Brahmagupta and Aryabhata (see MATHEMATICS, HISTORY OF). Present-day number theory draws on modern ALGEBRA, numerical and classical analysis, statistical techniques, and a rich history of methods for solutions to problems that have intrigued mathematicians for at least 4,000 years.

The development of powerful computers has given fresh impetus to many aspects of number theory, including the search for large prime numbers and the difficult problem of factoring large numbers. Primes and FACTORS are of particular importance in the development of codes for databank storage of sensitive information and for its safe transmission (see CRYPTOLOGY).

Numbers, Book of   Numbers, the fourth book in the Old Testament of the BIBLE, derives its name from the census lists at the beginning and middle of the book. Its Hebrew title, meaning "in the wilderness," better characterizes the work, however, because these lists as well as the book's otherwise unrelated narratives and scattered cultic legislation are all set in the wilderness. They continue the narrative, begun in the Book of Exodus, of Israel's journey from Egypt to Canaan. Although Numbers contains elements of the early traditions called *J* and *E* concerning challenges to Moses' leadership, the reconnaissance and abortive assault on southern Canaan, and the conquest of Transjordan, in addition to several fragments of extremely ancient poetry (1250–1050 BC), the present shape of the work is due largely to the source called *P* (*c*.450). *P* supplemented, edited, and occasionally altered the older sources to present his own view of the Mosaic period.

numeral   A numeral is the figure or character used to represent a NUMBER. Throughout history there have been many different representations for numbers and for the basic process of counting. At first there were spoken numbers and finger numbers (indicated by positions of the hands and fingers). For permanent recording and intermediate calculations, however, it was necessary to have written numerals.

A simple tally system uses a single symbol, such as a vertical stroke, that is repeated in calculations. For example, $||||+||=||||||$. In a modified system, five units are grouped together: $||||\ \ ||+||||=||||\ \ ||||\ \ |$.

The Egyptians used a refined tally system in which units of ten were grouped together and given a new symbol:

		$\begin{array}{c}|\\||\end{array}$	$\cap$	$|\cap$	$\cap\cap$	$\begin{array}{c}\cap\cap\\\cap\cap\end{array}$
1	2	5	10	11	20	40

There were special symbols for 100; 1,000; 10,000; and so on.

The Greeks and Hebrews used a similar system, except that the figures were the letters of their alphabet. The first nine letters were used for 1, 2, . . . , 9; the next nine were for 10, 20, . . . , 90; and the next nine for 100, 200, . . . , 900.

The Romans used the system of Roman numerals, which is still familiar today in certain applications. Here, I = 1, V = 5, X = 10, L = 50, C = 100, D = 500, and M = 1,000. A smaller number is added when it follows a larger number, but subtracted when it precedes the larger number. For example, VIII = 8, XXVII = 27, IX = 9 (10 − 1), and CM = 900 (1,000 − 100). Both situations may occur in the same number, as in CLXIV = 164 and MCMXCI = 1991.

The modern system of numeration (designation by the use of numbers) is derived from the Hindu–Arabic system. It uses a place-value system with 10 as the base (see BASE, mathematics). This system began in India around the 6th century, developed in the Arabian countries, and progressed into Europe and the rest of the world. Today all science and international trade use this system. The exact shape of the numerals has changed substantially over the years, but the introduction of printing has led to a standardization of shape.

numerical analysis

Numerical analysis is a branch of mathematics that deals with methods for calculating numerical answers to mathematical problems and analyzing the possible errors in the results. One large segment of numerical analysis involves a body of procedures, called ALGORITHMS. These are used to approximate roots of equations or systems of equations, to calculate areas under curves or the tangents to curves, to find solutions to differential equations, and to interpolate between known values of a FUNCTION. Because useful algorithms involve many computations, digital COMPUTERS have become one of the main tools of numerical analysts. Computers can store only a finite number of digits for each computation, however, so that approximations inevitably involve errors that may be magnified as the computation progresses. The understanding and the control of possible sources of error are, therefore, vital concerns in numerical analysis.

Founded on the calculating methods of ancient and medieval astronomers, numerical analysis became a modern science in the 17th century with the discoveries of the CALCULUS and LOGARITHMS, and the inventions of the slide rule and the mechanical computer. Today numerical analysis is an indispensible tool in mathematics, statistics, the physical and life sciences, and those areas of the social sciences which depend on numerical methods.

See also: ALGEBRA; ERROR.

Numidia

[noo-mid'-ee-uh]   Numidia, an ancient North African territory southwest of CARTHAGE, occupied much of what is now Algeria. The area was originally inhabited by Berber nomads; parts of it came under Carthage's control about 300 BC. MASINISSA, a Numidian tribal leader, who sided with Rome in the Second PUNIC WAR (218–201 BC), was rewarded with control over all Numidia. But Numidian king JUGURTHA warred with Rome, and after his defeat (105 BC), Numidia became a Roman client state.

Juba I (r. 60–46 BC), who supported POMPEY THE GREAT against Julius CAESAR, made the last effort to establish a strong, independent Numidian state. After Caesar defeated Juba in 46 BC, Numidia became a Roman province. It was conquered by the Vandals in AD c.430 and by the Arabs in the 7th century.

numismatics

Numismatics is the collecting and the study of coins and related forms of money, such as paper currency and tokens. As the products of human artistry and ingenuity, coins reflect human history through 2,500 years with a fidelity found in few other groups of objects. The application of numismatics as a sophisticated historical tool is a relatively new field, but it has immeasurably broadened the knowledge and conception of the past.

The systematic collecting of coins for their rarity or historical significance began during the Renaissance, when wealthy admirers of the ancient Greek and Roman civilizations made collections of coins from those eras. The numismatic enthusiasm of the time also resulted in the widespread counterfeiting of ancient coins, and, beginning in the 17th century, collections began to be cataloged, in part in an attempt to distinguish genuine from false coins. The growth of numismatics as a field of historical study dates from this period. By the 20th century the large-scale collecting of coins had become a specialty of museums and other endowed or wealthy institutions.

The use of numismatics for historical study is not restricted to ancient times, nor is it limited to coinage. Numismatists are becoming increasingly aware of the fact that the science can be employed to answer questions about more recent history and have found that paper money and tokens can be as informative as metal coins. One estimate puts the number of people in the United States who collect coins, bills, tokens, and MEDALS AND DECORATIONS at approximately 20 million; worldwide, the figure is likely to be four or five times as large.

In addition to their historical interest, coins are often collected as an investment. The value of collections of older coins usually increases with time, and many coins of even fairly recent vintage are now worth more than their face value because of their gold or silver content alone. (See MINTAGE for a discussion of the metal content of current coins.) Rarity is an important determinant of value; the physical condition of a coin is also a value factor, and coins are graded on a scale ranging upward as follows: poor, the design is almost worn away; good, features are worn but still discernible; very good, showing some signs of wear; fine, slightly worn but with sharp de-

Since the Renaissance, numismatists have collected and studied coins as historical records. Included in this group of coins are: (1) an electrum stater from Anatolia (late 7th century BC); (2) a Lydian stater (6th century BC); (3) a Greek tetradrachm (Athens, 5th century BC); (4) a Roman coin of Nero (1st century AD); (5) a 15th-century Italian florin (Florence); (6) a 16th-century Bohemian Joachimsthaler; (7) an English sovereign of Henry VII (1485–1504); (8) a 14th-century Chinese coin; (9) a Japanese "tempo tsuho" (19th century); (10) a Brasher's doubloon (United States, 1787); (11) a 17th-century Massachusetts shilling; (12) a rare U.S. $5 piece (1822).

tail remaining; very fine, showing minor wear; extremely fine, all details sharp, but without a polished finish; uncirculated, showing no signs of wear—in "mint" condition; and proof, the designation for coins that are specially struck for collectors.

nun   A nun is a member of a religious community of women ordinarily bound by the vows of poverty, chastity, and obedience. Nuns are generally thought of as Christian, but the term is also used in other religions. Roman Catholic church law uses *nun* to refer only to women with solemn vows and *sister* for those whose vows are not solemn.

See also: CONVENT; MONASTICISM; RELIGIOUS ORDERS.

Núñez Cabeza de Vaca, Álvar   see CABEZA DE VACA, ÁLVAR NÚÑEZ

Nuremberg   [noor'-em-bairk]   Nuremberg (German: Nürnberg) is a city located on the Pegnitz River about 145 km (90 mi) northwest of Munich in southern Germany. The population of Nuremberg is 467,400 (1987 est.).

The city's initial prosperity was due to its location at the junction of trade routes between Germany and Italy and between France and central eastern Europe. Commerce and shipping, which expanded after the opening (1972) of Nuremberg's port on the Rhine-Main-Danube Canal, are important. Principal products include precision instruments, machinery, vehicles, metalware, jewelry, pencils, gingerbread, and beer. The city is also a center for toy manufacturing.

Nuremberg was first mentioned in written sources in 1050. The fortified town received its charter as a free imperial city in 1219. During the Renaissance the city experienced both economic and cultural prosperity; Albrecht

Dürer lived there from 1509 to 1528. Melanchton established a school in the city in 1526. Nuremberg became part of Bavaria in 1806 and part of the German Empire in 1871. During the 1930s the city was a center of Nazi activity. Although more than half of the city was destroyed during World War II, the medieval landmarks and the modern city have been completely restored. The Nuremberg Trials of Nazi leaders accused of war crimes were held there from 1945 to 1946.

Nuremberg Trials At the end of World War II the victorious Allies (the United States, Great Britain, France, and the USSR) established an international military tribunal to try the surviving Axis leaders for WAR CRIMES. The trials took place in the German city of Nuremberg from November 1945 to October 1946.

In the main trial 22 German Nazi leaders were tried. Of these, 12 were sentenced to death, including Wilhelm KEITEL, Joachim von RIBBENTROP, Alfred ROSENBERG, Martin BORMANN (who was tried in absentia), and Hermann GOERING (who committed suicide); three, including Rudolf HESS, were given life sentences; four, including Karl DOENITZ and Albert SPEER, were sentenced to up to 20 years' imprisonment; and three, including Franz von PAPEN and Hjalmar SCHACHT, were acquitted. Lesser criminals were tried in 12 subsequent trials. The conviction of individuals for acts that were sanctioned by the government of the country they served raised legal issues that have made the Nuremberg Trials the subject of controversy.

Twenty-two Nazi officials were tried at the first of a series of war crime trials that began at Nuremberg in November 1945. Of these, 19 were convicted and 3 acquitted.

Nureyev, Rudolf [nu-re'-yef] Rudolf Hametovich Nureyev, b. near Irkutsk, USSR, Mar. 17, 1938, is perhaps the most celebrated male ballet dancer since Nijinsky. In 1958 he joined the KIROV BALLET as a soloist. Always a thorn in the side of the Soviet authorities, he decided to remain in the West when visiting Paris with the

Photo Linda Vartoogian

Rudolf Nureyev is seen performing with Anne McLeod in a production of Murray Louis's Canarsie Venus *(1978). Nureyev's brilliant technique and energetic style made him one of the most acclaimed dancers of the 20th century.*

Kirov in 1961. Nureyev has since appeared with many companies in Great Britain, the United States, Europe, and Australia. For many years he was primarily associated with Great Britain's ROYAL BALLET (RB) and, especially, with its ballerina Margot FONTEYN. Their partnership began with *Giselle* in 1962 and continued in such ballets as Frederick Ashton's *Marguerite and Armand*, created for them in 1963, and Marius Petipa's *La Bayadère*, act 4, "The Kingdom of the Shades," which Nureyev revived for the RB the same year. He has staged his own productions of ballet classics for many companies: *Raymonda* (1964), *Swan Lake* (1964), *Don Quixote* (1966), *The Sleeping Beauty* (1966), *The Nutcracker* (1967), *Romeo and Juliet* (1977), and *The Tempest* (1982).

Apart from his virtuosity and the glamour of his stage presence, Nureyev's great quality was his sheer appetite for dancing. He extended his range to include contemporary works and modern dance and appeared in dance films including *I Am a Dancer* (1972); Ken Russell's *Valentino* (1977), in the title role; and *Exposed* (1983). From 1983 to 1989 he was director of the Paris Opéra Ballet.

Nurhachi [noor'-hah-chee] A Manchurian tribal leader, Nurhachi, b. 1559, d. Sept. 30, 1626, consolidated various Manchu tribes into a powerful state during the early 17th century. His successors later overthrew (1644) the Ming dynasty and ruled China until 1911 as the QING dynasty. Nurhachi's greatest contribution was the creation of the banner system. Although primarily a mode of military organization, this system also divided the Manchu people into units for administration and taxation. Four banners were created in 1601 and another four in 1615; each had its own color. The banner system united the Manchu tribes into a military bureaucracy and was largely responsible for the Qing victories over the Ming dynasty.

Nurmi, Paavo [noor'-mee, pah'-voh]   Paavo Johannes Nurmi, b. June 13, 1897, d. Oct. 2, 1973, a Finnish track star of the 1920s, was one of the foremost runners in the history of the modern Olympic Games. He won nine gold and three silver medals in the 1920, 1924, and 1928 Olympics. Between 1920 and 1930, Nurmi set world records at distances of 1 mi (1.6 km), 2 mi (3.2 km), 3 mi (4.8 km), 6 mi (9.6 km), 10 mi (16 km), and 1,500, 2,000, 3,000, 5,000, 10,000, and 20,000 m. He also established a world record for the 1-hour run by covering 19.209 km (11 mi, 1,648 yd). Nicknamed the Flying Finn, Nurmi was declared ineligible for the 1932 Olympics when he lost his amateur status by accepting excessive expense money while on tour.

Nürnberg   see NUREMBERG

nursery rhymes   Usually anonymous and part of oral tradition, a nursery rhyme is a short poem of one verse or a number of verses recited or sung to entertain or instruct children. Many are centuries old, and several hundred exist in English. Some well-known nursery rhymes are "Humpty Dumpty," "Twinkle, Twinkle, Little Star," "London Bridge," "Ring-a-Ring o Roses," "Little Jack Horner," and "Little Miss Muffet." Two of the earliest published collections are *Tommy Thumb's Pretty Song Book* (1744) and *Mother Goose's Melody* (c.1760).

    See also: CHILDREN'S LITERATURE.

nursery school   see PRESCHOOL EDUCATION

nursing   Once defined as a religious vocation or womanly duty, nursing today emphasizes specialized education to support the work of health care. It has remained a female profession: in 1980, only about 2.7% of American nurses were male. Nurses teach preventive care and health maintenance, assist medical treatment, aid rehabilitation, and attend the dying. Most nurses work in HOSPITALS and NURSING HOMES, with others in public-health agencies, offices, schools, and industries. Nurses are also educators, supervisors, administrators, and independent practitioners.

    History. In the mid-19th century, most nursing care was done at home as part of women's unpaid domestic duties. Hospital patients, mostly destitute, were attended by women in religious orders or laywomen trained informally on the job.

    In the last half of the century, changing social conditions supported the development of a more sophisticated system of health care, one that created a place for the "trained nurse." In the United States the Civil War and the Spanish-American War both necessitated coordination of medical and nursing resources. The quickening pace of industrial work in the United States—accompanied by the world's highest rate of injury on the job—strained existing hospital resources. Urban growth brought new working-class and immigrant populations into cities, where poverty, overcrowding, and poor urban sanitation created formidable new health problems. For middle-class families, traditional unpaid nursing was replaced by a reliance on women paid to nurse the sick. By the end of the 19th century, anesthesia and antisepsis had increased the efficacy of medical care, and surgical intervention and hospitalization both became safer.

    Reform-minded women organized to respond to wartime conditions and growing urban populations. During the Civil War, Dorothea DIX sought respectable women to attend sick and wounded soldiers. After the war, women organized investigations of hospital care and established training programs for nurses, responding to Florence NIGHTINGALE's reforms of English nursing. In 1873 three schools of nursing opened, in New York City, Boston, and New Haven, Conn. Meanwhile, urban reformers concerned about the sick poor began to hire trained nurses to replace the charitable services of genteel laywomen.

    The rapid expansion of hospitals spurred the growth of nurses' training schools. Under the prevailing system of apprenticeship training, students performed most of the work of the hospital. In exchange they received training on the job, some classroom education, room, board, and a small stipend. By the late 1920s there were about 7,500 hospitals in the United States, and more than 2,000 had schools of nursing. Few hospitals employed their own graduates, and most nurses worked in private duty, hired by families to attend individual patients at home or in hospitals.

    In 1893 the American Society of Superintendents of Training Schools (ASSTS), composed of superintendents of the larger U.S. and Canadian schools, organized to try to regulate the burgeoning hospital training programs. In 1896 the Nurses' Associated Alumnae (NAA) formed, focusing its efforts on education reform, and state registration campaigns to enforce minimum standards of preparation. In 1900, the NAA began to publish *The American Journal of Nursing*. In 1911, when the group split into Canadian and U.S. sections, the U.S. division was renamed the American Nurses' Association (ANA), which remains the largest professional association in nursing. The National Association of Colored Graduate Nurses was organized in 1908 to represent African-American nurses. Public-health nurses banded together in the National Organization for Public Health Nursing, founded in 1912.

    The expanding health-care system reshaped nursing between 1910 and 1945. Some nurses found refuge from an overcrowded private-duty market in the vigorous public-health movement. Public health provided nurses with innovative roles and considerable autonomy; but as the agenda of public health expanded, its funding contracted.

    Responding to pressure from nursing organizations, increased demands for services, and the growing complexity of care, hospitals began to hire graduate nurses to staff their wards in the 1930s and 1940s. World War II brought nurses into positions of authority as they supervised male corpsmen and, for the first time, won the recognition of regular military rank. The U.S. Cadet Nurse Corps recruited thousands of young women into nursing.

    Nursing since 1945. War and postwar shortages moved

nursing toward a greater division of labor and specialization. Formal programs were developed for the so-called auxiliary nurses who had assisted registered nurses (RNs) on the wards, and they were licensed as practical nurses (LPNs), working under the supervision of RNs. As hospitals and medical care grew more specialized, services such as intensive care, cardiac care, burn units, and dialysis spawned new nursing specialties. Nursing leaders intensified the campaign to raise standards and to remove nursing education from the control of the hospitals. The Brown report, a 1948 assessment of the present and future of nursing, recommended college degrees as the minimum credential for professional nurses. The proposed standards caused bitter conflict in nursing ranks, and at first collegiate education made only slow inroads.

From the late 1930s to the late 1970s, nurses faced a curious dilemma. Hospital expansion supported a continuing demand for nurses, and the field had gained some authority from the prestige of medicine and from a shortage of nurses. Yet nurses continued to suffer the disadvantages of female workers in a sex-segregated work force. Their incomes lagged dramatically behind those of men with equivalent education, and nurses also earned less than women in comparable "female" jobs such as social work or teaching. On the job, many hospital-based nurses felt the tension of increased responsibilities, without commensurate authority.

In the late 1930s, unionization began to gain some support from nurses who were critical of what they perceived to be an overly passive and cautious American Nurses' Association. In response, in 1946 the ANA set national standards for minimum salaries and working conditions, and helped local associations to use those standards in negotiations with hospitals. Unionization gained momentum in the 1960s and '70s. The ANA changed its no-strike policy in 1968, and in 1974 the Taft-Hartley Act's prohibition of collective bargaining in voluntary hospitals was revoked.

Nurses have also responded to the frustrations of hospital work with a variety of revised and expanded forms of nursing practice. The development of a theory and practice of primary care has emphasized the need for continuity, and one nurse may now coordinate all the aspects of care for an individual patient. Nurses have also tried to establish career ladders that affirm the value of bedside nursing: the nurse-clinician can advance in salary and authority without leaving her patients for supervisory positions, the traditional route upward in nursing. Nurse-practitioners and nurse-midwives have tried to carve out independent domains, challenging medical-practice laws and reimbursement patterns that constrain autonomous nursing practice.

In the early 1980s, cost-containment efforts by the federal government and insurance providers resulted in layoffs and work speedups for hospital nurses. In the last years of the decade, however, severe nursing shortages—caused in part, perhaps, by the treatment the profession had received earlier and in part by low nursing salaries and better-paying opportunities in the many new fields now open to women—affected hospitals throughout the country.

Education. Most registered nurses in the United States prepare for their work in 2-year associate degree or 4- or 5-year baccalaureate programs. About 17 percent graduate from hospital schools. Licensed practical nurses are most often prepared in vocational schools or junior colleges, with some attending programs in hospitals, secondary schools, or government agencies. Nurses' aides and orderlies, who assist RNs and LPNs, train on the job without a structure of formal education or licensure.

nursing home   A nursing home is a long-term-care facility that functions primarily for elderly persons who are sick, for those who are too feeble to care for themselves and have no alternative source of care, and, often, for those who are too poor to provide for their own maintenance. About 23,000 long-term-care institutions function within the United States, housing more than 1.3 million persons. These institutions are classified by federal regulations either as skilled nursing facilities, which by law must provide around-the-clock supervision by a staff of skilled nurses assisted by physicians; intermediate-care facilities, which accept patients who are not so sick as to require a highly skilled medical staff; and extended-care facilities, which provide custodial care and do not employ skilled personnel.

Since the 1960s the number of residents in nursing homes in the United States has more than doubled. Several factors have contributed to this growth: an increase in the proportion of the population age 65 or older; changes in living styles that now often separate the elderly from their families; and, since 1965, the payment of over half the costs of nursing-home care through federal programs, primarily MEDICAID. Almost no private insurance plans pay for nursing-home costs, and patients whose savings or income make them ineligible for Medicaid often face yearly nursing-home bills of $50,000 or more. In the mid-1980s, private-pay patients were contributing half of total nursing home expenditures.

Both federal and state agencies set standards regulating levels of care and minimum staff skills in nursing homes. Nevertheless, the nursing-home industry has been the subject of periodic scandals involving inadequate patient care, fraudulent billing, and other illegalities.

In recent years the structure of the industry has changed radically, as more and more homes are operated by large nursing home chains that seek primarily to house the more profitable private-pay patients.

Regulations issued by the U.S. Department of Health and Human Services require that nursing homes assure their patients all possible privacy and allow them to receive visitors. Patients must also receive a regular physician's examination and be given routine dental care. Procedures to eliminate the misuse of psychoactive drugs are also outlined.

nut   Botanically, a nut is a one-seeded fruit enclosed in a leathery or woody covering, or the pericarp. A nut is classified as an indehiscent fruit—at maturity the pericarp does not split open to release the seed. The single seed is sometimes called a kernel. The acorn (from OAK trees), CHESTNUT, FILBERT (or hazel nut), PECAN, and WALNUT are true nuts. Many other kinds of dry, edible seeds or fruits with a woody shell are sometimes called nuts. The ALMOND, Brazil nut, CASHEW, PEANUT, and PINE NUT, although not true nuts, are considered nuts for commercial purposes as food.

Nut Cultivation. Nut crops grow primarily in the temperate and tropical regions of the world. Many species form vigorous trees that even without cultivation can compete on marginal land. Some species have been improved through selection and breeding and are subjected to complex cultural systems. Most marketed nuts come from cultivated orchard trees; the Brazil nut, however, is produced only by wild trees, and wild trees contribute to the production of many other species, such as the pecan and filbert.

The length of the growing season and the minimum winter temperature are two major limiting factors for nut-crop production, because—with a few exceptions, such as the Carpathian walnut, which bears even in New England—most commercially important nut trees are sensi-

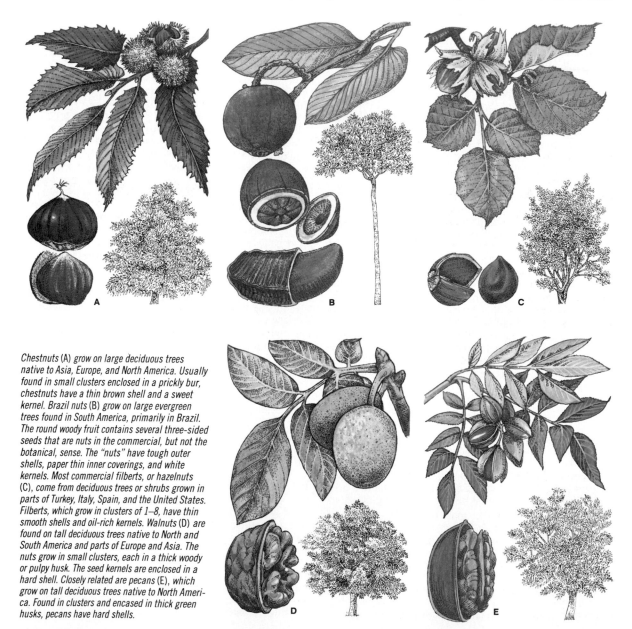

Chestnuts (A) grow on large deciduous trees native to Asia, Europe, and North America. Usually found in small clusters enclosed in a prickly bur, chestnuts have a thin brown shell and a sweet kernel. Brazil nuts (B) grow on large evergreen trees found in South America, primarily in Brazil. The round woody fruit contains several three-sided seeds that are nuts in the commercial, but not the botanical, sense. The "nuts" have tough outer shells, paper thin inner coverings, and white kernels. Most commercial filberts, or hazelnuts (C), come from deciduous trees or shrubs grown in parts of Turkey, Italy, Spain, and the United States. Filberts, which grow in clusters of 1–8, have thin smooth shells and oil-rich kernels. Walnuts (D) are found on tall deciduous trees native to North and South America and parts of Europe and Asia. The nuts grow in small clusters, each in a thick woody or pulpy husk. The seed kernels are enclosed in a hard shell. Closely related are pecans (E), which grow on tall deciduous trees native to North America. Found in clusters and encased in thick green husks, pecans have hard shells.

tive to frost and will not survive harsh winters.

Newly planted trees receive special care until they are established, because nut trees are generally difficult to transplant. HICKORY trees, for example, have a long taproot that is slow to regenerate new roots if it is damaged in transplanting. On the other hand, the filbert's root system is more fibrous, and filberts—which can be grown as shrubs or small trees—are easier to transplant. Most nut species require a moderately acid soil with a pH of about 5.5.

Nut trees are generally vegetatively propagated by grafting or budding, with the exception of filberts, which are propagated by layering. Trees are usually grown from seed only to obtain stocks for grafting, to raise seedlings for the selection of new varieties, or to produce large numbers of trees for wildlife or timber plantings.

Nutritional Content. Green nuts contain 50% or more water when harvested, but must be cured or semidried for proper storage. Fat content varies from about 70% in MACADAMIA NUTS and pecans to 4% in dried chestnuts. Carbohydrates are low in most tree nuts, although chestnuts are high in starch and, ground into a flour, are used in place of cereals in many Mediterranean countries. (Where acorns are still used as a food source, they are eaten in a similar manner.) Protein content ranges from approximately 3.4% in the coconut to 30% in the peanut. In general the food energy provided by nuts compares more than favorably with that of meat: about 600–700 calories per 100 grams from such nuts as walnuts, almonds, and pecans, compared with about 250 calories per 100 grams from a beefsteak with moderate fat content.

Uses. Nuts are used principally as a food and in some countries provide a considerable proportion of the diet. Many nuts are not commercially cultivated but are important foods where they are grown. Such nuts include LITCHI and ginkgo nuts in China; pine nuts, or pignolia, from certain pine species in North America and Europe; sapucaia, or monkey-pot nuts, which resemble Brazil nuts and also grow in the Amazon Basin; pili nuts, or java almonds, native to the Philippines and other Southeast Asian islands; the breadnuts of Jamaica; and the BEECH, BUTTERNUTS, black walnuts, and hickory nuts that grow wild in North America and Europe.

Edible fats and oils are important nut products derived principally from the COCONUT and peanut and from the kernel of the African oil PALM. Industrial oils are obtained principally from the tung nut, which is grown in Asia. Many nut-tree woods are highly valued for use in furniture making and for such special uses as (for hickory wood) tool handles.

nutation   A nutation is a small irregularity in the PRECESSION of the Earth's axis of rotation (nutation means "nodding"). The principal nutation, usually simply called *the* nutation, has a period of 18.6 years and carries the north celestial pole about 10 seconds away from the smooth precessional circle.

Because of its relative proximity, the Moon is twice as potent as the Sun in the contribution to precession. The plane of the Moon's orbit about the Earth is inclined at 5°

to the ecliptic, and itself precesses in space with a period of 18.6 years because of perturbations caused by the Sun. This motion is responsible for the principal nutation. Other nutations are the result of planetary perturbations.

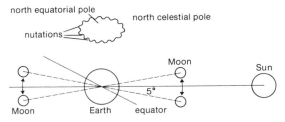

Changes in the Moon's orbit causing nutation

nutcracker   Nutcrackers, two species of birds in the crow family, Corvidae, are found in hilly to high mountainous coniferous forests of North America, Europe, and Asia. Sociable, noisy, and active, they are omnivorous but especially fond of pine seeds. They breed before winter has ended, and the female lays usually two to six pale green, brown-speckled eggs. Nutcrackers often hide seeds and are also able to store some in their crops as well as in a special pouch under the tongue. The Eurasian nutcracker, *Nucifraga caryocatactes*, is brown with white spots and averages about 32 cm (13 in) in total length and 200 g (7 oz) in weight. The slightly smaller Clark's nutcracker, *N. columbiana*, of western North America, is light gray with a white face and white patches in its black wings and tail.

nuthatch   Nuthatch is the common name for about 24 species of birds constituting the family Sittidae, order

The male white-breasted nuthatch (left) often crawls down tree trunks looking for insect prey. The male red-breasted nuthatch (right) is usually found in conifers and may be distinguished by its black eye stripe and reddish belly.

Passeriformes. They are called nuthatches from their practice of placing nuts or seeds in crevices and hacking them open. Nuthatches range from 9.5 to 19 cm (3¾ to 7½ in) in length. They have short tails, short legs, short necks, and large heads with thin, straight bills and often a dark stripe through the eyes. All but two species, which inhabit rocky cliffs, live in trees, where they crawl about, often head down, seeking food. Nuthatches usually nest in tree hollows, where the female lays and incubates 4 to 12 eggs. Most species are nonmigratory, but in some years the red-breasted nuthatch, *Sitta canadensis*, of North America's northern and western coniferous forests, moves in autumn to the southern and eastern United States.

nutmeg Nutmeg is the seed of the nutmeg tree, *Myristica fragrans*, of the nutmeg family, Myristicaceae. The tree is native to the Moluccas, also called the Spice Islands, of Indonesia, but is now cultivated in the West Indies and other tropical areas as well. The nutmeg tree is an evergreen growing to 20 m (65 ft) high, with long, oval leaves and small, pale yellow flowers; male and female flowers are borne on separate trees. The fruit, about 5 cm (2 in) long, splits open when fully ripe to expose the single, large, brown seed surrounded by a fleshy, reddish, netlike appendage (aril) of the seed stalk. The seed is the source of nutmeg; the dried aril is the source of another spice called mace. Both spices are considered toxic when consumed in excess, because they contain a hallucinogenic substance, myristicin. Nutmeg seed oil, which consists primarily of pinene and camphene, is used in perfumes and for flavoring sauces, tobacco, and medicines.

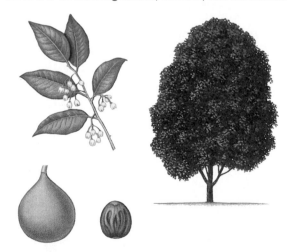

The tropical nutmeg tree grows golden yellow, apricotlike fruits. The spice, nutmeg, is the kernel of the fruit. Mace, another spice, is made from the kernel's thin, red outer covering.

nutria The nutria, *Myocastor coypus,* is an aquatic rodent and the only living species in the family Myocastoridae. It is also frequently classified in the family Capro-

The nutria digs its burrow along a riverbank or lakeshore. An able swimmer, it can remain submerged as long as 5 minutes.

myidae, along with the large, heavy-bodied rodents of the West Indies known as hutias. The nutria was formerly often called a coypu and its fur sold as *nutria* (the Spanish word for "otter"), but the latter name has now come into wide usage for both the animal and its fur. Nutrias resemble miniature beavers, but they have a rounded, tapered tail. They grow to 63 cm (25 in) long, plus a 40-cm (16-in) tail, and weigh more than 9 kg (20 lb). Their plush, dark gray fur is masked by reddish brown guard hairs. The hind feet are webbed. Native to central and southern South America, nutrias have been introduced into the United States and Europe, where they cause damage to crops and irrigation ditches.

nutrient cycles *Nutrient cycle* is the term used to describe the natural processes that keep all the chemical elements needed to support life circulating within the ecosphere.

Of the 88 naturally occurring ELEMENTS, about 20 are used in measurable amounts by most living organisms. Many of the remainder are used in small quantities by microorganisms in trapping energy, forming protoplasm and enzymes, and carrying out life activities. In order for life to survive, these elements must be constantly recycled in forms that plants and animals can use.

The water cycle, or HYDROLOGIC CYCLE, is necessary to the operation of all the nutrient cycles. Water is not only essential to all but a few of the simplest life forms, it is also the main mode of transport of many nutrients and the agent that leaches nutrients from rocks and soils. Two other basic cycles, the CARBON CYCLE and NITROGEN CYCLE, are discussed below.

Carbon. The carbon cycle clearly illustrates the complexity of relationships involved in the processes of recycling. Green plants have the unique ability to trap solar energy and to combine the inorganic substances carbon dioxide and water to make glucose and other carbohydrates through the process of photosynthesis, at the same time releasing surplus OXYGEN to the atmosphere. They also, immediately or later (or both), oxidize some of the foods they have produced to obtain the trapped solar energy. Even so, they consistently produce more food than they oxidize and would ultimately have all the available carbon dioxide tied up if it were not for animals that feed on them and return carbon dioxide to the atmosphere through respiration, excretion, fermentation, and decay (by bacterial action).

Nitrogen. Animals obtain the nitrogen needed for their body tissues by feeding on animal and vegetable proteins. Plants synthesize protein from inorganic compounds from the soil, or from free nitrogen in the air, with the aid of certain soil bacteria. In the last stage, decomposition by bacteria releases the amino group from protein as ammonia.

Sulfur. Sulfur is derived from volcanic gases and the weathering of iron sulfide minerals. In the sulfur cycle, anaerobic bacteria in the soil use sulfur in the same way that denitrifying bacteria use nitrogen. Other sulfur bacteria contain purple or green pigments that operate much as chlorophyll does and that enable the bacteria to break down carbon dioxide and hydrogen sulfide, using the Sun's energy to produce hydrocarbons.

Phosphorus. Phosphorus is basic to all life because it is a major component of deoxyribonucleic acid (DNA), the chemical that makes up the genetic material of all cells and controls reproduction of both the cell and the organism. Phosphates are taken up by the roots of green plants and used in organic synthesis. They are then passed to animals through food chains. Ultimately, phosphates are released to soil through bacterial and fungal decomposition after the death of an animal.

Wasting phosphorus has more serious implications

Phosphorus is essential to all life as a component of DNA and RNA and as part of the energy storage and utilization system at the cellular level. Inorganic sources of phosphates—phosphorus-containing salts—include granitic rocks. Organic sources include guano, waste from shallow-water fish, and sedimentary rocks. The phosphates are mined for use as fertilizer. Phosphates in the soil are taken up by plants, which are eaten by animals; they are released to the soil from animal excreta and from the tissues of dead animals and plants.

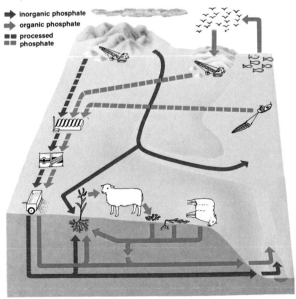

➡ inorganic phosphate
➡ organic phosphate
■■ processed
■■ phosphate

than the eutrophication of lakes. First, the supplies of usable phosphorus are relatively small compared to the demands of the ecosystem. Phosphorus running off the land or dumped into a river moves through waterways to the ocean, where some of it, along with other nutrients, is deposited in deep waters and becomes unavailable to plants and, therefore, to animals. In addition, phosphorus is recycled more slowly than other elements because large reserves exist in bones, teeth, and seashells, which take years to decompose.

Other Elements. In addition, iron, calcium, potassium, magnesium, cobalt, cadmium, copper, manganese, zinc, molybdenum, boron, sodium, chlorine, fluorine, iodine, and other less commonly used elements are all essential to one form of life or another. Several, such as iron and calcium, have complicated biogeochemical patterns that may strongly affect the availability of other elements.

Importance. The far-reaching nature of nutrient cycles has become obvious in recent years. One example was the discovery of DDT in the tissues of Antarctic penguins. The penguins obtained the DDT by eating shrimp that fed on oceanic plankton that, in turn, had taken up the pesticide when it washed off the land. Strontium-90 is another example. Derived from atomic explosions, it was transported by air currents, deposited in Arctic soil, taken up by lichens, eaten by caribou, and ultimately found in the tissues of people who hunt these animals.

Life depends on the interwoven and interdependent relationships of green plants and animals, supplemented by the activities of bacteria, and the constant transport of nutrients within the ecosystem and within organisms. Anything that disrupts or interrupts these cycles has far-reaching and potentially lethal effects.

See also: GEOCHEMISTRY.

---

nutrition, human   Nutrition is the science that interprets the relationship of food to the functioning of the living organism. It is concerned with the intake of food, digestive processes, the liberation of energy, and the elimination of wastes, as well as with all the syntheses that are essential for maintenance, growth, and reproduction. These fundamental activities are characteristic of all living organisms—from the simplest to the most complex plants and animals. Nutrients are substances, either naturally occurring or synthesized, that are necessary for maintenance of the normal function of organisms. These include CARBOHYDRATES, LIPIDS, PROTEINS, VITAMINS AND MINERALS, water, and some unknown substances.

The nutritionist, a scientist working in the field of nutrition, differs from the dietitian, who translates the science of nutrition into the skill of furnishing optimal nourishment to people (see DIET, HUMAN). Dietetics is a profession concerned with the science and art of human nutrition care, an essential component of the health sciences. The treatment of disease by modification of the diet lies within the province of the physician and the dietitian. Such modification can be, and often is, effected without the use of special foods, simply by changing the methods of food preparation or by restricting the diet. Special foods for particular dietary uses differ from ordinary foods by their specific composition or by physical, chemical, or other modifications resulting from processing. If there is an inability to metabolize one of the normal constituents of a diet, then this must be removed from the diet.

The foods consumed by humans must contain, in adequate amounts, about 45 to 50 highly important substances. Water and oxygen are equally essential. Starting only with these essential nutrients obtained from food, the body makes literally thousands of substances necessary for life and physical fitness.

Energy METABOLISM and requirements are customarily expressed in terms of the calorie, a heat unit. Adoption of the calorie by nutritionists followed quite naturally from the original methods of measuring energy metabolism. The magnitude of human energy metabolism, however, made it awkward to record the calorie measured, so the convention of the large calorie, or kilocalorie (kcal), was accepted. Atwater factors, also called physiologic fuel factors, are based on the corrections for losses of unabsorbed nutrients in the feces and for the calorie equivalent of the nitrogenous products in the urine. These factors are as follows: 1 g of pure protein will yield 4 calories, 1 g of pure fat will yield 9 calories, and 1 g of pure carbohydrate will yield 4 calories.

Essential Nutrients

Proteins. Proteins are widely distributed in nature, and no life-forms are known without them. They are made up of relatively simple organic compounds, the amino acids, which contain nitrogen and sometimes sulfur. Humans and animals build the protein they need for growth and repair of tissues by breaking down the proteins obtained in food into their component parts, the amino acids, and then building up these components into proteins of the type needed. The protein-rich foods from animal sources contain complete proteins, which supply all the amino acids in the proper proportions necessary in the human diet. Proteins of plant origin must be combined to get the proper complement of amino acids, a matter of concern to vegetarians.

Vitamins and Minerals. Most foods contain several vitamins and minerals. Vitamins are organic food substances, needed only in minute quantities but essential for the normal metabolism of other nutrients to promote proper growth and maintenance of health. Many vitamins and minerals act as catalysts or help form catalysts in the body. Minerals—such as calcium, iodine, iron, and boron—are an essential part of all cells and body fluids.

Fats and Carbohydrates. Fats, which are widely distributed in nature, are a concentrated food source of energy. Fats are glyceryl esters of fatty acids and yield glycerol and many different fatty acids when broken down by hydrolysis. Carbohydrates are the most abundant food sources of energy. Important dietary carbohydrates are divided into two groups—starches and sugars. The starches, which may be converted into utilizable sugars in plants or in the human body, are supplied in the grains, the pulses, the tubers, and some rhizomes and roots. The sugars occur in many plants and fruits, the most important being sucrose, which is obtained from sugarcane or the sugar beet.

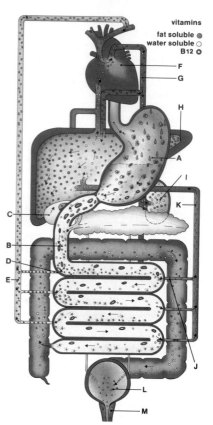

Vitamins are released from foods in the stomach (A). The fat-soluble vitamins, A, D, E, and K, are broken down in the small intestine (B) by bile from the gall bladder (C). The emulsified molecules pass through lymphatics (D) and veins (E) to the heart (F), which distributes them to the rest of the body through the arterial system (G). Excess fat-soluble vitamins are stored in the liver (H) and kidneys (I). The water-soluble vitamins, B-complex and C, are absorbed into the bloodstream through capillaries (J) in the small intestine. (Vitamin B_{12} cannot be absorbed unless it mixes with a special substance found in digestive juices.) Portal veins (K) carry the vitamins to the liver, heart, and arteries. Excess water-soluble vitamins are filtered out by the kidneys to be excreted in urine (L). Undigested excess vitamins are excreted in feces (M).

Dietary Fiber

Dietary fiber, also known as bulk or roughage, is also an essential element in the diet even though it provides no nutrients. It consists of plant CELLULOSE and other undigestible materials in foods, along with PECTINS and GUMS. The chewing it requires stimulates saliva flow, and the bulk it adds in the stomach and intestines during digestion provides more time for absorption of nutrients. Diets with sufficient fiber produce softer, bulkier stools and help to promote bowel regularity and avoid constipation and other disorders, such as DIVERTICULOSIS. Fruits, vegetables, whole-grain breads, and products made from nuts and legumes are all sources of dietary fiber (see BRAN). A diet overly abundant in dietary fiber, however, can cut down on the absorption of important trace minerals.

Food Groups

Foods can be classified into several groups: meat and meat substitutes, fruit-vegetable, milk, bread-cereal, and other foods.

Meat and Meat Substitutes. The meat-and-meat-substitutes group includes beef; veal; lamb; pork; variety meats, such as liver, heart, and kidney; poultry and eggs; fish and shellfish; and dried peas and beans and nuts. Meat contains 9% to 19% protein, making it a very useful protein source. The amount of fat depends on the kind of meat, the amount of trimming, and the method of cooking. The minerals copper, iron, and phosphorus occur in meats in significant amounts, as do the B vitamins thiamine, riboflavin, and niacin.

Fruits and Vegetables. Most fruits and vegetables are valuable sources of minerals, vitamins, and cellulose. Some, such as bananas and potatoes, contribute appreciable quantities of starch to the diet.

Milk. The milk group includes milk, cheese, and ice cream. Milk contains important amounts of most nutrients; calcium and phosphorus levels are very high. Vitamin A levels are high in whole milk, but in the production of skim milk this fat-soluble vitamin is removed. Riboflavin is present in significant quantities in milk unless the milk has been exposed to light. The composition of whole milk is approximately 4.9% carbohydrate, 3.5% fat, 3.5% protein, and about 87% water.

Bread-Cereal. The bread-cereal group includes all breads and cereals that are whole grain, enriched, or restored. Protein content is not high in cereals, but the large intake of cereals in some diets makes these products a significant source of protein. All cereals are very high in starch. Fat content generally is very low unless the germ is included in the food. The whole-grain products contribute significant quantities of fiber and such trace vitamins and minerals as pantothenic acid, vitamin E, zinc, copper, manganese, and molybdenum.

Other Foods. Other foods included in the diet are butter, margarine, other fats, oils, sugars, or unenriched refined-grain products. These foods supply calories and can add to total nutrients in meals.

Dietary Standards

The dietary standards used in the United States are the Recommended Dietary Allowances (RDA), which were developed by the Food and Nutrition Board of the National Research Council, National Academy of Sciences. The allowances are described as the levels of intake of essential nutrients considered—in the judgment of the Food and Nutrition Board on the basis of available scientific knowledge—to be adequate to meet normal nutritional needs.

Energy allowances are determined according to age and average heights and weights. Individual activity level is also used to determine the level of ideal calorie intake. For example, a decrease in recommended energy allowance with increasing age is consistent with the known decrease in basal metabolic rate that occurs with aging and with a possible decrease in physical activity.

Federal Guidelines

In 1980 the U.S. Department of Health and Human Services outlined certain guidelines for nutrition, which recommended that people eat a variety of foods daily, including fruits; vegetables; whole and enriched grain products; dairy products; meats, poultry, fish, and eggs; and dried peas and beans. The greater the variety of foods eaten, the less likely is a deficiency or excess of any single nutrient to develop. Women who are pregnant or of childbearing age, elderly people, and infants have special nutritional needs, but on the whole most people can derive essential nutrients by eating the type of foods mentioned in the guidelines.

The report emphasized that people should increase their consumption of complex carbohydrates—fruits, vegetables, and other unrefined foods—and naturally occurring sugars, while reducing consumption of refined and processed sugars. It encouraged reduced consumption of fats, particularly saturated fats. Reduced sodium intake by decreasing the amount of salt added to food was also recommended.

meat and meat substitutes

fruits and vegetables

dairy products

breads and cereals

The four basic food groups, which provide the nutrients not synthesized by the human body, are (clockwise from left) meat and meat substitutes, such as seafood and legumes; fruits and vegetables; cereals; and dairy products. Although the nutritional content of foods within each group varies somewhat, the groups generally represent foods containing similar amounts of proteins, vitamins, minerals, and other nutrients.

COMPONENTS OF A BALANCED DIET

Essential Nutrient	Daily Recommendations for Healthy Adults	Food Examples		
Fat	30% or less of calories (Saturated-fat intake, such as from dairy and meat products, should be less than 10% of calories.)	Butter Cream Bacon	Peanut butter Avocado Nuts	More than 75% of calories from fat
		Ice cream Cheddar cheese Tuna salad	Ham Pound cake Lamb chops	50–75% of calories from fat
		Skim milk Frozen yogurt Broiled cod Raw oysters	Dried beans Bread, pasta Fruits Vegetables	Less than 20% of calories from fat
Cholesterol	Less than 300 mg	3 oz lean beef 77 mg 2 frankfurters 112 mg 1 whole egg 215 mg 3 oz flounder 69 mg 1 tbsp butter 35 mg ½ cup ice cream 27 mg	1 cup whole milk 34 mg 1 muffin 21 mg 1 cup skim milk 5 mg peanut butter 0 mg fruits 0 mg vegetables 0 mg	
Carbohydrates	More than 55% of calories	**Percentage of Calories from Carbohydrates** Baked potato 90 Macaroni 81 Whole-wheat bread 79 Oatmeal 70 Kidney beans 70	Skim milk 57 Low-fat yogurt 42 Whole milk 30 Fishsticks 15 Peanut butter 13	
Protein	Between 0.8 and 1.6 g/kg of body weight (A 68-kg [150-lb] person should consume no more than 109 g per day.)	½ cup tuna in oil 33 g 1 cup cottage cheese 31 g 3 oz cooked veal cutlet 28 g 3.5 oz broiled swordfish 28 g 1 cup lima beans, cooked 10 g	1 cup milk, skim or whole 9 g 1 cup cooked spinach 6 g 1 medium hard roll 5 g 1 cup oatmeal 5 g 1 cup bran flakes 4 g	

Source: Compiled from a report of the Committee on Diet and Health, Food and Nutrition Board of the National Academy of Sciences (1989).

The dietary goals suggested reducing CHOLESTEROL intake by decreasing the amount of butterfat, eggs, and other sources in the diet. Controversy has arisen concerning cholesterol intake, however, even though abundant evidence indicates that dietary fat and cholesterol are factors that increase the risk of atherosclerosis and coronary heart disease, which leads to heart attacks. In a separate action, the Food and Nutrition Board concluded that the evidence warrants no specific recommendations about dietary cholesterol for the healthy person, who does not need to be concerned about fat intake.

Scientists and industry personnel are debating whether the diet of the U.S. population should be modified on the basis of these federal guidelines. The proportion of the population that would benefit from such changes is unknown, although early in 1984 the U.S. National Heart, Lung, and Blood Institute reported the results of a long-term study showing that persons with high cholesterol levels are clearly under greater risk of heart attacks and of developing heart disease than are persons with normal cholesterol levels.

Food Labeling

Nutritional labeling seems to be a solution to the problem of consumer ignorance of nutrients in foods. For a meaningful labeling program, the nutritional constituency in terms of percentage of the RDA for each nutrient and a system of freshness dating should be included on each label. This development would bring major changes in food labeling on the packages and would give information about serving size, number of servings, calories, proteins, carbohydrates, fats, vitamins, and minerals per serving. Since 1973 the U.S. Food and Drug Administration has required complete nutrition labeling, but only if a nutrient is added to a food or a nutrient claim is made by the manufacturer. Some manufacturers have also voluntarily supplied such information on packages.

nutritional-deficiency diseases Nutritional-deficiency diseases result primarily from a diet that does not have enough of the nutrients that are essential to health or development (see DIET, HUMAN). Another cause is that an individual may not be able to utilize properly the nutrients consumed in the diet. Deficiency diseases may result from a person's abnormally high metabolic needs for a nutrient or from some imbalance in the nutrients ingested. Certain drugs or medicines may also affect nutrient use.

Symptoms of many of these disorders include severe weight loss. The greatest tissue loss can occur in the intestines and liver. Most systems are affected, including the body's immune system. The skin appears dry and pale; the hair is dry and sparse and may fall out. Respiratory rate and heart output are reduced. Endocrine disturbances result in amenorrhea in women. DIARRHEA frequently occurs in undernourished individuals and can result in death.

Nutritional deficiency contributes to much of the ill health in developing countries. The most important forms of malnutrition there are protein-calorie malnutrition (PCM); endemic GOITER and cretinism because of iodine deficiency; vitamin A deficiency leading to xerophthalmia (abnormal eye dryness), which may impair vision; and nutritional ANEMIAS.

Deficiency Diseases

Humans obtain energy (measured in calories or joules) from carbohydrates, fat, and protein and also from alcohol. In the majority of societies the most available source of calories is carbohydrates, and fat and protein are less available. In general, as families or communities become more affluent, the proportion of fat and animal protein in the diet increases.

Protein-Calorie Malnutrition. A failure to consume adequate quantities of food energy may lead to loss of weight or growth failure in children, wasting of tissues, and eventually STARVATION. The production of enzymes and hormones is impaired in severe protein deficiency. Young children living in poorer communities throughout the world commonly have protein-calorie malnutrition. This condition is aggravated by common infections that cause diarrhea and sometimes by the irregular intervals at which a child may have food to eat.

The two clinical forms of PCM are nutritional marasmus and KWASHIORKOR. Marasmus is due primarily to an energy (calorie) deficiency; in kwashiorkor, protein deficiency predominates. Mild or moderate PCM is much more common than these two severe forms and leads to a slow rate of growth, to poor development, to increased susceptibility to infections, and eventually to permanent physical stunting.

Mineral Deficiency. The most important simple mineral deficiencies are iron deficiency, a common cause of anemia; iodine deficiency, leading to goiter and sometimes cretinism; and fluoride deficiency, which contributes to tooth decay.

Vitamin Deficiency. The major vitamin-deficiency diseases include xerophthalmia, which is due to vitamin A deficiency. It can result in ulceration of the cornea of the eye and increased susceptibility to infections and sometimes blindness. Beriberi, a thiamine, or vitamin B_1, deficiency, is commonly found among rice-eating peoples and alcoholics. Pellagra results from a deficiency in niacin and is associated with persons eating mainly a corn, or maize, diet. A riboflavin, or vitamin B_2, deficiency causes ariboflavinosis, in which there may be cracks of the lips and red, scaly lesions in the genital area. The macrocytic anemias (involving abnormally large red blood cells) result particularly from folic-acid deficiency during pregnancy and sometimes from B_{12} deficiency. RICKETS and osteomalacia (softening of the bones) are due to vitamin D deficiency, and SCURVY is due to vitamin C deficiency.

Treatment. The specific treatment for each of these deficiency states is usually the medical provision of appropriate doses of the nutrient in question and also an assurance that foods rich in these nutrients are consumed in the diet. This latter approach is also the basis for prevention of these diseases.

Problems of World Health

In recent years world concern has increased both about hunger and to some extent about malnutrition. In most parts of the world major FAMINES have led to international action to reduce the extent of starvation.

The World Health Organization (WHO), the Food and Agriculture Organization (FAO), and United Nations Children's Fund (UNICEF), all agencies of the UN, play important and different roles in trying to reduce the extent and seriousness of malnutrition, particularly in developing countries. (See also AGRICULTURE AND THE FOOD SUPPLY.)

Nyasa, Lake [ny-as'-uh] Lake Nyasa (also called Malawi), which lies in the southernmost part of the East African Rift System, is the third largest lake in Africa. Long (584 km/363 mi) and narrow (16–80 km/10–50 mi), the lake has a total area of 29,604 km² (11,430 mi²). Lying mainly in the landlocked nation of Malawi, which has developed an important fishing industry around the lake, Lake Nyasa is also owned by Tanzania (north and east) and Mozambique (east). Lake Nyasa drains into the ZAMBEZI RIVER.

Nyasaland see MALAWI

Nyerere, Julius K. [ny-uh-ray'-ray] Julius Kambarage Nyerere, b. March 1922, was president of Tanzania from 1964 to 1985. In 1954 he founded the anticolonial Tanganyika African National Union. He became prime minister (1961) and president (1962) of newly independent Tanganyika and president of Tanzania (1964) when Tanganyika was united with Zanzibar. Nyerere, who governed Tanzania along socialist principles, became a leading spokesperson for the frontline states opposing white rule in southern Africa. Under Nyerere, Tanzania achieved the highest adult literacy rate in Africa, although it experienced economic difficulties during the later years of his rule. Nyerere resigned from the presidency in 1985; his successor was Zanzibar president Ali Hassan Mwinyi.

nylon   Nylon, the general name of a group of synthetic fibers, was the first of the "miracle" yarns made entirely from chemical ingredients through the process of POLYMERIZATION. Discovered in the 1930s by a Du Pont Company research team headed by Wallace H. CAROTHERS, the fiber created immense excitement when the first nylon stockings were marketed in 1939. Unlike silk, which had been the fiber used for women's dress hosiery, nylon was strong even when knitted into the sheerest of fabrics and could be washed and dried quickly. Because of its strength, durability, and resistance to moisture and mildew, nylon became vital during World War II. It replaced silk in parachutes and cotton in webbing and sewing thread, and it was used for "flak vests" and reinforced aircraft tires.

At war's end, nylon was made into ropes, woven into boat sails, and used for lingerie and swimwear. The elasticity of nylon-textured yarn permitted the development of new forms of apparel, such as hosiery that could stretch to fit several foot sizes.

Nylon is synthesized from varying combinations of diamines and dicarboxylic acids. The most common form, nylon 66, is made from adipic acid and hexamethylene diamine. In its plastic form, the material can be extruded by spinnerets into filaments, formed into sheets, or molded into a variety of finished products. For textile use, nylon fiber is cold-drawn, or stretched, in a process that quadruples its length and reorients the material's molecules parallel to one another to produce a strong, elastic filament.

During the late 1950s the coincident development of equipment to tuft carpet yarns into a backing material and of a technique for imparting bulk or "loft" to nylon yarn by an air-texturing process opened a new era for the carpet industry. Carpets of nylon now account for nearly 80 percent of a market that was once the exclusive domain of wool fabrics.

The original Carothers theory that first produced nylon also laid the foundation for the development of other SYNTHETIC FIBERS, of which several billion kg are now produced annually in the United States.

nymph   Nymph is the name given to the immature stages of a variety of insects that undergo a simple metamorphosis from young to adult form. In these insects, which include the Orthoptera (grasshoppers and cockroaches) and Hemiptera (true bugs), the young are generally similar to the mature form and do not pass through a pupal stage to become adults. Nymphs of certain insects are aquatic and gill-breathing and are often referred to as naiads.

Nymphenburg Palace [nimf'-en-boork]   Nymphenburg Palace—the "Castle of the Nymphs"—was the summer residence near Munich of the Bavarian rulers. Designed in 1663 by Agostino Barelli as a five-story Italianate villa, it was considerably enlarged in the early 18th century. Beginning in 1716, Josef Effner redesigned the palace in the French *Régence* style and built three of the four exquisite garden pavilions in the extensive palace park: the Chinese-Dutch Pagodenburg (1716–23); the Badenburg (1718–21), with an opulent indoor swimming pool; and the meditational retreat called the Magdalenenklause (1725–28). Nymphenburg's finest works, a three-story Great Hall (*c.*1750) incorporated in the original villa and a rococo masterpiece, the Amalienburg Pavilion (1734–40), were designed by François CUVILLIÉS.

nymphomania   Nymphomania may be defined as a pathological degree of sexual desire in women. The term is no longer used by mental-health professionals because there is no way accurately to assess what a "normal" degree of sexual desire is. *Nymphomania* is also considered to be derogatory. The equivalent term for men, *satyriasis*, is rarely used.

nymphs   In Greek and Roman mythology nymphs were female nature spirits who were associated with such natural phenomena as seas, rivers, mountains, woods, meadows, and caves, as well as with specific localities. Young and beautiful, these mortal creatures figured frequently in myth, sometimes as the love objects of the Olympian god APOLLO or of various nature deities. Although characteristically gentle and benevolent, nymphs could also be vengeful and destructive, similar to SATYRS in their wildness. The main categories of nymphs included Naiads, or water nymphs, who lived in or near rivers and springs; Nereids, daughters of the sea-god NEREUS, and Oceanids, daughters of Oceanus, who lived and frolicked in the saltwater seas and oceans; and Dryads and Hamadryads, woodland nymphs, the latter of whom lived only so long as their particular trees remained intact.

Nyoro [nee-ah'-roh]   The Nyoro (also called Bakitara, Banyoro, Bunyoro, or Kitara) are a Bantu-speaking people of west central Uganda. In the late 1980s they numbered more than 2 million. The Nyoro kingdom, known as Bunyoro, evolved from the 14th-century kingdom of Kitara. The most powerful kingdom in the region in the 16th and 17th centuries, it came under British protection in 1896. When Uganda gained independence in 1962, it was a federation consisting of Bunyoro and three other major kingdoms; the kingships were not abolished until 1967.

Traditionally, the Nyoro were organized into numerous patrilineal clans that were divided into three castes: a nomadic herding group from which the king and subchiefs were chosen; a subordinate group of agricultural serfs; and an intermediate group permitted to intermarry with either of the other two. Before the British restricted hunting by declaring the northern part of Bunyoro a wildlife preserve (now Kabarega National Park), the Nyoro were skilled hunters who fashioned tools and weapons from local iron ore.

GERMAN-GOTHIC	RUSSIAN-CYRILLIC	CLASSICAL LATIN	EARLY LATIN	ETRUSCAN	CLASSICAL GREEK	EARLY GREEK	EARLY ARAMAIC	EARLY HEBREW	PHOENICIAN

O   *O/o* is the 15th letter of the English alphabet. Both the letter and its position in the alphabet were derived from the Latin alphabet, which in turn derived them from the Greek by way of the Etruscan. The Greeks converted a Semitic guttural consonant, *ayin*, to represent the sound of *O/o* that they called *omicron*. Although the Etruscan language had no *o* vowel, the Latin alphabet was derived from the Etruscan at an early date before the letter had been dropped from it.

In modern English, *O/o* has many pronunciations, and, as the words *love, cove,* and *move* show, giving consistent rules for how to pronounce it is impossible. Short *o* is like the *a* sound of most European languages, as in *fox* or *not*; long *o* is the sound heard in *stone*. Double *o* is usually pronounced like a long *u*, as in *moon*; this sound can also be represented by single *o*, as in *move*. *O/o* can also combine with all other vowels, as in *boat, foe, boil,* and *ought*. The diphthong *ou* (or *ow*) usually has the sound heard in *house*.

O. Henry   O. Henry was the pen name of William Sydney Porter, b. Greensboro, N.C., Sept. 11, 1862, d. June 5, 1910, an immensely popular American short-story writer. With little formal education, Porter left (1882) North Carolina for Texas, where he worked as a ranch hand, bookkeeper, bank teller, and eventually editor of a humorous weekly, *The Rolling Stone*. Indicted (1894) for embezzling from a bank in Austin and arrested in 1896, Porter protested his innocence but fled to Honduras and later to South America. He returned to Austin in 1897, stood trial, and was convicted (1898), after which he served more than three years in the federal penitentiary in Columbus, Ohio. There he wrote short stories under various pseudonyms; "O. Henry" finally superseded all others.

Following his release from prison, O. Henry lived in Pittsburgh for a short time but in 1902 settled in New York, a city he celebrated in his second collection of stories, *The Four Million* (1906), with its still-popular tale "The Gift of the Magi." (O. Henry's first collection, *Cabbages and Kings*, was published in 1904.) There followed in rapid succession eight more collections, published from 1907 to 1910. Financial problems and alcohol contributed to O. Henry's early death in 1910, yet enough material was left for three additional volumes of stories to appear posthumously. Hollywood recognized his talents by filming three of the stories in *O. Henry's Full House*

(1952). To memorialize his place in American literature, in 1918 the Society of Arts and Sciences established the O. Henry Award to be given to the authors of the best stories printed each year in American magazines.

O. Henry is the pseudonym of William Sydney Porter, an American short-story writer, who began writing while in prison for embezzling from a bank. O. Henry stories are noted for their careful plotting, ironic coincidences, and surprise endings.

Oahu [oh-ah'-hoo]   Oahu, third largest of the Hawaiian Islands, has an area of 1,575 km² (608 mi²) and a population of 836,231 (1990). It is 64 km (40 mi) long and 42 km (26 mi) wide. Of volcanic origin, Oahu consists of two rugged, parallel mountain ranges, the Koolau and Waianal, rising to 1,227 m (4,025 ft) and separated by a heavily cultivated central plain.

Tourism, the maintenance of military installations, especially at PEARL HARBOR, and the raising of pineapple and sugarcane are the major economic activities. Principal communities on the island include HONOLULU, Kailua, Kaneohe, Wahiawa, and Waipahu. Spectacular natural sights include the Nuuanu Pali cliffs and three extinct volcanic craters, one of which is Diamond Head. Oahu became the seat of the royal government by the middle of the 19th century.

oak   Oaks are deciduous or evergreen trees or, rarely, shrubs, of the genus *Quercus* in the beech family, Fagaceae. They are the most important and widespread hardwood trees in the northern temperate region, occur-

The oak tree is a temperate zone tree that has acorns and distinctive leaves. Red oak (top) and white oak (center) grow in eastern North America. Live oak (bottom) is native to the southern United States.

ring throughout North America and Eurasia and in higher elevations extending south into northwestern South America, Cuba, North Africa, and Indonesia. Of the approximately 450 species of oaks, 60 or more, some shrublike in form, are native to the United States and Canada. Oaks dominate the central and southern hard-

wood forests of the United States, and about 20 species in the eastern United States are commercially important. Oaks furnish more native timber annually than any other broad-leaved tree and in total lumber production are second only to the conifers. Oak lumber is used for flooring and wood trim in home construction and for railroad ties, barrels, boats, furniture, and fuel, including charcoal. Other oak products include cork, which is produced primarily from the bark of the European cork oak, *Q. suber*; tannin, a substance used in making leather, from the bark of such trees as the daimyo oak, *Q. dentata*, of the Orient; dyes, such as quercitron, which is derived from the bark of the black oak, *Q. velutina*; formerly, inks and dyes from oak galls, which are pea- to egg-sized growths rich in tannic acid, formed by oaks around developing gall-wasp larvae; and acorns, which are fed to hogs, used as human food if of the sweet variety, or, if from the valonia oak, *Q. macrolepis*, used as a source of tannin.

Oaks are monoecious, bearing separate male and female flowers on the same tree. The male flowers are small and are borne in drooping, tassellike clusters, called aments or catkins. The female flowers are borne either singly or in short spikes of several to many flowers. Each female flower is contained within a cuplike structure, the cupule, which is composed of modified leaflike bracts, or scales. The fertilized female flower matures into a nut, called an acorn, with the cupule enclosing its base. The oak's overwintering leaf buds and the leaves are usually clustered near the tips of twigs.

Oaks are divided into three groups: the red oaks, the white oaks, and the ringed oaks. In the last group, which has few members and is not found in North America, the scales of the acorn cupule are fused into a series of rings. The red oaks and white oaks generally can be distinguished by several characteristics. Red oaks have pointy-lobed leaves with spiny or bristly tips. The acorns are bitter, have hairy inner shells, and need two seasons to ripen. White oaks have round-lobed leaves that lack spines or bristles. The acorns are sweet, have smooth inner shells, and ripen in one season. Chestnut oaks, which have unlobed leaves with broadly toothed margins, are a subsection of the white oaks. The willow oaks, with narrow, unlobed, smooth-margined leaves, and the evergreen live oaks, with unlobed, smooth-margined, or toothed leaves, are subsections of the red oaks. The southern live oak, although placed with the red oaks because of similarities in wood anatomy, has sweet acorns that mature in one season.

Oakland

Oakland Oakland is a city in the San Francisco Bay urban complex of California and the seat of Alameda County. The population is 372,242 (1990). Oakland lies on the east shore of the bay opposite San Francisco, with which it is connected by bridge and the tunnel of the Bay Area Rapid Transit system (BART). Oakland is the core of the East Bay conurbation, which includes Alameda, Albany, Berkeley, Fremont, Hayward, Richmond, and San Leandro.

The city's commercial core and residential sections are the focus of a major urban-renewal program, and the surrounding hills have been developed into attractive neighborhoods. Oakland's highly diversified industries produce electrical equipment, glass, chemicals, office machines, and pharmaceuticals. The city is the leading port on the bay and the foremost container port on the West Coast. It has an almost totally artificial harbor, with 31 km (19 mi) of waterfront served by three major railroads. Points of interest include Jack London Square and Lake Merritt, a wildlife refuge and recreation area.

Horace Carpentier chose the site for Oakland in 1852 as a terminus for his ferry service to San Francisco. The city was incorporated in 1854. Harbor development was stimulated when Oakland became the terminus for the first transcontinental railroad in 1869. A severe earthquake in October 1989 caused the collapse of a portion of a double-decker highway, with heavy loss of life.

Oakley, Annie [ohk'-lee] The American sharpshooter Annie Oakley, b. Phoebe Anne Oakley Mezee, Patterson, Ohio, Aug. 13, 1860, d. Nov. 3, 1926, was famous for her amazing speed and accuracy with rifles and pistols. She began shooting as a child and by age 16 had challenged and beaten the well-known marksman Frank Butler, whom she later married. Oakley's special skill was stunt shooting: she could, for example, shoot a playing card in half, or from a distance of 27 m (90 ft) hit a dime in mid-air. From 1885 to 1902 she was a leading attraction in Buffalo Bill's Wild West Show. The popular musical *Annie Get Your Gun* was based on her life.

OAO The Orbiting Astronomical Observatory (OAO) program was a series of four U.S. scientific satellites launched between April 1966 and August 1972 that were designed to study astronomical phenomena at ultraviolet and X-ray wavelengths inaccessible to terrestrial observatories. The basic structure of the satellite, built by Grumman Aerospace Corporation, was an octagonal aluminum cylinder. The control, data processing, and telemetry systems were fitted into this shell, along with a cluster of telescopes. Attached to the cylinder were two paddlelike solar arrays.

The *OAO-1* satellite was successfully launched on Apr. 8, 1966; on its second day in orbit, however, the primary battery failed, rendering the satellite inoperative.

The successful *OAO-2* satellite, launched Dec. 7, 1968, carried a cluster of four 32-cm (12.5-in) ultraviolet telescopes, known collectively as the "Celescope," that were developed at the Smithsonian Astrophysical Observatory, and seven University of Wisconsin instruments, including a 41-cm (16-in) telescope, four 20-cm (8-in) photoelectric telescopes, and two ultraviolet spectrometers. The Smithsonian instruments mapped the sky in four ultraviolet wavelengths, and the Wisconsin telescopes studied the ultraviolet radiation of stars and gas clouds. The satellite operated until February 1973.

OAO-B, launched Nov. 30, 1970, failed to orbit when the nose fairing of the Centaur booster did not separate.

The *Copernicus* (*OAO-3*) satellite, launched Aug. 21, 1972, carried an 82-cm (32-in) reflecting ultraviolet telescope—at that time the largest telescope ever orbited—developed by astronomers at Princeton University, and three smaller X-ray telescopes developed at University College, London. *Copernicus* continued to function until early 1981.

An essential and unique feature of the OAO satellites was their ability to point the optics accurately in order to observe one star among the millions visible. Through the combined use of onboard star trackers and radio commands from Earth, the *Copernicus* satellite, from its nearly circular orbit 740 km (460 mi) above the Earth, could be pointed accurately to within a few tenths of a second of arc.

oarfish Oarfish, *Regalecus glesne,* are elongate marine fishes in the family Regalecidae. They are seldom seen unless washed ashore injured or sick but probably occur worldwide in temperate and tropical seas. Evidence indicates that more than one species may exist. Oarfish reach more than 7 m (23 ft) in length, live at moderate depths, and feed on small crustaceans. They have flat, broad, ribbonlike bodies, which are silvery or blue and transparent, and bright red fins. The pelvic fins are very long and slender. Little is known of their biology.

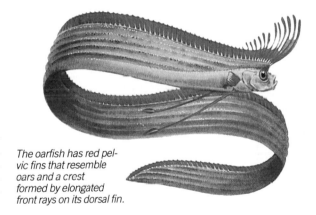

The oarfish has red pelvic fins that resemble oars and a crest formed by elongated front rays on its dorsal fin.

Oates, Joyce Carol [ohts] A powerful American writer whose vision of contemporary society is psychologically penetrating and often terrifying, Joyce Carol Oates, b. Lockport, N.Y., June 16, 1938, won popular recognition with *A Garden of Earthly Delights* (1967), the first in a loose trilogy of novels that spans American life from the 1920s to the 1960s. The second volume, *Expensive People* (1968), was followed by *them* (1969), which was set in a Detroit slum and which won the 1970 National Book Award. Oates has been called the most severe American realist: her works portray the darker aspects of life with a skill unmatched by any other contemporary author. She has produced about 20 novels, including gothics such as *A Bloodsmoor Romance* (1982); *Marya* (1986), *You Must*

Joyce Carol Oates is a contemporary American novelist, short-story writer, poet, playwright, and critic. Much of her fiction dramatizes the "phenomenon of violence and its aftermath, in ways not unlike those of the Greek dramatists," as she describes it.

Photo Jill Krementz © 1974

Remember This (1987), and other novels of the somewhat brutal here-and-now; an unending outpouring of short stories (*The Assignation*, 1989, is a recent collection), poems, and essays; and a book—*On Boxing* (1987)—on boxing.

Oates, Titus   A dismissed Anglican naval chaplain, Titus Oates, b. Sept. 15, 1649, d. July 12 or 13, 1705, schemed to exploit the intense anti-Catholic fears in England, fabricating the Popish Plot of 1678. He converted to Catholicism, studied in Jesuit seminaries in continental Europe, and, when he returned to England, revealed the "plot." Oates alleged that Jesuits planned to assassinate CHARLES II of England and place his Roman Catholic brother James, duke of York (later King JAMES II), on the throne. In the subsequent wave of anti-Catholic hysteria, Oates was gratefully rewarded, and about 35 innocent persons were executed. In 1685, however, after James acceded to the throne, Oates was convicted of perjury, flogged, and imprisoned. He was released and given a pension after James was deposed in the Glorious Revolution of 1688.

oath   An oath is a pledge by which a person swears, affirms, or acknowledges that he or she is bound because of religion or otherwise to perform an act faithfully and truthfully. Oaths are taken by witnesses in judicial proceedings, public officers who promise to perform their official duties faithfully, aliens in the naturalization process, and professionals such as physicians who pledge to conduct themselves according to the principles of their profession.

The oath undertaken by witnesses in judicial proceedings is generally administered by a judge or by a court officer in the presence of the presiding judge. Testimony will not be allowed from a witness who does not take some form of oath or affirmation, and anyone who offers false testimony under oath is subject to prosecution for PERJURY.

oats   A cereal grain used as a food primarily for livestock, oats are members of the genus *Avena* of the GRASS family, Gramineae. Their cultivation occurred relatively recently compared with that of other cereals, such as wheat. Oats were first grown in northern Europe in conjunction with the increasing use of horses as draft animals, perhaps in the 2d millennium BC. The plant is best suited to a moist, cool climate, and it has rarely been successfully cultivated in the southern regions of Europe. The variety known as red oats is heat tolerant and is grown in warm, moist climates. Oats, like rye, will produce yields in poor soils and are valuable as a rotation crop.

The slender oat stalk grows up to 1.2 m (4 ft) high, ending in branched spikelets that contain the flowers from which the husk-covered seeds develop. Oat seeds contain 8% to 14% protein, 63% to 65% carbohydrate, 2% to 3% fat, and 2% to 2½% minerals. The plant is vulnerable to rust and smut diseases, but resistant varieties have been developed.

Although they do not contain the gluten protein that makes wheat the major bread cereal, oats are nevertheless a nourishing food. Oat plants also make excellent straw, and the hulls are a source of furfural, an industrial chemical used in making resins and solvents.

The common oat, an important agricultural crop, is a grass that grows in temperate climates. Its spiky flower heads are enclosed in coarse hulls, which must be removed to obtain the edible seeds, or groats.

Oaxaca (city) [wah-hah'-kah]   Oaxaca de Juárez, the capital of the state of Oaxaca, in southern Mexico, lies at an altitude of 1,534 m (5,034 ft) in an area of gold and silver mines. It has a predominantly ZAPOTEC population of 157,284 (1984 est.). Oaxaca's industries produce textiles—including handmade serapes—as well as pottery, gold and silver jewelry, and leather goods. An important source of income is tourism. Famous pre-Columbian ruins are located nearby: 42 km (26 mi) to the southeast are the MIXTEC ruins at MITLA, and 5 km (3 mi) to the west is the complex of MONTE ALBÁN, a center of ancient Zapotec culture. Among the colonial buildings in the city proper, the most notable are a 17th-century cathedral and the church of Santo Domingo, begun about 1575. The birthplace of the Mexican president Benito Juárez, Oaxaca is the seat of the Benito Juárez University of Oaxaca (1955). Founded in 1486 as an Aztec garrison, Oaxaca was taken by the Spanish in 1522. The city was captured by Mexican revolutionaries in 1812.

Oaxaca (state)   Oaxaca is a mountainous state in southern Mexico along the Pacific Ocean, covering an area of 93,952 km^2 (36,275 mi^2). Its low-lying coast rises to several plateaus crossed by deep fertile valleys. The capital is Oaxaca, and the state's population is 3,021,513 (1990). Most of the people are ZAPOTEC and MIXTEC Indians. The economy is based on agriculture.

Ob River [awp]   The Ob River is a 3,682-km-long (2,287-mi) river in the USSR that flows north and northwest across western Siberia to the west branch of the Ob Bay of the Arctic Ocean. With its main tributary, the IRTYSH, the river is 5,413 km (3,362 mi) long, making this the fourth longest river system in Asia. The Ob and Irtysh drain an area of 2,975,000 km^2 (1,148,649 mi^2).

The Ob's headwaters, the Biya and Katun rivers, begin in the ALTAI MOUNTAINS of southwestern Siberia; they join at Biysk and flow north and northwest. At Novosibirsk the river is dammed to create the Ob Sea; beyond that point the river passes through the Tyumen petroleum and natural-gas fields. At Khanty-Mansiysk, the Irtysh joins the Ob, creating a 19-km-wide (12-mi) channel. About 320 km (200 mi) north of Khanty-Mansiysk the Ob divides into the Great Ob and Little Ob. They rejoin south of Salebhard and then split again at the river delta. The river is navigable from Biysk to its mouth, but it is frozen for 6–7 months each year.

Obadiah, Book of [oh-buh-dy'-uh]   The Book of Obadiah is the fourth book of the Twelve Minor Prophets in the Old Testament of the Bible. This brief collection of sayings reflects the fall of Jerusalem in 587 BC. Obadiah ("servant of the Lord") is particularly vehement toward the Edomites, long-standing enemies of Israel who cooperated with the Babylonian conquerors. He calls down divine judgment on the Edomites and predicts a final day of return from exile and triumph over Edom. The date of final compilation is uncertain.

obelisk   An obelisk is a monolithic stone monument whose four sides, which generally carry inscriptions, gently taper into a pyramidion at the top. The ancient Egyptians usually erected them in pairs and associated them with the rays of the Sun, which increase in width as they reach the Earth. The earliest known examples, excavated

at Abu Sir, Egypt, date from the Old Kingdom during the reign of Neuserre (2449–2417 BC). The unfinished obelisk in the quarry at Aswan shows how these monuments, some more than 32 m (105 ft) long, were cut as single pieces of red granite. Their transport on barges down the Nile is depicted on relief sculptures. So popular were these monuments among the Roman emperors that 13 of them were taken to Rome.

Oberlin, Johann Friedrich [oh'-bur-leen]   The Alsatian Lutheran pastor Johann Friedrich (Jean Frédéric) Oberlin, b. Aug. 31, 1740, d. June 1, 1826, was best known for his philanthropic efforts and educational innovations. Educated at Strasbourg, he was pastor of Waldersbach, Ban-de-la-Roche, in the Vosges from 1767 until his death. Influenced both by the Enlightenment ideas of Jean Jacques Rousseau and by the Christian mysticism of Emanuel von Swedenborg, he promoted engineering, administrative, agricultural, and educational reform within his parish. His work eventually won international recognition, especially his principles of infant education, as developed by Johann PESTALOZZI. Oberlin College in Ohio is named for him.

Oberlin College [oh'-bur-lin]   Established in 1833 as the first coeducational college in the United States, Oberlin College is a private 4-year liberal arts school in Oberlin, Ohio. The college's Conservatory of Music (1865) has 4- and 5-year programs.

Oberth, Hermann [oh'-bairt]   The Transylvania-born physicist Hermann Julius Oberth, b. June 25, 1894, d. Dec. 29, 1989, was one of the founders of modern astronautics. At the age of 11, Oberth's imagination was captured by Jules Verne's book *From the Earth to the Moon.* His early college years prepared him for a career in medicine, but he later switched to the physical sciences.

Before World War I, Oberth became interested in combat rockets, and in 1917 he proposed the development of

Hermann Oberth, one of the founders of astronautics, was a soldier in the Austro-Hungarian army when he designed his first long-range, liquid-propellant rocket. He developed rockets for Germany during World War II, later working for Switzerland, Italy, and the United States.

a liquid-propellant rocket (see ROCKETS AND MISSILES). He wrote *Die Rakete zu den Planetenräumen* (The Rocket into Planetary Space, 1923); it was only 92 pages long, but it explored all the major problems of human space travel. A 423-page version, *Wege zur Raumschiffahrt* (The Road to Space Travel, 1929), was accepted as his doctoral dissertation and received international acclaim. Oberth worked for the German army during World War II. Following the war he worked briefly for the U.S. Army under Wernher von Braun (a former student), but he returned to Germany in 1958.

obesity   Obesity, the excessive accumulation of body fat, is one of the most common metabolic problems. Public-health sources estimate that 40–50% of the population of the United States is obese. The principal cause of obesity is overeating, the intake of food in excess of the body's requirements. Obesity of significance can be generally defined as a body weight 20% above ideal weight for a given population.

Determination. The degree of obesity is usually determined by measuring the individual's height and referring to the standard height and weight tables assembled by the Metropolitan Life Insurance Company. There are fallacies in this system, however. For example, a football player who has a marked increase in musculature and normal carcass fat, and a person with fluid buildup in the tissues (see EDEMA) due to heart problems, may appear obese when measured by this standard when in actuality they are not. A more definitive method of measuring obesity is caliper measurement of skinfold thickness in such areas as the subscapular region or the triceps. A thickness of more than 23 mm (0.92 in) in males and 30 mm (1.2 in) in females constitutes obesity in persons 30 to 50 years of age.

Types. Two broad clinical types of obesity have been recognized. Persons with lifelong obesity tend to be grossly overweight, with the body fat distributed uniformly. The prognosis for these persons to return to normal body weight is not favorable. A second type is adult-onset obesity, comprising persons with obesity after age 20. This group is characterized by "middle-age spread," with distribution of body fat often centralized. With proper diet and adequate exercise these persons are more likely to achieve normal body weight.

Causes. Both genetic and environmental factors play a role in obesity. The juvenile obese patient has an increased number of fat cells, or lipocytes, which are probably genetically determined. Human studies have indicated that if both parents are obese, more than 80% of the offspring are obese. Furthermore, in most cases, individuals who are obese tend to return to the pre-weight-loss level even after successful reduction.

Endocrine-gland dysfunctions such as DIABETES mellitus and lesions of the hypothalamus can result in obesity, although rarely. Undoubtedly, most obesity is simple exogenous obesity, that is, too much consumption of food.

Complications. Insurance statistics have shown that there is an increased mortality rate with increased obesity.

Obesity has been associated with hypertension, diabetes, abnormalities in pulmonary function, and heart problems, and a 1990 report on weight and health in women indicated that being even mildly overweight increases the risk of heart attacks. Obesity may also cause psychological and emotional harm.

Treatment. The most effective treatment of obesity seems to be modification of dietary and exercise habits whereby total caloric intake is reduced and exercising is increased (see DIETING). Other methods include thyroid extracts, appetite suppressants, behavioral approaches, and psychotherapy. Surgical techniques such as intestinal bypass—that is, operations designed to decrease gastrointestinal absorption of food—are sometimes performed on grossly obese persons.

Obie Awards [oh'-bee]   Obie Awards, sponsored by the *Village Voice*, have been given annually since 1956 to outstanding artists in Off-Broadway theater. Award areas include playwriting, production, acting, and special achievement. Award winners are chosen by *Voice* critics and selected New York guest panelists.

oboe   The oboe is a soprano-range, double-reed woodwind instrument. About 0.5 m (2 ft) long, its wooden tube has a conical bore flaring at the end into a bell. Although the modern oboe's range extends from B-flat below middle C to the A nearly three octaves higher, its finest register sounds between D above middle C and the D two octaves above, where its pungent and penetrating quality pervades in all dynamics.

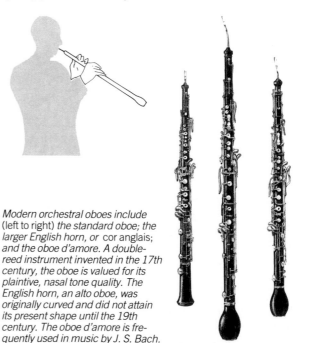

Modern orchestral oboes include (left to right) *the standard oboe; the larger English horn, or* cor anglais; *and the oboe d'amore. A double-reed instrument invented in the 17th century, the oboe is valued for its plaintive, nasal tone quality. The English horn, an alto oboe, was originally curved and did not attain its present shape until the 19th century. The oboe d'amore is frequently used in music by J. S. Bach.*

The immediate ancestor of the oboe was the loud, piercing treble SHAWM, an outdoor instrument. In order to satisfy the baroque need for refined expression, Jean Hotteterre, a French instrument maker and woodwind performer, created (c.1657) the oboe (French *hautbois*, "high wood[wind]"), probably with the assistance in reed making of Michel Philidor. The most important change was the abandonment of the shawm's lip rest. Attached to a staple, a longer, narrower reed could be held further forward where, controlled between the lips, a beautiful tone could be produced, with wide dynamic range.

This was the instrument used by Bach so effectively, particularly for obligatos to vocal solos. Only the necessity for more chromatic flexibility forced changes in the sweet-toned baroque instrument. By the time Beethoven had written his Ninth Symphony (1824), Joseph Sellner had produced his versatile 13-keyed oboe. The present German-style oboe, with its comparatively wider upper bore and its warm and sensuous tone, is essentially Sellner's oboe with mechanical improvements.

The French oboe, developed by the Triebert family between 1810 and 1878, now predominates in Western music, except in Vienna and some Viennese-influenced areas.

See also: BASSOON; ENGLISH HORN.

Obote, Milton [oh-boh'-tay] A political leader of Uganda, Apollo Milton Obote, b. Dec. 28, 1924, formed the Uganda People's Congress in 1957 and in 1962 became prime minister of newly independent Uganda. He sought to develop a centralized state but was thwarted by the existence within Uganda of the autonomous kingdom of Buganda. Obote suppressed Buganda in 1966, driving its king (kabaka) into exile, and assumed the presidency. In 1971, Obote was ousted in a coup led by Idi AMIN DADA. Invading Tanzanian forces and Ugandan exiles overthrew Amin in 1979. Obote was reelected president in December 1980 but was again overthrown in a military coup in July 1985.

Obrecht, Jacob [oh'-brekt] One of the leading composers of the Early Renaissance, the Dutchman Jacob Obrecht, c.1451–1505, was Josquin des Préz's greatest contemporary. An ordained priest, he wrote mostly sacred music: about two dozen masses and an equal number of motets. Most of the masses are based on a cantus firmus, either a plainsong melody or a secular song. He also wrote chansons, although the majority of his secular pieces have Dutch texts or titles.

Obregón, Álvaro [oh-bray-gohn'] A Mexican general, Álvaro Obregón, b. Feb. 19, 1880, d. July 17, 1928, served as president of Mexico in the early 1920s, bringing order to the country after a decade of political chaos. He was born into a working-class family and became a supporter of Francisco MADERO in the Revolution of 1910. He then joined Venustiano CARRANZA in the fight (1913–

Álvaro Obregón, a Mexican general, led the forces of Venustiano Carranza to victory in overthrowing Victoriano Huerta and then defeating Pancho Villa and Emiliano Zapata. Obregón deposed Carranza in 1920 and served as president until 1924.

14) against Victoriano HUERTA and eventually became the most powerful general in the Carranza camp. Obregón later defeated the forces of Pancho VILLA, thereby enabling Carranza to become president (1915).

For the next five years Obregón, who opposed Carranza's conservative policies, devoted himself to assembling a progressive alliance of the military and agrarian and labor organizations. This alliance overthrew Carranza in May 1920. Elected president on Dec. 1, 1920, Obregón effected a number of agrarian and labor reforms, and after leaving office in 1924 he remained an important political force. He was reelected president in 1928 but was assassinated before he could take office.

O'Brien, Edna An Irish writer who is banned in Ireland and now lives in London, Edna O'Brien, b. Dec. 15, 1932, has written novels, short stories, and plays centering on various aspects of the condition of women, particularly Irish Catholic women. Her first novel, *The Country Girls* (1960), began a trilogy that followed two Irish girls from their adolescent dreams of romance to disenchantment in marriage; the third volume was ironically titled

Edna O'Brien's novels, short stories, and plays are despairing comments on the spiritual and emotional solitude of women in a male-dominated society.

Girls in Their Married Bliss (1962). The second volume, *The Lonely Girl* (1962), was filmed as *The Girl with Green Eyes* (1964) from O'Brien's screenplay. Her later work, such as *August Is a Wicked Month* (1965), *Night* (1972), and the short-story collections *Mrs. Reinhardt and Other Stories* (1978) and *A Fanatic Heart* (1984), demonstrates a growing technical mastery along with an increasingly despairing view of the probabilities for happiness in women's lives.

O'Brien, Parry   Track-and-field star William Parry O'Brien, b. Santa Monica, Calif., Jan. 28, 1932, dominated the shot-put event during the 1950s. The first man to break (1954) the 18.3-m (60-ft) barrier, O'Brien held the world record several times, won two Olympic gold medals (1952, 1956), and was the 1959 Sullivan Award winner—as the finest U.S. amateur athlete.

obscenity   see PORNOGRAPHY

observatory, astronomical   An astronomical observatory is a scientific institution specially equipped for making observations of celestial objects. Among its most important instruments are the telescope (see TELESCOPE, OPTICAL), the PHOTOMETER, the spectrograph, and the photographic plate. The classic picture of an astronomical observatory as one or more large, white-domed buildings atop a remote mountain peak is at best incomplete. Astronomical observations are also made at radio observatories, which are seldom located on mountaintops. Observations are now made from high-altitude SOUNDING ROCKETS, BALLOONS, jet planes, artificial SATELLITES, and space probes.

Optical Observatories.   In the broadest sense of the term, astronomical observatories may have been in use in the 2d millennium BC, when STONEHENGE and other STONE ALIGNMENTS and stone circles may have been used to predict eclipses (see ARCHAEOASTRONOMY). The most important pretelescopic observatory was that of the Danish nobleman Tycho BRAHE, who established Uraniborg Observatory. His large instruments provided positional accuracies of better than 1 minute of ARC, enabling his student Johannes KEPLER to establish KEPLER'S LAWS.

Galileo's discoveries in 1609 with his handmade telescopes stimulated the construction of optical observatories. The PARIS OBSERVATORY was completed in 1672, the ROYAL GREENWICH OBSERVATORY began operation in 1676. In Russia, the Imperial Observatory of Pulkovo was opened in 1839.

In the 1880s and 1890s two major observatories were constructed in the United States—the LICK OBSERVATORY on Mount Hamilton, Calif., and the YERKES OBSERVATORY at Williams Bay, Wis. The Lick arrangement—a mountain observatory in an excellent climate operated by full-time professional astronomers—was so successful that it was repeated by the many subsequent large optical observatories. The first of these was the MOUNT WILSON OBSERVATORY with its 60-in (1.5-m) reflector, to which was added a 100-in (2.5-m) reflector in 1918. Its success justified,

The Palomar Observatory, located northeast of San Diego, Calif., at an elevation of 1,706 m (5,597 ft), houses the 200-in (5-m) Hale reflector, the second largest optical telescope in the world.

in turn, the building of the 200-in (5-m) Hale reflector at the PALOMAR OBSERVATORY, also in southern California, which was dedicated in 1948.

After World War II astronomers began to address the problem of the lack of telescopes in the Southern Hemisphere. In the 1970s, three large international observatories were built on the north central Chilean peaks of Cerro Tololo, La Silla, and Las Campanas (see CERRO TOLOLO INTER-AMERICAN OBSERVATORY; EUROPEAN SOUTHERN OBSERVATORY; LAS CAMPANAS OBSERVATORY), and the 153-in (3.9-m) Anglo-Australian Telescope at Siding Springs Observatory, Australia, was completed.

Large optical telescopes are usually put on high mountaintops in order to be free of lower cloud and dust layers and much of the atmospheric turbulence. A dry, cloudless, stable atmosphere is essential for optimum performance. The Andes mountains area about 500 to 650 km (300 to 400 mi) north of Santiago, Chile, inland from the city of La Serena, has been found to be one of the best observatory sites in the world. A consortium of Western European nations plans to build its Very Large Telescope (VLT) in Chile. The VLT will consist of four 314-in (8-m) telescopes that can operate in tandem to produce the resolution of a single 630-in (16-m) telescope. The VLT should be operable by the late 1990s. The 4,205-m (13,796-ft) summit area of Mauna Kea in Hawaii (see MAUNA KEA OBSERVATORY) is another prime site for recent and future telescope placements. The Keck Observatory, for example, was completed there in 1991. It houses the largest optical telescope in the world, employing a novel, segmented reflecting mirror.

The day-to-day operation of an optical observatory,

and its accessibility to researchers, varies with the location, the kinds of specialized instruments available, and the demand for using the instruments.

Radio Observatories. The second great stimulus to observatory building was initiated when astronomical observations were extended beyond the region of visible light seen by normal telescopes. This era began in 1931 with Karl JANSKY's discovery at Holmdel, N.J., of radio waves coming from a region in Sagittarius, marking the beginning of RADIO ASTRONOMY. An electrical engineer in Wheaton, Ill., Grote REBER, built a 31.5-ft (9.6-m) parabolic dish. With this backyard radio telescope, Reber proceeded to map the radio Milky Way. During World War II electronic techniques for detecting and analyzing radio waves were developed rapidly; many radio observatories were built, starting in the late 1940s. Although effective efforts are being made by Australian radio astronomers, most of the facilities are in the Northern Hemisphere.

Radio telescopes and radio observatories are a more heterogeneous group than their optical counterparts, and radio observations can usually be made day or night and in any weather. Radio observatories are often located in remote valleys, free from local radio and electrical interference. Some of these radio telescopes are very large. Examples include the Very Large Array (VLA) in New Mexico (see NATIONAL RADIO ASTRONOMY OBSERVATORY); the 305-m (1,000-ft) ARECIBO OBSERVATORY dish; the 5-km (3-mi) telescope at the MULLARD RADIO ASTRONOMY OBSERVATORY (MRAO) near Cambridge, England; and a Very Large Baseline Interferometer (VLBI) at England's NUFFIELD RADIO ASTRONOMY LABORATORIES. A continent-size Very Long Baseline Array (VLBA), consisting of 10 dishes ranging across the United States, is under construction; astronomers have experimented with a world-spanning 12,900-

The Pic du Midi Observatory, established in 1882 in the French Pyrenees at an altitude of 2,862 m (9,390 ft), was one of the first high-altitude astronomical observatories.

km (8,000-mi) VLBA and also proposed a VLBA incorporating space-based radio telescopes.

Space Observatories. Observations from the Earth's surface are impossible at wavelengths shorter than the ultraviolet because of atmospheric absorption. The third great stimulus to observatory building came after World War II with the advent of rockets that made it possible to put astronomical instrumentation above the atmosphere. Widely varying types of space observatories have been sent into orbit around the Earth or the Sun or launched toward other planets. These include the U.S. Orbiting Astronomical Observatory, Orbiting Geophysical Observatory, and Orbiting Solar Observatory programs (see OAO; OGO; OSO); entries in the EXPLORER series, such as IMP and UHURU; and planetary probes of the LUNAR ORBITER, MARINER, and VOYAGER programs. Similar Soviet series include COSMOS, LUNA, MARS, VENERA, and ZOND. Space observatories designed to operate in a particular region of the spectrum include the HIGH ENERGY ASTRONOMY OBSERVATORY (HEAO) satellites; the International Ultraviolet Explorer; the Infrared Astronomy Satellite (see IRAS; INFRARED ASTRONOMY); and *Exosat*, a European X-ray satellite. The SPACE TELESCOPE was orbited by the Space Shuttle in May 1990.

obsessive-compulsive disorder   Persons with obsessive-compulsive disorder manifest recurrent obsessive thoughts or compulsive behaviors. Obsessive thoughts are ideas, images, or impulses—often relating to violence or contamination—that are experienced as intrusive and senseless. Compulsions are repetitive, intentional behaviors that are performed in a stereotyped manner. Handwashing and counting are frequently occurring examples. Attempts to resist a compulsion often result in a mounting tension that is quickly relieved by engaging in the compulsive behavior. DEPRESSION and ANXIETY are common among sufferers. Many approaches are used to treat the disorder, including BEHAVIOR MODIFICATION and DRUG therapy (see PSYCHOPATHOLOGY).

The disorder occurs equally often in both sexes. Although it generally begins in adolescence or early adulthood, onset may occur in childhood. The illness is usually chronic, with symptoms fluctuating in intensity. Impairment is often moderate to severe, and sufferers with the most extreme cases allow the compulsion to become their dominant activity. The disorder was once considered rare, but recent research suggests that milder forms, such as perfectionism, may be more common.

obsidian [uhb-sid'-ee-uhn]   Obsidian, a volcanic glass, usually of rhyolitic composition, forms by rapid cooling of a viscous LAVA. Most obsidians are more than 70 percent silica and are low in volatile contents. Microscopic crystals of quartz or feldspar are sometimes included in the glass. Obsidian occurs as thick, short flows or domes over volcanic vents. It is usually black in color but occasionally red or brown (if iron-oxide dust is present), clear, or green (see IGNEOUS ROCK).

Obsidian displays a well-developed conchoidal frac-

Obsidian is a compact, glassy volcanic rock that results from such rapid cooling of molten lava that the quartz and feldspar minerals composing it do not crystallize out. Most obsidian is jet black, but it may be clear, red, brown, or green.

ture, which makes it an excellent material for arrowheads, knives, and other sharp tools and weapons. Archaeologists rely on obsidian tools in tracing trade routes, because such tools are relatively rare and each occurrence has a slightly different chemical composition. Thus the source of primitive obsidian tools may be located even if the tools have been traded across thousands of kilometers. Obsidian has also been used as a semiprecious gem because of its shiny luster.

Perlite, a hydrous form of obsidian, is used as a lightweight aggregate. When heated it expands into an artificial pumicelike material. Its potential expansion after transport is a major shipping advantage.

The rounded nodules of obsidian left after hydration and alteration of surrounding material into perlite are known as Apache tears. Looking like black teardrops, they are collector's items in the American Southwest.

obstetrics

obstetrics Obstetrics is the medical specialty that provides care for women during pregnancy, labor, and the first few weeks after childbirth (the puerperium). It is common for obstetricians also to be certified as gynecologists in order to provide comprehensive care for problems involving the reproductive systems of women before, during, and after pregnancy.

Although childbirth is most commonly without complication, an obstetrician is equipped through training and experience to handle difficult situations and to respond to emergencies that occasionally arise. Before delivery an obstetrician will often attempt by external manipulation to rotate the fetus into a head-downward position. This action will avoid the difficulties associated with a breech presentation (buttocks born first) or a transverse presentation (the fetus lying crosswise in the uterus). If this cannot be done, delivery by cesarean section may be required. During labor the obstetrician may have to use obstetrical forceps to assist the passage of the fetus and must be prepared to deal with unusual problems such as premature detachment of the placenta, placenta previa (a condition in which the placenta bleeds due to a low position of implantation), compression of the umbilical cord, or rupture of the uterus. (See also PREGNANCY AND BIRTH.)

O'Casey, Sean

O'Casey, Sean Sean O'Casey, b. Mar. 30, 1880, d. Sept. 18, 1964, was an important 20th-century dramatist and a major contributor to the IRISH LITERARY RENAISSANCE. Active in the Irish language and Irish labor movements, he also wrote the constitution of the Irish Citizen Army. Something of a cantankerous idealist, however, he had largely withdrawn from social involvement by the time of the Easter Rising (1916).

The first plays by O'Casey to be produced at the ABBEY THEATRE—*The Shadow of a Gunman* (1923) and *Juno and the Paycock* (1924)—proved instantly successful because of their droll comedy, moving pathos, and vivid recreation of slum life. His masterly *The Plough and the Stars* (1926), however, provoked several nights of riots in the theater with its allegedly unpatriotic portrayal of the events of 1916. Although it later became one of the most popular of all Irish plays, its initial reception caused O'Casey to move to England.

O'Casey's break with Ireland was followed by a break with the Abbey Theatre, occasioned by W. B. Yeats's rejection of his semiexpressionistic play about World War I, *The Silver Tassie* (1928). That play, rarely staged during O'Casey's lifetime, became highly regarded following posthumous productions in London and Dublin. O'Casey's middle period was, nevertheless, a time of uneven experimentation, and such plays as *Within the Gates* (1933), *The Star Turns Red* (1940), and *Red Roses for Me* (1942) failed to hold audiences. O'Casey then turned to writing a six-volume autobiography, of which *I Knock at the Door* (1939), *Pictures in the Hallway* (1942), *Drums under the Window* (1946), and *Inishfallen, Fare Thee Well* (1949) are particularly successful in their exuberant and eloquent prose.

In his later years O'Casey developed a new dramatic genre, the comic pastoral, to replace the tragicomedy of

Sean O'Casey, here photographed with his daughter, became a leading figure in the Irish Literary Renaissance with the Abbey Theatre productions of his tragicomedies Juno and the Paycock *(1924) and* The Plough and the Stars *(1926).*

his early plays. The best of these late plays—*Purple Dust* (1940), *Cock-a-Doodle Dandy* (1949), *Time to Go* (1951), and *The Drums of Father Ned* (1959)—evince a delight in language, a fertility of comic invention, and a fantastic theatricality. O'Casey's astringent dramatic criticism and essays appear in *The Green Crow* (1956), *Feathers from the Green Crow* (1962), and *Blasts and Benedictions* (1967).

Occam, William of   see WILLIAM OF OCCAM

—

Occam's razor [ahk'-uhmz]

Occam's razor is a logical principle attributed to WILLIAM OF OCCAM, although it was used by some scholastic philosophers prior to him. The principle states that a person should not increase, beyond what is necessary, the number of entities required to explain anything, or that the person should not make more assumptions than the minimum needed. This principle is often called the principle of parsimony. Since the Middle Ages it has played an important role in eliminating fictitious or unnecessary elements from explanations. In the development of logic, logicians such as Bertrand RUSSELL removed traditional metaphysical concepts by applying Occam's razor. Questions have been raised, however, as to whether a person can determine without any doubt that given entities or assumptions are not needed in an explanation. Unless this determination can be made, it is impossible to tell with complete certainty when the principle can be applied.

Occleve, Thomas   see HOCCLEVE, THOMAS

occupational diseases   see DISEASES, OCCUPATIONAL

—

Occupational Safety and Health Administration

The Occupational Safety and Health Administration (OSHA) was established by the U.S. Congress in the Occupational Safety and Health Act of 1970 "to assure so far as possible every working man and woman in the nation safe and healthful working conditions." The act covers every employer whose business affects interstate commerce. Because it is an agency of the Department of Labor, OSHA is administered by an assistant secretary of labor.

OSHA cooperates with the National Institute of Occupational Safety and Health (NIOSH), which carries out the research necessary to establish basic safety standards. OSHA inspectors carry out frequent, surprise inspections of workplaces to see that standards are maintained. Charges brought by OSHA are adjudicated by the Occupational Safety and Health Review Commission, and violators are obliged to pay fines. Among OSHA safety regulations are standards on worker exposure to acrylonitrile, cotton dust, asbestos, noise, toxic chemicals, lead, and pesticides.

—

occupational therapy

Occupational therapy, a subdiscipline of REHABILITATION MEDICINE, is the field of health care that utilizes various types of work to assist the physically or emotionally disabled in recovering competence. As a professional discipline occupational therapy has existed only since World War I. The use of therapeutic activities for the sick has a long history, however; it has long been known that recovery from illness is speeded if the convalescent is involved in some form of work.

In the late 19th century the use of recreational work as a tool for treating mental patients was first systematized. During World War I, varieties of occupational therapy came to be used for the wounded. Schools of occupational therapy were established during this time, and the first American professional association, the National Society for the Promotion of Occupational Therapy (now the American Occupational Therapy Association), was formed in 1925.

As in the related field of PHYSICAL THERAPY, occupational therapy is used to restore or to increase muscle strength and motor ability—although it employs tools and materials rather than mechanical exercise aids   and to train or to retrain handicapped people. For patients who have been hospitalized for long periods of time, this type of therapy serves not only as a means of restoring basic physical skills but also as a way of reestablishing contact with the world outside the hospital. For the elderly and those who are chronically disabled, the relearning of such elementary skills as handling a knife and fork or dressing is essential to eventual rehabilitation.

Numerous educational programs leading to a degree in occupational therapy have been accredited.

—

ocean-atmosphere interaction

The transfer of energy and matter between the oceans (see OCEAN AND SEA) and the ATMOSPHERE represents a major link between the weather and the ocean structure and circulation. The oceans and the atmosphere have substantially different characteristics, including different densities and heat capacities. The oceans are also dissimilar to land and ice, the other major interfaces with the atmosphere. Sunlight can penetrate the ocean to substantial depths (up to about 200 m/660 ft), and there is continuous movement, with currents transporting seawater both vertically and horizontally.

Exchange of Energy and Matter

The oceans are massive reservoirs of heat energy because of their large heat capacities relative to the atmosphere, their ability to mix, and their transparency to solar radiation. Whereas the atmosphere can, and often does, undergo large daily and seasonal temperature fluctuations, the sizes and rates of temperature changes in the oceans are much smaller because of their large thermal inertia. The oceans thus moderate short- and long-term climate changes. Exchange of heat and momentum between oceans and atmosphere also drives the deep ocean currents.

The exchange of heat between the atmosphere and the oceans is controlled by their relative temperatures. The water in an ocean colder than the atmosphere cools the air above it, forming a layer of relatively heavy, stable air that limits further exchange. The water in an ocean warmer than the atmosphere heats the air above, which rises, transferring heat from ocean to atmosphere. Because ocean temperature lags behind atmospheric temperature, the oceans have a seasonal effect on climate. In winter at middle and high latitudes the oceans are generally warmer than the atmosphere, and warm air rising from the surface may produce cumulus clouds and heavy precipitation. In summer at these latitudes the water is cooler than the air, a situation that can lead to persistent, low-lying fogs in land areas near the ocean.

The location of warm and cold pools of surface ocean water may also influence the location, movement, and intensity of storm systems in the atmosphere. The effects of such processes can be widespread. One such phenomenon, in particular, known as the EL NIÑO–Southern Oscillation, is initiated by a period in which unusually warm waters form off the equatorial coast of South America.

The oceans are also a reservoir of atmospheric constituents. Water vapor enters the atmosphere from the ocean interface through evaporation, both directly from the surface and from water bubbles ejected into the air after waves break in strong winds and along coasts. Liquid water is returned to the oceans primarily in the form of rain or snow falling on the water, and also by rivers.

The oceans absorb various gases from the atmosphere, including oxygen, nitrogen, and carbon dioxide. About half of the carbon dioxide produced by such human activities as combustion of fossil fuels and deforestation is dissolved in the ocean, which thus moderates the global warming that might result from a buildup of this gas (see GREENHOUSE EFFECT).

Ocean Currents and Waves

The oceans have a large inertia, or resistance, to changes in motion. Thus, only winds blowing over the water for long distances and periods of time are capable of generating the OCEAN CURRENTS that transport water from one location to another. The Gulf Stream and the Kuroshio Current, for example, are intense, warm currents driven by winds associated with the large high-pressure systems characteristic of the central parts of the Atlantic and Pacific. Along the eastern sides of the oceans the equatorward winds generated by these highs act to force the surface water offshore, to be replaced with colder, deeper ocean water in a process called upwelling (see UPWELLING, OCEANIC).

The wind also generates ocean waves, the size of which depends on the strength and fetch (the distance over which the waves are generated) of the wind, the depth of the water, and the length of time during which the wind has blown. WATER WAVES form when the wind exerts a shearing stress on the sea surface. Variations in wind speed cause pressure differences to develop, allowing some areas of water to rise higher than others. As the wind continues to blow, the differences in pressure between the trough and crest of the waves cause them to grow. After the wind speed decreases, waves subside, as their energy of motion is dissipated quickly along shore-

lines or lost slowly by internal friction. Waves that propagate beyond their region of formation are referred to as swells. During hurricane landfalls, the lower pressure of the storm, its wind circulation, and submarine topography combine to create a storm surge, inundating coastal areas under as much as 6 m (20 ft) of water.

---

ocean currents   The large-scale and permanent currents within the major ocean basins may be divided into those currents produced directly or indirectly by surface WIND stress and those produced by thermohaline convection (that is, by density differences resulting from temperature and salinity differences). The latter are mainly associated with the cooling and sinking of surface waters in high latitudes. The ultimate source of energy responsible for driving oceanic currents is solar radiation, and the major currents are a direct manifestation of the thermodynamics of the combined ocean and ATMOSPHERE system (see OCEAN-ATMOSPHERE INTERACTION). Both the wind-driven and thermohaline circulations depend in large measure on the circulation of the atmosphere; most of the heat energy required to drive the circulation in the atmosphere is, in turn, supplied to the atmosphere by the ocean.

Wind-Driven Circulation

Currents in the upper part of the water column, in almost all cases above a depth of 100 m (300 ft), are primarily wind-driven. They are affected by the horizontal circulation patterns in the atmosphere, by enclosing landmasses, and by the CORIOLIS EFFECT, which tends to accelerate flow to the right of its direction in the Northern Hemisphere and to the left in the Southern Hemisphere.

Idealized Three-Gyre Circulation. The wind-driven circulation patterns in all of the major ocean basins—the North and South Atlantic, the North and South Pacific, and the South Indian Ocean—have a number of features in common. Except for the Indian Ocean, considerable symmetry exists between circulation patterns in the Northern and Southern hemispheres for a given ocean. In high latitudes a cyclonic (in the same direction as the Earth's rotation—counterclockwise in the Northern Hemisphere) subpolar gyre is typically situated roughly from about 50° to 65°. In southern oceans this gyre is re-

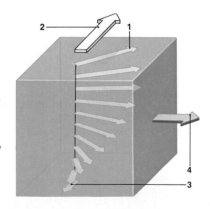

The Coriolis effect causes the surface flow (1) of an ocean current to be at an angle to the wind direction (2). Each subsequent lower water layer moves slower than the one above it and at an angle to it. At a certain depth, the flow is nearly zero and opposite to the wind direction (3). The resultant water flow is at right angles to the wind (4).

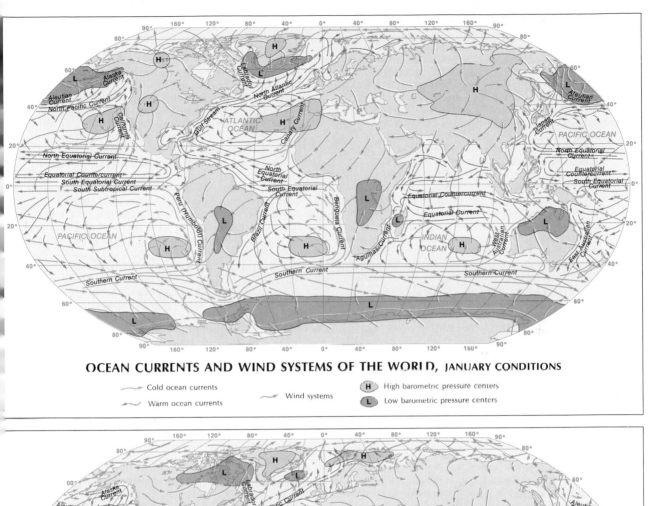

OCEAN CURRENTS AND WIND SYSTEMS OF THE WORLD, JANUARY CONDITIONS

⌒→ Cold ocean currents   ⌒→ Wind systems   (H) High barometric pressure centers

⌒→ Warm ocean currents   (L) Low barometric pressure centers

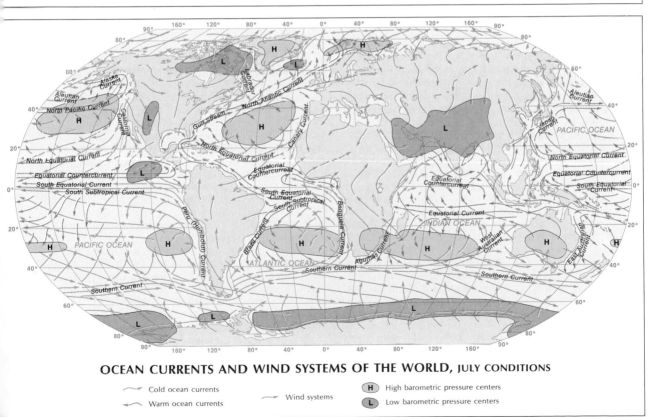

OCEAN CURRENTS AND WIND SYSTEMS OF THE WORLD, JULY CONDITIONS

⌒→ Cold ocean currents   ⌒→ Wind systems   (H) High barometric pressure centers

⌒→ Warm ocean currents   (L) Low barometric pressure centers

placed by the Antarctic Circumpolar Current, which flows without interruption around the Antarctic continent. In mid-latitudes, typically from about 15° to 50°, a major anticyclonic subtropical gyre occupies much of the ocean basin. In low latitudes a poorly defined cyclonic gyre may occur between the equator and about 15°. The basic features of each gyre are a zonal (east-west) current to the north and south, an intense and narrow western boundary current, and a broad and diffuse meridional (north-south) drift current occupying much of the central and eastern part of the gyre.

These features are either directly or indirectly produced by winds. To a very rough approximation, winds are zonal and symmetrical about the equator. In reality, winds do have a meridional component; they are not symmetrical about the equator but displaced a few degrees to the north. Weak polar easterlies—winds are labeled according to the direction from which they blow—occur in latitudes above approximately 60°. Strong westerlies, or roaring forties, prevail between approximately 30° and 60°. The trade winds (easterlies) are at their maximum strength at about 15°. Within the doldrums region in the vicinity of the equator are weak easterlies. These are all prevailing winds, but only the trades are steady. Seasonal changes and the associated monsoon winds are important near Asia.

To understand how these winds produce the current patterns described, consider the effects of the strong westerlies between 30° and 60° N latitude. These winds tend to move surface waters toward the east, but the Coriolis effect produces an acceleration to the right, that is, toward the south. The surface water, in turn, exerts a stress on, and thus produces motion in, the water immediately below it. Because of the Coriolis effect, this subsurface motion is deflected even farther to the right of the wind—a deflection that increases with depth. The magnitude of the deflection also depends on the latitude and on the speed of the water particles. Ideally, the resulting current structure describes a so-called Ekman spiral: that is, the currents at the very surface are deflected 45° to the right of the wind, the current magnitude decreases exponentially with depth, and the current deflection to the right of the wind increases linearly with depth. The net transport is directed 90° to the right of the wind (in this example of westerly winds, due south).

Between approximately 15° and 50° N latitude the surface Ekman transport converges; that is, the trade winds produce a surface transport to the north, and the westerlies centered on about 50° produce a surface transport to the south. The magnitude of the Ekman convergence depends on the rate of change of zonal wind stress with latitude.

Observed Surface-Current Patterns. Many of the features of the observed surface-current patterns fit within the idealized three-gyre circulation. Within each major ocean basin occurs a subtropical gyre, and within each subtropical gyre at least some evidence indicates a western boundary current flowing poleward. These include the Florida Current and the GULF STREAM, forming the Gulf Stream System; the Kuroshio, or Japan Current, in the

North Pacific; the Brazil Current in the South Pacific; the East Australian Current in the Southwest Pacific; and the Agulhas Current in the South Indian Ocean.

Subtropical gyres are bounded at high latitudes by a zonal, eastward-flowing current. These include the North Atlantic Current and the North Pacific Current in the Northern Hemisphere, and the Antarctic Circumpolar Current in the Southern Hemisphere. Subtropical gyres are bounded at low latitudes by a zonal, westward-flowing equatorial current.

The cold, western-boundary currents flowing toward the equator may be identified with circulation in a cyclonic subpolar gyre. They include the East Greenland Current and the Labrador Current in the North Atlantic, the Oyashio in the North Pacific, and the Falkland Current in the South Atlantic.

The equatorial current system in the Atlantic, although complicated, does exhibit westward-flowing North and South Equatorial Currents and an eastward-flowing Equatorial Countercurrent in the vicinity of the equator. A similar situation exists in the Indian Ocean during the period of northeast trade winds from November through March. This pattern is expected for an anticyclonic gyre north and south of the equator, as discussed earlier; the countercurrent would be positioned in the vicinity of the doldrums. Currents in the equatorial Pacific are more complicated because of details of the variation in the trade winds with latitude near the equator. They consist of westward-flowing North and South Equatorial Currents, eastward-flowing North and South Equatorial Countercurrents, and a westward-flowing Equatorial Current positioned near the equator. In addition, evidence indicates an eastward-flowing Equatorial Undercurrent in all three oceans centered on the equator. In the Pacific this current is called the Cromwell Current. Centered at a depth of about 100 m (300 ft), it is about 200 m (700 ft) thick and 300 km (200 mi) wide.

The Antarctic, or Southern, Ocean that surrounds the Antarctic continent is unique in that it has no meridional boundaries. Circulation consists primarily of continuous zonal currents around the continent. In a narrow zone (between 65° S and 70° S) surrounding the continent is a westward-flowing East Wind Drift maintained by easterly winds near the coast. From about 75° S to 45° S is the eastward-flowing Antarctic Circumpolar Current maintained by the westerly winds. The associated surface currents are called the West Wind Drift.

Besides these major currents, major eastern-boundary currents that flow equatorward and that are primarily the result of meridional winds often occur. These include the Peru (Humboldt) Current, the California Current, and the Benguela Current and Canaries Current along the west coast of Africa. They do not compare in intensity to the major western-boundary currents. The seasonal EL NIÑO current, which flows southward off the coast of Peru, can have a widespread, often devastating effect on climate patterns.

Thermohaline Circulation

Much of the circulation at depths greater than 1,000 m

(3,000 ft) is associated with thermohaline effects, whereby water cooled at high latitudes sinks to great depths (because of a change in density) and then flows horizontally. This deep circulation is not as well described as circulation in the upper layers. Two major sources apparently produce this deep flow. One source close to the Antarctic continent is the Weddell Sea, where the heaviest waters in the ocean are formed (Antarctic Bottom Water) during winter by cooling and by freezing out of ice, causing increased salinity. The other source is in the North Atlantic Ocean around Greenland; winter cooling and evaporation produce North Atlantic Deep Water. In the geological past, however, different conditions may have led to a reverse deep flow from warmer to cooler regions.

The volume transports associated with thermohaline circulation are apparently comparable to those in the upper layer. Much of the flow may occur in relatively narrow boundary currents along the western sides of the ocean basins. The sinking of the deep water is quite localized in high latitudes. It apparently flows horizontally and then rises very slowly over broad low- and middle-latitude areas. The thermohaline circulation appears to be extremely important in the maintenance of the ocean's vertical negative temperature gradient. Periodically, deep-current "benthic storms" stir up and rearrange sediments on the ocean bottom (see SEDIMENT, MARINE).

See also: OCEAN AND SEA.

Ocean Drilling Program

The Ocean Drilling Program (ODP), initiated in 1984, is an international program for drilling, recovering, and studying cores of the Earth's crust from beneath the deep oceans. Funded primarily by the U.S. National Science Foundation, it is managed for a consortium of oceanographic institutions and laboratories by the Scripps Institution of Oceanography in La Jolla, Calif. The ODP is the successor to the 15-year-long DEEP-SEA DRILLING PROJECT (DSDP), which ended in 1983 after obtaining more than 1,000 cores from the world's ocean floors. The ship used by the ODP, the *JOIDES Resolution,* has computerized controls and, unlike its predecessor, the smaller *Glomar Challenger,* is able to drill in the freezing waters around Antarctica. In addition to the United States, the countries taking part in the ODP include Great Britain, France, Germany, Canada, Japan, and a consortium of other European countries.

ocean liner

The ocean liner is an oceangoing passenger vessel that runs on a fixed schedule over a fixed route. (This distinguishes it from a tramp steamer, which will adjust its run to accommodate available business.) The three basic types are the superliner, the express liner, and the passenger-cargo liner.

The superliner was once found on services between Western Europe and the United States. This type of vessel offered the most luxurious passenger accommodations. It had a speed of about 28 knots, accommodation for about 2,000 passengers, and a gross registered tonnage (GRT) of more than 50,000. Superliners included the QUEEN ELIZABETH, *Queen Mary, United States,* and *France,* all of which had been withdrawn from service by 1974.

The express liner existed where mail and express cargo

The City of Paris, *launched in 1888, was one of the first twin-screw ocean liners. Its success foreshadowed the decline of sail-powered luxury liners.*

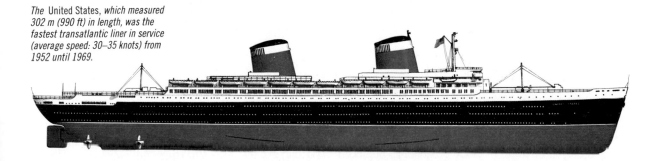

The United States, *which measured 302 m (990 ft) in length, was the fastest transatlantic liner in service (average speed: 30–35 knots) from 1952 until 1969.*

warranted a fast shipping service. Passenger accommodation totaled approximately 1,500 and the speed was up to 25 knots. A typical vessel was the *Southern Cross,* which served the Great Britain–Australasia trade.

The third category was the passenger-cargo combination, which generally operated on routes where cargo, rather than passengers, was the prime consideration. Such services were worldwide, and a typical ship had accommodation for 6,000 tons of general cargo and up to 500 passengers. (Vessels that carry freight only, with no passengers, are called freighters.)

The era of the great ocean liner has virtually ended; this is due primarily to the competition from airlines—which offer faster schedules and, often, lower fares—and the high cost of ship replacement and ship operation.

Today the ocean liner is smaller, with a GRT of about 20,000. It is used almost exclusively in the vacation-cruise trade. Even the *Queen Elizabeth II*—launched in 1969 as a replacement for the original *Queen Elizabeth*—is now a cruise ship and only occasionally plies its original transatlantic route, carrying affluent passengers who yearn for the grand old days.

---

ocean and sea Oceans and seas are the bodies of salt water that cover about 71 percent of the Earth's surface and are referred to in total as the world ocean. Several centuries ago the "seven seas" were considered the navigable oceans, namely the ATLANTIC, PACIFIC, INDIAN, and ARCTIC oceans, the MEDITERRANEAN and CARIBBEAN seas, and the Gulf of Mexico (see MEXICO, GULF OF). At present, however, oceanographers consider all other oceans and seas as belonging to the Atlantic, Pacific, or Indian oceans. The Arctic Ocean, the Mediterranean and Caribbean seas, and the Gulf of Mexico are considered marginal seas of the Atlantic Ocean. These, in turn, have their own marginal bays and seas. Narrow, shallow straits separate the marginal seas from the Atlantic: the Straits of Florida (Gulf of Mexico), the Strait of Gibraltar (Mediterranean; see GIBRALTAR, STRAIT OF), and many gaps between the islands of the Greater and Lesser Antilles for the Caribbean Sea.

The boundaries between the oceans are based on geographic criteria and have little to do with physical water-mass boundaries. The Atlantic is separated from the Indian Ocean by the 20° E meridian, and from the Pacific Ocean by a line extending from Cape Horn at the tip of South America to the South Shetland Islands off the tip of Antarctica in the south and by the narrowest part of the Bering Strait in the north. The dividing line between the Pacific and Indian oceans extends along an arc through the Malay Peninsula, Sumatra, Java, and Timor to Cape Londonderry in Australia, to Tasmania, and then along the 147° E meridian to Antarctica.

Reference is often made to the Antarctic, or Southern, Ocean, which encircles the Antarctic continent and consists of the southernmost sectors of the three principal oceans. In spite of the lack of definitive geographic boundaries, the meteorological and oceanographic conditions in the high southern latitudes combine to produce a well-defined circumpolar current called the West Wind Drift. This current distinguishes the Antarctic Ocean as a physical entity, but the ocean's geographic borders are less easily defined.

Origin

An explanation of the origin of the world's oceans must account for both the great ocean basins as well as the source of the water filling them.

The Water. The primordial ocean must have originated during the Earth's first billion years, because some of the earliest rocks found on Earth show evidence of deposition in a large body of water. The time required to accumulate the volume of water in the present oceans is unknown. The water was released as vapor from the crust and mantle during the cooling of the Earth. Soon afterward, at a remote stage of the Precambrian portion of GEOLOGIC TIME, it attained a volume not drastically different from that of the modern oceans.

The most recent changes in ocean volume have accompanied the ICE AGES during the last two million years. The northern polar ice cap has expanded and contracted with great regularity, and the volume of the oceans has fluctuated correspondingly as water is alternately locked into or released from the ice cap. These fluctuations, however, have accounted for changes in sea level of no more than 200 m (660 ft).

The Basins. The events of formation of the initial ocean basins that held the primordial ocean are unknown, because they have been destroyed by subsequent geologic events. The history of the present ocean basins, however, is well known. All of the continental landmasses as they are now known began to break up about 200 million years ago from two great supercontinents called Gondwanaland and Pangea. As the continents drifted to their present positions, the great ocean basins were left in their wake (see CONTINENTAL DRIFT).

Each ocean basin has evolved in a slightly separate manner, but the overall history of each basin has a similar series of events. The origin of the Atlantic Ocean basin is best known and serves as a good example of the processes involved. About 150 million years ago forces at work beneath the crust of the Earth split the supercontinents into large fragments. One such fragment contained North America joined to Eurasia, and another contained South America joined to Africa. By 135 million years ago North America had separated from Eurasia, leaving a small, restricted ocean basin with no open-ocean circulation. At the same time, the early South Atlantic basin was formed by the separation of South America and Africa. The two parts of the Atlantic were not connected with a pathway for deep circulation until about 65 million years ago, after the South Atlantic had widened to approximately 3,000 km (1,800 mi) and the North Atlantic had widened as a result of a separation between Greenland and Europe. The process continues today as new ocean crust is added by seafloor spreading at the Mid-Atlantic Ridge, widening the Atlantic Ocean.

The same process has formed the Pacific Ocean basin, but the relatively simple pattern outlined for the At-

DIMENSIONS OF THE OCEANS AND MARGINAL SEAS

Body of Water	Area thousands of kilometers²	Area thousands of miles²	Mean Depth meters	Mean Depth feet	Volume thousands of kilometers³	Volume thousands of miles³
Oceans						
Arctic	14,090	5,440	1,205	3,954	17,000	4,100
North Pacific	83,462	32,225	3,858	12,658	322,000	77,200
South Pacific	65,521	25,298	3,891	12,766	254,900	61,150
North Atlantic	46,772	18,059	3,285	10,778	153,600	36,850
South Atlantic	37,364	14,426	4,091	13,423	152,800	36,660
Indian	81,602	31,507	4,284	14,056	349,600	83,870
Antarctic (Southern)	32,249	12,451	3,730	12,238	120,300	28,860
Tributaries to the Arctic Ocean						
Norwegian Sea	1,383	534	1,742	5,716	2,408	578
Greenland Sea	1,205	465	1,444	4,738	1,740	417
Barents Sea	1,405	542	229	751	322	77
White Sea	90	35	89	292	8	2
Kara Sea	883	341	118	387	104	25
Laptev Sea	650	251	519	1,703	338	81
East Siberian Sea	901	348	58	190	53	13
Chukchi Sea	582	225	88	289	51	12
Beaufort Sea	476	184	1,004	3,294	478	115
Baffin Bay	689	266	861	2,825	593	142
Tributaries to the North Atlantic						
North Sea	600	232	91	299	55	13
Baltic Sea	386	149	86	282	33	8
Mediterranean Sea	2,516	971	1,494	4,902	3,758	902
Black Sea	461	178	1,166	3,826	537	129
Caribbean Sea	2,754	1,063	2,491	8,173	6,860	1,646
Gulf of Mexico	1,543	596	1,512	4,961	2,332	559
Gulf of Saint Lawrence	238	92	127	417	30	7
Hudson Bay	1,232	476	128	420	158	38
Tributary to the South Atlantic						
Gulf of Guinea	1,533	592	2,996	9,830	4,592	1,102
Tributaries to the Indian Ocean						
Red Sea	450	174	558	1,831	251	60
Persian Gulf	241	93	40	131	10	2
Arabian Sea	3,863	1,492	2,734	8,970	10,561	2,534
Bay of Bengal	2,172	839	2,586	8,485	5,616	1,347
Andaman Sea	602	232	1,096	3,596	660	158
Great Australian Bight	484	187	950	3,117	459	110
Tributaries to the North Pacific						
Gulf of California	177	68	818	2,684	145	35
Gulf of Alaska	1,327	512	2,431	7,976	3,226	774
Bering Sea	2,304	890	1,598	5,243	3,683	884
Sea of Okhotsk	1,590	614	859	2,818	1,365	327
Sea of Japan	978	378	1,752	5,748	1,713	411
Yellow Sea	417	161	40	131	17	4
East China Sea	752	290	349	1,145	263	63
Sulu Sea	420	162	1,139	3,737	478	115
Celebes Sea	472	182	3,291	10,798	1,553	373
Tributaries to Both the North and South Pacific						
South China Sea	3,685	1,423	1,060	3,478	3,907	937
Makassar Strait	194	75	967	3,173	188	45
Molukka Sea	307	119	1,880	6,168	578	139
Ceram Sea	187	72	1,209	3,967	227	54
Tributaries to the South Pacific						
Java Sea	433	167	46	151	20	5
Bali Sea	119	46	411	1,348	49	12
Flores Sea	121	47	1,829	6,001	222	53
Savu Sea	105	41	1,701	5,581	178	43
Banda Sea	695	268	3,064	10,053	2,129	511
Ceram Sea	187	72	1,209	3,967	227	54
Timor Sea	615	237	406	1,332	250	60
Arafura Sea	1,037	400	197	646	204	49
Coral Sea	4,791	1,850	2,394	7,855	11,470	2,752

Nearly three-fourths of the Earth's surface is covered by water. The Pacific, Atlantic, and Indian oceans account for 90 percent of this water area. The continental margins, or boundaries between the oceans and continents, consist of gently sloping continental shelves, steep continental slopes, and deep, gradually sloping continental rises that join extensive flat abyssal plains at depths of 5,000 to 6,000 m (16,000 to 20,000 ft). The most rugged areas on Earth are found on the abyssal plains and include numerous isolated mountain peaks, or seamounts, deep trenches, and huge mountain ranges. The Pacific Ocean is ringed by trenches. The largest of these are found in the western Pacific, are more than 10,000 m (32,800 ft) in average depth, and are closely associated with island arcs and zones of intense earthquakes. The central Pacific sector is dominated by northwest-directed ridges, or mountainous features, that are topped by

many islands, such as the Hawaiian island chain. Numerous east-west fracture zones dot the eastern region, along with the East Pacific Rise, which is a gently sloping ridge. The Indian Ocean is characterized by extensive abyssal plains and systems of ridges, including the longest straight ridge in the world—the Ninety East Ridge—which is 2,500 km (1,500 mi) long. The Mid-Oceanic Ridge is the longest volcanic mountain-range system on Earth. As the Mid-Atlantic Ridge, it extends for 65,000 km (40,000 mi) from the Arctic through the middle of the Atlantic and south around Africa into the Indian Ocean, where it branches. One branch continues northwest, and another curves southeast between Australia and Antarctica, continuing northward into the Pacific along the East Pacific Rise. In general, the ridges are below water, but they rise above the surface in such places as Iceland and the Azores. Many fractures, or fault zones, run perpendicular to the ridge system.

phytoplankton

flying fish

conger eel

green moray eel

pipefish

shrimps

zooplankton

cow-nosed ray

triggerfish

pearly nautilus

nutrient upwelling

gulper

killer whale

sardines

tuna

thornback ray

squid

viperfish

swallower

tuna

gray shark

scarlet prawns

gulper

mackerel

blackfish

coelacanth

deep-sea angler fish

crinoids

brittle stars

great barracuda

hatchet fish

luminous shark

marlin

Portuguese man-of-war

jellyfish

sperm whale

giant squid

photic zone

mesopelagic zone

bathypelagic zone

benthic zone

lantic Ocean has been complicated by other factors in the Pacific. The Pacific Ocean basin is surrounded by the great marginal trench systems, which are accompanied by volcanic island arcs and violent earthquake activity. These trenches mark the location where great slabs of oceanic crust are being reabsorbed back into the Earth by a process called subduction (see PLATE TECTONICS), which generates the seismic activity along the boundaries of the Pacific RING OF FIRE.

The history of the Indian Ocean basin has not been completely determined. India and Australia separated from Antarctica about 80 million years ago. India slid past Australia about 45 million years ago and rammed into Asia, leaving behind a deep ocean basin that widened in an east-west direction beginning about 35 million years ago. The pattern of seafloor formation, however, in this relatively small ocean basin has also not been completely determined, due to the complexities found there.

Physiography of the Seafloor

The seafloor is shaped into a host of tectonic features that grade from long submarine mountain chains, which are larger than their continental equivalents, to deep trenches that are thousands of times larger than those found on land. The shape of all these physiographic features is related to the origin of the slice of ocean floor on which they are found. The shape of the seafloor, in turn, affects the origin and distribution of some of the great oceanic circulation systems (see OCEAN CURRENTS). These systems play a role in the distribution of the OCEANIC NUTRIENTS that control biogenic productivity in the oceans.

Ridges, Plains, and Trenches. Perhaps the most striking feature on the seafloor is the MID-OCEANIC RIDGE system. Through its branches this system extends across all the major ocean basins, forming islands such as Iceland, the Azores, and the Galápagos Islands in the few places it extends above sea level.

The seafloor continues to deepen away from the crests of the mid-oceanic ridge system out to the extensive, flat abyssal plains, which constitute the largest segment of the seafloor. The depths of the individual plains are roughly uniform—the deepest of them occur in the Pacific Ocean (6,000 m/20,000 ft), and the shallowest occur in the Atlantic Ocean (5,000 m/16,000 ft).

In certain areas, usually at the margins of the ocean basins, the abyssal plains descend into steep OCEANIC TRENCHES, where the greatest depths in the oceans are found. Associated with most of the major trench systems are volcanic island arcs, such as the islands of Japan, that occupy a position on the landward side of the trenches.

Fracture Zones and Seamounts. Superimposed on the

In a marine food chain, energy from sunlight is converted into food by microscopic floating plants (phytoplankton) in the upper layers of the ocean. These support small animals, the zooplankton, and other herbivores. Nektonic, or actively swimming predators consume the zooplankton and small fishes. The sinking of organic debris provides food for inhabitants of the dark, sparsely populated, lower zones (mesopelagic and below). Coastal upwelling returns nutrients, which are released by decomposing organic matter on the bottom, to phytoplankton near the ocean surface.

features of the seafloor previously mentioned are many other smaller-scale, but very important, physiographic features. Segments of the mid-oceanic ridges are commonly offset laterally by parallel, linear fracture zones thousands of kilometers long. These oceanic fracture zones are characterized by ridges and valleys separated by steep rock cliffs that are hundreds to several thousands of meters high. These fracture zones can be traced out into the abyssal plains, where the traces of the cliffs are lost beneath the sediment.

The abyssal plains are also dotted with numerous isolated mountains called SEAMOUNTS, some of which rise above sea level and form islands. Characteristically, these seamounts belong to large groups of such features, which may be randomly dispersed over a large area or arranged in a line.

Continental Shelves, Slopes, and Rises. The margins of all the continents extend seaward as a broad, flat, shallow shelf. These continental shelves dip gently seaward and are mostly less than 200 m (660 ft) below sea level. The continental shelves comprise only a small portion (7.6%) of the seafloor, but their importance is disproportionately great because their shallow depths encourage exploitation of their natural resources.

The shelves abruptly end at the shelf breaks, where the seafloors rapidly descend along the continental slopes to the abyssal depths (see CONTINENTAL SHELF AND SLOPE). At the bases of the continental slopes, which cover about 15.3% of the oceanic area, are the continental rises, which represent a series of sediment slumps from the slopes above that have spilled down onto the deep seafloor or ocean basins. The basins themselves cover about 75.9% of the oceanic area. Only 1.2% of the ocean is more than 6,000 m (19,686 ft) deep.

Importance of the Oceans and Seas

Oceans and seas are now understood to be integral parts of the entire geologic process of continental weathering, runoff, and deposition, followed by either uplift and subaerial exposure or subduction into the depths of the Earth by plate-tectonic processes and seafloor spreading.

The oceans and seas, also known as the HYDROSPHERE, regulate many of the processes that operate on the surface of the Earth. Much of the precipitation that falls upon land areas is derived from oceanic evaporation. The hydrosphere acts as a tremendous heat reservoir, exerting a dominant effect on temperature extremes over large land areas. The movement of ocean currents also moderates the climate in areas where weather extremes might otherwise make life unpleasant (see OCEAN-ATMOSPHERE INTERACTION).

The oceans and seas represent a place of recreation and a storehouse of food, mineral resources, and energy. They provide, in addition, tremendous potential as a means of transportation. The major portion of goods distributed worldwide are shipped by water—the least expensive method of transport, and one that provides a livelihood for many people.

Biological Habitats. As a biological entity the oceans represent a highly productive environment. The chief biological habitats of the ocean can be divided into pelagic (water region) and benthonic (seafloor region) environments. The pelagic zone comprises the neritic zone (down to 200 m/660 ft and over the continental shelf) and the oceanic zone (below 200 m). The neritic and the upper oceanic regions correspond to the photic zone, in which there is enough light for photosynthesis. The benthonic habitat comprises the intertidal zone (between high and low tide), the sublittoral zone (down to 200 m; see LITTORAL ZONE), the bathyal zone (200 to 4,000 m), the abyssal zone (4,000 to 5,000 m/13,000 to 16,000 ft), and the hadal zone (deeper than 5,000 m). The photic zone is the most highly productive area, biologically, containing numerous benthonic, planktonic (free-floating), and nektonic (free-swimming) marine creatures. Below the photic zone the biomass decreases considerably, with the only food source for marine life being the constant rain of organic matter from above. The lack of light and scarcity of food has produced numerous adaptations in DEEP-SEA LIFE, resulting in the bizarre appearance of fish that live at these depths.

Throughout recorded history people have used the ocean as a source of food. But even at present rates of removal, the food-resource potential of the oceans has barely been touched. At present, most countries remove only certain choice species of fish from the ocean (see FISHING INDUSTRY). This practice has led to the depletion of fish populations of these few species, whereas at the same time other species have remained almost untouched. The depletion of fish populations in once-choice fishing grounds has caused considerable international dispute between the governments and fishing fleets of many countries—ultimately leading to expansion of offshore fishing limits in many parts of the world—and has also forced the development of techniques for FISH FARMING and the cultivation and seeding of many bottom areas in order to enhance shellfish production.

A change in attitudes about the consumption of various species of fish may also help alleviate fishing pressures on certain species and encourage a more balanced exploitation of fisheries resources. As a science, fisheries biology is still in its infancy, and the behavior, food requirements, and breeding habits of most fish are not well known. Future research may reveal ways in which the world's population can depend more heavily on the ocean as a food source without creating a drastic impact on the overall ecology of the ocean.

Water and Energy. The ocean is a source of drinking water in many highly arid, nearshore areas where the cost of transporting water from regions of abundant fresh water is greater than the cost of DESALINATION. The ocean also represents an almost unlimited source of energy, at least in theory. Current use of the oceans for generating power from this energy is restricted for the most part, however, to the use of seawater as a coolant in shoreside nuclear power plants, a use that environmental groups oppose as causing thermal pollution.

Some energy can be extracted from the ocean by making use of the change in sea level caused by tidal cycles. The use of this method, however, is thus far limited (see TIDAL ENERGY). Numerous other methods are mostly in experimental stages at present. Several of these make use of the temperature differential that exists across the thermocline (see OCEAN THERMAL ENERGY CONVERSION).

The Sun replenishes oceanic energy reserves faster than human beings could ever remove energy from the oceans. However, the problems of economically removing this energy, most of which is diffused over the entire ocean, are still too great to allow widespread dependence on this energy resource.

Oil and Minerals. In the past two decades the production of oil from offshore drilling on the continental shelves has increased dramatically to the point where it represents a substantial percentage of the world's production (see PETROLEUM INDUSTRY). More recent evidence indicates that oil deposits also reside on the continental slope.

Economically important minerals are constantly introduced into the ocean from a variety of sources, and most of the material accumulates on the ocean bottom. Rivers dump vast quantities of particulate mineral materials into the oceans each year. Volcanic eruptions and hydrother-

Serious ocean pollution is caused by the dumping of sewage sludge (right), *which contains heavy metals and toxic organic chemicals that are a long-term hazard to marine life. Nonbiodegradable garbage is also hazardous, as this ensnared gull demonstrates* (below).

mal solutions introduce many metals into solution and in solid form.

Heavy minerals, such as gold and platinum, have a tendency to accumulate in shallow, surficial PLACER DEPOSITS, and the deep sea, as well as nearshore environments, stores vast amounts of economically important mineral resources (see OCEANIC MINERAL RESOURCES).

Ocean Pollution

Oceans clearly play an essential role in life on Earth, yet because of their vastness humans have tended to use their waters as dumping grounds for many waste materials. This practice has increased as land areas for such wastes diminish. Oceans also receive all of the pollutants that are fed to them by the rivers of the world. Even when ships are not actively engaged in dumping wastes, they are themselves sources of pollution—most notably, the giant tankers that have caused numerous massive OIL SPILLS.

As a result, by the late 20th century ocean studies indicate that what had once been thought impossible is becoming a reality: the oceans as a whole are showing signs of pollution (see POLLUTION, ENVIRONMENTAL). Even surface waters are increasingly plagued by obvious litter. Some of this litter washes ashore to render beaches unsightly, while other such debris entangles and kills many sea birds and mammals every year. More insidious are the effects of toxic contaminants from wastes that are dumped. These chemicals can upset delicate marine ecosystems as they are absorbed by organisms all along the food chain.

The problems of ocean pollution have been recognized at national and international levels. The U.S. Congress, for example, passed an act in 1988 that would prohibit ocean dumping by 1991, and in that same year 65 nations agreed to cease burning toxic wastes at sea by 1994 should acceptable alternative practices be found. The latter action remains under debate, however, as several nations continue the practice of ocean burning of toxic wastes, and the U.S. act may prove as unenforceable as a prior one in 1977 that attempted the same prohibition. Worldwide, the problem of ocean pollution remains.

---

ocean sunfish The ocean sunfish, *Mola mola*, is a giant-sized fish in the mola family, Molidae, found in temperate and tropical seas. Related to the triggerfish, puffer, and porcupine fish, it is also called the headfish because the head appears to occupy the entire body. The ocean sunfish reaches up to 450 kg (1,000 lb) in weight and 3 to 4 m (10 to 13 ft) in length. It is frequently seen floating on its side and is a poor swimmer. In the western Atlantic the ocean sunfish appears to feed on jellyfish, small fish, and the larger plankton.

---

ocean thermal energy conversion Ocean thermal energy conversion (OTEC) is a process for converting the solar energy absorbed by tropical oceans into electricity, using a HEAT ENGINE, with warm surface water serving as the heat source and deep water as the heat sink. The process has aroused considerable interest because it utilizes a renewable resource, ocean water, and has a benign environmental impact. OTEC experts believe that the process is feasible for small (100-MW) stationary plants sited on shore, and for larger (400-MW) plants housed on ships cruising equatorial waters. Such "plantships" could also extract chemicals and minerals from seawater, as well as hydrogen for use as a fuel. This water could serve as a medium for culturing fish.

The French engineer Georges Claude experimented with OTEC technology as early as 1929. His system used low-pressure steam derived from seawater as the working fluid in an open-cycle method, where warm surface water was drawn into an evaporator and the steam produced was used to drive a turbo generator. Today's OTEC technology generates electricity through a closed-cycle heat engine, with ammonia as the working fluid.

Typically, surface water at 28° C (82.4° F) is pumped into evaporator tubes, and liquid ammonia is sprayed on the tubes' outer surfaces. The vaporized ammonia drives a turbine and is then returned to a liquid state in a condenser cooled by water at 4.5° C (40.1° F) pumped from a depth of about 1,000 m (3,300 ft).

Although several plants have undergone field tests, there are still significant unresolved problems. For plants housed aboard ship, the designs of the cold-water pipe, the platform, and the mooring system are crucial because of the complexity of the structures and the enormity of ocean forces. Both sea- and land-based plants must deal with the possibility of the "biofouling" of heat-exchanger surfaces by marine organisms. No tests have yet been conducted over periods long enough to prove the resistance of various designs and materials to oceanic currents, waves, and marine life.

The warm water needed to generate 1 kW is 4 liters/sec, and water volumes become enormous when, for instance, a 100-MW plant is considered. Capital costs for building such a plant are high enough to discourage the many developing countries that possess excellent thermal resources and could profitably use OTEC technology, rather than consume expensive fossil fuels for electricity generation.

No large-scale OTEC plants are yet in operation. Plans are underway for the first land-based U.S. OTEC facility, to be located in Hawaii.

See also: ENERGY SOURCES.

Oceania [oh-shee-an'-ee-uh] Oceania is a name used to refer to the widely scattered islands of the central and south Pacific; Australia and New Zealand are frequently included. Virtually all of the islands are volcanic peaks or tiny coralline atolls built on submerged volcanic bases. Some, such as New Guinea, are sizable land areas thrusting snowcapped peaks as high as 5,000 m (16,400 ft). The continent of Australia, however, shows no evidence of recent volcanism. Except for New Zealand and part of Australia, the whole of Oceania lies well within the tropics and enjoys continuous warm temperatures. The annual rainfall can reach 4,000 mm (157 in) in some locations. A number of equatorial atolls, the leeward sides of mountainous islands, and almost two-thirds of Australia tend to be arid.

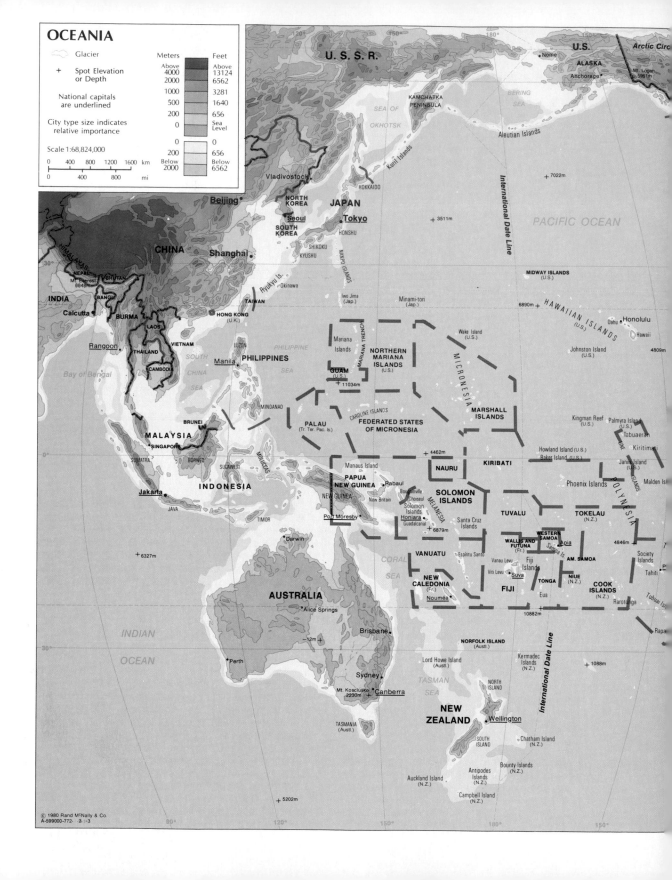

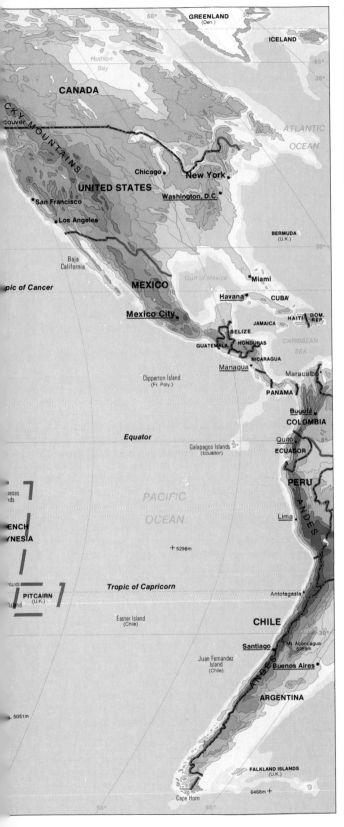

The port of Pago Pago is situated on the southeastern shore of Tutuila, the main island of American Samoa, opposite Mount Rainmaker. Pago Pago, the capital of the island group, has an excellent harbor.

Island Groups. Oceania is usually divided into three major island groups named by the French explorer Jules Dumont d'Urville: MELANESIA, MICRONESIA, and POLYNESIA. These names not only reflect the groups' locations but also their environment. Melanesia ("black islands") includes the large quasi-continental islands immediately north and east of Australia, from New Guinea to New Caledonia. Micronesia ("little islands") is almost exclusively composed of tiny atolls dotting the western Pacific. Polynesia ("many islands") is an immense region in the central Pacific—those islands farthest removed from Asia. It includes both large volcanic islands and coral atolls within a triangle connecting Hawaii, Easter Island, and New Zealand.

The variety of Oceania's flora and fauna is directly related to the distance from the Asiatic source region. Remote islands have no mammals except the bat, no amphibians or reptiles except the sea turtle, and few land birds. Isolation has also preserved ancient species.

Agriculture is the basis of the economy for most of Oceania. Coffee, cocoa, and copra are the main products. Tourism is expanding, whereas the once-important phosphate-mining industry is in decline.

History. About 30,000 years ago human habitation began in the western Pacific. The earliest peoples came via the partial land bridges and narrowed straits of Malaya-Indonesia that resulted from the lowered sea level during the ice ages. By about 1000 BC migration from Melanesia and Micronesia toward the Polynesian triangle was occurring.

Ferdinand MAGELLAN sighted Guam and one of the Tuamotus in 1521. Dutch explorers followed in the 17th century, and the English in the 18th century. Capt. James COOK, in his three voyages (1769, 1772–75, and 1776–79), explored most of Oceania. An influx of missionaries in the 19th century changed the political and cultural structure of the Oceanic peoples. Between 1842 and 1900 the area came under the control of European colonial powers. After World War I the German possessions were administered by the League of Nations.

During World War II the Japanese occupied much of the area, and many islands were the scene of battles. After the war some island groups were placed under UN trusts until independence or internal self-government could be achieved. Western Samoa gained independence in 1962, followed by Fiji and Tonga (1970), Papua New Guinea (1975), the Solomon Islands (1978), Kiribati and Tuvalu (1979), and Vanuatu (1980). The United States terminated its administration of the remaining trust territory, except for PALAU, on Nov. 3, 1986 (see PACIFIC ISLANDS, TRUST TERRITORY OF THE). The termination was approved by the UN Security Council on Dec. 22, 1990.

Oceania, art of

The art of Oceania encompasses the sculptural and pictorial traditions of the indigenous peoples of the central and southwestern Pacific islands, excluding the Asiatic-influenced civilizations of Japan, Taiwan, the Philippines, and Indonesia. Traditionally included within the boundaries of Oceania are the island societies of MELANESIA, POLYNESIA, and MICRONESIA. Although Australia usually is not considered to be a part of Oceania, this article also covers the artistic traditions of the Australian ABORIGINES.

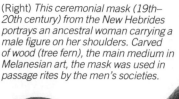

(Right) *This ceremonial mask (19th–20th century) from the New Hebrides portrays an ancestral woman carrying a male figure on her shoulders. Carved of wood (tree fern), the main medium in Melanesian art, the mask was used in passage rites by the men's societies.*

(Left) *This house-post ancestor figure is typical of carvings by the Maori sculptors of New Zealand. The Maori art of Polynesia is characterized by an original curvilinear style, carved in low relief.*

Art as a separable category has little meaning in an analysis of traditional Oceanic societies, in which artworks often are combined with music, dance, and oral literature in complex manifestations of social and religious themes. Aesthetics, in this context, denotes culturally specific ways of thinking about such forms.

Before contact (16th century) with Europeans, the use of metal was unknown in Oceania. Oceanic artists traditionally used tools made of stone, bone, shell, obsidian, shark's teeth, and fish skin; these cutting, incising, and filing elements were secured to wooden handles by fiber cords or wooden pegs. The widespread introduction of metal technology in the late 18th and early 19th centuries profoundly affected the Oceanic artistic traditions by bringing in more efficient tools and new visual images. The use of even the most primitive metallic elements, such as nails mounted as incising implements, encouraged a new efflorescence in wood carving, and the introduction of such other European trade goods as blankets and cloth often led to the evolution of their indigenous counterparts into refined prestige objects. Access to European goods meant that such traditional craft items as BARK CLOTH, BASKETRY, and wooden containers no longer had to be made for immediate use; they could be produced for sale to others.

Shifts in power owing to the introduction of guns altered the production and use of previously restricted goods, such as Hawaiian featherwork. Most destructive of all to Oceanic artistic traditions, however, was the introduction of the Christian god, in whose name not only did the production of images of the old gods cease, but also

This ceremonial shield (19th century), made of wicker and decorated with inlaid nautilus shells, exemplifies the intricate work of artisans from the central Solomon Islands in Melanesia.

New Guinea, the largest island of Oceania, has provided the richest source of Melanesian art. (Left) This ceramic head, sculpted by the Kwoma tribe of Papua New Guinea, was used as a ritual object in harvest ceremonies. (Below) This debating stool, used in formal clan activities, was carved in New Guinea's Sepik River area, a region noted for its highly developed religious and cultural traditions.

tourists. Basketry and bark cloth, produced in nontraditional forms, have now become high-quality crafts sold as souvenirs and decorative objects.

Melanesia. The traditional arts of Melanesia, an arc of islands in the southwest Pacific stretching from New Guinea to Fiji, can best be understood in relation to the pervasive political and social values placed on the community leaders known as bigmen. Melanesian societies characteristically were small independent groups headed by a bigman, a self-made political leader who gained power by aligning followers. Within these small social groupings, the creation of artistic works was often integrally associated with ceremonial cycles. Because each social group had its own traditional art forms, many different styles flourished throughout Melanesia.

Ceremonial cycles might involve the erection of a men's house; the manufacture and consecration of slit-gongs; the fabrication of masks, costumes, and musical instruments; or the production of representations of ancestors or legendary figures. The elaborate *malanggan* ceremonies of New Ireland, for example, called for the creation every few years of a new set of intricately decorated costumes, carved posts, and relief boards with complicated motifs that symbolized a particular clan's traditions and beliefs. The strong expressionism and the vivid interplay between line and color found in *malanggan* sculptures and costumes reflect the highly emotional and dramatic impact of much of Melanesian art.

Typical of Melanesian artistic traditions was the requisite destruction of many art objects once their ceremonial functions were fulfilled. Among the more permanent objects created by Melanesian artists are the polychrome pottery of the Sepik River basin and other areas of New Guinea; carved shell-discs, or *kapkaps*, of the Solomon Islands; and the carved and painted hardwood slit-gongs found in Vanuatu (formerly the New Hebrides). Other artistic media of varying durability include sculptures of soft stone, wood, or tree fern; masks of wood, bark cloth, mud, or spider webbing; ceremonial skulls molded with clay; face and body painting; and monumental, elaborately painted men's houses that were allowed periodically to fall into ruin, then to be destroyed and replaced.

Much of the Melanesian artistic tradition thus existed primarily as an artistic concept in the mind of the artist, who often worked without models or reminders when new objects of a particular type were to be produced for the next ceremony. This feature gave artistic works from Melanesia a spontaneous character and a creative individuality that have been much appreciated and emulated by various modern Western artists, notably the German expressionists and the surrealists.

Polynesia. A vast area in the central Pacific stretching from Hawaii in the north to New Zealand and Easter Island in the south, Polynesia differs from Melanesia in the greater homogeneity of its peoples, the less fluid and more hierarchical structure of its societies, and the more enduring and formalized nature of its art objects. Many Polynesian artworks were visual symbols of status, rank, and power that were passed as heirlooms from generation to generation. This emphasis on hierarchy and tradition

those which already existed were destroyed, both by the missionaries and by the converted islanders. Images of the new god were occasionally produced in traditional style, but for the most part, the making of religious art ended with the coming of Christianity. Today the production of images of the old gods has been revived for sale to

produced more formal and abstract art objects than those of Melanesia.

Throughout Polynesia, three-dimensional sculptural form as well as intricate relief incising were aesthetically important in themselves and did not depend on polychroming for an immediate dramatic impact. The highly stylized and conventional nature of most Polynesian sculpture is also characteristic of the sculptural tradition of EASTER ISLAND, whose artists meticulously carved small wooden figures as well as huge and solemnly powerful stone statues.

Except for New Zealand, where MAORI artists created ornately carved meeting houses, houses were relatively undecorated in Polynesia. The great oval houses of the chiefs, however, were distinguished by complex rafter formations and rafter lashings that often incorporated elaborate designs. The few but carefully conceived furnishings included bark-cloth bed coverings, plaited floor and sleeping mats, and carved wooden neck rests and decorated wooden bowls. Tools used in food preparation, such as stone pounders, tended either to be decorated with human images or to take on abstract forms beyond their functional purpose. Even fishhooks varied aesthetically in materials, shapes, and lashings.

As is typical in highly stratified societies, clothing and personal adornment were carried to elaborate heights in Polynesia. In Hawaii, feathered cloaks, capes, and helmets were worn on occasions of warfare and ceremony, whereas in New Zealand, flax fibers were woven into capes that bestowed on their owners both warmth and prestige. Ornaments and jewelry made of carved ivory, greenstone, human hair, shells, carved dog teeth, boar tusks, turtle shell, and feathers were worn in the hair or on the neck, arms, or legs.

The varied basketry traditions of Polynesia reached a high point in Tonga, where a variety of forms was made from creepers, coconut fiber, coconut leaves, or pandanus-leaf strips laced around bundles of coconut-leaf midribs. These art objects were passed from generation to generation along with stories about their owners and the occasions on which they were used. They served, in effect, as objectified histories and as models for new objects of the same type.

Micronesia. The arts of Micronesia, a widely scattered band of islands north of Melanesia and west of Polynesia, are as locally specialized and diverse as the social and linguistic systems that fostered them. For the most part, Micronesian artists displayed a keen awareness of the whims of the sea, on which their survival depended. Accordingly, canoes were not only functional objects but artistic constructions, with decorative elements, elaborate prows, and attached images whose purpose was to objectify or guard against sea spirits.

Architecture was sometimes monumental, including massive coral house posts in the Marianas and huge basalt prisms in Ponape. In Palau, large community houses incorporated stylized human figures in carved architectural parts such as sculptured house posts, gable ornaments, and incised and painted storyboards.

Other artistic high points of Micronesia include the

One of the artistic traditions of the Australian Aborigines is bark painting, in which intricate designs are painted on sheets of bark. The "X-ray" style, where the internal organs of the painted figures are shown, is often used.

body tattooing of the Marshall and Caroline islands; the loom-woven fabrics of banana and hibiscus fiber of Ponape and Kusaie; the widespread ornaments and "money" made of seashell or turtle shell; the sennit "armor" and shark-tooth weapons of the Gilbert Islands; the shell inlay of Palau; and the plaited bark-fiber ribbonwork used as personal adornment in many areas.

Australia. The culture and arts of the Australian Aborigines are much older than the parallel developments in the rest of Oceania and represent entirely separate traditions and origins. As nomadic hunters and gatherers closely adapted to the varied environments of the Australian continent, the Aborigines evolved highly complex social structures to govern the activities of their tribal groups. Painted or engraved forms include rock and cave paintings (see PREHISTORIC ART), bark paintings, ground paintings, *churingas* (carved ceremonial plaques), body decoration, elaborations on shields and other weapons, and *didjeridoo* (drone pipes). Perhaps the most striking of these two-dimensional artistic renderings are the bark paintings. Often incorporating totemic designs, bark paintings depict subjects as varied as hunting scenes and mythological principles. Characteristic of many western Arnhem Land paintings of animal and human forms is the so-called X-ray style, in which internal organs are shown.

Even where three-dimensional sculpture is found, as in the carved burial poles of Melville Island, the artistic impact of the work is supplemented by a painted, two-dimensional elaboration of the three-dimensional form. Designs in paintings and sculptures often are composed of complex combinations of small motifs organized into larger groupings that, in turn, form the overall composition. Similar design elements decorate engraved smoking pipes, spearthrowers, boomerangs, shells, and sacred rocks.

Oceania, languages of The native languages of Oceania—which comprise about one-third of the world's languages—are classified into three groups: the Aboriginal languages of Australia, the Austronesian (or MALAYO-POLYNESIAN) languages, and the Papuan languages. The Aboriginal languages of Australia and Tasmania all belong to a single family. They numbered about 250 at the end of the 19th century; today only 100 survive. The Austronesian family comprises between 600 and 1,000 languages spoken in Malaysia, Indonesia, Taiwan, the Philippines, Micronesia, Polynesia, and many islands of Melanesia. It extends beyond Oceania to include Malagasy, spoken in Madagascar, and a few minor languages scattered throughout Southeast Asia. Finally, Papuan languages, spoken in most of New Guinea and on a few neighboring islands, number approximately 800. Unlike Australian and Austronesian languages, Papuan languages do not constitute a clear genetic unit; rather, they form more than 60 probably unrelated families.

Archaeological evidence indicates that humans have inhabited the Indonesian archipelago since before the development of language, and that Australia and Papua New Guinea were already inhabited in 25,000–30,000 years ago. Other islands of the Pacific, in contrast, were settled only in the last 5,000 years by Austronesian-speaking populations originating from near Indonesia.

European colonization brought several European languages to Oceania, notably English and French, both of which are spoken today as first or second languages in much of the region. Several English-based creoles are also used as lingua francas in northern Australia, Papua New Guinea, the Solomon Islands, and Vanuatu.

Many Australian languages have disappeared or are in imminent danger of disappearing, with creole and English replacing the Aboriginal languages. In the 19th century the languages of Tasmania were wiped out with their speakers at the hands of European settlers.

See also: SOUTHEAST ASIAN LANGUAGES.

oceanic mineral resources Oceanic mineral resources include various metallic and nonmetallic materials of differing origin and economic potential that occur on or beneath the floor of the continental shelf and ocean basin. MINERAL resources of the continental shelf are similar to those of the adjacent continent because the continental shelf is underlain by continental rocks; the mineral resources are relatively accessible for exploitation because of the shallow water depths of up to hundreds of meters and the proximity to the continent. Mineral resources of the ocean basin are different from those of the continental shelf because oceanic rocks differ fundamentally from continental rocks. The mineral resources of the ocean basin also are less accessible for exploitation because of water depths of thousands of meters and large distances from shore. (See OCEAN AND SEA; ORE DEPOSITS.)

Oceanic mineral resources originate by various processes, chiefly erosion of continental rock (terrigenous); activity of living organisms (biogenic); chemical deposi-

The Orion, located in the North Sea, is one of more than 700 drilling rigs that are currently searching for or extracting oil or gas from seabeds. Such fixed platforms as the Orion are used in shallow waters; floating vessels are used in deeper waters.

tion from seawater (authigenic); chemical replacement (diagenic); and volcanic processes.

The mode of occurrence of an oceanic mineral resource determines the technique employed in its exploitation. Unconsolidated deposits in the form of sediment or nodules are recovered by dredging. Consolidated deposits that occur in hard rock may require drilling—if they are insoluble as are coal and metallic vein and lode deposits—or solution mining—if they are soluble as are sulfur deposits. Dissolved mineral salts require chemical and physical extractive techniques.

Only a small fraction of the potential mineral resources of the continental shelf and virtually none of the mineral resources of the ocean basins are currently utilized. Oceanic mineral resources have not yet been adequately assessed, and the cost of exploration and exploitation of most of these resources is not yet competitive with the cost of utilizing land mineral resources. As these factors change, the utilization of oceanic mineral resources should increase.

Continental Shelf

Unconsolidated terrigenous mineral deposits are widely distributed on continental shelves. Siliceous SAND and GRAVEL are the most utilized of these deposits. The potential for PLACER DEPOSITS—heavy mineral grains concentrated in sediments by virtue of their specific gravity (3.5 to 8)—exists seaward of sources on land. Utilized placer deposits include titanium sands off Brazil and tin gravels off Indonesia, Thailand, and Malaysia. The only offshore diamond mining was halted off South West Africa in 1972 for economic reasons. Unconsolidated biogenic and authigenic deposits include lime sediments, coral, and pearls.

Consolidated mineral deposits beneath the floors of continental shelves are generally seaward extensions of adjacent land deposits. Coal (see COAL AND COAL MINING), the most utilized of these deposits, is mined in seaweed extensions of coal fields in Canada, Chile, Great Britain,

Japan, and Turkey. Offshore extensions of metallic mineral deposits, such as BARITE off Alaska and bedded IRON ore off Canada and Finland, are also mined.

Extensive PHOSPHORITE deposits that exist in offshore areas of oceanic upwelling, such as off southwestern North America and western South America, have not yet been utilized because of the availability of phosphorite resources on land. Salt (halite), POTASSIUM, and SULFUR deposits exist beneath continents and adjacent continental shelves at sites of former EVAPORITE basins. Subsea production of sulfur, limited to two SALT DOME deposits offshore of Louisiana, yields about 20% of U.S. production of this mineral.

Oceanic mineral resources in fluid form recovered from continental shelves include PETROLEUM (oil and NATURAL GAS) and various minerals dissolved as salts or as elements in seawater. Salt is the largest product derived from seawater solutes. Subsea petroleum produced offshore of 25 countries has been contributing an ever-increasing percentage of the world's output and is now by far the most valuable oceanic mineral commodity being exploited (see PETROLEUM INDUSTRY).

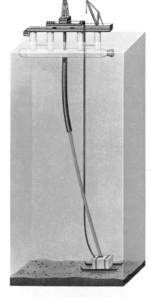

(Right) *One proposed means of mining manganese nodules involves the use of a self-propelled surface rig connected by means of an air-lift system to a skid-mounted collecting device on the seabed. Such a system could operate at a depth of 4,000 m (13,000 ft). (Below left) Such metals as manganese, nickel, copper, and cobalt are found in manganese nodules, which can densely accumulate in certain parts of the ocean floor, especially those where the sedimentation rate is low. The nodules were first discovered by the Challenger Expedition more than 100 years ago. (Below right) This cross section of a manganese nodule, enlarged to 37 times its actual size, reveals several nuclei—such as a shark's tooth near the top and a volcanic rock fragment below it—around which a ferromanganese crust forms. The nodules may grow to the size of golf or tennis balls.*

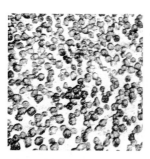

Ocean Basin

Unconsolidated mineral deposits of ocean basins comprise manganese nodules, which precipitate from seawater, and metalliferous sediments of volcanic origin. Golfball- to tennis-ball-sized manganese nodules are widely distributed on the floor of the ocean basin, where they vary in abundance and composition. In addition to manganese (up to 50% by dry weight), the nodules contain iron (1 to 18%) and cobalt, copper, and nickel (each up to 2%). The United States and several other nations have developed technologies for mining manganese nodules, but engineering and economic problems must be solved before mining can begin. Commercial exploitation is unlikely to occur until the 21st century, when more easily obtainable onshore resources are in short supply.

The formation of metalliferous sediments is primarily by hydrothermal processes related to volcanic activity at oceanic ridges (such as the Mid-Atlantic Ridge and the East Pacific Rise) and in rift zones where new ocean basins are forming (such as the Red Sea and the Gulf of California). The richest known metalliferous sediments, in several small basins near the center of the Red Sea at depths of about 2 km (1 mi), have an average metal content of 29% iron, 3.4% zinc, 1.3% copper, and 0.1% lead.

Consolidated mineral resources of ocean basins include manganese encrustations, massive hydrothermal copper-iron sulfide deposits, nickel-platinum sulfide deposits, and magmatic chromite deposits. The manganese encrustations of both authigenic and volcanic origins form patchy layers up to 2 m (7 ft) in observed thickness that adhere to hard-rock surfaces at the ocean bottom. The massive hydrothermal copper-iron deposits, nickel-platinum sulfide deposits, and magmatic chromite deposits have not yet been sampled in place.

See also: SEA, LAW OF THE.

oceanic nutrients   Seawater contains minute traces of inorganic and organic nutrients that are essential for the growth of phytoplankton, the microscopic organisms on which ocean life depends. Nutrients are used during the process of photosynthesis by phytoplankton in the ocean's surface layers, producing energy-rich compounds. The phytoplankton are eaten by herbivores, which in turn are eaten by carnivores. Nutrients are returned to the water by metabolic wastes and through the activity of bacteria, which decompose organic detritus, in the same manner that food-chain processes occur on land (see ECOLOGY).

Kinds of Nutrients. The most important inorganic nutrients are nitrogen and phosphorus, generally present as nitrate or ammonia and as phosphate. In the absence of these two elements plant growth decreases, limiting the numbers of zooplankton and fish. Other essential inorganic nutrients include carbon dioxide, silica, iron, manganese, magnesium, sodium, and calcium.

Organic nutrients are derived from the marine food chain. Trace amounts that are found in seawater include such growth factors as vitamin B$_{12}$, thiamine, and biotin as well as small amounts of such organic substrates as sugars and amino acids. The concentration of vitamins is important for the success of certain algal species, such as many of the Dinophyceae. The organic substrates promote the growth of bacteria.

Distribution. The concentration of all nutrients is much greater in coastal areas than in mid-ocean, and it is generally higher in deep water than at the surface. In tropical seas, in which little seasonal storm activity exists to mix surface and deep waters, nutrients are low throughout the year. In temperate oceans, storm activity during the winter brings a fresh nutrient supply to the surface, so that algal blooms occur frequently in the spring. Due to the pattern of OCEAN CURRENTS, areas of deep-water upwelling occur mainly off the western coasts of the continents and around Antarctica. These areas of periodically enriched nutrients are the sites of the world's largest fishing industries.

The quantity of nutrients in deep water of various oceans differs, depending on the time needed for nutrients to be derived from organic matter of the food chain. The deep Atlantic waters, for instance, contain about two-thirds of the nitrogen and phosphorus concentrations found in deep Pacific and Indian ocean waters. The oxidized form of nitrogen is most abundant in deep water as nitrate. In the surface waters, nitrate is taken up by plants that are in turn eaten by animals, which excrete nitrogen in the form of ammonia and in some cases urea. Many phytoplankton and bacteria use these forms of nitrogen and are thus rapidly recycled into the food chain.

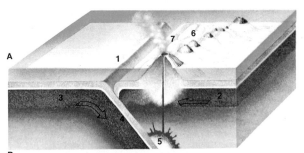

Oceanic trenches are long, deep, narrow depressions along ocean floors (A). A trench (1) is formed when two moving crustal plates (2, 3) meet and one slides beneath the other into the Earth's mantle (4). Friction between the plates results in a tremendous evolution of heat (5) and in the subsequent formation of a curving zone, or arc, of volcanoes (6). The remains of old volcanic arcs (7), carried toward the oceanic trench as the plates move together, are eventually swallowed up. A map (B) reveals that the oceanic trenches (red lines) are usually close to continental land masses or to island arcs.

oceanic trenches An oceanic trench is a long, narrow depression of the seabed with relatively steep sides (see OCEAN AND SEA). Trenches are generally deeper than 6,000 m (20,000 ft) and are the most abyssal, or deepest, regions on the face of the Earth. The deepest oceanic trench, the MARIANAS TRENCH, has a depth of about 11,034 m (36,201 ft) in the Challenger Deep subsector, the site of the BATHYSCAPHE *Trieste*'s abyssal dive in 1960.

Subduction Zones. Trenches, in a more restricted sense, are readily explainable in terms of PLATE TECTONICS. They are subduction zones, one of the three possible types of boundaries between the crustal or lithospheric plates that are drifting across the face of the Earth in relative motion at a rate of from 1 to 10 cm/yr (0.4 to 4 in/yr). As a portion of crust beneath the ocean basin ages beyond 150 million years, it becomes increasingly cold and therefore dense enough to be heavier than the underlying asthenosphere. The plate, about 100 km (60 mi) thick, will break and then commence subducting, or slowly descending beneath a more buoyant adjacent plate and into the Earth's hot mantle; this process is accompanied by EARTHQUAKE activity, the creation of an island arc, and volcanism (see VOLCANO). Along the line where the descending plate intersects the ocean floor, an oceanic trench forms as the surface expression of this subduction.

If a trench forms in mid-ocean, it tends to migrate toward and eventually collide with the margin of a conti-

nent. Therefore trenches tend to be peripheral to ocean basins. Such trenches surround virtually all of the Pacific Ocean (Aleutian, Japan, Marianas, and Peru-Chile trenches) and parts of the Indian Ocean (Indonesian Trench) and the Atlantic Ocean (West Indies and Scotia Arc trenches). Some trenches, however, such as the Romanche Trench in the equatorial Atlantic Ocean and the Vema and Diamantina trenches in the Indian Ocean, are far from any land. Such deep linear depressions are related to fracture zones and to rifts in the ocean floor that are axes of seafloor spreading; they are not true trenches in the strict sense.

Deeps and Troughs. A deep is a clearly defined subsector of any marine depression. The Challenger Deep in the Marianas Trench is an example. An elongate depression with sides that are less steep than those of a trench is called a trough.

oceanography Oceanography is the scientific study of the Earth's oceans and their boundaries. The interconnected world oceans, from which the continents rise like islands, cover 71 percent of the world's surface (see OCEAN AND SEA). Most human beings live on or near coastlines, and human history is closely linked to the oceans. They serve as a source of food, as the key to weather and climate (see OCEAN-ATMOSPHERE INTERACTION), and as the highways for ships of commerce. Much of the history of the planet itself is recorded in the bottom topography, geophysical properties, and sediments of the oceans. The 20th-century discoveries that have revolutionized geological thinking have in fact largely been the product of work in the ocean sciences (see PLATE TECTONICS; SEAFLOOR SPREADING).

Historical Background

Oceanography as a science began in the 19th century with the work of such men as U.S. naval officer Matthew Fontaine MAURY and his compilation of oceanographic data from ships' logs. The first major scientific expedition, and the one that firmly established the field of oceanography, was the around-the-world voyage of H.M.S. *Challenger*. Setting out from England in 1872, the Challenger Expedition returned 3-1/2 years later with a wealth of oceanographic data. In 1926 the South Atlantic voyage of the German ship *Meteor* in 1926 was the first to use an echo sounder to chart the ruggedness of the ocean bottom in a continuous manner.

Modern Oceanographic Disciplines

Modern oceanography, combining several fields of science, comprises the subdisciplines of physical, chemical, biological, and geological oceanography. Closely associated fields are those of marine technology, MARITIME LAW, and studies of the effects of ocean pollution (see POLLUTION, ENVIRONMENTAL).

   Physical oceanographers study the physical processes underlying such phenomena as currents; tides; WATER WAVES; water transparency, density, and temperature; and underwater acoustics and sound transmission. Chemical oceanographers are concerned with the chemistry of seawater, its major salts, and its many trace elements. Marine biologists study life in the sea, marine ECOLOGY, and the total organic production in the oceans (see OCEANIC NUTRIENTS). Ocean life comprises the floating or weakly swimming forms called PLANKTON and the rapidly swimming forms called nekton, as well as DEEP-SEA LIFE and

various bottom-dwellers. Marine geologists map the ocean floor, analyze shoreline problems, and study sediments of the ocean floor and rocks of the underlying crust (see OCEANIC MINERAL RESOURCES).

   As a whole, modern oceanography is mainly pursued at a few major centers around the world, such as the Scripps Institute of Oceanography, La Jolla, Calif. The research goals within such centers tend to focus on intense studies of smaller ocean areas by teams representing each of the broad oceanographic disciplines. In addition to work at such centers, a new era of oceanwide research was initiated when international scientific teams organized to tackle programs too vast in scope to be handled by individual institutions. One notable undertaking of this nature, the DEEP-SEA DRILLING PROJECT, was conducted from 1968 to 1983 by a consortium of U.S. institutions (JOIDES) and several European nations, the Soviet Union, and Japan. It was succeeded in 1984 by the more comprehensive OCEAN DRILLING PROGRAM.

Oceanographic Technology

The earliest technical devices used in the study of the oceans were weighted sounding lines, which obtained the local depth of water, and rope-suspended scoops or dredges, which brought sediment and bottom-dwelling marine life to a ship's deck. These were the main tools used in the water by the historic Challenger Expedition of the 1870s. By 1900, thermometers were devised that could be lowered to great depths and then "locked" on the temperatures recorded there as they were raised through waters of different temperatures. Water samples were taken from all depths by Nansen bottles, which were metal tubular containers with ends that could be shut by "messenger" devices. These tools could also be lowered in spaced groups, so that as each unit was triggered it released a new messenger to operate the next-lower unit.

   By the time of World War I, echo-sounding gear was available that timed the passage of a sound pulse to the ocean bottom and back (see HYDROPHONE). Thereafter a

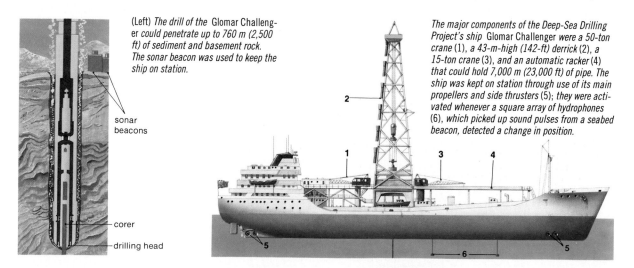

(Left) *The drill of the* Glomar Challenger *could penetrate up to 760 m (2,500 ft) of sediment and basement rock. The sonar beacon was used to keep the ship on station.*

sonar beacons

corer

drilling head

The major components of the Deep-Sea Drilling Project's ship Glomar Challenger *were a 50-ton crane (1), a 43-m-high (142-ft) derrick (2), a 15-ton crane (3), and an automatic racker (4) that could hold 7,000 m (23,000 ft) of pipe. The ship was kept on station through use of its main propellers and side thrusters (5); they were activated whenever a square array of hydrophones (6), which picked up sound pulses from a seabed beacon, detected a change in position.*

huge variety of specialized ocean instruments became available for both deep-ocean and nearshore experiments. Various forms of wavemeters provide elaborate data on ocean waves. Ocean currents are tracked offshore by constant-depth floats that report their positions acoustically, while sea-bottom currents are measured by devices called inclinometers.

Devices and sensors such as these must be designed in relation to their intended deployment. Most modern oceanographic vessels have at least one A-frame or crane that permits the lowered devices to go up and down in relatively heavy seas without striking the side of the ship. Some instruments may operate on floating buoys or aboard underwater buoys, recording their data on magnetic tape or transmitting them to surface vessels by radio signals.

Physical Measurements. Waterproofed photoelectric cells and Secchi disks report water turbidity by measuring the relative amount of sunlight that passes through a known depth of water. Such data are important to the management of all types of marine life, because the relative amount of solar energy absorbed by such life at any given depth is dependent on the turbidity of the water.

Water temperature is now usually measured by an electronic sensor, often a THERMISTOR (a temperature-sensitive electrical-resistance device). A device used for many years is the cable-lowered bathythermograph, which prints the temperature-versus-pressure curve on a smoked-glass plate. Depth is measured by an aneroid cell (a pressure-sensitive flexible compartment), and temperature by a bimetallic element in the device that also drives the scriber. Other physical measurements are of sound velocity, electrical conductivity, freezing point, and the amount of turbulence in the water mass.

Chemical Measurements. Standard chemical analyses are made of sampled seawater. At river mouths or estuaries, probably the most important chemical measurement is of the degree of salinity. Many dissolved substances, such as heavy-metal pollutants, occur in concentrations of only a few parts per billion, requiring sophisticated chemical analyses in onshore laboratories.

Another essential indicator of the degree of pollution of a water sample is the amount of dissolved oxygen it contains. Dissolved oxygen is often measured by allowing it to oxidize manganous hydroxide, which then reacts with an acid and potassium iodide to set free iodine that is measured. Many electronic dissolved-oxygen meters are now available.

Seabed Instruments. The seabed is usually examined by DREDGING or by coring. In simple coring procedures, coring tubes are lowered almost to the seafloor. The winch is then allowed to run free, and the corer drops into the sediment, penetrating it to a depth of as much as 10 m (30 ft). The material obtained is kept in an inner tube by a core catcher. Very deep coring samples are obtained by specially designed drilling derricks, as used aboard the *Glomar Challenger* of the Deep-Sea Drilling Project and the *JOIDES Resolution* of the Ocean Drilling Program. Deeper probes of the bottom are achieved by seismologic techniques using pulses of strong acoustic energy. The pulses can penetrate thousands of meters of bottom sedi-

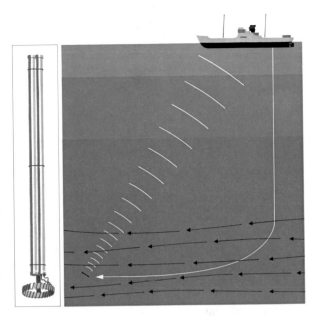

(Above left) *Deep-water currents can be detected with the remote-sensing device consisting of an oscillator attached to a float.* (Right) *As the device drifts with the currents, its ultrasonic signals are received and tracked by a nearby surface ship following its movements. In the western North Atlantic Ocean the drift of such a device revealed a strong north-south current flowing approximately 2,000 to 3,000 m (6,600 to 9,800 ft) beneath the opposite-flowing Gulf Stream current.*

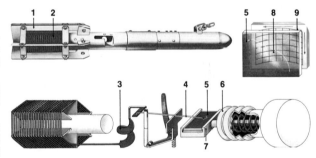

The mechanical bathythermograph simultaneously records temperatures and depths down to about 300 m (980 ft). Protective wings (1) cover 25 m (82 ft) of coiled-up, xylene-filled copper tubing (2). The xylene, because of the thinness of the wall and diameter of the tubing, assumes the ambient temperature. It expands upon contact with this temperature and distorts a Bourdon tube (3) to which the tubing is connected. The tube in turn is connected to a stylus (4), which makes a trace on a coated glass slide (5). The contraction of an air-filled bellows (6) with increasing water pressure and, consequently, depth pulls the stylus carriage (7) in a direction 90° from the stylus movement. The resulting bathythermogram, or depth-versus-temperature trace (8) on the slide, is read against a reference grid (9).

ment, sending back echoes that reveal the structure of underlying rock strata (see GEOPHYSICS).

Submersibles and Habitats. Oceanographers explore the ocean directly by using SCUBA DIVING gear or more complex diving suits (see DIVING, DEEP-SEA), but deeper de-

The U.S. submersible
Alvin, first launched
in 1964, is lowered
into the sea from a
special crane aboard
the research vessel
Atlantis II. Alvin is
able to carry a crew of
three deeper than
3,000 m (13,000 ft)
into the ocean. It has
been used to explore
hydrothermal vents
and, aided by robot
craft, to visit the
sunken Titanic, in
addition to its other
oceanographic re-
search assignments.

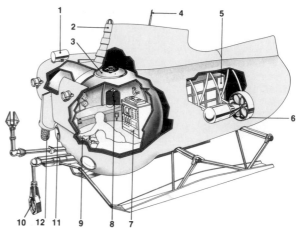

The Canadian-built submersible Pisces can reach depths of 2,000 m (6,560 ft). It houses a crew of two and is equipped with a speed log (1), transponder (2), hatch (3), radio aerial (4), batteries (5), propulsion motor (6), receiver (7), oxygen (8), control console (9), torpedo-recovery arm (10), port (11), and sonar transducer (12).

scents require some form of vessel. The first oceanographic device of this sort was the BATHYSPHERE, a hollow steel ball built in 1930, which had to be lowered and raised by cable. In the late 1940s French explorer Auguste PICCARD developed his first BATHYSCAPHE, a vessel

that could ascend and descend freely, and within a few years an advanced bathyscaphe had explored the world's deepest OCEANIC TRENCH.

Since that time several true submersibles, or steerable underwater craft, have been built for oceanographic use. A notable example is the *Alvin*, designed by Allyn Vine of the Woods Hole Oceanographic Institution. In the mid-1980s the *Alvin* was used to observe HYDROTHERMAL VENTS and also to visit the wreckage of the luxury liner *Titanic*. Such submersibles, and attendant robot craft operated by remote control (ROV, for Remotely Operated Vehicles), can be equipped with many instruments and cameras as well

Tektite I was an underwater habitat submerged to a depth of 4.9 m (16 ft) in the Caribbean Sea in 1969. The two cylinders were connected by an access tunnel (1) and contained living and sleeping quarters (2) for five marine scientists, a control and instrumentation room (3), an engine room (4), and an entry room (5). A shark cage (6) guarded the entrance to the habitat. A beacon light (7) and external lights (8) illuminated the areas viewed through the observation portholes (9). The scientists lived and worked in the habitat for a 14-day period.

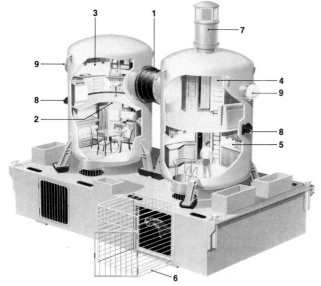

The underwater U.S. oceanographic laboratory Aquarius was installed off St. Croix in the Caribbean Sea in 1987 at a depth of 15 m (50 ft). The facility is 13 m (43 ft) long. Power and air are supplied by a surface vessel. Aquarius enables researchers to work in the vicinity for long periods.

as with mechanical arms for retrieving samples.

With the development of advanced breathing gear, various attempts have also been made since the early 1960s to use seafloor habitats. French oceanographer Jacques-Yves COUSTEAU conducted several such programs, and U.S. efforts have included the Tektite and Sealab projects. The current NATIONAL OCEANIC AND ATMOSPHERIC ADMINISTRATION (NOAA) habitat, called Aquarius, replaces the less-advanced Hydrolab that was used for nearly 200 missions before being retired in 1985. Oceanographic research can be conducted from the sites of these habitats, but their main value is for exploring how well humans can live and work underwater.

See also: HYDROLOGIC SCIENCES.

ocelot The ocelot, *Felis pardalis,* is found in forests and arid brushland from southern Texas to Paraguay. Large males reach a length of 1 m (40 in), plus a 45-cm (18-in) tail, and stand 46 cm (18 in) high at the shoulder; they weigh up to about 16 kg (35 lb). The tan or grayish coat is marked with black spots, black-bordered blotches that are elongated on the back and sides, and black stripes on the head and neck region. Ocelots hunt at any time, but mostly at night, and feed on small mammals, snakes, and birds. Gestation takes about 70 days, with usually two to four young born in a litter.

The ocelot is a proficient swimmer and climber.

ocher [oh'-kur] Ocher is a PIGMENT made from certain crushed and powdered iron-bearing ores. The most common sources are LIMONITE, which produces a yellow ocher, and HEMATITE, a red iron oxide. The application of heat to an ocher powder ("burnt ocher") will shift its color, producing a red or reddish brown. Related pigments are sienna, a brownish yellow that becomes orange red when burned, and umber, a dark brown.

Ochs, Adolph Simon [ahks] Adolph Simon Ochs, b. Cincinnati, Ohio, Mar. 12, 1858, d. Apr. 8, 1935, rescued the NEW YORK TIMES from almost certain death in 1896 and made it the most respected American newspaper. He founded the *Chattanooga* (Tenn.) *Times* in 1878 and acquired the *New York Times* in an effort to strengthen his finances. The slogan "All the News That's Fit to Print" came to symbolize the comprehensive policy of the paper. In the Ochs era the *Times* gave brilliant coverage to the Russo-Japanese War, the sinking of the *Titanic,* World War I, polar explorations, and the Lindbergh flight to Paris.

O'Connell, Daniel Daniel O'Connell, b. Aug. 6, 1775, d. May 15, 1847, created the first truly democratic political movement in Roman Catholic Ireland. A landowner and lawyer, he advocated the abolition of the last vestiges of the Penal Laws against Catholics. During the 1820s he organized a popular agitation that culminated in his election (1828) to a parliamentary seat, which, as a Catholic, he could not legally take. Rather than risk the disorders that were expected to follow refusal to seat O'Connell, Parliament granted CATHOLIC EMANCIPATION in 1829.

In 1837, disappointed at how little he could achieve with his bloc of Irish votes in the Commons, O'Connell launched a new agitation to repeal the Act of Union of 1800, which linked Britain and Ireland legislatively. The Repeal movement generated great enthusiasm in Ireland, but in the mid-1840s, O'Connell's influence declined.

O'Connor, Flannery The American writer Mary Flannery O'Connor, b. Savannah, Ga., Mar. 25, 1925, d. Aug. 3, 1964, was particularly noted for her macabre but strangely touching stories about life in the South. A native of Georgia, the setting for much of her fiction, O'Connor had a fine ear for Georgia dialect and a pitiless eye for the tawdry aspects of modern life. In her work, grotesque comedy and violence often mask a deeper seriousness of purpose and an abiding religious faith. For example, the backwoods protagonist of *Wise Blood* (1952; film, 1979), her first novel, is obsessed by the question of God's existence in a world peopled by freaks, nonentities,

Although she wrote only 2 short novels and 19 stories during her brief career, Flannery O'Connor made an important contribution to American fiction. A southerner and Roman Catholic, she mixed in her works a full-fledged gothic eeriness with an authentic feeling for the powers of grace and redemption.

and manipulators. Her second novel, *The Violent Bear It Away* (1960), also deals with a religious quest. O'Connor suffered from lupus, a debilitating disease of the tissues that left her an invalid in her thirties. Her short stories are collected in *A Good Man Is Hard to Find and Other Stories* (1955) and *Everything That Rises Must Converge* (1965). *Flannery O'Connor: The Complete Stories* (1971), appearing posthumously, received the National Book Award in 1972. O'Connor's essays and lectures were published as *Mystery and Manners* (1969).

O'Connor, Frank   Frank O'Connor is the pen name of the Irish writer Michael O'Donovan, b. 1903, d. Mar. 10, 1966. He fought as a republican in the Irish civil war, and during the 1930s he was director of Dublin's ABBEY THEATRE. His finest work appears in *The Stories of Frank O'Connor* (1952) and *More Stories by Frank O'Connor* (1967). *The Fountain of Magic* (1939) and *Kings, Lords, & Commons* (1959) contain excellent translations of Irish poetry. O'Connor also wrote a history of Irish literature and various literary studies.

O'Connor, John J.   John Joseph O'Connor, b. Philadelphia, Jan. 15, 1920, became the Roman Catholic archbishop of New York in March 1984 and was made a cardinal in May 1985. Ordained a priest in 1945, O'Connor joined the U.S. Navy as a chaplain in 1952 and rose to become the navy's chief of chaplains (1975–79). He served as auxiliary bishop of New York (1979–83) and bishop of Scranton, Pa. (1983–84). An upholder of traditional morality and a strong supporter of Vatican policies, Cardinal O'Connor has frequently taken stands on public issues.

O'Connor, Sandra Day   Sandra Day O'Connor, b. El Paso, Tex., Mar. 26, 1930, was appointed the first woman U.S. Supreme Court justice by President Ronald Reagan in 1981. A former Arizona state senate Republican majority leader (1972–74), she served as a judge in the Maricopa County (Ariz.) Superior Court (1974–79) and the Arizona Court of Appeals (1979–81), where she championed judicial restraint. She is usually, but not always, allied with the Court's conservative bloc.

octane number   see GASOLINE

octave   In Western music, an octave is the distance from one PITCH to the next higher or lower pitch of the same tone name (or letter designation), such as, for example, the interval between any C (as on a keyboard) and the next C above or below it. Use of the same letter to identify both pitches is appropriate because the two pitches are perceptibly different versions of the same tone. The term *octave* (Latin, "eight") is derived from the interval, or distance, between the two pitches, as they embrace a span of eight steps or degrees of the diatonic SCALE (such as in cdefgabc'). Acoustically, an octave results from

a vibration ratio of 2:1; that is, the higher pitch is produced by twice the number of vibrations as the lower pitch.

Octavia [ahk-tay'-vee-uh]   Octavia, 69–11 BC, was a Roman patrician, sister of Octavian (later the emperor AUGUSTUS) and wife of Mark ANTONY. A woman of tact and skill, she married Antony in 40 BC and for a time acted as a buffer between him and Octavian (who were then ruling Rome in a triumvirate with Marcus Aemilius LEPIDUS). Octavia aided her husband in talks that preceded the Pact of Tarentum (37 BC). They were divorced (32 BC) after Antony deserted her for CLEOPATRA.

octopus   Octopuses, marine mollusks of the class Cephalopoda, are characterized by a ring of eight arms around the mouth. Cephalopods are the most highly organized invertebrates, with complex internal systems and advanced learning capabilities. The approximately 150 species of octopuses inhabit nearly all seas. Most species are small, about 30 to 60 cm (1 to 2 ft) in span, but a few may span about 10 m (30 ft).

Many octopuses move by using the muscular suckers on their arms to crawl over the bottom. After attaching to some surface the suckers are expanded by muscular action, creating a partial vacuum that causes them to adhere to the surface. Like other cephalopods, octopuses also can use their exhalant siphons to provide jet propulsion. Water is taken into the mantle cavity—the space between the outer body musculature and the internal organs—and then is expelled forcefully through the siphon. The arms are typically joined at their bases by a web of tissue, but in some deep-sea octopuses the arms are joined by webbing along most of their length, and these forms swim much like jellyfishes by opening and closing this umbrellalike unit.

Octopuses are carnivorous. Prey is captured in the arms, brought to the mouth, bitten by the hard, chitinous,

The common octopus has eight arms, covered with suckers and used for locomotion and grasping prey. Its soft, saclike body contains a highly developed nervous system and brain. The octopus is considered an intelligent creature with a capacity for learning.

parrotlike beak, and injected with poison (tryamine) from the salivary glands. If the prey is a snail or similar hard-shelled animal, the octopus may use its tonguelike radula to drill a hole through the shell and then inject its poison.

Octopus eyes are very similar to the eyes of vertebrates, and are capable of image formation and shape discrimination. To escape enemies the octopus may discharge ink—a black liquid produced in the ink sac, which is attached to the digestive tract near the anus. The ejected ink cloud serves as a temporary decoy to distract the attacker, and alkaloids in the ink act to desensitize the attacker's scent detectors.

Reproduction in octopuses takes place by internal fertilization with the transfer of spermatophores, or packets of sperm. In male octopuses one arm, called the hectocotylus, is modified for the transfer of spermatophores from the male's funnel or mantle cavity to the mantle cavity of the female. In one genus of octopuses, *Argonauta,* called argonauts or paper nautiluses, the female secretes a papery egg case or brood chamber of calcium carbonate in which she not only deposits her eggs but also lives; however, this brood-case shell should not be confused with a true external shell.

ode   The ode, the most elevated and dignified kind of LYRIC poetry, was originally a ceremonious poem written to celebrate public occasions or exalted subjects. The earliest odes were probably the choric songs incorporated in classical Greek DRAMA. Among the many classical authors of odes, PINDAR and HORACE have exercised the greatest influence on later writers. Pindar's odes were written for musical accompaniment and have an extremely elaborate stanzaic structure. Those of Horace, although he called them *carmina,* or "songs," were not sung, but they retained graceful musical meters based on Greek models in two- and four-line stanzas.

Italian Renaissance poets were the first to imitate the classical ode, whose popularity quickly spread throughout Europe. In England, Ben JONSON imitated both the Pindaric and the Horatian ode with great success, but in the work of John Milton, Abraham Cowley, John Dryden, and Thomas Gray the Pindaric ode became a distinct genre. The less ecstatic, more reflective Horatian manner is perfectly exemplified by Andrew Marvell's "An Horatian Ode upon Cromwell's Return from Ireland" (1650). During the 19th century, romantic poets adopted the form, which then became virtually independent of classical models and reached a height of emotional expression in Samuel Taylor Coleridge's "Dejection: An Ode" (1802), William Wordsworth's "Ode: Intimations of Immortality from Recollections of Early Childhood," Percy Bysshe Shelley's "Ode to the West Wind" (1819), and the five great odes of John Keats, published in 1820.

Odense [oh'-thuhn-se]   The third largest city in Denmark (after Copenhagen and Århus), Odense is located on Fyn Island. A thriving commercial port on the Odense River and an industrial center, it has a population of 137,082 (1988 est.). In addition to its busy shipyards, Odense has metalworks and produces motor vehicles, processed foods, and dairy products. The city's most famous son, Hans Christian Andersen, is honored in two museums housed in his former homes. Other landmarks include the Danish Gothic cathedral of Saint Knud (begun *c.*1300) and the University of Odense (1966).

Named for the Norse god Odin, Odense was established and became the site of an episcopal see during the 10th century. The city had grown into a bustling port by the 17th century. Its growth was further stimulated by the opening of the Odense Canal in 1804.

Oder-Neisse line [oh'-dur-ny'-se]   The Oder-Neisse line marks the post–World War II boundary between Germany and Poland. It extends from Swinoujscie on the Baltic Sea south along the Oder and western Neisse rivers to the Czechoslovak border. First proposed by the USSR at the YALTA CONFERENCE of 1945, the division was reluctantly agreed to by the United States and Great Britain at the POTSDAM CONFERENCE the same year, after Soviet troops had occupied the disputed area. The border, however, remained a disputed issue until 1950 when Poland and East Germany signed a treaty; the West Germans did not formally recognize the line until 1970.

The map indicates the location of the Oder-Neisse line, the boundary between Poland and Germany since World War II. The line, agreed on by the Allies in 1945, brought a substantial portion of former German territory under Polish control.

Oder River   The 906-km-long (563-mi) Oder (Czech and Polish, Odra) is one of the principal rivers of Eastern Europe. The river rises in the Moravian highlands of northern Czechoslovakia and flows north into Poland and then northwest to its junction with the Neisse River, the principal tributary; it then flows along the German-Polish border. At Szczecin, Poland, it divides into two channels and finally drains into the Baltic Sea. The river drains an area of 119,140 km^2 (46,000 mi^2). Canals have made the river navigable for more than half of its length, but river traffic has declined since World War II.

Odessa (Texas) [oh-des'-uh]   Odessa, a city in the petroleum-rich Permian Basin of west Texas, is the seat of

Ector County; it has a population of 89,699 (1990). Its economy is centered on the petrochemical industry, and it is a market and distribution center for nearby truck-farming and ranching activities. One of the nation's largest known meteor craters is nearby, with remnants displayed in the Odessa Meteorite Museum. Established in 1886, Odessa developed as a rail distribution point for livestock but grew quickly after petroleum was discovered in the 1920s.

Odessa (USSR) [uh-dyes'-uh]   Odessa is the capital of Odessa oblast in Ukraine, a republic of the USSR. It is a major seaport on the northwest coast of the Black Sea, 32 km (20 mi) from the mouth of the Dnestr River. Its population is 1,115,000 (1989). The city's name is derived from that of a nearby ancient Greek colony known as Odessos.

Odessa is situated on terraced hills overlooking Odessa Bay, an inlet of the Black Sea that forms a natural harbor. From the central part of the city, a monumental stairway descends to the waterfront. It was made famous in the Russian film *Potemkin,* directed by Sergei EISENSTEIN, which depicts the naval mutiny that occurred during the Revolution of 1905. The city has beach resorts famous for therapeutic mud baths.

A diversified manufacturing center, Odessa produces a wide range of machinery and equipment, including machine tools, farm machinery, hoisting equipment, and refrigerators, as well as chemicals. Shipyards and a small petroleum refinery are important to the economy. Food processing is based on the city's proximity to rich Ukrainian farmlands.

Odessa is also a leading educational and cultural center and the seat of Odessa State University (1865). Its cosmopolitan atmosphere can be attributed to its importance as one of the USSR's principal foreign-trade ports and fishing-fleet bases, with traffic to and from the countries of the Mediterranean basin, Africa, the Middle East,

Odessa, a regional capital situated on the northwestern coast of the Black Sea between the mouths of the Dnestr and Dnepr rivers, is the USSR's principal port for the shipment of grain.

and Asia. Because of the growing role of foreign commerce in the Soviet economy, Odessa has spawned two large outer ports whose volume of shipping overshadows that of Odessa–Ilyichevsk, which became a city in its own right in 1973, and Yuzhny.

The city was founded in 1794 on the site of a Turkish settlement after the armies of Catherine II had wrested control of the Black Sea coast from the Turks. Odessa grew rapidly, especially in the late 19th century, when railroad construction in southern Ukraine made it Russia's principal port for grain exports. After the Bolshevik Revolution, the nation's economy turned inward, and Odessa stagnated. Its development was also set back during World War II, when it fell to German and Romanian forces in October 1941 after a 69-day siege. Growth resumed in the 1960s.

Odets, Clifford [oh-dets']   An American playwright who made his mark in the 1930s, Clifford Odets, b. Philadelphia, July 18, 1906, d. Aug. 14, 1963, is best known for his protest dramas, which also contain a strong romantic element. A member of the GROUP THEATRE from 1931, Odets became famous overnight with his first produced play, *Waiting for Lefty* (1935), a short, agitational work that attacked unemployment and unfair labor practices, problems that he returned to in later, full-length works. Two of these became American classics. *Awake and Sing!* (1935) is an optimistic play that comes down solidly on the side of both love and revolt. *Golden Boy* (1937; film, 1939), the most popular of all Odets's efforts, presents the tragedy of a young man who abandons the art of the violin to take up a brutal but profitable career in boxing. Two later plays were also successful: *The Country Girl* (1950; film, 1954) portrays an alcoholic actor's attempt to resume his interrupted career, and *The Flowering Peach* (1954) is a poignant adaptation of the story of Noah.

In Hollywood, Odets adapted several of his plays as films, wrote screenplays for many other movies (especially *Humoresque,* 1947, and *Sweet Smell of Success,* 1957), and directed two successful screen dramas, *None but the Lonely Heart* (1944) and *The Story on Page One* (1959).

Odetta [oh-det'-uh]   The American folksinger Odetta, b. Odetta Holmes, Birmingham, Ala., Dec. 31, 1930, was a student of classical music in Los Angeles when she discovered her talent for singing blues, ballads, and work songs and taught herself to play the guitar. Her rich contralto and her unusually sensitive delivery quickly won her a following. Her many performances have included concerts at New York's Town Hall and Carnegie Hall and frequent appearances at the Newport Folk Festival.

Odin [oh'-din]   In Norse mythology, as preserved in the Icelandic EDDAS (11th–12th century AD), Odin is the chief of the gods and the ruler of the universe. He was the son of the frost giant Bör and the giantess Bestla. Early in his career, together with his brothers Vili and Ve, Odin overthrew the primeval giant Ymir and fashioned the world from his remains.

Odin, his wife Frigg, and the other major Norse divinities—Thor and Tyr, sons of Odin—live in Asgard, near which is Valhalla, where Odin was believed to feast with the spirits of slain warriors. At Ragnarok, the "twilight of the gods," Odin will lead his army against the giants led by Loki. Odin will be devoured by the wolf Fenrir but then be avenged by his son Vidar. Odin's sacred bird is the raven, and his principal weapon—in addition to his powerful runes, or magical spells—is the spear. He is depicted as tall, bearded, and one-eyed, having exchanged his other eye for wisdom.

In pre-Christian Scandinavia the Odin cult was apparently characterized by human sacrifice, which was usually accomplished by hanging the victim from a tree. The German form of his name is Woden, or Wotan; the name Wednesday is derived from Woden's day.

Odoacer [oh-doh-ay'-sur] A Germanic warrior and king of Italy, Odoacer, also known as Odovacar, b. c.433, d. Mar. 15, 493, dethroned the young emperor Romulus Augustulus on Aug. 28, 476, bringing the moribund Western Roman Empire to a formal end. A member of either the Sciri or the Rugian tribe, Odoacer made few administrative changes in Rome. He recovered Sicily and Dalmatia, threatening the Byzantine emperor Zeno. In 488, Zeno sponsored the Ostrogothic king Theodoric against Odoacer. Theodoric overran Italy and assassinated Odoacer at a banquet, a week after Odoacer had surrendered.

Odoric of Pordenone [ahd'-ohr-ik, pohr'-den-oh-nee] An Italian missionary, Odoric of Pordenone, b. c.1286, d. Jan. 14, 1331, traveled extensively throughout the Far East and left a vivid account of his adventures. A member of the Franciscan order from about 1300, Odoric left Italy about 1316 on a journey to the Orient that lasted approximately 14 years. He visited India, the East Indies, and Southeast Asia before reaching China. He stayed for three years at Khanbalik, the Chinese capital, which Europeans called Cambaluc (modern Beijing), where Giovanni da Montecorvino had already established a Franciscan mission. On his return to Europe, Odoric probably visited Tibet, reaching Italy in 1330.

Odysseus [oh-dis'-ee-uhs] In Greek mythology Odysseus, king of Ithaca, was an epic hero whose arduous, ten-year voyage returning to Ithaca after the Trojan War is the subject of Homer's Odyssey. As a Greek commander in the Trojan War, he also appears in the Iliad. Noted for his cleverness—it was Odysseus who suggested the stratagem of the Trojan Horse—the Ithacan king served ably in the conflict with Troy. The goddess Athena, however, became angry with the Greeks because of the ill-treatment they had accorded the Trojan princess Cassandra at the end of the war. As a result, all of the victors had difficulties in returning to their homes in Greece.

None, however, encountered greater obstacles than Odysseus. For a decade he and his men wandered from place to place and had a great many adventures: they were turned into swine by the sorceress Circe; they almost succumbed to the temptations of the land of the Lotus-Eaters and the insidious song of the Sirens; they barely survived the dangers of the passage between Scylla and Charybdis, as well as their encounter with the fearsome one-eyed giant Polyphemus. Nevertheless, the wily Odysseus managed to survive.

With the help of the Phaecians, on whose shore Odysseus had been shipwrecked—his crew had long since perished—he finally arrived home in Ithaca only to find his faithful wife, Penelope, hounded by suitors, who believed him dead. Aided by his son Telemachus, he surprised Penelope's would-be husbands, killed them all, and was reunited with his family.

Odyssey [ahd'-i-see] The ancient Greek epic the Odyssey, by Homer, is thought to have been composed during the later 8th century BC. As with the Iliad, the poem's tight thematic control and organization belie its oral-formulaic origins. The poem describes the long and difficult return journey of the Greek hero Odysseus to Ithaca at the conclusion of the Trojan War. After ten years of war, followed by ten years of wandering, affliction, and distraction in perilous and semimagical surroundings, Odysseus arrives home only to find his wife, Penelope, besieged by suitors. By juxtaposing the fantastic worlds of the wanderings with the real world of Ithaca and by contrasting the despair of Odysseus while away from home with the joy he feels on returning, Homer focuses on what it is to be human and on the values and ideals that inform human existence. The Odyssey has served as the archetype for later applications of the theme of wandering, of which the first half of Vergil's Aeneid and James Joyce's Ulysses are the most distinguished.

Oe Kenzaburo [oh'-ay kayn'-zah'-boo-roh] Oe Kenzaburo, b. Jan. 31, 1935, is one of contemporary Japan's most highly acclaimed novelists. Deeply influenced by American and French literature, Oe invented a vivid, almost assaultive writing style—a far departure from traditional Japanese literary expression. At first a New Left critic of Japanese society, Oe changed when his first son was born with brain damage. He became obsessed with the figure of the damaged or deformed child, and much of his later work is concerned with both the literal and the symbolic significances of that figure. The novel A Personal Matter (1964; Eng. trans., 1968) is the first work dealing with this new theme. Others include stories in the collections Teach Us to Outgrow Our Madness (Eng. trans., 1977) and The Crazy Iris and Other Stories of the Atomic Aftermath (Eng. trans., 1985).

Oedipus [ed'-i-puhs] Most famous of the ancient Greek heroes of Thebes, the unfortunate King Oedipus inspired SOPHOCLES' great tragedies *Oedipus Rex* and *Oedipus at Colonus.* The son of Laius, king of Thebes, and Jocasta, the infant Oedipus was ritually wounded in the foot (hence his name, which means "swollen foot") and exposed on Mount Cithaeron, because of a prophecy that he would kill his father and marry his mother. Rescued by a shepherd, he was brought up by King Polybius of Corinth.

When grown, Oedipus heard the prophecy about himself and fled Corinth, believing that Polybius was his father. While on the road he killed a stranger, not knowing that it was Laius. Entering Thebes, he found the city dominated by a SPHINX who killed anyone who could not solve her riddle: "Who goes on four feet in the morning, on two at noon, and in the evening on three?" Oedipus vanquished her by replying, "Man, in the three ages of his life," and won the hand of the widowed queen.

Marrying Jocasta and thus fulfilling the prophecy, Oedipus reigned long in Thebes and raised two sons, Eteocles and Polynices, and two daughters, ANTIGONE and Ismene. When the secret of his birth came to light, Jocasta hanged herself, and Oedipus blinded himself in remorse, or was blinded. Under the regency of Jocasta's brother Creon, Oedipus was driven from Thebes. Antigone chose exile with him, the two seeking refuge at Colonus, near Athens. Both daughters helped prepare Oedipus for death in a grove sacred to the Eumenides. Many variations of the story occur in literature.

Oedipus complex   see COMPLEX (psychology)

Oehlenschläger, Adam Gottlob [url'-en-shlay-gur] Adam Oehlenschläger, b. Nov. 14, 1779, d. Jan. 20, 1850, is ranked as Denmark's greatest poet. His best-known works are epic poems and dramas drawn from Icelandic folklore. Enormously popular in their day, these works spurred new interest in ancient Icelandic literature. Oehlenschläger was at the forefront of the romantic movement in Danish literature, and one of his early lyric poems, *The Gold Horns* (1802; Eng. trans., 1913), became the keystone of that movement.

Oerter, Al [ohr'-tur]   Alfred A. Oerter, b. Astoria, N.Y., Aug. 19, 1936, an American discus thrower, won that Olympic Games event an unprecedented four consecutive times. He was 20 years old when he first captured the Olympic title, in 1956. In the 1960 Olympics, Oerter again won the event, but his 1964 victory was more impressive—he competed with a painful rib injury. Before he earned his fourth gold medal in 1968, Oerter was already recognized as the greatest discus thrower ever. In 1976, after a 7-year layoff, Oerter resumed competition and, despite his age, for a time, displayed Olympic potential once again.

O'Faolain, Sean [oh-fal'-uhn]   Sean O'Faolain, b. Feb. 22, 1900, d. Apr. 20, 1991, was an Irish writer best known for his short stories. His early novels, *A Nest of Simple Folk* (1934) and *Bird Alone* (1936), take place at the time of the EASTER RISING of 1916 and the "troubles" that followed World War I—events during which O'Faolain, discovering his Irish patriotism for the first time, played a small part. Changing his name from John Whelan to its Gaelic equivalent, and writing in Gaelic as well as in English, he embarked on the career that would make him a popular interpreter of Ireland. In addition to four novels, he wrote biographies of Irish notables; several works on Ireland, especially *The Irish: A Character Study* (1947; rev. ed., 1969); and the many short stories that established his fame. They are published in *The Collected Stories of Sean O'Faolain* (1983).

Off-Broadway theater   Beginning as a rebellion against the cautious policies and high costs of New York City's commercial theaters, Off-Broadway theater has since the 1950s served as a forum for the work of new authors, actors, and other artists, and as a center for experimental work of all kinds.

The Provincetown Players, originally organized as a playwrights' workshop and associated with early productions of plays by Eugene O'Neill, and the Washington Square Players were sporadically active in New York's Greenwich Village beginning in 1916. In the 1920s and '30s, "workers'" theaters proliferated Off-Broadway, producing primarily leftist dramas and plays that appealed to such special audiences as immigrants and trade unionists—*Pins and Needles* (1937), produced by the International Ladies' Garment Workers' Union, was an outstanding play of the period. The decade of the 1950s established such important theaters as Circle in the Square, the Phoenix Theater, Joseph PAPP's New York Shakespeare Festival, and the LIVING THEATRE. Performers who had been blacklisted on Broadway created *The World of Sholom Aleichem* (1953), which was staged in a hotel ballroom and ran for 305 performances.

Production costs for early Off-Broadway shows were minimal. Eventually, however, the actors' union Actors' Equity set working conditions and salaries for members performing off Broadway. Budgets soared along with the expectations of audiences, and Off-Broadway theater began to lose some of its creative edge. In the 1960s Joe Cino's Caffe Cino and Ellen Stewart's Café La Mama broke ground Off-Off Broadway. Theatre Genesis, Judson Poets, The Open Theatre, Bread and Puppet Theater, and other small companies developed important directors, writers, and performers. Equity again forced an agreement (1966) on salaries and working conditions, but Off-Off Broadway remains a home for the experimental (PERFORMANCE ART began and still flourishes there).

Offa, King of Mercia [ah'-fuh]   Offa, d. July 29, 796, ruled the Anglo-Saxon kingdom of MERCIA from 757 and succeeded in unifying England to a greater extent than ever before. Offa extended Mercia's power over Kent and Sussex, defeated King Cynewulf of Wessex, married off his daughters to the kings of Northumbria and Wessex, and took over East Anglia by having its king beheaded (794). Offa also repulsed a Welsh invasion and then built an earthwork called OFFA'S DYKE to defend the frontier between Mercia and Wales. Pope Adrian I allowed him to establish (788) a Mercian archbishopric at Lichfield in opposition to the Kentish one at Canterbury. Offa also negotiated as an equal with CHARLEMAGNE; the commercial treaty that they signed in 796 was the first such document recorded in English history.

Offa's Dyke   Offa's Dyke, one of the outstanding field monuments of the post-Roman period in Great Britain, extends about 195 km (120 mi) through the Welsh marches from the Dee estuary in the north to the Bristol Channel in the south. Its northern end is supplemented by a second linear earthwork to the east, known as Wat's Dyke, along with short lengths elsewhere, not all contemporary but nonetheless forming a complex frontier system between Welsh and English territories. Construction of the dyke is generally attributed to Offa, king of Mercia (757–96), to whom it was credited by the Welsh monk Asser in his *Life of King Alfred,* written less than a century later.

Offenbach, Jacques [aw'-fen-bahk]   The witty and satirical operettas of Jacques Offenbach, b. Cologne, Germany, June 20, 1819, d. Oct. 5, 1880, ridiculed the pompous aspects of life during the Second Empire in France, a period when all art, including the theater, was subject to censorship and musical life was dominated by grand opera. Offenbach was the son of the violinist and cantor Isaac Juda Eberst, who came from Offenbach am Main and was known as the "man from Offenbach." Originally named Jacob, he later adopted the French form Jacques, and in 1844 he became a convert to Roman Catholicism. In 1833 he entered the Paris Conservatory, where he studied cello, and in 1837 he joined the orchestra of the Opéra-Comique. He became conductor of

Jacques Offenbach, a 19th-century French composer whose comic operettas achieved immense success, created the genre that dominated the musical theater of his day. His fantasy opera Tales of Hoffmann (1880) *continues to be widely performed and enjoyed.*

the Théâtre Français in 1849 and opened his own small musical theater, Les Bouffes-Parisiens, in 1855.

Offenbach's first great success as a composer was *Orpheus in the Underworld* (1858; expanded, 1874), a tuneful travesty of the Greek myth. This opera is the source of Offenbach's famous cancan, which has been adapted for such ballets as *Gâité Parisienne.* He composed about 100 other works, including *La Belle Hélène* (1864), *La Vie parisienne* (1866), and *La Grande Duchesse de Gérolstein* (1867).

The Franco-Prussian War (1870–71) brought the Second Empire to an end, thus eliminating one of Offenbach's favorite targets. He died a few months before the triumphant premiere of his only grand opera, *The Tales of Hoffmann* (unfinished at his death; orchestration and recitatives by Ernest Guiraud). Unlike the operettas, which are so intricately connected with the concerns of Second-Empire Paris that they are often difficult to appreciate today, Offenbach's last work still has a firm place in the operatic repertoire.

Office of Strategic Services   The Office of Strategic Services (OSS) was a U.S. intelligence unit that operated during World War II. It was the military precursor of the CENTRAL INTELLIGENCE AGENCY. Set up on June 13, 1942, to collect and analyze information for the Joint Chiefs of Staff, the OSS replaced the office of Coordinator of Information. It was organized and directed by Maj. Gen. William J. "Wild Bill" Donovan (1883–1959). The organization utilized civilians and members of all branches of the armed forces. The personnel gathered and evaluated information from the major theaters of operations and from underground groups in enemy-occupied territories. The OSS also engaged in sabotage in order to damage the enemy's war-making capacities and morale. On Oct. 1, 1945, President Harry S. Truman discontinued the OSS, transferring some of the agency's functions to an Interim Research and Intelligence Service and delegating the remainder to the War Department.

offset lithography   Lithography is a printing process invented by Aloys Senefelder about 1800. This article treats applications of this process to commercial printing. Lithography, also a printmaking process, is planographic—that is, the image and nonimage areas are essentially on the same plane of the printing plate.

Although originally all LITHOGRAPHS were printed from a type of stone on a flatbed press, modern commercial printing uses paper, plastic, and metal plates on a rotary press. The difference between the image and nonimage areas on the plates is maintained chemically by the mutual repulsion of grease and water. In PLATEMAKING the image area is covered with an ink that is grease-receptive, and the nonprinting areas are made water receptive. In PRINTING on the press, the plate, which is mounted on a rotating cylinder, comes in contact with rollers wet with a water solution (dampening rollers) and rollers wet with ink. The water solution wets the nonprinting areas so that the ink wets only the image areas and is then transferred, or offset, to an intermediate cylinder covered with a rubber blanket. The paper or other substrate picks up the impression of the image as the paper travels between the rubber-covered blanket cylinder and an impression cylinder. The term *offset* comes from the transfer of the image to the intermediate rubber-covered cylinder. LETTERPRESS and intaglio printing processes can also use the offset principle, but because nearly all lithography is printed by this principle, the term *offset* has become synonymous with lithography.

Both web-fed and sheet-fed presses are used in offset lithography. In most web offset presses, the blankets of the two printing units oppose each other so that both sides of the web are printed at the same time.

Sheet-fed offset lithography is used for a wide variety of printing. Web offset is used for printing jobs such as newspapers, books, and magazines. Offset lithography is the fastest growing of the printing processes because of its ability to produce high-quality printing at relatively low cost.

offshore drilling   see PETROLEUM INDUSTRY

O'Flaherty, Liam [oh-flah'-u-tee, lee'-uhm]   Liam O'Flaherty, b. Aug. 28, 1896, d. Sept. 7, 1984, was an Irish writer whose powerful novel of betrayal, *The Informer* (1925; filmed by John Ford, 1935), set during the Irish "troubles" (civil war) of 1922, reflects his own experiences as a republican activist. This novel was followed by others on similarly violent episodes from Ireland's past, such as the psychological thrillers *Mr. Gilhooley* (1926) and *The Assassin* (1928) and a trilogy of naturalistic works dealing with the 19th century, *Famine* (1937), *Land* (1946), and *Insurrection* (1950). Many of O'Flaherty's short stories, collected in *The Stories of Liam O'Flaherty* (1956) and *The Wounded Cormorant and Other Stories* (1973), recall his native Aran Islands. He also wrote an autobiography, *Shame the Devil* (1934).

Ogaden [ah-guh'-dehn]   Ogaden, a semiarid, infertile region of southeastern Ethiopia, is bordered by Somalia on the north and east. Inhabited primarily by ethnic Somali nomads, it was claimed by Italian Somaliland in the 1890s and was the pretext for Italy's conquest of Ethiopia in 1935. It was returned to Ethiopia by Britain in 1948. In 1977, Somali troops invaded Ogaden in support of the Western Somalia Liberation Front's demands for self-determination. Ethiopia recaptured the area with the aid of Soviet and Cuban forces in 1978. Although Ethiopia and Somalia restored diplomatic relations in 1988, Somalia did not renouce its claim to Ogaden.

Ogden   Ogden, a city in northern Utah and the seat of Weber County, is located in the fertile front of the Wasatch Range at the confluence of the Weber and Ogden rivers. The city has a population of 63,909 (1990). Og-

den is best known for its aerospace facilities, but its industries produce building materials and processed foods. The Ogden Defense Depot and nearby Hill Air Force Base contribute to the city's economy, as do nearby ski resorts. The city is the site of Weber State College, a state industrial school, and a Mormon tabernacle. Ogden was established as a trading post in the 1820s and was settled by Mormons in the 1840s.

Oglethorpe, James [oh'-gul-thohrp]   The British general and philanthropist James Edward Oglethorpe, b. Dec. 22, 1696, d. July 1, 1785, founded the colony of Georgia and served (1733–43) as its first governor. In 1732, Oglethorpe and 19 associates secured a charter to colonize Georgia. He reached North America in 1733 and founded Savannah that year. He conceived the colony as a haven for Protestant dissenters and insolvent debtors who had served time in British prisons, and he hoped to provide economic incentives to reform the idle and criminal classes of England. He implemented acts prohibiting the sale of rum, outlawing slavery, and limiting the size of individual landholdings. Oglethorpe also organized Georgia as a colonial outpost against attacks from Spanish Florida (see FRENCH AND INDIAN WARS).

Oglethorpe's good intentions were frustrated by settlers who resented the economic restrictions placed on them. In 1743 he returned to England and largely severed himself from the Georgia venture. He and his associates yielded their charter in 1752, and Georgia became a royal colony.

OGO   The Orbiting Geophysical Observatory (OGO) was a series of six NASA scientific satellites launched between 1964 and 1969 that provided data on the Earth's atmosphere, ionosphere, and magnetosphere, and on Sun-Earth interactions.

The Spacecraft. The main body of the satellite, built by TRW Space Laboratories, consisted of a rectangular aluminum box that was 173 cm (68 in) long, 84 cm (33 in) wide, and 84 cm deep. Two rectangular panels covered with 32,000 solar cells provided 500 W of power, which recharged internal nickel-cadmium batteries. *OGO 1*, launched Sept. 4, 1964, carried 20 scientific instruments, including cosmic-ray counters, detectors, and telescopes; Geiger counters; ionization chambers; magnetometers; ion and electron traps; spectrometers; micrometeoroid detectors; and a photometer for studying the Gegenschein, or zodiacal light.

In succeeding satellites, the number of instruments varied from 20 to 25. OGO satellites thus varied in weight from 487 to 632 kg (1,073 to 1,393 lb). Three of them (*OGO 2*, *OGO 4*, and *OGO 6*) were launched in 1965, 1967, and 1969, repectively, from the Western Test Range at Vandenberg AFB, Calif., so that they could obtain a polar orbit. Three others (*OGO 1*, *OGO 3*, and *OGO 5*), launched from the Kennedy Space Center in Florida, were placed in highly eccentric orbits. None continue to function.

Scientific Contributions. OGO was a highly successful program. The spacecraft made many significant contributions to astrophysics: the first observation of protons responsible for a ring of electrical current that surrounds the Earth during magnetic storms; the provision of data for a proposed new magnetic field model for the International Geomagnetic Reference Field; the clear identification of the controlling influence of Earth's magnetic field on the number of ions in the magnetosphere; the verification of the existence of the plasmapause, the inward boundary surrounding the region of trapped radiation in the magnetosphere; and the first observations of a region of low-energy electrons totally enveloping the trapped-radiation regions.

OGO satellites also made the first observations of daytime auroras; provided data for the first worldwide map of airglow distribution; contributed to a greater understanding of Earth's bow shock, which is created by the impact of the solar wind on the Earth's magnetosphere; gave evidence of instabilities in the magnetospheric boundary; and provided fundamental data on the low-frequency radio waves known as whistlers.

O'Gorman, Juan   Juan O'Gorman, b. July 7, 1905, d. Jan. 18, 1982, was a Mexican architect and painter. As an architect he was one of the first in Mexico to follow the functionalist aesthetic of the International Style, an approach he later abandoned. O'Gorman's early interest in painting sparked his search in the 1950s for an indigenous architectural style that would integrate the plastic and the pictorial arts. A notable result was his mosaic-sheathed Library of the National University of Mexico (1953). O'Gorman also was an important muralist in the style of Diego RIVERA and an influential landscape painter whose imaginative interpretations of the Mexican countryside sometimes display strong symbolic elements and suggestions of surrealism.

Oh, Sadaharu   Sadaharu Oh, b. May 20, 1940, a citizen of the Republic of China (Taiwan), is the greatest home-run hitter in the history of Japanese baseball, comparable with Babe Ruth and Henry Aaron of the United States. In 1959, Oh joined the Yomiuri Giants as a left-handed-hitting first baseman. At bat, he lifted his right leg in the air in a style similar to that used by New York Giants' star Mel Ott. In 1977 he exceeded Aaron's total by clouting his 756th career home run. Oh was then rewarded with Japan's first National Hero Honors Order. He retired in 1980 with a total of 868 home runs.

O'Hara, Frank   The American poet and art critic Frank O'Hara, b. Baltimore, Md., June 27, 1926, d. July 25, 1966, began to write verse in the 1940s; he was equally interested, however, in the visual arts and associated with painters of the New York abstract expressionist school during the 1950s and '60s. His first volume of poems, *A City Winter*, was published in 1952, and his influential criticism of modern painting and sculpture began to appear in magazines at the same time. He was an enthusiastic champion of the painter Jackson Pollock, on whom he published a book in 1959. Some have noted affinities between O'Hara's disjointed, energetic style and the canvases of Pollock and Willem de Kooning. His *Collected Poems* (1971) were edited after his death by Donald Allen.

O'Hara, John   One of the most popular American novelists and short-story writers of the 20th century, John Henry O'Hara, b. Pottsville, Pa., Jan. 31, 1905, d. Apr. 11, 1970, established his gift for acute observation and ironic dialogue with his first novel, *Appointment in Samarra* (1934). In this and later novels, which include *Butterfield 8* (1935; film, 1960), *A Rage To Live* (1949; film, 1965), *Ten North Frederick* (1955; film, 1958), and *From the Terrace* (1958; film, 1960), O'Hara showed a thorough familiarity with American class, sex, and drinking patterns, especially as found in Gibbsville, Pa., a fictitious community modeled on his hometown. Volumes of his short stories include *Sermons and Soda Water* (1960), *The Cape Cod Lighter* (1962), *The Hat on the Bed* (1963), and *The Horse Knows the Way* (1964). A novel in the form of letters, *Pal Joey* (1940), was turned into a musical (1940; film, 1957).

O'Higgins, Bernardo   Bernardo O'Higgins, b. Aug. 20, 1778, d. Oct. 24, 1842, was the principal leader of Chile's struggle for independence from Spain and the first ruler of his country. The illegitimate son of Ambrosio O'Higgins, the viceroy of Peru, he went to England at age 17 and there he came under the influence of the Venezuelan republican Francisco de MIRANDA.

O'Higgins returned to Chile in 1802 and took part in the establishment of a Chilean national regime in 1810. Named to the revolutionary junta headed by José Miguel Carrera in 1812, he became commander of its army in 1814. After a defeat by the Spanish in October 1814, O'Higgins retreated to Argentina, where he joined forces with José de SAN MARTÍN. In February 1817 their army

Bernardo O'Higgins, a Chilean revolutionary leader, became the first ruler of Chile after the Spanish defeat in 1817 and formally declared its independence in 1818. His reforms lost him his former political support, and he was ousted from power in 1823.

OHIO

Land: Area: 107,044 km² (41,330 mi²); rank: 35th. Capital and largest city: Columbus (1990 pop., 632,910). Counties: 88. Elevations: highest—472 m (1,549 ft), at Campbell Hill; lowest—139 m (455 ft), at the Ohio River.

People: Population (1990): 10,887,325; rank: 7th; density: 101.7 persons per km² (263.4 per mi²). Distribution (1988 est.): 78.9% metropolitan, 21.1% nonmetropolitan. Average annual change (1980–90): +0.08%.

Government (1991): Governor: George V. Voinovich, Republican. U.S. Congress: Senate—2 Democrats; House—11 Democrats, 10 Republicans. Electoral college votes: 23. State legislature: 33 senators, 99 representatives.

Economy: State personal income (1988): $168.6 billion; rank: 8th. Median family income (1979): $20,909; rank: 16th. Agriculture: income (1988)—$3.6 billion. Forestry: sawtimber volume (1987)—22.4 billion board feet. Mining: value (1987)—$2.5 billion. Manufacturing: value added (1987)—$71.7 billion. Services: value (1987)—$39.4 billion.

Miscellany: Statehood: Mar. 1, 1803; the 17th state. Nickname: Buckeye State; tree: buckeye; motto: With God All Things Are Possible; song: "Beautiful Ohio."

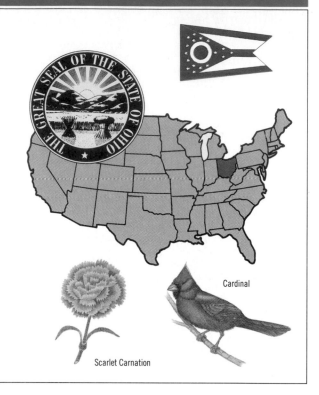

Cardinal

Scarlet Carnation

---

defeated the Spanish at Chacabuco. O'Higgins was appointed supreme director of Chile, and in 1818 he declared Chilean independence. The O'Higgins regime was autocratic, but he initiated many public improvements. The church and aristocracy resisted his liberal social reforms, while liberals regarded his rule as undemocratic, and in 1823, O'Higgins resigned. He then lived in Peru until his death.

Ohio   Ohio contains the edge of the Appalachian Mountains in the east and plains in the west. It is bordered by Indiana on the west, Michigan and Lake Erie on the north, and Pennsylvania and West Virginia on the east. The Ohio River follows the state's southern border with West Virginia and Kentucky. Almost equidistant in its north-south and east-west dimensions, Ohio has an area of 107,044 km² (41,330 mi²).

Because of its advantageous alignment with Lake Erie and the Ohio River, the Ohio country became the first destination for settlers and pioneers on their way further into the interior. In 1803, Ohio became the 17th state to join the Union and the first to be admitted from the Northwest Territory. Its name is derived from an Iroquois word meaning "beautiful."

Land and Resources

Ohio shares parts of two major physical provinces of the continental United States—the Appalachian Plateau and the Central Lowland. The boundary between these regions cuts the state in two along a northeast-southwest line extending from southwest of Cleveland to the Ohio River in Adams County. The two regions are distinguished by their relief and elevation, with higher, more rugged land in the plateau areas and less elevated, level terrain in the lowland province.

The effects of continental glaciation further divided the two major regions into five physiographic regions: the northern lake plain, the western till plain, the glaciated plateau, the unglaciated plateau, and the Lexington plain.

The lake plain encompasses the northernmost part of Ohio. It is as narrow as 8 km (5 mi) in the east but widens to ten times that distance toward the Indiana border. In the eastern plateau section, the land becomes increasingly hilly. The glaciated plateau occupies the northeastern part of the state, while relatively high relief adjacent to the Ohio River characterizes the unglaciated plateau to the southeast. The western till plain corresponds with the Central Lowland and is essentially of low relief and elevation except for Mount Campbell; its elevation of 472 m

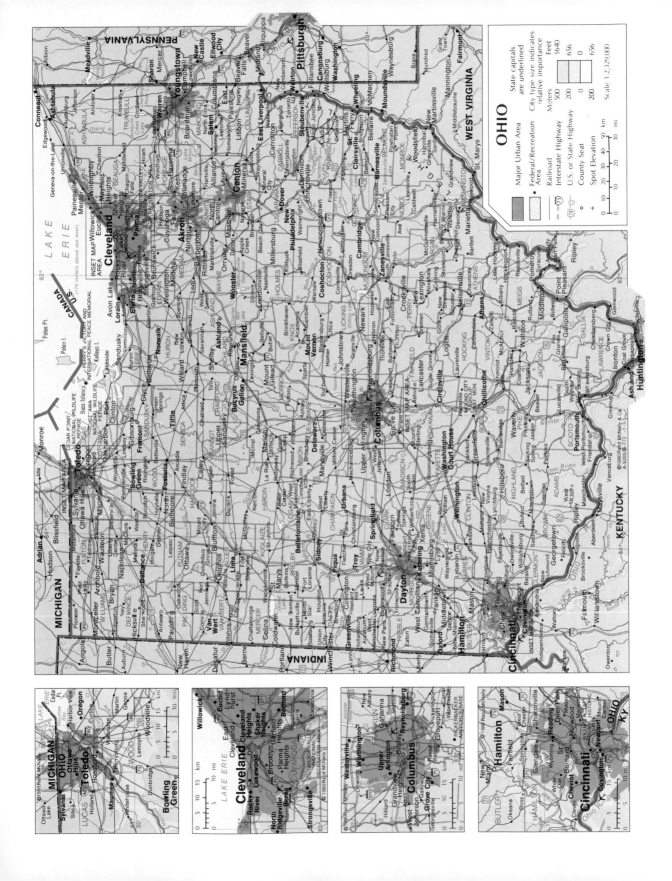

OHIO

(1,550 ft) is the highest in Ohio. The Lexington plain is a small northward extension into southwest Ohio of residual limestone soils of Kentucky's Bluegrass Basin.

Ohio's geology is relatively simple. Bedrock consists of basically undisturbed Paleozoic sediments. In western Ohio limestone and dolomite are widespread. Toward the east sandstones and shales are more prevalent.

Soils. Soils in Ohio have developed largely on transported glacial materials. Only in the unglaciated portion of southeastern Ohio can old, residual soils developed from bedrock be found. Soil thicknesses vary considerably but are greater in the glaciated areas. The residual soils of southeastern Ohio are thin, leached, and acidic, with low productivity.

Drainage. Only 29% of Ohio's waterways drain into Lake Erie (see ERIE, LAKE), including the Maumee-Auglaize system in northwestern Ohio and the Portage, Sandusky, Huron, Vermillion, Black, Cuyahoga, and Grand rivers. The southern—or OHIO RIVER—drainage region contains major streams and their drainage basins. The largest is the Muskingum River watershed, followed by the Scioto and the Miami. Other streams draining into the Ohio include the Little Miami, Raccoon, Hocking, and Mahoning rivers. While surface water provides the primary water source, aquifers constitute a perennial water reservoir.

Climate. Except for a small area along the Ohio River, a humid continental climate dominates the state. Large seasonal temperature changes are common, with January temperatures averaging below 0° C (32° F) and July temperature averages exceeding 24° C (75° F). Precipitation averages between 762 mm (30 in) and 1,016 mm (40 in). Slightly higher precipitation falls during the summer,

Farmland in central Ohio produces a rich harvest of oats and other field crops such as corn, wheat, and soybeans.

Cincinnatti's skyline incorporates the modern architecture and renovations of the city's riverfront downtown area. Riverfront Stadium, part of a major urban renewal project begun in 1962, dominates this view.

and autumns are relatively dry.

The Appalachian foothills have an important local climatic effect, creating frequent temperature inversions. This condition results in frosts in late spring and early fall. A more serious effect is the trapping of pollutants in highly industrialized portions of the upper Ohio River valley.

Vegetation and Animal Life. Unique vegetational areas included the swamp forest (Black Swamp) of the northwestern lake plain, and scattered prairie grasslands in the west central part. Settlement and intensive land use have totally altered these vegetational habitats. Today approximately 24% of Ohio is forestland.

Ohio's principal game fish is black bass followed by walleyed pike, Ohio muskellunge, white bass, perch, saugers, bluegills, rock bass, and channel catfish. Indigenous animals include the cottontail rabbit, white-tailed deer, quail, ruffed grouse, gray squirrel, and wild turkey. A few black bears can still be found. In western Ohio the ring-necked pheasant and Hungarian partridge have been introduced. Wild ducks inhabit the marshes along Lake Erie. Raccoon, muskrat, mink, opossums, and weasels are widely distributed.

Resources. Ohio's importance in natural resources is derived from its longtime production of coal. Coal resources are restricted to the east. Other nonmetallic minerals and mineral fuels include limestone, sand and gravel, clay, salt, sandstone, natural gas and petroleum, shale, gypsum, and peat.

Among other natural resources, water ranks high in Ohio; 95% of the water consumed comes from surface supplies. Included in this resource are Lake Erie, 28 km^2 (11 mi^2) of natural lakes, 417 km^2 (161 mi^2) of impounded water, and about 70,800 km (44,000 mi) of streams.

People

Ohio's heterogeneous population includes the descendants of colonial settlers as well as more recent European immigrants, chiefly German and Irish. Industrialization and urbanization encouraged the immigration of eastern and southern Europeans and an influx of large numbers of blacks. Population growth in Ohio has slowed considerably as the combined result of lower birthrates and out-migration. Although more than 80% of the population reside in the metropolitan areas, more than 50% of the metropolitan residents live outside the central cities. The largest urban centers in the state are AKRON, CINCINNATI, CLEVELAND, COLUMBUS (the capital), DAYTON, TOLEDO, all with populations exceeding 100,000, and YOUNGSTOWN. Because most of Ohio's major cities have relatively fixed political boundaries, rapid suburbanization has produced consistent declines in city populations. As an urban industrial state, Ohio has a racially and ethnically diverse population. Its African-American population exceeds 10% of the state total. Eastern and southern Europeans were attracted to Ohio's industrial cities and still form large contingents in the northern urban areas of CANTON, Akron, Cleveland, and Youngstown.

Education and Cultural Activity. An 1825 law required counties to fund education, but not until 1921 did schooling become mandatory for everyone between the ages of 6 and 18. Among Ohio's early educators, William Holmes MCGUFFEY and Horace MANN are famous, the former for his readers and the latter for his progressive educational methods.

Since 1804, with the establishment of Ohio University in Athens, public and private institutions of higher learning have grown to 140, among them Ohio State University (1870), with its main campus at Columbus, and the universities of Akron (1870), Cincinnati (1819), and Toledo (1872). Other state universities are Bowling Green State (1910), Cleveland State (1923), Kent State (1910), Miami University (1809) at Oxford, Wright State (1964), and Youngstown State (1908). Outstanding private institutions include ANTIOCH COLLEGE, Case Western Reserve University, Denison University, Kenyon College, OBERLIN COLLEGE, and the College of Wooster.

Supporting the educational process are about 250 public libraries and the academic libraries. The Cincinnati Public Library and the Ohio State University library contain more than 3 million volumes each.

Among Ohio's major cultural institutions are the CLEVELAND MUSEUM OF ART, the Cincinnati Symphony, and The CLEVELAND ORCHESTRA. The Ohio Historical Society, along with various county and municipal historical organizations, seeks to preserve prehistoric and historic sites.

The recreational traveler in Ohio is well rewarded. The Cuyahoga Valley National Recreation Area between Cleveland and Akron preserves the rural character of the Cuyahoga River Valley and the century-old Ohio and Erie Canal system. Major amusement parks include Cedar Point on Lake Erie and Kings Island near Cincinnati. Professional sports facilities can be found in Cincinnati and Cleveland.

Communications. Influential newspapers in the state are the *Cleveland Plain Dealer* and the *Cincinnati Enquirer.* There are also many television and radio stations. The first educational radio station in the nation was begun by Ohio State University in 1922.

Economic Activity

Ohio's economic function has historically been that of an outfitter, supplying food and materials to those farther west. The state's ability to assemble needed raw materials cheaply accelerated the industrial-urban process, making Ohio a principal manufacturing state with the attendant problems created by urbanization, dwindling energy supplies, and pollution of air and water.

A horse and buggy, typically used by Ohio's Old Order Amish, travels the roads of Wayne County, Ohio. The Amish, who began immigrating to the United States during the 18th century, have tried to maintain their traditional customs and agricultural way of life.

The closing of outmoded "smokestack industry" plants, such as this steel factory in Cleveland, during the 1980s adversely affected Ohio's economy. New factories opened during the decade, however, including a number owned by Japanese interests.

Agriculture. The northwest's field crops of corn and soybeans are typical of the agricultural economy in the Corn Belt, while southeastern Ohio has the general mixed-farming economy consisting of cattle grazing and minimal crop production more common in the East. As recently as the early 1970s more than half of all farm income came from livestock. Soon thereafter, however, Ohio farmers were deriving more money from crops. Corn and soybeans now bring the highest profits, followed by dairy products and cattle. Other important farm commodities are hogs, wheat, oats, popcorn, barley, hay, red clover, and rye. Vegetable growing is also important.

Forestry and Fishing. As agricultural land in Ohio has declined, forestland has increased. Most of the forestland is privately owned, while the remainder is within a number of state forests and Wayne National Forest. Valuable tree species include white oak, red oak, white ash, hard maple, tulip poplar, hickory, and beech. Trees often are not of sawtimber size but are an important pulpwood source for the paper industry in the southwest. Building materials and furniture are also products of the forest-based industries.

The waters of Lake Erie were once famous for large- and small-mouthed bass, white bass, yellow perch, bluegills, rock bass, and walleyed pike. Because of ecological changes resulting in the introduction of the sea lamprey and the alewife and from industrial and agricultural pollution, commercial fishing declined drastically. Recreational fishing, however, continues in the streams and lakes, including Lake Erie.

Mining. Coal is the most valuable mineral produced in Ohio, and Ohio's total reserves of coal have been estimated to be able to meet demand for about 500 years. Coal production is concentrated in the southeast. Limestone, which also ranks high in production value, is quarried throughout the state, but major deposits are located in northwestern Ohio. Sand and gravel are abundant on Ohio's western till plain and in the southern valleys that received generous outwash. Salt is produced along Lake Erie from rock salt and in the east from brine. The deep-est salt mine in the nation is near Fairport Harbor. Petroleum and natural-gas deposits in various parts of Ohio are important revenue producers.

Ohio sandstone constitutes the majority of the nation's supply. Production is scattered in the eastern half of the state. The best-known type of sandstone is Berea, or grit. Clay resources are more widespread than sandstone. The principal resource area is in the east central part of Ohio, where fire or refractory clays are quarried for the area's brick and tile industry.

Manufacturing. Ohio's favorable location and abundant natural resources, combined with a large labor supply, assured it early industrial prominence. Cincinnati, the state's first manufacturing city, had among its early industries barrel making and meat packing. Today Ohio's leading industries manufacture transportation equipment, rubber products, machine tools, soap, matches, cooking ranges, foundry and machine-shop products, pottery and porcelain ware, electrical machinery, chemical products, and pumps and steam shovels. Printing and publishing are also important in several of Ohio's larger cities.

Ohio ranks high among U.S. states in the value added by manufacture. Many layoffs in Ohio's steel and auto facilities occurred in the 1980s, but offsetting this trend, new factories opened, including Japanese-owned auto-assembly plants.

Tourism. Tourism is a major business in Ohio, adding substantially each year to the economy. State recreation areas and local parks cover many areas of the state. Ohio's presidential memorials and homes are leading attractions. The state's recreational sites are diverse and offer both summer and winter activities.

Transportation. Known historically as the "Gateway to the West," Ohio continues to benefit from its transportation advantages. Toledo and Cleveland are important Lake Erie ports. Toledo functions principally as an exporter of coal and coke. Cincinnati, the state's principal Ohio River port, also handles cargo.

Highways and railroads have replaced the earlier canal links. Ohio's early roads included Zane's Trace, built by Ebenezer ZANE for the U.S. government and opened in 1797, and the National (Cumberland) Road, important during the early 1800s. The state's major roads today include the Ohio Turnpike, which crosses the northern part of the state in an east-west direction; Interstate 71, which travels in a northeastern-southwestern direction from Cleveland to Columbus and Cincinnati; and I-70, which travels east and west through central Ohio. By 1860, Ohio had more miles of track than any other state. Railroad trackage has since declined, although freight service and some passenger service have been maintained. Ohio's many airports reflect an objective during the 1960s to establish an airport in every county.

Energy. Tied to national supply lines of petroleum and natural gas, Ohio's industry has relied on these energy fuels. Overdependence on distant and uncertain energy sources has created a renewed emphasis on developing in-state supplies of coal. Most electrical power already is derived from coal.

Government

Ohio's statehood in 1803 was preceded by a constitutional convention held in Chillicothe during November 1802. The resulting constitution favored the legislature and gave to it the power to appoint all state officials except the governor. A second constitution became effective in 1851.

Ohio's legislative power is vested in the general assembly, composed of a senate and a house of representatives. The 33 state senators are elected to 4-year terms. Each senatorial district has 3 representatives who are elected to 2-year terms. Although the number of senators and representatives is fixed, reapportionment takes place after each federal census.

The executive branch of the state government is headed by the governor, elected to a 4-year term. The governor is, however, limited to a maximum of two consecutive terms. Although both Democrats and Republicans frequently have held the governor's post, Ohio voters usually favor Republicans at the ballot box.

The state's judicial powers are vested in the supreme court, composed of a chief justice and 6 judges elected for 6-year terms. Lower courts consist of courts of appeals, courts of common pleas in each of Ohio's 88 counties, a division of domestic relations in several counties, and probate, municipal, county, juvenile, and police courts.

Counties, cities, villages, and townships constitute Ohio's smaller political units. Municipal governments conduct the affairs of cities and villages. City status is achieved when the population reaches 5,000, and a village may be formed through petition by 30 voters (a majority of them property owners) to the township trustees and a subsequent vote on the petition by the township residents.

History

Ohio's earliest occupants probably followed retreating glaciers into the area while hunting mastadon and giant beaver. The earliest inhabitants were followed by the more advanced MOUND BUILDERS who ranged over Ohio between 1000 BC and 800 AD. They were noted for their burial practices, evidence of which remains in about 6,000 burial and ceremonial mounds.

Probably the first European to set foot in the Ohio Country was either Robert Cavelier, Sieur de LA SALLE, or Louis JOLLIET. Between 1669 and 1670, La Salle explored the Ohio River area, and Jolliet journeyed along Lake Erie. Based on La Salle's exploration and resulting map, the French later laid claim to the entire Ohio Valley. Both French and English hotly contested their control of the Ohio territory before permanent American settlement.

Among the historic Indian groups in Ohio were the ERIE, HURON (Wyandot), OTTAWA, and TUSCARORA in the north; the Mingo (or IROQUOIS LEAGUE) in the east; the DELAWARE and SHAWNEE in the south; and the MIAMI in the west. Remnants of these tribes, led by the Shawnee chief Blue Jacket, were defeated at the Battle of Fallen Timbers in 1794. This U.S. Army victory led to the establish-

ment of the Greenville Treaty Line in 1795, which separated the Indian land to the northwest from the settlers' land to the east and south.

The Ohio Country became part of the NORTHWEST TERRITORY in 1787. With the passage of the Ordinances of 1785 and 1787, providing for stable government as well as land survey and sales in the territory, settlement by Anglo-Americans accelerated. Connecticut and Virginia retained title to Ohio land, forming the Connecticut Western Reserve in the northeast and the Virginia Military District between the Little Miami and Scioto rivers in the southwest. The OHIO COMPANY OF ASSOCIATES acquired 4,856 km^2 (1,875 mi^2) in southeastern Ohio and in 1788 founded Ohio's first town, MARIETTA, at the confluence of the Muskingum and Ohio rivers.

Ohio entered the Union in 1803. CHILLICOTHE was the state capital from 1803 to 1810, when it was replaced by ZANESVILLE. Chillicothe again was capital from 1812 to 1816, when Columbus assumed the honor.

The state's early years were characterized by dramatic population increases and military turmoil. Military problems resulted from Indian agitation and the campaigns of the WAR OF 1812. Two names forever to be connected with Ohio and its early struggles are TECUMSEH and William Henry HARRISON. The first was the great Shawnee chief who almost succeeded in rallying the Indians for a last stand against the white man. The latter was the victor in the fight to bring peace to the New West and was the first of several U.S. presidents with strong ties to Ohio.

Transportation opened Ohio to internal development. Favored by navigable waters north and south, overland transportation surged with completion of the NATIONAL ROAD through the state in 1838, and of the Ohio-Erie and Miami-Erie canals in 1832 and 1847, respectively. Ohio's railroad network was begun with the Dayton-Sandusky line in 1850. Efficient transportation gave impetus to the coal industry and boosted farm income and land values in the western and northern agricultural areas. By the Civil War period, Ohio had achieved national status as an agricultural and industrial state.

Preceding the Civil War, Ohio was strongly identified with abolitionist causes. The UNDERGROUND RAILROAD was active along the Ohio River and on Lake Erie. The abolitionist movement received wide support, and in 1848, Ohio repealed its Black Laws, which had been restrictive of blacks' civil rights. The Civil War was carried into Ohio during a cavalry foray led by Gen. John Hunt MORGAN. The "invasion" lasted from July 13 to July 26, 1863, ending with the surrender of Morgan and his men and their imprisonment as horse thieves rather than combatants.

After the Civil War, Ohio became a political power on the national level. Seven U.S. presidents were born in Ohio: Ulysses S. Grant, Rutherford B. Hayes, James A. Garfield, Benjamin Harrison, William McKinley, William Howard Taft, and Warren G. Harding.

As an industrial state, Ohio was in the forefront of the union-organizing movement. The American Federation of Labor was formed in Columbus in 1886, followed by the United Mine Workers in 1888. Violence connected with labor unrest became commonplace in the mining areas of southeastern Ohio. During a strike in 1884 several mine shafts in Perry County were set afire and have been burning ever since.

During the 20th century Ohio moved to the forefront of the industrial states under the business leadership of such men as Benjamin F. GOODRICH, Charles Franklin KETTERING, and John D. Rockefeller (see ROCKEFELLER family). Two world wars and conflicts in Korea and Vietnam triggered massive industrialization, rapid in-migration, and subsequent urbanization. Ohio's fortunes can, however, be rapidly reversed by economic relocation, such as a shift from coal to natural gas or by recession. These trends have had devastating results in the central cities and the traditional coal-mining districts in Appalachia, where unemployment and poverty are chronic ills. Beset by overcapitalization and outdated facilities, Ohio struggles to remain an industrial giant. Steel plants with excess capacity have shut down, as have outmoded automobile plants. New Japanese-owned factories have opened, however, partly offsetting the gloomy outlook.

Ohio Company   The Ohio Company, also called the Ohio Company of Virginia, was formed in 1747 by a London merchant and several prominent Virginians to promote settlement west of the Appalachian Mountains. A royal charter (1749) entitled the company to 200,000 acres (81,000 ha) of land in the upper Ohio Valley, and the members dispatched Christopher GIST to explore the region. Attempts to colonize the territory, which was claimed by France, helped lead to the outbreak (1754) of the last French and Indian War.

Ohio Company of Associates   The Ohio Company of Associates was formed in Boston on Mar. 1, 1786, to settle lands along the Ohio River that had recently been ceded to the U.S. government. The organizers, Generals Rufus PUTNAM and Benjamin Tupper, obtained support largely from veterans of the American Revolution. The company's activities encouraged Congress—which was desperately in need of revenue—to pass the Ordinance of 1787, which provided for the organization of the NORTHWEST TERRITORY. The Reverend Manasseh CUTLER served the company as lobbyist; in 1787 he allied himself with a group of New York speculators and negotiated the purchase of more than 1.5 million acres (600,000 ha) at less than 10 cents an acre. Cutler arranged these advantageous terms by involving a group of politicians in the Scioto Company, which was granted an option on some 5 million acres (2 million ha). The Scioto Company failed, however. Although the Ohio Company did not complete payments on all its land, it established (1788) MARIETTA, Ohio's first permanent settlement. The company ceased most of its land operations in 1796.

Ohio River   The Ohio River is a 1,579-km-long (981-mi) tributary of the Mississippi that originates at the con-

fluence of the Allegheny and Monongahela rivers in Pittsburgh, Pa. The Ohio flows through western Pennsylvania and along the West Virginia, Ohio, Kentucky, Indiana, and Illinois borders, discharging into the Mississippi at Cairo, Ill. The river's drainage basin of 528,000 km^2 (204,000 mi^2) is one of the world's most productive industrial-agricultural areas. The Ohio flows past the major cities of Cincinnati, Ohio; Louisville, Ky.; and Evansville, Ind. The river valley's major industries are coal, oil, steel, chemicals, pottery, and tobacco. The Ohio's many tributaries include the Beaver, Kanawha, Scioto, Kentucky, Green, Wabash, and Tennessee rivers.

Even though it is prone to severe spring floods and summer droughts, the Ohio is navigable year-round because of flood-control systems and continual dredging. The main traffic on the river consists of barges carrying bulk commodities.

The Ohio River valley was occupied by Mound Builders as early as 500 BC. The area was inhabited by Shawnee Indians when Robert Cavelier, sieur de La Salle, discovered the river in 1669. The French built forts along the upper river valley, causing a conflict with the British that culminated in the French and Indian War (1754–63). The river was an important route for pioneers moving west.

ohm   [ohm]   The ohm, named for the German physicist Georg Simon Ohm, is the unit of electrical resistance (see ELECTROMAGNETIC UNITS; RESISTANCE, ELECTRICAL; UNITS, PHYSICAL). The international ohm has been defined since 1893 as the resistance of a standard column of mercury; since 1948 the standard has been the absolute ohm, defined in terms of the wave impedance of a vacuum. When a steady current of 1 ampere flowing through a conductor produces a potential difference of 1 volt, the resistance of the conductor is 1 ohm. The ohm is also the unit of reactance and impedance.

See also: ELECTRICITY.

Ohm's law   Stated by the German physicist Georg Simon Ohm in 1826, Ohm's law establishes the mathematical relationship between voltage (V), current (I), and RESISTANCE (R) as $V = IR$, for both alternating and direct currents (AC and DC). Sometimes this linear relationship is written as $I = GV$, where G is called the conductance; the unit of conductance is the mho (inverse ohm). Other essentially equivalent forms of Ohm's law are also used, such as $J = \sigma E$ where J is the current density (current per unit area), E is the electric field, and σ is the conductivity.

In its original simple form, Ohm's law applied only to steady DC situations. In AC circuit theory, when the circuit contains resistors, inductors, and capacitors, $V = IZ$, where Z is a complex number called the IMPEDANCE. The standard procedure is to measure the ratio between voltage and current in ohms even if this ratio may sometimes be a complex number. Resistance may also vary with time, or resistance may be nonlinear (depending on the magnitude of the voltage or current). In these cases

Ohm's law for the instantaneous resistance R in a purely resistive circuit and the instantaneous impedance Z in a complex circuit is still valid.

See also: CIRCUIT, ELECTRIC.

oil see FATS AND OILS; PETROLEUM; PETROLEUM INDUSTRY

oil-drop experiment see MILLIKAN'S OIL-DROP EXPERIMENT

oil shale see SHALE, OIL

oil spill The accidental discharge of petroleum or petroleum products, an oil spill may occur on land from oil wells, oil transport trucks, or pipelines; on rivers or lakes from barges or other vessels; or at sea from offshore platforms, oil tankers, or oil-fueled vessels.

The size of an oil spill may have little bearing on its environmental effects. One of the largest recorded spills, the 1979 blowout of the Ixtoc I oil well in the Gulf of Mexico, released an estimated 530 million l (140 million U.S. gal), but ocean winds and currents prevented the slicks from drifting inland and the oil was dispersed and presumably disintegrated in the open sea. On the other hand, in 1978 a spill half this size, from the tanker *Amoco Cadiz* when it ran aground in the English Channel, fouled great stretches of the Brittany coast, creating an ecological disaster whose effects were felt for over a decade. Waterways with restricted circulation are especially vulnerable. The Persian Gulf, for example, became the scene of the world's worst oil spill during the war there in 1990–91, when destruction of Kuwaiti facilities caused millions of barrels of oil to pour into the gulf. The *Exxon Valdez* supertanker spill of 1989 is ranked as the worst U.S. oil disaster. Over 41 million l (11 million U.S. gal) of oil were released when the ship ran aground in Alaska's Prince William Sound.

Ecological Impacts. In addition to the scenic degradation of oil-fouled coastlines and the economic losses borne by fishing, tourist, and other industries dependent on the health of coastal waters, a major effect of oil spills is the mass killing of wildlife. Petroleum dissolves the protective waxes and oils in the feathers of waterfowl, and oil-coated birds die, primarily from freezing. Fur-bearing ocean mammals such as otter suffer the same fate. Clams, oysters, and crustaceans ingest oil-impregnated water and become tainted with an oily taste. Commercial shellfish beds must therefore be closed for a number of years following an oil spill. Where a spill occurs in a confined area, in regions where fish spawn, or on fish-migration routes, major fish kills may occur and, in some instances, as in Prince William Sound, fisheries have been wiped out or severely depleted.

Long-term effects, although not so obvious, may be equally devastating. The soluble fraction of the spilled oil may spread over vast areas, and toxic components may create chronic ecological damage, either by inhibiting reproduction or by causing genetic changes. A study of spill effects in the Caribbean found that coral organisms were severely hurt and coastal environments such as mangrove thickets were wiped out along with the creatures that inhabited them. A study of the Brittany coastline in the years following the *Amoco Cadiz* spill found massive death rates for such bottom-dwelling species as sea urchins, the practical elimination of other species, and the overall reduction of animal populations. Although oil-tainted environments probably recover eventually, not all species may return to their prespill status.

On land the effects of oil spills are less conspicuous. They receive less publicity and are not studied as intensively. One known effect results when gasoline from underground storage tanks leaks into the water table and thence into local water supplies. Some reports indicate that the ecological well-being of Alaska's North Slope may be at risk from the alleged negligence of companies exploiting the oil fields there.

Cleanup and Control Technology. Techniques for dealing with spills at sea include the use of floating booms to keep the oil contained until it can be collected by pumps or skimmers; spraying chemical dispersants, which break down the oil; and burning surface oil. All three techniques must be used quickly, before winds and waves thin and spread the slick. On land such methods as washing or steam-cleaning beaches and rocks have proven ineffectual.

During its Alaska cleanup, Exxon developed a promising technique for cleaning polluted rocky beaches using microbes. Naturally occurring microbes are known to consume oil, but they grow too slowly in cold climates such as that in Alaska. However, spraying the oil-covered rocks with fertilizer increases the microbes' reproduction rate, and fertilizer-sprayed shorelines (some of them treated several times over, for buried oil kept rising to the surface) became almost oil free.

See also: PETROLEUM INDUSTRY; POLLUTION, ENVIRONMENTAL.

Oistrakh, David [oy'-strahk] The Russian violinist David Feodorovitch Oistrakh, b. Sept. 30 (N.S.), 1908, d. Oct. 24, 1974, was among the leading virtuosos of his time. Beginning his studies at the age of five, he graduated from the Odessa Conservatory in 1926. He became known outside the USSR when he won first prize in a 1937 Brussels competition. The first Soviet artist to visit the United States during the cold war, he made his New York debut in 1955, playing Shostakovich's First Violin Concerto; this piece had been written for him, as was much of the violin music composed in the USSR during his career. Oistrakh's son Igor, b. Apr. 27, 1931, also became a prominent violinist.

Ojibwa [oh-jib'-way] The Ojibwa (or Chippewa) are a tribe of Algonquian-speaking North American Indians of the Upper Great Lakes. When first encountered in the 1600s by French explorers near Sault Sainte Marie, Canada, their small bands lived in tiny, self-governing villages without any tribal organization. Later, as they prospered in the fur trade and expanded their population and territory,

Strong Wind, a member of the Ojibwa, or Chippewa, tribe, was painted by George Catlin in 1843. By this time the Ojibwa, originally of the Great Lakes region, had expanded their territory as far west and north as present-day North Dakota and the Canadian provinces of Saskatchewan and Manitoba. (National Collection of Fine Arts, Washington D.C.)

the Ojibwa developed new tribal-level institutions, including the Midewiwin, or Grand Medicine Society.

By the late 18th century the Ojibwa had driven the Iroquois out of the Ontario peninsula. They also moved into western Wisconsin and northeastern Minnesota, driving away the powerful Santee Sioux after a long war, and expanded into the Canadian provinces of Ontario, Manitoba, and Saskatchewan. Generally located in areas remote from English and American frontier settlements, the Ojibwa managed to maintain many of their traditional cultural traits, such as skill in woodcraft and the use of birchbark canoes. The name Ojibwa is favored in Canada, but Chippewa is more often used in the United States. Chippewa on or near U.S. reservations numbered slightly more than 50,000 in 1989.

Ojukwu, Chukwuemeka Odumegwu [oh-jook'-wah, chook-woo-ay-may'-kah oh-doo-mayg'-wah]
Chukwuemeka Odumegwu Ojukwu, b. Nov. 4, 1933, a Nigerian soldier and politician, headed (1967–70) the Republic of BIAFRA during the Nigerian civil war. Ojukwu studied at Oxford University and subsequently served in the Nigerian administration and in the army. After a military coup in 1966, he was appointed military governor of the Eastern Region. There, in 1967, he led the IBO secessionist movement, and a bloody civil war ensued. When the war ended in the Ibo's defeat in 1970, Ojukwu fled to Ivory Coast. He returned to Nigeria in 1982.

Okanogan [oh-kuh-nah'-guhn]
The Okanogan, or Okinagan, are a North American Indian tribe of the Salishan family, who from earliest times occupied what is now the eastern and central border area between Washington State and British Columbia. The Okanogan were primarily salmon fishermen. Their permanent winter quarters were semisubterranean, conical dwellings covered with mats and earth. Their summer homes, adapted for the mobility that hunting and fishing required, were

tents and sheds. They used crude dugout and bark canoes. Copper-working and basketry were highly developed, but pottery was unknown. They made clothing from both deerskins and woven bark fibers. A technology of digging sticks, fish spears, hooks, traps, bag nets, and sinew-backed bows reflected their subsistence needs. They lived in small, extended families grouped into independent bands under their own chiefs. The accumulation of wealth was traditionally important. Today the Okanogan are part of the Confederated Tribes of the Colville Indian Reservation in Washington, which totaled 7,200 in 1989. The Okanogan in Canada numbered 1,084 in 1987.

okapi [oh-kap'-ee]
The okapi, *Okapia johnstoni*, in the giraffe family, Giraffidae, is unusual among mammals in that the female is larger than the male. She may stand 1.65 m (5.5 ft) at the shoulder and be 1.95 m (6.5 ft) long. The neck is tall, the muzzle pointed, and the ears large and erect. Males have small horns. The okapi can extend its long tongue to its eyes to wash them. The coat is purplish brown, with a light-colored face and bars of black and white on the upper legs and buttocks. Okapis live in dense eastern Congo rain forests. They are cud-chewers and eat fruits, leaves, and seeds.

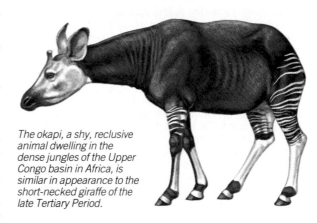

The okapi, a shy, reclusive animal dwelling in the dense jungles of the Upper Congo basin in Africa, is similar in appearance to the short-necked giraffe of the late Tertiary Period.

Okeechobee, Lake [oh-kee-choh'-bee]
Lake Okeechobee (Seminole: "big water"), one of the largest freshwater lakes in the eastern United States, is located in south central Florida, at the northern edge of the EVERGLADES, and covers about 1,813 km² (700 mi²). Fed by the Kissimmee River, the lake is 56 km (35 mi) long and up to 40 km (25 mi) wide; it has a mean depth of 2 m (7 ft) and a maximum depth of 5–6 m (15–20 ft). The lake drains south through the Everglades to the Gulf of Mexico. In 1937 the lake became part of the 250-km (155-mi) Cross-Florida Waterway. Flood-control projects, which reclaimed much of the fertile land around the lake, have been criticized for their effects on the fragile Everglades ecosystem.

Georgia O'Keeffe's Black Iris *(1926), one of a series of sensuous flower portraits, demonstrates the American artist's unique style of delicate contour and sharp linear form. (Alfred Stieglitz Collection, Metropolitan Museum of Art, New York City.)*

O'Keeffe, Georgia   The American painter Georgia O'Keeffe, b. Sun Prairie, Wis., Nov. 15, 1887, d. Mar. 6, 1986, was one of the most original members of the American avant-garde during the early decades of the 20th century. In 1915 her canvases, with their broad, summary forms, emphatic rhythms, and prismatic colors, came to the attention of the photographer and art exhibitor Alfred STIEGLITZ, who gave O'Keeffe her first one-person show at his 291 Gallery in New York City in 1917. She joined the circle of young artists around Stieglitz and married him in 1924.

Although her work sometimes turned to abstraction, O'Keeffe's subjects were usually derived from nature and included principally flowers, still lifes, and landscapes. Her famous flower paintings, characterized by bold magnification and an absolute clarity of form, first appeared in the mid-1920s. Later in that decade she also painted city scenes in the precise geometric style then prevalent. In 1929, O'Keeffe first visited New Mexico, where she established her home in 1949. During the intervening years her paintings had begun to reflect the atmosphere and scenery of the southwestern desert. A fine work of this period is the *Pelvis Series* (1943), austere studies of animal bones set against spare backgrounds.

O'Keeffe's highly individual and intuitive style, devel-oped over a long and prolific career, placed her in the forefront of American modernists.

Okefenokee Swamp [oh-kee-fuh-noh'-kee]   The Okefenokee Swamp is located in southeastern Georgia and northeastern Florida. Covering more than 1,554 km² (600 mi²), the swamp is drained by the Suwannee and Saint Marys rivers. The swamp is still in a relatively primitive state and contains virgin pine forests, stands of black gum and cypress, and grassland. Wildlife includes alligators and other reptiles, deer, bears, and several hundred species of birds. In 1937 most of the swamp was made a national wildlife refuge.

Okeghem, Jean d' [dahk'-uh-gem]   The Flemish composer Jean d'Okeghem, *c.*1430–*c.*1495, probably a native of Hainaut, was the most celebrated composer of his generation. He was a chorister (1446–48) in the chapel of Charles I, duc de Bourbon. From 1454 he acted as chaplain and composer to three successive French kings—Charles VII, Louis XI, and Charles VIII—becoming the king's chapel master in 1465. He also became (1459) treasurer of the prestigious Abbey of Saint Martin at Tours. His death occasioned the great *Déploration* by Josquin des Préz.

Okeghem's surviving works include approximately 20 chansons, 14 complete masses, and about 10 motets. His genius is most clearly seen in his masses, of which he is one of the foremost masters. He treated the mass in a variety of ways, including the use of the cantus firmus technique. His requiem is the earliest surviving setting of the text, Dufay's setting having been lost. His style reveals a romantic vitality and a love of the experimental and unexpected. He created a "seamless" texture achieved by continuous overlapping of phrases in different voice parts and by the avoidance of frequent cadences.

Okhotsk, Sea of [oh-kahtsk']   The Sea of Okhotsk, an inlet of the Pacific Ocean, lies north of Japan. The La Pérouse and Tatar straits connect the southern portion of the sea with the Sea of Japan. The sea is bounded by the USSR mainland in the west and north and the Kamchatka Peninsula and the Kuril Islands in the east. Sakhalin island separates the Sea of Okhotsk from the Sea of Japan. The 1,583,000-km² (611,200-mi²) sea is an important fishing ground, with an average depth of 777 m (2,550 ft). Just east of the Kurils, however, the trench drops to more than 3,334 m (10,938 ft). From November to June ice blocks shipping. The principal port is Magadan, USSR.

Okinawa [oh-ki-nah'-wah]   Okinawa is the largest of Japan's Ryukyu Islands in the western Pacific; it is 103 km (64 mi) long, and its average width is 11 km (7 mi). Okinawa has an area of 1,176 km² (454 mi²); its population is 1,222,000 (1989 est.). Naha serves as the chief

AT A GLANCE

OKLAHOMA

Land: Area: 181,185 km² (69,956 mi²); rank: 18th. Capital and largest city: Oklahoma City (1990 pop., 444,719). Counties: 77. Elevations: highest—1,516 m (4,973 ft), at Black Mesa; lowest—88 m (289 ft), at the Little River.

People: Population (1990): 3,157,604; rank: 28th; density: 17.4 persons per km² (45.1 per mi²). Distribution (1988 est.): 58.8% metropolitan, 41.2% nonmetropolitan. Average annual change (1980–90): +0.4%.

Government (1991): Governor: David Walters, Democrat. U.S. Congress: Senate—1 Democrat, 1 Republican; House—4 Democrats, 2 Republicans. Electoral college votes: 8. State legislature: 48 senators, 101 representatives.

Economy: State personal income (1988): $43.2 billion; rank: 28th. Median family income (1979): $17,668; rank: 35th. Agriculture: income (1988)—$3.4 billion. Forestry: sawtimber volume (1987)—6.7 billion board feet. Mining: value (1987)—$5.6 billion. Manufacturing: value added (1987)—$9.8 billion. Services: value (1987)—$9 billion.

Miscellany: Statehood: Nov. 16, 1907; the 46th state. Nickname: Sooner State; tree: redbud; motto: *Labor Omnia Vincit* ("Labor Conquers All Things"); song: "Oklahoma!"

Mistletoe

Scissor-tailed Flycatcher

city and port. The economy is based on the raising of sugarcane, rice, and sweet potatoes. Fishing is also important, as are services to U.S. military bases. The island has many World War II memorials and is the site of the University of the Ryukyus (1950) and Okinawa University (1956).

Sovereignty over Okinawa was disputed by Japan and China for centuries, but the Japanese established effective control in the 1870s. In World War II the island was the scene of a bitter three-month air, sea, and land battle in which Japanese kamikaze pilots took a heavy toll on U.S. ships. A decisive U.S. victory in June 1945 left the United States with air bases close to Japan. Okinawa remained in U.S. hands until 1972, when it was returned to Japan.

Oklahoma   Oklahoma, located near the central part of the conterminous United States, has an area of 181,185 km² (69,956 mi²) and ranks 18th in size among the states. It is bordered by Kansas and Colorado on the north, by New Mexico on the west, by Texas on the west and south, and by Missouri and Arkansas on the east.

Formed by the union of Oklahoma Territory and Indian Territory, Oklahoma was admitted as the 46th state on Nov. 16, 1907. *Oklahoma* is a Choctaw word meaning

"red man." Oklahoma has been nicknamed the "Sooner State" for the settlers who tried to enter the area and claim land sooner than it was legal to do so. The state is an important producer of agricultural products, especially wheat, beef, and cotton, and mineral fuels, notably petroleum products and coal.

Land and Resources

Oklahoma is located in the transitional zone between the eastern and western parts of the nation. The Ozark Plateau and the Ouachita Mountains are similar to the Appalachian highlands to the east; the central part of the state constitutes the southern part of the Central Lowlands; and northwestern Oklahoma is a part of the GREAT PLAINS. Elevation increases from 88 m (289 ft) near the southeastern corner of the state to 1,516 m (4,973 ft) on Black Mesa in the northwestern corner of the Panhandle.

The Ouachita Mountains are a series of long, steep-sloped, parallel ridges, many capped by a massive layer of sandstone. The OZARK MOUNTAINS, or Ozark Plateau, and the Ouachitas are separated by the Arkansas River. The Ozarks are composed of horizontal layers of rocks, mainly limestones and shales. The Wichita Mountains in the southwest are largely granite, rhyolite, and gabbro peaks, and much of the Arbuckle region in the south central part

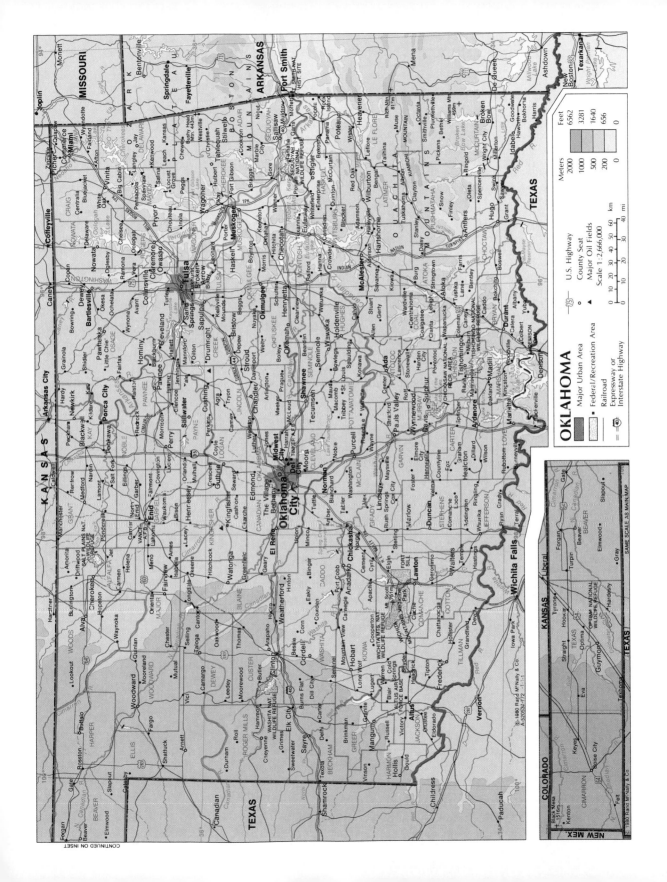

OKLAHOMA

of the state is formed of ribbed edges of limestone. The Osage Plains in central Oklahoma are underlain by nearly horizontal rocks that dip slightly westward. The Great Plains have elevations that increase westward from 610 to almost 1,525 m (2,000 to 5,000 ft). The northern limits of the Gulf Coastal Plain in the southeast constitute an area of soft sandstone, shale, and limestone.

Soils. About two-thirds of the soils developed under grass and the remainder under forest. The prairie soils in the west are extremely fertile when moisture is sufficient.

Rivers and Lakes. All drainage from Oklahoma occurs either by the ARKANSAS RIVER, which crosses the northeastern quarter of the state, or the RED RIVER, which follows the southern boundary. The CANADIAN RIVER, the Cimarron, the Neosho, and the Illinois are major tributaries of the Arkansas. The North Fork of the Red River and the Washita, the Kiamichi, and the Little rivers flow into the Red River. Eufaula Reservoir, covering 427 km^2 (165 mi^2) at normal level, is the state's largest artificial lake.

Climate. Oklahoma climate varies from the arid continental type in the west to the humid subtropical type in the southeast. Rainfall increases from less than 381 mm (15 in) annually in the western Panhandle to more than 1,270 mm (50 in) in the Ouachita Mountains. In the western part of the state, yearly temperatures range from −23° C (−10° F) in January to above 38° C (100° F) in July. In the southeast, temperatures vary from about 0° C (32° F) in winter to 32° C (90° F) in July.

Vegetation and Animal Life. Grasses are the dominant vegetation in the plains areas of Oklahoma. The Cross Timbers areas in the central part of the state are covered with blackjack oak and post-oak trees. Oak-hickory and oak-pine forests are located in the Ozark and Ouachita regions, respectively. Deer, coyotes, rabbits, and numerous smaller animals are common. The Wichita Mountain wildlife refuge has small herds of buffalo, long-horned cattle, moose, deer, and prairie dogs.

Natural Resources. Since 1896, Oklahoma has been a leading petroleum-producing state. Large coal reserves are located in eastern Oklahoma. Glass sand, salt, gypsum, lead, copper, limestone, dolomite, and granite are also found in great quantities. Much of Oklahoma's abundant hydroelectric-power potential has been harnessed since World War II. The fertile plains are covered with wheat farms and cattle ranches. Oklahoma's forests support a paper industry.

People

In 1990 the state's population was 82.1% white, 8.0% Indian, 7.4% black, and 2.7% Hispanic. Population growth in the period 1970–80 totaled 18.2%, most of which was the result of in-migration. Between 1980 and 1990 the growth rate slowed to about 4.4%. OKLAHOMA CITY and TULSA are the two largest cities. LAWTON, Norman, Broken Arrow, Edmond, and Midwest City have populations of greater than 50,000 each. The Southern Baptist and Methodist religious denominations have the largest memberships in the state.

Education. The first schools were established by mission groups and the governments of the Five Civilized Tribes in the 1830s. When Oklahoma was settled by whites, sections in each township were set aside for schools.

Oklahoma's state-supported system of universities includes the University of Oklahoma (1890) at Norman and Oklahoma State University (1890) at Stillwater. There are also more than a dozen privately supported colleges and universities. Oklahoma has a statewide system of public libraries.

Cultural and Historic Sites. Among Oklahoma's museums are the National Cowboy Hall of Fame and Western Heritage Center in Oklahoma City, the Gilcrease Institute of American History and Art and the Philbrook Art Center in Tulsa, and the Woolaroc Museum near Bartlesville. The Will Rogers Memorial is in Claremore. Indian City U.S.A. at Anadarko displays authentic Indian dwellings. Noted

(Left) *Wheat is Oklahoma's most valuable cash crop, although hay, sorghum grain, and soybeans are also important.* (Right) *The Wichita Mountains in southwestern Oklahoma were designated a wildlife refuge in 1905. In the same year the New York Zoological Society donated 15 bison to the preserve. Eventually numbering more than 1,000, the bison now wander over the entire refuge.*

The Glass Mountains, located in the Gypsum Hills of northwestern Oklahoma, are so named because their sides are covered with flakes of selenite, a form of gypsum, which glisten in the sun.

tional leader in fossil-fuel production, including coal as well as petroleum and related fuels. Many major petroleum firms have offices in Oklahoma, particularly in Tulsa, Bartlesville, and Oklahoma City. Nonfuel mineral production includes iodine, gypsum, limestone, and clays.

Energy. Oklahoma uses its abundant supplies of gas, oil, and coal to produce nearly all of its electric power. A small proportion of electricity is produced by hydroelectric plants.

Forestry. The Ouachita Mountains are densely forested with pine, oak, and hickory, and some cypress grows in the valleys of the Little and the Mountain Fork rivers. Pine-tree farming supplies a large paper mill in Valliant. Sawmills are common throughout both the Ouachita and Ozark regions.

Transportation and Tourism. Railroads, first built in Oklahoma in the 1870s, were an important factor in the state's development. Extensive road and highway networks, however, have increasingly supplanted railroads for freight transport as well as passenger travel. The McClellan-Kerr Arkansas River Navigation System (1971) links the Tulsa area with the Mississippi River and thus the Gulf of Mexico. Tourism is a growing economic activity.

Government

Oklahoma state government operates under its original 1907 constitution, as amended. The governor and state officers are elected for 4-year terms, as are state senators. State representatives serve 2 years. Supreme Court justices are elected to 6-year terms and are subsequently subject to nonpartisan, noncompetitive reelection. Although a large majority of Oklahomans are registered Democrats, it is not unusual for a Republican to be elected governor or U.S. senator.

Oklahoma has 77 counties, each electing its own officers. The chief officials in each county are the 3 county commissioners. In 1969 the Oklahoma legislature authorized the division of the state into 11 substate

historic sites include restored Fort Gibson, the Cherokee Village complex at Tahlequah, Spiro Mound near Spiro, and the Washita battlefield near Cheyenne. Oklahoma City and Tulsa have symphony orchestras. Oklahoma's numerous parks and wildlife refuges include the Ouachita National Forest and the Chickasaw National Recreation Area. Collegiate football is popular in the state.

Communications. Commercial radio broadcasting began in Oklahoma in 1921, and television broadcasting in 1949. The state has numerous daily and weekly newspapers.

Economic Activity

Since 1950 the economy of Oklahoma has changed dramatically. Oklahoma is no longer basically an agricultural state—mining (primarily oil), manufacturing, and service industries contribute much more to the gross state product than does agriculture. The worldwide decline in oil prices in the mid-1980s, however, combined with depressed farm prices, adversely affected the state's economy into the late 1980s.

Agriculture. Oklahoma's farms and ranches specialize in specific crops or animal production. The production of beef cattle contributes most to agricultural revenues. Winter wheat is the most important crop; other significant crops are hay, corn, sorghum grain, soybeans, and peanuts.

Manufacturing. Leading industries in Oklahoma include the manufacture of petroleum and coal products, nonelectrical machinery, food products, fabricated metal products, and rubber and plastics products. The chief manufacturing area lies in a belt from Oklahoma City northeast to the Kansas-Missouri-Oklahoma border.

Mining. Petroleum, natural gas, and natural-gas liquids (such as natural gasoline and butane) dominate the mining and energy sectors in Oklahoma. The state is a na-

Oklahoma City, the state's capital and largest city, was settled during a single day. On Apr. 22, 1889, the territory was opened to homesteaders, and 10,000 settlers rushed in to claim land.

planning districts to coordinate law enforcement, health and manpower planning, and community and economic development.

History

Indians lived in and migrated back and forth across what is now Oklahoma as they hunted for animals and food. The Spanish were the first Europeans to explore Oklahoma. Francisco Vázquez de CORONADO crossed the western part of the state in 1541. The French explored the streams in eastern Oklahoma, and the trader Auguste Pierre Chouteau (see CHOUTEAU family) established the first permanent settlement—now Salina—in 1817.

In 1803 the United States purchased the Louisiana Territory from France, but the limits of the purchased area were not known until the Adams-Onís Treaty was completed in 1819. The Red River and the 100° west meridian became boundaries of the American territory and today form the southern and most of the western boundary of Oklahoma. The Panhandle, extending westward to 103° west longitude, belonged to Spain until 1821, to Mexico from 1821 to 1836, and to the nation of Texas until 1850, when it became U.S. territory. The Panhandle remained unorganized territory until attached to Oklahoma Territory in 1890.

After the LOUISIANA PURCHASE the area was explored by traders. In 1808 the powerful OSAGE tribe ceded to the United States all of eastern Oklahoma north of the Arkansas River, and in 1818 the QUAPAW Indians ceded all claims to lands south of the Arkansas in present-day Oklahoma and Arkansas.

The government of the United States negotiated treaties with the Indians living in the Southeastern part of the nation whereby they would relinquish their Eastern lands in exchange for territory encompassing nearly all of present-day Oklahoma. The FIVE CIVILIZED TRIBES—CHEROKEE, CHICKASAW, CHOCTAW, CREEK, and SEMINOLE—were primarily successful farmers or professionals who adopted many cultural traits of the white settlers. Their removal (1830–40) over the various "trails of tears" resulted in many deaths and severe hardship.

To clear the way for the settlement of the Eastern Indians on Oklahoma lands, the United States government entered into a series of negotiations with the indigenous groups, culminating in a treaty signed Aug. 24, 1835. Under this treaty the COMANCHE, WICHITA, and associated tribes agreed not to make war on persons traveling through their territory and not to interfere with those Eastern Indians who wished to hunt in the territory. The KIOWA signed a similar document two years later.

In the new INDIAN TERRITORY the Five Civilized Tribes organized representative governments, established towns, and developed farms and businesses until the Civil War disrupted their way of life. Because many of the Indians were slaveholders, the people of the Five Civilized Tribes were divided in loyalty between the Union and the Confederacy. Following the Civil War the U.S. government declared these Indians to have been allies of the Confederacy and forced the Five Civilized Tribes to give up their western lands for considerations of 15 to 30 cents an acre. Much of the western area was then divided into reservations on which various Plains Indians—ARAPAHO, CHEYENNE, PAWNEE, Kiowa, Comanche, Wichita, and smaller tribes—were settled.

The Unassigned Lands near the center of Oklahoma, Old Greer County in the southwest, and the Panhandle were not alloted to any tribes. Texas veterans of the Civil War settled in Old Greer County, cattle raisers staked out ranches in the Panhandle, and the Unassigned Lands was opened (1889) to settlement. The Unassigned Lands was officially designated Oklahoma Territory on May 2, 1890.

With the establishment of the Oklahoma Territory and the rapid increase in population came pressure for statehood. Settlers also demanded that the Indians be confined to certain areas and that the remainder be opened to homesteading. Eventually the U.S. Congress appointed a commission, which entered ten years of negotiations with the Five Civilized Tribes. The Dawes Commission was successful in persuading the tribes to divide their lands among the individual members and to abolish their tribal governments.

Allotment of the Indian lands began on Apr. 1, 1899, and was not completed until 1910. By that time the two halves of Oklahoma had been joined in statehood on Nov. 16, 1907. Before this date Indian protest culminated in a meeting in Muskogee on July 14, 1905, when representatives of all sections of the Indian Territory adopted a constitution for a state to be called Sequoyah. Congress, however, refused to recognize the state.

Since statehood in 1907 many changes have taken place. Oklahoma has changed from a rural to an urban state, from an agricultural economy to one based on industry. Its population has increased with each census except 1930 and 1940, during the difficult times of the DUST BOWL and the Depression of the 1930s. Oklahoma has also become an important center for military activities. Petroleum production remains important, but since 1982 the industry has experienced a downturn that has contributed to Oklahoma's precarious economic condition of the 1980s.

Oklahoma City Oklahoma City, the capital and largest city of Oklahoma, is situated in the central part of the state on the North Canadian River. It is the seat of Oklahoma County and has a population of 444,719 (1990). The metropolitan-area population is 958,839. The city straddles a major oil field; rows of derricks mark its skyline.

Aviation—centered on the nearby Tinker Air Force Base, one of the world's largest air depots, and the Federal Aviation Administration Aeronautical Center—is the major economic industry. The city is also the processing and shipping hub for the state's livestock and grain products. Manufactures include drilling and electronic equipment, computers, and steel.

The city is the seat of Oklahoma City University (1904). Cultural resources include a symphony, theater companies, and the Oklahoma Art Center. The National Cowboy Hall of Fame and Western Heritage Center and the state historical museum preserve the city's Western heritage.

Oklahoma City was settled on the single afternoon of Apr. 22, 1889, when the area was first opened to homesteaders, and 10,000 land seekers charged into the area to stake out claims. The city flourished as the trade center for the Oklahoma Territory (created in 1890) and became the state capital in 1910. Discovery of petroleum resources under the city in 1928 sparked a new period of growth.

okra [oh'-kruh]   Okra, *Abelmoschus esculentus*, an annual plant belonging to the MALLOW family, Malvaceae, is grown for its edible capsule, or seedpod. In Creole cooking the vegetable is called gumbo and is used as an ingredient in creole soups and stews. Thought to be of African or Asian origin, okra was used by the Egyptians as early as the 12th century BC. A tropical plant, it grows best in warm temperatures and, planted from seed, needs about 60 days of midsummer weather to produce a crop. In northern climates it is usually transplanted into the garden as a hothouse-grown seedling.

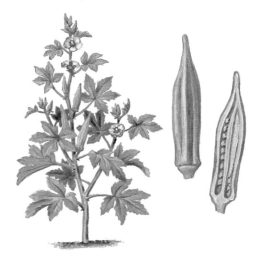

Okra is a vegetable originally from Africa or Asia. It bears hibiscus like flowers and large, star-shaped leaves. The pod, harvested when young and tender, is a basic ingredient in gumbo.

Okuma Shigenobu [oh'-koo-mah shee-gay'-noh-boo] The Japanese statesman Okuma Shigenobu, b. Feb. 16, 1838, d. Jan. 10, 1922, helped to overhaul Japan's antiquated tax structure and to launch parliamentary government after the MEIJI RESTORATION (1868). From 1869 until 1881 he was one of the key ministers involved in modernizing Japan's economy. Removed from the government, soon after he had proposed sweeping constitutional changes along Western lines, Okuma founded the Kaishinto, or Progressive, party in 1882 and helped arouse popular support for a constitution (promulgated 1889). Okuma served as foreign minister in 1888–89,

1896, and 1897. He became prime minister for a short time in 1898 as head of the new Kenseito, or Constitutional, party, formed by a merger of his party with the Jiyuto, or Liberal, party of ITAGAKI TAISUKE. Okuma retired in 1907 but again served as prime minister in 1914–16, a period of great economic advance for Japan. The country entered World War I on the side of the Allies, and Okuma's government forced China to grant territorial rights to Japan.

Okvik [ahk'-vik]   Okvik, an archaeological site on the northernmost of the Punuk islands, southeast of St. Lawrence Island, Alaska, is also the name of a prehistoric ESKIMO culture first identified there in 1934. Originally the Okvik was believed to have initiated (*c.*300 BC) an important cultural tradition concentrated on St. Lawrence Island and the opposite Siberian coast and to have been replaced by the OLD BERING SEA culture in the first half of the 1st millennium AD, followed by the Punuk culture about AD 600. This sequence is no longer accepted by some archaeologists, who now think that Okvik may have existed more or less contemporaneously with a developed form of the Old Bering Sea culture.

All three cultures show a clear specialization in seamammal hunting based on the use of sophisticated harpoons. Characteristic ivory artifacts—many decorated in the distinctive art style associated with each culture—include harpoon heads, ornaments, and human figurines. The last may have been used for ceremonies in connection with whaling, which was conducted in great skin boats (*umiak*).

Olaf I, King of Norway [oh'-lahf]   Olaf Tryggvesson, *c.*968–1000, was the king who initiated the Christianization of Norway. He joined in the VIKING raids on the English coast, and in 994 he and King SWEYN of Denmark collected 16,000 pounds of silver from King Æthelred II of England in return for peace. Already a Christian, Olaf formalized his conversion that year. The next spring, he launched an attack on Norway. He soon brought all except the inland districts under his rule. Olaf established Christian churches, especially in the south west, and proclaimed Norway a Christian kingdom. He died in battle against the Danes and Swedes.

Olaf II, King of Norway (Saint Olaf)   Olaf II Haraldsson, b. *c.*995, d. July 29, 1030, king and patron saint of Norway, promoted the establishment of Christian institutions during his reign. He spent eight years abroad as a VIKING and was baptized about 1014 by the archbishop of Rouen. King from 1016, Olaf checked Danish and Swedish encroachment into Norway, suppressed pagan religion, and established (1024) the church in Norway. King CANUTE of England and Denmark also claimed Norway, however, and he defeated Olaf at sea in 1028. Olaf took refuge in Russia; when he returned in 1030 he was killed at the Battle of Stiklestad. He was canonized the next year. Feast day: July 29.

Olaf V, King of Norway   The Norwegian king Olaf V, b. July 2, 1903, d. Jan. 17, 1991, reigned from 1957 until his death. He studied at the Norwegian Military Academy and the University of Oxford. Exiled to England with his father, King Haakon VII, during World War II, he became head of the Norwegian armed forces in 1944, regent in 1955, and king two years later. His son succeeded him as Harold V.

Olbers's paradox   "Why should the night sky be dark?" This paradox was recognized in the 1820s by the German astronomer Heinrich Olbers (1758–1840) after he attempted to calculate the background light received from the stars. If the universe were infinite and homogeneous, then the flux from all background stars would be infinite, and the night sky would be bright. Olbers cited absorption by interstellar dust as the solution to this paradox.

Olbers's paradox was subsequently used as an argument against an infinite universe. Later the paradox was thought to be resolved by the discovery of the cosmological RED SHIFT, which weakens the contribution of distant galaxies so that the combined light of all galaxies is less than 1% of the background light from the stars in our own galaxy. It has now been suggested, however, that the true explanation rests on the finite lifetimes of stars.

old age   Old age is now being experienced by more people for a longer period of time than ever before. Old age has increasingly significant political, medical, economic, social, and demographic consequences for all nations. While the percentage of persons age 60 and over now ranges from about 13% to 20% in industrialized nations and from about 4% to 8% in nonindustrialized ones, these percentages or the actual numbers they represent are expected to increase dramatically in the next few decades. It is predicted that the largest increase in the population of older people will occur in the industrializing nations of Latin America, Africa, Asia, and the Pacific—areas that may have the fewest resources.

Although every society appears to have a socially recognized category of "old person," definitions of what old age is vary according to era, place, and culture. In the West, old age is increasingly determined by the reaching of a specific chronological age—usually 65, which represents the common time of retirement from the work force and the age at which pensions, such as Social Security, usually commence. In many traditional and nonindustrialized societies, old age is not defined chronologically but depends on an array of "markers," such as physical change, loss of certain abilities, or change in social roles.

Problems of the Elderly. Although in theory the extension of the life span provides for unprecedented possibilities of achievement—such as multiple careers and lengthy periods of creativity—in fact the problems that face the elderly, both in the West and elsewhere, can be immense. In Western nations there has been growth in both the number and type of government-sponsored programs to aid the elderly. For example, as the result of income-assistance programs, the percentage of older persons living under the poverty line in the United States decreased from 22% in 1959 to 13% in 1980. Data indicate, nonetheless, that poverty, poor health, and reduced opportunities continue to affect many elderly—especially women and ethnic minorities.

In developing nations, with few governmental or institutional resources and widespread poverty, the elderly may fare poorly. Although supportive treatment of the elderly is common, one study found nonsupportive treatment of some older persons in about one-third of the societies in the sample.

In the West, older people find fewer social roles available to them. Some roles, such as that of paid employee, may be lost forever. Others may be transformed: for example, being the 70-year-old parent of a 50-year-old child is quite different from being the 40-year-old parent of a 20-year-old. Still other roles may be replaced or renewed, as through participating in the many volunteer activities available. Remarriage provides a role renewal for elders who have lost a spouse.

Attitudes and Myths. There is little doubt that society negatively values old age. Job discrimination and an emphasis on youth in public culture are two examples. Realities affect attitudes. Retirement usually brings a significant reduction in income. As one ages, the death of friends and peers occurs more frequently. About 9% of older Americans describe their health as "poor," in contrast to about 2% of other age groups.

A number of common myths about the elderly should be dispelled. Most families do not in fact abandon their older members but rather go to extraordinary lengths to care for them. The treatment of the elderly in non-Western societies is by no means uniformly ideal. Although older Americans are often said to be lonely, loneliness is not widespread among the aged. Contrary to a common impression, most elderly in the United States do not retire to the Sun Belt but remain where they have lived all their lives.

Help for the Aged. Despite government programs, old age is a family affair everywhere. In the United States, families are generally very diligent in trying to care for dependent elders at home. Only about 5% of the U.S. elderly are in institutions such as NURSING HOMES, and these represent both the sickest and those with the fewest family resources. For community-resident elderly, there is considerable international variation as to whether older people live with their children or independently. In the United States most older people maintain their own households, and about 30% of all older people live alone. In Japan, on the other hand, about 60% of all older people live with their children.

The SOCIAL SECURITY system established in the United States in 1935 and similar programs in other industrialized nations greatly improved the lives of older people, providing a stable income and increasing their economic and social independence. More recently, MEDICARE (a federal medical and hospital insurance program) and MEDICAID (a federal-state program for those with low incomes) have provided for much of the medical care of the elderly. The far-reaching Older Americans Act (1965) set up state and area agencies on aging that serve as focal points for channeling federal funds into local projects such as senior centers and in-home service programs (which may provide visiting nurses, homemaker help, and meals-on-wheels for homebound elderly). In the United States the political and social influence of older persons is increasingly apparent through such organizations as the AMERICAN ASSOCIATION OF RETIRED PERSONS (AARP) and the GRAY PANTHERS.

See also: AGING; GERIATRICS.

Old Believers   Sometimes designated as *Raskolniki*, a term meaning schismatics, the Old Believers are Russian Christians who refused to recognize the liturgical reforms introduced by NIKON, the patriarch of Moscow, in 1653. In conformity with the Greek practices of that time, these reforms included the obligation to make the sign of the cross with three fingers instead of two, and minor corrections in liturgical books. In rejecting the reforms, the Old Believers were not necessarily concerned with the substance of the changes but with the principle, which obliged them to consider contemporary Greeks, and also westernized Ukrainians, as having preserved the right usages.

The Old Believers were severely persecuted for their opposition to the official stance of the Russian Orthodox church, and many of them—including the archpriest (or *protopop*) Avvakum—died as martyrs for their beliefs. Since the only bishop who supported them—Paul of Kolomna—died in prison, their communities were deprived of a legitimate priesthood.

Old Bering Sea   Old Bering Sea refers to an early example of the Arctic Thule tradition (see ESKIMO) dating from about AD 100 to 500. Archaeological sites have been discovered on both the Alaskan and Siberian coasts and on the islands in between. Old Bering Sea culture may have been contemporaneous—and linked—with the OKVIK culture, but some experts question this.

Old Catholics   Old Catholics include several small local churches that have separated from the Roman Catholic church. The Church of Utrecht—which was established in 1724 in a dispute over papal charges of JANSENISM in Holland—was the first of these churches to separate from Rome. In the 1870s other Old Catholic churches were formed in Germany, Switzerland, and Austria by those Catholics who rejected the dogma of papal infallibility promulgated by the First Vatican Council (1870).

In the United States, Polish Roman Catholics, resentful of domination by non-Polish clergy, split in 1897 to form the Polish National Catholic church. Other Slavic groups have also become Old Catholics, as has the Philippine Independent Church (established 1902). Old Catholic churches are in communion with each other and with the Church of England and seek ecumenical relations.

Old English   The name given to the first period of the ENGLISH LANGUAGE, Old English, or Anglo-Saxon, spans the time from the Anglo-Saxon invasion of Britain during the 5th century to the Norman Conquest in 1066. The earliest writings in English consist of a few scattered inscriptions in the runic alphabet. With the introduction of Christianity in 597 by Saint AUGUSTINE OF CANTERBURY, the Anglo-Saxons began using the Latin alphabet.

Of the three Germanic tribes that invaded Britain, the Angles settled the middle and north of England (Northumbria, present-day East Anglia, and the Midlands), the Jutes colonized the southeast (KENT and the Isle of Wight), and the Saxons took the rest: ESSEX, MIDDLESEX, SUSSEX, and WESSEX. These ethnic and political divisions correspond well with the earliest distinguishable dialect areas, though documents of the 8th and 9th centuries indicate the existence of two Anglian dialects: Northumbrian—the variety of Old English spoken north of the Humber estuary—and Mercian—spoken in an area stretching from East Anglia to the West Midlands but centered on the kingdom of MERCIA.

English prose came into its own only during the last quarter of the 9th century with the educational program of King ALFRED. Earlier records are limited mainly to charters, inscriptions—notably the Ruthwell Cross (*c.*700) in Dumfriesshire—and English glosses of Latin words. With the assistance of a small coterie of scholars gathered from all parts of England and from Wales and the Continent, Alfred nevertheless produced a series of translations and original prose works in his own dialect of Old English, so-called Early West-Saxon.

After a 50-year pause English prose took another leap forward as a result of the 10th-century monastic revival led by Saints Æthelwold, Dunstan, and Oswald. Hundreds of homilies, saints' lives, and other religious pieces were composed in all parts of England, from York to Winchester, in a remarkably uniform written language known as Late West-Saxon.

As MIDDLE ENGLISH developed, the number of inflectional endings was gradually reduced, a process that was well under way in Old English, particularly in the north. Even in the south, scribes who copied manuscripts into Late West-Saxon, for instance, occasionally wrote the noun ending -*es* (genitive singular) for -*as* (nominative or accusative plural), indicating that both inflections had come to be pronounced alike.

Old English literature   see BEOWULF; ENGLISH LITERATURE; EXETER BOOK

Old English sheepdog   The Old English sheepdog, one of the most distinctive breeds, has shown an ever-increasing popularity, ranking among the top 40 favorite breeds in the United States. Males stand 65 cm (26 in) at the shoulder. Covered with a profuse coat, the dog bears an outer coat that should be hard in texture, not straight, but shaggy and free from curl. The undercoat is a dense, insulating, waterproof pile.

The Old English sheepdog is a large, shaggy working dog that originated about 1800 in the west of England, where it was raised primarily as a cattle and sheep drover.

The Old English was developed in the west of England. The breeds that were crossed to produce it are still in doubt, although it is believed that the Scotch bearded collie played a large role. The Old English is sometimes referred to as the bobtail; the tail is usually docked.

Old Faithful   Old Faithful is a geyser in YELLOWSTONE NATIONAL PARK in northwestern Wyoming. One of approximately 200 geysers in the park, Old Faithful erupts on an average of every 65 minutes, although intervals may range from 33 to 148 minutes. Each eruption spouts about 40 m³ (1,400 ft³) of water and steam to about 46 m (150 ft) in the air.

Old Ironsides   see CONSTITUTION

Old Man and the Sea, The   Ernest HEMINGWAY's novel *The Old Man and the Sea* (1952) tells the moving story of Santiago, an aged Cuban fisherman who endures immense hardships in conquering a gigantic marlin, only to lose his prize to a succession of voracious sharks during the long voyage home in a skiff too small to accommodate his catch. The novella was based on a true story that Hemingway had heard 15 years earlier. In the interim he charged the story with many ulterior meanings and invoked Christian symbolism to suggest that, in Santiago's words, "A man can be destroyed but not defeated."

Old Prussian language   see BALTIC LANGUAGES

Old Stone Age   see PALEOLITHIC PERIOD

Old Testament   see BIBLE

Old Vic Theatre   London's Old Vic Theatre is renowned for its productions of Shakespeare and other classical plays and for the many famous actors—Edmund Kean, John Gielgud, Laurence Olivier, and Alec Guinness among them—who have performed there. It opened as the Royal Coburg in 1818 and in 1833 became the Royal Victoria, or—as it was popularly known—the Old Vic. Beginning in 1912 the theater with its newly formed acting company specialized in Shakespeare, for which it became famous. Severely damaged by German bombs in 1941, the Old Vic was closed until 1950. The Old Vic Company disbanded in 1963, and until 1976 the theater was the home of the National Theatre Company. Rebuilt in 1982, the Old Vic is now one of London's commercial theaters.

Oldenbarnevelt, Johan van [ohl-den-bahr'-nuh-velt]   Johan van Oldenbarnevelt, b. Sept. 14, 1547, d. May 13, 1619, was, with William the Silent (see WILLIAM I, PRINCE OF ORANGE), a founder of the Dutch Republic, guiding it to a position of eminence among European states. In 1572, Oldenbarnevelt joined the rebellion to rid the Netherlands of Spanish rule. He sponsored the advancement of MAURICE OF NASSAU and achieved Spain's tacit recognition of Dutch independence in the Twelve Years' Truce (1609–21). In a conflict with Maurice over the position of the Calvinist (Reformed) church, Oldenbarnevelt supported the REMONSTRANTS, a more liberal Calvinist sect; this disagreement led to Oldenbarnevelt's trial (1618–19) for subversion and execution at The Hague.

Oldenburg [ohl'-den-boork]   Oldenburg (1985 pop., 138,400), a city in northwestern Germany in the state of Lower Saxony, lies on the Hunte River and the Hunte-Ems Canal, about 30 km (20 mi) south of the North Sea. A livestock-trading center, Oldenburg also has meat-processing plants and produces machinery, glass, textiles, and chemicals. Landmarks include the Lamberti Church (1270) and the palace (1607–15) of the counts, and then dukes, of Oldenburg, who long ruled the city. The city existed as early as 1108 and was chartered in 1345. From 1918 to 1946 it was the capital of the former Oldenburg state.

Oldenburg, Claes   A leading American pop artist, Claes Thure Oldenburg, b. Stockholm, Jan. 28, 1929, has wittily blurred the line between the mundane and the aesthetic with his oversized replicas of such ordinary objects as food, clothing, and household fixtures. With others who were trying to bring art into closer contact with daily life, Oldenburg became a planner of HAPPENINGS, events that involved the use of various mediums and were intended to break down the limits of art. By the late 1950s he had begun to exhibit props for these events as independent works of art—generally sculptures of everyday objects modeled from plaster or papier-mâché and heavily spattered with paint.

Although his work is more surrealistic, Oldenburg was linked with Roy Lichtenstein, Andy Warhol, Robert Indi-

Claes Oldenburg, one of the leading figures in the pop-art movement, is known for satiric sculptures such as Saw *(1970). Constructed on an exaggerated scale and in materials incongruous to the subject, Oldenburg's works are humorous visions of familiar objects. (Stedelijk Museum, Amsterdam.)*

ana, and other pop artists (see POP ART) who were presenting hard-edged, impersonal images of common objects. Oldenburg continued, however, to inject a strongly personal, often humorous quality into his art, as in his many versions of the steel-and-aluminum *Geometric Mouse,* first sculpted in 1969. His earliest sculpture transformed soft subjects into hard forms. During the 1960s this procedure was reversed. Hard objects were turned into soft, kapok-filled sculptures, for example, *Soft Typewriter* (1963), *Soft Toilet* (1966), and *Giant Soft Drum Set* (1967). These works have a toylike quality yet seem almost organic and even sensual.

Oldfield, Barney   Berna Eli Oldfield, b. Wauseon, Ohio, Jan. 29, 1878, d. Oct. 4, 1946, was a racing car driver who was instrumental in popularizing the sport in the United States. As a youth he was a professional bicycle racer; in 1902 he joined the Ford factory racing team and as the driver of the famous "999" became the first person to reach (1903) the speed of 60 mph (97 km/h). He was also the first person to drive a 100-mph (160-km/h) lap at the Indianapolis Speedway. At Daytona Beach, Fla., on Mar. 16, 1910, he established a world land speed record for the measured mile at 131.724 mph (211.944 km/h).

Oldowan   see PALEOLITHIC PERIOD

Olduvai Gorge   [ohl-duh'-vy]   Olduvai Gorge, an archaeological site on the Serengeti Plains in northern Tanzania, provides unique evidence of early human evolution and toolmaking from about 2 million to 100,000 years ago. Olduvai was discovered by Wilhelm Kattwinkel, a German entomologist, in 1911. Olduvai Gorge consists of four major geological beds formed by the sediments left by a shallow Lower Pleistocene lake that once covered a large area of the eastern Serengeti Plains. Early humanlike creatures camped by the banks of this ancient lake,

dropping their tools and the bones of the animals they hunted at their camp sites. In 1931 the British archaeologist Louis Leakey (see LEAKEY family) found stone tools in the gorge. In 1959, Mary Leakey found a skull of *Australopithecus boisei,* a primitive hominid (humanlike) fossil species, that was potassium-argon dated to about 1.75 million years before the present. Later a more gracile hominid, called HOMO HABILIS, was discovered in a level slightly lower than that of the original hominid find. The *Homo habilis* fragments were said to belong to a larger-brained hominid than AUSTRALOPITHECUS and included parts of a hand. A reconstruction of the hand bones revealed an opposable thumb capable of powerful gripping and precise manipulation. The 1.8-million-year-old skeletal remains of another *H. habilis* specimen were discovered at Olduvai Gorge in 1986.

The earliest occupation levels at Olduvai date from about 2 million years ago and contain crude Oldowan stone chopping tools with jagged edges as well as the bones of many extinct animals. Additional hominid fossils have come to light in the lower and the upper (later) levels of Olduvai, including a skull of HOMO ERECTUS dating from about one million years ago.

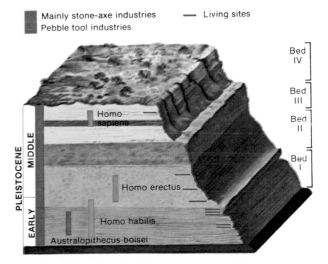

A cutaway drawing of Olduvai Gorge, in northern Tanzania, indicates the four major geological beds and the levels at which fossil hominids have been found. The earliest level in Bed I dates from about 2 million years ago; remains of modern humans, Homo sapiens, occur in Bed IV. The beds, formed from the sediments of a Lower Pleistocene lake, were exposed by an earthquake during the Upper Pleistocene.

■ Mainly stone-axe industries   — Living sites
■ Pebble tool industries

Homo sapiens

Bed IV
Bed III
Bed II
Bed I

PLEISTOCENE   MIDDLE   EARLY

Homo erectus

Homo habilis

Australopithecus boisei

oleander   [oh'-lee-an-dur]   Oleander, genus *Nerium,* is the common name for two species of evergreen shrubs belonging to the dogbane family, Apocynaceae. Native to Eurasia, oleanders are grown outdoors in mild climates and are drought-resistant. All parts of the plant are poi-

The common oleander, a decorative evergreen shrub found in mild climates, flowers throughout the summer. The blooms range from white to bright red. The plant grows up to 6 m (20 ft) tall. It is poisonous.

sonous if eaten. The common oleander, *N. oleander,* is the most widely grown species in the United States. Growing up to 6 m (20 ft) tall, it produces large, dark green, leathery leaves and large, showy flowers.

olefin   see ALKENE

oligarchy

Oligarchy (Greek, "rule by the few") is a form of government in which a small group of people holds ruling power. Aristotle wrote of several types of oligarchy: those in which property qualifications restrict voting or office holding to a few; those in which political power is based on birth; and those in which power is held by a small clique or junta. The military dictatorships in many countries of Latin America and Africa are examples of one type of oligarchy, as are the political machines that sometimes run local governments in democratic countries.

Oligocene Epoch   see EARTH, GEOLOGICAL HISTORY OF; GEOLOGIC TIME

olingo

Olingos, genus *Bassaricyon,* are mammals in the raccoon and panda family, Procyonidae, order Carnivora. They are slender, 33–46 cm (13–18 in) long, with a heavily furred tail 38–51 cm (15–20 in) long. The soft coat is golden pink to gray brown. The eyes are large, the muzzle is pointed, and the short legs have sharply curved claws. Olingos live in Central America and northern South America. They are found chiefly in tropical jungle regions and eat mainly fruit.

Oliphant, Patrick

[ahl'-i-fuhnt]   Patrick Bruce Oliphant, b. July 24, 1935, left Adelaide, Australia, for the United States in 1964 to become editorial cartoonist for the *Denver Post*; while working there he won (1967) a Pulitzer Prize. In 1975, Oliphant joined the *Washington Star.*

The *Los Angeles Times/Washington Post* Syndicate distributes his bitingly satirical cartoons to nearly 500 newspapers. In most of his work Punk the Penguin makes droll comments.

Olivares, Gaspar de Guzmán, Conde-Duque de

[oh-lee-vah'-rays]   The conde-duque de Olivares, b. Gaspar de Guzmán y Pimental, Jan. 16, 1587, d. July 22, 1645, who served as prime minister of Spain for 20 years, attempted to unify the Spanish kingdom and to expand Spanish power. In 1615 he became one of the personal attendants of the crown prince, who succeeded to the throne as PHILIP IV in 1621 and appointed Olivares prime minister in 1623. Hoping to bring much of Europe under the domination of the Spanish and Austrian Habsburgs, he involved Spain more widely in the THIRTY YEARS' WAR, with the result that Spain was overshadowed by French power. Olivares's centralizing policies also led to revolts in Catalonia and Portugal (beginning in 1640) and to a conspiracy (1641) in Andalusia. Olivares was forced to resign in 1643 and was later exiled to Toro.

olive

The olive, *Olea europaea,* of the family Oleaceae, a handsome, long-lived, evergreen, subtropical tree, has been cultivated for at least 40 centuries for its edible fruit and its valuable oil. It is native to the eastern Mediterranean region, where its culture may have begun as long ago as 3500 BC. The olive was introduced into the Western Hemisphere in 1560 by Spanish missionaries. Today California grows 99 percent of the olives produced in the United States.

Generally, the tree is medium in stature, about 8 m (25 ft) in height, although some trees may grow as tall as

The olive tree is an evergreen grown primarily in the Mediterranean region. It is cultivated for its fruit, the source of olive oil, and for its wood, which is exceptionally hard and fine grained.

18 m (60 ft). The narrow leaves are dull green above, silvery beneath, and paired on the stems. (Olive branches are ancient symbols of peace and victory.) The flowers are small, fragrant, and light cream-colored and cluster at the leaf axils. They are of two types: perfect, in which both the pistil and the stamens are functional; and staminate or imperfect, in which the pistil aborts but the stamens function normally. The small fruits vary in shape from round to oblong and are essentially black and very bitter at maturity.

In order to produce flowers and fruit, the trees must undergo chilling at temperatures below 7° C (44° F) for 2 to 3 months in regions where daily mean temperatures are below 10° C (50° F). The trees grow luxuriantly in the tropics but produce no fruit. They can be grown on a wide range of soil types, provided the soil drains well. Cultivars are propagated mainly by rooting cuttings. In California, commercially important olive cultivars include Manzanillo, Mission, Sevillano, Ascelano, and Barouni. The principal olive products are olive oil and both ripe and green olives for the table. The fruit is rendered palatable by special processing, which involves the use of lye (sodium hydroxide) and salt brine.

Oliver, King New Orleans cornet player Joseph "King" Oliver, b. near Abend, La., May 11, 1885, d. Apr. 8, 1938, won his title for his technical proficiency, endurance, and melodic inventiveness. Oliver made two significant contributions to the history of jazz: his inimitable Creole Jazz Band was the first black ensemble to be recorded (1923); and his influence on the young Louis Armstrong helped shape the renowned trumpeter's style and career. Two of Oliver's most famous compositions, "Dippermouth Blues" and "West End Blues," are preserved in the Smithsonian Collection of Classic Jazz.

Olivier, Laurence Kerr, Baron Olivier of Brighton One of the finest English actors of the 20th century, Laurence Olivier, b. May 22, 1907, d. July 11, 1989, performed superbly in diverse roles on stage and screen. He is probably best known for his films of Shakespeare's *Henry V* (1945), *Hamlet* (1948; Academy Award), and *Richard III* (1955). After acting (1926–28) with the Birmingham Repertory Company, he quickly achieved success on the London stage and in 1937 joined the OLD VIC THEATRE, where he won critical acclaim as an interpreter of Shakespeare. Equally successful in modern drama, he brilliantly portrayed Archie Rice in John Osborne's *The Entertainer* (1957; film, 1960) and the father in Eugene O'Neill's *Long Day's Journey into Night* (1972), among many other roles. From 1962 to 1973 he was director of the newly formed NATIONAL THEATRE Company. In addition to his Shakespeare films, Olivier acted in memorable screen versions of *Wuthering Heights* (1939), *Rebecca* (1939), and *Pride and Prejudice* (1940). His many television roles include an Emmy-winning performance in the 1982 series *Brideshead Revisited* and a production (1984) of *King Lear*.

Lord Olivier has been hailed as one of the most brilliant English actors of our time for such outstanding performances as his 1955 film portrayal of Richard III. The recipient of many awards, he was knighted in 1947 and created a baron in 1970.

olivine Olivines are common green or brown SILICATE MINERALS found in igneous and metamorphic rocks rich in magnesium and iron. Magnesium-rich olivines are used in refractory brick, and clear green crystals provide the gem PERIDOT.

The chemical formula of the olivines is $(Mg, Fe)_2SiO_4$, with the silica tetrahedra arranged so that each metal ion is surrounded by six oxygens. All varieties crystallize in the orthorhombic system. Most olivines contain principally magnesium. Magnesium and iron can substitute for each other freely, so that every composition between pure magnesium olivine, forsterite, and pure iron olivine, fayalite, is possible. Such compositional variation in minerals is called solid solution, and the olivines provide some of the best examples.

Formation. Olivine is the first mineral to start crystallizing as basaltic lava cools. As the temperature falls, olivine

Olivine is a magnesium-iron silicate mineral thought to be the most abundant material in the Earth's mantle. Olivine is commonly disseminated in dark-colored igneous rocks as small, rounded olive green vitreous crystals.

eventually stops crystallizing and reacts with the lava to form PYROXENE minerals. In the final rock, some olivine may remain, or all may have been consumed by the reaction.

If the lava cools slowly, the olivine may settle out and form a layer near the bottom. Thus the bottom part of the rock mass may be rich in olivine while the top part has none. (Rocks consisting of almost pure olivine are called DUNITES.) If such settling occurs underground and is followed by eruption of the still-molten lava, masses of solid olivine may be thrown out as volcanic bombs. Olivine bombs 15 cm (6 in) or more across have been found around ancient volcanoes in Arizona and New Mexico.

Occurrence. Olivines occur widely. Magnesium olivine is common in iron- and magnesium-rich basalt, which makes up much of the seafloor, as well as such volcanic islands as Iceland and Hawaii. Magnesium olivine is also abundant on the Moon, where it occurs in the basalts that make up the lunar maria.

Olivine is the major constituent of the rock PERIDOTITE. The geologic settings in which peridotite is found—along the mid-oceanic ridges and in mountain ranges—indicate that it is derived from the Earth's mantle, the zone that begins some 10 to 50 km (6 to 30 mi) beneath the Earth's surface. Olivine is also found in some stony meteorites and in rare meteorites called pallasites, which are made of about equal amounts of olivine and native iron.

Whereas forsterite (Mg_2SiO_4) is found chiefly in metamorphosed dolomites, fayalite (Fe_2SiO_4) occurs mainly in igneous rocks. Iron-rich olivines such as fayalite are rarer than magnesium-rich ones.

Olmec [ohl'-mek]   Olmec civilization, MESOAMERICA's first truly complex culture, flourished between 1200 and 400 BC, when it dissolved into a series of regional cultures. Centered on the southern Gulf coast of Mexico, Olmec economic and political influence extended into the central Mexican highlands and southeast along the Pacific coast to El Salvador and beyond. By 1200 BC, Olmec civilization was fully developed at SAN LORENZO, the first great civic-ceremonial center. About 900 BC, Olmec power shifted to LA VENTA. Massive public-works projects—clay building platforms and stone pavements and drainage systems—were built at both centers. Outside the heartland region the Olmec traded in exotic raw materials such as jade for the manufacture of luxury goods.

Notable works of Olmec art include colossal basalt sculptures of human heads and portable jade carvings. A few reliefs suggest the beginnings of the hieroglyphic writing associated with later Mesoamerican cultures. Strong continuities lead from Olmec, through IZAPA, to Classic MAYA art.

See also: PRE-COLUMBIAN ART AND ARCHITECTURE.

Olmsted, Frederick Law [ohlm'-sted]   Frederick Law Olmsted, b. Hartford, Conn., Apr. 26, 1822, d. Aug. 28, 1903, was one of the founders of landscape architecture in the United States. Best known as the designer, with Calvert VAUX, of Central Park in New York City, Olm-sted was part of a movement to bring the informal English garden style of the 18th century to North America and adapt it particularly to parks for public use.

The first to use the title landscape architect, Olmsted established a firm that planned metropolitan park systems and the ecologically sound use of watersheds and open spaces. He was the principal designer of the grounds of the World's Columbian Exposition of 1893 in Chicago. Other examples of his work include Prospect Park (1866–67) in Brooklyn, N.Y.; the plan of Stanford University's campus (1888), Calif.; Mount Royal Park (1877), Montreal; and the Biltmore estate (1890) in Asheville, N.C. Olmsted also worked to preserve such natural areas as what is now Yosemite National Park in California.

Olney, Richard   Richard Olney, b. Oxford, Mass., Sept. 15, 1835, d. Apr. 8, 1917, was U.S. attorney general (1893–95) and secretary of state (1895–97) under President Grover Cleveland. While attorney general he broke the 1894 PULLMAN STRIKE of railroad workers by obtaining federal injunctions against obstruction of the mails, thereby giving employers a major new weapon against unions.

As secretary of state Olney faced problems with Spain over Cuba and with Britain over the British Guiana–Venezuela border. In a note to the U.S. ambassador in London in 1895, Olney insisted on the right of the United States to intervene in this VENEZUELA BOUNDARY DISPUTE and called on Britain to accept arbitration. The position that the United States had the right to intervene in international disputes in the Western Hemisphere became known as the Olney Corollary to the MONROE DOCTRINE.

Olsen, Tillie   Tillie Olsen, b. Omaha, Nebr., Jan. 14, 1913, is a writer whose 1974 novel *Yonnondio: From the Thirties*, although it took 40 years to complete, was received as one of the most powerful indictments of the crushing effects of poverty ever to appear in American literature. After she had worked for many years in industry, Olsen received a series of grants that enabled her to begin writing full time. The title story of her collection *Tell Me a Riddle* (1961) won the 1961 O. Henry Award. The collection *Silences* followed in 1965.

Olson, Charles   A noted American critic and poet, Charles Olson, b. Worcester, Mass., Dec. 27, 1910, d. Jan. 10, 1970, first received recognition for his critical essay on Herman Melville, *Call Me Ishmael* (1947). Olson's poetry, with its steady insistence on the exact particulars of sensation and experience, had a clear impact on many of his contemporaries. *The Maximus Poems* (1953–68), for which he is best known, continued the tradition of Ezra Pound in using canto as historical collage. Olson's major influence was as a theoretician of the new "open form" of poetics that flourished after World War II, articulated in essays such as "Projective Verse" (1950; republished in expanded form, 1959).

Olympia (Greece) Olympia, on the northwest Peloponnesian peninsula, in southern Greece, was an important religious center and site of the OLYMPIC GAMES, the most important festival of the ancient Greek world. The site lies in the valley of the Alphaeus (now Alfiós) River, below wooded Mount Kronos, in the ancient province of Elis. Although the sacred precinct was never a city, it contained many of the finest treasures of Greek and Roman art and architecture. The games were officially established in 776 BC and held every 4 years.

A sacred place possibly as early as the Mycenaean period (*c.*1600–1100 BC), Olympia was a major sanctuary by the 8th century BC. Within the walls of the *Altis,* a sacred grove, are well-preserved Doric temples begun about 600 BC and dedicated to the Mother of the Gods (Metroön) and to Hera (Heraion). In the Heraion was found the famous *Hermes and the Infant Dionysus* (*c.*340 BC; Olympia Museum) of Praxiteles. The temple of Zeus, one of the largest in mainland Greece, was built about 470–456 BC by the architect Libon of Elis; it housed one of the SEVEN WONDERS OF THE WORLD, the gold-and-ivory statue of Zeus by Phidias.

On a terrace facing the temples is a row of small, 6th-century BC treasuries, representing various Greek cities and colonies. Other structures are the rotunda of Philip of Macedonia and the athletic buildings, including the gymnasium; palaestra, used for boxing and wrestling; and the hippodrome, where horse and chariot races were held. The stadium, dating from the 4th century BC, seated 40,000 spectators on grassy banks above a course 600 Olympian feet (190 m/630 ft) long.

The Olympic Games were suspended in AD 393. The sanctuary was demolished in 426 and obliterated by earthquakes and floods in the 6th century. Olympia was rediscovered in the 18th century.

Olympia (Washington) Olympia is the state capital of Washington and the seat of Thurston County. The city has a population of 33,840 (1990). Located in the west central part of the state at the southern end of Puget Sound on Budd Inlet, Olympia is a major port with a variety of industries and oyster fisheries, but its main business is government. The capitol buildings and their elaborate gardens attract many tourists, as do the Olympic National Park to the north and Mount Rainier to the east. St. Martin's College (1895) and Evergreen State College (1967) are there. Olympia was first settled in 1846 by Edmund Sylvester and Levi Lathrop Smith as Smithfield. It was platted in 1851 and was renamed for the nearby Olympic Mountains. In 1853 the city became the capital of the newly established Washington territory.

Olympic Games The Olympic Games are an international sports festival that began in ancient Greece. The original Greek games were staged every fourth year for several hundred years, until they were abolished in the early Christian era. The revival of the Olympic Games took

The athlete at the center of the painting on this Athenian cup (c.500 BC) is competing in a jumping contest, holding special weights to increase his distance.

place in 1896, and since then they have been staged every fourth year, except during World War I and World War II (1916, 1940, 1944).

Perhaps the basic difference between the ancient and modern Olympics is that the former was the ancient Greeks' way of saluting their gods, whereas the modern Games are a manner of saluting the athletic talents of citizens of all nations. The original Olympics featured competition in music, oratory, and theater performances as well. The modern Games have a more expansive athletic agenda, and for 2½ weeks they are supposed to replace the rancor of international conflict with friendly competition. In recent times, however, that lofty ideal has not always been attained.

The Ancient Olympics

The earliest reliable date that recorded history gives for the first Olympics is 776 BC, although virtually all historians presume that the Games began well before then.

(Left) *Pierre de Coubertin, a French baron, proposed a revival of the Olympic Games before a meeting of the Athletic Sports Union in 1892. Four years later de Coubertin realized his ambition through the staging of the first modern Olympiad* (below), *held in Athens, Greece.*

It is certain that during the midsummer of 776 BC a festival was held at Olympia on the highly civilized eastern coast of the Peloponnesian peninsula. That festival remained a regularly scheduled event, taking place during the pre-Christian golden age of Greece. As a testimony to the religious nature of the Games (which were held in honor of Zeus, the most important god in the ancient Greek pantheon), all wars would cease during the contests. According to the earliest records, only one athletic event was held in the ancient Olympics—a foot race of about 183 m (200 yd), or the length of the stadium. A cook, Coroibus of Elis, was the first recorded winner. The first few Olympics had only local appeal and were limited to one race on one day; only men were allowed to compete or attend. A second race—twice the length of the stadium—was added in the 14th Olympics, and a still longer race was added to the next competition, 4 years later.

When the powerful, warlike Spartans began to compete, they influenced the agenda. The 18th Olympics included wrestling and a pentathlon consisting of running, jumping, spear throwing (the javelin), discus throwing, and wrestling. Boxing was added at the 23d Olympiad, and the Games continued to expand, with the addition of chariot racing and other sports. In the 37th Olympiad (632 BC) the format was extended to 5 days of competition.

The growth of the Games fostered "professionalism" among the competitors, and the Olympic ideals waned as royalty began to compete for personal gain, particularly in the chariot events. Human beings were being glorified as well as the gods; many winners erected statues to deify themselves. In AD 394 the Games were officially ended by the Roman emperor Theodosius, who felt that they had pagan connotations.

(Left) *Gala festivities marked the opening- and closing-day ceremonies of the 23d Olympiad, held in Los Angeles in 1984. The Olympic torch is lit by a flame kindled on Mount Olympus, Greece, and then carried by a relay of runners to the site of each Olympiad.*

(Below) *Gymnast Olga Korbut* (left, in red) *watches as the Romanian Nadia Comaneci executes a flawless routine on the balance beam during the 1976 Olympics at Montreal.*

Jesse Owens received international acclaim for his performance in the 1936 Olympic Games at Berlin, where he won four gold medals in track and field.

While on the victory platform, Americans Tommie Smith and John Carlos, gold and bronze medalists in the 200-m sprint at the Mexico City Olympics (1968), bowed their heads and raised the "black power" salute during the playing of the U.S. national anthem to protest the treatment of U.S. blacks. Both athletes were suspended from the Games.

The Modern Olympics

The revival of the Olympic Games in 1896, unlike the original Games, has a clear, concise history. Pierre de Coubertin (1863–1937), a young French nobleman, felt that he could institute an educational program in France that approximated the ancient Greek notion of a balanced development of mind and body. The Greeks themselves had tried to revive the Olympics by holding local athletic games in Athens during the 1800s, but without lasting success. It was Baron de Coubertin's determination and organizational genius, however, that gave impetus to the modern Olympic movement. In 1892 he addressed a meeting of the Union des Sports Athlétiques in Paris. Despite meager response he persisted, and an international sports congress eventually convened on June 16, 1894. With delegates from Belgium, England, France, Greece, Italy, Russia, Spain, Sweden, and the United States in attendance, he advocated the revival of the Olympic Games. He found ready and unanimous support from the nine countries. De Coubertin had initially planned to hold the Olympic Games in France, but the representatives convinced him that Greece was the appropriate country to host the first modern Olympics. The council did agree that every 4 years the Olympics would move to other great cities of the world.

Thirteen countries competed at the Athens Games in 1896. Nine sports were on the agenda: cycling, fencing, gymnastics, lawn tennis, shooting, swimming, track and field, weight lifting, and wrestling. The 14-man U.S. team dominated the track and field events, taking first place in 9 of the 12 events. The Games were a success, and a second Olympiad, to be held in France, was scheduled. Olympic Games were held in 1900 and 1904, and by 1908 the number of competitors more than sextupled the number at Athens—from 311 to 2,082.

Beginning in 1924 a Winter Olympics was included—held at a separate cold-weather sports site in the same year as the Summer Games—the first held at Chamonix, France. (Starting in 1994, the Winter Games will be held two years after the Summer Games.) The Winter Games program includes Alpine and Nordic skiing, biathlon, ice hockey, figure skating, speed skating, bobsledding, and luge. But the Summer Games, with its wide array of

(Right) *Al Oerter of the United States, shown here at the 1956 Games, won four consecutive Olympic gold medals in the discus (1956–68).*

(Above) *The world's greatest decathlete in the 1980s was Great Britain's Daley Thompson, who won Olympic gold medals in both 1980 and 1984.*

(Below) *The American swimmer Mark Spitz won a record seven gold medals in the 1972 Olympics: four in individual events and three as a member of relay teams.*

(Left) *American athlete Carl Lewis, running in the 4 × 100-m relay at the 1984 Olympics, has been hailed as the greatest track star since Jesse Owens. Lewis duplicated Owens's feat at the 1936 Olympics by winning four gold medals in 1984—in the relay, the 100- and 200-m sprints, and the long jump.*

The American skater Eric Heiden emerged as the dominant athlete of the 1980 Winter Olympic Games. Winning every men's speed-skating event, Heiden accounted for five of the six gold medals won by the United States at Lake Placid.

events, are still the focal point of the modern Olympics. Among the standard events are basketball, boxing, canoeing and kayaking, cycling, equestrian arts, fencing, field hockey, gymnastics, modern pentathlon, rowing, shooting, soccer, swimming and diving, track and field, volleyball, water polo, weight lifting, wrestling (freestyle and Greco-Roman), and yachting. The Games are governed by the International Olympic Committee (IOC), whose headquarters is in Lausanne, Switzerland.

The ideology of nationalism has left its mark on the Olympics. Athletic nationalism was brought to a peak by Nazi Germany, which staged the 1936 Games in Berlin and used the Olympics to propagandize its cause.

The political overtones of the Olympics did not lessen with the fall of Nazi Germany. In 1956, Egypt, Iraq, and Lebanon boycotted the Melbourne, Australia, Games to

Soviet and American athletes battle for a loose puck during hockey competition at the 1980 Winter Olympic Games, in Lake Placid, N.Y. In a stunning upset, the U.S. team defeated the Soviet Union by a 4-3 score and went on to win the gold medal.

protest the Anglo-French seizure of the Suez Canal, and the Netherlands, Spain, and Switzerland boycotted to protest the USSR's invasion of Hungary. In Mexico City in 1968, 2 American blacks used the victory pedestal to publicize their disdain for U.S. racial policies. In Munich in 1972, 11 Israeli athletes were massacred by Palestinian terrorists. And in 1976 in Montreal, 33 African nations, to be represented by about 400 athletes, boycotted the Games to protest South Africa's apartheid policies.

In 1980, under strong pressure from the Carter administration, the U.S. Olympic Committee voted to boycott the Summer Games in Moscow to protest the 1979 Soviet invasion of Afghanistan. About 40 nations followed the U.S. lead (among them West Germany, China, and Japan). In 1984 the Summer Games, held in Los Angeles, were undercut by an Eastern-bloc boycott led by the USSR. Most commentators believed the reasons for the boycott to be political: a reflection of the poor state of recent U.S.-Soviet relations, simple revenge for the U.S. boycott of the Moscow Games, and possible embarrassment to the Soviets on worldwide television caused by planned anti-Soviet demonstrations and possible defections of Eastern-bloc athletes.

In 1988 the Winter Games—held in Calgary, Alberta, Canada—were completed without international incident. At the Summer Games, in Seoul, South Korea, East met West in Olympic competition for the first time since 1976, with only 6 nations (including Cuba and North Korea) boycotting. Despite some student demonstrations in Seoul, the spotlight returned to the athletes themselves. One cloud was the suspicion that the use of performance-enhancing drugs was widespread, especially after Canadian sprinter Ben Johnson tested positive and was stripped of his 100-m gold medal.

Olympus, Mount   Mount Olympus (Greek: Ólimbos) is the highest peak in Greece (2,917 m/9,570 ft). The great, snowcapped mountain rises in the Olympus range in northern Greece near the Aegean coast. In early Greek mythology, the cloud-covered mountain was believed to be the majestic home of the gods.

Olynthus [oh-lin'-thuhs]   Olynthus, an ancient Greek city on the Chalcidice Peninsula, was the center of Greek resistance to the power of Athens and Sparta in the 4th century BC. Leader of the Chalcidian League, Olynthus became by 382 a threat to Sparta, which besieged the city and dissolved the league (379). After Sparta's decline the league was reformed, and Olynthus stood against Athens in alliance with PHILIP II of Macedonia until, intimidated by Philip's growing power, it plotted against him with the Athenians. In 348, Philip attacked and destroyed the city.

Omaha (Indian tribe)   The Omaha, meaning "up-river," are North American Indians who once formed a large Siouan-speaking group with the Kansa, Osage, Quapaw, and Ponca. They may have originated on the Atlantic coast but by the 17th century had moved west to the Ohio and then the Missouri Valley. In 1780 they numbered about 3,000. On the Missouri the Omaha built earth lodges, cultivated maize and beans, and hunted bison in summer. Male leaders, priests, and curers formed a class above commoners. Ten patrilineal clans were organized into Earth and Sky moieties (complementary groups). Two sacred pipes along with a sacred bison pole were central to Omaha religion.

Fur trade with American settlers in St. Louis, Mo., in the 1800s followed earlier French trade. Smallpox and measles reduced the Omaha to only several hundred members by 1804. An 1815 peace treaty and vaccination saved them from total depopulation in the 1837 smallpox epidemic. Treaties between 1835 and 1854 ceded much Omaha land. Chief Joseph La Flesche led his people during this difficult period. In 1865 some Winnebago joined the Omaha; they accepted allotments and U.S. citizenship in 1887 to avoid being sent to INDIAN TERRITORY in present-day Oklahoma. Their best land was sold early in the 1900s. In 1987 an estimated 2,000 Omaha remained on or near the reservation in Nebraska.

Omaha (Nebraska)   Omaha is a city in eastern Nebraska on the Missouri River opposite Council Bluffs, Iowa. The seat of Douglas County and the state's largest city, Omaha has a population of 335,795 (1990), with 618,262 persons residing in the metropolitan area. Oma-ha is a major rail, trade, insurance, and food-processing center in a fertile agricultural region, as well as one of the country's largest livestock markets. It also manufactures railroad and agricultural equipment, electronic components, and petroleum products. Colleges include Creighton University (1878) and the University of Nebraska at Omaha (1908). Nearby are Offutt Air Force Base and Boys Town.

The site was occupied by the Omaha Indians until a treaty opened Nebraska Territory to settlement in 1854. The territorial capital from 1855 to 1867, Omaha grew as an outfitting point for the westward bound, with steamboats arriving regularly. In 1865 the Union Pacific, the first transcontinental railroad, began moving westward from Omaha. The railroad built stockyards there in the 1880s, and meat-packing houses followed. By the early 1900s the city was a great rail center.

Oman [oh-mahn']   The sultanate of Oman is an independent country occupying the eastern bulge of the Arabian Peninsula. It lies on the Gulf of Oman and the Arabian Sea and has land borders with the United Arab Emirates, Saudi Arabia (undefined), and Yemen. Oman includes an exclave on the Musandam Peninsula, which juts into the Strait of HORMUZ. A former Portuguese territory, Oman has maintained independence since 1650.

Land, People, and Economy

A coastal plain up to 19 km (12 mi) wide extends to a range of hills, which give way to a plateau with an average

AT A GLANCE

SULTANATE OF OMAN

Land: Area: 212,457 km² (82,030 mi²). Capital and largest city: Muscat (1982 est. pop., 85,000).

People: Population (1990 est.): 1,467,064. Density: 6.9 persons per km² (17.9 per mi²). Distribution (1986): 9% urban, 91% rural. Official language: Arabic. Major religion: Islam.

Government: Type: sultanate. Legislature: none. Political subdivisions: 50 *wilayats* (provinces).

Economy: GNP (1989 est.): $7.8 billion; $6,006 per capita. Labor distribution (1986): agriculture—23%; construction—28%; public administration and services—17%. Foreign trade (1988 est.): imports—$1.9 billion; exports—$3.6 billion. Currency: 1 Omani rial = 1,000 baiza.

Education and Health: Literacy (1990): 41% of adult population. Universities (1987): 1. Hospital beds (1987): 4,016. Physicians (1987): 1,243. Life expectancy (1990): women—58; men—56. Infant mortality (1990): 105 per 1,000 live births.

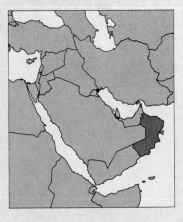

altitude of 305 m (1,000 ft). The mountainous north central area, the Hajar, reaches 3,035 m (9,957 ft) at Mount al-Sham in the Al-Akhdar Mountains. Most hills are barren, and the plateau is cultivated only at oases. The extreme southwestern province of Dhofar, however, is very fertile. Oman's climate is generally hot and dry, with temperatures ranging from 18° to 34° C (64° to 93° F) and rainfall ranging from 76 to 102 mm (3 to 4 in) per year.

The population is almost entirely Arab, with the exception of expatriate workers (mostly Indian and Pakistani), who constitute about 58% of the salaried labor force. Many inhabitants adhere to Ibadism, a Sunnite sect of Islam. The chief cities are Muscat, the capital, and the nearby port of Matra. In 1965, Oman had only three primary schools and one 12-bed hospital, but education and health-care facilities have increased dramatically since 1970. Sultan Qaboos University was opened in 1986.

Oman's economy is based on petroleum, which accounts for 99% of export revenues. Since 1970 petroleum revenues have been used to build roads and housing, provide electricity, expand irrigation, develop manufacturing, and modernize the fishing industry. A majority of the Omani population is engaged in subsistence farming, although water is scarce and less than 1% of the land currently is under cultivation.

Government and History

Sultan Qaboos bin Said wields absolute power. Oman has no constitution, legislature, or political parties. Provincial governors and members of the Consultative Assembly established in 1981 are appointed by and responsible to the sultan. In November 1990 the sultan announced that he would establish an elected assembly—the first in a Persian Gulf state—within a year.

An early link between the Mediterranean and the Far East, Oman was converted to Islam in the 7th century. In 1507, Muscat and its hinterland came under the control of the Portuguese, who held it until 1650, when the Omani successfully revolted and extended their influence as far south as Zanzibar. The Persians briefly gained control (1741–49), and then in 1798, Oman signed a treaty of friendship with Great Britain, though it remained independent.

From 1932 to 1970, Oman was ruled by the reclusive Sultan Said bin Taimur, whose repressive policies sparked a revolt in the Dhofar in 1965. In 1970 he was overthrown by his British-educated son, Qaboos, who then launched an ambitious modernization program. Regional security concerns, which prompted Oman and six other Persian Gulf countries to form the Gulf Cooperation Council in 1981, intensified with the 1990 Iraqi invasion of Kuwait and subsequent Gulf war.

Oman, Gulf of The Gulf of Oman is an arm of the Arabian Sea bordered on the north by Iran and on the south by Oman. It is about 565 km (350 mi) long and 320 km (200 mi) wide. The gulf, which is connected to the Persian Gulf by the Strait of Hormuz, is important as a petroleum shipping route from the Middle East.

Omar Khayyam [oh'-mahr ky-ahm'] The Persian poet Omar Khayyam, whose full name was Abu al-Fath Omar ben Ibrahim al-Khayyam, 1050?–1122, is best known in the West as a result of Edward Fitzgerald's popular translation of the long poem known as the Rubaiyat of Omar Khayyam. Among his contemporaries Khayyam was famous as a mathematician and astronomer. His work on algebra was known throughout Europe in the Middle Ages, and he also contributed to a calendar reform. His fame as a poet, however, has eclipsed his scientific achievements, even though verse forms used in the Rubaiyat existed in Persian literature before Khayyam, and the number of its verses that can be attributed to him with certainty is very small.

ombudsman An ombudsman (Swedish, "agent") is a public officer whose duty is to handle public complaints against actions of government. Ideally, the ombudsman acts as a public advocate, impartially and expeditiously handling public grievances. The ombudsman usually acts at the request of complaining citizens but may also initiate investigations of general public concern. The first ombudsman was established by the Swedish legislature in 1809; the official was to be a person of "known legal ability and outstanding integrity," chosen for a term of four

OMAN

- ┼ Oil Pipeline
- ▲ Major Oil Field
- + Spot Elevation or Depth

Meters	Feet
4000	13124
2000	6562
1000	3281
500	1640
200	656
0	0
200	656
Below 2000	Below 6562

Scale 1:12,000,000

© 1980 Rand McNally & Co.
A-564600-772 -1- -1-1

years. The work of the office has grown over the years. Other countries having ombudsmen include Finland (1919), Denmark (1955), New Zealand (1962), Norway (1963), and Britain (1967). In the United States, the U.S. Department of Commerce has an Ombudsman for Business, whose job is to handle complaints, suggestions, and inquiries from businesspeople dealing with the agency.

Omdurman [ahm-dur-mahn'] Omdurman (Arabic: Umm Durman), the largest city in the Sudan, is located opposite KHARTOUM on the left bank of the Nile River. The population is 526,287 (1983). A commercial and shipping center, the city exports hides, handicrafts, textiles, ivory, and gum arabic. Omdurman, Khartoum, and Khartoum North form the Three Towns metropolitan area. A small village until the late 19th century, Omdurman began to grow after the MAHDI made the city the headquarters of his anti-Egyptian rebellion in 1884. The Mahdi died in the city the following year, and his tomb became an important pilgrimage site. At the Battle of Omdurman (1898), Mahdist forces were defeated by Anglo-Egyptian troops under Lord KITCHENER, and the city came under British rule.

omen An omen, in popular and traditional belief, is a natural event thought to presage a future event. There are two basic kinds of omen: normal occurrences of nature (the cawing of ravens, hooting of owls, or howling of dogs, for example), which are interpreted in a specific context to augur good or bad fortune; and unusual occurrences, such as flights of sacred birds, or eclipses, or comets, that are believed to be direct manifestations of the gods.

See also: DIVINATION.

Omsk [awmsk] Omsk is the capital of Omsk oblast in Russia, a republic of the USSR. The population is 1,148,000 (1989). It is situated in southwest Siberia at the junction of the IRTYSH RIVER and the TRANS-SIBERIAN RAILROAD. The city is named for the Om River, which enters the Irtysh there. Omsk has a number of research institutes. Long limited to the processing of local agricultural products, in the 1950s and '60s it acquired a large petroleum-refining and petrochemical industry, whose significance was enhanced by the development of the West Siberian petroleum fields. The city arose as a fort in 1716. Its modern development and rapid growth date from World War II.

On Liberty *On Liberty* (1859) is a book by the English philosopher and social critic John Stuart MILL in defense of the individual's right to think and act independently. Although Mill starts with the utilitarian premise that the morally correct act is that which achieves the greatest good for the greatest number, he goes beyond utilitarianism in his concern for individual liberty—the freedom to think and act without external authority. He has a strong sense of individual responsibility as well: the individual is to exert his or her freedom only insofar as he or she does not hamper the freedom of others. Mill's solution to allowing individual creativity while maintaining order is a representative government.

on-line service   see DATABASE

Onassis, Aristotle Aristotle Socrates Onassis, b. Jan. 20, 1906, d. Mar. 15, 1975, was a Greek shipping magnate who accumulated a fortune of more than $500 million. Born of Greek parents in Turkey, he went to Buenos Aires in 1923 and became a telephone operator there. Soon Onassis established a tobacco import business, and by 1930 he was a millionaire. During the Depression of the 1930s he bought unused freighters at low prices and by the end of World War II had amassed great wealth in shipping. After the war he increased his fleet by purchasing surplus wartime freighters, and he pioneered the construction of oil supertankers. Onassis used his profits to acquire hotels and banks throughout the world, as well as Olympic Airways. Divorced in 1960, Onassis had a well-publicized friendship with the soprano Maria CALLAS. In 1968 he married Jacqueline Bouvier Kennedy.

Onassis, Jacqueline Bouvier Kennedy Jacqueline Bouvier Kennedy Onassis, b. Southampton, N.Y., July 28, 1929, was first lady of the United States during the administration (1961–63) of her first husband, John F. KENNEDY. She had been a newspaper reporter and photographer before their marriage in 1953. As first lady, she was a patron of the arts and an international fashion trendsetter. Under her supervision the White House was restored and redecorated and declared a national museum. She was riding beside President Kennedy when he was assassinated in Dallas, Tex., on Nov. 22, 1963. In 1968 she married the Greek shipping millionaire Aristotle Onassis. After her second husband's death, in 1975, she worked as an editor in book publishing.

Oñate, Juan de [ohn-yah'-tay] Juan de Oñate, c.1550–c.1630, a Spanish explorer and colonizer in America, was the first Spanish royal governor of New Mexico. Appointed in 1595, he founded the settlement of San Juan at the junction of the Rio Grande and the Rio Chama in 1598. Oñate explored as far north as Kansas (1601) and as far west as the Gulf of California (1605). Unable to find the vast riches the area was supposed to hold, Oñate fell into disfavor and was forced to resign in 1607. Subsequently accused of having disobeyed regal decrees and other offenses while governor, he was sentenced to perpetual banishment from New Mexico in 1614.

oncogene An oncogene is a segment of a cell's DNA (see GENE) that is involved in changing a normal nondividing cell or slowly dividing cell into a rapidly dividing CANCER cell. Two types of oncogenes appear to exist. One is a gene that is normally in control of cell division but then undergoes a mutation that tremendously increases the rate of cell division. This type of oncogene is most prevalent in colon and rectal cancers. The second type produces a cancer through a loss of function. The gene normally acts to suppress or reduce the rate of cell division, and the loss of this inhibitory activity releases the cell to divide rapidly. Such genes are found in retinoblastoma (eye cancer), Wilm's tumor (kidney cancer), small-cell lung cancer, and some forms of breast cancer (see GENETICS).

For both types of oncogenes, exposure of the cell to some external agent such as viruses, X rays, or chemicals seems to be needed for cancer formation to occur. In breast and ovarian cancer cells, the presence of an increased number of copies of a certain specific gene has been correlated with decreased life expectancy, as well. The increase in gene number, or amplification, perhaps plays a causative role in these cancers. If so, gene amplification represents a third method of oncogene production.

oncology Oncology is the scientific study of TUMORS, both benign and malignant (see CANCER). Such studies may be related to therapy (clinical oncology), or they may involve research on tumors in laboratory animals or on tumorous cells grown in tissue cultures (experimental oncology). Historically, tumor detection has progressed from reliance on physical examination to the use of microscopes, X rays, and other imaging techniques to study body cells.

Therapeutic procedures in oncology include surgery, chemotherapy, RADIOLOGY, and immunotherapy. Studies of tumor causes include examinations of the roles of various chemicals, of physical agents such as chronic irritation and ultraviolet light, and of biological agents such as viruses. More recently, attention has been drawn to the role of oncogenes in tumor formation and to the inheritance of tumor-forming tendencies (see GENETICS).

Onega, Lake [oh-nay'-guh] Lake Onega (Russian: Onezhskoye Ozero) is the second largest freshwater lake in Europe (after nearby Lake LADOGA). Onega lies about 320 km (200 mi) northeast of Leningrad in Russia, a republic of the USSR. The lake, which is frozen over for about six months each year, covers about 9,800 km^2 (3,800 mi^2). It is about 240 km (150 mi) long and 100 km (60 mi) wide.

Oneida [oh-ny'-duh] The Iroquoian-speaking Oneida tribe from earliest times inhabited a region of central New York State north of Binghamton, eastward to Raquette Lake, and southward to the Oneonta vicinity. They were members of the original Five Nations IROQUOIS LEAGUE and were represented on the League's Grand Council by nine sachems. The women farmed and gathered wild plant foods; men traded, cleared fields for gardens, hunted, and made war. Oneida villages were composed of bark-covered longhouses that sheltered families related through the female line. The matrilineal principle also served as a basis for their social and political institutions.

Greatly influenced by the Protestant missionary Samuel Kirkland, the Oneida alone among the Five Nations Iroquois sided with the colonists during the American Revolution. Despite their faithful support, they eventually lost their homelands and were removed to a reservation in what was then the Wisconsin Territory. Today small communities of Oneida live near Oneida and Red Hook, N.Y., as well as on reserves in Wisconsin (1987 est. pop., 4,550) and the province of Ontario, Canada (1987 pop., 2,046).

Oneida Community The Oneida Community was a Christian socialist society established in 1848 in Oneida, N.Y., by John Humphrey NOYES. Its members, who held property in common and believed in human perfectibility, were sometimes called Bible communists and perfectionists. They also practiced complex marriage, in which all adult members of the group were considered married to each other; this system aroused local hostility. The group prospered both in agriculture and by manufacturing steel traps and silverware, but it experienced intense internal disagreements and reorganized in 1881 as a joint-stock company; this ended the social experiment.

O'Neill, Eugene Eugene Gladstone O'Neill, b. New York City, Oct. 16, 1888, d. Nov. 27, 1953, America's preeminent playwright, led the fledgling early-20th-century U.S. theater into the mainstream of world drama. During a lengthy artistic career (1913–43) in which he won four Pulitzer Prizes and the Nobel Prize for literature (1936), the innovative O'Neill held up a mirror to American society and functioned as social critic and moral guide.

The third son of James O'Neill, a poor Irish immigrant who became a leading matinee idol, the young Eugene spent his early years in a theatrical milieu. His mother, Ella Quinlan O'Neill, was ill-equipped to endure the homelessness of constant tours. When Eugene was born, her miserly husband reportedly hired a quack doctor, who prescribed morphine for the sick woman, an error that led to Ella's 25-year drug addiction. The tragedy that ensued is

The celebrated American playwright Eugene O'Neill won the Nobel Prize for literature (1936) and four Pulitzer Prizes. A distinctly American dramatist, O'Neill produced about 40 plays, including The Iceman Cometh *(1946; film, 1973) and* Long Day's Journey into Night *(1956; film, 1962).*

dramatized in what many consider O'Neill's greatest play, the autobiographical *Long Day's Journey into Night* (1956), which recounts the recriminations of the four Tyrones (O'Neills) as each, guilt-ridden, lashes out at the other to assuage the pain and regret of a wasted life. Ella's alienation was compounded when James chose a summer residence, the family's only home, in New London, Conn., whose aristocratic Yankees ostracized the O'Neills. The Irish-Yankee conflict in New England becomes a dominant theme in the two extant cycle plays, *A Touch of the Poet* (1957) and *More Stately Mansions* (1962).

O'Neill's indoctrination to the harsh tenets of Irish Catholicism, in his home and while attending a Catholic boarding school and high school, left him with a deep spirituality that is manifested in his work. In 1906 he entered Princeton but was suspended for a prank. From 1907 to 1912 he held odd jobs and became a seaman, living in 1911–12 in a sleazy Manhattan waterfront saloon-hotel, Jimmy the Priest's, where he made a futile attempt to commit suicide. After working briefly as a reporter in New London, he was diagnosed in 1913 as having tuberculosis and sent to Gaylord Farm Sanatorium. There he read Strindberg's dramas and decided to write plays, enrolling in 1914 in Harvard's "47 Workshop," where he learned the fundamentals of his craft.

A major motif in O'Neill's work is the conflict between the sexes. O'Neill himself made a disastrous marriage (1909–12) to the pregnant Kathleen Jenkins, who bore him a son, Eugene Jr. In 1918 he married Agnes Boulton, who in 1920 bore a son Shane and in 1924 a daughter Oona. Marital happiness eluded the author, however, until in 1929 he divorced again and married Carlotta Monterey.

Bound East for Cardiff (1916) and *Thirst* (1916) were the first two of O'Neill's plays to be staged by the Provincetown Players. The group later presented the premieres of all the early plays in their Macdougal Street theater in New York. The author achieved international, as well as national, fame with two expressionistic works, *The Emperor Jones* (1920) and *The Hairy Ape* (1922), followed by *Desire Under the Elms* (1924). In his later plays in the 1920s, staged by the Theatre Guild, O'Neill used highly experimental devices: masks in *The Great God Brown* (1926), multiple settings in *Marco Millions* (1928) and *Lazarus Laughed* (1928), asides in the nine-act *Strange Interlude* (1928). The critically acclaimed trilogy *Mourning Becomes Electra* (1931), a New England version of the Greek *Oresteia* set during the Civil War, was instrumental in O'Neill's receiving the Nobel Prize.

Two dominant motifs emerge in the O'Neill canon: societal concerns, such as racial discrimination in America, as in *The Dreamy Kid* (1919), *The Emperor Jones*, and the controversial *All God's Chillun Got Wings* (1924); and reminiscences of family and friends, as in his two greatest plays, *The Iceman Cometh* (1946) and *Long Day's Journey into Night*, and two eulogies for his brother Jamie: *A Moon for the Misbegotten* (1947) and *Hughie* (1958), America's greatest one-act play.

O'Neill died not in 1953 but a decade earlier when the tremor in his hand prevented him from writing. His health deteriorated in the late 1940s, and he spent the last two years of his life in a Boston hotel.

O'Neill, Thomas P.   Thomas Philip "Tip" O'Neill, Jr., b. Cambridge, Mass., Dec. 9, 1912, served as Speaker of the U.S. House of Representatives from 1977 to 1987. A Massachusetts Democrat, he served in the state legislature before his election to Congress in 1952. O'Neill became assistant majority leader (1971) and majority leader (1973). As his party's highest-ranking official after January 1981—and a liberal—he opposed many of the Reagan administration's policies and legislative proposals.

onion   The onion, *Allium cepa*, of the family Amaryllidaceae, is by far the most important bulb vegetable. It is used both in its green stage as a scallion, or green onion, and in its mature stage as a bulb—the tightly packed

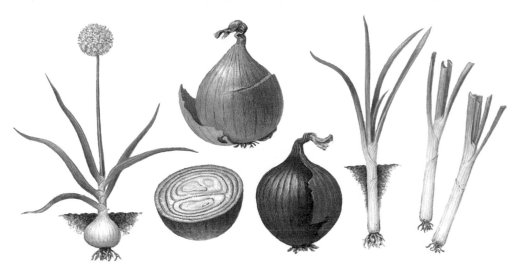

The onion is cultivated for its prominent bulb, which consists of the thickened bases of its cylindrical leaves. Mature bulb onions (center) develop a papery outer skin of dried leaves. When cut, the flesh is roughly circular and is separated by membranes. Scallions (right) are either bunch onions, which have cylindrical bulbs, or young bulb onions harvested before the bulbs mature. Both the bulb and leaves are eaten.

globe of food-storage leaves containing the volatile oil that is the source of the onion's pungent flavor. Thought to have originated in Asia, the onion has been cultivated since ancient times. Present-day cultivars include the Sweet Spanish, Bermuda, and globe onions. Onions vary in color, with white, yellow, and red predominating. Cultivars range from mild to pungent; valued for their flavor, onions are low in nutrients.

The onion plant is potentially a biennial, producing large bulbs the first year and seed the next. Plants may be grown from seed, as transplants of seedlings, or as small bulbs produced from thickly planted seed; when replanted, these bulbs reach maturity quickly. Mature onions are usually dried before marketing. Major world producers include China, India, the United States, and the Soviet Union.

See also: CHIVE; GARLIC; LEEK; SHALLOT.

Onondaga [ahn-uhn-daw'-guh]   The Onondaga ("people on the mountain" in their native tongue) are an Iroquoian-speaking tribe of North American Indians whose traditional homeland was in central New York around Auburn. An Onondaga site was the meeting place for the annual Grand Council of the IROQUOIS LEAGUE. Represented on the council by 14 sachems, the Onondaga were designated "keepers of the fire" and "wampum keepers," thus becoming the unofficial capital and the national archives of the league. They sided with the British during the American Revolution.

A calendric cycle of ceremonies mirrored Onondaga subsistence activities, which included the cultivation of maize, beans, and squash as well as the gathering of wild plant foods by women and hunting by men. Men also traded, cleared fields for gardens, and made war to accumulate honor and prestige. Kinship was reckoned through the female line. This matrilineal principle was extended to their social and political institutions. Descendants of the Onondaga are found at the reservation south of Syracuse, N.Y., and at the Six Nations Reserve, Ontario.

Ontario   The province of Ontario is located in central Canada, with Manitoba on the west, Quebec on the east, and the United States on the south. Ontario has Canada's largest population (1990 est., 9,747,600), and with an area of 1,068,580 km^2 (412,581 mi^2) is second in size only to Quebec. The word *Ontario* is of Iroquoian origin and was given to the most easterly of the Great Lakes in 1641. A fundamental contrast exists between southern Ontario, with the bulk of the province's population, manufacturing, and agriculture, and northern Ontario, which is sparsely settled and dependent on mining and forestry.

AT A GLANCE

ONTARIO

Land: Area: 1,068,580 km^2 (412,581 mi^2); rank: 2d. Capital and largest city: Toronto (1986 pop., 612,289). Municipalities: 839. Elevations: highest—693 m (2,274 ft), Ishpatina Ridge; lowest—sea level, along the Hudson and James bays.

People: Population (1990 est.): 9,747,600; rank: 1st; density: 9.1 persons per km^2 (23.6 per mi^2). Distribution (1986): 82.1% urban, 17.9% rural. Average annual change (1981–86): +1.14%.

Government (1991): Lieutenant Governor: Lincoln Alexander. Premier: Robert Keith Rae, New Democratic Party. Parliament: Senate—24 members; House of Commons—43 Liberals, 46 Progressive Conservatives, 10 New Democrats. Provincial legislature: 130 members. Admitted to Confederation: July 1, 1867, one of four original provinces.

Economy (monetary figures in Canadian dollars): Total personal income (1987): $187.16 billion; rank: 1st. Median family income (1987): $43,789. Agriculture: net income (1987)—$1.5 billion. Fishing: landed value (1985)—$40.6 million. Forestry: lumber production (1986)—2.2 billion board feet. Mining: value (1987 prelim.)—$5.6 billion. Manufacturing: value added (1986)—$54.8 billion.

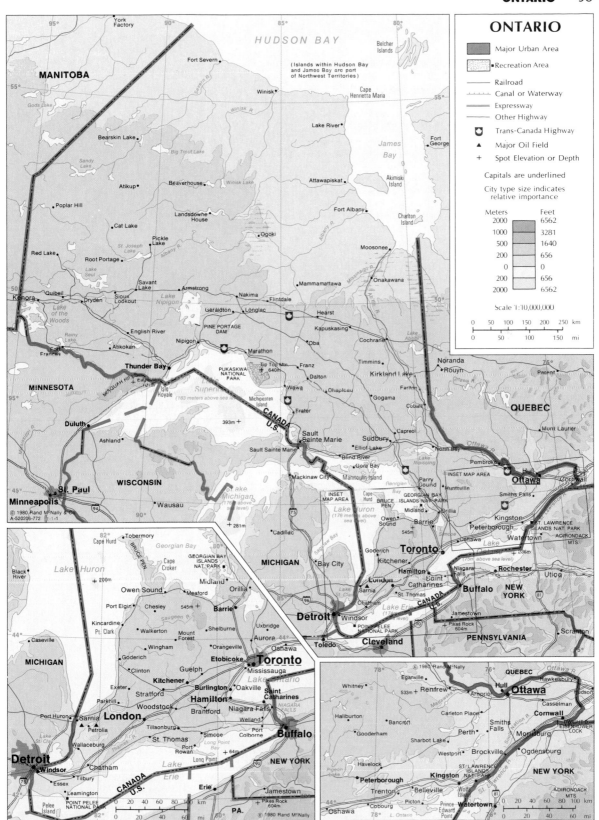

ONTARIO

Major Urban Area
Recreation Area
Railroad
Canal or Waterway
Expressway
Other Highway
Trans-Canada Highway
Major Oil Field
Spot Elevation or Depth

Capitals are underlined

City type size indicates
relative importance

Meters	Feet
2000	6562
1000	3281
500	1640
200	656
0	0
200	656
2000	6562

Scale 1:10,000,000

0 50 100 150 200 250 km
0 50 100 150 mi

Land and Resources

The dominant geological element in Ontario is the CANA-DIAN SHIELD with its Precambrian igneous and metamorphic rocks. The shield underlies much of the province. To the southwest of HUDSON BAY and JAMES BAY and between Lakes Erie, Huron, and Ontario, younger sedimentary rocks dominate. The most striking topographic feature is the Niagara Escarpment, which forms a transportation barrier from NIAGARA FALLS to the MANITOULIN ISLANDS.

Soils and Vegetation. The soils of Ontario are typical of humid temperate climates with coniferous forest growth. Southwestern Ontario has gray brown podzols underlying a deciduous forest that changes northward to a mixed forest. Brown podzols reach into northern Ontario, where coniferous forests dominate. The northern Ontario podzol-soil zone supports boreal forests with firs, spruces, tamaracks, and jack pines. Much of northern Ontario is bog and rock, and the Hudson Bay lowlands have tundra and deep bog soils interspersed with marshes and muskegs.

Climate. Ontario's average temperatures decrease with increasing latitude, and both temperature and precipitation are affected by the Great Lakes, by altitude, and by relief. January temperatures average –6° C (21° F), and those of July, 20° C (68° F). Annual precipitation decreases in amount from 864 mm (34 in) in the southwest to less than 508 mm (20 in) in the far north.

Rivers and Lakes. In northern Ontario the major rivers, including the Albany, Attawapiskat, and Moose, empty into James Bay, whereas the southern Ontario rivers flow into the GREAT LAKES. Ontario shares four of the five Great Lakes (Ontario, Erie, Huron, and Superior) with the United States. Other large lakes are Lake Nipissing at North Bay and Lake Nipigon near Thunder Bay.

Resources and Animal Life. The world's largest deposits of nickel and copper, with associated lead, zinc, gold, silver, and platinum, are in the Sudbury basin. North America's largest gold fields are north of Sudbury, at the towns of Porcupine and Kirkland Lake. One of the world's larg-

A rainbow hovers above Horseshoe Falls, situated near the west bank of the Niagara River, which separates New York State and southern Ontario.

est uranium fields is at Elliot Lake and major copper, zinc, and silver deposits are found near Timmins. Ontario also has considerable timber resources. Fur-bearing animals, such as mink, otters, and beavers, inhabit northern Ontario, as do moose, caribou, and other large game. Trout, whitefish, and pickerel are found in abundance.

People

Ontario's population at the 1986 census reflected a

Buildings of downtown Toronto, the capital of Ontario, rise near the city's waterfront on Lake Ontario. Canada's largest city, Toronto has developed into a manufacturing center and a vital lake port.

5.7% increase over that of the 1981 census. The growth rate of the cities of KITCHENER, LONDON, Mississauga, and Brampton exceeded the growth rate of the province. The cities of SUDBURY, SAINT CATHARINES, and THUNDER BAY decreased in population.

In the late 1980s about half the people were of British origin, followed by those of French, Italian, and German origins. The small Indian population is almost exclusively rural, and the small black population is concentrated in the Toronto area.

About one-third of Ontario's population are Roman Catholic. The principal Protestant denominations are the United Church, Anglican, Presbyterian, Baptists, and Lutheran.

Education. Primary education is provided by both public and Roman Catholic schools, and secondary education is offered by academic and vocational schools. The provincial government also supports a number of universities and other postsecondary schools. Ontario's oldest higher education institution is the University of Toronto (see TORONTO, UNIVERSITY OF).

Cultural Attractions and Historic Sites. The provincial and federal governments operate Canada's two largest museums at Toronto and Ottawa. Toronto is the center of Canada's English-language theater and supports the Toronto Symphony Orchestra. The O'Keefe Centre, now home of the Canadian Opera Company and the National Ballet of Canada, was opened in 1960. Ottawa acquired the National Arts Centre and Orchestra in 1969. The Stratford Festival, held annually during the summer, offers both dramatic and musical performances. The Shaw Festival at Niagara-on-the-Lake highlights the works of George Bernard Shaw.

Upper Canada Village in St. Lawrence Islands Park contains more than 40 reconstructed historic buildings. Fort Henry at Kingston and Fort George at Niagara Falls have been preserved. Toronto hosts the Canadian National Exhibition, Canada's largest annual fair.

Communications. Toronto is the headquarters of na-tional television and radio broadcasting, with a number of television stations and AM and FM radio stations. The province is served by such leading Canadian newspapers as the *Toronto Globe and Mail*, the *Toronto Star*, and the *Toronto Sun*.

Economic Activity

Ontario has changed from a primarily agricultural province to one dominated by manufacturing and mining. It is Canada's most prosperous as well as most populous province.

Manufacturing. Ontario's industries produce about half the country's total value of industrial production. Ontario particularly gained from a 1965 automobile trade pact with the United States, which almost tripled automobile production and resulted in comparable increases for related industries.

Mining. Mineral production in Ontario ranks second in value only to that of Alberta (although Alberta produced more than six times the value produced by Ontario). Ontario is first nationally in the production of nickel. Copper also contributes significantly. Other important minerals are iron, gold, uranium, salt, and silver.

Agriculture. Agriculture is one of the province's leading industries. Corn, mixed grains, barley, and winter wheat are among the major crops. About two-thirds of all farm income is derived from livestock raising. Dairy farming is also important.

Forestry. Vast forestlands are located in Ontario. The pulp and paper industry is concentrated along the shores of Lakes Superior, Huron, and Nipissing and where the railways cross the major Hudson Bay rivers. Most of the pulp and paper products are exported to the United States.

Energy. Virtually all the province's hydroelectric-power sites have been harnessed. Other sources of power include fossil-fuel or nuclear-powered plants. Ontario, always an importer of energy, meets some of its fuel needs through petroleum and natural-gas imports from western Canada. Coal is imported from the United States.

Transportation. The Great Lakes–St. Lawrence Seaway

Rows of winter wheat and barley are harvested on a farm in southeastern Ontario. Ontario is a leading province in cash receipts from farming operations.

system is vital in shipping bulk cargoes and prairie grains. A system of provincial roads supplements the Trans-Canada Highway. Canada's finest railroad network runs through southern Ontario. The system includes two transcontinental lines and one provincially owned railroad. The International Airport in Toronto is Canada's largest. SAULT SAINTE MARIE, Ottawa, London, and Thunder Bay also have commercial airports.

Government

A lieutenant governor, representing the queen, is at the head of the provincial government and governs with the advice and consent of his ministry, or executive council. The executive council is, in turn, responsible to the unicameral legislature, the Legislative Assembly, which is popularly elected every 5 years. The leader of the majority party in the legislative assembly is the premier. Ontario has 24 senators and 99 members of the House of Commons in the federal Parliament.

History

The original inhabitants of southern Ontario were HURON, Neutral, and Tobacco Indian farmers. Hunting was the major pursuit of the ALGONQUIN, CREE, and OJIBWA tribes of the north. The French explorer Étienne BRÛLÉ was the first European to travel among them on his expedition to the OTTAWA RIVER in 1610–11. When Samuel de CHAMPLAIN explored southern Ontario in 1615, he encountered the Huron. By 1648–49 the southern tribes were decimated as a result of the clash between the Iroquois and the French over the lucrative fur trade and because of the onslaught of European diseases.

In 1763, France ceded Canada to Great Britain. By the QUEBEC ACT of 1774, Ontario became part of an extended colony ruled from Quebec, and the territory was made a base for Loyalist and Indian attacks during the American Revolution. By 1784 between 6,000 and 10,000 LOYALISTS settled there.

The Constitutional Act of 1791 divided Quebec colony into Lower (French) and Upper (Loyalist) Canada. John Graves SIMCOE, the first lieutenant governor, fixed the capital of Upper Canada at York (now Toronto). In 1841, Upper and Lower Canada united, and the former Upper Canada became known as Canada West. The Robert BALDWIN–Louis Hippolyte LAFONTAINE ministry in 1848 introduced responsible cabinet government and the present systems of education and municipal government. Wheat and timber exports stimulated urban development by adding port functions and shipbuilding to the activities of towns along Lake Ontario's western shore. In the 1850s railways came, encouraging industrialization. On Confederation in 1867, Canada West became Ontario, and Toronto, the provincial capital.

In 1882 the Niagara Falls' hydroelectric power was harnessed, launching an era of industrialization. In the 20th century the chief concerns are economic development and the exploitation of minerals.

A central theme in the economy and the politics of Ontario is the interplay of centralizing and decentralizing forces. Those favoring more centralized control were in the forefront following the 1990 provincial election in which the New Democratic party gained control of the legislature, implementing the first democratic socialist government in Ontario's history.

(Below) *The Canadian Parliament Building and federal government offices occupy a bluff in Ottawa overlooking the Ottawa River. The city, in southeastern Ontario, was founded in 1827 and became the seat of Canada's government 30 years later.*

(Above) The Imperial Oil refinery is one of several large petroleum-related industries located in Sarnia, a county seat in southeastern Ontario.

white and black in the stone. Sardonyx has brown and white bands, and carnelian has red and white bands. The name *onyx* is Greek for "fingernail," referring to the color banding. India and South America provide the greatest quantities of minable onyx.

Ontario, Lake The smallest and most easterly of the five GREAT LAKES of North America, Lake Ontario is bordered on the north by Ontario, Canada, and on the south by New York State. The lake is 311 km (193 mi) long and extends 85 km (53 mi) at its widest point. The lake is mostly fed by the waters of Lake Erie, which is linked to Lake Ontario by the NIAGARA RIVER. Other rivers that enter the lake are the Genesee, Oswego, and Black rivers in New York and the Trent in Ontario. Lake Ontario drains into the ST. LAWRENCE RIVER in the northeast and is linked to the Atlantic Ocean by the ST. LAWRENCE SEAWAY. The lake is navigable for most of the year. Leading cities are Toronto, Kingston, and Oshawa (on the Canadian side) and Rochester and Oswego (on the U.S. side).

The first Europeans to visit the lake were the French explorers Étienne Brûlé and Samuel de Champlain (1615). The Canada-U.S. boundary was established after the American Revolution. Lake Ontario is the most polluted of the Great Lakes, although water quality is improving.

ontogeny [ahn-tahj'-uh-nee] Ontogeny is the development of an individual organism from its origin as a fertilized egg until its death. It is distinguished from PHYLOGENY, the evolutionary history of the group to which an individual organism belongs. During early embryonic life, however, the individual passes through developmental stages that resemble the embryos of ancestral species. This led the German naturalist Ernst Haeckel (1834–1919) to propound his Biogenetic Law, since refuted, which is commonly summed up by the statement "ontogeny recapitulates phylogeny."

ontology see METAPHYSICS

onychophoran see PERIPATUS

onyx [ahn'-iks] Onyx—considered the birthstone of July by the ancient Romans and Jews—is a semiprecious variety of CHALCEDONY, a silica mineral. Its largest use is in cameos and intaglios, which are carved to take advantage of the color contrast in the even, flat layers of alternating

Oort, Jan Hendrik [ohrt] The Dutch astronomer Jan Hendrik Oort, b. Apr. 28, 1900, has made major contributions to the knowledge of the structure and rotation of our GALAXY. Seeking an explanation for the discovery that our Galaxy's stars seem to move in two crossing "streams," Oort verified the theory, put forth by Bertil Lindblad the previous year, that our Galaxy rotates as a whole. Oort thereafter determined the direction and distance from the Earth of the center of our Galaxy, as well as the mass of our Galaxy. A pioneer of radio astronomy in the Netherlands, Oort, along with his colleagues, was able in the 1950s to determine the spiral structure of our Galaxy by radio means. He is also known for his theory of comets, published about 1950, which suggests that the Sun is surrounded by a distant cloud of comet material, and that comets are occasionally hurled into the solar system through gravitational perturbations by nearby stars.

op art Op (for optical) art was a movement that developed in the 1960s in Europe and in the United States.

Victor Vasarely's Cheyt-G *(1970) creates a surface of colored diamond shapes that appears to advance and recede. A master of optical techniques, Vasarely was a key figure in the development of op art. (Collection of the artist.)*

Because of its relationship to CONSTRUCTIVISM and FUTURISM, both European in origin, it was of greater importance in Europe. Op art was based on scientific principles of perceptual dynamics and retinal scintillation. Concentrating on the act of perception as the most important factor in art, this movement explored the potential of both color images and black-and-white linear arrangements to induce a visual experience. It also exploited illusionistic effects by opposing systems of perspective or color areas that contrast violently in hue but are of the same tonal value. Such confrontations created complex pulsations of light and movement. The European pioneers of the style were Josef ALBERS and Victor VASARELY. In the United States its main exponent was Richard ANUSZKIEWICZ.

opal   Opal, the birthstone for October and a semiprecious gem long valued for its play of colors and milky-to-pearly opalescence, is usually rounded and polished to display these properties best. Opal is composed of hydrated silica ($SiO_2 \bullet nH_2O$) and has a hardness of 5 to 6; its specific gravity varies from 1.9 to 2.2, depending on the water content. White and black opals gain their color from iridescence on, respectively, milky opalescent stones and dark green, black, or gray stones. Fire opals gain theirs from reddish orange flashes on a clear stone. The water, or hyaline, opal is an iridescent clear stone. Opals are porous; they lose their color and may crack if they dry out, or they may absorb body oils or other liquids. The finest opals—black opals—come from Australia.

Precious opal in the rough (left) *is a transparent to translucent, noncrystalline stone that shows flashes of colored light. The gem is usually cut* (right) *in cabochon, or rounded, form for jewelry.*

OPEC   see ORGANIZATION OF PETROLEUM EXPORTING COUNTRIES

open admission   Open admission is a policy that permits students to enroll in a college or university without regard to previous academic preparation. It gained a wide measure of acceptance in the United States during the 1960s. The policy is intended to enable students who may be capable and well motivated but are poorly prepared academically to receive higher education.

An essential key to the success of open admission lies in the remedial services—tutoring to improve reading and writing skills, for example—that are available to students, without which the attrition rate can be very high. Open admission is contrasted with traditional selective admission policies, which typically place great emphasis on high school grades or college-admissions test scores.

Advocates of open admission argue that selective admission policies exclude many students who could otherwise benefit from higher education and that a significant proportion of those students are from racial or ethnic minorities or from low socioeconomic backgrounds or both. Thus, they say, access to higher education with its subsequent economic rewards must be expanded through open-admission policies.

Critics of open admission fear that elimination of selective admission procedures will lead to a devaluation of the bachelor's degree. If the meaning of the degree is not to be changed, they say, many of the open-admission students will, of necessity, be forced out of college for academic reasons.

open classroom   The term *open classroom* refers to both a theory and a practical teaching method. The psychological theory, derived from Jean PIAGET, emphasizes that children learn through interaction with the natural and social world. They need experience in order to structure the world, to "learn to learn." They also need time to assimilate concepts. The educational needs of each child are stressed. The curriculum is adapted to individual interests and abilities, and schedules are flexible. Children often work in small groups or individually.

Open classrooms took root in England after World War II as part of a program of school reform. Up to one-third of primary classrooms in England developed integrated, or informal, curricula. Such classrooms were established in the United States in the 1960s in response to pleas for curriculum reform that would make learning more effective, rewarding, and pleasant.

Open Door Policy   In order to preserve its economic interests in China during the early 20th century, the United States advanced the Open Door Policy, the principle that equal trading rights in China should be guaranteed to all foreign nationals. By the treaties that followed the Chinese defeats in the OPIUM WARS (1839–42; 1856–60), China was forced to award trading concessions to the major powers, including Great Britain, France, Germany, Italy, Russia, Japan, and the United States. During the succeeding decades the European powers and Japan engaged in efforts to partition China into separate and exclusive spheres of influence.

Fearing that the United States was being frozen out of the China trade, Secretary of State John M. HAY set out the three-pronged Open Door Policy to the other powers: no country was to interfere with the rights of citizens of other countries; the Chinese tariff was to be the same for all traders; and any country possessing a territorial sphere of influence in China was to treat foreign merchants and industrialists the same as it did its own.

open-hearth process   see IRON AND STEEL INDUSTRY

open shop   An open shop refers to an employment situation where management is able to hire and retain employees even though they may not be members of a union. Thus union membership is not required to obtain or retain employment. It is the opposite of both a CLOSED SHOP and a UNION SHOP. (See also RIGHT-TO-WORK LAWS.)

opera   The 19th-century German composer Richard Wagner was speaking for composers of opera in all ages when he wrote of his aspiration to combine acting, singing, instrumental music, storytelling, poetry, painting, and architecture in a "complete art work" (*Gesamtkunstwerk*). With the addition of dancing, these are the elements that, in varying proportions, have gone into the drama with singing actors that has been known as "opera" since shortly after its inception about 1600. This elaborate art form has attracted many of the finest minds in literature, drama, music, and visual art, and it has given those arts much in return, including such musical forms as the SYMPHONY and the SUITE, and the proscenium stage and elaborate scenery of the European theater.

Origins: An Aristocratic Experiment

Opera stems from the courts of Renaissance rulers, who vied with each other in the magnificence of their private and public spectacles. Like many other art forms of the Renaissance, opera was created by reformers who wanted to replace scholasticism and complication in the arts with the simplicity and humanism of the ancient Greeks. A group of Florentine thinkers (the "Camerata"), in the last

The Italian composer Claudio Monteverdi (left) *created his first operatic work,* Orfeo, *in 1607 for the Duke of Mantua. Based on the myth of Orpheus and Eurydice, Monteverdi's innovative score* (right) *combined a dramatic recitative with an elaborate orchestral accompaniment.*

French composer Jean Baptiste Lully's Alceste (1674) *is performed at the palace of Versailles. As court musician to Louis XIV, Lully created a distinct French operatic style, the* tragédie lyrique.

third of the century, attempted to imagine what the ancient Greek drama sounded like, and came up with a declamatory solo vocal line with simple instrumental accompaniment. This *stile rappresentativo* ("theatrical style") was designed to project and enhance the words—in contrast with the contrapuntal madrigal, whose words were buried in a welter of competing voice parts.

In 1598 the poet Ottavio Rinuccini (1562–1621) and the composers Jacopo Peri and Jacopo Corsi (1561–1602) collaborated on a play set to music in the new style: *Dafne,* of which only two fragments survive, is considered the first opera.

Another Rinuccini-Peri collaboration, *Euridice,* based on the myth of Orpheus and Euridice and performed in 1600, is the first opera whose music has been preserved intact. Most of its vocal music is rhapsodic, speechlike monody, but some scenes end with songs in regular meter, which more closely approach the operatic ARIA.

The earliest operas included CASTRATO singers, males who had been castrated in boyhood so that their voices would remain in the soprano or contralto range. This practice produced adult voices of trumpetlike clarity and carrying power that, despite their high pitch, became associated with heroic male roles.

With *Orfeo* (1607), by Claudio MONTEVERDI, opera made the leap from an experiment in musical declamation to an integrated, vital art form. *Orfeo* combines monodic melody, madrigals, songs in a popular style, a large and varied orchestra, dramatic timing, scenic effects, and reprises of a leitmotivlike theme (*ritornello*) to create a still-vital music drama.

Until the middle of the 17th century, court opera was centered in Rome, where the powerful Barberini family of popes and cardinals sponsored the art. Works from this period contain, in rudimentary form, genres that would later be central to baroque instrumental music: the church SONATA, French OVERTURE, and Italian overture, or *sinfonia.*

Opera Goes Public

Opera became a popular art form virtually overnight in 1637, the year the first public opera house opened in

Venice. By the end of the century the citizens of Venice were supporting six opera companies and had seen nearly 400 operas. Monteverdi gave this phase a distinguished beginning with his last two operas, *Il ritorno d'Ulisse in patria* (The Return of Ulysses to His Country, 1640) and *L'incoronazione di Poppea* (The Coronation of Poppea, 1642).

Italian opera also spurred efforts in other countries to create a native music theater. From 1678 to 1738 a public opera house in Hamburg presented operas in German. The traditional English court masque began to resemble a pastoral opera, and the one true opera by Henry PURCELL, *Dido and Aeneas* (1689), provides a glimpse of the English-language operatic style.

In Paris, Jean Baptiste LULLY won an effective royal monopoly on opera, composing such works as *Cadmus et Hermione* (1673), *Alceste* (1674), *Atys* (1676), *Proserpine* (1680), and *Armide* (1686). Lully's operas are tailored to the French taste for dramatic verse and dancing. Two generations later, Jean Philippe RAMEAU enriched the Lullian formula with more contrapuntal writing for orchestra and chorus, adventurous harmonies, and a greatly expanded repertoire of dances.

The Eighteenth Century: Buffa versus Seria

By 1700 the public's taste for comic scenes led Alessandro Scarlatti (see SCARLATTI family) and others in Naples to compose entire COMIC OPERAS. Neapolitan *opera buffa* was imitated all over Europe; the Neapolitan composers Giovanni PAISIELLO and Domenico CIMAROSA would carry the tradition into the 19th century.

Court opera, meanwhile, reached once again for its antique roots through the dramatic poetry of Apostolo Zeno (1668–1750) and Pietro Trapassi, called metastasio. Their elegant and scholarly verse, which placed noble heroes of ancient times in highly conventionalized situations usually involving a conflict of love and duty, was

The Portuguese baritone Francisco d'Andrade (1859–1921) is depicted in the title role of Wolfgang Amadeus Mozart's Don Giovanni in this portrait (1902) by Max Slevogt. First produced in 1787, this popular opera deals with the legend of the Spanish libertine Don Juan. (Staatsgalerie, Stuttgart.)

turned into *opera seria*. This genre's music was as ritualized as its plots: characters invariably exited the stage at the end of their arias, and the arias were neatly classified according to the mood they illustrated (rage aria, lament, avowal of love, and so on).

The greatest weakness of *opera seria* was also its greatest glory: the long *da capo* arias repeatedly brought the drama to a halt, and yet the opportunities they provided for singers attracted a wide public to this most aristocratic of genres. George Frideric HANDEL made a successful venture of *opera seria* in London theaters, mounting new works virtually every year—from *Rinaldo* in 1711 to *Deidamia* in 1741.

The inevitable reaction took several forms. In England the dramatist John GAY and the composer John Christopher Pepusch (1667–1752) collaborated on *The Beggar's Opera*, whose success in 1728 spawned dozens more "ballad operas," which used spoken dialogue and popular tunes to poke fun at the pretentions of Handelian opera.

The French *opéra comique* developed along similar lines. An Italian influence arrived in Paris in 1752–54 with the performance of *La serva padrona*, an INTERMEZZO by the Neapolitan composer Giovanni Battista PERGOLESI. Defenders of the "high art" of Lullian *tragédie lyrique* and those of the "naturalness" of the Italian *buffa* style locked pens in the *"Querelle des Bouffons"* ("War of the Buffoons").

Later in the 18th century, a distinctively French style of *opéra comique* evolved, with sentimental plots, spoken dialogue, and casts of virtuous peasants, oppressive nobles, or other familiar stage types. André Grétry's operas pointed the way to such important works of the next century as *Faust* (1859) by Charles GOUNOD and *Carmen* (1875) by Georges BIZET.

The ideal of "naturalness" that underlaid the *opéras comiques* encouraged Christoph Willibald GLUCK to follow similar principles in serious opera. In the preface to his opera *Alceste* (1769) he wrote that his aim was "to re-

A contemporary caricature of a scene from George Frideric Handel's Italian opera Flavio (1723) represents (left to right) the singers Senesino (castrato), Francesca Cuzzoni (soprano), and Gaetano Berenstadt (bass).

strict music to its true office of serving poetry," a phrase reminiscent of the Florentine monodists. Gluck composed his first "reform" opera, *Orfeo ed Euridice*, in 1762.

The great composers of the Viennese classical period wrote operas with varying success. Those of Franz Josef HAYDN and Franz SCHUBERT suffer from a lack of theatrical instinct. BEETHOVEN's only opera, *Fidelio* (1804–14), carries on the *opéra comique* tradition of "rescue" operas by Grétry and Luigi CHERUBINI with music of symphonic complexity and eloquence.

Of this group, only Wolfgang Amadeus MOZART was a dramatist through and through. Mozart was at home in *opera seria* (*Idomeneo*, 1781; *La clemenza di Tito*, 1791); the German musical play, or Singspiel (*The Abduction from the Seraglio*, 1782; *The Magic Flute*, 1791); and comic opera (*The Marriage of Figaro*, 1786; *Don Giovanni*, 1787; *Così fan tutte*, 1790), these last three in collaboration with the master librettist Lorenzo DA PONTE. Mozart projected his insights into human nature with unprecedented color and depth.

The Popular Impulse

As the 19th century began, both serious and comic opera were becoming mass art. No one made operas more understandable and inviting than Gioacchino ROSSINI, who devised a formalized plan for the musical numbers in a scene, then clothed that plan in memorable tunes and ebullient orchestral writing. The final flowering of BEL CANTO ("beautiful singing") came in the operas of Gaetano DONIZETTI and Vincenzo BELLINI, which combined dramatic arias with subtle harmony and orchestral color.

Verdi dominated Italian opera for the rest of the 19th century. Whether his subject was politics (*Ernani*, 1844; *Macbeth*, 1847; *Don Carlos*, 1867), revenge (*Rigoletto*, 1851; *Otello*, 1887), tragic love (*La traviata*, 1853; *Aïda*, 1871), or the comic human predicament (*Falstaff*, 1893), he forged a realistic dramatic idiom that trans-

Tenor Luciano Pavarotti and mezzo-soprano Shirley Verrett appear in a modern production of Italian composer Gaetano Donizetti's La Favorita *(1840). This opera tells the story of the tragic love affair between the monk Fernando and Leonora de Guzman, mistress of the king of Castile.*

A scene from the last act of German composer Richard Wagner's Die Meistersinger *(1868) is performed in a contemporary German production.*

lates human passions directly into orchestral music and singing. Verdi was a practical man of the theater who demanded superb librettos from Arrigo Boito and others.

At the Opéra in Paris, a spectacle-loving middle class demanded ever-more-lavish productions in four or five acts, with epic-heroic stories, dazzling scenic effects, a large and active chorus, and a ballet. The term "grand opera," sometimes used to mean any opera without spoken dialogue, refers more specifically to this genre, brought to its peak by Giacomo MEYERBEER. (*Les Troyens* [1856–58] by Hector BERLIOZ is a grand opera in form, but it uses a purer French declamation and symphonic composing methods.)

New National Identities: Germany and Elsewhere

In Germany, romanticism dictated new subjects and musical idioms, and a free, open-ended method of musical development that was the opposite of static, formulaic *opera seria*. The landmark work here is *Der Freischütz* ("The Freeshooter," 1821), a Singspiel by Carl Maria von WEBER that seamlessly combines operatic arias and choruses with romantic elements such as folk song, coloristic scoring, scenes of country life, and supernatural horror.

Delving into literature, Teutonic mythology, philosophy, and the most advanced trends in nonoperatic music, Richard WAGNER vastly expanded opera's expressive canvas. In *Tristan und Isolde* (1865), *Die Meistersinger von Nürnberg* (1868), the four operas of the cycle *Der Ring des Niebelungen* (1853–74), and *Parsifal* (1882), set-piece arias gave way to "endless melody." In Wagner's hands the technique of leitmotiv—a recurring musical theme—grew into a multilayered system of musical references to characters, events, and concepts in the plot.

The Paris Opéra (1861–74) is one of the most ornate theaters in the world. It is also one of the largest, with 17 floors and a curtain weighing 7 tons. It houses the Académie Royale de Musique, established in 1669 by Louis XIV.

The Sydney Opera House, in Sydney, Australia, completed in 1973, is situated on a peninsula of the city's harbor. Designed as an arts center, the edifice also contains concert and exhibition halls, a theater, cinema, and recording studios.

Wagner also enlarged the orchestra and required a new kind of singer to convey the power and subtleties of his scores. He even designed his own opera house at BAYREUTH (opened 1876).

Although first billed as Wagner's operatic successor, and despite frequent collaborations with the literary-minded librettist Hugo von HOFMANNSTHAL, Richard STRAUSS followed instincts that were more theatrical than philosophical in such opulent works as *Salome* (1905), *Electra* (1909), *Der Rosenkavalier* (1911), and *Die Frau ohne Schatten* (1919).

Political nationalism in the late 19th century was reflected in the opera house, especially in eastern Europe. Russian and Central Asian folk music, Russian history, and Russian fairy tales imparted their unique color to the operas of Mikhail GLINKA, Modest MUSSORGSKY, Nikolai RIMSKY-KORSAKOV, and Aleksandr BORODIN. In Bohemia, Bedřich SMETANA and Antonín DVOŘÁK composed operas about village life with a strong Czech folk flavor; Leoš JANÁČEK cultivated a spare, contemporary idiom based on Czech speech in *Jenufa* (1894–1903).

The Twentieth Century: Opera as Classical Music

Landmarks of Italy's VERISMO ("realism") school, which arose to fill the vacuum left by Verdi's retirement in the 1890s, include *Pagliacci* (1892) by Ruggero LEONCAVALLO and *Cavalleria Rusticana* (1888) by Pietro MASCAGNI. The melting, sentimental idiom of Giacomo PUCCINI is not pure *verismo*, but his effective operas draw freely on this style, as well as on German and Russian models.

Verismo featured characters from everyday life, often in violent or tragic situations, which made it a fitting opening to the 20th century, during which operas have often occupied themselves with the moral and spiritual concerns of a violent age.

Claude DEBUSSY's only opera, *Pelléas et Mélisande* (1892–1902), remains a unique masterpiece of emotionally distanced symbolist poetry set to evocative music. Igor STRAVINSKY's operas (*The Nightingale*, 1909–14; *Mavra*, 1922; *The Rake's Progress*, 1951) outline his own progress from Russian late romantic to neoclassicist. Composers of the Second Viennese school deployed 12-tone harmony to expressive advantage in the opera house, Arnold SCHOENBERG in works of psychological or religious depth, Alban BERG in a dramatically effective combination of social protest and tender lyricism (*Wozzeck*, 1925; *Lulu*, 1929–35). Their prolific successor in the postwar period, Hans Werner HENZE, has composed grand operas, chamber operas, and comic operas in a serial idiom.

The elegance and clarity of French opera continued in the works of Francis POULENC and Darius MILHAUD. The lean yet expressive idiom of Benjamin BRITTEN, colored with English folk melody and tailored to the English language, came to full flower in *Peter Grimes* (1945). Since then, many English composers, including Britten, Michael TIPPETT, and Peter Maxwell Davies, have written successful operas.

In the United States, conservative composers such as Samuel BARBER and Gian Carlo MENOTTI have written melodious, effective works in English, following French and Italian models. In the 1930s, composers such as Aaron COPLAND and Virgil THOMSON used American folk song, jazz, and choral music in their operas. A celebrated composer of musical comedy, George Gershwin, built a bridge between Broadway and the opera house with a grand opera based on southern black life and music, *Porgy and Bess* (1935) (see GERSHWIN, GEORGE AND IRA). Later composers such as Leonard BERNSTEIN and Steven SONDHEIM have crossed back and forth on that bridge. Since World War II the proliferation of university opera workshops and regional companies has encouraged American composers to write operas. The "minimalist" operas of Philip GLASS (*Einstein on the Beach*, 1976; *Satyagraha*, 1981; *Akhnaten*, 1984) have attracted wide attention for their hypnotic use of non-Western musical and literary elements.

operating system   see COMPUTER

—

operetta   The word *operetta* means "little opera" in Italian. The progenitors of operetta were *The Beggar's Opera* (1728), an English ballad opera with a text by John Gay and a score of popular songs and folk tunes, and *La serva padrona* (The Maid as Mistress, 1733), by Giovanni Pergolesi. The German Singspiel also influenced operetta, because, like ballad opera, it combined music and songs with spoken dialogue. This formula distinguishes operetta from OPERA, in which dialogue is usually set to music.

Also related to COMIC OPERA and MUSICAL COMEDY, operettas tend to have light, even farcical plots, emphasizing love stories, often coupled with social and political satire. The characters are usually stereotypical aristocrats or idyllic peasants.

Many operettas have fallen into disfavor because their jokes and satire are no longer understandable. In addition, operetta makes greater musical demands on performers than does musical comedy and uses forms such as the waltz that sound old-fashioned to many theatergoers.

The most famous composers of operettas include the Frenchmen Jacques OFFENBACH, Alexandre Charles Lecocq (1832–1918), André Messager (1853–1929), and Reynaldo Hahn (1875–1947); and the Austrians Franz von Suppé, Johann Strauss II (see STRAUSS family), Franz LEHÁR, and Emmerich Kálmán (1882–1953). Robert Stolz (1886–1975), a Viennese composer, was writing operettas into the 1970s, and operetta theaters still flourish in Munich, Vienna, and Budapest.

England's contribution to the genre were the comic masterpieces of GILBERT AND SULLIVAN, and in the United States the most successful operettas were written by Victor HERBERT, Rudolf FRIML, and Sigmund ROMBERG.

—

operon [oh'-puhr-ohn]   In genetics, the term *operon* is used to specify the model of gene regulation proposed by French scientists François JACOB and Jacques Monod in 1961. Two types of gene are involved: control and structural. The control genes of each operon include a regulator, promoter, and operator gene, whereas the structural genes determine the amino acid sequences of various proteins. A great deal of experimental evidence exists for the operon model, which describes very well the regulatory mechanism of enzyme production in PROKARYOTES, such as bacteria and blue-green algae. Based on the conditions determining their production, two types of enzymes are involved: inducible and repressible.

Inducible Enzymes.   Inducible enzymes are involved in splitting complex molecules (substrates), a process known as catabolism, which provides energy or simple materials for the synthesis of other compounds. An inducible enzyme is produced only when the specific substrate on which it acts is present.

The inducible-enzyme system involves two types of genes: a regulator gene, which determines whether the enzyme will be produced; and one or more structural genes, which specify the amino acid sequence of the enzyme being produced. Two attachment loci on the structural genes control the movement of ribonucleic acid (RNA)-polymerase molecules onto the genes. In the absence of the substrate the regulator gene produces a repressor substance that attaches to the operator locus and prevents the RNA-polymerase molecules from attaching to the structural genes. When the substrate, known as the inducer, is present, the repressor substance combines with the inducer to form a molecule that is unable to attach to the operator locus. RNA-polymerase molecules can then transcribe information, and subsequent translation produces the inducible enzyme.

Another controlling element, the promoter locus, is the site of attachment of the RNA-polymerase prior to transcription. The speed with which RNA-polymerase molecules attach to the promoter locus determines the rate of production of messenger RNA (mRNA), and subsequently of enzymes.

Repressible Enzymes.   These enzymes are involved in the cell's synthetic processes and are produced only when the protein that they help metabolize is lacking. As an example, the enzymes involved in synthesizing the amino acid histidine are produced only when the amount of free histidine in the cell is drastically reduced.

The operon model of gene regulation for repressible enzymes has one important difference from the inducible-enzyme system. In the repressible system the repressor substance, produced by the regulator gene, cannot attach to the operator locus if the end product, or corepressor, is absent. When the end product is absent, transcription and subsequent translation occur. When the end product is present it combines with the repressor substance to form a molecule that can attach to the operator locus and end transcription.

Gene Regulation in Eukaryotes.   Gene regulation in EUKARYOTES (such as protozoans, molds, and all higher organisms) does not appear to follow the simple operon model, and no other general pattern has been found. In many higher organisms, hormones determine development and function; here too, however, no consistency of action is observed. For example, steroid hormones enter a cell, pass into the nucleus, and produce their effects by turning on the transcription of specific genes; peptide hormones remain on the cell surface and produce their effects through the activation of preformed genes.

Human hemoglobin provides a very complicated instance of gene regulation. Each hemoglobin molecule consists of two pairs of polypeptide chains. In early embryonic development the two types of chains are zeta and epsilon, but at about eight weeks after conception their production is terminated and two other types, called alpha and gamma, are produced. At birth, gamma production is replaced by production of so-called beta chains, for the rest of the individual's life, but alpha chains continue to be formed. Neither the programming of the hemoglobin types nor their significance is yet known.

See also: ENZYME; GENETICS; METABOLISM.

ophthalmology Ophthalmology is the branch of medicine concerned with the study of the anatomy, physiology, and diseases of the EYES. It should not be confused with optometry, the art and science of fitting patients with glasses or contact lenses, which does not require a medical degree. Ophthalmologists treat such EYE DISEASES as CONJUNCTIVITIS, plus infections and tumors that affect the interior of the eye. Through the use of an instrument called an ophthalmoscope, the ophthalmologist can look inside the eye and detect abnormalities in internal structures. Another instrument, the tonometer, determines fluid pressure in the eye. Ophthalmologists also detect and treat CATARACTS and GLAUCOMA, which can cause blindness.

Ophuls, Marcel [oh'-fuls]   Marcel Ophuls, b. Frankfurt, Germany, Nov. 1, 1927, is a French film director known for his lengthy, probing documentaries. The son of director Max Ophuls, he achieved critical success with *The Sorrow and the Pity* (1969), a 4½-hour-long examination of French attitudes during the Nazi occupation. The film was originally banned from French television by the de Gaulle government because of its controversial content. In the United States it received a special award from the National Society of Film Critics. *A Sense of Loss* (1972) focused on the war in Northern Ireland, and *The Memory of Justice* (1976) looked at the Nuremberg war crimes trials. In 1988, Ophuls presented *Hotel Terminus*, documenting the career of Klaus Barbie, Gestapo chief in Lyon during World War II, who—after three decades of hiding in Latin America—was convicted (1987) in a French court of crimes against humanity.

Ophuls, Max   Max Ophuls, b. Max Oppenheimer, May 6, 1902, d. Mar. 26, 1957, was a brilliant German film director, trained in the theater, whose work over 25 years displays a remarkable homogeneity. His first masterpiece, *Liebeli* (1932), made in Germany, has all the hallmarks of his mature style: a delicate tale of a woman tormented by love, the sensitive use of music, and a fluidly moving camera. Similar qualities are found in *La signora di tutti* (1934), made in Italy. His decorative tastes and formal elegance are apparent in his Hollywood films, *Letter from an Unknown Woman* (1948), *Caught* (1949), and *The Reckless Moment* (1949). In Europe he made yet another series of masterly works: the enormously successful *La Ronde* (1950), *Madame de...* (1953), and *Lola Montès* (1955).

opiate receptor   Most vertebrate animals have, in their central nervous systems, sites called opiate receptors, with which such opiate drugs as morphine interact. Opiate receptors are located in parts of the thalamus and the limbic system (which control pain and euphoria) and, to a lesser extent, the brain stem and pituitary. The body manufactures certain morphinelike chemicals called opiate peptides. These include endorphins, which are produced mainly in the pituitary and related regions of the hypothalamus, and enkephalins, which are produced in the adrenal glands, brain, and elsewhere in the body. Endorphins and enkephalins act through the opiate receptors by modulating nerve impulses across the synapses. Studies suggest that endorphins may also affect perception and blood cholesterol levels. Through study of these chemicals and their receptors, scientists learn more about drug addictions.

opinion polls   Opinion polls have been developed largely since the 1930s as a scientific way of learning what large numbers of people think and feel about various topics. They are used extensively in politics and MARKETING. In both fields many polling companies provide political candidates and manufacturers with confidential information that indicates how they are viewed by members of the public. This information is often used in developing advertising programs and planning the strategy of political campaigns.

Many national and statewide polls regularly sample public opinion on many different topics and publish the results in newspapers and magazines. In the United States the best known of these are the Harris Poll and the Gallup Poll. Academic organizations such as the Survey Research Center at the University of Michigan and the National Opinion Research Center at the University of Chicago also research and publish information on consumer behavior and political attitudes.

Historical Background. Opinion polls were used as early as 1824 by two newspapers, the *Harrisburg Pennsylvanian* and the *Raleigh* (N.C.) *Star*, to test the strength of political candidates. These were "straw polls," in which a haphazardly selected group of citizens were asked their opinions to see which way the "political wind" was blowing. In the 1920s and '30s the magazine *Literary Digest* became famous for its huge political polls. It sent as many as 18 million postcards to potential voters in the United States, asking their preference among the presidential candidates. About 2 million replies were received. The *Literary Digest* poll correctly predicted the presidential election winners up through 1932. In 1936, however, it predicted that Franklin D. Roosevelt would lose to Alf Landon, whereas Roosevelt actually won a landslide victory. Partly as a result of this error, the magazine soon went out of business.

Sampling Methods. In the 1936 election a more scientific SAMPLING method was introduced into politics—the method had been used in business since the 1920s—by three different polling pioneers, George GALLUP, Elmo Roper, and Archibald Crossley, all of whom correctly predicted Roosevelt's victory. They used the quota method of sampling, in which individual members of the sample are chosen in accordance with a quota so as to roughly match the national population on factors such as geographic area of the country, urban versus rural residence, sex, age, race, and socioeconomic status.

The major problem with the quota method of sampling is that the interviewers are allowed discretion in choosing the individual respondents within the quota categories. This discretion introduces a possible source of bias, because the resulting sample can largely omit some types of people, such as those who are difficult to contact. A much better approach is the probability method of sampling, in which specific respondents are chosen by random selection. The result of this method is that no type of individual is systematically omitted from the sample, and the likely amount of error in the resulting data can be calculated.

Statistical laws have established that no matter how large the population being studied (from a small city to a whole country), the size of the sample is the main factor that determines the expected range of error in a probability sample. Most current polls use samples ranging in size from 1,000 to 2,000 individuals. A sample of 1,500 has an expected (that is, a 95%-certain) margin of error of plus or minus 3%, and larger samples yield only slightly smaller errors. Many polling organizations have adopted probability methods in selecting their samples.

Validity of Poll Results. Several other factors, in addition to sampling methods, can cause errors in poll results. First, the pollster must determine whether respondents have any information about the topic on which to base their opinions. Second, the questions must be carefully worded and pretested in pilot studies to ensure their clarity and impartiality. Questions must avoid biases in wording that suggest a socially desirable answer or lead respondents to agree with one side of an issue. Finally, interviewers must be carefully trained to avoid influencing respondents' answers.

In political polling, several factors can cause errors in predicting election results. Would-be respondents who are not at home produce uncertainty in the data, and many respondents are often undecided which way to vote. Last-minute changes in voting intentions sometimes occur between the time of the poll and the election. Differential turnout on election day is also a problem, and pollsters have developed techniques for estimating respondents' likelihood of voting.

The major national polls in the United States and Great Britain have an outstanding record. Since the start of scientific polling in 1936, they have predicted only two national elections incorrectly—the 1948 U.S. presidential election in which Harry S. Truman scored a last-minute victory over Thomas E. Dewey, and the 1970 British election in which the Labour party was unexpectedly defeated.

opium A narcotic drug, opium is obtained from the juice of the immature fruits of the Oriental poppy (*Papaver somniferum*). There are more than 20 natural alkaloids of opium, including CODEINE and MORPHINE. The latter, the largest component, contributes most significantly to the physiological effects. HEROIN is the most important drug synthesized from these natural alkaloids. Opium and

Unripe seed pods of the oriental poppy yield crude opium, a milky sap containing more than 20 alkaloids. The opiate narcotics are used to relieve severe pain, and many, including heroin, codeine, and morphine, may lead to addiction.

some of its derivatives are highly addictive, and their use has led to serious DRUG ABUSE problems. The main producers and exporters of opium are Burma (see DRUG TRAFFICKING) and Afghanistan.

Opiates are still used widely in medicine. Their therapeutic effects include pain relief, depression of the cough reflex, slowing of respiration, and slowing of the action of the gastrointestinal tract.

Opiates have been used since ancient times both for medicinal purposes and for pleasure. Opium was taken orally, as a pill or added to beverages, for centuries in many countries of Asia, including India. Addiction did not become a wider problem until the practice of opium smoking was introduced from India into China in the 17th century. Opiates—particularly in the form of laudanum, a tincture of opium—had become widely used in Europe and North America in the 18th century because they were the most effective and reliable painkillers available.

On the street, opium is seen as a dark brown chunk or powder. It is either smoked, eaten, or injected as a solution. During the early phases of addiction, opium produces a feeling of euphoria, or well-being. With time, the addict becomes dependent through physical or emotional factors. The syndrome of tolerance develops: larger and larger doses of the drug are needed to produce the same effect. If denied the drug, an addict will experience the unpleasantness of withdrawal symptoms. Sudden withdrawal of heavily dependent addicts has occasionally been fatal. Addiction-related illnesses include respiratory complications, low blood pressure, malnutrition, and endocarditis (disease of the heart lining and valves).

Opium Wars The Opium Wars (1839–42, 1856–60), the first major military clashes between China and the West, ended the long Chinese isolation from other civilizations. For China, defeated in both conflicts, these wars represented the beginning of a century of humiliation by foreign powers through the imposition of unequal treaties that extracted commercial privileges, territory, and other benefits from the Chinese government.

The First Opium War stemmed from China's efforts to bar the illegal importation of opium by British merchants. Britain scored an easy military victory. By the treaties of Nanjing (1842) and the Bogue (1843), China opened the ports of Guangzhou (Canton), Xiamen (Amoy), Fuzhou (Foochow), Ningbo (Ning-po), and Shanghai to British trade and residence, ceded Hong Kong to Britain, and granted Britain EXTRATERRITORIALITY, (the right to try British citizens in China in British courts). The other Western powers soon received similar privileges.

The Second Opium War, or Anglo-French War, in China also resulted from China's objections to the opium trade. A joint offensive by Britain and France secured another victory. The Treaty of Tianjin was signed in 1858, but the Chinese refused to ratify it. Hostilities resumed, and Beijing was captured by the Western allies. In 1860, China agreed to the provisions of the treaty, which opened 11 more ports, allowed foreign envoys to reside in Beijing, admitted missionaries to China, permitted foreigners to travel in the Chinese interior, and legalized the importation of opium.

Oporto see PORTO

opossum Opossums are 65 species of marsupial mammals constituting the family Didelphidae. They are the only marsupials found outside the Australian region, and all but one species are found from Mexico south through Argentina. The only species established north of Mexico is the common opossum, *Didelphis marsupialis*, which ranges as far north as southern Canada. The common opossum grows to about 53 cm (21 in) long, plus a hairless 33-cm (13-in) tail; it stands about 18 cm (7 in) high at the shoulder and may weigh up to 6.3 kg (14 lb). The opossum's coat is coarse and commonly gray, with white guard hairs; the snout is white; and the tail is black for about half of its length or less. There are five toes on each foot, and the long, pointed muzzle contains 50 teeth and can be opened beyond 90°. Opossums are most active at night.

Oppenheimer, J. Robert [ahp'-uhn-hy-mur] His leadership in developing a strong tradition of theoretical physics in the United States, his direction of the laboratory that fashioned the atomic bombs used in World War II, and his prominent role as a government advisor on military weapons and policy in the postwar period made J. Robert Oppenheimer, b. New York City, Apr. 22, 1904, d. Feb. 18, 1967, one of the most influential American scientists of his day.

Between 1929 and 1942, Oppenheimer worked at both the University of California, Berkeley, and the California Institute of Technology, Pasadena, and at each he built large schools of theoretical physics from his following of graduate students and postdoctoral researchers. During this period, Oppenheimer studied quantum numbers of the nitrogen nucleus; Dirac's "holes," or positrons; nuclear forces; cosmic-ray showers; and neutron stars.

J. Robert Oppenheimer, a prominent American physicist, became known as the father of the atom bomb. During World War II he directed the Los Alamos laboratory in New Mexico, where the first atom bomb was designed and built.

The large common opossum uses its prehensile tail as an anchor while climbing. It hangs upside down by its tail only briefly before it drops to the ground.

World War II turned Oppenheimer's energies to a new line of research. Oppenheimer, among others, recognized that an explosive chain reaction could be sustained in nearly pure fissionable material (uranium-235 or plutonium) with fast neutrons. In 1942 he was asked to coordinate an investigation into this reaction. As part of the MANHATTAN PROJECT, research and development work on the ATOMIC BOMB was centralized at a remote laboratory in

Los Alamos, N.Mex. Even his critics concede that Oppenheimer, as director of the laboratory, performed brilliantly in developing the atomic bomb.

In 1947, Oppenheimer moved to Princeton, N.J., as director of the Institute for Advanced Study. Until 1952 he served as chairman of the board of scientific advisors of the Atomic Energy Commission (AEC). Because of his influence on the AEC, his sharp tongue, his sometimes controversial views on military strategy, and his belief in arms control, Oppenheimer incurred the enmity of various members of the military, politicians, and scientists who advocated fusion and a larger strategic arsenal. He was denied security clearance in 1953 primarily because of his opposition to the H-bomb, but also because of his contacts with Communists and fellow travelers. Under new rules for clearance, and in circumstances inflamed by the passions of the McCarthy era, Oppenheimer was a major casualty of blind worship of the security system.

optical activity In chemistry and mineralogy, optical activity is the ability of substances to rotate the plane of polarization of plane-polarized light. Ordinary light consists of light waves vibrating in many different planes. POLARIZED LIGHT consists of only those light waves which vibrate in a specific plane.

In 1811, Dominique Arago found that properly prepared quartz plates cause rotation of the plane of polarized light. Two kinds of quartz are known that differ only in that each possesses either a right-handed or a left-handed set of hemihedral facets (faces). These crystals are nonidentical mirror images of each other called enantiomorphs (Greek: *enantios*, "opposite"; *morphs*, "forms"). Jean Baptiste Biot, a French physicist, found that plates of the same thickness made from these different quartz forms rotated plane-polarized light in the same amounts but in opposite directions.

In 1815, Biot discovered that naturally occurring organic compounds such as sugar, turpentine, and tartaric acid are optically active and rotate the plane of polarized light whether they are in the liquid state, in the vapor state, or dissolved in solutions. Whereas optical activity in different crystal forms is due to a specific crystalline structure and disappears by melting or dissolving the solid, the ability of the organic substances to rotate the plane of polarization in solutions is inherent in the molecules themselves.

Molecules that exhibit optical activity cannot be superimposed on their mirror-image molecules. Such dissymmetry of molecular configuration is called chirality. Not until 1874, however, did Jacobus van't Hoff and Joseph Le Bel independently recognize that every optically active organic compound known at that time possessed at least one carbon atom united with four different atoms. Only if carbon had tetrahedral geometry could two different configurations (or crystal forms) exist. Louis Pasteur demonstrated (1848) that there are two types of crystals of sodium ammonium tartrate, one dextrorotatory (clockwise rotating) and the other levorotatory (counterclock-

wise rotating). Thus Pasteur, using a hand-lens tweezers, had achieved the first resolution of two configuration isomers (now called enantiomorphs).

See also: POLARIMETER.

optical communications and storage see COMPACT DISC; FIBER OPTICS

optical computing Optical computing is a method of computing (see COMPUTER) that uses PHOTONS, tiny "packets" of light, to process information. Traditional microprocessors incorporate tiny electronic switches, or logic circuits, for processing. Theoretically, an unlimited number of electronic switches can be added to a microprocessor; practically, however, the number is limited to the millions because of space limitations in wiring the circuits together. Photons, unlike electrons, have the special property of being able to pass through one another without affecting each other, thereby rendering wiring unnecessary. Photons also travel faster than electrons. Optical computers that are thousands of times faster than the most powerful electronic computers may someday be achieved.

Although researchers had attempted to design optical computers as early as the 1940s, significant progress was not made until the mid-1980s, and the technology is still in its infancy. In January 1990 a Bell Laboratories team led by Alan Huang unveiled the first optical computer—a table-top device consisting of an array of lasers, lenses, and mirrors—capable of simple addition. Miniaturization of the optical computer's individual elements is the biggest difficulty that researchers face.

optical isomer see STEREOCHEMISTRY

optics The word *optics*, from the Greek *optikes*, originally meant the study of the eye and vision. The term now refers to the study of all phenomena related to LIGHT. Geometrical optics is that branch which deals with reflection and refraction and the formation of images by optical instruments. It treats light as propagating in straight lines or rays. Physical optics is the study and explanation of optical phenomena in terms of the wave nature of light. This branch includes such phenomena as INTERFERENCE, DIFFRACTION, and polarization, as well as the subdivisions electrooptics, magnetooptics, crystal optics, and so on. Quantum optics has to do with the particle nature of light manifest in certain phenomena such as the PHOTOELECTRIC EFFECT.

Historical Overview

The science of optics has its roots buried in ancient times. In about 300 BC, EUCLID wrote a treatise entitled *Optics and Catoptrics* in which he gave the correct law of reflection and applied the law to the study of plane and curved mirrors. He also mentioned the phenomenon of refraction, but the true mathematical law governing refraction was not discovered until 1621 by Willebrord Snell.

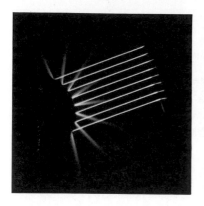 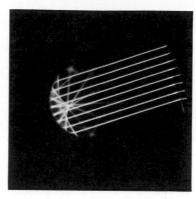 

A ray of light is reflected from a point on a surface at the same angle at which it impinges on the spot. The reflected-light pattern obtained from an incoming beam of parallel rays thus depends on the shape of the surface. Initially parallel light rays will diverge after striking a convex mirror (left) but converge after reflection from a concave surface (center). Parallel light rays will be refracted, or bent away, from their original path when they pass from air through a triangular glass prism and back to air again (right).

The first substantial contribution to the understanding of the visual process was made by Alhazen in the 11th century. He deduced that light coming from various portions of an illuminated object forms a visual image in the eye. The process of vision was one of the many things studied by Johannes KEPLER in the early 17th century. He was the first to give a reasonably complete description of the way that the lens of the eye forms an image on the retina.

One of the foremost figures in the development of the science of optics was Christiaan HUYGENS, whose *Treatise on Light* was published in 1690. Huygens considered light a wave disturbance rather than a stream of particles, and he formulated a useful method, now called Huygens's principle, for studying the propagation of light waves. Using this principle he was able to deduce the laws of reflection and refraction. He also applied the principle to the explanation of other optical phenomena such as double refraction. A contemporary of Huygens was Isaac NEWTON who, among his many accomplishments, performed numerous original experiments in optics. He discovered that white light, which can be broken into its component colors by means of a prism, can be recombined with a second prism. He perfected the reflecting telescope and investigated the phenomenon of interference. His famous book *Optiks* was published in 1704. Newton rejected the wave theory of Huygens; instead he advocated a corpuscular theory according to which a luminous body emits minute particles that propagate in straight lines.

The controversy over the wave theory versus the corpuscular theory continued for many years after Newton's death. In the early 19th century, largely owing to the work of Thomas YOUNG on the interference of light and later investigations of Augustin FRESNEL on diffraction and the interference of POLARIZED LIGHT, the wave theory gradually gained acceptance over the corpuscular theory. In the latter part of the 19th century the monumental work of James Clerk MAXWELL showed that virtually all optical phenomena known at the time could be explained in terms of his electromagnetic-wave theory. One of the fundamental results of this theory concerns the velocity of electromagnetic waves. This velocity can be calculated from purely electrical measurements and is precisely the same as the experimentally measured velocity of light determined by Armand Fizeau in 1849 and by many other investigators since then.

The final culmination of Maxwell's theory came about in the year 1888, when Heinrich HERTZ demonstrated the existence of electric waves (now known as radio waves), which travel at the same speed as visible light and other radiations. This demonstration was the experimental proof of Maxwell's wave theories. Ironically, Hertz also discovered in the previous year the photoelectric effect, a phenomenon best explained by treating light as a stream of particles, now called PHOTONS. This discovery turned out to be the first in a series of developments that eventually led to the quantum theory of light, which postulates

Light rays are refracted, or changed in direction, whenever they pass from water into air or from any medium into another of different density. Thus refraction causes a coin immersed in a glass of water (left) to appear to be at a different position from that of a coin located at the same point in an empty glass (right).

that light energy always occurs in discrete packets. The modern description of light is that it has a dual nature, wavelike in some circumstances and particlelike in others. Thus, in a sense, both Newton's and Huygens's views were correct.

Geometrical Optics

The fundamental concept of geometrical optics is the ray, which may be defined as the path along which a light wave propagates. The three basic laws of geometric optics are the law of rectilinear propagation, the law of reflection, and the law of refraction.

The law of rectilinear propagation states that in any medium of uniform composition light travels in straight lines, or rays. The law is exemplified by the formation of shadows. Another example is the pinhole camera, in which light rays coming from the various points of an extended object pass through the pinhole to form an inverted image on the photographic film.

The law of reflection states that the incident ray, the reflected ray, and a line perpendicular to the surface at the point of reflection (called the normal) all lie in a common plane and that the angles made with the normal by the incident and the reflected rays are equal to each other, or more simply, the angle of incidence is equal to the angle of reflection.

The law of refraction, also called Snell's law, states that the incident ray, the normal, and the transmitted, or refracted, ray also lie in the same plane and that the trigonometric sine of the angle of incidence bears a constant ratio to the sine of the angle of refraction. The numerical value of this ratio is called the relative INDEX OF REFRACTION.

When a ray passes from a medium of low density to one of higher density, such as from air to glass, the relative index is greater than unity, and the ray is refracted toward the normal. Conversely, if a ray passes from a medium of high density to one of lower density, such as from glass to air, the relative index is less than unity, and the ray is bent away from the normal.

The application of these three rules of geometrical optics to the study of optical instruments is known as ray tracing. The most elementary method of ray tracing is simple graphical construction. The more accurate methods employ mathematical calculations. Such calculations are needed in the design of complex LENS systems, such as camera lenses, and are now performed with the aid of high-speed computers.

Many optical instruments, including the microscope and the telescope, consist basically of two converging lenses combined in such a manner that one lens, called the objective, produces a real image of an object, and a second lens, called the eyepiece or ocular, forms a magnified virtual image of the real image. A real image is one that can be formed on a screen when the rays of light are brought to a focus. A virtual image cannot be formed on a screen but can be seen when focused by the eye. The enlarged image of an object examined by a magnifying lens is a virtual image.

In the microscope the objective lens has a short focal length and is placed correspondingly close to the object

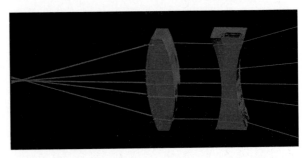

The path of light rays through a system of lenses depends on both the position of the light source and the types of lens. If the light rays issue from the focus of a double convex lens (left), they will emerge from the convex lens parallel to the central ray and will diverge from it as they pass through the double concave lens (right).

(microscope slide). In the telescope the objective has a long focal length and a large diameter for high light-gathering power. In practice the lenses are not single but are generally constructed of several components designed to correct the various defects (such as chromatic and spherical ABERRATIONS) of simple lenses.

In the case of the basic two-lens system, the image is inverted, a fact that is of no consequence for microscopes and astronomical telescopes. In order to produce a normal (or upright) image, a third optical element is required. In the terrestrial telescope this third element is simply another lens placed between the objective and the ocular. This lens forms an upright image of the original inverted one formed by the objective. Another method makes use of a special reflecting prism, called a Porro prism, that reinverts the original image by a series of reflections. This method is employed in the common field binocular.

Physical Optics

Any wave disturbance is produced by some sort of vibrating source. The wavelength, defined as the distance the wave progresses during one complete vibration, is determined by the wave velocity and frequency of oscillation according to the general equation

$$\text{wavelength} = \frac{\text{velocity}}{\text{frequency}}$$

Electromagnetic waves are generated by oscillating electrical charges, and these waves propagate through empty space with a velocity of 299,792 km/sec (186,282 mi/sec).

In the case of visible light the various colors perceived by the human eye correspond to wavelengths ranging from about 0.0004 to about 0.0007 mm. The shorter wavelength corresponds to violet, and the longer to red; the various colors of the spectrum fall between these limits. The visible spectrum occupies only a small portion of the range of known electromagnetic waves, which includes infrared, microwaves, and radio waves (all of

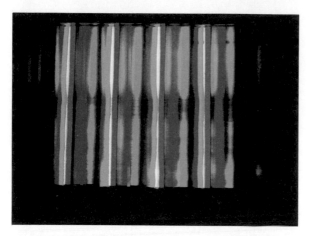

Four pairs of bright, continuous spectral images are obtained when four parallel beams of white light are passed through a diffraction grating. The light waves from each beam are diffracted and dispersed into their component colors. The diffracted waves from each beam then interfere with others from the same beam to produce spectral images on both sides of the beam's path.

which are longer than light waves) and ultraviolet, X rays, and gamma rays (which are shorter). (See ELECTROMAGNETIC RADIATION.)

Interference. When two identical wave disturbances are made to combine in such a way that the peaks of one wave coincide with the peaks of the other, the two waves will reinforce each other to produce a more intense disturbance. This process is known as constructive interference. On the other hand, if the peaks of one wave coincide with the valleys of the other, then the waves will tend to cancel one another. This process is called destructive interference.

Interference of light is used in many practical ways. The worldwide fundamental standard of length is based on the wavelength of a certain spectrum line of the gas krypton. Light from a krypton lamp is used in conjunction with an optical INTERFEROMETER to make precise measurements of length. Another use of interference is the antireflecting film; lenses and other optical parts used in all fine instruments are coated with thin transparent layers of material designed to reduce reflection losses by destructive interference. The light that would be otherwise reflected is transmitted. In multilens systems this process can increase the efficiency of an instrument considerably. Thin films are also used in such devices as the interference filter, which utilizes constructive interference in a way that allows light of one color to pass through the filter while reflecting all other wavelengths.

Diffraction. If an opaque object is placed between a point source of light and a white screen, careful examination will show that the shadow edge is not perfectly sharp, as predicted by the law of rectilinear propagation of geometrical optics. Rather, the viewer will find that a small amount of light spills over into the dark zone and that faint fringes appear in the illuminated zone. Another related phenomenon is the spreading of a beam of light af-

ter passing through a small pinhole or a narrow split. The name given to these departures from geometrical optics is diffraction. Geometrical optics provides useful results in most applications because the wavelength of visible light is small and diffraction effects are relatively unimportant in ordinary circumstances.

The essential features of diffraction phenomena can be explained by means of Huygens's principle, which states that each point on an advancing wave front can be considered the source of a new, or secondary, wave. These secondary waves combine to produce the new wave front. Diffraction is particularly apparent in the optical DIFFRACTION GRATING, a device used to separate light into its component wavelengths.

Polarization. The transverse nature of light waves is revealed by the phenomenon known as polarization (see POLARIZED LIGHT). Certain natural crystals, particularly the mineral tourmaline, have the special property known as dichroism; they absorb light whose electric vibrations are in one direction and transmit light whose vibrations are at right angles to this direction. The synthetic product Polaroid is dichroic. When ordinary light, which has random directions of vibration, is passed through a polarizer made of a dichroic material, the emerging light is polarized; in other words, it has its electric vibrations confined to one certain direction. When polarized light is sent through a second polarizer, the light will either be transmitted or

An ordinary unpolarized light beam is made up of innumerable electric and magnetic waves, each vibrating in its own plane at right angles to the direction in which the light travels. An end-on view (A) and a longitudinal view (B) reveal that the electric fields of the various electromagnetic waves oscillate in different planes. In a linearly polarized light beam (C, D), however, all the electric waves vibrate in the same direction. The electric waves of circularly polarized light (E, F) rotate along a circular path, whereas those of elliptically polarized light (G, H) follow an elliptical path.

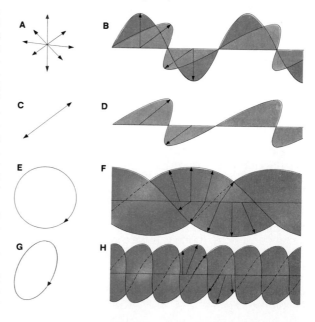

absorbed, depending on the relative orientation of the two polarizers. When natural unpolarized light is reflected from a smooth surface, such as the surface of a wet road, it becomes partially polarized. A suitably oriented dichroic sheet, such as that used in Polaroid sunglasses, can thus reduce the reflective glare by absorbing the polarized component of the light.

Quantum Optics. One of the optical phenomena that exhibits the particle nature of light is the photoelectric effect, mentioned above. When light falls on the surface of a metallic conductor, electrons are emitted by the metal. Careful experiments show that the energy of the electrons depends only on the wavelength (or frequency) of the incident light and not at all on the light intensity. Higher frequencies cause the ejection of more-energetic electrons. These facts can be explained by assuming that light energy is imparted to the metal in discrete packets called photons. Each emitted electron has absorbed a single photon. The energy E of a photon is proportional to the light frequency v: $E = hv$. Here h is a universal constant known as PLANCK'S CONSTANT.

See also: ABSORPTION; COLOR; DISPERSION; MICHELSON-MORLEY EXPERIMENT; MIRROR; REFLECTION.

---

option trading   Option trading is an important part of the financial system. An option contract describes a sale of a security or commodity that will occur at a specified later date and at a specified price if, and only if, one party to the contract—either the prospective buyer or the prospective seller—wants to go ahead with the sale. If the contract is a "call option," the buyer has the right to decide whether or not the sale happens; if the contract is a "put option," the seller decides.

The sale price stated in the option contract is called the "exercise price." The holder of an option contract can wait until the expiration date of the contract to decide whether to exercise the option. The holder of a call option (or of a put option) will exercise the option only if the exercise price is less (or is more) than the current market price for the security or commodity—otherwise, the holder could buy the same thing at a cheaper price (or sell at a higher price) in the open market.

The holder of an option pays a premium for this valuable right when the contract is first agreed to. The other party, known as the option writer, receives the premium. Since the contract requires the option writer to sell or buy upon request of the option holder, the option holder requires the writer to post collateral in a margin account as evidence of the writer's good faith.

The price of an option—its premium—depends on several things, including the price volatility of the item to be bought or sold. As the price volatility of the security or commodity increases, the option to buy it at a fixed price in the future becomes more valuable.

Options can be bought or sold on many different items. In the United States there are option markets for shares of stock, indexes based on stock portfolios, foreign currencies, bonds, precious metals, and FUTURES contracts on physical commodities and financial instruments.

---

oracle   In ancient Greece a priest or priestess who communicated the response of a god to a questioner was called an oracle. The term was also applied to the response itself and to the shrine of the god. The most famous oracles were at Dodona, where Zeus was thought to give answers through the rustling of the oak leaves, and at DELPHI, where Apollo supposedly spoke through a priestess. In both cases, oracular responses came in such ambiguous ways that it was difficult to prove them wrong. A famous Roman oracle was at Cumae, where the SIBYL was said to have drawn inspiration from Apollo.

---

oracle bones   Oracle bones are inscribed animal bones, especially tortoise plastrons (under shells) and cattle shoulder blades, on which are preserved the earliest examples of Chinese writing. They were originally used by the ancient Chinese as tools of divination, performed for the rulers of the SHANG dynasty (c.1600–1027 BC). The oracle bones were prepared for use by grinding small pits on their inner surface. A hot metal tool was touched to the pits, and a diviner foretold the future from the shapes of the cracks that appeared. Sometimes the questions or answers were inscribed next to the cracks. Individual bones were used many times, and after they could no longer be used they were buried together in pits, possibly as archives or perhaps only because of their sacred nature.

The oracle bones first came to the attention of scholars in 1899. The source of the bones was eventually traced to ANYANG, the last Shang capital, in Henan province. Excavations by archaeologists, begun in 1928, recovered thousands of examples. The oracle bones not only chronicle political and military events but also provide much information about the daily concerns of the Shang kings, for it was their questions that were asked and recorded. Most of the pictographic symbols can be translated.

Oraibi [oh-ry'-bee]   Oraibi, the oldest, largest, and most important village of the HOPI tribe of North American Indians, shares with ACOMA the distinction of being among the oldest settlements in the United States. Situated on Third Mesa, 130 km (80 mi) north of Winslow, Ariz., Oraibi was founded before AD 1150. Spanish contacts began in 1540, but the Oraibi population of about 1,200 along with other Hopi did not acknowledge Spanish rule until 1598. The repressive policies of SPANISH MISSIONS stimulated the people of Oraibi to join in the Pueblo Revolt of 1680. Under American rule (1846), conflict began between factions that favored resistance or acceptance of new ways. In 1906 the resistance group left to found Hotevilla and Bakavi. In 1910 the Christian Hopi also left and established New Oraibi. The original village had 335 inhabitants in 1986.

---

oral history   Oral history, information based on interviews with those who have taken part in historical events, is as old as the study of history itself. In the 5th century BC the Greek historians Herodotus and Thucydides, lacking the written sources on which modern historians have come to rely, questioned the survivors of the wars they described. In traditional societies without either a written language or widespread literacy, oral tradition passed down from generation to generation often serves as a substitute for written historical accounts.

The American historian Allan NEVINS along with other researchers at Columbia University began to preserve autobiographical accounts of the lives of prominent persons through tape-recorded interviews. Oral history has also been advanced by a growing interest in the lives of ordinary people and by the popular work of talented interviewers and compilers. A notable example is Studs Terkel, whose books of oral history are extraordinary documents of American life.

◾

oral literature Oral literature is the creation of people who do not possess a written language. Contemporary examples of such literatures might include the stories and songs of rural African tribespeople or the tale-tellings of native Americans. The most famous ancient examples are the *Iliad* and the *Odyssey*, attributed to the ancient Greek poet HOMER. The literary forms in which the most important creations of oral literature have passed down through the centuries are the heroic EPIC, SAGA, and FOLKTALE, but traditional songs, sayings, riddles, and a good many of the chants and rhymes of childhood also belong to the genre. The longest and most complex forms, the epics and sagas, were probably composite products created over time by individual bards or minstrels. In Homer they are called "singers."

The question of whether the *Iliad* and the *Odyssey* were composed by a single poet with no knowledge of writing seems to have been conclusively answered by American Homeric scholar Milman Parry (1902–35), who claimed that it should have been possible for a single poet to compose and recite works as monumental as these. They were, he said, the fruit of an age-long process of oral creation; their author was working within the framework of an oral technique he had heard from his childhood; and his listeners were familiar with the events of his story, since they belonged to the traditional history of their people.

The elaborate language of Homer's epics contains traditional verbal formulas, such as the Homeric epithet, that are used over and over again to characterize each of the poem's actors. Formulaic verbal patterns occur repeatedly to describe similar situations: battles, arguments, feasts. Early European poems believed to have been orally composed include BEOWULF, the NIBELUNGENLIED, the *Song of Roland* (see CHANSONS DE GESTE), and the *Poem of the Cid* (see EL CID).

◾

Oran [oh-rahn'] Oran (Arabic: Wahran), one of the leading ports of the North African republic of Algeria, lies on the Mediterranean Sea about 360 km (225 mi) west of Algiers. Oran has a population of 916,578 (1987 est.). Food-processing plants, foundries, and metalworks are located in the city. Wine, cereals, vegetables, and fruits are among the chief exports. The city's long history is reflected in its old Spanish fortress, the mosque, the French-built port facilities and Ville Nouvelle (New City), and the Université d'Oran (1965).

Although the site has been occupied since prehistory, Oran's founding dates to the 10th century, when Moors from Andalusia in Spain established a trading post there. The city, which for a time was a pirate stronghold, was held successively by the Spanish, Ottomans, and French, who captured the city in 1831. During the 1950s and early 1960s, Oran was a battleground, as Algerian nationalists fought the French to gain independence.

◾

Orange (dynasty) The house of Orange is the royal family of the Kingdom of the Netherlands. The dynasty originated in the medieval principality of Orange, in southern France. William the Silent, count of Nassau, who held estates in the Netherlands, became WILLIAM I, PRINCE OF ORANGE, in 1544 as heir of René of Chalon, and he carried this title as leader of the DUTCH REVOLT against Spain that created the Dutch Republic. His heirs and successors—MAURICE OF NASSAU; FREDERICK HENRY; WILLIAM II, PRINCE OF ORANGE; and WILLIAM III, KING OF ENGLAND, SCOTLAND, AND IRELAND—led the republic as stadholders of the principal provinces.

In 1797, William, stadholder of Friesland, a descendant of a daughter of Frederick Henry, was elected stadholder in the other provinces as **William IV** (1711–51). Although the principality of Orange had been ceded to France by the Peace of Utrecht (1713), he and his son and successor, Stadholder **William V**, b. Mar. 8, 1748, d. Apr. 9, 1806, carried the title of prince of Orange. Their branch of the family is known formally as the house of Orange-Nassau, and their descendants are the present royal family.

William V's son was created king of the Netherlands, as WILLIAM I, and grand duke of Luxembourg in 1815. He was succeeded by Kings WILLIAM II and WILLIAM III. In 1890, when Queen WILHELMINA succeeded in the Netherlands, Luxembourg passed to a collateral line of the family. Wilhelmina abdicated in 1948. Her successor, JULIANA, did the same in 1980, the throne passing to her eldest daughter, Beatrice (see BEATRICE, QUEEN OF THE NETHERLANDS).

◾

orange The sweet orange, *Citrus sinensis*, of the Rutaceae family, is the most important citrus fruit. The United Nations Food and Agriculture Organization ranks world orange production first among the tree fruits, with the apple next. Brazil, the United States, China, Spain, and Mexico are among the major producers of oranges.

Oranges grow on medium-sized evergreen trees, which under favorable conditions may yield fruit for 60 years or

The sweet orange tree is a compact evergreen that grows to 12 m (40 ft). Its small white flower is the state flower of Florida.

more. The pungent leaves have a glossy, wax-coated surface. The small white flowers, which are borne in clusters, appear in the spring in the subtropics but throughout the year in some tropical climates.

Botanically, the fruit is a berry known as a *hesperidium*. Oranges are round to ovular and covered by a thick, leathery peel that turns yellow orange to deep orange when ripened in subtropical climates. In the tropics ripe oranges are usually green to pale yellow. The inner pulp (endocarp) consists of 9 to 16 segments filled with juice vesicles. Ripe oranges normally contain 35 to 50 percent juice by weight, depending on variety, climate, and cultural conditions. Oranges may be seedless (navel), nearly seedless, or seedy. Extracted juice usually contains 9 to 12 percent total soluble solids (mostly sugar and citric acid); each fruit contains 20 to 60 mg (a small fraction of an ounce) of vitamin C.

Oranges are either eaten as table fruit or processed into related products, the most important being frozen juice concentrate. Other products are chilled and canned juice, canned sections, and dehydrated powder. The peel, seed, and pulp by-products of juice production are used in cattle feed, molasses, and special products such as peel oil.

Orange Free State

The Orange Free State, a province in east central South Africa, has an area of 127,338 km² (49,166 mi²). BLOEMFONTEIN is the capital. The population of the province is 1,776,903 (1985). The state lies on the Highveld, a plateau with an elevation of about 1,220 m (4,000 ft). Corn, sorghum, and wheat are grown, and cattle and sheep are raised. Mining yields gold, uranium, diamonds, and coal.

Originally inhabited by Bantu tribes, the area was settled by Boer (AFRIKANER) farmers in the early 19th century. The region was annexed by the British in 1848 but was granted its independence in 1854. In 1900, during the SOUTH AFRICAN WAR (1899–1902) between the Afrikaners and the British, the Free State was made the Orange River Colony of the United Kingdom. The colony regained its independence in 1907 and joined the Union of South Africa in 1910.

Orange River

The Orange River, the principal river of South Africa, flows west for about 2,100 km (1,300 mi) from its source in the Maluti Mountains of Lesotho to Oranjemund on the Atlantic Ocean. No part of the river is navigable, and much of it crosses thinly settled, semiarid land, including the KALAHARI and NAMIB deserts. In dry years the river does not reach the sea. Irrigation is important from Boegoeberg west to Aughrabies Falls and along the Vaal-Harts tributaries. The huge Orange River Project, begun in the early 1960s, provides hydroelectric power and water for irrigation.

Orangemen

The Loyal Orange Order is a worldwide Irish society dedicated to defending Protestant interests. It originated with a group of anti-Catholic rioters in County Armagh in the 1790s. Members proclaim loyalty to the British crown, on the condition that the monarchy remain Protestant. On July 12 every year Orangemen mark the anniversary of the victory of William of Orange (see WILLIAM III, KING OF ENGLAND, SCOTLAND, AND IRELAND) over the Catholic English king JAMES II in the Battle of the Boyne (1690); their celebrations have occasionally provoked sectarian violence. The order helped organize Ulster Protestant resistance to Home Rule for Ireland (see HOME RULE BILLS), and many observers believe that it exercised undue influence on the policies of the Northern Ireland regime of 1921–72.

orangutan

The orangutan, *Pongo pygmaeus,* a great ape, is native to the forests on the islands of Borneo and Sumatra. Its name is Malayan and means "man of the woods." Orangs have a shaggy coat of long, coarse, reddish brown hair. Adult males also have reddish blond beards and mustaches, well-developed cheek pads, and a large throat pouch that is used as a sound resonator to reinforce calls. Males are markedly larger than females, averaging about 75 kg (165 lb) in weight; females average about 40 kg (90 lb). A large male in the wild may weigh 100 kg (220 lb) and stand about 1.4 m (4.5 ft) tall. The orang's arms are very long relative to the body and legs and reach to the ankles when the animal stands erect.

Orangs often live in small groups of two to four animals, but adult males may be solitary. Orangs are arboreal, seldom leaving the trees, where they feed primarily on fruit but also on leaves, bark, and birds' eggs. They build simple sleeping nests, or platforms, on which they spend the night.

Full maturity is attained at 10 to 12 years of age; sexual maturity is reached at about 8 years. Gestation lasts

The orangutan is an arboreal ape native to Borneo and Sumatra. The adult male (above) *often develops large cheek pads— deposits of subcutaneous fat—and an enormous throat sac.*

about 9 months. Humans are the orangs' only significant enemy, and unless hunting and destruction of their forest habitat are curtailed, orangs will soon become extinct.

oratorio   An oratorio is an extended musical setting of a sacred text composed of dramatic, narrative, and reflective passages. Its music, which is like that of opera, is performed without scenery, costumes, or action. The oratorio was most intensively cultivated during the 17th and 18th centuries.

The oratorio originated at the Congregation of the Oratory, founded in Rome by Saint Philip Neri (1515–95). In a building called an *oratorio* ("prayer hall" or "oratory"), narrative-dramatic compositions based on stories from the Bible and the lives of saints were performed during worship services. About 1640, such compositions began to be called oratorios.

In the period from about 1650 to 1750 in Italy, oratorios emphasizing solo singing were performed in oratories in the palaces of the nobility and occasionally in churches. Outside of Italy the oratorio was cultivated primarily in Germany and England. Some works by Heinrich SCHÜTZ called *Historia* are similar to oratorios. Johann Sebastian BACH composed three oratorios and two extant Passions that are much like oratorios. George Frideric HANDEL composed more than 20 oratorios, most of them in English and emphasizing the chorus. His *Messiah* (1741) is the most influential and most widely performed oratorio.

Since the mid-18th century, major composers have composed fewer oratorios, but the genre has continued to be significant. Composers still tend to emphasize the chorus, as did Handel. Biblical subjects have predominated, but ethical subjects not strictly religious have also been used. Among the oratorios composed since 1750 are *The Creation* (1798) by Haydn; Beethoven's *Christ on the Mount of Olives* (1802); Mendelssohn's *St. Paul* (1836) and *Elijah* (1846); *The Childhood of Christ* (1854) by Berlioz; *Christus* (1856–67) by Liszt; Elgar's *The Dream of Gerontius* (1900); Honegger's *King David* (1921); Schoenberg's *Jacob's Ladder* (1917–22); Stravinsky's *Oedipus rex* (1926–27); Walton's *Belshazzar's Feast* (1931); *A Child of Our Time* (1944) by Tippett; *Song of the Forests* (1949) by Shostakovich; Ernst Krenek's *Spiritus intelligentiae sanctus* (1955), for two singers and magnetic tape; *The Raft of the Medusa* (1968) by Henze; and *The Transfiguration* (1969) by Messiaen.

oratory   SEE RHETORIC AND ORATORY

orbital   In atomic theory, an orbital is a region surrounding an atomic nucleus where an electron associated with the atom is most likely to be found. Although more of a mathematical representation than a physical reality, an orbital is generally visualized as a cloud with a specified size and shape determined, in general, by the energy level of the electron.

The classical picture of the ATOM proposed by Niels Bohr in 1913, in which electrons circled the nucleus in definite orbits, soon proved inadequate to explain certain complex properties of atoms. In the late 1920s, Werner Heisenberg, Erwin Schrödinger, Paul Dirac, and others developed an improved quantum theory (see QUANTUM MECHANICS) that included the discovery that electrons could have wavelike properties. A complex mathematical treatment of the atom led to a model that allowed an electron to be any distance from its nucleus. The model operates under the laws of probability; for any atom a minute but finite chance exists that some of its electrons are many meters away. Electrons, of course, are most likely to be found in close proximity to the nucleus. An orbital of a specified electron is the region in which about a 95% chance exists of finding the electron. Very little difference exists between this region and a 99% region.

Because no orbital can contain more than two electrons (Pauli's EXCLUSION PRINCIPLE), the number of orbitals of an atom increases with atomic number. The lowest-energy orbitals of each electron shell (*s* orbitals) are hollow spheres of somewhat indefinite thickness. Higher orbitals (*p, d,* and *f*) have more complex, lobed shapes. Covalent bonds are considered to be the overlapping of orbitals, which permits two nuclei to share an electron pair.

orbital elements   The elements of an orbit are quantities that define geometrically the orbit of one body moving around another in accordance with KEPLER'S LAWS. Seven elements are used in determining the orbit of a body and its position along that orbit. They are: the semimajor axis of the orbit, its eccentricity, the inclina-

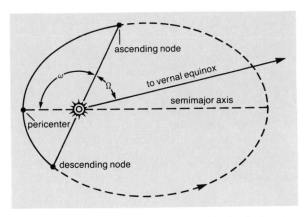

This diagram represents the orbit of a planet around the Sun. Its elements are defined in part by the Earth's orbital plane, represented here as the plane of the page surface. The orbit shown is tilted to this plane, lying partly below it (broken line) and partly above (solid line).

tion between the plane of the body's orbit and the plane of the Earth's orbit (the plane of the ECLIPTIC), the longitude of the ascending node, the longitude of pericenter, the time of pericenter passage, and the mean motion, or period.

The semimajor axis of an orbit is a measure of the size of the orbit (see ELLIPSE). The ECCENTRICITY is a measure of its shape, ranging from 0 for a circle to greater than 1 for a hyperbola.

The description of the orientation of an orbit in space requires three angles. One, the longitude of the ascending node (Ω), is measured (from the orbited body) between the vernal EQUINOX and the point (the ascending node) at which the orbiting body passes through the plane of the ecliptic. The second, the inclination, is the angle between the ecliptic plane and the plane containing the orbit. The third (ω), the longitude of pericenter, is measured (from the orbited body) between the ascending node and the pericenter, or point of closest approach of the orbiting to the orbited body.

Orbiting Astronomical Observatory   see OAO

Orbiting Geophysical Observatory   see OGO

Orbiting Solar Observatory   see OSO

—

orchestra and orchestration   An orchestra is a sizable assemblage of instruments drawn from four broad classes (strings, woodwinds, brass, percussion) in which each string part is performed by more than one player. It is distinguished from chamber-music ensembles, which use only one musician per part, and from bands, which lack stringed instruments.

Normal Complement
The full symphonic orchestra today employs about 100 musicians. The roster of instruments, listed in the order in which they appear in a modern printed score, rarely exceeds the following: 3 flutes and piccolo, 3 oboes and English horn, 3 clarinets and bass clarinet, 3 bassoons and contrabassoon (double bassoon); 4 horns, 3 trumpets, 3 trombones and tuba; a set of 4 timpani (tuned kettledrums), and other percussion (snare drum, bass drum, cymbals, triangle, xylophone, and so on); 2 harps; 16 to 18 first violins, 14 to 16 second violins, 12 violas, 10 cellos, and 8 contrabasses (double basses). In smaller orchestras the string groups are proportionately reduced; some compositions, however, call for a larger number of wind instruments or for other instruments not listed above.

History
The term *orchestra* comes from the ancient Greek theater; the term denoted the semicircular area in front of the stage, in which the chorus sang and danced. The word was adopted for the corresponding area (or pit) that housed the instrumentalists in European opera houses from the 17th century on and later came to designate the players themselves.

Orchestras of sorts functioned on ceremonial occasions in medieval and Renaissance times, but nobody knows exactly which instrument played which part. Giovanni Gabrieli's *Sacrae Symphoniae* of 1597 seemingly contains the first pieces to assign a specific instrument to each part.

Baroque Orchestra. Claudio Monteverdi, the first great opera composer, recorded the roster of instruments used at the premiere of his *Orfeo* (1607); this was an orchestra of about 40 players. Normally, a baroque orchestra was at full strength if it had as many as 20 to 25 players. The heart of the group was the body of strings, which after some experimentation came to be divided into four parts: first violins, second violins, violas, and a bottom line played in octaves by cellos and double basses. To these were added the wind sound of the double-reeded oboes and bassoons. Oboists were generally expected to play the flute as well. Other instruments could be added: trumpets and timpani for festive occasions, trombones for sacred music, horns for hunting scenes. A composer who raised orchestration to the level of true art, exploring the possibilities of each instrument, was Jean Philippe Rameau, who turned out a stream of remarkably scored operas from 1733 to 1764.

Classical Orchestra. In 18th-century performance the supreme group was the court orchestra at Mannheim, which flourished in the third quarter of the century. It had about 30 string players and helped to standardize the remaining forces: a pair each of flutes, oboes, bassoons, horns, trumpets, kettledrums and sometimes clarinets. Beethoven increased the technical demands on every orchestral instrument, and in his nine symphonies (1800–24) he occasionally augmented the classical orchestra by writing parts for piccolo, trombones, and contrabassoon.

Romantic Orchestra. As the 19th century progressed, the orchestra benefited from revolutionary changes in instrumental construction—notably the key mechanisms

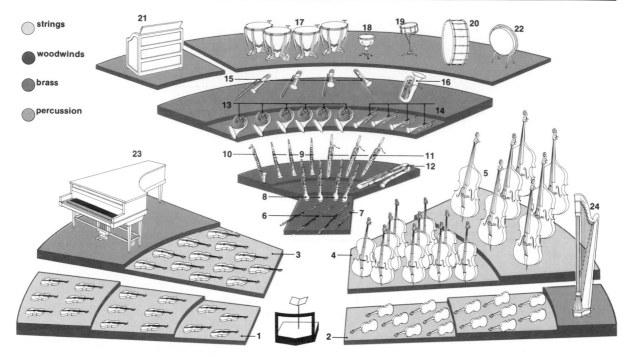

strings
woodwinds
brass
percussion

The modern symphony orchestra combines instruments drawn from four categories—strings, woodwinds, brass, and percussion—to form an ensemble capable of extremely varied musical expression. Although seating arrangements vary, the instruments are generally grouped by category in order to concentrate and blend the sounds of a given tone color. The strings, which include first (1) and second (2) violins, violas (3), cellos (4), and double basses (5), form the backbone of the orchestra. Their vibrant tones range from the sweetness of the violin to the deep resonance of the double bass. The woodwinds include the flute (6), piccolo (7), oboe (8), clarinet (9), bass clarinet (10), bassoon (11), and contrabassoon (12). Their tone quality is mellow, encompassing both the plaintive oboe and the clear, soft-spoken flute. Brass instruments, including French horns (13), trumpets (14), trombones (15), and tuba (16), contribute brilliance and clarity. The percussion instruments, which stress rhythm and provide emphasis, include the timpani (17); kettle (18), snare (19), and bass (20) drums; the celesta (21), a keyboard chime; and the gong (22). The piano (23) and harp (24) are standard solo instruments.

applied to the woodwinds and the valve systems built into horns and trumpets. With the enthusiastic support of Hector BERLIOZ, the tuba became the standard bass of the brass section, succeeding its deficient predecessors (serpent, ophicleide).

Berlioz, in fact, handled the entire orchestra with unprecedented imagination, daring, and skill, starting with his *Symphonie Fantastique* (1830). His *Requiem* (1837) even called for 4 auxiliary brass groups spatially deployed as well as 16 kettledrums played by 10 timpanists. He underscored his authority by publishing a still-invaluable treatise on instrumentation (1843), to which he later added a section on conducting.

Many romantic composers strove for ever greater orchestral expressiveness. This was achieved in part by paying increased attention to instruments capable of unusual nuances (clarinet, horn) and by enlarging the size of the orchestra. Richard Wagner came to prefer 8 horns, wrote for bass trumpet and contrabass trombone, and even designed a set of so-called "Wagner tubas"—to be played by hornists—that were later adopted by Anton Bruckner and Richard Strauss.

The trend toward gigantism reached its peak at the start of the 20th century in works by Strauss (*Domestic Symphony, Elektra*), Gustav Mahler (symphonies no. 2 and no. 8, the latter of which premiered with an orchestra of 171 and 858 singers), Arnold Schoenberg (*Gurre-Lieder*), and Igor Stravinsky (*Rite of Spring*). After Berlioz, Mahler exhibited the greatest virtuosity in orchestration; and his influence has been enormous on composers as disparate as Dmitry Shostakovich, Aaron Copland, and Benjamin Britten.

In the past half-century most composers have been content with orchestras of moderate size. This limit has not prevented them from exploring new ways to use traditional instruments, importing unusual sounds (siren, typewriter, car horn), incorporating instruments powered by electricity (the electric vibraphone, for instance), or using the sounds created by electronic instruments. Contemporary ELECTRONIC MUSIC is produced by instruments of such range that some of them are capable of creating the sound of an entire orchestra.

orchid Orchids comprise about 7 percent of all flowering plants. Some taxonomists recognize as many as

35,000 species in 1,000 genera. Other taxonomists recognize only about 20,000 species, but even this number ranks the Orchidaceae as the largest family of flowering plants. Orchids are perennials, with only one species, *Zeuxine strateumatica*, known to be an annual. They are also typically herbaceous, but some forms may be viny or somewhat woody. Orchid rootstock may become thickened to form overwintering tubers or pseudobulbs. From early classical times through the Middle Ages, terrestrial orchids with testiculate tubers were associated with human generative processes; in fact, the word *orchid* is derived from the Greek word for testicles, *orchis*.

Orchids are cosmopolitan, being found from the Arctic (*Habenaria hyperborea*) to the tropics and in almost every kind of habitat except desert. Most species, however, are tropical, and in the tropics most orchids are epiphytes, living upon other plants epiphytically but not parasitically. Temperate-zone orchids are mainly terrestrial, growing in soil. Some orchids are saprophytic, living on dead organic matter, such as leaf mold. A few grow completely underground. Cultivation of orchids is an important worldwide greenhouse industry. Thousands of hybrids have been created.

Flowers. Most orchids have small flowers, some as tiny as 3 mm (⅛ in), as in *Pleurothallis*. Others have large, broad-petaled flowers up to 23 cm (9 in) across, as in *Cattleya*, or long, threadlike petals that may span 60 cm (2 ft) from tip to tip, as in *Brassia*. Orchid flowers may be bisexual or unisexual, and they demonstrate a wide range of complexity that involves modifications for attracting or admitting only specific pollinators, such as certain butterflies or bees. Only about 200 species of orchids are known to be self pollinating, and none is known to be air- or water-pollinated.

The orchid flower's floral envelope consists of an outer whorl of three, usually equal-sized, petallike sepals and an inner whorl of three petals, two of which resemble the sepals; the third petal, called the lip or labellum, may be highly modified. The lip is in the upper position in the bud, but in most orchids it is eventually positioned in the lower part of the flower, a process called resupination.

The seed-bearing, or female, organ of the flower is the pistil. The top of the pistil, called the stigma, is three-lobed in orchids and serves as the deposition site for pollen. In most orchids a part of one of the three lobes is modified into a structure called a rostellum, used in transferring pollen from the anthers to the pollinating insect or other agent.

The male organ of the flower is the stamen, which possesses a pollen-producing head called the anther. A distinctive feature of the orchid flower is the fusion of the male stamen or stamens with the pistil into a single unit, or column.

Pollination. Pollen grains, produced by the anthers, are shed either singly or in attached groups. The groups range from four-unit tetrads to large pollen masses called pollinia. Pollination is effected by many kinds of insects and by hummingbirds and sunbirds. Because the pollen is commonly packeted and made unavailable, other means have been evolved to attract pollinators: the shape, color, and odor of the flowers and the presence of nectar and edible tissues. In some cases, to attract pollen eaters, the orchids form "pseudo-pollen" from grains of tissue. In certain instances the flower mimics the shape of the female of the pollinating insect, and males are sexually attracted to and try to copulate with the flower.

Seeds. The tiny seeds, perhaps as many as 4 million dustlike seeds in a single capsule of some species, are an excellent adaptation for dispersal by wind, but because of their small size the seeds contain no nutritive endosperm and no stored water. The embryo is unformed, consisting of only a few unorganized cells. Development of the seed leaf and other features does not occur until germination, and this commonly depends on the seed's association with certain mycorrhizal ("root") fungi. The fungi penetrate the seed and provide the embryo with carbohydrates

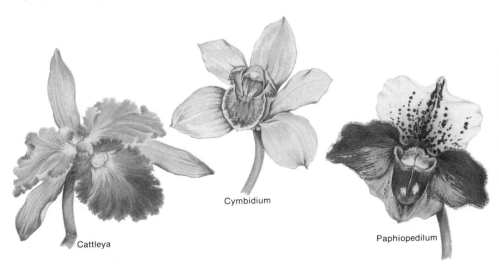

Cattleya

Cymbidium

Paphiopedilum

Popular commercial greenhouse orchids grown in the United States include Cattleya, *tropical American orchids that are commonly used for corsages and as ornamental plants.* Cymbidium, *native to tropical Asia and Australia, and* Cattleya *are grown for hybridization. Both* Paphiopedilum, *of tropical Asia, and* Cypripedium, *of North America, are called lady's slippers because they have a slipper-shaped lip.*

and other nutrients. Adult orchids ultimately digest some of the fungal threads.

Economic Use. Except for the horticulturally valuable species, this very large family has only one genus of economic importance: *Vanilla*, the source of the genuine vanilla of commerce. Other genera have minor uses. The boiled tubers of *Orchis* and *Satyrium* produce a starchy meal called salep. Faham tea is made from a fragrant *Angraecum*, and candy is made from pseudobulbs of *Cyrtopodium*. Other orchids are sources of food flavorings and primitive medicines.

Classification. The only certain orchid fossil, from rocks of the Eocene Epoch in Italy, is about 45 million years old, but orchids undoubtedly originated from the same ancestral stock as did the amaryllises (Amaryllidaceae) and the lilies (Liliaceae). Orchids are classified as the family Orchidaceae, order Orchidales, subclass Monocotyledonae. The family is generally divided into five subfamilies: Apostasioideae, Cypripedioideae, Orchidioideae, Neottioideae, and Epidendroideae.

Ordinance of 1787   see NORTHWEST TERRITORY

ordination   see MINISTRY, CHRISTIAN

ordnance   see AMMUNITION; ARTILLERY

Ordovician Period   see EARTH, GEOLOGICAL HISTORY OF; GEOLOGIC TIME

ore deposits
Modern industrial civilization is based primarily upon raw materials produced from various types of ore deposits. Machines are fabricated from metals, and even agriculture depends increasingly on metallic fuel-burning equipment and chemical fertilizers. Virtually all industrial energy is derived from coal, petroleum, and uranium.

An ore deposit is any geological, or nonrenewable, material that can be mined at a profit. Nonmetallic ores and fuels can be included in this economic definition, but only metallic ore deposits and their mineralogy, classification, distribution, genesis, and national importance will be discussed here. Although the size, assay (or tenor), shape, depth, and other geological characteristics of the deposit are important, nongeological factors also enter into this economic definition of ore. Nongeological factors include prices, geography, availability of transportation, labor contracts, and governmental policies.

An ore deposit has a high unit value if the ore minerals are so valuable that transportation costs do not greatly affect the economics of the mining operation. Conversely, if a mineral deposit must be close to a market in order to be economic, that deposit has a high place value. Most metals and fuels have high unit values; most nonmetallic deposits, especially sand and gravel, have high place values.

Ore Genesis

Metallic ore deposits are concentrations of metallic chemical elements well above their average crustal abun-

dance. For aluminum and iron the minimum necessary concentrations are only 2.2 and 3.4 times their crustal average. For many other metals, such as copper, molybdenum, nickel, uranium, and zinc, the concentration factor is between 100 and 1,000; for chromium and rare metals such as tungsten, lead, gold, silver, platinum, and mercury, ore deposits represent concentrations of more than 1,000 times the average crustal abundance.

Most ore minerals were precipitated from waters, gases, or magmas. Only a few kinds of deposits originated by the mechanical accumulation of chemically inert ore minerals (see PLACER DEPOSIT). The most common types of ore deposits are those which precipitate from hot, aqueous (hydrothermal) solutions. Most metals are soluble in hot, saline, sulfurous, and acidic waters; ores may be precipitated as these solutions cool and react with the rocks through which they pass (see ALTERATION, MINERAL). Thus hydrothermal ores are most commonly precipitated where former permeable zones or fissures intersected reactive rocks.

Classification

Ore deposits are rocks; thus they can be classified in the same manner as rocks. Since the Middle Ages, however, ore deposits have been and continue to be classified in a number of ways. Traditionally, they were classified according to shape, such as VEIN DEPOSITS, lodes, and stockworks.

Early in the 20th century scientists began classifying ore deposits according to environment of deposition. Most ore deposits were thought to have been precipitated from hydrothermal solutions derived from cooling granitic magmas. By the 1960s, however, heated groundwater and seawater had also been recognized as possible ore-forming solutions.

Some classifications of ore deposits rely on the age of the deposit compared to its surrounding rocks. Syngenetic deposits formed at the same time as the rocks were deposited; diagenetic deposits formed after deposition but before the rocks became lithified, or changed to stone; and epigenetic deposits formed after the rocks were lithified. Placer deposits are syngenetic; veins are epigenetic; and many base-metal deposits in sedimentary rocks appear to be syngenetic or diagenetic.

The present trend is to classify ore deposits descriptively without regard to origin. This classification uses type examples, such as Kambalda-type nickel deposits, or groups deposits into similar descriptive types. For example, porphyry copper deposit connotes various descriptive characteristics about copper deposits associated with granitic intrusions.

Distribution

Ore deposits are irregularly distributed within the Earth's crust. Their distribution depends primarily on the types of rocks present, the age of these rocks, the level of erosion with regard to these rocks, and, of course, nongeological factors. Processes that operate below the Earth's crust, such as subduction, may also be important (see PLATE TECTONICS). Each type of ore deposit is restricted to certain types of rocks. If erosion has removed the ore-bearing portion of these rocks, the area will be devoid of that particular type of ore deposit. Just as organic evolution restricted certain fossils to rocks of specific ages, evolution of the Earth's crustal lithologies, organisms, and atmosphere limited the time during which certain types of rocks and ore deposits formed. Lake Superior–type banded-iron formations and Witwatersrand-type conglomerates could no longer form when the atmosphere became oxygen-rich about 2.2 billion years ago.

Metallogenic provinces are portions of the Earth's crust that have unusual concentrations of one or more kinds of ore deposits. Examples are the porphyry-copper province of the southwestern United States and adjacent Mexico, the tin province of Southeast Asia, and the iron provinces of Kiruna, Sweden, and the Lake Superior region of the United States and Canada. The origin of metallogenic provinces is controversial, but rock types, the ages of the rocks, and the present level of erosion clearly are important factors.

Ore Reserves and Mineral Resources

The distinction between ore reserves and mineral resources is of prime economic and political importance. Reserves include all known deposits that can be profitably extracted under existing laws. To be identified as reserves, the material must have been actually sampled or be an inferred extension of sampled reserves. Resources are all identified mineral deposits that are uneconomic or illegal to mine plus estimates of undiscovered ores in known or undiscovered areas.

The estimation of reserves and identified resources is done by physically determining their size and assaying the deposits well enough to determine if they are ore or not. Conversely, unknown resources are estimated by various statistical methods, such as tabulating the amount of ore discovered per meter of drilling during the past year, the amount and rate of discoveries in past years, and the relative sizes of known deposits, and comparing the known or inferred geology of unprospected areas with the production and reserves of geologically similar known areas. Not surprisingly, the estimation of both reserves and resources is sensitive to changes in the price of the mineral commodity. A significant price increase, as in the case of uranium in the mid-1970s, may so encourage exploration that significant new reserves or resources are found.

Because the estimation of resources involves an estimation of the unknown, resources can never be known with certainty, and estimates of the same resources by

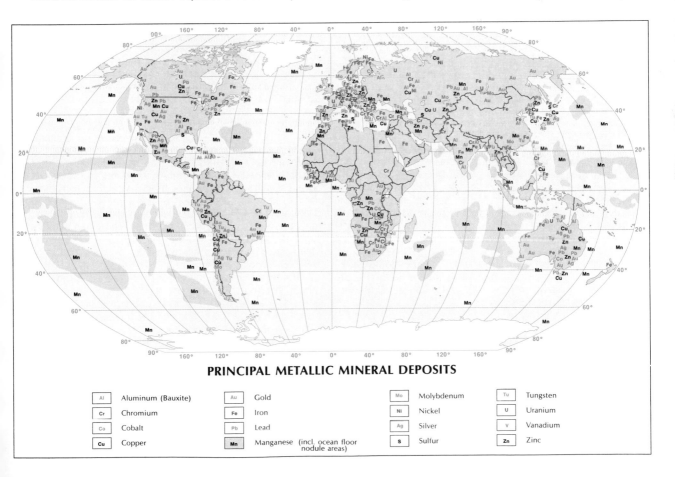

PRINCIPAL METALLIC MINERAL DEPOSITS

Al	Aluminum (Bauxite)	Au	Gold	Mo	Molybdenum	Tu	Tungsten
Cr	Chromium	Fe	Iron	Ni	Nickel	U	Uranium
Co	Cobalt	Pb	Lead	Ag	Silver	V	Vanadium
Cu	Copper	Mn	Manganese (incl. ocean floor nodule areas)	S	Sulfur	Zn	Zinc

different methods or by different experts may vary widely. Nonetheless, the estimation of resources has become increasingly important in determining the policies of nations whose economies depend heavily on the importation or exportation of minerals and fuels.

Research

Industry, government, and schools conduct research in an effort to increase reserves and resources. A new mining machine, drilling technique, or explosive may change previously uneconomic rock into ore. Much research is currently being conducted on new mining methods, especially the feasibility of leaching ores in place instead of extracting them by mechanical means. New techniques being developed for extracting ores from currently uneconomic deposits include grinding rock to ever finer particles to liberate the ore minerals, converting metals such as nickel in silicate minerals into synthetic sulfide minerals that can be routinely treated, and reducing iron ores to metallic iron in order to eliminate conventional smelting-stage techniques. New or improved geophysical techniques are being developed to detect hidden ore deposits. Simultaneously, exploration geologists look for known types of deposits that might have been uneconomic to mine in the past and for totally new types of deposits in geological environments that might not have been considered a few years earlier.

The most fundamental kind of research in mineral exploration is geological mapping of existing and prospective ore deposits. Mapping the distribution of rock types, alteration-mineral assemblages, mineralization, and geological structures such as faults, fractures, and folds of known deposits commonly leads to the discovery of previously unknown extensions of ore bodies. A thorough geological understanding of an existing ore deposit generally is the basis for discovering similar deposits in similar geological environments elsewhere.

Geochemical prospecting has become increasingly important since the 1960s because of the development of rapid and inexpensive instrumental techniques, especially atomic absorption, for determining trace amounts of several metals in large numbers of samples. Trace amounts of various metals in stream sediments are used in reconnaissance exploration just as previous prospectors used the gold pan to trace placer gold to the mother lode. Soils, plants, waters, and rocks also are analyzed for trace amounts of metals in hopes of finding concealed ore deposits (see GEOCHEMISTRY).

The airborne magnetometer, developed to detect submarines in World War II, is the basis for various airborne geophysical techniques that have been developed for mineral exploration. Geological, geochemical, or airborne geophysical anomalies commonly are checked by geophysical techniques on the ground. In most cases a combination of geological, geochemical, and geophysical techniques is necessary to verify and to evaluate the discovery of a deposit.

Once a potential ore deposit has been discovered, its size (tonnage) and grade (tenor) must be determined to decide whether it is economic to mine. Ultimately this involves extensive sampling of the deposit by drill holes, pits and trenches, exploratory shafts, and underground workings. If the ore reserves appear to be sufficient, additional engineering, marketing, and other feasibility studies are conducted on nongeological factors to determine whether the deposit can be mined at a profit.

Factors Peculiar to the Mining Industry

The mining industry (see MINING AND QUARRYING) differs from agricultural and manufacturing industries in a number of important ways. First, mineral deposits are nonrenewable; that is, once mined they are gone forever. This "one-crop" nature of mineral deposits is partially offset by the recycling or scrap return of most metals and some nonmetals. Second, the uneven distribution of ore deposits in the Earth's crust has historically promoted political problems between have and have-not nations and between the mining industry and groups wishing to preserve areas as wilderness. Finally, the capital investment required to find and develop ore deposits and bring them into profitable production must be undertaken over a time period longer than that needed for agricultural or other industrial enterprises; 3 to 7 years is not unusual.

Political and Economic Importance

Within the past century national power has become virtually synonymous with industrial power, and the growth of industrial power has almost always begun with the national possession of mineral resources.

A generalized model of industrial development based on the exploitation of mineral resources will show a correlation between the opening and development of mines, the building of smelters, the production of metal, and the economic growth of a region. During the initial period of mine development, ore deposits are discovered and mines built. During the next period output increases from fewer but larger mines, and expropriation by revolution, decree, or taxation may take place. In the third period, the abundant output of metals encourages a burgeoning of industry. The cost of raw materials decreases due to plentiful domestic supplies, and foreign minerals begin to be imported to meet the growing demand. As internal and foreign markets expand, the average standard of living rises. Growing dependence on foreign mineral resources and markets increasingly involve the country in international affairs.

The depletion of a cheap supply of domestic raw materials (the fourth period) usually signals the economic and political decline of a nation (fifth period). Dependence on foreign materials leads to increased manufacturing costs, which ultimately generate social problems and political unrest. The country that started with abundant, inexpensively minable resources has now become a have-not, or at least a "have-less," nation. Such a nation may improve its status by a variety of methods. In the past the most common were the acquisition of mineral resources by political alliance, economic domination, military conquest, or some combination of the three.

Great Britain has passed through all five periods and has now lost the position it held in the late 19th century as the world's leading mining, industrial, and military power. The United States lags one period behind Britain; it is still at the stage where it possesses mineral resources, but in diminishing quantities. Japan continues to be a major industrial power despite inadequate domestic mineral deposits and its unsuccessful attempt to obtain foreign deposits in World War II. A partial explanation of this anomalous condition is that Japan is the only major industrial power whose constitution forbids the maintenance of significant military forces. The money thus saved has been used to acquire foreign ore deposits, to expand the merchant marine, and to modernize industry.

oregano [uh-reg'-uh-noh]   Oregano is the name given to several species of plants whose leaves, when dried, impart a particular flavor to food. The common oregano of Europe and America is *Origanum heracleoticum,* of the Labiatae family, often mistakenly confused with wild marjoram, *O. vulgare.* The more pungent Mexican or Puerto Rican oregano is usually *Lippia graveolens,* of the VERBENA family, Verbenaceae.

Oregon   Oregon, one of the states of the northwest, lies along the Pacific Ocean coast. It is bordered by the state of Washington on the north, Idaho on the east, and Nevada and California on the south. Oregon ranks 10th in area among the U.S. states with 251,419 km^2 (97,073 mi^2), and 29th in population with 2,853,733 (1990). The capital is Salem. The origin of the name *Oregon* is uncertain, but one account traces the name to a corruption of the French word for Wisconsin (Ouisconsin). The name *Oregon* was first applied to a fictitious river, believed to rise in the upper Midwest and to flow westward to the Pacific. For many years the region was known as the "American West." During the 1840s it was defined as Oregon Territory, extending from the Rocky Mountain continental divide to the Pacific Ocean and from California to Alaska. Oregon, the Beaver State, was admitted to the Union in 1859, and the remaining part of the original territory now forms the Canadian province of British Columbia and the states of Washington and Idaho and western Montana.

Physiographic Regions. Seven distinct physical regions are generally recognized. The COAST RANGE (highest elevation: Marys Peak, 1,249 m/4,097 ft) extends along the state's coast in the west. Most of the surface is best described as rough, hilly land rather than as mountainous terrain. The Klamath Mountains, sometimes called the Siskiyou Mountains (highest elevation: Mount Ashland, 2,296 m/7,533 ft), extend southeast from the Coast Range near the California border. They are higher and more rugged than the Coast Range.

AT A GLANCE

OREGON

Land: Area: 251,419 km^2 (97,073 mi^2); rank: 10th. Capital: Salem (1990 pop., 107,786). Largest city: Portland (1990 pop., 437,319). Counties: 36. Elevations: highest—3,426 m (11,239 ft), at Mount Hood; lowest—sea level, at the Pacific.

People: Population (1990): 2,853,733; rank: 29th; density: 11.4 persons per km^2 (29.4 per mi^2). Distribution (1988 est.): 67.7% metropolitan, 32.3% nonmetropolitan. Average annual change (1980–90): +0.8%.

Government (1991). Governor: Barbara Roberts, Democrat. U.S. Congress: Senate—2 Republicans; House—4 Democrats, 1 Republican. Electoral college votes: 7. State legislature: 30 senators, 60 representatives.

Economy: State personal income (1988): $41.2 billion; rank: 30th. Median family income (1979): $20,027; rank: 21st. Agriculture: income (1988)—$2.1 billion. Fishing: value (1988)—$98 million. Forestry: sawtimber volume (1987)—378.6 billion board feet. Mining: value (1987)—$5.7 billion. Manufacturing: value added (1987)—$11.6 billion. Services: value (1987)—$9.1 billion.

Miscellany: Statehood: Feb. 14, 1859; the 33d state. Nickname: Beaver State; tree: Douglas fir; mottoes: The Union, and She flies with her own wings; song: "Oregon, My Oregon."

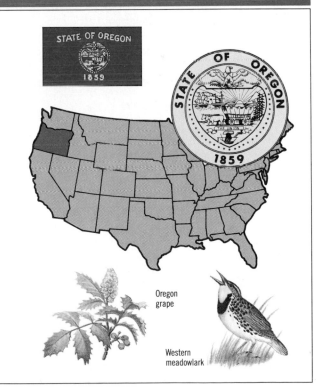

Oregon grape

Western meadowlark

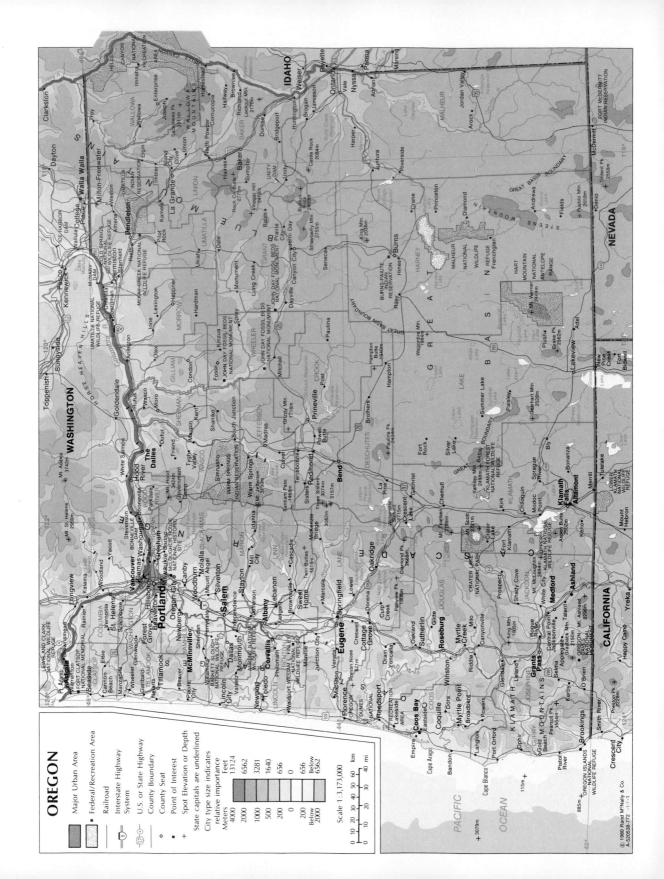

Portland, Oregon's largest city and principal port, lies at the confluence of the Willamette and Columbia rivers, with snow-capped Mount Hood in the distance.

The Willamette River valley (elevations generally below 130 m/430 ft) is located east of the Coast Range and is up to 80 km (50 mi) wide. The generally even surface is interrupted here and there by low isolated hills. Two-thirds of Oregon's population live in the valley.

The CASCADE RANGE (highest elevation: Mount HOOD, 3,427 m/11,245 ft) extends for the entire length of the state east of the Willamette River valley. Most of the range is forested, and melting snow supplies the adjacent lowlands with water during the dry summer. The Deschutes-Umatilla plateau (elevations up to about 2,100 m/6,900 ft) is located east of the Cascades. This plateau is Oregon's wheat belt. Northeast of the Deschutes-Umatilla plateau is the Blue Mountain region. Several distinct mountain masses and plateaus occur: the Wallowa Mountains and the Elkhorn and Greenhorn ranges. These were glaciated, and many lakes and spectacular landscapes resulted, including the 1.6-km-deep (1-mi) Snake River canyon.

Southeastern Oregon is made up of two distinct surfaces: the high lava plains, averaging about 1,200 m (4,000 ft) in elevation with many dry lake beds and some intermittent lakes; and further south the BASIN AND RANGE PROVINCE (highest point: Steens Mountain, 3,968 m/9,670 ft), with alternating broad basins and north-south-trending wooded ranges. Southeastern Oregon is sometimes called the Oregon Desert, but most of it is semiarid; only a few small areas have a desert climate.

Rivers and Lakes. The COLUMBIA RIVER flows through northern Oregon, creating the border with Washington; the river and its tributaries drain 58% of Oregon's land area. Most of the remainder drains directly to the Pacific Ocean. The lower Columbia River has a mean flow of over 7,000 m³/sec (247,000 ft³/sec), making it the third largest river in the United States. Its two principal tributaries are the SNAKE RIVER and WILLAMETTE RIVER.

Of Oregon's numerous lakes, 20 exceed 10 km² (3.8 mi²) in area, and 20 reservoirs are of comparable size. Klamath Lake is the state's largest; CRATER LAKE is the deepest in the United States (589 m/1,932 ft).

Climate. Rainfall and temperature are affected mainly by altitude and the distance from the ocean. At low altitudes the January temperature varies from 2° C to 10° C (35° F to 50° F); July temperatures range from 13° C to 24° C (55° F to 75° F). Precipitation ranges from less than 250 mm (10 in) in the southeast to more than 2,500 mm (100 in) on the western slopes of the Coast Range and Cascades. In the high mountains more than half of the precipitation is in the form of snow. Almost all the precipitation occurs during winter.

Vegetation and Animal Life. The coniferous trees include Douglas fir—which, as the principal timber tree, makes Oregon the leading lumber state—and ponderosa pine, Sitka spruce, and hemlock. The main hardwoods are oak, maple, and alder. Large areas in eastern Oregon are covered with grass or sagebrush. The heaviest forests are located in the Coast Range, Klamath Mountains, and Cascade Mountains, but large portions of these areas have been cut over. Animal life includes large game animals (deer, antelope, elk, and bear), as well as many kinds of small game, game birds, and waterfowl. Seals, sea lions, sea otters, and whales are seen in season along the coast.

Mineral Resources. Oregon has a variety of minerals, many of which occur in small deposits that are unprofitable to mine except in times of high prices. The recent increase in the price of gold has made it practicable to reopen some previously closed mines. Other metals include lead, silver, chromium, and copper. Oregon is the only major producer of nickel in the United States.

People

The population of Oregon is unevenly distributed. Large areas have less than 1 person per km² (2.6 per mi²),

Workers separate logs on a storage pond near Vaughn, Oreg. With coniferous forests covering approximately 50% of its total land area, Oregon has long been the nation's principal producer of wood products.

whereas areas near the large cities have more than 500 people per km^2 (1,300 per mi^2). More than a third of the population live in the 12 largest cities, each of which has more than 25,000 inhabitants. The leading cities are PORTLAND, EUGENE, SALEM, Corvallis, Springfield, MEDFORD, Beaverton, and Gresham. The Portland metropolitan area has a population of 1,239,842 (1990).

The population is predominantly Caucasian. The African-American, Asian-American, and Indian communities are not large but are increasing. Oregon's population is increasing more rapidly than that of the United States as a whole, largely because of an annual net in-migration. About one-third of Oregon's population claim church membership, but a dozen Christian denominations are well represented, including the Roman Catholics, Baptists, Methodists, Lutherans, Presbyterians, Mormons, and Episcopalians, as are the Jews.

Higher Education and Cultural Activity. The state system of higher education includes seven institutions, including the University of Oregon (1872) at Eugene. About half of the private colleges are located in or near Portland, including Reed College. The chief libraries are located at the universities, at the State Capitol in Salem, and at the Oregon Historical Society in Portland. Both Portland and Eugene have symphony orchestras and art museums.

Communications. Of Oregon's daily newspapers, Portland's *Oregonian/Oregon Journal* has the largest circulation. The *Eugene Register-Guard* is considered the state's best. Oregon has 12 commercial television stations and 117 such radio stations.

Economy

Oregon's economy has gradually shifted from an emphasis on agriculture to an emphasis on wood industries, manufacturing, and service industries.

Agriculture. Oregon's main crops are hay, wheat, barley, fruits, vegetables, grass seed, potatoes, and sugar beets. Livestock includes beef cattle, dairy cows, sheep, and poultry. The chief agricultural regions are the Willamette Valley and the Deschutes-Umatilla plateau.

Forestry and Fishing. Oregon's forests are the lifeblood of the state's economy. The harvest of timber and the processing of lumber, plywood, and paper are the largest sources of income. The Douglas fir tree is the chief source of timber, but other species such as ponderosa pine and spruce also contribute. Some alder, maple, and oak are used in the manufacture of furniture. About half of Oregon's timber reserve is on private land, and half is in national forests. Commercial fishing is a minor occupation in Oregon; salmon, halibut, hake, tuna, crab, and shrimp are the most important species.

Manufacturing and Energy. The wood industries—lumber, plywood, and paper—are the state's most important industries, although there have been some efforts at diversification of the economy. Food processing and metalworking are other major industries. Most of the state's industrial plant is concentrated in the Willamette Valley.

Oregon depends on hydroelectric power, imported oil, natural gas, and coal; wood waste; nuclear power; and, to a limited extent, geothermal power. Hydroelectric power provides about half of the state's energy needs. Most of the state's power plants are located on the Columbia River and on the margins of the Cascade Range. There is a power distribution grid interconnecting Oregon, Washington, and parts of Idaho and Montana.

Transportation. Oregon has two major interstate highways—I-5 and I-84—and is served by three major freight-carrying rail systems. There is rail passenger service to the larger Oregon cities of Portland, Salem, and Eugene. The international airport is at Portland, as is the state's major deepwater port. Other ports are at Astoria, Newport, and Coos Bay. The Columbia River is the state's major inland waterway.

Recreation and Tourism. Many thousands of Oregonians and visitors from other states and countries take

The Columbia River cuts through the basalt plateaus of Oregon's Cascade Range in a scenic gorge approximately 100 km (60 mi) long. The economically vital river is the primary source of hydroelectric power in the Northwest.

Herds of beef cattle are driven along a highway in the Blue Mountains of northeastern Oregon. The area's plateaus and rolling terrain contain the large ranches that make livestock so important to Oregon's agriculture.

advantage each year of the state's fishing, hunting, camping, skiing, cycling, and hiking facilities, helping to make travel and tourism one of Oregon's major employers. Among the state's various recreational establishments is Oregon's one national park—Crater Lake (established in 1902).

Government and Politics

Under the constitution adopted in 1857 and later amended, Oregon is governed by 3 branches: the legislative, with 30 senators and 60 representatives; the executive, including a governor elected for 4 years and 5 cabinet offices; and a judicial branch with a 7-member supreme court, a court of appeals, and circuit and district courts.

From the standpoint of politics Oregon is a constantly changing enigma. Voter registration usually shows a Democratic majority, but the vote often goes Republican. The state's U.S. senators and five congressional representatives regularly represent a party mix. Regional differences tend to change from time to time, but in general the coast counties are Democratic, the Willamette Valley is equally divided, and eastern Oregon is Republican.

History

Early History. Indians came to Oregon at least 10,000 years ago and included the BANNOCK, CHINOOK, KLAMATH, MODOC, and NEZ PERCÉ tribes. The first European fur traders, even before Lewis and Clark, were welcomed by the Indians for the trinkets, tools, guns, and whiskey they provided; but the Indians resented the arrival of permanent settlers, and many battles were fought before the Indians were subdued and placed on reservations.

Many ships touched the Oregon coast in the late 1700s and early 1800s, but these contacts provided little information about the interior. From 1805 to 1806, Meriwether Lewis and William Clark made the first land exploration (see LEWIS AND CLARK EXPEDITION). Their report created much excitement in the eastern United States, and

Americans began to think of taking possession of this distant land. Great Britain was also interested. In 1811, ASTORIA was founded as a fur-trading station by John Jacob Astor's AMERICAN FUR COMPANY, and the HUDSON'S BAY COMPANY soon thereafter began to trap and trade in the area.

Settlement and Economic Growth. The first white settlers arrived in the 1830s, and after 1840 immigration increased. A territorial government was formed in 1843, and provision was made to establish land ownership. A boundary dispute with Great Britain was settled in 1846, fixing the northern border of what was to become Oregon Territory as the 49th parallel (see OREGON QUESTION).

With the arrival of new settlers the population increased rapidly, from 12,000 (not counting Indians) in 1850 to 318,000 in 1890. The settlers brought with them a variety of seeds and livestock, even including hives of bees, with the intention of farming. Some, however, were diverted by the gold rush to California in 1849 and others by the discovery of gold in southwestern Oregon in 1850 and in eastern Oregon in 1860. Gold mining in the southwest and east stimulated farming and ranching.

In 1859, Oregon became the 33d state to be admitted to the Union. In the 1870s railroad building aided the timber and other industries and enabled Oregon fruits to be marketed fresh in the eastern markets.

The Modern Era. In the 20th century the population continued to grow, especially the urban population, as people moved to the cities from rural areas. State and local planners began to regulate the use of various resources, including forests, grasslands, fisheries, and power production. The present and future pose many problems—pollution, unemployment, depletion of resources, and the need to develop new sources of energy.

Oregon Question   The Oregon Question concerned ownership of the Oregon country—the Pacific Northwest between the parallels of 42° and 54°40' north, the area

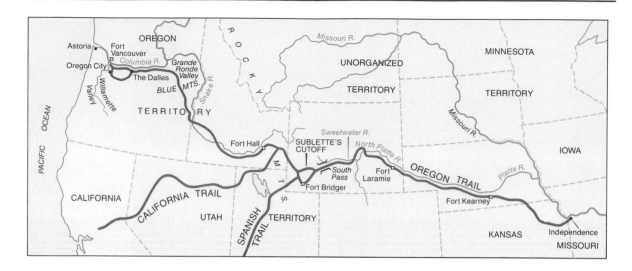

north of present-day California and south of the Alaskan panhandle. After a long dispute, the question was finally settled on June 15, 1846, by a treaty between the United States and Great Britain.

In the 18th century the area became an object of contention among France, Spain, Russia, Britain, and the United States. By the early 19th century, France and Spain had surrendered any claim to the area, and the Russians, by treaties of 1824–25, agreed to accept a southern boundary of 54°40' north for their Alaska territory. The United States and Britain agreed, by the Convention of 1818, to accept 49° north as the boundary between British North America and the United States, from the Lake of the Woods (between present Minnesota and Manitoba) to the Continental Divide; Oregon country west of the Rockies was open to joint occupation.

British trappers of the HUDSON'S BAY COMPANY dominated the area in the 1820s and '30s despite some incursions by MOUNTAIN MEN and missionaries from the United States. In 1843, however, the agricultural potential of the region began attracting large numbers of settlers afflicted with "Oregon fever." Arriving via the Oregon Trail, these settlers posed a threat to British fur-trapping interests. Britain wanted the northern U.S. boundary set at a line along the Columbia River but was willing to compromise at 49° north because the fur yield in the disputed area had diminished. (The Hudson's Bay Company had moved its major trading post north to Vancouver Island.) The United States, however, continued to demand the 54°40' line, although there were only a few American settlers in that area. American sentiment favoring 54°40' was rising. The Democrat James K. POLK was elected president in 1844 on an expansionist platform that seemed to claim "All Oregon." "Fifty-Four-Forty or Fight" became an emotional expansionist slogan, but in 1846, Polk accepted a boundary at 49°. Oregon Territory was created in 1848, its boundaries extending from the 42d to the 49th parallel.

Oregon Trail   During the 1840s and 1850s the Oregon Trail, which stretched about 3,200 km (about 2,000 mi) from Independence, Mo., to Fort Vancouver (on the site of modern Vancouver, Wash.), carried thousands of American pioneers to the rich farmland of the Willamette Valley in the Oregon country. The main trail ran west and then northwest to Fort Kearney (in present Nebraska), then west again along the Platte and North Platte rivers to Fort Laramie (now in Wyoming). It went through the Rockies via South Pass, turned north to Fort Hall, followed the Snake River to Fort Boise (both in what is now Idaho), and then moved northwest to the Columbia River. The trail's last stretch was the Columbia itself, usually navigated by raft to Fort Vancouver.

Explorers, fur trappers, and traders opened parts of the route during the early 19th century. A group of missionary families, led by Marcus WHITMAN, opened new stretches of the trail in 1836. Reports from these and other Protestant missions and from the Roman Catholic Pierre DE SMET encouraged others to make the trip to Oregon to establish farms. The resulting "Oregon fever" broke out in the spring of 1843, when about 1,000 men, women, and children gathered at Independence with their wagons to make the 6-month trek. By 1846 more than 6,000 people had used the trail. The discovery of gold in California in 1848 reduced the flow of traffic to Oregon, and by the 1860s use of the trail had dwindled considerably.

Orellana, Francisco de [ohr-ayl-yah'-nah]   Francisco de Orellana, b. c.1511, d. November 1546, was a Spanish explorer who discovered the Amazon River. He participated in Francisco Pizarro's conquest of Peru in the 1530s and set out from Quito on an expedition, led by Gonzalo Pizarro, to explore interior areas of South America. Orellana abandoned the main party and followed the Napo River to the Amazon. His party drifted down the river, reaching the Atlantic in August 1542. He told of encounters with female warriors, like the Amazons of classical legend.

Oresteia [ohr-es-tee'-uh]   The *Oresteia*, first produced in Athens in 458 BC, is the only surviving trilogy by AESCHYLUS, the earliest of ancient Greece's three great tragic dramatists. The plot is drawn from Greek myth, and the dramatic themes are vengeance, retribution, and divine justice. In the *Agamemnon*, King AGAMEMNON of Mycenae returns home after conquering Troy, unaware that he has been cursed by the gods for earlier misdeeds, including the sacrifice of his daughter IPHIGENIA. He meets his death at the hands of his wife, CLYTEMNESTRA, and her lover, Aegisthus, who then take over the throne. In the second play, the *Choephoroe*, or *Libation Bearers*, Clytemnestra and her lover are murdered by her son, ORESTES, acting on divine orders to avenge the death of his father. With this act of violence, Orestes and his sister ELECTRA also become victims of the curse that hangs over the house of ATREUS. In the *Eumenides*, the final play, Orestes, after being hounded by the avenging FURIES, is tried before the court of the Areopagus established by the goddess Athena and is there absolved of his guilt.

Orestes [ohr-es'-teez]   In Greek mythology Orestes was the son of CLYTEMNESTRA and AGAMEMNON, king of Mycenae and commander in chief of the Greeks in the Trojan War. Shortly after Agamemnon returned from Troy, Clytemnestra and Aegisthus, her lover, slew him. Despite the fact that matricide was a serious crime, Orestes avenged Agamemnon's death by killing Clytemnestra and her lover.

In Aeschylus's *Oresteia*, Orestes is ordered by Apollo to commit this act and is helped by his sister ELECTRA and his friend Pylades. At first Orestes is condemned by the gods for his actions, despite the favorable oracle from Apollo, but eventually he is exonerated by Athena and the FURIES, who, in the process, transformed themselves into the more benign Eumenides. Sophocles, Euripides, and later writers give slightly different versions of the story.

Orff, Carl [ohrf]   The German composer Carl Orff, b. Munich, July 10, 1895, d. Mar. 29, 1982, was one of the most successful composers of modern opera although he remained outside the mainstream of operatic fashions and trends. He also contributed to music education for the young through his widely used method that combines music with motion and incorporates the use of new and simple instruments, mostly percussion instruments.

Before 1937, Orff's works included songs, operas, theater scores, and orchestral and chamber music. His "scenic" cantata *Carmina Burana*, based on medieval poetry, was completed in 1937, also marking the begin-

ning of his exclusive attention to music for the theater. *Carmina Burana* was the first of a trilogy of works that also includes *Catulli Carmina* (1943) and *Trionfo di Afrodite* (1953). For his operas *Der Mond* (1937–38) and *Die Kluge* (1941–42), Orff wrote his own librettos based on fairy tales. He drew on classical antiquity for *Antigonae* (1947–48), *Oedipus der Tyrann* (1958; in German translations), and *Prometheus* (1968), which uses the original Greek text by Aeschylus.

Orff's last works include *Play from the End of Time*, which was premiered at the Salzburg Festival in 1973. Orff often used a large orchestra to convey word-engendered, highly rhythmic melodies and a dancelike rhythm that always served a dramatic purpose.

organ   The largest and most complex of all musical instruments, the conventional, or pipe, organ produces its sound when air, actuated by a keyboard, is blown through pipes of graduated sizes. (Electric and electronic organs substitute electromechanical or electronic devices to produce an organ sound, and may surpass the pipe organ in the variety of sounds they can create; see ELECTRONIC MUSIC.)

Mechanism

The pipes may be of the flue type, in which the air column inside the pipe is set into vibration by a stream of air passing over a sharp edge at the base of the pipe; or they may be of the reed type, activated by a beating reed, consisting of a slightly curved metal tongue vibrating in a slit in a metal tube (the shallot) set into the base of the pipe. The pipes are made in various cylindrical and conical shapes to produce distinctive timbres, or tone colors. Each rank, or set of pipes, consists of a series of pipes of one tonal design, gradated in size to produce all the pitches within the instrument's compass. In addition to sets of pipes at normal or "8-foot" pitch (so named because the pipe for the lowest note in such a rank, C, is approximately 8 feet long), there are sets of pipes constructed at 16 foot, 4-foot, 2-foot, and 1-foot pitches that sound, respectively, an octave below, or one, two, or three octaves above the note played. (There are also some ranks built at pitches other than the octave, for example, the quint [5⅓ feet], the twelfth [2⅔ feet], the tierce [1⅗ feet].)

The feet of the pipes are set into a channeled box, the "wind chest." A system of valves in the wind chest (the pallets), controlled through the action by a keyboard, admit air from the wind supply to sound the pipes. The wind supply may consist of manually or mechanically driven bellows or an electric blower. Linkage between the valves in the wind chest and the keyboard may be mechanical, pneumatic, electrical, or a combination thereof.

The organ is played by one or more keyboards, each of which usually controls one division of pipework, or more than one division through coupling, located on its own wind chest. In addition to manuals (keyboards played by the fingers of the hands) an organ usually has a keyboard for the feet, or pedal board. A thin batten called a slider passes under each rank of pipes. Controlled by stop knobs located near the keyboards, sliders govern the number of ranks, or stops, in use at any one time.

History

A mechanical adaptation of the primitive mouth-blown PANPIPES, the organ first appeared in the Hellenistic world. Ktesebios of Alexandria (3d century BC) is credited with

the invention of the hydraulus, or water organ, so called because the wind reservoir was immersed in water, the displacement of which served to maintain an even wind pressure.

Developments during the late Middle Ages include the balanced keyboard, the tracker-and-roller system of mechanical linkage between the pallets, and a keyboard that increased the size of the pipework possible in a given di-

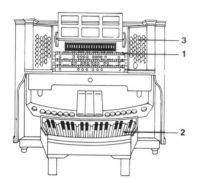

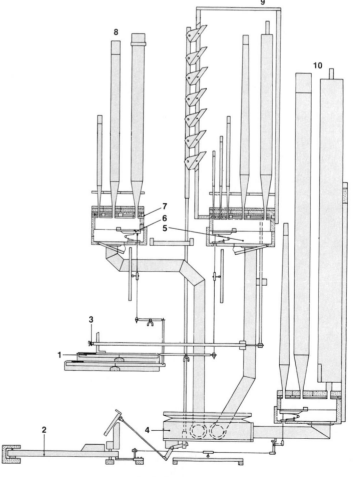

The pipe organ, which developed from a simple aerophone first known to the ancient Greeks, has become the most complex of all musical instruments. Although simpler organs, such as the 18th-century chamber organ (below left), use similar components, they lack the range and grandeur of the full pipe organ. Organs consist of three sections: the pipes, each of which produces a single tone; the console (above left), which contains keyboards or manuals (1), pedal board (2), and stops (3); and the action or mechanism, a system linking pipes to a constant wind supply and to the console. A schematic diagram (below) illustrates the operation of these parts through the traditional "tracker" mechanism, a system of levers controlling airflow. Air in a pressure-regulated reservoir (4) is admitted to wind chests (5) below the separate ranks, groups of pipes having the same tone quality. When a key (1) or pedal (2) is depressed, valves (6) admit air to specific pipes. Stops (3) regulate tone quality by moving pierced sliders (7) that can open or close ("stop") entire ranks of pipes. The organ's pipes are grouped in large divisions, which are controlled by separate keyboards and often differ in intensity and range. These include the great organ (8), the main division of pipes; the swell organ (9); and the deep pipes of the pedal organ (10).

vision. The following centuries (16th–18th) witnessed the consolidation and coordination of the various divisions of the organ. The main, or great, organ was characterized by the "principal chorus" of full-sounding flue pipes at various pitch levels. The choir organ, a separate instrument placed behind the player, had a somewhat softer-sounding complement of stops. In larger instruments there was frequently a third division positioned above and in front of the great organ. This division was later enclosed in a box with venetian shutters, the opening and closing of which made possible crescendo and diminuendo—hence the name *swell organ*. The instruments of northern Europe featured an independent division controlled by a pedal board.

The romantic organ of the 19th century emphasized a broad range of dynamics and tone colors, particularly stops that imitated orchestral instruments. The inventions of the pneumatic lever, the tubular pneumatic action, and the electromagnetic action allowed much greater flexibility in the size, layout, and location of the instrument than did the old mechanical action. During the 20th century, historical instruments have been restored and imitated, and new organs are usually designed to allow performance of music from various historical periods.

organ transplant see TRANSPLANTATION, ORGAN

organic chemistry The name *organic chemistry* originated at the beginning of the 19th century, when scientists wished to differentiate between those substances derived from plant and animal (organic) sources and those derived from inanimate (inorganic) materials. It was believed that organic substances had special qualities and could be created only in the presence of the "vital force" found in living organisms. Even though the vital-force theory was eventually disproved, the classification of chemical substances as organic or inorganic has continued to the present.

The modern usage of "organic chemistry" refers to the chemistry of compounds containing carbon. These organic substances are generally characterized by chains of connected carbon atoms. Millions of such organic compounds are known.

Many of these are "natural products," or compounds found in nature. The study of the large organic molecules found in living systems and their reactions, which make up the life processes, has come to be called biochemistry. A large number of the known organic chemicals have been synthesized in the laboratory, and our society is dependent on such synthetic materials as plastics, synthetic fibers, dyes, detergents, and insecticides. The chemical and allied-product industries contribute a large portion of the gross national product of the United States. The vast majority of synthetic products are derived from petroleum, and as the world's supply of petroleum decreases, new sources of carbon-containing raw materials will have to be found. Also, it has become apparent that many organic compounds, both synthesized and natural, have deleterious effects both on the environment and on

living organisms. Future developments in organic chemistry must take these effects into account.

History and Development

Organic chemistry began to evolve as a science in the early 19th century. Between 1769 and 1785, the Swedish chemist Carl Wilhelm SCHEELE had isolated and characterized a large number of chemical substances derived from living systems. Little was known about the chemical composition of these substances, however, until the French scientist Antoine LAVOISIER developed his classic combustion experiments in the late 18th century. Lavoisier devised a method of burning these compounds in pure oxygen gas and found that the combustion products were carbon dioxide, CO_2, and water, H_2O, indicating that the compounds contained carbon and hydrogen. Extensions of Lavoisier's work showed that all such compounds contained carbon and hydrogen and that many contained oxygen and nitrogen as well. These substances isolated from living organisms were first called organic compounds by the Swedish chemist Jöns Jakob BERZELIUS in 1807. So far it had proved to be impossible to prepare any of these compounds in the laboratory, and the belief was held that their synthesis involved a "vital force" present only in living organisms. Berzelius felt that the synthesis of organic substances was impossible. He was proved wrong, however, in 1828, when the German chemist Friedrich WÖHLER converted ammonium cyanate, NH_4OCN, a purely inorganic substance, into urea, $CO(NH_2)_2$, an end product of animal metabolism.

Wöhler's preparation of urea had another important consequence in that it furnished an example of two substances, urea and ammonium cyanate, which had the same chemical composition but very different properties. As experimental techniques improved, it became clear that there were other examples of more than one substance having the same composition. In the 1830s, Berzelius used the term *isomerism* (composed of equal parts) to describe this phenomenon, but an understanding of isomerism was not possible until the structure of these compounds became understood later in the century.

The mid-19th century saw the steady development of systematic organic research. A key step in this development was the establishment of the idea of radicals as the organic equivalent of atoms. Radicals were groups of atoms that retained their chemical identity during a chemical reaction. In simpler compounds these radicals contained only hydrogen and carbon (hydrocarbon radicals). In 1832, Wöhler and Justus von LIEBIG produced a series of compounds all containing the benzoyl radical, C_7H_5O, and their work encouraged others to discover new radicals by systematic reactions of organic compounds.

At about the time the radical theory was becoming firmly established, a new way of looking at organic reactions was introduced by two French scientists, Jean Baptiste Dumas and Auguste Laurent. The basis of this new theory was substitution. Dumas recognized that an atom of one element may replace that of another element in an organic compound. Laurent generalized Dumas's ideas, saying that radicals replace each other by substitution.

Although Laurent's idea was scoffed at by several noted chemists, he showed in 1837 that his theory was the basis for a classification of organic compounds. Laurent's associate, Charles Gerhardt, was another scientist who found little recognition for his ideas. An important contribution made by Gerhardt was the theory of "residues." He applied this theory in 1839 to reactions in which two organic molecules combine, eliminating part of each to form a simple compound such as H_2O or HCl while the organic "residues or radicals" combine together. An example he used was the reaction of benzene and nitric acid to form nitrobenzene with the elimination of water:

$$C_6H_5H + HONO_2 \rightarrow HOH + C_6H_5NO_2$$

Gerhardt also introduced the term *homologous series* to describe a series of compounds in which members differ by multiples of the molecular fragment CH_2. An example of such a series is methane (CH_4), ethane (C_2H_6), propane (C_3H_8), butane (C_4H_{10}), and so on.

A milestone in the development of structural organic chemistry came in 1858, when Friedrich August Kekulé in Heidelberg and Archibald Scott Couper in Paris independently introduced the general rules of valence bonds and the pictorial representation of a molecule as a group of connected atoms. They postulated that a carbon atom always has a constant valence of four; hydrogen and chlorine, one; oxygen, two; and nitrogen, three. Kekulé introduced a graphical representation of valence. In this representation, methane, CH_4, becomes

$$H - \overset{\displaystyle H}{\underset{\displaystyle H}{C}} - H$$

where a line between elements means that one valence of each atom has been used to establish a valence bond. The idea that carbon is tetravalent led Kekulé to propose that in many organic compounds carbon atoms are linked together. To support his theory of constant valence, Kekulé had to invent the multiple-bond concept. The valence of an atom then became the number of bonds that the atom can form. For example, in ethylene, C_2H_4,

$$\overset{\displaystyle H}{\underset{\displaystyle H}{C}} = \overset{\displaystyle H}{\underset{\displaystyle H}{C}}$$

carbon is bonded to only three atoms, but it still has a valence of four because of the double bond between the carbon atoms. Eventually the theory of constant valence was shown not to hold for many atoms. It does hold for carbon, however, and the structural ideas and multiple-bond concept to which it gave rise are extremely important in modern chemistry.

This new structural theory did not appreciate that molecules are three-dimensional. In 1874, however, Jacobus Henricus van't Hoff and Joseph Achille Le Bel independently proposed that the four bonds of carbon were located at equal angles to each other in space. This meant the four bonds were directed at the four corners of a tetrahedron, with the carbon atom at its center.

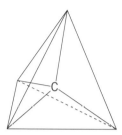

Their proposal was a correct description of the four carbon bonds, but at the time their ideas were not readily accepted.

The elucidation of the structures of organic molecules during the 19th century was an important step in the development of organic chemistry. In all this time, however, no clear understanding of the nature of the chemical bond had developed. It was not until 1917, when G. N. Lewis described CHEMICAL BONDS as electron pairs, that the modern period of organic chemistry can be said to have begun.

Properties and Classes of Organic Compounds

Why are there so many organic compounds, and why is only carbon capable of forming such a multitude of compounds? The answer lies in the electronic structure of the carbon atom. Carbon has four valence electrons and can share all four electrons to form a maximum of four chemical bonds. More important, carbon atoms are able to bond to one another, forming chains of carbon atoms in compounds that are stable because they are not readily attacked by air or water.

Some generalizations can be made about the properties and reactions of organic compounds. They are combustible, often charring to form elemental carbon. They are usually gases, liquids, or low-melting solids. The boiling points of compounds with similar structures increase with the number of carbon atoms: ethane, C_2H_6, boils at $-88°C$; propane, C_3H_8, at $-42°C$; and *n*-butane, C_4H_{10}, at $-0.5°C$. The highest melting points are found in symmetrical molecules. Since the electronegativities of carbon and hydrogen are similar, bonds between carbon and hydrogen are not very polar. Consequently, many organic molecules are not polar and are insoluble in the polar solvent water. Water-soluble organic compounds usually contain a polar group such as the hydroxyl group —OH. The nonpolar nature of many organic molecules also influences their chemical reactivity. Reactions between organic molecules are usually slow, because interactions between nonpolar molecules are weak. Heat is often required to speed up organic reactions. Also, organic reactions are generally not quantitative. The yield of the product seldom approaches the amount theoretically possible. Often the heat necessary to drive the reaction destroys some of the reactants and products, thus producing impurities along with the desired product. The occurrence of side reactions that produce undesired products also reduces the yield. In most reactions, the greater part of the carbon skeleton of a particular organic molecule remains unchanged, and much of the chemistry of organic compounds is really the chemistry of functional groups. These functional groups, which are attached to the hydrocarbon skeleton, generally contain atoms other than C or H.

Organic molecules can be classified into a number of groups. The simplest group includes compounds known as hydrocarbons, which contain only carbon, C, and hydrogen, H. Other organic compounds also contain elements such as oxygen, O, nitrogen, N, sulfur, S, or the halogens fluorine, F, chlorine, Cl, or bromine, Br, but all these compounds are based on the simpler hydrocarbons and are known as hydrocarbon derivatives.

The simplest group of hydrocarbons consists of the alkanes, in which each carbon atom is bonded to four other carbon or hydrogen atoms. Because the maximum number of atoms to which a carbon atom can bond is four, the valence of carbon in these compounds is said to be saturated, and the alkanes are also known as saturated hydrocarbons. The alkanes make up a homologous series having the general formula C_nH_{2n+2}, where n is an integer, 1,2,3.... The simplest member of the group is methane, CH_4, and each successive member of the series is related by the addition of a CH_2 unit. The next members of the series are ethane, C_2H_6, and propane, C_3H_8,

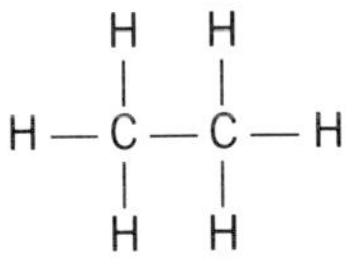

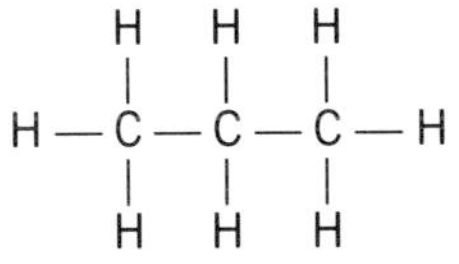

which can also be represented by their condensed formulas CH_3CH_3 and $CH_3CH_2CH_3$ (see CHEMICAL SYMBOLISM AND NOTATION). For methane, ethane, and propane there is only one structural form, but for butane, C_4H_{10}, there are two different structural forms that represent two distinct molecules:

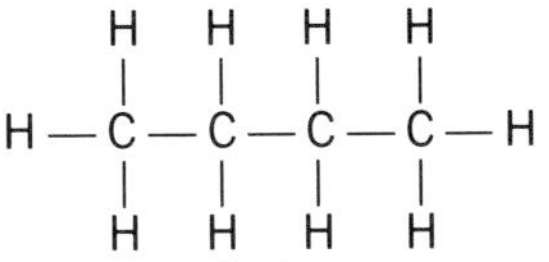

n-butane

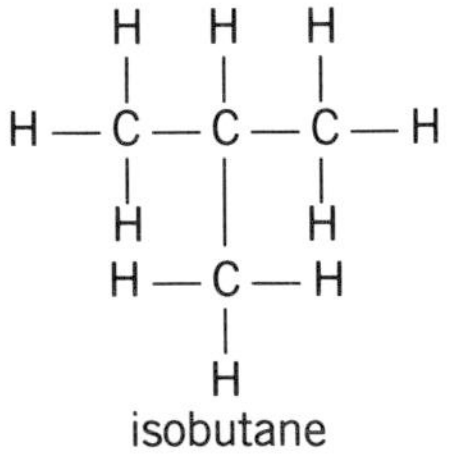

isobutane

Molecules having the same formulas but different structures are known as structural isomers. As the number of atoms in a molecule increases, so does the number of structural isomers. Decane, $C_{10}H_{22}$, for example, has 75 structural isomers. If three or more different types of atoms are present in a molecule, the number of isomers is even larger. The flat structural formulas depicted above suggest that the alkanes consist of flat chains of carbon atoms. The four bonds around each carbon atom are actually in a tetrahedral arrangement, however, so these chains are not flat but have a three-dimensional shape, as do all organic molecules.

The alkanes are very unreactive, but they will undergo substitution reactions in which one or more hydrogen atoms are replaced by other atoms or groups of atoms. The most common substitution reactions involve halogenation. Methane, for example, reacts readily with chlorine gas (Cl_2) to form methyl chloride, CH_3Cl.

Another group of saturated hydrocarbons comprises the cycloalkanes, in which the carbon-atom chain forms a ring. The cycloalkanes have the general formula C_nH_{2n}, the simplest one being cyclopropane, C_3H_6.

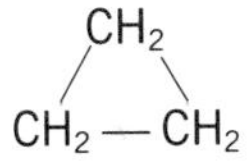

Another homologous series is the alkenes (or olefins), which also have the general formula C_nH_{2n}. Alkenes contain a carbon-carbon double bond, and since this means that not all the carbon atoms are bonded to four other atoms, the alkenes are known as unsaturated hydrocarbons. The simplest alkenes are ethylene (or ethene), $CH_2 = CH_2$ (C_2H_4), and propylene (propene), $CH_3CH = CH_2$ (C_3H_6). The presence of the double bond makes alkenes more reactive than alkanes.

The alkynes, which have the general formula C_nH_{2n-2} and are characterized by the presence of a carbon-carbon triple bond, make up another homologous series of unsaturated hydrocarbons. The simplest alkyne is acetylene, $HC \equiv CH$ (C_2H_2). The triple bond in alkynes makes these compounds very reactive.

The characteristic reaction of unsaturated hydrocarbons is addition: atoms or groups of atoms add to an alkene or alkyne by disrupting a double or triple bond. Chlorine, for example, adds to ethylene to form dichloroethane.

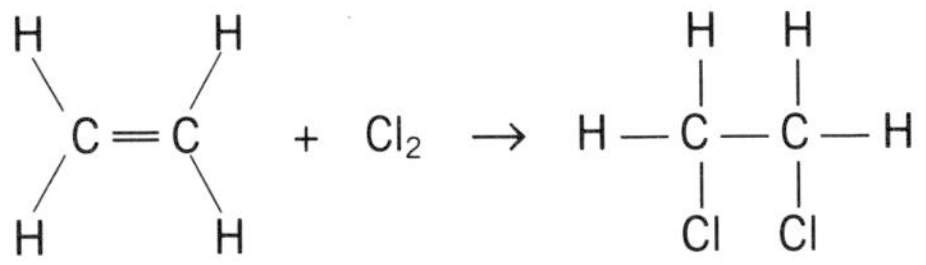

Under certain conditions alkenes will add to themselves, forming large compounds known as addition polymers. Many of the familiar plastics are polymers. Polyethylene, for example, is an addition polymer formed when many ethylene molecules add together.

$$n \, (CH_2{=}CH_2) \rightarrow ({-}CH_2{-}CH_2{-})_n$$

The alkanes, alkenes, and alkynes are collectively called *aliphatic* hydrocarbons. Another important group of compounds are called the *aromatic* hydrocarbons, the simplest of which is benzene, C_6H_6. The formula suggests that benzene is highly unsaturated, and it would therefore be expected to be very reactive. Instead, it is found to be fairly inert, and the explanation for this behavior lies in its structure. Benzene is a planar cyclic molecule represented by two so-called resonance structures

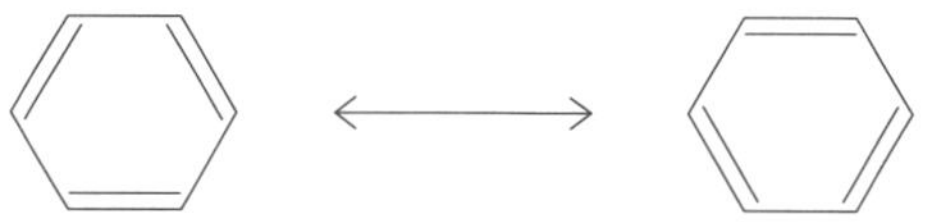

where each corner of the hexagon represents a CH group. These structures were first proposed in 1865 by Kekulé to demonstrate how each carbon atom in C_6H_6 can have a valence of four, and they are still known as Kekulé structures. Benzene is actually a single structure intermediate between these two (but difficult to draw). The pi-electrons of the double bonds are equally distributed around the ring (delocalized), giving stability to the molecule and decreasing its reactivity. Aromatic molecules, many of which are based on benzene, are generally characterized by their tendency to undergo substitution reactions rather than the addition reactions expected for unsaturated molecules.

There are a number of hydrocarbon derivatives containing other elements as well as carbon and hydrogen. These compounds are usually classified by their functional groups, which give them their characteristic properties. Several classes of molecules contain one or more oxygen atoms. One such class is the ALCOHOLS, in which an H atom in the corresponding hydrocarbon has been replaced by the hydroxy group —OH. The simplest alcohol is methanol, CH_3OH. In general, alcohols can be represented as R—OH, where R stands for a hydrocarbon group. Two alcohols can react together and eliminate a water molecule to form an ether, which is characterized by an O atom bonded to two hydrocarbon groups.

$$\mathrm{R{-}OH + HO{-}R' \rightarrow R{-}O{-}R' + H_2O}$$

Another common functional group containing oxygen is the carbonyl group, C═O. Molecules in which the carbon atom of the carbonyl group is bonded to two hydrocarbon groups are classified as KETONES, and those in which the carbon atom of the carbonyl group is attached to a hydrogen atom and a hydrocarbon group are classified as ALDEHYDES, for example,

$$\mathrm{R{-}\overset{\overset{\large O}{\|}}{C}{-}R'}\ \text{a ketone}\qquad \mathrm{CH_3{-}\overset{\overset{\large O}{\|}}{C}{-}CH_3}\ \text{an acetone}$$

$$\mathrm{R{-}\overset{\overset{\large O}{\|}}{C}{-}H}\ \text{an aldehyde}\qquad \mathrm{CH_3{-}\overset{\overset{\large O}{\|}}{C}{-}H}\ \text{an acetaldehyde}$$

A carbonyl group and a hydroxy group are combined in a carboxyl group, which is present in the compounds classified as CARBOXYLIC ACIDS:

$$\mathrm{R{-}\overset{\overset{\large O}{\|}}{C}{-}OH}\ \text{a carboxylic acid}\qquad \mathrm{CH_3{-}\overset{\overset{\large O}{\|}}{C}{-}OH}\ \text{an acetic acid}$$

Carboxylic acids and alcohols react to eliminate a molecule of water and form the compounds known as *esters*, for example, methyl acetate.

$$\underset{\text{methanol}}{\mathrm{CH_3OH}} + \underset{\text{acetic acid}}{\mathrm{HO{-}\overset{\overset{\large O}{\|}}{C}{-}CH_3}} \rightarrow \underset{\text{methyl acetate (an ester)}}{\mathrm{CH_3O{-}\overset{\overset{\large O}{\|}}{C}{-}CH_3}}$$

Organic compounds also form many esters with phosphoric acid (H_3PO_4), and such phosphate esters are important to the metabolism of plants and animals.

A number of functional groups also contain nitrogen. One class of nitrogen-containing organic compounds is the AMINES, represented by the general formulas RNH_2, RNHR′, and RNR'_2. Another class of nitrogen-containing organic compounds, the AMIDES, are formed when the hydroxyl group of a carboxylic acid is replaced by an amino group or a substituted amino group:

$$\mathrm{R{-}\overset{\overset{\large O}{\|}}{C}{-}NH_2}\ \text{an amide}\qquad \mathrm{R{-}\overset{\overset{\large O}{\|}}{C}{-}NH{-}R'}\ \text{a substituted amide}$$

The group of atoms of atoms composed of the carbonyl group bonded to an —NH— group is called an amide linkage and is found in such diverse molecules as proteins and nylons, which belong to a class of synthetic fibers known as condensation polymers. Nylons are polyamides that form when diacids (molecules containing two carboxylic acid groups) combine with diamines with the elimination of water molecules. Nitrogen is also present in organic compounds, as the inorganic nitro (—NO_2), nitrite (—ONO), and nitrate (—ONO_2) groups. Compounds containing these groups are unstable, and all conventional explosives are organic nitro and nitrate compounds. Two examples are trinitrotoluene (TNT) and glycerol trinitrate (nitroglycerine).

Halogen atoms are often found in organic molecules, forming the halocarbons R—Cl, R—F, and R—Br. Another element often present in functional groups is sulfur. Many organic molecules contain more than one functional group, and these functional groups are the ones that determine the chemical behavior of a particular molecule. A knowledge of the functional groups and their properties is fundamental to an understanding of organic chemistry.

Research in Organic Chemistry

There are several main areas of organic-chemical research. One of these is the synthesis of organic molecules, which involves converting available substances into desired product molecules. Such a process often requires a whole series of carefully controlled reactions. Many new molecules that have never appeared in nature are created in this way. Examples include plastics, synthetic fibers, and pharmaceuticals. Many chemists are also involved in synthesizing natural products, and it is now possible to synthesize some very complex molecules.

Another important area of research is the determination of the structure of organic molecules. When molecules are synthesized or natural products are isolated, their structures must be characterized. Often a careful study of the chemical reactivity and physical properties of a particular compound gives clues to its structure. Spectroscopic techniques, which take advantage of each molecule's characteristic interactions with light, also play an important role in structure determination. Still, a knowledge of the electronic structure is also necessary to really understand a molecule, and many scientists are engaged in research aimed at a more accurate theoretical description of chemical bonds in organic molecules.

Another field of research is the study of reaction mechanisms, the pathways through which chemical reactions proceed. It is possible to measure both the rate at which a particular reaction proceeds and the effects on the rate of such factors as temperature and concentration of reactants. Such measurements provide valuable insight into how a reaction or type of reaction proceeds, and this kind of information often leads to new synthetic methods.

Organic Chemistry, Health and the Environment

Organic research has produced many compounds that have benefited society as a whole. With extended use of synthetic organic compounds, combined with increasing sophistication of testing methods in the medical, biological, and environmental sciences, many have also been shown to have deleterious effects. In addition, numerous naturally occurring organic compounds have been identified as potentially harmful.

An ever-increasing number of organic compounds have proved to be carcinogenic, or cancer-causing. Since the induction period between exposure to a carcinogen and the onset of cancer can often be years, determining whether a substance is a carcinogen is not always a simple matter. Certain classes of compounds are known carcinogens, however. Potent natural carcinogens include aflatoxin, produced by molds in peanut butter and corn, safrole in oil from the sassafras tree, and benzopyrenes formed in charred meat and cigarette smoke. In some cases, evidence for carcinogenicity has come from human experience. For example, the synthetic hormone diethylstilbestrol (DES) was taken by a number of pregnant women to prevent miscarriage and later found to produce a rare form of cancer in these women's daughters. In other cases, evidence has come from animal testing. The once-popular artificial sweeteners known as cyclamates were banned in the United States in 1970, when they were shown to cause bladder cancer in rats, and they remain banned, although further studies have raised doubts

about the initial tests. The assessment of human risk based on animal test data continues to be an active area of research, with no universal agreement on methodology.

A group of chemicals that are not carcinogens but are still harmful includes various pesticides. The use of pesticides has served to increase the world's food supply and decrease disease-carrying pests, but many of these pesticides, particularly the polychlorinated hydrocarbons, have generated controversy because of their persistence in the environment. An example of such a "hard" insecticide is 2,2-di(p-chlorophenyl)-1,1,1-trichloroethane (DDT). DDT is extremely stable and persists for years in the environment. Consequently, it moves through the food chain and gradually builds up in plant and animal tissues. Although there is no evidence that normal use of DDT has ever harmed humans, it has proved harmful to fish and birds of prey, and the use of DDT has been severely limited.

Two other classes of pesticides are now widely used and are known as "soft" insecticides because they decompose more rapidly in the environment than the polychlorinated hydrocarbons. These groups are the organophosphates, two examples of which are malathion and Sevin, which is a carbamate. Even organophosphates must be used with care, however, since they are highly toxic. In fact, methyl isocyanate, a chemical used since 1979 in making Sevin, was responsible for one of the worst industrial accidents in history when a gas leak of the chemical at a plant in Bhopal, India, in December 1984 killed more than 2,000 people and injured 200,000 others.

There are also a number of organic chemicals that are not directly injurious to animals or humans but whose effect on the environment could prove to be detrimental. Synthetic detergents, for example, which have all but replaced soap (see SOAP AND DETERGENT), have a high phosphate content. This increases their cleaning efficiency but creates an environmental problem when they are discharged into streams and lakes from sewage systems. The phosphates increase the water's nutrient content, thus promoting excess growth of algae and weeds and depleting the oxygen supply in the water. This process is known as EUTROPHICATION. Phosphates have now been replaced by nonphosphate detergents in many applications.

Another group of chemicals that appears to be harmful to the environment includes chlorfluoromethanes such as CF_2Cl_2 and $CFCl_3$, which have been widely used as aerosol propellants and refrigerant gases. Their concentration in the upper atmosphere has been steadily increasing, and there is growing evidence that these compounds play a role in reactions that tend to destroy the Earth's OZONE LAYER.

Organic-Chemical Industry

The major sources of organic chemicals are petroleum and natural gas. The earliest organic raw materials suitable for industrial processes came from heating coal in the absence of air to yield coke and coal tar. Coal tar is a mixture of volatile compounds, including aromatics such as benzene, toluene, and naphthalene. These compounds are well suited as starting materials in the synthesis of dyes, and for this reason the synthetic-dye industry was one of the first major organic-chemical industries. The chemical industry developed first in Europe, but during World War I the United States became aware of how dependent it was on Europe for important chemicals. This awareness provided the impetus for the development of the chemical industry in the United States, and the organic-chemical industry has expanded rapidly. Important products are plastics, dyes, synthetic fibers, detergents, and pharmaceuticals. Industries maintain large research laboratories where new products are developed and production processes are improved.

Ninety percent of all organic chemicals are now made from starting materials derived from petroleum and natural gas. These are called petrochemicals. Crude petroleum is a mixture of hydrocarbons, including primarily alkanes as well as some cycloalkanes and aromatics. These are separated by distillation into a series of fractions according to boiling point, the higher boiling point belonging to molecules containing a larger number of carbon atoms. The different fractions include mixtures of hydrocarbons known as gasoline, kerosene, fuel oils, and asphalt. Since compounds do not occur in petroleum in the proportion that is most in demand, methods have been developed to break down larger molecules into smaller molecules and to combine smaller molecules to form larger ones. These processes are known as refining. In one of the refining processes, catalytic reforming, alkanes and cycloalkanes are converted to aromatics by passing them over suitable catalysts. More than 380 million liters (100 million gallons) of benzene are produced annually in this way. Major products of the refining process are the components of gasoline. Since branched alkanes burn more smoothly in gasoline than straight-chain alkanes, much of the refining process is aimed at producing branched alkanes. During a process known as isomerization, straight-chain alkanes are passed over catalysts and converted to branched-chain alkanes. In the cracking process large alkanes are heated to a high temperature in the absence of oxygen and are broken down into smaller alkanes.

A large proportion of the components of petroleum are eventually converted into polymers such as PLASTICS, SYNTHETIC FIBERS, and synthetic rubbers. Millions of tons of these products are produced annually in the world, and the production of polymers is second only to the production of steel as a measure of the vitality of a nation's economic system.

Organic chemicals also play an important role in the food industry, where they are used to color, flavor, preserve, and fortify the nutritional quality of foods. More than 1.8 million kg (4 million lb) of synthetic dyes are used annually to color food, and at least 750 synthetic flavorings are in use.

As stated above, the basic starting materials for the organic chemical industry come from petroleum and natural gas. In the past these have been abundant and cheap, but this situation is rapidly changing. As the supply of petroleum dwindles and its cost increases, the effects will be felt throughout the world. Society becomes ever more heavily dependent on these petrochemicals, and present and future chemists must either face the prospect of a decreased supply of starting materials or attempt to find new sources of carbon-containing raw materials. One attractive alternative may be the commercial generation of useful chemicals using living organisms. The relatively new field of molecular biology and its related technologies explore the use of cellular media and bacteria for the biochemical synthesis of compounds.

See also: BIOCHEMISTRY; CHEMICAL INDUSTRY; CHEMISTRY; PETROCHEMICALS.

Organization of African Unity

Organization of African Unity   The Organization of African Unity (OAU), an outgrowth of the Pan-Africa movement of the early 20th century, was established in Addis Ababa, Ethiopia, in 1963. The OAU charter defines its aims as the defense of the independence, sovereignty, and territorial integrity of its member states, the promotion of unity and mutual development, and the coordination of policy in matters of common interest, such as welfare, education, defense, and foreign affairs. The OAU is also dedicated to the eradication of all forms of colonialism. The heads of state and government of the OAU member nations convene at annual summit meetings to establish general policy and to settle disputes involving member nations.

Organization of American States

Organization of American States   The Organization of American States (OAS) is a regional political body of the Western Hemisphere. Traditionally, the OAS has been concerned with political matters, particularly the maintenance of peace in the Western Hemisphere and the settlement of disputes within the framework of the inter-American system. The OAS also implements the mutual-security Rio Treaty. Since the 1960s, largely at the insistence of the Latin American countries, economic cooperation has become increasingly important.

The OAS traces its origin to the First International Conference of American States held in Washington in 1889–90, when an International Union of American Republics was established, which later (1910) became known as the Pan-American Union. This organization constituted a system for the exchange of information and consultation on matters of common interest. In the following decades the scope of the organization was gradually widened. Eventually in 1948, the OAS was established at the Ninth International Conference of American States held in Bogotá, Colombia.

The OAS, which has 33 members, is now composed of the General Assembly—the highest organ, which meets annually—and the Permanent Council, the Inter-American Economic and Social Council, and the Inter-American Council for Education, Science, and Culture. Other organs of the OAS are the Meeting of Consultation of

Ministers of Foreign Affairs and various specialized agencies. The central organ of the OAS, the General Secretariat, is headed by a secretary-general elected by the assembly for a 5-year term.

Organization for Economic Cooperation and Development

The Organization for Economic Cooperation and Development (OECD) is an international organization set up to attain the highest possible sustainable rate of growth among its member countries consistent with maintaining financial stability, to expand world trade on a multilateral, nondiscriminatory basis, and to contribute via development to the expansion of employment and living standards everywhere.

Originally set up as the Organization for European Economic Cooperation (OEEC) to coordinate MARSHALL PLAN aid in 1948, the OECD took on its present form in 1961, once the task of reconstruction was accomplished. Today the membership includes 24 countries: Australia, Austria, Belgium, Canada, Denmark, Finland, France, Greece, Iceland, Ireland, Italy, Japan, Luxembourg, the Netherlands, New Zealand, Norway, Portugal, Spain, Sweden, Switzerland, Turkey, the United Kingdom, the United States, and Germany.

The OECD's organizational structure includes the Council, which may meet at the ministerial level, and which is in effect a permanent conference where problems of member countries are constantly reviewed. A secretary-general (and a Secretariat) is appointed by the Council and is responsible for assisting it in its day-to-day functions. The OECD headquarters is located in Paris.

Organization of Petroleum Exporting Countries

The Organization of Petroleum Exporting Countries (OPEC) was created by Iran, Iraq, Kuwait, Saudi Arabia, and Venezuela in Baghdad on Sept. 14, 1960, to counter price cuts of American and European oil companies. Qatar joined in 1961, Indonesia and Libya in 1962, Abu Dhabi (now part of the United Arab Emirates) in 1967, Algeria in 1969, Nigeria in 1971, and Ecuador and Gabon in 1973. In 1979 the OPEC countries produced 66% of world petroleum, but by the beginning of 1989 only 34%. OPEC production was further curtailed during the 1991 GULF WAR, when the Iraqi military set fire to about 500 oil wells in Kuwait.

In its first decade OPEC limited itself to preventing further reductions in the price of oil, but by 1970 it had begun to press for rate increases—there was a fourfold increase in 1973–74 alone. Prices stabilized between 1974 and 1978 but increased by more than 100% during 1979. These increases put severe strains on the international economic system, and efforts to cut consumption, combined with high production by Saudi Arabia, led to a surplus of oil in consuming countries by 1981. Since that time OPEC members have had difficulty reaching price or output accords that would increase oil prices by cutting production.

organized crime

Organized crime is an enterprise whose participants aim to secure profit and power by engaging in illegal activities. The organization is hierarchical. It avoids competition and strives to control particular activities on an industrywide or territorial basis. There is a willingness to use violence, bribery, and extortion to achieve ends or to maintain discipline. Membership is restricted.

Groups worldwide that have been identified as being involved in organized criminal activity include Japanese *yakuza*, Chinese triads, Neapolitan Camorra, Sicilian and American MAFIA, and Colombian cartels. Criminal activities include labor racketeering, loansharking, gambling, prostitution, and DRUG TRAFFICKING. Illicit profits are often invested in legitimate businesses.

Law-enforcement efforts against organized crime are limited by the constraints placed on democratic governments and by the secrecy to which criminals are sworn. U.S. legislation specifically designed to deal with organized crime and improved federal law-enforcement resources have resulted, nonetheless, in many successful prosecutions (see RICO ACT).

Orient Express

The Orient Express is a famous first-class train that ran between Paris and Istanbul in the last years of the 19th and the first half of the 20th century. When first inaugurated in 1883 the train ran from Paris via Strasbourg, Munich, Vienna, Budapest, and Bucharest to the Black Sea, with steamer service on to Istanbul. By 1889 the entire journey was by rail. By the mid-20th century service on much of the route was no longer first class. In the early 1980s, however, a fully restored Orient Express was providing first-class service between London and Venice.

Oriental Americans   see ASIAN AMERICANS

orienteering

Orienteering is an outdoor sport that combines the endurance of distance running with survival skills. It involves cross-country running between routing points using a map and compass for guidance. It is popular in the United States and Europe among amateur athletes of both sexes and of all ages.

Each runner carries a compass and a map of the terrain marked with routing points. There are two versions of the sport. In the first, runners must pass specified points in a sequence, the runner with the best time winning. In the second, runners must pass as many points as possible in a specified time. Each location has a point value determined by its distance from the starting point and the difficulty involved in reaching it; the high scorer wins. All routing points are marked by red and white flags visible from 50 m (54.7 yd) in any direction.

origami   see PAPER FOLDING

Origen [ohr'-i-jin]   Origen, c.185–c.254, is generally considered the greatest theologian and biblical scholar of the early Eastern church. At the age of 18 he was appointed to succeed Clement of Alexandria as head of the catechetical school of Alexandria, where he had been a student.

In 230 he traveled to Palestine, where he was ordained a priest by the bishops of Jerusalem and Caesarea. Demetrius, bishop of Alexandria, then excommunicated Origen, deprived him of his priesthood, and sent him into exile. Origen returned to the security of Caesarea (231) and there established a school of theology, over which he presided for 20 years. Persecution was renewed in 250, and Origen was severely tortured. He died of the effects a few years later.

Origen attempted to synthesize Christian scriptural interpretation and belief with Greek philosophy, especially Neoplatonism and Stoicism. He was the first major biblical scholar of the Christian church. Prior to Saint Augustine, he was also the most influential theologian of the church. Some of Origen's ideas remained a source of controversy long after his death, and "Origenism" was condemned at the fifth ecumenical council in 553 (see CONSTANTINOPLE, COUNCILS OF). Origen is one of the best examples of early Christian mysticism: the highest good is to become as like God as possible through progressive illumination.

Origin of Species, On the   see DARWIN, CHARLES

original sin   In Christian theology original sin refers both to the SIN of ADAM and EVE by which humankind fell from divine grace and to the state of sin into which humans since the fall have been born. The scriptural foundation for original sin is found in the epistles of Saint Paul. Christian theologians have argued a wide variety of positions on the nature of original sin and its transmission and on the efficacy of BAPTISM in restoring grace.

Orinoco River [oh-ree-noh'-koh]   The Orinoco River, one of the three great rivers of South America, has its source in the Parima Range along the Venezuela-Brazil border. The river flows north and then east. On part of its course the Orinoco follows the border between Venezuela and Colombia. After flowing through Venezuela, it enters the Atlantic Ocean via a large delta covering about 20,200 km^2 (7,800 mi^2) to reach the Atlantic 2,575 km (1,600 mi) from its source. The Orinoco drains a vast area of more than 1,000,000 km^2 (385,000 mi^2). Tributaries of the Orinoco include the Guaviare, Vichada, and Meta rivers in Colombia and the Arauca, Apure, Capanaparo, and Caroni rivers in Venezuela. The Casiquiare River connects the Orinoco to the Rio Negro, a tributary of the Amazon.

The mouth of the Orinoco was probably sighted by Christopher Columbus in 1498. In 1560, Lope de Aguirre, a Spanish adventurer, traveled most of its length, destroying Indian villages en route. The German naturalist Alexander von HUMBOLDT explored its upper reaches in 1799. Much of the land of those upper reaches still remains relatively unknown.

oriole [ohr'-ee-ohl]   Two families of perching birds of the order Passeriformes are known as orioles: 28 to 30 species of the Old World family Oriolidae and about 25 species of the New World family Icteridae. Members of family Oriolidae, which are closely related to crows and jays, typically inhabit tropical regions. Only the golden oriole, *Oriolus oriolus*, is found in more northern areas. Old World orioles measure 20 to 30 cm (8 to 12 in) in length and have brightly colored feathers, with yellows and greens predominating; some species also have brown, red, and black plumage. They have long, pointed wings and strong, usually slightly hooked bills. These solitary birds build their nests high in a tree and lay two to five eggs in a clutch.

New World orioles measure 15 to 25 cm (6 to 10 in) in length. These birds are distributed mostly in the tropics; they usually have striking plumages of black contrasted against orange or yellow. They lay two to six eggs, usually in a pendulous nest. The most widespread North American species is the northern oriole, *Icterus galbula*.

The Baltimore oriole, the state bird of Maryland, is a subspecies of the northern oriole. It prefers woodland habitats.

Orion (astronomy) [oh-ry'-uhn]   Orion, the Hunter, is the most spectacular and one of the most easily recognized constellations in the sky. The stars represent the figure of a warrior holding a shield in his left hand and a club in his right. The variable red star Betelgeuse, one of the largest stars known, marks his right shoulder,

Bellatrix his left shoulder, and Saiph and Rigel his two legs. The constellation is located near the celestial equator and can be seen from the Northern Hemisphere during the winter.

Orion (mythology)   In Greek mythology Orion was a famed Boeotian hunter. In one account he was the son of Poseidon; in others, he was born from the hide of an ox on which Zeus, Poseidon, and Hermes had urinated (hence his original name, Urion). Orion was blinded by Oenopion, whose daughter he had raped, but his vision was restored by the rising Sun. Stories concerning Orion's death vary. The most common relates that as he attempted to assault Artemis, or one of her nymphs, he was stung by a scorpion sent by Apollo or by Artemis herself. Both the scorpion and Orion later became constellations.

Orion nebula   The Orion nebula, also known as M42, is a galactic NEBULA consisting of gas and dust, which because of its brightness and angular size has been much studied by astronomers. The nebula is located at a distance of about 1,500 light-years. It has a strong emission-line spectrum. The main sources of its radiative energy are the two brightest stars in an area known as the Trapezium, a small group of six stars. Photographs taken with large telescopes show that the gas has a patchy, irregular structure.

Orissa [uh-ris'-uh]   Orissa is a state in eastern India located on the Bay of Bengal. It has an area of 155,788 km^2 (60,150 mi^2) and a population of 26,370,271 (1981). The capital is BHUBANESWAR. Most of Orissa is hilly except for a narrow, fertile coastal plain. The Eastern GHATS in the south are an important source of timber. In the North are valuable deposits of iron, manganese, coal, and mica. The state is chiefly agricultural.

Orissa was a center of the Kalinga kingdom as early as the 4th century BC. As the Kalinga's power declined, Orissa became the seat of Hindu dynasties. In 1568 it was invaded by the Afghans, but it soon passed under Mogul control. The British conquered Orissa in 1803. Following Indian independence, Orissa's area was increased, and it became a constituent state of India in 1950.

Orkney Islands [ohrk'-nee]   The Orkney Islands form an archipelago in the North Sea off the northeast coast of Scotland. The land area of the islands totals 974 km^2 (376 mi^2). Although less than one-third of the 67 islands are inhabited, the Orkneys have a population of 19,300 (1987 est.). Kirkwall, the administrative seat, is on Mainland (Pomona), the largest island. Of glacial origin, the Orkneys are low, almost treeless, windswept, and wet. North Sea petroleum dominates the economy.

The Orkney Islands were first inhabited by Neolithic peoples. By the 6th century AD the Picts had settled there. The Vikings invaded during the 8th century, and the islands were under the Norwegian crown until 1231, when they became a possession of the Scottish earls of Angus. Since 1472 the Orkneys have been ruled by the Scottish crown. During both world wars SCAPA FLOW was the main British naval base.

Orlando   Orlando is a city in east central Florida and the seat of Orange County, about 160 km (100 mi) northeast of Tampa. It has a population of 164,693 (1990). A transportation and distribution center, the economy is based on the area's citrus-fruit groves, aerospace industries, and tourism. Walt Disney World (see DISNEYLAND AND WALT DISNEY WORLD) is 24 km (15 mi) southwest. More than 50 lakes lie within the city limits. Orlando was settled about 1844 around an army post. It was known as Jernigan until the present name was chosen in 1857 to honor an army sentinel during the Seminole Wars. The city prospered after the arrival in 1880 of the South Florida Railroad.

Orlando, Vittorio Emanuele   Vittorio Emanuele Orlando, b. May 19, 1860, d. Dec. 1, 1952, was premier of Italy toward the end of World War I and headed its delegation to the PARIS PEACE CONFERENCE. A professor of law in Palermo, Sicily, he was elected to parliament as a Liberal in 1897. After the disastrous Italian defeat at the Battle of Caporetto in October 1917, the government resigned and Orlando became premier, rallying his nation to final victory.

At the peace conference, which convened in January 1919, Orlando's efforts to annex the seaport of Fiume (now Rijeka, Yugoslavia) led to a bitter clash with U.S. president Woodrow Wilson. Orlando resigned the premiership in June 1919.

At first a supporter of the Fascist government of Benito MUSSOLINI, Orlando turned against it in 1925 and resigned from parliament. After the overthrow of the Fascists, he was named (1944) to the Consultative Assembly. He served as president (1946–47) of the Constituent Assembly and as a member (1948–52) of the new Italian Senate. A candidate (1948) for the presidency of the republic, he was defeated by Luigi Einaudi.

Orléanais [ohr-lay-ah-nay']   Orléanais is a historical region and former province in north central France. Watered by the Loire, Loir, and Cher rivers, Orléanais is mainly an agricultural region producing fruits—especially wine grapes—and vegetables. The chief cities of the region are Orléans, the historic capital; CHARTRES, known for its cathedral; and Blois, once a favorite residence of France's kings and now a busy center of commerce and industry.

From the 10th century, Orléanais was part of the holdings of France's kings, and it became the appanage of the cadet branch of the royal dynasty (see ORLÉANS

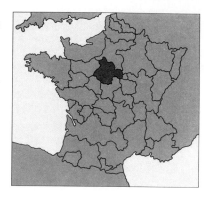

The shaded portion of the map indicates the location of Orléanais, a historical French province that is today divided among five administrative departments. This area in north central France is noted for its agricultural productivity.

family). In 1790 the province was divided into the departments of Loiret, Loir-et-Cher, Eure-et-Loire, and parts of Essone and Saarthe.

Orléans (family) [ohr-lay-ahn']   Orléans was the family name of cadet (or collateral) branches of both the Valois and Bourbon royal dynasties of France.

Valois-Orléans. The house of Valois-Orléans was founded by **Louis, duc d'Orléans**, b. Mar. 13, 1372, d. Nov. 23, 1407, who was granted (1392) the duchy of Orléans by his brother King CHARLES VI. When Charles went mad, Louis entered into a power struggle with PHILIP THE BOLD, duke of Burgundy. The murder of Louis precipitated civil war between his followers, called the Armagnacs, and the Burgundians. Louis's son, **Charles, duc d'Orléans**, b. May 26, 1391, d. Jan. 4, 1465, was titular leader of the Armagnacs, but he was captured by the English at the Battle of Agincourt (1415) and held prisoner until 1440. He is remembered primarily as a poet. Charles's son ascended the throne (1498) as LOUIS XII but died without having produced a son.

Bourbon-Orléans. The Bourbons first adopted the Orléans title in 1626, when Louis XIII granted the title and the Orléanais area to his brother, **Jean Baptiste Gaston, duc d'Orléans**, b. Apr. 25, 1608, d. Feb. 2, 1660. Gaston conspired against Cardinal Richelieu and was later a leader of the revolt known as the FRONDE. He was the father of the duchesse de MONTPENSIER but had no male heir.

The founder of the modern house of Bourbon-Orléans was **Philippe I, duc d'Orléans**, b. Sept. 21, 1640, d. June 9, 1701, brother of Louis XIV. Married to Henrietta, sister of King Charles II of England, he was a notorious libertine and had no political influence. He was the father of Philippe II, duc d'Orléans (see ORLÉANS, PHILIPPE II, DUC D'), and great-great grandfather of Louis Philippe Joseph, duc d'Orléans (see ORLÉANS, LOUIS PHILIPPE JOSEPH, DUC D'). The latter's son LOUIS PHILIPPE became king as a result of the July Revolution of 1830 but was overthrown in 1848.

Thereafter, although France was a republic (and briefly an empire under Napoleon III), the descendants of Louis Philippe continued to claim the throne. When the senior, or Legitimist, Bourbon line died out in 1883, its claim, too, settled on the house of Orléans. The last serious claimant

was **Louis Philippe Robert, duc d'Orléans**, b. Feb. 6, 1869, d. Mar. 28, 1926. Forced to live in exile, he became a notable explorer in the Arctic and East Africa.

Orléans (France)   Orléans is a city in north central France, on both banks of the Loire River, about 112 km (70 mi) southwest of Paris; it has a population of 102,710 (1982). A major city in the southern part of the Paris Basin, Orléans is a market center for a rich agricultural region with excellent vineyards.

Orléans is a railroad, road, and water transport center. Major industries process foods, beverages, and leather, and manufacture textiles and agricultural and electrical equipment. Noted landmarks include the Sainte-Croix Cathedral (rebuilt 17th–19th centuries) and the 16th-century Hôtel de Ville. The University of Orléans (1962) is there.

The Gallic Genabum was conquered by Caesar in 52 BC and was rebuilt by Emperor Aurelian as Aurelianum, from which the present name derives. It was the second leading city in France (after Paris) in the 10th and 11th centuries. The city is famous for JOAN OF ARC, the peasant girl who drove the English from Orléans in 1429, ending a siege of nearly a year during the Hundred Years' War. More than half the city was destroyed in World War II, first by the Germans in 1940 and then by Allied bombing in 1944.

Orléans, Louis Philippe Joseph, Duc d' (Philippe Égalité)   Louis Philippe Joseph, 5th duc d'Orléans, b. Apr. 13, 1747, d. Nov. 6, 1793, attempted the impossible task of allying himself with the FRENCH REVOLUTION. By birth a prince of the Orléans family, a cadet branch of the royal family, he was by inclination liberal. He acquired great popularity by promoting (1789) the union of the liberal nobles with the commoners, and later ostentatiously associated with the extreme Left. In 1792 he accepted the name Philippe Égalité and was elected to the National Convention, at which he voted for the death of LOUIS XVI. Already under attack by the GIRONDISTS, Égalité was arrested in April 1793, when his son, later King LOUIS PHILIPPE, defected to the Austrians with Gen. Charles François DUMOURIEZ. During the Reign of Terror, Égalité was guillotined.

Orléans, Philippe II, Duc d'   Philippe II d'Orléans, b. Aug. 2, 1674, d. Dec. 2, 1723, the freethinking and dissolute regent during the minority of LOUIS XV (1715–23), when France was reacting against LOUIS XIV's absolutism, made the Regency period synonymous in popular opinion with decadence. He was the son of Philippe I d'Orléans (see ORLÉANS family) and nephew of Louis XIV, whose legitimized daughter, Mademoiselle de Blois, he married. As regent, Orléans reversed the policies of Louis XIV and restored the right of the PARLEMENT—nullified since 1673—to remonstrate against legislation. Orléans also backed financier John LAW's ill-fated MISSISSIPPI SCHEME and checked antiregent intrigues by his former ally Philip V of Spain, a claimant to the French throne.

Orlon   see SYNTHETIC FIBERS

Orlov (family) [ur-lawf']   The Orlovs, a Russian family of five brothers, exerted considerable influence during the reign (1762–96) of CATHERINE II (Catherine the Great). **Grigory Orlov**, b. Oct. 17 (N.S.), 1734, d. Apr. 24 (N.S.), 1783, a member of a guards regiment, helped Catherine seize the throne in 1762. He was Catherine's lover and first in the list of her official favorites in the period 1761–71. Grigory actively promoted the Balkan project, designed to arouse the Orthodox Christian inhabitants of the Balkans to eject the Turks. **Aleksei Orlov**, b. Oct. 5 (N.S.), 1737, d. Jan. 5 (N.S.), 1808, also participated in the coup of 1762 and was widely assumed to have killed Catherine's husband, Peter III, during the coup. Aleksei became a renowned naval commander during the RUSSO-TURKISH WAR of 1768–74.

Ormandy, Eugene [ohr'-muhn-dee]   For more than four decades (1938–80), Eugene Ormandy, b. Budapest, Hungary, Nov. 18, 1899, d. Mar. 12, 1985, was permanent conductor of the PHILADELPHIA ORCHESTRA. He came to the United States in 1921 for a violin concert tour, which failed to materialize, and then became concertmaster of the Capitol Theater Orchestra in New York City, which he later conducted (1924–25). Brief assignments followed before he assumed (1931) leadership of the Minneapolis Symphony. In 1936 he was appointed associate conductor of the Philadelphia Orchestra, under Leopold Stokowski, whom he succeeded as music director and principal conductor in 1938. Subsequently, Ormandy's name became almost synonymous with that of the Philadelphia Orchestra. Ormandy maintained the lush "Philadelphia sound" and the orchestra's high level of virtuosity.

ornithology   Ornithology is the branch of zoology that deals with the study of birds (see BIRD), including living and fossil forms. The term derives from the Greek *ornis* for "bird." Professional ornithologists specialize in fields of pure science such as bird anatomy, behavior, ecology, and evolution, or in applied fields such as wildlife management and avian veterinary medicine. The American Ornithologists' Union was founded in 1883, and the first session of the International Ornithological Congress was held the following year. Amateur ornithologists can also participate in migration studies and other programs.

orogeny   see MOUNTAIN

Orozco, José Clemente [oh-rohs'-koh]   José Clemente Orozco, b. Zapotlán, Mexico, Nov. 23, 1883, d. Sept. 7, 1949, was one of Mexico's most important mural painters. He painted his first mural in 1922, and over the next five years he decorated the walls of several public buildings, including the National Preparatory School

The figures in this detail of José Clemente Orozco's fresco An Epic of American Civilization *(1932) attest to his social and political concerns. (Dartmouth College, Hanover, N.H.)*

(1922–27) and the House of Tiles (1925) in Mexico City, and the Industrial School (1926) in Orizaba. During a sojourn (1927–34) in the United States, he executed frescoes at the New School for Social Research in New York City (1930–31); at Pomona College in Claremont, Calif. (1930); and at Dartmouth College in Hanover, N.H. (1932).

Orozco returned (1934) to Mexico to develop a new American art that would imitate neither European nor pre-Columbian models. In major works such as his *Man in His Four Aspects: The Worker, the Educator, the Creative Thinker, and the Rebel* (1936; Assembly Hall, University of Guadalajara) and his famed *The Man of Fire* (1936–39; Hospicio Cabañas, Guadalajara), he created an expressionist style that reflected his sympathies for the miserable and the oppressed, whom he transformed into symbols of humanity. Along with the murals of Diego RIVERA, these paintings mark the high point of the socalled Mexican Renaissance of the 1930s and 1940s, in which a distinctly Mexican style of painting first appeared.

Orpheus [ohr'-fee-uhs]   In Greek mythology Orpheus was a Thracian musician whose magical skill on the lyre enabled him to charm the trees, rivers, and stones, as well as wild beasts. He was the son of Calliope, the muse of epic poetry, and a Thracian river-god (some versions say Apollo). Orpheus married the nymph Eurydice, but she soon died, bitten on the heel by a snake. Her grieving husband followed her to the underworld and, by playing on his lyre, charmed the deities into releasing her. The one condition was that he should escort her back to the upper world without looking at her. He did look, however, and Eurydice disappeared. Rejecting all women thereafter, Orpheus was torn to pieces by Thracian women; in one version, he was dismembered by MAENADS at the urging of Dionysus, who resented Orpheus's advocacy of the worship of Apollo. Orpheus's singing head and lyre floated to Lesbos, where an oracle of Orpheus was established.

Some legends make Orpheus the founder of the Orphic mysteries and the author of the sacred texts of that cult (see MYSTERY CULTS).

Orr, Bobby   The Canadian Robert Gordon Orr, b. Parry Sound, Ontario, Mar. 20, 1948, was a highly talented professional ice hockey player whose superb skating, scoring ability, and defensive play set the standard for other defensemen. Orr joined the Boston Bruins of the National Hockey League (NHL) while still in his teens. Named the league's Rookie of the Year in 1967, Orr set numerous NHL scoring records for a defenseman while playing (1967–76) for the Bruins. He received the James Norris Trophy 8 years in a row (1968–75) as the NHL's top defenseman and was awarded the Hart Trophy in 3 consecutive seasons (1970–72) as the NHL's most valuable player. In 1976, Orr joined the Chicago Black Hawks, but an old knee injury impaired his effectiveness. After his retirement (1979) he was elected to the Hockey Hall of Fame.

Bobby Orr, a defenseman for the NHL's Boston Bruins, set most of the scoring records for players at his position even though his career was cut short by injuries. He was the first defenseman to score 100 points in a season; the first to lead the league in scoring; and the first to amass more than 30 goals in a season. Orr had 270 goals and 645 assists in his career.

Ortega y Gasset, José [ohr-tay'-gah ee gah-set'] José Ortega y Gasset, b. May 9, 1883, d. Oct. 18, 1955, was a prominent Spanish essayist and philosopher. Ortega developed a philosophy that he called the "metaphysics of vital reason" and defended the place of "aristocratic" values in society. In 1923 he founded the *Revista de occidente* (Review of the West), a magazine through which he worked to overcome Spanish isolation from contemporary European culture. His outspoken participation in republican politics forced his exile during the Spanish Civil War, and Ortega was unable to return to Spain until 1948, when he founded the Institute of Hu-

manities in Madrid. *The Revolt of the Masses* (1929; Eng. trans., 1932), his most famous work, argues for the essential inequality of human beings and for the vital importance of intellectual elites in human history. Ortega's other writings include *The Dehumanization of Art* (1925; Eng. trans., 1925) and *Toward a Philosophy of History* (1941; Eng. trans., 1941).

Ortega Saavedra, Daniel [sah-vay'-druh] Sandinista National Liberation Front (FSLN) leader Daniel Ortega Saavedra, b. Nov. 11, 1945, was elected president of Nicaragua in 1984. Ortega joined the SANDINISTAS in 1963 and was instrumental in forging the alliance between the FSLN and middle-class opponents of the SOMOZA regime that led to the overthrow of President Anastasio Somoza Debayle in 1979. A member of the ruling junta since 1979, he was named the group's coordinator in 1981 and was inaugurated president on Jan. 10, 1985. In office Ortega faced a steadily declining economy. He stepped down as president after unexpectedly losing an early democratic election in March 1990 to opposition candidate Violeta Barrios de Chamorro.

orthodontics   In DENTISTRY, orthodontics is a specialty concerned with preventing and correcting TEETH and jaw abnormalities called malocclusions. These include crowded, overlapping, or crookedly positioned teeth, which often result from abnormal jaw growth. An orthodontist adjusts tooth positions by means of appliances such as braces, which are attached to teeth and tightened so as to move them over a period of time. Such corrections usually are made before the age of 18, when bones are less ossified. After receiving their doctorate in dentistry, dentists must take two years of postgraduate work before practicing orthodontics.

Orthodox church   One of the three branches of world Christianity and the major Christian church in the Middle East and Eastern Europe, the Orthodox church, also sometimes called the Eastern church, or the Greek Orthodox, or Orthodox Catholic church, claims to have preserved the original and apostolic Christian faith.

Structure and Organization. The Orthodox church is a fellowship of administratively independent, or autocephalous (self-governing), local churches, united in faith, sacraments, and canonical discipline, each enjoying the right to elect its own head and its bishops. Traditionally, the ecumenical patriarch of Constantinople (Istanbul) is recognized as the "first among equal" Orthodox bishops. He possesses privileges of chairmanship and initiative but no direct doctrinal or administrative authority. The other heads of autocephalous churches, in order of precedence, are: the patriarch of Alexandria, Egypt, with jurisdiction over Africa; the patriarch of Antioch, now residing in Damascus, Syria, and heading Arab-speaking Orthodox Christians in Syria, Lebanon, and Iraq; the patriarch of Jerusalem, with jurisdiction over Palestine; the patriarch

The Orthodox liturgy is celebrated at Mount Athos, Greece, a venerable center of Eastern monasticism. A theocratic republic, Mount Athos is the site of 20 monasteries, some of which date from the 10th century.

of Moscow and all Russia (Soviet republic); the patriarch-catholicos of Georgia (USSR); the patriarch of Serbia (Yugoslavia); the patriarch of Romania; the patriarch of Bulgaria; the archbishop of Cyprus; the archbishop of Athens and all Greece; the metropolitan of Warsaw and all Poland; the archbishop of Albania (presently suppressed); the metropolitan of Prague and all Czechoslovakia; and the archbishop of New York and North America.

Three autonomous churches also enjoy a large degree of independence, although the election of their primate is subject to nominal approval by a mother church. These are the churches of Crete and Finland, under Constantinople, and the church of Japan, under Moscow.

History. During the first eight centuries of Christian history most major intellectual, cultural, and social developments in the Christian church took place in Constantinople; for example, all ecumenical councils of that period met either in Constantinople or in its vicinity. Missionaries, coming from Constantinople, converted the Slavs and other peoples of Eastern Europe to Christianity (Bulgaria, 864; Russia, 988) and translated Scripture and liturgical texts into the vernacular languages used in the various regions. Thus, the liturgy, traditions, and practices of the church of Constantinople were adopted by all and still provide the basic patterns and ethos of contemporary Orthodoxy.

These developments, however, were not always consistent with the evolution of Western Christianity, where the bishop of Rome, or pope, came to be considered the successor of the apostle Peter and head of the universal church by divine appointment. Eastern Christians were willing to accept the pope only as first among patriarchs. This difference in approach explains the various incidents that grew into a serious estrangement. One of the most vehement disputes concerned the *filioque* clause of the Nicene Creed (see CREED), which the Western church added unilaterally to the original text.

The schism developed gradually. The first major breach came in the 9th century when the pope refused to recognize the election of PHOTIUS as patriarch of Constantinople. Photius in turn challenged the right of the papacy to rule on the matter and denounced the *filioque* clause as a Western innovation. The mounting disputes between East and West reached another climax in 1054, when mutual anathemas were exchanged (see SCHISM, GREAT). The sacking of Constantinople by the Fourth CRUSADE (1204) intensified Eastern hostility toward the West. Attempts at reconciliation at the councils of Lyon (1274) and Florence (1438–39) were unsuccessful. When the papacy defined itself as infallible (First VATICAN COUNCIL, 1870), the gulf between East and West grew wider. Only since the Second VATICAN COUNCIL (1962–65) has the movement reversed, bringing serious attempts at mutual understanding.

Doctrines and Practices. The Orthodox church recognizes as authoritative the decisions of the seven ecumenical councils that met between 325 and 787 and defined the basic doctrines on the TRINITY and the INCARNATION. In later centuries Orthodox councils also made doctrinal definitions on GRACE (1341, 1351) and took a stand in reference to Western teachings. The Orthodox church accepts the early traditions of Christianity, including the same sacraments as the Roman Catholic church—although in the Orthodox church infants receive the Eucharist and confirmation—and the episcopate and the priesthood, understood in the light of APOSTOLIC SUCCESSION. Married men may become priests, but bishops and monks may not marry. The veneration of MARY, as Mother of God, is central to Orthodox worship, and the intercession of saints is emphasized in the Orthodox liturgical tradition. After an early controversy on the subject (see ICONOCLASM), the images, or ICONS, of Christ, the Virgin Mary, and the saints are now seen as visible witnesses to the fact that God has taken human flesh in the person of Jesus. The LITURGY used by the Orthodox church is known as the Byzantine rite. It has been translated from Greek into many languages, including the Old Church Slavonic used by the Russian Orthodox church. The monastic republic of Mount ATHOS, Greece, is still viewed among Orthodox Christians as a center of spiritual vitality.

orthopedics Orthopedics is the specialty of medicine that deals with diseases and injuries of the locomotor system and its associated structures, including limbs, bones, muscles, joints, tendons, and ligaments. The term *orthopedics*, which literally means "straight children," goes back to the time when the profession was devoted to the treatment and correction of deformities in children, for example, CLUBFOOT. Now, however, orthopedists treat both children and adults for a variety of conditions, including fractured bones, torn tendons and ligaments, spastic muscles, congenital skeletal deformities, and bone and joint deformities arising from diseases such as arthritis and tuberculosis or from injury. They employ a variety of devices and techniques such as braces, splints, casts, drugs, and surgery to correct these conditions. Surgical procedures include repair of fractures, fusion of vertebrae to treat spinal deformities caused by disease or injury, correction of deformities by bone removal and bone grafting, and implantation of metal devices to strengthen or replace defective bone.

orthorhombic system [ohr-thoh-rahm'-bik] CRYS-TALS that can be referred to three mutually perpendicular axes of unequal length belong to the orthorhombic system. Crystals in this system are sometimes referred to as rhombic, a discouraged usage that leads to an obvious confusion with the rhombohedral division of the HEXAGO-NAL SYSTEM.

Orthorhombic crystals are distinguished by the presence of three twofold symmetry elements. These can be symmetry planes or axes, but three elements of the same rank must be present in order for a crystal to belong to this system. The orthorhombic system contains three classes. The highest order class in this system contains twofold axes (coincident with the crystallographic axis) with three symmetry planes perpendicular to each axis. The lowest-order class contains one twofold axis and two symmetry planes.

Crystals belonging to the orthorhombic system are biaxial. The three principal optical directions always coincide with the three crystallographic axes, and extinction or darkening of the crystal is always parallel to the crosshairs, or nicols, of a microscope. Minerals occurring in this system include epsomite, hemimorphite, topaz, sulfur, barite, and andalusite.

Orton, Joe   The talented English dramatist Joe Orton, b. Jan. 1, 1933, d. Aug. 9, 1967, wrote bizarre comedies notable for their violence, precise plotting, and comic dialogue. His plays include *The Ruffian on the Stair* (1964), the prizewinning *Entertaining Mr. Sloane* (1964), *Loot* (1966), and the posthumously produced *What the Butler Saw* (1969). His life and death—Orton was murdered by his male lover—described in John Lahr's biography *Prick Up Your Ears* (1978) and in the 1987 film made from the book, resemble his theatrical fantasies.

Orwell, George   The British author George Orwell, pen name of Eric Arthur Blair, b. Motihari, India, June 25, 1903, d. London, Jan. 21, 1950, achieved prominence in the late 1940s as the author of two brilliant satires attacking totalitarianism.

Orwell's parents were members of the Indian Civil Service, and, after an education at Eton College in England, Orwell joined (1922) the Indian Imperial Police in Burma, an experience that found expression in the novel *Burmese Days* (1934). His first book, *Down and Out in Paris and London* (1933), was a nonfictional account of several years of self-imposed poverty he had experienced after leaving Burma. He published three other novels in the 1930s: *A Clergyman's Daughter* (1935), *Keep the Aspidistra Flying* (1936), and *Coming Up for Air* (1939). His major works of the period were two documentaries: *The Road to Wigan Pier* (1937), a detailed, sympathetic, yet

The British writer George Orwell created two of the most influential and disturbing political satires of the mid-20th century, Animal Farm (1945), an allegory, and Nineteen Eighty-Four (1949), a dystopian novel.

objective study of the lives of nearly impoverished miners in the Lancashire town of Wigan; and *Homage to Catalonia* (1938), recounting his experiences fighting for the Loyalists in the SPANISH CIVIL WAR. Orwell, a socialist, joined an anarchist unit, was wounded, and when the Communists attempted to eliminate their allies on the far left, fought against them and was forced to flee for his life.

Orwell's two best-known books reflect his lifelong distrust of autocratic government, whether of the Left or Right: *Animal Farm* (1945), a modern beast-fable attacking Stalinism, and NINETEEN EIGHTY-FOUR (1949), a dystopian novel setting forth his fears of an intrusively bureaucratized state of the future. His wartime work for the British Broadcasting Corporation (BBC), published in the collections *George Orwell: The Lost Writings*, 1985, and *The War Commentaries*, 1986, gave him a solid taste of bureaucratic hypocrisy and may have provided the inspiration for his invention of "newspeak," the truth-denying language of Big Brother's rule in *Nineteen Eighty-Four*. The four-volume *Collected Essays, Journalism, and Letters of George Orwell* was published in 1968.

Osage [oh'-sayj]   The Osage are North American Indians whose traditional homeland lay in the Osage River area of western Missouri. A Siouan-speaking people, they combined bison hunting with cultivation of maize, beans, and squash. The Osage lived in wigwam-type mat-covered houses. Relatives in the male line formed clans that were grouped into two divisions, each headed by a hereditary chief. A council of male elders assisted the chiefs in ceremonial and political affairs.

After initial contact with Europeans in the 1670s, the introduction of the horse and the fur trader greatly transformed Osage life. Between 1750 and 1830 the Osage dominated the territory between the Arkansas and Red rivers for purposes of trade and raiding for horses. In treaties of 1808, 1818, and 1825 they ceded vast lands in Missouri, Arkansas, Oklahoma, and Kansas. Hard times forced them to sell reservation lands in Kansas and return to Oklahoma in 1872. When their reservation was subdivided (1906) the Osage Nation retained mineral rights to excess lands sold, and subsequent discovery and exploitation of oil greatly enriched them. They are currently reviving their traditional crafts and ceremonials. In 1987, an estimated 6,850 Osage lived on or near the reservation.

Osage orange Osage orange, *Maclura pomifera,* sometimes called mock orange, is a hardwood tree of the mulberry family, Moraceae. It is a medium-sized, often thorny tree, growing to 18 m (60 ft) high. Its orange, rot-resistant wood is used for bows, fence posts, and other outdoor applications. Its round, wrinkled, yellowish fruit somewhat resembles a large orange. Native to the Arkansas and Texas region, the drought-resistant Osage orange has been planted throughout the United States.

The Osage orange produces tough, flexible wood once used for bows by Osage Indians. Its inedible fruit appears in autumn.

Osaka [oh'-sah-kah] Osaka, one of Japan's largest cities, is located on Osaka Bay at the mouth of the Yodo River on Honshu Island. Its population is 2,635,156 (1989 est.). Osaka is a leading commercial and industrial center and is also known as the City of Water because of its maze of canals and waterways. Osaka is the transportation hub of the Kansai region, the western section of Japan's urban-industrial belt along the Inland Sea.

Osaka has well-developed heavy manufacturing industries producing steel, nonferrous metals, electrical appliances, chemicals, fertilizers, machinery, and petrochemicals. As one of Japan's leading ports, Osaka, with KOBE, handles much of the nation's exports.

HIDEYOSHI, the supreme military ruler of Japan in his time, built his castle in Osaka in 1583. The city was already a prosperous commercial, financial, and manufacturing center when preeminence passed to Edo (Tokyo) during the Tokugawa period (1603–1867). Osaka has ex-

perienced an industrial expansion and renewed prosperity since World War II.

Osborne, John The English playwright John James Osborne, b. Dec. 12, 1929, achieved immediate fame with his first play, *Look Back in Anger* (1956; film, 1958), and simultaneously became the spokesperson for a new generation of English writers, Britain's so-called Angry Young Men.

Look Back in Anger, whose 1956 production constituted a milestone in the English theater, introduces Jimmy Porter, the quintessential Osborne hero: an intellectual working-class youth who rails at establishment values in the welfare state, he wrecks his and his wife's lives through his excessive bitterness. *The Entertainer* (1957; film, 1960), a tour de force starring Laurence Olivier in the role of Archie Rice, a vulgar vaudeville hoofer, portrays three generations of music-hall entertainers. *Luther* (1961), a Brechtian historical drama, presents the Protestant reformer as an angry young man of the 16th century. *Inadmissible Evidence* (1964; film, 1968) dramatizes the life of a middle-aged failure. Osborne has also written screenplays, most notably for the film *Tom Jones* (1962). In 1981 he published an autobiography, *A Better Class of Person.*

Oscar see ACADEMY AWARDS

Osceola [ah-see-oh'-lah] Osceola, b. near the Tallapoosa River, Georgia, c.1803, d. Jan. 30, 1838, was a leader of the Florida Seminole Indians during the Seminole Wars. Under the terms of the Treaty of Payne's Landing (1832), the Seminole were to be removed to Indian Territory (present-day Oklahoma). Osceola, among others, resisted. In December 1835, President Andrew Jackson sent a U.S. army to Florida. Osceola struck, retreated, and struck again. In 1837 he was invited to peace talks under a flag of truce. The offer was a trick, however, and Osceola was captured and imprisoned. He died in a cell at Fort Moultrie in Charleston Harbor, S.C.

Osceola, an Indian leader during the Seminole Wars, was lured under a flag of truce to Saint Augustine, Fla., where he and other chiefs were seized and imprisoned by the U.S. government (1837). Osceola was sent to Fort Moultrie, S.C., where he died. (National Collection of Fine Arts, Washington, D.C.)

oscillator   An oscillator is an electronic circuit that can convert a steady, direct current into a given waveform while maintaining its frequency within stated limits. Oscillators are used in all transmitters, radar units, and television sets, and all but the simplest radios. Sinusoidal oscillators generate waveforms like those of a sine wave; relaxation oscillators can generate rectangular pulses (square waves) and sawtooth and peaked waveforms.

All oscillators have an active element, such as a TRANSISTOR or a vacuum tube, that functions primarily as an AMPLIFIER and also releases the proper amount of energy to the feedback circuit to maintain oscillations. Frequency is determined by the elements in the feedback circuit, a part of which may be composed of the distributed capacitances and inductances of the circuit itself.

oscilloscope   An oscilloscope is an electronic instrument that graphically displays an electrical signal as a glowing line on a phosphorescent screen. The instrument is based on the CATHODE-RAY TUBE. The pattern on the screen is actually a rapidly moving point of light. The oscilloscope has an electronic circuit, called a sweep circuit, that continuously and repeatedly sweeps this point across the face of the cathode-ray tube at a rate that exceeds the flicker response of the human eye. The electronic signal to be displayed deflects the electron beam perpendicular to the sweep axis (up or down) in proportion to the amplitude of the signal. The resulting pattern provides a graphic representation of the amplitude of the incoming signal as a function of time.

The oscilloscope has become an indispensable tool of the electronic technician and engineer and finds wide application in fields that require the visual monitoring of a fluctuating signal. For example, the electrical activity of the brain (see ELECTROENCEPHALOGRAPH) and of the heart (see ELECTROCARDIOGRAPH) can also be displayed on devices similar to the oscilloscope.

Oseberg ship burial [oo'-suh-bairg]   A ship burial discovered (1903) at Oseberg in southern Norway contained one of the finest VIKING boats yet unearthed. Buried in a peat mound 37 m (120 ft) in diameter, the vessel held the bodies of two women, who are believed on the basis of associated finds to have been interred during the period AD 850–900. The ship itself was older; it has been dated at AD c.800. The remarkably well-preserved burial finds have shed much light on the everyday life of the Vikings. They include pieces of furniture, bedding, tents, looms, a wall hanging, a four-wheeled carriage, sleds, and numerous smaller objects.

Oshawa [ahsh'-uh-wuh]   The city of Oshawa (1986 pop., 123,651) is located in southeastern Ontario on the northern shore of Lake Ontario. Oshawa is a major industrial center, with woolen mills, foundries, and pharmaceutical plants. Automobile production dates to the early years of the century, and General Motors of Canada has its headquarters in the city. The city was settled as a military outpost in 1795 and renamed Oshawa in 1842.

Oshkosh [ahsh'-kahsh]   Located in east central Wisconsin where the Upper Fox River enters Lake Winnebago, Oshkosh is the seat of Winnebago County and has a population of 55,006 (1990). The city is both a popular summer resort and a manufacturing center producing clothing, automobile parts, wood products, and machinery. A branch of the University of Wisconsin is located in the city.

In 1670 the French missionary Father Claude Allouez became the first European to visit the site. He was followed by French explorers, and in the early 19th century a fur-trading post was established there. First called Athens, the community was renamed Oshkosh (Menominee for "claw") in 1840 and incorporated in 1846.

Osiris [oh-sy'-ris]   Osiris, god of the dead and the underworld, was one of the most important deities in ancient Egypt. A fertility god in the Predynastic Period, he had by about 2400 BC become also a funerary god and the personification of dead pharaohs. With his sister-consort ISIS and their son HORUS, he formed the great triad of Abydos.

The only complete account of the Osiris myth occurs in Plutarch's *Of Isis and Osiris*, although Egyptian fragments support much of his version. The son of the earth-god Geb and the sky-goddess Nut, Osiris is credited with introducing the skills of agriculture to the Egyptians. He is murdered by his brother SET, but Isis recovers the 14 scattered parts of his dismembered body and restores him to life. Osiris, however, remains in the underworld as king, while his posthumous son Horus becomes the king of the living.

Osiris represented the resurrection into eternal life that Egyptians sought by arranging that after death their bodies would be embalmed and swathed like that of the beneficent god. Osiris is represented mummified in green stone statues, but in pictures the color of his flesh suggests that he was a black god. His body is customarily wrapped in white funeral cloths. In his hands he holds the crook and flail of kings and the scepter of the gods.

Osler, Sir William [oh'-slur]   The English-Canadian physician and medical educator Sir William Osler, b. Bond Head, Ontario, July 12, 1849, d. Dec. 29, 1919, greatly influenced the practice of internal medicine. He received his medical degree from McGill University in 1872, and in 1889 he was appointed professor of medicine and physician in chief at the newly created Johns Hopkins School of Medicine and Hospital in Baltimore, Md. He organized a clinic system at the hospital and is noted for his method of teaching medical students at the bedside, correlating their scientific studies with clinical observations. His publication *The Principles and Practice* of Medicine (1892) was highly influential and has become a standard text. Osler also pioneered in preventive medicine, advocating improved sanitation and other public-health measures. In 1905 he was named regius professor of medicine at Oxford University, and in 1911 he was named a baronet.

—

Oslo [ahz'-loh]   Oslo, the capital, chief port, and largest city of Norway, lies at the head of Oslo Fjord, about 97 km (60 mi) from the open sea. The city has a population of 457,818 (1990 est.).

Contemporary City. Today Oslo is a well-planned city with wide, straight streets. Government offices and the central business district are focused on Karl Johansgate, the main street. On the waterfront, facing the fjord and the downtown area, is the City Hall (completed 1950), which dominates the city and forms its most conspicuous landmark. The principal docks lie along the fjord, which must be kept open by icebreakers in winter.

Oslo is the principal business and financial center in Norway and the most important commercial port. Timber industries remain important, but in recent years they have been overshadowed by the processing of imported materials such as textiles and metals, shipbuilding, and the manufacturing of equipment needed in the North Sea petroleum fields.

Oslo is also the principal cultural center in Norway. The university, founded in 1811, is the largest in the country. The city is the site of the National Theater, a folk museum, and a museum of excavated Viking ships. On Holmenkollen, a mountain overlooking the city, is a famous ski jump, the focus of winter sports activities. Frogner Park contains the statuary of Gustav VIGELAND.

History. Oslo was founded about 1050 to the east of the present city. Early in the 17th century fire destroyed the wood-structured town. King Christian IV ordered the city rebuilt on the Akershus Peninsula below the fortress (built 1300), which could protect it. The new city was laid out on a grid plan and was named Christiania for its founder.

Oslo, the capital of Norway, has expanded rapidly since the 19th century to become the country's most populous city and principal port.

There was little growth before the 19th century. The population in 1814 was only 11,200. In 1814, Norway was separated from Denmark and became an independent state "united with Sweden under one king." Christiania became the national capital and at once began to grow. The Royal Palace was built, and the Storting (Parliament) and government offices were established. The population had reached 225,000 in 1910 and 270,000 by 1930. The name *Oslo* was readopted in 1925.

—

osmium [ahz'-mee-uhm]   Osmium is a bluish white, lustrous metallic chemical element, a member of the PLATINUM group of metals (Group VIII in the periodic table). The name is derived from the Greek *osme*, meaning "smell," which is descriptive of some of its compounds. Its chemical symbol is Os, its atomic weight is 190.2, and its atomic number is 76. It was discovered in 1803 by Smithson Tennant in the residue remaining when crude platinum was dissolved in aqua regia. Osmium is extremely hard and brittle even at high temperatures. It has a boiling point of 5,027° C and the highest melting point (3,045° C) of the metals of the platinum group. Although the metal is difficult to fabricate, in powdered form it can be sintered in an atmosphere of hydrogen at 2,000° C. Solid osmium is unaffected by air at room temperature, but in powdered or spongy form it slowly gives off osmium tetroxide (OsO_4), a strong oxidizing agent that is extremely toxic, has a pungent smell, and is used to detect fingerprints and to stain specimens for both electron and optical microscopy. The element exhibits variable oxidation states, the most common being +3, +4, +6, and +8. The metal finds its most widespread use in the production of very hard alloys with other members of the platinum group.

—

osmosis [ahz-moh'-suhs]   Osmosis is the process by which a liquid substance passes spontaneously through a semipermeable membrane, that is, a membrane that allows the liquid to pass through it but not dissolved substances. If the membrane is placed vertically between a pure solvent such as water and an aqueous solution, the water flows through the membrane into the solution. The volume of the solution is increased and its level raised. The flow of pure water into the solution can be prevented by applying a pressure on the solution, called the osmotic pressure. Alternatively, if osmosis is allowed to proceed unhindered, it ceases when the hydrostatic pressure due to the difference between the levels on each side of the membrane equals the osmotic pressure.

Osmotic Pressure. In chemistry the principal application of osmosis is the determination of molecular weights in the range of 10,000–100,000, which is difficult or impossible to determine by other means. The determination is based on the fact that osmotic pressure depends only on the number of dissolved molecules, and the method has been successfully applied to many proteins and artificial polymeric materials.

In technology the process called reverse osmosis has

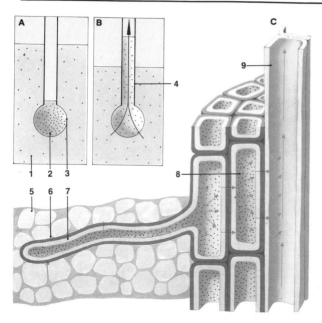

In osmosis (A, B), a solvent such as water passes from a dilute (1) to a concentrated solution (3) through a semipermeable membrane (2). The flow of solvent continues (4) until stopped by osmotic pressure. Red dots indicate solution concentration. A plant root (section, C), for example, absorbs water by osmosis. Water in the soil (5) flows into the more concentrated root-hair cytoplasm (7) through a semipermeable wall (6). Water passes from this cell to adjacent cells (8), also by osmosis, until it reaches water-conducting vessels (9).

become a practical means of removing salts from impure natural water. In this process the water is forced under pressure through tubes made of a membrane material that is not permeable to the ions; ion-free water can then be collected from outside the membrane. To make the water flow outward, the pressure applied mechanically must exceed the osmotic pressure of the solution being separated.

Biological Transport. In living organisms osmosis plays a crucial and pervasive role, because all cells, and most organelles within cells, are surrounded by semipermeable membranes. In general, biological membranes are more or less permeable to water, they do not pass substances having molecular weights of more than a few thousand, and they are quite selective with respect to the transport of positively charged ions. Thus, osmosis is involved, together with other processes, in determining and regulating what goes into and comes out of the cell or organelle (see MEMBRANE CHEMISTRY).

Osmosis is a special case of DIFFUSION, a process in which a substance always goes from a region of relatively high concentration to one of lower concentration. (Pure water passes into solutions where the water is less "concentrated.") In cells a substance often moves in the opposite direction, but such a process necessarily has to be powered by some metabolic reaction or reactions. That phenomenon is usually called ACTIVE TRANSPORT; it may be taking place at the same time as diffusion, but it must be clearly distinguished from it.

Osnabrück [ohs-nah-bruek'] Osnabrück is a city in northern Germany in the state of Lower Saxony with a population of 153,300 (1985 est.). Its location on the Hase River, with a link to the Ems-Weser Canal, has made it a shipping center as well as a rail and road hub. Osnabrück produces iron and steel, machinery, automobile bodies, textiles, and paper. Landmarks include the Rathaus (city hall; begun in the 15th century), the three-towered cathedral (begun in the 8th century), and the 17th-century bishops' palace. Settled by Saxons, Osnabrück was made an episcopal see by Charlemagne in 783. During the Middle Ages the city was a member of the Hanseatic League and a center of the linen trade. Allied bombings during World War II severely damaged the city.

OSO The Orbiting Solar Observatories (OSO) were a series of eight NASA satellites that provided a better understanding of the Sun's atmosphere and of the sunspot cycle. The satellites also investigated sources of X rays beyond.

The Spacecraft. The first seven satellites, built by Ball Brothers Research Corporation, were launched on Mar. 7, 1962; Feb. 3, 1965; Mar. 8, 1967; Oct. 18, 1967; Jan. 22, 1969; Aug. 9, 1969; and Sept. 29, 1971. (*OSO C*, launched Aug. 25, 1965, failed to achieve orbit after a premature third-stage ignition in the Delta launch vehicle.)

The upper, "sail" section of each OSO was a semicircular panel covered with 1,860 solar cells that were continuously pointed toward the Sun. On *OSO 1*, the scientific instrumentation in this upper section included three X-ray experiments, a gamma-ray detector, and a micrometeoroid detector. The lower, "wheel" section rotated at about 30 rpm to spin-stabilize the spacecraft. It contained nickel-cadmium batteries, telemetry processing equipment, a tape recorder, and two radio transmitters; its scientific instrumentation studied solar radiation (in the ultraviolet region) and solar cosmic rays, measured radiation levels in the Van Allen radiation belts, and detected neutrons. Various other experiments were incorporated into both the upper and lower sections of later OSO satellites. *OSO 8*, a 1,064-kg (2,346-lb) satellite built by the Hughes Aircraft Company and launched June 21, 1975, had a different configuration from its predecessors.

Astronomy and Astrophysics Contributions. The OSO satellites obtained the first full-disk photograph of the solar corona, the first X-ray observations from a satellite of solar streamers and of a solar flare in its initial stage of eruption, and the first white-light and extreme-ultraviolet observations of the corona.

osprey The osprey, *Pandion haliaetus*, is a large hawklike bird, often called the fish hawk, found near lakes, rivers, and seacoasts over most of the world. Ospreys are generally considered a single species, divided into six subspecies, and are usually classified in a family

The osprey may plunge completely underwater to capture a fish, which it grasps with its large talons. Also called the fish hawk, the osprey is found near freshwater and salt water.

the bichirs (about 10 species); and Actinopterygii, the ray-fins. The ray-fins comprise three infraclasses: Chondrostei, the sturgeons and paddlefishes (25 species); Holostei, the bowfins and gars (8 species); and Teleostei (18,000 or more species).

Bony-fish species are distributed by general habitat as follows: freshwater 41%, marine shore (warm) 40%, marine shore (cold) 6%, deep sea 11%, marine surface (epipelagic) 1.4%, and migratory between fresh and salt water 0.6%. Almost half the world's fish species are freshwater, despite the fact that 70% of the world is covered with salt water. The richest marine faunas inhabit the tropical Indo-Pacific, the Caribbean, and the temperate northeastern Pacific oceans. The richest freshwater faunas are in tropical South America, West Africa, and Southeast Asia.

of their own, Pandionidae. They may reach 60 cm (24 in) in length, with a 1.8-m (6-ft) wingspread, and 2 kg (4.6 lb) in weight; females are larger than males. Ospreys are blackish brown above and white on the undersides and on the head, with a blackish brown band through the eye and across the cheek, an irregular, spotted bank across the breast, and a barred tail.

Ospreys hunt by cruising over the water, hovering briefly when they see their prey, and then plunging feetfirst into the water. Large claws and feet studded with sharp spines enable the osprey to clutch its slippery prey. A mated pair of ospreys build a stick nest, which they use year after year, on top of a tree or other high point near water.

OSS see OFFICE OF STRATEGIC SERVICES

Ossian [ahsh'-uhn] Ossian (or Oisin), son of FINN MAC CUMHAIL, was the warrior hero of the Gaelic legends known as the Fenian cycle. In 1760 the Scots writer James MACPHERSON claimed that he had discovered the manuscripts of epics written by Ossian. Although his "translations" were rightly denounced as literary forgeries by Samuel Johnson, the Ossian poems were nonetheless admired by Goethe, Blake, and Byron and exercised a strong influence on the European romantic movement.

Osteichthyes [ahs-tee-ik'-thee-eez] The class Osteichthyes, the modern bony fishes, encompasses more than 95% of the vast array of living fishes, with about 430 families, approximately 4,000 genera, and more than 18,000 species. Bony fishes are characterized by the possession of bone, soft and usually segmented fin supports (rays), an air bladder or lungs present at least in the young, and a dermal maxillary and premaxillary bone forming the upper jaw. Four subclasses are often recognized: Dipneusti, the lungfishes (about 7 species); Crossopterygii, the coelacanth (1 species); Brachiopterygii,

Ostend [awst'-end] Ostend (Flemish: Oostende), is a city in northwestern Belgium on the North Sea with a population of 68,397 (1988 est.). Ostend is Belgium's leading fishing port; fishing, oyster culture, and shipbuilding are the leading industries. The city was settled as a fishing village in the 9th century and had become a well-known port by the 11th century. Fortified in 1583, Ostend became the last Dutch stronghold in Belgium but fell to Spain after a three-year siege in 1604. In 1745 the city was almost destroyed by the French; nevertheless, it became a prosperous commercial center. After Belgium won its independence in 1830, Ostend developed as a resort area. It was used as a submarine base by the Germans in World War I and suffered heavy damage during World War II.

Ostend Manifesto The Ostend Manifesto of Oct. 18, 1854, was a private letter drawn up by the American diplomats James BUCHANAN, John Y. Mason, and Pierre Soulé, accredited to London, Paris, and Madrid, respectively, urging U.S. Secretary of State William L. MARCY to consider the possibility of seizing Cuba. The United States had long been interested in Cuba, and when a U.S. ship, the *Black Warrior*, was seized by Spanish authorities in Havana in February 1854, Southern expansionists demanded war, hoping to secure the island as slave territory. In August, Marcy ordered Soulé, who had already issued an unauthorized ultimatum to the Spanish, to meet with Buchanan and Mason in Ostend, Belgium, and formulate a policy on Cuba. The resulting manifesto argued that the United States should attempt to buy the island to ensure that it would not come under control of the Cuban blacks or, if Spain refused to sell, to seize it. The manifesto's contents leaked to the public, and Northern protests caused the administration to repudiate it.

osteoarthritis [ahs-tee-oh-ahrth-ry'-tis] The most common form of ARTHRITIS, osteoarthritis is a degenerative disease involving the destruction of cartilage in joints and the enlargement of the joint ends of bones. It is also termed *degenerative joint disease*. A characteristic sign of osteoarthritis is the development of bony spurs near joints. Contributing genetic, metabolic, and endocrine factors have been suggested, but the cause is unknown.

Osteoarthritis is an accompaniment of aging that probably begins in the twenties. An estimated 90 percent of the population is affected to some degree after age 50. The main symptoms are pain aggravated by motion or the pressure of weight, stiffness after inactivity, and limitation of motion. Major disability can result from severe involvement of the hands, hips, knees, or spine.

osteomyelitis [ahs-tee-oh-my-uh-ly′-tis]   A bacterial, fungal, or rickettsial infection within bone and bone marrow, osteomyelitis is often associated with infections by the same organism in other parts of the body. Direct infection usually results from open fractures, wounds, or surgery. The infection begins suddenly in children, usually near the ends of long bones in the legs, and spreads through the marrow and other bone channels, causing high fever, chills, pain, and abscess. In adults the onset is more gradual, without acute fever, and usually affects the pelvis and the spine. Infection of vertebrae results in destruction of the ends of vertebrae and of the disks between vertebrae. Later, new bone may form between adjacent vertebrae and cause them to fuse. Unless treated with antibiotics, bone destruction can result. Also, organisms may remain in the bone and cause a recurrence years later.

osteopathic medicine   Osteopathic medicine combines the treatment of disease not only with drugs and surgery but also with manipulative procedures in which a physician palpates, by hand, areas of the body that are under tension or are distorted. Underlying osteopathy are the ideas that body structure and function are closely interrelated and mutually interdependent and that the body is an integrated whole.

The first school of osteopathy was founded by Dr. Andrew T. Still in 1892 at Kirksville, Mo. Today 15 schools are located throughout the United States; training involves four years of study in medical sciences and an internship. Although trained in the manipulative techniques, a Doctor of Osteopathy (D.O.) is qualified to prescribe drugs and to use the medical instruments commonly used by medical doctors. More than 200 osteopathic hospitals and numerous clinics provide care in the United States. The American Osteopathic Association is the official organization of these physicians.

osteoporosis   Osteoporosis is a condition of bone characterized by excessive porosity, or bone-tissue reduction. Absorption of old bone exceeds deposition of new bone; the result is an enlargement of spaces normally present and a thinning of the bone from the inside. No change occurs in the outside dimensions, except in compression of weight-bearing bones. Senile and postmeno-pausal, or primary, osteoporosis, the most common type, is found only in elderly persons and in women who have passed through menopause. It is characterized by compression of the vertebrae with resultant back pain and loss of height, and by susceptibility to fractures. Disuse, or secondary, osteoporosis involves bones that have been immobilized by paralytic disease or traumatic fractures, or that have been subjected to prolonged weightlessness during spaceflight. Other osteoporoses are associated with endocrine diseases and nutritional disorders. Exercise programs, calcium supplements, and fluorine tablets are used in prevention and treatment. Older women may receive estrogen therapy.

Ostia [ohs′-tee-uh]   Ostia, the harbor of ancient Rome, was situated at the mouth of the Tiber River, 27 km (17 mi) downstream from the capital. First occupied (c.340 BC) to guard the coast and serve as a naval base, the site became an important commercial center with the increase of Roman power in the 2d century BC. The emperor Claudius had an artificial harbor (the Portus) constructed (AD c.40). Within the carefully planned town were shops, offices, and warehouses, along with public baths and lavatories, a theater, and a gymnasium. Later expansion of the harbor by Trajan sparked a building boom marked by high-density apartment buildings as tall as five stories.

ostracoderm [ahs-truh-koh-durm′]   Ostracoderms are extinct jawless fishes that existed from late Cambrian to late Devonian times, about 510 million to 350 million years ago. The name means "shell-skinned," and these fishes were typically armored with scales and bony plates; the head was commonly protected by a solid shield of bonelike material. Most ostracoderms had only a tail fin and usually some variety of single-line fins along the back or belly; however, a number of forms had a pair of low-set fins just behind the head. Ostracoderms were generally about 13 cm (5 in) long, but a few reached 60 cm (2 ft). Ostracoderms discovered in 1978 in northeastern Wyoming are the earliest known vertebrate fossils.

Ostrava [aws′-trah-vah]   Ostrava, an important mining and industrial center and a regional capital of northern Moravia, is the fourth largest city in Czechoslovakia. The city is located about 275 km (170 mi) east of Prague. The population is 328,373 (1987 est.). Surrounded by the Ostrava, Karviná, and Orlová coalfields, Ostrava is a center of anthracite and bituminous coal mining, metallurgy, machine building, and chemical and hydroelectrical power production. A college of mining and metallurgy is located there. Points of interest include the Church of Saint Wenceslaus, dating from the late 13th century, the Old Town Hall (1687), and the opera house.

Ostrava was founded in 1267, and coal deposits were first discovered in 1767. The Vítkovice steel works, with the region's first blast furnace, was built in 1829. Industrial development boomed thereafter until the German occupation during World War II, when the city sustained heavy damage. Rapid industrial expansion followed the war.

ostrich   The ostrich, *Struthio camelus*, is the largest living bird. It may stand 3 m (10 ft) tall and weigh more than 150 kg (330 lb). Although flightless, the ostrich is able to take 3.5-m (12-ft) strides and to run at a sustained speed of 50 km/h (30 mph) for 15 minutes or more. In short bursts it may reach 70 km/h (43 mph). If cornered, it can also kick dangerously with the two clawed toes on each of its long, featherless legs. Its long neck is sparsely covered with hairlike feathers; the head is small, with large eyes and a short, flat bill. Its body is covered with large, soft, loosely structured feathers, and its wing and tail feathers are plumelike. The female is grayish brown; the male is black, with white wings and tail. Alone among birds, ostriches eliminate urine and feces separately.

Ostriches live in arid, open country, where they feed on plant matter as well as on occasional insects, lizards, birds, and mice. They can go for long periods without water. Ostriches commonly live in small, loosely organized flocks. Sometimes, due to food or water conditions, flocks may temporarily join to form a group of several hundred birds.

The most common mating pattern is one male and three females in a family unit. The male usually makes a nest by scraping out a depression in sandy ground. All the females lay their eggs in the same nest, and both sexes incubate the eggs. A family of females may lay from 15 to 30 eggs, but not all hatch. The eggs are larger than those of any other living bird; they may be 150 mm (6 in) long and 127 mm (5 in) wide, have a shell 1.97 mm ($\frac{5}{64}$ in)

The ostrich is the world's largest bird, standing up to 3 m (10 ft) tall. It is flightless but capable of running rapidly. Ostriches in captivity may have life spans as great as those of humans. Farm birds are the source of most of the ostrich feathers and skin (leather) used in the fashion industry.

thick, and weigh up to 1,600 g (3.5 lb). The young hatch in 42 days and are able to run almost immediately. Both young and adult ostriches hide by sitting with their heads and necks stretched out on the ground, which may have given rise to the erroneous belief that ostriches bury their heads in the sand. Ostriches reach full size in about 6 months but do not attain sexual maturity until 3 to 4 years of age. They may live for 30 years in the wild and much longer in captivity.

The ostrich is the only living species in the family Struthionidae and in the order Struthioniformes. It originated in the Asiatic steppes during the Eocene Epoch, 40 million to 50 million years ago, and once ranged through Asia, Europe, and Africa. Its natural range is now limited to Africa, where it is separated into four subspecies.

Ostrogoths   see GOTHS

Ostrovsky, Aleksandr Nikolayevich [uh-strawf'-skee]   A prolific Russian playwright, Aleksandr Nikolayevich Ostrovsky, b. Apr. 12 (N.S.), 1823, d. June 14 (N.S.), 1886, was in the forefront of social drama written in the realist tradition. His early plays include *The Bankrupt*, retitled *It's All in the Family* (written 1849; produced 1860; Eng. trans., 1917); *The Poor Bride* (1852; Eng. trans., 1933); and *Poverty Is No Crime* (1854; Eng. trans., 1917). His masterpiece, *The Storm* (1860; Eng. trans., 1889), is a powerful tragedy about superstition, ignorance, and a doomed marriage in a provincial Volga town. His best-known work in the West is *Diary of a Scoundrel* (1868; Eng. trans., 1923), a comedy of manners exposing hypocrisy.

Ostwald, Wilhelm [awst'-vahlt]   The German physical chemist and philosopher Friedrich Wilhelm Ostwald, b. Sept. 2, 1853, d. Apr. 4, 1932, was the cofounder and the most active organizer of PHYSICAL CHEMISTRY as a special discipline. After receiving (1878) his doctorate in chemistry from the University of Dorpat, he taught (1882–87) at the Polytechnic Institute in Riga. In 1887, Ostwald started a laboratory of worldwide influence in Leipzig and coedited the first journal of physical chemistry. His major studies of the kinetics of chemical reactions and equilibrium states later incorporated the Swedish chemist Svante ARRHENIUS's theory of ionization. In his studies of catalysts, Ostwald established that catalysts do not affect the overall energy relations between the reacting chemicals and their products. He received the 1909 Nobel Prize for chemistry.

Oswald, Lee Harvey   Lee Harvey Oswald, b. Dallas, Tex., Oct. 18, 1939, d. Nov. 24, 1963, was the lone assassin of President John F. KENNEDY, according to the WARREN COMMISSION report on the killing. After serving in the U.S. Marines, Oswald lived (1959–62) in the Soviet Union. In October 1963 he began working at the Texas School Book Depository in Dallas. Shots apparently fired from the Depository on Nov. 22, 1963, killed President Kennedy. Charged with the assassination and the subsequent killing of a policeman, Oswald himself was shot and killed by Jack Ruby, the operator of a Dallas nightclub.

Oswald, Saint   Saint Oswald, d. 641, was king of the Anglo-Saxon kingdom of NORTHUMBRIA from 633. He was converted to Christianity while on the Scottish island of Iona during the reign of his uncle Edwin, who had overthrown (616) Oswald's father, Æthelfrith. After Edwin's death Oswald recovered his father's throne and introduced Celtic Christianity to Northumbria. He was also recognized as overlord by the southern English kingdoms. Killed in a battle with the pagan king Penda of Mercia, Oswald was venerated as a martyr. Feast day: Aug. 5 (Aug. 8 or 9 in some places).

Othello   *The Tragedy of Othello, the Moor of Venice* (c.1604) is SHAKESPEARE's only venture into the popular genre of domestic tragedy, in which the protagonists are not great nobles. Othello is a professional soldier, a person on whom the city of Venice depends; he is also an African Moor, however, and thus an alien figure in Venetian society. After marrying Desdemona, the daughter of Brabantio, a senator, Othello is tricked into killing his loving wife through the diabolic machinations of Iago— Shakespeare's most highly developed villain. The play is based on an Italian story in Giraldi Cinthio's *Hecatommithi* (1566), but Shakespeare may have worked from a French translation (1584).

Otis, James   James Otis, b. West Barnstable, Mass., Feb. 5, 1725, d. May 23, 1783, was a distinguished American lawyer and political leader in prerevolutionary Massachusetts. In 1760 he appeared on behalf of Boston merchants challenging the legality of the writs of assistance empowering royal customs officers to search any house for contraband. Otis lost the case, but in his impassioned argument that the writs were unconstitutional as well as contrary to the laws of nature, he articulated concepts later central to the colonial opposition to the British Parliament.

As a member of the Massachusetts legislature (1761–69), Otis continued to attack the writs in eloquent speeches and pamphlets. He also joined the protest against the STAMP ACT (1765). After receiving a serious head injury in a tavern brawl in 1769, however, he ceased to play a significant political role.

Oto   [oh'-toh]   The Oto, a tribe of North American Indians, lived in Wisconsin in prehistoric times. They spoke a Siouan language of the Hokan-Siouan stock. Along with the MISSOURI and the IOWA, they separated from the WINNEBAGO to settle near the Iowa River. After a factional fight on Grand River, the Oto went farther up the Missouri; in the late 18th century they numbered more than 1,000 in several villages along the Platte River in Nebraska. The Oto lived in oven-shaped earth houses when cultivating along the river but used tepees while on excursions into the plains to hunt bison. Society was organized in nine clans based on male ancestry, cut across by voluntary associations, such as the Medicine, Buffalo, and Curing Lodges. Mystical vision quests were important male rites.

After the Civil War about 400 Oto and 50 Missouri moved onto a reservation in northwest Kansas, ceding much land in Nebraska. In 1881, they sold their reservation and moved to INDIAN TERRITORY, where they became members of the NATIVE AMERICAN CHURCH. During World War I, oil was discovered on their land, but its irregular production has failed to provide the Oto with a substantial income source. The Otoe-Missouria tribe numbered about 1,250 in 1987.

otolaryngology   see MEDICINE

Ottawa   (Indian tribe) [aht'-uh-wuh]   The Ottawa (Algonquian for "traders"), a group of five independent Algonquian-speaking clans of North American Indians, had such skill in trading that the French used their name to refer to all Algonquians with whom they traded. When Samuel de CHAMPLAIN first met them near the mouth of the French River in 1615, they were closely allied with the HURON confederacy of Ontario. Their language was mutually intelligible with OJIBWA and nearly so with POTAWATOMI.

Refugees from the Ottawa River valley in eastern Ontario and Quebec, Canada, the Ottawa had settled by the 17th century on Manitoulin Island in Lake Huron and later along Chequamegon Bay in northern Wisconsin, where for many years they dominated trading relations between the French and the interior tribes. Their great leader Pontiac, in 1763, led an unsuccessful attempt to drive out the English (see PONTIAC'S REBELLION). Some Ottawa remain on Manitoulin Island today, and others live in Michigan, Wisconsin, and Oklahoma.

Ottawa   (Ontario)   Ottawa, the capital of Canada and seat of the Ottawa-Carleton municipal region in Ontario, is in the southeastern part of the country. Ottawa is the fourth largest metropolitan area in Canada, with a population of 819,263 (1986), of which 300,763 (1986) live within the city limits. The city is located at the junction of the Ottawa, Rideau, and Gatineau rivers. The Ottawa River marks the provincial boundary between Ontario and Quebec, with the city of Ottawa on the Ontario side and the large secondary city of Hull on the Quebec side. Ottawa was named for the Ottawa Indian tribe, although the name had previously been applied to the river. In recent years it has been one of the fastest growing major urban centers in the nation. The populace of Ottawa-Hull is representative of the Canadian ethnic mix; about one-third of the total are French Canadian. As probably the most bilingual city in Canada, Ottawa is also the epitome of the Canadian bicultural "ideal."

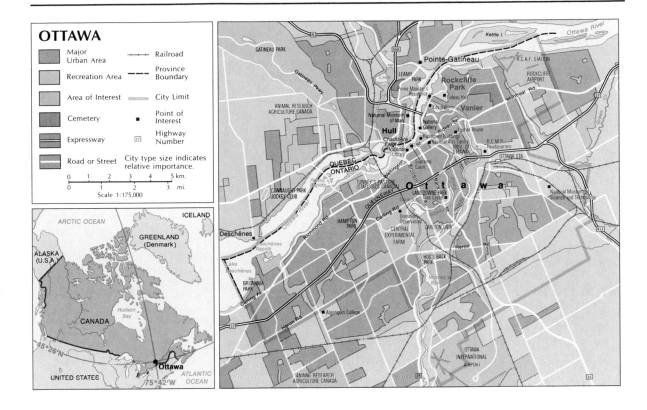

OTTAWA

Major Urban Area

Recreation Area

Area of Interest

Cemetery

Expressway

Road or Street

Railroad

Province Boundary

City Limit

Point of Interest

Highway Number

City type size indicates relative importance.

0   1   2   3   4   5 km.
0   1   2   3 mi.
Scale 1:175,000

The industrial heritage of early Ottawa is still maintained in the forest-products plants and hydroelectric facilities on both sides of the river. Industries include paper mills and appliance, furniture, and cement manufacturing. In addition, Ottawa has considerable commercial activity, based in part on a prosperous agricultural hinterland, a number of financial institutions, and an important tourist industry. The major employer in Ottawa, however, is the federal government.

Ottawa is noted for its parks, gardens, scenic drives, and monuments. Points of interest include the Parliament Buildings, National Library, National Museum of Science and Technology, and the new National Gallery (1988). Carleton University and the University of Ottawa are in the city.

Although the area was explored by Samuel de Champlain in 1613, the city's development did not begin until 1826 when Lt. Col. John By and his Royal Engineers arrived to construct the Rideau Canal (as a bypass for Rideau Falls). The community that developed around the construction headquarters was called Bytown, which in 1855 was declared a city with the new name of Ottawa. The first railroad also arrived in that year, but the river maintained its prime importance for the developing lumber industry. Ottawa was chosen as the capital for United Canada in 1857, despite bitter opposition from four rival cities. The choice was confirmed when the new Dominion of Canada was established in 1867.

Ottawa River The Ottawa River flows through southeastern Ontario and southern Quebec, Canada. Its length of about 1,120 km (700 mi) makes it the second longest river in eastern Canada after the St. Lawrence River, of which it is the chief tributary. The Ottawa's drainage basin is about 142,000 km² (55,000 mi²). From its source in Lake Capimitchigama in southwestern Quebec the river flows west through several lakes into the northern end of Lake Timiskaming. After leaving the lake at its southern end, the Ottawa flows in a southeasterly direction along the Ontario-Quebec border. It passes Ottawa and flows east through farmlands to Montreal, where it empties into the St. Lawrence. The Ottawa is connected to Lake Ontario by the Rideau River and Canal.

otter   Otters are long-bodied, semiaquatic members of the weasel family, Mustelidae. This group includes the sea otter, genus *Enhydra*; the river otters, *Lutra*; the giant otter, *Pteronura*, of South America; the African clawless otter, *Aonyx*; and the small-clawed otters of Asia, *Amblonyx,* and Africa, *Paronyx,* both of which are often classified with the clawless otter.

The river otters, *Lutra,* comprise 11 or 12 species found on all the continents except Australia and Antarctica and include the North American otter, *L. canadensis,*

The approximately 12 species of river otters are swimmers that can close their ears and nostrils to make themselves watertight.

and the European otter, *L. lutra.* They have broad snouts, small ears, short legs with fully webbed feet, and a thick but tapering tail. Their underfur is short and dense, brownish or grayish in color, and is overlain with darker, coarser guard hairs. Male river otters reach about 1 m (3 ft) in length, plus a 50-cm (19-in) tail; they weigh up to about 14 kg (30 lb). Females are smaller.

River otters feed on fish, crustaceans, amphibians, turtles, and even birds and small land mammals. Northern populations of river otters mate in summer, and the young are not born until 9½ to 12½ months later. This prolonged gestation is due to the delayed implantation, or attachment, of the newly developing embryo to the wall of the uterus.

otter hound   The otter hound is a large dog, similar in size and shape to the bloodhound, with a domed skull and long, hanging ears, but with a rough coat. It is the only hound breed developed specifically for hunting in water. It has webbed feet and an oily, double coat consisting of a dense, woolly undercoat and a coarse, crisp outer coat, 7.5 to 15 cm (3 to 6 in) long. Otter hounds stand from 56 to 69 cm (22 to 27 in) high at the shoulder and weigh from 29.5 to 52 kg (65 to 115 lb). Any coat color is permissible. Reports on otter hunting with dog packs exist from the time of King John's reign (1199–1216), but the modern otter hound is a product of the late 19th century.

Otterbein, Philip William   [oht'-ur-byn]   One of the founders of the Church of the United Brethren in Christ (1800), Philip William Otterbein, b. Dillenburg, Germany, June 3, 1726, d. Nov. 17, 1813, was a German Reformed pastor and itinerant evangelist. After attending the Reformed Seminary at Herborn, he immigrated to Pennsylvania in 1752 as a missionary to the German settlers. Throughout his ministry he traveled as an evangelist in Pennsylvania and Maryland. A friend of the Methodist Francis ASBURY, he also worked closely with Martin BOEHM, with whom he drew together the United Brethren. The two were elected the first bishops of the church (which later became the EVANGELICAL UNITED BRETHREN CHURCH).

Otto, Rudolf   The German theologian and philosopher Rudolf Otto, b. Sept. 25, 1869, d. Mar. 6, 1937, was noted for his analysis of the central religious experience of the holy. His thought was influenced both by the theology of Friedrich Schleiermacher and by the philosophy of Immanuel Kant. In his best-known work, *The Idea of the Holy* (1917; Eng. trans., 1923), Otto claimed that the holy has a complex character that includes both rational and nonrational elements. The nonrational element, often overlooked, he called the numinous. This is characterized by mystery, awesomeness, and fascination (*mysterium tremendum fascinans*). The analysis is supported by a wealth of evidence from the Bible and nonbiblical religions.

Otto I, King of Germany and Holy Roman Emperor   Otto I, b. Oct. 23, 912, d. May 7, 973, the greatest of the Saxon kings of Germany, founded the HOLY ROMAN EMPIRE. Otto succeeded his father, HENRY I, in 936, inheriting a state that centered mainly on the duchies of Saxony and Franconia. In 937 he established his dominion over Burgundy. In 940, Otto allied with the powerful CAPETIAN Hugh the Great against LOUIS IV of France but later intervened (950) to preserve a balance of power between the French monarchy and the Capetians. Otto also commissioned the Saxon nobles Hermann Billung and Gero to conquer the Wends, a Slavic group living across the Elbe from Saxony. By defeating the MAGYARS at Lechfeld (955), he won the allegiance of most of the German people.

Otto brought the church tightly under his control; he gave the archbishoprics of Cologne and Mainz to his brothers Bruno and William respectively, rewarded churchmen lavishly, and exacted administrative and military service. His three expeditions into Italy (951–52, 961–65, 966–72) greatly increased his power. On the first he secured the crown of Lombardy. On the second Pope John XII crowned him Roman emperor in 962; later embellished with the adjective *holy,* this title was enjoyed by German kings until 1806. The third expedition brought Otto into conflict with the Byzantines in southern Italy and thus consolidated his authority over the papacy.

Known as Otto the Great, he stimulated German cultural life, encouraging the Ottonian Renaissance. His son Otto II succeeded him.

See also: OTTONIAN ART AND ARCHITECTURE.

Otto II, King of Germany and Holy Roman Emperor   Otto II, b. 955, d. Dec. 7, 983, was crowned German king in 961 and Holy Roman emperor in 967. His reign was not peaceful. In 974, Duke Henry II of Bavaria revolted against him, obtaining support from Prince Mieszko I of Poland and from Prince Boleslav II of Bohemia. This revolt was suppressed in 978.

After a war with France over Lorraine, Otto led an expedition into Italy in 980. He restored Pope Benedict VII, who had been driven from his see by a Roman faction, but his campaign against the Arabs (Saracens) in south-

This illustration from the Registrum Gregorii, a manuscript of the late 10th century, shows either Otto II or Otto III receiving homage from figures representing four subject peoples of his empire: the Germans, the Italians, the French, and the Slavs. (Musée Condé Chantilly.)

ern Italy ended (982) with a decisive defeat. In 983 he learned of invasions of his domains by both the Danes and the Slavs, but he died before returning to Germany. His son Otto III succeeded him.

Otto III, King of Germany and Holy Roman Emperor

Otto III, b. July 980, d. Jan. 23, 1002, succeeded his father, Otto II, as German king in 983 and was crowned emperor in 996. Until 995, guardians ruled for him: his Byzantine mother, Theophano, his grandmother Adelheid, and Archbishop Willigis of Mainz. After coming of age he was strongly influenced by the ecclesiastics Adalbert of Prague and Gerbert of Aurillac.

Otto gave more attention to imperial and Italian affairs than to Germany. Proclaiming the restoration of the ancient Roman Empire, he settled in Rome in 998 and surrounded himself with antique artifacts and Byzantine ceremony.

In 996, Otto appointed the first German pope, Gregory V; in 999 he made Gerbert pope as Sylvester II. Otto visited Poland in AD 1000; he had good relations with BOLESŁAW I and gave Poland a native church organization by creating the archbishopric of Gniezno. Otto left no descendants and was succeeded by his third cousin HENRY II.

Otto IV, King of Germany and Holy Roman Emperor

Otto IV, b. 1182, d. May 19, 1218, was the only member of the powerful WELF family, longtime rival to the imperial HOHENSTAUFEN dynasty, to become Holy Roman emperor. Called Otto of Brunswick, he was a son of HENRY THE LION. After Emperor HENRY VI died in 1197, the anti-Hohenstaufen princes elected Otto king of Germany on June 9, 1198 in opposition to PHILIP OF SWABIA, Henry's brother. By many concessions, Otto won Pope INNOCENT III's support, and when Philip was murdered in 1208, all Germany acknowledged Otto as king.

Immediately breaking his promises to the pope, Otto invaded the Sicilian lands of Henry VI's son, the future emperor FREDERICK II. Innocent, therefore, persuaded Frederick to assert his rights in Germany, where the princes elected him king in 1212. Otto secured the alliance of his uncle King JOHN of England, while Frederick allied with PHILIP II of France. Defeated by Philip in the Battle of Bouvines (July 27, 1214), Otto retired to his Brunswick estates. Frederick succeeded him as emperor.

Otto, King of Greece

Otto, or Otho, b. Austria, June 1, 1815, d. July 26, 1867, was the first king of the Hellenes. The second son of LOUIS I of Bavaria, Otto was chosen to occupy the new throne of Greece in 1832 by a conference of the European powers in London; the choice was confirmed by the Greek National Assembly. He arrived in Greece in 1833, accompanied by a Bavarian council of regency. Greek resentment toward Otto's regime grew, and a military coup forced him to accept a constitutional monarchy in 1843. At the beginning of the CRIMEAN WAR, Greece invaded (1854) Turkish territory, but the British and French retaliated by occupying Piraeus. Deposed in October 1862, Otto returned to Bavaria. To replace him the Greeks chose a Danish prince, crowned as GEORGE I.

Ottokar II, King of Bohemia (Přemysl Ottokar)

[oht'-oh-kahr] Ottokar II, b. c.1230, d. Aug. 26, 1278, son and successor of WENCESLAS I, was one of the greatest kings of medieval Bohemia. During his father's reign, Ottokar won (1251) the title duke of Austria. After succeeding to the Bohemian throne in 1253, he defeated (1260) Béla IV of Hungary to seize Styria, and he later acquired (1269) Carinthia, Carniola, and Istria.

As the most powerful prince in the Holy Roman Empire, Ottokar was a leading contender for the German kingship in 1273. Rudolf of Habsburg won the election, however, and became king as RUDOLF I. In 1275 and 1276, Rudolf deprived Ottokar of his Germanic lands, and in 1278, with the support of Ladislas IV of Hungary, he defeated Ottokar in the Battle of Marchfeld (or Dürnkrut). Ottokar's heroic death in the battle was immortalized in Czech folklore. His son succeeded him as WENCESLAS II.

Ottoman Empire

The Ottoman Empire was a Muslim Turkish state that encompassed Anatolia, southeastern Europe, and the Arab Middle East and North Africa from the 14th to the early 20th century. It succeeded both the BYZANTINE EMPIRE and the Arab CALIPHATE, whose mantle of descent from Muhammad it claimed after conquest of Egypt in 1517. The Ottoman Empire was broken up at the end of World War I, when its heartland of Anatolia became the Republic of TURKEY.

Expansion. The Ottoman Turks were descendants of Turkoman nomads who entered Anatolia in the 11th century as mercenary soldiers of the SELJUKS. At the end of the 13th century, Osman I (from whom the name Ottoman is derived) asserted the independence of his small

SULTANS OF THE OTTOMAN EMPIRE

1290 – 1326	Osman I		1623 – 40	Murad IV
1326 – 62	Orkhan		1640 – 48	Ibrahim
1362 – 89	Murad I		1648 – 87	Mehmed IV
1389 – 1402	Bayezid I		1687 – 91	Suleiman II
1402 – 13	Interregnum		1691 – 95	Ahmed II
1413 – 21	Mehmed I		1695 – 1703	Mustafa II
1421 – 44	Murad II		1703 – 30	Ahmed III
1444 – 46	Mehmed II		1730 – 54	Mahmud I
1446 – 51	Murad II (restored)		1754 – 57	Osman III
1451 – 81	Mehmed II (restored)		1757 – 74	Mustafa III
1481 – 1512	Bayezid II		1774 – 89	Abd al-Hamid I
1512 – 20	Selim I		1789 – 1807	Selim III
1520 – 66	Suleiman I		1807 – 08	Mustafa IV
1566 – 74	Selim II		1808 – 39	Mahmud II
1574 – 95	Murad III		1839 – 61	Abd al-Mejid
1595 – 1603	Mehmed III		1861 – 76	Abd al-Aziz
1603 – 17	Ahmed I		1876	Murad V
1617 – 18	Mustafa I		1876 – 1909	Abd al-Hamid II
1618 – 22	Osman II		1909 – 18	Mehmed V
1622 – 23	Mustafa I (restored)		1918 – 22	Mehmed VI

principality in northwestern Anatolia. Within a century his dynasty had extended its domains into an empire stretching from the Danube to the Euphrates.

The empire was temporarily disrupted by the invasion of the Tatar conqueror TIMUR, who defeated and captured the Ottoman sultan BAYEZID I at the Battle of Ankara (1402). However, Mehmed I (1389?–1421), the Restorer, succeeded in reuniting much of the empire, and it was reconstituted by MURAD II and MEHMED II. In 1453, Mehmed II conquered Constantinople, the last Byzantine stronghold. Both sultans developed the *devshirme* system of recruiting young Christians for conversion to Islam and service in the Ottoman army and administration; the Christians in the army were organized into the elite infantry corps called the JANISSARIES.

The empire reached its peak in the 16th century. Sultan SELIM I (r. 1512–20) conquered Egypt and Syria,

gained control of the Arabian Peninsula, and beat back the Safavids of Iran at the Battle of Çaldiran (1514). His successor, SULEIMAN I (the Magnificent, r. 1520–66), took Iraq, Hungary, and Albania and established Ottoman naval supremacy in the Mediterranean.

Institutions. Under the structure formalized in the 16th century, the Ottoman Empire was dominated by a small ruling class that achieved its power and wealth as a result of the status of its members as slaves (*kapikullari*) of the sultan. This elite group included both the older Turko-Islamic aristocracy and the newer *devshirme* class of Christian converts and their descendants. The sultans played these two groups off against each other to enforce standards of honesty and obedience. The ruling class was organized into four administrative institutions: that of the palace, which was in charge of supporting the sultan and making sure that the system worked; and those of administration and finance, the military, and culture and religion. The vast subject class was organized in autonomous religious communities called *millets*—for the Jews, the Armenian Christians, the Greek Orthodox Christians, and the Muslims—and in artisans' guilds and popular mystic orders and confederations.

Decline. The decline of the empire, which began late in the 16th century, was caused by many factors, including the division of the *devshirme* class into many political parties that fought for power, manipulated sultans, and used the government for their own benefit. In the 17th century, a few members of the ruling class temporarily remedied the abuses by forcefully restoring Ottoman institutions and practices. Chief among these traditionalist reformers were Sultan Murad IV (r. 1623–40) and the Köprülü family of grand viziers (chief executive officers), who dominated the administration from 1656 to 1702.

The empire experienced its first major defeat by Europeans in the Battle of LEPANTO (1571). Nonetheless it recovered dominance of the eastern Mediterranean, capturing Crete from the Venetians in 1669. In the east, Murad

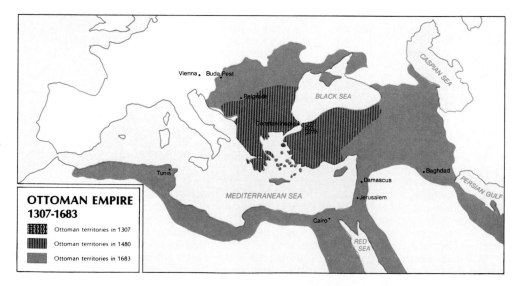

Shaded portions of the map indicate the expansion of the Ottoman Empire during a period of almost four centuries (1307–1683). The Ottoman Empire achieved its deepest penetration into Europe when Turkish forces besieged Vienna in 1529 and 1683.

**OTTOMAN EMPIRE
1307-1683**

Ottoman territories in 1307
Ottoman territories in 1480
Ottoman territories in 1683

(Left) *In the Battle of Lepanto, fought in 1571 off the coast of Greece, a multinational Christian fleet overwhelmed a Turkish fleet led by Ali Pasha and checked Ottoman expansion.*

(Right) *The Janissaries, the elite corps within Ottoman armies for centuries, were originally Christians who were forcibly converted to Islam and conscripted into service in the sultan's armies.*

IV reconquered (1638) part of Persia, which had asserted its independence under Shah ABBAS I. Following its failure to take Vienna (1683), however, the Ottoman army collapsed. Major territories were lost to its European enemies in the ensuing war, which culminated in the Treaty of Karlowitz (1699). During the 18th century, wars with Russia (see RUSSO–TURKISH WARS) and Austria accelerated the decline and loss of territory.

Reform Attempts. Sultan SELIM III (r. 1789–1807) attempted to reform the Ottoman system by destroying the Janissary corps and replacing it with the *nizam-i jedid* (new order) army modeled after Western military institutions. This attempt so angered the Janissaries and others with vested interests that they overthrew him and massacred most of the reform leaders. Defeats at the hands of Russia and Austria, the success of national revolutions in Serbia and Greece, and the rise of the powerful independent Ottoman governor of Egypt, MUHAMMAD ALI PASHA, so discredited the Janissaries, however, that Sultan MAHMUD

II was able to massacre and destroy them in 1826.

Mahmud's subsequent reforms included the destruction of the traditional institutions and their replacement with new ones imported from the West. These reforms culminated during the Tanzimat reform era (1839–76) and the reign (1876–1909) of ABD AL-HAMID II. Despite the reform efforts, the Ottoman sultanate had become known as the "Sick Man of Europe" by this time. European diplomacy focused on the so-called EASTERN QUESTION—how to dispose of the Sick Man's territories without upsetting the European balance of power. Abd al-Hamid II rescued the empire, at least temporarily, by reforming the Ottoman financial system, manipulating the rivalries of the European powers, and developing the pan-Islamic and pan-Turkic movements. The sultan also granted a constitution and parliament (1876), but he soon abandoned them and became so despotic that liberal opposition arose under the leadership of the YOUNG TURKS.

Overthrow. In 1908 a revolution led by the Young

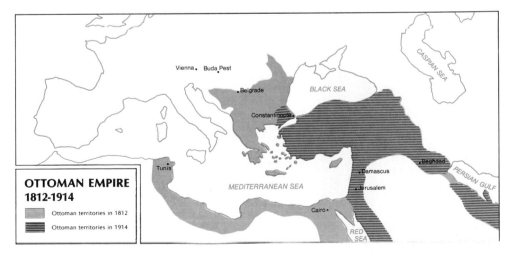

OTTOMAN EMPIRE
1812-1914

Ottoman territories in 1812
Ottoman territories in 1914

Vienna • Buda Pest
• Belgrade
Constantinople
BLACK SEA
CASPIAN SEA
Tunis •
MEDITERRANEAN SEA
Damascus •
Baghdad •
PERSIAN GULF
Jerusalem •
Cairo •
RED SEA

The map indicates the contraction of Ottoman territories between the end of the Russo-Turkish War of 1806–12 and 1914, when the Ottoman Empire entered World War I as a German ally. The Ottoman Empire lost almost all of its Balkan territories during this period.

Turks forced Abd al-Hamid to restore the parliament and constitution, and in 1909 Abd al-Hamid was dethroned completely. He was replaced by Mehmed V Rashid (r. 1909–18), who was only a puppet of those controlling the government.

Rapid modernization continued during the Young Turk era (1908–18), with particular attention given to modernizing the cities, agriculture and industry, and communications and also to the secularization of the state and the emancipation of women. However, the Young Turk leader Enver Pasha (1881–1922), who was virtual dictator from 1913, involved the empire in World War I on the side of Germany and Austria-Hungary. The defeat of these Central Powers led to the breakup and foreign occupation of the Ottoman Empire. The Turks accepted the resulting independence of their Arab and Balkan provinces, but the attempt of the victorious Allies to control the Anatolian territory led to the Turkish war for independence (1918–23). Under the leadership of Kemal ATATÜRK, the Turkish nationalists overturned the postwar settlement embodied in the Treaty of Sèvres (1920) and established the Republic of Turkey, formally recognized by the Treaty of Lausanne (see LAUSANNE, TREATY OF) in 1923.

Ottonian art and architecture [ah-toh'-nee-uhn]

The term *Ottonian* defines the art and architecture produced (*c*.950–1050) in Germany under the Saxon rulers of the Holy Roman Empire, the first three of whom were named Otto. Drawing inspiration primarily from CAROLINGIAN ART AND ARCHITECTURE and BYZANTINE ART AND ARCHITECTURE, Ottonian artists created a distinctive and influential body of work that not only laid the groundwork for much of ROMANESQUE ART AND ARCHITECTURE but also introduced a strain of expressionism that would recur throughout the subsequent history of GERMAN ART AND ARCHITECTURE.

The principal art centers of the early Holy Roman Empire were key bishoprics such as Mainz, Speyer, and Bamberg, and monastic centers. After the imperial court, the clergy were the principal patrons of Ottonian art. The most often used church type, as at Saint Cyriakus (961–65) in Gernrode, was an adaptation of the Carolingian basilican plan: a three-aisled nave, a pronounced transept,

Saint Peter Receiving the Keys, *a detail from the* Pericopes of Henry II (c.1020), *exemplifies the illuminated manuscript style developed at the Benedictine Abbey at Reichenau during the reign of the Ottonian emperors. (Bayerische Staatsbibliothek, Munich.)*

and a single apse. Ottonian builders increased the size and regularized the proportions of the western entrances, or westworks, and alternated pier and column supports to divide the interior into a harmonious system of spatial cells. In the series of great imperial cathedrals built in the Rhineland, particularly those at Mainz (begun 1009) and at Speyer (begun 1029), the arcaded wall elevations and the articulated spaces achieve enormous scale and foreshadow basic features of Romanesque architecture.

Ottonian churches were decorated with sculptural works remarkable for their animation, expressionism, and technical virtuosity. The wooden *Gero Crucifix* (970–76; Cologne Cathedral) reintroduced into Western sculpture the type of modeled-in-the-round monumental figure that had all but disappeared after the classical period.

Ottonian manuscript illumination flourished in monasteries throughout the empire (see ILLUMINATED MANUSCRIPTS). During the late 10th century Trier became the principal center for production of important manuscripts, and out of the Trier school emerged the leading artist of the century, the Gregory Master, who created illuminations unequaled in the early Middle Ages in conveying space and atmosphere. The next great school of Ottonian manuscript painting, that of the island of Reichenau in Lake Constance, adapted both Byzantine and Carolingian motifs into brilliantly colored patterns that convey the spiritual intensity of the mature Ottonian style.

Otway, Thomas

Thomas Otway, b. Mar. 3, 1652, d. Apr. 14, 1685, an English Restoration dramatist, is best remembered for his blank-verse tragedies *The Orphan* (1680) and *Venice Preserved* (1682). Their mixture of pathos and domestic drama ensured their popularity until the 19th century. Two tragedies in rhymed verse, *Alcibiades* (1675) and *Don Carlos* (1676), preceded them. His three comedies are not highly regarded.

Ouagadougou [wah-guh-doo'-goo]

Ouagadougou (1985 pop., 441,514), the capital and largest city of Burkina Faso, is situated in the center of the country. It is the administrative, transportation, and commercial hub of the country. Its industries include handicrafts and the processing of beverages and foods—mainly peanuts. Founded in the 11th century as the seat of the Mossi empire, Ouagadougou was until 1971 home of the reigning *moro naba,* the traditional ruler, whose palace still stands.

Ouija [wee'-juh]

Ouija is a board game in which two players ask questions of and receive answers from a seemingly supernatural source. The board, which has letters and numbers printed on it, is placed across the players' knees. Players lightly rest their fingertips on the message indicator, a three-legged, heart-shaped device with a clear viewfinder. One player poses a question, and the message indicator is then supposed to spell out an answer. Originally called "Ouija Talking Board," the game was developed in the late 1890s by William Fuld.

Our Town   see WILDER, THORNTON

Outcault, Richard Felton   see COMIC STRIP

Outer Mongolia   see MONGOLIA

—

outlaws   As the American FRONTIER moved westward in the 19th century, outlaws and lawlessness posed serious problems in many of the newly settled areas. The criminals' threat to frontier society, however, should be kept in perspective. Lawlessness was not limited to the fringes of civilization. During the years between the Civil War and the end of the century, when some of the most famous criminal episodes of the West occurred, the rate of serious crimes apparently was increasing throughout the United States. Neither should the extent of outlawry on the frontier be exaggerated. Most westerners probably lived out their lives without ever witnessing a serious crime. Mining camps and cattle towns experienced more crime than agricultural regions, but even in the former the rate of crime was less than might be expected from popular accounts.

Regional Factors. Different causes produced the lawlessness in the various regions of the frontier. The wealth of the mining towns of California and the Rocky Mountains held a natural attraction for those who would rather steal gold or silver than dig for it. Moreover, because the populations of the camps were highly mobile, many of the residents showed little interest in law enforcement aimed at future stability. As a result, these places were preyed on by outlaws such as Henry Plummer (c.1837–1864), who operated in California and later in Idaho and Montana; he posed as a lawman while leading a gang responsible for more than 100 robberies and murders.

The huge herds of cattle raised on the Great Plains and in the Southwest tempted some to try their hand at rustling. Butch Cassidy (Robert Leroy Parker; 1866–1911 or 1937) stole cattle in Wyoming before turning to bank and train robbery. The struggles among cattle ranchers for control of the range sometimes included killings by famous Western "badmen." The Lincoln County war (1878–81) in eastern New Mexico made the reputation of William H. Bonney, alias BILLY THE KID, and the gunslinger John Henry Selmon (1839–96) was involved briefly in the same conflict.

Outlaws took advantage of the vast distances and the isolation of frontier life, whether on the plains, mountains, or deserts. These conditions demanded long and unprotected lines of transportation to move goods, people, and money, a situation that road agents (stage robbers) and train robbers exploited. Black Bart (Charles E. Boles; 1830–1917?) held up WELLS, FARGO AND COMPANY stages and eluded California law officers for more than 8 years before being captured and sent to prison in 1883. Some of the West's best-known outlaws, including Sam BASS, the Dalton Gang, and Butch Cassidy and the Sundance Kid (Harry Longbaugh; d. 1911 or 1957) occasionally robbed trains carrying supplies and payrolls to western communities.

Finally, prejudice and ethnic tensions contributed to

The Wild Bunch (left), led by Butch Cassidy (sitting, far right), terrorized the western frontier from South Dakota to New Mexico.

Billy the Kid (below) led a gang in the Lincoln County, N. Mex., cattle war of the late 1870s.

A wanted poster for stagecoach robber Black Bart (left), issued by Wells, Fargo and Co., carries a message, in verse, from the outlaw.

lawlessness on some parts of the culturally diverse frontier. The banditry of Joaquín Murrieta (c.1830–1853?) in California during the early 1850s, for instance, may have been motivated by outrages commited by Anglos on his fellow Mexicans.

Coping with the Problem. From the start efforts were made to cope with the problem of lawlessness on the frontier, and in time criminals were brought under a reasonable degree of control. Where official agents of the law were slow to arrive or ineffective, frontiersmen sometimes banded together in vigilance committees to meet the threat themselves. The VIGILANTES, particularly in the mining camps, banished or executed some of the most blatant offenders; for example, Henry Plummer was hanged by the Virginia City and Bannack vigilance committee in Montana. Private law enforcement could take more permanent forms. Cattle ranchers organized associations that hired range detectives to apprehend rustlers. Some business firms, of which the Pinkerton Detective Agency was the most famous, protected frontier enterprises and pursued outlaws for a fee. At various times Pinkerton agents were on the trail of Sam Bass, Jesse JAMES and his brother Frank, and YOUNGER BROTHERS' gangs, and Butch Cassidy's "wild bunch." Banks, mining companies, railroads, and stage lines hired guards and detectives to protect property and customers.

As the West's inhabitants increased and its communities matured, local, state, and federal law-enforcement agencies became increasingly effective. In time western lawlessness became little different from that elsewhere in the nation.

ovary SEE PREGNANCY AND BIRTH; REPRODUCTIVE SYSTEM, HUMAN

ovenbird Ovenbird is the common name for several birds that build roofed-over, dome-shaped nests resembling Dutch ovens. The ovenbird, *Seiurus aurocapillus,* of the wood warbler family, Parulidae, is about 15 cm (6 in) long, olive brown above and dark-streaked white below, and has a distinct ring around each eye and a black-bordered orange brown patch on the head. It generally inhabits wooded areas with little undergrowth, where it searches the ground for insects and similar prey. It breeds from central Canada to the southern United States and winters from the Gulf Coast to Colombia.

The genus *Furnarius,* in the ovenbird family, Furnariidae, comprises six species of South American birds. They average about 20 cm (8 in) in length and are usually plainly colored, dark above, light below, with a light-colored eye stripe.

The ovenbird, a sparrow-sized wood warbler, builds a domed nest on the floor of the forest. Its flight song, as well as its streaked breast and striped crown, helps to distinguish this bird.

overture The musical overture (literally, "opening") is an instrumental composition in one movement, often in sonata form, that precedes an opera or other dramatic work. Although the overture has its antecedents in the short introductions of early 17th-century Italian operas, its history may be said to begin with the operas of Jean Baptiste Lully, whose overtures, starting slowly, continuing with a faster fugal section, and frequently concluding with a dance, were long regarded as models.

Christoph Willibald Gluck in *Iphigénie en Tauride* (1779) and Mozart in *Don Giovanni* (1787) and *Così fan tutte* (1790) were the first composers to incorporate music from the opera itself in its overture. Beethoven's first three overtures to *Leonore* (ultimately *Fidelio*, 1805–14) are less prefaces to the opera than vivid tone poems on its

subject. From Beethoven also came overtures for stage plays and the first concert overtures not connected to any drama. Richard Wagner, beginning with *Lohengrin* (1850), provided his operas not with overtures but with preludes that lead directly into the music of the first scene. Many opera overtures, notably those by Carl Maria von Weber and Gioacchino Rossini, have become popular concert pieces, although the operas they were written for have failed to stay in the repertoire.

Ovid [ahv'-id] One of the most prolific poets of Rome's Golden Age, Ovid, the name by which Publius Ovidius Naso is commonly known, specialized in the witty and sophisticated treatment of love in all its permutations. Born Mar. 20, 43 BC, a year after the murder of Julius Caesar, Ovid passed his youth in his native Sulmo, untouched by the civil wars. Shortly after peace resumed, when Augustus ruled unthreatened, Ovid went to Rome to continue his education. Before he was 20, he was reading his poems to appreciative audiences, and by age 30 he was Rome's most successful poet. Success followed success for two more decades, when Augustus suddenly dispatched Ovid, then 50, into exile. The place of exile was Tomis (modern Constanța, in Romania), a rather primitive town on the Black Sea. Arriving there in spring of AD 9, Ovid fought his loneliness and longing for his friends and beloved Rome by writing poetry about exile. The last datable poems refer to the year 16, and presumably he died soon after, an unhappy man of 60.

Ovid's principal poetry reflects his concern with love's complexities. Beginning under the influence of his friend Propertius, Ovid in the *Amores*, written between 10 and 1 BC, depicted a witty lover who refuses to be tormented and instead turns love into a sport. Ovid's next great poetic endeavor, the *Heroides*, also developed a situation suggested by Propertius. Here Ovid imagines famous heroines like Ariadne or Dido writing passionate letters to the men who have abandoned them. In the *Art of Love* (c.1 BC), Ovid assumes the role of "professor" to teach men how to seduce women in Rome.

Ovid proposed in the *Fasti* (AD 8) to deal wittily with the events (holidays, national heroes, seasonal changes) suggested by the Roman calendar, devoting one book to each month. When exiled, he had completed six. In the METAMORPHOSES (AD 8), his greatest poetic achievement, Ovid isolated love as the agent of change. In his last years Ovid addressed five books of elegiacs, *Tristia* (8–12 AD), to anonymous Roman friends, and four books of elegiac letters, *From the Black Sea* (12–16 AD), to named ones.

Oviedo [oh-vee-ay'-doh] Oviedo, a city in Spain, lies about 370 km (230 mi) northwest of Madrid. Its population is 186,363 (1988 est.). Located near vast deposits of coal and iron, Oviedo is the industrial, commercial, and cultural hub of the area. It has metallurgical industries and also produces armaments, chemicals, alcoholic beverages, processed foods, and textiles. Founded in about 760, Oviedo was the capital of the kingdom of ASTURIAS in the 9th century. Places of interest include the Gothic cathedral, which contains the tombs of the Asturian kings, and the University of Oviedo (founded 17th century).

Ovimbundu The Ovimbundu, the largest ethnic group in Angola (nearly 40% of the total population), speak a Bantu language, Umbundu. They moved southward into what is now Angola in the 1600s and were organized into a number of independent or autonomous chiefdoms before their conquest by the Portuguese in the early 1900s. During the struggle for independence, the Ovimbundu were the chief supporters of the National Union for the Total Liberation of Angola (UNITA), led by Jonas SAVIMBI, but civilians in the Ovimbundu heartland of west central Angola suffered greatly during UNITA's long postindependence struggle against the central government.

oviparity Oviparity is the bringing forth of offspring by means of laying eggs. The eggs may be fertilized before they are laid (birds and reptiles) or after they are laid (fish and amphibians). Such animals are said to be oviparous, in contrast to viviparous animals, whose young are born live (see VIVIPARITY).

Owen, Daniel Daniel Owen, b. Oct. 20, 1836, d. Oct. 22, 1895, is usually considered the most important Welsh novelist. Although trained as a Methodist minister, he practiced as a tailor in his hometown of Mold. His works include *Rhys Lewis* (1885) and *Profedigaethau Enoc Huws* (The Trials of Enoc Huws, 1891; Eng. trans., 1894–96)—penetrating studies of contemporary Welsh life full of memorable scenes and characters. *Gwen Thomas* (1893; Eng. trans., 1937) is considered his best work.

Owen, Robert Robert Owen, b. May 14, 1771, d. Nov. 17, 1858, was a Welsh industrialist and social reformer who had a strong influence on 19th-century utopian socialism. Owen believed that human character would be greatly improved in a cooperative society rather than in the traditional family.

In 1799, Owen and two partners purchased the New Lanark textile mills in Lanarkshire, Scotland. Owen set about improving the living and working conditions of his employees. He opened (1816) the Institute for the Formation of Character, which included schools for child laborers, community rooms, and England's first nursery school. Owen also set up a fund for the support of sick workers, shortened working hours, and increased industrial output by new management techniques.

Owen was influential in the passage of the Factory Act of 1819, intended to protect children in industry. He also proposed that the unemployed be gathered in self-supporting Villages of Cooperation of about 1,000 people each. To further his idea of self-contained communities, Owen gave up the management of New Lanark and established cooperative communities at NEW HARMONY in Indiana (1825–27) and at Queenwood in Hampshire, England (1839–45). Both experiments failed because of dissension among the participants. Owen then became involved in trade unionism, but the movement was soon crushed. He spent the rest of his life propounding his ideas on education, marriage, and religion.

Owen, Robert Dale The Scottish-born American social reformer and legislator Robert Dale Owen, b. Nov. 9, 1801, d. June 24, 1877, promoted public education, reform of marriage laws, and slave emancipation. In 1825 he and his father, the famous reformer Robert Owen, came to the United States to establish a socialist community in NEW HARMONY, Ind. After the experiment failed in 1827, he associated with Frances WRIGHT in an agnostic, socialistic group called the Free Enquirers.

After serving in the Indiana legislature (1836–38), Owen went to Washington for two terms (1843–47) as a Democratic representative. While there he worked for the establishment of the Smithsonian Institution. As a delegate to the 1850 Indiana constitutional convention he played a major role in securing expanded state responsibility for public education, property rights for married women, and liberalized divorce laws. After serving as U.S. minister to Italy (1855–58), Owen became a leading advocate of freeing the slaves; arguments in his *Policy of Emancipation* (1863) reportedly influenced Abraham Lincoln.

Owen, Wilfred Of the English poets killed in World War I, Wilfred Owen, b. Mar. 18, 1893, d. Nov. 4, 1918, has become the most admired. *Poems* (1920) was published after his death by his friend Siegfried Sassoon. Owen produced his finest work in the space of a year, during which he saw action almost daily. His last work, which includes "Dulce et Decorum Est," "Futility," and "Anthem for Doomed Youth," is both elegiac and realistic in its descriptions of "these who die as cattle."

Owens, Jesse James Cleveland "Jesse" Owens, b. Danville, Ala., Sept. 12, 1913, d. Mar. 31, 1980, was an

Jesse Owens, an American track star, gave a memorable performance during the 11th Olympic Games (1936), at Berlin. Before an audience anticipating a strong German showing, Owens won four gold medals.

African-American track star. Though best remembered for his Olympic performance, Owens achieved the finest one-day showing in track history on May 25, 1935, when he equaled the 100-yd (91.4-m) dash world record at 9.4 sec; set a new long-jump record of 8.13 m (26 ft 8.25 in), which stood for 25 years; and set records in the 220-yd (201.2-m) dash and 220-yd low hurdles with times of 20.3 sec and 22.6 sec, respectively. Owens won the 100-m and 200-m races and the long jump and was on the winning 4 x 100-m relay team in the 1936 Olympics, which Adolf Hitler had proclaimed as the showcase for Aryan "supremacy."

Owensboro   Owensboro is a city in northwestern Kentucky, along the Ohio River about 200 km (130 mi) west of Louisville. The seat of Daviess County, it has a population of 53,549 (1990). Its industries manufacture electronic, tobacco, and food products, as well as aluminum, steel, and bourbon whiskey. Settled about 1800, it was known as Yellow Banks to river-flatboat captains; the present name was adopted in 1866 to honor a Kentucky war veteran, Col. Abraham Owen.

owl   Owls are a widely distributed group of birds of prey broadly characterized by large heads, flat faces, forward-directed eyes, hooked beaks (the size of which is obscured by facial feathers), strong legs, sharp claws, and soft feathers. The owl order, Strigiformes, comprises three families. One of these, the Protostrigidae, is extinct. These owls lived in North America during the Eocene Epoch, about 45 million years ago. The remaining two families are the barn owls and the typical owls.

The barn owl family, Tytonidae, contains two genera, *Tyto* and *Phodilus*, with 10 or 11 living species and 11 known fossil species. The earliest record of the barn owls is from France and dates back to the Miocene Epoch, about 19 million years ago. Barn owls range from 27 to 53 cm (11 to 21 in) in length and have relatively small eyes, a heart-shaped face, a comblike margin on the middle claw, and a light coloration and sparse markings on the underparts of the body. The typical owls, family Strigidae, comprise 25–31 genera, three of them extinct, with 124–137 living species and 25 extinct species. The earliest known typical owls first lived in Europe during the late Eocene or early Oligocene, about 38 million years ago. Typical owls range from 13 to 71 cm (5.1 to 28 in) in length and have large eyes, a rounded or gogglelike face, feathered toes in many species, two tufts of head feathers resembling ears or horns in many species, and usually dark coloration and heavy markings on the underparts of the body.

Most owls are nocturnal, but several, including the pygmy owls, genus *Glaucidium,* are crepuscular, or twilight active, hunting mainly at dawn and dusk. A few owls, such as the burrowing owl, *Speotyto cunicularia,* and the short-eared owl, *Asio flammeus,* are also active during the day. The smallest owls are probably the pygmy owls, some of which are only 13 cm (5.1 in) long, have a

The North American saw-whet owl (above) is found in moist, coniferous forests.

The short-eared owl (above) is found worldwide in open country. The crested owl (right) is found in New World tropical forests. The Teng-malm's owl (below) is found in far northern regions.

The barred owl (right) and the ferruginous pygmy owl (below) are native to New World forests.

32-cm (12.6-in) wingspan, and weigh only 50 g (1.76 oz). The largest owls are the eagle owls, *Bubo bubo* and *B. lacteus,* which may reach 71 cm (28 in) long, have a wingspan of just over 2 m (6.6 ft), and weigh about 4 kg (almost 9 lb).

Most owls see well in poor light, but all see well in bright daylight—something that even the most nocturnal northern species have to do during the arctic summer. The owl's eyes are almost immovable, and the owl must turn its head to look elsewhere; however, some species can rotate their heads horizontally 270°, or about ¾ of a circle, and can turn their heads completely upside down (180°). The eyes are more forwardly directed in owls than in other birds, and the visual fields of the two eyes therefore overlap, creating a binocular span of 60° to 70°, or about ⅙ of a circle. The overlapping visual fields of the two eyes are a prerequisite for instantaneous stereoscopic vision, or depth perception.

The owl's ear openings are located behind and to the side of the eyes. They are covered by sparse, sound-transparent feathers that form the flat face. Most owls have an ear opening about the size of the eye, whereas a few species have extremely large ear openings that occupy the whole height of the head. Nine genera of owls have a remarkable anatomical asymmetry in the ear openings—the ear openings differ in position and shape so that one is not the mirror image of the other. Owls can determine the direction of a sound source on a horizontal level by comparing the intensity of a sound heard in the two ears: generally, the ear nearest the sound source will receive the highest intensity. Owls also need to know the vertical direction of a sound to be able to strike prey concealed by vegetation or snow, and this ability is provided by the asymmetrical ears. The soft feathers contribute to a noiseless flight, enabling owls to surprise their prey.

ox An ox is a fully grown castrated bull; a younger castrated bull is called a steer. A number of breeds or types of cattle have been bred to produce large, powerful oxen for use as draft animals, as was done by the Afrikaners of South Africa and is now being done by Dutch-Americans in the vicinity of Holland, Mich. The term *ox* also refers to members of the subfamily Bovinae, in the family Bovidae, and includes the Asiatic buffaloes, genera *Bubalus* and *Anoa*; the African buffalo, *Syncerus*; true cattle, *Bos*; and bisons, *Bison*. More specifically, *ox* refers to the true cattle, or members of the genus *Bos.*

The kouprey, a wild ox native to Cambodia, was discovered in 1936. Rare even then, the kouprey has been driven to virtual extinction by the prolonged warfare in Indochina.

oxbow lake An oxbow lake develops on a river FLOOD-PLAIN when a change in course cuts off and isolates one or more meander loops of a river system (see MEANDER, RIVER). Such a change occurs when a river that is flooding short-cuts the narrow neck of the meander. Clay, silt, sand, and organic matter gradually fill the abandoned loop, giving rise to a clay plug.

See also: LAKE (body of water) ; RIVER AND STREAM.

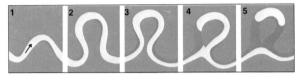

As a river deposits debris on inside bends and erodes outside bends (1), its loops become longer (2), and the open loop ends become narrower (3). Sediment seals off one loop side (4) and then both sides from the main stream, leaving an oxbow lake (5).

Oxenstierna, Axel, Count [ook'-suhn-shahr-nah] Axel Gustafsson Oxenstierna, greve (count) of Södermöre, known as Count Oxenstierna, b. June 16, 1583, d. Aug. 28, 1654, was chancellor of Sweden during that country's rise to greatness. Entering the state council under CHARLES IX, he helped establish a stable government based on cooperation between the crown and the higher level of aristocracy. GUSTAV II ADOLF named him chancellor in 1612.

The king commanded the army while Oxenstierna handled its finances and supply, and together they decided on policy. This combination made Sweden a great power during the THIRTY YEARS' WAR. During the 12-year minority (1632–44) of Queen CHRISTINA, Oxenstierna ran Swedish affairs almost as though he were a sovereign. He formulated the Swedish position at the Peace of Westphalia (see WESTPHALIA, PEACE OF), although he did not take part in the negotiations.

Oxford Oxford, a city with a population of 115,400 (1988 est.), is situated about 85 km (55 mi) northwest of London in the heart of Oxfordshire, England, where the River Thames is joined by the Cherwell. An ancient university town, Oxford is the administrative center for the county. The buildings of Oxford University, which dates to the mid-12th century, include the Sheldonian Theatre (designed by Christopher Wren), the Old Clarendon Building, the Old Bodleian Library, and the Divinity School, as well as the individual colleges. Oxford has grown in recent years and now includes industrial sites.

Town and gown now live together amicably, but many students were killed in clashes with townspeople during the 14th century. A memorial commemorates the 16th-century martyrs Thomas Cranmer, Hugh Latimer, and Nicholas Ridley, who were burned at the stake for their opposition to the Roman Catholic church. Charles I used Oxford as his headquarters during the English Civil War, and his forces surrendered there in 1646.

Oxford English Dictionary, The Perhaps the most extensive and ambitious dictionary ever published, *The Oxford English Dictionary* (*OED*) was originally called *A New English Dictionary on Historical Principles* (*NED*); however, after one volume was published with the present title, in 1895, that title became more commonly used. Begun in 1857 as a modest project of the Philological Society of England, it was intended to supplement existing dictionaries. The guiding genius behind the dictionary was Sir James MURRAY, who edited almost half of it. The first of 125 separate parts appeared in 1884, and the completed work, in 12 volumes, in 1928. A supplement of one volume was published in 1933, and another, in four volumes edited by R. W. Burchfield, appeared in 1972–86. In 1989 the second edition, the so-called *OED 2*, was published in 20 volumes, edited by John A. Simpson and Edmund S. C. Weiner. The *OED 2* defines more than 500,000 words and contains 22,000 pages; it is also available in electronic, CD-ROM format.

In addition to defining words, the *OED* traces their etymology—from first appearance to obsolescence. Definitions are supported by quotations—most drawn from literary sources; nearly 2.5 million quotations appear in the *OED 2*.

Oxford movement A movement to reform the Church of England begun at Oxford University in 1833, the Oxford movement was led by John KEBLE, John Henry NEWMAN, and Richard Hurrell Froude. All were fellows of Oriel College, Oxford, passionately loyal to the church and deeply disturbed by the British government's interference in its affairs. In addition, they were influenced by the patristic writings and attracted to the ritual and worship of the early and medieval church.

Newman believed the movement began when, on July 14, 1833, Keble preached on "National Apostasy," a sermon prompted by an attempt in Parliament to suppress ten Irish bishoprics. More important was the publication of *Tracts for the Times* by Newman. The first three were published on Sept. 9, 1833; and the last, *Tract 90,* which aroused a storm of controversy, in 1841. The tracts aimed at recalling the English to true churchmanship, to an understanding of the church as an organic, independent body, not a creature of the state, and to a sacramental ministry and life. The Tractarians, as they came to be called, envisioned the movement as a middle way between Roman Catholicism and evangelicalism. The movement was soon under attack. Liberals protested its dogmatism, and evangelicals its Roman tendencies. Gradually some of its members, including William Ward and Henry MANNING, joined the Roman Catholic church. In 1845, Newman was converted and the movement came to a point of crisis. Leadership passed to Keble, Edward PUSEY, and Charles Marriott. The movement's principles were maintained by Anglo-Catholics who were much influenced by ritualism, Christian Socialism, and liberalism. The Oxford movement had a strong influence on the established church, and its principles continue to inform the entire Anglican Communion.

Oxford University One of the world's oldest universities and greatest architectural treasures, Oxford University, in Oxford, England, dates from the 12th century. In the 13th century the first of its 35 self-governing colleges and 5 private halls was established, heralding its development into a federal, self-governing university.

Undergraduates normally enter from secondary school to study (generally for 3 years) for the degree of bachelor of arts, with honors. Entrance is by examination; standards are high, and competition is intense. Individual colleges assume responsibility for the students' welfare and academic progress—through allocation to a personal tutor—while the university provides lectures, libraries, laboratories, examinations, and degrees appropriate to their course of study.

The university is financed by government grants, student fees, endowments, and private fund-raising. Congregation, consisting of all university teachers and senior administrative staff, is its governing body. The titular head of the university is the chancellor, an honorific life appointment.

At Oxford is the Ashmolean Museum, with one of the world's most important collections of European and Near Eastern archaeological finds. Library facilities include the BODLEIAN and the colleges' own libraries. Oxford University Press was founded in 1478.

Oxford's Colleges, coeducational unless otherwise noted, include **All Souls College** (1438; for male fellows), **Balliol College** (1263–68), **Brasenose College** (1509), **Christ Church** (1546; for men), **Corpus Christi College** (1517), **Exeter College** (1314), **Green College** (1979; primarily for postgraduate medical students), **Hertford College** (1740), **Jesus College** (1571), **Keble College** (1870), **Lady Margaret Hall** (1878), **Linacre College** (1962; for graduates), **Lincoln College** (1427), **Magdalen College** (1458), **Merton College** (1264; for men), **New College** (1379), **Nuffield College** (1937; for graduates), **Oriel College** (1326; for men), **Pembroke College** (1624), **The Queen's College** (1340), **St. Anne's College** (1893), **St. Antony's College** (1950; for graduates), **St. Catherine's College** (1868), **St. Cross College** (1965; for graduates), **St. Edmund Hall** (*c.*1278), **St. Hilda's College** (1893; for women), **St. Hugh's College** (1886; for women), **St. John's College** (1555), **St. Peter's College** (1929), **Somerville College** (1879; for women), **Trinity College** (1554–55), **University College** (1249), **Wadham College** (1612), **Wolfson College** (1965; for graduates), and **Worcester College** (1283).

Permanent private halls include **Campion Hall** (1896; primarily for members of the Society of Jesus), **Greyfriars** (1910; especially for members of the Franciscan Order), **Mansfield College** (1886), **Regent's Park College** (1927–40; primarily for Baptist theological students), **St. Benet's Hall** (1897; especially for members of the Benedictine community).

Oxfordshire Oxfordshire (abbreviated as Oxon) is a county in south central England. Part of the River Thames basin, its 2,608-km^2 (1,007-mi^2) area is bounded on the northeast and southeast by hills. The population is 578,900 (1988 est.). OXFORD is the county town. Farming is important. Sand and gravel, ironstone, and limestone are mined, and automobiles, steel, paper, and blankets are manufactured. The region has many ancient relics. The best known is the Uffington White Horse, carved into a chalk hillside and believed to date to the Iron Age. Settled since Paleolithic times, Oxfordshire was once part of the Anglo-Saxon kingdoms of Mercia and Wessex. It was occupied by the Danes (10th–11th centuries), and was the site of battles during the English Civil War (1642–51).

oxidation and reduction Oxidation and reduction are complementary chemical processes that involve a loss of electrons (oxidation) by one reactant and a corresponding gain (reduction) by another. Both processes must occur simultaneously and in equivalent amounts. The most familiar oxidative processes utilize oxygen from the atmosphere; these include the rusting of iron (see CORROSION), COMBUSTION, and respiration (see METABOLISM). In each case oxygen is reduced. Reductive processes include the recovery of metals from their ores, the photosynthetic production of carbohydrates, and the hydrogenation of fats.

Oxidizing Agents. The substance that acquires electrons during an oxidation-reduction reaction is an oxidizing agent. In the course of the reaction, the oxidizing agent is reduced; a strong oxidizing agent reacts and becomes a weak reducing agent. Of the chemical elements, the most electronegative elements (see ELECTROMOTIVE SERIES) have the greatest tendency to participate in reactions as oxidizing agents, because they form negative ions (gain electrons) very readily. Fluorine, with the most highly electronegative atoms, is the most active oxidizing agent among the elements. It reacts to form the fluoride ion (F^-), the weakest reducing agent. Oxygen (O_2) is highly active, particularly so as ozone (O_3). All of the halogen elements can act as strong oxidizing agents.

Certain oxygen-containing compounds readily give up oxygen to another reactant, becoming reduced in the process. Some examples are hydrogen peroxide, nitric acid, concentrated sulfuric acid, potassium nitrate, and the permanganate, dichromate, chlorate, and hypochlorite ions.

Reducing Agents. Elements that readily form positive ions are active reducing agents and, as expected from their low electronegativities, the most active are the alkali metals followed by the alkaline earth metals. Lithium is the strongest reducing agent of the elements. Useful reducing agents in organic chemistry include hydrogen, lithium aluminum hydride, and sodium borohydride.

In general, the strength of a reactant in an oxidation-reduction process depends on the reaction conditions. To oxidize or reduce certain functional groups on a complex molecule but leave others unaffected, a chemist must carefully select the appropriate agent, catalyst, concentrations, temperature, and pressure.

Biological Oxidation and Reduction. The vast majority of living organisms rely on oxygen to generate oxidative power. The actual mechanism is not a direct chemical reaction but a series of electron transfers through a number of intermediate compounds that readily accept and release electrons, alternating between an oxidized and a reduced form. This route is called the electron transport chain and is similar in all organisms. As the strongest oxidizing agent of the chain, oxygen is the final electron acceptor. Its vital role in living organisms is essentially as a substance on which to "dump" electrons. Many microorganisms are anaerobic; that is, they do not require oxygen for survival. These organisms are able to utilize other substances, such as sulfur and some of its compounds, as oxidizing agents.

All organisms generate reducing power through the reversible biochemical reactions of substances such as nicotinamide-adenine dinucleotide (NAD), flavins, and cytochromes, which can exist in an oxidized or reduced form. By participating in the electron transport chain, the reduced form is continually regenerated from the oxidized form.

oxide minerals The chemically diverse oxide minerals, or naturally occurring oxides, comprise a wide range of mineral species. They are, in general, dense (specific gravity of 3.5–5.5 grams per cm^3), hard, and poor conductors of electricity and heat. They have high refractive indices and may be strongly colored. Chemically, oxides are relatively inert and insoluble.

Occurrence. One or more species of oxide minerals occur in at least traces in practically every kind of rock on the Earth and Moon and in many meteorites. Oxide minerals are ubiquitous in IGNEOUS, METAMORPHIC, and SEDIMENTARY ROCKS and in many veins and ORE DEPOSITS. High concentrations of chromite, magnetite, and ilmenite occur in layered igneous intrusive bodies and peridotites of the Alpine type; segregations of titanomagnetite occur in anorthosites and granitic masses; and rutile, brookite, and magnetite bodies occur with alkali igneous rocks and carbonatites. Magnetite and HEMATITE occur in banded iron formations of sedimentary origin, and various manganese oxides occur in layered sedimentary and metamorphic rocks and as nodules on the deep seafloor (see OCEANIC MINERAL RESOURCES).

Oxide minerals are important ores of metals such as iron (hematite, magnetite), titanium (rutile, ilmenite), tin (cassiterite, SnO_2), copper (CUPRITE; tenorite, CuO), chromium (chromite), manganese (pyrolusite; psilomelane), zinc (zincite), and niobium and tantalum (from several multiple oxides, including columbite, $(Fe,Mn)(Nb,Ta)_2O_6$).

oxidizing agent see OXIDATION AND REDUCTION

Oxus River see AMU DARYA

oxygen Oxygen and its compounds play a key role in many of the important processes of life and industry. Oxygen in the biosphere is essential in the processes of respiration and metabolism, the means by which animals derive the energy needed to sustain life. Furthermore, oxygen is the most abundant element at the surface of the Earth. In combined form it is found in ores, earths, rocks, and gemstones, as well as in all living organisms.

Oxygen is a gaseous chemical element in Group VIA of the periodic table. The chemical symbol for atomic oxygen is O, its atomic number is 8, and its atomic weight is 15.9994. Elemental oxygen is known principally in the gaseous form as the diatomic molecule O_2, which makes up 20.95% of the volume of dry air. Diatomic oxygen is colorless, odorless, and tasteless.

Two 18th-century scientists share the credit for first isolating elemental oxygen: Joseph PRIESTLEY and Carl Wilhelm SCHEELE. It is generally believed that Scheele was the first to isolate oxygen but that Priestley, who independently achieved the isolation of oxygen somewhat later, was the first to publicly announce his findings.

The interpretation of the findings of Priestley and the resultant clarification of the nature of oxygen as an element was accomplished by the French scientist Antoine-Laurent LAVOISIER. Lavoisier's experimental work, which extended and improved on Priestley's experiments, was principally responsible for the understanding of COMBUSTION and the establishment of the law of conservation of matter (see CONSERVATION, LAWS OF).

Lavoisier gave oxygen its name, which is derived from two Greek words that mean "acid former." Lavoisier held the mistaken idea that oxides, when dissolved in water, would form only acids. It is true that some oxides when dissolved in water do form acids; for example, sulfur dioxide (SO_2) forms sulfurous acid: $SO_2 + H_2O \rightarrow H_2SO_3$. Some oxides, however, such as sodium oxide (Na_2O), dissolve in water to form bases, as in the reaction to form sodium hydroxide: $Na_2O + H_2O \rightarrow 2NaOH$.

Natural Occurrence

Oxygen is formed by a number of nuclear processes that are believed to occur in stellar interiors. In the terrestrial environment oxygen accounts for about half of the mass of the Earth's crust, 89% of the mass of the oceans, and 23% of the mass (and 21% of the volume) of the atmosphere. Most of the Earth's rocks and soils are principally silicates (see SILICATE MINERALS). The silicates are an amazingly complex group of materials that typically consist of greater than 50 (atomic) percent oxygen in combination with silicon and one or more metallic elements.

Several important ores are principally oxides of the desired metals, such as the iron-bearing minerals hematite (Fe_2O_3), magnetite (Fe_3O_4), and limonite (hydrated Fe_2O_3) and the most important aluminum-bearing mineral, BAUXITE (a mixture of hydrated aluminum oxides and iron oxide).

Physical and Chemical Properties

If oxygen at a pressure of one atmosphere is cooled, it will liquefy at 90.18 K ($-182.97°$ C), the normal boiling point of oxygen, and it will solidify at 54.39 K ($-218.76°$ C), the normal melting point of oxygen. The liquid and solid forms of oxygen have a pale blue color.

Oxygen gas exhibits a slight but important solubility in water. Molecular oxygen dissolved in water is required by aquatic organisms for their metabolic processes and is ultimately responsible for the oxidation and removal of organic wastes in water. The solubilities of gases depend on the temperature of the solution and the pressure of the gas over the solution. At 20° C (68° F) and an oxygen pressure of one atmosphere, the solubility of O_2 in water is about 45 grams of O_2 per cubic meter of water, or 45 ppm (parts per million).

Molecular diatomic oxygen is a fairly stable molecule with a dissociation energy (the energy required to dissociate one mole of molecular O_2 in its ground state into two moles of atomic oxygen in its ground state) of 493.6 kilojoules per mole. The molecule is dissociated by ultraviolet radiation of any wavelength shorter than 193 nm. Solar radiation striking stratospheric oxygen dissociates it into atomic oxygen for this reason. The atomic oxygen formed in this fashion is capable of reacting with O_2 to form OZONE, O_3.

Corrosion. The deterioration and destruction of materials by exposure to the environment is known as CORROSION. One important type of corrosion is the chemical reaction of metals with oxygen. The most familiar example of metal corrosion is the rusting of iron and steel, an electrochemical process that requires the presence of oxygen, moisture, and impurities in the metal. Because the corrosion product, a hydrated iron oxide, falls away from the metal to expose a fresh surface, an entire object can be consumed by rusting. In contrast, aluminum is protected from deterioration because aluminum oxide (Al_2O_3) adheres to the aluminum surface and protects it from further oxidation.

Biological Oxidation. Biological oxidation reactions are ultimately the sources of energy for the higher plants and animals, are responsible for the cleansing of streams of biodegradable wastes, and are responsible for the natural decomposition of organic material. Waste products and dead plants and animals decompose (are oxidized) principally through the agency of microorganisms, and energy-bearing foods are metabolized (oxidized) by enzyme-controlled biochemical reactions.

Reactivity. Many substances that do not react rapidly with oxygen in air at temperatures below 100° C will do so at 1000° C with a strong evolution of heat (exothermically). For example, coal and petroleum can be stored indefinitely at the temperatures encountered under normal climatic conditions, but they readily oxidize, exothermically, at elevated temperatures.

The most common compounds of oxygen are those in which the element exhibits a valence of two. This fact is associated with the electronic structure of atomic oxygen, which requires two additional electrons to fill its outermost energy level. Examples of divalent oxides are numerous among well-known substances such as water (H_2O); carbon dioxide (CO_2); aluminum oxide (Al_2O_3); silicon dioxide (SiO_2); the silicate calcium carbonate ($CaCO_3$); and sulfur dioxide (SO_2). Oxygen is also known to have other valences, such as in the PEROXIDES, of which hydrogen peroxide (H_2O_2) is an example.

The direct reaction of oxygen with another element frequently does not occur rapidly or at all at room temperature but is strongly exothermic, and once oxidation is initiated the evolved heat raises the temperature of the reactants such that the reaction is self-sustaining. Examples of such reactions are with the elements magnesium, carbon, and hydrogen:

$$2Mg + O_2 \rightarrow 2MgO$$
$$C + O_2 \rightarrow CO_2$$
$$2H_2 + O_2 \rightarrow 2H_2O$$

Magnesium and carbon burn in air once the reaction is initiated, and a hydrogen-oxygen mixture can react explosively when the reaction is initiated by a flame or spark.

Uses

Pure oxygen is used extensively in technological processes. It is used in the welding, cutting, and forming of metals, as in oxyacetylene welding, in which oxygen reacts with acetylene to form an extremely hot flame. Oxygen is added to the inlet air (3% to 5%) in modern blast furnaces to increase the temperature in the furnace; it is used in the basic oxygen converter for steel production, in the manufacture of chemicals, and for rocket propulsion.

Oxygen is also used in the partial combustion of methane (natural gas) according to $2CH_4 + O_2 \rightarrow 2CO + 4H_2$, or coal (taken here to be carbon) according to $H_2O + O_2 + 3C \rightarrow 3CO + H_2$, to make mixtures of carbon monoxide and hydrogen called synthesis gas, which is in turn used for the manufacture of methanol. Processes in which combustible liquids are produced from coal will become increasingly important as petroleum resources become further depleted.

Production

Oxygen is conveniently produced in the laboratory by heating mercuric oxide (HgO) or potassium chlorate ($KClO_3$) to moderately high temperatures. It can also be produced in the laboratory by the electrolysis of water, a process that reverses the violent hydrogen-oxygen reaction discussed previously. When a current is passed through water the liquid is decomposed at the electrodes according to $2H_2O$ $(l) \rightarrow 2H_2$ $(g) + O_2$ (g). This method is also used to produce oxygen on a commercial scale when a high-purity product is desired.

The more economical, and therefore preferred, method for the commercial production of oxygen is the liquefaction and distillation of air. The air is cooled until it liquefies, principally by being made to do work in a rotating expansion turbine, and the resulting liquid air is fractionated by a complex distillation process. The gaseous oxygen produced in this fashion is shipped in pressurized cylinders or, as is often the case when large amounts are involved, through pipelines to nearby industrial plants.

Relationship to Life Sciences

Most organisms depend on oxygen to sustain their biological processes. The great majority of living organisms fall into two categories. In the first category are the higher plants and the photosynthetic bacteria. These organisms utilize light energy through PHOTOSYNTHESIS to combine carbon dioxide and water (or, infrequently, other inorganic substances in place of water) into more complex materials characterized as CARBOHYDRATES while at the same time releasing oxygen into the atmosphere. In the second category are the higher animals, most microorganisms, and photosynthetic cells that live in the dark. All these second-category organisms use complex series of enzyme-catalyzed OXIDATION AND REDUCTION reactions with materials such as glucose as the fuel and oxygen as the terminal oxidizing agent (see METABOLISM). The end products of metabolism in these organisms are carbon dioxide and water, which are returned to the atmosphere.

The net result of these complementary functions is the oxygen cycle, in which the photosynthetic organisms, using solar energy, synthesize carbohydrates from water and carbon dioxide and give off O_2 as a by-product, while the aerobic organisms oxidize ingested organic materials, using up O_2 and giving off carbon dioxide and water through a complex series of metabolic processes. It has been estimated that 3.5×10^{11} tons of carbon dioxide are cycled annually via these processes (see CARBON CYCLE, environment).

In the vertebrates—and in humans in particular—oxygen is thus necessary to sustain metabolism and hence life. Air is inhaled, and oxygen in the air is exchanged in the lungs between the atmosphere and the hemoglobin in the blood. The blood carries the oxygen, complexed with hemoglobin, to all parts of the body in which metabolic processes occur. It also carries carbon dioxide back to the lungs, where the CO_2 is exchanged with the atmosphere and exhaled.

If the oxygen concentration were to drop to about half its value in the atmosphere, humans could no longer survive. For this reason an important component of the life-support systems of divers and astronauts is a source of oxygen gas. Similarly, persons with respiratory diseases that interfere with normal respiration, such as pneumonia and emphysema, are often kept in oxygen-rich atmospheres to improve the exchange of oxygen with the blood. OXYGEN TENTS and HYPERBARIC CHAMBERS, the latter administering high-pressure oxygen, may be used to treat a variety of ailments.

Important Compounds

In the realm of inorganic chemistry there are numerous oxygen-containing compounds. There are very few elements for which no oxides are known, and there are several metallic elements (such as titanium, vanadium, and praseodymium) for which a wide variety of solid oxides exist. The solid oxides of the metallic elements can generally be synthesized by the direct reaction of the elements at high temperatures. In many cases such reactions will result in the formation of a single oxide of the metal in its most oxidized form. Typical examples are the metallic oxides of sodium, Na_2O; calcium, CaO; lanthanum, La_2O_3; and titanium, TiO_2.

Ternary oxides, consisting of two metallic elements plus oxygen, are of great interest to solid-state scientists. For example, compounds with the general formulas AB_2O_4, such as $MgAl_2O_4$ (the SPINELS) and $ABO3$, such as $BaTiO_3$ (the PEROVSKITES), are studied extensively because of their interesting magnetic and electrical properties. Examples of important ternary oxides are the magnetic FERRITES, whose magnetic properties can be tailored, making them useful in computer memory units. The ferrites are prepared by firing compacted mixtures of iron oxide and one or more metal oxides (such as those of nickel, copper, zinc, magnesium, and manganese).

Also of importance in inorganic chemistry are the oxides of the nonmetals. Most of the nonmetals are known to form a wide variety of compounds with oxygen. For example, carbon forms CO_2, CO, and C_3O_2; nitrogen forms N_2O, NO, N_2O_3, N_2O_4, NO_2, N_2O_5, and NO_3; and fluorine forms OF_2 and O_2F_2. The nitrogen oxides are undesirable by-products of high-temperature combustion in air (as in an internal-combustion engine) and can cause serious environmental pollution.

See also: OXIDE MINERALS.

oxygen furnace   SEE IRON AND STEEL INDUSTRY

---

oxygen tent   A clear, nearly airtight plastic canopy that encloses the whole patient or only the patient's head, an oxygen tent provides higher than normal concentrations of oxygen to maintain a patient without the use of an endotracheal tube or face mask. The oxygen tent also permits relative control of environmental humidity and temperature. Cooled, filtered air is circulated within the confines of the oxygen tent; temperature is regulated by an air-conditioning system attached to the oxygen supply. Oxygen tents are used when other modes of oxygen delivery are not practical. Such an occasion would arise with small children in disease status who require simply an environment of high humidity and who may or may not need additional oxygen. Oxygen tents are the mainstay of today's oxygen delivery, particularly for patients suffering from heart and lung disorders that reduce the delivery of oxygen to the body.

oxytocin   SEE HORMONE, ANIMAL; PREGNANCY AND BIRTH

---

oyster   Oysters are mollusks of the class Bivalvia (or Pelecypoda). The term includes the true oysters, family Ostreidae, in the order Eulamellibranchia; and the winged and pearl oysters, family Pteriidae (or Aviculidae), the spiny oysters, family Spondylidae, and the saddle oysters, family Anomiidae, all in the order Filibranchia. The true oysters, which include the edible oysters, are characterized by rough and irregularly shaped shells that are closed by only one muscle.

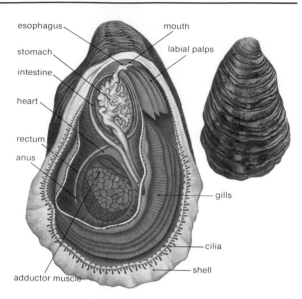

The edible American oyster is found along the Atlantic coast of North America and has been introduced into Pacific coastal waters. The drawings show both internal anatomy (left) and external appearance (right).

Oysters are found in shallow, brackish, or tidal waters throughout all but very cold regions of the world, often in large colonies called oyster beds; where oysters are produced as a food crop, such beds may be artificially established. Adult oysters live attached to an object, either by means of tough, horny strands called byssal threads, or the byssus, or by cementing one shell to the object. Oysters lack a foot or have a reduced foot, and they have a reduced head and associated sense organs. In the true oyster, the upper shell is larger and hollowed to contain the oyster's body; the lower shell is usually flat. Oysters are filter feeders, using their extensive gills and associated hairlike cilia to trap and move tiny food particles to the mouth. In some oysters fertilization is external; in others the female retains and broods the eggs, which are fertilized by sperm drawn in from the outside. Oysters hatch as free-swimming larvae.

See also: PEARLS AND PEARLING.

---

oystercatcher   Oystercatchers are six species of widely distributed shorebirds constituting the family Haematopodidae. They average between 43 and 53 cm (17 and 21 in) in total length and 500 g (1 lb) or more in weight. Oystercatchers are characterized by pink legs and a long, bladelike, bright orange red bill. They feed on worms, crabs, snails, and shellfish such as mussels or oysters. The American oystercatcher, *Haematopus palliatus,* of North and South America, has a brownish black back and head with a white belly. The black oystercatcher, *H. bachmani,* of western North America, lacks white markings.

The American oystercatcher (foreground) *and the black oyster-catcher* (background) *use their elongated bills to pry open shell-fish and mollusks found in shallow coastal waters.*

Oz, Amos   One of Israel's most talented authors, Amos Oz, b. May 4, 1939, writes tales in Hebrew that portray life in contemporary Israeli society. Oz's first novel, *Elsewhere, Perhaps* (1966; Eng. trans., 1973), examines the tangled life of a kibbutz family. His next novel, *My Michael* (1968; Eng. trans., 1972), portrays the drab life of a married couple in besieged Jerusalem. His other works include *Unto Death* (1971; Eng. trans., 1975), consisting of two novellas, and two more novels, *Touch the Water, Touch the Wind* (1973; Eng. trans., 1974) and *A Perfect Peace* (1982; Eng. trans., 1985). In *In the Land of Israel* (1983; Eng. trans., 1983), Oz visits various Israeli ethnic and economic groups, discovering startlingly differing attitudes toward the Arabs and the occupation of the West Bank.

Ozaki Yukio [oh-zah'-kee yoo'-kee-oh]   Ozaki Yukio, b. 1858, d. Oct. 7, 1954, was a leading Japanese liberal statesman. A journalist, he became a follower of OKUMA SHIGENOBU, who appointed him education minister in 1898. He became mayor of Tokyo in 1903 and in 1915 served in Okuma's second cabinet as minister of justice. Elected to every diet (parliament) from 1890 to 1952, Ozaki fought consistently for further democratization in Japan. He opposed militarism and was imprisoned during World War II. He was responsible for a gift of Japanese cherry trees to Washington, D.C., in gratitude for U.S. mediation efforts during the Russo-Japanese War of 1904–05.

Ozark Mountains [oh'-zahrk]   The Ozark Mountains (Ozark Plateau) are a series of hills and knobs in the south central United States, covering about 130,000 km^2 (50,000 mi^2) in southern Illinois, Missouri, northern Ar-kansas, eastern Oklahoma, and southeastern Kansas. The highest peaks, exceeding 600 m (2,000 ft), are in the Boston Mountains of Arkansas. The area is drained by the Black, White, Osage, and Gasconade rivers. The major economic activity of the Ozarks is tourism. The damming of the Osage and White rivers created the Lake of the Ozarks and Taneycomo Lake, which provide hydroelectric power and recreation. Lumbering, farming, and lead and zinc mining are also important. Part of the Ozark National Forest is in the mountains.

Ozawa, Seiji [oh-zah'-wah, say'-jee]   Seiji Ozawa, b. Manchuria to Japanese parents, Sept. 1, 1935, is the first Oriental conductor to reach international prominence. He moved to Japan as a child and later studied Western and Oriental music. In 1960 he won the Koussevitzky Prize at the Berkshire Music Center at Tanglewood in Lenox, Mass.; the next year he became assistant conductor with the New York Philharmonic. Subsequently, he was conductor of the Chicago Symphony Orchestra at the Ravinia Festivals (1963–68), principal conductor of the Toronto Symphony (1965–69), and music director of the San Francisco Symphony (1969–76). In 1973 he became music director of the Boston Symphony Orchestra—the youngest in the orchestra's history.

Ozick, Cynthia [oh'-zik]   Novelist, short-story writer, and translator Cynthia Ozick, b. New York City, Apr. 17, 1928, has carved for herself a unique place in American letters. Ozick's complex fiction is a mélange of elements from which tensions emerge: Jewish mysticism, folklore, and supernaturalism in a modern, secular world, more often than not New York City; realism infused with cruel irony and dry humor; a controlled style replete with symbolism and rhetorical fantasy. Ozick's works include *Trust* (1966), *The Cannibal Galaxy* (1983), and *The Messiah of Stockholm* (1987), novels; *The Pagan Rabbi* (1971), *Bloodshed and Three Novellas* (1976), *Levitation* (1982), and *The Shawl* (1989), collections of short fiction; and *Art and Ardor: Essays* (1983) and *Metaphor and Memory: Essays* (1989).

ozone   Ozone is a form of OXYGEN in which three atoms combine to form a molecule (O_3), instead of the usual diatomic form of the element (O_2). It is a blue gas with a pungent odor, noticeable when the gas is formed by an electrical discharge. Ozone is a powerful oxidizing agent and an effective antiseptic and bleaching agent; in high concentrations it is severely irritating. Ozone in the upper atmosphere forms an important barrier against solar radiation, but ozone produced in the lower atmosphere by industry and automobile exhaust is a pollutant, causing significant crop damage.

ozone layer   The ozone layer, a region of the upper atmosphere about 20 to 25 km (12 to 15 mi) above the

Earth's surface, is characterized by peak concentrations of the unstable form of oxygen called ozone. The ozone layer protects life on Earth by strongly absorbing ULTRAVIOLET LIGHT from the Sun. Without such protection the incidence of human skin cancers and cataracts would rise, and food production would fall worldwide.

The natural forces at work in this high-altitude layer maintain a mixture of gases that includes atomic oxygen (O), ordinary oxygen (O_2), and ozone (O_3). The quantities of each form fluctuate diurnally and seasonally in response to solar radiation, temperature changes, and other catalytic influences.

Within the ozone layer, the rate of formation of ozone equals the rate of its consumption. These rates have apparently stayed in general balance over a long period of geological time. Human activities, however, now appear to be affecting that balance through the introduction of certain destructive chemicals into the layer. The potential harm caused by the resulting loss of ozone has become a matter of international concern.

The chemicals concerned are producers of FREE RADICALS, which are atoms and molecules with an unpaired electron. Free-radical chlorine is an example. When a chemical that can form free-radical chlorine is introduced into the ozone layer, the chlorine will react with the ozone in the following manner: $O_3 + Cl \rightarrow OCl + O_2$, and $OCl + O_3 \rightarrow Cl + 2O_2$.

Decreases in ozone concentrations were first detected in the late 1970s. The largest decreases have occurred over Antarctica, where ozone concentrations temporarily decline each spring, resulting in an ozone "hole." Its size appears to be increasing, and similar seasonal losses are apparently on the increase in the Arctic region as well.

The chemicals that have been linked most directly to this phenomenon are the chlorofluorocarbons, or CFCs (see FLUOROCARBON), which are widely used as AEROSOL propellants, refrigerants, foaming agents for plastic packaging, and cleaning fluids. In 1987, in response, an international treaty called the Montreal Protocol on Substances that Deplete the Ozone Layer mandated a reduction in the use of CFCs. In 1989, 93 nations further agreed to phase out their production and to aid poorer nations in revising their technologies accordingly. The chemicals thus far devised as replacements are less versatile and more expensive than CFCs.

Ozu, Yasujiro [oh'-zoo, yah-soo'-jee-roh] Japanese filmmaker Yasujiro Ozu, b. Dec. 15, 1903, d. Dec. 12, 1963, originated a style of filmmaking that has been called "transcendental cinema." His films generally deal with the Japanese middle class and present detailed, wryly humorous observations on parent-child relationships and the problems of growing up. Their underlying and more serious theme is the unending cycle of death and rebirth that occurs in nature.

A rigorous, traditional craftsman, Ozu started in films as a scriptwriter and collaborated early in his career with the noted scriptwriter Kogo Noda and the actor Chishu Ryu. In his own films he did not use sound until 1936 and color until 1958. In all, he directed 54 films, among them such classics as *Hitori Musuko* (The Only Son, 1936); *Soshun* (Early Spring, 1956); and *Samma No Aji* (An Autumn Afternoon, 1962).

Pp

GERMAN-GOTHIC	RUSSIAN-CYRILLIC	CLASSICAL LATIN	EARLY LATIN	ETRUSCAN	CLASSICAL GREEK	EARLY GREEK	EARLY ARAMAIC	EARLY HEBREW	PHOENICIAN

P *P/p* is the 16th letter of the English alphabet. Both the form of the letter and its position in the alphabet were derived from the Latin alphabet, which in turn derived it from the Greek by way of the Etruscan. The Greeks called the letter *pi,* and the name, form, and position of the letter were taken by them from a Semitic writing system, in which the name of the sign was *pe.*

P/p is a voiceless labial stop, as in *pin, park,* and *lip.* It is the voiceless counterpart of the voiced labial stop *b* and is also related to the labial continuants *f* and *v.* When *p* is followed by *h* in the same syllable, the combination is usually pronounced as *f,* as in *phone* or *graph.*

P-38 Lightning The P-38 was one of the most distinctive-looking of U.S. Army Air Force planes. It was a single-seat monoplane fighter with a 15.8-m (52-ft) span. Its twin Allison V-1710 liquid-cooled engines were installed at the front of the pair of slim tail-supporting booms, and it had tricycle landing gear and powerful nose-mounted armament. The plane originated as the winner of the February 1937 U.S. Army Air Corps design competition for a high-performance pursuit plane capable of intercepting enemy aircraft at high altitude. Eventually, the P-38 operated in several variants throughout World War II in all theaters.

P-40 The Curtiss P-40 series of fighter planes included several single-seat, low-wing monoplane variants produced between 1938 and 1944. Originating in July 1937 as a development of the P-36, the P-40 was equipped with a larger 1,040-horsepower engine; production began in April 1939. Named Tomahawk Mk.I and Mk.IIA, the airplane was supplied to the Royal Air Force, which later received 930 of the improved Mk.IIB. One hundred of this batch of P-40Bs—90 of which eventually arrived— were diverted by the U.S. government to China to provide initial equipment for the American Volunteer Group (AVG), directed by Gen. Claire Lee CHENNAULT; it was there that the three squadrons gained renown fighting the Japanese, becoming known as the Flying Tigers. The P-40 design was developed through 12 main variants, with later designs known as the Warhawk and Kittyhawk.

The Curtiss P-40B, the first American monoplane fighter, was used by the Flying Tigers, an American volunteer group, to help China defend its Burma Road supply line against the Japanese in 1941-42. Painted-on shark's teeth and Chinese Nationalist colors identified these planes.

Pa Hsien   see BA XIAN

Pa-ta Shan-jen   see ZHU DA

Pabst, G. W. [pahpst] A major contributor to the German cinema during its experimental silent and early sound eras, director George William Pabst, b. Bohemia, Aug. 27, 1885, d. May 30, 1967, is especially identified with the straightforward portrayal of human degradation, as in *Joyless Street* (1925) and *Pandora's Box* (1929). His first sound films were the pacifist *Westfront 1918* (1930) and *Kameradschaft* (1931) and his version of *Dreigroschenoper* (Threepenny Opera, 1931). His *Don Quixote* (1933) starred the renowned Russian singer Chaliapin in his only film role. Following World War II, Pabst made *The Trial* (1947) and *Ten Days to Die* (1955), an account of Hitler's end.

paca The paca, *Cuniculus paca,* is a nocturnal rodent of the family Dasyproctidae that lives in forests from central Mexico to southern Brazil. It measures 51 to 76 cm (20 to 30 in) in length and weighs about 9 kg (20 lb). The body is chunky and has white-spotted brown fur, and

The paca, recognized by the rows of white spots on its coat, is a delicacy to South American Indians, who hunt it for its meat.

the squarish head has large cheekbones. The paca feeds on fruit and other plant materials.

pacarana   see FALSE PACA

pacemaker, artificial An artificial pacemaker is implanted in the human body when the natural pacemaker—a knot of tissue in the HEART muscle that initiates the rhythmic heartbeat—does not function properly (see HEART DISEASES). The device, invented in 1958 by American biomedical engineer Wilson Greatbatch, is a small, flat, plastic disk powered by a tiny battery. It is implanted somewhere in the body, usually in the subcutaneous fat layer, and connected by wires to the heart through a surgically formed tunnel. It emits rhythmic electric impulses that trigger heart action. The impulse rate is either controlled from an external switch or preset specifically for the particular patient. Researchers are developing pacemakers that are sensitive to changes in body temperature and to increases in oxygen need.

Pachacamac [pah-chah-kah-mahk'] Pachacamac was an important religious pilgrimage center of pre-Columbian Andean civilization. Located on the central coast of Peru south of modern Lima, it was noted as the site of a famous oracle. An important center by the 5th century AD, it had become a substantial city by the year 1000. In the 14th and 15th centuries the INCA built an elaborate temple there with a house of "chosen women" to serve it. Like other native religious centers the temples of Pachacamac were badly damaged by the Spanish as part of their attempts to Christianize the natives. The oracle itself was reported to have been a carved wooden post, and people came from many parts of the Andes to consult and worship it. An art style portraying eagle designs in polychrome ceramics and tapestries seems to have originated at Pachacamac and spread over most of the central Peruvian coast during the 7th and 8th centuries AD.

Pachacuti [pah-chah-koo'-tee] Pachacuti, r. c.1440– c.1470, was the ruler responsible for the INCA expansion into an empire, although legend credits MANCO CAPAC with founding the royal dynasty. Pachacuti is the first of the Inca rulers whose historical identity is unquestionable. The details of his conquests may have been distorted by the glorification of Pachacuti in official Inca oral history, but it is clear that he was brilliant both as a strategist of conquests and as an organizer of empires. During the final stage of his rule, Pachacuti was assisted by his son and successor Topa Inca. Together they expanded the empire to nearly the size encountered by the Spanish in 1532.

Pachelbel, Johann [pah'-kul-bel]   German organist and composer Johann Pachelbel, b. August 1653, d. Mar. 3, 1706, is noted by music historians for his influence on Johann Sebastian Bach. Pachelbel was himself a composer of importance, and his works are still played. His best works are his chorale variations and chorale preludes.

Pacher, Michael   The Tyrolean artist Michael Pacher, b. c.1453, d. August 1498, was among the first northern European painters to adapt the techniques of Italian Renaissance art successfully to his own work. The influence of Jacopo Bellini and, in particular, of Andrea Mantegna is obvious in his work—for example, in the use of such devices as the placement of large figures in exaggerated perspective against a low horizon line. His sculpture and the architectural elements in his paintings, however, are in the German Flamboyant Gothic style.

Most of Pacher's numerous altarpieces were made for Tyrolean parish churches and have remained in them. His finest surviving work is the large polyptych (multiwinged) high altar (signed and dated 1481) at Sankt Wolfgang am Ambersee, Austria. All of the wings are carved on the outside and painted on the inside, with the carved *Coronation of the Virgin* as a central shrine.

Pachuca [pah-choo'-kah]   Pachuca (full name: Pachuca de Soto) is the capital of Hidalgo state in central Mexico. Located in the ore-rich western foothills of the Sierra Madre Oriental, about 90 km (55 mi) northeast of Mexico City, Pachuca has a population of 135,248 (1983 est.). The basis of the city's wealth and many of its industries is mining, especially of silver. Pachuca is the home of the University of Hidalgo (1869). Among the city's landmarks are a 16th-century church and convent. The Spanish settled on this ancient Toltec site in 1534.

Pacific, War of the   The War of the Pacific (1879–84), also called the Chile-Peruvian War, was a conflict between Chile and the allied armies of Peru and Bolivia. It began as a result of an argument between Chile and Bolivia over ownership of nitrate-rich land in Bolivia's Atacama province. Chilean companies had been exploiting these nitrates freely in the area until 1878, when the Bolivians levied an export tax. Chileans operating at the port of Antofagasta refused to pay the tariff, leading to seizure (February 1879) of the territory by the Bolivian government. In retaliation a Chilean invasion force easily captured Antofagasta on Feb. 14, 1879. Chile then invaded Peru—which had formed a secret alliance with Bolivia in 1873—and occupied Lima in January 1881. By the Treaty of Ancón (October 1883), which ended hostilities between Chile and Peru, Chile was granted Peru's Tarapacá province and the right to continue its occupation of the Peruvian provinces of Tacna and Arica for ten years (see TACNA-ARICA DISPUTE). The truce with Bolivia, signed at Valparaíso in April 1884 and finalized in 1904, provided Chile with Atacama, Bolivia's only coastal territory.

Pacific Islands, Trust Territory of the   The Trust Territory of the Pacific Islands, in the tropical western Pacific Ocean, was a United Nations trusteeship administered by the United States. It included the MARSHALL ISLANDS, the MARIANA ISLANDS (excluding GUAM), and the CAROLINE ISLANDS (see also MICRONESIA, FEDERATED STATES OF; and PALAU). Fewer than 200 of the more than 2,000 small islands and atolls, which are scattered across a water area of 7,770,000 km² (3,000,000 mi²) and have a land area of about 1,300 km² (500 mi²), are inhabited. The population is 175,000 (1988 est.).

The islands of the trust territory were first sighted by Europeans in the early 16th century, when Ferdinand Magellan sailed through the area. Formerly German possessions—the Mariana and Caroline groups from 1899 and the Marshall Islands from 1885—the islands came under Japanese mandate following World War I and were the scene of bitter fighting during World War II. In 1947 they became a UN trusteeship administered by the United States. The United States has military bases there and used two of the islands, BIKINI and ENIWETOK, for nuclear-weapons testing after World War II.

The trust territory was later divided into four internally self-governing units; local constitutions came into effect in the Northern Marianas in 1978, in the Marshall Islands and the Federated States of Micronesia (eastern Carolines) in 1979, and in the Republic of Palau (Belau) in 1981. The inhabitants of the Northern Marianas voted in 1975 to become a U.S. commonwealth. Compacts of free association with the United States, under which each would become a sovereign state with the United States retaining responsibility for its defense and providing economic assistance, were approved in plebiscites in the Marshall Islands and the Federated States of Micronesia in 1983. The situation in Palau, where a similar compact failed to receive the 75% approval needed to override the nuclear ban in the Palauan constitution in numerous plebiscites, remained unresolved after the United States ended its trusteeship arrangements with the Marshall Islands (Oct. 21, 1986) and with the Federated States of Micronesia and the Commonwealth of the Northern Mariana Islands (Nov. 3, 1986). The trust territory, with the exception of Palau, was formally terminated by the UN Security Council on Dec. 22, 1990.

Pacific Ocean   The Pacific Ocean, the world's largest water body (see OCEAN AND SEA), occupies a third of the Earth's surface. Extending approximately 15,500 km (9,600 mi) from the BERING SEA in the Arctic north to the icy margins of Antarctica's Ross Sea in the south, the Pacific reaches its greatest width at about 5° north latitude, where it stretches approximately 19,800 km (12,300 mi) from Indonesia to the coast of Colombia. The Pacific contains about 25,000 islands (more than the rest of the world's oceans combined), almost all of them south of the equator. The Pacific covers an area of 179.7 million km^2 (69.4 million mi^2). The lowest known point on Earth, in the MARIANAS TRENCH, lies within the Pacific.

Along the Pacific Ocean's irregular margins lie many seas, the largest of which are the Celebes Sea, CORAL SEA, East China Sea, Sea of Japan (see JAPAN, SEA OF), SULU SEA, and YELLOW SEA. The Strait of Malacca (see MALACCA, STRAIT OF) joins the Pacific and the Indian oceans on the west, and the Strait of Magellan (see MAGELLAN, STRAIT OF) links the Pacific with the Atlantic Ocean on the east.

Ocean Bottom

The ocean floor of the central Pacific basin is relatively uniform, with a mean depth of about 4,270 m (14,000 ft). The major irregularities are the extremely steep-sided, flat-topped submarine peaks known as SEAMOUNTS. The western part of the floor consists of mountain arcs that rise above the sea as island groups and deep trenches (see OCEANIC TRENCHES). Most deep trenches lie adjacent to the outer margins of the wide western Pacific continental shelf.

Along the eastern margin of the Pacific basin is the East Pacific Rise, which is a part of the worldwide mid-oceanic ridge. About 3,000 km (1,800 mi) across, the rise stands about 3 km (2 mi) above the adjacent ocean floor.

Water Characteristics

Water temperatures in the Pacific vary from freezing in the poleward areas to about 29° C (84° F) near the equator. Water near the equator is less salty than that found in the midlatitudes because of abundant equatorial precipitation. Near the poles salinity is also low, because little evaporation of seawater takes place in these areas.

The surface circulation of Pacific waters is generally clockwise in the Northern Hemisphere and counterclockwise in the Southern Hemisphere (see OCEAN CURRENTS). The North Equatorial Current, driven westward along latitude 15° north by the trade winds, turns north near the Philippines to become the warm Kuroshio, or Japan, Current. Turning eastward at about 45° north, the Kuroshio forks, and some waters move northward as the Aleutian Current, while the rest turn southward to rejoin the North Equatorial Current. The Aleutian Current branches as it approaches North America and forms the base of a counterclockwise circulation in the Bering Sea. Its southern arm becomes the south-flowing California Current.

The South Equatorial Current, flowing west along the equator, swings southward east of New Guinea, turns east at about 50° south latitude, and joins the main westerly circulation of the Southern Pacific, which includes the Earth-circling Antarctic Circumpolar Current. As it approaches the Chilean coast, the South Equatorial Current divides; one branch flows around Cape Horn, and the other turns north to form the Peru, or Humboldt, Current.

Climate

Only the interiors of the large landmasses of Australia, New Guinea, and New Zealand escape the pervasive climatic influence of the Pacific. Within the area of the Pacific, five distinctively different climatic regions exist: the midlatitude westerlies, the trades, the monsoon region, the typhoon region, and the doldrums. Midlatitude westerly air streams occur in both northerly and southerly latitudes, bringing marked seasonal differences in temperature. Closer to the equator, where most of the islands lie, steadily blowing trade winds allow for relatively constant temperatures throughout the year. The monsoon region, with its marked seasonality of cloudiness and rainfall, lies in the far western Pacific between Japan and Australia. Typhoons often cause extensive damage in the west and southwest Pacific. Two major doldrum areas noted for high humidity and frequent calms lie within the ocean, one located off the western shores of Central America and the other within the equatorial waters of the western Pacific.

Geology

The Andesite Line is the most significant regional distinction in the Pacific. It separates the deeper, basic igneous rock of the Central Pacific Basin from the partially submerged continental areas of acidic igneous rock on its margins. The Andesite Line follows the western edge of the islands off California and passes south of the Aleutian arc, along the eastern edge of the Kamchatka Peninsula, the Kuril Islands, Japan, the Mariana Islands, the Solomon Islands, and New Zealand. The dissimilarity continues northeastward along the western edge of the Albatross Cordillera along South America to Mexico, returning then to the islands off California. Indonesia, the Philippines, Japan, New Guinea, and New Zealand—all eastward extensions of the continental blocks of Australia and Asia—lie outside the Andesite Line.

Within the closed loop of the Andesite Line are most of the deep troughs, submerged volcanic mountains, and oceanic volcanic islands that characterize the Central Pacific Basin. Outside the Andesite Line, volcanism is of the explosive type; the so-called Pacific rim of fire is the world's foremost belt of explosive volcanism.

Landmasses

The largest landmass in the Pacific is the continent of Australia. About 3,200 km (2,000 mi) southeast of Australia is the large island group of New Zealand. Almost all of the smaller islands of the Pacific lie between 30° north and 30° south latitude. They are classified into three groups: MELANESIA, MICRONESIA, AND POLYNESIA.

Islands in the Pacific Ocean are of four basic types: continental islands, high islands, coral reefs, and uplifted coral platforms. Continental islands lie outside the

SIBERIA

STANOVOY MTS.

YABLONOY MTS.

Sea of
Okhotsk

KAMCHATKA

Bering
Sea

Alaska

Bering
Abyssal
Plain

3908 m.

5569 m.

Aleutian Islands

ALEUTIAN TRENCH

Aleutian
Abyssal Plain

MENDOCINO FRACTURE ZONE

7822 m.

Kuril Islands

KURIL TRENCH

JAPAN TRENCH

6088 m.

EMPEROR SEAMOUNTS

Emperor Trough

SHATSKY RISE

ASIA

Gobi Desert

Sakhalin
Island

Amur

10542 m.

Sea of
Japan

Midway

HAWAIIAN RIDGE

MOLOKAI FRACTURE ZONE

Yellow
Sea

East
China
Sea

JAPAN

9810 m.

MAPMAKER
SEAMOUNTS

Yangtze R.

CHINA

RYUKYU TRENCH

PHILIPPINE TRENCH

Philippine
Ridge

MARIANA TRENCH

Mariana
Islands

Wake Island

MID-PACIFIC MOUNTAINS

Hawaiian
Islands

CHRISTMAS RIDGE

Philippine
Sea

4740 m.

CLIP

South
China
Sea

RYUKYU

PHILIPPINES

PARECE VELA

10497 m.

11022 m.

Caroline
Islands

Bikini Atoll

Marshall
Islands

Mekong

Sumatra

INDONESIA

Borneo

Java Sea

Java

Arafura Sea

Bismarck

New Guinea

NEW BRITAIN TRENCH

NEW HEBRIDES TRENCH

9140 m.

8717 m.

Coral Sea

Solomon
Islands

New
Hebrides

Gilbert
Islands

Ellice
Islands

North
Tokelau
Trough

MANIHIKI
PLATEAU

Society
Islands

Samoa
Islands

Fiji

New
Caledonia

South
Fiji
Basin

Tonga

TONGA TRENCH

10882 m.

TUAMOTU RIDGE

Cook
Islands

INDIAN
OCEAN

AUSTRALIA

LORD HOWE RISE

10047 m.

KERMADEC TRENCH

Tasman Abyssal Plain

Great Bight
Abyssal Plain

Tasmania

Tasman
Sea

Southeast
Australian
Basin

NEW ZEALAND

NEW
ZEALAND
PLATEAU

Chatham
Islands

5559 m.

SOUTHEAST INDIAN
OCEAN RIDGE

MACQUARIE RIDGE

MACQUARIE SWELL

Bounty
Trough

Antipodes
Islands

South   Indian   Basin

The relief map shows features of the Pacific Ocean floor. Many geologists believe that the seafloor spreads from the East Pacific Rise and is reabsorbed into the Earth's mantle along oceanic trenches.

Andesite Line and include New Guinea, the islands of New Zealand, and the Philippines. These islands are structurally associated with the nearby continents. High islands are of volcanic origin, and many contain active volcanoes. Among these are Bougainville, Hawaii, and the Solomon Islands.

The third and fourth types of islands are both the result of coralline island building. Coral reefs are low-lying structures that have built up on basaltic lava flows under the ocean's surface. One of the most dramatic is the GREAT BARRIER REEF off northeastern Australia. A second island type formed of coral is the uplifted coral platform, which is usually slightly larger than the low coral islands.

History and Economy

Important human migrations occurred in the Pacific in prehistoric times, most notably those of Polynesians from Tahiti to Hawaii and New Zealand. The ocean was sighted by Europeans early in the 16th century, first by Vasco Núñez de Balboa (1513) and then by Ferdinand Magellan, who crossed the Pacific during his circumnavigation (1519–22). For the remainder of the 16th century, Spanish influence was paramount. During the 17th century the Dutch, sailing around southern Africa, dominated discovery and trade; Abel Janszoon Tasman discovered (1642) Tasmania and New Zealand. The 18th century marked a burst of exploration by the Russians in Alaska and the Aleutian Islands, the French in Polynesia, and the British in the three voyages of James Cook—to the South Pacific and Australia, Hawaii, and the North American Pacific Northwest. Growing imperialism during the 19th century resulted in the occupation of much of the Pacific by the Western powers. Significant contributions to oceanographic knowledge were made by the voyages of the H.M.S. *Beagle* in the 1830s, with Charles Darwin aboard; the H.M.S. *Challenger* during the 1870s; the U.S.S. *Tuscarora* (1873–76); and the German *Gazelle* (1874–76). Although the United States took the Philippines in 1898, Japan controlled the western Pacific by 1914. By the end of World War II the U.S. Pacific Fleet was the virtual master of the ocean.

Fourteen independent nations are located in the Pacific: Kiribati, Nauru, Papua New Guinea, Taiwan, Tuvalu, Western Samoa, Australia, Fiji, Japan, New Zealand, the Philippines, the Solomon Islands, Tonga, and Vanuatu. Also within the Pacific are the U.S. state of Hawaii and several island territories and possessions of Australia, Chile, France, Japan, New Zealand, the United Kingdom, and the United States.

The exploitation of the Pacific's mineral wealth is hampered by the ocean's great depths. In shallow waters off the coast of Australia, petroleum and natural gas are extracted.

pacifism and nonviolent movements   Pacifism is the belief in peaceful reconciliation of human differences. It opposes not only war between nations but also violent revolution and the use of coercive violence by governments. For some individuals, such as CONSCIENTIOUS OBJECTORS, pacifism is a matter of private morality. In modern times, however, pacifism has more often been associated with groups working for political ends and dedicated to nonviolent methods of achieving them.

Origins of Pacifist Ideas

The beliefs that lie at the core of pacifism—a respect for life and a consequent repugnance toward killing—are ancient. They can be found in the Chinese Daoist doctrine of *wuwei*, or nonaction, although this doctrine suggests passivity rather than pacifism in the modern political sense. In ancient India the doctrine of *ahimsa*—nonharming—was shared by the Buddhists, by certain Hindu elements, and by the Jains. Not until the appearance of Mahatma GANDHI at the end of the 19th century, however, did *ahimsa* take on the social and political aspects associated with pacifism. Earlier it had been regarded simply as a question of action or nonaction that might affect the individual's karma, or destiny. Early Buddhist monarchs such as Asoka in India and the kings of Ceylon sought to rule peacefully, but no Buddhist realm in history has forsworn violence altogether.

A truer pacifism was to be found among the early Christians, who were inspired by such Gospel exhortations as "Love thine enemies" and "Blessed are the peacemakers; for they shall be called the children of God," and among the Jewish ESSENES, who preached withdrawal from the realm of war and politics. Even in the first centuries, however, Christians were divided in their attitudes toward war and violence; the question whether a Christian could remain a soldier was long debated. Some Fathers of the Church, like TERTULLIAN, took an essentially pacifist stand. For the church as a whole to be pacifist became politically impossible after the Emperor Constantine's conversion in the early 4th century and the adoption of Christianity as the state religion of the Roman Empire. In the 5th century, when orthodox Christianity in North Africa was threatened by the Vandals, who supported the rival sect of Arian Christians, Saint AUGUSTINE devised the doctrine of the Just War, a doctrine that has been sustained by institutional Christianity ever since.

The pacifist strain reemerged in such medieval sects as the ALBIGENSES and the BOGOMILS, some of whom renounced the use of violence. After the Reformation, pacifism was adopted by a number of Western European sects, including the MENNONITES; the Quakers, or Society of FRIENDS; and some of the ANABAPTISTS. In 17th-century Russia the Great Schism in the Orthodox church encouraged the emergence of radical sects such as the DOUKHOBORS and the Molokans, who opposed participation in war and employed passive resistance against the authorities seeking to coerce them.

Among Christian pacifists, a distinction must be made between those who resist participation in war merely to save their consciences (see MILLENARIANISM), and those who see their pacifism as part of an attempt to transform the world here and now, as do the Quakers. In the late

17th century the Quakers waged a painful campaign against the English law forbidding dissenters to meet publicly; nearly 400 Quakers died in the pestilential prisons of the time. The Quakers provide an early example of a successful nonviolent movement.

Nonviolent Political Movements

Pacifism emerged from its religious context and became a political philosophy during the 19th century. American abolitionists led by William Lloyd GARRISON preached the use of nonviolent methods in the fight against slavery. Many of the suffragettes who struggled for women's rights in Britain and North America adopted nonviolent resistance. Count Leo TOLSTOI, after his conversion to a radical kind of Christianity, advocated a pacifist rejection of war and the use of CIVIL DISOBEDIENCE as an alternative to violent revolution in books such as *The Kingdom of God Is Within You*. A Tolstoian movement developed in tsarist Russia, surviving for some time after the Revolution of 1917.

Nineteenth-century socialists were often antimilitarist in the sense that they opposed capitalist or imperialist wars. Many socialists advocated an international general strike should war be declared, but when World War I began in 1914 the only resistance came from dedicated pacifists and a few revolutionary socialists. The labor movements on both sides abandoned their internationalism to support their own governments.

The horrors of World War I led to an upsurge of pacifist sentiment in the West. International pacifist organizations such as the Fellowship of Reconciliation flourished. In Britain the students at Oxford University passed a resolution pledging not to fight "for king and country," and the Peace Pledge Union founded in 1935 had gained a membership of 133,000 by 1937. Most of this resistance melted when world war again came in 1939. Pacifism swelled again in the 1960s: in Britain mass demonstrations and acts of civil disobedience were organized by

The Indian nationalist leader Mahatma Gandhi made the principle of ahimsa *(noninjury to all living beings) the basis of his campaigns of passive resistance* (satyagraha) *to achieve social and political reforms.*

Martin Luther King, Jr. (center), was photographed while leading the 1965 Freedom March from Selma to Montgomery, Ala. Advocating passive resistance, King organized the first large-scale civil rights movement in U.S. history.

the Campaign for Nuclear Disarmament, and in the United States the Vietnam War brought widespread resistance. The pacifism of the 1960s, however, attracted many nonpacifists who turned to nonviolent forms of action because they were expedient.

Gandhi's Campaigns. Perhaps the most successful campaigns of nonviolence were those led by Mahatma Gandhi in South Africa before World War I and in India afterward. Gandhi based his theories of civil disobedience partly on the writings of Westerners such as Tolstoi and Henry David Thoreau and on the Christian Gospels and partly on Indian teachings of *ahimsa*. Out of these he developed his own approach, called *satyagraha* (truth-force), which in practice took many different forms: strikes, street demonstrations, withdrawal of cooperation, and symbolic breaches of law such as the manufacture of salt—all within the context of a movement based on self-discipline, self-sacrifice, and moral purity. Gandhi directed his nonviolent campaigns not only against British rule but also against abuses within Indian society such as discrimination against the casteless group called Untouchables. His campaigns were the most important factor leading to the British withdrawal from India in 1947.

Martin Luther King. Nonviolence also characterized the campaigns that Martin Luther KING, a disciple of both Gandhi and Thoreau, led in the 1950s and '60s against racial segregation in the United States. King and his immediate associates were Protestant ministers who interpreted Christianity in a pacifist way, but they were also influenced by the tradition of nonviolence stemming from William Lloyd Garrison and the abolitionists. A boycott by blacks of the Birmingham, Ala., bus service in 1955 succeeded in forcing the bus company to change its segregated seating policy. The cause gathered public support, and white as well as black activists joined in peaceful demonstrations throughout the South. King became the most prominent leader in the CIVIL RIGHTS movement of the 1960s, which succeeded in desegregating public facilities in the South and also in obtaining civil rights legislation from Congress.

As with Gandhi, however, not all who followed Martin Luther King were pacifists. When it became clear that much social inequality remained, particularly in employment and housing, many in the civil rights movement turned to other forms of action. When King himself, like Gandhi before him, was assassinated in 1968, riots in the Northern black ghettos followed.

Although pacifist resistance has yet to succeed in stopping a war, movements using nonviolent methods in peacetime have been able to gain political and social ends where other movements have failed. The popular campaigns that succeeded in overturning the Communist regimes of Eastern Europe in 1989 were for the most part nonviolent.

Pacino, Al [puh-chee'-noh] Alfred Pacino, b. New York City, Apr. 25, 1940, in a relatively short time established himself solidly as an actor both on stage and screen. His role in *The Indian Wants the Bronx* earned him a 1968 Obie Award, and his Broadway debut in *Does a Tiger Wear a Necktie?* (1969) brought him a Tony Award. Highly regarded for his 1972 film portrayal of the young Michael Corleone in *The Godfather*, Pacino followed with successful performances in such films as *Serpico* (1973), *The Godfather, Part II* (1974), *Dog Day Afternoon* (1975), *Sea of Love* (1989), *Dick Tracy* (1990), and *The Godfather III* (1990).

pack ice Pack ice, made of frozen seawater, is composed of pieces of ice of various shapes, sizes, and ages that are free to drift under the influence of winds and ocean currents. An individual piece of ice in the pack is called a floe and can vary from a few meters to more than 10 km (several feet to more than 6 mi) in length. The two largest areas of pack ice are in and near the Arctic Ocean and in the Antarctic region.

Arctic Pack. The Arctic pack, which averages 3 to 6 m (10 to 20 ft) thick during winter, circles the Arctic Ocean in a clockwise direction. Most floes stay in the Arctic Ocean for 5 or more years, but they eventually escape, mainly between Spitzbergen and Greenland, and may float as far south as Iceland before completely melting away.

In certain places in the Arctic pack, the jamming and crushing of floes form pressure ridges and hummocks that may rise 5 m (16 ft) or more above the general level of the pack. Irregular openings in the pack, called polynyas, occur in other places. It was through one of these that the submarine U.S.S. *Skate* surfaced (1959) close to the North Pole.

Antarctic Pack. The Antarctic pack entirely surrounds the Antarctic continent at the end of winter and may extend for several hundred kilometers north of the coast. Its edge advances northward during the winter months and retreats southward during the summer. The Antarctic pack is 1 to 2 m (3 to 7 ft) thick, and the individual floes are 1 or 2 years old.

packaging   A package is a container used for the storage and protection of a commodity. In addition to containing material, it may serve as a measure, such as a quart bottle, or a dispenser, such as an aerosol spray can. Packaging minimizes loss by leakage or evaporation and reduces spoilage and contamination by dirt, insects, bacteria, mold, moisture, or oxygen. The package can be a sales medium whose attractive colors and design encourage the purchase of the product.

Development of Packaging. The emergence of automatic production equipment toward the end of the 19th century brought packaging into common use. The standard can for processed food was first used in the early 1900s (see CANNING). The beginnings of CELLOPHANE manufacture in the 1920s opened the era of transparent wrappings. Films made of polyethylene, polyester, and other plastics came into use after World War II. Plastic bottles and AEROSOLS were first introduced in 1945.

New packaging technologies have enormously diversified the ways in which goods are merchandised, bought, and consumed. Plastic boil-in-the-bag food pouches, for example, contain foods that are ready to eat within minutes after they have been put in a pot of boiling water. Plastic blisters with peel-off covers now provide "portion packs" of jellies, pills, or ointments. The foam-plastic sleeves on soft-drink bottles, which reduce breakage, are also being adopted for toiletry and pharmaceutical bottles. Vacuum-metallized plastic films are supplanting foil laminations for products that must be protected from moisture or oxygen. Milk containers come in glass, paperboard, and plastic. The rise of the microwave oven has been accompanied by a new type of food package that can be used as a cooking vessel.

The Industry. The package-making industry, with about a million workers, is the largest industrial employer in the United States and the third largest industry in terms of sales. The total value produced by the industry is about 10 percent of the value of all finished goods.

The Social Costs of Packaging. Packaging is a major source of litter and solid waste. The amount of packaging materials used and eventually thrown away grows yearly and, in the late 1980s in the United States, was estimated at well over 54.4 million metric tons (60 million U.S. tons). Much of this waste will remain, unchanged, in LANDFILLS and garbage dumps.

In an effort to reduce the enormous volume of solid wastes, many states have enacted legislation requiring the payment of deposits on all beverage containers. Communities have made serious efforts to collect waste materials in order to carry out the RECYCLING OF MATERIALS such as aluminum cans and other metal materials, glass, paper, and some types of plastic.

The more sophisticated packaging technologies have required ever-larger investments in packaging equipment and have led to higher costs both for manufacturers and for consumers. Small entrepreneurs have been effectively shut out of their markets by packaging developments. Several decades ago, for example, large numbers of bottlers of soft drinks operated in local markets throughout the country. The advent of throwaway cans and bottles forced most of them out of business, because only the largest bottlers can afford to invest in the costly machinery needed to make the new containers.

paddle tennis   Paddle tennis is a ball and paddle game contested by 2 or 4 players. It is popular mainly in the United States, where it is played on special courts with a 15- to 17-in-long (38- to 43-cm) laminated wood paddle and a punctured tennis ball.

The sport was devised in 1898 by Rev. Frank P. Beal, who later introduced it to New York City. Beal wanted an ideal playground game for children. He reduced the dimensions of a regulation tennis court by half to yield a playing area 39 by 18 ft (11.8 by 5.5 m) and applied most of the rules of tennis to the game. The wooden paddles had short handles for easier control by children, but the striking area was the same size as that of a tennis racket. A sponge-rubber ball was substituted for the tennis ball. Paddle tennis also became popular with adults. Before World War II, interest in the game stagnated because adult players found the court size a constraint on strategy. Overhead serves and the tactic of rushing the net made sustained rallies difficult.

In 1959 new rules were introduced, and a renaissance began in the sport. A larger court area 50 by 20 ft (15.2 by 6.1 m), a 31-in-high (78.7-cm) net, the punctured tennis ball, and the elimination of the overhead serve helped make the game extremely fast and enjoyable to watch. This court contains 4 service areas, each 22 ft (6.7 m) long and 10 ft (3 m) wide, with baselines 3 ft (91.4 cm) beyond the service areas.

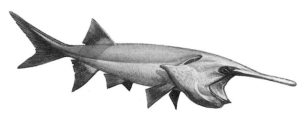

The Mississippi paddlefish is a survivor of a group of fishes that dates back more than 100 million years.

paddlefish Belonging to the family Polyodontidae and distantly related to the sturgeons, the two known species of paddlefish are characterized by the large paddle shape of their extended snout and by their large gill covers. The true function of the paddle is unknown, but it is not used to root in the river bottom, as is sometimes supposed. It may function as a hydrofoil, balancing the downward drag of the huge mouth as it sweeps the water straining tiny food organisms. A large fish—specimens weighing more than 45 kg (100 lb) have been reported—*Polyodon spathula* is found in the Mississippi River and *Psephurus gladius* in the Chang Jiang (Yangtze River).

Paderewski, Ignace Jan [pah-dair-ef'-skee, een-yahs'] A great Polish statesman as well as a pianist and composer, Ignace Jan Paderewski, b. Nov. 18, 1860, d. New York City, June 29, 1941, was given, by presidential decree, a state burial at Arlington National Cemetery. He made his mark initially as a pianist more as a result of his majestic appearance and magnetic appeal than of his musicianship; nevertheless, shortly after his U.S. debut in 1891, he became the most loved pianist since Franz Liszt and was paid fabulous sums for his recitals. He established scholarship endowments for young musicians, and he donated all of his concert receipts from 1914–18 to Polish war victims. After World War I he served first (1918–19) as the Polish representative to Washington and then (1919–20) as his nation's prime minister. He also led (1940–41) the exiled Polish government during the German occupation of World War II. Although he composed many piano pieces, a symphony, an opera, songs, and chamber music, few of his works—other than the Minuet in G and Piano Concerto, op. 17—are still performed.

Padua [pa'-juh-wuh] Padua is a city in northeast Italy with a population of 223,907 (1988 est.). It is located west of Venice on the Bacchiglione River. The city's industries produce machinery, motorcycles, textiles, and processed foods. Padua is known for its university (1222), which is the second oldest in Italy. GIOTTO painted (1304–06) the frescoes in the Scrovegni Chapel. Frescoes by Andrea MANTEGNA adorn the 13th-century Eremitani Church, and bronzes by DONATELLO can be seen in the six-domed Basilica of St. Anthony (1232–1307).

According to legend, Padua was founded by the Trojan hero Antenor. The town prospered under the Romans, who called it Patavium; Livy was born there. Destroyed by the Lombards in 601, Padua recovered rapidly to become a prosperous and politically important free commune from the 12th to the 14th century. Padua's growth continued under rule by the Carrara family (1318–1405) and Venice (1405–1797). Padua was controlled (1815–66) by Austria until it became part of the unified Kingdom of Italy.

Paducah [puh-doo'-kuh] Paducah, a port city in southwestern Kentucky, is the seat of McCracken County. On the left bank of the Ohio River, the city has a population of 27,256 (1990). It is a distribution and trade center for tobacco, livestock, fruit, and timber. Nearby coal deposits and hydroelectric power support industries that produce clothing, auto parts, and concrete. Named for a Chickasaw Indian chief, Paducah was settled in 1827.

Paestum [pest'-uhm] Paestum is the Roman name for the ancient Greek city of Poseidonia, a colony established (c.600 BC) on the Tyrrhenian coast of southern Italy, about 100 km (62 mi) south of present-day Naples. Famed for its riches and its fine classical architecture, Paestum flourished until it was conquered (c.400 BC) by the Lucanians, who in turn were ousted (273 BC) by the Romans. Thereafter the city declined in importance until the site was abandoned completely (9th century). Among its architectural remains are two of the best-preserved Doric temples extant.

Páez, José Antonio [pah'-ays] José Antonio Páez, b. June 13, 1790, d. May 7, 1873, Venezuelan caudillo and revolutionary, served as the republic's first president and as supreme dictator. An associate of Simón BOLÍVAR in the independence struggles against Spain, Páez led the *llaneros* (plainsmen) in their successful effort to drive the Spanish out of Venezuela. Later, he led the separatist movement that broke up Gran Colombia, Bolívar's unified republic, of which Venezuela was a part. After gaining Venezuela's independence, Páez became its first president (1831–35, 1839–43) and ruled it as a conservative CAUDILLO until 1848. Forced into exile, Páez returned in 1861 as supreme dictator but had to flee again two years later. He died in exile in New York City.

Pagan [puh-gahn'] Pagan, a village on the Irrawaddy River in central Burma, was once a great walled city of old Burma. Founded in AD 849, it flourished until overrun (1287) by the Mongols. King Anawratha (r. 1044–77) made Pagan his capital, summoning foreign artisans from eastern India and from the MON kingdom of southern Burma to build and decorate Buddhist shrines and royal palaces there. Many still stand, making Pagan the largest surviving complex of the medieval brick and stucco buildings that once flourished throughout Southeast Asia. The main architectural types are tall, bell-domed stupas; square shrines with terraced roofs and curvilinear towers (the great Ananda Temple, built in 1091, is still in use); and halls and libraries often adorned with flamboyant ornament.

Paganini, Niccolò [pah-gah-nee'-nee]   Niccolò Paganini, b. Genoa, Oct. 27, 1782, d. Nice, May 27, 1840, was an Italian violinist and composer considered by many the greatest violinist of all time. His influence on the growth of virtuosity and showmanship in the romantic era was parallel to that of the pianist Franz Liszt, and his feats of skill were legendary. Much of his music is a vehicle for the display of technique, although some of it is musically interesting. His compositions include concertos, capriccios, and chamber music, much of it never published.

Paget, Sir James [paj'-it]   The English surgeon Sir James Paget, b. Jan. 11, 1814, d. Dec. 30, 1899, is often considered the founder of PATHOLOGY. At Saint Bartholomew's Hospital in London he described several diseases, including osteitis deformans, now known as Paget's disease. Paget made recommendations on treatment, including removal of bone tumors rather than amputation.

Paget's disease   Paget's disease, also known as osteitis deformans, is a chronic, progressive BONE DISEASE in which the balance between bone absorption and replacement is disrupted; the processes occur rapidly and randomly, resulting in deformity as well as chemical and physical abnormality. The disease usually is localized in bones that bear weight.

Pago Pago [pahn'-goh pahn'-goh]   Pago Pago, the capital of American Samoa, is a village on Tutuila Island. It has a population of 3,058 (1980). Located in the middle of the island at the head of one of the finest natural harbors in the Pacific, Pago Pago was chosen by the U.S. Navy in 1872 as a strategic base and repair station.

pagoda   In Oriental architecture, a pagoda is a type of freestanding tower associated principally with Chinese or Japanese Buddhist temple precincts. The term *pagoda*, from *Bhagavati* (Sanskrit, "divine female"), was originally used to designate the spired towers of Hindu shrines in India. After the introduction (AD 68) of Buddhism in China, the Chinese created their own pagodas, of two basic kinds: one was derived from an indigenous structure, the other from Indian towers. The former, the *ting* pagoda, is rectangular in plan and consists of several levels of open pavilions, each with its own upward curving roof. A characteristic example is the pagoda of the 7th-century Ho-

The Gojunoto, or five-story pagoda, of the Horyuji complex near Nara, Japan, is a prototypical Japanese pagoda dating from the 7th century. The structure of this pagoda most clearly reflects the architecture of the Chinese Tang dynasty in the stone foundation and exterior bracketing. The Chinese pagoda was itself derived from the Indian Buddhist stupa.

ryuji Temple in Nara, Japan. The second kind has a square, multilevel plan with ascending niches on each side to accommodate Buddha images. The White Goose Pagoda (AD 652; Chang'an, China) exemplifies this type. By the 8th century, as Buddhist influence in China waned, the pagoda lost much of its original significance as a religious shrine. Eventually, the term came to mean any monument resembling the Buddhist tower.

Pahlavi   see MUHAMMAD REZA SHAH PAHLAVI; REZA SHAH PAHLAVI

Paige, Satchel   Leroy Robert "Satchel" Paige, b. Mobile, Ala., July 7, 1906, d. June 8, 1982, an American professional baseball player whom some experts consider the best pitcher ever, pitched in the Negro leagues before the major leagues were integrated. After the color line was broken, Paige, at the age of 42, became the first black pitcher in the American League when he joined (1948) the Cleveland Indians. Paige played until 1953, when he retired. Although he had only 28 major league wins, by some accounts Paige had pitched a total of 2,500 games during his career. He was inducted into the Baseball Hall of Fame in 1971.

Paik, Nam June [payk]   Famous as an originator of VIDEO ART, Nam June Paik, b. Korea, July 20, 1932, has also created musical and multimedia HAPPENINGS and highly dramatic mixed-media works. Paik's video art, which usually employs assemblages of television sets, is always humorous, often impressive in its technical wizardry, and replete with chance juxtapositions, strange collections of sounds, and seemingly spontaneous on-screen improvisations. His monumental *Fin de Siècle II* (1989) is composed of a wall of over 200 TV sets whose rapidly changing screen images are generated by computer.

pain Pain is an unpleasant sensory and emotional experience that is normally associated with injury or threat of injury to body tissues. The behavior of a person in pain must be understood as a complex interaction of physiological, psychological, and sociological factors. For example, differences can be observed between individuals and between members of different cultures in their degree of response to injury. In everyday life, acute pain performs a valuable function in minimizing the harm of accidental injury or minor disease—persons who are born without the ability to feel pain or who develop such an inability through disease are at great risk of the consequences of unrecognized injury. On the other hand, the severe pain associated with surgery, accidental injury, or childbirth can trigger reflexes that affect breathing, heart function, and blood pressure, sometimes with serious consequences.

Acute pain may become chronic—persisting indefinitely and serving no beneficial purpose—when it is not effectively treated or when healing is incomplete. Such pain is very resistant to medical intervention and may cause prolonged suffering and discouragement.

Sensory Mechanisms

The basic elements of pain are the sensory impulses generated by injury-sensitive receptors in the NERVOUS SYSTEM. These sense organs, called nociceptors, convert mechanical, thermal, or chemical stimulations that injure or threaten tissues into impulses that are transmitted along peripheral nerves to the SPINAL CORD and from there to higher brain centers.

Injury may excite two different kinds of nociceptors, known as A-delta and C fibers. The A-delta fibers generate a fast, bright, and short-lasting pain sensation that is well localized. The C fibers slowly and persistently send diffuse and particularly unpleasant sensations. A sharp blow to the toe, for example, results in a bright flash of pain, followed by a longer-lasting burning sensation. The flash is due to A-delta nociceptors, whereas the slow pain comes from C fibers.

When injury occurs, spinal reflexes are also activated. These reflexes are rapid stimulus-response circuits that function between nociceptors and the spinal cord. Thus motor reflexes cause muscles surrounding an injury to go into spasm. The spasm, in turn, produces cramping pain, which adds to the pain of the injury. Other reflexes diminish the microcirculation of blood in the tissues surrounding the injury and cause the release of certain chemical substances that may cause pain when they come into contact with the nociceptors. These reflexes protect the injury victim by minimizing blood loss, but they often contribute to the degree of pain.

Spinal-Cord Pathways

At junctions called synapses, the sensory nerves transmitting injury signals connect with spinal-cord pathways that carry information to higher brain centers, where sensory, emotional, and thinking mechanisms produce the conscious experience of pain. Two kinds of pathways carry injury signals in the spinal cord. One has long nerve fibers that connect directly with a central relay station, the thalamus (see BRAIN), from which other neurons reach to the cerebral cortex. This system conducts injury information rapidly and transmits information concerning the site, intensity, and duration of damaging stimulation—information that is perceived as a sharp, localized pain. The other pathway has long and short fibers with many synapses that slow the signal transmission to the thalamus; projections from this pathway go to brain centers responsible for unpleasant feelings and emotions. Impulses traveling along this pathway cause certain physiological reactions to injury that are linked to these unpleasant feelings.

INFLAMMATION at the site of injury enhances pain signals by producing chemicals that sensitize the nociceptors so that they fire in response even to minor mechanical stimulation. In contrast, impulses are damped when repetitive signals from the nerve endings that detect touch and pressure close a "gate" in the spinal cord that blocks the transmission of injury impulses. Gating also occurs when certain pain-inhibiting neurons that descend from the base of the brain (brain stem) are activated, either by MORPHINE and similar drugs or by certain naturally occurring substances called endorphins that are produced within the brain.

Chronic Pain

Sometimes the pain of an injury or disease never completely disappears with healing, or HEADACHES or other pains appear for no apparent reason and then recur or never subside. Many surgeries to which sufferers resort only make the situation worse, as does the overuse of prescription medication. Multidisciplinary pain clinics have been established, and teams of medical specialists, psychologists, and social workers are often able to help patients with chronic pain.

Relief of Pain

Many ways exist for controlling or relieving pain. The use of ANESTHETICS for surgery is familiar, and ACUPUNCTURE and HYPNOSIS have also been tried. For other relief of pain, ANALGESIC drugs such as aspirin, acetaminophen, and ibuprofen can be used in cases where inflammation is present. Opioid drugs (see OPIUM) work by mimicking the naturally produced substances that activate pain-inhibiting systems in the brain stem and spinal cord. Electrical-stimulation treatments, massage, and other such therapies may also be helpful.

Paine, John Knowles American composer, organist, and music teacher John Knowles Paine, b. Portland, Maine, Jan. 9, 1839, d. Apr. 25, 1906, pioneered in the establishment of music as an academic discipline in the United States. His training and aesthetic outlook were German, and his own compositions were derivative of German models. He was, however, the first major American composer of large-scale orchestral works. He became a lecturer and recitalist in the Boston area and was appointed an instructor of music at Harvard in 1862. In 1875 the course became accredited, and he was made the nation's first full professor of music. Paine's works include two symphonies, symphonic poems, choral works, a never-performed opera, chamber music, songs, and organ and piano pieces.

Paine, Thomas   The Anglo-American revolutionary writer Thomas Paine, b. England, Jan. 29, 1737, d. June 8, 1809, called for American independence in his 1776 pamphlet COMMON SENSE, which was widely distributed and had a profound influence on public opinion in America. An English excise officer, Paine was dismissed (1774), probably for agitating for a salary increase, and emigrated to America on the recommendation of Benjamin Franklin. In Philadelphia from 1774, Paine became a journalist and essayist. After the publication of *Common Sense,* which sold 100,000 copies in three months, he continued to inspire and encourage the patriots during the Revolutionary War in the series of pamphlets called *The Crisis* (1776–83).

Paine returned (1787) to England after the war and published *The Rights of Man* (1791–92), in which he defended the French Revolution in response to Edmund Burke's *Reflections on the Revolution in France* (1790). Outlawed for treason, Paine fled (1792) to France, became a French citizen, and was elected to the National Convention. Imprisoned (1793–94) during the Reign of Terror, Paine wrote the first part of *Age of Reason* (1794), a deistic statement of his religious views. All Paine's works reflect his belief in natural reason and natural rights, political equality, tolerance, civil liberties, and the dignity of man. His *Age of Reason* and his criticism of George Washington in *Letter to Washington* (1796), however, made him unpopular. Paine returned to the United States in 1802 and died in poverty.

Thomas Paine, an 18th-century political writer, received immediate recognition in America for his Revolutionary War pamphlet Common Sense *(1776). The first issue of his series of pamphlets called* The Crisis *was so inspiring to patriots that Washington ordered it read to his troops at Valley Forge.*

paint   Paints encompass an extensive variety of materials intended for application to surfaces for the purpose of protecting them or enhancing their visual appearance or both. With few exceptions, paint is applied in liquid form and dries to a thin, hard, continuous nontacky film either by the evaporation of volatile components or by chemical reaction.

All paints have a solid phase known as the PIGMENT, which is responsible for the color, and a liquid phase called the vehicle or binder. LACQUERS, stains, and VARNISHES are classified separately because of their transparency, but, when heavily pigmented, they are basically paints.

Composition of Paints

Paint binders differ greatly in consistency; they range from thin, pourable liquids such as linseed oil to hard, often brittle solids typified by synthetic polymers and natural resins.

Solvent-Based Paints. To be usable, resinous binders require petroleum solvents such as alcohols or esters. Upon exposure to air or heat, the solvent portion evaporates, depositing the pigment and vehicle as a continuous film. The film deposited may require further change to chemically convert the binder to a nontacky solid. Oils or resins containing oils are converted when exposed to air by chemical oxidation and polymerization reactions. This process is accelerated by heat and also by the addition of compounds of cobalt, manganese, lead, and other metals called driers.

Water-Based Paints. Water has always been viewed as an attractive alternative to solvents because of its low cost and low odor, the absence of a fire hazard, and ease of cleanup. Unfortunately, the materials that are soluble in water tend to retain this solubility in their dried films.

Easily emulsified resins tend to form soft films. Higher-molecular-weight resins, which offer superior qualities, are reacted directly in water by a process called emulsion POLYMERIZATION. This method is used to produce the vinyl and acrylic water-based emulsions now used in all areas of coating technology.

Upon application, the water evaporates and deposits a heterogeneous blend of pigment and vehicle particles that is pulled together by capillary attractions, adhesion, and cohesion. Through the addition of small quantities of strong solvents called coalescing aids, the films form a relatively continuous structure.

Variations in Finish

Gloss is derived from the paint binder. To maintain maximum gloss, addition of pigment must be limited to relatively low volumes. Any fine-sized pigment may be employed, at concentrations not exceeding 20% by volume of the binder (excluding solvent or water).

Increased pigment concentrations create a crowding effect within the dried film whereby the pigment particles alter the profile of the surface, creating a reduction in reflected gloss. Eggshell and semigloss paints are available that exhibit little reduction in resistance properties due to preservation of a continuous film. Further addition of pigment produces additional crowding in the dried film and gradually overwhelms the ability of the film to encapsulate the pigment totally. Dry pigment particles protrude above the surface, producing a flat finish. This effect is particularly exaggerated if coarse particles are present.

The tiny cracks and crevices formed by the protruding particles in flat paints permit stains and other surface contaminants to become deeply embedded in the film and, therefore, difficult to remove. An added deficiency of such systems is the tendency for the exposed pigment particles to be loosely bound and, therefore, to be easily removed by mild abrasion. This produces burnishing, whereby a glossy or polished area is created in an otherwise flat background.

Types of Paint

Primers. Primers are ideally vehicle-rich coatings intended for application as foundation and adhesion-promoting coats only. On exterior wooden surfaces they are designed to penetrate deeply into a firm surface to provide maximum adhesion, seal off stains prior to topcoating, and yet be flexible enough to expand and contract with the wood.

Metal primers do not require the flexibility of exterior primers. Their function is to form a firm adhesive bond with the surface and also an impermeable barrier between the environment and the metal surface. Where active rust-prevention is essential, rust-inhibitive pigments, which chemically retard oxidation, are used.

Primers intended for use as undercoats for enamels and automotive paints contain hard resins and high pigment loadings that permit them to be sanded prior to topcoating.

Exterior Coatings. Exterior coatings require vehicle and pigment having long-term performance capabilities. Appropriate vehicles have excellent adhesion plus resistance to moisture and to ultraviolet exposure. Most systems incorporate pigments or additives that actively combat the formation of unsightly mildew accumulations. Linseed oil or oil-modified alkyd resins are almost exclusively used for solvent-based paints. Vinyl and acrylic latexes offer exceptional lightfastness in water-based coatings. Factory-coated metal siding often contains highly durable silicone-modified alkyds, acrylics, and vinyl resins.

Interior Wall Paints. These coatings are developed for maximum hiding ability, usually with a single coat. Color, sheen uniformity, and ability to be touched up without major color or sheen differences are important features of a quality wall paint. Flat paints contain high pigment concentrations. As sheen levels increase, the films become more durable, although hiding ability diminishes slightly.

Floor Paints. These coatings are formulated with hard, water- and alkali-resistant vehicles such as epoxy and phenolic modified alkyds, varnishes, or chlorinated rubber.

Texture Paints. Sand-finish or rough coatings contain sand, volcanic ash, styrene particles, nut shells, or other rough, granular material. They are often used to rejuvenate walls and ceilings that are in poor condition.

paintbox   The paintbox is a video painting device that allows the user to apply many techniques of two-dimensional art to the video screen. It is used primarily by pro-

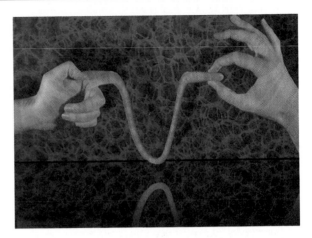

Paintbox artist Henry Baker created the whimsical Fingerstretch *by manipulating images, shapes, and colors on a Quantel paintbox.*

duction facilities to create original artwork, to enhance existing visuals, or to assist in the production of special effects.

The paintbox consists of a mainframe, a disk drive, and a work station—a high-quality video monitor, a sensitized tablet, a pressure-sensitive pen, and a keyboard. The artist watches the video screen while drawing with the pen on the tablet, controlling the video output via the keyboard.

Paintbox artists work with single frames of video information, which may be either used as stationary images or edited together to produce animation. The modes of operation are selected from a menu display on the video monitor. By selecting different modes, the artist may make the pen a paintbrush, airbrush, or chalkstick, choosing from any size and every color. The paintbox can be used to create geometric shapes, or even to cut out a shape and paste it up in another place on the painting. All styles and sizes of typeface can be used for typesetting. Virtually every operation performed by traditional illustrators and pasteup artists is possible, entirely within the video medium of the paintbox.

See also: COMPUTER GRAPHICS; VIDEO ART.

Painted Desert   The Painted Desert, a badlands region in northeastern Arizona between the Grand Canyon and Petrified Forest National Park, covers an area of about 19,425 km^2 (7,500 mi^2). Its elevation is 1,375–1,980 m (4,500–6,500 ft). Rainfall is about 175 mm (7 in) annually, and temperatures range from −32° to 41° C (−25° to 105° F). The desert's name is derived from the layers of red and yellow sediment and variously colored clays exposed by the erosion of sand on the COLORADO PLATEAU.

painted turtle   The painted turtle, *Chrysemys picta*, family Emydidae, is an attractively marked turtle that

The painted turtle is perhaps the most numerous small-pond turtle found in the northern United States and southern Canada. Its shell usually has bright red or yellow markings.

measures 10–25 cm (4–10 in) in length, with females attaining a larger size than males. This species has red markings on the margin of its shell, dark limbs that are streaked with red or yellow, and a black head marked with yellow. The smooth, oval carapace is unserrated along its posterior margin. The males have long claws on the forefeet that presumably are used in courtship display.

Painted turtles are found throughout the northern United States and southern Canada; part of their range extends to Florida, Louisiana, and Arizona. They prefer quiet, shallow waters with a heavy growth of vegetation. These turtles are fond of basking. They usually hibernate underwater, buried in the mud, but in southern states may not hibernate every year. They are mainly carnivorous.

painting   The art of painting encompasses all forms of applying pigments to a surface in order to produce images with decorative value, representational value, or both. At its most basic level, the act of painting consists of two components: DRAWING, or the conscious design of a pictorial image; and the use of color or hues and light tones to augment the beauty or effectiveness of the image. Although some modern painters, such as the abstract expressionists, have dispensed with the drawing component, most painters throughout the history of Western civilization have used color and line to explore the outer world of natural things and events and the inner, private world of feelings and fantasies. For considerations of non-Western painting, see articles elsewhere in the encyclopedia, as follows: AFRICAN ART; CHINESE ART AND ARCHITECTURE; INDIAN ART AND ARCHITECTURE; INDIANS OF NORTH AMERICA, ART OF THE; ISLAMIC ART AND ARCHITECTURE; JAPANESE ART AND ARCHITECTURE; LATIN AMERICAN ART AND ARCHITECTURE; MOGUL ART AND ARCHITECTURE; PERSIAN ART AND ARCHITECTURE; PRE-COLUMBIAN ART AND ARCHITECTURE.

Prehistoric and Ancient Painting. The earliest painted images still extant, the rock paintings discovered in caves in Lascaux, France, and in Altamira, Spain, probably were created as magic talismans to ensure a fruitful hunt. Exe-

cuted perhaps 15,000 years ago, the bulls, horses, and deer depicted on the cave walls still retain an animation and vitality imparted by bold contours and crudely powerful forms (see PREHISTORIC ART).

Egypt was the earliest historical culture of the Western world to produce an important body of painting. Isolated by desert and sea in a corner of northern Africa, Egyptian civilization developed along fairly stable lines for fully three millennia, beginning about 3000 BC. Although not without subtle changes over the centuries, Egyptian painting reflects the deeply rooted traditions of its culture in the iconographic conventions that govern its images. These conventions—visual signs that represent real objects and relationships—often approximate but rarely reproduce the actual qualities of the real world; rather, they form an internally cohesive system that, once grasped, makes the work comprehensible. The 18th-dynasty *Fowling Scene* (1570–1349 BC; British Museum, London), for example, can be read by its conceptual logic rather than its perceptual fidelity: the central figure is larger than the rest because he is more important. Reflecting the artist's concern with choosing the most easily understood presentation for each anatomical part rather than with mirroring reality, the figure's legs, arms, and head are shown in profile, whereas the torso and eye are depicted frontally.

Virtually nothing remains of the painting of the various Mesopotamian civilizations that rose and fell during the Egyptian era. A radically different aesthetic concept does appear, however, in the surviving fragments of frescoes and mosaics executed by Cretan artists of the Minoan civilization that flourished about 2000 BC. In these works, the rigid conventions of Egyptian painting give way to fluid design and spirited action. The immediacy and directly

This 18th-dynasty Fowling Scene *in the tomb of Menena at Thebes reveals the ancient Egyptian stylistic trait of depicting the human body with a combination of frontal and profile views.*

representational emphasis of Minoan painting were developed in GREEK ART, but, unfortunately, all large-scale Greek painting has been lost. Written accounts of Greek artists as well as a considerable body of painted vases reveal the increasing naturalism of Greek painting, and a new and different worldview—one in which the timeless and hierarchical Egyptian conception of humankind yields to a recognition of the flux and activity of life.

Through the medium of Hellenistic art, the vitality and naturalism of Greek painting greatly influenced ROMAN ART AND ARCHITECTURE. Roman wall paintings and mosaics reveal sophisticated experiments with the creation of illusionistic depth and the suggestion of realistic atmosphere and lighting—obvious concerns of painters attempting to represent objective reality with accuracy.

Early Christian and Byzantine Painting. The coming of the Christian era and the dissolution of the ancient civilizations brought profound changes in the style and purpose of painting. Christian culture, like that of Egypt, was concerned with the symbolic importance of worldly things, not with their physical appearance. Accordingly, EARLY CHRISTIAN ART AND ARCHITECTURE and BYZANTINE ART AND ARCHITECTURE tended toward the static, hierarchical, and convention-governed style of Egyptian painting, although the naturalism and representational bias of classical painting was never completely absent from Christian art. Church decoration was generally done in MOSAIC, which in art history is considered a form of painting.

For the first 1,000 years of Christian civilization in western Europe, ILLUMINATED MANUSCRIPTS were the principal medium for painted images. In Ireland, where classical art had little or no influence, manuscripts were produced during the 7th and 8th centuries with incredibly detailed designs that interlaced abstract line and color with stylized animal motifs, as in the BOOK OF KELLS (*c.*760–820; Trinity College, Dublin). Equally beautiful illuminations, although more influenced by Byzantine and classical art, were produced in the 9th and 10th centuries in the continental centers of CAROLINGIAN and OTTONIAN ART AND ARCHITECTURE.

Gothic and Flemish Painting. By the end of the 14th century GOTHIC ART AND ARCHITECTURE, radiating outward from France, had fostered the development of a progressively more precise and articulate naturalism that recorded the subtleties of light and atmosphere and reintroduced human figures of grace and elegance. This gradual reinvention of the classical principles of direct representation was particularly advanced in early-15th-century northern Europe, where a profoundly original style and technique evolved in Flemish art (see FLEMISH ART AND ARCHITECTURE). Paintings on the manuscript page began to assume internally consistent spatial systems. Even more important, painters discovered new purposes for their art, such as altarpieces and portraits, and new patrons to commission their efforts in the growing bourgeois class. The result was the rise of panel painting and a new quest for the accurate depiction of the objective world, which reflected the materialist concerns of the merchant-patrons. Aiding these new trends immensely was the development of oil glazes, which permitted a far more exact

In his wedding portrait of the Arnolfini (1434) Jan van Eyck gave new emphasis to depicting accurate detail. He also created a complex symbolism for the work, relating to its role as a marriage record, including the dog to mean fidelity and a single lighted candle signifying God's presence. (National Gallery, London.)

registration of light and color than could be had from FRESCO or TEMPERA painting. The revolutionary character of 15th-century Flemish painting is well represented in Jan van EYCK's *Wedding of the Arnolfini* (1434; National Gallery, London).

The Italian Renaissance. In Italy, painting through most of the Gothic era reflected Byzantine influence. Gold-leaf backgrounds and stylized drapery folds were characteristic of iconographical panel paintings (see ICONOGRAPHY). By the beginning of the 14th century the gradual growth of Renaissance humanism had begun to influence Italian painters (see ITALIAN ART AND ARCHITECTURE). These emergent ideas inspired the Renaissance.

The first landmark of RENAISSANCE ART AND ARCHITECTURE was GIOTTO DI BONDONE's *Lamentation* (1304–13; Arena Chapel, Padua), in which the modeling of the heavy, folded drapery clothing the figures is combined with a dramatic positioning of the figures to create the impression of weight and three-dimensionality in a stage-like space. Along with DUCCIO, Simone MARTINI, and other 14th-century Italian painters, Giotto introduced into Italian painting those elements of drama, monumentality, and coherent spatiality that would characterize almost all Italian Renaissance painting.

The ruling members of the Italian city-states competed for the services of noted artists, who, for the first time, were sought after as creators rather than employed as mere artisans. Florence, a noted center of the arts since the days of Giotto and Dante, led the way in the early 15th century with important advances in the mathematical and optical simulation of the space of the world—in other words, in PERSPECTIVE.

Renaissance artists also studied anatomy and evolved new ways to show figures in action. The frozen figures of Giotto or the contemplative ones of Fra Angelico gave way to the vitality of Antonio del Pollaiuolo's (see POLLAIUOLO FAMILY) *Saint Sebastian* (1475; National Gallery, London) and the muscular animation of MICHELANGELO's over-

Raphael's monumental School of Athens *(1510–11) depicts the ancient philosophers within an architectural setting. Raphael included portraits of himself* (lower right), *Leonardo* (center), *and Michelangelo* (seated, center foreground). *(Vatican Palace, Rome.)*

whelming ceiling frescoes in the SISTINE CHAPEL (1508–12; Vatican City). RAPHAEL's *School of Athens* (1510–11; Stanza della Signatura, Vatican palace) is one of many frescoes done by papal commission between 1490 and 1520. Its architectural setting provides another instance of a spatial "window" that seems to demand that the viewer look through, rather than at, the painting's surface. Although the growing freedom of the artist, a concern for coherent pictorial space, and the development of portraiture allied Florentine and Roman Renaissance painting with Flemish art, the Italian emphasis on monumentality rather than on detail and the preference for fresco rather than oil differentiated it from northern European painting. The full potential of oil paint was finally realized in the radiant atmospheric color developed by such early-16th-century Venetian painters as TITIAN and GIORGIONE, who realized the potential of color as an expressive tool. Shape, line, contour—the tools of precision and clarity in pictorial representation—give way in the works of the Venetians to the deep shadows and resonances of Giorgione's *Fête Champêtre* (c.1510; Louvre, Paris).

As the 16th century progressed, a late Renaissance style, sometimes called MANNERISM, emerged. Mannerism is exemplified in the works of ROSSO FIORENTINO and PONTORMO, in which the classical proportions of the figures become exaggerated, the colors harsh, and the composition agitated and asymmetrical. In Spain, EL GRECO worked in a distinctly personal version of the Mannerist style.

Northern Renaissance and Baroque. In Germany, the importation of Italian ideas helped to form the style of Albrecht DÜRER, the preeminent master outside Italy at the time of the High Renaissance and a major influence on all northern European artists. Later in the 16th century the Dutch painter Pieter Bruegel the Elder's (see BRUEGEL family) Mannerist depictions of peasant life expanded the range of subjects available to painters, just as Hieronymus BOSCH's bizarre pictures had earlier legitimatized the pictorial rendering of inner fantasies.

During the 17th century, BAROQUE ART AND ARCHITECTURE dominated European painting. Baroque paintings often exploited strong directional light and asymmetrical compositions to achieve dramatic illusionistic effects (see ILLUSIONISM), typically using a diagonal sweep into deep space. In Italy, CARAVAGGIO masterfully used CHIAROSCURO (contrasts of light and dark) to achieve the convincing tactility of his robust, earthy figures. The large scale of 17th-century Italian painting—a heritage of the monumental frescoes of Renaissance masters such as Michelangelo and LEONARDO DA VINCI—was also important in the flamboyant aesthetics of the baroque. Broader brushstrokes, with resultant blurred contours, became the hallmark of a painterly style that contrasted vividly with Renaissance linearity—that is, the artist's skill in the use of paint became more important than skill in drawing.

In Caravaggio's Conversion of Saint Paul *(1601–02) the contrasts of light and shadow emphasize the drama of this scene of religious revelation. Caravaggio's powerful images, realism and simplicity, and use of strong chiaroscuro greatly influenced such later artists as Rembrandt. (Santa Maria del Popolo, Rome.)*

Considerable differences in national as well as personal style characterize the painters of the baroque era, which coincided with the final breakup of medieval Christendom along religious and nationalistic lines. Dynamic energy and elaborate action combine with fluid handling in the Flemish painter Peter Paul RUBENS's many large canvases, whereas the classical repose of the Frenchman Nicolas POUSSIN's cool, pensive depictions of mythological subjects recalls the order and serenity of Renaissance masters. With the founding (1648) of the Académie Royale de Peinture et de Sculture (see ACADEMIES OF ART) in Paris came the beginning of the codification and institutionalization of Renaissance ideas that was to guide, then smother, later generations of French artists.

In Roman Catholic southern Europe, baroque painters exhibited a grandness of scale and treatment that was used to advance aggressively the ideals of the Roman Catholic Counter-Reformation. Painters from the Protestant north explored new secular motifs. The delicate light of Jan VERMEER, which illuminates small-scale works depicting domestic life in mid-17th-century households, seems capable of infinite subtlety. REMBRANDT's *Self-Portrait* (1669; National Gallery, London), in contrast, makes full use of deep golden tones and warm browns to reveal the essential humanity and introspective personality of the artist. Other 17th-century Dutch artists, most notably Jacob van RUISDAEL and Jan STEEN, reflected a recognition that many commonplace aspects of the world were worthy of depiction by elevating GENRE PAINTING and LANDSCAPE PAINTING to esteemed roles in European art.

Neoclassicism and Romanticism. During the 18th century, Paris rose in importance in European painting as the dramatic baroque gave way to the decorative ROCOCO STYLE of light and elegance. Rococo artists frequently portrayed pastoral subjects in aristocratic and decorative terms, as in Antoine WATTEAU's *A Pilgrimage to Cythera* (1717; Louvre, Paris).

Eventually, the lightness of the rococo style degenerated into frivolity, and serious-minded painters, inspired by the momentous events of the French Revolution, pursued the more lofty ideals of NEOCLASSICISM and ROMANTICISM, both of which evolved in France in the late 18th century. Set in the context of the French Revolution, Jacques Louis DAVID's painting took on political significance, as opposed to what was perceived as the self-indulgence and aristocratic sensuality of the rococo *ancien régime*. David's ideals, developed further by his gifted pupil Jean Auguste Dominique INGRES, eventually froze into rigid academic prescriptions that came to stifle officially sanctioned French art.

Romanticism opened to pictorial exploration the subjective emotions and visions of individual personalities. The world of the mythic imagination is central to the works of William BLAKE, whereas Eugène DELACROIX explored the exoticism of distant lands, the primal powers of animals, and the image-rich tales of tragedy. Germany produced the eerie symbolic landscapes of Caspar David FRIEDRICH, while in Spain Francisco de GOYA confronted and pursued the dark and destructive side of human nature. With the elevation of the individual sensibility in the romantic era came a new freedom in the techniques of painting. Nowhere was this freedom in handling more arresting than in the romantic landscapes of the English painters John CONSTABLE and J. M. W. TURNER.

Realism and Impressionism. In the middle of the 19th century neoclassicism and romanticism were challenged by essentially new aesthetic currents in France (see FRENCH ART AND ARCHITECTURE). Gustave COURBET's realism rejected both the exoticism of the romantics and the idealism of the classicists in favor of an art that portrayed or-

(Above) *Rembrandt's* Self-portrait *(c.1664), one of the Dutch master's most forceful and beautiful late works, combines dazzling technique with unsentimental observation. (Iveagh Bequest, Kenwood House, London.)*

(Below) *In this version of* A Pilgrimage to Cythera *(c.1717) Antoine Watteau created a* fête galante, *a rococo fantasy on the theme of love. (Staatliche Museen, Berlin.)*

(Above) In J. M. W. Turner's Rain, Steam, and Speed (1844) the concrete form of the train dissolves into a blur of glowing light and rain. The sense of motion is emphasized by the receding tracks. (National Gallery, London.) (Below) In Déjeuner sur l'herbe (1863) Édouard Manet combined the pose of the central figures, taken from a 16th-century engraving of a work by Raphael, with his own proclivity toward bold, flat areas of color. (Musée d'Orsay, Paris.)

went even further. For Claude MONET, the prime exponent of IMPRESSIONISM, the world was composed not of objects to conceive but of reflected light to perceive. Painting *en plein air* (out-of-doors) rather than in the confines of a studio, he worked directly on the canvas without preliminary sketches.

Toward the end of the 19th century, Georges SEURAT attempted to render scientifically the impressionist perception of light with the use of small dabs or dots of paint in a style called pointillism. Paul CÉZANNE developed painted analogues for the structure of the material world, eschewing the atmospheric dissolution of objects in impressionist painting, and Vincent VAN GOGH explored the emotionally seething inner world of the psyche (see POST-IMPRESSIONISM).

Modern Painting. The first decade of the 20th century brought an explosion of artistic experimentation in Paris that soon pervaded artistic thought throughout Europe and North America. Of the various schools of painting that coalesced, including FAUVISM, EXPRESSIONISM, and FUTURISM, the movement that was to have the greatest impact on subsequent painting was CUBISM. Developed simultaneously by Pablo PICASSO and Georges BRAQUE, cubism considered the nature of space and the construction of objects from a position of detached analysis. Picasso's *Girl with a Mandolin* (1910; Nelson Rockefeller Collection), for example, reduces the human form to a series of angular, interpenetrating brown and gray planes. The figure appears recomposed in a fluctuating spatial environment.

By reordering reality according to the wishes of the artist, the cubists prepared the way for truly ABSTRACT ART—that is, paintings based entirely on subjective conceptions, with no reference to the objective world. Both Wassily KANDINSKY (from 1910 on) and Piet MONDRIAN (from *c*.1916 on) created strictly nonobjective paintings

dinary people leading ordinary, unromantic lives. Building on Courbet's defiance of the ideal and the sublime, a group of artists in Paris in the 1860s began to formulate a completely new theory of pictorial representation.

The modern stereotype of artists as cultural leaders unaccepted by their reactionary audience harks back to Édouard MANET, whose *Déjeuner sur l'herbe* (1863; Musée d'Orsay, Paris) was rejected for exhibition by the state-sanctioned SALON; it was then shown in a defiant exhibition mounted expressly to display works refused by the Salon. Manet's nude figures were deemed "not proper" because they were shown as ordinary people rather than as Greek goddesses or exotic odalisques.

Inspired by Manet and Edgar DEGAS, a group of young artists who were labeled *impressionists* by a hostile critic

Pablo Picasso's portrait of French art dealer Daniel Henry Kahnweiler (1910) exemplifies analytical cubism. The facets of the subject are recombined into superimposed planes to reveal simultaneous points of view. (Art Institute of Chicago.)

in which even the tenuous cubist connection with perceived reality was severed. Another vein of MODERN ART was explored in the 1920s by the proponents of SURREALISM, for whom the images generated by dreams and the subconscious had a potent reality surpassing that of conscious life.

In the United States the stylistic revolutions in Paris gradually came to supplant the native tradition of naturalism represented in the 19th-century works of Winslow HOMER, Thomas EAKINS, and the members of the HUDSON RIVER SCHOOL and the related movement called LUMINISM (see AMERICAN ART AND ARCHITECTURE).

As the European movements lost cohesion, American painters combined various principles of surrealism and nonobjectivity into a new aesthetic synthesis that made New York the artistic center of the Western world. Calling their synthesis ABSTRACT EXPRESSIONISM, young American painters of the 1940s and '50s used large canvases and energetic brushstrokes and dribbled paint to create works that could be taken either as the record of the creative act or as forceful, cogent form rendered simply for its own sake.

Representation had been absent long enough from American art for the reintroduction of recognizable images and objects to be an important event of the 1960s. POP ART, which was invented by British artist Richard HAMILTON in 1956, combined common objects and revered stereotypes of popular culture to satirize the artificial, mass-produced quality of consumer society. The fertile 1960s also produced OP ART—visually startling works that depend on optics for their effects. At the same time, cool and emotionally remote nonobjective paintings fur-

Jackson Pollock's Circular Form *(1948) displays the spontaneity of the gestural wing of American abstract expressionism. Pollock refined the technqiue of dripping paint across a canvas to create random patterns. (Sidney Janis Collection, New York City.)*

ther explored the possibilities of color (see COLOR-FIELD PAINTING) and largeness of scale. Then, toward the end of the 1960s and through the 1980s, realist painting emerged once again as PHOTOREALISM. At the same time, the neoexpressionism that flourished in Europe—in the work of the German Anselm Kiefer, for example, or the Italian Sandro Chia—began to be seen in works by American painters such as Julian Schnabel.

The surreal quality of Salvador Dali's Soft Construction with Boiled Beans: Premonition of Civil War *(1936) is enhanced by the shocking imagery and meticulous execution. (Philadelphia Museum of Art.)*

Paisiello, Giovanni [pah-eez-ee el'-loh] Giovanni Paisiello, b. May 9, 1740, d. June 5, 1816, was one of the most important Italian opera composers of his time. After composing more than 50 operas between 1763 and 1776, he was invited to become conductor at the court of Catherine the Great of Russia. He subsequently served the courts of Ferdinand IV of Naples (1784–99) and Napoleon in Paris (1802–04) before returning to Naples, where he died.

Paisiello wrote both serious and comic operas and made significant contributions to both types. He broadened the scope of comic opera, as in *Il Re Teodoro in Venezia* (1784), and introduced the concerted finale—which had previously been used only in comic opera—into serious opera. In addition to almost 100 operas and a great deal of religious music, Paisiello composed symphonies, concertos, string quartets, and other instrumental music.

Paisley [payz'-lee] Paisley, a city in the Scottish region of Strathclyde and seat of the former county of Renfrew, lies 11 km (7 mi) west of Glasgow on the White Cart Water, a stream. Paisley has a population of 84,789 (1981). One of the world's leading producers of cotton thread, Paisley was once famous for patterned paisley shawls. The city's industries also include shipbuilding and the manufacture of automobiles, boilers, chemicals, jam, and soap. The town grew around Paisley Priory, an abbey that dates from 1163. The abbey was destroyed and rebuilt several times. The present structure was erected during the 15th century.

---

paisley   In textile design, the name *paisley* signifies a particular type of pear-shaped, curvilinear design that originated in India and was admired on the cashmere shawls brought back from the subcontinent around 1800 by British soldiers. The textile industry in Paisley, Scotland, began to manufacture fine wool shawls, adapting this design. Manufacturing ended about 1850, and the few genuine paisley shawls still extant have become museum pieces. Paisley designs, however, have since been used on many different fabrics and decorative items.

Paisley, Ian   The Reverend Ian Richard Kyle Paisley, b. Apr. 6, 1926, is a leading spokesperson for the militant Protestant faction of Northern Ireland. Paisley established the Free Presbyterian Church of Ulster in 1951, using his pulpit to attack Roman Catholicism and defend Protestant supremacy in the North. After the outbreak of fighting between Protestants and Catholics and the intervention of the British army there in 1969, he helped found (1972) the Democratic Unionist party. A member of the British Parliament since 1970 and of the European Parliament since 1979, Paisley has continued to uphold the Unionist cause.

Paiute [py-oot']   The Paiute are North American Indians who were traditionally divided into northern and southern groups that spoke different Shoshonean languages. The Northern Paiute occupied portions of Oregon, Idaho, Nevada, and California; the Southern Paiute were in parts of Utah, Arizona, Nevada, and California. Sparse food resources in the Great Basin area forced the Northern Paiute to live in small groups. Temporary leaders were chosen for rabbit drives, war, and dance festivities. Individual families lived in sagebrush or rush huts, called WICKIUPS. The Southern Paiute subsisted principally by digging for roots; those occupying the high plateau skirting the Grand Canyon area planted maize and squash in irrigated fields.

After 1850, ranchers and the railroads disrupted Paiute life, and the United States seized their lands in 1863. Now scattered on reservations and small tracts in California, Nevada, Oregon, and Utah, the Paiutes numbered between 4,000 and 6,000 in the late 1980s.

Pakistan [pak'-is-tan]   Pakistan occupies a strategic location in South Asia between China to the north, India to the east, and Afghanistan and Iran to the west and northwest. The Arabian Sea is to the south. A populous and ancient center of Islam, Pakistan became independent on Aug. 14, 1947, by partition of British India. It originally consisted of two separate land areas located about 1,600 km (1,000 mi) apart to the east and west of India, but the eastern portion seceded in 1971 as the nation of BANGLADESH. The name *Pakistan*, coined in 1933, is derived from Urdu words meaning "Land of the Pure."

Land and Resources

One-third of the land consists of plains along the INDUS valley in the south and east. The remainder, in the west and northwest, is a continuation of the eastern HIMALAYAS. The plains are irrigated and densely settled where water is available but give way to Pakistan's portion of the THAR DESERT on the east and to the arid tableland of the Balochistan (BALUCHISTAN) Plateau in the southwest. To the north the land rises to elevations between 300 and 600 m (1,000 and 2,000 ft) in the Himalayan foothills and elevations of more than 6,000 m (20,000 ft) in the rugged mountains of the HINDU KUSH and Kashmir's KARAKORAM RANGE, where K2, the world's second highest peak, rises to 8,611 m (28,250 ft).

Soils are high in calcium and low in humus. They are alluvial in the Indus valley and range elsewhere from loess in Balochistan to sandy desert loams. The Indus and its Pakistan tributaries, including the SUTLEJ, provide irrigation water for PUNJAB and Sindh (Sind) provinces.

Climate and Vegetation. Pakistan's climate is hot and dry, with cooler temperatures and greater rainfall in mountain areas. Annual temperatures average about 24° C (75° F) on the plains and 7° C (45° F) in the mountains. Most rain falls during the summer monsoon (July–September). Lahore receives only 460 mm (18 in) of precipitation per year, and Karachi, only 200 mm (8 in).

The natural vegetation is predominantly drought resistant, with tough grasses and scrub trees in semiarid areas giving way to desert vegetation in the Thar Desert and Balochistan Plateau. Where water is available, however, a wide variety of plants flourishes. Forests occupy about 3% of the land, and that minimal amount is much depleted by overcutting.

Resources. There are substantial deposits of natural gas but very limited resources of petroleum. Limestone, used to manufacture cement, is important. There are also limited reserves of lignite and low-grade iron ore.

People

Pakistan's diverse population reflects many centuries of invasion and settlement. The Punjabis, the largest ethnic group, constitute about 58% of the total population. The largest ethnic minorities are the Sindhis, who form a majority in Sindh, and the PATHAN (Pushtuns), who predominate in the North-West Frontier province and have strong ties to Afghanistan. In Balochistan are the Balochi (BALUCH), and the Brahuis. During the 1980s more than 3 million Afghans took refuge in Pakistan. After the final Soviet withdrawal from war-torn Afghanistan in 1989, the Pakistani government sought a broad political settlement there that would allow the refugees to return home.

Language and Religion. English, widely used in busi-

AT A GLANCE

ISLAMIC REPUBLIC OF PAKISTAN

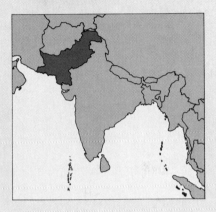

Land: Area: 803,940 km^2 (310,403 mi^2). Capital: Islamabad (1983 est. pop., 359,000). Largest city: Karachi (1989 est. pop., 7,191,240).

People: Population (1990 est.): 114,649,406. Density: 142.6 persons per km^2 (369.4 per mi^2). Distribution (1990): 28% urban, 72% rural. Official languages: English, Urdu. Major religion: Islam.

Government: Type: federal republic. Legislature: National Assembly, Senate. Political subdivisions: 4 provinces, federally administered tribal area, federal capital area.

Economy: GNP (1989): $46 billion; $436 per capita. Labor distribution (1990): commerce and services—30%; manufacturing—13%; agriculture and fishing—51%; construction—6%. Foreign trade (1990 est.): imports—$6.9 billion; exports—$5.0 billion. Currency: 1 Pakistan rupee = 100 plasa.

Education and Health: Literacy (1991): 33% of adult population. Universities (1987): 20. Hospital beds (1988): 64,471. Physicians (1988): 55,238. Life expectancy (1990): women—57; men—56. Infant mortality (1990): 110 per 1,000 live births.

ness and government, and Urdu are official languages. One of the INDO-IRANIAN LANGUAGES, Urdu is derived mostly from a Sanskritic base but is written in a script similar to Arabic and has many words borrowed from Persian. The principal regional languages of Pakistan are Punjabi, Sindhi, Pushtu, and Baluchi.

Islam, the official religion, is professed by about 97% of the population. Most Pakistani Muslims are members of the SUNNITE sect, but economically significant minorities, such as the ISMAILIS, Memons, and Bohras, are SHIITES.

Demography. Pakistan has one of the highest birthrates in the world, and rapid population growth has placed strains on the developing economy. The largest cities are KARACHI and LAHORE; other important urban centers are ISLAMABAD and RAWALPINDI, Lyallpur (now Faisalabad), HYDERABAD, MULTAN Gujranwala, Peshawar, and Quetta. Population densities are highest in agricultural areas of Punjab and Sind.

Education and Health. Primary education is free, but less than half of all children attend school. Most educational facilities are overcrowded, and some, especially in rural areas, are poorly equipped. Among the larger centers of higher learning are the University of Karachi (1951) and the University of Punjab (1882) in Lahore.

Preventive medicine has contributed to increased life expectancy, but doctors, nurses, and hospital beds remain in short supply. Tuberculosis, dysentery, typhoid, and other diseases related to polluted water supplies and unsanitary conditions are widespread.

The Arts. Pakistan's culture is a mixture of Western traditions, inherited from the British, and Islamic traditions acquired during seven centuries of earlier Muslim-Mogul rule. Poetry, mostly in Persian (the language of most Muslim rulers) and Urdu, is the dominant literary form; Pakistan's leading 20th-century literary figure is the poet Sir Muhammad IQBAL. Painting and dance forms prized by the elite in old Muslim society are popular with today's growing middle class.

Economic Activity

While part of British India before 1947, Pakistan's economy was integrated with that of India. Partition truncated regional economic systems, cut across road, rail, and irrigation systems, and left most of the subcontinent's manufacturing industries in India. Recovery began in 1955, but the economy has grown at a slower pace than the population.

Agriculture. Slightly more than 25% of the land is cultivated, about 80% of it with the aid of irrigation. In the 1960s, Pakistan significantly raised yields of wheat (the major food grain), rice, cotton, and sugarcane in a GREEN REVOLUTION. Meat, dairy products, wool, skins, and hides provide about one-third of total farm income.

Manufacturing and Energy. Manufacturing has expanded since 1947. Predominant industries are the manufacture of cotton textiles and the processing of agricultural

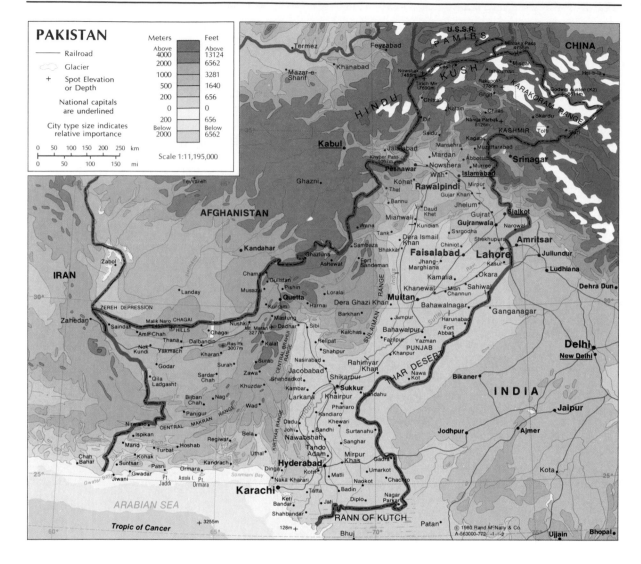

products. Heavy industry includes the production of fertilizers, tools, chemicals, pharmaceuticals, machinery, and steel.

Hydroelectric power is important, much of it produced in association with irrigation projects. Natural gas is piped from gas fields in Balochistan and Sindh to most major cities and is widely used in industry. There is a nuclear power plant in operation at Karachi and another under construction at Chasma. Many countries have refused to supply Pakistan with nuclear technology because it has not signed the Nuclear Non-Proliferation Treaty.

Transportation and Trade. An extensive rail network, created by the British, is now government owned and operated. Roads provide access to most areas, but more than half are unimproved dirt tracks. Government-owned Pakistan International Airlines (PIA) serves domestic and international routes. Karachi and Muhammad Bin Qasim

are the leading ports.

Pakistan has an unfavorable balance of trade that is partly offset by remittances from Pakistanis working abroad. The principal exports are raw cotton, cotton textiles, rice, carpets, and rugs. The leading imports are wheat, machinery, industrial raw materials, and petroleum.

Government

Pakistan's third constitution (effective 1973) was suspended in 1977. President ZIA UL-HAQ made substantial changes in this constitution in 1985. The principal change was to enhance greatly the powers of the previously figurehead presidency. The directly elected prime minister thus shares leadership with an indirectly elected president. The incumbents of the two offices after Zia's death repeatedly clashed, and the president dismissed the prime minister in 1990.

History

Pakistan's long history dates to the ancient INDUS CIVILIZATION preserved at Harappa and Mohenjo-daro (ending *c*.1500 BC) and was subsequently influenced by Indic cultures while part of the Magadha (beginning *c*.542 BC), MAURYA (*c*.321–236 BC), Kushan (AD *c*.78–176), and GUPTA (AD 320–*c*.535) empires. Islam was introduced into Sindh in the 8th century and gained wider acceptance after MAHMUD OF GHAZNI initiated 700 years of Turko-Afghan rule in the 11th century. The MOGUL dynasty assumed control in the 16th century. British influence grew after the 1750s, direct British rule being imposed in 1858 (see INDIA, HISTORY OF).

Creation of Pakistan. The idea of partitioning British India into separate Hindu and Muslim areas originated in the 1930s and became the goal of the MUSLIM LEAGUE under the leadership of Muhammad Ali JINNAH in the 1940s. Independence was achieved on Aug. 14, 1947, and Pakistan assumed sovereignty over two separate regions—East Bengal (later East Pakistan) and West Pakistan. The separation from Hindu-dominated areas granted to India was accompanied by widespread Hindu-Muslim rioting, the transfer of about 8,000,000 Hindus and Sikhs from Pakistan (especially from the Punjab) to India, and the forced relocation of about 6,000,000 Muslims from India to Pakistan. War erupted with India over control of Muslim-dominated Jammu and Kashmir (see KASHMIR) and ended in 1949 with a cease-fire line recognizing Pakistani control of about 40% of the disputed state (see INDIA-PAKISTAN WARS).

Internal differences between East and West Pakistan—united by little other than religion—frustrated efforts to create a central government and delayed adoption of the first constitution until 1956. During these trying years the military grew increasingly politicized and on Oct. 7, 1958, seized control of the government. Martial law was imposed, with Gen. (later Field Marshal) Muhammad AYUB KHAN as chief martial-law administrator. In

The huge Islamabad Mosque is in Islamabad ("City of Peace"), Pakistan's capital since 1967. The city, which is in the north of the country, is completely modern; construction began in 1960.

Traditions mingle in Peshawar. This city, near the Afghanistan border at one end of the Khyber Pass, had the world's largest refugee population during the Soviet occupation (1979–89) of Afghanistan.

1962 he proclaimed a new constitution and became president. Discontent and rioting, especially in the eastern wing, forced Ayub Khan to resign in March 1969. Gen. Muhammad Yahya Khan assumed control, and martial law was temporarily reimposed.

Creation of Bangladesh. Political activity was allowed to resume in 1970. National Assembly elections gave an overall majority to East Pakistan's Awami League, led by Sheikh MUJIBUR RAHMAN, which pledged to seek greater autonomy for East Pakistan; a majority in less populous West Pakistan was won by Zulfikar Ali Bhutto's (see BHUTTO family) Pakistan People's party. Yahya Khan twice postponed convening the new assembly; then, in March 1971, the election results were disregarded, the Awami League outlawed, and Sheikh Mujibur Rahman arrested. East Pakistan then declared its independence as the People's Republic of Bangladesh, and civil war ensued. The army moved in to end the civil war but was defeated after India intervened.

Modern Hisory. Civilian rule was restored in West Pakistan (now Pakistan), with Bhutto as president. A third constitution was adopted in 1973, under which he became prime minister of the demoralized nation. Bhutto was reelected prime minister in 1977, but the army again seized control of the government, on July 7, 1977. Gen. Zia ul-Haq became chief martial-law administrator and in 1978 assumed the office of president. Bhutto was arrested and later hanged. Zia, who twice postponed elections, embarked on a program of Islamization, which was approved in a probably fraudulent referendum in December 1984, a vote that he took as approval for his continuance in office for a period of five years. Following legislative elections in 1985, a civilian prime minister was appointed. After legislative sanction for the acts of the martial-law period, martial law was ended on Dec. 30, 1985. Zia dismissed the prime minister, the lower house of parliament, and the provincial governments in May 1988. On August 17, Zia was killed in a plane crash. In November elections, the Pakistan People's party, led by Bhutto's daughter Benazir, won a plurality of seats. She was appointed prime minister on December 1 by President Ghulam Ishaq Khan, Zia's successor. Bhutto faced ethnic and linguistic strife and opposition from groups favorable to the Zia legacy and fundamentalists unhappy with her opposition to the imposition of Islamic law. On Aug. 6, 1990, the president dismissed Bhutto and dissolved the National Assembly. The army-backed conservative Islamic Democratic Alliance, headed by Nawaz Sharif, decisively won new elections held on October 24. As prime minister, Sharif introduced legislation to make Islamic law the supreme law of the land.

Palacký, František [pah'-laht-skee, frahn'-tih-sek] František Palacký, b. June 14, 1798, d. May 26, 1878, a Czech historian, is known as the father of modern Czech nationalism. He wrote a five-volume history of medieval Bohemia (1836–67) that contributed significantly to the rise of Czech patriotism. At first Palacký supported Austro-Slavism and worked for a reorganized, federalized, and Slavic-dominated Austrian Empire, but the failure of the Revolution of 1848 crushed his hopes. Palacký then turned gradually toward Russia and Russian-led PAN-SLAVISM.

Palamas, Kostis [pah-lah-mahs', kohs-tees'] The prolific Greek poet Kostis Palamas, b. Jan. 13, 1859, d. Feb. 27, 1943, was the undisputed leader of Greek literature in his time. His best collection of lyric poems, *Life Immovable* (1904; Eng. trans., 1919), the philosophical epic-lyric *The Twelve Words of the Gipsy* (1907; Eng. trans., 1969), and the nationalistic epic *The King's Flute* (1910; Eng. trans., 1967) attempt a synthesis of ancient and Byzantine culture with the contemporary folk tradition.

Palamedes [pal-uh-meed'-eez] In Greek mythology Palamedes was a hero of the TROJAN WAR and was also credited with such inventions as the alphabet, numbers, measures, coinage, and the method for telling time. He was also noted for cunning. When ODYSSEUS pleaded insanity to avoid fighting in the Trojan War, Palamedes exposed his trickery. In the Euripidean tragedy Odysseus sought revenge by hiding gold in Palamedes' tent and forging a letter from King Priam of Troy indicating that Palamedes would betray the Greeks for gold. The Greeks believed the forgery and stoned Palamedes to death.

In Arthurian legend Palamedes was a Saracen knight who was repeatedly defeated in both battle and love by Tristran, who converted him to Christianity.

Palatinate [puh-lat'-i-nayt] The Palatinate, a major principality of the HOLY ROMAN EMPIRE, comprised an area astride the middle Rhine now incorporated in the German state of Rhineland-Palatinate. The oldest German university was founded in 1386 in its capital, HEIDELBERG.

In 1156, Holy Roman emperor Frederick I conferred the title count palatine on his half brother Conrad, who controlled extensive territories along the Rhine. In 1214 the title and territories passed to the WITTELSBACH family, which divided (1329) into two major branches: one holding the Rhenish Palatinate and the area now in northeastern Bavaria called the Upper Palatinate; the other, Bavaria. In 1356 the counts palatine were designated electors of the Holy Roman Empire.

In 1562, Elector Frederick III made the Palatinate Calvinist, and it became the center of radical religious movements in Germany. The election of FREDERICK V (the Winter King) to the throne of Bohemia in 1619 helped to precipitate the THIRTY YEARS' WAR. The Palatinate became one of its principal battlegrounds, and Frederick lost the Upper Palatinate to the duke of Bavaria. At the Peace of Westphalia (1648; see WESTPHALIA, PEACE OF) a new electorate was created for Frederick's son, Charles Louis.

The Palatinate was devastated in 1688–89 by the troops of Louis XIV in the War of the GRAND ALLIANCE. In 1803, under Napoléon's auspices, the Palatinate was divided between Bavaria and Baden.

Palau [puh-low'] Palau (Belau), the westernmost of the CAROLINE ISLANDS in the western Pacific, has a total land area of 460 km² (178 mi²). The predominantly Micronesian population of 14,106 (1988 est.) is concentrated on Koror, the capital. Palau came under U.S. administration after World War II (see PACIFIC ISLANDS, TRUST TERRITORY OF THE). In 1982 it signed a compact of free association with the United States, but the compact failed the win the 75% approval needed to override the nuclear ban in the Palauan constitution in repeated plebescites. On Dec. 22, 1991, the UN Security Council terminated the trusteeship arrangement over all of the islands of the trust territory except Palau. Palau was to remain under trusteeship until it could resolve its differences with the United States.

Pale [payl] The term *pale* (from the Latin *palus*, "stake") is used to designate a district set off by distinct boundaries from the surrounding territory. In imperial Russia the Jewish population was confined to a Pale of Settlement, established in 1792, that consisted of Russian Poland, Lithuania, Belorussia, the Crimea, Bessarabia, and much of the Ukraine. In late medieval Ireland the Pale was the area around Dublin first conquered and settled by the English in the 12th century. The English also occupied (1347–1558) a pale around Calais, France.

Palembang [pah-lem-bahng'] Palembang, a port city in southern Sumatra, Indonesia, lies along a swampy area of the Musi River. Its population is 873,900 (1984 est.). The city is a shipping center and rail junction. Petroleum refining, canning, and the production of fertilizers, textiles, and building materials are major industries. Exports include petroleum, rubber, timber, and coffee. Between the 7th and the 12th century, Palembang was the center of the Hindu empire of Srivijaya. It subsequently became the capital of Palembang sultanate (abolished in 1825). The Dutch established a trading post there in 1617 and built a fort in 1659.

Palenque [pah-layng'-kay]

Palenque, in northern Chiapas, Mexico, was one of the great centers of Classic MAYA civilization. By AD 600 the site had grown from a modest civic-ceremonial center into the capital of a large regional state. It flourished during the 7th and 8th centuries but shortly after 800 became the first great Maya center to collapse. Palenque's impressive ruins include a series of elegant temples and a palace complex with an unusual tower that may have been an astronomical observatory. Stone and painted-stucco reliefs adorn the walls of major buildings.

paleobotany

Paleobotany, the study of the geologic history of the plant kingdom, is a major branch of paleontology, the study of ancient life. The most ancient fossils yet discovered, those of the Archeozoic Era, are over 3 billion years old and are evidently allied to microscopic plants of simple form (see Evolution of Plants under PLANT). The study of the origins and development of all plants and plantlike organisms—from yeasts and bacteria to redwoods and orchids—from these ancient beginnings is included in the science of paleobotany. Study of microscopic plant fossils, particularly pollen, has grown into an important specialization known as palynology.

Adolphe Brongniart (1801–76) pioneered the use of plant fossils for geologic age determination. Important contributions to 19th-century paleobotany were also made by W. C. Williamson, who studied calcareous concretions called coal balls in which plant tissue structures were preserved in almost perfect condition. Early in the 1900s, A. C. Seward made very important contributions to Gondwana paleobotany (see CONTINENTAL DRIFT) and to recognition of floristic diversifications. Modern research has been amplified by extensive palynologic investigations of sediments of all ages.

The advent of Precambrian (Proterozoic and Archeozoic eras) paleobotany is one of the most significant recent developments. In 1965, E. S. Barghoorn established the existence of well-preserved, diversified blue-green algae in chert deposits of the Gunflint Formation of Ontario, approximately 1.9 billion years old. Later studies have demonstrated similar fossil algae in a large number of other similar deposits, mostly associated with calcareous or sometimes siliceous algal structures called stromatolites. These occurrences are likely to provide a basis for

Swamp forests of the Carboniferous Period, about 300 million years ago, covered many land areas in the Northern Hemisphere. Plant life included tree-sized ferns, horsetails, lycopods (ancestors of the modern club mosses), and gymnosperms. Remains of these plants decomposed in deltas and lagoons under oxygen-deficient conditions to form peat deposits. These deposits were buried and, over millions of years, converted into coal fields. Most of the world's productive coal deposits originated in the Carboniferous Period.

paleontological age determination during the later Precambrian (Proterozoic). Such a result would have been unthinkable a generation ago when all suggestions of Precambrian fossils were greeted skeptically. These results have far-reaching biological implications about the antiquity of life on Earth and the origin of nucleated organisms from which sexual diversification originated. The immensity of Precambrian research potential is indicated by the fact that Precambrian time represented approximately ⅞ of the history of the Earth.

See also: POLLEN STRATIGRAPHY.

Paleocene Epoch   see EARTH, GEOLOGICAL HISTORY OF; GEOLOGIC TIME

---

paleoclimatology   Paleoclimatology is the study of past climates throughout geological time and of the causes of their variations. CLIMATE involves complex interrelationships between the ATMOSPHERE, the oceans (see OCEAN-ATMOSPHERE INTERACTION; OCEAN AND SEA), and the continents (particularly continental ice) over time scales from thousands to several hundred million years. Climatic change involves alterations in the long-term mean values, and variations about the means, of such atmospheric elements as temperature, precipitation, and pressure.

Overview

Viewed in the context of the past 600 million years of Earth history, the widespread glaciation of the Pleistocene Epoch is a rare event (see GLACIERS AND GLACIATION; ICE AGES). During about 95 percent of GEOLOGIC TIME, the Earth experienced warmer average temperatures than those prevailing today; equator-pole temperature gradients were more modest, and circulation was less vigorous. The Paleozoic Era, cold and glacial to begin with, increased in warmth until the Silurian and Devonian peri-

---

Paleoclimatology, or the study of ancient climates, has revealed that temperatures at various latitudes have changed markedly since Permian times, about 280 million years ago. Warm-weather residues, such as evaporite deposits, coral reefs, desert sandstones, and animal fossils indicate that most of Europe, Asia, and North America were closer to the paleoequator of the Permian period. Glacial features however, disclose that Australia, India, South Africa, and parts of South America were once in much colder latitudes.

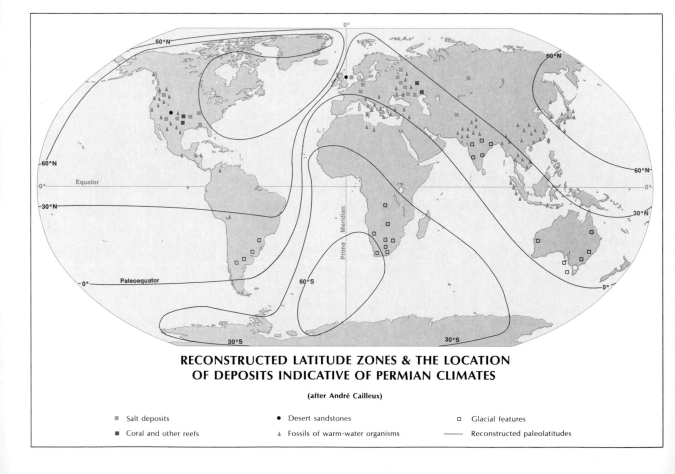

RECONSTRUCTED LATITUDE ZONES & THE LOCATION OF DEPOSITS INDICATIVE OF PERMIAN CLIMATES

(after André Cailleux)

| ■ Salt deposits | ● Desert sandstones | ▫ Glacial features |
| ■ Coral and other reefs | ▲ Fossils of warm-water organisms | —— Reconstructed paleolatitudes |

ods, and then cooled to the Carboniferous-Permian glaciation. The Mesozoic Era was generally warm and equable but moderated somewhat during the early Cenozoic Era. The late Tertiary Period experienced marked cooling, estimated at 5 to 10 C degrees (9 to 18 F degrees) or more on the average, presaging the Quaternary glaciations. Within the Quaternary Period at least four major glacial-interglacial cycles are recognized, with multiple minor fluctuations. Variations within the Recent Epoch are recognized, but their number and nature are still debated.

Climatic Evidence and its Interpretation

The nature of the evidence is such that the farther into the past one looks, the less information is obtained. The geologic record consists of incomplete data accumulated and integrated over long periods of time. Interpretations, therefore, tend to be qualitative and sometimes ambiguous.

Most types of evidence of glaciation and cold climates tend to be transitory on geologic time scales. Alpine landforms can disappear within a hundred million years. Only deposits that are incorporated into the stratigraphic record may persist through geologic time as markers of cold climates. The most common such deposit is tillite, or lithified glacial TILL (see TILL AND TILLITE).

Numerous deposits have been interpreted as indicative of warm paleoclimates, but not all are unequivocal. Coal deposits have been considered as representative of warm, humid forests, such as modern tropical mangrove swamps. Coal measures are often succeeded in the geologic column by red sandstones of Permian-Triassic age, interpreted as representing conditions varying from hot, arid DESERTS to warm, humid deltas. Carbonate rocks formed from CORAL REEFS represent warm tropical seas. Shifts in position of coral deposits through time might reflect CONTINENTAL DRIFT, but changes in the width of individual coral belts are more likely indicative of temperature changes in the sea.

EVAPORITE sequences are certain indicators of ARID CLIMATES in which evaporation exceeded precipitation. Lake brines tend to be too highly variable in physical and chemical properties, but marine evaporites may serve as paleothermometers, based on geochemical studies of the sequence and intensity of precipitation of various salts as functions of temperature.

Use of Fossils. Several techniques allow high-resolution quantitative estimates of Quaternary paleoclimate. Estimation of a variety of paleoclimatic parameters is achieved with multivariate statistical-transfer functions, whereby the relationship between modern faunal and floral assemblages and their environments is used to interpret fossil assemblages. The technique has proved successful in studies of oceanic FORAMINIFERA and of terrestrial pollen (see POLLEN STRATIGRAPHY), and it provides resolution of several years to a century or so for the past few thousand to few hundred thousand years. For example, revegetation of and vegetation change in eastern North America can be mapped from pollen studies, and climatic changes can in turn be estimated. Similar techniques also permit the analysis of annual tree-ring series (see DENDROCHRONOLOGY). A year-by-year record for nearly the entire Recent

Epoch now exists for BRISTLECONE PINE (*Pinus longaeva*) in the White Mountains of California. Among the parameters estimated in addition to temperature and precipitation are DROUGHT indices and pressure fields.

Isotope Chemistry. The fractionation in oceans of heavy and light ISOTOPES of oxygen in water, carbon dioxide, and calcium carbonate is temperature- and salinity-dependent. Measurement of the isotope ratios in the carbonate tests of fossil foraminifera provides a measure of sea temperatures and of ocean volumes, both of which correspond to changes in ice-sheet and glacier volumes. Isotope ratios in glacial ice provide a measure of average air temperatures. Continuous records have now been constructed for nearly the entire Quaternary Period.

Historic Data. The few centuries of the historic period provide a wealth of qualitative and quantitative data. For the period prior to the keeping of instrumental records of meteorological parameters, indices of climatic severity or temperance have been constructed from such social records as private diaries, tithe and tax accounts, harvest records, cherry-blossom festival dates, travelers' notes, and freeze-thaw dates for lakes and rivers. When such qualitative data are supplemented by quantitative data, some calibration is possible.

Mechanisms of Climatic Change

Many mechanisms have been proposed for climatic change. The theory of continental drift removes many previously intractable problems. For example, a major principle of paleoclimatology is that the poles have never been very warm. Continental drift can explain how coal beds in Antarctica were deposited at the same time that lands that are now near the equator were being glaciated.

Most theories of climatic change aim to explain the phenomenon of glaciation. Most promising of the many theories seem to be those of orogeny and of continental masses in polar positions (see PALEOGEOGRAPHY). Mountains perturb the mid-latitude atmospheric circulation and are associated in geologic time with steepened hemispheric temperature gradients. Continents around or at a pole can isolate the pole from heat flux from neighboring regions and can collect sufficient snow and ice to form glaciers. Long-period variations in the parameters of the Earth's orbit (eccentricity, obliquity, and precession) can alter the seasonal values of solar insolation and may act as pacemakers of glacial events when the requisite geography is present.

Concern over possible human alterations of climate arises from considerations of atmospheric transparency. The addition of carbon dioxide, a product of fossil-fuel combustion, can increase the amount of terrestrial radiation trapped by the atmosphere, thereby heightening the GREENHOUSE EFFECT.

See also: EARTH, GEOLOGICAL HISTORY OF; FOSSIL RECORD; METEOROLOGY; PALEOBOTANY.

paleoecology Paleoecology is the study of the relationships between fossil organisms and their environments. Paleoecology combines a knowledge of both the

A trilobite fossil, an extinct marine arthropod, dates from the Paleozoic Era (600 to 225 million years ago). On the basis of body form, paleoecologists deduce that most trilobites were bottom dwellers.

biology and the ecology of living organisms—which indicates how ancient animals and plants may have looked and lived—and of geological processes—which account for why their remains are found where they are.

paleogeography Paleogeography, the study of the Earth's past geography, is a major subfield of historical geology. Relying on a broad spectrum of information made available from many other fields in geology and the natural sciences, it analyzes, interprets, and synthesizes the former configuration and distribution of oceans and lands, mountains and plains, climatic belts, paleobiological provinces, paleoecological conditions, and many related features.

Early Concepts

Development of paleogeography has proceeded along several courses. Charles LYELL, in his *Principles of Geology* (1830–33), stated that every part of the land had once been beneath the sea and that every part of the ocean had once been land, in an endless cycle from land to sea and back again.

James Dwight DANA proposed (1873) that continents had always been continents but from time to time had been flooded by shallow, epicontinental seas. Dana showed that the margins of continents (at least of eastern North America) were covered by much thicker deposits than were the centers of the continents. He applied the term GEOSYNCLINE to these long, linear belts of thicker sediments. Dana believed that the Earth was cooling—a common hypothesis of the 1800s and early 1900s—and therefore that the Earth's surface was shrinking. He believed that this shrinking, like a shriveling orange skin, was the cause of most of the structural deformation of the Earth's crust.

Charles Schuchert (1858–1942), a dominant figure in paleontology in North America during the first quarter of

this century, developed the concept of paleogeographic maps in order to show how relationships changed over successive intervals of geologic time.

During the last quarter of the 19th and the early part of the 20th century, a number of European geologists became interested in paleogeography in order to understand the distributions of certain fossils (see FOSSIL RECORD). Henry Francis Blanford (1834–93) and Edward SUESS found close similarities between fossils from parts of South America, Africa, Australia, and India. Suess proposed that these areas had once been connected by land areas that had subsequently foundered in the South Atlantic and Indian oceans. Later geologists included Antarctica among these areas. Suess called this large theoretical supercontinent Gondwana. He also originated the name *Tethys* for the east-west sea that extended across southern Europe and Asia during the Mesozoic Era.

Continental Drift

An extremely controversial hypothesis was first proposed by Alfred Lothar WEGENER in 1912. Because he rejected the ideas of the permanence of ocean basins and the fixity of continents, he did not need to consider the foundering parts of continents in ocean basins. He believed that

Most of the present continents were combined into two large supercontinents about 500 million years ago (top). About 225 million years ago (bottom) the two landmasses collided, forming Pangea and deforming the margins of the continents, as well as producing geosynclines, mountain chains, and areas of volcanic activity.

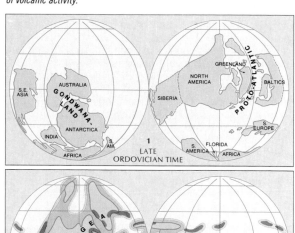

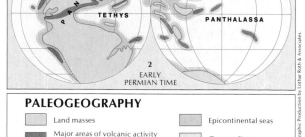

PALEOGEOGRAPHY

Land masses

Epicontinental seas

Major areas of volcanic activity and mountain forming

Geosynclines

Cartographic Production by Lothar Roth & Associates

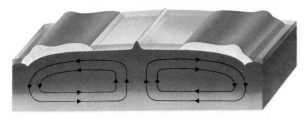

According to the theory of seafloor spreading, hot lava from Earth's interior rises through rifts in ocean ridge systems and creates new seafloor crust. The new crust forms and spreads on both sides of a ridge, pushing back older crust into the mantle along ocean trenches.

continents drifted like rafts across the surface of the Earth, and that occasionally they had joined together to form landmasses having different shapes, coordinates, and geometries than those at present. Evidence of CONTINENTAL DRIFT was assembled as a synthesis of data from many fields and was reasonably convincing but lacked a geologic mechanism.

The ideas of the permanence of ocean basins and the fixity of continents and the reluctance to accept continental drift in its original form also influenced the interpretations of the origins and dispersals of present day faunas and floras (see PALEOBOTANY). Alfred Russel WALLACE published (1875) a two-volume study of present-day animal distributions. His general map, based mainly on the distribution of families of organisms, has been only slightly modified by later studies, although the environmental and phylogenetic bases for his maps have been significantly clarified. In order to explain many present-day distributions, various possibilities for dispersals were studied through the stimulation developed by George Gaylord SIMPSON between the 1930s and the 1960s. Land bridges, isthmian links, island hopping, and long-distance (sweepstakes) dispersals received increasingly close attention and commonly drew on statistical methods and probability theory to lend support to various models of

species and generic dispersals. During the course of such studies a great deal has been learned about the processes that control dispersals and about the present geographic distribution of plants and animals.

Modern Interpretation

The actual amount of departure from the present configuration of continents and ocean basins during the geologic past was unclear for many years. During the 1960s and '70s intensified studies by geophysicists, sedimentologists, and paleontologists of the ocean basins and their PALEOMAGNETISM, EARTHQUAKE patterns, and heat flow (see EARTH, HEAT FLOW IN) demonstrated that the earlier understanding of ocean-continent relationships had not been correct. The result was the theories of seafloor spreading and PLATE TECTONICS. These studies showed that the oldest parts of the Atlantic Ocean basin originated during the Late Jurassic or Early Cretaceous periods, and that the oldest parts of the Pacific and Indian Ocean basins were formed during the Late Triassic or Early Jurassic periods. The ocean basins are geologically very young in comparison to the continents. Very different arrangements for continents prior to the Jurassic were thus possible. Seafloor spreading and plate tectonics can be used as the mechanisms to construct the continental configuration of the supercontinent Pangea for the Carboniferous, Permian, and part of the Triassic periods. The steps that led to the gradual accretion of continental fragments to form such a supercontinent during Early and Middle Paleozoic time are currently being explored; the Precambrian relationships are not completely known.

Other Paleogeographic Tools

The reconstruction of Late-Paleozoic Pangea is based mainly on fitting together the geometric shapes of the broken edges of continental fragments, tracing the geosynclines and orogenic belts and comparing their histories, and determining apparent pole positions through paleomagnetic studies (see POLAR WANDERING). These criteria

About 200 million years ago (A) continental drift caused Pangea—a supercontinent—to separate into two large landmasses: Laurasia (1) and Gondwanaland (2). Near the end of the Cretaceous Period, about 75 million years ago (B), Gondwanaland broke up into Africa (3), Madagascar (4), India (5), New Zealand (7), and a continental group (6) containing South America, Antarctica, and Australia. By the beginning of the Eocene Epoch 50 million years ago (C), the continents had separated and moved close to their current positions.

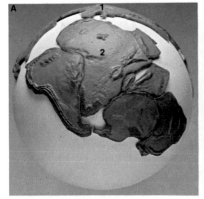
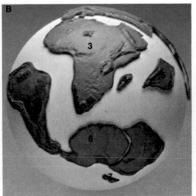
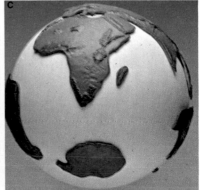

are less readily interpreted for pre-Carboniferous times.

Climatic belts similar to those that exist today were present in the geologic past; thus climatic indicators are helpful in interpreting approximate latitudinal positions (see PALEOCLIMATOLOGY). Glacial deposits such as tillites (see TILL AND TILLITE), glaciomarine strata, and glacially grooved surfaces (see GLACIERS AND GLACIATION) generally indicate cold climates. On the other hand, thick, light gray limestone deposits, particularly large reef, bank, and shoal deposits that are rich in calcareous algae and large calcareous foraminifers, indicate warm, tropical, or subtropical water. Beds of red sandstone may indicate warm, moist lateritic climates or warm, oxygen-rich depositional environments, or both. Dune sands (see SAND DUNE) may indicate nearness to a beach, desert, or some other type of eolian environment. Coal deposits (see COAL AND COAL MINING) commonly represent reducing environments where oxidation of carbon compounds is slow. Coals may occur in many latitudes, but those having fossil plants with annual growth rings are considered to have formed outside tropical latitudes. EVAPORITES suggest warm to hot, dry climates. Thick clastic wedges of coarse sediment are the erosional product of nearby mountain ranges or orogenic uplifts.

Faunal provinciality is another tool of paleogeographers. Phylogenetic similarities, particularly at the species and generic level, between geographically different fossil assemblages of the same age and same ecological communities suggest interbreeding or only recently separated fossil populations. When entire fossil faunas are compared on this basis, an evaluation of common elements and general similarities can be made. In a broad way, close similarities indicate geographic continuity of favorable ecological environments. Also, the number of species is usually greater among tropical communities than among polar communities. The resulting species-diversity gradient forms an additional basis for estimating latitudinal position.

Paleolithic Period

The Paleolithic Period, or Old Stone Age, is the earliest and longest stage of human cultural development, lasting from about 2.5 million to about 10,000 years ago. The concept of a Paleolithic Period was proposed in 1865 by the English antiquarian Sir John Lubbock. Like most of the archaeologists at the time, Lubbock had accepted the chronological validity and comprehensiveness of the three-age system first proposed (1836) in Denmark by C. J. Thomsen (1788–

1865)—a scheme which stated that stone implements had preceded bronze tools, which in turn had preceded iron use in antiquity. Lubbock and his colleagues working elsewhere in Europe soon realized that the Stone Age itself should be divided into a later NEOLITHIC PERIOD (New Stone Age), characterized by ground stone tools, and an earlier, much longer Paleolithic Period, newly recognized by them and represented by chipped stone implements, sometimes associated with the bones of extinct species such as mammoth and cave bear. The transition between Lubbock's two periods was later termed the MESOLITHIC PERIOD (Middle Stone Age).

On the basis of observations made especially in France, the Paleolithic Period was divided by the late 19th century into three phases: the Lower, or Early, Paleolithic, characterized by the use of bifaces, or hand axes; the Middle Paleolithic, when flake tools largely replaced bifaces; and the Upper, or Late, Paleolithic, distinguished by the use of blade tools. This scheme is still in use today in Old World ARCHAEOLOGY, although the scheme is evidently not valid for all areas nor does it imply necessarily that the passages from one phase to another took place simultaneously.

Time Span. The Paleolithic Period spans the end of the Pliocene and the totality of the Pleistocene, a geological epoch characterized by a series of marked oscillations of the climate. Until recently, in the absence of reliable techniques, Paleolithic sites were dated by reference to a sequence of glacial and interglacial periods established in the geological examination of river terraces, loess deposits, and glacial advances in the Alps and through faunal and palynological correlations. Recent studies of climatic oscillations during the Pleistocene using sea-core sediments, geomagnetic data, and radiocarbon and argon-potassium dating methods have indicated that the classic glacial sequence is neither complete nor detailed enough—especially before the last glaciation (Würm)—and must be replaced by a more precise scheme.

The common use of the traditional archaeological periodization based on changes in the shape of stone implements should not obscure the fact that other materials, such as wood, bone, and antler, were also used for tools throughout the Paleolithic. Since these materials decay relatively quickly unless special conditions exist, archaeological specimens are much rarer than their stone counterparts. Roughly split or flaked bone fragments with signs of wear have nevertheless been found in the earliest hominid sites such as OLDUVAI GORGE and Zhoukoudian, and such tools continued to be used even when tech-

This bifacially flaked point was produced with the help of a bone or wood hammering tool. Dating from about 300,000 years ago, it belongs to the Acheulean tool industry of the Lower Paleolithic Period.

This scene reconstructs a lower Paleolithic camp that was excavated in 1966 at Terra Amata, in Nice, France. Remains of the earliest huts have been dated about 400,000 years ago. These oval-shaped dwellings measured 8–15 m by 4–6 m (26–49 ft by 13–20 ft) and contained hearths, the walls, made of branches, were braced by stones on the outside and supported by central posts. The huts were occupied by nomadic hunters for a brief period each year, probably in late spring and early summer. Evidence indicates that these visitors hunted such animals as the wild boar (1), Merk's rhinoceros (2), stag (3), wild ox (4), ibex (5), and elephant (6); they also caught fish, shellfish, and turtles. A variety of early Acheulean tools, including scrapers (7) and bifaces (8), have been found at the Terra Amata site.

niques had been developed to shape bone or antler into specialized implements during the Upper Paleolithic. Although wood is even less resistant to decay, fragments of wooden artifacts were found at Torralba in Spain dated to at least 300,000 years ago, and they were doubtless always important.

Importance of Stone. Stone was, nevertheless, the most fundamental element because it provided the strong edge necessary to shape the other materials and to process the gathered plants and killed animals that constituted human subsistence. One of humankind's first major technological achievements was the relatively rapid and extensive exploitation of stones and minerals that possessed the required properties for use as tools. Hardness, the first of these, was indispensable for a strong working edge. Brittleness, the second most important quality, was necessary so that the selected material could be shaped with relative ease. The third property common to all prehistoric stone artifacts was structural isotropy or homogeneity. Isotropic materials have no natural cleavage planes,

and the stone-tool makers, or flint knappers, could therefore determine the plane of fracture by manipulative skill alone. These three properties exist to different degrees in all stones used during the Paleolithic. Siliceous materials such as flint (see CHERT AND FLINT) and quartzite were generally preferred because they possess all three of these qualities to a relatively high degree and tend to be readily available. Igneous stones such as basalt or obsidian, also widely exploited, are less hard but more brittle or isotropic.

Throughout the Paleolithic, two major trends can be distinguished in the manufacture of stone implements. The first was an increase in the number of tool types that evolved from a relatively few unstandardized and multipurpose forms to more numerous, uniformly shaped implements adapted to specific tasks. The second trend was a reduction in the size—and, consequently, in the waste—of the stone materials used.

Lower Paleolithic Period. Core and flake tools constitute the two basic kinds of Lower Paleolithic stone imple-

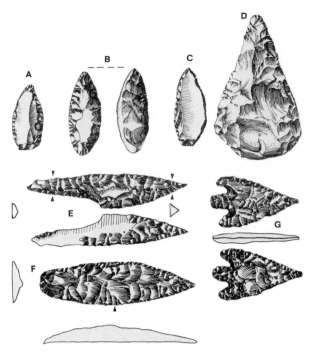

These points (A; B, both sides; C) *belong to the Mousterian (c.125,000–32,000 years ago), a Middle Paleolithic tool culture. This Acheulean (Lower Paleolithic) hand ax* (D) *was produced about 250,000 years ago. The Solutrean (c.20,000–17,000 years ago) is an Upper Paleolithic tool industry of France and northeastern Spain; implements* (surfaces and cross sections shown) *include a shouldered point* (E), *a leaf-shaped point* (F), *and a tanged and barbed point* (G).

ments. A core tool is relatively massive and is made by removing flakes from a piece of stone until it is trimmed down to the desired shape. To form the flake tools a piece of stone core is used as a nucleus, that is, a source of flakes. The flakes are used for cutting, either as they are obtained or after being further retouched (trimmed) along the edges into specialized tools.

Simple examples of these basic tools discovered at the earliest-known hominid sites of the Upper Pliocene and Early Lower Pleistocene, in the Omo Valley in Ethiopia, date from about 2.5 million years ago. They are also present in the area east of Lake Rudolf in Kenya and, especially, in the Olduvai Gorge of Tanzania, where the earliest sites (Bed I) are about 1.8 million years old. These assemblages, called Oldowan, include core tools, specifically choppers, made by striking a few flakes from the two faces of a pebble along part of its edge. Oldowan core tools and flakes were used for cutting or were fashioned into scrapers by chipping part of the edge to strengthen it. These tools are sometimes found in association with large quantities of broken bones and rows of arranged stones, indicating animal-butchering or habitation sites, and with remains of the earliest hominids such as the early human species Australopithecus and Homo habilis.

Assemblages similar to those of Oldowan type have been observed in northwest Africa and, of later date, in southern Europe at Vallonet Cave, in eastern Europe at Vertesszöllös, and in the western European Clactonian sites. The East and Southeast Asian chopper and chopping tool tradition, illustrated for instance at Zhoukoudian, is essentially similar to the chopper and flake tradition in Africa and Europe but lasted in relative isolation into the Upper Pleistocene. The Olduvai Gorge sequence has revealed that a developed Oldowan tradition with a greater number of specialized flake tools continued until about 400,000 years ago into the Middle Pleistocene; further examples of this complex have also been identified at Sterkfontein and Swartkrans in South Africa. This evolved Oldowan tradition seems to have existed concurrently, starting at least 1.5 million years ago, with a newer tool tradition, the Acheulean, where choppers were replaced by bifaces. From the earliest Acheulean sites in Africa, such as at Olduvai (Bed II) and Aïn Hanech, the biface tradition—including its first phases, sometimes referred to as Abbevillian or Chellean—spread during the Middle Pleistocene over most of the Old World. Acheulean artifacts dating from c.700,000 years ago at 'Ubeidiya in Israel constitute the oldest known occurrence of bifaces outside of Africa. Many European Middle Pleistocene sites illustrate that the Acheulean biface tradition developed parallel with the European chopper and flake tradition.

Acheulean bifaces are of two kinds: hand axes and cleavers. Hand axes measure, on the average, about 10–15 cm (4–6 in) and vary in form from oval to triangular. The working edge is obtained by flaking a pebble bifacially along its entire edge. Cleavers, often made on large flakes, are similarly shaped except that they have at one end a wide and sharp cutting edge set perpendicularly to the long axis of the implement. This cleaver edge represents the intersection of a large flake scar with the other face of the tool.

The bifaces were probably used for butchering but presumably also for many other tasks, as suggested by the great variation in size, thickness, and form of these core tools. The major flake implements found with Acheulean bifaces include scrapers, flakes with notched or denticulated edges, backed knives (flakes with one blunted edge), and borers made by chipping part of the flake's edge into a strong point. These tools and the many other unretouched flakes used for cutting are of varied shapes and outlines due to the limited degree of control that could be attained during the knapping of the stone nuclei. Eventually, the Acheulean biface users developed independently in both Africa and Europe the Levallois technique (see Levalloisian). By this method flakes of roughly predetermined size and shape could be obtained through careful preparation of the nucleus.

The production of specialized flake tools and bifaces with increasingly straight working edges and more regularly tapered and thinner cross sections marked a major advance in lithic technology; this factor no doubt favored the spread of the early human biface makers into new regions. Another important element that contributed to the success of these early humans, generally identified as the species HOMO ERECTUS, was their use of fire both in hunting and in domestic hearths for heat and the preparation of food.

Middle Paleolithic Period. At the beginning of the Upper Pleistocene, approximately 100,000 years ago, flake tools increased in number and variety until they became the predominant stone implements by the onset of the last glaciation. This marks the beginning of the Middle Paleolithic, or MOUSTERIAN, in Europe, Southwest and Inner Asia, and North Africa and the start of the Middle Stone Age in sub-Saharan Africa (see AFRICAN PREHISTORY). The sites from this period have yielded remains of NEANDERTHALERS and of some hominids even closer to modern humans, including in some cases evidence of funerary practices, such as at Shanidar in Iraq. The major kinds of Mousterian flake tools include a variety of scrapers as well as points, denticulates, borers, and backed flakes. In addition to the Levallois technique in evidence throughout the Middle Paleolithic, another efficient method of knapping was developed at this time. This method was the Mousterian discoidal nucleus technique, which consists of flaking the periphery of a rounded hunk of flint and using the resulting flake scars as successive striking platforms, from which large numbers of flakes could be successively removed.

Upper Paleolithic Period. The most striking feature of the Upper Paleolithic assemblages is the great number and variety of well-defined tools made on blades. Manufactured by CRO-MAGNON MAN, these blades were first removed in parallel series from specially prepared tabular or prismatic nuclei and then knapped either by direct percussion with stone or antler hammers or by indirect percussion using an intermediary bone or antler punch. Among the many kinds of Upper Paleolithic blade tools, the most common are the backed blades, the end scrapers, and the burins. The backed blades with their abruptly trimmed edge are analogous in manufacture and use to the backed flakes of earlier periods. The end scrapers were made by retouching one end of the blade into a rounded scraping edge, whereas the burins were formed with a thick chisel end. The burins, of which there are many varieties, made it possible to work bone, antler, and ivory efficiently; consequently, many new implements were produced in these strong and durable materials, such as spear points, barbed harpoon heads, and spear-throwers as well as engraved and sculpted ornaments and figurines. Many of these artifacts are decorated with carvings of hunted animals, such as bison, horse, and reindeer; such images were also often painted on cave walls (see PREHISTORIC ART).

The high level of prosperity and cultural complexity of the Upper Paleolithic toolmakers is well illustrated by their spread over the entire habitable world (including the New World), the increasing size of their settlements—exemplified by the open-air site of DOLNÍ VĚSTONICE—and the extraordinary refinement of their technology and art. About 10,000 years ago the climate changed; the glacial sheets retreated to the highest mountains, the sea level rose, and the steppes and tundras with their large herds of herbivores were replaced by forests. New ways of life were progressively developed, which reflected, during the succeeding Mesolithic Period, a different ecological and cultural adaptation.

See also: PREHISTORIC HUMANS.

---

paleomagnetism   The study of the history of the Earth's magnetic field is called paleomagnetism. Certain rocks record the intensity and direction of the geomagnetic field as magnetic fossils; the most reliable magnetic fossils are the thermoremanent magnetization (TRM) of igneous rock and detrital (or depositional) remanent magnetization (DRM) of sedimentary rocks and oceanic deposits. TRM arises when igneous rock is cooled from a high temperature in a magnetic field. The direction of TRM is parallel to that of the applied magnetic field, and its intensity is proportional to that of the applied field.

Igneous rocks generally contain a large number of small grains of an iron oxide mineral called magnetite. These small grains of magnetite have spontaneous (permanent) magnetization that, however, disappears at temperatures higher than a critical temperature called the Curie point (see MAGNETISM). At high temperatures, thermal agitation overcomes the energy of alignment of atomic magnetic moments within the magnetic mineral.

When an assembly of a large number of magnetite grains within an igneous rock is cooled from a temperature higher than the Curie point in the presence of a magnetic field, the spontaneous magnetizations of these grains tend to statistically align along the applied field direction. When their temperature is cooled further past another critical point, the blocking temperature, the aligned grains become tightly blocked in this alignment. The assembly of blocked spontaneous magnetizations thus forms the thermoremanent magnetization, which is very stable at atmospheric temperature against mechanical and magnetic disturbances.

The magnetic fossil in sedimentary rocks, the detrital remanent magnetization (DRM), is acquired during the processes of deposition and sedimentation of magnetite grains (together with other nonmagnetic silicate grains) in oceans or lakes in the presence of a magnetic field. Because these grains are able to rotate in water, the spontaneous magnetizations of tiny magnetite grains tend to align statistically along the applied magnetic field, and they become blocked when the sediments coagulate.

Other kinds of remanent magnetization of natural rocks often cause misleading paleomagnetic interpretations. Isothermal remanent magnetization (IRM) is obtained by applying a strong magnetic field at atmospheric temperature, such as the field accompanying a lightning stroke. Chemical remanent magnetization (CRM) is produced when tiny magnetite grains are chemically formed in rocks in the presence of a magnetic field. Viscous remanent magnetization (VRM) is slowly accumulated during a long geologic period even at atmospheric temperature.

One of the remarkable discoveries of paleomagnetism

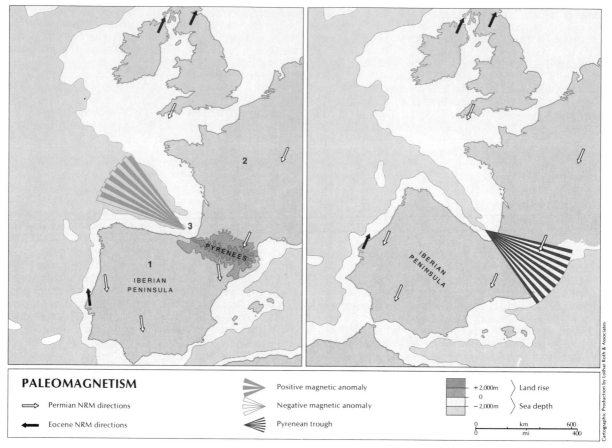

PALEOMAGNETISM

⇒ Permian NRM directions

← Eocene NRM directions

▶ Positive magnetic anomaly

▷ Negative magnetic anomaly

◀ Pyrenean trough

+2,000m / 0 / −2,000m ⟩ Land rise / Sea depth

0 ——— km ——— 600
0 ——— mi ——— 400

(Left) *Paleomagnetic studies of rocks from Spain (1) and from the rest of Europe reveal the same reversal of Earth's magnetic poles between the Permian and Eocene periods. The Spanish rocks, however, indicate a different north pole direction. These results disclose that Spain rotated away from France (2) after the Eocene period. The rotation opened up the Bay of Biscay (3) and created a rift, leading to seafloor spreading. The discovery of alternating bands of opposite magnetic polarity along the bay floor supports this conclusion. In addition, the rotating Spanish plate uplifted the crust along the French border and formed the Pyrenees Mountains. (Right) A computer-generated paleographic map indicates the probable configuration of Europe before Spain began to rotate.*

is that frequent reversals of the geomagnetic field have taken place. When the geomagnetic field polarity is the same as it is at present, it is called the normal polarity; otherwise it is called the reverse polarity. The normal and reverse pattern of geomagnetic field polarity as a function of time in the past has been adopted as the paleomagnetic time scale.

See also: EARTH, GEOMAGNETIC FIELD OF.

——

paleontology   The term *paleontology,* derived from the Greek words for "ancient life," refers to the science that deals with the study of prehistoric life. The main objects of study in this field are fossils—the remains or traces of prehistoric organisms—and hence paleontology can also be defined as the study of fossils. Through the study of fossils paleontologists can date rocks, determine ancient environments, and trace the EVOLUTION of life. In so doing, they utilize principles from both geology and bi-

ology, making paleontology a point of fusion between these sciences.

See also: EVOLUTION; FOSSIL RECORD; PALEOBOTANY; PALEO-ECOLOGY; PALEOGEOGRAPHY; POLLEN STRATIGRAPHY; STRATIGRA-PHY.

Paleozoic Era   see EARTH, GEOLOGICAL HISTORY OF; GEOLOGIC TIME

——

Palermo [pah-lair'-moh]   Palermo (ancient *Panormus*) is the capital of the Palermo region of Sicily in southern Italy. It has a population of 751,483 (1989 est.). Located on the northwestern coast of Sicily, on the Bay of Palermo, the city is the major commercial center and foremost seaport of Sicily. Shipbuilding, food processing, and winemaking are important industries. Textiles, chemicals, steel, paper products, and furniture are also manufactured. The University of Palermo (1777) is located in the city. Important buildings include the cathedral (begun 1185), the Church of Saint John of the Hermits (1132), Abatellis Palace (15th century), and the Chiaramonte Palace (1307).

Palermo was founded by the Phoenicians, probably between the 8th and 6th centuries BC. It was successively conquered by the Romans (254 BC), the Byzantines (AD 535), the Arabs (831), and the Normans (1072), who made it the capital of Sicily. The city's greatest cultural and commercial flowering took place during the reign (1220–50) of Holy Roman Emperor FREDERICK II. Control subsequently passed to the French Angevin dynasty. The revolt of the SICILIAN VESPERS (1282) against the Angevins began in Palermo. Spanish rule, beginning in 1302, brought on the city's decline. The Bourbons ruled Palermo from 1734 until 1860, when Giuseppe GARIBALDI liberated it. The city was badly damaged by bombings during World War II.

Palermo Stone   The Palermo Stone is a fragment of a hieroglyphic inscription that, when complete, bore the names of the kings of Egypt from predynastic times to the 5th dynasty (c.2450 BC) and recorded, year by year, the chief events in the reigns of the dynastic kings. It has been in the Palermo Museum since 1877; it is believed to have been taken from Egypt to Sicily in a ship's ballast and then discarded. Events mentioned in the annals include royal progresses by river; sacred festivals; the making of statues of kings or deities; the building of ships, temples, or palaces; and military campaigns. Beneath each annual entry is a record of the highest level of the Nile in that year.

Palestine [pal'-es-tyn]   Palestine, a historic region on the east coast of the Mediterranean, also known as the Holy Land, was the site of the ancient kingdoms of Israel and Judah and comprises areas of the modern states of Israel and Jordan. In the 20th century, Arab and Jewish nationalists have made conflicting claims to the region. The borders of Palestine have fluctuated throughout history but have generally included the territory lying between the southeastern Mediterranean coast on the west, the Jordan/Dead Sea Valley on the east, the Negev Desert on the south, and the Litani River on the north—an area only about 280 km (175 mi) long by 128 km (80 mi) wide. This land has been coveted throughout history because, by local standards, it is relatively well watered and strategically located on major land routes linking western Asia and northern Africa.

Early History. The name *Palestine* is an adaptation from a Greek word that was in turn derived from the Hebrew word for "the land of the Philistines." Palestine was first peopled by wandering Stone Age hunters; permanent agricultural settlements appeared at JERICHO about 8000 BC. A mixed society of agricultural villagers, sheep- and goat-herding nomads, and urban artisans evolved. The principal influx of Hebrew tribes (see JEWS) from the desert to the east into Palestine occurred between the

This engraving of Jerusalem shows the city as it appeared in the late 16th century. Jerusalem's walls were completed (1542) by Suleiman I, sultan of the Ottoman Empire at the height of its power.

14th and 12th centuries BC. At roughly the same time the PHILISTINES invaded from the sea. Eventually, the Hebrew tribes dominated the area politically by forging a union c.1000 BC under the warrior kings SAUL, DAVID, and SOLOMON. This unity was fragile, however, and the kingdom split into two small states, Israel and Judah (see ISRAEL, KINGDOM OF; JUDAH, KINGDOM OF). Israel was destroyed by Assyria (721 BC) and Judah by Babylonia (587 BC). Afterward, except for a period of independence (143–63 BC) under the MACCABEE family, Palestine was dominated by a succession of foreign rulers including the Persians, Alexander the Great, and the Hellenistic Ptolemies and Seleucids.

The last vestige of ancient Hebrew statehood was shattered in AD 70, when the Romans responded to a revolt by occupying the capital city of JERUSALEM, destroying the Temple, and placing Palestine under Roman governors. During the succeeding 500 years of Roman and Byzantine rule, Palestine became overwhelmingly Christian. The Arab conquest of 641 brought Palestine under the sway of the Islamic CALIPHATE. By the 10th century most Palestinians had embraced Islam. After the decline of the central caliphate, the region endured another period of political instability. In 1099 the Crusaders took Jerusalem and established a feudal kingdom (see JERUSALEM, LATIN KINGDOM OF), which was itself destroyed in 1291 when the Europeans were expelled by the MAMELUKES of Egypt. The rule of the Turkish OTTOMAN EMPIRE (1516–1918) brought some stability but also stagnation.

In 1918, Palestine's population included about 500,000 Muslim Arabs, 100,000 Christian Arabs, and 60,000 Jews. All but a few thousand of the Jews had arrived since the 1880s, when immigrants from Europe, inspired by ZIONISM, started establishing agricultural settlements. Zionism's program called for a Jewish "national

Winston Churchill (right) visited Jerusalem in 1921. The next year, during which the British government issued a White Paper reaffirming its commitment to the establishment of a Jewish "national home," the League of Nations approved the British mandate for Palestine.

reaction to Nazi persecution of Jews in Europe, Jewish settlement jumped dramatically. Between 1935 and 1939, Britain advanced proposals to stabilize the population with an Arab majority. The Arabs resented these schemes, and Zionists rejected them.

Between 1936 and 1939 the Arab Higher Committee, formed to unite Arab opposition to Jewish claims and led by the grand mufti (chief Islamic judge) of Jerusalem, Amin al-HUSAYNI, carried on a virtual civil war. Thousands were killed, and many of the Arab Palestinian leaders were deported or forced to flee. The conflicts exposed serious Arab social fragmentation, as well as military deficiencies, that contrasted with the solidarity and organizational efficiency displayed by the Jews, who formed a paramilitary organization, the Haganah, during the period of unrest.

Britain's last serious attempts to reach a compromise were the inconclusive London Round Table Conference (1939) and the White Paper of that year, which promised the establishment within 10 years of an independent Palestine retaining an Arab majority. The White Paper also limited Jewish immigration to 1,500 per month until 1944, when Jews would no longer be admitted to Palestine. This limit was a devastating blow to the Jews of Hit-

home" in Palestine supported financially and politically by a worldwide organization.

British Occupation. Toward the end of World War I, British troops led by Gen. Sir Edmund ALLENBY invaded Palestine, capturing Jerusalem in December 1917 and ending four centuries of Ottoman sovereignty. In 1922 the League of Nations approved a British mandate over Palestine and neighboring Transjordan. The Arab state of Transjordan (later Jordan) became autonomous in 1923 and was recognized as independent in 1928. In Palestine, however, independence was delayed while conflicting Arab and Jewish claims were weighed. In 1916 an ambiguous political accord between HUSAYN IBN ALI, sharif of Mecca, and Henry McMahon, British high commissioner in Cairo, had led the Arabs to believe that the British would support the creation of an independent Arab state that would include Palestine. On Nov. 2, 1917, however, the British government issued the BALFOUR DECLARATION, which promised support for Zionist aims.

In July 1919, the General Syrian Congress in Damascus demanded independence for a Syrian state that would include Palestine, categorically rejecting the concept of a Jewish national home. In 1920, Emir Faisal (later FAISAL I, King of Iraq), military commander of an Arab revolt (1916–18) against Ottoman rule, was declared king of this Syrian state. That April the Allied supreme council assigned France the mandate over Syria, and in July, French troops took Damascus, deposing Faisal. Anti-Zionist riots broke out among Arab Palestinians in April 1920 and were followed by even more serious violence in May 1921. Another serious clash erupted at the Wailing Wall in Jerusalem in 1929. That year the Zionists formed the Jewish Agency to help develop quasi-governmental institutions among Palestine's Jews.

The Palestine crisis deepened in the 1930s when, in

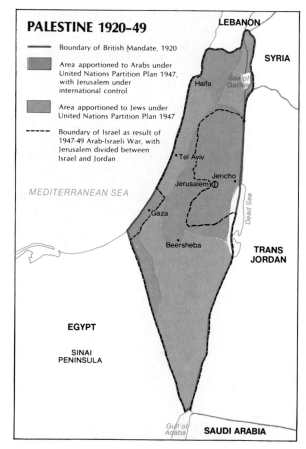

ler's Europe, and, after the outbreak of World War II, Zionists transferred their major efforts to attract support from Britain to the United States. After World War II, when large numbers of European concentration-camp survivors sought homes in Palestine, Britain's resistance to reviving large-scale Jewish immigration prompted a revival of widespread disorder.

Birth of Israel. By 1947 the exhausted British referred the problem to the United Nations, which voted in November to split Palestine into Arab and Jewish states. Despite violent Arab protests, Palestine's Jews proclaimed the creation of the independent state of ISRAEL, comprising more than half of Palestine's territory, on May 14, 1948. Armies of the adjacent Arab states quickly entered Palestine. This war, the first in a series of ARAB-ISRAELI WARS, ended in 1949 with an Israeli victory that included possession of territories won on the battlefield; the migration of more than 700,000 Arab Palestinian refugees out of Israeli territory into adjacent areas controlled by various Arab states; the confiscation of the property left by the Arab refugees and its redistribution to Israelis; and the eclipse of Palestine as a political entity. Most of the territory west of the Jordan River that the United Nations had designated as Arab came under the control of Transjor-

dan, renamed Jordan, which formally annexed it in 1950. After the 1967 Arab-Israeli War, however, this WEST BANK territory was occupied by Israel. In 1974 the UN General Assembly reaffirmed the right of the Palestinians to self-determination; Jordan formally severed its links to the West Bank in 1988 in favor of the PALESTINE LIBERATION ORGANIZATION (PLO).

The Palestinian Arabs reacted to the loss of their homeland with despair, shame, and anger, and most still seek identifiable statehood within the boundaries of historic Palestine. Since the early 1950s a bewildering array of organizations, programs, strategies, and leaders—ranging from moderates favoring a secular Palestine that would guarantee equality for Jews and Arabs, to militant revolutionaries advocating the destruction of Israel and the creation of an independent Arab state in Palestine—have tried to realize this aim. An uprising launched in December 1987 by Palestinians in the West Bank and Gaza Strip and the 1991 GULF WAR gave renewed impetus to the search for peace, but no solution acceptable to all parties has been found.

Palestine Liberation Organization   The Palestine Liberation Organization (PLO) is an umbrella organization composed of several groups of Palestinians engaged in a struggle to "liberate" their homeland from what they view as an illegitimate Israeli state. The PLO has been linked to and has taken credit for numerous terrorist acts around the world. The PLO considers itself the political and military arm of Palestinian Arabs, many of whom fled their homes following the United Nations partition of Palestine and the subsequent ARAB-ISRAELI WARS. In 1974 the PLO was proclaimed the sole legitimate representative of the Palestinian people by the Arab states at the Rabat Conference, and the UN General Assembly recognized the PLO as "the representative of the Palestinian people." Israel has refused to negotiate with an organization dedicated to Israel's destruction.

The PLO was formed in 1964 to represent Palestinian Arabs; its charter vests supreme policy-making authority in the Palestine National Council, a kind of Palestinian parliament-in-exile. The PLO's financial holdings, with an estimated value of $5 billion in 1985, are managed by the Palestine National Fund. Yasir ARAFAT became chairman of the PLO in 1969. His Al Fatah guerrilla organization is the most powerful of the diverse groups loosely allied under the PLO umbrella. Since 1983 the PLO has been deeply but informally split into pro- and anti-Arafat factions, the latter backed by Syria.

Expelled from Jordan in 1971, PLO guerrillas established a virtual state-within-a-state in Lebanon from which they launched attacks on Israel. They were driven from their Beirut headquarters by the Israeli army in 1982 and scattered throughout the Arab world. On Feb. 11, 1985, Jordan's King Hussein and Arafat announced that the PLO had accepted the idea of a negotiated settlement of the dispute. This move was accompanied by rising violence, including disputes within the PLO and Israeli retaliation for PLO terrorist activities, and the effort col-

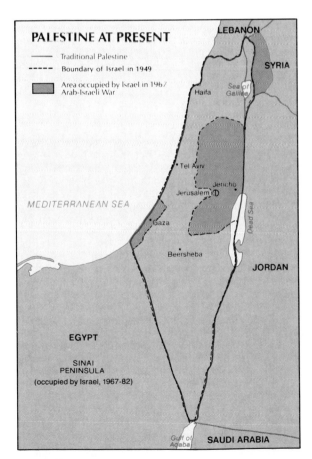

PALESTINE AT PRESENT

——— Traditional Palestine

- - - - Boundary of Israel in 1949

▨ Area occupied by Israel in 1967 Arab-Israeli War

LEBANON
SYRIA
Haifa
Sea of Galilee
MEDITERRANEAN SEA
Tel Aviv
Jericho
Jerusalem
Gaza
Dead Sea
Beersheba
JORDAN
EGYPT
SINAI PENINSULA
(occupied by Israel, 1967-82)
Gulf of Aqaba
SAUDI ARABIA

lapsed in 1986. Pressured by a Palestinian uprising in occupied territories that began in December 1987 and by Jordan's formal severing of its links to the West Bank in July 1988, the Palestinian National Council formally declared a Palestinian state in November 1988 and conditionally accepted UN Resolution 242, which implicitly recognizes Israel. Arafat, who recognized Israel's right to exist and renounced terrorism in December, was appointed president of the Palestinian state in April 1989. In June 1990, however, the United States suspended its dialogue with the PLO after it refused to denounce a May terrorist attack on Israel. Prospects for a peaceful settlement subsequently dimmed as PLO leaders tilted away from Egypt, which favored diplomacy, toward Iraq. The PLO was among the very few supporters of Iraq during the 1991 GULF WAR.

Palestrina, Giovanni Pierluigi da [pal-es-treen'-uh] Giovanni Pierluigi da Palestrina, b. Palestrina, near Rome, c.1525, d. Feb. 2, 1594, was an illustrious Italian composer of church music. Palestrina's musical career kept him mostly in Rome, where he enjoyed the grace and favor of popes and cardinals. Director of the Julian Chapel Choir from 1551 to 1555, he became a singer in the pontifical choir in the latter year and began to compose for the papal chapel. From 1555 until 1560 he was in charge of the choir at Saint John Lateran, moving in 1561 to Santa Maria Maggiore. In 1571 he returned to the Julian Chapel as director of music.

Palestrina's works are exclusively vocal and almost totally liturgical, the only exceptions being a solitary book of madrigals and a collection of spiritual madrigals. He wrote 105 masses (for four to eight voices) most of which are of the "parody" type—that is, they take their starting point from compositions of his own or of other composers. Many of his masses are based on plainsong tenors, while 9 make use of alternating chant and polyphony. More than 250 of his motets are extant, few being based on

Giovanni da Palestrina was the foremost composer of liturgical music of the 16th century. His polyphonic and contrapuntal musical techniques influenced both Bach and Handel. His first published work (1554) was a volume of masses dedicated to Pope Julius III.

plainsong tenors, although the chant is sometimes paraphrased within the overall texture. Illustrative musical touches are found in the 29 motets based on the Song of Solomon. There are also 68 offertories, 13 complete sets of Lamentations, 12 litanies, 20 psalms, and 35 magnificats. Palestrina's tremendous output never fell below a remarkably high level of musical accomplishment.

Paley, Grace [pay'-lee] Grace Paley, b. New York City, Dec. 11, 1922, is a short-story writer whose dialogue captures the idiosyncrasies and idioms of New Yorkers in love and at war with each other. Her carefully developed characters include ordinary as well as eccentric people who continually introduce insights into the workings of the human heart. Her collected stories include *The Little Disturbances of Man* (1959), *Enormous Changes at the Last Minute* (1974; a film of that name, based on three of the stories, was released in 1985), and *Later, the Same Day* (1985).

Paley, William S. After six years in the family cigar business, William Samuel Paley, b. Chicago, Sept. 28, 1901, d. Oct. 26, 1990, purchased a network of radio stations in 1928 and thus created the nucleus for the Columbia Broadcasting System (see RADIO AND TELEVISION BROADCASTING). His acute sense of entertainment programming for mass audiences enabled Paley to build his network into the powerful conglomerate CBS, Inc. Paley served (1928–46) as president of CBS and then as chairman of the board until 1983 and again from 1986. He wrote *As It Happened* (1979).

Palisades [pal'-i-saydz] The Palisades, a series of vertical cliffs 60 to 165 m (200 to 540 ft) high, rise from the west bank of the HUDSON RIVER for a distance of about 24 km (15 mi) from Fort Lee, N.J., to Piermont, N.Y. The columnar structure of the diabasic cliffs is believed to be the result of the cooling of molten material at the end of the Triassic Period. Since 1900 the area has been protected by the Palisades Interstate Park Commission.

Palladio, Andrea [pahl-lah'-dee-oh] One of the most illustrious architects of the Italian High Renaissance, Andrea Palladio, b. Andrea di Pietro della Gondola, Nov. 30, 1508, d. Aug. 19, 1580, was active in Venice, in Vicenza, and throughout the Veneto. He fashioned a vocabulary of architectural proportions and motifs that he first discovered in ancient Roman ruins and then rationalized in his own distinctive way. So far-reaching and influential were his ideas, which he articulated not only in buildings but in writings, that he is the only architect to have given his name to an architectural style.

Palladio made five lengthy visits to Rome, where he measured and sketched ancient buildings. In 1554 he published his findings in a treatise, or guidebook, *Le An-*

Andrea Palladio's Villa Rotunda (c.1549–53) in Vincenza, Italy, incorporates the domed cylindrical structure of the Roman Pantheon in its symmetrical, blocklike form.

tichità di Roma, on the antiquities of classical Rome.

Later, through his buildings and his most famous treatise, *The Four Books of Architecture* (1570; Eng. trans., 1738; 1965), Palladio's influence permeated Western architecture. Under careful preparation for over 20 years, the *Four Books* gave plans, elevations, and decorative schemes for his designs and went through many editions and numerous translations. From northern Italy, Palladianism reached England through Inigo JONES, who introduced this radical architectural style in a country still under the sway of late Tudor Gothic. Thus Palladio's buildings—through such intermediary architects as Jones—served as models for various architects to the end of the 18th century, especially in designs for aristocratic and royal patrons. Palladio's civic and ecclesiastical buildings, urban palaces, and country villas were imitated and adapted by architects not only in England but in Ireland, North America, in every European nation, and even in the West Indies and Imperial Russia.

Although sources for some of Palladio's architectural designs can be found in the works of Jacopo Sansovino, Donato Bramante, and Michelangelo, the dominant influences were Palladio's own rationalizations, which he based on his direct study of ancient Roman buildings.

See also: ARCHITECTURE.

Palladium [puh-lay'-dee-uhm] In Greek mythology the Palladium was a wooden statue of the goddess ATHENA, or Pallas Athene, that was sent from heaven by Zeus to Dardanus, the founder of Troy. It was said to protect the city from enemies. During the Trojan War, Odysseus and Diomedes stole it, after which Troy fell to the Greeks. Roman myths relate that Aeneas brought the Palladium to Rome, where it was credited with the same protective powers that it had afforded Troy.

palladium Palladium is a soft, white, ductile metallic chemical element and a member of the PLATINUM group of metals. Its chemical symbol is Pd, its atomic number is 46, and its atomic weight is 106.4. The English chemist William Wollaston, who discovered palladium in 1803, named the element for the asteroid Pallas, which had been discovered the previous year. Palladium often occurs in nature in an alloy with platinum or gold or as a selenide. Its physical characteristics resemble those of platinum. Because of its low contact resistivity, palladium is used as a low-current electrical contact, primarily in telephone equipment and in printed circuits. It is also used to strengthen gold-based dental alloys.

Palladius, Saint [pah-lay'-dee-uhs] Saint Palladius, d. 432?, sometimes mistakenly identified with Saint PATRICK, was a 5th-century Roman deacon appointed (430) first bishop of Ireland by Pope Celestine I. He was therefore the forerunner of Saint Patrick. When his work against PELAGIANISM and to reorganize the church in Ireland met with little success, he began to preach the gospel in Scotland. Feast day: July 6.

Pallas's cat Pallas's cat, or manul, is classified as *Felis manul* or sometimes *Otocolobus manul*. Pallas's cat inhabits the dry, cold steppes of Central Asia from Siberia to Tibet, where it feeds on rodents, hares, and birds. It has a broad head, small and low-set ears, and a long coat; some people believe that it may be the ancestor of the Persian cat. Its coat is commonly pale brown, grizzled with white or gray; a few dark stripes may be present across the body. Pallas's cat reaches 65 cm (25 in) in length, plus a 30-cm (12-in) tail, and weighs up to 3.4 kg (7.5 lb).

palm Palms are perhaps the most striking plants in tropical floras. Their often tall, usually straight, unbranched, woody stems topped by a spreading crown of long-stalked, sometimes huge, featherlike or fanlike, pleated leaves distinguish them from nearly all other forms of vegetation. The palm family is the only family in the order Arecales and is one of the oldest of flowering plants. The palms' fossil record traces back to the Triassic Period, about 220 million years ago. Strict application of the International Code of Botanical Nomenclature would make Arecaceae the valid name for the palm family, but the name Palmae has been accepted as a legitimate alternative. The palm family comprises nearly 2,500 species in 200 or more genera. They are widely distributed in the tropics and subtropics; few species occur in warmer temperate regions.

One of the hardiest of the tree palms is the windmill palm, *Trachycarpus fortunei,* of eastern Asia, which is cultivated outdoors in milder maritime climates as far north as Vancouver, Canada. The most cold-tolerant palm

Tree palms found in the United States, include the desert fan palm (A), which has fan-shaped leaves (1), bisexual flowers (2), and oval to round fruit (3); and the Florida royal palm (B), which has feathershaped leaves (4), unisexual flowers (5) borne in triads (two male with one female), and round fruit (6).

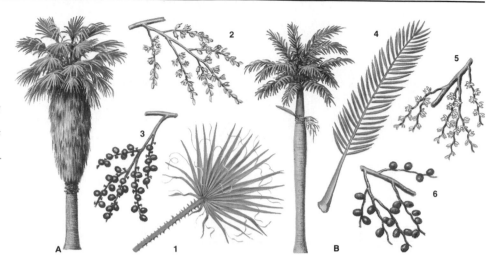

is the needle palm, *Rhapidophyllum hystrix*, of the southeastern United States: it has been known to survive temperatures of −21° C (−6° F).

In addition to the commonly recognized treelike forms, which may reach 30 m (100 ft) high, there are those with prostrate or creeping stems (*Rhapidophyllum*), those with stems completely underground (*Nypa*), and those with vinelike stems (*Desmoncus*). The long, thin, ropelike stems of the rattan palms, *Calamus* and *Daemonorops*, which may climb 60 m (200 ft) into the treetops, are the rattan cane used commercially. The leaves of the raffia palms, *Raphia*, are the largest in the plant kingdom, exceeding 20 m (65 ft) in length, and are the source of raffia fiber.

Palm flowers are typically small and may be borne singly, in pairs, in threes (triads), in small clusters (cincinni), in small lines (acervuli), or in large clusters (panicles). The flower cluster, or inflorescence, is enclosed by a bract that ranges from thick and woody to paper thin. This serves to protect the inflorescence and allows it to develop to maturity with little outside interference, such as animal or insect predation. Palm flowers may be bisexual but are usually unisexual. Palm trees are normally monoecious, bearing both male and female unisexual flowers on the same tree, but some species are dioecious, with separate male and female trees, or polygamous, with both unisexual and bisexual flowers on the same tree. Palm fruit is botanically a berry, nut, or drupe, depending in part on the structure of the flower ovary. The COCONUT (with husk) is a drupe, a fruit technically like that of the peach but dry and fibrous instead of fleshy.

Since prehistory, palms have provided thatch for shelter; fibers for weaving, plaiting, and basketry; timber for constructing buildings, tools, and utensils; leaves for clothing and food; and sap for beverage. Foremost among African palms is the date palm, *Phoenix dactylifera*. The oil palm tree, *Elaeis guineensis,* also native to Africa, is the most important source of palm oil, which is used in foods, pharmaceuticals, soaps, candles, and lubricating greases.

Palm Beach

Palm Beach (1990 pop., 9,814), situated on the northern end of a 29-km-long (18-mi) island off the southeast coast of Florida, in Palm Beach County, is an extraordinarily wealthy resort community. The first house was built there during the U.S. Civil War. The railroad tycoon Henry M. Flagler purchased property there in 1893 and began the development that established Palm Beach as a winter resort.

Palm Springs

Palm Springs (1990 pop., 40,181) is a desert city in Riverside County, southern California, about 160 km (100 mi) southeast of Los Angeles; it is a fashionable winter resort. First occupied by Cahuilla Indians, Palm Springs grew around a stagecoach stop established in 1872.

Palm Sunday

In the Christian calendar Palm Sunday is the Sunday before EASTER, the sixth and last Sunday in LENT, and the first day of Holy Week. It recalls the triumphal entry of Jesus into Jerusalem, a week before the Resurrection, when the people strewed palm branches in his path.

Palma [pahl'-mah]

Palma de Mallorca is the capital of the Balearic island of MAJORCA and of the Baleares province of Spain in the western Mediterranean Sea. It is a commercial and tourist center and has a population of 306,840 (1987 est.). Port activities are important to the economy. Points of interest include Bellver Castle (14th century), a Gothic cathedral (1230–1601), and several museums and art galleries. Air and sea links connect Palma with the mainland.

Palme, Olof [pahl'-muh]

Leader of the Swedish Social Democratic party, Sven Olof Joachim Palme, b. Jan.

30, 1927, d. Feb. 28, 1986, was prime minister of Sweden from 1969 to 1976 and from 1982 to 1986. Palme entered parliament in 1958 and held a succession of cabinet posts before becoming premier. During his first ministry, which governed with Communist support, he rejected full Swedish participation in the European Community and was an outspoken critic of U.S. involvement in Indochina. His second term of office, marked by a sagging economy and labor unrest, was cut short when he was shot to death by an assassin on a Stockholm street.

Palmer, A. Mitchell

Alexander Mitchell Palmer, b. Moorehead, Pa., May 4, 1872, d. May 11, 1936, was a U.S. attorney general (1919–21) best known for initiating the 1919–20 Palmer Raids against alleged radicals and subversives during the Red Scare period following World War I. A lawyer, he served (1909–15) in the House of Representatives and gave Woodrow Wilson crucial support at the 1912 Democratic convention. Because of his Quaker beliefs, Palmer declined Wilson's offer of the post of secretary of war. His postwar raids, spurred by fear of revolution in the wake of Russia's Bolshevik Revolution of 1917, resulted in the arrests of thousands of citizens and aliens and the deportation of several hundred aliens.

Palmer, Alice Freeman

Alice Elvira Freeman Palmer, b. Colesville, N.Y., Feb. 21, 1855, d. Dec. 6, 1902, was an American educator. At the age of 24 she became a professor of history at WELLESLEY COLLEGE, and at 27 its youngest president. During her six-year tenure she put the college on a sound financial footing, increased enrollment, and raised academic standards. From 1892 to 1895 she was nonresident dean of women at the University of Chicago. Palmer founded the precursor of the AMERICAN ASSOCIATION OF UNIVERSITY WOMEN. During her term (1889–1902) on the Massachusetts State Board of Education she advocated higher standards and better pay for teachers.

Palmer, Arnold

Arnold Daniel Palmer, b. Latrobe, Pa., Sept. 10, 1929, an American professional golfer, almost singlehandedly brought that sport to its current state of popularity in the United States with his exciting brand of play. In 1954, after winning the National Amateur title of the United States Golf Association (USGA), he turned professional. Later he became the first professional golfer to earn more than $100,000 in one year and the first to earn $1,000,000 in his career—excluding his business earnings, which are extensive.

Friendly and personable, Palmer attracted a great many fans who became known as "Arnie's army," and he provided many thrills for them as he came charging from behind to win important tournaments. Palmer's 61 U.S. tournament career victories rank him fourth behind Jack Nicklaus, Sam Snead, and Ben Hogan. Worldwide, including his Senior Tour victories, he has won more than 90 tournaments. Palmer won the Masters 4 times (1958,

The American golfer Arnold Palmer holds the trophy from the 1975 Penfold Championship in England, his 79th professional victory. Just as Palmer's immense popularity ensured success for the PGA tour in the late 1950s and the 1960s, his participation during the 1980s on the Senior PGA tour (for golfers ages 50 and over) ensured that agenda's success.

1960, 1962, 1964), the British Open twice (1961–62), and the U.S. Open once (1960). He also played on 5 Ryder Cup teams and 6 victorious World Cup teams.

Palmer, Nathaniel Brown

Nathaniel Brown Palmer, b. Stonington, Conn., Aug. 8, 1799, d. June 21, 1877, a U.S. sea captain, was probably the discoverer of the Antarctic continent. While searching for new seal rookeries in 1820, he sighted what is now known as the Antarctic Archipelago (also Palmer Archipelago) and the Antarctic Peninsula (the southern tip of which is named Palmer Land) about 1,130 km (700 mi) southwest of Cape Horn.

Palmer, Samuel

The English landscape painter and etcher Samuel Palmer, b. Jan. 27, 1805, d. May 24, 1881, developed a personal, mystical style that greatly influenced later artists. In 1826, Palmer moved from London to the country, where he painted and engraved landscapes of great poetic intensity, such as *The Harvest Moon* (1833; collection of Mr. and Mrs. Paul Mellon). After visiting Italy for two years (1837–38), a period during which his work became more representational, Palmer began to etch, producing some outstanding works in that medium. Among his important later watercolors are a series illustrating John Milton's shorter poems.

Palmerston, Henry John Temple, 3d Viscount

The British statesman Henry John Temple, Viscount Palmerston, b. Oct. 20, 1784, d. Oct. 18, 1865, served in Whig governments as foreign secretary (1830–34, 1835–41, 1846–51) and home secretary (1852–55) and was twice prime minister (1855–58, 1859–65). A towering figure in British diplomacy, he pursued his country's interests by his outspoken support of liberal and national movements in Europe and by his often belligerent use of force throughout the world. Although much criticized by the crown and Parliament, he was very popular with the

Lord Palmerston, a 19th-century British statesman, aggressively pursued a nationalistic foreign policy that often antagonized his colleagues while making him a national hero.

electorate, serving in the House of Commons from 1807 until his death (with only a brief break in 1835).

From 1830 to 1832, Palmerston successfully promoted Belgian independence from the Netherlands while barring French intervention. In 1846–47 he prevented both Austrian and French intervention in the Swiss civil war, and he sent arms to Sicilian insurgents in 1848.

Seeking to preserve the Mediterranean balance of power, Palmerston in 1840 prevented the French-backed Egyptian ruler, MUHAMMAD ALI PASHA, from conquering the Ottoman Empire. He initiated the First OPIUM WAR (1840–42) to advance British commercial interests in China. In 1850, Palmerston ordered the seizure of Greek ships to force the Greek government to pay an ostensible debt to a British citizen. Defending his action in a famous parliamentary speech, he asserted that, like ancient Roman citizens, British subjects should be protected throughout the world. Prime Minister Lord John RUSSELL dismissed him from the foreign office in 1851 for welcoming the coup of Napoleon III before consulting other members of the government.

Many felt that the CRIMEAN WAR (1854–56) could have been avoided if Palmerston had remained in the foreign office; he became prime minister in the wake of criticism of the handling of that conflict. As prime minister he pursued a vigorous policy in the war, suppressed the INDIAN MUTINY of 1857, and supported the Italian RISORGIMENTO. His foreign policy met setbacks, but he always bounced back until 1864, when Otto von BISMARCK called his bluff over the Schleswig-Holstein question.

palmetto The name palmetto refers to nearly 20 species of PALMS in the genus *Sabal* of the family Palmae. These fan-leaved palms are native to the southeastern United States, Bermuda, the West Indies, and northern South America. Palmetto leaves are used for thatching roofs, and the buds of some species, known as palm hearts, are eaten.

palmistry see FORTUNE-TELLING

Palmyra [pal-my′-ruh] Palmyra, an ancient oasis settlement in the Syrian Desert 230 km (140 mi) northeast of Damascus, was an important trading point between the Roman and Parthian empires. Tadmor, the Semitic form of the name, appears in Akkadian tablets from the early 2d millennium BC, but the site's prominence dates from the Hellenistic period, when much trade took place between the Mediterranean and Mesopotamian worlds. Because of its isolated position, Palmyra became associated with the Roman Empire only in AD 14–17 and always preserved significant local autonomy. A tariff on the caravans passing through the city was the source of Palmyra's growing wealth and influence in the 1st and 2d centuries AD. Before his death in 267, Prince Odaenathus assembled a small empire stretching from the Red Sea to southern Anatolia. His wife ZENOBIA later added Anatolia and Egypt to Palmyra's sphere of influence and even won partial recognition from the Roman emperor Aurelian before her open revolt provoked the destruction of the city and her imprisonment in 273.

Aramaic was the language of Palmyra, whose populace was of mixed Amoritic, Aramaic, and Arabic stock; its art and architecture reveal a blend of Hellenistic Greek and Parthian elements. A broad colonnaded street crossed the center of the city, connecting the Great Temple of Bel to the palace. The cemeteries surrounding the city were characterized by impressive tomb towers holding numerous individuals, who were identified through inscribed plaques carrying portrait busts.

Palo Alto [pal′-oh al′-toh] Palo Alto (1990 pop., 55,900) is located on the western shore of San Francisco Bay in Santa Clara County, northern California. The economy is dominated by the aerospace, electronics, and communications industries. Palo Alto was founded in 1891 as a residential community for Stanford University, located in nearby Stanford.

palo verde [pal′-oh vur′-dee] Palo verde is a small shrubby tree, *Cercidium floridum*, of the pea family, Leguminosae, native to Arizona, southern California, and northern Mexico. It remains leafless most of the year and is also known as the blue palo verde because of its smooth blue gray or blue green bark. It grows to about 9 m (30 ft) high and has spiny twigs, two-stalked (bipinnate) leaves with two to four pairs of leaflets (pinnae) on each stalk, small yellow flowers, and flat, brownish seedpods. The similar yellow palo verde, *C. microphyllum*, of the same general region, has a yellowish green bark, bipinnate leaves with four to seven pairs of leaflets on each pinna, and cylindrical seedpods that are constricted between the seeds.

Palomar Observatory [pal′-oh-mahr] Palomar Observatory houses the 200-in (5.08-m) Hale reflector, the largest telescope in the world from 1948 to the late

1970s. The observatory, located 144 km (90 mi) south-east of Pasadena, Calif., atop Palomar Mountain, at an elevation of 1,708 m (5,600 ft) above sea level, is operated by the California Institute of Technology. From 1970 to 1980 it was part of Hale Observatories, operated by Cal Tech and the Carnegie Institution of Washington (D.C.) and named for astrophysicist George Ellery Hale. Palomar also has a 60-in (1.92-m) photometric reflector and a 48-in (1.22-m) SCHMIDT TELESCOPE.

Work done at the observatory included the confirmation that nebulae outside the Milky Way are galaxies like our own. Ongoing work at Palomar includes studies of the rate of expansion of the universe and the production of major sky surveys (see ASTRONOMICAL CATALOGS AND ATLASES).

palomino see HORSE

palpitation Palpitation is a rapid, forceful, or irregular beating of the heart. In most cases, it is caused by nervous preoccupation with one's own heart action, either from fear of heart disease or from emotional disorders.

Palpitation can also be a symptom of a number of organic diseases of the heart or other organs, such as the thyroid gland. Sinus tachycardia is a disorder characterized by a heart rate of more than 100 beats per minute. Premature ventricular systole creates the false sensation of the heart skipping a beat, because of premature contraction of the heart ventricles after a previous contraction and a prolonged compensatory pause before the next regular contraction. Paroxysmal tachycardia is a rapid but regular heartbeat that causes a fluttering sensation in the chest. Paroxysmal atrial fibrillation is a rapid, irregular pounding caused by temporary loss of rhythm in the atria, or auricles, of the heart.

palsy [pawl'-zee] The term *palsy*, originally defined as PARALYSIS, has been extended to apply to several conditions characterized by loss of muscular control. Included are diseases that cause jerky movements, tremors, or spasticity, a condition of muscle rigidity. CEREBRAL PALSY causes lifelong disability. PARKINSON'S DISEASE, or shaking palsy, is caused by degenerative changes in the central nervous system. Other forms include wasting palsy (as in MUSCULAR DYSTROPHY), progressive bulbar palsy (as in respiratory POLIOMYELITIS), and Bell's palsy, a paralysis of facial muscle.

palynology see POLLEN STRATIGRAPHY

Pamirs [puh-meerz'] The Pamirs, a region of high mountains and valleys in central Asia sometimes called "the roof of the world," form the core of several of the highest ranges on Earth—the HINDU KUSH, the KUNLUN MOUNTAINS, the KARAKORAM RANGE, and the TIAN SHAN. Most of the area lies in Tadzhikistan, in the USSR, but it extends into northeastern Afghanistan and Xinjiang province, China. The average elevation exceeds 4,000 m

(13,000 ft), and the highest point is atop K2. Geologically complex, the Pamirs contain rocks of the Precambrian, Paleozoic, and Mesozoic eras. More than 1,000 glaciers cover an area of 8,042 km^2 (3,105 mi^2). Because of the severely cold and arid climate, vegetation is sparse. Tadzhiks raise sheep and goats in the lower valleys and farm the small plots of arable land.

Crossed by Marco Polo in 1271, the Pamirs were first explored by the Russian A. P. Fedchenko in 1871. In the 1930s a warm-weather highway traversing the region was built.

Pampas [pam'-puhz] The Pampas (from the Quechua word for "plain") is a vast savanna in southern South America extending from the Atlantic coast to the Andes. With an area of about 764,000 km^2 (295,000 mi^2), the Pampas lies mostly in Argentina and extends into Uruguay. The land gradually rises from 6 m (20 ft) above sea level in the east to 600 m (2,000 ft) in the west and is divided into eastern humid Pampas and western dry Pampas. The PARANÁ and the URUGUAY are the main rivers.

One of the richest agricultural areas in the world, the eastern Pampas supports most of Argentina's population. From the Pampas come 80% of Argentina's farm products, especially beef and wheat, but also linseed oil, corn, and dairy products. Meat-packing and food-processing industries are centered in the cities, the largest of which are BUENOS AIRES and LA PLATA. Cattle, introduced in the mid-1500s, have been traditionally tended by gauchos, the Pampas cowboys. Much of the area remained sparsely populated until the mid-19th century, when European immigration and railroads spurred its growth.

Pamplona [pahm-ploh'-nah] Pamplona, the capital of the Navarra autonomous community in northern Spain, lies about 320 km (200 mi) northeast of Madrid. Situated 40 km (24 mi) from the French border on a pass through the Pyrenees, it is a thriving commercial and agricultural center. Its population is 178,666 (1987 est.). Cereal products, textiles, furniture, paper, and handicrafts are manufactured there. Historical landmarks include the cathedral (1397–1427) and the old royal treasury (1364). The annual Fiesta de San Fermín, during which bulls run through the streets, is the major tourist attraction.

According to tradition, Pamplona was founded by the Roman general Pompey in 75 BC and named Pompaelo. It became the capital of the kingdom of Navarre in the 11th century and was annexed to Castile in 1512. The French occupied the city in 1808, but the British drove them out in 1813.

Pan In Greek mythology Pan, son of HERMES, was an Arcadian god of shepherds and their flocks, hunters, forests and wildlife, and fertility—in essence, the god of nature. Portrayed as having the body of a man but the beard, horns, ears, and legs of a goat, Pan frequented lonely rustic areas and inspired terrible fear in travelers who encountered him (hence the word *panic*). He was playfully lecherous and continually chased the nymphs. When he was pursuing the nymph Syrinx, he reached out to embrace her and she vanished, leaving in her place a bed of reeds. Pan fashioned these into a shepherd's pipe, or syrinx, which he often played.

Pan-American Games The Pan-American Games are the regional equivalent of the Olympic Games in the Western Hemisphere. The Games are held every four years, one year before the Olympics. The Games are open to amateur athletes of both sexes from the nations of North America, Central America, South America, and the Caribbean. Most of the Olympic events are included in the program. The Pan-American sports are archery, baseball, basketball, boxing, bowling, canoe/kayak, cycling, equestrian events, fencing, field hockey, gymnastics, judo, roller skating, rowing, shooting, soccer, softball, swimming and diving and synchronized swimming, table tennis, Tae kwon do, team handball, tennis, track and field, volleyball, water polo, weightlifting, wrestling, and yachting. The Pan-American Sports Organization, consisting of the Olympic committees of all participating countries, conducts the Games with the cooperation of the International Amateur Athletic Federation.

The Olympic committees of 16 nations met in 1940 to make plans for the first Pan-American athletic contests, to be held in 1942. World War II intervened, however, and the Games did not take place until 1951.

Pan American Highway The Pan American Highway is an international road system extending from the U.S.-Canadian border to Santiago, Chile. Its projected length is almost 26,000 km (16,000 mi). Still to be constructed is the segment between the Panama Canal and northern Colombia. Planned at the Fifth International Conference of American States in 1923, the highway was under construction by 1936. Mexico financed its own part of the network, but the Central American nations received financial assistance for construction from the United States.

Pan American Union see ORGANIZATION OF AMERICAN STATES

Pan-Slavism [pan-slahv'-izm] Pan-Slavism, a 19th-century political, religious, and cultural movement, attempted to unite the Slavs of Eastern Europe. Its first advocates were Slavs living within the Austrian and Ottoman empires, but, by the middle of the 19th century, Russian Slavophilism had taken control of the movement (see SLAVOPHILES AND WESTERNIZERS). Pan-Slavists believed that the Latin and Germanic cultures of the West were dying and must yield to the young and vigorous Slavic culture.

As German nationalism grew, Pan-Slavism became more political. In 1869, Nikolai Danilevsky wrote in *Russia and Europe* that the struggle for survival among the great civilizations required the unification of the Slavs under Russian hegemony—by force, if necessary. This implied threat led to the widely held but unsupported belief that the subsequent Balkan Wars and even Russian entry into World War I flowed from the Russian design to master all of eastern Europe.

Panama [pan'-uh-mah] The Republic of Panama occupies the Isthmus of Panama, the 725-km-long (450-mi) neck of land that joins North America to South America. It is bounded on the north by the Caribbean Sea and on the south by the Pacific Ocean. To the west lies Costa Rica and to the east, Colombia. The PANAMA CANAL has been the dominant factor in the life of this former Spanish colony since it became independent from Colombia in 1903. Treaties negotiated between the United States and Panama in 1977 provided for eventual Panamanian control of the canal and for the virtual abolition of the PANAMA CANAL ZONE. Concerns for the security of the canal contributed to a December 1989 invasion of Panama by U.S. forces that ousted Panamanian dictator Manuel NORIEGA.

Land and People

The dominant topographical feature of Panama is a low mountain chain, heavily forested and virtually uninhabited, that runs the length of the country. The highest point in the region is Baru Volcano (formerly called Chiriquí Volcano; 3,475 m/11,400 ft) near the western border. A wide belt of fertile volcanic soil along the Pacific side of the central highlands is the leading agricultural region of the country.

Panama has a tropical climate, with high humidity and heavy rainfall. The annual precipitation varies from an average of 1,753 mm (69 in) on the Pacific side of the isthmus to 2,489 mm (98 in) on the Atlantic side. Average temperatures in the lowland along the Pacific coast are about 27° C (81° F).

The Chagres River is the most important of Panama's many short rivers. By damming its waters, the engineers of the Panama Canal Commission were able to form Gatun Lake, the central feature of the Panama Canal. Most of the country is covered with dense tropical forest, and animal life includes anteaters, armadillos, tapir, small tigers, and monkeys.

Panama's population is classified at 62% *mestizo* (mixed), 14% black, 10% white, and the remainder Indian and others. The most significant racial and cultural division is between the mestizo population and the blacks from Jamaica and Barbados, who were brought into the country to help construct the Panama Canal. The blacks speak English rather than Spanish, the official language (although many Panamanians can speak English). About 85% of all Panamanians adhere to Roman Catholicism.

Approximately one-third of the country's population reside in the metropolitan area of PANAMA CITY, the capital and largest city. COLÓN is a major port and the Caribbean terminus of the Panama Canal.

AT A GLANCE

REPUBLIC OF PANAMA

Land: Area: 75,517 km² (29,157 mi²). Capital and largest city: Panama City (1990 est. pop., 411,549).

People: Population (1990 est.): 2,315,047. Density: 31 persons per km² (79 per mi²). Distribution (1988): 52% urban, 48% rural. Official language: Spanish. Major religion: Roman Catholicism.

Government: Type: republic. Legislature: Legislative Assembly. Political subdivisions: 9 provinces, 1 territory.

Economy: GNP (1989): $4.2 billion; $1,780 per capita. Labor distribution (1989): agriculture—30%; public administration, defense, and services—29%; trade—15%; manufacturing—10%; other—16%. Foreign trade (1989 est.): imports—$830 million; exports—$220 million. Currency: 1 balboa = 100 cents.

Education and Health: Literacy (1990): 90% of adult population. Universities (1990): 3. Hospital beds (1988): 7,776. Physicians (1988): 2,761. Life expectancy (1990): women—76; men—72. Infant mortality (1990): 22 per 1,000 live births.

Economic Activity

Since the completion of the Panama Canal in 1914, Panama's economy has been greatly influenced by this world transportation artery. The canal provides revenues and jobs; the dominant service industries, including an international finance and banking sector, function basically near the canal. Cash crops include bananas, sugarcane, and coffee. The main food crops are rice, corn, and beans. Cannabis is illegally produced for the world drug trade. Industry is limited.

Panama has one of the highest per capita foreign debts in the world. The economy outside the service sector, which was increasingly based on legal but shady ventures allowing foreign companies to circumvent the laws of other countries, had been in decline since 1978. By some estimates, the economy contracted by 40% from 1987 to 1989 due to the imposition of U.S. sanctions, corruption, and the virtual collapse of the banking system. Unemployment rose dramatically, the invasion itself caused further devastation, and the release of Panamanian assets frozen by the United States and additional U.S. aid were unlikely to solve the overwhelming economic problems. The government sought to rebuild through a revival of the private sector rather than public works projects.

Government

Prior to constitutional reforms in 1983, the government was controlled by Gen. Omar TORRIJOS HERRERA. The Panama Defense Force (restructured as the Public Force in 1990) exerted a strong (even controlling) role under Torrijos and later under Gen. Manuel Antonio Noriega, although the nation had a civilian government headed by a president. Noriega annulled the May 1989 elections and dissolved the national assembly, but constitutional government was restored later that year with U.S. intervention. The president is directly elected for a five-year term. Two elected vice-presidents and an appointed cabinet assist the president. Members of the unicameral Legislative Assembly are elected to five-year terms.

History

The first European known to have visited Panama was the Spaniard Rodrigo de Bastidas in 1501; in 1502, Christopher Columbus explored the eastern Panamanian coast on his fourth trip to the New World. In 1513, Vasco Núñez de BALBOA crossed the isthmus and saw the Pacific Ocean. Panama's early importance centered on its position as a transshipment route between Spain and its New World colonies. Panama was, as a result, one of Spain's wealthiest colonial centers during the 17th century.

Panama declared its independence from Spain in 1821 and joined Simón BOLÍVAR's Gran Colombia. The economy lagged until the late 19th century, when interest in transportation schemes across the isthmus developed. In the 1880s a French company headed by Ferdinand de LESSEPS began to excavate a canal across the isthmus but later sold the rights to the United States. U.S. president Theodore Roosevelt supported a Panamanian independence movement, hoping for more favorable treaty terms for canal construction. These efforts led to a Panamanian

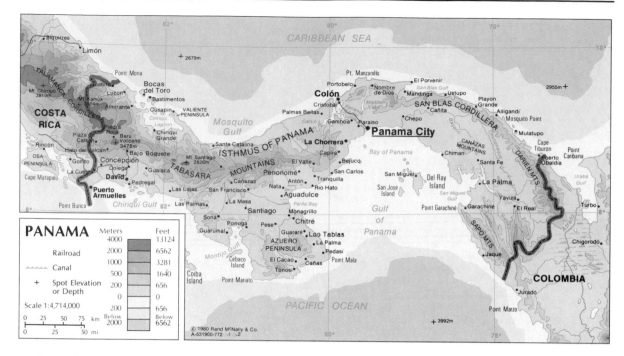

revolt and declaration of independence from Colombia on Nov. 3, 1903. The new government immediately concluded the Hay–Bunau-Varilla Treaty with the United States, creating the U.S.-controlled Panama Canal Zone.

Much subsequent Panamanian history was dominated by the issue of whether the republic would someday gain sovereign control over the Canal Zone. None of several U.S.-Panamanian–negotiated modifications of the 1903 treaty satisfied Panamanian desire for full control, and in 1977 an agreement was reached on two new treaties.

Gen. Torrijos, who negotiated the treaties, seized power in a 1968 military coup and was Panama's most powerful leader until his death in 1981. Aristides Royo, president from 1978 to 1982, was succeeded by Ricardo de la Espriella. Nicolás Ardito Barletta, president in 1984–85, was apparently forced out by Noriega. His successor, Eric Arturo Delvalle, was ousted in 1988 by Noriega, who then installed Manuel Solís Palma as president. The United States suspended aid and imposed economic sanctions in 1987 following anti-American demonstrations orchestrated by the government. Sanctions were intensified in 1988, after two U.S. courts indicted Noriega on drug charges, and again in 1989, after Noriega annulled elections held in May and installed Francisco Rodríguez as president. As anti-American incidents increased, U.S. forces invaded Panama on Dec. 20, 1989, and deposed Noriega. Guillermo ENDARA, generally viewed as the victor in the May election, was installed as president. He sought U.S. aid to rebuild the shattered economy.

Panama, Isthmus of [is'-muhs]   The Isthmus of Panama, coextensive with the Republic of Panama, is the narrow, 725-km-long (450-mi) neck of land connecting North and South America and separating the Atlantic and Pacific oceans. The first European to cross the isthmus was Vasco Núñez de Balboa in 1513. For several centuries travelers crossed on foot to avoid the long sea voyage around South America. The Panama Railroad was built in 1850–55. The Panama Canal was finished in 1914.

Panama Canal   The Panama Canal, an artificial waterway across the Isthmus of Panama in Central America, connects the Atlantic and the Pacific oceans. At the time of its opening it was universally acknowledged as the greatest engineering feat of the modern age, and it is still so regarded by many observers. The passage through this waterway shortens the trip from the Atlantic to the Pacific by 11,270 km (7,000 mi).

Description. The total length of the canal is 64 km (40 mi) from shoreline to shoreline and 82 km (51 mi) from deep water in the Caribbean to deep water in the Pacific. The maximum width is about 90 m (300 ft), and the minimum depth is 12 m (41 ft). The canal has six pairs of locks, with concrete chambers 305 m (1,000 ft) long and 34 m (110 ft) wide. Cristóbal is its Atlantic terminus, and Balboa, its Pacific.

On the Atlantic side, three flights of the Gatun Locks raise the water level to 26 m (85 ft) at Gatun Lake, which was created by damming the Chagres River. After traversing the Gatun Lake, the canal route crosses the Continental Divide in the 13-km-long (8-mi) Gaillard Cut (formerly the Culebra Cut). The Pedro Miguel Locks then bring the level of the canal to that of Miraflores Lake, 16 m (54 ft) high. Finally, two sets of Miraflores Locks lower the water to the level of the Pacific. The transit takes 7 to 8 hours.

The canal was a commercial success from the time of its opening, but it is unable to accommodate modern bulk tankers and supertankers. Plans to widen the Gaillard Cut have been discussed, and the Trans-Isthmus Pipeline, opened in 1982, transported 600,000 barrels of oil in 1988. That same year, the canal handled more than 12,000 ships and 156.9 billion metric tons (173 billion U.S. tons) of cargo.

History. The idea of an artificial waterway connecting the Atlantic and the Pacific dates from the early 16th century. In 1878 a French company headed by Ferdinand de LESSEPS won from Colombia (of which Panama was then a part) the concession for building a sea-level canal through the isthmus. Work began in 1881, but was hampered by malaria, yellow fever, and treacherous terrain. The company went bankrupt, and work ceased in 1887.

In 1902, after prolonged negotiations (in which Philippe BUNAU-VARILLA played a prominent role), the United States bought out the French interests and began talks with Colombia for the rights to build a canal. Because Colombia proved intransigent, the United States gave its tacit support to a rebellion in Panama. After the rebels declared Panama independent in 1903, President Theodore Roosevelt immediately recognized the new republic, within two weeks the Hay–Bunau-Varilla Treaty (see also HAY-PAUNCEFOTE TREATY) was signed. It called for the cre-

A freighter en route from the Pacific to the Atlantic Ocean enters the Pedro Miguel Locks of the Panama Canal. The canal, opened to commercial navigation in 1914, will come under full Panamanian control in the year 2000.

ation of the Panama Canal Zone under the complete control of the United States "in perpetuity." In return, the United States agreed to pay Panama $10 million and an annual rent (later increased) of $250,000.

Work on the canal began in 1904 and continued for ten years. The idea of a sea-level waterway was abandoned, and a lock canal was designed. Dr. William C. Gorgas succeeded in ridding the area of malaria and yellow fever. George Washington Goethals, appointed chief engineer in 1907 by President Roosevelt, is generally credited with the success of the project. As many as 40,000 workers at one time were employed at the site. The cost was $336,650,000.

Panama Canal Accords of 1978 and Later Developments. Despite the liberalization of the Hay–Bunau-Varilla Treaty over the years, the U.S. presence was regarded by Panama as imperialistic. Negotiations for a new treaty began in the 1950s. The Panama Canal Neutrality Treaty (which guaranteed the canal's neutrality after the year 2000) and the Panama Canal Treaty (which stipulated that the United States would operate the canal, with increasing Panamanian participation, until Panama assumed legal control in 2000) were approved by Panamanian voters in 1977 and ratified by the U.S. Senate in 1978. The U.S.-Panamanian Panama Canal Commission took over operation of the canal in October 1979. By 1990, when a Panamanian became head of the commission, more than 80% of the canal's employees were Panamanian.

Panama Canal Zone The Panama Canal Zone, until 1979 a U.S. government reservation, was a 1,678-km^2 (648-mi^2) area that ran through the middle of the Republic of Panama from the Atlantic to the Pacific Ocean. It extended for 8 km (5 mi) on each side of the Panama Canal. Approximately 25% of the zone's territory consisted

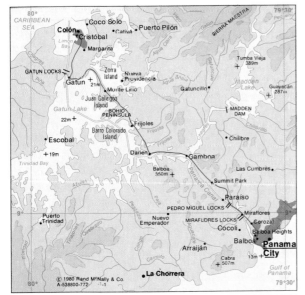

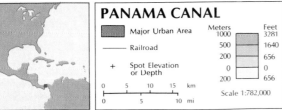

PANAMA CANAL

Major Urban Area
Railroad
+ Spot Elevation or Depth

Meters	Feet
1000	3281
500	1640
200	656
0	0
200	656

0 5 10 15 km
0 5 10 mi

Scale 1:782,000

of the Gatun Lake, formed during the construction of the Panama Canal in 1912. The zone was divided into townsites; the two largest were Balboa on the Pacific side and Rainbow City on the Atlantic.

The zone came into existence with the ratification of the Hay–Bunau-Varilla Treaty in 1903, which granted the United States powers "as if it were sovereign" within its boundaries forever. A governor appointed by the U.S. president administered the zone; he was also the ex-officio president of the Panama Canal Company, a corporate U.S. agency responsible for the day-to-day operation of the Panama Canal.

In 1977, U.S. president Jimmy CARTER and Panamanian general Omar TORRIJOS HERRERA negotiated two treaties calling for full Panamanian sovereignty within the zone and Panamanian control over the canal itself by the year 2000, with guarantees of the canal's neutrality. In 1979, when the treaties came into effect, the zone itself was abolished. The United States returned about 60% of the former zone to Panamanian jurisdiction, including the ports, 11 of 14 military bases, and the Panama City–Colón railway.

Panama City

Panama City (1990 est. pop., 411,549), the capital and chief industrial, financial, and cultural center of the Republic of Panama, is located alongside the Pacific terminus of the Panama Canal. The PAN AMERICAN HIGHWAY goes through the city, which is also the Pacific terminus of the Panama Railroad and the Trans-isthmian Highway. Industries manufacture clothing, furniture, food products, shoes, cement, and beer. Notable landmarks are the 17th-century Church of San José and the cathedral (completed in 1760). The University of Panama (1935) and the Santa María University (1965) are there.

Panama City, founded by the Spanish in 1519, was an important base for Spain's conquest of the Pacific coastal areas of South America. The English privateer Henry Morgan completely destroyed it in 1671, but the city was quickly rebuilt. After a decline in the 18th and early 19th centuries, Panama City was revitalized by the opening of the Panama Railroad in 1855. It became the national capital when Panama seceded from Colombia in 1903 and a leading transportation center after the Panama Canal opened in 1914.

pancreas

[pan'-kree-uhs]   A long, thin organ in humans, the pancreas has both digestive and endocrine functions and for this reason contains two completely different types of cells. Measuring about 12–15 cm (5–6 in) long, it is nestled within the curve of the duodenum and stretches transversely across the posterior abdomen behind the stomach, in front of the spine and aorta.

The digestive, or exocrine, cells of the pancreas consist of a number of small lobules, or acinar cells, joined together into small ducts that, in turn, join the two major ducts of Santorini and Wirsung, which empty through small muscular openings into the duodenum. The lobules

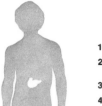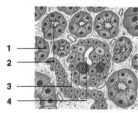

The pancreas is found in the lower abdomen, behind the stomach. Its exocrine tissue consists of lobules that contain alveoli (1), or acini (shown in cross section). The alveoli secrete digestive enzymes into ducts (2) that lead into the main pancreatic duct opening into the duodenum. Scattered through the tissue are the so-called islets of Langerhans (3), which secrete hormones into the bloodstream through capillaries (4). They contain alpha cells (stained orange or red), the source of glucagon, and beta cells, the source of insulin.

contain numerous cells that secrete pancreatic secretions containing electrolytes and three important digestive enzymes, trypsin, amylase, and lipase. These enzymes digest proteins, split fat, break down highly polymerized nucleic acids, and break down polysaccharides such as starch, amylopectin, and glycogen. The protein-splitting enzyme trypsin becomes active only when the duodenal enzyme enterokinase is mixed with it, or in the presence of diseases such as pancreatitis or cancer. In a similar manner the activity of the other enzymes is enhanced by the admixture of intestinal secretions and bile.

The endocrine function of the pancreas is to release hormones secreted by small groups of cells called the islets of Langerhans into the blood. The hormone secretin controls the amount of fluid secretion. The hormones pancreozymin and gastrin, as well as the vagus nerve, control the amount of enzymes secreted. The islets of Langerhans secrete two hormones that regulate carbohydrate metabolism. Insulin causes a decrease in blood suger; glucagon increases blood sugar. Other hormones control intestinal motility or interact with the thyroid, adrenal, or pituitary glands. In the absence of these islet cells a person develops DIABETES mellitus.

pancreatitis

[pan-kree-uh-ty'-tis]   Pancreatitis is an acute or chronic inflammation of the pancreas. In an acute attack, inflammation is brought on when the activated digestive enzymes of the pancreas escape into the organ's tissues instead of entering the intestine. This leads to autodigestion of pancreatic tissues. The initial inflammation results in EDEMA and, if severe, to localized tissue death. Symptoms of the onset of acute pancreatitis include abdominal pain, repeated vomiting, and, if the attack is severe, signs of shock. Other complications include respiratory insufficiency and abscesses. Acute attacks are usually due to gallstones or alcohol abuse. Treatment includes prevention of pancreatic stimulation and support of vital functions.

Chronic pancreatitis is a long-term inflammation, most commonly due to alcoholism. Its main feature is upper abdominal and back pain. Progressive injury may result in loss of pancreatic digestive fluid, with failure of digestion, weight loss, and loss of insulin production, leading to DI-ABETES mellitus. Other complications include cystic collections of pancreatic secretions and obstruction of the bile ducts. Surgical relief may be required.

panda   Pandas comprise two species of mammals, each the sole member of its genus. The giant panda, *Ailuropoda melanoleuca*, is commonly classified as a bear, family Ursidae; the lesser, or red, panda, *Ailurus fulgens*, is usually placed with the raccoons, family Procyonidae.

The giant panda, a rare and closely protected animal, lives in the cool, damp bamboo forests of mountainous central China, generally at elevations of 1,500 to 4,000 m (5,000 to 13,000 ft). Its thick, woolly coat is black or brownish black and yellowish white; the darker color forms patches around the eyes, covers the ears, legs, and chest, and forms a band across the shoulders. Giant pandas grow to 1.5 m (5 ft) long, plus a short tail, and weigh 150 kg (330 lb) or more. Bamboo constitutes most of their diet. One or two young are born.

The lesser panda is found in the forested mountains of western China at elevations of 1,800 to 4,000 m (6,000 to 13,000 ft). Its dense, woolly coat of reddish brown has lighter-colored bands on the tail and dark red brown to black undersides. The face is white, with a reddish brown stripe on each cheek. The animal grows to 112 cm (44 in) long, including a 48-cm (19-in) tail, and weighs up to 5 kg (11 lb).

The panda population has declined sharply in the last decade, due to human encroachment of the pandas' natural habitats in bamboo thickets. Pandas are being forced to move into isolated communities, resulting in inbreeding and a loss of food. The Chinese government has established 12 panda reserves with new breeding centers in an attempt to prevent the panda's extinction. Breeding of pandas in captivity has had limited success, however, because their sexual habits are poorly understood.

Pandora [pan-dohr'-uh]   In Greek mythology Pandora (meaning "all gifted") was the first woman on Earth. The gods bestowed on her such gifts as beauty and charm but also gave her great curiosity. Zeus, seeking to punish man for accepting the gift of fire that Prometheus stole from heaven, gave Pandora a box containing all the troubles and diseases that the world now knows. She was warned not to open the box, but her curiosity overcame her. Only Hope remained in the box as she quickly closed the lid again.

Pangea   see CONTINENTAL DRIFT; PALEOGEOGRAPHY

pangolin [pang-goh'-lin]   The pangolins, or scaly anteaters, constitute the mammmalian order Pholidota, which contains a single living family, Manidae, with a single genus, *Manis*. There are seven species: four in tropical Africa and three in the region of southern Asia. Their large, overlapping scales, dark brown to yellowish, are flattened and horny elevations of the skin. Pangolins range in size from the Chinese pangolin, *M. pentadactyla*, which may be only 71 cm (28 in) long, including a 25-

The giant panda is a rare, bearlike animal of central China. Its survival is threatened by the flowering-and-dying phase in the century-long life cycle of its principal food—bamboo.

The small-scaled tree pangolin, a scaly mammal of Africa, hangs upside down from a tree branch by its strong, flexible tail. The long tongue of the pangolin is controlled by a complicated musculature that is anchored to an elongated breastbone, which extends back to the pelvic region. The name pangolin is from a Malay word for "round cushion" and refers to the animal's defense of curling up into an armored ball.

cm (10-in) tail, to the giant pangolin, *M. gigantea*, which may be 1.5 m (5 ft) long, including a 65-cm (26-in) tail.

Pangolins are toothless, but their tongues, used to lick up their food of ants or termites, may be as much as 25 cm (10 in) in length. The tongue can be withdrawn into a movable sheath and pulled into the chest cavity.

___

panic, financial　A financial panic occurs when there is widespread public fear that banks and other monetary institutions are in imminent danger of collapse. It is usually preceded by a period of feverish speculation in securities markets in which prices are driven to unsupportably high levels. When the speculative bubble bursts, prices fall drastically and investors scramble for liquidity (to convert their holdings to cash). Banks, whose loans are based on fractional reserves, are then placed in a precarious position that can lead to failure. The effect can be cumulative as defaulted obligations wipe out the value of assets on which they are based.

A frequent aftermath of the financial panic, which refers only to the last stage of a financial debacle, is the decline in real output that ensues as business firms, banks, and consumers attempt to retrench. Loans are made with greater caution, spending declines, unemployment increases, and general economic depression follows. The DEPRESSION OF THE 1930s was preceded by the great panic of 1929.

The history of financial panics, however, is complex. In many earlier periods, their effect was largely limited to the financial sector without serious consequences in consumer or capital-goods industries. Noted historical panics include the Mississippi Bubble (see MISSISSIPPI SCHEME) of 1720 in France, the SOUTH SEA BUBBLE of 1720 in England, and in the United States, the panics of 1819, 1837, 1857, 1869 (BLACK FRIDAY), 1873, 1893, and 1907. The strong U.S. Federal Reserve System and post-1929 legislation establishing the Securities and Exchange Commission, federal deposit insurance, Social Security insurance, and unemployment insurance now function to prevent overall economic breakdown following a panic. Limits on computerized trading and other reforms were instituted in financial markets after the plunge in stock prices of Oct. 19, 1987.

___

Pankhurst (family)　The Pankhurst family led the fight to achieve women's suffrage in Britain (see SUFFRAGE, WOMEN'S). In 1903, **Emmeline Goulden Pankhurst**, b. July 4, 1858, d. June 14, 1928, founded the Women's Social and Political Union (WSPU) to agitate for voting rights for women. She was joined in the movement by two daughters: **Christabel Harriette Pankhurst**, b. Sept. 22, 1880, d. Feb. 13, 1958, who became organizing secretary of the WSPU; and **Estelle Sylvia Pankhurst**, b. 1882, d. Sept. 27, 1960. The WSPU adopted increasingly militant tactics to draw attention to its cause, and its members—including the Pankhursts—were frequently arrested.

When World War I started (1914), the Pankhursts called a halt to their suffrage campaign, and Emmeline and Christabel turned to war work. After the war they went separate ways: Emmeline died while running for Parliament as a Conservative, a few weeks after the passage of the law that gave women full voting rights; Sylvia became a radical socialist and championed Ethiopian independence; and Christabel became an evangelist in the United States.

Panofsky, Erwin [pan-awf'-skee]　The art historian Erwin Panofsky, b. Hanover, Germany, Mar. 30, 1892, d. Mar. 15, 1968, is best remembered for his studies of the ways in which images and themes acquire symbolic meaning in works of art—a field known as iconology. He taught at the Institute of Fine Arts, New York University, and, beginning in 1935, at the Institute for Advanced Studies, Princeton, N.J., becoming one of the dominant figures in his field. In his early writings he concentrated on Italian Renaissance art; in later years he turned his attention more to Netherlandish and German painting of the 15th and 16th centuries. Among Panofsky's major works are *Studies in Iconology* (1939; 2d ed. 1962), *Early Netherlandish Painting* (1953), *The Life and Art of Albrecht Dürer* (1955), *Renaissance and Renascences in Western Art* (1960), and *Idea: A Concept in Art Theory* (Eng. trans., 1968).

___

panpipes　Panpipes consist of a set of tubes (usually seven), graduated in size and blown from the top. They

Panpipes, a series of graduated pipes bound together, have been made of such diverse materials as stone and plastic, with wooden pipes such as these perhaps the most common. Originating in China, they are popular throughout the world. Panpipes are played in a vertical position, as shown.

were called *syrinx* by the ancient Greeks, after the nymph beloved of Pan. Built of various materials, the tubes are often made to look like reeds. Their best-known use is in Mozart's opera *The Magic Flute*, and they occasionally are used as a toy. More complex forms of the pipes are found in China, Romania, South America, and Southeast Asia, where they are widely used.

pansy   The garden pansy, a short-lived perennial, *Viola tricolor* (also classified as *V. wittrockiana*), is a member of the violet family, Violaceae. It is considered a descendant of the European wild pansy, *V. tricolor*, crossed with one or more other species of violets. The European wild pansy now also grows wild in North America, where it is known as the field pansy or Johnny-jump-up. The garden pansy grows to 23 cm (9 in) tall and bears rounded, flattened, five-petaled, velvety flowers of various colors and up to 13 cm (5 in) across. A number of species in the genus *Achimenes*, in the gesneria family, Gesneriaceae, are called orchid pansies, Japanese pansies, or monkey-faced pansies.

The garden pansy is a hybrid of the wild pansy and one or more European violets. The flowers have five velvety, overlapping petals; color varieties include violet, blue, purple, red, yellow, rose, and white. Other names for the pansy include heartsease and love-in-idleness.

pantheism   Pantheism is the belief that everything is divine, that God is not separate from but totally identified with the world, and that God does not possess personality or transcendence.

Pantheism generally can be traced to two sources. The first is the Vedic tradition (see HINDUISM), which begins with the belief that the divine principle from which everything arises is a unity and that the perception of multiplicity is illusory and unreal. In the Vedanta, Brahman (see BRAHMA AND BRAHMAN) is the infinite reality behind the illusory and imperfect world of perception. The

knowledge of humans is imperfect because they experience subject and object as distinct.

In the Western tradition the cosmology of the Stoics and, more importantly, the emanationist hierarchy of NEO-PLATONISM tend toward pantheism. In Judeo-Christian thought the emphasis on the transcendence of God inhibits pantheism. The most important modern version of pantheism is that of Baruch SPINOZA. For him nature is infinite, but because the only being capable of genuine infinity is God, God must be identical, in essence, with nature.

Pantheon [pan'-thee-ahn]   Built in Rome, AD *c.*118–28, in the reign of Emperor Hadrian, the Pantheon is the best preserved and most impressive of all Roman buildings. The Pantheon asserts the primacy of space as contained volume over structure; it has exerted an enormous influence on all subsequent Western architecture.

The Pantheon was designed and built by Hadrian. The existing structure is an immense round temple covered by a single dome, fronted by a transitional block and a traditional temple portico. The temple is deceptively simple in appearance, consisting of a circular drum carrying a hemispherical dome with an inside diameter of 43.2 m (142 ft). The proportions are such that, if extended to the floor, the curve of the inner surface of the dome would just "kiss" the

The Pantheon, surmounted by a perfectly hemispheric dome, was built (AD c.118–28) by the Emperor Hadrian in Rome. The conventional portico has granite columns (1) with white marble Corinthian capitals. The intermediate block (2) leads to the rotunda (3). The main exedra (4), of which there are seven, has a semidome. The floor (5) is made of granite, porphyry, and marble. The attic (6), faced with paneling and pilasters, has decorated rectangular coffers (7) rising above it. The central oculus (8) is the only source of light.

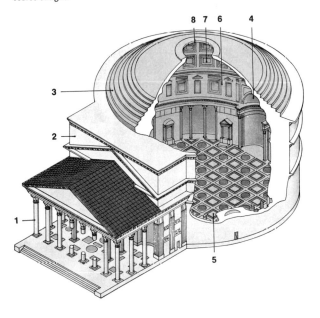

floor; thus, a perfect sphere is contained, a symbolic reference to the temple's dedication to all the gods—*pan* ("all") plus *theos* ("god")—in the sphere of the heavens.

The visually compressive effect of the dome on the inside is lessened by deep coffers (indentations) radiating down from the central oculus ("eye")—9.1 m (30 ft) in diameter—the only window in the building. The Pantheon was converted into a church dedicated to Mary (Santa Maria Rotunda) in 609, and therefore it escaped destruction.

panther   see CAT; LEOPARD

pantomime   see MIME AND PANTOMIME

Paoli, Pasquale [pah'-oh-lee]   The Corsican patriot Pasquale Paoli, b. Apr. 26, 1725, d. Feb. 5, 1807, led Corsica's movement for independence from Genoa from 1755. While waging an effective war, first against Genoa, then against France, he also introduced liberal reforms. In 1768, Genoa sold Corsica to France, and Paoli fled (1769) to England. The French revolutionaries made him governor of Corsica in 1790. Opposing Jacobin extremism he broke with France in 1793 and accepted British sovereignty over Corsica the next year. Disappointed at not receiving office, Paoli retired (1795) to England.

Pap test [pap]   The Pap test is a procedure used to detect the most common type of cervical CANCER, which occurs in the squamous cells of the cervix. The test is named for a Greek doctor, George N. Papanicolau, who first described the concept in 1928, although the Pap test did not become a standard procedure until the 1940s. The test involves scraping cells from the cervix and the vaginal wall, staining them, and examining them under a microscope.

Professional opinion has varied as to how often Pap tests should be given. In 1987 the American Cancer Society recommended yearly tests and pelvic examinations for all women once they have reached 18 years of age, and for younger women also if sexually active. If three tests in a row prove normal, the interval between tests may be increased to two years or so, at the physician's discretion. Tests for PAPILLOMA virus are now being used as adjuncts to Pap tests.

papacy [pay'-puh-see]   The papacy denotes the office of the pope, or bishop of Rome, and the system of central ecclesiastical government of the ROMAN CATHOLIC CHURCH over which he presides. Believed by Roman Catholics to be the successor of the apostle PETER, the pope grounds his claim to jurisdictional primacy in the church in the so-called Petrine theory. According to that theory, affirmed by the Council of Florence in 1439, defined as a matter of faith by the First VATICAN COUNCIL in 1870, and endorsed by the Second VATICAN COUNCIL in 1964, Jesus Christ conferred the position of primacy in the church upon Peter alone. In solemnly defining the Petrine prima-

This 13th-century bronze statue of Saint Peter, sculpted by Arnolfo di Cambio, stands in the main nave of Saint Peter's Basilica in the Vatican. Saint Peter holds the keys to the Kingdom of Heaven, the traditional symbol of papal authority.

cy, the First Vatican Council cited the three classical New Testament texts long associated with it: John 1:42, John 21:15 ff., and, above all, Matthew 16:18 ff. The council understood these texts, along with Luke 22:32, to signify that Christ himself constituted Saint Peter as prince of the apostles and visible head of the church, possessed of a primacy of jurisdiction that was to pass down in perpetuity to his papal successors.

Although the pope's priestly powers as bishop come from the sacramental act of ordination, the pope derives his papal authority from an act of election, which since 1179 has been the right of the Sacred College of Cardinals (see CARDINALS, COLLEGE OF). It is by virtue of their decision that each new pope inherits his official titles, ancient and modern, secular and sacred: bishop of Rome, vicar of Jesus Christ, successor of the prince of the apostles, supreme pontiff of the universal church, patriarch of the West, primate of Italy, archbishop and metropolitan of the Roman province, sovereign of the state of VATICAN CITY, servant of the servants of God.

The Early Papacy. By the 3d century the Roman bishops were representing themselves as having succeeded to the primacy that Peter had enjoyed among the apostles and as wielding within the universal church a primacy of authority in doctrinal matters. During the 4th and 5th centuries, after the Roman emperor CONSTANTINE's grant of toleration to Christianity (the Edict of Milan, 313) and its rise to the status of an official religion, a series of popes, most notably LEO I (r. 440–61), translated that claim into a primacy of jurisdiction over the church. That claim was matched, however, by the rival claim of the church at Constantinople to a jurisdictional primacy in the East equal to that of Rome in the West. In fact, for at least another century, it was the Byzantine emperor of Constantinople who could actually claim to be functioning as the supreme leader of Christendom in spiritual as well as temporal matters.

The Medieval Papacy. From the 6th to the 16th century the papacy rose to a position of unique prominence within the Christian community in three broad phases. The first, extending from the late 6th to the late 8th century, was marked by the turning of the papacy to the West and its escape from subordination to the authority of the Byzantine emperors of Constantinople. GREGORY I (r.590–604) was forced to confront the collapse of imperial authority in northern Italy. As the leading civilian official of the empire in Rome, it fell to him to undertake the civil administration of the city and its environs and to negotiate for its protection with the Lombard invaders threatening it. In the 8th century, after the rise of Islam had weakened the Byzantine Empire and the Lombards had renewed their pressure in Italy, the popes finally sought support from the Frankish rulers of the West and received (754) from the Frankish king PEPIN THE SHORT the Italian territory later known as the PAPAL STATES. With the crowning (800) by LEO III of CHARLEMAGNE, first of the Carolingian emperors, the papacy also gained his protection.

By the late 9th century, however, the Carolingian empire had disintegrated and the bishopric of Rome had fallen under the domination of the nobles. Once again the papacy sought aid from the north, and in 962, Pope John XII crowned as emperor the German king OTTO I. In this revived empire, soon called the HOLY ROMAN EMPIRE, the pope theoretically was the spiritual head, and the emperor the temporal head. The relationship between temporal and spiritual authority, however, was to be a continuing arena of contention.

The second great phase in the process of the papacy's rise to prominence extended from the mid-11th to the mid-13th century. It was distinguished, first, by GREGORY VII's bold attack after 1075 on the traditional practices whereby the emperor had controlled appointments to the higher church offices, an attack that spawned the protracted civil and ecclesiastical strife in Germany and Italy known as the INVESTITURE CONTROVERSY. It was distinguished, second, by URBAN II's launching in 1095 of the CRUSADES, which, in an attempt to liberate the Holy Land

This miniature by Jean Fouquet portrays the coronation of the Frankish ruler Charlemagne by Pope Leo III in 800. The event marked the beginning of a long and often strained relationship between papacy and empire.

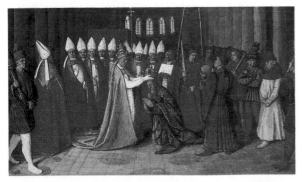

Pope Alexander III received the submission of Holy Roman Emperor Frederick I (Barbarossa) after the emperor's defeat (1176) at Legnano. This short-lived papal triumph was part of a prolonged struggle between popes and emperors during the Middle Ages.

from Muslim domination, marshaled under papal leadership the aggressive energies of the European nobility. Both these efforts, although ultimately unsuccessful, greatly enhanced papal prestige in the 12th and 13th centuries. Such powerful popes as ALEXANDER III (r. 1159–81), INNOCENT III (r. 1198–1216), GREGORY IX (r. 1227–41), and INNOCENT IV (r. 1243–54) wielded a primacy over the church that attempted to vindicate a jurisdictional supremacy over emperors and kings in temporal and spiritual affairs.

This last attempt proved to be abortive. If Innocent IV triumphed over Holy Roman Emperor FREDERICK II, a mere half-century later BONIFACE VIII (r. 1294–1303) fell victim to the hostility of the French king PHILIP IV. In 1309, Pope CLEMENT V left Rome and took up residence in Avignon, the beginning of the so-called Babylonian Captivity (1309–78), during which all the popes were French, lived in Avignon, and were subject to French influence, until GREGORY XI returned the papacy to Rome. During the 13th and 14th centuries, therefore, papal authority over the universal church was exercised increasingly at the sufferance of national rulers and local princes of Europe. This fact became dismally clear during the Great Schism of the West (1378–1418; see SCHISM, GREAT), when two, and later three, rival claimants disputed for the papal office, dividing the church into rival "obediences"; in their desperate attempts to win support, the claimants opened the way to the exploitation of ecclesiastical resources for dynastic and political ends. The years of schism, then, and the related efforts of the general councils of Constance and BASEL to limit the papal authority (see CONCILIARISM), saw the onset of the process whereby the papacy was reduced to the status of an Italian principality. Its supreme authority over the universal church had come to

POPES

Name	Reign Dates
Peter	d. 64 or 67
Linus	67?–76?
Anacletus I	76?–88?
Clement I	88?–97?
Evaristus	97?–105?
Alexander I	105?–15?
Sixtus I	115?–25?
Telesphorus	125?–36?
Hyginus	136?–40?
Pius I	140?–55?
Anicetus	155?–66?
Soter	166?–75?
Eleuterus	175?–89
Victor I	189–99
Zephyrinus	199–217
Callistus I	217–22
Urban I	222–30
Hippolytus (antipope)	???–35
Pontian	230–35
Anterus	235–36
Fabian	236–50
Cornelius	251–53
Novatian (antipope)	251–58?
Lucius I	253–54
Stephen I	254–57
Sixtus II	257–58
Dionysius	260–68
Felix I	269–74
Eutychian	275–83
Caius	283–96
Marcellinus	296–304
Marcellus I	308–09
Eusebius	309–10
Miltiades	311–14
Sylvester I	314–35
Marcus	335–36
Julius I	337–52
Liberius	352–66
Felix II (antipope)	353–65
Damasus I	366–83
Ursinus (antipope)	366–67
Siricius	384–99
Anastasius I	399–401
Innocent I	401–17
Zosimus	417–18
Boniface I	418–22
Eulalius (antipope)	418–19
Celestine I	422–32
Sixtus III	432–40
Leo I	440–61
Hilarius	461–68
Simplicius	468–83
Felix III	483–92
Gelasius I	492–96
Anastasius II	496–98
Symmachus	498–514
Laurentius (antipope)	498–505
Hormisdas	514–23
John I	523–26
Felix IV	526–30
Boniface II	530–32
Dioscurus (antipope)	530
John II	533–35
Agapetus I	535–36
Silverius	536–37
Vigilius	537–55
Pelagius I	556–61
John III	561–74
Benedict I	575–79
Pelagius II	579–90
Gregory I	590–604
Sabinian	604–606
Boniface III	607
Boniface IV	608–15
Deusdedit	615–18
Boniface V	619–25
Honorius I	625–38
Severinus	640
John IV	640–42
Theodore I	642–49
Martin I	649–55
Eugene I	655–57
Vitalian	657–72
Adeodatus	672–76
Donus	676–78
Agatho	678–81
Leo II	681–83
Benedict II	684–85
John V	685–86
Conon	686–87
Theodore II (antipope)	687
Paschal I (antipope)	687–92
Sergius I	687–701
John VI	701–05
John VII	705–07
Sisinnius	708
Constantine	708–15
Gregory II	715–31
Gregory III	731–41
Zacharias	741–52
Stephen II	752–57
Paul I	757–67
Constantine (antipope)	767
Philip (antipope)	767
Stephen III	767–72
Adrian I	772–95
Leo III	795–816
Stephen IV	816–17
Paschal I	817–24
Eugene II	824–27
Valentine	827
Gregory IV	827–44
John VIII (antipope)	844
Sergius II	844–47
Leo IV	847–55
Benedict III	855–58
Anastasius III (antipope)	855
Nicholas I	858–67
Adrian II	867–72
John VIII	872–82
Marinus I	882–84
Adrian III	884–85
Stephen V	885–91
Formosus	891–96
Boniface VI	896
Stephen VI	896–97
Romanus	897
Theodore II	897
John IX	898–900
Benedict IV	900–03
Leo V	903
Christopher	903–04
Sergius III	904–11
Anastasius III	911–13
Lando	913–14
John X	914–28
Leo VI	928–29
Stephen VII	929–31
John XI	931–35
Leo VII	936–39
Stephen IX (VIII)	939–42
Marinus II	942–46
Agapetus II	946–55
John XII	955–63
Leo VIII	963–64
Benedict V	964
John XIII	965–72
Benedict VI	973–74
Benedict VII	974–83
John XIV	983–84
Boniface VII	984–85
John XV	985–96
Gregory V	996–99
John XVI (antipope)	996–98
Sylvester II	999–1003
John XVII	1003
John XVIII	1003–09
Sergius IV	1009–12
Benedict VIII	1012–24
Gregory VI (antipope)	1012
John XIX	1024–33
Benedict IX	1033–45
Sylvester III	1045
Gregory VI	1045–46
Clement II	1046–47
Damasus II	1048
Leo IX	1049–54
Victor II	1055–57
Stephen IX	1057–58
Benedict X	1058
Nicholas II	1058–61
Alexander II	1061–73
Honorius II (antipope)	1061–64
Gregory VII	1073–85
Clement III (antipope)	1080–1100
Victor III	1086–87
Urban II	1088–99
Paschal II	1099–1118
Theodoric (antipope)	1100–02
Albert (antipope)	1102
Sylvester IV (antipope)	1105
Gelasius II	1118–19
Gregory VIII (antipope)	1118–21
Callistus II	1119–24
Honorius II	1124–30
Celestine II (antipope)	1124
Innocent II	1130–43
Anacletus II (antipope)	1130–38
Victor IV (antipope)	1138
Celestine II	1143–44
Lucius II	1144–45
Eugene III	1145–53
Anastasius IV	1153–54
Adrian IV	1154–59
Alexander III	1159–81
Victor IV (antipope)	1159–64
Paschal III (antipope)	1164–68
Callistus III (antipope)	1168–78
Innocent III (antipope)	1179–80
Lucius III	1181–85
Urban III	1185–87
Gregory VIII	1187
Clement III	1187–91
Celestine III	1191–98
Innocent III	1198–1216
Honorius III	1216–27
Gregory IX	1227–41
Celestine IV	1241
Innocent IV	1243–54
Alexander IV	1254–61
Urban IV	1261–64
Clement IV	1265–68
Gregory X	1271–76
Innocent V	1276
Adrian V	1276
John XXI	1276–77
Nicholas III	1277–80
Martin IV	1281–85
Honorius IV	1285–87
Nicholas IV	1288–92
Celestine V	1294
Boniface VIII	1294–1303
Benedict XI	1303–04
Clement V	1305–14
John XXII	1316–34
Nicholas V (antipope)	1328–30
Benedict XII	1334–42
Clement VI	1342–52
Innocent VI	1352–62
Urban V	1362–70
Gregory XI	1370–78
Great Schism	
Urban VI (Roman line)	1378–89
Clement VII (Avignon line)	1378–94
Boniface IX (Roman line)	1389–1404
Benedict XIII (Avignon line)	1394–1423
Innocent VII (Roman line)	1404–06
Gregory XII (Roman line)	1406–15
Alexander V (Pisan line)	1409–10
John XXIII (Pisan line)	1410–15
End of Schism	
Martin V	1417–31
Eugene IV	1431–47
Felix V (antipope)	1439–49
Nicholas V	1447–55
Callistus III	1455–58
Pius II	1458–64
Paul II	1464–71
Sixtus IV	1471–84
Innocent VIII	1484–92
Alexander VI	1492–1503
Pius III	1503
Julius II	1503–13
Leo X	1513–21
Adrian VI	1522–23
Clement VII	1523–34
Paul III	1534–49
Julius III	1550–55
Marcellus II	1555
Paul IV	1555–59
Pius IV	1559–65
Pius V	1566–72
Gregory XIII	1572–85
Sixtus V	1585–90
Urban VII	1590
Gregory XIV	1590–91
Innocent IX	1591
Clement VIII	1592–1605
Leo XI	1605
Paul V	1605–21
Gregory XV	1621–23
Urban VIII	1623–44
Innocent X	1644–55
Alexander VII	1655–67
Clement IX	1667–69
Clement X	1670–76
Innocent XI	1676–89
Alexander VIII	1689–91
Innocent XII	1691–1700
Clement XI	1700–21
Innocent XIII	1721–24
Benedict XIII	1724–30

POPES

Name	Reign Dates	Name	Reign Dates	Name	Reign Dates	Name	Reign Dates
Clement XII	1730–40	Pius VII	1800–23	Leo XIII	1878–1903	John XXIII	1958–63
Benedict XIV	1740–58	Leo XII	1823–29	Pius X	1903–14	Paul VI	1963–78
Clement XIII	1758–69	Pius VIII	1829–30	Benedict XV	1914–22	John Paul I	1978
Clement XIV	1769–74	Gregory XVI	1831–46	Pius XI	1922–39	John Paul II	1978–
Pius VI	1775–99	Pius IX	1846–78	Pius XII	1939–58		

be no more than theoretical, the power over the national and territorial churches having passed to kings, princes, and rulers of such city-states as Venice.

The Papacy in the Age of Reformation. The seeming inability of Leo X (r. 1513–21) and those popes who succeeded him to comprehend the significance of the threat posed by Martin Luther—or, indeed, the alienation of many Christians by the corruption that had spread throughout the church—was a major factor in the rapid growth of the Protestant Reformation. By the time the need for a vigorous, reforming papal leadership was recognized, much of northern Europe was lost to Catholicism.

Not until the election (1534) of Paul III, who placed the papacy itself at the head of a movement for church-wide reform, did the Counter-Reformation begin. Paul established a reform commission; appointed several leading reformers to the College of Cardinals; initiated reform of the central administrative apparatus at Rome; authorized the founding of the Jesuits, the order that was later to prove so loyal to the papacy; and convoked the Council of Trent, which met intermittently from 1545 to 1563. The council succeeded in initiating a far-ranging moral and administrative reform, including the reform of the papacy itself, that was destined to define the shape and set the tone of Roman Catholicism into the mid-20th century. The 16th century also saw the development of foreign missions, which were encouraged by the popes and enhanced their prestige.

The Papacy in the 18th and 19th Centuries. Their diplomatic skills notwithstanding, the 17th- and 18th-century popes proved unable to reverse the long-established trend toward increasing royal control of national clergies and increasing autonomy of the national and local doctrines. National doctrines of French, German, and Austrian provenance (known respectively as Gallicanism, Febronianism, and Josephism, and all of them in some measure promoting the limitation of papal prerogatives) helped reduce these popes progressively to a state of political impotence.

After the Napoleonic Wars the Congress of Vienna (1815) restored the Papal States, but they were forcibly annexed to the new Kingdom of Italy in 1870, and not until 1929 with the Lateran Treaty was the "Roman Question"—the problem of nonnational status for the pope—solved. The treaty, which created in the heart of Rome a tiny, sovereign Vatican state, restored to the papacy a measure of temporal independence but left it with political influence rather than actual political power.

Paradoxically, the eclipse of papal temporal power during the 19th century was accompanied by a recovery of papal prestige. The monarchist reaction in the wake of the French Revolution and the later emergence of constitutional governments served alike, though in different ways, to sponsor that development. The reinstated monarchs of Catholic Europe saw in the papacy a conservative ally rather than a jurisdictional rival. Later, when the institution of constitutional governments broke the ties binding the clergy to the policies of royal regimes, Catholics were freed to respond to the renewed spiritual authority of the pope.

The popes of the 19th and 20th centuries have come to exercise that authority with increasing vigor and in every aspect of religious life. By the crucial pontificate of Pius IX (r. 1846–78), for example, papal control over worldwide Catholic missionary activity was firmly established for the first time in history. The solemn definition of the papal primacy by the First Vatican Council gave clear theoretical underpinnings to Pius IX's own commitment to an intensified centralization of ecclesiastical government in Rome. The council's companion definition of papal Infallibility strengthened the energetic exercise of papal magisterial power.

The Papacy in the 20th Century. Never before had popes been quite so active in moral and doctrinal teaching, and the great encyclicals of Leo XIII (r. 1878–1903) and Pius XII (r. 1939–58) especially, dealing with an imposing range of topics from sexual morality and eucharistic teaching to economic, social, and political ideas, became

Pope John Paul II, the first non-Italian pontiff in 456 years, has been widely acclaimed for his strong leadership. His conservative stance on certain doctrinal and organizational issues has, however, disappointed some groups in the Roman Catholic church.

determinative in shaping the development of Catholic thinking. The theological innovation and energetic reform evident at the Second Vatican Council, convened by JOHN XXIII (r. 1958–63), found expression in its decrees on ecumenism, religious liberty, the liturgy, and the nature of the church. The ambivalence of some of those decrees, however, and the disciplinary turmoil and doctrinal dissension following the ending of the council, brought about new challenges to papal authority. The establishment of national conferences of bishops tended to erode it to some degree, and PAUL VI's encyclical *Humanae Vitae* (1968), reaffirming the prohibition of artificial birth control, was met with both evasion and defiance. By the late 1970s papal authority itself had become a bone of contention.

John Paul II, who became pope in 1978, reaffirmed the decrees of the Second Vatican Council. He concentrated his main efforts, however, on strengthening papal authority, which was perceived as having waned under Pope Paul.

Papago [pah'-puh-goh]   Most of the Papago, a tribe of North American Indians, still live in their traditional homeland, a barren desert country in southern Arizona. Like their relatives the PIMA, they speak dialects of the Aztec-Tanoan linguistic family. *Papago* means "bean-eating people" in the Pima language. The Papago learned to use all available water, conserving the overflow from summer storms in primitive reservoirs, or *charcos*, and growing maize, beans, and squash. The *charcos* would be dry by harvest time, and the Papago would camp by springs in nearby mountains. Under these difficult conditions they were able to raise about 25 percent of their food, supplementing their crops with rabbits and edible wild plants.

Although Spanish missionaries came to the area in the late 17th century, the Papago remained remote and were seldom visited by whites until recent decades. Consequently, they have retained far more of their native culture than have the Pima.

In 1986 the Papago Nation officially changed its name to Tohono O'odham ("desert people"). On or near the reservation they numbered about 16,500 in 1989.

Papal States [pay'-pul]   The Papal States, or States of the Church, were the portion of central Italy under the temporal control of the papacy from the mid-8th century until 1870. They comprised the modern Italian regions of Lazio, UMBRIA, the MARCHE, and part of EMILIA-ROMAGNA. Awarded to Pope Stephen II in 756 by the Frankish king PEPIN THE SHORT, the territory was loosely ruled by the popes until the middle of the 11th century, when Pope GREGORY VII and his successors began to tighten papal control over central Italy. With the restoration of a strong papacy after the end (1417) of the Great Schism, the popes became almost absolute monarchs. Through their governors, including the ruthless Cesare Borgia (see BORGIA family), they brought the area under direct papal government.

In the early modern era, the curbing of local feudal families and the crushing of brigands brought a measure of peace and security to central Italy. During the Napoleonic Wars the French occupied Rome, but the Congress of Vienna (1815; see VIENNA, CONGRESS OF) restored papal rule. In 1860, during the RISORGIMENTO, the kingdom of Italy annexed Marche and Umbria, and in 1870 it conquered Rome, which was made the capital of newly unified Italy. The papacy continued to contest the loss of its territorial sovereignty until 1929, when the Lateran Treaty created the independent state of Vatican City.

Papandréou, Andreas [pah-puhn-dray'-oo]   Andreas Georgios Papandréou, b. Feb. 5, 1919, was prime minister of Greece from 1981 to 1989. His father, Georgios Papandréou, had been prime minister three times (1944–45, 1963, 1964–65). During World War II, Papandréou emigrated to the United States, where he taught economics at several universities. He returned to Greece in 1959 to enter politics in association with his father but went into exile again after the military coup of 1967. In 1974 he founded the Panhellenic Socialist Movement. As premier, Papandréou initiated socialist reforms, confiscated church land, and tried to improve relations with Turkey. Charges of official corruption helped bring about the fall of his government in June 1989. In September he was ordered to stand trial for criminal misconduct.

papaw [paw'-paw]   The papaw, *Asimina triloba,* is a small North American fruit tree ranging from 3 to 12 m (10 to 40 ft) tall. Its tropical relatives include the CUSTARD APPLE, the soursop or guanabana, and the fragrant ilang-ilang. Papaws grow naturally from the southern United

The papaw tree is native to the United States; it is sometimes confused with the tropical papaw.

States north to New York and west to Michigan and Kansas. The smooth, leathery fruit, brown when mature, is irregularly oblong-shaped and from 5 to 15 cm (2 to 6 in) long. Its creamy, highly aromatic flesh surrounds numerous large, smooth seeds. The edible wild fruit tends to vary from bitter to sweet.

papaya [puh-py'-ah] The papaya, *Carica papaya*, family Caricaceae, often called the melon tree and sometimes the papaw, is a soft-wooded, palmlike evergreen tree indigenous to the tropical lowlands of Central America. It is cultivated in tropical countries around the world for its palatable fruit and for the latex of the green fruit, which contains papain, a protein-digesting enzyme that is used commercially as a meat tenderizer.

Papaya trees, which are male, hermaphroditic, or female, have palmate leaves clustered at the top of the trunk. White, cream-colored, yellow, or purple-tinged flowers are borne in inflorescences on the trunk in the axils of the leaves. Both male and female trees must be present to produce fruit; hermaphroditic trees are self-fruitful. Fruit ranges in shape from globose to long-ovoid, in weight from 113.4 g (4 oz) to 9.1 kg (20 lb) or more, and in color from light yellow through deep yellow, orange, and pink to red.

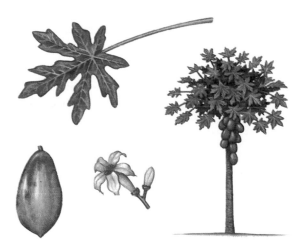

The soft-stemmed papaya tree bears clusters of soft, melonlike fruit. Papaya is an important food in tropical countries.

Papen, Franz von [pahp'-en] Franz von Papen, b. Oct. 29, 1879, d. May 2, 1969, German chancellor from June to December 1932, helped Adolf HITLER come to power the following year. A right-wing member of the Center party, he sat in the Prussian Diet from 1921 to 1932. While chancellor, he tried in vain for National Socialist backing to obtain a Reichstag majority. In January 1933, Papen, believing he could control the Nazis,

worked out an arrangement for a majority coalition with Hitler as chancellor and himself as vice-chancellor. Papen was subsequently ambassador to Austria (1934–38) and Turkey (1939–44). Acquitted at the Nuremberg Trials (1946), he was later sentenced to several years' imprisonment by a German denazification court but was released in 1949.

paper Paper is a sheet of interlaced fibers—usually cellulose fibers from plants, but sometimes from cloth rags or other fibrous materials—that is formed by pulping the fibers and causing them to felt, or mat, to form a solid surface.

The evolution of writing materials culminated in the development of paper. The oldest written records still surviving are Sumerian clay tablets dating from the 4th millennium BC. PAPYRUS came into use about 3500 BC. PARCHMENT, made from the skins of animals, was another important material used in Europe from about the 2d century BC. Almost any portable surface that would retain the marks of brush or pen was also used as a writing surface (see WRITING SYSTEMS, EVOLUTION OF).

The Development of Paper Manufacture

The invention of paper is generally attributed to a Chinese court official, Cai Lun, in about AD 105; he was the first to succeed in making a paper from vegetable fibers—tree bark, rags, old fish netting. The art of making paper was kept secret for 500 years; the Japanese acquired it only in the 7th century.

In AD 751 the Arab city of Samarkand was attacked by marauding Chinese. Among the Chinese prisoners taken were several skilled in papermaking. They were forced by the city's governor to build and operate a paper mill, and Samarkand soon became the papermaking center of the Arab world.

The Spread of Papermaking in Europe. Knowledge of papermaking traveled westward, spreading throughout the Middle East. The Moorish invasion of Spain led to the

Until the end of the 18th century all paper was made by hand. As seen in this Japanese painting, linen rags were pulped in a large mortar (right), and the pulp was mixed with water. The mixture was then scooped into a rectangular copper sieve (center) and allowed to drain, after which the paper was hung to dry (left).

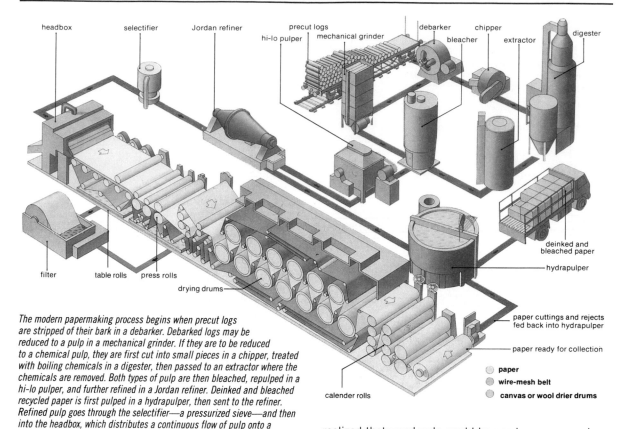

headbox   selectifier   Jordan refiner   precut logs   debarker   chipper   digester
hi-lo pulper   mechanical grinder   bleacher   extractor

deinked and bleached paper

hydrapulper

paper cuttings and rejects fed back into hydrapulper

paper ready for collection

filter   table rolls   press rolls

drying drums

○ **paper**

◐ **wire-mesh belt**

◑ **canvas or wool drier drums**

calender rolls

The modern papermaking process begins when precut logs are stripped of their bark in a debarker. Debarked logs may be reduced to a pulp in a mechanical grinder. If they are to be reduced to a chemical pulp, they are first cut into small pieces in a chipper, treated with boiling chemicals in a digester, then passed to an extractor where the chemicals are removed. Both types of pulp are then bleached, repulped in a hi-lo pulper, and further refined in a Jordan refiner. Deinked and bleached recycled paper is first pulped in a hydrapulper, then sent to the refiner. Refined pulp goes through the selectifier—a pressurized sieve—and then into the headbox, which distributes a continuous flow of pulp onto a wire-mesh belt moving at high speed. Table rolls remove the water, which passes through a filter for recycling. The web of paper is pressed in press rolls, dried on drying drums, and given its finish by the calender rolls.

erection (*c.*1150) of the first European paper mill, at Játiva in the province of Valencia. Knowledge of the technology spread quickly, and by the 16th century paper was being manufactured throughout most of Europe.

Vegetable fibers were shredded and reduced to a pulp in water; a screen was dipped in the pulp and removed with a thin layer of pulp. As the water drained off, the pulped fibers meshed and matted into a sheet, which was then dried and pressed.

Development of Papermaking Machinery. The first mechanical papermaking process was invented (1798) by Nicolas Louis Robert (1761–1828), a Frenchman. Eventually, a practicable, commercially successful machine was built (1805) by the Fourdrinier brothers, Henry (1766–1854) and Sealy (d. 1847), and Bryan Donkin (1768–1855).

19th-Century Improvements. Papermaking technology improved rapidly throughout the 19th century. The introduction of chlorine for bleaching meant that white paper could now be manufactured from colored linen and cotton rags, thus increasing the range of available raw materials. Esparto grass from Spain and North Africa became a valued commodity for papermaking. Only when it was

realized that wood pulp could be used as a source, however, did large-scale paper manufacture become possible. A machine was developed that could pulp logs using grindstones revolving in water, but because the pulp contained large amounts of impurities, the first wood pulp papers were of very poor quality. It was found that these impurities could be removed by boiling the wood pulp with various chemical reagents: soda and sulfite in the 1850s, sulfate in the 1880s.

The Papermaking Process

Papermaking is a continuous process that begins with the tree and ends with the cut sheet of paper.

Although wood fiber is the basic ingredient, only a little more than half of the fiber used comes from trees cut specifically for paper manufacture. The remaining fiber is made up of secondary material obtained by recycling used newsprint, spent packaging, and other waste paper. The waste residues of lumber operations and wood chips from saw mills provide additional material.

Pulp Processing. The principal functions of pulping are to dissolve the lignin that holds the cellulose fibers together and to separate the fibers. The logs that will be reduced to pulp go through one of two processes: either they are mechanically ground into pulp, or they are reduced to a pulp by being chipped and then cooked in a chemical solution. Cheaper grades of paper are generally produced from mechanically made pulp, which often contains some unwanted residues. Chemical methods remove more of the residues. In the chemical process, wood chips are first cooked in a digester, a closed tank operated at high temperature and pressure. In the sulfite process, the chips are pulped under steam pressure in a solution of sulfite salts; in the sulfate, or kraft, process, the chemical solution consists of caustic soda and sodium sulfide. In both processes, the lignin, the material that holds wood cells together, is dissolved, and the cellulose fibers separate.

In order to make the fibers more flexible, thereby increasing their matting, or felting, capacity, the pulp next goes through a mechanical pounding and squeezing process called beating, which is carried out with high-speed conical or disk beaters, or refiners. Pigments or dyes are added to the pulp at the beating stage, along with filler materials that help to preserve the paper or give it a better opacity and finish. Sizing materials, such as rosins, starches, and gums, that will make the paper resistant to the water in water-based writing inks may also be added during beating.

Paper Machines. The two most common machines in current use are the Fourdrinier and the cylinder machine. Both produce paper sheet from pulp in a continuous process. In the Fourdrinier the pulp-and-water mixture flows at a controlled rate through a headbox and onto a moving wire-mesh screen. As the screen moves away from the headbox, various suction devices drain the water from the pulp, leaving a sheet of matted pulp that still contains a high proportion of water. A wire-covered roll holding a wire design, and called the dandy roll, may travel over the sheet surface to impress a watermark. The sheet then moves on to a woolen felt screen, which takes it through a series of presses, where more water is removed. Finally, the sheet passes over a number of heated drums that evaporate the remaining water.

The Fourdrinier machine forms processed pulp into sheets. At the initial section (background), *the wet stock is projected at high speed onto a wire-mesh or synthetic-fiber belt, where most of the water drains away. Here the fibers first form the sheet of paper.*

The cylinder machine differs from the Fourdrinier principally in the "wet end," or forming operation. Instead of the moving wire screen, a screen-covered rotary cylinder is half-submerged in the pulp vat. As the cylinder rotates, a sheet of matted pulp is formed on its exterior surface and is then picked up by a moving belt, where it is treated to remove the remaining water, as in the Fourdrinier process. A series of cylinders may be used, each one depositing an additional layer of pulp on the belt, so that thicker, multilayer sheets are built up.

Finishing. As it leaves the paper-forming machine, the dried paper is wound onto large reels. The rolled paper may be slit to the widths required, cut into sheets, trimmed, and packaged. Other finishing operations include calendering, coating, or operations that convert the paper roll into special products.

Acid Content of Paper. Many of the sizings used to improve the "feel" and printability of paper are acidic and over time cause the cellulose fibers that constitute paper to degenerate, turning pages yellow and brittle. Books made in the last 150 years have been particularly affected by acidic deterioration. Alkaline sizing agents have been developed to neutralize this acidity, and many high-quality books are now printed on such acid-free paper.

Paper Products

In addition to the papers used for writing and PRINTING, paper is made into a wide variety of end products, from the absorbent papers used for toweling, toilet, and blotting papers to paperboards that are made up into containers; papers used in building construction (such as roofing paper); and special papers that are designed for other particular uses.

Pollution Problems

Because of their need for water and lumber for pulp, paper mills are often located on the banks of rivers, in remote, forested areas. Papermaking processes require the heavy use of chemicals, and the by-products have included dioxins and other toxins, which have been components of the wastewater that is flushed into the river.

Working with the industry and with paper-manufacturing states, the Environmental Protection Agency (EPA) has been developing new standards for paper-mill effluents in order to reduce pollution.

World Paper Production

Production of pulp and paper is for the most part concentrated in areas that have abundant wood resources and a large industrial base, such as the United States, Scandinavia, Canada, and the USSR. Paper recycling is increasing, especially in the United States (see RECYCLING OF MATERIALS).

paper folding Paper folding, the craft of folding paper into objects without cutting, pasting, or additional decoration, has been practiced in the Orient for centuries. Although its origins are unknown, it may have been de-

Paper folding is most beautifully expressed in the forms, such as the crane, of the Japanese art of origami. The crane, a symbol of good fortune and longevity in Japan, is the most popular of the animal forms in origami and is the basic shape for the others.

rived from the older tradition of cloth folding. In Japan, paper folding—called origami—evolved into a highly sophisticated mode employing hundreds of intricate folds and was valued for its ceremonial and decorative functions. For decorative playthings, origami commonly takes the form of flowers, birds, fish, insects, animals, and figures, sometimes with movable parts.

In the West, the educator Friedrich Froebel (1782–1852) introduced paper folding into his kindergarten movement in Germany during the 19th century. Later the Bauhaus utilized the craft for training its students in functional design. In the United States and England, paper folding enjoyed a vogue as a type of mathematical construction. A characteristic example is the flexagon (1939); when correctly flexed, this paper structure undergoes radical alterations in its faces.

papier-mâché [pay'-pur-muh-shay']   A substance made from paper that has been soaked in such binding materials as flour paste, glue, or resin, papier-mâché had been used as an art material in the Orient for centuries before its first use in 18th-century France. (The term is French and means crushed or mashed paper.) Sheets of paper that have been glued together and dried in a mold as well as soaked-and-shaped paper pulp have been used to produce papier-mâché, which dries into a strong, hard material. During the 19th century, when it reached a peak of popularity, articles made of papier-mâché ranged from decorated boxes and trays to furniture, jewelry, and sculptures.

papilloma   Papilloma is the common name for various benign tumors that grow on the skin or glands, and for a VIRUS group associated with many of these tumors and with WARTS. The development of clusters of papillomas is fairly common and is called papillomatosis. One type, confluent and reticulated papillomatosis, is genetically determined; it causes an eruption on the trunk and elbows at puberty, usually in girls.

Although benign, the tumors must be surgically removed when they interfere with the functioning of an organ. Juvenile papillomas, which grow in the larynx, often appear in clusters so thick that the airway is blocked. Exophytic papillomas, which occur in the nasal cavity, have fingerlike projections and often must be removed repeatedly. Inverted papillomas, which invade the mucosa of the nasal cavity with similar projections, are unusually persistent; removal of surrounding healthy tissue is frequently required. Other papillomas include cockscomb papilloma, which grows on the cervix during pregnancy and regresses after delivery; intraductal papilloma, which occurs in the duct system of the breast; and villous papilloma, which grows in the urinary bladder, the breast, or the brain.

More than 50 types of human papilloma viruses are known. A few have been found associated with rapidly growing cancers and may contribute to their development, although possibly the viruses simply invade cancerous tissues. Type 18, in particular, has been associated with cervical cancers; its presence may help in the early identification of women at risk of rapidly growing cervical cancer.

papillon [pah'-pee-ohn]   The papillon breed of dog takes its name from the French word for butterfly, an apt description of its widely set and erect but angled ears. The older variety of papillon, which has hanging, or drop, ears, has been known since at least the 1500s. The erect-eared type apparently first appeared in Belgium about 1900. Papillons have a short skull, a pointed muzzle, dark eyes, a long tail carried over the back, and an abundant, long, silky coat. The dog stands from 20 to 28 cm (8 to 11 in) high at the shoulder and weighs from 1.5 to 5 kg (3.5 to 11 lb), with lighter dogs preferred.

The papillon (French for "butterfly") is a toy dog named for its erect, fringed, winglike ears. Once called the dwarf spaniel and favored as a lapdog in the court of Louis XIV, the papillon appears in paintings by Boucher, Fragonard, Rubens, and Watteau. According to the American Kennel Club, its coat should be white with patches of any two colors.

Papineau, Louis Joseph [pah-pee-noh'] Louis Joseph Papineau, b. Montreal, Oct. 7, 1786, d. Sept. 23, 1871, was a French-Canadian lawyer, politician, and rebel. Elected (1808) to the House of Assembly of Lower Canada (now Quebec), he joined the Parti Canadien and served as speaker of the House from 1815 until 1837. A French-Canadian nationalist, he supported the liberal principle of representative government. He also supported the Roman Catholic church and the seigneurial system as the basis of Lower Canadian society. Fearing the assimilation of the French, he fought the proposed union of Upper Canada (now Ontario) and Lower Canada.

Papineau spurred the assembly's 92 Resolutions of February 1834, which called for greater self-government. British rejection of Canadian demands led to organized resistance by some of Papineau's followers, resulting in violence on Nov. 23, 1837, when an attempt was made to arrest Papineau (see REBELLIONS OF 1837). He fled to the United States and then into exile in France but returned to Canada in 1845 and was a member (1848–54) of the unified Canadian legislative assembly.

Papp, Joseph A colorful and creative director-producer, Joseph Papp, b. Joseph Papirofsky in Brooklyn, N.Y., June 22, 1921, has exerted a major influence on the American theater since the early 1950s. In 1954 he helped to found the New York Shakespeare Festival, an enormously popular summer theater that gave free performances first in ghetto areas and later in Central Park. From this success evolved Papp's Public Theater (1967), now the New York Shakespeare Festival Public Theatre.

Known for his innovative and dynamic approach to drama, Papp has introduced countless new playwrights, performers, and directors to the American stage. His most memorable productions include *A Midsummer Night's Dream* (1964), *Hair* (1967), *Sticks and Bones* (1971), *That Championship Season* (1972), *A Chorus Line* (1975), *The Threepenny Opera* (1977), *The Pirates of Penzance* (1980), and *The Mystery of Edwin Drood* (1985).

paprika SEE PEPPER (VEGETABLE)

Papua New Guinea [pap'-yoo-uh, gin'-ee] Papua New Guinea, an independent country in the southwest Pacific Ocean, comprises the eastern half of the island of NEW GUINEA, the BISMARCK ARCHIPELAGO, the northern part of the SOLOMON ISLANDS, and hundreds of small offshore islands.

Land, People, and Economy

Papua New Guinea has a rugged, mountainous landscape and is frequently subject to seismic activity. Mountain ranges on New Guinea run from northwest to southeast. Snow-capped Mount Wilhelm reaches a height of 4,509 m (14,793 ft). The main river systems are the Sepik,

---

AT A GLANCE

PAPUA NEW GUINEA

Land: Area: 462,840 km² (178,703 mi²). Capital and largest city: Port Moresby (1987 est. pop., 152,100).

People: Population (1990 est.): 3,822,875. Density: 8.3 persons per km² (21.4 per mi²). Distribution (1990): 13% urban, 87% rural. Official language: English. Major religions: Roman Catholicism, Protestantism, traditional religions.

Government: Type: parliamentary state. Legislature: National Parliament. Political subdivisions: 20 provinces.

Economy: GDP (1989): $3.57 billion; $938 per capita. Labor distribution (1988): commerce and services—45%; manufacturing—9%; agriculture and fishing—27%; construction—5%; government and public authorities—14%. Foreign trade (1990 est.): imports—$1.35 billion; exports—$1.3 billion. Currency: 1 kina = 100 toea.

Education and Health: Literacy (1990): 32% of adult population. Universities (1988): 2. Hospital beds (1985): 13,560. Physicians (1987): 283. Life expectancy (1990): women—56; men—54. Infant mortality (1990): 68 per 1,000 live births.

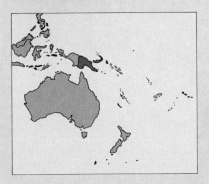

PAPUA NEW GUINEA

+ Spot Elevation or Depth

0 100 200 300 400 km

0   100   200   mi

Scale 1:22,400,000

© 1980 Rand McNally & Co.
A-592200-772 -1-1-1

the two, but the Papuans tend to occupy interior regions. More than 700 languages and dialects are spoken, making this one of the most complicated linguistic areas in the world. Pidgin English and Motu are the most widespread languages. Education, controlled by the government, is not compulsory. The most important city is PORT MORESBY, the capital.

The vast majority of the inhabitants practice subsistence farming based on yams, taro, bananas, and sweet potatoes. Commercial crops include copra, coffee, tea, and cocoa. Papua New Guinea has some of the world's richest gold and copper deposits, and high-grade petroleum was discovered recently. In the 1990s it faced an economic crisis, precipitated by the closing by separatist rebels in May 1989 of the huge Paguna copper mine on Bougainville (which had provided 17% of government income and 40% of exports) and compounded by falling prices for agricultural exports and declining tourism.

History and Government

Papua, or southeastern New Guinea, was sighted by the Portuguese explorer Jorge de Meneses in 1526–27. The British annexed it in 1888, and it passed to Australia in 1905. Northeastern New Guinea, the Bismarck Archipelago, and Bougainville were administered by Germany until World War I, when Australian forces occupied the area. The United Nations placed it under Australian administration as a trust territory in 1946. Australia combined the two territories in 1949. The country became self-governing in 1973 and gained full independence on Sept. 16, 1975. The British monarch, represented by a governor-general, is head of state, but real leadership is exercised by the prime minister. Michael Somare served as prime minister from 1972 to 1980 and again from 1982 to 1985 and was the government's chief negotiator during the nation's most serious crisis since independence, the separatist movement on Bougainville. In a peace accord signed on June 24, 1991, the government agreed to grant the rebels immunity from prosecution and restore basic services in exchange for their surrender, but unrest continued, and talks on the future political status of Bougainville were deferred.

Papuan languages   see OCEANIA, LANGUAGES OF

---

papyrus [puh-py'-ruhs]   From about 2400 BC or earlier, the people of Egypt, Palestine, Syria, and southern Europe used the pith of the sedge *Cyperus papyrus* to make a writing material known as papyrus. The material continued to be regularly used during the time of the Roman Empire but began to be replaced by the cheaper PARCHMENT in the late Empire.

To make papyrus, moistened strips of thinly sliced pith with the rough outer covering removed were laid side by side on a board, and another layer was superimposed at right angles. The two layers were then pressed and carefully beaten with hammers until the plant tissue ruptured; the exuding sap glued the strips together as the

Ramu, and Markham. The islands of BOUGAINVILLE, NEW BRITAIN, NEW IRELAND, and Manus are also hilly and mountainous, with valleys and gorges inland. Soils are generally leached and infertile. Average rainfall exceeds 2,030 mm (80 in) in all areas, with some averaging over 5,080 mm (200 in). Temperatures average 27° C (81° F) in the coastal lowlands and 16° C (61° F) at 1,830 m (6,000 ft). Most of the country is covered with tropical rain forest, but drier areas are covered in savanna or reed grass.

The inhabitants constitute two major population groups: the Melanesians (15%) and the Papuans (84%). There are few physical and cultural differences between

Port Moresby, the capital of Papua New Guinea, is named for Capt. John Moresby, who explored the area in 1873. The city has become Papua New Guinea's most important commercial center.

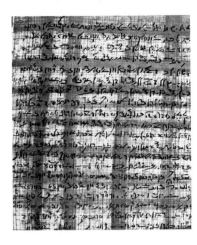

This papyrus sheet was made by stripping the reed of its outer stalk and then laying slices of the reed in two transverse layers. The starchy juice of the plant bonded the slices as they were pressed together.

papyrus was dried in the sun. The resulting sheet, which was very strong, was rubbed smooth with stones. To make a scroll, many sheets were joined together and rolled on a wooden rod.

---

parable [par'-uh-bul] A parable—from the Greek *parabole*, "a setting beside"—is a brief moral tale that uses the devices of ALLEGORY. The parable resembles the FABLE, but whereas a fable is a straightforward narrative, a parable is an extended metaphor that alludes to spiritual truth through a simple story. Jesus Christ frequently used parables; well-known biblical examples include the stories of the Prodigal Son and of the Good Samaritan.

---

parabola [puh-rab'-uh-luh] A *parabola* is a special type of plane curve. It may be defined in a number of ways. A parabola is formed by a plane that intersects a right circular cone and is parallel to one of its elements; that is, it is a CONIC SECTION. A parabola may also be defined as the locus of points that are equidistant from a fixed point (the focus) and a fixed line (the directrix).

The ECCENTRICITY of a parabola is 1, because it is the ratio of the distances to the directrix and the focus, and these two distances are equal. All parabolas are similar, because their eccentricities are the same. A parabola may be defined as the conic section with an eccentricity of 1.

The equation for a parabola with vertex at the origin and focus at $(a, 0)$ is $y^2 = 4ax$. Such a parabola opens to the right and is pictured in the figure. Similar equations can be written for parabolas opening upward ($x^2 = 4ay$), to the left ($y^2 = -4ax$), or downward ($x^2 = -4ay$).

The parabola has a very special geometric property that makes it useful as a reflector of light and sound. Light rays (or sound waves) passing through the focus and being reflected from the parabola will emerge in a direction parallel to the axis of the parabola; conversely, rays approaching the parabola parallel to the axis will be reflected so that they pass through the focus. This property may be referred to as the focal property, optical property, acoustical property, or simply as the reflection property of a parabola. The parabola also arises in problems involving moving bodies subject to the force of gravity.

When a parabola is rotated about its axis, it generates a surface called a paraboloid of revolution. This surface has the same reflection property as the parabola and is used in automobile headlights, reflecting telescopes, and loudspeakers.

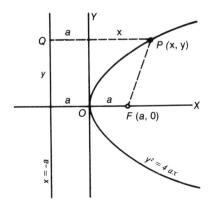

Paracas [pah-rah'-kahs] The ancient Andean culture of Paracas flourished in the Ica and Nazca valleys on the south coast of Peru from about 900 to 200 BC or somewhat later, when the art styles of the area evolved into those of the later NAZCA culture. The apex of Paracas artistic and technological achievement was exceptionally fine weaving and embroidery. Both cotton and wool were made into richly colored textiles of great beauty and intricacy. Enormous mantles were embroidered with hundreds of tiny figures, usually representing animals, employing complicated color schemes. The finest examples of Paracas fabrics accompanied burials; important examples were recovered from Paracas cemeteries at Cerro Colorado.

Paracas ceramics, sometimes called Ocucaje style, are characterized by resin-painted polychrome designs applied after firing and therefore not set by the firing process. Especially during its early phases the Paracas style was influenced by that of Chavín (see CHAVÍN DE HUÁNTAR).

Paracelsus [par-uh-sel'-suhs] The German physician and chemist Theophrastus Philipus Aureolus Bombastus von Hohenheim, b. Nov. 10 or 14, 1493, d. Sept. 24, 1541, who called himself Paracelsus, was a medical reformer who introduced a new concept of disease and the use of chemical medicines. Paracelsus studied at several Italian universities and began to practice medicine and surgery in the 1520s. A difficult personality, he created controversy because of his wholesale condemnation of traditional science and medicine. Paracelsus's new concept of disease emphasized its causes to be external agents that attack the body, contrary to the traditional idea of disease as an internal upset of the balance of the body's humors. Therapy, according to Paracelsus, was to be directed against these agents of disease, and for this he advocated the use of chemicals rather than herbs. ALCHEMY became the means of preparing such chemicals; in this way Paracelsus changed the emphasis of alchemy from making gold to making medicines.

parachute   A parachute is a folding, umbrella-shaped device made of fabric that is used to slow down a rapidly moving object by creating additional wind resistance while being dragged behind it. Stored in compact, folded form, it is released and unfurled when needed. Until about 1950 it was used solely as an aerodynamic brake for a falling body, but today it is also used to slow aircraft after landing, to slow the final descent of space capsules, and in sports such as drag racing. Leonardo da Vinci sketched a parachute c.1495. André Garnerin jumped from a balloon using a parachute in 1797. In 1808 a parachute was first used in an emergency to save a human life.

For a century the basic parachute has been assembled from approximately triangular gores, or panels, first of silk and later of nylon, joined together to form an almost hemispherical canopy across which pass the rigging lines. The assembly packs into a small fabric container from which it is withdrawn by pulling the rip cord, which opens the pack. A small auxiliary parachute, called the pilot parachute, pops out and pulls out the main canopy. Aircrew wear the pack as a seat cushion or on the chest; parachute troops usually wear the pack on the back.

Since World War II most combat airplanes have been fitted with ejection seats, which are fired by cartridges and often have rocket assistance and various stabilization systems. A drogue (small pilot parachute) slows the seat while a main seat parachute is deployed. The occupant is then released and descends with a parachute separately from the seat.

In recent years, sport parachuting, or SKYDIVING, has become increasingly popular.

Paradise Lost   *Paradise Lost* (1667), the finest work of John MILTON, is a poem in 12 books whose subject is the Christian story of "man's first disobedience," temptation, and fall, and the promise of redemption by "one greater man"—Jesus Christ. The poem, which draws on Milton's profound knowledge of Greek, Latin, and Hebrew tradition, offers its majestic style and subject as a Christian alternative to the pagan heroism of classical epic. Adam is Milton's hero, Satan his adversary. The poem begins with an invocation of the "Heavenly Muse"; describes Satan's expulsion from heaven and the war of the angels, the building of hell, and the creation of Satan's offspring, Sin and Death; and concludes with the sorrowful departure of Adam and Eve from Paradise.

paradox (literature) see FIGURES OF SPEECH

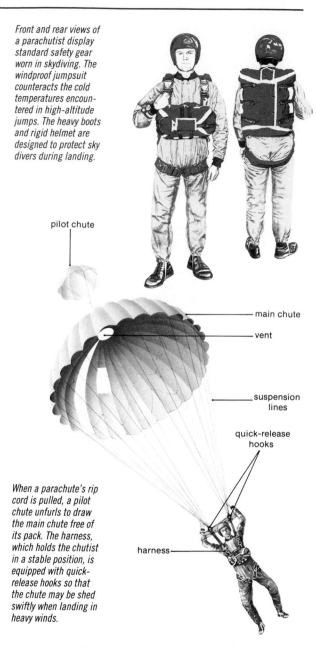

Front and rear views of a parachutist display standard safety gear worn in skydiving. The windproof jumpsuit counteracts the cold temperatures encountered in high-altitude jumps. The heavy boots and rigid helmet are designed to protect sky divers during landing.

pilot chute

main chute

vent

suspension lines

quick-release hooks

When a parachute's rip cord is pulled, a pilot chute unfurls to draw the main chute free of its pack. The harness, which holds the chutist in a stable position, is equipped with quick-release hooks so that the chute may be shed swiftly when landing in heavy winds.

harness

paradox (mathematics)   In the strict sense, a paradox arises when a contradiction follows from seemingly obvious premises. There is paradox in a looser sense when the conclusion is not a contradiction but clashes strongly with intuition or common sense. Logical paradoxes have puzzled thinkers for many centuries, and some, such as ZENO'S PARADOXES, remain well known. The ability to handle paradoxes is an important test of a logical theory (see LOGIC). Logical paradoxes shook the foundations of SET

THEORY between 1895 and 1930 and importantly influenced the foundations of mathematics generally.

Another group of paradoxes involves notions of meaning and truth and are called semantical paradoxes. The simplest, known from ancient times, is the Liar paradox: if a person says "What I am now saying is false," then the truth of that statement implies its falsehood, so then it seems true after all.

Paradoxes can be "solved" in different ways by rejecting different assumptions or presuppositions. Such pluralism (the existence of many different possibilities) flourishes particularly for the semantical paradoxes.

Paraguay [par'-uh-gway] The Republic of Paraguay is a landlocked country of central South America, bordered by Argentina, Bolivia, and Brazil. Paraguay means "a place with a great river" in the Guaraní Indian language, and most of its boundaries are marked by rivers. Primarily agricultural, Paraguay produces mainly livestock and cotton. The country gained independence from Spain in 1811, and much of its subsequent history has been dominated by wars.

Land and Resources

Paraguay is divided into eastern and western regions by the PARAGUAY RIVER. Most of the eastern region is the low-lying, densely forested Paraná Plateau. The highest elevation, in the Villarica Mountains, is only 700 m (2,297 ft). The plains to the west of the Paraguay River are known as the CHACO. Soils in the eastern parts are fertile but little cultivated. The western region is less suited to agriculture because of seasonal flooding and occasional drought.

Most of Paraguay has a subtropical climate. Weather conditions are also affected by hot, moist winds from the Amazon basin and cool, dry winds from the Argentine Pampas. Average annual rainfall in the Chaco is about 813 mm (32 in), but the high rate of evaporation produces seasonal aridity. In the eastern region precipitation increases from about 1,321 mm (52 in) at Asunción to 2,007 mm (79 in) along the Brazilian border. The average annual temperature is about 23° C (74° F).

Drainage in the eastern area is provided by the PARANÁ RIVER and the Paraguay. The Chaco is drained by the Paraguay and Pilcomayo rivers. Vegetation in eastern Paraguay is alternately hardwood forests and grasslands, whereas the Chaco is dominated by rough grasses, cacti, and thorny shrubs. Wildlife ranges from the jaguar and puma to peccary and deer, and Paraguay is noted for its tropical and coastal birds.

People

Most Paraguayans (95%) are mestizos (of mixed Indian and Spanish descent); prominent among the European minorities is a German community. Although Spanish is

AT A GLANCE

REPUBLIC OF PARAGUAY

Land: Area: 406,752 km² (157,048 mi²). Capital and largest city: Asunción (1990 est. pop., 607,706).

People: Population (1990 est.): 4,279,500. Density: 11 persons per km² (27 per mi²). Distribution (1989): 43% urban, 57% rural. Official language: Spanish. Major religion: Roman Catholicism.

Government: Type: republic. Legislature: Senate, Chamber of Deputies. Political subdivisions: 19 departments.

Economy: GNP (1988): $4.8 billion; $1,180 per capita. Labor distribution (1986): agriculture—44%; industry and commerce—34%; services—18%; government—4%. Foreign trade (1989): imports—$613 million; exports—$970 million. Currency: 1 guaraní = 100 céntimos.

Education and Health: Literacy (1989): 77% of adult population. Universities (1990): 2. Hospital beds (1988): 3,498. Physicians (1988): 2,536. Life expectancy (1990): women—72; men—67. Infant mortality (1990): 48 per 1,000 live births.

Beef cattle, raised on large ranches throughout Paraguay, are one of the nation's chief sources of export earnings.

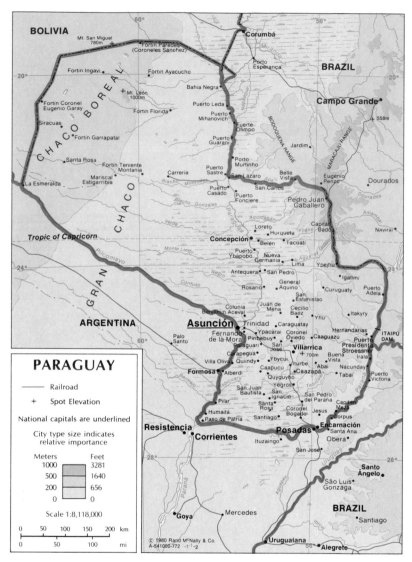

PARAGUAY

— Railroad

+ Spot Elevation

National capitals are underlined

City type size indicates relative importance

Meters		Feet
1000		3281
500		1640
200		656
0		0

Scale 1:8,118,000

0	50	100	150	200 km
0	50		100	mi

© 1980 Rand McNally & Co.
A-541000-772 -1-1-2

the official language, a majority speak Guaraní. Roman Catholicism is the state religion, claiming the adherence of 96% of the inhabitants. More than 90% of the people live in the eastern region, with nearly 15% in Asunción, the capital.

Education is free in a centralized public system. The National and Catholic universities are located in Asunción. Health-care facilities are concentrated in urban areas.

Economic Activity

Agriculture, forestry, and fishing are historically the dominant economic activities in Paraguay. Although 27% of the total land area is arable, only 5% is used for crops. Cassava, maize (corn), sugarcane, tobacco, and rice are leading food crops, and livestock raising is the chief activity in the Chaco. Forest products include citrus, palm

hearts, maté, and lumber. Paraguay's traditional exports, meat and lumber, have been adversely affected by trade restrictions; by 1989, cotton, soybeans, and vegetable oils provided more than 70% of export revenues. Paraguay has no mineral fuels but has abundant hydroelectricity. The country's first steel plant, at Villa Hayes north of Asunción, was inaugurated in 1986.

In the late 1970s and early 1980s, construction of the giant Itaipú Dam on the Paraná River, the world's largest hydroelectric installation, helped to give Paraguay the highest economic growth rate in Latin America. When construction ended, however, the rate of development and foreign investment in Paraguay slowed dramatically, despite the construction of another huge hydroelectric project on the Paraná, Yacyretá Dam, which was expected to become operational in the mid-1990s. Factories built

Asunción, the capital and largest city of Paraguay, was founded (1537) by the Spanish and rapidly became a regional trade center. Located on the Paraguay River, the city is Paraguay's major port.

in the 1970s were operating far below capacity, and unemployment increased steadily in the 1980s.

Government

Paraguay is a unitary republic. Under the constitution of 1967 the president and members of the bicameral legislature are elected to concurrent 5-year terms by universal adult suffrage. In the legislature the party receiving the largest number of votes is allotted two-thirds of the seats in each chamber. Gen. Alfredo STROESSNER came to power in 1954 and in 1988 was reelected to his 8th term as president. In February 1989, however, he was deposed in a coup led by Gen. Andrés Rodríguez, the second-in-command of the armed forces. For most of Stroessner's tenure, all or part of Paraguay was ruled under a state of siege (lifted, 1987).

History

The conquering Spaniards encountered little resistance from the local GUARANÍ Indians and established themselves in Paraguay after 1537. Relatively few Spaniards, however, reached the country. Those who did mixed rapidly with the Guaraní, giving the population a mestizo element from the outset.

Paraguay became independent in 1811, and the despotic José Gaspar Rodríguez de FRANCIA emerged as dictator of the fledgling republic (in office 1814–40). The country has been ruled by similar dictators ever since. One of these, Francisco Solano LÓPEZ (in office 1862–70), provoked Brazil, Argentina, and Uruguay into the War of the Triple Alliance (1865–70; see TRIPLE ALLIANCE, WAR OF THE) against Paraguay. The war left the country occupied by Brazil until 1876.

The next conflict was with Bolivia over sovereignty of the Chaco. In the CHACO WAR (1932–35), Paraguay won most of the disputed territory but again faced a long period of recovery. Postwar instability ended in 1954, when Gen. Alfredo Stroessner seized power. Although Paraguay generally prospered under Stroessner's authoritarian rule,

internal and external pressures for change increased in the 1980s, and in February 1989, Stroessner was deposed in a coup. The coup, led by Gen. Andrés Rodríguez, followed a power struggle between the militant and traditionalist factions of the Colorado party, the political arm of the Stroessner regime. Setting himself up as provisional president, Rodríguez pledged to bring democracy to Paraguay and moved to end press censorship and legalize banned political organizations. He also guaranteed free assembly, released political prisoners, welcomed returning political exiles, and launched an economic privatization program. In May 1989 he was elected president of Paraguay for a 5-year term.

Paraguay River   The Paraguay is a 2,550-km-long (1,585-mi) river in Brazil and Paraguay. It rises near Diamantino in Mato Grosso state, south central Brazil, and flows south into Paraguay to Asunción. Following the border between Paraguay and Argentina, the river joins the PARANÁ RIVER north of Corrientes, Argentina. The Paraguay drains a relatively empty and little-developed area of 1,100,000 km^2 (425,000 mi^2). Of major importance to landlocked Paraguay, the river is navigable by large vessels as far as Corumbá, Brazil.

parakeet   Parakeet is the common name for a number of small, usually slender birds of the parrot family, Psittacidae, order Psittaciformes, characterized by long, pointed tails. The best-known parakeet, widely known as the budgerigar, is *Melopsittacus undulatus,* native to the grasslands and sparsely wooded areas of central and southern Australia, where individuals sometimes gather in enormous flocks. Budgerigars are about 18 cm (7 in) long and, in the wild, are finely barred yellow and gray above, with pale green undersides and a bluish tail. The cere, a

Parakeets include the budgerigar (right) *and the crimson rosella* (left), *both native to Australia.*

raised area around the nostrils, is blue in adult males, brown in adult females, and pink in the young. Many budgerigars have been raised in captivity, and they are now available in many color varieties.

The monk, or green, parakeet, *Myiopsitta monachus,* native to southern South America, is among the hardiest of the parrot family. Permanent breeding populations are present in the region around New York City and are believed to have originated from escaped birds. Monk parakeets grow to about 28 cm (11 in) long and are green above, gray below, with dark blue feathers in the tail. They feed on fruit and grain and build large stick nests that may house up to six pairs of birds.

The only member of the parrot family native to the United States was the Carolina parakeet, *Conuropsis carolinensis,* which lived in flocks in heavily wooded wet areas east of the Great Plains from Virginia south. It was about 30 cm (12 in) long, with a greenish body and a yellow and orange head. Overhunting and habitat destruction caused its extinction.

paralegal services   *Paralegal services* refers to the employing of nonlawyers to assist lawyers and clients in law-related matters. Paralegal services were developed to increase access to legal services at reduced cost. Paralegals work under the supervision of lawyers and may not give legal advice requiring the exercise of independent legal judgment, represent clients in litigation, or fail to disclose that they are not attorneys.

Formal training in paralegal skills began in the late 1960s. Thousands of paralegals currently are employed by law firms and agencies, trained on the job or in programs in schools, colleges, and universities, many of which are approved by the American Bar Association.

parallax [par'-uh-laks]   Parallax is the difference in the apparent position of an object against a background when viewed by an observer from two different locations. These positions and the actual position of the object form a triangle from which the apex angle (the parallax) and the distance of the object can be determined if the length of the baseline between the observing positions is known and the angular direction of the object from each position at the ends of the baseline has been measured.

The traditional method in astronomy of determining the distance to a celestial object is to measure its parallax. Because of the large distances involved, astronomers choose as long a baseline as possible to obtain the greatest precision. For the Sun and the Moon the baseline is the Earth's equatorial radius, with the parallax defined as the difference in direction as seen by an observer at the equator and from the center of the Earth with the Sun and the Moon on the horizon. In practice two widely separated points on the Earth are chosen. The parallaxes of the Moon and the Sun are 57'02.448" and 8.794", respectively.

For parallaxes of objects beyond the solar system, the semimajor axis of the Earth's orbit is adopted as the

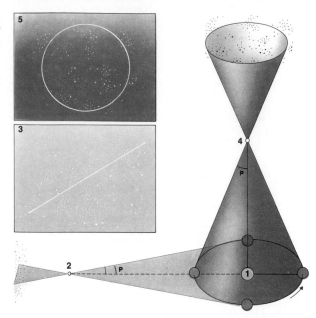

To a terrestrial observer a nearby star appears to shift its position among farther, relatively fixed background stars as the Earth orbits the Sun (1). The apparent motion, or parallax, is defined as the angle P at which the star subtends the radius of the Earth's orbit. A star (2) located in the plane of the Earth's orbit, or ecliptic, appears to oscillate in a straight line (3). A star that lies at a pole (4) of the ecliptic moves in a nearly circular path (5).

baseline. The parallax of the nearest star, Alpha Centauri, is 0.763". Approximately 60 separate stars are known with parallaxes equal to or larger than 0.50". In addition to Alpha Centauri they include the bright stars Sirius, Procyon, and Altair; the remainder are faint telescopic objects.

See also: DISTANCE, ASTRONOMICAL.

parallel processing   Parallel processing is a computer processing technique in which many operations are performed simultaneously, as opposed to serial processing, in which the computational steps must be performed in a sequential order. Conventional COMPUTERS are generally designed around a single CENTRAL PROCESSING UNIT; parallel processors utilize many interconnected microprocessors. A "coarse-grained" parallel processor contains a relatively small number of powerful processors; a "fine grain," or "massively parallel," machine contains thousands of microprocessors. Computers that utilize more than 65,000 microprocessors have been manufactured.

Proponents claim that parallel processors can solve large and complex problems much quicker—and that they are much cheaper to build—than the most powerful conventional computers. They expect parallel processors to be particularly adept at solving problems with a large number of variables, such as weather forecasting, quantum chromodynamics, voice recognition, and a variety of military applications. Parallel processors have already proven successful in the business world in such applications as assessing loan applications. Critics point to the tremendous programming difficulties (see COMPUTER PROGRAMMING) that parallel processors present. They caution that more basic research needs to be done before parallel processors achieve their wide potential.

parallelogram A parallelogram is a four-sided, closed, plane figure (a QUADRILATERAL) with its opposite sides equal in length and parallel. The lines passing through nonadjacent vertices are called diagonals. Either diagonal will divide the parallelogram into two congruent triangles. A perpendicular from any vertex to the opposite side is called an altitude of the parallelogram. The perimeter of a parallelogram is equal to $P = 2l + 2w$, where l and w denote any pair of adjacent sides. The area of a parallelogram can be obtained from the product of the base and the altitude drawn to that base. Special types of parallelograms include the SQUARE and RECTANGLE.

paralysis Paralysis is the temporary or permanent loss of function, usually motor but occasionally sensory, due to impairment of the nervous system or the muscles. If the damage is to the neural pathway between the muscle and the spinal cord, the victim experiences flaccid paralysis. The muscles lose tone and wither. When paralysis is due to brain injury or disease that affects an upper motor neuron from the cortex to the spinal cord, the extremities retain a reflex arc through the spinal cord and become hyperactive on a single fiber basis, tightening up in spastic paralysis and eventually becoming fixed in flexion due to contractures. The muscles do not waste away, or atrophy. Paralysis is most commonly encountered as a result of birth trauma (see CEREBRAL PALSY), accidents, strokes, brain tumors, and terminal muscle disease.

Paramaribo [par-uh-mar'-i-boh] Paramaribo (1988 est. pop., 67,905) is the capital of Suriname (formerly Dutch Guiana), on the northeastern coast of South America. It lies on the Suriname River about 24 km (15 mi) from the Atlantic Ocean. Tourism and small-scale industry are main sources of income. The older buildings in the city reflect Dutch influences. Originally a small Indian village, Paramaribo was occupied by the French and the English during the 17th century and came under Dutch rule in 1816.

Paramecium [par-uh-mee'-shuhm] *Paramecium* is a genus of single-celled protozoans with cilia, in the class Ciliophora. Found free-living in fresh water, paramecia are easily recognized under the microscope by their distinctive slipper shape. The body surface is covered with numerous cilia used for the organism's spiraling locomotion. The water currents thus produced help funnel bacteria, the paramecium's usual food, into the mouth, which is situated at the end of the oral groove, a ciliated

channel. A food vacuole forms around the food and travels in a cyclic manner in the cytoplasm. The vacuole's contents are subjected to digestive enzymes, and the products of digestion are diffused into the cytoplasm. Undigested material is released at the posterior end of the body. Liquid wastes and excess water are discharged through several permanently located contractile vacuoles, which produce star-shaped tubes in the water-collecting process.

Sexual reproduction in *Paramecium* is achieved through an exchange of chromosome-containing nuclei between two temporarily united paramecia. Genetic characters are passed to offspring by nuclear reorganization and duplication followed by a simple pinching into two cells. Paramecia also reproduce asexually through binary fission.

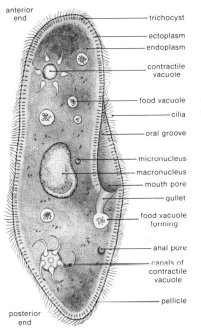

anterior end

trichocyst
ectoplasm
endoplasm
contractile vacuole
food vacuole
cilia
oral groove
micronucleus
macronucleus
mouth pore
gullet
food vacuole forming
anal pore
canals of contractile vacuole
pellicle

posterior end

(Left) Paramecium moves by means of cilia, which also sweep food particles through an oral groove into the gullet. A thick outer membrane, or pellicle, surrounds the cell ectoplasm. Unlike other protozoans, ciliates possess two types of nucleus: the larger macronucleus, and the micronucleus, which functions in reproduction. Contractile vacuoles regulate the water content of the cell.

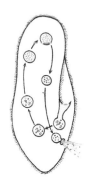

(Right) A food vacuole forms around food particles at the end of the gullet. As the vacuole circulates through the endolpasm, its contents are digested by enzymes. Undigested materials exit through an anal pore.

paramedic A paramedic is a highly skilled medical worker who is trained to carry out some of the more routine duties of a physician. Physician assistants, who are graduates of intensive 2-year programs, are paramedics skilled in taking case histories, giving medical examinations, making diagnoses, and providing basic medical care. Emergency medical technicians (EMTs), who function as ambulance workers, must complete 110 hours of classroom and clinical training and pass examinations. They are qualified to provide emergency firs aid and other life-support services. Advanced EMT-paramedics must complete an additional 700 to 1,000 hours of training.

American paramedics were originally specially trained military medical technicians who were first utilized during the Korean War. In many cases, these specialists were parachuted into locations where they were urgently needed: hence the term *para-medic* (a medical corpsman who was also a parachutist). Today the term is used to signify personnel who function as subsidiaries or supplements to physicians (the prefix *para* now is taken to mean "closely resembling; beside").

Paraná [pah-rah-nah'] Paraná, an important commercial and cultural center, is the capital of Entre Ríos province in northeastern Argentina. Located about 350 km (220 mi) northwest of Buenos Aires, the city has a population of 178,000 (1985 est.). Situated along the Paraná River opposite Santa Fe, Paraná has a well-developed port nearby. Cement and glass are manufactured, and an air force base is a major employer. Historical landmarks include the cathedral (completed 1883) and the Senate buildings (1858) of the Argentine Confederation. Founded in 1730, Paraná did not gain importance until 1853, when it was designated the nation's capital. The seat of government was moved to Buenos Aires in 1862, and in 1883, Paraná was made the capital of the province.

Paraná River The Paraná River, comprising a river system about 4,880 km (3,030 mi) long, is South America's second longest river. The Paraná proper is about 3,900 km (2,450 mi) long, and it drains an area of roughly 2.8 million km^2 (1,080,000 mi^2). The main tributaries are the Paraguay, Tiete, Paranapanema, Iguaçu, and Salado rivers. Beginning at the junction of the Paranaíba and Grande rivers in south central Brazil, the Paraná follows Paraguay's borders with Brazil and Argentina. At Corrientes, Argentina, it turns south and flows through its delta into the Río de la Plata. A shallow river broken at several points by falls, the Paraná is navigable by large ocean vessels only as far as Rosario.

paranoia [par-uh-noy'-uh] Paranoia, in psychology, is a state of mind characterized by delusions of grandeur or by an unfounded belief that one is being persecuted by others, or both. Although even healthy individuals may be subject occasionally to mild forms of paranoia, those with chronic cases tend to form rigid belief systems, often misinterpret the behavior of others as confirming their delusional views, and exhibit a great deal of anger and hatred. It is unknown what causes the escalation to paranoia from the natural "vigilance" with which most people regard their sometimes hostile environment. Some theorists suggest, however, that paranoid individuals project onto others attributes that they dislike in themselves. Organic causes are also possible. Social isolation—whether by choice or circumstance—seems to exacerbate paranoia.

Paranoid personality disorder is a diagnostic category (see PSYCHOPATHOLOGY) that encompasses chronic sufferers of paranoia. Delusional (paranoid) disorder is the term used to describe acute paranoia cases of a month or less in duration, which may be brought about by other emotional problems. The usual course of treatment for both is PSYCHOTHERAPY. Paranoia is also a characteristic of a subtype of SCHIZOPHRENIA known as paranoid schizophrenia. In addition to having the symptoms described above, persons with paranoid schizophrenia have frequent auditory hallucinations that reinforce their delusions. The course of treatment for paranoid schizophrenia often includes drug therapy (see PSYCHOPHARMACOLOGY).

parapsychology Parapsychology is the study of the ability of the mind to perform psychic acts. Psychic phenomena, as the term is applied to the human mind, generally fall into two broad categories: EXTRASENSORY PERCEPTION (ESP) and psychokinesis. ESP is the ability to acquire information without the benefit of the senses. It is generally divided into two subcategories: telepathy, the perception of someone else's thoughts; and clairvoyance, or remote perception, the sensing of an object or event out of range of the senses. Psychokinesis is defined as the ability to move or alter animate or inanimate matter by thought alone. Most scientists outside of the parapsychological field do not accept the existence of psychic phenomena.

History

Parapsychology is an outgrowth of the SPIRITUALISM movement in the late 1800s in Great Britain and the United States. The British Society for Psychical Research,

Parapsychological research in areas such as mental telepathy and clairvoyance is now being performed with modern apparatuses. In this photograph, a subject is being tested by machine, using a five-figure test developed by Karl Zener. The machine records how many of the same figures are selected by both subject and examiner when all contact between them has been eliminated.

founded in 1882, and the American Society for Psychical Research, founded in 1885, both sought to establish whether mediums who conducted spiritualistic séances actually contacted the dead or were merely fakes. Much of the early evidence cited by the psychical societies and others for the existence of psychic phenomena tended to be highly unscientific.

Psychologist J. B. RHINE intended to change this state of affairs when he began his investigations into parapsychology at Duke University in North Carolina in 1927. It was Rhine who coined the term *extrasensory perception*. Although he was not the first worker in the field to use statistical methods in his investigations, his methodology was regarded as more rigorous and sophisticated than those of earlier investigators. In a typical clairvoyance experiment, Rhine would seat the test subject in one building and the experimenter in another. The experimenter would shuffle a deck of Zener cards (a specially designed ESP testing deck, each card having one of five boldly printed symbols—star, square, circle, plus sign, and three wavy lines). Then the experimenter would draw a card and place it face down on the table. After a minute the experimenter would repeat the procedure. The subject, who had earlier synchronized watches with the experimenter, would try to guess, minute by minute, which card was lying on the table. Hundreds, and sometimes thousands, of trials would be made and the results tabulated.

Rhine claimed that in one test 1,850 guesses were recorded and that the test subject made 588 "hits," well above the probabilistic average of 370. Such results on a single test do not contravene the rules of chance, however. In the history of psychical research, promising results have tended to be nonrepeatable. (Repeatability of results is a benchmark of whether an experiment is considered scientifically valid.)

Since Rhine's ground-breaking experiments, parapsychologists have developed more sophisticated devices and safeguards. One device, for instance, uses a Geiger counter to measure random bursts of radiation from a radioactive substance and, depending upon the reading, light up one of four light bulbs on a panel. The subject tries to guess which light bulb will light up next.

Other researchers have tried to uncover qualitative information about the psychological state of subjects who supposedly perform well on ESP tests. They claim that subjects who believe in parapsychological phenomena tend to do better on the tests, as do subjects who are given immediate feedback after each guess. Some work has also been performed on subjects in "altered states" of consciousness, such as under hypnosis or under the influence of drugs.

Criticism

In 1955 chemist G. R. Price launched a famous attack against Rhine's work, calling it fraudulent (he later claimed he had been unfair in his judgment). This type of criticism has often been leveled at parapsychologists. Rhine himself once discovered that one of his senior researchers had been faking results, and he dismissed the

man. Parapsychologists maintain that they have policed their own ranks well.

A more serious charge is that parapsychologists are not trained well enough to be able to tell if a subject is committing fraud against them. The Committee for Scientific Investigation of Claims of the Paranormal, based in Buffalo, N.Y., has demonstrated on several occasions that even an amateur magician can fool a psychic investigator.

Others have charged that in many parapsychological research projects, statistical inferences have been made, experimental design has been shoddy, and data have been misread. A 1988 study by the National Research Council found that no scientific research conducted in the previous 130 years had proved the existence of parapsychological phenomena, although the council did find probabilistic anomalies in some experiments that could not readily be explained. Parapsychologists have countered that the study was unfair because the members of the study committee were prejudiced against parapsychology.

A final criticism is that for phenomena such as extrasensory perception and psychokinesis to be true, fundamental physical laws would have to be broken. Some parapsychologists adopt the view that psychic phenomena are outside the realm of science, whereas others believe that breakthroughs in particle physics may one day provide explanations for such phenomena.

---

parasite Parasitism, a symbiotic relationship, involves a species of organism (parasite) that infects a host species and depends on the host for nutrition and other basic metabolic needs. In highly evolved types of parasitism, minimal damage may be done to a host population, except that less-fit or disabled members may be weeded out. At the other end of the spectrum, highly virulent parasites cause diseases, such as rabies, and are referred to as pathogens.

Almost every life-form is affected by parasitism. Even bacteria are infected by certain viruses known as bacteriophages. Many parasites cause considerable agricultural damage. Tapeworms, which live in the gastrointestinal tract, are among the parasites that cause human illness.

---

parasitic diseases More than 100 parasitic organisms are known to be causes of serious diseases in human beings. Such diseases present a particular danger to people living in subtropical and tropical areas, as well as to children everywhere. A substantial percentage of the world's population is permanently debilitated to some degree by parasitic diseases.

Strictly speaking, any infectious organism could be considered a parasite (see INFECTIOUS DISEASES), but the term is conventionally applied only to those larger organisms which cause diseases, as contrasted to bacteria and viruses. The three major groups of parasitic organisms, then, are the protozoans (see PROTOZOA), various parasitic worms referred to collectively as helminths, and a number of ARTHROPODS.

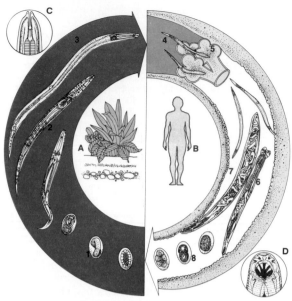

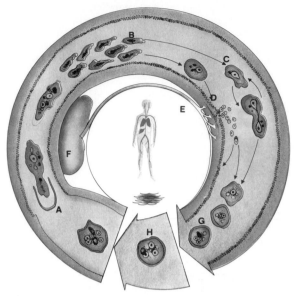

The hookworms Ancylostoma duodenale *and* Necator americanus *are common nematode parasites of humans. Their life cycle consists of stages in the soil (A) and in humans (B). Eggs (1) passed in the feces of an infected human hatch within 48 hours and develop into noninfective rhabditiform larvae (2). These molt to become filariform larvae (3) capable of infecting another human. After penetrating the skin, the larvae (4) enter the bloodstream, migrate to the lungs (5), and are coughed up into the throat and swallowed. They reach the intestine and mature into male (6) and female (7) adult worms, which attach to the intestinal wall with their sharp mouthparts (D; compare mouth of filariform larva, C). Adult hookworms live on human blood and produce thousands of eggs (8), eliminated in the host's feces.*

Amoebic dysentery is caused by the protozoan Entamoeba histolytica, *a food-transmitted human parasite. Ingested* Entamoeba *cysts pass to the small intestine, where the cyst wall dissolves (A). This liberates amoebas that divide to produce vegetative forms called trophozoites (B), which move to the large intestine. Noninfective trophozoites (C) feed on intestinal bacteria; infective trophozoites invade the gut wall (D), multiply, and dissolve intestinal tissues using protein-digesting enzymes. If they enter the blood circulation (E), the amoebas may be carried to the lungs (F), liver, or brain, where they cause abcesses. Amoebas released from the intestinal wall often form cysts (G), which pass out of the host's body with the feces. Cysts may infect another human who ingests contaminated food or water (H).*

Protozoal parasites include AMOEBAS, GIARDIA and other flagellates, ciliates (see CILIATA), and sporozoans (see SPOROZOA). Helminths include trematodes (FLUKES), cestodes (TAPEWORMS), and NEMATODES (roundworms, including filariids). In the case of protozoans and helminths, infections by the organisms and their resulting effects on the body constitute the parasitic disease involved. In the case of arthropods, however, including arachnids (MITES and TICKS) and insects (for example, the BEDBUG, FLEA, LOUSE, MOSQUITO, TSETSE FLY), some of the organisms may in fact live as parasites on the body and produce various debilitating effects and disorders. They are of more concern to epidemiologists, however, as the vectors for a wide range of serious human illnesses, including many of the diseases caused by parasitic protozoans and helminths.

Among the major diseases caused by protozoan infestations are AMEBIASIS, balantidiasis, amoebic DYSENTERY, kala-azar, LEISHMANIASIS, MALARIA, TOXOPLASMOSIS, trichomoniasis, and TRYPANOSOMIASIS. Among the helminths, SCHISTOSOMIASIS—also known as bilharziasis or snail fever—is the only human disease known to be caused by a fluke. Other major helminth infections include ASCARIASIS; various forms of FILARIASIS, including EYE WORM and RIVER BLINDNESS; and TRICHINOSIS. The many diseases transmitted by biting arthropods include trypanosomiasis (sleeping sickness) carried by tsetse flies, malaria and filariasis carried by mosquitoes, leishmaniasis and kala-azar carried by sand flies, Chagas's disease carried by triatomid bugs, and river blindness carried by blackflies. (Other, nonparasitic diseases transmitted by such arthropods are described in individual entries on those life-forms.)

Other routes of infection for parasitic diseases vary according to the parasite. Food-transmitted human parasites include *Entamoeba histolytica*, the cause of amoebic dysentery, and *Trichinella spiralis*, the cause of trichinosis. Soil- and water-transmitted diseases include ascariasis, schistosomiasis, and hookworm. Human parasitic diseases classified as ZOONOSES are diseases transmitted to humans from other animals. Toxoplasmosis, for example, is an infection caused by a protozoan normally parasitic in felines and rodents, and trichinosis normally occurs in pigs and rats.

Immune responses are part of the human body's internal defense mechanisms against parasitic invasion. A successful parasite must overcome host IMMUNITY. The antigen-antibody interactions involving metazoan parasites are more complex than those involving bacteria and viruses because of the multiplicity of the metazoan parasite's antigen system. Production of parasite antigens resembling host antigens, or the binding of host antigens to the parasite body surface, may prevent the host's body from recognizing the parasite as an invader. This may explain why parasites can be so successful.

See also: DISEASES, ANIMAL; DISEASES, PLANT.

parathyroid The parathyroid glands are small, bean-shaped endocrine glands found in mammals, lizards, and birds. Humans usually have four, lying just behind or within the THYROID GLAND in the lower part of the front of the neck. The parathyroid hormone, called parathormone, regulates the concentrations and balance of calcium and phosphate ions in the blood. Parathormone secretion, stimulated by a reduction in the level of blood calcium, causes the level to be restored to normal by the release of calcium from bone. At the same time, phosphate is excreted in urine to maintain the correct balance between the two ions. If too much parathormone is secreted (hyperparathyroidism), the result is a softening of bones from decalcification, and low blood-phosphate levels. If too little is secreted (hypoparathyroidism), the result is low blood calcium, high blood phosphate, and nervous excitability leading to tetany (rapid and involuntary muscle contraction).

See also: ENDOCRINE SYSTEM; ENDOCRINE SYSTEM, DISEASES OF THE.

paratroops SEE AIRBORNE TROOPS

parchment A writing material made from the skins primarily of sheep, calves, or goats, parchment was probably developed in the Middle East more or less contemporaneously with PAPYRUS. The material came into wide use, however, only in the 2d century BC when, in the city of Pergamum in Anatolia, a method was perfected for making a parchment that could be used on both sides. Skins were depilated, scraped and polished, stretched, and then rubbed with chalk and pumice.

Early parchments were yellow and were often tinted with a purple dye to point up the silver and gold inks used in lettering. Later, techniques were developed for whitening the skins. Fine skins from young calves or kids were called vellum, and the name was often used for all parchment manuscripts. The use of parchment grew—gradually supplanting papyrus—until it became the most important writing material in the Western world. Even after the invention of printing made paper a more economical material for bookmaking, parchment continued in use for special manuscripts.

pardon A pardon, in law, is a release from punishment given by the head of a government. The president of the United States has the constitutional power to "grant reprieves and pardons for offenses against the United States." President Gerald Ford pardoned former president

Richard Nixon following the latter's resignation in connection with the WATERGATE scandal. Ford also extended a conditional AMNESTY, or group pardon, to draft resisters and deserters from the armed forces of the Vietnam War period, provided they agreed to work in public-service jobs for a specified period.

In the United States, governors are called on for pardons much more frequently than are presidents, because the individual states have jurisdiction over most crimes. In general, pardons are granted to mitigate the harshness of the law, as with an elderly sick prisoner, to recognize evidence of reform on the part of the guilty person, or to acknowledge belief in the innocence of the accused.

parent A parent is the legally recognized father or mother of a person. In its narrowest sense and under the old common law, the term refers only to biological mothers and fathers. By statute in most American jurisdictions, however, people who adopt children are also considered to be parents.

The status of parenthood results in certain rights and duties existing between parents and minor children. Modern statutes in the United States provide that both the father and the mother are natural GUARDIANS of their offspring. If it becomes necessary for the law to appoint alternative guardians, these people are known as guardians by law. Parents are responsible for the health, financial support, and education of their children. (If either parent fails to provide support for his or her minor children, it is generally a criminal offense.) Illegitimate children are usually given into the custody of the mother, with the father providing support.

See also: ADOPTION AND FOSTER CARE; DIVORCE; FAMILY.

Parents and Teachers, National Congress of The National Congress of Parents and Teachers (also known as the National PTA), founded in 1897 and headquartered in Chicago, is a private organization of parents, teachers, and school administrators that promotes the educational, social, and economic welfare of school-age children. Concerns include the development of reading skills, children's safety and emotional health, juvenile protection, and raising the quality of education.

Pareto, Vilfredo [pah-ray'-toh, veel-fray'-doh]   Vilfredo Pareto, b. Paris, July 15, 1848, d. Aug. 20, 1923, was a theorist of economics and sociology whose most important contribution to those fields was to insist on the use of scientific methods of analysis and theory construction. Pareto pioneered the use of mathematical statistics in constructing a formal theory to explain how an economy operates. Although many of his original formulations have been modified, he set the basis for the contemporary field of ECONOMETRICS and devised the classic law of income and wealth distribution known as Pareto's law.

Pareto viewed the study of sociology as an extension of economics. According to Pareto, sociology deals primarily with the nonlogical components of social action, such as values, desires, and illusions, which are not handled by disciplines such as economics. In attempting to link these nonconcrete elements of behavior with the logical components of social action, Pareto developed a complex, formal view of society as a system. The most important empirical application of Pareto's abstract sociological theories was his perspective on the role of ELITES in society. Pareto was professor of political economy at the University of Lausanne, Switzerland, from 1893 to 1907.

Parícutin [pah-ree'-koo-teen] Parícutin, an active volcano in Michoacán, west central Mexico, first erupted Feb. 20, 1943. Before the eyes of an Indian farmer about to plow his cornfield, the flat land opened, and within the first 24-hour period the volcano formed an 8-m-high (25-ft) cinder cone. In eight months it reached a height of 457 m (1,500 ft) above its base, 2,774 m (9,100 ft) above sea level. The town of Parícutin was buried, and San Juan Parangaricutiro was partially covered, by 18 km^2 (7 mi^2) of lava and volcanic ash. The initial eruptions ceased in 1952.

Paris (France) Paris, the capital of France, is located in northern France on both banks of the SEINE RIVER, 145 km (90 mi) from the river's mouth on the English Chan-

nel. A total of 2,146,900 (1990) inhabitants live in Paris proper, and 10,210,059 persons (1984 est.) live in greater Paris, one of Europe's largest metropolitan areas. A city of world importance, Paris is the business, historic, intellectual, diplomatic, religious, educational, artistic, and tourist center of France and dominates the historic region of ÎLE-DE-FRANCE.

Contemporary City

Paris is more than 2,000 years old and has been one of the major cities of Europe since the Middle Ages, but its greatest growth came during a 40-year period after 1850, when the population doubled. Since 1921, when the population of the city proper reached a peak of 2,906,500, most growth has occurred in the suburbs.

The economic activities of Paris overshadow those of any other part of France in importance and complexity. About 65% of the nation's bank and corporate headquarters are in the city. Much of the industry in central Paris is small scale and often family owned; many of these operations make luxury items such as perfumes, furs, gloves, jewelry, toys, clothing, and wooden articles. Book printing and publishing are major activities in central Paris. Heavier industries are situated in the suburbs. These include the manufacture of automobiles, machine tools, railroad rolling stock, electric and electronic products, chemicals, and processed foods. Construction and the production of building materials are also important. Tour-

The Eiffel Tower, built for the Paris Exposition, the centenary of the French Revolution, rises 300 m (984 ft) above the city. When completed in 1889, it was the world's tallest structure.

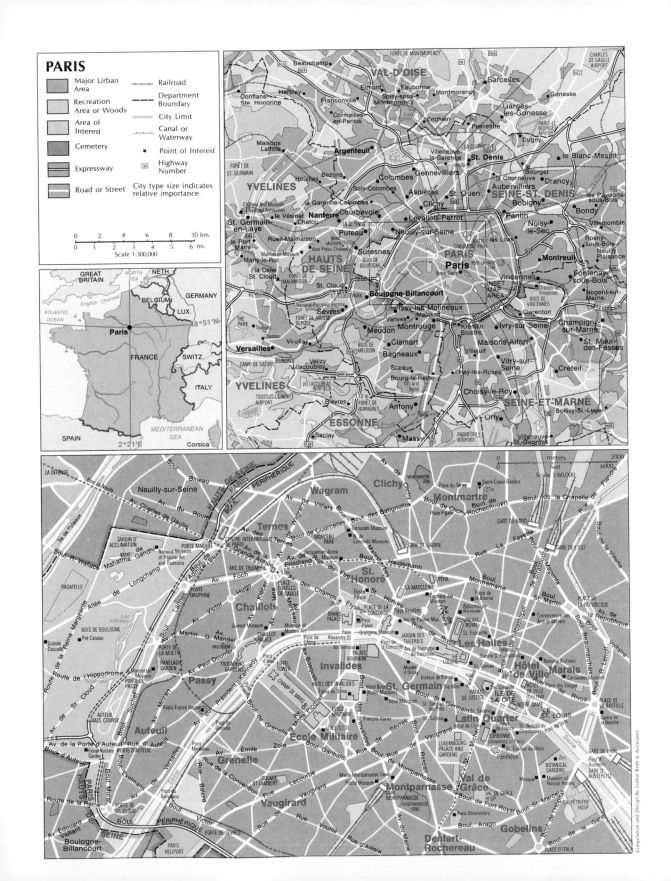

ism, however, is by far the city's largest source of income.

Government. Paris is divided into 20 *arrondissements*, or districts, each with its own mayor. Each of these is again divided into four sections. Two prefects and a mayor administer the city as a whole with the help of a general council.

Transportation. Paris is the head of barge and ship navigation on the Seine and is the fourth most important port in France (after Marseille, Le Havre, and Dunkerque). The Loire, Rhine, Rhône, Meuse, and Scheldt rivers can be reached by canals connecting with the Seine. Paris is also a major rail, highway, and air-transportation hub. Two international airports, Orly and Charles de Gaulle, serve the city. The city's subway system, the Métro, was opened in 1900.

Layout and Landmarks. The street plan and total urban development of Paris are divided into two parts by the Seine and connected by 31 bridges. The major street pattern is the result of the 19th-century plan of Baron Georges HAUSSMANN, prefect under Napoleon III. He positioned the main streets and boulevards so that they are long and straight and focus on the major traffic circles, intersections, and architectural landmarks throughout the city. Between the major thoroughfares are the narrow, winding, congested streets.

The Rive Gauche, or Left Bank (when facing downstream), contains the governmental and university sectors of the city. It is the site of the most famous landmark of Paris, the EIFFEL TOWER (1889). Nearby are the Musée d'Orsay (1986) and the Hôtel des Invalides, which dates from the time of Louis XIV and includes a church containing the tomb of Napoleon I. The Latin Quarter is the home of students because the Sorbonne (part of the Universities of Paris, founded in 1150) is there. Montparnasse, toward the outskirts of the city, was once frequented by avant-garde artists, writers, and poets.

Situated in the Seine, the Île de la Cité is the focal point of the city and is dominated by the majestic Cathedral of NOTRE DAME DE PARIS (begun 1163).

The Rive Droite, or Right Bank, contains the retail center, large department stores, hotels, banks, the theater district, and government buildings. The urban axis known as the Triumphal Way begins at the LOUVRE, continues past the TUILERIES Garden to the elegant Place de la Concorde and up the Champs-Élysées to the ARC DE TRIOMPHE DE L'ETOILE, continuing from there along the Avenue Charles de Gaulle to the Arc de La Défense (completed in 1989) at the city's western edge. North of the Champs-Élysées is the Garnier Opéra, and beyond that the Montmartre district with the Sacré-Coeur basilica. The Place de la Bastille, on the Right Bank near the Île de la Cité, marks the location of the fortress destroyed during the French Revolution (see BASTILLE) and is the site of the Bastille Opera house, opened in 1990.

History

Gauls of the Parisii tribe founded a fishing village on the present-day Île de la Cité between 250 and 200 BC. Known as Lutetia (Lutèce) in ancient times, Paris was conquered by Julius Caesar in 52 BC and was a regional

The Cathedral of Notre Dame, the oldest church in Paris, lies at the eastern end of the Île de la Cité. The cornerstone of this church, one of the first built in the French Gothic style, was laid in 1163, but its initial construction was not completed until the 14th century.

center under the Romans and in the early Middle Ages. In 987, HUGH CAPET, Count of Paris, became king of France, and under his successors, the CAPETIANS, the city's position as the nation's capital became established. The people of Paris first declared themselves an independent commune under the leadership of Étienne Marcel in 1355–58. The storming of the Bastille in 1789 was the first of a series of key actions by the Parisian people during the FRENCH REVOLUTION. Paris also played a major role in the revolutions of 1830 and 1848. In 1871, during the FRANCO-PRUSSIAN WAR, the city was besieged for four months until France surrendered. After German troops withdrew, French radicals briefly established the COMMUNE OF PARIS. During World War I the Germans were prevented from reaching Paris, but they occupied the city during World War II from 1940 to 1944.

Paris today maintains its importance, character, and charm, though its appearance is being transformed by structures such as the BEAUBOURG and by the ambitious *grands projets* building program carried out under the presidency of François Mitterrand. In addition to La Défense arch and the Bastille Opera, Mitterrand's projects have included the renovation of the Louvre by architect I. M. Pei, the La Villette complex in the northeast, and, in the southeast, the Bibliothèque de France, begun in 1991.

Paris (mythology)   In Greek mythology Paris was the handsome Trojan prince, son of PRIAM and HECUBA, whose seduction of HELEN caused the TROJAN WAR. As an infant Paris was exposed on a hillside and left to die by his parents because an oracle had predicted that he would bring about Troy's downfall. He was found and raised by some shepherds and, as a young man, returned to Troy. His athletic prowess was so great—he earned the epithet Alexandros or "champion"—that his true heritage was recognized, and he was reunited with his family.

Paris was greatly favored by the goddess Aphrodite, whom he had selected as the fairest of the goddesses over HERA and ATHENA; she led him to Helen, wife of King MENELAUS of Sparta and the "most beautiful woman in the world." During the Trojan War, Paris was despised for his cowardice. He survived a duel with Menelaus and, with a poisoned arrow guided by Apollo, slew ACHILLES. He eventually died from a war wound that his first wife, the nymph Oenone, refused to treat.

Paris, treaties of

Paris, the capital of France, has been the site of many important treaty negotiations. The SEVEN YEARS' WAR was concluded by the Treaty of Paris of Feb. 10, 1763, signed by Britain, France, and Spain. France lost to Britain all of its North American possessions (except Louisiana, which it had ceded to Spain); the treaty excluded French troops from Bengal, effectively ending the French imperial drive in India; and, in Africa, France yielded Senegal to the British. The only colonies retained by France were Saint Pierre and Miquelon (in the Gulf of St. Lawrence); Saint Lucia, Haiti, Guadeloupe, and Martinique (in the West Indies); and Pondichéry and Chandernagor (in India). Spain recovered Cuba and the Philippines but ceded Florida to Britain.

If the 1763 treaty was a landmark in the growth of the BRITISH EMPIRE, another Treaty of Paris (Sept. 3, 1783) marked Britain's first major colonial loss. By that treaty, which ended the AMERICAN REVOLUTION, Britain recognized the independence of the United States. The treaty also made navigation of the Mississippi free to all signatories (which included France, Spain, and Holland), restored Florida to Spain and Senegal to France, and gave the United States fishing rights off Newfoundland.

By the Treaty of Paris of May 30, 1814, concluded after the initial defeat and abdication of Napoleon I, the Allies (Britain, Austria, Prussia, and Russia) imposed a fairly lenient settlement on a France exhausted by the NAPOLEONIC WARS. After the return and second defeat of Napoleon, the same countries signed a second Treaty of Paris (Nov. 20, 1815), which reduced France to its 1790 boundaries.

The Treaty of Paris of Mar. 30, 1856, brought the CRIMEAN WAR to an end. Russia agreed to neutralization of the Black Sea and ceded the mouth of the Danube and part of Bessarabia to what was to become Romania. In addition, the European powers guaranteed the integrity of the Ottoman Empire (Turkey).

The SPANISH-AMERICAN WAR ended in another Treaty of Paris (Dec. 10, 1898). Spain ceded the Philippines, Guam, and Puerto Rico to the United States and granted independence to Cuba.

For the treaties concluding World War I that were negotiated in Paris, see PARIS PEACE CONFERENCE.

By the treaties of Paris following World War II (Feb. 10, 1947), the victorious Allies imposed territorial adjustments on Italy, Romania, Hungary, and Finland. In addition, these countries and Bulgaria were forced to pay indemnities.

The most recent important treaty signed in Paris was the cease-fire agreement of Jan. 27, 1973, in the VIETNAM WAR. That pact called for U.S. withdrawal from South Vietnam, release of all prisoners of war, recognition of the right of the South Vietnamese people to determine their own future, and establishment of an international peacekeeping force in South Vietnam. Although U.S. troops withdrew, the war did not end until the North Vietnamese overran South Vietnam in 1975.

Paris, Universities of

The 13 Universities of Paris were founded in 1970 as a result of a 1968 act that reformed French institutions of higher learning. Eight of the universities are in Paris; the other 5 are in Nanterre, Orsay, Créteil, Saint-Denis, and Villetaneuse. All operate under the Ministry of Education and are financed by the state. The original University of Paris, founded c.1170, grew out of the schools of the cathedral of Notre Dame. It became northern Europe's most famous seat of learning, especially in theology, and by the 13th century it also had faculties in canon law, medicine, and the arts.

The university came to be composed of a federation of colleges, a format that influenced the organization of other European and, especially, English universities. Around 1257, Robert de Sorbon endowed a college for theological studies that came to be known as the Sorbonne. The name *Sorbonne* became synonymous with the theological faculty of the university and later with the university itself. The Sorbonne now incorporates three units of the Universities of Paris and is made up of three general faculties of letters and sciences and of administrative offices. In 1808, Napoleon reorganized the University of Paris and other French institutions, freeing them from political and religious control.

By the mid-20th century the University of Paris had distinguished faculties of letters, law, medicine, pharmacy, and sciences. Free education was available for men and women who passed the baccalaureate examination given at the end of secondary school. Growing discontent with overcrowding, the lack of student and faculty participation in university decisions, and the rigid faculty and university structure led to a massive student protest at the Sorbonne in May 1968 and to the reorganization of 1970.

Paris Observatory

Paris Observatory (Observatoire de Paris) is the oldest astronomical observatory still in use. It was built (1667–72) in Paris under Louis XIV by the architect Claude Perrault at the instigation of Jean Picard and J. B. COLBERT. The observatory's first director was Giovanni Domenico Cassini. In 1887 a congress at Paris agreed to create the *Carte du Ciel* (Map of the Heavens; see ASTRONOMICAL CATALOGS AND ATLASES). Today the Paris Observatory has observational sites outside Paris. One is the Meudon Observatory founded by Jules Janssen in 1876. Instruments at Meudon include a 3.3-ft (1-m) reflector and a 16-in (40-cm) wide-angle Schmidt camera telescope. A radio astronomy observatory is also attached to the Paris Observatory, as well as a site on the plateau of Calern.

Paris Peace Conference The Paris Peace Conference was organized by the victors at the end of WORLD WAR I to settle the issues raised by that conflict. Because the 27 nations represented often had conflicting plans for peace, the resulting treaties were controversial. The conference convened on Jan. 18, 1919. Germany and the other defeated Central Powers were not permitted to sit at the conference tables. The four major victorious powers, Britain, France, Italy, and the United States, dominated the proceedings. U.S. president Woodrow WILSON favored a conciliatory settlement based on the liberal principles of his FOURTEEN POINTS. French premier Georges CLEMENCEAU, trying to secure his country against future German attack, was often at odds with Wilson. David LLOYD GEORGE, the British prime minister, and Vittorio ORLANDO, the Italian premier, were the other "Big Four" leaders of the Supreme Council that controlled the conference. Advisory committees worked on specialized areas such as REPARATIONS, economics, and future international organization.

France conceded its key demand, that the left bank of the Rhine be detached from Germany and put under French military control, in exchange for British and American promises of future support. The Treaty of Versailles, presented to Germany in May 1919 and signed on June 28, was, however, still criticized as a harsh "dictated peace." Germany was compelled to admit war guilt, to give up territory, and to disarm; its Saar and Rhineland districts were placed under Allied occupation; and it was supposed to pay heavy reparations.

The Versailles treaty did not conform to the Fourteen Points, but Wilson was pleased with the other major result of the conference, the covenant of the LEAGUE OF NATIONS, which was given final approval on Apr. 28, 1919. The Treaty of Saint Germain with Austria (September 10) and the Treaty of Neuilly with Bulgaria (November 27) were also signed at Paris. Treaties with Hungary and Turkey were not completed at the conference, which ended on Jan. 16, 1920, with the formal inauguration of the League of Nations.

parity (economics) *Parity* is an economic term referring to the measurement of equivalent categories. In agriculture, it is the price for a farm product that will give farmers the amount of purchasing power obtained during the so-called golden years of U.S. farming (1909–14). Government agriculture programs attempted to keep farm prices at a percentage (usually 60–90%) of parity, either by direct subsidy or by purchasing surplus crops. Parity was superseded by other price-support measurements in the 1980s.

Parity (or par value) also refers to the value of one country's currency as expressed in the equivalent value of another currency (see EXCHANGE RATE) or in terms of some precious metal.

parity (physics) In physics, parity is bilateral SYMMETRY, or symmetry under reflection across a plane. All higher animals exhibit this symmetry, appearing symmetric about a plane through the middle. Corresponding to each point on one side of the plane there is an identical point on the other side at the same distance. A symmetrical object, when reflected in a mirror, has an identical image except that its left and right side are interchanged. Therefore, parity symmetry is often called reflection symmetry, or left-right symmetry. Some physical quantities, such as velocity, electric field, and polarity of magnets, reverse under parity reflection, whereas others, such as rotational velocity and magnetic field, remain unchanged. Proper account of this has to be taken in the study of the reflection symmetry of systems involving these quantities.

The Basic Laws of Physics. The laws of electricity and magnetism, determined by Maxwell, Faraday, and others, are invariant under reflection, as are the laws of gravity of Newton and Einstein. In the subatomic domain, the strong force between protons and neutrons is also known to obey the parity symmetry. It was assumed for a long time that all laws of nature are left-right symmetric. Through further studies of the weak force that is responsible for nuclear BETA DECAY and other decays of subatomic particles, however, inconsistencies were found. This prompted the Chinese-American physicists T. D. Lee and C. N. Yang, in 1956, to suggest that parity symmetry is violated in weak interactions, which was quite a revolutionary idea. The suggestion was confirmed the following year in studies by researchers of the beta decay of the cobalt nucleus.

The Neutrino. Why is the weak interaction so different from all other forces? It has been speculated that this is related to the properties of an elusive particle called the NEUTRINO, which has no electric charge and has no other form of interaction but weak interaction. It is emitted in the process of beta decay, which involves the conversion of a neutron into a proton and an electron. This particle is supposed to have no (or only a very tiny) mass and to have an intrinsic rotation (or spin) always antiparallel to its direction of motion. The other state of the neutrino, in which the spin is parallel to the particle's direction of motion, is not found in nature. Therefore, by its very existence the neutrino defines a screw sense. Because it participates only in weak interactions, only those laws of motion violate parity. The final word on this has not yet been said.

There exists an alternative proposal, which restores the left-right symmetry to weak interaction and explains the observed parity violation in beta decay as being a result of asymmetric boundary conditions that become manifest at large nuclear distances. According to this theory, when beta-decay experiments are carried out in high-energy accelerators, traces of the intrinsic parity symmetry should appear. This theory requires the neutrino to have some mass. Its appeal is that it puts the weak force on a par with and provides a more unified description of the other forces of nature.

Linked with the question of parity invariance are the questions of invariance under reversal of time direction and under matter-antimatter substitution. It is strongly believed that simultaneous parity, time reversal, and matter-antimatter transformations leave all physical laws unchanged. Because parity is violated in weak interactions and time-reversal invariance is thought to hold, matter-antimatter symmetry must also be violated in beta decay to keep the product of all three transformations symmetrical.

Park Chung Hee   Park Chung Hee, b. Nov. 14, 1917, d. Oct. 26, 1979, was president of South Korea from 1963 until his assassination. Park, a South Korean army general, masterminded the overthrow of the civilian government in 1961 and became chairman of the ruling junta. He was elected president in 1963 and reelected in 1967 and 1971. Park instituted martial law in 1972 and assumed dictatorial powers. Great economic advances were made in South Korea under Park, but political opposition to him increased in the 1970s. In 1974, Park's wife was killed in an assassination attempt on Park. Five years later Park was killed by Kim Jae Kyu, the head of the South Korean Central Intelligence Agency.

Parker, Alton Brooks   Alton Brooks Parker, b. Cortland, N.Y., May 14, 1852, d. May 10, 1926, a prominent American jurist, was the Democratic candidate for president in 1904. A power in New York State Democratic politics, Parker served as a judge on several New York State benches between 1885 and 1904 and rendered liberal decisions in cases involving the rights of labor. In 1904 the Democratic presidential convention, although badly split, chose Parker on the first ballot. To contrast him with the Republican nominee, progressive Theodore ROOSEVELT, the party presented Parker as a conservative. Parker carried only the South, receiving 140 electoral votes out of 476.

Parker, Bonnie   see BARROW, CLYDE

Parker, Charlie   Charles Christopher "Bird" Parker, Jr., b. Kansas City, Kans., Aug. 29, 1920, d. Mar. 12, 1955, was an alto saxophonist who became one of the seminal influences in the jazz movement known as BEBOP. Although he played in big bands, most notably in the band led by Jay McShann, Parker was happiest in small jazz groups. In 1945, while he was playing in New York's 52d Street jazz clubs, he and Dizzy GILLESPIE made the first definitive bop recordings. Bop's ragged, rhythmically erratic and harmonically extended style exerted enormous influence on jazz musicians, and Parker is now recognized as one of the jazz greats.

Parker, Dorothy   An American critic, satirical poet, and short-story writer, Dorothy Rothschild Parker, b. West End, N.J., Aug. 22, 1893, d. June 7, 1967, is remembered as much for her flashing verbal exchanges and malicious wit as for the disenchanted stories and sketches in which she revealed her underlying pessimism. Starting her career as *Vanity Fair*'s drama critic (1917–20) and

Dorothy Parker's terse style, acid wit, and sharp perception won her recognition as one of the most agile critics, poets, and short-story writers in the United States during the mid-20th century. Among her most acclaimed works are Enough Rope *(1927), her first volume of poetry, and the short story "Big Blonde."*

continuing as the *New Yorker*'s theater and book reviewer (1927–33), Parker enhanced her legend in the 1920s and early 1930s through membership in the Algonquin Hotel's celebrated Round Table.

Parker published her first light verse in *Enough Rope* (1927) and *Death and Taxes* (1931). These were followed by the short-story collections *Laments for the Living* (1930) and *After Such Pleasures* (1933), containing her most famous story, "Big Blonde." Parker scripted films in Hollywood from 1933 to 1938 and in 1937 covered the Spanish Civil War for the *New Masses*. In collaboration with others she also wrote two Broadway plays: *Close Harmony* (1924), with Elmer Rice, and *Ladies of the Corridor* (1953), with Arnaud d'Usseau.

Parker, Ely S.   Ely S. Parker (Do-ne-ho-ga-wa), b. Oct. 13, 1829, d. Aug. 31, 1895, a SENECA Indian of the Wolf clan, served under President Ulysses S. GRANT on the Board of Indian Commissioners. Parker's clan grandfather was RED JACKET, a famous warrior chief and champion of the Indian manner of life, and his grandnephew was Arthur C. Parker, an anthropologist and founding member of the NATIONAL CONGRESS OF AMERICAN INDIANS.

Ely Parker was born in western New York and educated in mission schools. As a child, he lived for a time in traditional Iroquoian style in the Canadian woods. Later, he worked in New York with anthropologist Lewis Henry MORGAN on a study of Iroquois culture. Before 1850, Parker had gone to Washington, D.C., as an advocate for Seneca land claims. A captain in the Union forces during the Civil War, Parker served as military secretary to General Grant, and after the war President Grant appointed Parker an Indian commissioner. Parker and others came under attack in an investigation of corruption in the Bureau of Indian Affairs. Although government records seem to exonerate him, he resigned his position.

Parker, Francis Wayland   Francis Wayland Parker, b. Bedford, N.H., Oct. 9, 1837, d. Mar. 2, 1902, was an

American leader of PROGRESSIVE EDUCATION. He began teaching at the age of 16 and continued until 1872, when he went to Germany to study the new methods of Johann F. HERBART and Friedrich FROEBEL. As superintendent of schools (1875–80) in Quincy, Mass., he introduced science and the arts into the curriculum and encouraged pupil self-expression. After holding supervisory positions in the school systems of Boston (1880–83) and Cook County, Ill. (1883–99), Parker founded (1899) the Chicago Institute, a private school that became the University of Chicago's school of education in 1901.

Parker, Matthew   As archbishop of Canterbury, Matthew Parker, b. Aug. 6, 1504, d. May 17, 1575, identified himself with the moderate reform of the Elizabethan church. He had been made chaplain to Anne Boleyn and later to Henry VIII and received several preferments under Edward VI but, upon Mary I's accession (1553), was forced to go into hiding. Under Elizabeth I, Parker was chosen archbishop (1559). Along with his scholarly editions of medieval works, he helped issue the THIRTY-NINE ARTICLES (1563) and the "Bishops' Bible" (1568).

Parker, Quanah   The Comanche war leader Quanah Parker, b. northern Texas, c.1845, d. Feb. 21, 1911, was the son of Peta Nocona, chief of the Kwahadi band in Texas, and Cynthia Parker, a white captive. From 1867 to the time of his defeat at Adobe Walls in 1874, he led raids against white settlers. After this defeat the Indian camps were destroyed and their inhabitants were forced onto the reservation at Fort Sill, Okla. In June 1875, Quanah settled there and counseled his people to adapt to the white man's control without surrendering their Comanche customs and heritage. Quanah, an appointive judge (1886–98) of the Court of Indian Affairs and a successful businessman, rode in Theodore Roosevelt's inauguration parade.

Parker, Theodore   Theodore Parker, b. Lexington, Mass., Aug. 24, 1810, d. May 10, 1860, was a preacher and social reformer whose activist ministry has been an example to succeeding generations of ministers. He became the focus of controversy in 1841 when he preached a sermon—"The Transient and Permanent in Christianity"—which undercut Christianity's claim as a unique revelation from God. His religious philosophy, strongly influenced by transcendentalism, was the basis for vigorous attacks on the popular theology and for advocacy of social and ecclesiastical reforms. An abolitionist, Parker risked imprisonment in attempting to free a fugitive slave by force.

Parkes, Sir Henry   Henry Parkes, b. England, May 27, 1815, d. Apr. 27, 1896, premier of New South Wales (1872–75, 1877, 1878–83, 1887, 1889–91), emigrated to Sydney in 1839 and gained political prominence in 1849 as the leader of opposition to the transpor-

tation of convicts from Britain to Australia. He was a liberal reformer whose achievements as premier included the establishment of free trade, the creation of a free and compulsory secular school system, and the curbing of Chinese immigration. In 1889, Parkes became the chief advocate of federation for the six Australian colonies, and he led the Australian federal convention in 1891. He was knighted in 1877.

Parkinson's disease   Parkinson's disease, or parkinsonism, is a chronic disorder characterized by involuntary tremulous motion beginning in the hands at rest. Movements become slow as the muscles become rigid, causing a masklike face, and the torso tilts forward. Onset is between the ages of 40 and 70. The disease progresses to severe physical limitations, and the intellect may ultimately be compromised.

The disease can be induced by certain chemicals, suggesting that parkinsonism might have an environmental origin. The·injury to the body occurs in the region of the upper brain stem where the NEUROTRANSMITTER dopamine is normally produced. Lack of this brain chemical causes the onset of the disease's symptoms. Drug treatments include use of the dopamine precursor levadopa—dopamine itself cannot cross the blood-brain barrier—but levadopa causes severe side effects. When it is used in combination with a more recent drug, deprenyl, these effects are reduced.

Doctors in Mexico pioneered a radical approach in 1986 when they transplanted cells from the adrenal gland into the brain of a patient, with the aim of stimulating brain cells to manufacture dopamine. The results of such transplants have not proved very promising, but doctors are finding more hope in another procedure in which fetal brain cells are introduced into a patient's brain for the same purpose. SHOCK THERAPY has also been tried with some success.

Parkinson's law   Parkinson's law states that work expands to fill the time available for its completion. This comic "law" was expounded by Cyril Northcote Parkinson in *Parkinson's Law: The Pursuit of Progress* (1957), a work that ridicules the excesses of bureaucracy. Parkinson laid down similar dicta in a later work, *The Law and the Profits* (1966): for example, expenditure rises to meet income.

Parkman, Francis   Francis Parkman, b. Boston, Sept. 16, 1823, d. Nov. 8, 1893, one of America's great historians, vividly described the American wilderness and the Anglo-French struggle for mastery of North America. Born to a wealthy family and educated at Harvard University, Parkman fought poor health and failing eyesight to write his histories. His masterwork, *France and England in North America* (1865–92), comprises seven separate studies describing the French explorers and their empire in North America.

Parkman took pains to visit the sites of the episodes

Francis Parkman, one of the greatest U.S. historians, wrote many volumes on the American West. Although Parkman was ill during most of his life, his research was meticulous: prior to writing his history of the Oregon Trail, he traveled the route and lived among the Sioux Indians.

he described. He spent seven months making the difficult westward trek across the continent before writing his classic *The California and Oregon Trail* (1849). During his trip, Parkman lived briefly with the Sioux Indians; he used this experience to advantage in the *History of the Conspiracy of Pontiac* (1851).

parlement The French parlements, regional supreme courts of criminal and civil law (*c.*1250–1789), included the original prestigious Parlement of Paris for central France and, at the end of the 18th century, 12 less powerful parlements in the outlying provinces. At first the parlements were staffed by royal appointees who supported medieval monarchs, but later, members of the parlements purchased hereditary judgeships and formed a new nobility, called the *noblesse de robe*. They obstructed the powerful monarchs of the 17th and 18th centuries through their right of remonstrance—that is, the right to point out breaches of tradition in royal legislation.

Following the revolt of the FRONDE (1648–53), LOUIS XIV reduced the powers of the parlements to judicial functions, but the right of remonstrance was restored in 1715. The parlements forced LOUIS XVI to convoke the popular STATES-GENERAL in 1788–89. They lost that body's favor, however, when the pronoble Parlement of Paris ruled futilely that the States-General should vote by social order, not by individual delegates. In a move that started the FRENCH REVOLUTION, the Third Estate of the States-General proclaimed itself the National Assembly on June 17, 1789. One of the assembly's first acts was to abolish the parlements.

Parliament The Parliament of Great Britain is the legislative body of that nation. Formally, Parliament consists of the monarch, the House of Commons, and the House of Lords. In common usage, however, the term refers to Commons and Lords only. Virtually all power rests with the House of Commons. The power exercised by Parliament is unlimited, making it in fact the sovereign of the nation.

Membership and Responsibilities. The House of Commons has 635 elected members. The maximum period between elections is 5 years, but the actual timing of an election is usually decided by the PRIME MINISTER. The total membership of the Lords is about 1,150, but the majority of peers take no active part in the proceedings of the house. Members of the Lords include hereditary peers, life peers, the 10 senior judges, the archbishops of Canterbury and York, and 24 bishops of the Church of England. Normally the largest party in Commons forms the government, and the leading members of this party are appointed to senior ministerial positions (the cabinet).

All important legislation is introduced into Parliament by the government. The House of Lords can initiate amendments on bills (except money bills) and delay legislation. Because the government usually has a majority in Commons, it can normally ensure that its major policies are accepted by Parliament. Party loyalty and discipline in Commons are strong. When the government does not have an actual majority in Commons (because of third-party members), it must enlist enough support from minority members to get legislation passed. When such coalitions fail on an important vote, the government falls. The prime minister and cabinet resign, and if no other party leader is able to form a government, Parliament is dissolved and a new election is called.

History. Parliament evolved from the Curia Regis, or Great Council of the Realm, which began in the Middle Ages as an advisory body to the monarch. Originally it

King Edward I of England, flanked by the rulers of Scotland and Wales, conducts a session of Parliament in this medieval miniature.

comprised the great landholders, the chief nobles, and the church prelates. Beginning in the 13th century the monarch occasionally would call up representatives of the other classes, mainly the knights, the lower clergy, and the burgesses. The two bodies met separately, however, and eventually evolved into, respectively, the House of Lords and the House of Commons.

Parliament's history is one of long competition with the monarchy, and eventual supremacy. Important milestones in that competition include assertion of control by the early Commons over grants of revenue to the monarch; the ENGLISH CIVIL WAR, during which Parliament ordered the beheading of the king; the GLORIOUS REVOLUTION of 1688, during which Parliament succeeded in establishing its sovereignty over the crown; the growing dependence of the prime minister on Parliament (instead of on the monarch) during the 18th century; the great reforms of the 19th century (see REFORM ACTS), which extended suffrage to most of the adult male population and established the secret ballot; the Parliament Act of 1911, which abolished the veto power of the Lords; and the Representation of the People Acts of 1918, 1928, 1948, and 1969, which extended the suffrage to women, established the principle of one person one vote, and lowered the voting age from 21 to 18.

---

parliamentary procedure　Parliamentary procedure is an established and systematic body of principles, motions, and practices used by deliberative assemblies to govern the conduct of their business. First applied in the early English Parliament and developed over ensuing centuries, the procedure enables an organization to accomplish its purposes in a manner that is efficient, fair, and in accordance with democratic traditions. To do so the organization will usually designate a specific manual, such as *Robert's Rules of Order* or *Sturgis's Standard Code of Parliamentary Procedure,* as its authority on parliamentary procedure.

Principles of Deliberation

Parliamentary procedure is based on the principles of full and fair discussion and debate, orderliness and decorum, and majority rule, among others.

Full and Fair Discussion. To ensure full and fair discussion, parliamentary procedure distinguishes between motions that are amendable and debatable, and those which are not. For example, both a proposed main motion and a proposed amendment to it are debatable. A motion to lay on the table, however—that is, to suspend business temporarily—is not, because debate would defeat its parliamentary purpose.

To ensure fairness in debate, standard procedure requires that speakers on opposing sides of a question be recognized alternately, that discussion of personalities or motives be avoided, and that points of order, parliamentary inquiries, and requests for information be promptly resolved.

Orderliness and Decorum. Orderliness is achieved by the general practice of permitting only one motion and

one speaker to be in order at a time. A main motion may be set aside temporarily, but until it is disposed of—referred to committee, postponed, tabled, or approved or disapproved by the assembly—it is a pending question, and no other principal question can be taken up. The conventional standard of conduct is that members do not randomly interrupt speakers or engage in dialogues with them without the permission of the chair.

Majority Rule. The traditional rule observed in parliamentary procedure is that the majority of members of an organization are empowered to make decisions binding on all. Usually, a majority means a simple majority of one-half the members plus one, or a plurality of the members voting. Some proposals, however, such as those dealing with constitutional revisions, closing of debate, or suspension of rules, require an extraordinary majority (such as a two-thirds vote).

Main Motions

To make a motion of any kind, a member rises and addresses the chair to request recognition, and, on being recognized, states the motion. The chair determines whether the motion is in order and whether it requires a second. The chair then states the motion and either invites discussion or debate, or, if no debate is required, asks for an immediate vote by the assembly. Main motions are substantive proposals for consideration and action, whereas secondary motions facilitate discussion and consideration of main motions and are conducted under a ranked system of priority.

Parma [pahr'-mah]　Parma is the capital city of Parma province in the Emilia-Romagna region of Italy, on the ancient Aemilian Way and the Parma River. The population is 175,301 (1988 est.). Parma is an important road and rail junction and an agricultural trade center. The world-famous Parmesan cheese, canned goods, and sausages are the city's chief food products; farm machines and fertilizers are manufactured. Home of the state University of Parma (1064), the city is also rich in artistic and architectural monuments, including the octagonal Romanesque-Gothic baptistery (1196–1260), the Romanesque cathedral (12th century), and the Camera del Correggio (in the Convent of Saint Paul, with CORREGGIO's frescoes, done in 1519). The National Gallery houses 15th–17th-century paintings.

Founded by the Romans in 183 BC, Parma had three great historical periods. The first was as a free commune during the 12th and 13th centuries; the second was during the 16th century when Pope Paul III created (1545) the duchy of Parma and Piacenza; and the third began in 1749, when the duchy passed to Spain. In 1861, Parma joined united Italy. It suffered heavy Allied bombing during World War II.

Parmenides [pahr-men'-i-deez]　Parmenides of Elea, *c.*515–*c.*450 BC, was one of the most important of the pre-Socratic philosophers (see PRE-SOCRATIC PHILOSOPHY).

In his long two-part poem he turns philosophy away from questions of cosmos formation to what he sees as a prior question: What must the world be like if it is to be intelligible? The poem argues that the world must be unitary, indestructible, indivisible, and unchangeable. The world as it presents itself to the senses—full of change and variety—is "unthinkable and unsayable." Parmenides' influence can be seen in the work of his followers ZENO OF ELEA and Melissos (see ELEATIC SCHOOL).

Parmigianino [pahr-mee-jah-nee'-noh]

The Italian painter Francesco Mazzola, b. Jan. 11, 1503, in Parma (from which he takes the name Parmigianino), d. Aug. 24, 1540, was one of the creators and greatest exponents of MANNERISM. His early works include frescoes of the legend of Diana and Actaeon (1523; Cittadella di San Vitale, Fontanellato) and the daringly foreshortened *Self-Portrait in a Convex Mirror* (1524; Kunsthistorisches Museum, Vienna). The major accomplishment of Parmigianino's sojourn (1524–27) in Rome is *Madonna and Child with Saints John the Baptist and Jerome* (1526–27; National Gallery, London). About 1535 he executed his masterpiece, the *Madonna with the Long Neck* (Uffizi, Florence).

Parmigianino's art is distinguished by a new emphasis on ornament and grace. During the course of his career he developed a supremely elegant, artificial style, characterized by vibrant color, elongated forms, and distorted spatial relationships. His numerous drawings and engravings, even more than his paintings, led to his widespread influence in Italy and abroad.

The Madonna with the Long Neck *(1534–40), by the Italian painter Parmigianino, exemplifies the Mannerist style developed by him in reaction to the classicism of the High Renaissance. Parmigianino's paintings are characterized by elongated figures and ambiguity of spatial perspective. (Uffizi, Florence.)*

Parnassians [pahr-nas'-ee-uhnz]

The Parnassians, taking their name from the Greek mountain sacred to the muses, were a group of 19th-century French poets who embraced the "Art for Art's sake" doctrine of poet and critic Théophile GAUTIER. Théodore de Banville outlined the group's doctrine in his *Petit Traité de poésie française* (Brief Treatise on French Poetry, 1872). Led by Charles Marie LECONTE DE LISLE, and including José Maria de Heredia and Sully Prudhomme, the Parnassians attempted to create formally perfect, "objective" poems.

Parnassus [pahr-nas'-uhs]

Parnassus (modern Greek: Parnassós) is a barren massif in the Pindus Mountains of central Greece. Its limestone summit, overlooking central Greece and the northern Peloponnesus, rises to 2,457 m (8,061 ft). The ancient Greeks and Romans venerated the mountain as the home of APOLLO and the MUSES. One of the summits was sacred to DIONYSUS, and Bacchanalia were held around the Corycian Grotto. Poets considered the mountain's fountain of Castalia a source of inspiration. DELPHI is located at the mountain's base.

Parnell, Charles Stewart [pahr-nel']

The Irish nationalist politician Charles Stewart Parnell, b. June 27, 1846, d. Oct. 6, 1891, turned self-government for Ireland from an impractical dream into an attainable goal. Born into a Protestant landed family, Parnell was elected to Parliament in 1875. As he rose to leadership of the Irish nationalist party, he skillfully associated himself with the popular agitation for land reform, becoming president of the Irish Land League in 1879. Although the government treated him as an advocate of violence, he induced many FENIANS (members of a secret revolutionary society active in both Ireland and the United States) to support constitutional methods. He also reached informal understandings with the Roman Catholic hierarchy.

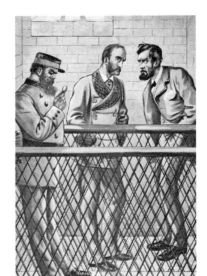

Charles Stewart Parnell (center), an Irish nationalist leader, consults with a colleague, John Dillon (right), during their imprisonment at Kilmainham jail in this 1881 magazine illustration. Parnell, leader of the Irish party in Parliament, was jailed (1881–82) for inciting Irish tenant farmers to resist their landlords.

In the 1885 general election Parnell's party won 86 seats, exactly the number of votes separating the Liberals (335) from the Conservatives (249). William E. GLADSTONE announced his support for a HOME RULE BILL and with Irish support became prime minister for the third time. But the bill that Gladstone introduced in 1886 split his Liberal party and was consequently defeated. Parnell seemed politically invincible until 1890, when a divorce court revealed that he had been living with the wife of another politician. Gladstone forced the Irish party to choose between Parnell's leadership and his own support for a Home Rule bill. The majority in the party, together with the Catholic bishops, turned against Parnell. Parnell died soon after.

parochial schools   see PRIVATE SCHOOLS

parody

Parody is the artful and subversive use of mimicry to expose pretension or falsity in the original that it imitates. Though it is a literary technique, its uses are not confined to literature; any distinctive use of language—by advertisers, journalists, or politicians—is vulnerable. Parody usually intends to deflate its victim but also has more complex, creative purposes that it shares with pastiche. Vladimir Nabokov's *Pale Fire* (1962) is a notable modern parody of academic commentary that disarms its potential critics and explicators by including footnotes and mock-learned explanations. Parody is also an aspect of the MOCK EPIC satire of Alexander Pope's *The Rape of the Lock* (1712), in which it is used not to mock epic poetry but to invoke lofty standards of human behavior. Henry Fielding's *Shamela* (1741), written to expose the absurdities of Samuel Richardson's *Pamela,* is such a slapstick parody that it verges on BURLESQUE AND TRAVESTY. Jane Austen's analysis of the foolishness of Gothic romance in *Northanger Abbey* (1818) explores the subtler possibilities of extended parody.

parole

Parole, in criminal law, is a conditional release from prison in which the prisoner is excused from serving the remainder of a sentence provided he or she maintains good behavior. Parole may be granted prisoners who have received indefinite sentences (such as from 3 to 10 years) after the minimum sentence has been served. A parole board makes the decision after reviewing a prisoner's record.

A parolee is usually required to observe minimum standards of conduct, to stay within a certain area, and to report regularly to a parole officer. Any violation may result in a return to prison. The supervision of parolees may vary from a monthly check by a police officer to skilled counseling by professional caseworkers. The underlying philosophy is that many offenders need help rather than punishment.

Parole differs from PROBATION, in which the offender is conditionally excused from prison at the time of sentencing.

Parousia   see SECOND COMING OF CHRIST

parrot

In common usage, *parrot* signifies any bird of the more than 300 species of the order Psittaciformes. Parrots are easily distinguished by their short, curved beaks; large heads; short necks and feet; and reversed toes (two before, two behind), which aid, along with the beak, in grasping seeds and climbing. Most are fruit and seed eaters, with well-developed crops to soften food. Parrots also have a fleshy and often feathered projection, called a cere, at the base of the upper bill. They have long been favorite cage birds and are among the oldest domesticated animals. All parrots have loud and often raucous calls, and some species are especially noted for imitating sounds that they hear. Such imitation, however, is not typically observed among these animals in the wild. It is more likely a practice adopted by domesticated birds when they are kept without companions.

The order Psittaciformes is usually classified into three families. Lories and lorikeets form the family Loridae, and COCKATOOS the family Cacatuidae. All other kinds are grouped in the family Psittacidae, including the true parrots, MACAWS, PARAKEETS, budgerigars, conures, lovebirds, owl and pygmy parrots, and such unusual forms as keas and vulturine parrots. The order worldwide has a southern distribution. Most species are found in South America, with many fewer farther north and in Africa and India. Nearly all the northern species are in the tropical lowlands, with a few in the Himalayas and the mountains of Mexico. The most unusual genera inhabit New Zealand, Australia, and New Guinea.

Other than sharing certain characteristics of bill and beak, parrots vary greatly in appearance. They range in size from the 10-cm (4-in) pygmy parrots of New Guinea to the 1-m (3.3-ft) hyacinth macaw, *Anodorhyncus hyacinthinus*, of Brazil, much of whose length is an elaborate tail. Many parrots are brightly colored in reds, yellows, and blues, but the most common color is green, which serves as camouflage.

Parrots also vary in habits. They often gather in flocks, within which they are commonly in pairs, and they may form roosting groups at night. Some species are daytime birds that live in trees, whereas others are nocturnal and remain mostly on the ground. Nearly all parrot species are monogamous, normally mating for years, if not for life. The young develop slowly, and in captivity some members of the larger species have lived to an age of 70 to 80 years.

Because parrots tend to gather in flocks, and because they sometimes feed on farm products, some populations of the birds have been destroyed by overhunting. Other

(Opposite page) *The scarlet macaw* (1) *can break nutshells with its strong beak. Unlike most other parrots, the rainbow lorikeet* (2) *feeds primarily on softer foods, such as berries, and has a tongue with a brushlike tip adapted for feeding on pollen and nectar. The red-tailed cockatoo* (3) *raises its broad crest feathers in an aggressive display when threatened. The thick-billed parrot* (4) *is native to the mountains of northern Mexico, and the slaty-headed parakeet* (5) *is found in the Himalayas. Like all lovebirds, the masked lovebird* (6) *exhibits a strong attachment to its mate.*

species are being decimated through encroachment on their habitat by human activities. Several species have become extinct in the 20th century, including the only one ever resident in the United States, the Carolina parakeet, *Conuropsis carolinensis*. Some rare species have also become endangered through private collecting activities.

parrot fish   The parrot fishes (family Scaridae) are some of the largest and most gaudily colorful of tropical reef fishes, with bright blues, greens, reds, and yellows characterizing the males more so than the females. Their parrotlike beak is used to scrape algae and living coral from the substrate, causing much reef erosion but, at the same time, producing sand, which is ecologically important. All parrot fishes are diurnal and by night retire to caves.

Parry, Sir William Edward   Sir William Edward Parry, b. Bath, England, Dec. 19, 1790, d. July 8, 1855, was a noted explorer of the Arctic who led a number of unsuccessful expeditions in search of the NORTHWEST PASSAGE to the Orient. He made his first expedition in 1818 as second in command to Sir John Ross. The following year, in command of his own ships, Parry reached latitude 114° west in Baffin Bay, discovering on the way Barrow Strait, Prince Regent Inlet, Viscount Melville Sound, M'Clure Strait, and Wellington Channel. Two more expeditions followed in 1821–23 and 1824–25. In 1827, in an effort to reach the North Pole, Parry traveled across the ice from Spitsbergen, to latitude 82° 45' north, an accomplishment unequaled for the next half century. Parry was knighted in 1829.

parsec   see DISTANCE, ASTRONOMICAL

Parsifal [pahr'-si-fahl]   In the Arthurian legends, Parsifal— or Perceval—was a knight of the Round Table who, after youthful blunders, became a model of chivalry and won a glimpse of the Holy Grail. The Parsifal figure was based to some extent on the historical Welsh hero Peredur. Parsifal was replaced in the 13th century by Galahad as the hero of the Grail romances. Richard Wagner made him the hero of his last opera, *Parsifal* (1882).

Parsis [pahr'-seez]   The Parsis are descendants of Zoroastrians (see ZOROASTRIANISM) who fled from Persia to India in order to escape Muslim persecution in the 10th century. The Parsis have retained almost unchanged the beliefs and customs of their ancestors. They observe the prohibitions against the contamination of the sacred elements of fire, water, and earth; their lives are governed by rituals and sacrifice that deal with every aspect of life from birth to death; and they practice the stringent precepts of morality laid down by Zoroaster. Death is regarded as the ultimate impurity, and Parsis refuse to defile the earth with burial; instead, the body is exposed within a circular, unroofed tower (*dakhma*), where it is devoured by vultures.

The Parsis are a closed community and permit neither intermarriage nor proselytization by other faiths. They are noted for their wealth and generosity; they have founded many hospitals, orphanages, and schools.

parsley Parsley is a biennial herb, *Petroselinum crispum* of the carrot family, Umbelliferae. It is native to southern Europe and is widely cultivated for its fragrant foliage, which is used as a food garnish and as an ingredient of *fines herbes*, a mixture of chopped fresh herbs essential to French cooking. Special curative and maleficent powers were long attributed to parsley, in part, perhaps, because it is difficult to grow from seed.

Parsley is a popular herb characterized by its deep-green curled leaves. Fresh parsley is often used as a garnish on a variety of dishes.

parsnip The parsnip, *Pastinaca sativa*, of the family Umbelliferae, forms a long, yellowish, edible root that can

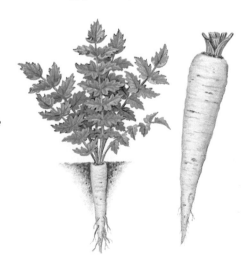

The parsnip is used as a cooked vegetable. Its sweet, edible root (detail, right) is a good source of vitamin C. Pinnate leaves on a grooved stem characterize its sizable upper growth.

reach lengths of 40 cm (16 in). It is native to Eurasia and was cultivated by the Greeks and Romans. Because it grows best in cool weather, most of the North American parsnip crop is a product of the northern United States and Canada. Plants require a long growing season, but because they can withstand freezing they may be left in the field over winter, or the roots can be dug up and stored at temperatures of about 0° C (32° F). Quality depends on exposure to temperatures below 5° C (41° F); this exposure encourages starch-to-sugar changes. Parsnips are also used as a livestock feed.

Parsons, Talcott Talcott Parsons, b. Colorado Springs, Colo., Dec. 13, 1902, d. May 8, 1979, was the major theorist in American sociology following World War II. His functional approach to the study of society not only shaped American sociology through the 1950s and '60s but also had a profound influence on anthropology, psychology, and, to a lesser degree, history. In his first book, *The Structure of Social Action* (1937), Parsons introduced the ideas of three major European thinkers—Émile DURKHEIM, Vilfredo PARETO, and Max WEBER—while presenting his own theory, which was derived from their work. Beginning with *The Social System* (1951), Parsons developed his functional approach to the study of society, explaining any society as a total system of interrelated institutions each of which fulfilled functions necessary for the continuing operation of the whole. Parsons taught his theory in Harvard University's department of social relations, which he founded in 1946.

Partch, Harry Harry Partch, b. Oakland, Calif., June 24, 1901, d. Sept. 3, 1974, an avant-garde composer, inventor of musical instruments, and speculative theorist, developed a significant system of musical aesthetics and notation in which he balanced ideas and techniques in both music and theater (discussed in his book *Genesis of a Music*, 2d ed., 1974). Partch used diverse sources, including Asiatic, African, North American, and Western European styles and techniques. He synthesized them into unique sounds, as can be heard in such works as *And on the Seventh Day Petals Fell in Petaluma* (1963–64; rev. ed. 1966), *Delusion of the Fury* (1963–66), and *Revelation in the Courthouse Park* (1961).

parthenogenesis [pahr-thuh-noh-jen'-uh-sis] Parthenogenesis is the development of an unfertilized egg into an adult organism. Activation of development normally occurs after an egg is fertilized by a sperm; in parthenogenesis, however, the stimulus for the egg to cleave occurs spontaneously or can be induced experimentally. The mechanism or events occurring during egg activation are not known but apparently include certain changes in the egg membrane.

In a female, an egg undergoing the first meiotic division produces two cells, both of which contain a diploid number of chromosomes. One of these cells atrophies; in this state it is known as the first polar body and remains attached to the other cell. Parthenogenetic activation occurs at this stage of development. During parthenogenesis, the egg commences the second meiotic division in either of two ways: either the paired chromosomes separate and one of each homologous chromosome is extruded in the second polar body, leaving a haploid complement of chromosomes; or the extrusion of the second polar body does not occur, consequently leaving a diploid number of chromosomes in the egg. Parthenotes—individuals developed from parthenogenesis—most frequently arise from the latter form of activation.

Parthenogenetic development occurs regularly among such social insects as bees or ants. In these cases, unfertilized eggs that the queen lays develop into drones, which are male. In amphibians, adult parthenote frogs (*Rana japonica, R. nigromaculata,* and *R. pipiens*) can develop from unfertilized eggs that have been pricked with a needle. Parthenogenesis among higher animals, on the other hand, is rare. The lizard species *Lacerta saxicola* and *Cnemidophorus uniparens* are entirely parthenogenetic. Occasionally chickens and turkeys develop by such means.

Parthenon   see ACROPOLIS

Parthia [pahr'-thee-uh]   Parthia was the ancient country of central Asia located in what are today the Iranian province of Khurasan and Turkmenia, one of the 15 constituent republics of the USSR. A land of deserts, plains, and mountains, Parthia is first mentioned as a province of the ACHAEMENID Persian empire; its governor Hystaspes was the father of DARIUS I.

Parthia became important only after Alexander the Great's defeat of the Persians and the parceling out of their empire among his successors. The impetus for expansion came from the Parni, nomads from the north who invaded Parthia, adopted the local language, and led the Parthians in revolt (*c.*238 BC) against their SELEUCID masters, thus beginning a dynasty called ARSACID after the first ruler, Arsaces. Their capital was at first at Dara and then at Nisa, both now in Turkmenia; CTESIPHON served as capital in the 2d century BC. Parthia reached the height of its power and influence in the 1st century BC, when it controlled the heartland of the old Persian empire as well as ARMENIA and when the Parthian tongue had spread from Afghanistan to the borders of Syria. Parthia remained Rome's major opponent throughout the 1st and 2d centuries AD. The Parthians, never completely united, were defeated by the SASSANIANS in AD 224, and the last of the Arsacid kings died in battle three years later. The Iranian national epic, the *Shah Namah,* by the poet FIRDAWSI, reflects the feudalism and chivalry of the Parthian era.

See also: PERSIA, ANCIENT.

participle   see PARTS OF SPEECH

particle accelerator   see ACCELERATOR, PARTICLE

particle detector   see DETECTOR, PARTICLE

partridge   Partridges are small to medium-sized (15–45 cm/6–18 in long) birds in the pheasant and quail family, Phasianidae. They include primarily the 40 to 45 species of the genera *Perdix, Alectoris,* and *Francolinus.* Partridges are distributed over much of Africa and Eurasia, from sea level to 4,600 m (15,000 ft), and occupy a wide variety of habitats. Plumage patterns vary considerably, with browns and red brown, as well as black and gray, predominating. Like other galliforms, partridges are primarily terrestrial, often moving about in small coveys. Nests are shallow depressions in the ground lined with grass and twigs. Usually 4 to 12 eggs are laid.

The gray partridge is a small, gray and rust-colored upland ground bird. Founded in parts of Europe, Asia, and North America—particularly in heavily irrigated areas—this bird is hunted as game.

parts of speech   In the 1st century BC the Greek scholar Dionysius Thrax isolated the fundamental categories that are generally believed to be found in all languages: nouns, verbs, pronouns, and conjunctions. These categories, called parts of speech, are basic tools used in understanding GRAMMAR and SYNTAX.

The list devised by Dionysius has been extended and modified in various ways; the parts of speech most commonly used by grammarians in describing the syntax of Western languages are the following: nouns (and pronouns), verbs, adjectives, adverbs, conjunctions, and prepositions. In the sentence "The old woman and her husband walked slowly up the stairs," *woman, husband,* and *stairs* are nouns, *her* is a pronoun, *and* is a conjunction, *walked* is a verb, *old* is an adjective, *slowly* is an adverb, and *up* is a preposition. Analyzing a sentence grammatically in this way is called "parsing."

Nouns and Pronouns. A noun (from the French: *nom,* "name") is a word designating a person, place, entity, or quality. Nouns have two main subcategories. They may be proper nouns, such as *John, Mary,* or *The United States of America*—that is, names of specific persons, places, or things; or they may be common nouns, such as *boy, river, country,* or *abstraction*—that is, names for classes of entities. Nouns typically are the heads (main words) of phrases that function as arguments of predicates—that is, noun phrases are typically subjects of verbs, objects of verbs, or objects of prepositions. Pronouns are words such as *he, she, this,* or *him,* used to stand for nouns or whole noun phrases to avoid repetition.

Verbs. A verb is a word that describes an action or a state of being. The word *verb* is from the Latin *verbum,* meaning "word"—short, one may suppose, for "action word." Verbs have many subcategories in all languages. A transitive verb normally requires an object noun phrase: for example, *hit* [the ball], or *vacate* [the house]. An intransitive verb (*arrive,* for example) does not allow an object noun phrase. A copular verb such as *be, seem,* or *appear* links the subject to some other noun phrase or to a modifier. Auxiliary verbs such as *have* or *be* in *has gone* or *is leaving* express some special aspect of an event; modal verbs such as *must, may,* or *can* express an attitude toward an event. An impersonal verb expresses an event not involving willful performance by an individual person (for example, rain in "It's raining"). Just as nouns are the heads of noun phrases that may include additional material such as articles and modifiers of various sorts, verbs are the heads of verb phrases that may include noun phrases as objects and other kinds of additional material that fill out the meaning of the verb. These additions are called complements. For example, in "She admitted reluctantly that she was exhausted," both *reluctantly* and *that she was exhausted* are complements of the verb *admitted.*

Adjectives. An adjective is a word that modifies a noun. *Adjective* means "thrown toward," in this case thrown toward the noun. Many scholars prefer the term *adnominal,* meaning "attached to the nominal (noun)," parallel to the term *adverb,* meaning "attached to the verb." Like nouns and verbs, adjectives are the heads of adjective phrases: for example, *sharp as a newly honed razor* is an adjective phrase of which the head is the adjective *sharp.* The adjectival function, that of specifying in greater detail the meaning of some head noun, is also capable of being fulfilled by a clause, called a relative clause, more accurately an adjectival (adnominal) clause, such as *whom we visited yesterday* in the noun phrase *the doctor whom we visited yesterday.*

Adverbs. Modifiers of all words except nouns are called adverbs. Perhaps most commonly, adverbs modify verbs, as in "The plumber worked *hard*" (manner), "The plumber worked *all night*" (duration), "The plumber arrived *at noon*" (point in time), or "The plumber worked *for a living*" (reason or cause). Adverbs may also modify an entire clause (for example, *obviously* in "Obviously this sentence is unintelligible"). An adverb may also modify an adjective or another adverb as in "It is *extremely* obvious that he is *very* intelligent." Like nouns, verbs, and adjectives, adverbs

may serve as the heads of adverbial phrases (for example, *early* in "He arrived *early in the morning*").

Prepositions, Conjunctions, and Interjections. Words such as *on, by, with, in, except, of,* and *for* are prepositions, used to form prepositional phrases that function as adjectives or adverbs. A prepositional phrase is a preposition plus a noun phrase (for example, *on the table, over the rainbow,* or *by five o'clock*). The name *preposition* indicates that, in English, these words are placed before (prepositioned) a noun phrase. In some languages, however, they occur after the noun phrase; for this reason many grammarians prefer to call them adpositions, a name that is appropriate whether they occur before or after the object.

Conjunctions are connecting words such as *and, or,* and *but;* they mark equal phrases such as *John and Mary, milk or honey,* and *dull but nice.* Conjunctions differ from prepositions in that they do not have a subordinate relation to the material to which they are related. Interjections are phrases such as *Holy smokes!* or *Okay* that do not fit structurally into the rest of a sentence.

---

parvovirus [pahr'-voh-vy-ruhs] Parvovirus is best known as a contagious disease of dogs. Also called canine parvoviral enteritis, it affects puppies more often than older dogs. The fatality rate is extremely high. The disease is caused by one of a group of extremely small viruses that also affect rodents, pigs, cattle, humans, and other animals. In humans, parvoviruses apparently combine with the larger adenoviruses, causing upper respiratory tract infection and eye inflammation (CONJUNCTIVITIS).

Canine parvovirus infects the entire intestinal tract of a dog, causing diarrhea, vomiting, dehydration, and malaise. Puppies typically develop a high fever, but older dogs may have subnormal temperatures. Some dogs also develop a cough or swelling of the cornea of the eye. The illness usually begins suddenly, and without treatment the animal often dies within a few days. A vaccine is now available, and veterinarians recommend that all puppies be immunized and that dogs receive booster injections annually.

Pasadena [pas-uh-dee'-nuh] Pasadena (1990 pop., 131,591) is a suburban city in southern California, located just north of Los Angeles. The CALIFORNIA INSTITUTE OF TECHNOLOGY (1891) and its JET PROPULSION LABORATORY have influenced the city's economic base—research and the manufacture of scientific instruments and aerospace components. Each January 1, Pasadena hosts a postseason college football game in its famous Rose Bowl, as well as a parade. The city was founded in 1874.

Pascal, Blaise [pahs-kahl', blez] The French thinker, mathematician, and scientist Blaise Pascal, b. June 19, 1623, d. Aug. 19, 1662, has been credited not only with imaginative and subtle work in geometry and other

The scientific investigations of 17th-century French thinker Blaise Pascal led to invaluable contributions in mathematics and physics. He is also remembered for his introspective religious and philosophical writings, most notably his Pensées.

branches of mathematics, but also with profoundly influencing later generations of theologians and philosophers. A prodigy in mathematics, Pascal had mastered Euclid's *Elements* by the age of 12. Pascal invented and sold the first ADDING MACHINE (1645). His study of hydrostatics led to his invention of the syringe and hydraulic press (see PASCAL'S LAW). In 1647, a few years after publishing *Essai pour les coniques (Essay on Conic Sections),* he suddenly abandoned the study of mathematics. Because of his chronically poor health, he had been advised to seek diversions from study and attempted for a time to live in Paris in a deliberately frivolous manner. His later interest in probability theory has been attributed to his calculation of the odds involved in the gambling games he played during this period.

At the end of 1654, after several months of intense depression, Pascal had a religious experience that altered his life. He entered the Jansenist monastery at Port-Royal (see JANSENISM), although he did not take orders. He never published in his own name again. The Jansenists encouraged him in his mathematical studies, which he resumed. To assist them in their struggles against the Jesuits, he wrote, under a pseudonym, a defense of the famous Jansenist Antoine ARNAULD in the form of 18 epistles. Known as *Lettres provinciales,* they were likely responsible for the subsequent reputation of the Jesuits as hypocritical and casuistic. In 1658 he broke with the Jansenists and left the monastery.

Pascal died at the age of 39 in intense pain from cancer. His most famous work is the *Pensées* (*Thoughts*), a set of deeply personal meditations in somewhat fragmented form on human suffering and faith in God.

Pascal's law

Blaise Pascal stated (1653) that in a fluid at rest, the pressure on any surface exerts a force perpendicular to the surface and independent of the direction of orientation of the surface. This law is sometimes assumed to include the principle that any additional pressure applied to the fluid will be transmitted equally to every point in the fluid, which was stated separately by Pascal. Pascal's law is often used in machines involving HYDRAULIC SYSTEMS.

Paschal II, Pope

[pas'-kul] Paschal II, d. Jan. 21, 1118, was pope from 1099 to 1118. His original name was Ranerius. Succeeding URBAN II as pope in the middle of the prolonged INVESTITURE CONTROVERSY, Paschal renewed previous papal decrees against lay investiture of bishops. He reached compromises on this issue with HENRY I of England and PHILIP I of France in 1107. In 1111, in the compact of Sutri, the German king HENRY V agreed to renounce investiture, and in return Paschal promised that the German bishops would surrender all their lands to the crown. This agreement was rejected by the bishops, however. Paschal, after failing to reconcile church reformers and the king, again condemned lay investiture in 1116.

Pašić, Nikola

[pah'-shich, nee'-koh-lah] A Serbian statesman, Nikola Pašić, b. Dec. 31 (N.S.), 1845, d. Dec. 10, 1926, was repeatedly prime minister and foreign minister of Serbia from 1891 on. Pašić founded (1878) the Serbian Radical party and dreamed of a greater Serbia uniting all the lands inhabited predominantly by Serbs. After the overthrow (1917) of the Russian monarchy, Pašić negotiated the formation of the Kingdom of the Serbs, Croats, and Slovenes (later Yugoslavia). In the 1920s, Pašić grew increasingly conservative, and he relinquished his last premiership in 1926.

Pasolini, Pier Paolo

[pah-zoh-lee'-nee] One of 20th-century Italy's foremost intellectuals, Pier Paolo Pasolini, b. Mar. 5, 1922, d. Nov. 2, 1975, was known primarily as a filmmaker of remarkable persuasiveness and ingenuity. A Marxist since his twenties, Pasolini made his first film, *Accatone,* in 1961. *Mamma Roma* (1962) was followed by a down-to-earth retelling of the New Testament story, *The Gospel According to Saint Matthew* (1964). An interest in myth led to two of his most powerful films, *Oedipus Rex* (1967) and *Medea* (1969). He also filmed adaptations of Boccaccio's *The Decameron* and Chaucer's *Canterbury Tales* (both 1971). He is perhaps at his best in two scathing studies of the affluent class, *Teorema* (Theorem, 1968) and *Il Porcile* (Pigsty, 1969), in which sexual perversion and religious experience are equated. Pasolini's last film, an adaptation of De Sade's *120 Days of Sodom* (1975), is set in Salò, seat of Mussolini's short-lived Fascist Republic.

passacaglia and chaconne

[pah-suh-kahl'-yuh, chah-kuhn'] The passacaglia and the chaconne are dance forms dating from the 16th century that subsequently were widely used in instrumental, vocal, choral, and balletic contexts, often within the larger framework of opera. Insofar as their origins can be traced, both dances appear to be of relatively humble status, if *chaconne* is associated with the Spanish *chacota* (a peasant song) and *passacaglia* with *pasacalle* (a street song, or piece to be sung while strolling through town). Because both forms use a ground bass, or ostinato, in 3/4 time, the terms have often been freely interchanged. If any distinction can be made between the two, it is that a passacaglia usually relies on an ostinato bass, over which a chain of variations is laid (as in Bach's organ *Passacaglia in C minor*), whereas the chaconne is normally built on the old harmonic sequence produced by four notes descending from the tonic in any minor key, although this motive could be extended to six, eight, or more notes.

passage, rites of   *Rites of passage* is a term coined by the great French ethnologist and folklorist Arnold van GENNEP in his seminal study, *Rites de passage* (1909; Eng. trans., 1960). The concept has attained a central place in social theory. Van Gennep observed that all societies must impose cultural order both upon the changing statuses of persons as they move through different social positions and upon the constant alternations of days, seasons, and years that impose their own flux on social relations. Despite the fact that these social rituals and calendrical ceremonies vary in content from society to society, van Gennep discerned broad, common features. Most may be reduced to a tripartite structure: a process of separation from an existing form; a transitional or liminal stage that is neither what preceded nor what is to come; and a process of aggregation or reincorporation into a new state. The most obvious examples of this structural process appear to be such biological, or "natural," changes as birth, puberty, and death, but his theory applies as well to such processes as MARRIAGE and adop-

In a traditional Hindu wedding ceremony, offerings of roasted grain are cast into a sacrificial fire, which is then circumambulated by the bride and groom to solemnize their marriage bond. Marriage, a long-term mating approved by the community, involves ritual as well as economic and political linkage between two kin groups. Many taboos and restrictions apply at or before marriage.

tion or induction into an occupation, religious office, or secret society.

Van Gennep held that there is a complex interplay between the individual and the group, between natural and social factors, and that the symbols inextricable to ritual weld together natural and cultural worlds. Birth, death, the seasons, years, and even space gain full, clear significance only when articulated through group ritual and according to unchanging structural forms. His concept is pertinent to comprehending the ways by which an African boy is initiated first as a novice and then as a warrior, but also for seeing how a Christian society goes from Lent through Good Friday to Easter. It also describes the process by which an unshorn, civilian-garbed, unnumbered, unsentenced person gradually becomes a shorn, uniformed, and numbered convict, or how a troublesome eccentric with many legal rights becomes incarcerated as a lunatic. One of the central features of van Gennep's thought is that these processes deal not only with transitions in the ways that persons and things are defined, but with their movements between the realms of the profane or prosaic and the sacred, between that which is safe and that which is dangerous. For van Gennep the transitional, or liminal phase, represents a sector of profound disorder or danger requiring careful segregation from ordinary social life by means of complex restrictions and TABOOS.

More recent research on such transitional rituals has sought to relate the ways in which particular symbols are orchestrated in various societies so as to provide not only cognitive but sensual reinforcement of values and beliefs. Hence, new relations between bodily and cognitive processes have been suggested by some studies. Other studies indicate ways in which such rituals reaffirm or redefine the changing configurations of social relations as the

The Mudmen of the Asaro Valley, in the eastern highlands of Papua New Guinea, celebrate communal initiation rites that establish the social status of male societal members.

persons linking groups change their positions or pass off the scene through marriage, installation in office, divorce, or death. Such rites may thus serve as social dramas by which the lines of authority, power, and group membership are made manifest. Still other research points out how such ceremonies provide important occasions for the accumulation and distribution of resources. The domains of individuals and persons, of beliefs and values, and of natural resources as modulated through time are all analyzable through this single complex paradigm.

Rites of passage is one of the core concepts in social analysis. Its importance proclaims the complex and at times circular interdependence between social and physical reality, ultimately indicating that even what seem to be the most obvious features of existence must be defined repeatedly through the activities and acknowledged terms of a group.

See also: PRIMITIVE RELIGION.

A Balinese priest blesses the ritual offerings made during a cremation ceremony. Death is a universal transition, one that often arouses anxiety or terror. It often disrupts the community and typically evokes complex ritual.

Passaic [puh-say'-ik] Passaic (1990 pop., 58,041), an industrial city in northeastern New Jersey, lies along the Passaic River, about 16 km (10 mi) west of New York City. The once-great textile center now manufactures television cables, rubber goods, and clothing. Originally an Indian camping ground, Passaic was settled by Dutch traders in 1678. Its name was changed from Acquackanonk Landing to Passaic in 1854.

Passamaquoddy [pas-uh-muh-kwah'-dee] The Passamaquoddy, a small Algonquian-speaking Indian tribe that was part of the ABNAKI confederacy, traditionally lived along the boundary between Maine and New Brunswick, Canada, around Passamaquoddy Bay. Closely related to their neighbors the Malecite (Maliseet), they lived in villages of WIGWAMS (an Abnaki word).

In the 16th century the Passamaquoddy became allied with New France by intermarriage with French settlers on their lands, and this alliance led to a lasting enmity with the English colonists to the south. With the defeat of the Abnaki confederacy and the independence of the United States, most Passamaquoddy remained south of the international boundary. Beginning in the late 1950s, the Passamaquoddy and the PENOBSCOT sued Maine for lands lost in the 1790s through illegal state treaties. In 1980, through a negotiated settlement of this land claim, the two tribes were awarded $27 million and 121,400 ha (300,000 acres). In 1989, Passamaquoddy on or near the reservation numbered about 1,500.

passerines see PERCHING BIRDS

Passion cycle The events of the Passion are among the most frequent subjects of religious art. They are popular because the sacrifice of the Crucifixion is central to Christian belief. Some scenes from the Passion appeared in Christian art as early as the 4th century. These subjects became especially common, however, in the late Middle Ages and at the beginning of the Renaissance, probably because depictions of Christ's suffering were in keeping with the heightened religious emotion that followed the Black Death and the Hundred Years' War. Also during this period the Pietá was introduced and developed. Although without biblical authority, this scene became part of the Passion cycle. The wide appeal of the Passion cycle is clearly shown by Albrecht DÜRER's woodcut cycles known as the *Small Passion* (1509–11) and the *Large Passion* (1510–11) as well as another sequence called the *Engraved Passion* (1507–13).

passion play see MEDIEVAL DRAMA

passionflower The passionflower, genus *Passiflora*, is any one of about 400 species of evergreen or semievergreen flowering vines in the family Passifloraceae. It is primarily native to tropical America and has been introduced into the U.S. South. Its vines may become pests by becoming entangled in other vegetation. The edible berries, also called passion fruit, sweet granadilla, and sweet calabash, are economically important in the tropics.

The passionflower, a climbing vine of tropical America, produces fragrant, intricately formed flowers (A), which are symbolically linked with the passion of Jesus Christ. The egg-shaped, juicy fruit (B) matures from large buds (C).

Passover   Passover (in Hebrew, *Pesach*) is one of the most important Jewish festivals. Celebrated in late March or early April (by the Jewish calendar, Nisan 15–22), it commemorates the Exodus—the deliverance of Israel

A ceramic platter (1673) used for the seder, celebrated at the beginning of Passover, commemorates aspects of Jewish history and tradition.

from slavery in Egypt. The name *Passover* is interpreted in the Mishnah to refer to the statement (Exod. 12:23) that God would pass over the houses of the Israelites in killing the firstborn of Egypt. In the Bible, however, the name is applied to a festival involving the sacrifice of a lamb or kid and the eating of unleavened bread; this was probably an ancient spring festival.

The Passover is celebrated for seven days (outside Israel, traditionally observant Jews add an extra day), the first and last days being full holidays when work is not to be done. Throughout the week only unleavened bread (*matzo*) is eaten; the scrupulously observant abstain from all leavened food and even from nonleavened food not prepared for the festival with special care. Samaritans still perform the ancient Passover sacrifice; all other Jews gave up this rite when the Temple was destroyed. Instead, the first two evenings of Passover are marked by a festal meal, called the SEDER, at which the story of the Exodus is retold through the reading of the Haggadah (story) and the symbols of the occasion—unleavened bread, bitter herbs, and others—are explained.

passport   A passport is a government-issued document that permits the holder to cross international borders. Most passports formally establish the holder's identity with a sealed photograph, indicate nationality, and request safe passage for the traveler. A passport may contain one or more visas, which are endorsements permitting the holder to travel in a certain foreign country.

Although passports have been used for centuries, they did not become compulsory in many countries until after World War I. Regulations governing their use were simplified and relaxed after World War II, when worldwide tourism became common. In some countries citizens are required to carry "internal passports" for registration purposes.

pasta   Pasta, a large family of shaped, dried wheat pastes, is a basic staple in many countries. Its origins are obscure. Rice pastes were known very early in China; pastes made of wheat were used in India and Arabia long before they were introduced into Europe in the 11th or 12th century. According to legend, Marco Polo brought a pasta recipe with him in 1295 from Asia. Pasta quickly became a major element in the Italian diet, and its use spread throughout Europe.

Pasta is made from durum wheat flour, which, because of its high gluten content, makes a strong, elastic dough. Hard durum wheat has the highest wheat protein value. The flour is mixed with water, kneaded to form a thick paste, and then forced through perforated plates or dies that shape it into 1 of more than 100 different forms. The shaped dough is dried to reduce the moisture content to about 12 percent; properly dried pasta should remain edible almost indefinitely. Pastas can be colored

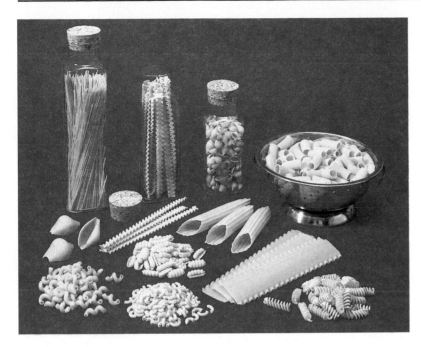

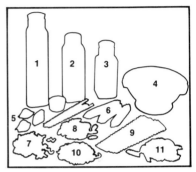

Various forms of pasta, manufactured by forcing highly elastic dough through shaped dies, were developed for such properties as heat retention and aesthetic appeal. Ribbon-shaped forms, such as mafaldi (2) and lasagna (9), are the traditional specialty of northern Italy, where pasta is often made with eggs; such tubular forms as spaghettini (1), rigatoni (4), manicotti (6), elbow twists (7), and elbow macaroni (10) are standard in southern districts. Other shapes include shells (3), jumbo shells (5), and such twisted forms as cavatelli (8) and tortiglioni (11).

with spinach or beet juice. The addition of egg produces a richer, yellower pasta that is usually made in noodle form and is often sold undried.

pastel   Pastel is an art medium in which crayonlike sticks of soft pigment are applied to paper. These pigments, ranging from pure colors to mixtures with white, are held together by a gum substance. Although the colors are permanent, they do not penetrate the paper and are easily rubbed off or blurred. They must therefore be protected by glass or sprayed with a fixative. Sharp lines can be made with the edge of the stick and broad strokes with its side. Because many pastels contain white, the term *pastel* has come to designate light, creamy colors.

Pastels first became popular in 18th-century France, when the Venetian portrait painter Rosalba CARRIERA arrived in Paris (c.1720) and her pastel portraits became fashionable. In the 19th century, Edgar DEGAS used pastels for his portrayals of ballet dancers. He is reputed to have used turpentine on his paper to make the pastels sink into the surface (a practice frowned upon by purists). Mary CASSATT, an American who spent most of her life in France and was a close associate of Degas, specialized in portraying mothers and children in both her paintings and pastels. Odilon Redon produced many still lifes of flowers, using an impressionistic technique well suited to the medium.

Pasternak, Boris [pas'-tur-nak]   The winner of the 1958 Nobel Prize for literature, Boris Leonidovich Pasternak, b. Feb. 10 (N.S.), 1890, d. May 30, 1960, won international recognition as a major novelist, although he was much criticized in his native Russia. His father was a well-known painter and his mother a concert pianist, and he grew up in a highly cultivated atmosphere. At a time when most Soviet poets wrote verse designed to inspire ordinary people to work for the Communist cause, Pasternak's intellectual lyrics probed the meaning of life and the mystery of death.

Many of Pasternak's poems and some of his prose works have strong religious overtones. Pasternak was not interested in social issues in themselves, except as they influence individual human destinies. This lack of interest was often criticized by the Soviet press, and for many years Pasternak's verse was not allowed to appear in print. Like many other silenced Soviet writers during the 1930s and '40s, Pasternak sought refuge in translation.

Boris Pasternak, one of the Soviet Union's most prominent poets, was awarded the 1958 Nobel Prize for literature largely as a result of the publication of his epic novel, Doctor Zhivago (1958).

He is well known for his Russian versions of Goethe, Shakespeare, and Soviet Georgian poets.

In Pasternak's prose, as in his verse, mood is more important than plot, and contemplation of such problems as death, fate, and the role of poetry and music is more important than ordinary events. These qualities persist from an early collection of tales, *The Adolescence of Zhenya Luvers* (1925; Eng. trans., 1961), to the autobiographical *Safe Conduct* (1931; Eng. trans., 1958), to Pasternak's most famous work, the novel *Doctor Zhivago* (1958; Eng. trans., 1958; film, 1965).

Doctor Zhivago was rejected by Soviet publishers as anti-Soviet. It was smuggled out to the West by an Italian Communist publisher and was soon printed in many languages. Actually, the novel is studiously apolitical. It is, essentially, the story of two lovers who attempt to insulate their private lives from the Revolution of 1917 and the civil war that followed. The award of the 1958 Nobel Prize to Pasternak unleashed in the USSR a campaign of vilification that lasted until his death. Although Pasternak's poetry has been published in the USSR, *Doctor Zhivago* was first printed—as a serial in a literary journal—only in 1988.

French chemist Louis Pasteur's research on fermentation led him to develop pasteurization, a controlled heating process that protects liquids from spoilage caused by microorganisms. Pasteur was also the first to develop and use vaccines against anthrax and rabies.

Pasteur, Louis [pahs-tur']

The French chemist Louis Pasteur, b. Dec. 27, 1822, d. Sept. 28, 1895, is considered the founder of MICROBIOLOGY. Although Pasteur was not the first to argue that infectious diseases are caused by germs, his work was of paramount importance in demonstrating the relevance of germ theory to infectious disease, surgery, hospital management, agriculture, and industry. In 1884, Pasteur became professor of chemistry and in 1863 dean of the Lille Faculty of Science.

Studies of the industrial fermentation of beet juice led him to the hypothesis that fermentation was dependent on living "germs" or "ferments." Pasteur demonstrated that yeast was a microorganism that converts sugar into alcohol. Previous speculations about the role of yeasts in fermentation had been ridiculed by eminent organic chemists who argued that fermentation was a purely chemical process and that microorganisms were the product rather than the cause of fermentation. In *Mémoire sur la fermentation appelée lactique* (History of Lactic Acid Fermentation; 1858), Pasteur stated that specific kinds of fermentation were caused by the activities of specific microscopic living organisms, and that many diseases were also caused by specific germs. Thus he laid the foundation of the germ theory of disease.

Fermentation studies led to Pasteur's battle against the doctrine of SPONTANEOUS GENERATION. Pasteur demonstrated that microbes arise from other microbes and do not spontaneously develop in a sterile medium, and any evidence to the contrary was the result of careless technique and experimental artifacts. He further showed that spoilage of perishable substances can be averted by destroying microorganisms to prevent contamination, resulting in the process of pasteurization.

An investigation of the diseases of silkworms provided a transition between research on fermentation and the diseases of higher animals. Working with the ANTHRAX bacillus, Pasteur established the role of earthworms in the dissemination of anthrax and developed a preventive vaccine in 1881. In 1882 he showed that RABIES is caused by a transferable agent too small to be seen with a microscope, and in 1885 he developed the first vaccine against the disease. Pasteur became the first director of the newly established Pasteur Institute in 1888. His numerous accomplishments were achieved despite a paralyzing stroke at the age of 46.

pasteurization [pas'-chur-i-zay-shuhn]

The pasteurization of food and beverages by heating destroys microorganisms that cause disease and spoilage without significantly impairing the flavor and appearance of the food. This process was developed by and named for Louis Pasteur, the French scientist who in the early 1860s demonstrated that wine and beer could be preserved by heating above 57.2° C (135° F). In the United States federal laws require pasteurization of milk and most milk and egg products.

The high-temperature, short-time (HTST) pasteurizers used today typically have a stack of thin, stainless-steel plates separated by rubber gaskets. Milk is pumped in one direction through passages between the plates, and water through alternate passages in the opposite direction. The milk is rapidly heated by this method, and 80 to 90 percent of the heat is reused because milk leaving the pasteurizer gives up heat to incoming cold milk. HTST standards for milk are 71.7° C (161° F) for 15 seconds; for whole, liquid eggs, 60° C (140° F) for 3.5 minutes. After pasteurization, the milk is cooled immediately to below 10° C (50° F) to prevent contamination.

A direct injection or infusion of steam is also used to pasteurize food; both processes allow nearly instantaneous heating to well above the boiling point. Steam is introduced into the milk, which is pumped into a vacuum changer; there the steam condenses, cooling the milk. If the temperature is held at 137.8° C (280° F) for two seconds, the product can be labeled ultrapasteurized—a process that allows milk or cream to be preserved without refrigeration. Consumer concern has been expressed, however, about the effect of this process on the taste of the product.

pastoral literature

Pastoral—a term derived from the Latin word *pastor* ("shepherd")—is a literary genre established by the classical Greek poet Theocritus and perpetuated by the Roman poet Vergil, whose *Eclogues* (39 BC) were widely imitated during the Renaissance by Italian and English writers. Theocritus described the idyllic life of the bucolic country dweller, praising the simplicity of a rural existence and implicitly denigrating the complexity and haste of civilized urban behavior. The assumption that humanity and nature remain essentially innocent until corrupted by civilization is central to the genre.

Important Renaissance pastorals in verse and in prose include Jacopo Sannazaro's *Arcadia* (1504), Torquato Tasso's *Aminta* (1581), Giovanni Battista Guarini's *Il Pastor Fido* (1583), and Sir Philip Sidney's *Arcadia* (1590). Conventions established by these works were used by William Shakespeare in *As You Like It* (1599). Edmund Spenser, in the *Shepheardes Calendar* (1579), used a pastoral allegory to discuss the social evils of his time, and John Milton, exploiting the metaphorical resonance of the word *pastor*, included criticism of corrupt clergy in his pastoral elegy, *Lycidas* (1637).

Noting that pastoral literature commonly juxtaposes the simple with the complex in order to question social custom, the critic William Empson used the term *pastoral* to describe works that stand outside the formal limits of the genre. His book *Some Versions of Pastoral* (1935; repr. 1968) contains a celebrated essay on Lewis Carroll's *Alice in Wonderland* (1865), in which Alice, Empson pointed out, applies a child's innocent common sense to the pedantic rules and foolish prejudices of her elders.

Patagonia

[pah-tah-gohn'-ee-ah]   Patagonia, the southern 30% of South America, lies poleward of 40° south latitude. Most of this cool, windy, arid region is in Argentina between the Andes and the Atlantic Ocean. Patagonia means "big feet," referring to the TEHUELCHE Indians who, when first seen by Ferdinand Magellan in 1520, were wearing oversize boots. The area is estimated at 673,400 km^2 (260,000 mi^2) and consists of plateaus rising to 1,525 m (5,000 ft) in the Andean foothills. Scrub grass and tuftlike bushes predominate.

Patagonia is primarily a sheep-raising area. Fruits, cereals, and potatoes are grown in irrigated areas. In 1907 petroleum was discovered near Comodoro Rivadavia, the principal city of Patagonia. Some iron and coal is mined.

After Magellan's coastal explorations, the Spanish dominated the area until British sheep ranchers settled there in the 1880s. In 1833, Charles Darwin discovered and explored the Chubut River aboard the H.M.S. *Beagle*.

patent

A U.S. patent, known as letters patent, gives its owner (the patentee) or joint owners the right to exclude others from making, using, and selling in the United States the owner's invention for 17 years (design patents have different terms). Anyone who makes, uses, or sells, without the consent of the patentee, what is covered by any claims of a patent is liable for damages and may be enjoined from infringing the patent.

Patents are granted to encourage inventions and their disclosure to the public. Patent laws vary among countries. The U.S. patent system is derived from that of England, where Parliament abolished (1624) the practice of granting patents as favors to the king's friends in favor of granting patents only to inventors of "any manner of new manufacture."

The U.S. Constitution (Article I, Section 8) grants Congress the power to establish a patent system. The first U.S. patent law was passed in 1790, and a basic system was enacted in 1836 (revised in 1870 and 1952). The Patent Office, also established in 1836 (now the Patent and Trademark Office, part of the Department of Commerce), is administered by a commissioner, who can issue patents and register TRADEMARKS. The office has granted about 4 million patents since 1836.

Only certain classes of inventions are patentable: machines or apparatuses, articles of manufacture, compositions of matter, processes and methods, ornamental designs, and certain types of botanical plants. In 1980 the Supreme Court ruled that genetically engineered organisms could be patented, and methods of genetic engineering have since received patents as well. Internationally, however, patenting in the field of biotechnology does not yet follow uniform rules. Processes and methods now being patented include COMPUTER SOFTWARE programs and complex mathematical ALGORITHMS. To be patentable an invention must be new and useful and must not have been obvious to a person of ordinary skill in the art at the time it was made. An invention is not considered patentable if it was known or used by others in the United States, or described by anyone (including the applicant) in a publication, or was in public use or on sale anyplace in the world more than one year before application for a patent.

Pater, Walter

[pay'-tur]   One of the most important writers of late-Victorian England, Walter Horatio Pater, b. Aug. 4, 1839, d. July 30, 1894, abandoned the search for an absolute standard of truth and morality that had preoccupied earlier Victorian writers and asserted that all truth was relative. His view was that the individual's only responsibility is to enjoy experience—particularly aes-

Walter Pater, a 19th-century British critic and author, is remembered largely for his volumes of cultural criticism, such as Studies in the History of the Renaissance *(1873). Pater wrote several fictional works, the most notable of which remains* Marius the Epicurean *(1885), a novel set in ancient Rome.*

thetic experience—as intensely as possible. His adherence to the doctrine of art for its own sake influenced a generation of writers at the turn of the century, notably Oscar Wilde and William Butler Yeats.

Pater was educated at Oxford University, where he was elected a fellow of Brasenose College in 1864, a post he held for the rest of his life. A bachelor, he led a retired and uneventful life. He achieved fame, however, with the publication of a collection of essays, *Studies in the History of the Renaissance* (1873). Many of the essays in the book, later called *The Renaissance*, had already appeared in the *Fortnightly Review*.

Marius the Epicurean (1885) was a fuller and more careful exposition of his views, written partly because Pater feared the morally subversive effect of misinterpretations of his hedonistic conclusion to *The Renaissance*. He later published some shorter pieces of philosophical fiction (*Imaginary Portraits*, 1887), a collection of critical essays (*Appreciations, with an Essay on Style*, 1889), and lectures (*Plato and Platonism*, 1893).

Paternoster   see LORD'S PRAYER

Paterson [pat'-ur-suhn]   Paterson, located in heavily urbanized northeastern New Jersey 23 km (14 mi) north of Newark, is the seat of Passaic County and has a population of 140,891 (1990). Paterson's industries manufacture silk and rayon textiles, machinery, machine tools, chemicals, and plastics. One of the first submarines, built by John P. Holland in 1881, is exhibited in Paterson's West Side Park.

In the late 18th century the 21-m-high (70-ft) Great Falls of the Passaic River so impressed Alexander Hamilton that he organized the Society for Establishing Useful Manufactures in 1791 and founded the city in 1792, naming it for William Paterson, then governor of New Jersey. The first cotton-spinning mill was built there in 1792. The city's initial cotton-textile industry was supplemented by the silk industry, developed in the 1840s. Samuel Colt produced his first revolvers there in 1836.

Paterson's textile mills have experienced much labor unrest. Under the leadership of the Industrial Workers of the World, workers struck the mills in 1912 and again in 1913. The second strike lasted five months.

Paterson, William   The American statesman William Paterson, b. Ireland, Dec. 24, 1745, d. Sept. 9, 1806, represented New Jersey at the federal CONSTITUTIONAL CONVENTION in 1787, where he proposed the New Jersey, or small states', plan for a unicameral federal legislature, with each state voting equally. He served New Jersey as U.S. senator (1789–90) and governor (1791–93) and was appointed to the U.S. Supreme Court in 1793.

Pathan [puh-tahn']   Pathan, or Pashtun, is the ethnic name of more than 60 tribes speaking various dialects of an Iranian language (Pashtu) in Afghanistan and Pakistan. One of the largest tribal groupings in the world, the Pathan population is estimated at nearly 8 million in Afghanistan and 15 million in Pakistan. Their traditional homeland is the mountainous borderland between those two countries, although they are now distributed throughout most of Afghanistan and the plains of Pakistan. The largest tribes are the Ghalzai and the Durrani.

The Pathan are the culturally dominant people of Afghanistan and of the North West Frontier Province of Pakistan, but they have never been politically united. From the 1950s the Afghanistan government backed the establishment of an independent state (Pashtunistan) for the Pathan, which would include a large part of Pakistan. Although most Pathans are settled agriculturalists, pastoral nomadism and migrant trading have always been important among them. The traditional Pathan way of life was badly disrupted by the Soviet occupation of Afghanistan (1979–89) and subsequent civil war. Large numbers of Pathan fled from Afghanistan to refugee camps in Pakistan, increasing tensions in the border area.

Pathet Lao [path'-et lah'-oh]   The Pathet Lao (Lao Country) functioned as a leftist nationalist political party and revolutionary organization in Laos from about 1950 to the mid-1970s. As major powers contended for control of Indochina, Pathet Lao activities became intertwined with larger conflicts (see VIETNAM WAR).

After World War II, some Laotian nationalists, including Prince SOUPHANOUVONG, were dissatisfied with French plans to establish a semi-independent state in Laos and formed the Pathet Lao, which joined the VIET MINH in an invasion of northern Laos in 1953. The GENEVA CONFERENCE of 1954 recognized Pathet Lao control over two northern provinces of Laos.

When Souvanna Phouma, Souphanouvong's half brother, became premier in 1956, the Pathet Lao became a legal political party (United Lao Patriotic Front), serving in several coalition governments. Rightist leaders objected to this, and a full-scale civil war in which the United States and North Vietnam became increasingly involved was soon under way. The Pathet Lao "liberated" Vientiane on Aug. 23, 1975, and established the Lao People's Democratic Republic in December.

pathology   Pathology is a branch of medicine that deals with the causes and processes of disease and its effects on the structure and function of the human body. All physicians are involved to some extent in pathology, but a pathologist specializes in interpreting processes of disease by examination of tissues and body fluids obtained during surgery or AUTOPSY.

The two major branches of pathology are tissue, or anatomical, pathology and clinical pathology. Anatomical pathology is based on the direct examination of organs and tissues to determine the nature, extent, and prognosis of a patient's disease, as in a biopsy, or to explain the cause of a patient's death, as in an autopsy.

Clinical pathology involves laboratory procedures to determine the concentration of various biochemical substances in body fluids; the numbers and types of cells in blood, bone marrow, and other tissues; the functioning of organs such as the liver and kidneys; the status of the immune system; and the identification of infectious organisms. The head of a hospital clinical laboratory is usually a clinical pathologist.

Forensic pathologists obtain medical evidence for legal purposes in criminal cases or suspicious deaths.

Patman, Wright [pat'-muhn]   John William Wright Patman, b. Patman's Switch, Tex., Aug. 6, 1893, d. Mar. 7, 1976, served as Democratic representative from Texas from 1929 until his death and chaired (1963–75) the powerful Committee on Banking and Currency. Patman opposed bank and corporate concentration of financial power. He coauthored the ROBINSON-PATMAN ACT (Fair Trade Practices Act) of 1936 and sponsored the 1953 legislation establishing the Small Business Administration.

Paton, Alan [pay'-tuhn]   One of South Africa's most important novelists, Alan Stewart Paton, b. Jan. 11, 1903, d. Apr. 12, 1988, achieved international fame

Alan Paton, a South African writer and political figure, gained international attention with his novels Cry, the Beloved Country *(1948) and* Too Late the Phalarope *(1953), moving and eloquent accounts of racial conflict in South Africa.*

with his first novel, CRY, THE BELOVED COUNTRY (1948), which portrays the precarious relationship between blacks and whites in that country. A spokesperson for liberal forces in South Africa, Paton further explored the tensions between blacks and whites, and older and younger generations, in *Too Late the Phalarope* (1953); this novel also became an international best-seller. Paton's other works include such nonfiction as *The Land and the People of South Africa* (1955) and *Hope for South Africa* (1958), the short-story collections *Tales from a Troubled Land* (1961) and *Knocking on the Door* (1975), and a two-volume autobiography, *Towards the Mountain* (1980) and *Journey Continued* (1988).

Patras [pah-trahs']   Patras (Greek: Pátrai), the largest city and the cultural, industrial, and commercial heart of the Peloponnesus, is located on the northern shore of that Greek peninsula, about 180 km (100 mi) west of Athens. Its population is 142,163 (1981). The city has a fine natural harbor and is a major shipping center for agricultural products. Power resources and excellent road and rail connections with Athens contribute to the city's economic importance. The University of Patras was founded there in 1966.

A commercial center by the 5th century BC, Patras participated in the Achaean League in about 280 BC. It was colonized by Romans in 31 BC. According to tradition Saint Andrew was martyred there in AD 70. The Greek revolt against the Turks began in Patras in 1821.

patriarch   Originally used by Jews to refer to the head of a family or tribe, *patriarch* later became a Christian ecclesiastical title, denoting the occupants of several prominent episcopal sees who exercised leadership over their fellow bishops. The development of patriarchates was one of the significant features in the history of the church after it became established in the Roman Empire and adopted a more centralized ecclesiastical administration, patterned after the organization of the state.

Today, in the ORTHODOX CHURCH, the title is used by the heads of the churches of Constantinople, Alexandria, Antioch, Jerusalem, Russia (USSR), Georgia (USSR), Serbia (Yugoslavia), Romania, and Bulgaria. The canonical prerogatives of each patriarch are limited to presidency and moral leadership in the synod of bishops of each church. The title is also used by the heads of the several EASTERN RITE CHURCHES.

patricians   Patricians were members of the hereditary aristocratic order of ancient Rome, entitled to privileges denied other citizens. Only patricians could hold civil and religious offices, and until 445 BC they were forbidden to intermarry with PLEBEIANS. The plebeians fought for and obtained increased power, substantially diminishing the patricians' privileged position by the 3d century BC. Under the empire, the distinction between the two classes became blurred, and *patrician* eventually became an honorific title.

Patrick, Saint   Saint Patrick, c.389–461, the patron of Ireland, was a bishop and missionary. He was born in Roman Britain and, at the age of 16, was captured and sold into slavery in Ireland. During his captivity he turned to religion. After 6 years of labor as a shepherd, Patrick escaped to the Continent. He returned to Britain at the age of 22, determined to convert the Irish to Christianity. This goal led him to Gaul, where he studied, was ordained (c.417) to the diaconate, and spent 15 years in the church of Auxerre. His first nomination as bishop to the Irish was rejected because of a sin in his youth. On the death of PALLADIUS—appointed first bishop of the Irish in 431 by Pope Celestine I—Patrick was ordained a bishop (432) and set out for Ireland.

Although opposed by priests of the indigenous religion, Patrick secured toleration for Christians and, through active preaching, made important converts among the royal families. He developed a native clergy, fostered the growth of monasticism, established dioceses, and held church councils. Feast day: Mar. 17.

Saint Patrick, a British bishop who had escaped from slavery in Ireland as a youth, returned to convert the heathen Irish to Christianity. Despite some differences with his ecclesiastical superiors, Saint Patrick was highly successful in this mission and is today revered as the patron saint of Ireland. (National Museum of Ireland, Dublin.)

patrilineal   see LINEAGE

patristic literature   Patristic literature refers to the writings of the Fathers of the Christian church (the Greek word *patristikos* means "relating to the fathers") between the latter part of the 1st century and the middle of the 8th century. It can therefore be distinguished from New Testament theology at one end and from medieval SCHOLASTICISM and Byzantine systematization at the other. It reflects the philosophical and religious thought of the Hellenistic and Roman world from which it derived the bulk of its concepts and vocabulary. The themes of this vast literature are manifold, but the theological reflection of the Fathers focused for the most part on questions of Christology and the Trinity.

Patristic literature falls into three main periods. The ante-Nicene period (before 325) includes the writings of the Apostolic Fathers, the apologetic and antiheretical literature, and the beginnings of speculative Greek theology. The major figures of this period include CLEMENT OF ALEXANDRIA, CYPRIAN, IRENAEUS, JUSTIN MARTYR, ORIGEN, and TERTULLIAN. The period between the councils of Nicaea (325) and Chalcedon (451) was the golden age of the Nicene fathers (including EUSEBIUS OF CAESAREA, the first major church historian), the Alexandrians (most notably ATHANASIUS and CYRIL OF ALEXANDRIA), the Cappadocians (BASIL THE GREAT, GREGORY OF NAZIANZUS, and GREGORY OF NYSSA), and the Antiochenes (John Chrysostom and THEODORE OF MOPSUESTIA). This was also the period of the great Latin fathers: HILARY OF POITIERS, AMBROSE, JEROME, and, above all, AUGUSTINE. The final period of patristic literature ends with GREGORY I (the Great) in the West and JOHN DAMASCENE in the East.

patronage   Patronage refers to the practice in which jobs and favors are distributed on a political basis to the politically faithful rather than according to merit. It originated in the *spoils system*, a term introduced during the presidency of Andrew Jackson. In the United States patronage fueled the political machines of the late-19th and 20th centuries and is closely associated with the influx of large numbers of immigrants to America's rapidly industrializing urban centers. Political machines and their powers of patronage provided these immigrants with an avenue of economic and social advancement. Patronage was distributed to those who followed the lead of the political BOSS and the local political organization. Following that lead might include faithful service, electoral support, and financial contributions. In recent decades, formal credentials, merit examinations, and bidding statutes have combined to make the distribution of patronage more difficult and much less common.

patroons   *Patroon* was the title given to a landlord in the Dutch North American colony of NEW NETHERLAND. In 1629 the members of the Dutch West India Company were granted estates with 26-km (16-mi) frontages along the colony's navigable rivers on the condition that they send 50 settlers in 4 years to occupy the land. With the exception of the prosperous estate of the VAN RENSSELAER family in the area of modern Albany, N.Y., the patroon system worked poorly because the patroons were unable to manage their estates effectively from Holland. The system gradually fell into disuse after New Netherland came under English control (1664).

pattern recognition   Pattern recognition refers to the analysis of the complex processes involved in recognizing patterns. The senses and the brain perform these tasks in the human being. The field of pattern recognition

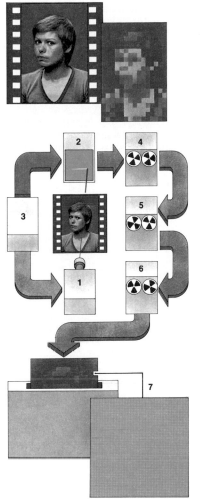

Pattern recognition is the ability of the brain to resolve a set of visual signals into an identifiable object. Research is now being done to determine how much visual information is needed for recognition. This picture of a woman (top left), on a 35-mm transparency, was broken down into a grid pattern with the aid of a computer. First, the picture is scanned by a beam of light (1), which analyzes the opacity and color variation in each of 1,024 lines. This information is transmitted to a light-sensitive photomultiplier tube (2). A synchronizer (3) coordinates the action of the beam and the tube. In a series of computer operations (4, 5, 6), the lines are divided into discrete points, each of which is assigned a numerical value corresponding to its brightness and color. Finally, these numbers are plotted on a grid (7). The picture emerges from the computer as a pattern of colored squares, an abstract version of the original photograph.

lies in developing ROBOTS that can interpret optical input while in motion. This application would be useful, for instance, in space exploration.

Sound-pattern recognition involves translating sound from its continuous wave, or analog, form to a digital form that can be analyzed by a computer (see DIGITAL TECHNOLOGY). Researchers in this area are primarily interested in problems related to voice recognition. Systems have been developed and marketed that can be "trained" to recognize a limited vocabulary from a single speaker. Computer programming advances and the availability of more powerful computers will eventually bring about systems that will recognize a large vocabulary and understand any speaker.

Pattern recognition is not limited to the recognition of sensory input, but also applies to information already in store. This entails looking, for example, at a set of events and trying to detect a recurring pattern or some other feature that makes prediction possible. STOCHASTIC PROCESS is the name for a statistical technique that provides for just such an analysis.

Patterson (family) [pat'-ur-suhn]   The Patterson family of newspaper publishers traces its roots to **Joseph Medill** (1823-99), who from 1855 to 1899 transformed the *Chicago Tribune* into a leading American daily. The families of his two daughters, the Pattersons and the McCormicks, carried on this tradition. One Medill grandchild, **Joseph Medill Patterson**, b. Chicago, Jan. 6, 1879, d. May 26, 1946, founded the *New York Daily News* (initially as the *Illustrated Daily News*) in 1919, the first American tabloid newspaper. Joseph Medill Patterson's sister, **Eleanor Medill Patterson**, b. Chicago, Nov. 7, 1884, d. July 24, 1948, later became owner of the *Washington Times-Herald*. Joseph's daughter **Alicia Patterson Guggenheim**, b. Chicago, Oct. 15, 1906, d. July 2, 1963, founded the popular suburban New York tabloid *Newsday* in 1940.

Joseph Patterson and his associate and cousin Robert Rutherford McCormick began their careers on the *Chicago Tribune*, assumed joint control in 1911, but later parted ways. By 1924, Patterson's *New York Daily News* led the nation in circulation with 750,000 readers. After Patterson's death in 1946 the *New York Daily News* came under McCormick's control.

Patterson, Floyd   Floyd Patterson, b. Waco, N.C., Jan. 4, 1935, was the first world heavyweight boxing champion to regain his title after losing it in the ring. He won (1951, 1952) the Golden Gloves championship in the 160-lb (72-kg) division; he then won the Olympic gold medal in 1952 as a middleweight. Patterson turned professional, and on Nov. 30, 1956, he defeated Archie Moore to win the heavyweight championship.

On June 26, 1959, Patterson lost his title to Ingemar Johansson but regained it on June 20, 1960. After losing the championship in 1962 to Sonny Liston, Patterson retired; he attempted a comeback in 1970 but was defeated in 1972 by Muhammad Ali.

is involved especially with the manufacture of artificial systems that achieve similar ends, whether using the same methods or not. In particular, much research has been done on mimicking sight (optical pattern recognition) and hearing (sound pattern recognition).

There are generally three stages in optical pattern recognition: IMAGE PROCESSING, pattern classification, and scene analysis. Image processing takes many forms but is concerned with sharpening the edges of patterns to make classification easier. Pattern classification interprets specific items in the processed image such as chairs, tables, or letters of the alphabet. Many such systems have been devised and are in wide use. Optical character readers, or scanners (see SCANNING), recognize printed characters. In the military, computer systems have been developed that analyze radar images to detect friendly or unfriendly aircraft. Law-enforcement agencies use optical pattern recognition in matching fingerprints found at crime sites with those in computer files. One important research goal

Gen. George Patton, one of the most able American field commanders of World War II, makes a dramatic arrival at Gela, Sicily, in 1943, shortly before his capture of the island's principal city, Palermo.

Patton, George S. [pat'-uhn]

George Smith Patton, Jr., b. San Gabriel, Calif., Nov. 11, 1885, d. Dec. 21, 1945, was one of the foremost American combat generals of World War II. Scion of a prominent military family from Virginia, he graduated from West Point in 1909 and saw tank service in France in World War I. The colorful, tough-minded, outspoken officer—he wore ivory-handled revolvers on his hips—was a chief proponent of the adoption of armored weapons and mobile tactics.

After the outbreak of World War II, Patton played a major part in the invasion (1942) of North Africa and in the capture (1943) of Sicily. His career climaxed in 1944–45 when, after the Allies' Normandy invasion, Patton's Third Army swept across France and into Germany. One of the war's ablest tank commanders, he played a pivotal role in helping to halt the German counterattack in the Battle of the BULGE (December 1944–January 1945). Relentlessly hard-driving and combative, "Old Blood and Guts" Patton incurred unfavorable publicity for slapping a combat-exhausted soldier in a hospital, although he later apologized publicly for the incident. Patton was fatally injured in an automobile accident near Mannheim, Germany.

Paul, Saint

The Apostle Paul, one of the most successful early Christian missionaries, is chiefly known for his letters (epistles) to various churches, which are preserved in the New Testament of the Bible and had a major influence on later Christian theology. Of Jewish origin, Paul became a leading champion of Gentile CHRISTIANITY, denying the need for Christians to observe Jewish law.

Life. Most of what is known about Paul's life comes from the New Testament, especially from his own letters and the ACTS OF THE APOSTLES. He was born at Tarsus in what is now Turkey, probably about the beginning of the 1st century, and was originally named Saul. Raised as a pious Jew, he was a zealous opponent of the Christians until about AD 34, when he had a profound mystical experience—a vision of Jesus Christ on the road to Damascus—that converted him to Christianity. This transforming experience was followed by missionary activity in Arabia, Syria, and his native Cilicia. In the early 40s, supporting himself as a tentmaker, he worked with Christians from Antioch in the first organized mission to Cyprus and south Galatia. This has been called his first missionary journey. Then, on a second journey, he and a group of colleagues spread the Christian message in north Galatia, Macedonia, and Greece, founding many churches along the way.

About 51, Paul took part in a meeting of church leaders at Jerusalem (sometimes called the Apostolic Council), where he defended the right of Gentile Christians to be free from the Jewish law, particularly from circumcision. The success of his missionary activities was acknowledged by the leaders of the Jerusalem church, but the militant Judaizers—those who believed in the necessity of circumcision—continued to oppose him. The last ten years of his life were marked by conflicts with them and with other missionaries, as well as by internal disputes between rival factions in his churches. After a third missionary journey, Paul delivered a gift of money collected from the other churches to the church of Jerusalem, intending this as a gesture of mutual love between Gentile and Jewish Christians. Hostility aroused by his attitude toward the law, however, led to a riot in Jerusalem and to Paul's arrest and imprisonment. He was executed in Rome in AD 62 or possibly later.

The Pauline Letters. The first of Paul's letters were the Epistles to the THESSALONIANS, in which he warned against thinking of the expected SECOND COMING OF CHRIST as an

Saint Paul was largely responsible for the development of Christianity from a Jewish sect to an independent religion. The churches he established brought the teachings of Jesus, originally directed to a Jewish audience, to the larger, Gentile world. This portrait is taken from a 6th-century mosaic in the church of San Vitale in Ravenna, Italy.

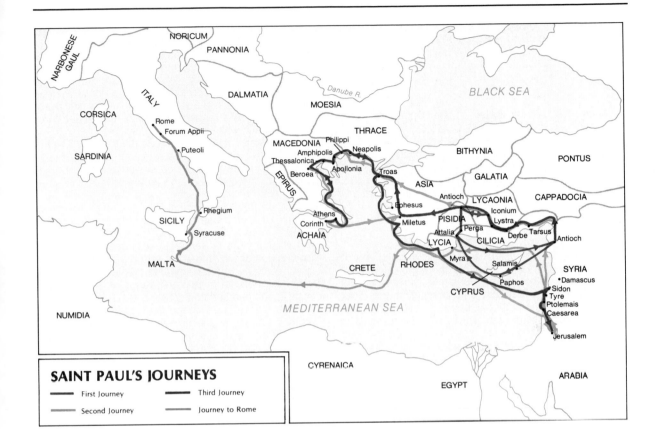

SAINT PAUL'S JOURNEYS

—— First Journey   —— Third Journey

—— Second Journey   —— Journey to Rome

easy escape from trouble. Written about AD 50, 1 Thessalonians is the earliest Christian document known to exist.

The Epistle to the GALATIANS was written, probably in 53, to counter the influence of Judaizers who were active in the Galatian church.

The Epistle to the PHILIPPIANS, written after Galatians, probably while Paul was a prisoner in Ephesus, promotes a theology of self-emptying love as an antidote to partisanship and a response to adversity.

Paul's extensive correspondence with the churches of Corinth in Greece are now incorporated in the two Epistles to the CORINTHIANS. In them Paul developed an innovative view of bodily responsibility based on the premise that body and soul were interdependent. He rejected prostitution as a violation of the body that had been joined to Christ, defended marriage as a covenant between equal partners to meet bodily desires, and articulated a wide-reaching concept of the autonomy of the individual conscience.

In his longest and most influential letter, the Epistle to the ROMANS, written between 56 and 58, Paul developed a systematic argument showing that salvation comes through faith rather than through conformity to human standards.

Feast day: June 29 (with Saint Peter).

Paul, Alice The American feminist Alice Paul, b. Moorestown, N.J., Jan. 11, 1885, d. July 9, 1977, was a leader in the fight for women's suffrage (see SUFFRAGE, WOMEN'S). A tough-minded reformer, Paul worked (1907–10) with militant women suffragists in England while pursuing graduate education. After her return to America she was dismissed from the gradualist National American Woman Suffrage Association because she applied militant tactics to the suffrage cause. She formed (1913) the National Woman's party and used protest marches and other forms of direct action to focus attention on the movement. From 1920, when the 19th Amendment granting the vote to women was ratified, she worked for enactment of an Equal Rights Amendment.

Paul, King of Greece Paul I, b. Dec. 14, 1901, d. Mar. 6, 1964, king of the Hellenes (1947–64), was the third son of King CONSTANTINE I. When the monarchy was restored in 1935, Paul returned to Greece as crown prince. He married (1938) Princess Frederika-Louise, daughter of the duke of Brunswick and granddaughter of German emperor William II. When the Germans invaded (April 1941) Greece, Paul escaped, taking refuge in

South Africa. He returned home in September 1946 and ascended the throne on Apr. 1, 1947, after the death of his elder brother King GEORGE II. As king he was criticized for intervening in political affairs. He was succeeded by his son CONSTANTINE II.

Paul of the Cross, Saint   Saint Paul of the Cross, b. Ovada, Italy, Jan. 3, 1694, d. Oct. 18, 1775, founded the Barefooted Clerks of the Cross and Passion (the Passionist order). A vision in 1720 inspired him to found the order, which was not granted papal approval until 1741. He also founded (1771) the Passionist nuns. Paul was canonized in 1867. Feast day: Oct. 19 (formerly Apr. 28).

Paul I, Emperor of Russia   Paul I, b. Oct. 1 (N.S.), 1754, d. Mar. 23 (N.S.), 1801, was emperor of Russia (1796–1801). He was the son of CATHERINE II by an early lover, although the Romanov dynasty insisted that his father was Catherine's husband, Emperor Peter III, who was killed in Catherine's coup of 1762. Paul was isolated from his sons (later emperors ALEXANDER I and NICHOLAS I), who were raised by Catherine. A vociferous opponent of many of Catherine's policies, Paul thwarted her efforts to disinherit him and pass the crown to Alexander. After Catherine's death (1796), Paul attempted to rule in German autocratic style, imposing harsh disciplinary measures on the military, thereby alienating the prestigious guard regiments. Allied with Austria, he launched the first Russian military campaigns against Napoleonic France. His erratic behavior led to a conspiracy to oust him from power. Paul was assassinated in the course of a coup d'état in 1801.

Paul III, Pope   Paul III, b. Feb. 29, 1468, pope from 1534 until his death on Nov. 10, 1549, was the first and most important pontiff of the COUNTER-REFORMATION. Born into the influential Farnese family (he was originally named Alessandro Farnese), he was created a cardinal-deacon in 1493. He led a worldly life, fathering four illegitimate children, but underwent a conversion prior to his ordination to the priesthood in 1519. After being elected pope, Paul vigorously promoted the reform of the church and attempted to conciliate the Lutherans through the efforts of Cardinal Gasparo Contarini. He approved the Society of Jesus (see JESUITS) and, in 1545, convoked the Council of TRENT. Paul was also a patron of Michelangelo and other Renaissance artists. His ambition for the advancement of his children and grandchildren marred his record even while pope and led to distrust of his motives, especially by Holy Roman Emperor CHARLES V.

Paul VI, Pope   Paul VI, b. Sept. 26, 1897, d. Aug. 6, 1978, originally named Giovanni Battista Montini, was pope from 1963 to 1978.

In 1937, Montini became under secretary of state for ordinary or internal affairs under his patron, Cardinal Pacelli, the future pope PIUS XII. Papal favor ended in 1954 when Montini recommended Vatican financial reforms in a report citing the profitable activities of Pacelli's nephews. He was appointed archbishop of Milan, where he was identified with social reforms, and finally became a cardinal in 1958, heading Pope JOHN XXIII's first list of new cardinals. Montini helped John at the Second VATICAN COUNCIL and was his chosen successor.

On the death of John in 1963, Paul VI was elected pope and promised to continue Vatican II and the policies of his predecessor. Though conservative in his understanding of Catholic teaching, Paul nevertheless realized that the church had to soften some features that were blocking ecumenical reunion. On the other hand, he staunchly defended priestly celibacy and papal primacy. His 1968 encyclical on contraception, *Humanae Vitae*, surprised many progressives in the church by supporting its prohibition based on natural law.

Paul delegated certain deliberative and consultative powers to synods of bishops convened at Rome and to priests' councils mandated within the dioceses. He reorganized the Roman Curia and demanded resignation of bishops at age 75. At the same time, he enlarged the College of Cardinals and named new members to it from Third World and Communist countries, thus weakening the Italian vote. He relaxed regulations on fasting and interfaith marriages. Paul's 1967 encyclical, *Populorum Progressio*, attacked laissez-faire capitalism and the "international imperialism of money."

Pope Paul VI reigned (1963–78) during a period of great dissension in the Roman Catholic church. Although he supported moderate reform, his conservative stance on such issues as priestly celibacy, contraception, and papal authority evoked much criticism.

Pauli, Wolfgang [pow'-lee]   The Austrian theoretical physicist Wolfgang Ernst Pauli, b. Apr. 25, 1900, d. Dec. 15, 1958, was one of the founders of modern physics. He is most famous for his "Pauli EXCLUSION PRINCIPLE," which states that no two electrons in an atom can have the same four quantum numbers (see QUANTUM MECHANICS). For his work in this area he was awarded the 1945 Nobel Prize for physics.

While an undergraduate student in physics at Munich, Pauli wrote a comprehensive article on the theory of relativity that became the classic treatment of the subject. In

The Austrian-American physicist Wolfgang Pauli was awarded (1945) the Nobel Prize for physics for his discovery of the atomic exclusion principle. Pauli is renowned for his pioneering work in the field of quantum mechanics.

proposed the alpha helix as the basic structure of proteins and narrowly missed discovering the double-helix structure of DNA. In 1954 he was awarded the Nobel Prize for chemistry for his contributions toward understanding chemical bonding.

After the war Pauling became deeply concerned about the dangers of radioactive fallout from nuclear-weapons tests. In 1958 he presented a petition to the United Nations signed by more than 11,000 scientists. On Oct. 10, 1963, the effective date for the U.S.-Soviet test-ban treaty, Pauling was awarded the 1962 Nobel Peace Prize.

Pauling's later career has centered on medical issues. He has shown that sickle-cell disease is a hereditary molecular disease and has investigated megavitamin therapy (the use of large amounts of vitamins for health purposes). In particular, he has advocated a large intake of vitamin C for treatment of the common cold.

1924 he proposed a new quantum number (related to spin) for electrons, and the following year he enunciated the exclusion principle. In 1931 Pauli predicted that conservation laws demanded the existence of the NEUTRINO, a particle later found. After being at Princeton University during World War II, Pauli became a U.S. citizen, but he spent his last years in Zurich.

Linus Pauling, winner of two Nobel Prizes, wrote The Nature of the Chemical Bond *(1939), a landmark of 20th-century science. The American chemist later gained attention for his advocacy of larger doses of vitamin C to fight colds.*

Paulicians   The Paulicians, a dualistic sect regarded as heretical, derived their name either from Saint Paul, in the interpretation of whom they followed MARCION, or from a Manichaean preacher called Paul (see MANICHAEISM). The first Paulician community was founded (c.657) in Armenia by Constantine of Mananalis (also known as Silvanus), who, after 27 years of preaching, was tried for heresy and stoned to death (c.684). The sect fragmented after persistent persecution. Those who fled to the Balkans appear to have merged with the BOGOMILS in the 10th century.

The Paulicians believed in two gods, one good and one evil, and taught that all matter was evil. They denied the humanity of Jesus and rejected the Old Testament, Catholic hierarchical order, and the notion of tradition. The Paulicians claimed that Christ was an angel and therefore incapable of crucifixion.

Pauling, Linus Carl [paw'-ling]   The American physical chemist Linus Carl Pauling, b. Portland, Oreg., Feb. 28, 1901, has made extensive contributions to structural chemistry and molecular biology. He received his Ph.D. from the California Institute of Technology (1925) and taught there until 1964. In 1939, having applied quantum mechanics to chemistry he published *The Nature of the Chemical Bond*, one of the most influential scientific books of the 20th century.

In the mid-1930s, Pauling became interested in biological molecules. His research projects were interrupted by World War II, during which he worked on explosives and developed an oxygen detector. In the early 1950s he

Pausanias [paw-say'-nee-uhs]   The Spartan general Pausanias, d. c.470 BC, commanded the Greek forces in their victory (479) over Persia at PLATAEA during the PERSIAN WARS. Later, as admiral of the Greek fleet, he won victories in Cyprus and the Bosporus, capturing Byzantium in 478. He fell under suspicion, however, because of his alleged Persian sympathies and was accused of secret intrigues with the Persian king. Pausanias was later accused of attempting to seize power by inciting the helots to revolt and was starved to death after he had taken sanctuary.

Pavarotti, Luciano [pah-vah-roht'-tee, loo-chee-ah'-noh]   An Italian tenor whose lyrical voice can take on a thrilling metallic ring, Luciano Pavarotti, b. Oct. 12, 1935, is one of the principal singers with the Metropolitan Opera, La Scala, and other leading companies. He made his debut as Rodolfo in Puccini's *La Bohème* at the Teatro Municipale in Reggio Emilia in 1961. He repeated the role in a film directed by Franco Zeffirelli and at his

Metropolitan Opera debut in 1968. Pavarotti is also acclaimed for Edgardo in Donizetti's *Lucia di Lammermoor*, Nemorino in the same composer's *L'Elisir d'Amore*, and the Duke of Mantua in Verdi's *Rigoletto*.

Pavia [pah-vee'-ah]   Pavia is a city in the Lombardy region of northern Italy on the Ticino River. It is connected by a canal to Milan, 32 km (20 mi) north. Pavia has a population of 85,056 (1981). Manufactures include sewing machines, foundry products, textiles, chemicals, and food products. Notable buildings include the cathedral (15th–19th century), the 12th-century Romanesque Church of San Michele, and the 12th-century Church of San Pietro. The University of Pavia (1361) is there.

Originally a Papirian settlement named Ticinum, it was conquered by Rome about 220 BC. In the 6th century it was the capital of Lombard Italy, and it was a free commune from the 11th to the 14th century. In 1525, Holy Roman Emperor CHARLES V defeated and captured FRANCIS I of France nearby. Beginning in the 18th century Pavia was dominated by Spain, France, and Austria. It joined a united Italy in 1859.

Pavlov, Ivan Petrovich [pahv'-luhf]   Ivan Petrovich Pavlov, b. Sept. 26 (N.S.), 1849, d. Feb. 27, 1936, was a Russian physiologist best known for his discovery of the conditioned reflex. He investigated the physiology of the cardiovascular system, the digestive system, and the central nervous system. In 1904 he was awarded the Nobel Prize for his work on digestion. In his experimentation Pavlov used live animals and studied each system as a continuing process.

The discovery of conditioning was accidental. For his research on digestion, Pavlov needed to collect saliva from his laboratory animals, dogs. He stimulated saliva flow by placing meat powder in the dog's mouth; soon he noticed the dog would begin salivating at the sight of the experimenter, in the expectation of receiving meat powder. Pavlov tried to pair other stimuli with the meat and found the dog would indeed salivate to stimuli such as the sound of a bell.

Through his work on higher nervous activity ("behav-

ior") and the discovery of the principle of conditioning, Pavlov helped to turn psychology away from the study of the mind to the study of overt behavior. He applied his model of a functioning system to human behavior in his concept of language as "a second system of signals" developing out of the first system of conditioned reflexes, and in his concept of mental diseases, such as schizophrenia, as an imbalance of the central nervous system. He also developed a classification of human temperaments on a similar basis. Pavlov's discovery of methods of experimental neuroses in dogs was a major step toward the study of human psychiatry in mental hospitals, work to which he devoted the last years of his life. His work continues to be a major influence in Soviet physiology, psychology, and psychiatry.

Pavlova, Anna [pahv'-luh-vah]   Anna Pavlova, b. Jan. 31, 1881, d. Jan. 23, 1931, was one of the world's best-known ballerinas. In 1899 she was accepted by the Imperial Ballet. From dancing solo roles in her first years, she graduated in 1903 to the title role in *Giselle* and achieved ballerina status in 1906. Pavlova excelled in those roles which required virtuoso technique and beautiful line. She first performed *The Dying Swan,* a solo choreographed for her by Mikhail FOKINE, in 1907, and it became her signature piece for the rest of her life. The role depended on extraordinary fluidity of movement and the expression of poetic feeling for its effect.

Pavlova toured outside Russia beginning in 1908, sometimes on her own and occasionally appearing with the BALLETS RUSSES DE SERGE DIAGHILEV. She settled in London and purchased Ivy House in 1912, in which she established a dance school. She organized her own dance company and toured throughout the world during the next decade. As a result of these extensive tours, she became the most famous and the wealthiest dancer of her time. Her performances in these years were mostly *pas de deux*

Ivan Petrovich Pavlov (right), a Russian physiologist and experimental psychologist, discovered the conditioned reflex while conducting physiological research on digestion. In his famous experiment, laboratory dogs were conditioned to salivate at the sound of a bell.

Anna Pavlova, a Russian dancer, was one of the most gifted and highly acclaimed ballerinas of the 20th century. Her lyrical interpretations of classical roles, most notably those of The Dying Swan and Giselle, *won her international recognition.*

(duets) with a partner and a *corps de ballet* (ensemble), usually derived from classical ballets, and solos in which Pavlova portrayed a bird, a dragonfly, and, of course, a swan. She was responsible for popularizing ballet throughout the world, and in her lifetime Pavlova became a synonym for this art form.

pawnbroker A shopkeeper engaged in lending small sums of money on pledges of personal property is called a pawnbroker. In the United States the pawnbroker is regulated at the state level to assure low interest rates and adequate protection for the articles pledged.

Historically, pawnbrokers date from ancient times, and in the Middle Ages this trade was pursued exclusively by the moneylenders of Lombardy, Italy, and by the Jews. The traditional symbol of the pawnbroker shop is three gold balls, which originally came from the armorial bearings of the Medici family, the richest moneylenders of Florence.

Pawnee [paw-nee'] The Pawnee Indians of North America possess one of the oldest native American cultures of the Great Plains. Sometime after about AD 1200 these Caddoan speakers entered the plains from east of the Mississippi River and settled near the Platte River in present-day Nebraska. Four independent Pawnee bands lived in villages composed of large, sturdy earth lodges adjacent to their maize fields. After planting and after harvest they made two tribal migrations a year to hunt the plains bison herds for meat and skins. Their highly developed religion, directed by an organized priesthood, taught that all energy derived from the stars and constellations; it may have been influenced by ancient Mexican civilizations. The chief of each village received instructions from a celestial body, whose sacred objects he held. One of the many Pawnee rituals demanded that every spring a young female captive be sacrificed to the Morning Star.

Attacked by nomadic hunting tribes who were fleeing from European colonization farther east, pressed also by incursions of the westbound pioneers, and weakened by smallpox and cholera, the Pawnee accepted a reservation in Nebraska in 1857. They later joined their relatives the WICHITA in Indian Territory (present-day Oklahoma) in 1876. Estimated at 10,000 in 1790, the Pawnee now number 2,428 (1988).

Pawtucket [puh-tuhk'-it] Pawtucket is a city in Providence County, R.I., on the Blackstone River near Providence. It has a population of 72,644 (1990). The city's mills make synthetic and natural-fiber textiles, yarns, and threads. Other industries manufacture machinery, wire, and glass fiber.

Pawtucket was settled in 1671 by Joseph Jencks, Jr., an ironmaker who set up his forge at the Blackstone River falls in what is now the city's business district. The city was the site of the first waterpowered cotton mill in North America, built by Samuel Slater in 1793 and now a National Historic Site.

Paxton, Sir Joseph [paks'-tuhn] An English landscape gardener and architect, Sir Joseph Paxton, b. Aug. 3, 1803, d. June 8, 1865, gained international renown for building the CRYSTAL PALACE (1850–51), which housed the Great Exhibition of the Works of Industry held in 1851 at Hyde Park in London. Inspired by work on a special greenhouse for the duke of Devonshire at Chatsworth, Paxton designed for the exhibition an enormous building made of a prefabricated cast-iron framework sheathed in glass. Paxton's achievement set off a craze for ferrovitreous (iron-and-glass) construction that resulted in notable examples in other cities.

Payton, Walter The running back Walter Jerry Payton, b. Columbia, Miss., July 25, 1954, was one of the National Football League's greatest performers. After attending Jackson State (Miss.) University, Payton played his entire career (1975–87) with the Chicago Bears. He set NFL career records for rushing (16,726 yds), all-purpose yards (21,803), and number of games in which he gained at least 100 yds rushing (77). Payton was the NFL's MVP in 1977, and his 275 yds gained rushing in a single game is another NFL record. He scored 125 career touchdowns.

Paz, Octavio [pahs] Winner of the 1990 Nobel Prize for literature, Mexican poet, essayist, and literary critic Octavio Paz, b. Mar. 31, 1914, has also served as a diplomat. Although his earliest collection of verse, *Luna silvestre* (Wild Moon, 1933), is characterized by lyric simplicity, his mature poetry, which shows the influence of the French surrealists, explores the themes of erotic love, solitude, and the essence of poetic expression. Important verse collections include *Early Poems, 1935–55* (1973), *Sun Stone* (1957; Eng. trans., 1963), and *Collected Poems, 1957–87* (1987). Paz is particularly known for his essays on the Mexican character in *The Labyrinth of Solitude* (1950; Eng. trans., 1962). Other essays are in *Conjunctions and Disjunctions* (1982) and *Convergences* (1987).

Paz Estenssoro, Victor [es-ten-sohr'-oh] Victor Paz Estenssoro, b. Oct. 2, 1907, served three terms (1952–56, 1960–64, 1985–89) as president of Bolivia. An economist, Paz Estenssoro was a founder in 1941 of the leftist Nationalist Revolutionary Movement (MNR). In his first presidential term he nationalized tin mines and effected agrarian and other reforms. After a period of coups, his third term was notable for relative stability and economic improvement.

PBS see RADIO AND TELEVISION BROADCASTING; TELEVISION, NONCOMMERCIAL

PCB   see POLLUTANTS, CHEMICAL

pea   The garden pea, the vine *Pisum sativum* of the legume family, Leguminosae, is among the most widely grown vegetables, both for its high protein content and because it can easily be preserved by drying. Native to Eurasia, the pea was grown at least as long ago as the Bronze Age and, like certain other plants that have been cultivated for millennia, it can no longer be found growing in its original, wild form. Most peas are raised for their seeds, which are contained within pods and are harvested while they are young and tender. Snow, or sugar, peas have tender pods that can also be eaten. The field pea, variety *arvense*, is grown for drying and is also used as a green manure and a forage crop. Most commercial pea plantings are processed for canning or freezing.

Cool temperatures are essential for good pea production. Seeds are usually planted very early in the spring, as they will germinate at temperatures even below 5° C (41° F). Frosts, however, will injure plants, blossoms, and pods. Temperatures above 25° C (77° F) can reduce the quality of taste and texture, as can a delayed harvesting, which produces peas that are tough and starchy.

Leguminous relatives of the garden pea include the black-eyed pea, or COWPEA, the chick-pea, and the LENTIL, all of which provide food and fodder; and the SWEET PEA, an ornamental plant grown only for its flowers.

The garden pea has been cultivated for centuries for its edible green seeds, which grow in pods. Greger Mendel conducted experiments with pea plants that led to the science of genetics.

Peabody, Elizabeth   Elizabeth Palmer Peabody, b. Billerica, Mass., May 16, 1804, d. Jan. 3, 1894, was an American educator associated with UNITARIANISM and TRANSCENDENTALISM. At age 16 she opened a school at which she taught for two years. From 1825 to 1834 she was secretary to the Unitarian preacher William Ellery CHANNING, and from 1834 to 1836 she worked with Bronson ALCOTT's Temple School in Boston. A bookstore she opened in Boston in 1839 became the intellectual center of the city and of the transcendentalist community. Peabody wrote many articles for the *Dial*, the transcendentalists' literary quarterly, as well as for education journals. The kindergarten she started in Boston in 1860 was the first in the United States—just one of many she inaugurated.

Peabody, George   A merchant and financier, George Peabody, b. South Danvers (later Peabody), Mass., Feb. 18, 1795, d. Nov. 4, 1869, was one of the foremost philanthropists of his time. His fortune was accrued through a dry-goods enterprise in Baltimore and an investment-banking business in Boston and London, where he lived from 1837 until his death.

His philanthropies included the Peabody Institute of Baltimore, comprising the Peabody Conservatory of Music and a large reference library; a natural-history museum at Yale University; an archaeology and ethnology museum at Harvard University; and the establishment (1867) of the Peabody Fund to improve education in the South.

Peace Corps   The Peace Corps was established in 1961 by the U.S. government to send American volunteers abroad to help meet the needs of developing countries for trained manpower. The underlying goal is to promote better understanding between Americans and people of other nations. From 1971 to 1981 the Corps was part of the ACTION governmental agency, after which it became an independent agency again.

Any U.S. citizen over the age of 18 may volunteer for the Peace Corps. The normal tour of duty, after training, is two years. Volunteers, who receive living-expense allowances, live among the people with whom they work, as part of the community. Many volunteers are teachers; others work in agriculture and rural development, health projects, and small-business development.

peace pipe   see CALUMET

Peace River   The Peace River is a 1,925-km-long (1,195-mi) river in western Canada. It is formed by the joining of the Finlay and Parsnip rivers at Finlay Forks in east central British Columbia. The Peace then flows east through the Rocky Mountains and into Alberta to the town of Peace River, and then northeast to Fort Vermilion, entering the SLAVE RIVER north of Lake Athabasca. Its main tributaries are the Smoky and the Wabasca. The W. A. C. Bennett Dam in British Columbia provides hydroelectric power and flood control. The river is named for Peace Point, Alta., site of a territorial settlement between Indian tribes.

peach   The peach tree, *Prunus persica*, of the family Rosaceae, belongs to the genus that includes the plum,

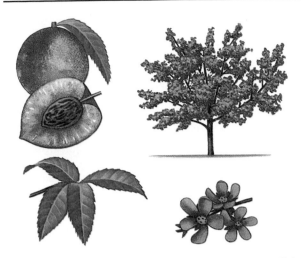

The peach tree is grown as an ornamental because of its beautiful flowers and in orchards for its fruit. The peach is second in popularity to the apple as a temperate-climate dessert fruit.

cherry, apricot, nectarine, and almond. From its native China, culture of the fruit gradually spread westward. The tree was given the specific name *persica* in the belief that it originated in Persia. Grown very extensively, the peach is cultivated commercially in most temperate apple-growing regions, and—because it can withstand heat and because less cold is required to break the tree's rest period—it is also grown closer to the equator.

Peach trees require a certain amount of chilling—the number of hours at temperatures below 7° C (45° F) that is necessary to break their dormancy and ensure proper spring budding. For many varieties, the chilling period is at least 750 hours. Peach varieties have been developed, however, for states in the American South that have mild winters. On the other hand, peach flower buds are extremely tender and will not tolerate winter temperatures below −23.3° C (−10° F).

peacock   Peacocks, more appropriately called peafowl (peacock refers to the male), are large pheasants, family

The blue, or common Indian, peafowl is native to dry, open woods of India and Sri Lanka. The male peacock is celebrated for its beauty. Its tail is fully displayed during courtship of the peahen.

Phasianidae, of the Indian-Asian region. They are found in dry forests, usually in small groups consisting of one male and several females. Peafowl rarely fly; rather, they run from danger. They are omnivorous, obtaining most of their food by scratching the leaf litter with their strong feet. The male displays by fanning its elongate upper tail coverts (not the actual tail) over its back. True peafowl include the blue peacock, *Pavo cristatus*, of India and Sri Lanka, well known in captivity, and the green peacock, *P. muticus*, of Burma and Indochina. A rare and aberrant form, the Congo peacock, *Afropavo congensis*, is found only in forests of the Congo basin in Africa.

Peacock, Thomas Love   Thomas Love Peacock, b. Oct. 18, 1785, d. Jan. 23, 1866, was an English poet, novelist, and essayist. He is best known for such short, comic novels as *Nightmare Abbey* (1818) and *Crotchet Castle* (1831). These novels satirize many of the literary, philosophical, and political fashions of the early 19th century and include caricatures of Lord Byron, Samuel Taylor Coleridge, Percy Bysshe Shelley, and other romantic writers. The action is often farcical and is subservient to the witty dialogue. Peacock's essay "The Four Ages of Poetry" (1820) is an ironic criticism of romantic poetry, and it prompted Shelley's *Defence of Poetry* (1840).

Peale (family) [peel]   Charles Willson Peale, his brother James, and the children of each form the most distinguished family of American painters.

Charles Willson Peale, b. Queen Anne, Md., Apr. 15, 1741, d. Feb. 22, 1827, painted portraits of famous Americans—about 60 of George Washington alone. Opening a portrait gallery in Philadelphia in 1782, he later installed in Independence Hall a museum with stuffed animals, Indian artifacts, minerals, and portraits—the first institution of its kind in the United States. In Philadelphia he helped establish (1794) the country's first public art exhibition and later (1805) the Pennsylvania Academy of Fine Arts. His most-often-reproduced work is the *Staircase Group* (1795; Philadelphia Museum of Art), which depicts his sons Raphael and Titian climbing a stairway.

Charles Willson had four sons who painted. **Rembrandt**, b. Richboro, Pa., Feb. 22, 1778, d. Oct. 3, 1860, specialized in portraits of famous Americans, especially Washington, but he later turned to classical subjects and moral allegories. **Rubens**, b. Philadelphia, May 4, 1784, d. July 17, 1865, painted nature subjects and opened (1825) a museum in New York City. **Titian Ramsay**, b. Philadelphia, Nov. 17, 1799, d. Mar. 13, 1885, was an explorer and naturalist who did scientific illustrations. Of Charles's children, **Raphaelle**, b. Annapolis, Md., Feb. 17, 1774, d. Mar. 25, 1825, was the most talented, and his still lifes are among the earliest and best in American art.

Charles Willson's brother, **James Peale**, b. Chestertown, Md., 1749, d. May 24, 1831, is known for his still

According to legend, Raphaelle Peale painted After the Bath *(1823) to tease his jealous wife, who had accused him of working with nude models to achieve his extraordinary naturalism. (Atkins Museum of Fine Arts, Kansas City, Mo.)*

lifes and miniatures on ivory as well as numerous large portraits, history paintings, and landscapes. Two of James's five daughters achieved success as painters: **Anna Claypoole**, b. Philadelphia, Mar. 6, 1791, d. Dec. 25, 1878, excelled in painting bright, meticulously brushed miniatures; **Sarah Miriam**, b. Philadelphia, May 19, 1800, d. Feb. 4, 1885, achieved a vigorous style of portraiture suited to her preferred subject—well-known individuals in public life.

peanut   The peanut, *Arachis hypogaea*, of the legume family, Legum inosae, is a tender, herbaceous viny plant that produces edible seeds, also called peanuts (or goobers, pindars, groundnuts, or grass nuts). Native to South America, the plant was introduced into Africa by European explorers and reached North America with the slave trade. Its value as a food crop was recognized only in the late 19th century.

Cultivation. Peanuts grow best in slightly acid, sandy soil. Soil calcium is essential; its lack impairs plant development or aborts seed. Plants require a long growing season to mature seeds and will not tolerate frost. Although they form underground, the edible portions are not tubers but seeds housed in a capsule—a nutlike shell. The plant bears yellow male flowers and inconspicuous female flowers. After fertilization, the flower stalk elongates, forcing the growing seedpod underground, where it matures. Peanuts are broadly classified into two major types: runner varieties grow small, round, pink-skinned seeds in two-seeded pods; bunch types produce larger, deep-red seeds in three-seeded pods.

Most commercially grown peanuts are mechanically harvested, artificially cured, and automatically handled and shelled. Although peanuts may be held for up to five years under optimum conditions, poor storage practices can produce inedible nuts within a month. Mold, insect infestation, discoloration, absorption of foreign flavors, and staleness or rancidity are major causes of stored-peanut loss. Peanuts and peanut meal are particularly susceptible to infestation by the molds that produce the poisonous substance aflatoxin.

The Peanut Industry. Peanut growing in the United States began in the post–Civil War era, when Southern farmers, beset by the ravages of the boll weevil, sought a substitute crop for cotton. As peanut acreage grew, numerous uses for the plant and its seed were gradually found. The most famous researcher into the potential for the peanut crop was George Washington CARVER, whose discoveries helped establish the industry.

The peanut contains about 28% protein, 50% oil, 18% carbohydrates, and 4% ash. Few agricultural plants have as many potential uses. In the United States, peanut butter is the most important peanut product; very little peanut butter is consumed in other countries. Worldwide, about two-thirds of the peanut crop is crushed for oil, and peanut oil supplies about 8% of the world's vegetable-oil production. Peanut products are used in food processing and in animal-feed products. Plants left in the ground provide excellent forage for cattle and swine and are valuable as a green manure.

The peanut, a herbaceous vine native to Brazil, is cultivated for its seeds, which grow in underground pods.

pear   North American pear trees belong to one of three botanical groups: *Pyrus communis,* the common European pear; *P. pyrifolia,* the Oriental sand pear; and various cultivars that are crosses between the two species. Like the peach and apple, the pear was brought to North America by colonists who planted the European varieties, known collectively as butter pears because of their smooth, silky flesh. Fire blight, a bacterial disease that kills fruit and new tree growth, attacked butter-pear orchards. Oriental-pear types—called sand pears because of their gritty flesh—were found to be resistant to the disease. Eventually, hybrid varieties were developed that combined butter-pear quality with sand-pear resistance to fire blight. Kieffer and Leconte pears are the best known of these hybrids. Bartlett, Anjou, Bosc, and Comice are among the cultivars developed from European types.

The pear is usually propagated by budding the desired variety into seedling stocks. Dwarf trees are produced by grafting pear onto quince roots. Most pear varieties require cross-pollination. Trees begin to produce at 5 to 7 years, reaching full production when they are 12 to 15 years of age. The pear's growth and flowering habits resemble those of the apple, but the pear is not as hardy.

The pear tree produces most of the common dessert-pear varieties. Closely related to the apple, the sweet-fleshed pear is more perishable and is usually harvested before maturity.

Pearl Harbor   The Japanese bombing of Pearl Harbor, on Oahu island, Hawaii, the operating base of the U.S. Pacific Fleet, in 1941 resulted in the immediate entry of the United States into WORLD WAR II and opened the Pacific phase of the war.

In late 1941 more than 75 U.S. warships, including battleships, cruisers, destroyers, and submarines, were based at this "Gibraltar of the Pacific." All U.S. aircraft carriers were elsewhere. On November 26 a Japanese task force, including 6 carriers and 2 battleships under command of Vice

Adm. Chuichi Nagumo, departed in secret from the Kuril Islands. Observing radio silence, it reached a launching point at 6 AM, December 7. At 7:50 AM, the first wave of Japanese planes struck Pearl Harbor, bombarding airfields and battleships moored there. A second wave followed. The surprise attack was over before 10 AM.

The results were devastating; 18 U.S. ships were hit, and more than 200 aircraft destroyed or damaged. The battleship *Arizona* was a total wreck; the *West Virginia* and *California* were sunk; and the *Nevada* was heavily damaged. Approximately 2,400 Americans were killed, 1,300 wounded, and 1,000 missing. Japanese losses were fewer than 100 casualties, 29 planes, and 5 midget submarines. The Japanese scored a brilliant tactical victory, apparently crippling U.S. naval power in the Pacific.

The attack was, however, a colossal political blunder, for it mobilized U.S. public opinion against the Japanese and served as the catalyst that brought the United States into

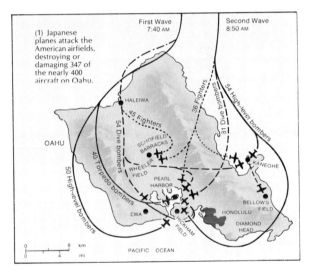

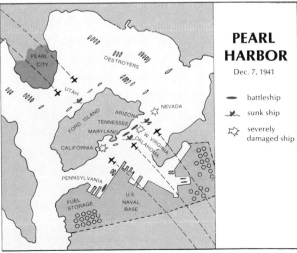

the war. "December 7, 1941," said President Franklin D. Roosevelt, is "a date which will live in infamy." A monument has been built across the hull of the sunken U.S.S. *Arizona*; it was dedicated as a national memorial in 1962.

pearls and pearling

The pearl, a hard, round object valued as a gem, is produced as an abnormal growth within the shells of certain bivalve mollusks: saltwater pearl oysters, saltwater and freshwater mussels, and some species of clams and abalones. All these mollusks have an inner layer of shell made of a lustrous material called nacre, or MOTHER-OF-PEARL. It is composed of the mineral aragonite and an organic, cartilaginous substance, conchiolin. When a bit of foreign matter enters the shell—a grain of sand, for example—the mollusk isolates it by gradually coating it with layers of nacre. The process is slow; it may take three years or more for a mature mollusk to produce a pearl large enough to be commercially valuable.

The most-prized pearls are taken from saltwater mollusks and are classed as Oriental. They have a high degree of iridescence and luster; the refraction and reflection of light is caused by the overlapping arrangement of various crystals on their surface. Freshwater pearls usually lack a significant degree of iridescence. Color, which is identical to the color of the nacreous shell-lining, is also important in determining value. Pearl color varies from white through pale shades of rose, yellow, blue, and green to brown or the dark gray that is the color of a black pearl. The most valuable colors are white, cream, rose, and black. Pearl shape is rarely perfectly round; irregular shapes, called baroque, are less prized.

Saltwater Pearls. The pearl oyster is found in the Red Sea; the Persian Gulf; the South Pacific, including the waters around northern Australia; the Caribbean Sea; and the Gulf of California. The oldest pearl fisheries, those off the north coast of Sri Lanka, have been producing for 2,000 years.

Oysters are gathered by dragnets or by pearl divers, who often must descend to great depths. Of the thousands of oysters gathered, only a small fraction bear pearls, and an even smaller fraction—perhaps one in ten thousand—bear pearls of gem quality. The nacreous shell of the pearl oyster, however, if it is thick enough, is valuable for its mother-of-pearl.

Freshwater Pearls. Freshwater pearls, which have become rare, are found in mussels inhabiting lakes and

Gem pearls are organic products found in specific species of oyster or mussel. They may occur in various colors and shapes (left). *The most prized pearls are white and round* (right).

streams in Europe, Asia, and the Americas.

Cultured Pearls. Cultivation—the art of artificially inducing pearl growth—begins with the insertion of mother-of-pearl beads into the shells of 3-year-old oysters. The oysters are placed in cages in the waters of a sheltered bay, and nacre forms around the beads. The oysters are harvested from 10 months to 3½ years after the bead insertion. The thickness of the nacre deposit is usually only one-sixth to one-tenth of the pearl's total diameter, but only a professional can distinguish between a cultured and a natural pearl.

Pearson, Drew

[peer'-suhn]   Drew Pearson, b. Evanston, Ill., Dec. 13, 1897, d. Sept. 1, 1969, was a controversial newspaper and radio commentator. He and Robert S. Allen anonymously published a book, *Washington Merry-Go-Round* (1931), which was so successful that they launched their column of the same name the next year. In later years Pearson's associate was Jack Anderson. Pearson's charges that Sen. Thomas Dodd misappropriated campaign funds led to the formation of the Senate Ethics Committee.

Pearson, Karl

Karl (born Carl) Pearson, b. Mar. 27, 1857, d. Apr. 27, 1936, a British applied mathematician and philosopher of science, was one of the major developers of the science of STATISTICS. A graduate (1879) of Cambridge University, he spent most of his career as a

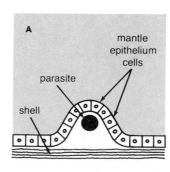

A pearl begins to form when foreign matter (A) *enters the mantle, or tissue, under a pearl oyster's shell. Epithelium cells on the tissue surface secrete successive layers* (B) *of lustrous calcium carbonate (nacre) and conchiolin (a cementing material) to form a pearl* (C).

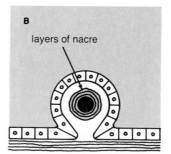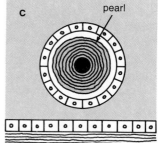

professor at University College, London, serving (1911–1933) as the first Galton professor of eugenics. Well known for his *The Grammar of Science* (1892), a study of science that anticipated some of the outlooks of relativity theory, he became interested in developing mathematical methods for studying the processes of heredity and evolution. In his work he originated such basic statistical concepts and procedures as standard deviation, the random walk, and the chi-square test.

Pearson, Lester B.

Lester Bowles Pearson, b. Toronto, Apr. 23, 1897, d. Dec. 27, 1972, was a Canadian statesman and prime minister. Pearson attended the University of Toronto and then Oxford, earning a master's degree in history; he returned to teach (1924–28) at Toronto. For the next seven years he served as first secretary in the Department of External Affairs and became assistant undersecretary of state (1941), Canadian ambassador to the United States (1945–46), and undersecretary of state (1946).

Two years later he entered Parliament and was named secretary of state for external affairs by Prime Minister Louis St. Laurent. Pearson won (1957) the Nobel Peace Prize for his role in the Suez Crisis of 1956. In January 1958 he became leader of the Liberal party, which suffered a disastrous defeat in the election of March 1958. He was named prime minister in 1963 on the defeat of the Conservative leader John G. Diefenbaker. Pearson's ministry was noteworthy for the establishment of the Canada Pension Plan, which became effective in 1966, and for the adoption of the Canadian flag (1965). He resigned as prime minister in 1968.

Lester Pearson, a Canadian statesman, achieved international prominence through his diplomatic skills. Pearson played a vital role in defusing the Suez Crisis of 1956, receiving a Nobel Peace Prize for his mediation efforts. In 1963 he led the Liberal party to victory in national elections and served as prime minister until 1968.

Peary, Robert Edwin

[peer'-ee]   Robert Peary, b. Cresson, Pa., May 6, 1856, d. Feb. 20, 1920, was a U.S. Arctic explorer and is generally considered the first person to have reached the North Pole. Peary was a land surveyor and draftsman before becoming (1881) a civil engineer in the U.S. Navy. His interest in the Arctic seems to

Robert E. Peary, an American explorer and naval officer, was the first person to reach (Apr. 6, 1909) the North Pole, on his last attempt. Peary's application of Eskimo survival techniques contributed to his success.

have been aroused by reading about Greenland.

In 1886, with Matthew Henson, he made a sledge journey into interior Greenland. In 1891 and 1892 he explored and mapped the northern coastline of Greenland. His third and fourth voyages (1893–95 and 1898–1902) were efforts to reach the North Pole. During another voyage (1905–06), he reached a position 280 km (174 mi) from the Pole.

In March 1909, Peary set out once again; he claimed to have reached the North Pole on April 6. Five days before the world learned of his feat, Frederick A. Cook announced that he had conquered the Pole in 1908. Cook's claims were later generally dismissed, but controversy surrounded Peary's accomplishment for decades. A new study made public in 1989, however, supported the legitimacy of Peary's claim. Peary retired with the rank of rear admiral in 1911.

peasant

The term *peasant* generally describes a farmer practicing small-scale and traditional forms of agriculture in a society with a history of rigid social stratification. Europe, Asia, Africa, and Latin America have had many farmers of the peasant class. The United States, Australia, and New Zealand, on the other hand, have never had a peasantry because the social distinctions implied by the term have not existed there.

Peasants practice essentially subsistence agriculture, producing what they and their families need in order to live, with perhaps some surplus to sell. Whether they own or rent their land, peasants have a degree of security in the resources they use, unlike farmhands or migrant workers. Peasant communities are typically small, closed groups that have developed their own customs and traditions.

The peasant in Europe was the social descendant of the serf under MANORIALISM in the Middle Ages. The lord of the manor ruled his estate; the serfs farmed it, and the lord in return gave them protection and permission to farm a portion for their own subsistence. Serfs were bound to the land, a condition that persisted in Russia until 1861, when the serfs were emancipated. The term *peasant* continues to imply a fixed relationship to the land, although not actual bondage. Improved technology and educational opportunities are gradually eroding the peasantry as a class.

Peasants' Revolt   The Peasants' Revolt (1381) was the only major outbreak of social rebellion in medieval England. Reduced population as a result of the Black Death (1349) encouraged impoverished peasants as well as prosperous artisans and urban workers to demand abolition of serfdom, an easing of the restrictions of the manorial courts, and repeal of the Statute of Labourers (1351), which aimed at imposing a maximum wage. Unrest peaked when a poll tax of a shilling a head was imposed (1380). Its collection sparked revolt simultaneously in Kent and Essex in June 1381. The Kentish leaders, including Wat Tyler and John Ball, a rebel priest, entered London on June 13. The boy king RICHARD II met them on June 14 and granted their demands for abolition of serfdom, elimination of wage restrictions, and low rents. At a later meeting with the king, Tyler was slain by the mayor of London. The rebels then dispersed, and the king's concessions were withdrawn.

Peasants' War   The Peasants' War (c.1524–26) was the last and most widespread of the long series of socioreligious revolutionary movements of the later Middle Ages in central Europe. From the Alpine lands to Thuringia, peasants and small-town artisans and laborers sacked castles and monasteries, issuing lists of demands, of which the Twelve Articles is the most notable. The insurgents called for the abolition of serfdom, the reduction of rents and taxes, and the resumption of the rights of village communities over common land. Martin LUTHER, whose teachings had inspired the revolt, condemned all rebellion. The peasants were ultimately defeated by the German princes' professional armies.

peat [peet]   Peat is a more or less obscurely stratified natural deposit of plant remains that has been protected from dissipation by a high water table. It is commonly used as a fuel in European countries when air-dried and converted into blocks or briquettes; in the United States, it is used as an agriculture top dressing or as a soil conditioner. Peat is chiefly a product of environments such as bogs and marshes where plants abound with little chance for detrital mineral contamination. Some peat also accumulates in bayous, lakes, and estuaries, but in such areas mineral contamination is likely to be greater. Under some circumstances peat may be a precursor to coal; all coal beds, in fact, originated from peat (see COAL AND COAL MINING). If the water table is lowered or drained, however, the peaty accumulation is further degraded by fungi and is oxidized. The residue contributes to the humus of the soil.

peat moss   Peat moss, or bog moss, an order of mosses of the genus *Sphagnum*, grows in bogs, ponds, and lakes. A primitive plant form, it has a network of large, inflated, thin-walled dead cells that absorb and retain water, at the same time replacing the plant's minerals with acid. The plant's saturation retards the passage of air, slowing its decomposition.

Because of its moisture-retaining capacity, porosity, and acidity, peat moss is used to improve soil. It also serves as packing for plants and nursery stock and, because it absorbs odors as well as moisture, as animal litter. Sterile, and with slightly antiseptic and antibiotic qualities, it was employed as late as World War I in surgical dressings.

pecan   The nut-bearing pecan tree, *Carya illinoinensis*, of the walnut family, is classified botanically as a HICKORY. The tallest and fastest growing of the hickories, the trees produce the best-selling nut in the United States—the delicately flavored, fat-rich pecan. This nut is the basis for pralines, pecan pie, and other foods originating in the southern United States, where the tree grows and yields most abundantly.

Pecan trees may reach a height of 25–30 m (75–90 ft). Because of their deep taproots they are difficult to transplant except as very young trees, and they need 8 to 10 years to produce a crop. Pecans bear best in warm, moist regions.

The pecan is a tree native to the Mississippi valley and is the tallest tree of the hickory genus. The pecan's thin-shelled nut is prized for its rich, sweet taste.

peccary [pek'-uh-ree]   The peccary is an ARTIODACTYL (even-toed) mammal native to the Western Hemisphere, from Texas to Patagonia. The family, Tayassuidae, consists of two genera, *Catagonus* and *Tayassu*. Peccaries are closely related to the SWINE family and fill similar ecological niches. They differ from pigs in several ways, however, including the possession of a dorsal musk gland. The body is 75–90 cm (30–35 in) long and weighs up to 30

The collared peccary lives in deserts, dry woodlands, and rain forests from the southwestern United States to Argentina, most often in groups of 5 to 15 animals.

kg (66 lb). The slim legs end in sharp, two-toed hooves. The snout is cylindrical, and spearlike upper canine teeth give peccaries the alternative name javelina. The animals can run quickly. They live in groups in a wide range of habitats and feed on insects and small animals.

Pechstein, Max [pek'-shtyn]   The expressionist painter and printmaker Max Pechstein, b. Dec. 31, 1881, d. June 29, 1955, was a member of DIE BRÜCKE (The Bridge), a group of German expressionist painters, active just before World War I, who reacted against the impressionism of the Secession movement. Pechstein shared the bold color and expressionist distortion of the Brücke artists but in a less extreme and more decorative form than that practiced by the group's leaders, as is evident in his colorful *The Red Turban* (1911; Carnegie Institute, Pittsburgh, Pa.). Primitive art inspired Pechstein as much as French postimpressionism and led him to visit the Palau Islands in 1913–14. In his later career Pechstein executed many designs for stained glass and mosaics. He taught (1923–33) at the Berlin Academy before being removed by the Nazis, who condemned expressionism as degenerate. He was reinstated in 1945.

Peck, Gregory   Known for his ability to project quiet strength and dignity, the actor Gregory Peck, b. La Jolla, Calif., Apr. 5, 1916, became a star with his second film, *The Keys of the Kingdom* (1944). Some of his best subsequent roles were in *Spellbound* (1945); *The Yearling* (1946); *Duel in the Sun* (1946); *Gentleman's Agreement* (1947); *The Man in the Gray Flannel Suit* (1956); *Moby Dick* (1956); *The Big Country* (1958); *To Kill a Mockingbird* (1962; Academy Award); *MacArthur* (1977); *The Boys from Brazil* (1978); and *Old Gringo* (1989). In 1989 he received the American Film Institute lifetime achievement award.

Peckinpah, Sam [pek'-in-paw]   The filmmaker David Samuel Peckinpah, b. Fresno, Calif., Feb. 21, 1925, d. Dec. 28, 1984, had his first critical success with the western *Ride the High Country* (1962). With *The Wild Bunch* (1969), however, Peckinpah reached a wide public and acquired his reputation for bloody screen violence, often depicted in slow motion and intended to force spectators to examine their own violent impulses. *Straw Dogs* (1971) fed the controversy about his work, but he proved in *Junior Bonner* (1972) that he could develop his

themes—the worldview of men outliving their times or living on the fringe—in a nonviolent context.

Pecos Bill [pay'-kohs]   A legendary cowboy hero of the American Southwest, Pecos Bill was actually Edward O'Reilly's literary creation, first appearing in *The Century Magazine* in 1923. Weaned on moonshine, Pecos Bill grew up among the coyotes along the Pecos River in Texas. After a career as a cowboy, train robber, and Indian fighter, he went to Arizona, where he found his horse, Widow-Maker, and raised him on nitroglycerin and dynamite. His greatest feat was riding a cyclone bareback; the rain this caused washed out the Grand Canyon, and Bill's landing created Death Valley.

Pecos River   The Pecos River rises in north central New Mexico in the Sangre de Cristo Mountains and flows generally southeast for about 1,490 km (925 mi) before emptying into the RIO GRANDE 56 km (35 mi) northwest of Del Rio, Tex. It drains a relatively arid and sparsely populated region and provides water for irrigation in Texas and New Mexico.

Pécs [paych]   Pécs, a city in southwestern Hungary's coal-mining region, about 170 km (105 mi) southwest of Budapest, is a trade and handicrafts center and a rail and road junction with a population of 183,082 (1989 est.). Petroleum piped from the USSR is refined there. Wine, leather goods, ceramics, and furniture are produced. The main landmark is the cathedral, begun in 1009 when Pécs was made a bishopric by Stephen I, the first king of Hungary.

Under the Roman emperor HADRIAN (r. 117–38), the city—called Sopianae—was a provincial capital. Hungarians conquered it in the 9th century, and Louis I (Louis the Great) founded Hungary's first university there in 1367. Between 1543 and 1686, Pécs was under Turkish rule.

pectin [pek'-tin]   Pectin is the name given to a group of complex carbohydrates that occur in certain vegetables and ripe fruits. It is the gelling agent used in making fruit jams and jellies. When cooked with the proper amounts of sugar and water, pectin-rich fruits such as apples, pears, lemons, or oranges form a gel. (In overripe fruits pectin becomes pectic acid and does not gel.) Commercial pectin, derived from apples or citrus fruits, is used to make jellies from fruits that have little natural pectin. As a pharmaceutical, pectin is considered helpful in healing wounds and in treating diarrhea.

pediatrics   Pediatrics is the branch of medicine concerned with the treatment and prevention of disease in infants and children. Pediatricians generally provide medical care for children from infancy through adolescence. Pediatrics arose as a medical specialty because many diseases and other medical problems occur exclusively in children or tend to be more prevalent among them (see DISEASES, CHILDHOOD). In addition, children and adults exhibit major anatomical, physiological, and behavioral differences. Children also change rapidly, presenting characteristic medical problems at each stage of development. In infants, for example, the pediatrician is likely to encounter infectious diseases, inherited defects, birth injuries, or problems arising from prematurity, whereas in older children medical problems are more likely to arise from infectious diseases and accidents.

The prevention and treatment of infectious diseases is a major part of pediatric practice because children are much more susceptible to such diseases than are adults. This vulnerability arises from absent or incomplete immunity to certain diseases and the greater opportunity for contagion provided by the concentration of children in schools and playgrounds. Pediatricians routinely immunize infants and young children against the more serious childhood infections, such as DIPHTHERIA, POLIOMYELITIS, TETANUS, and WHOOPING COUGH. Children are also more susceptible to nutritional deficiencies because of their rapid growth.

pedophilia   Pedophilia is a psychosexual disorder (see PSYCHOPATHOLOGY) characterized by a sexual desire for and sexual acts with prepubescent children. Onset of the disorder can occur from adolescence through old age, and it occurs predominantly in males. About two-thirds of pedophiliacs are attracted to children of the opposite sex. Based on evidence from criminal court records, pedophiles usually know the children that they abuse. Most pedophiles resort to deception rather than force. Although more is known about pedophilia than any other psychosexual disorder, pedophiles are difficult to treat and recidivism rates are high.

Pedro   for Spanish and Portuguese kings of this name, see PETER

Pedro I, Emperor of Brazil   Pedro I (Antonio Pedro de Alcântara), b. Oct. 12, 1798, d. Sept. 24, 1834, was the first emperor of independent Brazil. Son of the prince regent, later King JOHN VI of Portugal and Brazil, Dom Pedro fled with the royal family from Lisbon to Rio de Janeiro after the French invaded the Iberian Peninsula in 1807. When John reclaimed the Portuguese throne in 1821, Pedro remained in Brazil as prince regent. On Sept. 7, 1822, Pedro declared Brazil an independent monarchy.

Pedro resisted Portugal's efforts to restore the colonial regime yet granted economic concessions to Britain that compromised Brazilian sovereignty. Although he appeared to be liberal, he dissolved the Constituent Assembly in 1823 and the following granted a new constitution that satisfied neither republicans nor monarchists. A disastrous war (1825–28) with Argentina, preoccupation with affairs in Portugal—where his daughter's right to the crown was being challenged by his brother, Miguel—and a revolt in Rio de Janeiro precipitated Pedro's abdication

Pedro I, first emperor of Brazil, declared Brazil's independence from Portugal in 1822. His reign was beset by a series of military and constitutional crises. After his forced abdication in 1831, he returned to Portugal as King Peter IV.

(1831) in favor of his five-year-old son, Pedro II. Pedro I then returned to Portugal, where he engineered the defeat of his brother and had his daughter declared of age to be crowned Queen MARIA II.

Pedro II, Emperor of Brazil   Pedro II (Pedro de Alcântara), b. Dec. 2, 1825, d. Dec. 5, 1891, second and last emperor of Brazil (1831–89), was a liberal minded reformist best remembered for overseeing the abolition of slavery in Brazil. Pedro, who succeeded his father, Pedro I, was far more successful as a linguist and scientist than as a ruler; his reign was marred by a number of internal revolts and conflicts with neighboring countries. Unrest among planters, the military, and the republicans culminated in a coup that overthrew the emperor and established (1889) the first republic.

Peel, Sir Robert   The British statesman Sir Robert Peel, b. Feb. 5, 1788, d. July 2, 1850, founded Great Britain's CONSERVATIVE PARTY and was prime minister three times. Peel entered Parliament as a Tory in 1809 and served (1812–18) as chief secretary for Ireland. His hardline opposition to the admittance of Roman Catholics to Parliament earned him the nickname Orange Peel. In

Sir Robert Peel, three times prime minister of Great Britain, is often regarded as the founder of that nation's Conservative party. Initially an opponent of reform, he came to support Catholic Emancipation, conciliation toward Ireland, and repeal of the Corn Laws.

1819, Peel headed a commission that reinstituted the gold standard, and in the 1820s he displayed administrative capacity as a reforming home secretary. By securing passage (1829) of the Metropolitan Police Act he helped reorganize the London police force, whose members are called "Bobbies" in his honor. Modifying his earlier views, he earned the enmity of Tory extremists when he and the duke of WELLINGTON pushed the CATHOLIC EMANCIPATION through Parliament in 1829. To recover Tory support, Peel opposed the Whig parliamentary reform bills of 1831–32 (see REFORM ACTS). He served a brief term as prime minister (late 1834–April 1835), founding the Conservative party on a basis outlined in his election speech known as the Tamworth Manifesto of 1834.

During his second and third periods as prime minister (1841–45, 1845–46) he was viewed as a political healer. In 1842 and 1845 he advanced toward free trade, abolishing tariffs and reintroducing the income tax; helped pass the Bank Charter Act (1844), establishing the foundations of Great Britain's banking and fiscal policies; and advocated a combination of toughness and conciliation toward Ireland. In keeping with his increasing sympathy toward the Irish, Peel became convinced of the necessity of repealing the CORN LAWS. When the Irish potato disease struck and famine followed in Ireland, Peel pressed harder for repeal of the Corn Laws, alienating many of his followers and precipitating his resignation (late 1845). Restored to office within days, he repealed the Corn Laws with the aid of opposition votes and was again cast (1846) from office.

peerage   see TITLES OF NOBILITY AND HONOR

▬

Pegasus [peg'-uh-suhs]   In Greek mythology Pegasus was the winged horse of the Muses, born of the blood of the decapitated MEDUSA. He was tamed by BELLEROPHON with the aid of a golden bridle given him by Athena. When Bellerophon tried to ride the horse to heaven, Pegasus, stung by a gadfly sent by Zeus, threw him to his death and continued the ascent alone, becoming the constellation bearing the same name.

▬

pegmatite [peg'-muh-tyt]   Pegmatite is a common plutonic rock (see IGNEOUS ROCK), of variable texture and coarseness, that is composed of interlocking crystals of widely different sizes. Crystals up to many meters long are found in such rocks.

Some pegmatite bodies are small irregular patches less than 1 cm (0.4 in) across in larger masses of plutonic or metamorphic rocks. Others may be thousands of meters in length and hundreds of meters thick. Some appear as dikes, veins, or sills. Many have irregular outlines.

Composition. Pegmatites may be composed of any type of plutonic material. Names such as granite pegmatite, gabbro pegmatite, syenite pegmatite, or names with any other plutonic rock type as prefix are appropriate. Compositions in the range from granodiorite to GRANITE are the most usual, with large crystals of quartz, potassium feldspar, sodium-rich plagioclase, and micas also present.

Simple pegmatites contain few, if any, exotic minerals. The center zones of complex pegmatites, however, may contain a wide variety of minerals such as tourmaline, topaz, garnet, spodumene, scapolite, beryl, apatite, fluorite, zircon, and various rare minerals. Many valuable metallic elements are among the substances obtained from pegmatite deposits, which have also provided radioactive minerals for use in RADIOMETRIC AGE-DATING of many rock complexes.

Origin. As a result of the bewildering variety of shapes, sizes, appearances, and field relationships, many origins have been proposed for pegmatites. Some dikelike bodies showing clear intrusive relationships must be of igneous origin. These frequently cut across all other associated rocks and therefore represent material from late stages of crystallization of plutonic complexes. They were probably rich in volatile materials such as water, fluorine, chlorine, phosphorus, and sulfur.

Other pegmatites grade into other rocks and show no intrusive relationships. Such bodies may represent material produced by melting (anatexis) during metamorphism at high temperatures and pressures.

Pegmatites are very hard, extremely coarse, light-colored igneous rocks made up of large crystals of feldspar, quartz, and mica. The rocks may be found in almost any shape but are usually tabular or flat. Pegmatites are among the richest sources of gemstones, such as moonstone, tourmaline, aquamarine, topaz, and rose quartz.

▬

Pegu [pe-goo']   Pegu (1983 pop., 150,447), a city in southern Burma on the Pegu River, is about 76 km (47 mi) northeast of Rangoon. It is a major rail junction and a distribution and processing center for rice and lumber from the surrounding region. Pegu was founded as the capital of the MON kingdom about 825. It declined when the Burmese conquered the area in the 11th century but became the capital of the revived Mon kingdom in 1369. It was the capital of the united Burmese kingdom from 1539 to 1599 and from 1613 to 1634. The city was largely destroyed after a Mon revolt in the mid-18th century.

Pei, I. M. [pay]   The Chinese-American architect Ieoh Ming Pei, b. Guangzhou (Canton), China, Apr. 26, 1917, is one of the most prolific contemporary architects. He went to the United States in 1935 to study architecture at the Massachusetts Institute of Technology and at Harvard University's Graduate School of Design, where he also taught. He became a U.S. citizen in 1954.

Pei first practiced architecture in Boston and in 1955 established his own firm in New York City. He soon received such major commissions as Denver's Mile High Center (1956). Pei's Kips Bay Plaza apartment towers (1960–65; New York City) are much admired for their practical simplicity, as are many of his smaller buildings of particular grace and elegance.

Several of Pei's large and costly projects of the 1970s have met with criticism: the John Hancock Tower (1973; Boston) has been plagued with technical problems; the East Building (1978) of the National Gallery of Art, Washington, D.C., although hailed for its brilliant use of an awkward site, has been called an elitist extravagance. Pei, however, has also continued to create chaste and beautiful buildings. In 1978 the Chinese government commissioned him to design a new luxury hotel in Beijing. The Fragrant Hill (Xiangshan) Hotel, completed in 1983, is a modest low-rise building that blends traditional Chinese vernacular and Western architectural styles. Although the recipient of many honors, Pei stirred controversy with his design of a glass pyramid for the new main entrance of the Louvre museum in Paris (completed in 1988). His angular 70-story Bank of China headquarters (1990) in Hong Kong also attracted wide attention.

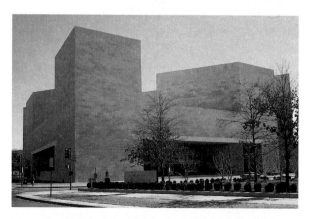

The geometric forms of I. M. Pei's East Building (1978), a wing added to the National Gallery of Art, Washington, D.C., are tailored to its triangular site and repeated throughout the interior.

Peipus, Lake [py'-puhs]   Lake Peipus is located in the USSR on the boundary between Estonia and Russia. The lake has an area of about 3,600 km² (1,390 mi²) and a maximum depth of 15 m (50 ft). Connected to Lake Pskov by a 24-km (15-mi) strait, Lake Peipus empties into the Gulf of Finland via the Narva River. ALEXANDER NEVSKY defeated the TEUTONIC KNIGHTS on the frozen lake in 1242. World War II battles were fought there in 1941 and 1944.

Peirce, Charles Sanders [purs]   An American philosopher, mathematician, and physicist, Charles Sanders Peirce, b. Cambridge, Mass., Sept. 10, 1839, d. Apr. 19, 1914, is best known as the founder of the pragmatic movement (see PRAGMATISM) in American philosophy. Peirce worked as an astronomer and as a physicist, at the same time pursuing his interests in philosophy and publishing numerous papers.

As the founder of American pragmatism, Peirce developed a criterion of meaning in terms of conceivable effects or consequences in experience and a view of beliefs as "habits of action." His metaphysics embraces a theory of cosmic evolution and a theory of causal laws. He also wrote extensively on logic, epistemology, scientific method, cosmology, semiotics, and mathematics.

Peisistratus [py-sis'-truh-tuhs]   Peisistratus, c.605–527 BC, became tyrant of Athens in 561 BC after acquiring popularity as a military hero. Because of attacks on him he was assigned a bodyguard of club-wielding rural citizens, with whose help he seized the Acropolis and became ruler of the city. Twice he fell from power because of opposition from a coalition of rival aristocratic families. After his final return in 546 he remained in firm control until he died 19 years later. He was succeeded by his sons, HIPPARCHUS and Hippias. Hipparchus was assassinated in 514, and Hippias was driven out in 511–10.

Peixoto, Floriano [pay-shoh'-toh]   General Floriano Peixoto, b. Apr. 30, 1842, d. June 29, 1895, was Brazil's second president (1891–94). With other military leaders he helped found the Brazilian republic in 1889 by overthrowing Emperor PEDRO II. He became president in 1891, when Manuel Deodoro da FONSECA resigned. Two years later Peixoto's dictatorial rule provoked a revolt. It was crushed by April 1894, but in November, Peixoto handed power to an elected civilian president, Prudente José de Moraes Barros.

Peking   see BEIJING

Peking man   The HOMO ERECTUS specimens commonly referred to as Peking man were excavated (1927–37) from Middle Pleistocene deposits at the site of ZHOUKOUDIAN, near Beijing, in northern China. Skeletal remains of 44 individuals were found jumbled together with thousands of splintered and burned animal bones and numerous stone tools. Many experts consider the smashed and fragmentary condition of the hominid fossils as evidence of cannibalism. Huge mounds of hackberry seeds and many hearths within the deposits indicate that the cave at Zhoukoudian served as a home for the early humans who lived there between 460,000 and 230,000 years ago.

In 1941, at the outbreak of World War II, the Peking man fossils were lost. Through the work of Franz Weidenreich and Davidson Black, however, plaster casts and detailed descriptions of the specimens are available. Since the 1950s, when the Chinese reopened excavations at Zhoukoudian, several new fossils have been discovered.

Peking Opera   see BEIJING OPERA

Peking University   see BEIJING UNIVERSITY

Pekingese [pee'-kin-eez]   The Pekingese is one of the most popular purebred dogs in both England and the United States. First brought West by the British in 1860, following the sacking of the Imperial Palace in Beijing, the breed dates back to the Tang dynasty of the 8th century. The Chinese apparently classified the Pekingese into three types: lion dogs, named for their massive fronts and heavy manes; sun dogs, with golden red coats; and sleeve dogs, the smallest specimens, which were readily carried in the sleeves of their masters' garments. The Pekingese has a long, profuse coat and is short-legged and small. The tail is heavily plumed and carried over the back. The dog weighs between 3.2 and 5.4 kg (7 and 12 lb). The foreshortened head gives the breed its unique expression. All colors are found.

The Pekingese was the royal dog of China and the exclusive property of Chinese emperors. It was taken to England in 1860 after the British invaded the Imperial Palace at Beijing.

Pelagianism [puh-lay'-jee-uhn-izm]   Pelagianism is the name given to the teachings of Pelagius, a British Christian active in Rome in the late 4th and early 5th centuries. Pelagius stressed the human ability to fulfill God's commands. In Rome he became the center of an aristocratic group whose aim was to pursue the most rigorous form of the religious life in contrast to the indifferent morality of other Christians. Pelagianism may thus be considered a reform movement within late Roman Christianity.

Pelagius emphasized the freedom of the human will and the ability to control one's motives and actions under the guidance of God's law. In contrast, AUGUSTINE insisted that no one can control his or her own motivation and that each person requires the assistance of God's GRACE if he or she is to will and to do good. In the resulting controversy Augustine's views prevailed and became dominant in Christian teaching. Pelagius was excommunicated (417) by Pope Innocent I, and his views were condemned as heresies by a series of church councils.

Pelé (athlete) [pay-lay']   Edson Arantes do Nascimento, b. Oct. 23, 1940, a native of Brazil better known as Pelé, was perhaps the greatest of all soccer players. A supremely gifted athlete, Pelé made his debut with the major league Santos club in 1956 at the age of 15. A year later he was selected to play for the Brazilian national team, and in 1958 he led them to victory in the World Cup. Brazil won the World Cup again in 1962 and 1970 with Pelé on the team. In his long professional career, Pelé scored 1,281 goals in 1,363 games, even though he was invariably given special coverage by the opposition. A muscular, compact man standing 1 m 72 cm (5 ft 8 in) tall and weighing 68 kg (150 lb), Pelé possessed the perfect blend of physical power, dazzling ball handling, and an instinct for discerning an opponent's weakness. Pelé retired in 1974 but returned to play in 1975 for the New York Cosmos. He helped popularize soccer and establish the sport in the United States. Pelé retired permanently in 1977.

Pelé, a soccer player who became one of the wealthiest and most famous athletes in the world, led the national team of his native Brazil to three World Cup championships (1958, 1962, 1970).

Pele (mythology) [pay'-lay]   In Polynesian mythology Pele was the fire goddess who inhabited the crater of Kilauea Volcano on the island of Hawaii. Her jealous rages were believed to cause Kilauea's eruptions.

Pelée, Mount [puh-lay']   Mount Pelée, an active volcano located 6 km (4 mi) inland from the northern coast of the island of Martinique in the West Indies, rises to a height of 1,397 m (4,583 ft). After recorded eruptions in 1792 and 1851, the volcano suddenly came to life again on May 8, 1902. Lava and ash quickly engulfed the plantations on its slopes and the town of Saint-Pierre at its base, and ships in the bay capsized in the boiling, seething water. Within 7 hours more than 30,000 persons were killed. Auguste Ciparis, a prisoner in a deep dungeon, was the only person found alive. Pelée erupted again in 1929 and remained active for 3 years, but no lives were lost.

Pelham, Henry   Henry Pelham, b. 1696, d. Mar. 6, 1754, headed a Whig ministry during the reign of GEORGE

II. He was the younger brother of Thomas Pelham-Holles, duke of NEWCASTLE. Pelham entered Parliament in 1717 and served under Robert WALPOLE as secretary of war (1724–30) and paymaster general (1730–43) before his own tenure (1743–54) as prime minister. The Pelham administration negotiated (1748) the end of the War of the AUSTRIAN SUCCESSION; reduced the national debt; and carried out (1752) the conversion to the Gregorian calendar in British territories.

pelican   Pelican is the common name for the large aquatic birds of the family Pelecanidae, which reach 180 cm (72 in) in length. They have long necks, short tails, long, broad wings, and huge bills with deeply expansible

The brown pelican (right) *dives from a great height, striking the water with an enormous impact. The bird is approximately 130 cm (50 in) long and has a wingspan of 2.5 m (90 in). It is protected from the shock of its dive by air pockets that line the flesh beneath its breast.*

The Old World white pelican (left) *of southeastern Europe, Asia, and Africa is found near lakes, marshes, and streams. It is approximately 170 cm (67 in) long. In flight, a line of pelicans may move as choreographed dancers, beating their wings, gliding, and dipping in unison. Pelicans also hunt cooperatively.*

skin pouches in the lower mandible; the upper mandible serves as a lid for covering the pouch. Widely distributed, predominantly over the warmer regions of the world, pelicans are strong fliers and swimmers, feeding on fish and crustaceans captured by diving into the water from the air or while swimming on the surface. They are sociable animals, often nesting in colonies of up to several thousand birds. Females produce two to three plain, bluish or yellowish eggs, although usually only one egg survives the 30- to 42-day incubation period. The young are born naked, and plumage appears after 8 to 14 days. Sexual maturity occurs after the third or fourth year.

Pella [pel'-uh]   The ancient city of Pella, located about 39 km (24 mi) northwest of modern Thessaloniki, Greece, was the capital of ancient Macedonia and the birthplace of the great Macedonian conquerors Philip II and Alexander the Great. After King Archelaus (r. 413–399 BC) moved the Macedonian capital from Aigai to Pella, the city flourished until Macedonia was conquered (168 BC) by Rome, after which it declined rapidly in importance and eventually fell into ruins. Rediscovered in 1954, the site has since yielded fine examples of Hellenistic art and architecture. Most renowned is the House of the Lion Hunt (late 4th century BC).

pellagra   see NUTRITIONAL-DEFICIENCY DISEASES

Pelli, Cesar Antonio [pel'-lee]   The American architect Cesar Pelli, b. Argentina, Oct. 12, 1926, is one of the foremost designers of public spaces. He makes his building complexes open-ended, accommodating industrial growth and change as natural conditions. A strong interaction is evident between Pelli's interior work systems and exterior landscapes, as in his Comsat Headquarters (1967; Clarksburg, Va.) and Teledyne Headquarters (1967; Northridge, Calif.). In 1968, Pelli became partner in charge of all architectural design for the California-based Gruen Associates. From 1976 to 1984 he was chairman of the department of architecture at Yale University. Pelli designed the Museum of Modern Art's extension and apartment tower in New York City (completed 1984). Subsequently, he helped design Battery Park City, also in New York.

Peloponnesian War [pel-oh-puh-nee'-zhuhn]   The Peloponnesian War (431–404 BC), a mighty struggle between ATHENS and SPARTA and their respective allies, resulted in Athens being defeated and stripped of its empire and in Sparta becoming the acknowledged leader of the Greek world. The underlying cause was Spartan fear of Athens's expansive power, but the war was triggered by hostility between Athens and Corinth, Sparta's major ally, when Athens interfered with Corinth's colonies and placed an embargo on nearby Megara.

Because the Spartans had a superior army, the strategy of the Athenian leader PERICLES was to avoid land bat-

PELOPONNESIAN WAR

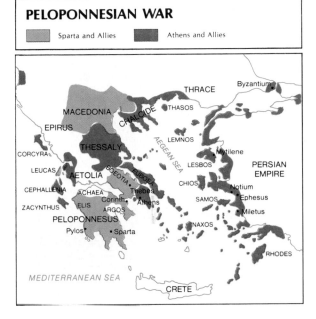

Sparta and Allies   Athens and Allies

THRACE
Byzantium
MACEDONIA   THASOS
EPIRUS   CHALCIDE
LEMNOS
THESSALY   AEGEAN SEA
CORCYRA   Mytilene
LEUCAS   LESBOS   PERSIAN EMPIRE
AETOLIA   CHIOS
CEPHALLENIA   ACHAEA   BOEOTIA   Notium
Thebes   EUBOEA   SAMOS   Ephesus
ZACYNTHUS   ELIS   Corinth   Athens   Miletus
ARGOS
PELOPONNESUS
Pylos   Sparta   NAXOS

RHODES

MEDITERRANEAN SEA
CRETE

tles and rely instead on control of the sea. When the war broke out, most Athenians crowded into the city, leaving the outlying areas of Attica open to invasion. Sparta's strategy was to invade yearly, hoping to break Athens's will and to encourage its subjects to rebel.

The first stage of the war ended in a stalemate in 421 BC with the Peace of NICIAS. Athens had remained firm and had suppressed the dangerous rebellion of Mytilene in 427. It was most damaged by the onset (430) of plague, which killed about a quarter of the Athenian population, including Pericles.

The peace was unstable. In 415 BC, a year after destroying the inoffensive island-state of Melos, Athens attempted to conquer Syracuse, largely at the urging of ALCIBIADES. The expedition ended disastrously for Athens in 413, and the debacle enticed Sparta into fighting once more. Aided by Persian resources, Sparta became a naval power. It encouraged the rebellion of Athens's allies and gradually overcame the Athenian navy. LYSANDER won the decisive battle of Aegospotami in 405; Athens was blockaded and surrendered (April 404). Athens gave up its fleet, submitted to the destruction of its fortifications, and suffered the rule of an oligarchy, the Thirty Tyrants. The imperial city never recovered from the blow, although the Thirty Tyrants were deposed in 403. Thucydides' *History of the Peloponnesian War* is the principal source for the events of the war up to 411 BC.

Peloponnesus [pel-oh-puh-nee'-suhs]   The Peloponnesus (also Peloponnese) is the southernmost part of mainland Greece, a broad, mountainous peninsula of about 21,440 km² (8,278 mi²). It has a population of 1,012,528 (1981). It is bordered on the west, south, and east by the

Ionian, Mediterranean, and Aegean seas, and is connected to the mainland by the narrow Isthmus of Corinth, which is cut by a canal. PATRAS is the largest city and major port.

In ancient times the Peloponnesus was the center of some of the world's most powerful civilizations; CORINTH and SPARTA were the chief cities. The Peloponnesian War (431–404 BC), fought between Sparta and Athens, spurred the decline of the Greek world. Spartan domination of the peninsula was followed by Macedonian rule. The Romans conquered it in 146 BC. The peninsula thereafter passed to Byzantium. In 1204 the leaders of the Fourth Crusade took over most of the Peloponnesus, which subsequently came under Venetian and Ottoman control. In the 19th century, the peninsula was included as part of independent Greece.

Pelops [pee'-lahps]   In Greek mythology Pelops was founder of the Pelopid dynasty at Mycenae; the Peloponnesus was named for him. Pelops won the hand of Hippodamia in a famous chariot race against her father, Oenomaus, by driving winged horses given him by Poseidon and by bribing Myrtilus, Oenomaus's charioteer, to take a bolt out of his master's chariot. Pelops then drowned Myrtilus to avoid paying the bribe. The misfortunes of the house of ATREUS, Pelops's son, were attributed to the curse of the dying Myrtilus.

pelvis   The pelvis, a cup-shaped structure of bone, distributes the weight it receives from the upper body to the legs, forms the basis for many muscle attachments, and supports the organs of the lower abdomen. The pelvis in the HUMAN BODY consists of two hipbones that form the lateral and front walls. Each hipbone is composed of the fusion of the ilium, ischium, and pubic bones termed *innominate bone*. The innominate bones are held together at the bottom by the pubic symphysis, a joint. The posterior wall of the hipbone is fused to the sacrum, coccyx (tailbone), and fifth lumbar vertebra of the spine.

The pelvic cavity, like the abdomen, is lined by a moist membrane, called the peritoneum. Found within the cavity are the urinary bladder, sigmoid colon, and rectum. In females, the reproductive organs are also found there. The pelvis is wider, not as deep, and lighter in structure in women than in men, and thus has a greater capacity.

Pemba [pem'-buh]   Pemba, the world's leading source of cloves, is an island of Tanzania in the Indian Ocean about 50 km (30 mi) off the coast of East Africa. The island, which is 68 km (42 mi) long and 23 km (14 mi) wide, has a total area of 906 km² (350 mi²) and a population of 265,039 (1988). Important towns include Wete and Chake Chake. Coconuts are exported, and fishing is important.

Settled by mainland Africans in the 10th century, the island of Pemba was taken by Portugal in the 16th century but was seized a century later by the Arabs. In 1822, Sayyid Said, later sultan of Zanzibar, conquered Pemba. It was part of the British protectorate of Zanzibar, which gained independence in 1963 and merged with Tanganyika to form Tanzania in 1964.

Pembroke Welsh corgi

The Pembroke Welsh corgi is a long-bodied, short-legged working dog. The breed apparently resulted from the crossing of small schipperkelike dogs (brought to Wales by Flemish weavers about 1107) with the local breeds, probably early Cardigan corgi types. The Pembroke has erect ears, a characteristic foxy face, and a tail docked completely. The dog stands 25 to 30 cm (10 to 12 in) at the shoulder and weighs 10.8 to 12.7 kg (24 to 28 lb). The coat is of medium length and double. The undercoat is short, dense, and weather resistant; the outer coat is somewhat longer and coarse.

The Pembroke may be red, sable, black, or tan, with or without white markings on the legs, chest, neck, muzzle, or underparts, and may have a blaze on the head.

The Pembroke Welsh corgi is a small working dog of a type known in Wales for centuries. Originally developed to work with cattle, it has been a favorite pet of the royal family of England since Princess Elizabeth received a pair as a gift from her father, George VI.

Pembrokeshire   see DYFED

pen

A pen is a hand-held instrument used to apply ink to a writing surface. Many types of writing instruments have been used since the first writing systems were developed. The ancient Egyptians used reeds, rushes, and hollow pieces of bamboo. The Chinese drew ideograms with camel's- or rat's-hair brushes; the Greeks used metal styli to mark waxed tablets. For later western civilizations the quill became the preferred writing tool.

Quill pens were made primarily from the wing feathers of the goose and swan. Points were shaped and sharpened by the quill user.

Metal pen points, or nibs, had been used occasionally in Europe, but no efficient manufacturing method was devised until the 1830s, when machinery was developed to stamp out and shape the points.

The fountain pen, incorporating its own ink reservoir, is an 1884 invention of an American, Lewis E. Waterman.

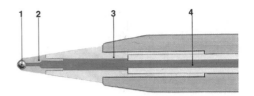

(Above) *The writing mechanism of a ball-point pen consists of a porous metal ball (1) that rotates in a socket inside a brass point (2). The point is attached to the barrel of the pen by a plastic holding device (3). A reservoir tube feeds ink (4) directly to the ball, which deposits it on the writing surface. Except for the point and ball, all parts are constructed of plastic.*

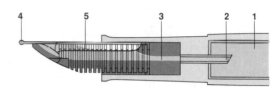

In a cartridge-fed fountain pen, an ink cartridge (1), inserted into the pen's barrel, is pierced by a tube (2), which channels a flow of ink through the feed structure (3) of the nib to the writing tip (4). An air vent (5) brings air into the cartridge to replace the used ink. Surface tension keeps the ink in the nib's comb until it is drawn down by pressure on the nib.

The basic elements of modern fountain pens still resemble those Waterman assembled: a nib or writing point; an ink reservoir and a device for filling it; and an external housing, or shell. Waterman's reservoir was filled by squeezing ink into it with an eye dropper.

The first patent for a ball-point writing tip was issued in 1888 to an American, John H. Loud. His concept, coupled with advances in ball grinding and measuring technology, allowed Lazlo Biro, a Hungarian, to make a ballpoint pen that wrote easily on paper. The so-called Biro appeared in England in 1944.

The success of the first soft-tip pen, a Japanese product introduced in 1964, has led to a proliferation of pens, or markers, that use new tip materials and a wide range of brilliantly colored inks.

penance   see CONFESSION (religion)

Penang

[puh-nang'] Penang (Pulau Pinang) is an island of Malaysia located off the northwestern coast of the Malay Peninsula. Part of Pinang state, the island is 285 km² (113 mi²) in area, with a mountainous interior and narrow coastal plains. George Town (1980 pop., 250,578), the state capital, is the leading seaport of Malaysia. The rest of the island is rural and sparsely populated. Industries include electronics, textiles, and coconut and bamboo processing. Rice, tin, and rubber are exported. Penang, settled in 1786 by Francis Light of the British East India Company, was the first English community on the Malay Peninsula. A bridge linking the island to the mainland opened in 1985.

penates [puh-nay'-teez]   Penates (Latin: "those who live in the cupboard") were the ancient Roman gods who watched over the household. Responsible for guarding the domestic stores, they were linked with the general welfare of the family members and were worshiped at the hearth, where food was sacrificed to them. In Roman mythology the penates were originally the household gods of AENEAS, which he brought with him from the destroyed city of Troy.

pencil   A pencil is a hand-held device for writing, marking, or drawing; it consists of a core of solid marking substance contained in a holder. Graphite is the marking substance used in "lead" pencils. Powdered graphite, clay, and water are blended, extruded into small-diameter rods, dried, and finally kiln-fired at about 1,038° C (1,900° F). The rods are impregnated with wax to impart smoothness. Varying the amount of clay determines the degree of hardness. Wood for pencils must be straight-grained and of a texture that can be cut against the grain with a pencil sharpener. About 98% of today's pencils are made of North American incense cedar.

Penderecki, Krzysztof [pahn-dair-ets'-kee, kshish'-tawf]   Krzysztof Penderecki, b. Poland, Nov. 23, 1933, is a specialist in the exploration of new instrumental and vocal sounds. His treatment of large numbers of strings, as in *Threnody for the Victims of Hiroshima*, for 52 strings (1960), and *Polymorpha*, for 48 strings (1961), is especially striking. His monumental *St. Luke Passion* (1966) and his first opera, *The Devils of Loudun* (1968), are widely acclaimed. Important later works—which turn toward what he calls a "new romanticism"—include *Utrenya*, for solo voices, chorus, and orchestra (1971); the sacred drama *Paradise Lost* (1978); the choral piece *Polish Requiem* (U.S. premiere, 1986); and the opera *Black Mask* (1986).

Pendergast, Thomas Joseph [pen'-dur-gast]   American political boss Thomas Joseph Pendergast, b. Saint Joseph, Mo., July 22, 1872, d. Jan. 26, 1945, ruled Democratic politics in Kansas City, Mo., for more than 30 years. Acknowledged as city boss in about 1910, he later exerted a dominant influence in state politics as well. Harry S. Truman got his start in politics under the sponsorship of the Pendergast machine. In 1939, Pendergast was convicted of income-tax evasion and sent to Leavenworth prison. He was paroled in 1940 on condition that he stay out of politics for 5 years.

Pendleton, Edmund   Edmund Pendleton, b. Caroline County, Va., Sept. 9, 1721, d. Oct. 26, 1803, was a leading Virginia statesman. Elected to the House of Burgesses in 1752, he led the conservative "Cavalier" faction during the colonial period. In the years before and during the American Revolution, he supported resistance to Britain but opposed the violent measures advocated by Patrick HENRY and other radicals. Pendleton, Thomas JEFFERSON, and George WYTHE revised (1776–79) Virginia's law code, and from 1779 until his death Pendleton was president of Virginia's Supreme Court of Appeals.

Pendleton, George Hunt   George Hunt Pendleton, b. Cincinnati, Ohio, July 29, 1825, d. Nov. 24, 1889, was a prominent American politician who sponsored CIVIL SERVICE reform in Congress. He served in the Ohio state senate (1853–54) and the U.S. House of Representatives (1857–65). Pendleton was the Democratic party's vice-presidential nominee in 1864 and 4 years later was a leading contender for the Democratic presidential nomination. His advocacy of redeeming government bonds in GREENBACKS instead of coin, however, led key eastern Democrats to oppose him. Elected U.S. senator in 1878, he was chairman of the Senate committee that sponsored legislation, later known as the Pendleton Act of 1883, establishing a system of competitive examinations supervised by a federal civil service commission. Pendleton was U.S. minister to Germany from 1885 until his death.

pendulum   A pendulum consists of a weight that is suspended from a point and is free to swing back and forth. The interesting properties of a pendulum (which apply only if the angle of swing is less than about 10°) are that the pendulum executes simple harmonic motion (see MOTION, HARMONIC), and that the period of each swing is constant, independent of the mass of the weight and the displacement, and depends only on the pendulum's length. The uniformity of time marked by a swinging pendulum led Christiaan HUYGENS in 1656 to incorporate the principle into the first practical pendulum clock. In such timepieces each swing of the pendulum releases the clock's escapement mechanism, allowing the hands to advance at the proper rate. Energy lost by friction is resupplied by descending clock weights or by a coiled spring.

The period of oscillation (T) of a pendulum is $T = 2\pi\,L/g$, where L is its length and g is the acceleration of gravity (980 cm/sec^2).

See also: FOUCAULT PENDULUM.

Penelope [puh-nel'-uh-pee]   In Greek mythology Penelope was the faithful wife of ODYSSEUS, king of Ithaca. During Odysseus's 20-year absence, Penelope was besieged by an ardent band of suitors. Neither she nor her son Telemachus ever quite gave up hope of Odysseus's return, however, so she devised a clever scheme to keep her suitors at bay. Announcing that she would remarry as soon as she finished weaving a funeral shroud for her aged father-in-law, Laertes, Penelope unraveled it secretly every night. After 3 years of this deception, her maids revealed her secret; but, when all seemed lost, Odysseus returned and, with the aid of Telemachus, slew his wife's suitors.

(Left) *Like all penguins, the black-footed penguin is an expert swimmer and diver. Unlike other species, however, it feeds only on fish, consuming about half a kilogram (1 lb) each day.*

(Above) *The rockhopper penguin is a crested penguin that moves on land and ice by standing upright and hopping on both feet.* (Left) *Largest of all living penguins, the emperor penguin reaches 1.2 m (4 ft) in height and weighs as much as 40 kg (90 lb).*

from the surface at speeds approaching 40 km/h (25 mph). Although penguins feed mainly on small crustaceans (krill), fish, and squid near the surface, the emperor penguin may descend up to 260 m (850 ft) in search of food.

Penguins gather into large colonies to breed, returning year after year to the same rookery. The female emperor penguin lays her egg in May and then goes to sea to feed while the male incubates continuously for two months without eating. He stands on the Antarctic ice in the perpetual darkness of winter, holding the egg on his feet under a fold of abdominal skin. When the female returns to care for the newly hatched chick, the male goes to sea to regain his lost weight. The downy chicks herd together into crèches for warmth and protection as they get older. Chicks feed by reaching into their parents' throats for food that is brought from the sea.

penicillin   Since 1929, when the Scottish biologist Alexander FLEMING first observed the effects of penicillin on bacteria, penicillin has become a generic term for a very important group of ANTIBIOTICS. Fleming recognized the therapeutic potential of penicillin, but a separate group of biologists, including H. W. Florey (1898–1968), first purified the drug in 1941 and established its effectiveness in treating infectious diseases in humans.

Penicillin was initially obtained from Fleming's strain of *Penicillium notatum*, but most commercial penicillins today are produced from a strain of *P. chrysogenum*. The main form produced is benzylpenicillin, or penicillin G. Penicillin is effective against most gram-positive bacteria, including those which cause syphilis, meningococcal meningitis, pneumococcal pneumonia, and some staphylococcal and streptococcal infections. Most gram-negative bacteria are resistant to penicillin, a notable exception being the causative bacteria for gonorrhea. A synthetic penicillin, ampicillin, is active against both gram-positive and gram-negative bacteria. Penicillin acts by interfering with the synthesis of a microorganism's cell wall, leaving the internal structures vulnerable.

Although penicillin causes few side effects, allergic reaction can result, and sensitive patients must be given an alternative antibiotic. With the widespread use of penicil-

penguin   Penguins are stout-bodied, short-legged, flightless birds superbly adapted for swimming underwater. Their wings resemble flippers and their bodies are covered with short, scaly feathers with downy bases. All 6 genera and 18 species, in the family Spheniscidae, are blackish above and white below, but some are banded across the breast (*Spheniscus*) and others have ornamental yellow crests (*Eudyptes*). Penguins are found in the colder waters of oceans of the Southern Hemisphere, breeding near the equator on the Galápagos Archipelago, in southern South America and Africa, in Australia and New Zealand, and on many islands. Only two species, the adélie and the emperor, breed in Antarctica.

Penguins swim underwater with powerful strokes of their wings and use their webbed feet and stiff tail as rudders. Sometimes they make a series of porpoiselike leaps

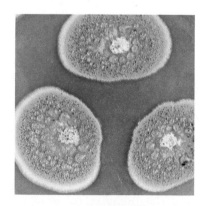

The mold P. chrysogenum *yields the antibiotic penicillin, used to treat many bacterial infections. Most penicillin is produced commercially from high-yielding strains grown in large aerated tanks. Several species related to* P. chrysogenum *also synthesize penicillin.*

lin, resistance by many microorganisms, particularly staphylococci, has become increasingly common.

Peninsular Campaign

The Peninsular Campaign of the U.S. Civil War was an unsuccessful Union advance against Richmond, Va., the Confederate capital, that began in early April 1862 when Gen. George B. McCLELLAN moved his force of 110,000 toward the peninsula between the York and James rivers. A month later McClellan and his army captured Yorktown; in response, Gen. Joseph E. JOHNSTON, the Confederate commander, moved most of his troops south to defend Richmond, sent a force down the peninsula, and contested McClellan's advance with roughly equal numbers of troops. McClellan expected help from Gen. Irvin McDOWELL's 40,000 men. Gen. Robert E. LEE, however, acting as advisor to President Jefferson DAVIS, dispatched Gen. Stonewall JACKSON to the Shenandoah Valley, an action that resulted in the diversion of McDowell's troops.

Johnston attacked McClellan at Seven Pines (Fair Oaks), a few miles east of Richmond, May 31–June 1, 1862. In heavy fighting Johnston was wounded and his men were driven toward Richmond. President Davis gave command of the Confederate army to Lee, who immediately planned to attack McClellan.

In the Seven Days Battles (June 26–July 2, 1862) that followed, Lee hurled his 85,000 men against McClellan's 100,000. Successive clashes at Beaver Dam Creek, Gaines's Mill, Savage's Station, and Glendale brought the armies to the terrible battle of Malvern Hill on July 1. McClellan retreated to the Union base at Harrison's Landing, and the campaign ended in failure.

Peninsular War   see NAPOLEONIC WARS

penis   see REPRODUCTIVE SYSTEM, HUMAN; SEXUAL INTERCOURSE

Penn, Arthur

With the hugely influential *Bonnie and Clyde* (1967), filmmaker Arthur Penn, b. Philadelphia, Sept. 27, 1922, strikingly embodied the antiestablishment impulses and latent violence that characterized the American scene in the late 1960s. Previously, Penn had directed for the Broadway theater such plays as *Two for the Seesaw*, *Toys in the Attic*, and *All the Way Home*. The films *The Left-Handed Gun* (1958) and *The Miracle Worker* (1962) were expanded versions of earlier theater and television work. Penn's films, which have often addressed counterculture concerns, include *Alice's Restaurant* (1969), *Little Big Man* (1970), *Night Moves* (1975), *Four Friends* (1981), and *Dead of Winter* (1987). In 1982 he returned to Broadway to direct *Monday after the Miracle*.

Penn, William

William Penn, b. Oct. 14 (O.S.)/Oct. 24 (N.S.), 1644, d. July 30 (O.S.)/Aug. 10 (N.S.), 1718, was a prominent English Quaker and reformer and the

William Penn, an English Quaker, campaigned vigorously for religious toleration and freedom of conscience. The Commonwealth of Pennsylvania, founded by Penn in 1681, was intended by him to be a haven of liberty and democracy.

founder of Pennsylvania. Penn's Puritan leanings led to his expulsion (1661) from Oxford, prompting his father, Admiral Sir William Penn, to send him on a continental tour.

Returning to England in 1664, he joined (c.1666) the Quakers (see FRIENDS, SOCIETY OF), while managing his father's estates in Ireland. He soon began to preach and write in defense of his new faith, and his unorthodox tract *The Sandy Foundation Shaken* (1668) resulted in his imprisonment until 1669.

In 1676, Penn became one of the proprietors of West Jersey, and in 1681 he and 11 other Friends became the proprietors of East Jersey. Owing a debt to Penn's father, King Charles II in 1681 gave the younger William Penn a territory that was named Pennsylvania for Penn's father. In 1682 the duke of York (later James II) added the area subsequently known as Delaware.

Penn's Frame of Government (1682) and the early laws he proposed for Pennsylvania guaranteed settlers an elective assembly and council, religious freedom for all believers, and traditional English liberties. On his first visit to America (1682–84), Penn helped plan Philadelphia, met with the Indians and established the basis for peaceful relations, and summoned the assembly. Though Penn wanted his colony to be a "Holy Experiment," quarrels among factions and settlers' disputes with him soon caused its utopian quality to fade.

Mismanagement of his estates and his steward's fraudulent activities led to Penn's incarceration (1717–18) in debtor's prison. Quarrels with the colonists continued, and during negotiations with the crown to sell the rights of government of Pennsylvania, Penn suffered (1712) a stroke. He remained partially incapacitated until his death.

Pennacook

[pen'-uh-kuk]   The Pennacook, an Algonquian-speaking tribe of North American Indians, numbered about 5,000 members in the early 17th century, when they occupied a territory that covered most of present-day New Hampshire, eastern Vermont, northern coastal Massachusetts, and parts of coastal Maine. Until about 1670 they were also known as the Merrimac Indians. The seminomadic Pennacook hunted game and cultivated maize and other crops. The dwellings in their pali-

saded, semipermanent villages ranged from conical tepees to domed wigwams and, in some areas, rectangular
barrel-roofed longhouses. The basic unit of social organization was the extended family. Independent political
units were integrated through confederacies designed for
mutual defense. Tribal sachems were advised by councils
of lesser chiefs.

During the colonial period the Pennacook sided with
the French during the French and Indian Wars but later
turned against the colonists altogether. They formed an
alliance with the ABNAKI and in the early 18th century migrated with them to Saint-François, Quebec. The Abnaki
bands in Quebec numbered nearly 1,400 in 1989.

Penney, J. C.

James Cash Penney, b. Hamilton, Mo.,
Sept. 16, 1875, d. Feb. 12, 1971, founded the chain of
department stores in America and Europe that bears his
name. In 1897, Penney moved to Longmont, Colo., for
the sake of his health. He found work there in a dry-goods
store and 5 years later was sent to Kemmerer, Wyo., to
open a branch. He purchased one-third of this operation,
soon bought out his partners, and by 1909 had a chain of
three stores. By 1924, Penney had 500 stores. By the
time of his death, the firm had 1,660 stores, making it
the country's fifth largest merchandising corporation.

Pennines [pen'-ynz]

The Pennines, a chain of hills in
north central England, extend 260 km (160 mi) from the
Cheviot Hills on the border of Scotland to the valley of the
River Trent in the south. Called "the backbone of England," the Pennines act as a watershed for England's
northern rivers. They reach their greatest elevation in
Cross Fell (893 m/2,930 ft). The flat-topped hills are
composed of limestone and shale. Deep caverns and
chasms are found in the range.

Pennsylvania [pen-sul-vayn'-yuh]

Pennsylvania, one
of the Middle Atlantic states, is bounded by Lake Erie and
New York on the north, New Jersey on the east, Delaware
and Maryland on the south, West Virginia on the south
and west, and Ohio on the west. The state ranks 5th in
population, exceeded only by California, New York, Texas,
and Florida, but it ranks 33rd in size among the states.
Pennsylvania, or "Penn's Woods," was named by King
Charles II of England in honor of Admiral William Penn,
father of William PENN, the founder of the colony. The
state did not assume its present boundaries until 1792,
when the "Erie triangle" in the extreme northwest was
added, giving the state a larger outlet to Lake Erie. The
MASON-DIXON LINE set the state's southern boundary.

Pennsylvania has played a leading role in the nation's
development. The First CONTINENTAL CONGRESS met in Philadelphia, and the Declaration of Independence was signed
there. In the 19th century Pennsylvania became a major
industrial state of the nation, but in recent years it has
faced slowing industrial growth and population decline.

Pennsylvania is known as the Quaker State or the Keystone State. The latter name suggests its location along
the arch of the 13 original states.

Land and Resources

Nearly all of the topographic features common to the
eastern United States are found in Pennsylvania. Along
the DELAWARE RIVER in southeastern Pennsylvania is a narrow strip of the Atlantic Coastal Plain. From the Coastal
Plain westward, the Piedmont Lowlands slope upward to
a maximum elevation of about 150 m (500 ft) at the base
of the Blue Mountains. Where the Coastal Plain borders
the higher land to the west, hard rock and steeper slopes
mark the FALL LINE. The Blue Mountains are rugged, discontinuous highlands that extend from northeast to south
central Pennsylvania.

To the west of the Blue Mountains is the Great Valley,
which extends beyond Pennsylvania through New Jersey
and Virginia. The Ridge and Valley Province, about 70 km
(40 mi) wide, extends in a northeast-to-southwest direction to the north and west of the Great Valley. The ridges
rise to an elevation of approximately 490 to 610 m
(1,600 to 2,000 ft) above sea level.

Adjoining the Ridge and Valley Province on the west
and north is the Appalachian or Allegheny Plateau, a rugged hill country that covers more than half the state. The
plateau contains the highest elevations in Pennsylvania,
including Mount Davis, 979 m (3,213 ft), the highest
summit. The high eastern edge of the plateau is known as
the Allegheny Front. In the northwest is the narrow Erie
Lake Plain, part of the Central Lowlands.

The rocks in Pennsylvania vary from young sedimentary
rocks to very ancient complex rocks. The Atlantic Coastal
Plain is composed of recent sedimentary deposits, primarily sandstones and shales. The Piedmont and Blue Mountains consist mostly of granites and schists. To the west of
the older rocks of southeastern Pennsylvania are younger
sedimentary sandstones, shales, and limestones.

Soils. Pennsylvania's distribution of soil types corresponds to its physiographic regions. In the Atlantic Coastal
Plain and the Erie Lake Plain are sandy soils. In the upland
areas infertile sandy soils are most common, whereas the
river valleys are covered with fine, fertile alluvium.

Rivers and Lakes. Two major river basins dominate
Pennsylvania. Nearly half of the state is drained by the
SUSQUEHANNA RIVER system. The major branches of the
Susquehanna are its North Branch and West Branch and
the Juniata River. In western Pennsylvania the ALLEGHENY
RIVER and the MONONGAHELA RIVER are part of the OHIO RIV-
ER system and form the second largest river basin in the
state. The Delaware River—with its major tributaries, the
Lehigh and Schuylkill—follows the eastern boundary of
the state. The POTOMAC RIVER in the south and the Genesee in the north have small parts of their basins in Pennsylvania. The state has numerous lakes, the largest of
which is Lake Wallenpaupack in the northeast. Artificial
lakes include Allegheny Reservoir on the Allegheny River
and Pymatuning and Shenango River reservoirs on the
Shenango River.

Climate. Pennsylvania has a humid continental climate, but topographic differences result in local anoma-

AT A GLANCE

PENNSYLVANIA

Land: Area: 117,347 km² (45,308 mi²); rank: 33d. Capital: Harrisburg (1990 pop., 52,376). Largest city: Philadelphia (1990 pop., 1,585,577). Counties: 67. Elevations: highest—979 m (3,213 ft), at Mount Davis; lowest—sea level, at the Delaware River.

People: Population (1990): 11,924,710; rank: 5th; density: 101.6 persons per km² (263.2 per mi²). Distribution (1988 est.): 84.8% metropolitan, 15.2% nonmetropolitan. Average annual change (1980–90): +0.05%.

Government (1991): Governor: Robert Casey, Democrat. U.S. Congress: Senate—2 Republicans; House—11 Democrats, 12 Republicans. Electoral college votes: 25. State legislature: 50 senators, 203 representatives.

Economy: State personal income (1988): $194.8 billion; rank: 6th. Median family income (1979): $19,995; rank: 24th. Agriculture: income (1988)—$3.3 billion. Forestry: sawtimber volume (1987)—52.2 billion board feet. Mining: value (1987)—$3.5 billion. Manufacturing: value added (1987)—$57.7 billion. Services: value (1987)—$49.7 billion.

Miscellany: Statehood: Dec. 12, 1787; the 2d state. Nicknames: Keystone State and Quaker State; tree: hemlock; motto: Virtue, Liberty, and Independence; song: none.

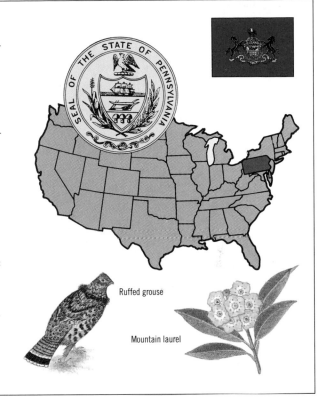

Ruffed grouse

Mountain laurel

lies. The southeast has long, hot summers and comparatively mild winters, whereas the Appalachian Plateau experiences longer, colder winters and shorter, milder summers. Because Pennsylvania lies close to the Atlantic Ocean, precipitation is more than adequate, averaging 890 to 1,270 mm (35 to 50 in). Pennsylvania has extremely variable weather due to the passage of successive low- and high-pressure areas across the state from west to east. Average annual snowfall varies from about 760 mm (30 in) in southeastern Pennsylvania to 1,370 mm (54 in) or more in the northwest.

Vegetation and Animal Life. Pennsylvania lies in a transition zone between northern and southern forests. Mixed deciduous hardwoods, such as oak, maple, ash, elm, and sycamore, dominate southeastern and central Pennsylvania. On the Appalachian Plateau are mixed stands of conifers and hardwoods, characteristic of northern forests. About 60% of the state is forested.

White-tailed deer, black bears, beavers, rabbits, squirrels, raccoons, and woodchucks are found in the forested regions. The state's many species of songbirds include orioles, eastern meadowlarks, bobolinks, robins, and cardinals. Game birds include woodcocks, wild turkeys, ring-necked pheasants, bobwhite quail, Canada geese, and ducks.

Resources. Pennsylvania is a leading mineral-producing state. Large reserves of bituminous coal underlie the western portion of the state, and anthracite can be found in northeastern Pennsylvania. Petroleum reserves are located in western Pennsylvania. Major deposits of iron ore are found at Cornwall and Morgantown, near READING. Limestone provides the basis for a large cement industry in the Lehigh Valley. Clay, sand, and stone are valuable nonmetallic minerals.

People

Between 1980 and 1990, Pennsylvania slipped from 4th to 5th position (overtaken in population by Florida) among the most populous U.S. states. It is one of the more densely populated states, characterized by fewer young people and a larger population of persons 65 and older than in the nation as a whole. Pennsylvania's birthrate is lower than the U.S. average, while its death rate is somewhat higher than the national average. The population is nearly 90% white and about 9% black, although blacks make up a greater percentage in the state's largest urban areas.

About 96% of the population are native-born. Most of the state's foreign-born population originated in Italy, Poland, and Germany. Hispanic Americans, mainly from Puer-

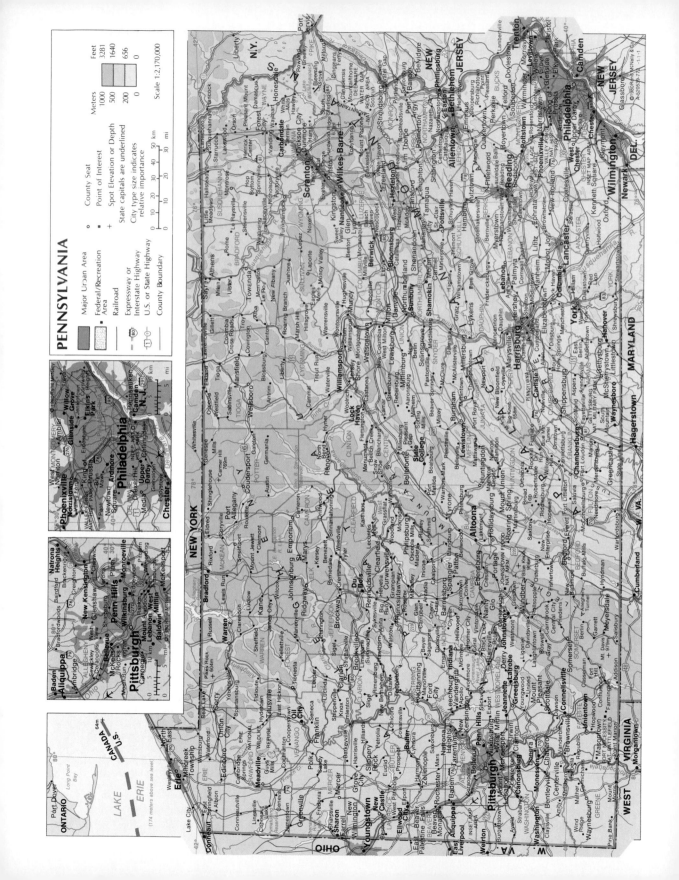

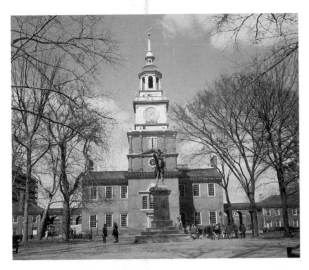

Independence Hall, a Philadelphia landmark, was the site of the Second Continental Congress, the signing of the Declaration of Independence, and the Constitutional Convention.

to Rico, and Asian peoples are also represented. A concentration of MENNONITES is located in Lancaster County in the southeast, an area often called the land of the PENNSYLVANIA DUTCH.

The Roman Catholic church has the largest membership of any single religious group. Most Protestants belong to the Lutheran, Methodist, or Presbyterian denomination.

Pennsylvania has two Consolidated Metropolitan Statistical Areas centered on PHILADELPHIA and PITTSBURGH. Philadelphia, Pittsburgh, ALLENTOWN, and Erie have more than 100,000 residents each.

Education. Pennsylvania established a public school system in 1790, but the system really did not begin to develop until the 1830s. Today education is compulsory for all children from age 8 to age 17. Among Pennsylvania's institutions of higher education are the state-supported higher-education system and four state-related universities. These include The Pennsylvania State University (1855) at University Park, the University of Pittsburgh (1787), and Temple University (1884) in Philadelphia. Private institutions located in the state include such schools as Bryn Mawr College, BUCKNELL UNIVERSITY, CARNEGIE–MELLON UNIVERSITY, HAVERFORD COLLEGE, SWARTHMORE COLLEGE, the University of Pennsylvania (see PENNSYLVANIA, UNIVERSITY OF), and VILLANOVA UNIVERSITY.

Cultural Institutions. Pennsylvania has a large number of cultural institutions. The PHILADELPHIA ORCHESTRA and the Pittsburgh Symphony Orchestra are two of the nation's finest. The Philadelphia Orchestra has been led by such famous conductors as Eugene ORMANDY and Leopold STOKOWSKI. The famed Curtis Institute of Music is also in Philadelphia. Major museums in the state include the Andrew Carnegie museums of natural history and art in Pittsburgh and, in Philadelphia, the PENNSYLVANIA ACADEMY OF THE FINE ARTS, the Philadelphia Museum of Art, the Natural Sciences Museum, and the University Museum.

Pennsylvania folk art is preserved in the Farm Museum at LANCASTER, the William Penn Memorial Museum at HARRISBURG, the Mercer Museum at Doylestown, and the Hershey Museum at Hershey.

Historical Sites. Many historical sites and museums commemorate the long history of the state of Pennsylvania. These include Revolutionary War and Civil War sites, such as VALLEY FORGE, INDEPENDENCE HALL, the GETTYSBURG Battlefield, and Washington Crossing. The early economic history of the state is recalled at such places as the Cornwall Furnace, Hopewell Village, Drake Well Museum, the Lumber Museum, and the Railroad Museum.

Communications. The colony's first newspaper, the *American Weekly Mercury*, was established in 1719. Nine years later the *Pennsylvania Gazette* was founded; it was purchased in 1730 by Benjamin Franklin, the colony's most renowned publisher. The world's first commercial radio station, KDKA, began operation in Pittsburgh on Nov. 2, 1920. Today the state has many radio and television stations, and the *Philadelphia Inquirer* is a leading newspaper.

Economic Activity

Pennsylvania has a highly diversified economy, with manufacturing the state's single most important economic activity. Philadelphia and Pittsburgh are the leading manufacturing centers. Coal and oil and valued commodities. Agriculture, tourism, and growing service-related industries also contribute to the state's economic well-being.

Agriculture. Most of Pennsylvania's farm income is derived from livestock production, including beef cattle, milk cows, hogs, and sheep. Pennsylvania is a leading U.S. state in the production of milk and milk products, chickens, eggs, and apples and is the nation's leading producer of mushrooms. Principal field crops produced in the state include corn, hay, oats, soybeans, wheat, and barley. Important fruits grown are peaches, grapes, tart cherries, toma-

Pittsburgh's Golden Triangle, the city's central business district, is located where the Monongahela and Allegheny rivers join to form the Ohio River.

toes, and pears. Some of the nation's richest farmland is found in southeastern Pennsylvania, and much agricultural production is centered in Lancaster County.

Forestry. Once a leading state in forest-related industries, Pennsylvania has experienced a decline in lumbering because of overcutting during the 19th century. Most of the forested land is commercially owned, and most timber is cut for pulp and paper. Forestry activity takes place generally in the northern part of the state.

Mining. Pennsylvania is a leading mineral-producing state and one of the major coal-producing areas in the United States. Both anthracite (hard coal) and bituminous (soft) coal are found, with anthracite mined in Pennsylvania's eastern counties and bituminous coal mined in the western and other parts of the state. Pennsylvania is the only major producer of anthracite in the United States. Oil and natural-gas wells are found in northwestern Pennsylvania.

The most valuable nonfuel mineral is portland cement. Other important minerals found in Pennsylvania include masonry cement, pig iron, sand and gravel, lime, sandstone, clays, mica, and peat.

Manufacturing. Pennsylvania is one of the nation's major manufacturing states. Most manufacturing is concentrated in the southeastern and southwestern parts of Pennsylvania. Highly diversified manufacturing has developed in the southeast, based on large local and regional markets. The southwestern portion of the state is noted for its heavy industries, attracted initially by large coal reserves. Major industries found in Pennsylvania are the primary-metals industries, involved in steel production and in the manufacture of nails and other basic metal products; and the manufacture of food products, nonelectrical machinery, electrical machinery and equipment, chemicals, fabricated-metal products, transportation equipment, paper, printed materials, and clothing. Oil refining is also important.

Tourism and Recreation. Tourism and recreation are major sources of employment for the people of Pennsylvania. Millions of recreational travelers and vacationers are drawn each year to the state's wide variety of tourist attractions, forested mountains, green valleys, and clear lakes. Pennsylvania has numerous state parks, recreation areas, national historic sites, and national historical parks. Outdoor sports are developed extensively, particularly in the Pocono Mountains, where a number of ski areas operate between December and April, and along the Delaware Water Gap. Game lands and waterways are well maintained and well stocked. Major league baseball, and professional football, basketball, and hockey teams play in Pittsburgh and Philadelphia. College basketball is especially popular in Philadelphia.

Transportation. Pennsylvania is a Middle Atlantic state within the populous Eastern Seaboard, and it is a gateway to the Midwest. The state's strategic location is enhanced by a comprehensive transportation network. One of Pennsylvania's most important roadways is Interstate 80, also known as the Keystone Shortway. This east-west superhighway opened central Pennsylvania to industrial development by providing a link to the Midwest and the Atlantic Coast. Another major highway is the Pennsylvania Turnpike, the first high-speed multilane highway in the United States. Several major railroads offer freight-carrier service, and Amtrak provides rail passenger service in the state. Pennsylvania's waterways offer the unique feature of triple port coverage: a deepwater port at Philadelphia, a Great Lakes port at Erie, and an inland-water port at Pittsburgh. Pennsylvania has numerous public airports served by various commercial airlines.

Energy. Pennsylvania's energy needs are supplied by coal, petroleum, natural gas, nuclear power, and hydropower. Although Pennsylvania has some nuclear power plants in operation, the 1979 accident at the Three Mile Island power plant near Harrisburg brought into question the safety of NUCLEAR ENERGY as a source of electrical power. The accident sent a radioactive stream into the atmosphere and caused the temporary evacuation of thousands of people.

Government and Politics

Pennsylvania is governed under the amended constitution of 1873. Executive authority is vested in a governor, a lieutenant governor, an attorney general, an auditor general, and a treasurer, all elected for 4 years. The governor may serve only two 4-year terms in succession.

The general assembly is the legislative branch of the government. The senate's 50 members are elected for 4 years, and the 203 members of the house of representatives are elected for 2 years.

The state's supreme court dates from 1722; its justices are elected for 10 years and form the court of last resort. The superior court, with judges also elected for 10-year terms, hears appeals from the courts of common pleas. The commonwealth court, created in 1968, has jurisdiction over civil actions involving the state.

Counties, townships, cities, boroughs, and other civil subdivisions derive their power of self-government from the state. Pennsylvania has 67 counties.

Pennsylvania, overwhelmingly Democratic between 1800 and 1860, came out of the Civil War strongly Republican. Between the Civil War and 1934, Democrats won the governor's seat only twice, but they have increased their strength in recent decades. Labor, African Americans, and Roman Catholics, concentrated in the cities, have boosted membership in the state's Democratic party. Democratic governors have been elected from time to time since 1934, and today the balance between the two major parties in Pennsylvania is very close.

History

Colonial Period. Before white settlement Pennsylvania was the home of about 15,000 Indians, most of whom belonged to the DELAWARE, SHAWNEE, and SUSQUEHANNA tribes, as well as scattered groups of the IROQUOIS LEAGUE. As early as 1614 the Dutch explored the lands along the Delaware River. In 1643 a party of Swedes called the territory NEW SWEDEN and established the first permanent colonies at Tinicum and New Göttenburg near modern CHESTER. In 1655, Peter Stuyvesant, the governor of New Netherland, led an expedition against the Swedes and

The Ephrata community, in southeastern Pennsylvania, was founded in the 18th century by J. C. Beissel, leader of a German Protestant group called the Seventh Day Baptists.

imposed Dutch rule. Dutch authority was terminated when, in 1664, a British force seized New Netherland (present day New York). In 1681, William Penn, a prominent British Quaker, obtained from Charles II a grant of the territory known as the Providence of Pennsylvania. The first permanent British colony was established at present-day Philadelphia in 1682.

Penn planned to make his new colony the "Holy Experiment." He immediately drew up "The Great Law of Pennsylvania," under which male suffrage extended to those who professed a belief in God and met moderate property requirements. No man was deprived of life, liberty, or estate except by trial before a jury of 12. Children were to be taught to read, to write, and to learn a skill or trade. Penn's seal read, "Mercy, Justice, Truth, Peace, Love, Plenty."

Penn signed a treaty of friendship with the Indians of Pennsylvania, setting a high standard in relations. His successors extended this friendship to an alliance with the Iroquois, and as a result the settlers enjoyed 70 years of peaceful relations with the Indians. By 1750, however, this era of friendship was nearing an end, as land purchases for white settlements encroached on Indian territory.

In the 1750s, British traders and settlers poured into western Pennsylvania, eager for land and furs. The French built a chain of forts from Lake Erie to the Forks of the Ohio River and then brought pressure on the Indians to break relations with the British. The FRENCH AND INDIAN WAR of 1754–63 ensued. After the British victory at FORT DUQUESNE the French withdrew, and the British general John FORBES built Fort Pitt in 1759–61 on the site of present-day Pittsburgh.

Revolutionary Era. Pennsylvania figured significantly in the Revolutionary War. As early as 1766, Benjamin FRANKLIN, the colonial agent in Great Britain, vigorously opposed the STAMP ACT before the House of Commons. When war broke out, Pennsylvania troops took part in many of the campaigns of the revolution, including the

siege of Boston in 1775. The battles of the BRANDYWINE, Paoli, Fort Mifflin, and Germantown were fought in Pennsylvania. Valley Forge, where Washington and his men spent the winter of 1777–78, is located 40 km (25 mi) west of Philadelphia.

Philadelphia was a major center of political activity in the colonies. In July 1774 a provincial congress convened at Philadelphia and elected delegates to the First Continental Congress, which met in the city. The Second Continental Congress also met there, signing the Declaration of Independence in 1776. In 1787 delegates to the CONSTITUTIONAL CONVENTION in Philadelphia drafted the U.S. Constitution.

The independent western Pennsylvanians were often at odds with both the rest of the state and the federal government. In 1794 open insurrection broke out over the right of the federal government to tax local industry, especially whiskey distilling. When the settlers refused to pay the tax, President Washington called out the Pennsylvania Militia. The uprising, the WHISKEY REBELLION, ended without bloodshed.

In 1799, Lancaster was chosen the state capital. Harrisburg was selected as the capital in 1812.

Civil War. Pennsylvania was a pivotal state in the Civil War struggle, not only because the state had men and materiel but also because key routes from the South led to Harrisburg, Philadelphia, and Pittsburgh. In order to control these routes the Confederate Army of Northern Virginia invaded Pennsylvania in 1863. Gettysburg became one of the most decisive as well as one of the bloodiest battles of American history. Almost a third of the Union army in the Battle of Gettysburg (see GETTYSBURG, BATTLE OF) was from Pennsylvania.

Industrial Development. After the Civil War, Pennsylvania experienced a tremendous industrial expansion based on the increased use of metals, especially steel. By 1870, Pittsburgh had become the chief center of the steel industry, producing two-thirds of the national total. Of the steel magnates Andrew CARNEGIE played a dominant role, creating a giant steel empire at the end of the 19th century. In 1901, Carnegie sold his vast industrial complex to financier J. Pierpont Morgan (see MORGAN family). Morgan used Carnegie's company to create the United States Steel Corporation (now USX), headquartered in Pittsburgh. As Pennsylvania grew industrially, the labor movement expanded, giving rise to the AMERICAN FEDERATION OF LABOR AND CONGRESS OF INDUSTRIAL ORGANIZATIONS, which had its origin in the state. During World War II, Pennsylvania played a significant role in terms of both industrial production and military manpower. In recent decades, while the state remains a leader in steel and coal production, there has been a comparative decline in those industries due to a decline in demand for coal and to labor and other problems related to the steel industry.

Pennsylvania, University of Established in 1740 by Benjamin Franklin, the University of Pennsylvania is a private coeducational institution in Philadelphia. It is a member of the IVY LEAGUE and was the first American school to be designated a university. The Wharton School of Finance and Commerce (1881) and the medical school (1865) are the oldest in their fields. The University Museum has important collections of Near Eastern, Classical, and Egyptian art and sponsors archaeological expeditions.

Pennsylvania Academy of the Fine Arts

The Pennsylvania Academy of the Fine Arts in Philadelphia was founded in 1805. It is the country's oldest art school in continuous existence and was the first public art museum in the United States. The Academy is the direct descendant of the Columbianum, which was, in turn, the successor of a drawing school started in 1791 by Charles Willson Peale (see PEALE family). Its importance as an art school and museum has continued to this day.

Pennsylvania Dutch

The Pennsylvania Dutch, also called Pennsylvania Germans, are descendants of German-speaking immigrants from the German Rhineland, Switzerland, and Alsace who went to America in the late 17th and 18th centuries and settled in eastern Pennsylvania. They are concentrated in the counties of Lancaster, Lehigh, Lebanon, York, Northampton, and Berks. Many of the early immigrants spoke different regional dialects and brought competing German customs to the New World, factors that in the beginning tended to fragment their efforts in America. They immigrated principally between 1683 and 1806. Some later German arrivals or other neighbors joined the community, largely through marriage into the group. Although a few Holland Dutch joined the Rhineland Germans to establish Germantown as their initial settlement in Pennsylvania, as a group the Pennsylvania Dutch are not Dutch, but ethnically and culturally German. The common use of the term *Dutch* to identify them was a derogatory name used by the English colonists who mispronounced *deitsch*, the German dialect word meaning "German."

Two main currents of Pennsylvania Dutch settlers entered Pennsylvania: the "plain" or pietist German sectarians, and the "fancy" or Church Germans. Among the so-called Plain Folk, a visible minority by their plain dress and their disdain even today for electricity, automobiles, and other modern devices, are the BRETHREN, MENNONITES and Amish, and Dunkers (German Baptists). Lutheran, German Reformed, and Evangelical church Germans wear no distinctive garb and have blended into the American mainstream. The latter group, also called the Gay Dutch, constitutes approximately 90 percent of Pennsylvania Dutch. Both groups are still concentrated in large numbers in southeastern Pennsylvania. Their dialect is spoken by an estimated 175,000 persons and understood by an estimated 350,000 others.

Folk art was highly developed among the Pennsylvania Dutch. Fraktur drawing and sgraffito ceramic plates incorporated folk symbols such as the heart, tulip, tree of life, and distelfink, a characteristically stylized bird. These motifs are repeated in varied ways on artifacts ranging from intricately hand-lettered and embellished *taufscheine* (baptismal certificates) and molded iron stove plates of the 18th and 19th centuries, to hand-stitched quilts and decorated piecrusts of the present day.

Pennsylvanian Period   see GEOLOGIC TIME

Penobscot

[puh-nahb'-skaht]   The Penobscot are a tribe of North American Indians whose homeland lies along

Lancaster County, in southeastern Pennsylvania, ranks among the most productive agricultural areas in the United States. The most valuable crop harvested in this center of Pennsylvania Dutch culture is a variety of leaf tobacco used as a filler in cigars.

the Penobscot River and Penobscot Bay in Maine. Speakers of an Algonquian language, they are most closely affiliated with the PASSAMAQUODDY, fellow members in the ABNAKI confederacy. An agricultural and fishing people, the Penobscot were traditionally organized into about 14 villages, each consisting of a few hundred people. In the early 16th century the first European fishermen visited the tribe. By the next century European writers described the tribe as the "kingdom of Norumba," and so it appeared on maps.

In the struggles between colonial powers the Penobscot sided with the French until 1749, when they made peace with the English. This move saved them from having to migrate into Canada like other Abnaki tribes, and they have continued to live in Maine. With the Passamaquoddy, they have a nonvoting representative in the Maine legislature. In the 1950s the Penobscot joined the Passamaquoddy in a suit against Maine to recover lands granted by illegal treaties in the 1790s; the suit was successfully settled in 1980. Penobscot on or near the reservation number 1,073 (1989 est.).

Penobscot River   The 563-km-long (350-mi) Penobscot River is Maine's longest stream. Rising in the lakes of central Maine, the river flows generally south into Penobscot Bay, 37 km (23 mi) south of Bangor. The first European, an English explorer, to travel on the river did so in 1603.

Pensacola [pen-suh-koh'-luh]   Pensacola, a city in northwestern Florida on Pensacola Bay, is the county seat of Escambia County. It has a population of 58,165 (1990). Pensacola's deep, natural harbor has made it a shipping and commercial fishing center. It also manufactures synthetic fibers, paper products, naval stores, and chemicals. The U.S. Naval Air Station, established in 1913, is a leading navy flight-training center. The University of West Florida (1967) is located in the city.

The area was discovered by the Spanish in 1516. The first permanent settlement was established on the site in 1698. The city was held by the British, the French, and the Spanish until it was captured from the British by Andrew Jackson in 1818. It became part of the United States in 1821.

Pensées, Les   see PASCAL, BLAISE

pension   A pension is an income payable after a worker retires, usually at the age of 60 or above, depending on the provisions of the particular retirement plan. Pensions can also be paid out earlier if a worker becomes disabled, or to the survivors of a worker who dies. About 90 percent of all U.S. workers are covered for retirement and disability under SOCIAL SECURITY. Most of the others are members of some public-employee retirement system. Fewer than half of all workers in the private sector are covered by private pension or profit-sharing plans.

Modern retirement plans come in two general forms.

The traditional form is the defined-benefit plan, under which the employer promises specific pension benefits based on an employee's earnings and length of employment. Generally, employees do not pay any earnings into defined-benefit plans. In defined-contribution plans, however, workers may pay into the plan along with employers. In this type of plan, pension benefit amounts are not specified, and depend upon such unknowns as the returns on investments made with the pension fund during a participant's employment tenure.

Governmental Retirement Systems. Governments at the various levels sponsor two kinds of pension arrangements: social insurance and retirement systems for public employees. The federal government sponsors two interrelated social-insurance systems under the provisions of the Social Security Act of 1935 and the Railroad Retirement Act of 1937. Under these systems most workers in the United States are part of a mammoth social-insurance arrangement providing old-age pensions as early as age 62 and disability pensions at any age.

Private Pension Plans. In the private sector, most pension plans are sponsored by employers. In some cases a plan may have been arrived at in collective bargaining with a labor union, and it may be part of a larger plan that covers the employees of other companies. Adjustments for inflation are often part of collective-bargaining negotiations.

The Employee Retirement Income Security Act (ERISA) of 1974 was enacted to protect employees' pension rights. It specified certain conditions that a pension plan in the private sector must meet. It also established the Pension Benefit Guaranty Corporation to insure private plans, through premiums paid by employers, and to guarantee payment of pensions in the event of employer bankruptcy. There are, nonetheless, substantial problems with retirement arrangements in the United States. Among them are provisions allowing companies to use excess pension-fund assets for purposes unrelated to pensions (for example, as cash for the many mergers and takeovers of the 1980s) and to end, or change the terms of, retirement plans for new employees. Pension benefits are often lost when a worker changes jobs.

Future congressional changes in pension laws may include a ban on a company's use of excess pension-fund assets (assets that have accrued beyond the minimum required to fulfill a fund's responsibilities) for other than pension needs, and provisions for allowing accrued pension benefits to be transferred from one employer to another when a worker changes jobs.

Management of Pension Plans. Private pension plans and state or local governments accumulate substantial amounts of money awaiting distribution in the form of pensions. These dollars are invested in virtually every kind of income-producing resource, including stocks, bonds, mortgages, and real estate. Pension-fund assets, and the money they earn through investments, are not taxable; in 1989 they totaled $2.6 trillion in the United States.

Pentagon, The [pen'-tuh-gahn]   The Pentagon, located in Arlington, Va., across the Potomac River from Washington, D.C., is a five-story, five-sided building that is headquarters for the departments of Defense and of the Army, the Navy, and the Air Force. Designed by architect G. E. Bergstrom with the intent to conserve structural steel, which was in short supply during World War II, this building was completed in January 1943, after 16 months of round-the-clock work. It consists of five pentagon-shaped buildings that form concentric rings joined by corridors. The Pentagon, having approximately 343,740 m^2 (3,700,000 ft^2) of office space, also has its own fire department, police force, radio and television stations, and phone exchange.

Pentagon Papers

The Pentagon Papers is the popular name given to a secret study done in 1967–69 by a team of analysts for the U.S. Department of Defense. The 47-volume study (officially called "HISTORY OF THE U.S. Decision-Making Process on Viet Nam Policy") sharply criticized the U.S. policies in Southeast Asia that had led to the Vietnam War and stated that the government had misrepresented its role there to the American people. In 1971, Daniel Ellsberg, who had access to the study, released it to the *New York Times*, which began publishing excerpts in a series of articles. The Department of Justice ordered publication halted, citing as a reason a threat to national security. The U.S. Supreme Court ruled, however, in *New York Times Company* v. *United States* (1971), that the constitutional right to freedom of the press outweighed other considerations and that publication could be resumed. The articles were published in book form in 1971. Ellsberg was indicted for theft, espionage, and conspiracy, but in 1973 the charges were dismissed.

pentane

A colorless, inflammable liquid, pentane (C_5H_{12}) is a HYDROCARBON recovered from petroleum. Practically insoluble in water, pentane boils at 36° C. It is called *n*-pentane to distinguish it from two other 5-carbon isomers, isopentane and neopentane. A constituent of gasoline and ligroin (petroleum ether), pentane is valued as a starting material for making petrochemical products.

Pentateuch   see BIBLE

pentathlon

[pen-tath'-lahn]   The pentathlon is any combination of five athletic events in which the winner is the high scorer according to a specially designed point system. The pentathlon can be traced back to the ancient Greek Olympics of 708 BC. The traditional men's pentathlon—long jump, javelin throw, 200-m sprint, discus throw, and 1,500-m run—was a part of the modern Olympics until 1924.

The women's pentathlon was in the Olympics from 1964 to 1980 and consisted of five track-and-field events held over the course of two days: the 100-m hurdles, the shot put, the high jump, the long jump, and the 200-m sprint. In the 1984 Olympics the javelin and 800-m run were added, making the event the heptathlon.

The modern men's pentathlon, which has been an Olympic event since 1912, combines quite different events, testing survival skills. It takes five days, and the events are an 800-m show-jumping obstacle course for horse and rider, an épée fencing match, pistol shooting, a 300-m swim, and a 4,000-m cross-country run.

Pentecost

[pen'-tuh-kawst]   Pentecost refers to the Jewish Feast of Weeks, or SHAVUOTH, and to the Christian feast celebrating the coming of the HOLY SPIRIT upon the disciples of Jesus. The first Christian Pentecost occurred, according to Acts 2, when the disciples were gathered together for this feast after the ASCENSION OF CHRIST. They were filled with the Holy Spirit, manifested as the sound of wind and tongues of fire, and began to speak in tongues unknown to themselves but recognized by the foreign pilgrims in Jerusalem (see TONGUES, SPEAKING IN). Peter then preached a sermon that began the sequence of conversions that fills Acts. Pentecost, also called Whitsunday or Whitsun, is celebrated 50 days after EASTER and is one of the major feasts of the Christian year.

Pentecostalism

[pen-tuh-kaws'-tul-izm]   Pentecostalism, a worldwide Protestant movement that originated in the 19th-century United States, takes its name from the Christian feast of Pentecost, which celebrates the coming of the Holy Spirit upon the disciples. Pentecostalism emphasizes a postconversion experience of spiritual purification and empowering for Christian witness, entry into which is signaled by utterance in unknown tongues (glossolalia; see TONGUES, SPEAKING IN).

Although Pentecostalism generally aligns itself with FUNDAMENTALISM and EVANGELICALISM, its distinguishing tenet reflects roots in the American Holiness movement, which believed in the postconversion experience as entire sanctification.

Pentecostalism grew from occurrences of glossolalia in the southern Appalachians (1896), Topeka, Kans. (1901), and Los Angeles (1906). Working independently, Holiness movement preachers W. R. Spurling and A. J. Tomlinson in the South, Charles Fox Parham in Topeka, and William Seymour in Los Angeles, each convinced of general apostasy in American Christianity, preached and prayed for religious revival. Generally rejected by the older denominations, Pentecostals long remained isolated and were reluctant to organize. Now, however, several groups belong to the National Association of Evangelicals in the United States and to the World Council of Churches.

See also: CHARISMATIC MOVEMENT.

pentlandite

[pent'-luhnd-yt]   The nickel and iron isometric SULFIDE MINERAL pentlandite [$(Fe,Ni)_9S_8$] is the principal ore of nickel. Forming light bronze yellow, granular aggregates in basic igneous rock, it is nearly always intimately associated with and hard to distinguish from pyrrhotite. Hardness is 3½–4, luster is metallic, streak is light brown, and specific gravity is 4.6–5.0. At nickel mines in Sudbury, Ontario, and elsewhere, the pentlandite-pyrrhotite aggregate is crushed, and the pyrrhotite is magnetically separated from the nonmagnetic pentlandite.

Penzias, Arno   see WILSON, ROBERT W., AND PENZIAS, ARNO A.

---

peony [pee'-uh-nee]   Peony, genus *Paeonia,* is the common name for about 33 species of perennial flowering plants in the peony family, Paeoniaceae. The large, showy flowers range from white through pink and red to the darkest purple, plus a few yellow types. The hardy plants also have decorative foliage. Two classes of peonies exist: the herbaceous types are derived from *P. lactiflora,* and the tree peonies are forms of *P. suffruticosa.* Peonies thrive in any soil, particularly a fertile loam. They are native to north temperate Eurasia and western North America.

The peony P. officinalis has spectacular flowers and, once established in the garden, may bloom for decades. Its seeds were, at one time, supposedly used in herbal teas to ward off nightmares.

Peoria [pee-ohr'-ee-uh]   Peoria is the seat of Peoria County in north central Illinois, on the Illinois River where it forms Lake Peoria. The state's third largest city, it has a population of 113,504 (1990). Peoria is located in the heart of the state's central farm country and is a manufacturing and distribution center for heavy machinery, especially earth-moving equipment, steel, and chemicals; distilling is also important. In addition, Peoria is an important rail center. Bradley University was established there in 1896.

Father Jacques Marquette and Louis Jolliet sailed along Lake Peoria in 1673, and near there Robert Cavelier, sieur de La Salle, established Fort Crèvecoeur in 1680. That fort was abandoned, but, in 1691, Fort Saint

Louis, located upstream, was moved to Lake Peoria. Although the settlement was not continuously occupied, French traders frequented the area thereafter. In 1813, Fort Clark was erected and became the nucleus of the present settlement.

Pepin the Short, King of the Franks [pep'-in]   Pepin, also known as Pepin III, *c.*714–68, was the first CAROLINGIAN king of the Franks (*rex francorum*) and the father of CHARLEMAGNE. Pepin and his brother Carloman succeeded (741) their father, CHARLES MARTEL, as mayors of the palace; after they crushed a half dozen revolts in Bavaria, Alamannia, Saxony, and Aquitaine, Carloman entered (747) a monastery. Three years later Pepin arranged with Pope Zacharias to support the papacy in return for papal sanction of Carolingian usurpation of the Frankish kingship. Thus Pepin deposed (751) King Childeric III and was anointed king of the Franks. To preserve his bond with the papacy, Pepin crushed the Lombards when they threatened Rome (754, 756). He ceded conquered territories to the pope (the Donation of Pepin), thus establishing the basis for the PAPAL STATES. Pepin was succeeded by his sons, Charlemagne and Carloman.

---

pepper (spice)   Pepper is the dried fruit of a vine, *Piper nigrum,* that is native to the East Indies and is cultivated in Indonesia, Malaysia, India, Brazil, Madagascar, and Sri Lanka. A pungent spice and a stimulant, pepper has been highly valued for centuries. European demand for pepper was a factor in the 15th-century search for ocean routes to the spice-growing East. Black pepper is the dried, unripe berry, or peppercorn; white pepper, which has a milder flavor, is the dried ripe fruit from which the dark hull has been removed.

The pepper is a climbing vine that bears fruit on stalks. The dried fruit is a highly valued spice.

pepper (vegetable)   The garden vegetable pepper, *Capsicum annuum*, of the Solanaceae, or NIGHTSHADE, family, is grown throughout the world, and the species includes not only the green, bell-shaped, sweet peppers that are common garden varieties but also the hot peppers used for such spices as paprika, chili, and cayenne. Most cultivated peppers belong to one of two major groups. The Grossum group yields the globose, mild-flavored, sweet peppers and the pimiento, or Spanish pepper. The Longum group produces the "hot" chili and cayenne peppers, several hundred varieties of which are cultivated in warmer regions. Longum peppers are characterized by their extreme pungency. They may be highly irritating when eaten fresh, and in Western cuisines they are used for the most part in the form of spice powders made from the dried fruit. Paprika is obtained from a milder variety of hot pepper.

The Tabasco pepper, *C. frutescens*, is a small-fruited hot type grown principally for use in commercial hot sauces.

The pungency of hot peppers is caused by a crystalline substance, capsaicin. The hottest peppers may contain as much as 1 percent capsaicin. Peppers are native to tropical regions of the Western Hemisphere.

The garden pepper is available in several varieties. Shown are a pepper plant (left), with several sweet, bell-shaped green peppers (also bottom, enlarged), as well as one pepper that has turned a ripe red; a flower (top center); two elongated hot peppers (top right) in different stages of ripeness; and a cherry pepper (center).

peppermint   Peppermint, *Mentha piperita*, a hybrid of SPEARMINT and water mint, *M. aquatica*, is the most important commercial species of the mint family, Labiatae. A perennial, it is distinguished from spearmint by the greater length of its leaf stalks. The leaves contain an oil that is distilled out and used for flavoring in chewing gum, toothpaste, candy, and medicines. The United States is the world's leading producer of this oil.

Peppermint, a perennial herb, is commercially cultivated for its leaves, which are widely used to flavor tea, candy, mouthwashes, and drugs. Its purple flowers, which grow in spiked heads, bloom in autumn.

Pepperrell, Sir William [pep'-ur-ul]   Sir William Pepperrell, b. June 27, 1696, d. July 6, 1759, was a New England merchant, official, and soldier. He served for many years in the Massachusetts legislature and on the governor's council. A colonel in the colonial militia, Pepperrell led an expeditionary force of New England troops that, together with ships of the Royal Navy, seized (June 17, 1745) the French fortress of LOUISBOURG. For this action he was made (1746) a baronet, a title never before awarded to an American-born British subject.

peptide   Peptides are polymers of AMINO ACIDS that occur naturally in living tissues and play an important role in many biological processes. The amino acids in a peptide are linked by the bonds, called peptide bonds, between their carboxyl (-COOH) and alpha amino ($-NH_2$) groups. Small peptides are classified according to the number of amino acids they contain; larger ones are called polypeptides. Polypeptides with more than 50 amino-acid groups are usually classified as PROTEINS. Among the more familiar peptides are hormones such as adrenocorticotropic hormone, antidiuretic hormone (vasopressin), glucagon, and oxytocin.

Pepys, Samuel [peeps]   The English public servant and writer Samuel Pepys, b. Feb. 23, 1633, d. May 26, 1703, is remembered primarily for his diary, a lively record of 17th-century London, including eyewitness accounts of the Plague and the Great Fire. Written in a code, the diary focuses on Pepys's private life rather than on his distinguished public career.

Pepys was a member of Parliament (1673–79) and president of the Royal Society (1684). Twice secretary of the admiralty (1673–79, 1684–89), he was famed for his naval reforms. Pepys acquired a considerable silver collection and a valuable library, now housed at Magdalene College, Cambridge.

Perceptions accord more often with objects' properties than with the sensory stimulation; for example, a man's perceived height remains constant even though his retinal image size changes as he approaches an observer. There are many such perceptual constancies, which usually cause one to perceive the world more correctly than would be expected from sensory stimulation.

Illusions are cases in which perception accords neither with how the receptors are stimulated nor with the characteristics of the objects themselves. For example, in brightness contrast, an object's reflectance—in fact constant—appears to change when its surroundings change. In these geometrical illusions, the appearance of size or length is drastically altered by the addition of a few slanting lines (in Figure 1, a = b).

Figure 1

Line segment (a) appears to be shorter than line segment (b). In fact, the segments are identical in length.

Pequot [pee'-kwaht] The Algonquian-speaking North American Indians known as the Pequot (from *Pekawatawog*, "the destroyers") were once the most feared tribe of New England. Numbering several thousand, they were part of the MOHEGAN under Chief Sassacus; following the revolt of UNCAS the Pequot faction split away and embarked on a campaign of conquest. Because of Pequot aggression, other tribes sided with the colonists against them. In 1637 the Pequot War, the first major conflict between Indians and whites in New England, ended when the English and their allies destroyed the major Pequot town. The 3,000 surviving Pequot were resettled among their former Indian enemies but were treated so badly that in 1655 the colonists moved them to two reservations on the Mystic River. Current estimates (late 1980s) of their population range between 900 and 1,600.

perception Perception is the process and experience of gaining sensory information about the physical world. In Hermann HELMHOLTZ's classical approach to perceptual theory, the first step was to divide sensory experience into modalities such as vision, touch, and smell, and to subdivide the modalities into elementary sensations (see SENSES AND SENSATION) from which all more complex perceptual experiences—such as those of objects and events—were presumed to be constructed. Sensations were to be explained in terms of their physiological bases (the receptor neurons) and the physical energies to which the receptors are specially adapted to respond.

Constancies, Illusions, and Organizational Phenomena

Three sets of phenomena cause difficulties for classical perceptual theory and have been responsible for most research in perception: constancies, ILLUSIONS, and organizational phenomena.

Whereas experience with the world might teach people to perceive things correctly, as shown by the constancies, it is less evident why experience should result in illusions. Illusions are in fact pervasive phenomena.

The organizational phenomena rest on the perceptual distinction between figure and ground: when a contour gives shape to one area (figure), the region bounded by the other side of the contour (ground) usually has no recognizable shape. Figure 2a is usually perceived as a vase (2b) or as two faces (2c), but not as both simultaneously. Which area becomes figure is therefore critical to what object will be perceived. GESTALT PSYCHOLOGY opposed classical perceptual theory by considering the form (the Gestalt) of the stimulating energies to be the essential attribute. Gestaltists sought laws of organization such as the "law of good continuation," which states that people perceive the figure-ground organization that interrupts the fewest smoothly continuing lines.

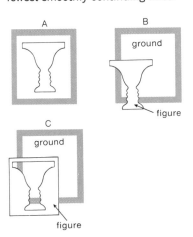

An optical illusion is an image that can be interpreted by the brain in more than one way. The image in this illustration (A) appears alternately as a vase (B) or as a pair of faces turned toward each other (C). Each interpretation vies for dominance in the visual signal sent to the brain.

One explanation of the constancies and illusions that has continued to gain support since Helmholtz is that both reflect the same processes. That is, one perceives those objects or events which would normally be responsible for the sensory stimulation received. In this way, a person's visual system acquires associations that reflect the normal structure of the physical world. For example, the perceptual system learns to take distances into account when estimating the sizes of objects. Such sophisticated inferences are surely not conscious, if in fact they are made at all, so this theory is often phrased as "unconscious inferences based on unnoticed sensations." The theory is difficult to test, because the sensations cannot be directly observed.

Classical Perceptual Theory Revised

Because the elementary experiences (sensations) in classical theory must be considered unobservable and unpredictable (as the constancies, illusions, and organizational phenomena demonstrate), Egon Brunswik restated (1956) Helmholtz's position as follows: Because of the regularities in the physical world, the light at the eye normally contains packets of cues to any property of the physical world. The correlations are usually less than perfect—that is, the cues are only probabilistic. The organism presumably learns to rely on any cue to a degree proportional to the cue's correlation with an object's attributes. Few studies of such correlation have been undertaken, however.

Recent Physiological Findings

Recent physiological and psychophysical study of the nervous system suggests that the latter contains receptive units much more complex than a mere mosaic of photoreceptors (in vision), and that these allow for a more direct perceptual theory than the classical version. Ernst MACH and Ewald Hering, contemporaries of Helmholtz, made early proposals to account explicitly for at least some perception of an object's lightness, form, and distance in terms of innate sensory mechanisms. These proposals have recently gained immensely in popularity with the discovery of lateral connections between the receptors, as well as in the higher levels of the nervous system, that provide for more direct response to object properties. For example, NEURAL NETWORKS exist that respond directly to the *ratio* of the light coming from some object relative to the light from its immediate surroundings. Such responses would normally remain constant with changes in illumination, because any change in lighting of both target and background would proportionally change the light that each of them sends to the eye, leaving the ratio itself intact.

James Jerome Gibson has proposed theories in which the properties of the scenes and events in the perceived world are direct responses to information in the light at the eye. A particular aspect of Gibson's theory—that the visual system registers differences in textural gradients between near and far surfaces and uses these impressions to comprehend depth—has been used successfully in developing computer vision systems.

New Directions in Research

Other lines of research that might test this general theory are in progress. Primary among these is the study of perceptual development. A fair amount of evidence exists that some animals can respond innately to depth cues, thus showing that the classical analysis of sensory processes was at least incomplete in that regard.

In perceiving shape, one sees detail only at the fovea (a small region in the center of the retina), so the eye makes successive rapid, aimed movements, called saccades, at different parts of any object or scene. With each eye movement, of course, the image of the scene shifts on the retina. The shifting retinal images are normally not noticed, a form of constancy that is often explained as a compensation for the eye movements. The question of how individual successive glances are perceived has been studied extensively. Similarly, research on brief "tachistoscopic" glimpses has studied the effects of attention, expectation, familiarity, and motivation. Words with which the viewer is more familiar, has reason to expect, or that accord with his or her interest and concerns will be detected at briefer exposures. Explanations for these effects remain under debate. In any case, however, such research does not address the most serious problem posed by eye movements—how one uses the sequence of partial glimpses to perceive completed objects and scenes.

The process of how one fills out and stores momentary glimpses is close to (and may be identical with) that of mental imagery—that is, experiences of objects not actually stimulating the sense organs. In classical theory, as noted, mental images provided the vehicle for transforming raw sensations into perceptions of the world, but research on imagery proved so unreliable that the problem was set aside for many years. Objective work on imagery has increased on many fronts since the 1970s. Neurologists are studying how neural networks in the brain process perceptual information, and computer scientists continue work (with varying degrees of success) on developing computer analogs of these networks. Studies of people who have suffered brain trauma have also yielded information on perceptual processing centers in the BRAIN. Finally, the field of COGNITIVE PSYCHOLOGY has produced important insights into perception.

See also: SENSORY DEPRIVATION.

———

perch   Perch is a commonly used name for a wide variety of teleost (bony) fishes found in many distantly related families. The Sacramento perch is a SUNFISH (family Centrarchidae), the Rio Grande perch (*Cichlasoma cyanoguttatum*) is a cichlid, and the zebra perch is a sea chub (family Kyphosidae). Surf perches (family Embiotocidae) are among the few viviparous (live-bearing) marine fishes. Other notable perches include the pirate perches (family Aphredoderidae) and trout perches (family Percopsidae) of North America, and the Nile perches (genus *Lates,* family Centropomidae) of Africa. The ocean perch (*Sebastes marinus,* family Scorpaenidae) is a commercially important food fish of the North Atlantic. The white

The yellow perch, like other true perches, has a spiny dorsal fin that precedes a separate, soft-rayed dorsal fin.

perch (*Morone*) is a popular food fish in North America related to the striped bass (*Roccus,* family Serranidae).

To ichthyologists the true perches are members of the family Percidae. Percids are freshwater fishes found in the Northern Hemisphere. They range in size from the darters, such as the least darter (*Etheostoma microperca*), which matures at 2.5 cm (1 in) in length, to the walleye, which may reach 90 cm (36 in) and 11.25 kg (25 lb). Percids are carnivorous.

The family Percidae is composed of two major groups. The subfamily Percinae includes the yellow perch (*Perca flavescens*) and its relatives in Europe and Asia (genus *Perca*), and the darters (several genera, all North American). The darters are recognized by some ichthyologists as a separate subfamily, the Etheostominae. The subfamily Leucopercinae includes the North American pike perches (*Stizostedion*) and two genera of European darterlike fish (*Romanichthys* and *Zingel*).

The yellow perch has six to nine dark bars along its sides. It inhabits lakes, ponds, and slow-moving streams. Originally found only east of the Rocky Mountains, it has been widely introduced as a sport fish. The yellow perch matures between 11.25 and 30 cm (4.5 and 12 in) in length; its average weight is 0.45 kg (1 lb). The species tends to breed in the spring and can produce as many as 300,000 eggs, depending on the size of the female.

The leucopercids include two popular North American game fishes: the walleye (*Stizostedion vitreum*) and the sauger (*S. canadense*), which resembles the walleye in general appearance but is a smaller fish.

Percheron   see HORSE

perching birds   The perching birds comprise the largest bird order, Passeriformes, which includes approximately 5,100 species, or more than one-half of all living species of birds. Commonly called passerines, they first appear in the fossil record in the Eocene Epoch (54 to 38 million years ago). During the Cenozoic Era they have undergone an explosive ADAPTIVE RADIATION, culminating in their present great diversity. The reasons for their evolutionary success are poorly understood, but an important factor is their generally small size.

In passerines the bones of the palate are arranged in a manner found only rarely in other birds. The foot is of a characteristic form, with three toes directed forward and the large first toe (hallux) directed backward and placed at the same level as the other toes. The opposing hallux adapts the foot for grasping perches, although some species are ground dwellers as well. In the wing, passerines have ten primary feathers arising from the hand, although in some the outermost primary is reduced to a vestige. Passerines in general have a well-developed syrinx, or voice organ, and many of these birds produce extremely complex vocalizations.

There are several suborders. The suborder Tyranni includes nine families, of which one, Tyrannidae, reaches North America. The Tyranni include the cotingas, manakins, sharpbill, plantcutters, pittas, asities, and, with uncertainty, the New Zealand wrens and the broadbill.

The suborder Furnarii, an entirely New World group, ranges through South and Central America. It includes the woodcreepers, ovenbirds, antbirds, and tapaculas.

The suborder Menurae includes two families endemic to Australia: the Atrichornithidae (scrubbirds) and the Menuridae (lyrebirds). The suborder Passeres (or Oscines, also called SONGBIRDS) is the largest group, with about 4,000 species.

percussion instruments   see MUSICAL INSTRUMENTS

Percy (family)   The Percy family, descended from Normans who were first settled by William I (the Conquerer) in Yorkshire, played an important role in English political history. The acquisition (1309) of Alnwick Castle by **Henry Percy**, 1272–1315, made the family a power on the Scottish border. Another **Henry Percy**, b. 1342, d. Feb. 20, 1408, an associate of JOHN OF GAUNT's, was named 1st earl of Northumberland in 1377. He and his son Henry—nicknamed **Hotspur**—b. May 20, 1364, d. July 21, 1403, supported HENRY IV against Richard II in 1399, but the Percys later quarreled with Henry over the ransom of Scottish prisoners. Both died in rebellions against Henry IV—Hotspur at Shrewsbury and Northumberland at Bramham Moor. During the Wars of the Roses (1455–85), the Percys supported the Lancastrian king Henry VI.

The family retained strong Roman Catholic ties after the Reformation. **Thomas Percy, 7th earl of Northumberland**, 1528–72, was beheaded for supporting Mary, Queen of Scots, in the Northern Rebellion (1569), and another **Thomas Percy**, b. *c.*1560, d. Nov. 9, 1605, was involved in the Gunpowder Plot (1605). In 1766 the Percy family acquired the title duke of Northumberland, a title they have retained, along with the ancestral Alnwick Castle.

Percy, Walker   The American novelist Walker Percy, b. Birmingham, Ala., May 28, 1916, d. May 10, 1990, practiced medicine for a year before contracting tuberculosis. Reflecting the existentialist philosophers that he read during his recuperation, Percy's first novel, *The Moviegoer* (1961; National Book Award), is about a deeply alienated man. In *Love in the Ruins* (1971), Percy deals allegorically with the redemption of a failed man living through civilization's technological collapse. *Lancelot* (1977) wryly tackles questions of religious faith, and *The Second Coming* (1980) deals with a prosperous Southerner's mental breakdown. Dr. Thomas More, protagonist of *Love in the Ruins*, reappears in *The Thanatos Syndrome* (1987), Percy's first thriller.

peregrine falcon   see FALCON

Pereira, Nuno Álvares [pay-ray'-rah]
Nuno Álvares Pereira, 1360–1431, was a military leader allied with JOHN I, the first Portuguese monarch of the house of Avis. Nuno Álvares led John's forces to victories against Castilian invaders in the Battle of Aljubarrota (1385) and in later confrontations that helped to ensure John's kingdom. Known as the Holy Constable, he retired to a Carmelite monastery and was beatified in 1918. Through his daughter Beatriz, Nuno Álvares was an ancestor of Portugal's Bragança dynasty.

Perelman, S. J. [purl'-muhn]
Sidney Joseph Perelman, b. Brooklyn, N.Y., Feb. 1, 1904, d. Oct. 17, 1979, was an American humorist, playwright, and Hollywood screenwriter whose pieces appeared regularly in the *New Yorker* after 1931. Perelman's most successful Broadway play, the musical comedy *One Touch of Venus* (1943), was written in collaboration with Ogden Nash and Kurt Weill. Making use of parody, hyperbole, outrageous puns, and an extensive vocabulary, Perelman satirized everything from fiction and films to advertising and current fads in such archly titled volumes as *The Road to Miltown; or, Under the Spreading Atrophy* (1957) and *Eastward Ha!* (1977). His humor can be sampled in *The Best of S. J. Perelman* (1947).

Peres, Shimon [pair'-ez, shee'-mohn]
Shimon Peres, b. Poland, Aug. 16, 1923, was prime minister of Israel in a Labor-Likud government from 1984 to 1986 and finance minister in the same coalition, with Likud's Yitzhak SHAMIR as prime minister, from 1986 to 1988. After the 1988 election this coalition was renewed, with Peres as finance minister. It collapsed in March 1990 due to disagreements over peace policy, but Peres survived a challenge to his party leadership from Yitzhak RABIN after Shamir formed a right-wing government. In Palestine from 1934, Peres became active in the Jewish underground and the Mapai party. A protégé of David BEN-GURION and a defense expert, he was elected to the Knesset in 1959 and helped found (1968) the Labor party. He held cabinet posts under Golda MEIR and Yitzhak Rabin and served (1977–84, 1990–) as opposition leader.

perestroika [pe-re-stroy'-kah]
Perestroika (Russian: restructuring) is the term used by Soviet president Mikhail GORBACHEV to describe his program of political and economic reforms, implemented in the late 1980s. Closely linked to his concepts of GLASNOST (openness) and democratization, *perestroika* was declared by Gorbachev to be a second revolution that would further the aims of the Bolshevik revolution of 1917. His political reforms included a restructuring of the central government of the USSR, the introduction of multicandidate elections, a relaxation of censorship, and, most radically, an end to the Communist party's monopoly of political power. Among his economic changes were a reintroduction of limited private enterprise, a more flexible price structure, and decentralization of economic decision making. In foreign policy, *perestroika* led to the breakup of the Soviet satellite system in Eastern Europe and the end of the cold war with the West. By 1990, however, the loosening of political and economic controls had permitted the emergence of separatist movements in the Soviet republics and work stoppages in the industrial sector, as well as causing major disruptions in the system of supply, severe shortages of consumer goods, and dramatic increases in retail prices.

Peretz, Y. L. [pair'-ets]
The major Yiddish writer Yitzchak Leibush Peretz, b. May 18, 1852, d. Apr. 3, 1915, forms, together with Mendele Mokher Sefarim and Sholem Aleichem, the classical triumvirate of Yiddish literature. Peretz received a religious education in his native Polish village, wrote prolifically between 1870 and 1878, then studied and practiced law until the Russian authorities revoked his license in 1887. He thereafter began a literary career in Warsaw, writing first in Polish and Hebrew but finally choosing Yiddish as the most effective medium in which to address a Jewish audience.

Peretz excelled in every form—poetry, drama, essays, but especially the short story. He first attracted wide attention with his ballad *Monish* (1888), the tragedy of a man engaged in a desperate struggle with demonic forces within himself. He published his first collection of Yiddish stories in 1890. *Stories and Pictures* (1901; Eng. trans., 1906), *Hasidic Tales* (1908), and *Folk Tales* (1909) were subsequently translated into many languages. His most active period as a playwright (1906–09) culminated in *The Golden Chain* (1909; Eng. trans., 1953), a powerful drama of a great personality who tries to raise ordinary mortals into a messianic realm of holiness.

Pérez de Cuéllar, Javier [pay'-res de kway'-yar, hah-vee-air']
The Peruvian diplomat Javier Pérez de Cuéllar, b. Jan. 19, 1920, succeeded Kurt Waldheim as secretary-general of the United Nations (UN) in January 1982; he began a second term in 1987. A former ambassador to the USSR, Pérez de Cuéllar led (1971–75) Peru's delegation to the UN and also served as UN under-secretary-general for special political affairs.

performance art
Performance art is a term applied to a great variety of "action art" presentations that nearly always involve several media. The HAPPENINGS of the

1960s were precursors of the hybrid performance pieces that developed in the 1980s. Visual and sound elements are two customary components of performance art, but these can be combined in many ways.

Laurie Anderson is the most widely known of the American multimedia performance artists. Her *Empty Places* (1989), like the earlier *United States* (1983), blends songs, anecdotes, film, slides, and electronic music in interconnected fragments. Such American writer-monologuists as Karen Finley, Eric Bogosian, and Spalding Gray are often called performance artists.

perfume   Compounds of fragrant essences obtained from plants and other odorous substances, perfumes have a history as ancient as Egypt, where tomb remains reveal the use of fragrant ointments and oils. Avicenna, an Arab physician, is said to have discovered the distillation process that greatly reduced the cost of making the ESSENTIAL OILS used in perfumery.

The first modern perfume, made of scented oils blended in an alcohol solution, was made in 1370 at the command of Queen Elizabeth of Hungary and was known throughout Europe as Hungary Water. The art of perfumery prospered in Renaissance Italy; in the 16th century, France became the European center of perfume and COSMETIC manufacture.

In the 1920s the great clothing designers of Paris began to promote fragrances that carried their house names: Worth, Chanel, Patou. American fashion designers are presently using the same technique.

Fragrances. The essential oils that are the foundation for perfumes are taken from a large variety of plants. The most important, however, are bitter orange blossoms, jasmine, and rose. Citrus oils are obtained from the peel, leaves and shoots, and flowers of various citrus fruits, especially the pear-shaped, inedible BERGAMOT.

Aromatic synthetic chemicals supply new odors not found in natural substances. Some synthetics are used to create floral fragrances resembling those of flowers that do not yield oils.

Fixatives. Fixatives are used to bind the various fragrance elements together and to equalize their rate of evaporation. They are obtained from balsams, resins, and animal secretions. The most important are those from the scent glands of the civet cat (civet); from the male musk deer (MUSK); from the beaver (castor); and from AMBERGRIS, a fatty substance that is the product of the sperm whale.

Fragrances and fixatives are diluted and blended in pure alcohol, chilled and filtered, and then aged for up to a year.

Pergamum [pur'-guh-muhm]   Pergamum was an ancient Greek city on the Aegean coast of ANATOLIA, at the site of present-day Bergama. The territory surrounding the city was granted to the Greek settlers by the Persian emperors Darius I and Xerxes I. In the turbulent era following the death of Alexander the Great (323 BC), Pergamum became the capital of a flourishing Hellenistic kingdom and one of the principal centers of Hellenistic civilization, with a library that rivaled Alexandria's, a famous school of sculpture, and important public buildings. Under Kings ATTALUS I and EUMENES II, Pergamum reached the height of its independent powers; at the same time it began to look to Rome for alliance against the warring Hellenistic rulers. After Attalus III bequeathed (133 BC) his domains to the Romans, the city retained its position as the pre-eminent artistic and intellectual center of Anatolia but declined in political and economic importance.

Pergolesi, Giovanni Battista [per-goh-lay'-zee] The founder of Italian comic opera (opera buffa), Giovanni Battista Pergolesi, b. Jan. 4, 1710, d. Mar. 16, 1736, had one of the shortest life spans among notable composers. In his youth he was sent to a Naples conservatory and began his career as a composer soon after, writing church music and both serious and comic operas for Naples and Rome. He became deputy music director of the city of Naples and served various noble patrons before illness (possibly tuberculosis) cut short his career, then his life. His reputation soared after his death. His short comic opera *La serva padrona* (The Maid as Mistress, 1733) swept Europe; its performance in Paris in 1752 provoked a pamphlet war between the partisans of French and Italian opera (the "War of the Bouffons") and led to the founding of French *opéra comique*. Pergolesi's fame today rests primarily on this work and a sacred piece, his *Stabat Mater* (1736). His music was influential in the formation of the rococo style.

pericarditis   SEE HEART DISEASES

Pericles [per'-i-kleez]   Pericles, c.495–429 BC, was the political leader of Athens from about 460 to 429, the period in which Athenian culture and military power were at their height. His name is associated with the greatest artistic creations of the age, and he initiated the great

Pericles was the leading Athenian statesman during the golden age of Greek culture. A brilliant and cultured leader, Pericles strengthened the military power of Athens, broadened its democracy, and patronized its great artists and writers. (Roman copy of 5th-century BC Greek bust. Museo Vaticano, Rome.)

public building program that produced the Parthenon.

Pericles entered politics in 463 BC by prosecuting CI-MON. Shortly afterward, in association with Ephialtes, he implemented major democratic reforms. After a war against Sparta and its allies was concluded in 446–445, he tightened Athens's control of its empire, crushing major rebellions, imposing democratic governments, and dispatching colonies of Athenian citizens to strategic areas.

Convinced of the inevitability of war with Sparta and the Peloponnesians, Pericles made (433 BC) an alliance with Corinth's enemy, Corcyra (modern Corfu). He also refused Sparta's demand that he revoke the Megarian decree, which denied Megara access to the harbors of the empire. These actions led to the PELOPONNESIAN WAR (431–404), in which Pericles' strategy was to rely on the fleet and the empire's resources, and to avoid a pitched battle with the Peloponnesians in Attica. He fell victim to the plague, however, never to know that the war he initiated would result in the disastrous defeat of Athens. The historian THUCYDIDES nevertheless admired his singular control of the Athenian democracy.

peridot [per'-i-doh]   Peridot [$(Mg,Fe)_2SiO_4$]—the birthstone for August—is gem-quality OLIVINE, a ferromagnesian SILICATE MINERAL. Olivine forms transparent to translucent, olive green to brownish or yellow crystals (orthorhombic system) and compact or granular masses. Transparent stones of olive green color are denoted peridot; yellowish material is chrysolite. The hardness of peridot is 6½–7, luster is vitreous, and specific gravity is 3.3–3.4. The finest peridot has been produced from the mines on Saint John's Island in the Red Sea since at least AD 70. Burmese peridot is noted for the size of its crystals.

Peridot is a transparent, green gem variety of olivine, a magnesium-iron silicate that crystallizes in the orthorhombic system (left). *It is usually cut with a series of facets* (right) *and set with other jewels in necklaces, brooches, and earrings.*

peridotite   Large sections of the Earth's mantle are thought to be peridotite, a plutonic IGNEOUS ROCK composed mainly of coarse grains of OLIVINE (a variety of which is called peridot, from which the rock's name is derived). Peridotites may also contain substantial

amounts of pyroxene, hornblende, and mica, and small amounts of apatite, chromite, garnet, magnetite, and pyrrhotite. Peridotites are often partially or largely altered to serpentinite. Some are of economic value, providing ores of chromium and asbestos (pyroxene peridotite) and diamonds (mica peridotite, or KIMBERLITE).

period-luminosity relation   see VARIABLE STAR

periodic motion   see MOTION, HARMONIC

periodic table   The periodic table is a classification and tabulation of the chemical ELEMENTS in the order of their atomic numbers that permits systematic explanation and prediction of many of the elements' chemical and physical properties.

Development of the Periodic Table

As the 19th century began, chemistry had progressed to the point of defining an element as a substance that could not be decomposed into a simpler substance by any known means. The number of substances thus defined increased rapidly, but there was no way of telling how many remained to be discovered or where they might be expected to be discovered. As the number increased, however, it became evident that certain groups of elements could be classified into families with similar chemical properties. Thus, the reactions of lithium, sodium, and potassium resembled each other closely, as did those of chlorine, bromine, and iodine.

The actual discovery of the periodic law came in the years between 1868 and 1870 and was made almost simultaneously by Lothar Meyer in Germany and Dmitry Ivanovich Mendeleyev in Russia. Meyer arranged the 57 elements known to him in the order of their atomic weights, leaving blank spaces where the properties of the elements seemed to indicate that one was missing. He was particularly concerned with the physical properties of the elements, such as their atomic volumes, and he saw that similar values for these recurred periodically after every seventh element in his table.

At the same time, Mendeleyev, who was engaged in writing a chemistry textbook that later became world famous, reached a conclusion similar to that of Meyer but based instead largely on the chemical properties of the elements. He also left blank spaces where elements were obviously missing, and he went well beyond Meyer in his published tables (1869 to 1870). In several cases the atomic weights of elements, as they had been determined at the time, indicated misplacement of the position of the elements in these tables. Mendeleyev did not hesitate to say that these atomic weights were incorrect. Even more boldly, he predicted in detail what the chemical and physical properties of the missing elements would be when they were found. Using the Sanskrit word for the numeral one, *eka*, he prefixed the names of known elements that were situated above missing ones in his table. Thus he described the properties of what he called ekaaluminum, ekaboron, and ekasilicon. Mendeleyev's pre-

	IA	IIA	IIIB	IVB	VB	VIB	VIIB	VIII	VIII	VIII	IB	IIB	IIIA	IVA	VA	VIA	VIIA	O
1	1 H																	2 He
2	3 Li	4 Be											5 B	6 C	7 N	8 O	9 F	10 Ne
3	11 Na	12 Mg											13 Al	14 Si	15 P	16 S	17 Cl	18 Ar
4	19 K	20 Ca	21 Sc	22 Ti	23 V	24 Cr	25 Mn	26 Fe	27 Co	28 Ni	29 Cu	30 Zn	31 Ga	32 Ge	33 As	34 Se	35 Br	36 Kr
5	37 Rb	38 Sr	39 Y	40 Zr	41 Nb	42 Mo	43 Tc	44 Ru	45 Rh	46 Pd	47 Ag	48 Cd	49 In	50 Sn	51 Sb	52 Te	53 I	54 Xe
6	55 Cs	56 Ba	57 58 La to 71	72 Hf	73 Ta	74 W	75 Re	76 Os	77 Ir	78 Pt	79 Au	80 Hg	81 Tl	82 Pb	83 Bi	84 Po	85 At	86 Rn
7	87 Fr	88 Ra	89 90 Ac to 103	104 Unq	105 Unp	106 Unh	107 Uns	108 Uno	109 Une									

● Metals   Nonmetals

Lanthanide series	58 Ce	59 Pr	60 Nd	61 Pm	62 Sm	63 Eu	64 Gd	65 Tb	66 Dy	67 Ho	68 Er	69 Tm	70 Yb	71 Lu
Actinide series	90 Th	91 Pa	92 U	93 Np	94 Pu	95 Am	96 Cm	97 Bk	98 Cf	99 Es	100 Fm	101 Md	102 No	103 Lr

In the periodic table the chemical elements are arranged in horizontal rows (periods) by increasing atomic number, listed above the symbol for each element. The vertical columns represent groups of elements that have similar chemical properties because they have the same number of valence electrons. Elements in blue are metals; those in yellow are nonmetals. Elements 104 onward are being given names that are the Latin form of their number, such as "unnilquadium" for 104.

dictions were soon confirmed. New atomic-weight determinations corrected the values he had questioned, and the discovery of the actual elements gallium, scandium, and germanium showed that these had almost exactly the properties that he had indicated for them.

Arrangement of the Periodic Table

From that time on, the periodic table—as it began to be called—assumed the basic form that, in spite of some modifications, it has retained ever since. Hydrogen, recognized as an anomalous element, is placed by itself at the beginning of the chart. The elements that follow are arranged horizontally so that each vertical column comprises a family of elements having similar chemical properties.

Originally, there were seven families, designated by Roman numerals I to VII. Later, the numeral VIII was assigned to a group of transition metals with similar properties, and separate A and B columns were created to reflect property differences. Two distinct systems for naming families became common. The U.S. system is represented by the table given here, except for the zero designation of the inert gases, which is part of the European system; the U.S. system labels them VIIIA. The European system also reverses the A and B suffixes on families III through VII. In order to have a truly single system, a simple numbering of the columns from left to right as 1 through 18 has been recommended by the authoritative body, the International Union of Pure and Applied Chemistry. This new system has been accepted by some, but not yet by all.

Periodicity and Atomic Theory

Although the table fit observed facts very well by the end of the 19th century, it still lacked a theoretical underpinning. The next major step was to explain the positions of the elements in the table. This was accomplished by physicists rather than chemists. At the end of the 19th and the beginning of the 20th century great progress was made in elucidating the structure of the ATOM itself.

The most direct application of the new atomic theories to the periodic table came from the work of Henry G. J. Moseley in 1913. Moseley bombarded a number of different target metals with a stream of electrons and observed that X rays were produced. The frequency of these X rays varied in a characteristic manner from element to element. The shift could be expressed mathematically by a unit number, which Moseley called the ATOMIC NUMBER. The order of these numbers was exactly the same as the order of elements in the periodic table, except that the discrepancies in the order based on atomic weights for argon and potassium, iodine and tellurium, and cobalt and nickel disappeared and each element took its proper place in the order of elements. It was quickly realized that the atomic number represented the positive charge of the atomic nucleus and that this charge increased by one as the elements advanced along the table. ATOMIC WEIGHTS were later recognized as having some variation because they are actually averages of the atomic weights of all the naturally occurring ISOTOPES with the same atomic number.

The concept of the atomic number also indicated exactly where missing elements occurred in the periodic table, and the chemical properties of each missing element as shown by the table itself indicated where those elements should be sought in nature. Using these criteria as guides, hafnium and rhenium were soon discovered, though all attempts to discover elements 43 (an analog of rhenium), 61 (a rare earth), 85 (a HALOGEN), and 87 (an ALKALI METAL) remained unsuccessful. With these exceptions, the table from hydrogen, atomic number 1, to uranium, 92, was complete.

As the structure of the atom became clearer, so did the theoretical explanation for the periodic table. Atomic structure was based on the picture proposed by Niels BOHR in 1913. The atomic number was identified with the number of protons—positively charged particles—present in the nucleus of each atom. Balancing this is an equal number of negatively charged electrons orbiting the nucleus in a series of shells designated by the letters $K, L, M,$ and so on. The innermost shell, $K,$ holds either one electron, corresponding to hydrogen, or two, corresponding to the inert gas helium. When the K shell is complete, a new shell, $L,$ accommodates 8 electrons, accounting for the next 8 elements to the next inert gas, neon, atomic number 10. A similar progression fills the next shell and gives the 8 elements from sodium (Na) through argon (Ar).

Beginning with the fourth period, space must be made in the table for series of elements (the TRANSITION ELEMENTS) in which electron shells can accommodate not 8 but 18 and then 32 electrons. In this arrangement, elements with similar chemical properties fall in the same columns across the entire table. This periodicity of properties is accounted for by the arrangements of electrons in atoms—atoms of elements in the same column have identical or very similar arrangements of their electrons.

Chemists now recognize that the chemical properties of an element are determined by the number of electrons occupying the outermost electron levels of its atoms (see ELECTRON CONFIGURATION). Thus, for example, the inert gases (Group 0) are not reactive, because their outermost electron levels are filled with 8 electrons. In contrast, the halogens (Group VIIA) are very reactive because they have 7 outermost electrons and readily gain 1 more. For elements in the A groups, the group number indicates the number of outermost electrons.

Radioactivity

The final vindication of the periodic table came from the study of RADIOACTIVITY, the spontaneous emission of energy as particles or electromagnetic radiation by atoms with unstable nuclei. It was found that radioactive elements are undergoing spontaneous conversion (transmutation) into different elements with more stable nuclei. For example, emission of an alpha particle (a helium ion, which has two protons) moves an element two places to the left in the periodic table, as expected for a decrease by two in the atomic number.

Artificial Transmutation

Once the idea of the interconversion of elements had been accepted, it became apparent that artificial transmutation might be possible if some sort of charged particle could be introduced into a nucleus to make it unstable. In the 1930s the Joliot-Curies succeeded in creating artificially radioactive isotopes by bombarding metals with alpha rays.

With the development of the cyclotron by Ernest Lawrence, much more powerful bombarding particles became available. In 1937, Emilio Segré succeeded in making missing element 43, the first artificially produced element. It was named technetium from the Greek word for "artificial." Soon, other gaps in the periodic table were filled by production of the radioactive elements promethium (element 61), astatine (element 85), and francium (element 87).

The even more exciting prospect of creating new elements heavier than uranium was realized in 1940, when Edwin M. McMillan produced element 93. He named it neptunium, the first element beyond uranium, just as Neptune is the first planet beyond Uranus. Under the direction of Glenn Seaborg, McMillan's colleague, element 94 was produced as part of the atomic-bomb project. Following publication of this work in 1964, the production of TRANSURANIUM ELEMENTS has been actively pursued. Thus far, elements 95 to 109 have been synthesized. The transuranium elements complete the ACTINIDE SERIES of elements that parallel the rare earths—the LANTHANIDE SERIES. The lanthanides and actinides are placed together at the bottom of the periodic table. Transuranium elements of atomic number 104 and higher fall in the seventh period in the main part of the table.

---

periodical   Periodicals are bound, paper-covered magazines or other publications issued regularly—usually weekly, fortnightly, monthly, or quarterly—to inform, instruct, or entertain. The word *magazine* is derived from the French *magasin,* "storehouse," and evidently was first used (1731) by the *Gentleman's Magazine* of London.

More than 11,500 periodicals were published in the United States at the end of the 1980s. Three-quarters of the U.S. adult population buys one or more magazines in the course of a year, and increasingly, readers subscribe, usually for a year's worth of issues, rather than buy single issues as they are published. Advertisers bought an annual $6 billion in magazine advertising in the late 1980s, a sum representing slightly more than 5 percent of total advertising expenditures. (In contrast, newspapers received more than 25 percent.)

History

The first periodical was perhaps the French *Journal des*

Scavans (1665–1792). British periodicals such as the *Gentleman's Magazine* and the *London Magazine* became models for magazines in the colonies. The first magazine published in the colonies was Andrew Bradford's short-lived *American Magazine* of Philadelphia, issued on Feb. 13, 1741, which was followed three days later by Benjamin Franklin's *General Magazine.*

Until the late 19th century, low circulation and little if any advertising kept revenues down and prevented most magazines from surviving for more than a few years. *Godey's Lady's Book,* later *Godey's Magazine* (1830–98), however, with its sentimental fiction, poetry, and light essays, as well as colored fashion plates and art engravings, was published for more than five decades; *Harper's* (1850) and the *Atlantic Monthly* (1857) still survive. A boom in new magazines after the Civil War increased the number of periodicals from 700 in 1865 to 3,300 in 1885.

Late-19th-Century Developments. The modern magazine of low price, popular appeal, and national circulation was born in the 1890s. Among the reasons for this development were the growth of industry, which produced brand-name merchandise for a national market and, consequently, the rise of advertising; technological advances in printing, which allowed large press runs; a redistribution of income, increasing the number of potential readers and therefore the number of potential buyers of advertised products; and an increase in literacy.

Publishers responsible for the birth of the modern magazine included Cyrus H. K. CURTIS, Frank Andrew MUNSEY, and S. S. McClure. In 1883, Curtis started the 10-cent *Ladies' Home Journal,* and under the brilliant editorship of Edward William BOK it achieved sales of nearly a million by the century's end. In 1897, Curtis acquired the weekly *Saturday Evening Post,* which rapidly became a leader in circulation and advertising. According to one estimate, the 3,500 magazines that ex-

isted in 1900 had combined sales of 65 million.

The trade and technical press had several forerunners—lists of current prices issued as early as 1609 in Amsterdam and 1744 in Charleston, S.C., and the early-19th-century American shipping lists, reports of public sales, and local commercial newspapers. Periodicals for specialized occupations appeared as early as the 1830s.

The 20th Century. The period between the two world wars saw the establishment of the news weekly TIME and the picture weekly LIFE, the two magazines on which publishing magnate Henry R. LUCE established his empire; and the founding (1922) of *Reader's Digest,* which reprinted condensed versions of articles from other magazines and became the prototype for the many pocket-style periodicals that followed (see WALLACE, DEWITT).

The rapid social changes that have occurred in the past decades have been mirrored in the growth of new kinds of publications: *Playboy* (1953) successfully responded to the new mores of the time; *Ms.* (1972), among others, answered to the changing role of women in the United States; *Ebony* (1945), *Jet* (1951), and *Essence* (1970) echoed African-American pride; *Interview* (1969) exploited Americans' obsession with celebrity; *Premiere* (1987) plumbed its obsession with movies and movie stars. The phenomenally successful *Sports Illustrated* (1954) and the dozens of specialized sports publications that followed focused on the American enthusiasm for excellence in every variety of game.

In the 1960s the movement toward narrower audiences led to the proliferation of city magazines. In 1925, Harold Ross had established the *New Yorker* for a sophisticated, affluent, metropolitan audience, and publishers across the United States tried in vain to duplicate its success. From the early 1960s, however, a number of privately owned local magazines catering to the interests of urban communities have achieved high sales. Among the

Before the widespread use of photographs in journalism, popular weekly magazines vied for attention with colorful cover illustrations. Maxfield Parrish contributed to Collier's (left), *and Norman Rockwell's paintings appeared in the* Saturday Evening Post (center). *This tradition is continued by the* New Yorker (right).

most successful are *New York Magazine, Atlanta, Chicago, Philadelphia,* and *Washingtonian.* Other such monthlies cover individual states.

By the late 1970s, because of sharp increases in postal rates, major magazines were exploring alternative systems for delivery of copies to subscribers. With a decline in the number of newsstands, supermarkets became a major outlet for single-copy sales. Rising costs led periodicals to pass on to their readers a larger share of their costs. When television emerged as a competitor for audiences and advertising in the mid-1950s, periodicals strove for ever-larger circulations; in the last years of the 1980s, however, high costs and the power of television had reduced magazine advertising significantly.

New Publication Technologies

A series of fundamental changes in periodical publishing has occurred within the past decade. Computerized transmittal of text and pictures over improved telephone systems has meant that news magazines, for example, can be almost as current as newspapers. Computerized typesetting and page layout has further shortened the time needed to produce an issue. Finally, by mixing computerized printing with new binding operations, it has become possible to print and bind different pages within the same edition of a magazine, creating market specificity.

▬

periodontics [per-ee-oh-dahn'-tiks] Periodontics is a specialty of DENTISTRY concerned with the health of the tissues that surround and support teeth. Periodontal disease is caused by bacterial plaque, a gummy film that coats the surface of teeth. If not removed, the bacteria produce toxins that cause inflamed gums that bleed easily. This early stage of gum disease is called gingivitis. Plaque that migrates below the gum line causes advanced gum disease called periodontitis, or PYORRHEA. This disease causes gums to pull away from teeth; pockets to form that fill with pus and cell debris; and jawbone degeneration.

Early stages of periodontal disease can be effectively treated with regular oral hygiene. A dental specialist, the periodontist, treats more advanced periodontal diseases with a variety of methods: thorough cleaning to remove plaque, antibiotics that kill disease-causing bacteria, and surgery to remove infected tissues and to reshape pockets.

▬

Peripatetics [per-i-puh-tet'-iks] The Peripatetic school of philosophy, founded by ARISTOTLE, was named for the prominent *peripatos,* or covered walking place, that belonged to the school building, the Lyceum, in Athens. The school was a center for critical research and rivaled Plato's Academy. Following Aristotle's death (322 BC), his successor THEOPHRASTUS elaborated on metaphysical and psychological theory and stressed the study of the natural sciences. Strato, head of the school from 287 to 269 BC, did some interesting work in physical theory, but the school soon lost touch with Aristotle's major works (either through

indifference or unavailability) and began to decline.

The recovery of Aristotle's manuscripts in the 1st century BC and the new edition of his logical works—called *Organon* ("instrument") and produced in Rome by Andronicus of Rhodes—reawakened interest in Aristotelianism. In the third century AD, however, the Peripatetic school was absorbed by NEOPLATONISM, proponents of which used Aristotle's works as their methodological base.

▬

Peripatus [puh-rip'-uh-tuhs] *Peripatus* is a genus of segmented, wormlike animals sometimes called walking worms because of the presence of 14 or more pairs of stumpy, nonjointed legs. *Peripatus* and its relatives constitute the phylum Onychophora, which is of great biological interest because the members of this group possess features of both the annelid worms and the arthropods. The body wall, for example, is annelidlike, but its outer covering, or cuticle, is arthropodlike in general structure and chemical composition; penetrating the cuticle are the scattered openings of the arthropodlike tracheal-tube breathing system. The most obvious external evidence of body segmentation in *Peripatus* is the long, regularly spaced series of paired legs. *Peripatus* is found in the humid tropics of the Western Hemisphere, as far north as central Mexico. The largest onychophoran is a species of *Peripatus* that sometimes attains 15 cm (6 in) in length.

peripheral nervous system   see NERVOUS SYSTEM

▬

periscope   The periscope is an optical instrument that allows its user to see what is not directly within viewing range. The simplest type of periscope, used in trench warfare from the 19th century, is a tube with two mirrors set parallel to one another. The top mirror reflects the scene at the tube top; the observer views the scene from the bottom mirror. Far more complex periscopes are in use in submarines and tanks, and to achieve remote viewing in inaccessible areas such as nuclear reactors, rocket engines, or—as miniature instruments—inside the human body (see ENDOSCOPE).

Light enters the standard periscope through a top prism that shifts its direction downward. Reflected through several lenses, it reaches a bottom prism that restores the rays to the horizontal and thence into an eye lens. In remote viewing, bundles of glass fibers relay images, often along curved paths (see FIBER OPTICS).

▬

perissodactyl [puh-ris-uh-dak'-tul] The mammalian order Perissodactyla includes 3 families of medium-sized to large herbivores: horses (Equidae), tapirs (Tapiridae), and rhinoceroses (Rhinocerotidae), with 6 living genera and 17 species. They are all odd-toed animals, with either one or three hoofed toes on each hind foot. The name Perissodactyla comes from the Greek *perissos,* "odd," and *daktylos,* "finger," and distinguishes the odd-toed ungulates (hoofed herbivores) from the even-toed, or Artiodactyla.

Perissodactyls bear most of their weight on the central toes. The third toe is the longest, and this is the only functional digit. The RHINOCEROS walks on all three toes of each foot. The TAPIR has four developed digits on the front feet and three on the hind feet. Like the artiodactyls, perissodactyls are good runners, especially the HORSE.

The mammary glands are located in the groin area. The cheek, or grinding, teeth are well developed, complex, and massive, whereas canine teeth are small if present at all. Perissodactyls graze (eat grass) and browse (munch shoots and leaves from bushes and trees).

Horses, asses, and zebras are the most numerous of the perissodactyls. Living species of horses and asses are native to Europe and Asia but are now found worldwide. Zebras are indigenous to Africa. Rhinoceroses are native to Africa and Asia. Tapirs live in Central and South America and in Southeast Asia.

Perissodactyls of today are the sparse descendants of phenacodontids, which flourished in the Paleocene and Eocene epochs (65 million to 54 million years ago) and played a leading role in the animal life of that time.

peristalsis [per-i-stal'-sis]   Peristalsis is one of several types of patterns of movement associated with the gastrointestinal tract. It can be described as a moving, coordinated wave of muscular contraction that is propulsive in

Diagramed (above left) is the portion of the human digestive tract from the pharynx (1) to the rectum (2). The walls of most of the tract contain an inner circular muscle coat (3) and an outer longitudinal muscle coat (4). As a ball of food (5) enters the pharynx, a reflex action is initiated. The peristaltic reflex consists of waves of muscle contractions behind the food and muscle relaxation in front of it. The circular and longitudinal muscles function together to push the food through (A, B) the digestive tract and toward eventual elimination. Peristalsis occurs in the esophagus, stomach, and intestines.

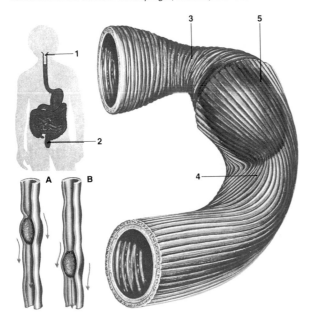

nature, forcing the contents of the digestive tract ahead of it. Peristalsis occurs most frequently in the esophagus, where it is stimulated by a swallow (primary peristalsis) and moves the entire length of the esophagus to the stomach. A peristaltic wave may also occur in the absence of a swallow (secondary peristalsis). A secondary peristalsis is elicited when the esophagus is distended— if the primary wave fails to clear the esophagus of food, or if gastric contents reflux into the esophagus. Peristaltic waves also occur in the small intestine but rarely travel more than 4 cm (1.6 in). In the large intestine peristalsis is responsible for the two or three mass movements that occur daily. Peristalsis is controlled largely by central and local nerves.

peritonitis [per-i-tuh-ny'-tis]   Peritonitis, an acute inflammation of the membrane (peritoneum) that lines the abdominal cavity, is usually caused by infection from bacteria entering the cavity through a perforation in the gastrointestinal tract. Bacteria that cause the infection include *Escherichia coli*, streptococci, and pneumococci. The perforation can result from wounds, blood clots, or such disorders as colitis, gastric ulcer, appendicitis, and chronic liver disease. Uterine infections, particularly those caused by rupture or injury of the uterus during instrument abortions, may spread into the abdominal cavity. Peritonitis can cause intestinal paralysis, severe abdominal pain, and distension of the abdominal cavity with fluids from the bloodstream. The resultant fever, diarrhea, dehydration, or shock can be fatal if left untreated. Treatment may include antibiotics, surgery, and restoration of body fluids.

periwinkle   Periwinkles, genus *Vinca*, are about 12 species of plants in the dogbane family, Apocynaceae. They have evergreen, shiny leaves and simple flowers that are usually blue, white, or purple. The alkaloids vincristine and vinblastine, extracted from two common periwinkles, *V. major* and *V. minor*, are used to treat various cancers.

perjury   Perjury is the willful giving by a person under oath and in a judicial proceeding of false testimony or information important to the matter at issue. In most instances perjury is a felony, and a convicted perjurer may be sent to prison. A person who, in good faith, gives mistaken testimony is not deemed to have committed perjury. A person who persuades another to give false testimony may be prosecuted for subornation of perjury.

Perkin, Sir William Henry   see DYE

Perkins, Frances   The first woman cabinet member in U.S. history, Frances Perkins, b. Fannie Coralie Perkins in Boston, Apr. 10, 1882, d. May 14, 1965, served as secretary of labor (1933–45) during the administration of Franklin D. Roosevelt. An advocate of social reform, she

Frances Perkins, U.S. secretary of labor under Franklin D. Roosevelt, was a tireless champion of social reform. She was instrumental in achieving enactment of the Social Security Act, minimum-wage laws, and other New Deal legislation.

was especially drawn to the problems of blue-collar workers. As secretary of the New York Consumers League (1910–12), Perkins investigated conditions in factories, especially those employing women and children, and lobbied for reduction of their workweek. She was named (1919) to the New York state industrial commission, chaired (1926–29) the state's industrial board, and was state industrial commissioner during Franklin D. Roosevelt's governorship (1929–33).

As secretary of labor Perkins strengthened an almost defunct department. She championed such reforms as social security, federal public works and relief, and legislation for minimum wages and maximum hours and the abolition of child labor.

Perkins, Maxwell   Maxwell Evarts Perkins, b. New York City, Sept. 20, 1884, d. June 17, 1947, as an editor and later (1935) vice-president of Charles Scribner's Sons, was instrumental in publishing the works of such writers as F. Scott Fitzgerald, Ernest Hemingway, and J. P. Marquand. One of Perkins's most notable achievements was editing Thomas Wolfe's rambling manuscript for *Look Homeward, Angel.*

Perlman, Itzhak [purl'-muhn] Israeli-born Itzhak Perlman, b. Aug. 31, 1945, overcame polio to become one of the most respected violinists of his generation. Perlman went to the United States in 1958 to attend the Juilliard School in New York City, made his Carnegie Hall debut in 1963, and won the Levintritt Competition in 1964. Since then his brilliant technique and delineation of detail have been evident in his growing repertoire, especially in 19th- and 20th-century works.

Perls, Friedrich S. [pairlz] Friedrich Salomon "Fritz" Perls, b. Berlin, July 8, 1893, d. Chicago, Mar. 14, 1970, and his wife, Laura, founded Gestalt therapy (see GESTALT PSYCHOLOGY). Perls was trained as a Freudian psy-

choanalyst and was subsequently influenced by Wilhelm Reich before drawing upon Gestalt psychology in working out his own ideas. His writings include *Ego, Hunger, and Aggression* (1947) and *Gestalt Therapy Verbatim* (1959).

Perm [purm]   Perm (1988 est. pop., 1,087,000) is the capital of Perm oblast in Russia, a republic of the USSR. It is situated on the left bank of the Kama River, on the western slopes of the Ural Mountains. The city is a major machine-manufacturing and petrochemical center, producing gantry cranes, excavators, and mining dredges. Perm arose in the 18th century on the site of an old copper works. The city was called Molotov from 1940 until 1957.

permafrost   Permafrost is naturally occurring earth material that maintains a temperature below 0° C (32° F) continuously for two or more years. This layer of frozen ground is so designated exclusively on the basis of temperature, rather than on the presence of any moisture in the ground. Part or all of the ground's moisture may not actually be frozen, depending on the chemical composition of the water and depression of the freezing point by capillary forces. Most permafrost is, however, consolidated by ice.

Occurrence. Permafrost underlies an estimated 20% to 25% of the world's land surface and is a widespread phenomenon in polar and subpolar regions. It occurs in about 50% of the USSR and Canada, 82% of Alaska, 20% of China, and probably all of Antarctica. The permafrost is 1,600 m (5,250 ft) thick in northern Siberia and 650 m (2,100 ft) thick in northern Alaska, and it thins progressively toward the south.

Origin. Permafrost in the Northern Hemisphere is generally differentiated on land into two broad zones—continuous and discontinuous—depending on its lateral continuity. Permafrost forms in those parts of the world where the mean annual air temperature is colder than 0° C. Some of the ground frozen during the winter will not completely thaw in the summer; therefore a layer of permafrost will form and continue to grow downward in small increments until the upward-flowing internal heat of the Earth becomes equal in amount to the difference between the freezing point and the mean annual surface temperature.

Effect on Human Activities. Permafrost profoundly affects human activities in the Arctic and subarctic regions. Agriculture, mining, water supply, sewage disposal, and construction are seriously affected by subsidence of the ground surface caused by thawing of the perennially frozen ground as well as by associated problems brought on by soil flowage and FROST ACTION. Civil engineers must thoroughly understand the thermal and mechanical problems unique to permafrost if they are to design passable roads, usable air strips, safe buildings, and reliable pipelines in far northern areas.

Permian Period   see EARTH, GEOLOGICAL HISTORY OF; GEOLOGIC TIME

permutation and combination   In mathematics, the terms *permutation* and *combination* refer to the handling of objects in a set, such as a set of numbers (see SET THEORY). For a given set S, a permutation is any one of all the possible ordered selections of objects from S, and a combination is any one of all the possible unordered selections of objects from S. (Repetitions of selections sometimes are also involved.) The branch of mathematics that deals with such arrangements of objects in a set is called combinatorial theory. It is of great importance in computer science, CRYPTOLOGY, NUMERICAL ANALYSIS, and PROBABILITY studies.

A basic example of a permutation is the ordered selections of two objects from the set S containing objects a, b, and c. Three possible choices exist for the first object, but only two for the second. Multiplying the possibilities, $3 \times 2 = 6$, gives the total number for that given permutation of S. The actual possibilities are ab, ac, ba, bc, ca, and cb. Because permutations are *ordered* selections, ab is not equivalent to ba, and so on.

For a basic example of a combination, choose two objects from the same set. Because combinations are *unordered*, only three combinations exist instead of six. That is, ab is now equivalent to ba, and so on.

Perón, Eva   [pay-rohn']   Eva Duarte de Perón, b. May 7, 1919, d. July 26, 1952, popularly known as Evita, was the second wife of Argentine president Juan Perón and a strong political force in Argentina. Eva Duarte was a well-known radio and film actress before marrying Perón in 1945. When Perón won the presidency in 1946, Evita, a persuasive orator, became in effect his copresident. She helped achieve women's suffrage, initiated educational reforms, and concerned herself with the welfare of the poor. Evita was to have run for vice-president with her husband in 1951, but despite the near idolatry of the people, the military opposed her and forced her to withdraw. Her death from cancer was a serious blow to the Perón regime.

Perón, Juan D.   Juan Domingo Perón, b. Oct. 8, 1895, d. July 1, 1974, twice president of Argentina (1946–55, 1973–74), was that country's outstanding political figure of the 20th century. Perón played an important role in the right-wing military coup of 1943 that overthrew President Ramón S. Castillo. He was named secretary of labor and social welfare and a year later was appointed vice-president and war minister. Perón used his labor post to establish rapport with the labor movement, and the social legislation he sponsored guaranteed him popular support among the *descamisados* ("shirtless ones"). His political successes were resented by a rival military faction, and Perón was briefly imprisoned in 1945. The *descamisados,* however, mobilized by Eva ("Evita") Duarte, soon to be Perón's second wife, spurred his return with massive demonstrations. In 1946 he was elected to the presidency.

As president of Argentina from 1946 to 1955, Juan Perón established a strong regime based on the political mobilization of workers—in which he was much aided by his popular second wife, Eva—and repression. Overthrown in 1955, he retained sufficient loyalty among the people to return to power in 1973–74.

Perón's reform program, known as *peronismo,* blended economic nationalism with private ownership in a totalitarian framework reminiscent of German nazism and Italian fascism. Perón also had the support of the Roman Catholic church. His second administration, which began in 1952, was far less successful. The death of his wife Evita was a severe blow—her popularity was far greater than Perón's. The economic situation deteriorated, and the church withdrew its support and eventually excommunicated him. Perón's regime was overthrown in September 1955.

Perón settled (1960) in Spain, where he continued to direct the movement bearing his name. After the interim election of Peronist Héctor Campora, Perón was reelected president in 1973. Perón, however, came back to a different Argentina, and he himself was aging. Factionalism and violence marred his short second tenure, and within nine months the ailing Perón succumbed to a heart attack. His third wife, Isabel Martínez de Perón, succeeded him in office but was deposed in 1976.

perovskite   [pur-ahf'-skyt]   The calcium titanate mineral perovskite, $CaTiO_3$, frequently contains iron, sodium, and rare earths (chiefly cerium) as impurities. Perovskite occurs in basic igneous rocks and associated pegmatites; in altered limestones; and in chlorite, talc, and serpentine schists.

The term *perovskite* is also used to classify other minerals and synthetic compounds that have a similar chemical structure. The ideal perovskite form is ABX_3, in which A and B are metallic cations (ions with a positive charge), and X is a nonmetallic anion (ion with a negative charge). Magnesium silicate perovskite, $MgSiO_3$, which makes up much of the lower mantle, is thought to be the Earth's most abundant mineral. Perovskites synthesized in the laboratory have shown promise as high-temperature superconductors.

peroxide   [puh-rahk'-syd]   A peroxide is a chemical compound characterized by the presence of two linked oxygen atoms. Several hundred different peroxides, or peroxy compounds, are known, of which a few dozen have commercial value.

The most widely used peroxy compound is hydrogen peroxide, H_2O_2, sometimes written as HOOH to indicate the structure. It is a colorless liquid that freezes at about the same temperature as water. Hydrogen peroxide is normally sold as an aqueous solution in concentrations of 30–90% by weight. Because hydrogen peroxide is a strong oxidizing agent, it has been used as a rocket fuel, but this property has made it even more valuable as a bleaching agent. Of all the hydrogen peroxide commercially produced, about 70% is used to bleach natural and synthetic fibers and paper. Dilute solutions of hydrogen peroxide are used as household antiseptics.

All the alkali metals and alkali earth metals, as well as many others, can form peroxides. The most important in an industrial sense is sodium peroxide, Na_2O_2, a pale-yellow solid used as an oxidizing and bleaching agent. Other metal peroxides are used in pyrotechnics and disinfectants and are incorporated into various pharmaceutical and cosmetic preparations.

Perpendicular Gothic style   see GOTHIC ART AND ARCHITECTURE

perpetual motion machine   A perpetual motion machine is one that would do external work (move resisting forces) without the aid of any power other than that created by the machine itself, or one that is self-contained and once started would continue moving forever without an external supply of energy. No such machine has ever been successfully demonstrated; perpetual motion is considered impossible to achieve.

The United States Patent Office receives about 100 applications each year for devices that involve some form of perpetual motion; applications must be accompanied by a working model. The British Patent Office refuses to consider any application that involves perpetual motion on the ground that this concept violates the laws of physics.

Machine efficiency is defined as the ratio of work output to energy input. The two can never be equal, because of friction within the machine or because of losses that occur when one form of energy is changed to another. A perpetual motion machine would have to have an efficiency of 100 percent or greater.

Perrault, Charles [pair-oh']   Although the French poet and critic Charles Perrault, b. Jan. 13, 1628, d. May 16, 1703, is today better remembered for his *Tales from Mother Goose* (1697; Eng. trans., 1729), during the 17th century he was the leading champion of contemporary French writers in the "quarrel between the ancients and the moderns." In the poem *Le Siècle de Louis le Grand* (The Century of Louis XIV, 1687) he argues the superiority of Régnier, Molière, and Malherbe over the poets of classical antiquity.

Perrot, Nicolas [pair-oh']   Nicolas Perrot, b. Burgundy, c.1644, d. Aug. 13, 1717, was a French explorer and administrator in the Great Lakes region. He went to Canada in 1660, visited various Indian tribes, and learned their languages. As early as 1667 he began trading out of Green Bay on Lake Michigan, where in 1685 he became French commandant. He founded forts Saint Antoine and Saint Nicolas on the upper Mississippi. Until 1698 he explored and traded in the region of present-day Wisconsin and conducted diplomacy with the tribes of the area. In 1685 he negotiated peace between the Fox and Chippewa tribes, and in 1692 he aided the governor of New France, the comte de FRONTENAC, by enlisting several western tribes as allies against the Iroquois League.

Perry, Fred   Frederick John Perry, b. May 18, 1909, giant of British tennis during the 1930s, was his country's best player ever. A tenacious competitor with a spectacular forehand, Perry was the last British man to win (1934–36) at Wimbledon. Not until Björn Borg won 5 straight Wimbledon crowns (1976–80) did a modern player better Perry's 3 consecutive titles. Perry also won the Australian (1934) and French (1935) singles championships, as well as winning 39 of 41 singles matches for Britain in Davis Cup competition.

Perry, Gaylord   In May 1982, Gaylord Jackson Perry, b. Williamston, N.C., Sept. 15, 1938, became the 15th pitcher in baseball history to win 300 games. Despite his notoriety for throwing the illegal "spitball" (and for not getting caught at it), Perry demonstrated his skill by winning 2 Cy Young awards (1972, 1978) during his long career (1962–83), one in each league. Perry had a won-lost record of 314-265, an earned run average of 3.09, and 3,534 strikeouts.

Perry, Matthew Calbraith   The American naval officer Matthew Calbraith Perry, b. Newport, R.I., Apr. 10, 1794, d. Mar. 4, 1858, "opened" Japan to the West in 1854. He was the younger brother of Oliver Hazard Perry. Commissioned a midshipman in 1809, Perry served in the War of 1812 and after the war helped establish Liberia as a refuge for free American blacks. During the 1830s he devised an apprentice-training system for enlisted men, organized the first naval engineer corps, and fostered the introduction of steam warships. Promoted (1841) to commodore, Perry commanded (1843–44) the U.S. African squadron, an implementation of the Webster-Ashburton Treaty designed to suppress the slave trade. He later led the U.S. naval forces in the Mexican War.

In 1852 the U.S. Department of the Navy selected Perry to lead a naval mission to Japan with the purpose of gaining a treaty to protect shipwrecked American seamen and expand U.S. commerce. He began his negotiations with Japan only after making an impressive show of U.S. naval force in Tokyo Bay. On Mar. 31, 1854, Perry signed

Commodore Matthew Perry, commander of the U.S. naval expedition that "opened" isolationist Japan, anchored his force in Tokyo Bay on July 8, 1853, and refused to leave until the Japanese government agreed to receive U.S. requests.

a treaty with representatives of the Japanese government by which Japan agreed to protect shipwrecked American sailors, to sell coal to U.S. ships, and to open two ports to American merchants. In doing so, he set in motion the process by which Western ideas and commerce gradually penetrated Japan.

Perry, Oliver Hazard   Oliver Hazard Perry, b. South Kingstown, R.I., Aug. 23, 1785, d. Aug. 23, 1819, an American naval officer, earned the appellation Hero of Lake Erie during the WAR OF 1812. He was the older brother of Matthew Calbraith Perry. Appointed a midshipman in 1799, Perry first served aboard the *General Greene*, captained by his father. During the Tripolitan War he made two cruises to the Mediterranean (1802–03 and 1804–06).

Given command of the U.S. naval forces on Lake Erie in February 1813, Perry built a small fleet and on Sept. 10, 1813, set sail from Put-in-Bay, Ohio, to meet an attacking British squadron. Fighting from one ship until forced to transfer his flag to another, Perry held out until the British surrendered. "We have met the enemy and they are ours," he said, to report history's first capitulation of an entire British naval squadron. His victory made the Ohio Valley immune to British attack and opened part of Upper Canada to U.S invasion.

Perse, Saint-John [pairs]   The French poet Saint-John Perse (pen name of Alexis Saint-Leger Leger), b. Guadeloupe, May 31, 1887, d. Sept. 20, 1975, won the Nobel Prize for literature in 1960. An extraordinary technician, Perse wrote poems that exhibit both great erudition and a deeply felt lyricism. *Anabasis* (1924), translated by T. S. Eliot in 1930, established his reputation in the English-speaking world. *Exile* (1942; Eng. trans., 1949), *Winds* (1946; Eng. trans., 1953), and *Seamarks* (1957; Eng. trans., 1958) are typical of Perse's richly allusive style, evocative imagery, and thematic concerns.

Persephone [pur-sef'-uh-nee]   In Greek mythology Persephone (also called Kore) was the beautiful daughter of ZEUS and DEMETER who represented both nature's growth cycle and death. HADES, god of the underworld and brother of Zeus, was lonely in his underworld kingdom; therefore Zeus, without consulting Demeter, told him to take Persephone as his wife. Thus, as Persephone was picking flowers one day, Hades came out of the Earth and carried her off to be his queen. While the grieving Demeter, goddess of grain, searched for her daughter, the Earth became a barren wasteland. Zeus finally obtained Persephone's release, but because she had eaten a pomegranate seed in the underworld, she was obliged to spend four months (winter) of each year there, during which time barrenness returned to the Earth. With her mother, Persephone was a central cult figure in the ELEUSINIAN MYSTERIES. In Roman mythology she was called Proserpina.

Persepolis [pur-sep'-uh-lis]   Persepolis (in Greek, "city of Persia"), located near modern Shiraz in southwestern Iran, was the principal royal residence and ceremonial center of the Achaemenid empire of Persia (550–330 BC) and one of the greatest architectural complexes of the ancient world. Work on the site was begun (518 BC) by Darius I (r. 521–486 BC) and substantially completed under Xerxes I (r. 486–465 BC) and Artaxerxes I (r. 464–425 BC), although various units were added to the complex as late as the reign (359–338 BC) of Artaxerxes III. Fabled throughout the ancient world for its wealth and splendor, Persepolis was looted and burned (330 BC) by the troops of Alexander the Great, and today only ruins remain on the site.

As was typical of Assyrian and Persian palace complexes, Persepolis was built atop a huge limestone platform that served to level off the site and provide a secure foundation for its structures. At the time of its destruction, the terrace at Persepolis contained the palaces of Darius, Xerxes, and Artaxerxes III, along with a harem, a labyrinthine treasury, and several ornamental gateways approached by double stairways that converged at the top. Other impressive structures included the great Apadana (audience hall) of Darius and the so-called Hall of One Hundred Columns, or Throne Hall, of Xerxes.

Perseus [pur'-see-uhs]   In Greek mythology Perseus, the son of Zeus and DANAE, was the hero of many exciting adventures. Danaë's father, King Acrisius, fearing the fulfillment of a prophecy that he would die at the hands of his grandson, tried to dispose of mother and child by enclosing them in a chest and throwing them into the sea. The chest floated to safety on the island of Seriphus, where Perseus grew to manhood. Its ruler, King Polydectes, fell in love with Danaë and schemed to get rid of Perseus. He set Perseus the almost impossible task of killing the Gorgon MEDUSA. With the aid of a cap that made him invisible, Perseus succeeded in slaying the monster.

In Ethiopia, before reaching home, he encountered ANDROMEDA, whom he saved from a fearful sea monster and then took as a bride. After returning to Seriphus, he rescued his mother from Polydectes by turning him to stone with Medusa's head and then gave the head to the goddess Athena. Later, while participating in athletic games, Perseus threw a discus far beyond its target, hitting and killing Acrisius, who was a spectator. Thus the prophecy was fulfilled.

Perseus, King of Macedonia [pur'-see-uhs]   Perseus, c.212–c.165 BC, was the last king of Macedonia, succeeding his father, PHILIP V, in 179. Suspected by Rome, he established connections with other royal families and won friends in Greece and in neighboring countries. He avoided provoking Rome, but the Romans deluded him by their diplomacy and finally attacked him in 171. The ensuing Third Macedonian War ended with Perseus's defeat by Lucius Aemilius Paullus in 168 and the abolition of the monarchy.

Pershing, John J. [pur'-shing]   John Joseph "Black Jack" Pershing, b. Laclede, Mo., Sept. 13, 1860, d. July 15, 1948, commanded the American Expeditionary Forces (AEF) in World War I. An 1886 graduate of West Point, he returned there in 1897 as a member of the tactical staff.

During the Spanish-American War, Pershing distinguished himself at Kettle and San Juan hills. He went (1899) to the Philippines, where he led a series of important expeditions among the hostile Moros. In 1905 he became military attaché in Tokyo and then went to Manchuria as an observer of the Russo-Japanese War.

In 1906, President Theodore Roosevelt elevated Pershing in rank from captain to brigadier general. Pershing took command of Fort McKinley near Manila and then became (1909) governor of Moro province in the southern Philippines, thoroughly defeating the Moros by 1913. Given command of the 8th Brigade in 1914, he led (1916–17) the difficult punitive expedition against Pancho VILLA in Mexico. Experience and seniority brought him command of the AEF in 1917.

In France during World War I, Pershing had to organize, train, and supply an inexperienced force that eventually numbered more than 2 million. AEF successes in the war were largely credited to him, and he emerged from the war as its most celebrated American hero. Congress created a new rank for Pershing, general of the armies. His memoirs, *My Experiences in the World War* won him the 1932 Pulitzer Prize for history.

Gen. John J. Pershing commanded the U.S. forces in Europe during World War I. A veteran of campaigns in the Philippines and Mexico, General Pershing was responsible for training the American Expeditionary Forces, whose offensives at Meuse-Argonne and St. Mihiel hastened the Allied victory.

Persia, ancient [pur'-zhuh]   The name *Persia* (from the ancient province of Persis; modern Fars, Iran) was given by the Greeks to the entire area occupied by various Iranian tribes from which the ACHAEMENID dynasty arose. It is the land of present-day IRAN and AFGHANISTAN, geographically the Iranian plateau.

The various groups who occupied the area assume a historical identity only with the advent of written records in cuneiform. In the south were the Elamites (see ELAM), whose principal city, Susa, was in MESOPOTAMIA. The Elamite language, though not yet fully deciphered, was unlike any of the later languages of the region. To the north in the mountains lived KASSITES, who also descended onto the plains of Mesopotamia. In present-day Azerbaijan province lived people called Manneans. South of the sea that bears their name lived the Caspians. The art objects of these peoples reveal the high material culture then existing. Bronze funereal objects from Luristan especially are evidence of great artistic originality.

By the end of the 2d millennium BC invaders from the north had begun to spread over the Iranian plateau. These were Indo-European speakers, Iranians who called themselves ARYANS. They had war chariots pulled by horses, but the Iranians soon found that cavalry was more effective in mountain areas. By the 9th century they had entered the Zagros Mountains; the Medes, the most prominent of the Iranian peoples, are mentioned in Assyrian sources as being there by 836 BC. More than a century later the Parsa, or Persians, appeared in the south.

The Median Kingdom. The first Iranian kingdom was created by the Medes in western Iran about 700 BC. The rise of MEDIA was hindered by invasions from north of the Caucasus Mountains, first by a Thracian people called Cimmerians, then by Iranian nomads called SCYTHIANS. About 625 BC a new attempt was made by the Medes under Cyaxares to form a united kingdom, and after defeating the Scythians the Medes turned against Assyria. An alliance between the Babylonians and the Medes stormed and destroyed the Assyrian capital, Nineveh, in 612 BC, a date used today by the KURDS, who claim descent from the Medes, to begin their era of time reckoning.

The Achaemenids. The Medes also subdued the Persians and other Iranians on the plateau, but the Median empire lasted only until 549, when the last Median king, Astyages (r. 584–549), was defeated by his Persian vassal CYRUS THE GREAT, who became the heir of the Median king and ruled an even greater empire from 549 to 530 BC. His son Cambyses II, ruling from 530 to 522, invaded Egypt. Following an interregnum of a year, DARIUS I took power by killing the usurper Smerdis and established the Achaemenid empire on a firm basis. He consolidated and

A royal guardsman is depicted in this glazed brick relief from the palace of Artaxerxes II at Susa, the administrative capital of the Achaemenid king Darius I and his successors (521–331 BC).

further extended Persian conquests (so that the empire stretched from Egypt and Thrace in the west to northwestern India in the east); established the system of satraps (local governors) under strong centralized control; encouraged the spread of ZOROASTRIANISM; and was a great patron of the arts (see PERSIAN ART AND ARCHITECTURE). Darius's son XERXES I (r. 486–465), after his defeat by the Greeks in the PERSIAN WARS, retired from active government, thus setting a precedent for future kings who were kept in power by the efficient bureaucracy organized by Darius. Constant revolts were put down, but the weakness of the empire was apparent under ARTAXERXES I (r. 465–424), Xerxes II (r. 424–423), and Darius II (r. 423–404). Under ARTAXERXES II (r. 404–359), the revolt of his brother CYRUS THE YOUNGER almost cost him his throne. Artaxerxes III (r. 359–338), an able although cruel monarch, saved the empire from disintegration by reconquering the provinces of Phoenicia and Egypt, which had previously regained their independence. The last prince of the Achaemenid family, Darius III Codomannus, assumed the throne in 336. He was defeated twice by ALEXANDER THE GREAT and was murdered by his followers in 330.

The Seleucids. In the fighting among Alexander's successors, the Diadochi, Iran fell to SELEUCUS I, who created a new era of time reckoning by his march into Babylon in 312 BC. The SELEUCIDS established many Greek settlements in the east, and under them Hellenism mixed with local cultures to form a syncretic civilization in Iran. The Seleucids never controlled all of the Iranian plateau, and the south, present-day Fars province, was ruled by an independent local dynasty. In the northern province of Azerbaijan, a Persian satrap from the Achaemenid period called Atropates established a local dynasty. In the east the Greeks who settled in BACTRIA established an independent kingdom about 246 BC, and the Parthians (see PARTHIA) declared their independence from Seleucid rule about the same time.

Although the Seleucids temporarily regained the allegiance of both sets of rebels during the reign of ANTIOCHUS III (r. 223–187 BC), the Parthians were to emerge as their heirs.

The Parthians. The ARSACIDS, rulers of the Parthians, called themselves phil-Hellene on their coins, and they continued using Greek until the end of the dynasty in AD 224. The Parthians were famous as cavalry soldiers who used bows and arrows against their Roman adversaries, and they lived in a feudal society. The many small courts of the nobility provided the background for the development of the Persian national epic, which is filled with heroic stories from the Parthian period. Under the Parthians many lesser kingdoms, including ARMENIA, existed in uneasy allegiance to an Arsacid king of kings. The Parthians had to fight the Romans in the west and the Sakas, or Scythians, followed by the Kushans, in the east. The lack of unity among the Parthian princes aided the rise of the Sassanian dynasty.

The Sassanians. The SASSANIANS were not phil-Hellene like their predecessors but sought to establish a national Persian renaissance in both culture and ideology. From the outset Ardashir I, who killed his Parthian overlord in AD 224, proclaimed a revival of ancient glory, although the Sassanians had only the faintest memory of the Achaemenids. The early buildings of Ardashir in Fars province were massive, proclaiming imperial grandeur. The centralization of power in the hands of the king of kings contrasted markedly with the Parthians' practice. After Shapur I's victory over the Romans and capture of Emperor Valerian in 260, he proclaimed his power in a series of rock reliefs in Fars depicting his victories. Roman prisoners were employed in building dams and irrigation projects in various parts of the Sassanian empire. During Shapur's reign Zoroastrianism became the official state religion.

Shapur's immediate successors all sought to strengthen dynastic power over the nobility. Under SHAPUR II (r. 309–79) and other 4th-century kings, wars with Rome alternated with struggles against nomadic invaders from the east. Yazdegird I (r. 399–421) relaxed the persecution of Christians, who had been suspected of being secret allies of the Romans. Bahram V (r. 421–39) was surnamed Gur because of his skill in hunting the onager. Many stories are told about him in the national epic, *Shah Namah*, by

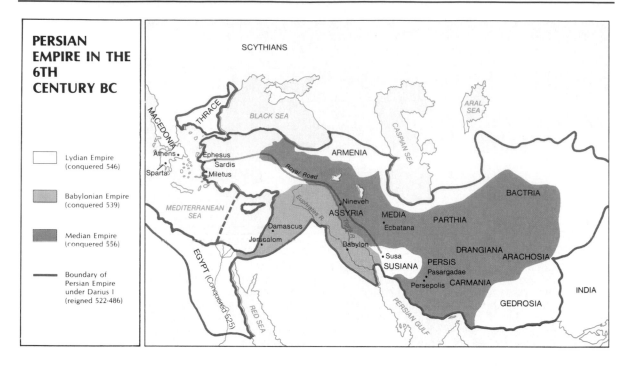

PERSIAN EMPIRE IN THE 6TH CENTURY BC

Lydian Empire (conquered 546)

Babylonian Empire (conquered 539)

Median Empire (conquered 556)

Boundary of Persian Empire under Darius I (reigned 522-486)

FIRDAWSI. In the 5th century, Sassanian kings had difficulties with the Hephthalites (White Huns) in present-day Afghanistan. Under Kavad (r. 488–531), a communistic socioreligious movement led by the "prophet" Mazdak gained adherents. It was savagely suppressed by KHOSRU I (r. 531–79), who has been called the greatest ruler of the dynasty. Bahram Chobin (r. 590–91), the only successful rebel against the Sassanian house, was overthrown by Khosru II (r. 591–628), the last great Sassanian ruler. He tried to reestablish the frontiers of the Achaemenid empire, but initial success was followed by his defeat at the hands of the Byzantine emperor HERACLIUS and assassination by his son. A succession of rulers culminated in Yazdegird III (r. 632–51), under whom the exhausted Sassanian empire succumbed to the attacks of the Muslim Arabs.

Persian art and architecture Persian art and architecture reflect a 5,000-year-old cultural tradition shaped by the diverse cultures that have flourished on the vast Iranian plateau occupied by modern Iran and Afghanistan. The history of Persian art can be divided into two distinct eras whose demarcation is the mid-7th century AD, when invading Arab armies brought about the conversion of the Persian people to Islam. Whereas during the pre-Islamic centuries artistic expression was at the service of the kings and the worship of fire was preeminent, during the Islamic period the arts served Allah, and religious structures and artifacts were the focal points of artistic interest.

Despite this sharp break between the ancient and Islamic eras, Persian art throughout the centuries displays an underlying unity. Persian design almost invariably has stressed decorative forms—geometrical and floral—rather than the human figure. This continuity of forms—executed in such media as stone, plaster, brick, tiles, pottery, and textiles—is the most distinctive feature of Persian art.

Ancient Era

Newly discovered prehistoric sites on the Iranian plateau date back to at least 5000 BC, and handsome, decorated pottery, some of which is eggshell thin, has been found in great quantities at sites dated 3000 BC and later. In Luristan countless bronzes have been recovered from the graves of a people who bred horses, served as mercenaries in the armies of Assyria, and employed smiths who made (c.2000 BC–c.700 BC) marvelous works in cast bronze, including bits and other horse trappings, weapons, religious totems, embossed shields and belts, and hosts of miniature animals.

Early Kingdoms. Excavations of the Elamite capital of Shush, or Susa, have yielded numerous art objects that reflect Mesopotamian influence. At the height of Elamite power, King Untash-napirisha (r. 1275–1240 BC) built a grandiose religious complex at Dur-Untash, to the southeast of Susa. Its most striking feature is a well-preserved temple tower, or ZIGGURAT, called Choga Zanbil. Measuring 105 m (344 ft) on each square side, Choga Zanbil originally rose in a series of stepped stages to a height of 52 m (171 ft). At both Dur-Untash and Susa, archaeological finds have included masses of cuneiform inscriptions and statuettes of gods, kings, and guardian animals.

Shortly after Ashurbanipal, an Assyrian ruler, took and

burned (646 BC) Susa, Assyria itself was ravaged by the Medes, who together with the Persians dominated the Iranian plateau in the 7th century BC. The architecture of the Medes is largely unknown except for an impressive fire temple (c.750 BC) at Nush-i Jan whose walls still rise to a height of 8 m (26 ft).

Achaemenid Period. Under Cyrus the Great, a Persian who formed a lasting union of the Persians and the Medes, the entire plateau fell under the sway of the Achaemenid Empire (c.550 BC–330 BC). Cyrus ordered construction undertaken at a valley site known to the Greeks as Pasargadae, where palaces, audience halls, and a towerlike structure with the folk name of Solomon's Prison were built.

Under one of Cyrus's successors, Darius I, work began (c.518 BC) at PERSEPOLIS, or Parsa, a royal complex located about 80 km (50 mi) south of Pasargadae that was completed by Xerxes I and Artaxerxes I. The entire complex was built atop a lofty terrace reached by a double stairway that led to the monumental Gate of Xerxes. Both Mesopotamian and Greek influences are apparent in the carved reliefs that decorate the double stairway of the Audience Hall, on which are depicted peoples from the 23 lands of the empire bringing tribute on New Year's Day.

The monumental style of the Achaemenid period was refined further at Naqsh-i Rustam, located about 10 km (6 mi) west of Persepolis, where the facades of the tombs of four Achaemenid rulers of the 5th century BC are carved into the face of a cliff. Relief scenes above these tomb-facades depict Ahura Mazda, god of fire and of the sun and moon, hovering in the air over a ruler who presents sacrificial offerings to a fire burning on an altar. In front of the tombs stands a towerlike fire temple known as the Shrine of Zoroaster. Excavations have unearthed a wide variety of elaborately decorated art objects—many

This glazed-brick relief of a winged bull, part of the decoration of the palace of Darius I (r. 522–486 BC) at Susa, reflects the synthesis of Mesopotamian styles characteristic of Achaemenid art. (Louvre, Paris.)

made by artisans brought to Persia from Greece—including silver and gold vessels, tableware in stone, statuettes in semiprecious materials, and jewelry.

Sassanian Period. After the death of Alexander the Great (323 BC), Iran fell under the sway of a Hellenistic kingdom founded by Seleucus, one of Alexander's generals. The Seleucid kingdom, in turn, was conquered (141 BC) by Iranian nomads who called themselves Parni and Aparni but who were known to the Greeks and the Romans as the Parthians. Parthian art and architecture reflects an uneasy and at times graceless combination of Achaemenid, Hellenistic, and Central Asian motifs. When the Parthians gave way (224) to the Sassanian dynasty, however, a new artistic spirit took hold.

The Sassanians thought of themselves as the heirs of the Achaemenids and carried on such early traditions as the worship of fire and the cult of Ahura Mazda. Surviving in ruin are several imposing Sassanian palaces and approximately 40 fire temples.

The Sassanian architects used masonry vaults and domes, which had been introduced by the Parthians. The Sassanian fire temple was a square chamber crowned by a dome and punctuated by wide-arched openings in each wall. The transition from the square of the chamber to the circular base of the dome was achieved by means of squinches, Persian-invented corbeled supports that spanned each corner of the chamber.

The most important works of Sassanian sculpture are the nine rock-cut reliefs depicting Ahura Mazda holding out a beribboned diadem to a king, thereby recognizing his right to the throne. Among the minor arts of the period, the most striking objects are silver plates decorated with relief scenes depicting the rulers hunting and enjoying courtly pleasures.

Islamic Period

Following the Arab conquest (completed 651), Iranian culture was preserved by native dynasties. Mahmud of Ghazni was the patron of Abu'l Qasim FIRDAWSI, whose 60,000-couplet epic titled *Shah Namah*, or *Books of Kings* (c.1010)—along with other epic and poetic works—was copied over and over again in manuscripts abundantly illustrated with exquisitely detailed miniature paintings.

Islamic art was encouraged under the Seljuks, a Turkish group that ruled Iran from 1038 until 1194, but widespread destruction and a cessation of most artistic activity followed the 13th-century invasion by the Mongols. The Mongol dynasty (1256–1336) gave way to the reign (1370-1502) of Timur and his descendants, who sponsored a great artistic revival that blossomed further under the Safavids (1502–1736), a true Iranian dynasty.

Architecture. Within Iran a distinctive MOSQUE type had been developed by the time of the Seljuks. Adopted from Sassanian architecture was the basic plan of a square sanctuary chamber surmounted by a dome, and the *ivan*, a large barrel-vaulted hall open at one end. In later Iranian mosques, an *ivan* was the main element of a towering entrance portal; in addition, *ivans* were located on both sides of the open court and in front of the domed sanctu-

An illustration of a polo match from a 15th-century manuscript of the Shah-namah *displays the highly stylized, decorative forms characteristic of Persian miniature painting. The* Shah-namah, *or Book of Kings, created (completed c.1010) by Abu'l Qasim Firdawsi, is a mythical and historical account in verse form of the legends and adventures of ancient Persian kings and heroes.*

ary. The most renowned example of this type, the Masjidi Shah at Isfahan, built (1612–30) for Shah Abbas I, is one of the world's architectural masterpieces. The mosque plan was also used in the construction of madrasahs, or religious schools, such as the so-called Madrasah-i Mader-i Shah (1706–14; Isfahan).

Among the great Iranian religious shrines, the most famous is the complex of structures that comprises the shrine of the Imam Riza at Mashhad, particularly the Masjid-i Gowhar Shad (completed 1418). The religious architecture of the Timurid period was most highly developed at Samarkand, the capital of the realm, where the supreme monuments include the Gur-i-Mir (completed 1405), Timur's mausoleum; the Masjid-i Jami', or Congregational Mosque (completed c.1404); the Madrasah of Ulugh Beg (1417–20); and the Shah-i Zinda Necropolis (completed 1405), in which more than a dozen domed tombs line a narrow hillside lane.

Secular architecture was far less important in Islamic countries than religious structures. Iranian palaces were often built of mud-brick, rather than the baked brick employed for mosques and madrasahs, and they soon disappeared as a result of the onslaught of the elements.

The ancient Persian tradition of floral and geometric decoration found its fullest expression on the wall and dome surfaces of Iranian religious structures. Early mosques were adorned with brick bonding patterns, which were supplanted (12th century) by decorative patterns cut into wet plaster, or stucco. Beginning in the Timurid period, glazed tiles of several colors were used to line entire wall surfaces, most stunningly in the so-called Blue Mosque at Tabriz (1437–68). Mosaic faïence, in which large-scale patterns were formed out of myriad tiny pieces, reached a glowing climax in Safavid architecture of the 17th century.

The Arts. Calligraphy, manuscript illumination, miniature painting, ceramics, textiles, carpets, and metalwork all achieved great distinction in the Islamic art of Iran. Calligraphy enjoyed the status of a major art. Although most inscriptions, including the large-scale ones used in mosques, were written in Arabic rather than Persian, both languages employed the Arabic script, which had limitless decorative possibilities. Over the centuries a vast number of Korans were handwritten and illuminated in color, primarily in gold and blue. Illustrations in

The Masjid-i-shah, or Royal Mosque, was built (1612–30) by Shah Abbas I at Isfahan, the new Safavid capital. One of the most magnificent Islamic monuments in the world, the Masjid-i-shah reflects the earlier architectural conventions of the Seljuks in its use of the four-ivan mosque plan and features lateral courts, pools, and prayer chambers. The entire surface, both interior and exterior, is faced with brilliantly colored faïence mosaic and glazed tilework.

A 16th-century miniature portrays the death of Shirin, one of the principal characters of the Khamseh, *a 12th-century epic written by the poet Nizami. (Private collection.)*

epics and works of poetry were peopled with kings and courtiers, men and women, without regard for the alleged Islamic prohibition against the portrayal of living beings. Lacking the perspective drawing familiar in the West, Persian miniature paintings offer views of the world that seem frozen in time and space, their exquisitely drawn figures statically posed against timeless azure skies.

The development of manuscript illumination was spurred by Baysunghur, who, while governor of Herat (1415–33), established a famed academy of book production. Baysunghur's interest was carried on by Husayn Bayqara, at whose court worked (after 1480) Kamal al-Din BIHZAD, acknowledged to be the greatest of all Persian miniaturists.

Persian metalwork was executed in gold, silver, copper, and brass, which were used to fashion objects such as ewers, basins, salvers, cups, pen cases, and astronomical instruments. Many splendid pieces surviving from the Seljuk and later periods are engraved with bands of inscriptions and often contain such added features as the

signs of the zodiac and scenes of hunting and of life at the courts.

The Safavid period is renowned for its vast output of rich textiles and magnificent carpets, which were produced by master designers in Isfahan, Kerman, Kashan, Herat, Tabriz, and other towns. The textile designs associated with these centers are often quite reminiscent of contemporary miniature paintings. The most famous Persian carpet, now in London's Victoria and Albert Museum, is more than 10 m (34 ft) long and 5 m (17 ft) wide; it was woven (1539) by Maqsud Kashan for the shrine of the Safavid family at Ardabil.

See also: CALLIGRAPHY; ISLAMIC ART AND ARCHITECTURE; POTTERY AND PORCELAIN; RUGS AND CARPETS.

Persian cat   see LONGHAIRED CATS

Persian Gulf   The Persian Gulf is an arm of the Arabian Sea separating Iran from the Arabian Peninsula. Connected to the Gulf of Oman by the Strait of HORMUZ, the gulf is about 990 km (615 mi) long and 56–338 km (35–210 mi) wide; it has an area of about 240,000 km² (92,500 mi²). The gulf is bordered by Iran, Iraq, Kuwait, Qatar, Saudi Arabia, and the United Arab Emirates. Bahrain is the largest of the islands in the gulf.

Many islands, shoals, and reefs break the surface of the shallow waters, whose average depth is only 26 m (84 ft). The coasts are either sandy or gravelly plains, except at the northern end, where Iran's mountains plunge steeply to the gulf. The main tributary is the SHATT-AL-ARAB. Petroleum is the most important product of the gulf region. The principal ports are ABADAN, Bandar-e Khomeini, and Bushire in Iran; Kuwait; Ras Tanura and Dammam in Saudi Arabia; Manama in Bahrain; DOHA in Qatar; and DUBAI and Sharjah in the United Arab Emirates. Shipping on the gulf was disrupted by the IRAN-IRAQ WAR, and a major oil spill occurred there during the 1991 GULF WAR.

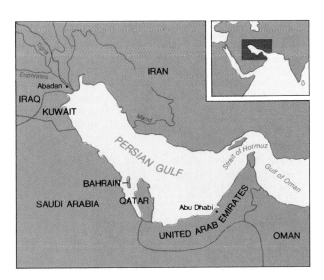

Persian language   see INDO-IRANIAN LANGUAGES

Persian literature   Persian literature has its roots in the culture of pre-Islamic Iran, although it was strongly influenced by the Arabic language and culture of its conquerors. Classical Persian literature—the form of Persian that developed in Iran after the Arab conquest—dates from the mid-9th century; it flourished until reaching an apex during the 14th century. A subsequent period of ebb lasted until the 19th century, when there arose a conscious movement to imitate the classical verse and prose forms of the 10th to the 12th century. This trend was weakened by the adoption of Western subject matter and was followed by a gradual modernization of the literary forms themselves.

The first centuries of the classical literary development saw the adoption of the ode, a rigid Arabic literary form. The 10th-century poet Daqiqi used it as a panegyric to eulogize the Persian prophet Zoroaster, and under his successors it developed into an intricate stylized form. Its images eventually became lifeless through repetition, although its use continued in formal poetry until the 20th century. Originally a part of the ode, the lyric poem was isolated by the Persians, who used it for various subjects but especially for love in both its profane and mystical manifestations. Sheykh Moslehoddin SADI and Mohammed Shamsoddin HAFEZ were the most important poets in this tradition. By the 14th century the lyric, too, had become highly intricate and stylized. Epic poetry, by contrast, was an indigenous Iranian literary form. FIRDAWSI's heroic epic the *Shah Namah*, or *Book of Kings* (c.1010), was the first and greatest national epic. Both romantic and mystical themes appeared (c.1180–1230) in the epics of Nezamoddin Ilyas NEZAMI and Farid al-Din Abu Hamid Attar (1119–c.1230), but after Jami (1414–92) the epic—and classical Persian poetry—declined.

During the 19th century a short-lived effort was made to return to the purity of earlier literary forms and diction that were, however, rapidly becoming obsolete as the impact of the West began to make itself felt. Among those adopting Western literary forms in the early 20th century, Muhammed Ali was particularly important for introducing the form of the short story. Other writers followed him in the use of fiction as a means of expressing social discontent. Although the classical forms of poetry have endured, Nima Yushij (1895–1959), the most influential figure of the modernistic movement, in the 1920s broke completely with traditional poetry in both form and content, a break perpetuated and even expanded by his successors.

Persian Wars   Although wars between Greeks and Persians occured throughout the ACHAEMENID period (549–330 BC), the term *Persian Wars* applies more specifically to those wars waged by DARIUS I and XERXES I, which ended in GREECE's victory in 478 BC. Conflict began with the conquest of Lydia by CYRUS THE GREAT, who triumphed over CROESUS at Sardis in 547. Cyrus then gained control of the Ionian towns along the Aegean formerly subject to Lydia. Most of these towns revolted and had to be subdued. When the Ionian towns again rebelled, Athens supported them by sending a fleet in 499, although by 493 the uprising had been suppressed. In retaliation, Darius in 490 sent a fleet with an invasion force against Athens, which defeated the Persian army at MARATHON.

Darius's son and successor, Xerxes, determined to punish Athens, invaded Greece in 480. At first successful, the huge Achaemenid army annihilated LEONIDAS and his Spartan forces at THERMOPYLAE, then marched to Athens and burned the city. The Greeks, however, decisively defeated the Persian fleet off the island of SALAMIS. Xerxes returned to Persia, leaving an army to subdue Greece. The Greeks' defeat of this army at PLATAEA in 479 ended the danger of Persian invasion.

For the next 30 years the Greeks fought under Athenian leadership, winning back territory from the Persians in Thrace and Anatolia, although Greek intervention in Egypt ended in disaster. During the PELOPONNESIAN WAR (431–404 BC) between Athens and Sparta the Persians played one opponent against the other. In 411, Sparta made peace with the Persians and recognized Persia's claims to the Ionian towns. The more comprehensive King's Peace of 387–386 left under Achaemenid rule only those Greek cities which were in Asia. Even this did not end Persian intrigues, which ceased only with ALEXANDER THE GREAT's conquest of the Persian empire in 330 BC.

The *History* of HERODOTUS is the principal source of information on the Greco-Persian conflicts, while XENOPHON's *Anabasis* describes an expedition (401 BC) by Spartan mercenaries in the service of CYRUS THE YOUNGER.

persimmon   The several varieties of trees that bear the edible persimmon fruit are members of the EBONY

The Japanese persimmon grows up to 12 m (40 ft) tall and has yellowish white flowers. The fruit is orange to red with orange flesh.

family, Ebenaceae. The Japanese persimmon, or kaki, *Diospyros kaki*, native to China and Japan, is the most important commercially. The black sapote, *D. digyna,* native to tropical Mexico and Central America, was important in the pre-Columbian diet there. One U.S. species, the common persimmon, *D. virginiana*, which grows from Connecticut to Florida and west to Kansas, bears fruit that is edible when fully mature. Another, the Texas persimmon, *D. texana*, bears inedible fruit. Persimmons are also grown as ornamentals or for their wood.

personal property   see PROPERTY

personality   The study of personality in psychology incorporates the results of research in developmental psychology, learning theory, and social psychology, focusing on individual differences and on consideration of the total person. Personality theorists attempt to formulate general principles that will explain and predict individual differences in behavior. Theories of personality generally cover such areas as the structure of personality; the psychological processes involved in the individual's interaction with his or her environment; the development of personality; disturbed or pathological aspects of personality; and principles of personality change. Just as questions can be asked concerning the structure of the human body and the functioning of bodily processes, the personality theorist can ask comparable questions about an individual's psychological functioning.

Approaches to Personality

Many competing theories of personality have been formulated, offering different approaches to several critical issues. One such issue is whether to emphasize characteristics of the individual that tend to remain stable across situations and over time or to emphasize the ways in which environmental stimuli elicit behavior that changes considerably as the individual moves from situation to situation.

A second issue involves opposing views of human nature—one of which emphasizes the positive, actualizing aspects of human beings; the other, their aggressive, destructive aspects. A third question is whether the conscious or unconscious aspects of personality should be stressed. Some theorists argue that the courses of human behavior are primarily unconscious; other theorists deny that the unconscious exists.

Personality Theories

Psychoanalytic Theory. The psychoanalytic-psychodynamic point of view is based on the work of Sigmund FREUD. Psychoanalytic theory (see PSYCHOANALYSIS) suggests that the basic personality structure or character is determined during the early years of life, especially during the first five years. Early experiences in eating, toilet training, and sexual feeling are critical in shaping the developing personality structure. The structure is manifest throughout life in the individual's view of himself or herself, in relationships with others, and in general ways of relating to the environment.

Since the development of psychoanalytic theory by Freud, a number of analysts, such as Carl JUNG and Alfred ADLER, have developed differing psychoanalytic or psychodynamic theories. Karen HORNEY, Erich FROMM, and Harry Stack SULLIVAN have departed from Freud in their greater emphasis on cultural and interpersonal forces.

Followers of Freud such as Erik ERIKSON have attempted to stress the social as well as the biological aspects of the individual's development and the importance of periods later than infancy and early childhood. Although many differing schools of psychoanalytic thought exist, the theory developed by Freud remains the cornerstone of these approaches.

Trait Theory. Trait theory also stresses those characteristics of an individual which persist through varying conditions, such as sociability, dominance, impulsiveness, and anxiousness. According to trait theory, a trait represents a basic predisposition to respond in a particular way. For example, a person high in the trait of sociability is more likely to initiate social encounters, and to respond positively to social overtures, than is a person low in sociability. Although manifest in a wide range of situations, traits do not necessarily operate constantly: an individual high in dominance may not dominate every situation. In addition, an individual's behavior is determined by the joint action of many traits rather than by the action of any single trait.

Humanistic Personality Theory. The existential-humanistic approach to personality (see HUMANISTIC PSYCHOLOGY) evolved in part as a response to what was seen as an excessive emphasis on the biological, the destructive, and the unconscious by psychoanalytic theory. In contrast, the existential-humanistic approach emphasizes the growth and self-actualization of the individual and his or her conscious, phenomenological perception. The primary interest focuses on the way in which the person experiences the self and the surrounding world rather than in the unconscious significance of such experiences. Whereas the existential-humanistic approach has its roots in European philosophy, this school has had many advocates in the United States, including Carl ROGERS and Abraham MASLOW.

Social Learning Theory. The approach of social LEARNING THEORY has its roots in American learning theory, with its emphasis on laboratory experimentation. Social learning theorists of personality consider personality as patterns of behavior that have been learned as a result of observing others and being reinforced by others. People vary from situation to situation, it is held, because they are capable of recognizing that the rewards for behavior differ in different situations.

Cognitive Personality Theory. Another approach, cognitive personality theory (see COGNITIVE PSYCHOLOGY), represents a general orientation rather than a specific theory that can be associated with a number of individuals. Some of its aspects represent the most recent developments in personality theory, although others are to be found in earlier theories. Cognition refers to the ways in which the individual thinks and organizes information about the world. It includes the manner in which he or she perceives, remembers, thinks, and makes use of language. Spurred by advances in computer science, many psychologists have become interested in how the individual processes information both about the self and the surrounding world. Some personality theorists seek to discover how the individual interprets or construes the world and, like a scientist, how he or she attempts to predict and control events. Some researchers stress the individual's capacity to discriminate among situations and organize information concerning characteristics of these situations. Other investigators emphasize how some people tend to think in a complex, abstract way whereas others think in a simple, concrete way. Finally, some theorists stress the manner in which people organize information to make long-range plans and to regulate their behavior in accordance with these plans.

personality, multiple The central feature of the extremely rare multiple-personality disorder is the existence of two or more apparently distinct personalities in one individual. Each of the personalities is associated with unique ways of thinking, behaving, and expressing emotion. In some cases the multiple personalities are fully developed in the sense that they are associated with distinctly different types of identities and have different memories for past events. In other cases characteristics of the personalities overlap so that they share some traits and memories. Either way, a person with the disorder responds differently on psychological tests—and may even demonstrate different patterns of brain activity—for each personality. The transition from one personality to another typically is abrupt and is precipitated by a stressful experience or environmental cue.

Patients with multiple-personality disorder vary in the extent to which they are aware of their condition. Some are unaware that they manifest dramatic changes in personality, whereas others are conscious of the fact that they show distinct personalities. The extent of the functional impairment in these patients varies from mild to severe. The cause of the disorder is as yet unknown. PSYCHOTHERAPY is the most common form of treatment for multiple-personality disorder.

Studies of multiple-personality disorder report that it occurs from three to nine times more frequently in females than in males. Onset of the disorder often occurs in childhood, and in almost all cases the disorder is preceded by some form of abuse or other traumatic event.

See also: PSYCHOPATHOLOGY.

personality disorders see PSYCHOPATHOLOGY

personification see FIGURES OF SPEECH

perspective In art, perspective comprises the techniques used to represent three-dimensional spatial relationships on a two-dimensional surface. The three principal types of perspective are visual perspective, in which depth is suggested by overlapping and by the smaller size of distant objects; linear perspective, in which lines converge as they approach the horizon; and aerial perspective, in which distant colors become cooler and outlines gradually fade.

A degree of visual perspective is often seen even in primitive art, but linear perspective was not important before the ancient Greeks, who reportedly made extensive studies in perspective (none of which survive). Later the Romans made copies of Greek works and achieved some perspective skills. With the coming of Christianity and its emphasis on the spiritual, artists lost interest in depicting the natural world, and perspective was largely ignored until, in the 14th century, a radically new conception of space and form was first reflected in the art of GIOTTO and Pietro Cavallini and then in that of the Lorenzetti brothers. This trend was consolidated in the early 15th century, when a renewed interest in optics and mathematical laws contributed to the resources of ILLUSIONISM. Filippo BRUNELLESCHI was one of the first to experiment with perspective theory. Leon Battista ALBERTI, in his treatise *On Painting* (1435),

Andrea Pozzo's painting on the ceiling of Sant' Ignazio, Rome, The Triumph of Saint Ignatius *(1691–94), is a masterpiece of* quadratura, *or illusionist architectural decoration, employing aerial perspective.*

set forth all that was then known on the subject. LEONARDO DA VINCI's *Last Supper* (1494–95; Santa Maria delle Grazie, Milan) achieves a perfectly realized combination of narrative and perspective (both linear and aerial) ideas.

In the Netherlands the approach tended to be less rigidly mathematical and the compositions—often set in vastly receding landscapes—less self-contained. After the early 1400s, painters everywhere took pleasure in extreme refinements and visual trickery of various kinds; for example, in Jan van Eyck's *Arnolfini Wedding* (1434; National Gallery, London), a convex mirror in the background reflects the scene back to the viewer.

Perth (city in Australia) [purth]   Perth, the capital of Western Australia, is located 19 km (12 mi) from the Indian Ocean on the Swan River near the southwest corner of Australia. Its port city is Fremantle. Perth's population is 1,118,800 (1988 est.). The city is the commercial, financial, and cultural center of Western Australia. Perth's industries, most of which are in the suburbs of Fremantle, Kwinana, and Welshpool, include shipbuilding, oil refining and storage, food processing, and lumber milling. Minerals mined nearby are shipped from Perth. Perth is the seat of the University of Western Australia (1911) and Murdoch University (1975). An arts festival is held there each year.

Perth was founded in 1829 as an English claim to the Australian continent and became a city in 1856. In the 1890s the discovery of gold at KALGOORLIE, 400 km (248 mi) to the northeast, transformed Perth into an important commercial center.

Perth (city in Scotland)   The city of Perth, on the River TAY in central Scotland, is the seat of Perth and Kinross district. It has a population of 43,009 (1981). Perth is known for its dye works, its wool and linen factories, and its cattle markets. Perth's first settlers may have been Romans in about AD 80. Between the 11th century and 1437, Perth was Scotland's capital. In 1559, John Knox preached a famous sermon against idolatry at the Church of Saint John the Baptist, the oldest building (c.1440) remaining in Perth.

Perth (county in Scotland)   Perth is a former county in the Tayside and Central regions of east central Scotland, most of which has been part of Perth and Kinross district since the government reorganization of 1975. The rivers TAY and FORTH and their tributaries drain the area, a scenic region of lakes and mountains. Farming dominates the economy, but whiskey distilling and the manufacture of glass and fish products are also important. From the mid-9th century to 1651 the coronation of many Scottish kings took place in the village of Scone. Pitlochry is a major tourist center.

perturbation   In astronomy, two bodies, constructed as rigid spheres, subject only to their mutual gravitational attraction and moving in accordance with Newton's laws, will describe what is called Keplerian motion. Departures from Keplerian motion are called perturbations.

At any instant the orbit of the Moon around the Earth can be described as Keplerian. The Earth is not a sphere, however, nor is it rigid, and the Moon is also subject to attraction by other bodies, most notably the Sun. In addition, the rules of Newtonian mechanics and gravitation must be modified in accordance with relativity. These factors are responsible for perturbations in the Moon's orbit.

Observations of perturbations permit the analysis of bodies causing them. The existence of Neptune was predicted before it had been observed, because Uranus showed perturbations that could not be accounted for by known bodies. Gravity anomalies on the Moon were discovered by observing the perturbed motion of satellites orbiting the Moon. Most of the existing knowledge about the gravitational field of the Earth comes from analysis of the perturbed motion of artificial Earth satellites.

See also: ORBITAL ELEMENTS.

Peru [puh-roo']   The Republic of Peru extends 2,414 km (1,500 mi) along the western coast of South America. The country is bounded on the north by Ecuador and Colombia, on the east by Brazil and Bolivia, on the south by Chile, and on the west by the Pacific Ocean. Peru declared its independence from Spain in 1821.

Land and Resources

The ANDES Mountains divide Peru into three regions: a coastal lowland in the west; the Andean highlands, or Sierra; and the upper Amazon basin, the Montaña, in the east.

Coastal Lowlands. The narrow lowlands, about 10% of the total land area, include the west flank of the Andes (below 1,525 m/5,000 ft). The average temperature at Lima is 18° C (65° F), and the annual rainfall is 41 mm (1.6 in)—making this one of the world's coolest and driest low-latitude deserts.

Highlands. The Andean highlands, 27% of the total land area, extend southeast from the Ecuadorean border the entire length of Peru. Elevations on the plateau reach up to 4,575 m (15,000 ft), and Huascarán, the highest peak in the country, rises to 6,768 m (22,205 ft). Amazon tributaries have cut deep, longitudinal valleys into the surface of the plateau. Lake TITICACA is located in the southeastern Sierra. At Cuzco (3,364 m/11,037 ft) the average annual temperature is 16° C (60° F), and annual rainfall averages about 813 m (32 in). The Sierra is rich in fodder grasses and temperate-zone trees and plants, and the animals include the alpaca, llama, the wild guanaco, and vicuña. Most of Peru's mineral wealth is found in the Sierra.

The Montaña. The Montaña region in the east, constituting 56% of the total area, consists of the eastern slopes of the Andes and the AMAZON RIVER basin. Average rainfall exceeds 2,540 mm (100 in) annually, and the average annual temperature is 25° C (77° F). Ebony and mahogany grow in the vast tropical forest, and wild animals include the puma and jaguar.

REPUBLIC OF PERU

Land: Area: 1,285,216 km^2 (496,224 mi^2). Capital and largest city: Lima (1989 est. pop., 5,659,200).

People: Population (1990 est.): 22,332,000. Density: 17 persons per km^2 (45 per mi^2). Distribution (1989): 69% urban, 31% rural. Official languages: Spanish, Quechua. Major religion: Roman Catholicism.

Government: Type: republic. Legislature: Congress. Political subdivisions: 24 departments, province of Callao.

Economy: GNP (1988): $39 billion; $1,850 per capita. Labor distribution (1989): agriculture—34%; services—27%; trade—15%; manufacturing—10%; other—14%. Foreign trade (1988): imports—$3.1 billion; exports—$2.7 billion. Currency: 1 inti = 1,000 soles.

Education and Health: Literacy (1988): 87% of adult population. Universities (1986): 35. Hospital beds (1987): 32,648. Physicians (1988): 20,931. Life expectancy (1990): women—66; men—62. Infant mortality (1989): 83 per 1,000 live births.

People

Peru's inhabitants are predominantly Indian (54%) and mestizo (of mixed European and Indian heritage, 32%). Europeans make up 12% of the population, and the remainder are mostly black, Japanese, or Chinese. The country is preponderantly Roman Catholic. In 1975, QUECHUA, the Inca language spoken by about one-half of the population, became the second official language. Fifteen percent of the population speak AYMARA.

LIMA, the capital and major city, and its port of CALLAO are the principal cities of the coastal lowlands; Cuzco and Arequipa are the principal cities of the Sierra; and Iquitos on the Amazon is the chief city of the Montaña.

Education is free and compulsory for children from ages 7 to 16. The National University of San Marcos (1551) in Lima is the oldest university in South America. Progress has been made in reducing epidemic diseases, improving sanitation, and expanding medical care, but massive rural-to-urban migration has strained social services. An epidemic of cholera in early 1991 claimed more than 1,000 lives.

Economic Activity

Peru, one of the poorest countries in Latin America, has experienced serious economic problems for years. By 1989, with an inflation rate of 8,000% and more than half the work force unemployed or underemployed, the country faced its worst economic crisis of the century. The failed economy spurred the disruptive activities of leftist guerrillas.

Farmers in the Sierra grow corn, wheat, barley, and potatoes for food and coca (the source of cocaine), which has become Peru's leading cash crop even though its cultivation is illegal. Joint Peruvian-U.S. efforts to eradicate coca plants have been resisted by planters and guerrillas. Commercial irrigated farming in the coastal oases produces cotton, sugar, and coffee for export. Peru's fish catch was the largest in the world from 1962 until 1972, when the warm EL NIÑO current caused cool-water species to move elsewhere temporarily.

Exports of copper, silver, lead, zinc, and iron provide about 40% of all export income. Petroleum is extracted near Talara on the coast and near Pucallpa in the Amazon basin.

The chief export industries are metal refining and smelting and the processing of agricultural and fish products. The textile, sugar-refining, paper, chemical, automotive, and shipbuilding industries are concentrated on the coast, while the processing of forest products and petroleum refining are the leading industries in the Montaña.

The PAN AMERICAN HIGHWAY runs along the Peruvian coast from Ecuador to Chile. The Central Railroad—the highest standard-gauge railroad in the world—crosses the Western Cordillera at 4,817 m (15,805 ft).

Government

In 1968 a coup led by Gen. Juan Velasco Alvarado deposed the civilian government of Fernando BELAÚNDE TERRY, and the 1933 constitution was suspended. In 1978 an assembly was elected to draw up a new constitution for a return (1980) to civilian rule. Belaúnde Terry, leader of the left-wing Popular Action party (AP), was returned to office by a wide margin. The 1985 presidential election was won by Alan García Pérez of the left-center Popular Revolutionary Alliance (APRA). The 1990 election, won by political newcomer Alberto Fujimori of the Cambio 90 movement, underlined voter disenchantment with traditional politicians. The legislature consists of a 180-member Chamber of Deputies and a 60-member Senate.

History

Early Period. When the Spanish arrived in Peru in 1531, they found the flourishing empire of the INCA. By the arrival (1532) of Francisco PIZARRO, civil war had so weakened the empire that it was easily conquered by the Spanish. In 1535, Pizarro founded Lima, and in 1544 it became the capital of the viceroyalty of Peru. This viceroyalty comprised all the Spanish territory in South America until the creation of the viceroyalties of New Granada (1718) and La Plata (1776).

Independence. Following the suppression of a major Indian revolt led by Tupac Amarú in 1781–82, Spanish authority in Peru remained strong. The independence movement, therefore, was led by foreigners. The Argentine general José de SAN MARTÍN entered Lima in July 1821 and proclaimed (July 28) Peru's independence. The task of wiping out the remaining Spanish forces was then left to Simón BOLÍVAR and his general, Antonio José de SUCRE, in the battles of Junín and Ayacucho (both 1824).

A succession of power-hungry generals kept Peru in

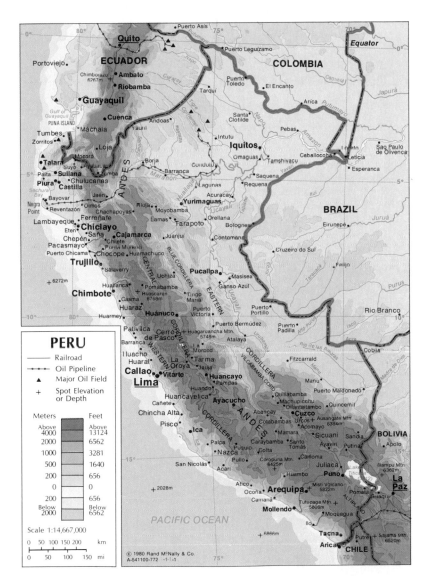

Cuzco, in a valley of the Andes in southern Peru, was the capital of the ancient Inca empire until it fell to the Spanish in 1533. It is a major archaeological site, its remains including the nearby 15th-century fortress of Sacsahuaman. Cuzco, with a predominantly Indian population, is the marketing center of an agricultural region.

(Below) *Indian women from Peru's Sierra region wear the heavy woolen clothing necessary in the cold highlands.*

(Above) *The Plaza de Armas, at the center of Lima, Peru's capital, is surrounded by several of the city's few remaining structures dating from the Spanish colonial era. The largest city in Peru, Lima was founded in 1535 by the Spanish conquistador Francisco Pizarro.*

turmoil until 1845. From 1836 to 1839, Peru was united with Bolivia under the presidency of Andrés SANTA CRUZ. A period of civil war (1842–45) ended with the emergence of Ramón CASTILLA, who, during his two terms as president (1845–51, 1855–62), brought about extensive economic and political reforms.

With the help of Ecuador, Bolivia, and Chile, Peru defeated a Spanish invasion in 1866, and in the 1879 peace treaty Spain recognized Peru's independence. The president of the first civilian government, Manuel Pardo, allied with Bolivia against Chile, which led to Peru's participation (1879–83) in the War of the Pacific (see PACIFIC, WAR OF THE). This war resulted in the loss of the valuable nitrate fields and led to the prolonged TACNA-ARICA DISPUTE.

20th Century. The first third of the 20th century was dominated by Augusto Bernardino Leguía y Salcedo, who served (1908–12) as civilian president and ruled later (1919–30) as a virtual dictator, despite adoption (1920) of a new and more liberal constitution.

Resistance to the government increased after 1924, when APRA was founded by Víctor Raúl HAYA DE LA TORRE. In 1945, after being barred from elections for 20 years, the APRA candidate, José Luís Bustamante y Rivera, was elected president, but he was deposed in 1948 by a military junta. Haya himself then won in the 1962 presidential elections, and again the military seized power. Fernando Belaúnde Terry was elected president in 1963; in 1968, however, he was deposed by the military.

The junta led by Velasco Alvarado instituted a land-distribution program, establishing farm cooperatives on formerly private estates, and also nationalized many industries, including the petroleum industry. A new military junta led by Gen. Francisco Morales Bermúdez took power in 1975. In July 1980 this junta yielded power to Belaúnde Terry's civilian government, which contended with increasing resistance from leftist guerrillas and continuing economic problems. Taking office in 1985, García Pérez took various measures to forestall economic collapse. He also intensified the war against the Maoist Shining Path guerrillas. Despite such efforts, by 1990 as Alberto Fujimori assumed office, Peru's economic and political problems seemed increasingly entrenched.

Perugia [pay-roo'-jah]   Perugia, the capital of the Umbria region in central Italy, overlooks the Tiber River about 135 km (85 mi) north of Rome. It has a population of 147,602 (1988 est.). The city's picturesque hilltop setting and its striking medieval appearance make it an important tourist center. Chocolate candy, pottery, textiles, and pharmaceuticals are its main products. The city is the home of the state University of Perugia (1200). Perugia is rich in art and architecture, including the medieval Maggiore Fountain, the Gothic Priors' Palace, the 15th-century Collegio del Cambio, the Renaissance Oratory of San Bernardino, and the medieval and Renaissance Umbrian paintings housed in the National Gallery of Umbria.

Perugia was a flourishing Etruscan settlement before it was conquered by Rome in 310 BC. It was a free commune in the Middle Ages, and by the 14th century it had come to dominate most of Umbria. In 1540 the city was forcibly incorporated into the Papal States and generally remained under papal rule until the unification of Italy in the 1860s.

One of Perugino's most acclaimed works is the fresco Christ Giving the Keys to Saint Peter *(1481– 82). The painting displays a characteristic spatial freedom, serene mood, and symmetrical composition. The three clearly defined ground planes, culminating in a landscape framed by architecture, reflect the artist's emphasis on spatial perspective. (Sistine Chapel, Vatican City, Rome.)*

Perugino [pay-roo-jee'-noh]   Perugino, b. Pietro di Cristoforo Vannucci, c.1445–1523, was the most eminent Umbrian painter of the Renaissance. Little is known of his training, although he may have worked with Verrocchio. In 1472 he was listed among the painters of the Company of Saint Luke in Florence. By October 1481, Perugino was in Rome, called there together with Cosimo Rosselli, Sandro Botticelli, and Domenico Ghirlandaio by Pope Sixtus IV to decorate the Sistine Chapel. One of Perugino's surviving Sistine frescoes— *Christ Giving the Keys to Saint Peter* (1481–82)—demonstrates his most notable contribution to Italian painting: an expansion of space to suggest a new, luminous sense of infinity, thus transcending the rationalized, circumscribed framework defined by Florentine artists earlier in the century. Another early work, the altarpiece *Crucifixion with Saints* (1481; National Gallery of Art, Washington, D.C.), exemplifies Perugino's vast, mountainous landscapes, adorned by feathery trees and inhabited by tranquil, graceful figures.

Pescadores [pes-kuh-dohr'-uhz]   The Pescadores (Chinese: P'eng-hu) are a group of about 64 islands in the Formosa Strait 50 km (30 mi) west of Taiwan and 140 km (85 mi) east of China. Only 20 of the islands are inhabited. A county of Taiwan, the Pescadores have a land area of 127 km^2 (49 mi^2) and a population of 96,232 (1990 est.). More than half of the people live on the largest island, P'eng-hu, where a large Taiwanese naval base and the largest town, also P'eng-hu, are located. The islands' economy is based on fishing, farming, and phosphate mining.

Inhabited by Chinese since the 12th century, the islands were named Pescadores by Portuguese explorers in 1590. The Dutch seized the islands in 1622. They were under Japanese control from 1895 until 1945, when Japan returned them to China. In 1950 the Pescadores were made a county of Taiwan.

Pestalozzi, Johann Heinrich [pes-tah-loht'-tsee] Johann Heinrich Pestalozzi, b. Jan. 12, 1746, d. Feb. 17, 1827, was a Swiss educator whose ideas laid the foundation for the reform of 19th-century popular education and influenced the development of progressive pedagogy in Europe and the United States. A lifelong champion of the poor and underprivileged, he established a school for pauper children at Neuhof, Switzerland, in 1773—an experience important in formulating his educational ideas. In 1780, Pestalozzi wrote *The Evening Hour of a Hermit*, a book of aphorisms influenced by Jean Jacques Rousseau that contained the heart of his educational philosophy. His most widely read book, the novel *Leonard and Gertrude* (1781–87; trans. & abridged ed., 1801), attempted to show how social, moral, and political regeneration can be achieved through education. In 1805, Pestalozzi founded a boarding school at Yverdon, near Neuchâtel, that attracted such visitors as Friedrich FROEBEL and Johann Friedrich HERBART. Pestalozzi believed that all children have a right to education and the capacity to profit from it and that their innate faculties should be developed in accordance with nature. He advocated emphasis on accurate observation of concrete objects, moving from the familiar to the new, and the creation of a loving and emotionally secure environment.

pesticides and pest control   Life forms that in some manner cause injury to human food supplies or living areas or that act as parasites or disease vectors are considered pests, and efforts to deal with these life-forms are known as pest control. Although various techniques are available or being developed, the most familiar and widespread technique in the 20th century is the use of pesticides. These chemical agents can be classified as insecticides (for insect control), HERBICIDES (for weeds), acaricides (mites and ticks), molluscicides (snails and slugs), fungicides (molds, mildews, rusts, and smuts), nematocides (nematodes), and rodenticides (rodents).

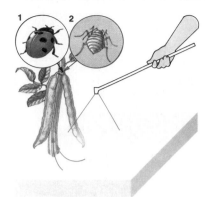

Systemic insecticides are absorbed by plants and kill the insects that feed on these plants. Systemic agents have little effect on such predatory insects as ladybirds (1), which feed on the plant surface, but they are useful against aphids (2) and other pests that feed on plant juices.

History

Since ancient times pesticides have been used to control pests that attack crops, stored foods, domestic livestock, arable lands, domiciles, and the human body. Homer (c.1000 BC) refers in the *Odyssey* to the "pest-averting sulfur," and Cato (c.200 BC) describes the boiling of bitumen (asphalt) to produce insecticidal fumes that controlled pests in vineyards.

Dioscorides (AD 40–90), a Greek physician considered the father of toxicology, recognized the value of arsenic in pest control. After tobacco was introduced into Europe during the 17th century, crude extracts were used to control various insects, such as lace bugs on pear trees. During the 1800s several pesticides were discovered and widely employed, most consisting of copper and arsenic salts and copper oxide and used as fungicides and insecticides.

Botanical pesticides were at first crude dusts made from dried and ground leaves, flowers, stems, and roots, all of which contained some active pesticidal agents such as alkaloids, esters, glycosides, coumarins, or essential oils such as the terpenoids.

Metallic Compounds. By 1930 rapid advances in chemistry led to the development and application of pesticides based on various metallic compounds. Many of these compounds are inorganic, such as lead arsenate, mercury bichloride, and potassium permanganate. They have been largely superseded by the many organic pesticides that were developed between 1925 and 1970.

The first organic pesticides were organometallic fungicides, such as phenylmercuric acetate (PMA). These compounds are applied to soil, seed, corms, foliage, fruit, and equipment, depending upon each individual compound's biological spectrum, toxicity to plants or animals, and biodegradability.

Organic Compounds and DDT. By 1940 interest centered on purely organic pesticides, which are structured on a carbon-hydrogen framework and may include such elements as oxygen, sulfur, phosphorus, chlorine, bromine, fluorine, and nitrogen. Characteristically, these compounds are degraded, at varying rates, by physical factors and by organisms into smaller, and usually less harmful, molecules, compared to the metals that tend to accumulate.

In 1939, Paul Müller observed that an organic chlorine compound, DDT (dichlorodiphenyltrichloroethane), first synthesized in 1874, had extraordinary insecticidal properties. DDT became very important, for example, in the control of malaria. It remained the most effective of all the analogues tested and stimulated the synthesis of a whole series of other organochlorines, many of which emerged as practicable pesticides in their own right.

After World War II, industrial research developed hundreds of different organophosphate molecules, many of which found use as pesticides.

Herbicides. Coincident with the development of the insecticides and fungicides, substantial interest arose in synthesizing herbicides. A whole series of organic weed-control chemicals emerged that revolutionized crop production by replacing time-consuming cultivation to suppress weeds.

Controversy and Legislation

Opposition by environmentalists to pesticide use in general and to certain groups of compounds in particular has grown in recent years (see CONSERVATION), based on the contention that pesticides present a threat to the environment and to health. First aroused by the book *Silent Spring* (1962), by Rachel CARSON, the antipesticide movement has had a substantial influence both in the U.S. Congress and in several state legislatures. As a result severely restrictive legislation has banned the use of many pesticides and restricted the use of several others.

Reputed Dangers of Pesticides

Environmentalists, scientists, and workers in the pesticide industry have also contended that some pesticide compounds are hazardous to human health. Workers in factories that produce some of these compounds have, in the process of bringing legal suits against some manufacturers, received financial compensation for illnesses allegedly caused by exposure to these chemicals. Agricultural workers have also brought suits, claiming that they have suffered physical damage as a result of pesticide exposure. Some pesticide chemicals—for example, DBCP (dibromochloropropane), which affects the production of sperm, Kepone (chlordecone), which causes a peripheral neuropathy, and EDB (ethylene dibromide), which is suspected of causing cancer—have had their manufacture severely restricted. Long-range potential dangers of pesticide bioaccumulation in the body are also beginning to concern experts.

Some other problems are attracting public attention. Certain pesticides are lethal to bees, and it is estimated that heavy pesticide use has caused substantial reduction in some local hive populations. Also, some pesticides that have been banned in the United States are still being sold to developing countries, where uncontrolled applications may cause damage and contaminate foods that are consumed locally and exported.

Finally, it has been suggested that the buildup of nondegradable pesticides in the soil and in the food chain may be more hazardous, in the long run, than these immediate problems. At this point, even the claims made against DDT—which was banned in the United States because of its supposed deleterious effects and its bioconcentration in the food chain—are still denied by some experts. Nevertheless, by the mid-1980s the ENVIRONMENTAL PROTECTION AGENCY had made pesticide pollution its most urgent problem, and chemical industries and public-interest groups were reaching some accord on ways to deal with pesticide regulation.

Alternative Methods of Pest Control

Those who oppose the use of pesticides contend that their function can often be replaced by nonchemical methods. Such alternatives as planting resistant cultivars, crop rotation, pest-avoidance plantings and harvest times, proper sanitation, and irrigation have been used by competent growers for decades; many observers, however,

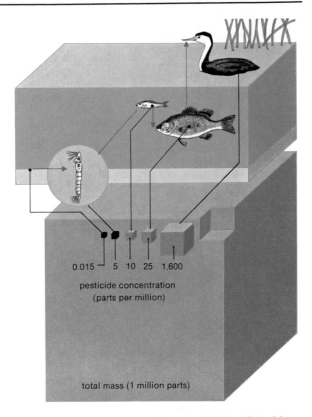

Some chlorinated hydrocarbon pesticides accumulate in body fat and decompose slowly. Concentrations (cubes) of the pesticide increase during each step of the food chain, from plankton through fish-eating birds, reaching hazardous levels (red) in many fishes and birds.

0.015 — 5 10 25 1,600

pesticide concentration
(parts per million)

total mass (1 million parts)

Broadcast spraying (1) of certain insecticides controls the harmful carrot fly (2) but also kills the ground beetle (3), which preys on the harmful cabbage fly (4). Sowing of carrot seed with insecticide granules (5) kills carrot flies but allows ground beetles to live.

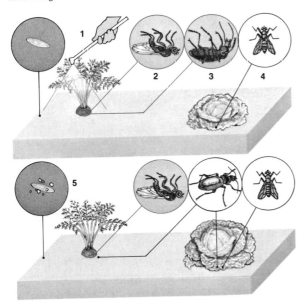

think that these methods do not achieve total or even adequate pest control. The use of natural predators, parasites, and pathogens has shown success in some cases. To date, such methods can control only a small percentage of insect-pest species out of about 10,000 known species. Such methods are not effective in combating fungal, bacterial, nematodal, and viral diseases.

Modern, highly sophisticated insect-control measures involving the release of large quantities of sterile males, the use of sex-attractant pheromones, and the application of physiologically disruptive pest hormones reveal some promise and, in certain cases, have accomplished phenomenal results. Such measures, however, are highly specific, limited in number, often expensive, and must be applied continuously over broad geographic areas to be fully effective.

Integrated pest management (IPM) seeks to integrate all available nonchemical methods with a minimal use of pesticides to effect crop and livestock pest control. IPM, a growing science, is now applied to several cultivated crops.

Whatever the political and administrative developments in the use of pesticides may be, for the time being their application continues in the production of crops and livestock for food, feed, fiber, shelter, and the maintenance of public health. In the use and disposal of pesticides, as with all chemicals, users should read the label before application and follow the instructions precisely. All chemicals can be hazardous to humans and to the environment unless they are employed with knowledge, caution, and appropriate restraint.

PET   see POSITRON EMISSION TOMOGRAPHY

Pétain, Henri Philippe [pay-tan']   Henri Philippe Pétain, b. Apr. 24, 1856, d. July 23, 1951, a World War I French military hero, headed the VICHY GOVERNMENT in France during World War II. A student and later a teacher at the École de Guerre, Pétain attained the rank of general after the outbreak of World War I. He became a hero after the Battle of Verdun (1916; see VERDUN, BATTLE OF), in which he halted the advance of German troops despite massive French losses, and later became commander in chief of armies in the field (1917) and a marshal of France (1918).

After France's defeat (1940) by the Germans, the French government fled to Bordeaux, and Pétain became premier. He concluded an armistice with Germany and became chief-of-state in the fascist-oriented Vichy Government of unoccupied France. Although at first he was nominally independent, he found it increasingly difficult to resist German demands. In December 1940, Pétain dismissed his foreign minister Pierre LAVAL, a collaborator who had helped to bring him to power, but in 1942 he recalled Laval at German insistence.

Following the war, the French brought Pétain to trial. He was sentenced to death, but the provisional president Charles de Gaulle commuted the sentence to life imprisonment.

Henri Philippe Pétain, marshal of France, was called the "hero of Verdun" for his defense of that city in the Battle of Verdun (1916). Pétain was made head of France's Vichy Government during World War II. His cooperation with the Germans led to his conviction for treason in 1945.

Peter, Epistles of   The two Epistles of Peter are part of the section of the New Testament of the BIBLE called the General Letters (Catholic Epistles). They are the 21st and 22d books of the canon. Early tradition supports 1 Peter's claim to authorship by Saint Peter (1 Pet. 1:1), although the attribution has been challenged. The

book was possibly written from Rome ("Babylon" of 1 Pet. 5:13) to Christians in Anatolia (1 Pet. 1:1) just before AD 64. Its purpose was to strengthen Christians suffering persecution. Peter explained the suffering as a test of faith and pointed the persecuted Christians to their living hope founded on God, who raised Jesus from the grave.

Authorship of 2 Peter, although also ascribed to Peter (2 Pet. 1:1), has been questioned by many scholars. No mention of the letter occurs until about the 3d century. Probably written for the same Anatolian audience as was 1 Peter, the book warns against false teachers in the community and gives affirmative assurance that Christ will return (2 Pet. 3:1–10).

Peter, Saint   Saint Peter was the most prominent of Jesus Christ's disciples. Originally named Simon son of Jonah (Matt. 16:17), he was given the Aramaic name *Cephas* by Jesus or the early church; the name means "rock" and is translated into Greek as Peter.

All that is known of Peter's life before he was called by Jesus is that he was a Galilean fisherman with a brother named ANDREW. Peter is mentioned numerous times in the Gospels and first 15 chapters of Acts. He is pictured as a leader and spokesman of the disciples; he identifies Jesus as Messiah (Mark 8:27; Matt. 16:16) and is selected as the rock on which the church will be built (Matt. 16:18). He is several times mentioned with the brothers James and John, with whom he witnesses the TRANSFIGURATION and Jesus' agony in Gethsemane. After Jesus' arrest Peter denies knowing him three times and later repents his denial (Matt. 26:69–75; John 18:10–27).

A bronze relief (c.1433–45) from the central doors of Saint Peter's Basilica, Rome, depicts the head-down crucifixion of the apostle Peter.

In Acts, Peter is a leader in the Jerusalem church and engages in missionary activity in Samaria, Galilee, Lydda, Sharon, and Joppa. He favors admission of Gentiles into the church but occupies a middle position between JAMES (the "brother" of Jesus), who wants to keep Christianity very Jewish in practice, and PAUL, who wishes to minimize requirements for Gentile converts.

The New Testament says nothing about Peter's life after his presence at the meeting in Jerusalem with James and Paul (Acts 15). Later sources say that Peter went to Rome, was martyred (c.64–68) under Nero, and buried on Vatican Hill. Evidence concerning his presence, activity, and death in Rome is slight. Feast day: June 29 (with Saint Paul).

Peter Chrysologus, Saint [kris-ahl'-uh-guhs] Saint Peter Chrysologus, c.400–c.450, bishop of Ravenna, is remembered primarily for his sermons. Although *chrysologus* means "golden worded," his sermons are characterized more by brevity and classical rhetoric than by eloquence or theological depth. In a sympathetic letter to EUTYCHES, father of MONOPHYSITISM, he advised obedience in matters of faith to Rome. He was declared a Doctor of the Church in 1729. Feast day: July 30 (formerly Dec. 4).

Peter Damian, Saint [day'-mee-uhn] Saint Peter Damian, b. 1007, d. Feb. 22, 1072, was an Italian churchman and reformer. In 1035 he entered the Benedictine monastery at Fonte Avellana, where he became prior in 1043 and acquired a reputation for his sermons denouncing worldliness, simony, and other clerical abuses. In 1057 he was named a cardinal. He continued his work of ecclesiastical reform and served as a papal envoy to France and Germany. Peter Damian was never formally canonized, but in 1828 Pope Leo XII extended his feast day, February 23, to the universal church and declared him one of the Doctors of the Church.

Peter Lombard [lahm'-bahrd] Italian theologian Peter Lombard, b. c.1100, d. Paris, July 21 or 22, 1160, was known as the Master of the Sentences because of his principal work, *The Four Books of Sentences*. Composed between 1148 and 1158, before his election as bishop of Paris in 1159, the *Sentences* served as the fundamental textbook for beginners in theology for more than 350 years. The *Sentences* met with opposition from more traditional theologians; thus, Walter of Saint-Victor regarded Peter as one of the four "pests of France" responsible for creating SCHOLASTICISM.

Peter Martyr see VERMIGLI, PIETRO MARTIRE

Peter Pan A perennially popular children's play, James M. BARRIE's *Peter Pan* (1904) is about a boy who refuses to grow up or to leave his home in Never-Never Land. Peter introduces the three Darling children—Wendy, Michael, and John—to flying and to adventures involving his friends Tinker Bell and Tiger Lily and the wicked pirate Captain Hook. The play's creation was influenced by Barrie's friendship with the five sons of his friend Llewelyn Davies; later, Barrie reworked it into a story, *Peter Pan and Wendy* (1911). Maude Adams, Eva Le Gallienne, Mary Martin, and Sandy Duncan have been among the many actresses who have played the role of Peter Pan.

Peter the Hermit A French monk, Peter the Hermit, b. c.1050, d. July 8 or 11, 1115, was one of the most effective preachers of the First CRUSADE. In 1096, with the knight Walter the Penniless, he led a large band of peasants across Europe to Constantinople. He lost control of his followers, who crossed into Anatolia before the arrival of the main Crusader army and were massacred. Peter, who had returned to Constantinople to seek help, took part in the conquest of Jerusalem in 1099 and later helped found the Augustinian monastery of Neufmoutier (Huy) in Belgium.

Peter III, King of Aragon (Peter the Great) [air'-uh-gahn] Peter III, b. c.1240, d. Nov. 11, 1285, king of Aragon from 1276, conquered Sicily and served as its king from 1282 until the end of his life. Known as Peter the Great, he was the son and successor of JAMES I of Aragon. After the rebellion known as the SICILIAN VESPERS (1282) he took Sicily from CHARLES I, king of Naples. Pope Martin IV excommunicated Peter and urged the French to launch a crusade against him. By strengthening feudal rights through the General Privilege (1283), Peter won the support of the nobles in Aragon against the French, whose invasion he defeated in 1285.

Peter I, King of Castile (Peter the Cruel) [kas-teel'] Peter I, b. Aug. 30, 1334, d. Mar. 23, 1369, king of Castile (1350–69), acquired the epithet Peter the Cruel because of his harsh treatment of his wife, his relatives, and his subjects. He succeeded his father, Alfonso XI, as king. Imprisoning his wife, he aroused the opposition of the nobility led by his illegitimate half brother, Henry of Trastamara. Henry challenged Peter's right to rule but was defeated in 1367; subsequently, however, Henry defeated Peter at Montiel and murdered him, then assuming the Castilian crown as Henry II.

Peter I, King of Portugal Before he was crowned (1357) king of Portugal, Peter I, b. Apr. 8, 1320, d. Jan. 18, 1367, was a participant in an episode that has been frequently romanticized in Portuguese literature. His father, Alfonso IV (r. 1325–57), caused the murder (1355) of Peter's mistress (and perhaps later wife), Inez de Castro, and the prince subsequently led a brief revolt against him. After Peter became king, he condemned the murderers to horrible deaths.

Peter II, King of Portugal   King Peter II, b. Apr. 26, 1648, d. Dec. 9, 1706, promoted the economic development of Portugal. Regent for his incompetent brother Alfonso VI from 1667, he became king on Alfonso's death (1683). Peter signed an important trade agreement with England (Treaty of Methuen, 1703); as a result Portugal was drawn into the War of the SPANISH SUCCESSION.

Peter I, Emperor of Russia (Peter the Great)   Peter I, known as Peter the Great, b. June 9 (N.S.), 1672, d. Feb. 8 (N.S.), 1725, was tsar of Russia (1682–1725) and the first Russian emperor (from 1721). His military achievements and westernizing reforms laid the foundation of the modern Russian state.

The youngest son of Tsar ALEXIS by a second marriage, Peter was not expected to rule. He associated with and learned from foreigners, especially the Dutch, in the foreign quarter of Moscow. After Alexis's death (1676), Fyodor III, Peter's half brother, became tsar. Fyodor died in 1682, however, and Peter became co-tsar with his half brother Ivan V, under the regency of his half sister, Sophia. Peter gained effective control of the government in 1689. After becoming sole tsar on Ivan's death (1696), he traveled (1697–98) to Europe—the first journey of its kind for a Russian ruler—to examine the latest technical advances and to recruit engineering and military experts for his service.

Peter began his reign in earnest in 1700, when he joined a European alliance that initiated the Great NORTHERN WAR (1700–21) against Sweden. He hoped to annex territories along the Baltic coast and thereby open warmwater ports to give Russia a "window to the west." CHARLES XII of Sweden defeated Peter at the Baltic city of Narva in 1700, but Peter's retrained and reequipped

Peter the Great, one of Russia's ablest tsars and its first emperor, ruled from 1682 to 1725. Peter was a bold leader whose attempts at expansion and Westernization were ruthlessly carried out. His efforts did much to make Russia a major European power.

army then overwhelmed Charles at Poltava in Ukraine in 1709. The Peace of Nystadt (1721) gave Russia its new Baltic coastline and proclaimed Peter emperor of all the Russias.

The Great Northern War required Peter to reorganize his empire. He needed troops for his army, necessitating a census and a system of conscription; artillery, which meant mines to be explored, transport to be arranged, and forges to be built and run by Western experts; and a fleet, which required special training for Muscovites who had not sailed before. The nobles, previously uneducated and attached to their distant lands, were required to attend schools and to devote their lives to civil or military service. The Guards Regiments, aristocratic units that were the core of Peter's army, became especially powerful. Peter also coerced the Russian Orthodox church into service to the state, making it a part of government administration through the creation of a Holy Synod controlled by the tsar.

The emperor's heavy emphasis on military and technical development spurred the growth of manufacturing and accelerated the commercial life of Russia, especially through its new Baltic ports. Peter also speeded the trend toward the secularization and modernization of culture. He built a new capital, Saint Petersburg (see LENINGRAD), which he intended to be a symbol of the new Russia. Peter promoted secular education, encouraged Western dress, modernized the calendar and alphabet, and edited the first Russian newspaper.

Peter's attempt to arrange the succession to the throne, however, met with difficulties. After his death his second wife ruled, ineffectually, as CATHERINE I and was followed by his sickly grandson Peter II (r. 1727–30).

Peter I, King of Serbia   Peter I, b. July 11 (N.S.), 1844, d. Aug. 16, 1921, was king of Serbia (1903–18) and subsequently the first monarch of the Kingdom of the Serbs, Croats, and Slovenes (1918–21), later Yugoslavia. Exiled from 1858 to 1903, he fought for France in the Franco-Prussian War (1870–71) and provided assistance for the Serbian uprising against the Turks (1875–76). Peter, a member of the Karadjordjević family, promoted the growth of constitutional government. During World War I he retreated before the advance of the Central Powers. At the war's end, Peter was proclaimed king of the South Slavs. He was succeeded by his son ALEXANDER, who became king of Yugoslavia.

Peter II, King of Yugoslavia   Peter II, b. Sept. 6, 1923, d. Nov. 3, 1970, the second and last king of Yugoslavia (1934–41), succeeded to the throne under the regency of Prince Paul, a cousin of his father, King ALEXANDER. Paul's neutralist government was overthrown in March 1941, and Peter was declared of age. He was forced, however, to flee the country within weeks following a German invasion. The postwar Communist regime abolished the monarchy in 1945, and Peter settled in the United States.

Peterborough   Peterborough is a city in Cambridgeshire in east central England. Situated on the River Nene about 120 km (75 mi) north of London, Peterborough is a diversified industrial center. The city's population is 151,200 (1987 est.). Historical landmarks include Saint Peter's Cathedral (12th to 13th century) and Saint Thomas's Chapel (14th century). The city is also the burial place of Catherine of Aragon. Peterborough grew up around a monastery and was chartered in 1541. After the reclamation of The Fens, Peterborough prospered as a marketing center. From 1884 to 1965 the city was part of an administrative unit called the Soke of Peterborough within Northamptonshire. It was then part of the county of Huntingdon and Peterborough until the redistricting of 1974 placed it within Cambridgeshire.

Petersburg   Petersburg is an independent city in southeast Virginia on the Appomattox River. It has a population of 38,386 (1990). Petersburg is an important tobacco market. Its industries manufacture cigarettes, textiles, wood and leather products, and boats. Historic landmarks include the Petersburg National Battlefield and the Old Blandford Church, the cemetery of which contains the graves of 30,000 Confederate soldiers. Fort Lee, a U.S. Army post, is nearby.

Petersburg was established in 1748 on the site of Fort Henry (1646) and figured importantly in the American Revolution. British forces under Benedict Arnold and William Phillips captured Petersburg in April 1781, and the following month the British general Charles Cornwallis began there the campaign that culminated in his surrender at Yorktown. The Union siege of the city was the last major campaign of the Civil War.

Petersburg campaign   During the U.S. Civil War, the city of Petersburg, Va., an important railroad center south of Richmond, was besieged by Union forces from June 1864 to April 1865. The Confederate general P. G. T. BEAUREGARD was a hero of the early assaults, holding his lines against the more numerous Union troops until the arrival (June 18, 1864) of reinforcements led by Gen. Robert E. LEE. A siege ensued during which Union generals George MEADE and Ulysses S. GRANT threw increasing forces against the more than 32 km (20 mi) of Confederate trenches. A huge mine exploded (July 30, 1864) by the Federals in a tunnel under the city's defenses failed to breach the Confederate line. The soldiers of both sides became the battle's real heroes, enduring daily horror and privation. Grant finally broke Lee's lines on Apr. 2, 1865; Petersburg and Richmond fell the following day, and Lee surrendered at APPOMATTOX COURT HOUSE a week later.

Peterson, Oscar   The Canadian jazz pianist Oscar Emmanuel Peterson, b. Montreal, Aug. 15, 1925, made a spectacular American debut in 1949 at a "Jazz at the Philharmonic" concert at Carnegie Hall in New York City and since that year has ranked among the most popular of jazz artists. A virtuoso performer, Peterson has an encyclopedic range—from 1920s stride piano to modern jazz. He has recorded with his famous trio and with many of the major musicians of the post-1940s era.

Pétion, Alexandre Sabès [pay-tee-ohn']   Alexandre Sabès Pétion, b. Apr. 2, 1770, d. Mar. 29, 1818, was a Haitian independence leader. A well-educated, freeborn mulatto, he first supported but then opposed the revolutionary leader François TOUSSAINT L'OUVERTURE in the 1790s. He later fought (1802–03) alongside the ex-slave Jean Jacques DESSALINES against French colonial rule.

Once Haiti achieved its independence (1804) from France, Dessalines repudiated their alliance and proclaimed himself emperor. Pétion then conspired with Henri CHRISTOPHE to assassinate him. After Dessalines's death (1806) the conspirators became opponents. In the north, an assembly proclaimed Christophe ruler of Haiti, but the mulatto-dominated senate in the south elected (1807) Pétion president of a separate, southern republic. Pétion was made president for life in 1816.

Petipa, Marius [pe-tee-pah', mahr-ee-oos']   A gifted dancer, a skilled mime, and an uncompromising teacher, the Frenchman Marius Petipa, b. Mar. 11, 1819, d. July 1 (N.S.), 1910, dominated Russian ballet throughout the last half of the 19th century. The more than 60 ballets that he created during his lifetime define classical ballet as it is now known, and many of his full-length ballets, such as *The Nutcracker, The Sleeping Beauty,* and *Swan Lake,* are in the permanent repertoires of Soviet and Western companies.

Petipa partnered several famous European ballerinas, including Carlotta Grisi and Fanny Elssler, before joining (1847) the Imperial Theater in Saint Petersburg as premier danseur. He became chief ballet master of the Saint Petersburg Ballet in 1869 and soon began to create the full-length ballets for which he is famous—*La Bayadère* (1877), *The Sleeping Beauty* (1890), the revised *Swan Lake* (1895; with Lev Ivanov), and *Raymonda* (1898).

Petit, Roland [puh-tee']   Roland Petit, b. Jan. 13, 1924, has been a major force in French dance since World War II. From 1939 to 1944, while dancing with the Paris Opéra Ballet, he began choreographing; in 1945 he founded the Ballets des Champs-Elysées with Boris Kochno. Some of his more successful works from this period are *Les Forains* (1945), *Le Jeune Homme et la Mort* (1946), *Les Demoiselles de la Nuit* (1948), and *Carmen* (1949). Les Ballets de Paris de Roland Petit (1948) presented works for several years, with interruptions while Petit and his wife, Zizi (Renée) Jeanmaire, worked on films. He is the founder (1972) and director of the Ballet National de Marseilles. He choreographed *The Blue Angel* (1985) specifically for dancer Natalia Makarova.

Petőfi, Sándor [pe'-tur-fee, shahn'-dohr]   Hungarian lyric poet Sándor Petőfi, b. Jan. 1, 1823, enriched the artistry and extended the range of his nation's poetry beyond any predecessor and created a new synthesis of poetic techniques and realistic subjects. His epics were powerful blends of folk topics, attitudes, and verse forms, and his lyric poems stood out as aesthetic expressions of genuinely felt experiences. His language, images, and characters were rooted in the Hungarian Great Plains. He participated in Hungary's War of Independence (1848–49) and disappeared on July 31, 1849, in a battle against Russian forces.

Petra [pee'-truh]   Petra, located in southern Jordan, was the capital of the ancient Arabic kingdom of Nabataea from the 4th century BC to the 2d century AD. Walled in by towering rocks except for a deep, narrow cleft, and with an ample supply of pure water, it was a major city on the caravan trade route from southern Arabia. Subject to strong Hellenistic cultural influence, Petra was conquered by the Roman emperor TRAJAN in AD 106 and became part of the Roman province of Arabia. Later declining in economic importance, Petra was forgotten until its ruins were identified in 1812 by Jakob BURCKHARDT. It is now a major archaeological and tourist site, famous for its rock-cut temples and tombs.

Petrarch [pee'-trahrk]   The great Italian Renaissance poet, scholar, and humanist Francesco Petrarca, b. July 20, 1304, d. July 19, 1374, is generally known in the English-speaking world as Petrarch. In 1312 his father, a Florentine notary in political exile, moved with the family to the French city of Avignon, then a papal residence. Petrarch began (1316) legal studies in nearby Montpel-

The Italian poet and humanist Petrarch is depicted in his studio in this 14th century portrait. Petrarch's lyric poetry and perfecting of the sonnet form influenced the course of Western literature, and recognition by his contemporaries culminated in his coronation (1341) as poet laureate in Rome.

lier, and from 1320, with his brother, Gherardo, he attended the University of Bologna. After their father's death in 1326, both returned to Avignon, where Petrarch for some time lived the life of a fashionable young man-about-town and came in contact with members of the Roman Colonna family, who became his patrons.

On Apr. 6, 1327, in the Church of Santa Clara, Petrarch saw, and fell in love with, a woman he called Laura but whose true identity remains uncertain. To her he wrote the love lyrics of his *Canzoniere* (Songbook, 1342). Having decided to enter the church, he took the minor orders in 1330 and was employed by Cardinal Giovanni Colonna. In 1341 he was crowned poet laureate in Rome.

Although it is known that he revised them at least ten times, Petrarch referred to his *Canzoniere* as a work of little importance, calling them *Rerum vulgarium fragmenta* ("short pieces in the vernacular"). This, however, is the work for which he is primarily remembered and which, for centuries to come, constituted the standard model for love poetry. *Petrarch's Secret* (1353–58; Eng. trans., 1911) is an intimately confessional work that gives dramatic form to the conflict between flesh and spirit that troubled Petrarch throughout his life. The work is a dialogue in Latin between the poet and his second self in the guise of Saint Augustine. In a pitiless analysis, Augustine berates Petrarch's inability to resist the earthly temptations of love and fame and urges him to save his soul.

Petrarch's *Africa* (1338–41; Eng. trans., 1977), an epic in Latin hexameters on the second Punic War and the exploits of Scipio Africanus, remained unfinished. In the Italian triple rhyme of his *Triumphs* (1344; Eng. trans., 1962), Petrarch conceived in the form of a vision a series of triumphs, one superseding the other, so that Love in the end is overcome by Time and Eternity. *The Life of Solitude* (begun 1346; Eng. trans., 1924) is a Latin treatise that compares the leisure of a country life with the fatigue of a city life, whereas *De remediis utriusque fortunae* (Remedies against Fortune, 1354–66) is a disquisition on the stoical acceptance of favorable as well as adverse fortune. Petrarch's Latin letters, *Epistolae familiares, Epistolae seniles* (1363–66; Eng. trans., 1967), comprise letters to famous contemporaries and to the vast circle of his friends, including some fictional letters to classical authors.

petrel [pet'-rul]   Petrels are wide-ranging oceanic birds that spend most of their lives at sea and come to land only to breed. They are related to albatrosses. The various petrel species are scattered through three families, found mainly in the Southern Hemisphere but also along northern shores. The family Procellariidae, the large petrels, also includes the fulmar, prions, and SHEARWATERS. The family Hydrobatidae consists of the storm petrels—so named because sailors once believed that their presence presaged coming storms—and the family Pelecanoididae comprises the diving petrels.

All petrels are strong fliers with long wings. They have close-set, tubular nostrils on their hooked bills, which are deeply grooved. The body ranges from black to shades of

Wilson's petrel breeds from December through February in Antarctica and on subantarctic islands. At other times it ranges far north in both the Atlantic and Pacific oceans. It is the most common of the storm petrels.

gray or brown, with patches of white. The tail is broad and short, and the webbed feet bear claws and a vestigial hind toe. Storm petrels and diving petrels usually are from 14 to 25 cm (5.5 to 10 in) long, whereas large petrels may be more than three times this size. Some petrel species nest in burrows excavated in sandy soil on islands; others nest in crevices in rocky cliffs. They lay a single large egg, which is cared for by both sexes.

Petrie, Sir Flinders [pee'-tree]

In his generation, the British archaeologist Sir William Matthew Flinders Petrie, b. June 3, 1853, d. July 28, 1942, was the outstanding excavator in Egypt, not only because of his discoveries there but also as a leading innovator of scientific methods in excavation. He was largely self-taught, never having attended any school or university. His father, a civil engineer, taught him surveying, and his first mission to Egypt (1880–82) was to make a systematic survey of the Great Pyramid and its two neighboring pyramids at Giza. Between 1884 and 1926 he explored more than 30 different sites; two of his best-known discoveries were a commemorative inscription of Merneptah (*c.*1236–1223 BC), which contains the only known reference to Israel by name in Egyptian literature, and a rich collection of jewelry at Illahun that had belonged to a princess of the 12th dynasty (*c.*1880 BC).

Petrified Forest National Park

see NATIONAL PARKS

petrified wood

Petrified wood is the result of a process called petrifaction (or petrification), meaning "to change into stone." The process involves mineral emplacement, in which dissolved minerals are carried by groundwater into the porous parts of buried wood (or shells or bones), where they crystallize out and settle, filling the pores. An object so impregnated with minerals is denser, heavier, and more resistant to destruction than it was originally.

During the Triassic Period, from about 225 million to 190 million years ago, conifers often grew in large forests, in marshes, and in other very humid habitats. At the end of the Triassic, shallow seas returned and submerged these forests. The drifting logs or upright stumps of the forest remains were eventually buried in volcanic ash or other sediments, and the process of petrifaction began. The waters penetrating the sediments were rich in mineral salts, which reacted with the plant matter inside the cell walls of the trees. The most common of these minerals were silica (SiO_2), occurring as quartz, of which chalcedony and jasper were part; and calcium carbonate ($CaCO_3$), occurring as calcite. Iron and magnesium OXIDE MINERALS (Fe_2O_3, MgO, and others) gave petrified wood colors of red, yellow, and orange.

As the mineral salts penetrated into the cells and started to crystallize, they usually left the cell walls almost completely intact. Thus petrified wood, although of rocklike density and weight, consists of both organic (1% to 15%) and mineral matter. Complete crystallization of the cell cavities was a very rapid and extremely efficient process that left fossils so well preserved, with such excellent clarity and transparency, that they can be studied through a microscope in the same manner as recent organic material.

Petrified wood consisting largely of *Araucarioxylon ari-*

The famous Petrified Forest in Arizona contains numerous remains of ancient trees in which the wood has been completely replaced by silica and mineral impurities.

zonicum (related to the pinelike *Araucaria* of the Southern Hemisphere) can be seen in the Petrified Forest National Park in Arizona. Among other interesting exposures of petrified wood is the one located in Yellowstone National Park, Wyoming.

petrochemicals   Petrochemicals are chemicals produced from natural gas, natural-gas liquids, or refinery products derived from crude-oil distillation, or cracking (see PETROLEUM INDUSTRY). First-stage petrochemicals, including ethylene, propylene, butylenes, benzene, toluene, and xylenes—the petrochemical "building blocks"—are produced as a starting point for a number of secondary petrochemicals that, in turn, are transformed into a variety of petrochemical end products: PLASTICS, SOLVENTS, SYNTHETIC FIBERS, elastomers, and other essential commodities.

The Rise of the Petrochemical Industry

Some of the products referred to as "petrochemicals" were in the past produced from charcoal, coal-tar distillation by-products, ACETYLENE, or fermentation alcohol. The science of petrochemicals is based on industrial ORGANIC CHEMISTRY. The growth of the refining industry in the United States, based on abundant petroleum and natural-gas resources as well as on the development of sophisticated thermal and catalytic oil-cracking processes, created the conditions for the present petrochemical industry. Although the main focus of the refining industry has always been the supply of motor and heating fuels, the oil-transformation processes that were developed in the 1920s and 1930s also provided by-products in the form of highly reactive hydrocarbons—the petrochemical "building blocks"—that were quickly seen to be economical feedstocks for many organic chemicals.

World War II greatly accelerated the rise of the U.S. petrochemical industry. First, the suddenly increased demand for high-octane aviation gasoline led to a surge in refinery capacity, with a concomitant increased production of reactive hydrocarbons. Second, the need for synthetic rubber required the development of a large-scale technology for producing BENZENE, styrene, butylenes, butadiene, and ACRYLONITRILE. The war was also responsible for creating a demand for many other petrochemical products. At the end of the war, pent-up consumer demand kept petrochemical plants running.

By the late 1960s growth in the European industry had narrowed the U.S. lead in petrochemicals, and Japan's industry also began to develop. In the 1970s oil-rich nations such as Saudi Arabia, Iran, Canada, Algeria, and Norway began building their own petrochemical plants.

Petrochemicals Production

First-stage petrochemicals are produced either as part of petroleum refining operations, where they are by-products, or in plants built specifically for making these materials. Thus, some ethylene and substantial amounts of propylene and butylene—all of which are hydrocarbons (molecules containing only carbon and hydrogen atoms)

A typical cracking installation in an oil refinery is a maze of towers and pipelines. Products from the initial distillation of petroleum are reformed in these units into gasoline and other useful products.

with a double-bond structure—are still the products of oil-cracking operations carried out for the specific purpose of producing higher-octane gasoline. Naphtha reforming, a petroleum-refinery operation that occurs at elevated pressures and temperatures over a catalyst, produces large amounts of BTX (benzene, toluene, xylene) aromatics, which can be used to raise gasoline octane rating or for further processing into a variety of derivatives. The most important primary petrochemical production process is "steam cracking," in which such petroleum-derived feedstocks as ethane, propane, naphtha, and higher-boiling crude fractions are cracked into ethylene, propylene, butylenes, butadiene, and BTX aromatics. The production of ammonia and methanol via steam reforming of hydrocarbons is another key petrochemical process.

The petrochemicals produced in these operations are then further transformed, via conventional chemistry, into a huge variety of intermediates and end products.

Petrochemical Uses

ETHYLENE is the most widely used raw material for the petrochemical industry. A by-product of the cracking process, it is used to make ethyl glycol, which serves as an antifreeze and as the basis for the production of styrene, a major constituent of synthetic rubber; polyethylene, a translucent plastic with countless uses; fabric finishes; latex paints; and many others.

The ACETYLENE family of chemicals also provides material for the petrochemical industry. Obtained from METHANE, the main component of natural gas, acetylene and its derivatives are used to make acetate fiber, vinyl acetate, and vinyl chloride used in adhesives, plastics, and coatings.

The range of petrochemical use is enormous. Major needs met by the petrochemical industry include almost every consumer field, some of which follow.

Agriculture and Food. The most important petrochemical product in this area is ammonia, for which natural gas is the preferred feedstock. Ammonia is used to make nitrogen fertilizers. Other products include crop-protection chemicals, single-cell proteins, and feed and food additives.

Housing. Polyvinylchloride siding, polyurethane insulation, caulking materials, vinyl adhesives, furniture fabrics, carpeting, paints, and wallpapers are major products.

Clothing. Of the 20 major synthetic fibers, only three—acetate, rayon, and acetic anhydride—are not based on petrochemicals.

Transportation. These products include polyester car and truck bodies, acrylic automobile finish coats, styrenic car bumpers, synthetic elastomers for tires and hoses, vinyl seat covers, methacrylate traffic lights and road signs, and vinyl road paints. (Many automobile models use several hundred kilograms of plastic, which is strong but much lighter than metal.)

Medicine. A large number of medicines are the product of petrochemicals, including many antihistamines, decongestants, antihypertensives, and analgesics.

Industry Problems

Two major problems arose as the petrochemical industry grew in scale and became a producer of an ever-increasing number of chemical derivatives: plant emissions and toxicity. Although over the years the industry has taken a number of steps to mitigate these problems, they remain important issues.

Petrochemical plants discharge gaseous, liquid, and solid waste streams into their surroundings as a part of normal operations. Furnaces and steam boilers may emit carbon or sulfur oxides and other products of combustion. Process water used for direct cooling and for equipment cleaning usually contains organic wastes. These waste streams can be responsible for various forms of atmospheric pollution, contamination of streams and lakes, and harmful additions to landfill.

Additional problems have arisen as consumers discharge nonbiodegradable detergents into sewers or septic tanks, generate plastic waste, and use aerosol sprays containing chlorofluorocarbons, which destroy the OZONE LAYER.

Federal, state, and local regulations, together with concerted efforts by the chemical community, have substantially reduced the magnitude and toxicity of plant emissions, and are reducing or eliminating the production of chemicals whose discharge is particularly harmful to the environment. A number of identified sites remain where major cleanup operations must take place, with costs borne by the industry.

Incineration and RECYCLING OF MATERIALS are beginning to make an impact in reducing the amount of plastic waste in LANDFILLS, where biodegradability is a major issue.

Toxicity is equally important as an industry issue. It was discovered too late that prolonged worker exposure to vinyl chloride fumes can be directly linked to certain types of cancer; that certain chlorinated insecticides contain highly toxic dioxins; and that chlorinated wastes, dumped into landfills that later become housing sites, can be responsible for birth defects (see POLLUTANTS, CHEMICAL).

Emissions and toxicity can combine in a disastrous manner, as they did in a pesticides plant in BHOPAL, India, in 1984, where the accidental injection of water into a tank of methyl isocyanate caused the release of a toxic gas that killed 2,500 and injured hundreds of thousands.

---

petroleum Petroleum—the oil and gas in the Earth's crust—is of immense importance to humans. The word *petroleum*, derived from the Latin *petra* and *oleum*, means literally "rock oil." Petroleum occurs widely in the sedimentary rocks of the Earth's crust and may occur as a gas, liquid, semisolid, or solid, although mixtures of gas and liquids are most common. From a chemical standpoint, petroleum is an extremely complex mixture of hydrocarbon compounds with minor amounts of nitrogen, oxygen, and sulfur as impurities. Forms of petroleum include crude oil, or unrefined liquid petroleum; NATURAL GAS, consisting of the compound methane, with lesser proportions of ethane, butane, and propane; asphalt, a solid or semisolid bituminous substance obtained as a residue from certain petroleums (see TAR, PITCH, AND ASPHALT); and gilsonite, one of a number of solid asphaltlike compounds. Commercially, crude oil is the most important form of petroleum, and natural gas is second.

Physically, crude oil is a mixture of different compounds that boil at different temperatures. The lightest fraction consists of gases that boil below atmospheric temperature. The next fraction, normally refined into GASOLINE, boils between about 30° and 200° C (85° and 390° F). The fraction boiling between about 140° and 320° C (285° and 610° F) is termed KEROSENE. The fraction boiling above about 320° C is commonly refined into heating, diesel, and lubricating oils (see LUBRICATION). The remaining and heaviest fraction is the residue, which supplies waxes, asphalts, and some fuel oils.

Petroleum is enormously important from an economic, technological, and social standpoint. Fuels that are derived from petroleum supply more than half of the world's total supply of energy. Gasoline, kerosene, and diesel oil provide fuel for automobiles, tractors, trucks, aircraft, and ships (see AUTOMOTIVE INDUSTRY). Fuel oil and natural gas are used to heat homes and commercial buildings. Petroleum is the source of PETROCHEMICALS used in the manufacture of synthetic fibers for clothing, and in plastics, paints, fertilizers, insecticides, soaps, and synthetic rubber. Growth in the use of petroleum as a source of petrochemicals in manufacturing shows no signs of abating.

Origin

The origin of petroleum has provoked extensive argument, and major gaps exist in understanding the process of its formation. Geologists generally agree, however, that petroleum is formed through progressive chemical change of materials provided by microscopic aquatic organisms

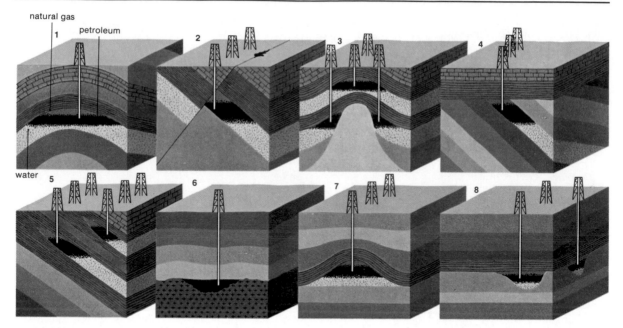

Pools of natural gas, petroleum, and water are found in traps consisting of reservoir, or porous, rocks capped by impervious rock layers. Traps are formed in anticlinal, or uplifted, formations (1), in areas (2) in which the oil-bearing reservoir rocks have been moved by faulting and blocked by impervious strata, between salt plugs and the surrounding upturned rock layers (3), and in tilted porous beds (4) overlain by horizontal impervious strata. Reservoir rocks may also become thinner, or pinch out, to form traps along their highest points (5). The oil may collect in water-free hollows in basement rocks (6), in fossil coral reefs (7), and in long, winding fossil river channels (8).

incorporated in marine sedimentary rocks, where most of the world's petroleum occurs. These organisms apparently include microscopic marine plants and animals that settled to the sea bottom and were incorporated in the sediments.

Transformation of some of this sedimentary material to petroleum probably began soon after deposition, with bacteria playing some role in the initial stages, and clay particles serving as catalysts.

The transformation processes have been strongly influenced by temperature. Temperatures within the Earth's crust increase more or less directly with depth. Some evidence indicates that most petroleum has formed at temperatures not exceeding about 100° to 120° C (210° to 250° F), with the generation of petroleum hydrocarbons beginning as low as 65° C (150° F). At temperatures above 175° to 200° C (345° to 390° F) most liquid hydrocarbons are destroyed.

Migration

The processes by which petroleum migrates into pools are also poorly known. Commercial deposits of oil and gas occur in pools or fields in which the oil or gas occupies pore space in the rock. Some pools are large, extending laterally over many square kilometers and their vertical extent ranging from several meters to as much as several hundred meters. The oil or gas occupying the pore space in the pool has displaced the water that was initially present in the pores. The presence of a pool of oil or gas therefore implies that the oil or gas has migrated into the pool.

When sediments such as mud and clay are deposited, they may contain a large amount of water with suspended hydrocarbons. As layer upon layer of sediment accumulates, the progressively increasing load of material causes the sediment to compact, expelling some of the water in the pores. Migration of hydrocarbons probably begins at this stage. Oil and gas are propelled by buoyancy to migrate in an upward direction through permeable rocks. Buoyancy results because oil and gas are less dense than water. The route of migration may involve a substantial horizontal component such as, for example, along the upper surface of a gently sloping permeable sandstone bed overlain by a relatively impermeable bed of mudstone or shale.

Reservoir Rocks and Traps

Besides being a source of the oil or gas, an oil or gas pool requires a reservoir rock that is porous and permeable and a trap to contain the oil or gas. Migration is thus essential to convey the oil or gas from its source, into and through the reservoir rock, and to the trap, where it finally accumulates.

Most traps are created by a structural relationship in which a relatively permeable reservoir rock is bounded above by impermeable rock. Traps are of many forms, and the search for petroleum is to a large extent the search for traps. Even when a trap has been identified, drilling may prove it to be dry, that is, without any accumulation of oil and gas.

A common type of trap is a dome, or anticline, that dips away in all directions. An anticlinal trap is a form of structural trap because its trapping properties are due to deformation or folding of the layers of rock after they were deposited. Other common structural traps are created by relationships involving faults.

Stratigraphic traps are alternative forms of traps, resulting from variations in the layers, or strata, that were created when the strata were deposited. Examples of stratigraphic traps include sandstone lenses, limestone reefs, and wedge-outs formed by depositional variations. SALT DOMES, formed by flowage of salt at substantial depths, have created numerous traps that are both structural and stratigraphic.

Virtually all types of sedimentary rock form reservoir rocks under certain conditions. Most reservoir rocks, however, consist of SANDSTONE or LIMESTONE. A good reservoir rock is one that is both permeable and porous. A sandstone that is composed of large, rounded grains that are more or less uniform in size is an ideal reservoir rock, because both its permeability and porosity are high.

Although most petroleum is produced from underground reservoirs, petroleum occurs in a variety of forms at the surface. Surface seepages of oil and gas are common in many regions. Seeps range from mere traces, such as a film of oil or gas bubbling through water, to deposits large enough to be commercially valuable.

Exploration for Oil and Gas

The petroleum industry is worldwide, because every country depends on petroleum. Many countries produce petroleum, but some countries that are large consumers of petroleum produce less than they consume. Access to sources of petroleum is thus of critical economic and military importance. Petroleum is truly global in its distribution, but the relative abundance of petroleum is extremely variable, some regions being much more richly endowed than others.

Exploration for oil and gas is conducted on a worldwide basis, both on land and on the continental shelves. Seismic surveys are often conducted in advance of exploratory drilling. Under favorable conditions, seismic surveys provide a remarkably detailed overview of the geologic, structural, and stratigraphic conditions beneath the surface. Under exceptional conditions, seismic surveys may reveal directly the presence of gas. More often, however, drilling is necessary to confirm the presence or absence of commercially producible quantities of gas and oil. Geologic information is also provided by DRILLING and is obtained through the use of modern borehole logging techniques, which may be incorporated with seismic data. Drilling technology has been substantially advanced in recent decades, particularly with respect to the capability of drilling from ships or from platforms that rest on the seafloor.

It is believed that by the year 2010 only about 30 percent of the world's energy will be supplied by oil, while coal, natural-gas, solar, and nuclear sources will increase in

TABLE 1: ESTIMATED PROVED WORLD RESERVES OF CRUDE OIL AND NATURAL GAS*

Region	Crude Reserves at Year-end (million barrels)			Natural-gas Reserves at Year-end (billions of ft³)		
	1989	1988	% Diff.	1989	1988	% Diff.
North America	85,233	86,955	− 2.0	332,958	335,193	− 1.0
South America	70,820	70,566	0.4	162,559	158,357	2.7
Western Europe	16,781	17,315	− 3.1	197,564	198,509	− 0.5
Eastern Europe	59,771	62,882	− 4.9	1,571,023	1,522,031	3.2
Africa	60,814	58,668	3.7	221,629	206,194	7.5
Middle East	592,752	585,314	1.3	1,341,167	1,325,579	1.2
Asia	43,586	43,959	− 0.9	263,815	258,692	2.0
Australia/Pacific	3,169	3,149	0.6	81,918	78,290	4.6
World Total	932,925	928,799	0.4	4,172,632	4,083,882	2.2

Source: *World Oil,* August 1990.   *Excludes natural-gas liquids.

TABLE 2: DISTRIBUTION OF WORLD OIL AND GAS RESERVES
(As of August 1990)

Region	Country	Oil (In millions of barrels)	Gas (in billions) m³	ft³
North America		85,233	9,428	332,958
South America		70,819	4,603	162,559
	United States	26,324	4,621	163,204
	Venezuela	60,516	2,993	105,689
	Mexico	51,983	2,060	72,744
	Canada	6,769	2,746	96,985
	Argentina	2,158	744	26,271
	Ecuador	1,413	113	3,996
Western Europe		16,781	5,594	197,564
	United Kingdom	3,808	560	19,776
	Norway	11,037	2,635	93,051
	Netherlands	157	1,725	60,918
Middle East		592,752	37,978	1,341,169
	Saudi Arabia	260,054	5,222	184,395
	Kuwait	96,000	1,377	48,643
	Iran	62,500	16,990	600,000
	UAE Abu Dhabi	54,360	5,174	182,700
	Neutral Zone	4,887	226	7,970
	Oman	4,291	280	9,875
	Qatar	2,556	4,587	162,000
	Syria	2,000	157	5,542
Africa		60,814	6,276	221,629
	Libya	22,800	827	29,200
	Nigeria	16,700	1,343	47,440
	Algeria	9,230	3,235	114,225
	Tunisia	1,802	88	3,120
	Egypt	4,300	325	11,473
	Congo	710	70	2,475
	Angola	2,100	51	1,800
Eastern Europe		59,771	44,572	1,571,023
	USSR	57,875	43,891	1,550,000
Asia, Australia, and Pacific		46,755	9,790	345,733
	China	21,500	935	33,022
	Indonesia	11,970	2,427	85,700
	India	4,345	590	20,850
	Malaysia	3,675	1,516	53,542
	Australia	2,831	2,080	73,455
	Brunei	1,152	346	12,200
	Pakistan	305	650	22,950
	World total	932,925	118,156	4,172,632

Source: *World Oil,* August 1990.

importance. The United States, whose domestic oil reserves and production both dwindled during the 1980s, may soon begin seriously to cultivate other energy sources.

World gas reserves at the end of 1989 were believed to be much larger than reserve estimates made only five years earlier, increasing by almost 20 percent. Although some experts suggest that the bulk of the world's oil and gas has already been discovered, and that declining production is inevitable, others believe that substantial amounts of oil and gas remain to be found and, furthermore, that unconventional sources will eventually be exploited. Unconventional sources include methane dissolved in subsurface waters, which will possibly provide an immense resource of natural gas; the extraction of oil from TAR SANDS—which contain billions of barrels of the fuel—and from oil shales (see SHALE, OIL); and the liquefaction and gasification of coal (see SYNTHETIC FUELS). All attempts to utilize these sources have proved so far to be noneconomic in competition with oil and natural gas. (The U.S. synthetic fuel program, which was begun with great fanfare in the late 1970s, ended in 1986 when federal funding was withdrawn.) Future technologies may, however, find ways of extracting fuel from these substances more efficiently.

petroleum industry

petroleum industry   The world petroleum industry, which includes both oil and NATURAL GAS, divides functionally into five main phases: exploration, production, transportation, refining, and consumption. Production of petroleum is concentrated in eight major areas: the Middle East, the USSR, North America, South America, Africa, China, the Far East, and Europe's North Sea region. Consumption of oil is centered in four major areas: North America, Western Europe, Japan, and the USSR. Because the production levels of North America, Western Europe, and Japan are much lower than their consumption levels, the majority of the world's oil is shipped to these areas from producing countries (see PETROLEUM for a discussion of exploration).

Production

The first commercial production of oil in modern times began in 1857 in Romania, where shallow reservoirs were developed. The modern petroleum industry, however, may be said to have begun in 1859, at Titusville, Pa., where oil was first produced in commercial quantity from a drilled well.

Most wells are now drilled by the rotary method. A steel bit attached to a drill pipe is revolved at the bottom of a hole. This action breaks up the rock by chipping and cutting it. Meanwhile a special mud mixture runs down through the multichannel drill pipe, lubricating the bit, carrying rock cuttings upward to the surface, and creating a pressure that prevents subsurface water from infiltrating the well area. When the drill reaches oil-bearing formations, a casing pipe containing special tubing is lowered into the hole and used to withdraw the fluid.

After the crude oil and natural gas are brought to the surface, the gas is separated from the crude oil in special pressurized gas separators. Water, suspended solids, and sand are also separated out from the oil. The oil is then stored temporarily in steel tanks until it is transported to the refinery by pipeline or tanker.

Oil Production.   The USSR remains the world's largest producer of crude oil; the United States ranks second. The largest petroleum exporters are countries in the Middle East—particularly Saudi Arabia, Iran, and Iraq—whose largest customer is the United States. Beginning in the 1970s, oil from North Sea deposits also became significant in export markets, as did products from Mexican oil fields.

The Iranian revolution of 1979 and the Iran-Iraq war (1980–88) resulted in an initial massive decrease in Iran's oil production, although by the mid-1980s Iran had recovered its production capacity. The impact of unrest in the Middle East was felt even more forcefully in 1990, when Iraq invaded Kuwait. The United States felt its interests so threatened that it dispatched a large force to Saudi Arabia. United Nations sanctions against Iraq stopped the flow of oil from that country, the region's second-largest producer, and from occupied Kuwait, creating the potential of a major oil shortage on world markets. Surplus production capacity in Saudi Arabia, however, helped maintain normal oil shipments to the West, and a cease-fire was reached in early 1991, with oil availability and prices showing only minor and temporary distruptions.

Natural-Gas Production.   The production and use of natural gas, which is often found near oil deposits, have been increasing steadily. Gas has become important almost everywhere in the world. This is a new development for the Eastern Hemisphere, although the United States has been producing and using gas for a long time. The worldwide growth rate for natural gas exceeds that for any other fuel, including oil. Between 1980 and 1988, natural-gas consumption had grown by almost 30 percent; it may double by the year 2000. The Soviet Union is by far the largest producer and consumer of natural gas, the United States ranks second in both categories, and the fuel is increasingly important in Canada and in Europe.

Still another new development of major interest is the extraction of liquefied petroleum gas (LPG) from a high-value portion of the natural gas. In contrast to liquefied natural gas (LNG), which is composed largely of methane, LPG consists primarily of propane and butane, is easily transportable, and remains liquid at a moderate temperature. LNG is difficult to handle because extremely low temperature or high pressure is required for its transport. It can be dangerous for this reason, but its huge potential supply makes the solution of these problems imperative.

Transportation

Natural gas, crude oil, and refined petroleum products are transported by various means, but primarily by pipelines (see PIPE AND PIPELINE) and TANKERS, and in some

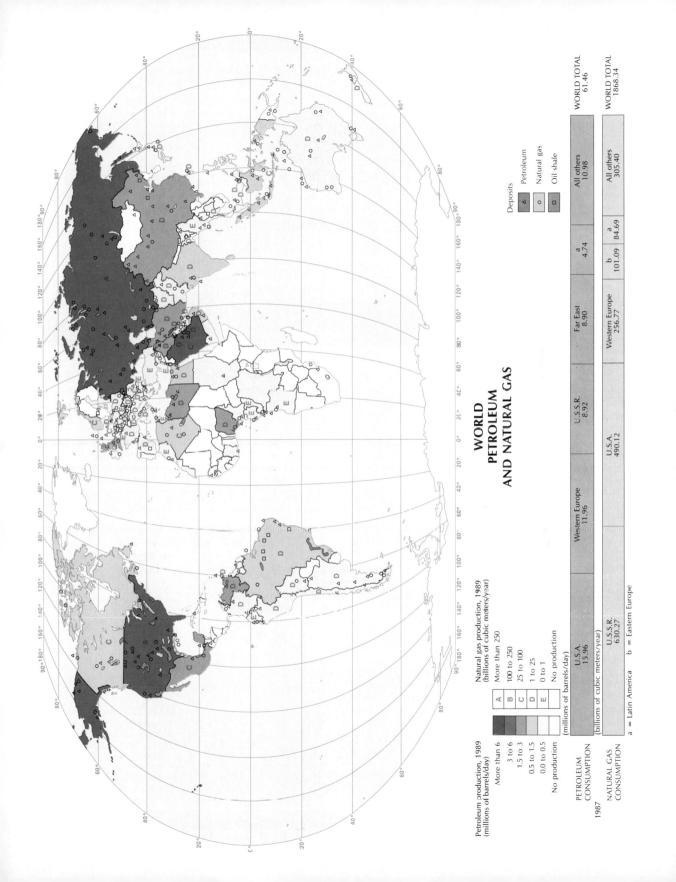

WORLD
PETROLEUM
AND NATURAL GAS

Petroleum production, 1989
(millions of barrels/day)

More than 6 — A
3 to 6 — B
1.5 to 3 — C
0.5 to 1.5 — D
0.0 to 0.5 — E
No production

Natural gas production, 1989
(billions of cubic meters/year)

More than 250
100 to 250
25 to 100
1 to 25
0 to 1
No production

Deposits

△ Petroleum
○ Natural gas
□ Oil shale

	(millions of barrels/day)					
PETROLEUM CONSUMPTION 1987	Western Europe 11.96	U.S.A. 15.96	U.S.S.R. 8.92	Far East 8.90	a 4.74	All others 10.98	WORLD TOTAL 61.46

	(billions of cubic meters/year)						
NATURAL GAS CONSUMPTION	U.S.A. 490.12	U.S.S.R. 630.27	Western Europe 256.77	b 101.09	84.69	All others 305.40	WORLD TOTAL 1868.34

a = Latin America   b = Eastern Europe

This deep-sea oil rig is located in the Santa Barbara Channel, off California. Drilling platforms are either anchored to the seafloor with pylons or kept afloat by their own buoyancy. The petroleum is pumped through a borehole well driven through layers of rock.

cases by trucks and rail tank cars. In the United States and the USSR, where commodities must be transported overland for great distances, most of the crude oil and natural gas, as well as some bulk products, moves by pipeline.

Pipelines. Oil pipelines were first used in the United States in the early oil fields. Modern pipelines are now in operation in the Middle East, Africa, Europe, South America, and Asia, as well.

The latest and most important technological improvements in pipeline operation include (1) automation, which reduces the number of operators required, allowing savings in operating costs; (2) transportation of a wider range of products; and (3) use of new materials, such as aluminum, plastics, and thin-wall steel pipe.

Oil Tankers. Transportation of oil by tanker, a relatively cheap long-distance method of transport, has contributed significantly to the important position of oil in the world's current pattern of energy use. An important attribute of ocean-tanker transport is flexibility. Tankers can be transferred to any of the trade routes where they are needed; they can carry any type of oil; and they are able to meet seasonal requirements with surplus capacity.

Tanker capacity is measured by deadweight tonnage (dwt), which is the total weight the tanker is able to carry. For the crude-oil trade, oil companies employ the largest tankers possible. Most can pass through the Suez and Panama canals, but some are so large that they must avoid all canals. Large tankers are the largest vessels afloat. Their capacity now exceeds 500,000 dwt. By 1990 over half the world's total consumption of oil was being transported by tanker. Attention has focused on the danger of OIL SPILLS caused by tanker accidents, particularly since the rupture (1989) of the tanker *Exxon Valdez* in Alaskan waters.

Liquefied Natural-Gas (LNG) Tankers. The utilization of

natural gas from remote regions has been made possible by liquefying the gas and transporting it under atmospheric pressure. Large unused natural-gas reserves in such areas as Alaska and the Middle East are now being tapped, and the gas is being transported to distant population centers far away from these large natural-energy sources.

Until the 1960s pipelines were the only means of transporting natural gas. This method of gas transport costs three times as much as pipeline movement of crude

(Left) *The first U.S. oil well, shown in an 1866 photograph, was sunk in Titusville, Pa., under the direction of Edwin L. Drake, a retired railroad conductor (foreground, right).*

(Opposite page) *An aerial view of a modern oil refinery reveals numerous clusters of tank farms, groups of large tanks that store crude oil and refined products. The tanks are connected to an enormous complex of refining plants and distillation towers by a network of pipelines.*

oil of equivalent energy content. In the 1960s the technology was developed for storing and transporting the gas as a liquid, by cooling it to a temperature below its boiling point (-161° C; -258° F). At low temperatures liquid natural gas (LNG) takes only about 1/600 of the space it occupies as a gas. Because ordinary metals become brittle when this cold, LNG is kept in cryogenic tanks made of magnesium-aluminum or nickel-steel alloys. With the addition of heat, the liquid reverts to a gaseous state. LNG is kept in insulated storage tanks for use during peak winter heating days, when supplies of pipeline-transported gas are insufficient. It can also be transported in cryogenic tank trucks.

Pipeline versus Tanker. The investment required for tankers is appreciably lower than that for pipelines—pipelines entail high fixed charges, a large initial investment, and payment of royalties to the countries transited in certain areas. Important savings are made by the use of big pipelines and big tankers; a supertanker, for instance, is estimated to transport oil at less than half of the per-ton cost of the standard "T-2" tanker, and unit pipeline costs decrease with the increase in pipeline diameter (although costs increase with volume, they do so at a lower rate). Tankers lose turnaround time while they are being filled or emptied. Because tanker costs continue whether the vessel is transporting cargo or merely loading or discharging, the impact of lost turnaround time can be severe, particularly if the length of the voyage is short. On the other hand, pipelines operate continuously around the clock; thus they suffer no such lost time. The differences in the two means of transportation are fundamental: pipeline cost per kilometer scarcely changes with distance, whereas, for other transport means, the shorter the distance, the higher the cost per kilometer.

Refining

In many countries—particularly the United States, where demand for gasoline is high—petroleum refining is a complex art calling for highly trained specialists who devote their careers to perfecting the refining process. Basically, the refining process separates the many types of hydrocarbons of which petroleum is composed. These molecules range in size from the simplest with one to four carbon atoms, which are gases when isolated, through the larger molecules, which are liquids, to the heaviest, which are solids (bitumens).

The refinery thus takes a barrel of crude oil and transforms it into many products for different uses. A barrel of petroleum may be thought of as a log of wood, and the refining process may be seen as sawing up the log. A large part—sometimes more than half, depending on the heaviness of the crude oil—is cut off the bottom; this portion represents the residual fuel oils, which are heavy, unrefined, and also the cheapest to produce. The next part cut off the log—the lighter oils such as diesel oil and light fuel oils—is a smaller portion. The next is gasoline, a smaller piece of the log worth still more. The remainder of the log represents a range of other petroleum products. Whereas gasoline occurs as only a minor natural constituent of crude oil, it is commonly created by further refining less desirable fractions.

The tall metal towers that characterize petroleum refineries are distillation, or fractionating, towers. Distillation is the method most frequently used to refine petroleum. When heated crude oil is fed into the lower part of a tower, the lighter oil portions, or fractions, vaporize. Losing temperature as they rise, they condense into liquids, which flow downward into the higher temperatures

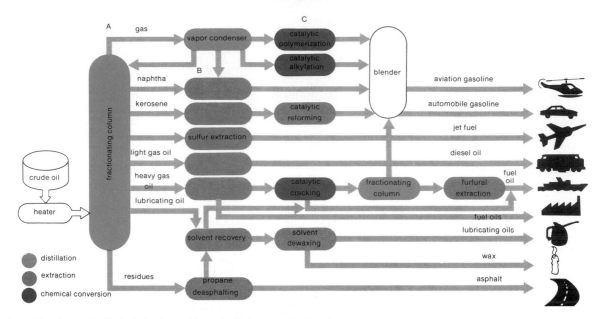

In a refining plant, crude oil is heated and passed into a distillation column (A). Nonvolatile residues are drawn off from the bottom, and liquid fractions with higher boiling points are removed at progressively higher levels. Uncondensed gases are taken out from the top of the tower. Extraction solvents (B) are used to remove sulfur compounds and other contaminants or to separate mixtures, such as oil and asphalt or oil and wax. Catalytic chemical processes (C) convert unwanted fractions into the various useful products indicated.

and are revaporized. This process continues until the various fractions have achieved the appropriate degrees of purity. The lighter fractions are tapped off from the top of the tower; heavier fractions, like fuel and diesel oils, are taken from the lower half.

The less valuable products of distillation are refined once again through various conversion processes. Thermal cracking, using heat and pressure, and catalytic cracking, employing a finely powdered catalyst, both reformulate heavy petroleum compounds into lighter fractions, such as gasoline. The chief refinery products are liquefied petroleum gas (LPG); GASOLINE and jet fuel; petroleum solvents; KEROSENE; diesel and fuel oils; and asphalts (bitumens). Petroleum products can be used to produce PETROCHEMICALS, which are the costliest of all petroleum derivatives (see CHEMICAL INDUSTRY).

Political History of the Industry

Since its inception the petroleum industry has shown a strong tendency to organize itself into huge units. This characteristic has contributed heavily to its stormy political history. In the United States, John D. Rockefeller (see ROCKEFELLER family) organized the Standard Oil Trust, which by the year 1880 controlled 90% of U.S. oil production. In 1911 the U.S. Supreme Court found the monopoly guilty of violations of the SHERMAN ANTI-TRUST ACT and ordered it broken up into 34 smaller companies. Despite this development, in the following decades the U.S. industry, bolstered by the huge oil demands of two world wars, was dominated by just five companies, three of

which were the offspring of Standard Oil. Two non-U.S. companies, Royal Dutch-Shell and British Petroleum, completed the list of the so-called majors, which by 1966 controlled 76% of world oil production.

In the absence of government regulation, the tremendous quantities of oil discovered after World War I presented the danger of periodic surpluses and shortages on the world market. Thus while the majors competed fiercely during this period for control of production—for example, in the recently discovered Middle East oil fields—they also reached secret agreements among themselves that helped to regulate production and, thereby, prices.

The Restructuring of the World Oil Industry. Mexico nationalized its oil industry in 1938, expropriating the foreign companies that had developed its oil fields and that—under the concession system used by the companies wherever they did not actually own the fields—controlled production and took a large share of the profits. In 1951 the Iranian premier Muhammed MOSADDEQ did the same with the Iranian oil industry, and although he was later ousted and jailed (partially at the instigation of Western interests) the industry remained nationalized. The shah of Iran, MUHAMMED REZA SHAH PAHLAVI, negotiated contracts with a consortium of oil companies in 1954 that were to set new standards for future oil-field nationalizations in other countries.

In 1959 a glut of oil on the world market led the major oil companies to lower prices, a move that sharply reduced the revenues of the oil-producing nations. In 1960, Venezuela and several Middle Eastern countries formed the ORGANIZATION OF PETROLEUM EXPORTING COUNTRIES (OPEC), later joined by many other countries, in order to control oil prices. Through the 1970s, OPEC took an increasingly militant posture, bringing about a rapid decline in the relative power of the private oil companies and a drastic increase in oil prices, which rose by about 1,000% between 1973 and 1980.

In Western countries the oil industry operates under several widely differing forms of ownership and control. In the United States and Canada private oil firms are free to compete for drilling sites. In South America oil industries are now controlled for the most part by government-created authorities, who may lease development rights to foreign companies but maintain ownership of the oil. The relatively new oil fields in the North Sea are divided among the United Kingdom, Norway, the Netherlands, Germany, and Denmark.

Challenges to U.S. Oil Firms. At the same time that their power was being eroded at the production end of the system, the U.S. oil companies were encountering political challenges in their own country. They were sharply criticized for their record profit increases during the world oil shortages of 1973 and 1979, although by that time they had seemingly surrendered most of their control over prices to OPEC. They also took a disproportionate share of the blame for U.S. dependence on foreign oil producers. The controversial depletion allowance, a tax benefit for the oil companies, was repealed in 1975, and in 1980 a tax was levied on "windfall profits" resulting from the U.S. government's decontrol of domestic oil prices. The system of foreign tax credits, which permits some multinational oil concerns to pay little or no domestic tax on foreign profits, also came under attack. In addition, environmental issues surfaced in the public consciousness in the 1960s and '70s, and the oil industry was accused of a lack of concern for problems caused by its operations, such as tanker spills and "blowouts" from offshore drilling rigs, pollution from petrochemical production, and ecological disruption associated with the TRANS-ALASKA PIPELINE.

The Oil Glut. The average rate of yearly increase in the demand for oil products was 7.8% during the period 1960–70. This rate of increase began to slow to about 4% yearly during the 1970s and to only about 1% in the mid-1980s. In 1950, U.S. oil consumption was about twice that of the rest of the world, but by 1979 world consumption was approximately 62.5 million barrels daily, of which the United States used only about one-seventh (8.5 million barrels).

Oil consumption peaked in 1979. Between 1979 and 1984, consumption in non-Communist countries dropped by 14%. The fall in demand was caused in large part by successful conservation efforts, the increased use of substitute fuels, and the development of more fuel-efficient automobiles. Slow growth in the industrial countries also contributed to lowering demand. To keep their markets, oil-producing nations began to cut prices, weakening the power of OPEC, which by the mid-1980s was producing at only one-half its capacity.

The U.S. oil industry was sharply affected by lowered demand and prices. To cut costs, oil companies shut down refineries and curtailed their retail operations.

The prosperity of the late 1980s combined with lower oil prices to increase U.S. oil consumption dramatically. The West's renewed dependence on Middle East oil once again became a matter of public concern with the 1990 invasion of Kuwait by its neighbor Iraq, but the end of the conflict in 1991 brought oil supplies and prices back to prewar levels, with only temporary disruptions.

See also: ENERGY SOURCES.

petrology   Petrology, a subdivision of geology, deals with the origin, structure, occurrence, and history of ROCK, as opposed to petrography, which is limited to rock description and classification. Petrology is generally concerned with metamorphic rocks and igneous rocks. Among other things, petrologists study how the densities of various rock types are affected by the pressures and temperatures found at various depths within the Earth. Phase changes—changes of density at specific temperatures and pressures—are studied to reveal their effects on earthquake waves traveling through layers of varying density in the Earth. Stresses and strains on rocks are examined for their effects on rock strength.

Petronius Arbiter   [puh-troh'-nee-uhs ahr'-bi-tur]
The preeminent Roman writer of romance Gaius Petronius Arbiter, d. AD 66, is the reputed author of the *Satyricon* and was a favorite at the court of the emperor Nero. There, according to Tacitus, he became the "arbiter of elegance." Although reported to have lived a hedonistic life and to have encouraged Nero's extravagances, Petronius proved himself an able administrator in positions of public responsibility. Tacitus reports that, after he fell out of favor with Nero, Petronius committed a leisurely suicide by cutting his wrists and spent his last moments compiling a list of Nero's vices.

Pettit, Bob   Hall of Fame member Robert E. Lee Pettit, b. Baton Rouge, La., Dec. 2, 1932, a great forward in the National Basketball Association, began as a center for Louisiana State University (All-American, 1954). The 6-ft 9-in (2-m 6-cm) Pettit joined the NBA's Milwaukee Hawks (who then moved to St. Louis) in 1955, winning Rookie of the Year honors. He played 11 seasons for the Hawks, leading them to one NBA title (1958) while earning Most Valuable Player awards and the league scoring championships in 1956 and 1959. A 1st-team All-NBA selection 10 times, Pettit had 20,880 career points (26.4 per game) and 12,851 rebounds (16.2 per game, 3d in NBA history).

Petty, Richard   Richard Petty, b. Level Cross, N.C., July 2, 1937, was, through the 1970s, the most successful Grand National stock car driver in the United States. His father, Lee Petty, was the winner of 3 National Association for Stock Car Auto Racing (NASCAR) Grand National championships. The younger Petty, who started racing in 1958, now holds many NASCAR records. Through the 1980s, Petty won nearly 20% of the races he entered. He captured 7 NASCAR Winston Cups (formerly called the Grand National championship) and 7 Daytona 500 titles (the last in 1981) while earning over $7 million in purses.

petunia

Petunia is a genus of annual or perennial flowering plants that number about 30 species in the nightshade family, Solanaceae. The showy, fragrant petunia blooms have single or double petals, ruffled or fluted, in a wider variety of colors than almost any other flower. *P. hybrida* (common garden petunia) has many varieties and strains; a compact dwarf strain exists that is well suited for rock gardens. *P. axillaris* is a spreading or erect perennial that grows up to 60 cm (2 ft) tall, with cylindrical tube and white flowers. *P. violacea* has purplish flowers resembling violets.

Native to South America, petunias are widely grown as annuals in northern gardens. The many varieties of garden petunia are popular as both bedding and window-box plants.

Pevsner, Antoine

[pee-evz'-nur]   The Russian sculptor and painter Antoine Pevsner, b. Jan. 18 (N.S.), 1886, d. Apr. 12, 1962, is best known for the role that he played, with his brother Naum GABO, in the abstract art movement CONSTRUCTIVISM. They studied in Russia and lived in Paris (where they took an interest in both cubism and futurism) and in Oslo. Pevsner and Gabo returned (1917) to Moscow, where—with Vladimir Tatlin and Kasimir Malevich—they developed the principles of constructivism. These, published in their *Realist Manifesto* (1920), proposed an art based on the concepts of modern physics rather than the representation of what is seen by the eye.

Pevsner, Sir Nikolaus

[pevz'-nur]   The architectural critic and historian Sir Nikolaus Bernhard Leon Pevsner, b. Jan. 30, 1902, d. Aug. 18, 1983, began his career in his native Leipzig but was forced to leave Germany for Britain in 1933. He wrote widely on architectural history. His first major work, *Pioneers of Modern Design* (1936; repr. 1974), established him as an important spokesman for theories of design and architecture associated with the BAUHAUS. His other main concern, especially in later years, was British 18th- and 19th-century architecture. Beginning in 1945 he was editor of two historical series: *The Pelican History of Art* and *The Buildings of England.* The latter work, in 46 volumes largely written by Pevsner himself, attempts to describe county by county all the significant buildings in England.

pewee

[pee'-wee]   Pewee is the common name for several birds of the family Tyrannidae, the tyrant FLYCATCHERS. The name is an imitation of their whistle. The eastern wood pewee, *Contopus virens*, and western wood pewee, *C. sordidulus*, of North America are small (about 17 cm/6.5 in) and dull olive gray with whitish wing bars, light gray breasts, and off-white undersides. Woodland dwellers, they catch insects on the wing.

The western wood pewee is a small North American flycatcher.

pewter

[pue'-tur]   Pewter is an alloy of tin mixed with a small proportion of another metal, generally lead but sometimes copper, antimony, or bismuth. Silver gray in color, it is a comparatively soft metal, worked by casting, hammering, and turning.

The origins of pewter technology have not been determined, but it has been in common use in Europe since the Roman period. Pewter was used extensively to make household utensils and ecclesiastical vessels until the mid-19th century, when it began to be replaced by new alloys (Britannia metal and German silver), which were more durable and suitable for silver-plating, as well as by cheaper and more practical industrial pottery and glassware. A revival of decorative pewterware occurred in the late 19th and early 20th centuries. As a decora-

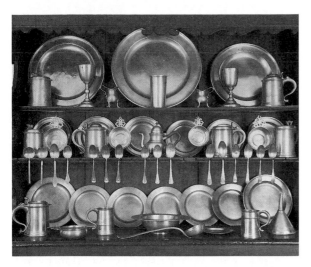

Pewter tableware was widely produced in the American colonies from the early 18th century. The simple decorative forms were often derived from silverware designs. (Winterthur Museum, Delaware.)

tive art, pewter reached its European zenith in the 16th century.

peyote [pay-oh'-tee]   Peyote, or mescal, is the common name of the spineless cactus *Lophophora williamsii*, found in the southwestern United States to central Mexico. Peyote is used in religious rituals primarily for its hallucinogenic effects (see HALLUCINOGENS). At the end of the 19th century a German chemist, Arthur Heffter, demonstrated that mescaline (3,4,5-trimethoxyphenethylamine) was responsible for peyote's pharmacological effects. Mescaline is related to the amphetamines. When ingested it can produce hallucinations, frequently of a visual nature. It stimulates the autonomic nervous system and can cause nausea, vomiting, sweating, tachycardia (rapid heartbeat), pupillary dilatation, and anxiety.

Use of peyote by native Americans was noted by Europeans as early as the 16th century. Its use in elaborate religious rites began in the late 19th century, and it was incorporated as a sacrament into the NATIVE AMERICAN CHURCH in 1918. In the user's view, peyote symbolizes spiritual power and is eaten to induce a hallucinogenic trance and communion with God. Some controversy ensued in 1990 when the U.S. Supreme Court ruled that religious practice did not exempt peyote users from state laws against illegal drugs.

Peyotism   see NATIVE AMERICAN CHURCH

pH   The pH of an aqueous solution is a value expressing the solution's acidity or basicity (see ACIDS AND BASES) in terms of the relative amounts of hydrogen ions (H^+; protons) and hydroxide ions (OH^-) present. A pH value may fall anywhere on a scale from 0 (strongly acidic) to 14 (strongly basic or alkaline), with a value of 7 representing neutrality.

The measurement and control of pH is important in the manufacture of foods, paper, and chemicals. In agriculture, testing and maintenance of soil pH are necessary for good yields of crops (see GARDENING). Maintenance of WATER QUALITY and the study of ACID RAIN illustrate the application of pH measurement methods in environmental science.

Definitions. According to its simplest definition, introduced by Søren Sørenson in 1909, pH is the negative logarithm of the molar CONCENTRATION of H^+ ions: $pH = -\log[H^+]$ or $[H^+] = 10^{-pH}$. Each pH unit downward represents, therefore, a tenfold increase in the H^+ concentration. A pH of 3, for example, indicates a 10^{-3} molar concentration of hydrogen ions. Because the H^+ ion associates very strongly with water molecules, the pH may more correctly be said to represent the concentration of hydronium ions (H_3O^+).

Measurement. Measurement of pH, a crucial tool in QUANTITATIVE CHEMICAL ANALYSIS, can be done by using INDICATORS—substances that change color with a change in pH—or certain types of electrodes that exhibit a pH-dependent electrical potential. The exact amount of base required to neutralize an unknown acid (see TITRATION) and the pH at the halfway point of the neutralization of an acid (pK_a) are characteristic of that particular acid and may allow its identification or quantification. The pH of a BUFFER—a solution of a weak acid or base and its salt—changes only slightly when stronger acids or bases are added. A buffer is often used as a standard for pH measurement.

Phaedra   see HIPPOLYTUS

Phaethon [fay'-uh-thuhn]   In Greek mythology Phaethon, the son of HELIOS, persuaded his father to let him drive the chariot of the Sun for a day. He lost control of the horses, however, and they rushed too near the Earth, burning the large area that is today known as the Sahara Desert. Zeus struck Phaethon dead with a thunderbolt to prevent him from burning up the entire planet.

Phaistos [fy'-stuhs]   Phaistos, in southern Crete, is the site of a Bronze Age palace, second only in size and splendor to that at KNOSSOS. The palace stood on the eastern end of a ridge overlooking the fertile Mesara plain. The harbor of Phaistos may have been at Ayia Triadha (Hagia Triada), a nearby settlement below the ridge to the west. That site, as well as the palace and parts of the city at Phaistos, has been excavated since 1900.

Recent work has revealed quantities of fine decorated pottery of the Early (First) Palace at Phaistos, which was destroyed by fire *c*.1700 BC. The Later (Second) Palace was an entirely new building, which appears to have been designed by a gifted architect; it was burned down in the course of the Mycenaean conquest of Crete (*c*.1450 BC).

phalanger [fuh-lan'-jur]   Phalangers, family Phalangeridae, are a diverse group of arboreal MARSUPIAL mammals—including the CUSCUS and KOALA—whose name re-

The vulpine phalanger, or brush-tailed possum, is a small marsupial native to Australia. Highly adaptable, it lives in trees, caves, city parks, and on the roofs of houses.

fers to the grasping ability of some of the finger and toe bones (phalanges), which enables the animals to climb trees. The phalangers are the most widely distributed of all marsupials, ranging from Australia and New Guinea to the Solomon Islands and parts of Indonesia. They have been introduced into New Zealand. Seventeen genera and about 42 species are known. Phalangers vary from 10 to 122 cm (4 to 48 in) in total length. Their mode of locomotion also varies greatly, from that of the slow-moving koala to that of the gliding opossum. The fur is usually dense and woolly and is valuable in commerce. The tail is commonly long, though vestigial in the koala, and sometimes prehensile. Some genera have membranes for gliding through the air. Most phalangers live in trees; a few inhabit plains areas.

phalarope [fal'-uh-rohp]   Phalaropes comprise three shorebirds, of the family Phalaropodidae, in which many

Wilson's phalarope is an uncommon shorebird that inhabits inland pools rather than coastal waters. The female (foreground) is larger and more colorful than the male.

of the usual breeding roles of the sexes are reversed. The females wear the brighter plumage and establish and defend territories; males do most or all of the incubating of the eggs. Two species, the Arctic-breeding red (*Phalaropus fulicarius*) and northern (*Lobipes lobatus*) phalaropes, spend time on the oceans between breeding seasons, wintering mainly in the Southern Hemisphere. The Wilson's phalarope, *Steganopus tricolor*, of North and South America infrequently goes to sea.

phallic worship   Phallic worship, or phallicism, refers to the veneration of the phallus, a representation or symbol of the male generative organ. The practice often includes a similar veneration for representations of the female generative parts as well. Phallicism is ancient, some form of it having existed in almost all religions, although the worship of the phallus has never constituted the totality of the religious meaning of any group. Classical examples appear in the ancient Greek myths of Demeter and Eleusis and in the Roman cult of Priapus. Although phallicism is traditionally associated with agricultural societies (and is still found among the folkloric practices of various societies of India, Japan, and central Europe), it is also highly developed in nonagricultural societies of the South American Indians and of the Australian Aborigines.

Pham Van Dong [fahm vahn dawng]   A leader of North Vietnam during the Vietnam War, Pham Van Dong, b. Mar. 1, 1906, became prime minister of the unified Socialist Republic of Vietnam in 1976 and chairman of the Council of Ministers in 1981. He was one of the founders of the VIET MINH movement in 1941. A close comrade of HO CHI MINH, he played a leading role in the war against the French in the early 1950s. He attended the Geneva Conference in 1954 and became prime minister of North Vietnam in 1955. He resigned from the party politburo in 1986 and was replaced as prime minister by Pham Hung (d. 1988) in 1987.

pharaoh [fair'-oh]   From the New Kingdom onward the title *pharaoh*, from an Egyptian word meaning "the royal palace," was given to the kings of ancient Egypt (see EGYPT, ANCIENT). It was later added to the king's name as part of his title. Egyptian kings were thought to be divine, incarnations of the god HORUS. Pyramids and the tombs in the Valley of the Kings at Thebes were built to ensure the survival of the king's influence after his death. Ideas regarding the king's divinity eventually changed, however. By the New Kingdom a distinction was usually made between the institution of divine kingship and the individual pharaoh.

Pharisees [fair'-i-seez]   The Pharisees were a major Jewish sect from the 2d century BC to the 2d century AD. The seeds of Pharisaism were planted during the Babylonian Captivity (587–536 BC), and a clearly defined party emerged during the revolt of the MACCABEES (167–165 BC) against the Seleucid rulers of Syria-Palestine.

The Pharisees' chief rival sect was the SADDUCEES. Whereas the Sadducees were drawn mainly from the conservative and aristocratic priestly class, the Pharisees tended to be middle class and open to religious innovation. In the interpretation of the law the Pharisees differed from the Sadducees in their use of oral legal tradition to supplement the Torah, although their interpretations, once given, were scrupulously adhered to. Pharisaic emphasis on divine providence led to a marked fatalism, and followers adopted a belief in resurrection and an elaborate angelology. All this was rejected by the Sadducees.

In the New Testament the Pharisees appear as Jesus' most vocal critics. Their insistence on ritual observance of the letter rather than the spirit of the law evoked strong denunciation by Jesus; he called them "white washed tombs" (Matt. 23:27) and self-righteous lovers of display (Matt. 6:1–6, 16–18). The Pharisees are portrayed as plotting to destroy Jesus (Matt. 12:14), although they do not figure in the accounts of his arrest and trial. Despite Jesus' attacks on the Pharisees—which were possibly on unrepresentative members of the sect—he shared many beliefs with them, including the resurrection of the dead.

The Pharisees held the Jews together after the destruction of the Temple in AD 70. The sect continued into the 2d century, working on the redaction of the TALMUD and looking for the restoration of Israel through divine intervention.

pharmaceutical industry

The pharmaceutical industry is made up of hundreds of companies that discover, develop, produce, and sell drug products. These products are used by health professionals to prevent or to cure some diseases or to relieve symptoms of other ailments. Throughout the 20th century and especially from the 1940s on, members of the industry have discovered new drugs that cure previously incurable diseases, prevent diseases that are epidemic in nature, reduce the frequency and length of hospital stays, and increase life expectancy.

Manufacture. Both over-the-counter and ethical, or prescription-only, drug products must be made according to Good Manufacturing Practice regulations. Each lot of raw materials, containers, and closures received in a plant is sampled and tested before it can be used in a pharmaceutical product. The products are made according to strictly written batch records. Each batch is sampled, tested, and approved before it is released for shipment to drug wholesalers, hospitals, and pharmacies.

In the United States each drug manufacturer must register with the FOOD AND DRUG ADMINISTRATION (FDA), providing a list of each product it makes. Every two years the FDA inspects the manufacturer for compliance with federal regulations. The research and development of a drug product and its actual production are heavily regulated by the FDA and similar agencies throughout the world (see PHARMACY).

Generic drug products are those produced by more than one company and are known by their pharmaceutical name rather than by a trade or brand name. These products must meet the same manufacturing requirements of the FDA.

Research. Besides the more traditional research and development (R & D) of chemical pharmaceuticals, such highly advanced techniques as recombinant DNA and computer-aided design are being used. The ethical-drug industry spends more than 50 percent of its multibillion-dollar profits for R & D activities; safety and efficacy tests account for up to 60 percent of the total. For each new product, companies must obtain an approved New Drug Application from the FDA. Clinical tests are used to prove the drug safe, after previous ANIMAL EXPERIMENTATION has been done.

pharmacist   see PHARMACY

pharmacology

Pharmacology, a term derived from the Greek word *pharmakon* ("medicine"), may be broadly defined as the study of DRUGS. The study includes three major and intimately related disciplines: TOXICOLOGY, pharmacodynamics, and therapeutics, each of which has developed into a specialized area of study. In a restricted sense, *pharmacology* and *pharmacodynamics* are used synonymously and comprise the study of the biochemical and physiological effects of drugs on a living organism, from their administration, absorption, and distribution to their metabolism and excretion. The mechanism by which the drugs produce their effects is also studied. Therapeutics considers the use of drugs in the prevention, diagnosis, and treatment of disease.

Pharmacology as an experimental science began in the 19th century with the work of François Magendie (1783–1855) who studied the mechanism of absorption and distribution of drugs in the human body and their localization at the site of their action. Since that time a close relationship has existed in the fields of chemistry, physiology, pathology, and microbiology to study drug action.

pharmacopoeia

[fahr-muh-kuh-pee'-uh]   The term *pharmacopoeia,* derived from the Greek words *pharmakon* ("medicine") and *poiein* ("to make"), has been used over the years to refer to a variety of books containing information about the preparation of remedies. Although drug preparations have been acknowledged since Babylonian times, the first official pharmacopoeia was the *Dispensatorium* of Valerius Cordus, published in 1546. The first pharmacopoeia published in the United States was the *Lititz Pharmacopoeia,* compiled by Dr. William Brown in 1778 for use in military hospitals during the American Revolution.

In December 1820, *The Pharmacopoeia of the United States of America* was published, a result of the deliberations of the Pharmacopoeial Convention (Washington, D.C.; Jan. 1, 1820), which was attended by representatives of U.S. medical societies and colleges. The Pharmacopoeial Convention has reconvened every 10 years thereafter, and the *Pharmacopoeia* itself has been revised every 5 years since 1940. A supplementary formulary of medicinal preparations, the *National Formulary*, was published in 1888 by the American Pharmaceutical Association. Since 1906 the *United States Pharmacopoeia* and the *National Formulary* have been recognized as legal standards for all drugs therein.

pharmacy Pharmacy is a service within the HEALTH-CARE SYSTEM that is related to drugs, their preparation, and their proper use to treat illness by cure, control, and prevention. Modern pharmacy is so complex and rapidly changing that no one can know or practice all of it. In only one part of the health-care system do pharmacists alone dominate—in the dispensing of drugs prescribed by physicians.

The concerns of pharmacy and pharmacists begin with drug discovery and end with evaluating and improving drug effectiveness in a single patient at a given time. Drugs are created either through synthesis by pharmaceutical chemists or through collection and purification from natural sources by experts in pharmacognosy. The scientific study of drug effects is called PHARMACOLOGY. Biopharmaceutics and pharmacokinetics study and describe how drugs reach and are removed from their sites of action in the body.

Chemicals that possess desirable drug effects must be put into a finished product, such as a tablet or an injection. The drug product must meet many requirements related to stability, safety, and effectiveness. Most drugs that are marketed today are mass-produced by the PHARMACEUTICAL INDUSTRY. In earlier times this was the realm of the APOTHECARY.

The modern pharmacist is responsible for the quality of the drugs compounded for and dispensed to a patient. The pharmacist is also responsible for helping to ensure that a drug program is appropriate for a patient, based partly on how much detailed and timely knowledge of the patient's condition is at hand. Further, he or she should inform the person administering or taking the drug about its proper use, side effects, and dangers.

History. The oldest accounts relating to pharmacy come from ancient India and China, where healing was based on the belief that disease was caused by the presence of spirits in the body. The concept of purification from sin by a purgative existed in Babylonia, Assyria, Egypt, and parts of Greece. Galen, in 2d-century Rome, classified drugs in terms of their supposed effects on the four humors—blood, phlegm, yellow bile, and black bile; though widely followed, this system unfortunately was scientifically incorrect. From the 7th century until the Middle Ages, Arabs contributed a large body of knowledge concerning available drugs.

By 1240, Emperor Frederick II issued three regulations that separated the profession of pharmacy from medicine, instituted government supervision of pharmacy, and obliged pharmacists to take an oath to prepare drugs reliably. During the 19th century, pharmacy developed in the United States, including pharmacy organizations, formal education of pharmacists, and official texts, or pharmacopoeias, setting standards of identity and purity of drugs.

Pharmacists began to organize to further their professional, economic, and political goals with the formation (1852) of the American Pharmaceutical Association. The U.S. pharmaceutical industry has been represented since 1958 by the Pharmaceutical Manufacturers Association. The Fédération Internationale Pharmaceutique, established in 1910, is a worldwide organization of pharmacists based in the Netherlands.

Legal Regulation. The federal FOOD AND DRUG ADMINISTRATION (FDA) is the strongest force determining directions for U.S. pharmacy because it controls drug manufacturing and distribution. The individual states have the most influence on the practice of pharmacists through their licensing power. Federal law decides which drugs are safe for self-medication and which drugs must be prescribed because of their potential danger. States decide who may prescribe.

The regulatory procedures of the FDA are generally considered the strictest of any government. The advantages of this were seen in the 1960s, when FDA nonapproval of the drug THALIDOMIDE averted the birth defects produced in other nations by the antinausea drug. Some observers cite FDA strictness, however, as the reason why many drug companies tend to develop "me-too" variants of established medicines rather than risking research costs on unproved kinds of drugs.

Before FDA release, the distribution and use of an investigational new drug are tightly controlled until the drug has been scientifically proved to be safe and effective. Although each package of a drug has an FDA-cleared information insert, much knowledge does not reach the professionals and patients who need to know it. Sometimes when a drug has obvious dangers and taking it is optional, the FDA requires the pharmacist to provide the patient with an authorized information sheet. Nonprescription drugs must have package labeling with adequate information about what the drug does, its dosage, and its dangers.

Pharmacists can be sued for malpractice if their professional activities cause injury and result from performance below standard. The American Pharmaceutical Association code of ethics requires pharmacists to be ethical in their solicitation of services and to respect the confidentiality of records. Although the FDA closely controls manufactured drugs, it considers the filling of a single compounded prescription as a practice of pharmacy and out of its jurisdiction. Refilling a prescription usually requires authorization of the prescriber.

Pharos of Alexandria see SEVEN WONDERS OF THE WORLD

phase equilibrium In chemistry, a phase is a recognizable and physically separable state of matter such as gas, liquid, and solid. Solids themselves can have different phases, such as the rhombic or monoclinic forms of

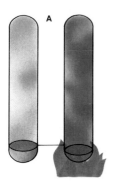
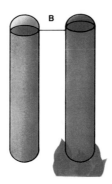
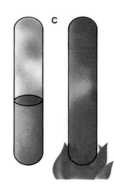

For every substance a critical temperature and pressure exist at which the liquid and gas phases coexist and are equal in density. The density under these specific conditions of temperature and pressure is known as the critical density. If the average density of a liquid and its vapor in a sealed tube is less than the critical density (A), heat will cause evaporation to occur, and the liquid level will drop. No vaporization will result if the density is greater than the critical density (B), and the level of the heated liquid will rise. If the average density is equal to the critical density (C), the densities of the two phases will approach each other as heat is applied and will become identical when the critical temperature is reached.

sulfur. Oil floating on water is an example of a two-phase liquid system.

Phases can exist together in equilibrium. At equilibrium all forces or variables that control the system are balanced. An infinitesimal force applied in one direction will change an infinitesimal amount of one phase into another. Equilibrium implies reversibility; that is, an infinitesimal force in the opposite direction will restore the system to its original condition. An example of a system with two phases at equilibrium is ice and water under the pressure of one atmosphere and at 0° C. The application of a little heat will change a little ice into water, and a small amount of refrigeration will change a little water into ice.

For a pure substance that can exist as a gas (known as the vapor of that substance), a liquid, or a solid, common types of phase equilibria are vapor-liquid, vapor-solid, and liquid-solid pairs. There can also be solid 1–solid 2 pairs.

One-Component Systems

The simplest phase-equilibrium system has one component. A typical pressure-temperature diagram of a single substance has three regions where the solid, liquid, and vapor phases exist, according to the temperature and pressure conditions. In each such region there is one phase and only one component present. At the boundaries between these regions, two phases are in equilibrium.

Triple Point. The unique point where three phases are in equilibrium is the triple point. This point occurs at the intersection of the pressure-temperature curves for

the three phase pairs. At the triple point, the temperature and pressure are fixed, definite, and reproducible. The invariance of the triple point of water is used as a calibration point for the Kelvin temperature scale. The temperature of this point is 273.16 K, or 0.01° C (32.018° F), at 4.58 mm Hg pressure.

Critical Point. The liquid-vapor curve ends in a point called the critical point, the coordinates of which are those of the critical temperature and pressure. Beyond this temperature no liquid can exist, no matter how great the pressure. In addition, the highest vapor pressure a liquid can have is the critical pressure. If a liquid is heated in a half-filled sealed test tube, the meniscus disappears at the critical point. There is then only one phase present.

Two-Component Systems

A simple two-component system is the solution of a gas in a liquid. There are two phases, the solution and the gas above it, and equilibrium is determined by two variables, the temperature and the pressure. When temperature is held constant, the effect of pressure in determining the mass of gas dissolved is given by Henry's law: mass = constant × pressure.

Unless chemical reactions occur, Henry's law holds for a wide range of pressures. If the two components react, there will be a positive deviation from the law; that is, more gas will dissolve. This happens when ammonia gas is dissolved in water. A negative deviation occurs when the solvent contains impurities. A technique for expelling a gas from a solution is to "salt it out" by adding an ion-forming substance.

Miscible Liquids. Another simple two-component system is a solution of two miscible liquids. The vapor pressure of such a solution is the sum of the partial pressures of both components of the solution (see DALTON'S LAW). The partial pressure of a component, however, is not the same as its vapor pressure before mixing, but is less and in proportion to the component's mole fraction in the solution. (The mole fraction is the ratio of the moles of the component to the total moles of the system.) For ideal solutions the partial pressure of a component is given by Raoult's law: $P_A = x_A P_A^o$, where P_A^o is the vapor pressure of pure component A, and x_A is the mole fraction of A in the solution.

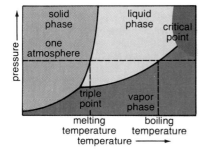

In a phase diagram of a one-component system the curves denote the conditions of temperature and pressure where two phases are in equilibrium. They meet at the triple point, where all phases are in equilibrium.

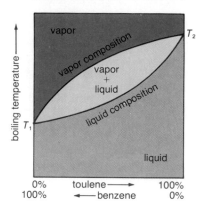

The boiling point of two miscible liquids, benzene and toluene, is diagrammed. T_1 is the boiling point of pure benzene and T_2 the boiling point of pure toluene. At the specific boiling point for any given mixture, the top curve gives the vapor composition, and the bottom curve the liquid composition.

Deviations from Raoult's law can occur in either direction—positive or negative. The partial pressure can become greater than expected, for example, when the constituents of the mixture differ in polarity. Negative deviations from Raoult's law occur less often. They are usually caused by the two components forming a compound. There are three variables that determine equilibrium in the solution of two miscible liquids: temperature, composition, and pressure. Solutions, however, are often studied under the constant pressure of one atmosphere. With only two variables remaining, the system can be illustrated by a two-dimensional phase diagram relating the boiling temperature to the composition of the solution or vapor. When the solution boils, both components enter the vapor state, but it is important to note that the composition of vapor and solution are different. By drawing a horizontal line representing a boiling temperature and comparing the vapor and liquid compositions, it is clear that the vapor is richer in the lower-boiling component. Stepwise condensation of the vapor and redistillation of the condensate can, in principle, separate the solution into its pure components. Such a FRACTIONATION procedure is widely used in the chemical industry—for example, to separate crude oil into its components or to increase the alcoholic content of spirits.

Azeotropic Mixtures. Not all miscible-liquid systems behave in this ideal manner. Some have phase diagrams that display maxima or minima, unique points where the two curves touch tangentially. At these points the composition of the liquid and vapor is the same, and the solution, called an azeotrope, cannot be separated into its

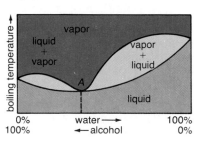

The ethyl alcohol and water system forms an azeotrope, or constant boiling mixture, at composition A. Because the vapor has the same composition as the liquid, the composition of the boiling liquid at A remains unchanged.

components by distillation. Ethyl alcohol and water form a solution with a minimum boiling point. Boiling a water-alcohol solution of any composition causes it to continually change until the azeotropic composition is reached. Thereafter the solution will boil unchanged.

Solid-Liquid Mixtures. A common binary system is one that has two components that are not miscible as solids but are completely miscible as liquids. Assuming constant pressure (usually one atmosphere), a phase diagram for the system can be constructed that has four regions: all-solid, all-liquid, and two regions in which the liquid exists in equilibrium with each of the respective solid components.

From the solid-liquid diagram, it is clear that cooling the liquid will cause one of the solid components to precipitate out. Which pure component will be obtained depends on the original composition of the liquid. As the remaining solution is now richer in the other component, continued cooling enriches it further until the eutectic point is reached. The last of the mixture will freeze and a mixture, not an alloy, of the two solid components will separate out. The eutectic point is the lowest temperature at which a liquid can exist. This temperature is lower than the melting point of either solid. At the eutectic temperature three phases exist in equilibrium.

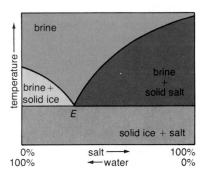

The salt-ice-brine system indicates a eutectic point, the lowest possible temperature at which the liquid phase can exist, at point E. Metal systems (alloys) typically have eutectic points.

One such system, the salt-ice-brine system, is used to attain a temperature colder than that of melting ice. The eutectic temperature of this system was chosen as the zero point on the Fahrenheit temperature scale. This system also operates in the oceans at the Arctic regions. When the surface of the sea freezes there, pure ice is formed.

pheasant   The approximately 175 species of birds in the avian family Phasianidae, order Galliformes, are referred to as pheasants. The term *true pheasants* is used for the 50 species of 16 genera in the subfamily Phasianinae, which includes peafowl, jungle fowl, and pheasants. These medium- to large-sized birds have spurs on their legs. The males are usually extremely colorful, whereas females have dull plumage. Many species have long, ornate tails; their heads often have featherless areas with patches of brightly colored skin and may be ornamented with wattles or sawtoothed combs. Most of these birds are polygamous (a male

The flamboyant ring-necked pheasant is commonly seen in fields and brush through-out the northern United States, where it feeds on seeds, berries, and grains. The female is camouflaged by protective dull coloration.

associated with several females), and the males are not involved in nest building or care of young. Males exhibit an elaborate courtship display.

Species of true pheasants are native to central and southern Asia (particularly India) and adjacent islands, as well as to west central Africa. For centuries pheasants have been kept in captivity, and the ring-necked, or common, pheasant (*Phasianus colchicus*), treasured in aviaries of ancient Greece, Rome, and Egypt, has been successfully introduced into Europe, North America, Hawaii, and New Zealand. It eats berries, seeds, and grains and prefers open country with brush cover.

phenacetin   see ANALGESIC

phenobarbital [feen-oh-bahr'-bi-tawl]

Phenobarbital, one of the earlier derivatives of barbituric acid, is used as a hypnotic, sedative, and anticonvulsant. First introduced in 1912 under the trade name Luminal, phenobarbital is one of the long-acting BARBITURATES; thus it is taken two to four times daily. It is a central-nervous-system depressant, and prolonged use can produce habituation or addiction; overdose can cause coma or death. Because of its persistent effect, phenobarbital is rarely used for inducing sleep and is used more commonly for daytime sedation or prevention of convulsions.

phenol [fee'-nawl]

Also known as carbolic acid and hydroxybenzene, phenol, chemical formula C_6H_5OH, was originally obtained as a by-product from coal tar but is now chiefly manufactured from benzene, chlorobenzene, or isopropyl benzene. It is a colorless solid that turns red on air oxidation and melts at 40.8° C. Phenol is slightly soluble in water and has weakly acidic properties (pH of about 6). It is toxic and corrosive, but it has antiseptic properties and is the standard by which antiseptics are evaluated. Its chief use is in the manufacture of plastics, dyes, and disinfectants.

phenomenology

Phenomenology is a school of philosophy whose principal purpose is to study the phenomena, or appearances, of human experience while attempting to suspend all consideration of their objective reality or subjective association.

Phenomenology took its present shape at the beginning of the 20th century with the writings of Edmund HUSSERL. Husserl intended to develop a philosophical method that was devoid of all presuppositions. His aim was to discover the essential structures and relationships of the phenomena as well as the acts of consciousness in which the phenomena appeared, and to do this by as faithful an exploration as possible, uncluttered by scientific or cultural presuppositions.

Husserl intended by this suspension, or bracketing, of extraneous commitments to go beyond the usual choices of IDEALISM and realism (see REALISM, philosophy) to "the things themselves." In his later work, however all beliefs about the external existence of the objects of consciousness were bracketed. This suspension of all reference to the reality of the thing experienced left the philosopher with nothing but the experiencing itself, which Husserl divided into the "noesis" (act of consciousness) and the "noema" (object of consciousness). Here the line between idealism and phenomenology became blurred, although the suspension of belief in the reality of an object of consciousness is not the same thing as denying that it exists.

There is considerable diversity in the use that Husserl's successors have made of his method. Max SCHELER, an early assistant of Husserl, adapted it to religious and ethical experience, and Martin HEIDEGGER, a student of Husserl, applied it to such experiences as dread and fear and thereby generated what is now known as existential phenomenology. The French philosophers Jean Paul SARTRE and Maurice MERLEAU-PONTY also employed the methods of phenomenology for their existential programs, as did the German philosopher Karl JASPERS (see EXISTENTIALISM). Through these philosophers, especially Jaspers, the phenomenological method has influenced psychological thought, particularly that of certain European psychiatrists, such as Ludwig Binswanger. Phenomenology has also influenced neo-Thomist religious thought.

phenotype   see GENETICS

phenyl group [fen'-ul]   The phenyl group, C_6H_5, is the chemically combining form of benzene, C_6H_6. It is a structural unit of numerous organic chemical compounds. When the phenyl group reacts, it does so as a stable, intact unit. All compounds that contain the phenyl group are AROMATIC COMPOUNDS.

phenylketonuria [fen-ul-keet-uh-noor'-ee-uh]   Phenylketonuria (PKU) is a genetic disease that, if undetected at birth, affects brain maturation and results in mental retardation. The disease is caused by defective activity of the enzyme phenylalanine hydroxylase, which results in a higher-than-normal blood level of the amino acid phenylalanine. If left untreated, accumulation of this amino acid can produce seizures, extreme hyperactivity, and neurological problems that prevent walking and talking. The IQ of an untreated child with PKU rarely rises above 70. The incidence of PKU in the United States is about 1 in 14,000 births, but fortunately most cases are identified at birth with a mandatory heel-prick blood screening test. An infant identified with PKU is placed on a special low-protein, formula-based diet that severely limits phenylalanine intake and allows normal, healthy development. The child stays on this diet through adolescence and in some cases into adulthood. Women with PKU need to stay on the restricted diet when pregnant, because abnormal amounts of phenylalanine can injure a fetus. One person in 60 carries one gene for PKU. A child of two carriers has a 25 percent chance of developing the disease. In 1983 a genetic-marker technique was introduced to detect carriers and affected fetuses in families that have a history of PKU.

pheromone [fair'-uh-mohn]   Pheromones (from the Greek *pher*, "to carry" and *horman* "to stimulate") are chemicals released by organisms into the environment, where they serve as signals or messages to alter behavior in other organisms of the same species. As such, they differ from hormones, which designate internal secretions carried in the blood. Pheromones are secreted as liquids by specialized cells or glands and are transmitted as liquids or gases. Their use has been demonstrated in insects, algae, nematodes, spiders, crustaceans, fishes, and mammals. They act as signals for reproductive behavior (sex and assembling pheromones), alarm and defense, territory and trail-marking, social regulation and recognition, and control of caste differentiation. Thus pheromones emanating from a queen honeybee in the hive stimulate congregating, feeding, and grooming behavior by worker bees. Scent-marking substances are frequently deposited in the urine of dogs and cats.

Insect pheromones have received much greater attention than any others from scientists in the field of ANIMAL COMMUNICATION. Most of the knowledge gained concerns the sex pheromones. It is almost certain that such pheromones are required by all species of the family Lepidoptera (moths and butterflies), whose members are long-distance fliers. Release by the female of an infinitesimal amount of pheromone is detected by a flying male located downwind at a distance as great as 3.2 km (2 mi).

Pheromones are a means of chemical communication between members of the same species. The antennae of this male emperor moth are covered by thousands of tiny olfactory receptors that can detect sex-attractant pheromones released by a female miles away.

Animals have managed to persist in hostile surroundings because they have developed extraordinary adaptations or abilities, one of which is a highly specialized sense of smell. It is this sense that enables them to make use of sex and aggregation pheromones to locate one another and to stimulate courtship and mating; of alarm pheromones to warn of impending danger; and of trail pheromones to direct others to suitable food or egg-laying or resting sites. Mammals use pheromones for family and clan cohesion, for individual range and territorial maintenance (marking of living and breeding space), and for aggression and social dominance.

Phi Beta Kappa [fy bay'-tuh kap'-uh]   Phi Beta Kappa, an acronym for the Greek words *philosophia biou kubernetes,* meaning "philosophy the guide of life," is an American honorary academic society. Organized in 1776 at the College of William and Mary as a secret literary society, it has about 240 chapters across the United States. College juniors and seniors who have achieved certain academic requirements stipulated by their colleges are elected to the society.

Phidias [fid'-ee-uhs]   Often considered the greatest of the ancient Greek sculptors, Phidias, *c.*490–430 BC, was renowned for the majesty of his figures. An Athenian sculptor, he worked primarily in bronze or in gold and ivory, creating statues of divinities, heroes, and athletes for the major city-states and sanctuaries. In ancient times his fame was centered on his chryselephantine (gold and ivory) cult statues, none of which survive. These include the *Athena Parthenos* that stood in the Parthenon and a colossal Zeus for the temple at Olympia, one of the SEVEN WONDERS OF THE WORLD. An idea of these originals can be obtained only from coins, gems, and small Roman copies, or from ancient descriptions.

Phidias is also credited with being the overall supervisor of the artistic works on the ACROPOLIS in Athens. Some of his designs may have survived in the architectural sculpture of the Parthenon, most of which is in the British Museum in London.

Philadelphia [fil-uh-del'-fee-uh]   Philadelphia, the largest city in Pennsylvania and the fifth largest in the United States, is situated in southeastern Pennsylvania on the west bank of the Delaware River. The Schuylkill River flows through the city. Philadelphia gets its name from two Greek words meaning "city of brotherly love."

Philadelphia has a population of 1,585,577 (1990). During the 1980s the city slipped from its fourth-place rank among most populous U.S. cities as its population declined by 6%. The Philadelphia metropolitan area, which includes portions of the state of New Jersey, has 4,856,881 people. Philadelphia County and the city are coextensive and cover an area of 334 km^2 (129 mi^2).

Contemporary City. Philadelphia is one of the nation's

City Hall (center), *Philadelphia's tallest building, rises to a height of 167 m (548 ft). On top of the building rests a massive sculpture of William Penn, the colonial leader who laid out the original plan for the city.*

major financial and insurance centers. Tourism and conventions are important to the economy. Philadelphia is an important port and the center of a major industrial area.

The Philadelphia Harbor, including ports in the Philadelphia metropolitan area, ranks as one of the most important in the United States. Textiles and apparel, petroleum products, food processing, chemicals and pharmaceuticals, printing and publishing, and machinery are the city's leading industries.

Rail service connects the city with all parts of the country, and more than 250 truck lines serve the area's industry and commerce. The Philadelphia International Airport is one of the nation's busiest.

The private University of Pennsylvania (see PENNSYLVANIA, UNIVERSITY OF) is one of the nation's most prestigious schools. Other schools include the Curtis Institute of Music, Drexel University (1891), St. Joseph's University (1851), the Philadelphia College of Textiles and Science (1884), Temple University (1884), and La Salle University (1863).

Among Philadelphia's learned societies are the PENNSYLVANIA ACADEMY OF THE FINE ARTS, the American Philo-

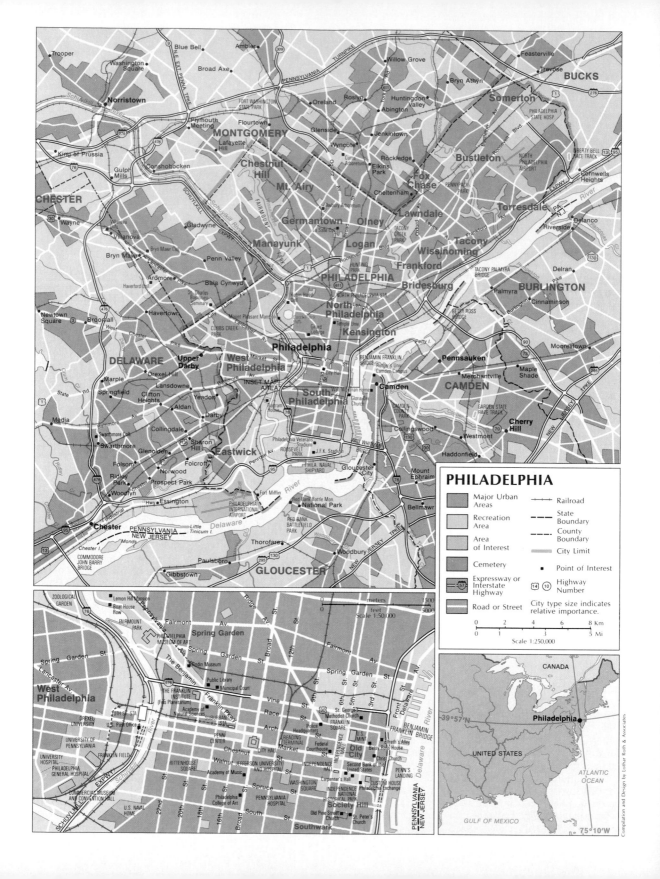

PHILADELPHIA

▨	Major Urban Areas	
▨	Recreation Area	
▨	Area of Interest	
▨	Cemetery	
╍57╍	Expressway or Interstate Highway	
	Road or Street	

┼┼┼	Railroad
╌╌╌	State Boundary
╍╍╍	County Boundary
▬	City Limit
■	Point of Interest
14 10	Highway Number

City type size indicates relative importance.

0   2   4   6   8 Km
0   1   2   3   4   5 Mi

Scale 1:250,000

Compilation and Design by Lothar Roth & Associates

meters
0   1500
feet
0   5000

Scale 1:50,000

sophical Society, and the Academy of Natural Sciences.

The PHILADELPHIA ORCHESTRA is world famous, as are the Pennsylvania and Milwaukee Ballet and the Opera Company of Philadelphia. Museums include the Franklin Institute Science Museum, the Philadelphia Museum of Art, the University (of Pennsylvania) Museum, and the Rodin Museum.

Philadelphia's main tourist attractions are INDEPENDENCE HALL, the LIBERTY BELL, Carpenters' Hall, and Congress Hall, within Independence National Historical Park. Other points of interest are the Betsy Ross House, Christ Church, the U.S. Mint, and Gloria Dei Church.

The city supports professional baseball, football, ice hockey, and basketball teams. The Army-Navy football game is played there each year (except for a 1983 Rose Bowl foray).

History. Philadelphia was founded in 1681 by William PENN, an English Quaker, who planned it as the center of his ambitious colonizing scheme for what would become the state of Pennsylvania. The town quickly prospered, thanks to peace treaties Penn signed with the Delaware Indians that permitted the Quakers (and other religious dissenters) to settle the area.

Philadelphia's second major figure was Benjamin FRANKLIN. He arrived in Philadelphia in 1723 as a young man and went on to become the city's leading citizen. By 1775 the city was the colonies' largest, with more than 25,000 inhabitants, and it played an important role in the American Revolution and in the early years of independence. The two greatest documents of U.S. history—the Declaration of Independence and the Constitution—were both drawn up and signed in Philadelphia. The city was the seat of the Continental Congress and thus served as the capital of the colonies during the Revolution (except when it was under British occupation) and then became the capital of the new republic from 1790 to 1800.

Philadelphia continued to grow during the 19th and 20th centuries, although it lost its position as the first city to New York. During the second half of the 20th century, Philadelphia has suffered urban ills common to many large, older cities. Ambitious urban-redevelopment programs have been inaugurated to cope with those problems.

Philadelphia Orchestra, The

The Philadelphia Orchestra, noted for its virtuosity and tone quality, ranks as one of the greatest orchestras of the world. In the spring of 1900 conductor Fritz Scheel formed an orchestra for benefit concerts; the following autumn, it became the 85-member Philadelphia Orchestra. Scheel was succeeded briefly (1907–12) by Karl Pohlig, who then gave way to the flamboyant Leopold STOKOWSKI. During his turbulent reign (until 1938), Stokowski brought the orchestra international recognition, drawing into it some of the world's finest instrumentalists and creating the distinctive "Philadelphia sound." Stokowski was succeeded in 1938 by his assistant conductor Eugene ORMANDY, who proved more sedate than Stokowski but no less capable.

In 1980, Ormandy was succeeded as music director by Riccardo MUTI. Muti announced (1990) plans to give up the position in 1992.

Philadelphia Zoological Garden

The oldest zoo in the United States, the Philadelphia Zoological Garden opened in 1874 and is especially noted for the naturalistic environment created for its bird collection and for having the largest building in the United States for the exhibit of members of the cat family.

philanthropy   see FOUNDATIONS AND ENDOWMENTS; FUND-RAISING

philately

philately [fil-at'-uh-lee]   The avocation of philately, or stamp collecting, began shortly after May 6, 1840, when the world's first adhesive postage stamp, the Penny Black, was issued in London. A two-pence, blue, followed on May 8. Shortly thereafter stamps were issued by Brazil (1843), the Swiss cantons of Zurich and Geneva (1843) and Basel (1845), and the United States (1847). By the 1860s stamp collecting had become a popular hobby, and the first stamp catalog for the use of collectors was published in 1864.

The word *philately*, which was coined by a Frenchman in the 19th century from a combination of Greek words whose sum means "the love of being tax free," alludes to the fact that, before postage stamps, letters were sent collect.

For many years the 1840 British stamps set the pattern for the stamps of other countries: generally about 2.5 cm (1 in) in height, slightly less in width, and usually printed with a sovereign's portrait in a single color. The United States stamps of 1847 were somewhat larger and pictured Benjamin Franklin and George Washington. Brazil's first stamps were ovals with large denomination numerals imprinted on horizontal rectangles and were called Bull's Eyes.

Stamps have appeared in various shapes. A few have been smaller than the 1840 originals, and in recent years some have been up to five times the size of the originals. Except for the first issues, in which stamps had to be scissored from printed panels, most stamps are perforated around their sides for easy separation.

Stamps have been issued not only for ordinary postal uses but also for special uses, such as to expedite official and military mail and to indicate a tax on certain commodities.

Included in a philatelist's collection might be stamp-imprinted envelopes, postal cards, letter sheets such as the current aerograms, day-of-issue stamped envelopes (first-day covers), plate blocks, and complete panes of stamps as they come from the printer. Stamp collections are housed in albums that are usually loose-leaf. Stamps are affixed to the page by gummed hinges or are slipped into pochettes, transparent pockets that are used primarily for mint-condition stamps—stamps that have never been used.

(Left) *The Penny Black, issued by Great Britain in 1840, was the world's first adhesive postage stamp.* (Center) *Brazilian Bull's Eye stamps were issued in 1843 in denominations of 30, 60, and 90 reals.* (Right) *The British Guiana one-penny magenta (1856), the only known stamp of its issue, sold for $850,000 in 1980.*

The 1918 U.S. airmail "invert," with the flying machine Curtiss Jenny *mistakenly printed upside down, is among the most celebrated errors in stamp production. Only 100 of these stamps were issued.*

This proof of the U.S. airmail stamp commemorating the first lunar landing was canceled by astronauts during the Apollo 11 *flight and again on the first day of issue.*

Contemporary postage stamps, as these recent issues show, commemorate historical events and political figures and reproduce works of art.

Stamps are valued according to their rarity and condition. Among the world's most valuable stamps is a one-penny 1856 British Guiana stamp; it brought $280,000 at a 1970 auction and was resold for $850,000 in 1980. Stamps printed with errors are rare and often valuable. One hundred U.S. airmail stamps were issued in 1918 with the picture of an airplane accidentally printed upside down. One of these sold at auction in 1979 for $135,000. A world record price was set in 1987 with the $1.1 million sale of a two-cent stamp purchased in Pittsburgh in 1852 and known as the "Lady McGill" stamp.

See also: postal services.

Philby, H. St. John [fil'-bee] The British explorer Harry St. John Bridger Philby, b. Apr. 3, 1885, d. Sept. 30, 1960, traveled through parts of Arabia that no European had previously visited; he wrote extensively of his discoveries. He first visited the region in 1917 on a special mission for the British foreign service. Philby later became a Muslim with the name Hajj Abdullah and served as an advisor to King IBN SAUD of Saudi Arabia for about 30 years.

The explorer's son, Harold Adrian Russell Philby, b. Jan. 1, 1912, d. May 11, 1988, known as Kim, gained notoriety as a member of a Soviet spy ring that included Guy Burgess, Donald MacLean, and Anthony Blunt within the top reaches of British intelligence. He defected to the USSR in 1963.

Philemon [fil-ee'-muhn] A Greek playwright who wrote in Athens and became a citizen of the city c.307 BC, Philemon, c.365–c.264 BC, is sometimes credited with the introduction of New Comedy to the Greek stage. A rival of Menander for popular favor at the annual dramatic festivals, Philemon produced 97 comedies, of which at least 60 titles are known. About 200 fragments of his works exist.

Philemon, Epistle to The Epistle to Philemon, the 18th book of the New Testament of the Bible, is Saint PAUL's eloquent appeal on behalf of a runaway slave, Onesimus, whom he had converted to Christianity. The letter, which was probably written during Paul's Ephesian imprisonment in AD 56 or during his Roman imprisonment five years later, shows the depth of his Christian humaneness. In it he asks Philemon—a wealthy Christian of Colossae whom he had converted—for Onesimus's quiet return to his former station or, in another interpretation, for his complete freedom to become an evangelist.

Philip, Prince see EDINBURGH, PHILIP MOUNTBATTEN, DUKE OF

Philip, Saint Saint Philip, one of Jesus' first apostles, brought Nathanael (or BARTHOLOMEW) to Jesus (John 1:43–51). He was present at the feeding of the 5,000 (John 6:5–7) and acted as an intermediary for Gentiles wishing to meet Jesus (John 12:20–22). Feast day: Nov. 14 (Eastern); May 3 (Western).

Philip the Bold, Duke of Burgundy Philip the Bold, b. Jan. 17, 1342, d. Apr. 27, 1404, the youngest son of JOHN II of France, served as a regent for his nephew, King CHARLES VI, and was virtual ruler of France after Charles became insane (1392). Philip was captured (1356) with his father at the Battle of Poitiers and became duke of Burgundy in 1363. Six years later he married Margaret, heiress to the counties of Flanders, Burgundy, Artois, and Nevers. He ruled these lands as count after 1384, beginning a system of marriage alliances that was to bring important parts of the Low Countries adjacent to Flanders into his family's realm. He thus created the Burgundian state that brought nominal unity to the Netherlands. In his later years Philip was challenged by his nephew and rival, Louis, duc d'Orléans (see ORLÉANS family).

Philip the Evangelist Philip the Evangelist was one of the first seven men chosen by the apostles to be a Christian deacon and missionary (Acts 6:2–6). Philip converted the Ethiopian eunuch and the Samaritan followers of SIMON MAGUS (also one of his converts; Acts 8:4–13, 26–40). Feast day: Oct. 11 (Eastern); June 6 (Western).

Philip the Good, Duke of Burgundy Philip the Good, b. July 31, 1396, d. June 15, 1467, succeeded his father, JOHN THE FEARLESS, as duke of Burgundy in 1419 when John was assassinated in Montereau during a meeting with the French dauphin (later King CHARLES VII). Philip passively supported the effort of the English king HENRY V to usurp the French throne, but he avoided his father's deep involvement in French politics.

Philip's two predecessors extended Burgundian influence in the Low Countries, and Philip reaped the benefits of this policy. Already count of Flanders and Artois, Philip successively acquired Namur, Hainaut, Brabant, Holland, Zeeland, and Luxembourg between 1420 and 1443. In 1435 he also obtained a strategic part of Picardy.

Famous for his patronage of chivalry and the arts, Philip founded the order of the Golden Fleece in 1430. His court reflected the splendor of the early northern Renaissance, and he was perhaps the most powerful ruler of his day.

Philip of Hesse The German prince Philip of Hesse, b. Nov. 13, 1504, d. Mar. 31, 1567, also called Philip the Magnanimous, introduced the Reformation into Hesse. As a youthful landgrave, he founded (1527) Marburg, the first Protestant university. After he failed to reconcile Swiss Protestant reformer Ulrich Zwingli with Martin Luther, Philip signed (1530) the AUGSBURG CONFESSION, a declaration of the Lutheran doctrines of faith. In response to Emperor CHARLES V's threat to crush Lutheranism, Philip helped form (1531) the Schmalkaldic League, which enabled the Reformation to take hold throughout Germany. Philip's bigamous marriage (1540) to Margaret of Saale cost him the support of many reformers, forcing him to make peace with Charles in 1541. In the Schmalkaldic War (1546–47), however, Charles destroyed the league and imprisoned Philip.

Philip of Swabia   Philip of Swabia, b. *c.*1178, d. June 21, 1208, reigned as one of two German kings after a disputed election. The youngest son of Holy Roman Emperor FREDERICK I, Philip was duke of Tuscany and Swabia under his brother, HENRY VI. When Henry died (1197), leaving a three-year-old son who later became emperor as FREDERICK II, Philip backed the boy. The German princes, however, wanted an adult king. Most of them chose Philip, on Mar. 6, 1198, and later crowned him king; on June 9 others elected Otto of Brunswick, who ruled as German King and Holy Roman Emperor OTTO IV. In the ensuing civil war, Philip was on the verge of victory—despite opposition from Pope INNOCENT III— when he was assassinated. Otto became sole king after Philip's death.

Philip I, King of France   Philip I, b. 1052, d. July 29 or 30, 1108, was king of France from 1060 to 1108. He was 8 years old when he succeeded his father, HENRY I. For 7 years he was under the guardianship of Baldwin V, count of Flanders. Philip ruled only a very small part of France and was in constant trouble with the church because of a bigamous marriage, resistance to church reform, and slothful, sensual behavior. After 1100 his son LOUIS VI gradually took over the government.

Philip II, King of France (Philip Augustus)   Philip II, b. Aug. 21, 1165, d. July 14, 1223, the son of LOUIS VII and Adèle of Champagne, was king of France from 1180 to 1223. Philip made France the strongest monarchy in Europe and is usually considered that country's greatest medieval king. Through his marriage to Isabella of Hainaut he obtained Artois, and later he also acquired Vermandois. The royal lands remained surrounded, however, by three strong states—CHAMPAGNE, FLANDERS, and the possessions of HENRY II of England, notably ANJOU and NORMANDY. Royal penetration of Flanders was aided when Count Baldwin IX went on the Fourth Crusade in 1202. Champagne, ruled by Philip's maternal relatives, was usually friendly toward the French monarch. Against the Plantagenet family of England, Philip followed his father's policy and supported the rebellious sons of Henry II.

On the Third CRUSADE (1188–92), Philip quarreled with RICHARD I of England, but this dangerous enemy was killed in 1199. Richard's brother, JOHN, who succeeded him as king, agreed to hold the family lands in France as Philip's vassal but was summoned before the royal court in 1202 on the complaint of one of his own vassals. When John ignored the summons, Philip occupied

Philip II Augustus, king of France, conducted a lifelong campaign against the Plantagenet kings of England, who claimed extensive territorial holdings in France. He fortified Paris, subdued the nobility, and instituted a system of administrative officers to maintain order in the provinces.

(1204–06) Normandy and Anjou. John, allied with Emperor OTTO IV, attempted to regain these lands, but Philip defeated his coalition at Bouvines in 1214. Philip then embarked on the crusade against the ALBIGENSES in southern France.

Philip III, King of France (Philip the Bold)   Philip III, b. Apr. 3, 1245, d. Oct. 5, 1285, the son of LOUIS IX and Margaret of Provence, became king of France in 1270. Philip's great achievement was the smooth and peaceful absorption of the counties of Toulouse, Poitiers, and Auvergne, following the death of his uncle Alphonse in 1271. Another uncle, CHARLES I of Naples and Sicily, persuaded Philip to undertake an ill-advised crusade in 1285 against the king of Aragon, PETER III. Philip died in the course of this unsuccessful expedition and was succeeded by his son Philip IV.

Philip IV, King of France (Philip the Fair)   Philip IV, b. 1268, d. Nov. 29, 1314, succeeded his father, Philip III, as king of France in 1285, the same year he married Jeanne of Champagne, queen of Navarre. Although his reign was one of the most important in French history, Philip's actual role has been disputed. He is no longer considered a mere figurehead dominated by his aggressive officials, but debate continues as to whether he was ruthless and cynical or a deeply religious man. His belief in the sacred majesty of French kingship led him into conflict with the church and the nobility as well as with foreign powers.

Philip went to war with England in 1294 and attempted several unpopular fiscal measures to support this effort. He prevailed in a dispute with Pope BONIFACE VIII about taxation of the clergy and won initial victories over England and Flanders. In 1301, Philip charged Bernard Saisset, bishop of Pamiers, with treason, precipitating a bitter quarrel with the pope. In a vicious propaganda attack on the pope, Philip used large assemblies later known as the STATES-GENERAL.

Philip issued (1303) an ordinance of reform and made concessions to England in order to free his hand for the defeat of the Flemings and a stroke against the pope. After Boniface's death (1303), Philip secured the election of a French pope, CLEMENT V, who established himself at Avignon.

To replenish the royal treasury, depleted after many years of warfare, Philip expelled the Jews in 1306, confiscating their property and the moneys owed to them. He also destroyed the TEMPLARS, a wealthy crusading order.

Philip VI, King of France

Philip VI, b. 1293, d. Aug. 22, 1350, succeeded his father, Charles, as count of Valois, Anjou, and Maine in 1325. Three years later he became the first king from the house of VALOIS. Philip's opponents—mostly from the northwestern nobility—gave their homage to EDWARD III of England after the HUNDRED YEARS' WAR broke out (1337). The war went badly for Philip: he was defeated at Crécy in 1346, and his program for a well-financed army was ruined by the Black Death of 1348. Philip gradually relinquished authority to his son, JOHN II.

Philip II, King of Macedonia

Philip II, b. c.382 BC, d. June 336 BC, the father by Olympias of ALEXANDER THE GREAT, forcibly united Greece. Succeeding to a troubled kingdom in 359, he defeated neighboring tribes, gradually conquered the Greek coastal cities, notably OLYNTHUS (348), and asserted royal control over the barons of Upper Macedonia. Conquest of a mining area in Thrace gave him huge resources for reorganizing his army into an efficient fighting force and for pursuing a vigorous policy in Greece.

After conquering Thessaly, Philip intervened decisively in the long war over Delphi. In virtual control of Delphi by 346 BC, he forced Athens into an inglorious peace and alliance. He then aimed at attacking Persia, using the convenient slogan of a Hellenic Crusade, which was created by intellectuals such as ISOCRATES. While DEMOSTHENES succeeded in rallying Athens against Philip, Artaxerxes III rebuilt Persian power, and their common action defeated (340–339) Philip at Byzantium. In 338, however, Philip's defeat of the forces of Athens

Philip II of Macedonia, depicted on an ancient coin, established his state as a dominant military power in the Balkans and set the stage for the subsequent conquests by his son Alexander the Great.

and Thebes at Chaeronea made him master of Greece.

After installing friendly governments in most cities and garrisons in some, Philip forced the Greeks to join in a Hellenic league that swore allegiance to him and his dynasty. In 336 he invaded Asia, but dynastic troubles supervened, leading him to divorce Olympias and to exile Alexander temporarily before his assassination under mysterious circumstances later the same year.

Philip V, King of Macedonia

Philip V, 238–179 BC, king of Macedonia from 221, was Rome's last powerful opponent in Greece. Carthaginian victories in the Second PUNIC WAR led him to side with HANNIBAL and to attack Roman allies in Illyria. Defeated by Roman forces, he was involved by Roman diplomacy in war against Aetolia and Pergamum, from which he emerged with favorable peace treaties (206–205).

Made overconfident by success, Philip brutally expanded his power eastward and resumed provocation in Illyria. Pergamum and Rhodes united against him, and in 201–200 Rome joined them in the Second Macedonian War. The Roman general Titus Quinctius FLAMININUS, uniting Greece against Philip, finally defeated him in 197 at Cynoscephalae.

Deprived of his Greek possessions, Philip retained his throne and supported Rome against the Seleucid ANTIOCHUS III, but even so constantly lost territory as a result of Roman arbitration. Roman intrigues to give the Macedonian throne to his younger son Demetrius led to the latter's execution, and Philip was succeeded peacefully by his son PERSEUS.

Philip I, King of Castile

(Philip the Handsome) [kas-teel'] Philip I, b. July 22, 1478, d. Sept. 25, 1506, king of Castile (1506), founded the HABSBURG line of Spanish kings. Son of Holy Roman Emperor MAXIMILIAN I and MARY OF BURGUNDY, Philip married (1496) JOAN THE MAD, daughter of FERDINAND II of Aragon and ISABELLA I of Castile. On her mother's death (1504) Joan inherited Castile, and in June 1506, Philip assumed control but died suddenly shortly thereafter. Philip and Joan's son later became Holy Roman Emperor CHARLES V.

Philip II, King of Spain

Philip II, b. May 21, 1527, d. Sept. 13, 1598, HABSBURG king of Spain, ruled a vast domain that included Spain and its possessions in America and Italy, the Low Countries, and (from 1580) Portugal and its empire. He acquired these territories (except Portugal) when his father, Holy Roman Emperor CHARLES V, abdicated in 1555–56.

From the beginning Philip had to contend with potentially hostile powers, especially France and the Ottoman Empire. The French were defeated (1557) at Saint Quentin and were later distracted by civil wars, but Turkish incursions in the western Mediterranean remained a problem throughout Philip's reign.

Revolt broke out in the Low Countries in 1566 (see

Philip II, king of Spain, devoted all the military and political resources of his empire to the preservation of Roman Catholicism in Europe. His reign, although fraught with court intrigue and continual wars, saw the start of the Golden Age of Spanish literature.

DUTCH REVOLT), and Philip became enmeshed in a struggle that lasted until 1648. English and French efforts on behalf of the rebels led him to attempt (1588) an invasion of England—with disastrous results (see SPANISH ARMADA)—and to engage in a series of inconclusive adventures in France after 1589. The expense of these efforts and of the struggle with the Turks was more than even the enormous resources of his empire could bear. Although his forces defeated (1571) the Turks at the Battle of LEPANTO, regained the southern part of the Netherlands, and were generally successful in protecting his American possessions, the glories of the "golden age" were dearly bought.

Hardworking, meticulous, and suspicious, Philip ruled his vast patrimony first from Madrid and then from the great monastery-palace at the ESCORIAL. His insistence on orthodoxy and obedience, which he demonstrated in the suppression of rebellions by the MORISCOS (1568–70) and the Aragonese (1591), was tempered by a concern for justice, and he was generally beloved by his Spanish subjects. Philip asserted his claims to Portugal in 1580, when the Portuguese king Henry died without heirs. He confirmed the privileges of his new subjects and permitted them to retain control of their institutions.

Philip's first wife, Maria of Portugal, died (1545) after two years of marriage, leaving him with a son, Don Carlos, whose violence and instability forced Philip to imprison him. A second marriage (1554–58), to MARY I of England, was unhappy and barren. In 1568, when Don Carlos died in prison and Philip's third wife, Elizabeth of Valois, died a few months later, Philip was wrongly accused of murdering them both. Elizabeth left him with two daughters to whom he was devoted. In 1570, Philip married Anne of Austria; they had four sons, three of whom died in childhood. Their surviving son, Philip III, inherited a powerful but exhausted empire.

Philip III, King of Spain   Although Spain outwardly remained a major power throughout the reign of Philip III, b. Apr. 14, 1578, d. Mar. 31, 1621, his accession (1598) marked the beginning of increasing social and economic crises. The only surviving son of Philip II, he also ruled Portugal (as Philip II). A virtual nonentity, Philip left the government to his favorite, the duque de Lerma. Lerma concluded peace with England in 1604 and a truce with the Dutch in 1609, but he did little to halt Spain's disastrous economic decline. The expulsion of the MORISCOS (1609–14), although popular at the time, further weakened the Spanish economy. At the end of Philip's reign, Spain became involved in the THIRTY YEARS' WAR. Philip was succeeded by his son, Philip IV.

Philip IV, King of Spain   During the reign of Philip IV, b. Apr. 8, 1605, d. Sept. 17, 1665, Spain declined from its position as a major world power. Philip IV, who succeeded his father, Philip III, in 1621, also ruled Portugal (as Philip III) until 1640. Fond of hunting and a patron of the arts, he left the government to his favorite, the conde-duque de OLIVARES, during the first two decades of his reign. The strain of participation in the THIRTY YEARS' WAR and other military adventures crippled the economy and led to revolts (1640) in Catalonia and Portugal.

Olivares was dismissed in 1643, and Philip soon fell under the influence of Don Luis de Haro, Olivares's nephew. Haro reduced Spain's foreign commitments, but he was unable to reform the tottering fiscal and administrative structure of the empire. The last years of the reign were devoted to a futile war leading to Portugal's independence. Intelligent and well-meaning, but lacking in force, Philip left a disastrously weakened kingdom to his son, the sickly CHARLES II.

Philip V, King of Spain   The founder of the BOURBON dynasty in Spain, Philip V, b. Dec. 19, 1683, d. July 9, 1746, ascended the throne in 1700 and presided over the resurgence of much of Spain's earlier influence as a world power. Philip received a strong moral and religious

Philip V was the first Bourbon king of Spain. Because he was also in the line of succession to the French throne, Philip's claim to Spain was contested by other European powers in the War of the Spanish Succession.

upbringing under the Abbé François FÉNELON. In 1700, King CHARLES II of Spain died without heirs, naming Philip, a grandson of King LOUIS XIV of France, as his successor. Philip accepted, but Louis insisted that Philip retain his rights to the French throne, leading Austria, England, Portugal, and the Dutch Republic to declare war against France and Spain. In the ensuing War of the SPANISH SUCCESSION (1701–14), Philip's courage made him popular among his subjects. By the treaties of Utrecht (1713; see UTRECHT, PEACE OF), and Rastadt (1714), Philip retained Spain and Spanish America but lost other Spanish territories in Europe. In 1702 he married María Luisa of Savoy, and after her death in 1714 he married the ambitious Elizabeth FARNESE. Philip was more interested in hunting, music, and religion than in governing Spain, and he let himself be guided by his wives and by his prime ministers. Spanish foreign policy in the 1730s was directed mainly at winning territories in Italy for Elizabeth's son Charles. In later life Philip became insane. He was succeeded by his sons FERDINAND VI and CHARLES III.

___

Philippi [fil-ip'-y]   At Philippi, a city of ancient Macedonia near the modern town of Kavalla, Mark ANTONY and Octavian (later Emperor AUGUSTUS) won a famous victory over BRUTUS and CASSIUS LONGINUS in 42 BC. Fortified by PHILIP II of Macedonia in 356 BC, it boasts an extant temple and amphitheater. Philippi was the scene of Saint Paul's first preaching in Europe.

___

Philippians, Epistle to the [fil-ip'-ee-uhnz]   The Epistle to the Philippians, the 11th book in the New Testament of the BIBLE, was written by Saint PAUL to the Philippians—a Christian community in eastern Macedonia—from prison in Ephesus in AD 57 or, as some scholars believe, in Rome in the early 60s. Some scholars think that the present letter is a composite of three different ones. In one (4:10–20), Paul thanks the Philippians, with whom he had good relations, for a gift they sent him. In another (1:1–3:1), Paul gives them a hopeful report of his legal situation and encourages them to Christian living. In a third (3:2–4:3), he attacks a Judaizing gnostic group trying to mislead the Philippians. The epistle is noted for the hymn to Christ in 2:6–11 and for its generally joyful tone.

___

Philippines [fil'-uh-peenz]   The Philippines is an independent island nation in the western Pacific about 800 km (500 mi) off the coast of mainland Southeast Asia. Over centuries, foreign elements have been added to the indigenous Malay culture, creating a cultural mosaic that reflects both Eastern and Western influences.

Land and Resources

Many of the more than 7,000 volcanic islands that constitute the Philippine archipelago are uninhabited; the 11 largest islands account for more than 94% of the total land area. The archipelago extends for more than 800 km (500 mi) from LUZON in the north, through the Visayan Islands (including Negros, CEBU, Leyte, Samar, and Panay) in the center, to MINDANAO and the SULU ARCHIPELAGO in the south. The terrain is generally mountainous, rising to a high point of 2,954 m (9,692 ft) at Mount Apu, a volcano on Mindanao. Only Luzon and Mindanao have extensive lowland areas. Rivers are generally short, swift flowing, and seasonal.

Climate. The Philippines has a tropical climate, with a mean annual lowland temperature of about 27° C (80° F). Temperatures vary more between day and night and high and low altitudes than between seasons. About 90% of the country receives more than 1,780 mm (70 in) of rainfall a year.

Resources. Much of the land is hilly, eroded, and unfit for human habitation, but extremely fertile volcanic soils are found on Luzon, Mindanao, and parts of Negros. The forests that once covered 80% of the land are being rapidly depleted. Native wildlife includes water buffalo, monkeys, reptiles, and a variety of tropical birds. The country has substantial deposits of chromium, copper, gold, silver, manganese, lead, and iron ore and considerable hydroelectric-power potential.

People

Although the people of the Philippines speak a variety of MALAYO-POLYNESIAN LANGUAGES and are scattered across many islands, they have a relatively high degree of cultural homogeneity. There is a strong sense of national identity despite the continuing importance of kinship ties. Least assimilated are the Muslims (Moros) of the south, the upland hill tribes (see NEGRITO), and recent Chinese immigrants.

Ethnically, most Filipinos are a mixture of Malay and Mongoloid racial elements, with some admixture of Chinese, Indian, Spanish, and American elements. The Spanish term *mestizo* is used to describe anyone of mixed blood. The most important ethnolinguistic groups are the Tagalogs, Ilocanos, Pampagos, Bicolanos, and Hiligaynon of Luzon and the Cebuanos, Ilongos, and Waray-Waray of the Visayan Islands. These groups, constituting about 90% of the population, are predominantly Roman Catholic, although the Philippine Independent Church (see AGLIPAY, GREGORIO) and the Iglesia ni Christo command significant followings. The hill tribes practice tribal religions, and Islam is strongest in the Sulu Archipelago, Palawan, and parts of southern Mindanao.

Demography. The population of the Philippines is increasing rapidly, placing great strains on the economy and on social services. About half of the people live on Luzon, with sizable populations on Cebu, Mindanao, Leyte, and Negros. Most Filipinos live in small rural villages. Recent years, however, have seen large-scale migration from rural areas to the cities, especially MANILA, the capital. Nearly one in eight Filipinos lives in Metro Manila, which includes QUEZON CITY (the capital from 1948 to 1976), Caloocan, and Pasay. Other large cities are CEBU, DAVAO, and Zamboaga.

Education and Health. The Philippines has one of the highest literacy rates in Asia. Primary education is free

REPUBLIC OF THE PHILIPPINES

Land: Area: 300,000 km^2 (115,831 mi^2). Capital and largest city: Manila (1990 est. pop., 1,876,194).

People: Population (1990 est.): 66,117,284. Density: 220.4 per km^2 (570.8 per mi^2). Distribution (1990): 43% urban, 57% rural. Official language: Pilipino. Major religions: Roman Catholicism, Protestantism, Islam.

Government: Type: republic. Legislature: National Assembly. Political subdivisions: 13 regions, 73 provinces, 61 chartered cities.

Economy: GNP (1989): $40.5 billion; $625 per capita. Labor distribution (1989): commerce and services—36%; manufacturing—21%; agriculture and fishing—10%; construction—7%; government and public services—26%. Foreign trade (1990 est.): imports—$11.5 billion; exports—$8.0 billion. Currency: 1 peso = 100 centavos.

Education and Health: Literacy (1990): 83% of adult population. Universities (1986): 52. Hospital beds (1988): 85,943. Physicians (1989): 54,000. Life expectancy (1990): women—66; men—63. Infant mortality (1990): 48 per 1,000 live births.

and compulsory. The many colleges and universities include the University of the Philippines (1922) and the University of Santo Tomás (1611). Higher education is greatly valued, although the economy cannot absorb all college graduates.

Manila has excellent medical facilities, but a shortage of trained medical personnel exists in rural areas. Malnutrition-related infant deaths remain high.

Culture. The rich body of indigenous artistic traditions includes folktales, music, and the folk dances made famous by the Bayanihan Dance Troupe. Painting and sculpture often combine Asian and Western elements. Spanish and English have been the vehicles for such writers as José Rizal, N. V. M. González, Bienvenido Santos, and F. Sionil José.

Economic Activity

The Philippines is primarily an exporter of raw materials and an importer of manufactured goods. Rice and corn, the staple food crops, occupy 80% of all cropland. Commercial crops, led by coconuts and sugarcane, include bananas, pineapples, abaca (Manila hemp), tobacco, coffee, and cotton.

Land is unequally distributed; about 70% of all peasants are landless, and large landowners exercise economic and political power to the detriment of the peasantry. Land reform has been on every government's agenda since 1946, but little meaningful redistribution has taken place.

Industry provides about one-fourth of the gross domestic product. The processing of agricultural products accounts for almost half of all industrial production, followed by electronic and electrical equipment, chemicals, petroleum refining, and textiles. Industry is concentrated in the Manila area. Copper, gold, nickel, and chromium are mined for export and coal for domestic use. Fishing, forestry, tourism, and remittances from overseas workers are also important.

Government

The constitution of 1935, based on that of the United States, was suspended when martial law was imposed in 1972. A new constitution ratified in 1973 changed the government from presidential to parliamentary form, but this document did not come fully into effect until 1981, by which time it had been amended to place supreme power, including the right to rule by decree, in the hands of the president.

Corazon AQUINO, who took de facto control of the government on Feb. 25, 1986, assumed legislative powers on March 25 under a transitional "freedom constitution." The legislature was abolished, many officials were replaced by Aquino appointees, and a committee was appointed to draft a new constitution. This constitution, overwhelmingly approved in a Feb. 2, 1987, plebescite, allowed Aquino to remain in office until June 1992. She pledged not to run in 1992, and subsequent presidents were restricted to a single 6-year term. On July 27, 1987, Aquino turned legislative power over to a Senate and House of Representatives that had been elected in May. Local elections were held in 1988.

History

The Philippines, thought to have been peopled chiefly by waves of migrants from Indonesia, have been inhabited for more than 30,000 years. Extensive trade with India, Indonesia, China, and Japan developed; Islam was introduced to the southern islands from Indonesia in the 15th century.

When Ferdinand MAGELLAN claimed the islands for Spain in 1521, there was no central government to mount effective resistance. The first permanent Spanish settlement was made by Miguel López de Legazpi on Cebu in 1565. In 1571 the islands were renamed in honor of King Philip II, and the capital was moved to Manila. The colonial administration was headed by a governor-general responsible to the viceroy of Mexico, but the parish priest was often the only visible symbol of Spanish authority in rural areas. Trade in Chinese luxury items, gathered in Manila and sold in Acapulco in exchange for silver, was the economic foundation of the colony until the 19th century, when the independence of Spain's New World colonies forced a shift to a cash-crop economy.

In the 1880s the writings of José Rizal (1861–96) helped spur Filipino demands for reform. Rizal's execution made him a national hero and sparked an unsuccessful revolution led by Emilio AGUINALDO. On June 12, 1898, after the outbreak of the SPANISH-AMERICAN WAR, Aguinaldo declared the Philippines independent in the mistaken belief that the United States supported his struggle. Instead, Spain ceded the Philippines to the United States. From 1899 to 1901, Aguinaldo led a war against his country's new colonial rulers.

In 1935 the Philippines became a self-governing commonwealth under President Manuel Luis QUEZON, but World War II delayed full independence. Japan attacked the Philippines on Dec. 8, 1941, defeating U.S. and Filipino forces at BATAAN and CORREGIDOR in 1942. The struggle against Japan, culminating in Gen. Douglas MACARTHUR's return in 1944, came to symbolize U.S.-Philippine solidarity. On July 4, 1946, the Philippines gained full independence with Manuel ROXAS Y ACUNA as president.

After World War II the infrastructure of the Philippines was a shambles. Inadequate land distribution and unequal taxation fed the Hukbalahap (Huk) guerrilla revolt against the government, which was defused in the early 1950s by a resettlement and amnesty program devised

Manila, located on the western coast of Luzon, on Manila Bay, is the capital, largest city, and main port of the Philippines. The city, founded in 1571, is bisected by the Pasig River.

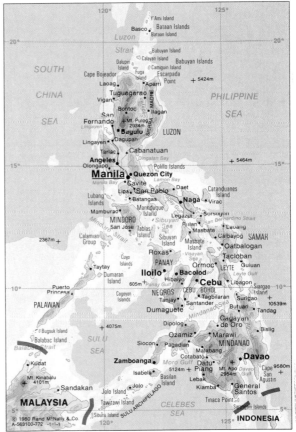

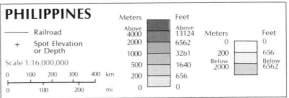

by Ramón MAGSAYSAY, who succeeded Elpidio QUIRINO as president in 1953.

Ferdinand MARCOS became the first president to win (1969) a second term after defeating President Diosdado Macapagal in 1965. In 1972, facing a Muslim revolt in the south, a leftist rural insurgency, and student unrest, Marcos declared martial law. He restored law and order, promoted social and economic reforms (often at the expense of his political foes), and created a political machine that remained dominant after martial law was lifted in 1981. On Aug. 21, 1983, Marcos's chief political rival, Benigno S. Aquino, Jr., was assassinated as he returned to the Philippines from exile. Marcos loyalists were accused of complicity in the killing, which touched off waves of popular protest. Marcos called early presidential elections, which were held on Feb. 7, 1986. Opposition leader Corazon Aquino, Benigno's widow, was backed by much of the business community and the influential Roman Catholic church. When the National Assembly declared Marcos the victor, Aquino launched a campaign of nonviolent resistance to secure the post many believed she had won. On February 22, when defense minister Juan Ponce Enrile and army deputy chief of staff Lt. Gen. Fidel Ramos resigned, huge crowds of ordinary Filipinos turned out to protect the dissident military leaders, and U.S. pressure on Marcos to step down increased. On February 25, Marcos left for exile in the United States, which quickly recognized Aquino as president.

Aquino took steps to restructure the government and the military, restore civil liberties, promote free enterprise, and retrieve public moneys illegally appropriated by Marcos and his cronies. Despite popular support, Aquino was unable to reach a negotiated settlement with Communist insurgents and was criticized for failing to halt corruption. Marcos died in 1989, but Aquino was challenged by many former allies, including Enrile and Vice-President Salvador Laurel, who became head of the opposition Nacionalista party in 1989. Aquino survived a seventh coup attempt in October 1990.

Philistines [fil'-uh-steenz] The Philistines were one of a number of SEA PEOPLES who penetrated Egypt and Syro-Palestine coastal areas during 1225–1050 BC. Of Aegean origin, they settled on the southern coastal plain of Canaan, an area that became known as Philistia. The Philistines rapidly adopted Canaanite language and culture, while introducing tighter military and political organization and superior weaponry based on the use of iron, over which they had a local monopoly. The chief Philistine cities were Ashkelon, Ashdod, Ekron, Gath, and Gaza. The military rulers of the Philistines extended their rule in Canaan, constantly warring with Israel. The Israelite king DAVID, who had earlier been a Philistine vassal, finally defeated them, succeeding where SAMSON and SAUL before him had failed.

Phillip, Arthur A British naval officer, Arthur Phillip, b. Oct. 11, 1738, d. Aug. 31, 1814, established the first permanent European colony in Australia. Phillip interrupted his naval career to farm in England from 1763 to 1776. In 1787 he founded a settlement in New South Wales and populated it with more than 700 convicts and about 300 free persons. As the colony's governor (1788–92), he created a permanent community despite rebellion and the threat of famine. He returned to England and was promoted to admiral in 1814.

Phillips, Wendell The American reformer Wendell Phillips, b. Boston, Nov. 29, 1811, d. Feb. 2, 1884, was a radical opponent of slavery and a supporter of women's rights, labor reform, and temperance. Handsome, a compelling speaker, and Harvard-educated in the law, Phillips declared his allegiance to the doctrine of immediate slave emancipation in 1836. He quickly established a reputation as the abolition movement's most eloquent platform speaker, "abolitionism's golden trumpet," and became an associate of abolitionist William Lloyd GARRISON.

A powerful leader in the American Anti-Slavery Society, Phillips also developed extended theories on the justice and necessity of women's rights. As the Civil War approached, Phillips increasingly emphasized the need to employ violence if slavery were to be abolished, and when the war came, he continued in the forefront of the struggle to secure emancipation and equal rights for blacks.

During the postwar years Phillips demanded that stringent measures be taken to protect blacks and loyal whites in the defeated South. He also became increasingly committed to workers' struggles for union recognition and higher wages.

Philo of Alexandria [fy'-loh] Philo of Alexandria, also called Philo Judaeus, c.20 BC–AD c. 50, was the greatest Jewish philosopher and theologian of the Greco-Roman period whose writings survive. Their preservation was due largely to their influence on early Christian thought, especially the theologies of Clement and Origen, both Alexandrians. Philo was a member of a delegation sent (AD 40) to Rome to persuade Caligula to grant the Jews of Alexandria the right to follow their own laws and not worship the emperor.

Philo was a significant figure in the development of Middle Platonism, a philosophy that included elements of Stoicism in a matrix largely derived from Plato. His principal contribution was his allegorical interpretation of the Bible within this philosophical context, one of the first attempts to reconcile Greek philosophy with biblical religion.

Philoctetes [fil-ahk-tee'-teez] The Greek legendary hero Philoctetes was the recipient of HERCULES' famous bow and poisoned arrows. On the way to fight in the TROJAN WAR, Philoctetes was bitten by a serpent. His cries of pain and the smell of the festering wound led the Greeks to abandon him on the island of Lemnos. When a captured Trojan seer told the Greeks that they could not conquer Troy without Hercules' bow and arrows, ODYSSEUS and NEOPTOLEMUS went to Lemnos and healed Philoctetes' wound. Philoctetes killed Paris (see PARIS, mythology) with one of the arrows.

philodendron [fil-oh-den'-druhn]   The nearly 200 species of the genus *Philodendron* are popular evergreen vine- and shrub-type foliage plants classified in the arum family, Araceae. More than 120 species of philodendrons occur in the tropical regions of the Americas, many as dense vines supported by trees. Philodendrons can be divided into two major types, climbing and nonclimbing. Both are useful as indoor plants with attractive foliage. They do best in warm temperatures and indirect sunlight.

The philodendron P. hastatum, a vine with large, shiny leaves, grows well as a potted plant in places with poor lighting. The name, which is derived from a Greek word meaning "lover of trees," was given because the plant originally was found in South America as a vine on trees.

Philomela and Procne [fil-oh-mee'-luh, prahk'-nee]   In Greek mythology Philomela and Procne were the daughters of King Pandion of Attica. Procne married the Thracian king Tereus, who raped Philomela and cut out her tongue to silence her. Philomela managed to tell her sister what happened by weaving the story into some cloth. Procne then punished Tereus by feeding him their son, Itys. The sisters fled, with Tereus in pursuit. The gods intervened by changing Tereus into a hawk (or hoopoe), Procne into a nightingale, and Philomela into a swallow.

philosophes [fee-loh-zawf']   The philosophes were a group of French intellectuals whose ideas formed the core of ENLIGHTENMENT thought in France. The principal figures involved were MONTESQUIEU, VOLTAIRE, Denis DIDEROT, Jean Jacques ROUSSEAU, CONDILLAC, ALEMBERT, Baron d'HOLBACH, TURGOT, and CONDORCET. They shared a belief in reason, scientific inquiry, and human progress.

In religion the philosophes encouraged toleration and skepticism; in politics their writings often reflected and furthered the democratic spirit. The doctrines of natural and consensual law, which they helped to popularize, were codified in the Declaration of the Rights of Man and of the Citizen (1789) and in the American Bill of Rights

(1791). Their appetite for rational investigation of the natural world is exemplified by Diderot's *Encyclopédie* (1751–66), to which many of them contributed.

philosophy   Philosophy is the oldest form of systematic, scholarly inquiry. The name comes from the Greek *philosōphos,* "lover of wisdom." The term, however, has acquired several related meanings: (1) the study of the truths or principles underlying all knowledge, being, and reality; (2) a particular system of philosophical doctrine; (3) the critical evaluation of such fundamental doctrines; (4) the study of the principles of a particular branch of knowledge; (5) a system of principles for guidance in practical affairs; and (6) a philosophical spirit or attitude.

All of these meanings of philosophy are recognizable in the intellectual traditions of ancient Greece. The pre-Socratics (see PRE-SOCRATIC PHILOSOPHY) sought to find fundamental, natural principles that could explain what individuals know and experience about the world around them. As the Greek thinkers codified their pictures of the world, they saw that for each science or study of some aspect of the world there could be a corresponding philosophy of this science or study, such as the philosophies of science, art, history, and so on. Each of these involves examining the fundamental principles of a discipline to see if they are logical, consistent, and—most important—true.

The pre-Socratic thinkers dealt primarily with a metaphysical question: What is the nature of ultimate reality as contrasted to the apparent reality of ordinary experience? They tried to determine whether some ultimate constituents of the world would be the real and basic elements, whereas everything else would be ephemeral and merely a surface appearance.

Over time, some aspects of the attempt to delineate reality became separated from the metaphysical quest and became the subject matter of the various natural sciences. This development has accelerated since the 17th century. The areas of study that have been peeled off from philosophy and assigned to the natural sciences include astronomy, physics, chemistry, geology, biology, psychology, and others.

Another constant philosophical quest, from Greek times up to the present, has been to try to establish the difference between appearance and reality. Once people learned about sense illusions, the question arose of how to tell what seems to be from what really is. Skeptical thinkers have pressed the claim that no satisfactory standard can be found that will actually work for distinguishing the real from the apparent in all cases.

Another type of question raised by philosophers is: What is truth? Various statements about aspects of the world seem to be true, at least at certain times. Yet experience teaches that statements that have seemed to be true have later had to be qualified or denied. Skeptics have suggested that no evidence would be able to tell, beyond any doubt, that a given statement is in reality true. In the face of such a challenge, philosophers have sought a criterion of truth, especially one not open to skeptical challenge.

Philosophers have also traditionally raised questions

(Right) The School of Athens, *a 16th-century Vatican fresco by the Renaissance painter Raphael, includes the Greek philosophers Plato and Aristotle* (center). *Western philosophy traces its origins to Greece, beginning with the pre-Socratics.*

(Left) The Apotheosis of Saint Thomas Aquinas, *a 14th-century painting by Francesco Traini, portrays Aquinas seated between Plato and Aristotle. Aquinas combined Aristotelian philosophy and Augustinian theology.*

about values: What is good? How can good be distinguished from bad or evil? What is justice? What would a just society be like? What is beauty? How can the beautiful be distinguished from the ugly? These questions all deal with matters of evaluation rather than fact. The values that are at issue are not perceived in the same way as facts. If they were, much more agreement would exist about the specific answers to value questions. The philosopher seeks to find some means of answering these sorts of questions, which are often the most important ones that a person can ask and which will exhibit the basis of a theory of values.

Philosophical Methods

In view of the kinds of questions that philosophers deal with, what methods does the philosopher use to seek the answers? The philosopher's tools are basically logical and speculative reasoning. In the Western tradition the development of LOGIC is usually traced to ARISTOTLE, who aimed at constructing valid arguments and also true arguments if true premises could be uncovered. Logic has played an important role in ancient and modern philosophy—that of providing a clarification of the reasoning process and standards by which valid reasoning can be recognized. It has also provided a means of analyzing basic concepts to determine if they are consistent or not.

Logic alone, however, is not enough to answer philoso-

phers' questions. It can show when philosophers are being consistent and when their concepts are clear and unambiguous, but it cannot ascertain if the first principles or the premises are correct. Here philosophers sometimes rely on what they call intuition and sometimes on a speculative reasoning process. From their initial premises, philosophers then try to work out a consistent development of their answers to basic philosophical questions, following the rules of logic. Irrationalist philosophers, however, such as the Danish thinker Søren KIERKEGAARD, have contended that the less logical the solution to philosophical problems, the better. Philosophers such as these sometimes argue that the most important elements of existence and experience cannot be contained by logic, which is, after all, an element of experience itself. The part, they argue, cannot explain the whole.

Philosophy's Relation to Other Disciplines

Philosophy is both related to most disciplines and yet different from them. Almost from the beginning of both mathematics and philosophy in ancient Greece, relations were seen between them. On the one hand, the philosophers were strongly impressed by the degree of certainty and rigor that appeared to exist in mathematics as compared to any other subject. Some, such as the philosopher-mathematician PYTHAGORAS OF SAMOS, felt that mathematics must be the key to understanding reality. PLATO claimed that mathematics provided the forms out of which everything was made. Aristotle, on the other hand, held that mathematics was about ideal objects rather than real ones; he held that mathematics could be certain without telling us anything about reality.

In more modern times, René DESCARTES and Baruch SPINOZA used mathematics as their model and inspiration for formulating new methods to discover the truth about reality. The philosopher-mathematician Gottfried Wilhelm von LEIBNIZ, the codiscoverer (with Isaac Newton) of calculus, theorized about constructing an ideal mathematical language in which to state, and mathematically solve,

(Left) The 17th-century French philosopher René Descartes is depicted in an engraving from a contemporary edition of his works. Often regarded as the father of modern philosophy, Descartes advanced a philosophy based on certitude, from which his famous "Cogito, ergo sum" ("I think, therefore I am") was derived.

John Locke, the founder of British empiricism, was a seminal influence in the history of philosophy and political theory. In his major philosophical work, An Essay Concerning Human Understanding (1690), Locke argued against a doctrine of innate ideas and expounded the empirical theory that all knowledge is based on sense experience.

all philosophical problems.

Philosophy has both influenced and been influenced by practically all of the sciences. The physical sciences have provided the accepted body of information about the world at any given time. Philosophers have then tried to arrange this information into a meaningful pattern and interpret it, describing what reality might be like. Western philosophers over much of the last 2,500 years have provided basic metaphysical theories for the scientists to fit their data into, and as the data changed, their metaphysical interpretations have had to be adjusted. Thus the scientific revolution of the 17th century, encompassing the scientific work of Johannes Kepler, Galileo, and Newton, was accompanied by a metaphysical revolution led by such thinkers as Descartes, Spinoza, and Leibniz.

In the late 18th and early 19th centuries, the prevailing philosophers in England and France came to the conclusion that the sciences are, and ought to be, completely independent of traditional metaphysical interpretations. Instead, the sciences should simply attempt to describe and codify observations and experiences. This approach has led in the last two centuries to a divorce of philosophy from the sciences. What has developed in response is a new branch of philosophy, the philosophy of science, which examines the methods of science, the types of scientific evidence, and the ways the sciences progress.

A third intellectual area that has been intimately involved with philosophy is religion. In ancient Greece some philosophers such as ANAXAGORAS and SOCRATES scandalized their contemporaries by criticizing aspects of Greek religion. Others offered more theoretical approaches about the evidence for the existence and nature of God or the gods.

When Christianity entered the Greek world, attempts were made to develop a philosophical understanding of Christianity. Finally, toward the end of the 4th and beginning of the 5th century, Saint AUGUSTINE achieved a synthesis of some of the elements of Platonic philosophy with the essentials of Christianity. Throughout the Middle Ages, philosopher-theologians among the Jews, Muslims, and Christians sought to explain their religions in rational terms. They were opposed by antirational

theologians who insisted that religion is a matter of faith and belief and not of reasons and arguments. After the Reformation, philosophers such as Spinoza and David HUME began criticizing the traditional philosophical arguments used by theologians. Hume and Immanuel KANT sought to show that all of the arguments purporting to prove the existence of God and the immortality of the soul were fallacious. Philosophers attempted to explain why people were religious on nonrational grounds, such as psychological, economic, or cultural ones. The defenders of religion found themselves estranged from the philosophers, who kept using the latest results of science and historical research to criticize religion. Some, such as Kierkegaard, made a virtue of this estrangement, insisting that religious belief is a matter of faith, and therefore not a matter of reason.

Branches of Philosophy

The several different branches of philosophy correspond to the different problems being dealt with. One of the most basic is EPISTEMOLOGY, the theory of knowledge (episteme is Greek for knowledge). It deals with what can be known, how it can be known, and how certain the individual can be about it. It has special branches such as the philosophy of science. The kinds of answers that emerge from a particular epistemology usually structure its METAPHYSICS. Metaphysics is the study of the nature of reality, the study of what features of experience are real and which are apparent. Aristotle called metaphysics the study of being as such; the term ontology is often used to describe this branch of philosophy today.

Other branches of philosophy such as ETHICS, AESTHETICS, and political philosophy deal with evaluative aspects of the world such as what is good conduct, what is beautiful, and what is socially and politically just.

History of Western Philosophy

The Pre-Socratics. Western philosophy began in Greece, in the Greek settlement of Miletus in Anatolia. The first known philosophers were THALES OF MILETUS and his students, ANAXIMANDER and ANAXIMENES. Present-day knowledge of this Milesian school is based on fragments attributed to them by later writers. These first philosophers were metaphysicians, seeking for an element or force behind appearance that explained everything. Greek philosophy before Socrates was principally concerned with these metaphysical questions (see Monism; Pluralism).

Socrates. Socrates, an Athenian, was primarily interested in value questions that affected what a person should do. At the time in Athens, the paid teachers, the Sophists, taught people how to live successfully; they did not raise the Socratic question of what was the right way of life, however. Socrates did not write anything, but he is vividly portrayed in the Dialogues of Plato (a pupil of Socrates) as being the "gadfly" of Athens, forever asking people why they were doing what they were doing and making people realize that general principles were necessary to justify their conduct.

Plato. Socrates' disciple Plato developed the first comprehensive philosophical system and founded the Academy, the first formal philosophical school. Plato contended that knowledge must be of universals (that is, of general types or kinds) and not of particulars. To know a particular cat, Miranda, the individual must first know what it is to be feline in general. Otherwise he or she will not be able to recognize the particular feline characteristics in Miranda. These universals, Plato claimed, were the basic elements from which the world was formed. They are called the Forms, or Platonic Ideas. Mathematics provides the most obvious cases of these Forms. They are known not by sense perception but by reasoning. They are known by the mind, not by the bodily organs. The world of Platonic Ideas is the unchanging Forms of things. The philosopher should turn away from this world of appearance and concentrate on the world of Forms. (See Republic, The.) The school of Neoplatonism, which began a few centuries after Plato's death, stressed these otherworldly and mystical elements, identifying the idea of the Good with God.

Aristotle. Plato's leading student, Aristotle, developed the most comprehensive philosophical system of ancient times. Aristotle broke with Plato, stressing the importance of explaining the changing world that humankind lives in as opposed to the Platonic Ideas. Aristotle spent years studying the natural sciences and collecting specimens, and about 90 percent of his writings are on scientific subjects, mostly biological ones. Aristotle believed he could account for the changes and alterations in this world without either having to deny their reality or having to appeal to another world. For Aristotle all natural objects were composed of form and matter, and the changes that take place in matter are the substitution of one form for another. This substitution takes place because every natural object has a goal, or *telos*, which it is its nature to achieve. Thus stones, because they are essentially material, seek the lowest point, which is why they fall down. Each species is ultimately trying to achieve a state of perfection, which for Aristotle was a state of perfect rest.

Hellenistic and Roman Periods. In the period from about 300 BC to AD 200 the central philosophical concerns shifted to how an individual should conduct his or her life. The Stoics (see Stoicism), the skeptics (see Skep-

ticism), and the Epicureans (see Epicureanism), although they dealt with the classical epistemological and metaphysical issues, emphasized the question of how humans should conduct themselves in a miserable world. All these theories stressed withdrawal, whether physical, emotional, or intellectual, from the turmoils of the day.

Medieval Period. Greek philosophy was the major formative influence on the later philosophical traditions of Judaism, Islam, and Christianity. In all three, the theories of the Greeks, particularly those of Plato and Aristotle, were employed to clarify and develop the basic beliefs of the religious traditions.

Philo of Alexandria introduced Platonic ideas and methods into Jewish thought, particularly into the interpretation of Scripture about the beginning of the Christian era. In Judaism, as in Islam and Christianity, religious speculation and philosophy developed in close connection. This development is particularly evident in the Jewish mystical tradition, the Kabbalah. The esoteric teachings of these schools have influenced much later Jewish thought, including that of Spinoza, the most important Jewish philosopher of the early modern period. Drawing both on his religious background and on the geometric method of Descartes, Spinoza developed a philosophical Pantheism of great depth.

In the Islamic tradition the starting point was the work of Plato and Aristotle. The 9th-century Neoplatonist al-Kindi was followed by al-Farabi, who drew on both Plato and Aristotle to create a universal Islamic philosophy. The most important of the medieval Muslim philosophers, however, was Avicenna (Ibn Sina). Starting from the distinction between essence and existence, Avicenna developed a metaphysics in which God, the necessary being, is the source of created nature through emanation. Both his metaphysics and his intuitionist theory of knowledge were influential in the later Middle Ages as well as in the later history of Islamic thought.

The first systematic Christian philosophy was that of Origen, but for the European Middle Ages no authority could rival Saint Augustine. Augustine elaborated a Neoplatonist vision combining the metaphysics of Plotinus with an elaboration of the Christian doctrine of the Trinity. To this he added an epistemology in which knowledge is achieved through illumination by grace. No substantial movement arose beyond Augustine until the 12th century, when new interest arose in logic and theory of knowledge. In this connection the most important figures are Saint Anselm and Peter Abelard.

In the late 12th and early 13th centuries the writings of Aristotle were reintroduced into the West, first in translations from the Arabic and later in direct translation. After some initial resistance Aristotle became the dominant philosophical authority and remained so until the Renaissance. First Saint Albertus Magnus and then Saint Thomas Aquinas combined Aristotle's philosophy with the tradition of Augustinian theology to produce a synthesis holding that Aristotle was right about those things which are within the grasp of reason, whereas what was beyond reason could be known only by faith. Thus reason could prove that God exists, but his nature could be known only by faith.

Modern Period. The synthesis of Christianity and Aristotelianism was a major form of SCHOLASTICISM, which dominated European philosophy into the 17th century. The methods of the new scientific schools conflicted with, and thus brought into question, the principles inherited from the Middle Ages. René Descartes proposed a method for guaranteeing knowledge. He argued that in order to provide a secure foundation for knowledge it was necessary to discover "clear and distinct ideas" that could not be doubted and could serve as a basis for deriving further truths. He found such an idea in the proposition "I think, therefore I am." Using this as a paradigm, Descartes drew a distinction between thinking substance and extended substance, or mind and matter.

Descartes, Spinoza, and Leibniz were all rationalists (see RATIONALISM) in their epistemologies; they stressed a world of metaphysical truths that could be discovered by reason. In contrast to this kind of philosophizing, a quite different approach developed in Great Britain, stressing the importance of sense experience as the basis of knowledge (see EMPIRICISM). Starting with Sir Francis BACON, the empirical theory of knowledge was propounded both as a way of eliminating various metaphysical and theological difficulties and as a way of genuinely advancing knowledge. The most important statement of this theory was made by John LOCKE. He claimed that all knowledge comes from sense experience.

David Hume showed that a thoroughly consistent empirical theory of knowledge leads to a complete skepticism. Hume's major contribution was to show that an individual cannot gain any causal information about experience, or about what is beyond immediate experience, from empirical knowledge. He or she can neither deduce nor induce the cause or the effect of experience (see CAUSALITY). Individuals thus have no basis for accepting that the future must resemble the past. It is only habit or custom that leads them to expect and believe that the items found constantly conjoined in experience will remain so in the future. Hume also argued that from empirical data humans could have no real knowledge of substance, mind, or even God. They are reduced to complete skepticism except that habits or customs make them unjustified believers.

Kant and Hegel. The German philosopher Immanuel Kant claimed that reading Hume awoke him from his dogmatic slumbers and made him realize the depths of the problem of knowledge that cried out for a solution. Kant insisted that humans do possess genuine knowledge. The problem was to show how, in the face of Hume's critique, knowledge was possible. Kant first insisted that although all knowledge begins in experience, this does not mean that all knowledge comes from experience. The human mind provides the forms and the categories that can be used to describe experience. Because these are the necessary conditions of all possible human experience, experience will have certain characteristics. But this knowledge cannot be extended to what is beyond all possible experience—to real substances (things-in-themselves, or noumena), to the self, or to God.

After Kant a new metaphysical movement developed in Germany starting from Kant's claim that the individual

The German philosopher Georg Wilhelm Friedrich Hegel figured prominently in the development of modern philosophy, influencing such movements as pragmatism and existentialism. His concept of Geist, or world-spirit, was explored in The Phenomenology of the Spirit *(1807).*

contributes the form of all possible experience. Georg Wilhelm Friedrich HEGEL advanced the idea that the basic element of reality (The Real) is not a principle of organization interior to the mind but a process that acts through individuals and unfolds itself in the history of the world (see DIALECTIC). Hegel worked out a metaphysics in which all of human history was rational. His ideas were influential throughout Europe in the 19th century, particularly on the ideas of Karl MARX.

20th Century. Twentieth-century philosophy has been characterized in part by its revolt against Hegelianism. PRAGMATISM in the United States and the modern empiricism of Bertrand RUSSELL, LOGICAL POSITIVISM, and linguistic philosophy in both Britain and America all rejected Hegelian metaphysics. The pragmatists wanted an earthy theory—that the truth is that which works—as an expeditious way of solving problems. From William JAMES to John DEWEY pragmatism dominated American thought in the first half of this century. Logical positivism, based on modern developments in logic and an empiricism like Hume's, was the joint result of British thinkers such as Russell and an Austrian group called the Vienna circle, whose most influential member, Ludwig WITTGENSTEIN, had been a student of Russell's at Cambridge. The British and Austrian positivists and linguistic philosophers challenged any form of metaphysical thinking and insisted that something could be said to be true if (and only if) it could be verified by logical or scientific procedures. No metaphysical claim, they insisted, could meet this test (see ANALYTIC AND LINGUISTIC PHILOSOPHY).

Quite different kinds of philosophy developed in France and Germany. One of the most extreme reactions to Hegel came from the Danish thinker Søren Kierkegaard. Kierkegaard believed that all metaphysical systems are unsuccessful, but that to avoid despair an individual had to opt for some sort of belief, by taking a "leap of faith." Kierkegaard's emphasis on subjectivity, confrontation, and despair has greatly influenced the school of thought called EXISTENTIALISM. Martin HEIDEGGER developed a philosophy of "being-in-the-world," which also influenced Jean Paul Sartre and other existentialists.

The British philosopher and mathematician Bertrand Russell introduced modern empiricism into 20th-century philosophy. Russell emphasized logical analysis based on an integration of philosophy with the precise methodology of mathematics.

In the countries of Eastern Europe, MARXISM was the dominant form of philosophical thought during the period of Communist rule in the decades after World War II.

Eastern Philosophy

The Indian Tradition. The philosophical traditions of India have their beginnings in reflection on the VEDAS and specifically in attempts to interpret the UPANISHADS. A wide variety of schools emerged, including some that specifically reject the authority of the Vedas. Thus the Indian philosophy is commonly divided into two traditions: the orthodox schools of HINDUISM that accept Vedic authority, and the nonorthodox schools that do not accept that authority. Within the first category are six major schools: Samkhya, YOGA, Vaisheshika, Nyaya, Mimamsa, and VEDANTA. The second category consists of Charvaka, JAINISM, and BUDDHISM.

Samkhya, one of the oldest and most influential of the schools, is traditionally held to have been founded by Kapila, who may have lived as early as the 7th century BC and to whom the *Samkhya-sutra* (Principles of Samkhya) is attributed. Samkhya metaphysics is based on the distinction between prakriti and purusha, which may be rendered as the objective, or nature, and the subjective, or self. The bondage to suffering that is the common starting point of all Indian philosophical thought arises from the involvement of purusha with prakriti. Release comes when ignorance is overcome; that the attachment of purusha to the changing empirical world is illusory becomes apparent.

The means by which this ignorance is overcome are elaborated by the Yoga school. The knowledge acquired through meditation is an intuitive, nonrational, and direct cognition of the nature of things. This intuition is the cessation of individuality and the identity of the self with the eternal purusha. Some form of Yoga is recognized as a practical method of enlightenment by most of the other Indian schools.

The Vaisheshika system is thought to have been developed by Kanada in the 3d century BC. The essential aspect of Vaisheshika is a complex pluralistic metaphysics that recognizes nine substances: earth, water, fire, air, ether, space, time, self, and mind. Liberation is achieved through the cessation of action, and achievement of a state beyond pleasure, pain, and experience in general.

Nyaya is closely associated with Vaisheshika, and they are often grouped together. The emphasis in Nyaya is on methods of argument, and particularly on the elaboration of logical theory, which is used to justify Vaisheshika metaphysics. Nyaya distinguishes various forms and origins of knowledge, as originally put forward by the school's founder, Gantama (2d century BC). In the course of time Nyaya developed a variety of arguments for the existence of God, as conceived by Vaisheshika, some of which parallel the classic arguments in the Western traditions.

The Mimamsa in general is concerned with establishing the nature and demands of religious law or duty (DHARMA) as it is found in the Vedas. As such it tends to emphasize the practical, although Mimamsa thinkers have made important contributions to logic and theory of knowledge. The Mimamsa is closely associated with Vedanta and sometimes treated simply as a school within the Vedantic tradition. Vedanta means "the end of the Vedas" and in general suggests analysis and contemplation of the theory and vision of the Vedic material. Central to the Vedanta schools is the interpretation of Brahman (see BRAHMA AND BRAHMAN) and its relation to atman (self). The best known of the schools is the nondualist, or advaita, Vedanta of Shankara (AD 788–820), for whom Brahman is undifferentiated, eternal, and unchanging and the world is illusion, or maya.

Of the three nonorthodox schools, Charvaka is known only from fragments referred to in the works of its opponents. Jainism, on the other hand, is an ethical religion that arose in the 6th century BC. It insists on the distinction between matter and soul and argues for a realistic atomism in the context of an atheistic universe. Salvation is achieved through the three jewels of faith, knowledge, and practice of the virtues, which are nonviolence, truth telling, not stealing, chastity, and not being attached to worldly goods and concerns.

Buddhism originated as a sectarian movement in India in the 6th–5th century BC, but it spread over much of China, Southeast Asia, and Japan. In the course of its history Buddhism has developed diverse philosophical traditions. The central teaching of Buddhism is the dharma. This term can mean a variety of things, including "the nature of things," "the law," and "the true view of reality." Dharmas, in the plural, are usually held to be the genuine constituents of reality as opposed to the mere appearance.

Many scholars hold the Madhyamika school to be the central philosophy of Buddhism. The name itself means "traveler on the middle way" and suggests a position that attempts to mediate between the extremes of the other schools. The founder and leading intellect of Madhyamika was Nagarjuna (2d century AD). Nagarjuna mounted a detailed critique of the theory of knowledge that held knowledge to be expressible only in terms of propositions. These propositions are derived from individual concepts and from perceptions and are in some sense a construction of the individual rather than a genuine representation of reality in itself. Understanding is reached when the relativity of these conceptual constructions is recognized and claims to absolute knowledge and truth are given up. The highest wisdom is in seeing this ephemeral relativity and acquiring direct awareness of reality itself, unconditioned by concepts. Many later schools are related to the Madhyamika, including the Zen schools (see ZEN BUDDHISM), although the relations are difficult to uncover in many places.

The Chinese Tradition. Philosophical thought in China has largely concerned itself with social and political philosophy. This assertion is not to say that cosmological and metaphysical speculation has been absent. The I CHING reflects a complicated vision of the universe. The oracles of the *I Ching* began to assume their present written form perhaps as early as the 7th century BC, and the book as a whole played an important role throughout the subsequent development of Chinese philosophy.

The first recognized philosopher in China, however, was Confucius (541–497 BC). Confucius taught that the goal of the philosopher was to become learned, but this concept means more than merely knowing a large number of facts. Rather, on the basis of a broad learning in the classic texts, the canon of which he essentially formulated, Confucius held that a person, regardless of his or her social status, could become aware of the moral order of the cosmos and of his or her proper place in it (see CONFUCIANISM).

The first figure in the Confucian tradition to move toward a philosophical system was MENCIUS (4th–3d century BC). Mencius argued for the essential goodness of persons—that divergence in moral responsibility is a result of a bad upbringing or environment. The results of a poor moral training can be overcome by education, and society is thus essentially perfectable. The duty of government is to foster the well-being of the people and bring society to perfection, a goal with which the genuine ruler is in accord due to his inborn goodness and moral sense.

A strain in Confucianism diametrically opposed to the idealism of Mencius arose a generation later in the thought of Xunzi (330–225 BC). Xunzi argued that, far from good, the inborn nature of persons is evil, or uncivil. Rather than eliciting innate moral virtues through education, Xunzi insisted on the need to impose them from without.

The second important indigenous Chinese tradition is DAOISM. The teaching of the *Daode Jing*, a work attributed to the semilegendary LAOZI (6th century BC), is elusive and complex and can perhaps best be characterized as teaching the eternal principle of reality and the way in which all things are governed by and find their true natures in it.

Also exercising wide influence in Chinese thought were the Moists, who taught the existence of a Supreme Spirit that possessed equal and universal love for all people; the Legalists, who advocated a practical philosophy of political domination; and the Buddhists, who became important from the 4th century AD on.

Phips, Sir William [fips]   Sir William Phips, b. near Pemaquid, in present-day Maine, Feb. 2, 1651, d. Feb. 18, 1695, was the first royal governor of Massachusetts. He became a Boston shipbuilder and was knighted in 1687 after recovering sunken Spanish treasure. In 1688, Phips joined Increase Mather in pressing Britain for an end to the Dominion of New England government. He captured Port Royal in 1690 during King William's War, but his campaign against Quebec in 1691 was a failure. As governor of Massachusetts under its 1691 charter, Phips stopped the SALEM WITCH TRIALS after several months of hesitation, during which the trials went on and 20 persons were put to death.

phlebitis [fluh-by'-tis]   Phlebitis, or inflammation of a vein, can lead to thrombophlebitis—the formation of blood clots (thrombi) at the site of the inflammation. The clots can break loose and be carried through the bloodstream to the heart or lungs, where they can cause serious damage or death to tissues by blocking their blood supply (embolism).

Phlebitis can occur as a result of traumatic injury to a vein or from the spreading of infection or other inflammation to a vein from adjacent tissues. It can also occur in varicose veins or result from the use of oral contraceptives. Inactivity is an important predisposing factor to thrombophlebitis.

Thrombophlebitis may be painful and produce swelling if it occurs in veins near the surface; it may be painless if it occurs in a deep vein. The principal treatment for thrombophlebitis is the administration of anticoagulant drugs, such as heparin, to reduce blood clotting.

phloem   see PLANT

phlogiston theory [floh-jis'-tahn]   According to the phlogiston theory, every combustible substance consisted of a hypothetical principle of fire known as phlogiston, which was liberated through burning, and a residue. The word *phlogiston* was first used early in the 18th century by the German chemist Georg Ernst STAHL. Stahl declared that the rusting of iron was also a form of burning in which phlogiston was freed and the metal reduced to an ash or calx. The theory was superseded between 1770 and 1790, when the French chemist Antoine LAVOISIER showed that both burning and rusting involved oxygen and concluded that both ash and rust were compounds of oxygen.

phlox [flahks]   The phlox family, Polemoniaceae, comprises about 300 species of popular flowering annual, biennial, and perennial plants native mainly to North America but also found in South America, Europe, and Asia. Close clusters of showy flowers are produced in tones of red, pink, violet, blue, buff, or white. The perennial species are popular garden plants. Dwarf creep-

Annual phlox, an herbaceous plant native to Texas, is frequently planted in border or rock gardens.

ing varieties are also planted in rock gardens and used as edging plants, and tall, hardy varieties are used for midsummer perennial gardens. Two species commonly planted for this purpose are *Phlox suffruticosa* and *P. paniculata*.

Phnom Penh [nahm pen]   Phnom Penh, the capital of Cambodia, is in the south central part of the country at the confluence of the MEKONG and Tonle Sap rivers. It has a population of 750,000 (1987 est.). The city has a deepwater outlet at Kompong Som and is the hub of the nation's highway and rail network.

Until the Communist takeover in 1975, Phnom Penh was the commercial, cultural, and educational center of the country. Among the city's landmarks are the royal palace and many famous pagodas, including the Preah Morokot.

Phnom Penh was settled during the 14th century and became the capital of the Khmer Empire in about 1434. It was made the permanent capital of Cambodia in 1867. After the KHMER ROUGE victory in 1975, Cambodia's rulers virtually emptied the city, sending its inhabitants to the countryside. The city was repopulated after the installation of a Vietnamese-backed Communist regime in 1979.

phobia [foh'-bee-uh]   A phobia is an irrational, obsessive, and intense fear that is focused on a specific circumstance, idea, or thing. Phobic disorders, according to modern classification, are a subcategory of anxiety disorders (see ANXIETY; PSYCHOPATHOLOGY). Some common phobias are fear of public places, high places, closed spaces, social situations, death, the dark, animals, foreigners or other groups of people, meteorological events, and electricity. Phobia sufferers may experience a variety of symp-

toms, including dizziness, palpitations, nausea, and immobilization.

The cause of phobia is unknown, but numerous theories have been advanced: that phobias result from a single frightening experience with the thing feared; that phobias mask anxieties dating from childhood (see PSYCHOANALYSIS); that phobias are "learned" gradually, over a long period of time; and that phobias result from distorted thoughts about the thing feared. Various treatments have been developed for phobia sufferers, each with similar high levels of success. Psychoanalysts strive to help their patients remember suppressed thoughts about childhood traumas. Behaviorists (see BEHAVIOR MODIFICATION) may use one of two treatments—gradual exposure to the thing feared, or intense exposure (flooding). Cognitive psychologists seek to alter the way their patients think about what they fear. Drugs and other forms of PSYCHOTHERAPY have also been used in successfully treating phobia sufferers.

Phobos [foh'-buhs]   Phobos is the larger and innermost of the two satellites of Mars (the other is DEIMOS), both of which were discovered by Asaph Hall at the U.S. Naval Observatory in 1877. It lies at a mean distance of only 9,378 km (5,824 mi) from the center of Mars. Its period of revolution is less than one-third of Mars's rotation period, and the moon appears to rise in the west as seen from Mars.

Intensive photographic and infrared studies of Phobos were made by a VIKING orbiter during February 1977. Phobos is a body of very irregular shape, roughly $27 \times 21.5 \times 19$ km ($18 \times 13 \times 12$ mi), and it always keeps its long axis pointed toward Mars. The surface of the satellite is covered with craters and exhibits elongated depressions, peculiar parallel linear striations, and chains of craters, all tending to parallel the orbital plane. Phobos may be a captured asteroid rather than a natural satellite of Mars.

Phocion [foh'-shuhn]   Phocion, c.402–318 BC, elected general by the Athenians 45 times, served brilliantly in campaigns against the Macedonians between 348 and 322. Even so, he urged Athens to seek accommodation with PHILIP II and ALEXANDER THE GREAT. Phocion headed (322–318) an aristocratic government backed by Macedonia, and when the democratic party regained power (318), he was executed as a traitor for permitting the Macedonian seizure of Piraeus.

Phocis [foh'-sis]   Phocis, an agriculturally rich district of central ancient Greece, lay in the Cephissus valley and Crisa plains and contained DELPHI, Elatea, and Mount Parnassus. In the First Sacred War (c.590 BC), Phocis lost control of the coveted shrine, the oracle at Delphi, to a Greek league of states; but a strong internal federation, along with Athenian aid, enabled Phocis to regain control

(457 BC) at the beginning of the Second Sacred War. Allied with Sparta during the Peloponnesian War (431–404), Phocis came under Theban control in the 4th century BC. The city sought independence from Thebes in the Third Sacred War (355–346 BC), but by the war's end it was controlled by PHILIP II of Macedonia.

phoebe [fee'-bee]   Phoebe commonly refers to three species of North American birds comprising the genus *Sayornis* in the tyrant flycatcher family, Tyrannidae. The eastern phoebe, *S. phoebe,* is 17 cm (7 in) long, dark olive-gray above with whitish undersides, and constantly flicks and wags its tail. Chiefly insectivorous, the phoebe winters in the southern United States and Mexico and is one of the first migrants to move north in spring. It is represented in the West by the Say's phoebe, *S. saya,* and in the Southwest and Mexico by the nonmigratory black phoebe, *S. nigricans.*

Two species of North American phoebe are Say's phoebe (left) and the eastern phoebe (right). Unlike other flycatchers, phoebes perch in open areas on low branches and, with the exception of Say's phoebe, are usually found near water.

Phoenicia [fuh-nee'-shuh]   Phoenicia was the ancient Greek name for the long and narrow coastal strip of Palestine-Syria extending from Mount Carmel north to the Eleutherus River in Syria. The Phoenicians were linguistically and culturally related to the Semitic inland peoples who are traditionally called Canaanites.

Already inhabited in Paleolithic times, Phoenicia developed into a manufacturing and trading center early on. Cedars from its mountainous hinterland were imported by the Old Kingdom Egyptians (c.2800–c.2200 BC). By the 2d millennium BC a number of Phoenician and Syrian cities—including SIDON, TYRE, UGARIT, Arvad, Berytus (modern Beirut), and BYBLOS—achieved preeminence as sea-

ports and vigorously traded in purple dyes and dyestuffs, glass, cedar wood, wine, weapons, and metal and ivory artifacts.

Divided by the Lebanon Mountains into small, loosely leagued city-states, Phoenicia was never politically strong. Its cities may have experienced brief periods of independence but were usually forced into tribute-paying submission by their larger neighbors. Initially under Egyptian cultural domination and then under imperial control (to c.1200 BC), Phoenicia was autonomous for about 350 years before it fell successively to the Assyrians (860), the Neo-Babylonians (612), the Achaemenid Persians (539), Alexander the Great (333) and his Seleucid successors, and finally Rome (64).

During Phoenicia's period of independence, individual Phoenician cities interacted with the rising state of Israel. In the 10th century BC, King SOLOMON—who employed men and materials supplied by Hiram of Tyre to build his Temple at Jerusalem and fortify the cities of Megiddo, Gezer, Hazor, and Jerusalem—joined with Hiram in sending sailing expeditions into the Red Sea and possibly also into the Mediterranean. The Bible also records personal and political contacts between the kings of the northern kingdom of Israel and Phoenician rulers.

During the early years of the 1st millennium BC, Phoenicians explored the Mediterranean as far as Spain and into the Atlantic, establishing colonies in Sicily, Malta, the Tunisian coast at CARTHAGE (c.800), and beyond the Strait of Gibraltar at CÁDIZ. Phoenician enterprise turned the Mediterranean, from the Levant to Gibraltar, into the greatest maritime trading arena of antiquity. During this period Phoenician culture—a cosmopolitan blend of Egyptian, Anatolian, Greek, and Mesopotamian influences in religion and literature—reached its peak. Phoenician artists excelled at ivory carving, metal engraving, ornamental sculpture, and gold jewelry; their art was eclectic, drawing forms and motifs from

This Phoenician galley, with two banks of oars and a single sail, was capable of lengthy voyages. The ancient Phoenicians were famed for their navigational and trading skills, colonizing areas from Greece to southern Gaul. (British Museum, London.)

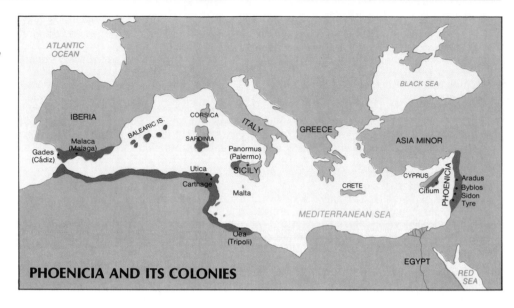

Shaded portions of the map represent territories controlled by the Phoenicians, a Semitic people who extended their influence throughout much of the ancient world through commercial activities. Several trade posts established by the Phoenicians developed into powerful city-states, the most notable of which was Carthage.

ATLANTIC OCEAN

BLACK SEA

IBERIA

CORSICA

ITALY

GREECE

ASIA MINOR

BALEARIC IS.

SARDINIA

Malaca (Malaga)

Panormus (Palermo)

Gades (Cádiz)

SICILY

CYPRUS

Aradus

Utica

Byblos

Carthage

Malta

CRETE

Citium

Sidon

PHOENICIA

Tyre

MEDITERRANEAN SEA

Oea (Tripoli)

EGYPT

RED SEA

PHOENICIA AND ITS COLONIES

the art of their Egyptian, Assyrian, and Aegean neighbors. The Phoenician alphabet, devised in the 2d millennium BC and adapted by the Greeks about 800 or earlier, was subsequently transmitted to Western Europe through Rome.

Phoenix (Arizona) [fee'-niks]   Phoenix is the capital of Arizona, the seat of Maricopa County, and the largest city in the state. It is situated in the south central part of the state on the Salt River. The city has a population of 983,403 (1990). In recent years it has struggled with serious air-pollution problems caused mainly by automobiles and precipitated by the city's rapid population expansion. The population increased about fourteenfold between 1940 and 1990, with much of that growth the result of in-migration. Metropolitan Maricopa County includes the communities of MESA, Tempe, and Scottsdale and has a population of 2,122,101 (1990). The populace is largely Caucasian and has a prominent Hispanic component.

A broadly based economy has supplanted the city's earlier heavy dependence on agriculture (especially citrus fruits, cotton, and cattle) and tourism. Industrial, commercial, and service activities have expanded rapidly, making Phoenix a leading industrial, wholesale, and retail center. Its industries produce aircraft, chemicals, textiles, electrical equipment, and processed foods. Phoenix is also a major transportation crossroads, particularly for highway and air traffic. Several colleges are located in the metropolitan area, and Phoenix has a symphony orchestra, numerous museums, and community and professional theaters. The Desert Botanical Gardens and Papago Park are there; the World's Championship Rodeo is an annual event.

Prehistoric Hohokam Indians had established a primitive irrigation system in the area, but they had disappeared long before white settlers arrived (1867). The initial farming community was incorporated in 1881 and was first reached by a railroad in 1887, two years before it became the territorial capital. On Arizona's admission to the Union (1912), the city became the state capital.

Phoenix (mythology)   Phoenix was the Greek name for the mythological bird that was sacred to the Sun-god in ancient Egypt. An eaglelike bird with red and gold plumage (as described by Herodotus), the phoenix lived in Arabia and had a 500-year life span. At the end of that period the bird built its own funeral pyre, on which it was consumed to ashes. Out of the ashes a new phoenix arose. The cycle was repeated every 500 years. Symbolic of the rising and setting of the Sun, the phoenix later appeared in medieval Christian writings as a symbol of death and resurrection.

Phoenix Islands   The Phoenix Islands are a group of eight uninhabited islands in the central Pacific just south of the equator. Their area is 28 km^2 (11 mi^2). Since 1979 the group has been part of the independent nation of KIRIBATI. Previously, the six smaller atolls had been part of the British Gilbert Islands colony; the two largest islands, Canton and Enderbury, had been jointly administered by the United States and Great Britain.

The islands were discovered in the first half of the 19th century by British and American sailors and were annexed by Great Britain in 1889. They became important as a refueling stop for airplanes after transpacific flights began in the 1930s. In 1938 the United States claimed Canton and Enderbury and in 1939 signed an agreement with Great Britain to administer the islands jointly for 50 years. Attempts in the late 1930s to relieve crowded conditions in the Gilberts by resettling people in the Phoenix Islands failed.

___

phonetics Phonetics is the branch of LINGUISTICS devoted to the study of the events associated with the production of human speech sounds. By extension, it is also the study of the perception of these sounds, and of their physics. Phonetics is therefore anchored in anatomy, physiology, psychology, and neurology. Phonetics, however, is basically *not* concerned with meaning, and in that respect it differs from all other branches of linguistics.

Traditionally, phonetics has dealt with the positions and activities of the parts of the human body that produce speech sounds, with the transition from one position to another, and with the qualities and direction of the airstream that is emitted when a person speaks. All of these considerations come under the heading of articulatory phonetics. Left out of account are the speaker's brain, which triggers speech acts, and the listener's brain, which interprets the vocal message. Ideally, phonetics should begin with the study of the encoding of the speech sounds in the speaker's brain, and end with the study of their decoding in the hearer's brain.

The Organs of Speech. First the brain issues a command to the lungs to initiate an airstream. Before this airstream can become speech, however, it must pass through, or by, the larynx, pharynx, tongue, teeth, lips, and nose—all of which can modify the airstream in various ways.

The larynx contains the vocal cords, or vocal lips, which can be closed to stop the advance of the air, and which also can be made to vibrate or made taut. The pharynx is a tube at the very back of the mouth, where the throat begins. It, too, can be made taut—the result being a stage whisper.

The mouth has one all-important movable organ, the tongue, which is rooted in the throat but can move in every direction. The front of the tongue is especially plastic and can be controlled with great precision by the nervous system. To produce vowels, the tongue, by assuming different positions within the mouth, creates a great variety of resonance chambers. To produce consonants, the tongue collaborates with other parts of the mouth to make partial or complete closures, either forcing the air through a narrow constriction (as in the pronunciation of the *th* sound of *breathe*) or stopping its progress altogether (as with the *d* sound of *breed*).

For some sounds, like the *p* in *pay*, the lips are first closed for a fraction of a second, stopping the progress of the air, then opened, releasing the air. To pronounce the *f* of *file*, however, only the lower lip is used—positioned against the upper teeth.

Comparison of the initial sounds of *pile, bile, file, vile,* and *while* with that of *mile* shows that the nose, too, plays an important role in speech. The sounds *p, b, f, v,* and *wh* are all released through the lips; for the *m* of *mile*, however, a valve in the pharynx channels the airstream into the nose.

Families of Sounds. Sounds can be catalogued according to the place where, and the manner in which, they are produced. Thus the initial sounds in *pile, bile, file, vile, while,* and *mile* are all labials—that is, they are formed by the lips. The final sounds in *hack, hag,* and *hang* are all velars—formed by pushing the tongue against the back of the roof of the mouth, called the velum. The final sounds in *writhe, ride,* and *write* are dentals, so called because they are formed by bringing the tongue into contact with the upper teeth. Some of these consonants, such as *b* and *d*, are called stops, because the airstream momentarily comes to a complete halt; for others, such as *v* and *th*, known as aspirants or fricatives, the airstream flows continuously.

It is more important, however, to understand how sounds are made than to give them labels. Besides, a so-called phonetic transcription—series of letters enclosed in square brackets to indicate pronunciation—can provide no more than a rough visible record of the succession of noises that is human speech. The International Phonetic Alphabet is the best-known system for phonetic transcription but is losing favor because of the unusual symbols it requires.

Voiced and Unvoiced Sounds. The vocal cords are responsible for producing [h]—called a glottal fricative because the space between the vocal cords is called the glottis—and a few other sounds; but they also account for the voiced/voiceless distinction between sounds produced by other organs. In producing labial consonants [b] and [v], for instance, the vocal cords vibrate; for [p] and [f], however, they are inert and silent. The vowels of most languages are voiced, but voiceless vowels do exist, as in whispered speech.

Accent or Stress. In phonetics the term *accent,* or *stress,* refers to prominence given to a vowel and the consonants that surround it. Such prominence is achieved by increasing the loudness of the vowel or modulating the pitch of the vowel or doing both. Some languages, like Japanese, have only pitch accent, but others, like English, use both loudness and pitch.

Acoustic Phonetics. Ideally, it should be possible to establish a one-to-one correspondence between events occurring during sound production in the human body and records of the events as they are intercepted in the air by delicate equipment. In fact, the sound spectrograph allows investigators to intercept sound waves, analyze them, and print visual images representing the main physical events that make up a given sound.

Phoneticians now know and can represent the two principal formants, or concentrations of energy, for each vowel. A formant may be low (few cycles per second) or high. Each vowel has many formants, but the two lowest ones—the so-called first and second formants—are essential for its identification. Both the absolute position of each formant and the relative position of the two principal formants to each other depend on the shape of the resonance chamber—that is, on the position of the speech organs at the moment when the vowel is being pronounced and recorded for analysis. Thus [i] has a low first formant and a high second one; [a] has a higher first formant than [i], but a lower second one than [i]; and both formants of [u] are low.

The formant method of characterizing sounds can also be applied to consonants, because they, too, are the correlates of specific physiological events—of energy passing through resonance chambers of specific shapes. The sound spectrograph is also highly useful in studying such features of speech sounds as voice, length, nasalization, and aspiration. A few other features, such as pitch (high versus low), require other equipment.

The science of phonetics is now a vital part of the investigation of the physical chemistry of hearing, the diagnosis and correction of speech disorders, the teaching of speech to the deaf, or the study and treatment of aphasia (the partial or complete inability to speak).

phonograph The term *phonograph* was coined by inventor Thomas EDISON for his cylinder sound-recording apparatus. In the United States the term became synonymous with *record player* and was used for all record-playing equipment. Emile Berliner, who invented the first commercially practical disk recording system, used the term *gramophone* (originally Gram-O-Phone) for it, and that term was adapted in most of the world to distinguish the disk system from the cylinder phonograph system.

Origins

There were a number of precursors to the invention of the phonograph. Unequivocally, however, the credit for the first documented device that would both record and reproduce sound goes to Thomas Edison. The basic concepts occurred to him during the summer of 1877, when he was at work on telegraph repeating equipment. He realized that an embossed disk, tape, or cylinder could be used to record acoustic vibrations in permanent form and to activate a playback system that, in moving over the embossed surface, would create an acoustic facsimile of the original sound. He even suggested electromechanical devices that predated much later developments. When he

Francis Barraud's His Master's Voice *(1900) became internationally famous as the trademark of RCA (Record Company of America) Victor.*

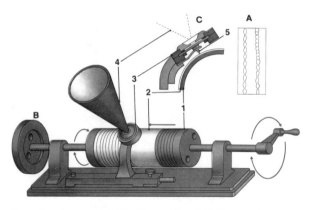

The earliest phonograph, built by Thomas Edison in 1877, recorded sound on a grooved brass cylinder (1) covered with foil (2). The vibrations of his voice were transmitted through a metal diaphragm (3) by a conical mouthpiece (4) into a steel stylus (5), which embossed them on the foil (A). The sound could be played back through the apparatus. Front (B) and side views (C) are diagramed.

sketched a device for his machinist, John Kruesi, to build as a working model, probably in November of that year, it was in the form of a hand-turned, grooved metal cylinder, oriented with its axis horizontal. A sheet of tinfoil was stretched over the cylinder. Sound pressure against a diaphragm pressed a stylus into the surface of the tinfoil, embossing it; in playback, the tinfoil in turn pushed against the stylus, which moved the diaphragm to produce sound. The model, finished in December, was the first operating sound-recording apparatus. A patent was issued on Feb. 19, 1878.

At the Volta Laboratory in Washington, D.C., Chichester Bell and Charles Tainter developed several variants of Edison's phonograph. The most important, substituting a wax-covered cardboard cylinder for the tinfoil, was patented in 1885. This patent, which specified that the groove was engraved (implying the removal of some wax, rather than its mere indentation as in the embossing of Edison's tinfoil), was later used by those who then controlled it to outflank Edison.

The disks Emile Berliner made in 1888, by contrast, used an etching process. The master disk was of zinc, covered by an acid-proof resist. In recording, this resist was scratched by the stylus to expose the zinc. The master was then immersed in acid, which removed the exposed zinc to create the groove. A mold, or stamper, made from the master was then used to form hard-rubber (later, shellac) disks.

In Edison's arrangement the groove had been impressed vertically into the recording surface, with the stylus (in either recording or playback) riding up and down in response to—or in re-creation of—the sound wave (vertical modulation); Berliner's stylus had to move from side to side across the surface of the disk (lateral modulation). By 1920 most companies were using Berliner's lateral cut exclusively.

By 1926 the acoustic process—in which sound pressure alone created the groove modulation, and groove modulation alone created the sound waves in playback—had been superseded by the electrical process, in which electrical signals acted as an intermediary between the essentially mechanical properties of sound and of the record groove.

Later Developments

The next major technological change took place in 1948 in the United States, when Columbia Records introduced the long-playing record (LP), which was recorded and played back at a speed of 33⅓ revolutions per minute (rpm), and had fine, closely spaced grooves called microgrooves.

Soon thereafter, RCA Victor introduced a 45-rpm disk that also used the microgroove; eventually the 45 became the medium for popular "single" recordings. By this time stereophonic sound had also become available—that is, in 1958 the recording industry adopted a variant in which, in effect, one groove wall held the left-channel signal and the other the right-channel signal.

The late 1970s saw the development of pulse-code modulation (PCM), a recording technique that reduces the noise and distortion that had been unavoidable in earlier recording methods. In the recording process, PCM analyzes sound and stores it as a series of digital pulses. These pulses are reconverted into acoustic signals to produce conventional records. The COMPACT DISC (CD), an innovation that first appeared in the early 1980s, uses a new technology that inscribes PCM information—that remains in digital form—directly on a disc with a laser beam, instead of the groove-cutting stylus of earlier recording. The CD, however, requires its own player.

See also: SOUND RECORDING AND REPRODUCTION.

---

phonology and morphology Phonology is the system of deployment of a language's phonetic resources. Morphology is the aggregate of patterns and other regularities involving word formation within a given language. Because the majority of phonological patterns in most languages probably can be stated in terms of morphology, with only limited recourse to SYNTAX, this article will first discuss morphology and then phonology.

Morphology

Morphology, as a branch of LINGUISTICS, is the study of word formation. Although linguists are nearly unanimous in their belief that all languages have elements called words, they have yet to agree on a universal definition of word. The common definition, that a word corresponds to a stretch of writing with spaces fore and aft, is not cogent for various reasons. For instance, many languages lack a writing system, or orthography. Others have systems that do not use spaces or other word-isolating devices (see WRITING SYSTEMS, EVOLUTION OF). Some languages have two orthographies that differ as to how to isolate words, for example, the Arabic and Roman orthographies for Swahili. Even within one orthographic system, arbitrary conventions or inconsistencies exist. (Is the correct spelling firehouse, fire-house, or fire house?)

Morphemes. The -ed of walked is an example of a morpheme—a minimum meaning-bearing constituent of a word. If a word has no smaller meaning-bearing parts, the word itself is a morpheme. Because -ed bears the meaning "past" and cannot itself be resolved into smaller meaning-bearing parts, it is a morpheme. For the same reasons walk is a morpheme, whether coterminous with a word in a sentence like I will walk or part of a word, as in I walked.

Compounding. Just as morphemes can be strung together to make words, so words can be joined to make compound words, or compounds. Firehouse, for example, contains the two independent words fire and house.

Affixation. Perhaps the most common morphological process among the world's languages is affixation, in which an affix morpheme, normally with a grammatical, as opposed to a lexical, function, is added to a stem morpheme. In English and most European languages the type of affixation used in verb inflection is suffixation (for example, walk-ed, walk-s, walk-ing); many other languages use prefixation (for example, Swahili tembea, "walk," [a-] li-tembea, "[he] walked"). Rarer is infixation, in which the stem morpheme is interrupted by the affix (for example, Tagalog [Philippine] lakad, "walk," l-um-akad, "walked").

Other Morphological Processes. Certain types of morphology do not lend themselves to clear segmentation into morphemes. Ablaut involves a series of two or more vowel replacements—as in sing, sang, sung—or, less commonly, consonant replacements—as in Irish póg, "kiss," tóg (spelled phóg), "kissed." Portmanteau morphology involves two or more morphemic functions invested in what is apparently one minimal form. (What part of was marks past tense?) Series such as crash, bash, smash constitute phonesthemes, which represent an especially difficult case of unique morphs, or nonclassifiable residues of morphemic segmentation. For example, cranberry ostensibly contains the morpheme berry, but the intractability of cran to further classification makes it a classic example of a unique morph.

Inflection and Derivation. Word formation may be classified in terms of form (affixation, compounding, ablaut, and so on) or function. The most common functional classification of morphology is that of inflection and derivation.

Inflectional morphology characteristically involves relatively tight systems of grammatical marks—most commonly but not always affixes—on one lexical item without change in part of speech. In grammars the inflected forms of a given lexical item are frequently grouped into paradigms. English has relatively modest inflection, both of nouns (singular-plural-possessive: boy-boys-boy's-boys') and of verbs (present and past; active and passive participial: speak, speaks, spoke; speaking, spoken). English and other relatively uninflected languages, such as Chinese, compensate for inflection periphrastically, that is, by syntactic means. For example, English uses nine words—If I had known I would not have waited—for what Latin can convey in four—Sī scīvissem nōn mansissem.

Phonology

To say that a language's phonology involves the deployment of that language's phonetic resources within the framework of its morphology and syntax is virtually tantamount to saying that a language's phonological system cannot be identified with either its phonetic or morphosyntactic system but rather mediates between those systems. This situation can be illustrated by a few English words: *mopper, mop, slobber, pop.* First, the plural suffix *-s* is pronounced differently in *moppers* and *mops,* like the *z* of *booze* in the former but like the *s* of *moose* in the latter. Moreover, these differences in pronunciation of the plural *-s* are not idiosyncratic facts about the words *mopper* and *mop* (as, for example, could be claimed for *dice* as the plural of *die*), but rather bespeak a pervasive regularity of English. The *z* pronunciation of *-s* is the norm for nouns ending in a voiced sound—that is, a sound articulated with concomitant vibration of the vocal cords (see PHONETICS). Similarly, the *s* pronunciation of *-s* is the norm for nouns ending in a voiceless sound—a sound made with the vocal cords at rest.

Phonological Rules. The manner in which phonological rules are formulated and the names and symbols used vary considerably from linguistic school to linguistic school and from theory to theory. The phonological element that serves as input to the rule is variably called a morphophoneme, underlying segment, or phoneme. Despite differences of other sorts, all theories of phonology recognize the importance of distinctiveness in the organization and function of sound systems, normally by taking phonemes to be distinct from one another, with nonphonemic differences in sound following from phonemic distinctions. Thus it is usually assumed that *mob* and *mop* differ distinctively (phonemically) in the difference between *b* and *p*, while the difference in vowel length follows from that (the pronunciation of *o* being longer before *b* than before *p*).

Segmental and Suprasegmental Phonology. Segmental phonology is the phonology of vowels and consonants; suprasegmental or prosodic phonology involves phenomena such as stress (intensity) and tone (pitch). An accentual pattern involves the deployment of suprasegmentals within a word (for example, the stress differences between the noun *ínsert* and the verb *insért*, whereas an intonational pattern involves suprasegmentals within the framework of a sentence (for example, all the words in *Máry wórries Mártin* are accentually stressed on the first syllable, but the stress in *Mártin* is intonationally most prominent). Because the sentence characteristically constitutes the framework for intonation and because sentences are fundamentally syntactic constructs, intonation is one phonological phenomenon whose domain goes beyond morphology.

phonon [foh'-nahn]   The phonon is the unit of sound or mechanical vibration and is named in analogy to the photon, the unit of electromagnetic vibration. For example, the atoms in a crystal vibrate in energy levels defined by quantum mechanics as multiples of hv, where h is PLANCK'S CONSTANT and v is the frequency of the vibration. Such a quantized vibration is a phonon, sometimes thought of as a packet of sound waves. Like the photon, the phonon has particlelike characteristics.

Phonons are the excitations of vibrations carrying energy as they travel through materials. In insulators, heat is transported by phonons. In metals, heat is conducted by both phonons and electrons, so that the thermal conductivity of metals is 10 to 100 times greater than that of nonmetals. In a solid made up of more than one type of atom, phonons of different frequencies exist; these different phonons have different properties. Optical phonons are responsible for infrared absorption and acoustical phonons for sound propagation.

phosphate minerals   Phosphate MINERALS are those which contain the phosphate ion (PO_4^{3-}) as a major constituent. Because of chemical and structural similarities, arsenate (AsO_4^{3-}) and vanadate (VO_4^{3-}) minerals are traditionally classed with phosphates. Several hundred minerals, mostly rare, are in this important class, of which approximately 250 are phosphates. Appreciable solid solution may occur between phosphates and arsenates and between arsenates and vanadates, but the differences between phosphorus and vanadium are sufficiently great that little substitution occurs between phosphates and vanadates.

Occurrence. Phosphate mineralogy is overwhelmingly dominated by the APATITE group of minerals, common in all types of rock. The bulk of the world's phosphate resides in marine PHOSPHORITES and other phosphate rocks. These vast sedimentary deposits of massive, fine-grained apatite are usually called collophane. To a mineralogist, the most interesting phosphate occurrences are in PEGMATITES, in which a wide variety of phosphate minerals are found in complex paragenetic sequences and several massive magnetite-apatite deposits.

Phosphates also occur in various forms in living organisms. The hard bone and tooth material of vertebrates is essentially carbonate- or hydroxyl-apatite. Apatite and the rarer phosphates brushite, hannayite, monetite, newberyite, struvite, and whitlockite have been identified in human kidney and urinary stones.

Uses. Because phosphorus is an essential plant nutrient, most phosphate is used in the production of fertilizer. Other uses include animal feed supplements, detergent, insecticides, and medicines. Some less common phosphate minerals have economic value as semiprecious stones (TURQUOISE) or as ores of rare metals (MONAZITE). Several important uranium minerals are phosphates, arsenates, or vanadates.

phosphor   A phosphor is a solid material that emits visible light when activated (excited) by an external energy source such as an electron beam, heavy charged particles, or ultraviolet light. A characteristic feature of such emission is the persistence of the emitted light after the excitation is removed. Many phosphors have been developed having emission in various parts of the visible spectrum and persistence times ranging from a few billionths of a second to many hundreds of seconds. Major applications include coatings of fluorescent light bulbs, cathode-ray tubes, radar screens, television picture tubes, and luminous instrument dials.

See also: BIOLUMINESCENCE; FLUORESCENCE.

phosphorescence Phosphorescence is a form of light emission caused by the excitation of atoms by an outside source. Phosphorescence differs from FLUORESCENCE only by the long persistence of the emitted light after the excitation is turned off. The initial excitation can arise by electron beam bombardment, impact by charged particles from radioactive decay, chemical reactions, and absorption of ultraviolet light. The process involves the excitation of electrons to intermediate metastable energy levels, or "electron traps," from which the electrons rarely decay directly to the original ground state. Instead, processes such as infrared absorption or thermal excitation usually transfer the excitation energy to other levels that then rapidly decay by emitting light.

Practical applications of phosphorescent emission are based on the long-term energy-storage aspect, the efficiency of the energy-conversion process, and the averaging effect provided by the long-term persistence. The latter is especially important in television picture tubes and oscilloscopes.

See also: LUMINESCENCE; PHOSPHOR.

phosphorite Minable deposits of the calcium PHOSPHATE MINERALS in the APATITE family, phosphorites provide nearly all the phosphate for fertilizers and the elemental phosphorus and phosphoric acid used in industry. The largest phosphorite deposits—blankets of pellets and nodules that have precipitated on the seafloor—may be more than 4.6 m (15 ft) thick and cover hundreds of square kilometers. Phosphorite also occurs extensively in apatite deposits in intrusive igneous rocks, and as residual deposits in tropical, humid climates where phosphate-rich limestones decompose. Other phosphorites are rocks, particularly limestone, that have been acted on by phosphatic water; pellets from the residual deposits that accumulate in streams; and seafowl or bat GUANO.

phosphorus Phosphorus is a nonmetallic chemical element that is a member of Group VA in the periodic table. The chemical symbol for phosphorus is P, its atomic number is 15, and its atomic weight is 30.975. Phosphorus was first prepared by the German alchemist Hennig Brandt in 1669; in the course of his search for the philosopher's stone he obtained from a residue of evaporated urine a white solid that glowed in the dark and ignited spontaneously in air. The name *phosphorus* (from the Greek for "light-bringing"), which at that time was used for any substance that glows of itself, was eventually appropriated to this element. Phosphorus does not occur in elemental form in nature; it is found most commonly in apatite minerals such as fluorapatite (see PHOSPHATE MINERALS).

Allotropes of Phosphorus. About ten forms of the element are known. White phosphorus consists of molecular

P_4 and is a waxlike substance, very toxic and extremely flammable. When it is exposed to air in the dark, it emits a greenish light and gives off white fumes. It can ignite spontaneously. White phosphorus is used in incendiary and napalm bombs and in rat poison.

Red phosphorus, a more stable form than white, can be obtained by heating white phosphorus to 250° C in a closed vessel. Red phosphorus is often considered a mixture of white and black phosphorus. It neither phosphoresces nor spontaneously burns in air. It is used in industry as part of the coating of safety matches and in the manufacture of tracer bullets, smoke screens, and skywriting compounds.

When heated to temperatures near 300° C for several days, red phosphorus is converted to black phosphorus. Black phosphorus is flaky, like graphite, and has some metallic properties. It is the least reactive of the forms.

Phosphates. Nearly all the phosphorus used in commerce is in the form of phosphates, the salts derived from phosphoric acid, H_3PO_4. Large amounts of phosphate-containing fertilizer are used to enhance soil fertility. Sodium triphosphate, $Na_5P_3O_{10}$, is used in detergents because it softens water and disperses inorganic soiling substances. A serious disadvantage of using phosphates in detergents, however, is the fact that the phosphates later end up in natural bodies of water, where they act as fertilizers, causing algae in the water to proliferate (see BLOOM, ALGAL). Phosphates are also used in toothpastes and as polishing agents. Monocalcium phosphate, $Ca(H_2PO_4)_2$, and sodium acid pyrophosphate, $Na_2H_2P_2O_7$, are leavening agents used in baking powder.

Biological Role of Phosphorus. Phosphorus, exclusively in the form of phosphates, is found in all forms of life. Phosphates are essential to the energy-transfer reactions (see METABOLISM) necessary to sustain life processes, to a number of coenzymes, and to nucleic acids.

Phosphates are also important ingredients of bone; the human skeleton contains about 1.4 kg (about 3 lb) of phosphates as calcium phosphates, $Ca_3(PO_4)_2$. A phosphorus deficiency is rare, except in people with certain gastrointestinal malabsorption syndromes, such as CROHN'S DISEASE. A mild deficiency causes fatigue, weakness, and a decreased attention span. A severe deficiency may lead to seizures, coma, or even death.

See also: FERTILIZER; SOAP AND DETERGENT.

Photius [foh'-shuhs] A saint of the Orthodox church, Photius, b. *c.*820, d. Feb. 6, 891?, patriarch of Constantinople (858–67, 877–86), was the greatest scholar of medieval Byzantium. When Photius was elevated to the patriarchate, he soon entered into a conflict with Pope NICHOLAS I. Nicholas was eager both to extend the growing power of the papacy over Byzantium and interested in the jurisdiction over the Bulgarians, converted (864) to Byzantine Christianity under Photius. The conflict acquired doctrinal undertones when the pope's emissaries introduced a text of the Nicene Creed in which the Holy Spirit was said to have proceeded "from the Father and the Son" (*filioque*), instead of the original "from the Father."

In 867, Photius summoned a council that deposed Nicholas. In 879–80 a great council, presided over by Photius, was held at Hagia Sophia, with legates of Pope John VIII present. The council, with the legates' approval, confirmed the original form of the creed, and normal relations between Rome and Constantinople were restored. Photius was forced to retire in 886. Feast day: Feb. 6.

Photo-Secession   see PHOTOGRAPHY, HISTORY AND ART OF

---

photochemistry

Photochemistry is the study of chemical processes that are exclusively brought about by the interaction of light with matter. On the basis of experience and observations, two fundamental laws of photochemistry have been propounded. The law stated by Theodor Grotthus (1817) and rediscovered by John William Draper (1843) states that only light that is absorbed by a system can cause a photochemical reaction; the law of Johannes Stark and Albert Einstein (c.1910) says that in a photochemical process a molecule absorbs a single quantum of light energy called a PHOTON. Modern experiments with lasers (see LASER; MASER) have shown that these rules are not always strictly obeyed. Under certain circumstances a molecule can simultaneously absorb two (and sometimes more) photons, but only under very high light intensities such as can be achieved with lasers. In another deviation from the photon rule, two molecules sufficiently close to each other can jointly absorb one quantum of light.

When a quantum of light energy (a photon) is absorbed by a molecule, the direct, immediate consequence of this interaction is that the molecule is raised to an electronically excited state. For most molecules this is caused by the absorption of visible or ultraviolet light and takes place in an extremely short period of time, about 10^{-15} second. The electronically excited state can be viewed as a molecule in which the distribution of the electrons about the atoms that compose the molecule is changed relative to the normal, or ground, state of the molecule. Because the electronic distribution affects such properties as bond strengths and molecular geometry, many changes can take place in an electronically excited state that cannot occur (or that take place very slowly) in the ground state.

Photophysical Processes

The consequences of the absorption of light by a chemical species—and the subsequent formation of an electronically excited state—can be grouped into two main classes: physical processes and chemical processes. In a photophysical process, a molecule undergoes no direct change in its chemical identity. For example, some of the ways in which an electronically excited molecule can physically dispose of the energy absorbed from the photon are by (1) reemitting light (FLUORESCENCE and PHOSPHORESCENCE); (2) converting the electronic excitation energy into vibrational (thermal) energy; (3) transferring the electronic excitation energy to another (identical or different) molecule; and (4) ejecting an electron (the PHOTOELECTRIC EFFECT).

In fluorescence and phosphorescence, visible, ultraviolet, or sometimes infrared radiation is given off by the electronically excited molecules. The emission causes each molecule to return to its normal, or ground, state. A common example of this process at work is fluorescence imparted to papers and fabrics for brightening or identification purposes. Phosphorescence is usually observed in the visible (or sometimes in the infrared) region of the spectrum and generally occurs efficiently only when the molecule is contained in a solid matrix or is at a very low temperature.

The only difference between fluorescence and phosphorescence is the time the molecule remains in the excited state. While the time required for light absorption is very short (about 10^{-15} sec), the time it takes for molecules to reemit light as fluorescence or phosphorescence is substantially longer. The half-life is defined as the time it takes a collection of electronically excited molecules to decrease in population by 50%. For molecular fluorescence, half-lives are usually between one billionth (10^{-9}) and one millionth (10^{-6}) seconds, depending on the molecule; for phosphorescence, half-lives are much longer, generally between one thousandth (10^{-3}) of a second and 10 seconds.

Photochemical Processes

In a photochemical process, some change takes place in the bonding arrangement of the atoms in the molecule. This change can be brought about directly as a result of light absorption and the production of an excited state, or indirectly through energy transfer from the excited state of one molecule to another, different molecule. The molecule that receives the energy can then react photochemically. A reaction that is brought about in this way is said to be *sensitized*.

Photoinitiated chemical reactions are sometimes further classified as being primary or secondary processes. In a primary photochemical process, the reaction takes place immediately from the excited state created by light absorption. A secondary process occurs when a molecular fragment, produced in a primary process, reacts with another molecule to form a product. Another useful term for describing a photochemical reaction is *quantum yield* (or quantum efficiency). This is a number that reflects the success (or failure) of a certain photochemical process and is defined as the ratio of the number of product molecules formed in the processes to the number of photons absorbed by reactants. For primary processes, the quantum yield can range from 0 to 1 (that is, from 0% to 100% efficiency). For reactions that involve secondary processes, quantum yields can sometimes be as large as 1 million, because a fragment produced in a primary process may go on to start a chemical CHAIN REACTION with other molecules. This is what happens in photopolymerization, in which many molecules become bonded together to form a polymer.

Simple photochemical reactions involve the breaking or rearranging of a chemical bond, or both. The fact that light has the potential to rupture a chemical bond can be realized by noting that blue violet light, having a wavelength of 400 nm, corresponds to an energy of about 71 kcal. This exceeds the amount of energy needed to break several types of chemical bonds. Ultraviolet light having a wavelength of 250 nm is intrinsically energetic enough to break most chemical bonds.

Photobiological Processes

Photochemical reactions play a vital role in certain biological systems. Two important photobiological processes are vision and photosynthesis. The initial photochemical steps that occur when light strikes the retina of the eye, eventually causing a neural impulse to be sent to the brain, are not yet fully understood. The basic idea, however, is that light causes cis-trans isomerization (see ISOMER) to occur on a portion of the light-absorbing protein, rhodopsin, and that an eventual change in the shape of the protein results in the production of a neural impulse.

PHOTOSYNTHESIS is also a highly complicated process that involves many separate chemical reactions. The initial step involves light absorption by chlorophyll molecules that are arranged in specific groups called lamellae. The light supplies the energy needed to convert oxidized carbon (in the form of CO_2) ultimately to reduced carbon (as carbohydrate $C_6H_{12}O_6$). Several quanta of light are needed to achieve the generation of one carbohydrate molecule.

Atmospheric Photochemistry

Photochemical reactions abound in many layers of the Earth's atmosphere. For example, in the stratosphere (20–40 km/12–25 mi altitude), short-wavelength ultraviolet radiation from the Sun produces OZONE, O_3, from oxygen molecules, O_2:

$O_2 + UV \rightarrow O + O$ [primary step—photodissociation]
$O + O \rightarrow O_2$ [recombination]
$O + O_2 \rightarrow O_3$ [secondary step—ozone formation]

The ozone thus formed plays the vital role of absorbing much of the Sun's harmful ultraviolet radiation, thereby preventing that radiation from reaching the Earth's surface (see OZONE LAYER).

Another atmospheric photochemical process that is of interest at sea level is the formation of photochemical smog. One of the exhaust products of the internal-combustion engine is nitric oxide, NO, which can be oxidized in air to nitrogen dioxide, NO_2: $2NO + O_2 \rightarrow 2NO_2$. Nitrogen dioxide is a red brown gas that can photodissociate to form oxygen atoms and nitric oxide: $NO_2 + $ sunlight $\rightarrow NO + O$. The reactive oxygen atoms then form ozone, whose pungent odor can sometimes be easily detected at street level: $O + O_2 \rightarrow O_3$.

Infrared Photochemistry

Experiments with infrared lasers have shown that certain specific chemical reactions can be induced by exceptionally high-intensity infrared sources. These reactions take place from highly excited vibrational states of the molecule. They are, in some cases, distinct from those chemical reactions which are brought about by the ap-

plication of heat (that is, purely thermal excitation).

An interesting application of infrared photochemistry is the isotopic enrichment of certain elements. This enrichment is done by using the high power and sharp wavelength resolution of the laser source to excite to very high vibrational levels only those molecules possessing atoms of a certain isotope. The molecules that are excited in such a way break apart, and subsequent scavenging of the fragments of the molecules containing the desired isotope is then accomplished.

See also: POLYMERIZATION; POLLUTION, ENVIRONMENTAL.

---

photoelectric cell A photoelectric cell is a device that is activated by electromagnetic energy in the form of light waves. Three basic kinds of photoelectric cells exist, corresponding to the three different forms of the PHOTO-ELECTRIC EFFECT employed: the photoconductive cell, the photoemissive cell, and the photovoltaic cell, or solar cell. The first two are passive devices, depending on an external current or voltage. The photovoltaic cell is an active device, converting light energy directly into electricity.

Photoconductive Cell. The photoconductive cell is the oldest photoelectric device, having first been developed in basic form in the later 19th century. It is also known as a photoresistor. Photoconductive cells are familiar in supermarkets as the sensor that scans codes on grocery items at checkout counters. In photography they are designed as the light meters used to measure the intensity of illumination (see ACTINOMETER).

A modern photoconductive cell uses the energy of light to free electrons from their valence bonds in a SEMI-CONDUCTOR material. The number of free charges in a semiconductor is relatively limited at room temperature, so the addition of light-released electrons raises its conductivity (reduces its resistance). The resistance may change from several hundred thousand ohms in the dark to a few hundred ohms in sunlight.

Photoemissive Cell. The photoemissive cell, or phototube, first appeared in the 1920s. Such cells are familiar as the "electric eyes" that trigger the automatic opening of doors when a person intercepts a beam of light. In the form of PHOTOMULTIPLIER tubes, they are used in astronomy to measure electromagnetic radiation from celestial objects.

A photoemissive cell is constructed with a wire anode and a semicylindrical cathode with an emitting surface, sealed in an evacuated or gas-filled bulb. Photons that strike the cathode transfer their energy to the surface electrons; some electrons can overcome the binding force and be emitted into space. These emitted electrons are attracted to the positive anode as a photocurrent of microampere order.

Photovoltaic Cell. The first photovoltaic cells appeared shortly after the photoemissive cell. They are now used in a wide range of electronic systems, an example being modulated-light systems such as FIBER OPTICS communications arrays. When the Sun is the source of light they are known as SOLAR CELLS, and their many applications are described more fully in that entry (see also SOLAR ENERGY).

Photovoltaic cells employ a solid-state diode structure

with a large area on a silicon wafer. The surface layer is very thin and transparent so that light can reach the junction region of the silicon sandwich. In that region the photons are absorbed, releasing charges from their atomic bonds. These charges migrate to the terminals, raising the potential. Typical efficiencies for solar cells currently run from 10 to 15 percent. Efficiencies of 30 percent have been achieved, however, and researchers hope eventually to reach as high as 40 percent.

photoelectric effect   The photoelectric effect is the release of electrons from certain metals or semiconductors by the action of light or other ELECTROMAGNETIC RADIATION. The three different photoelectric effects are the photoemissive, the photoconductive, and the photovoltaic.

Photoemissive Effect. In the photoemissive effect, radiant energy striking the prepared surface of a metal such as cesium imparts sufficient energy to the electrons so they are emitted from the surface into space. In a photoelectric cell operating by this principle, the emitted electrons are collected by a positive electrode. Under the influence of an applied voltage they create an electric current linearly proportional to the incident light intensity.

Photoconductive Effect. In the photoconductive effect, light changes the electrical conductivity of a material. In semiconductors, most of the electrons are fixed in the valence bonds of the atoms, but a few electrons with higher energies will have broken bonds and will be free to serve as mobile charges in conduction. The energy differential needed to break a bond is called the gap energy. If light carries sufficient energy, then absorption of light will free an electron, and it will take part in conduction in the semiconductor. The increase in the electrical conductivity is proportional to the light intensity received and causes an increase in the current of an external circuit.

Photovoltaic Effect. In the photovoltaic effect the light energy is applied to the junction region of a SEMICONDUCTOR diode. The incident photons break electron bonds in the junction region, creating free charges as electron-hole pairs. These free charges migrate to the two sides of the junction, increasing the charge density there and raising the junction voltage. Materials are available to provide sensitivity through the visible and into the infrared region.

Basic Theory. The explanation of the photoelectric effect by Albert Einstein in 1905 accelerated the transition from classical to modern physics. The electromagnetic theory of light predicts a relationship between the intensity of incident light and the energy of the emitted electron. The intensity of the light wave depends on the square of its amplitude and is independent of frequency. Careful measurements showed that increasing the intensity of light causes the release of more photoelectrons with no increase in their energy. Furthermore, the energy was shown to be dependent on wavelength (or frequency); shorter wavelengths cause electrons of higher energy to be emitted.

To explain the effect, Einstein made use of Max Planck's concept of the quantum unit of radiation, now called a PHOTON. A surface energy barrier binds electrons within a metal, but this binding can be overcome and electrons emitted to space if the electron energy, or outward velocity, is increased sufficiently. Only photons striking the surface with great enough energies will produce emission. Einstein's photoelectric equation $E = hv$, where h is PLANCK'S CONSTANT, v is the freqency of the radiation, and their product is the energy of a single quantum, was found to explain the observed photoelectric effect.

See also: LIGHT.

photoengraving   Photoengraving is the technology of making LETTERPRESS printing plates that reproduce illustrations through the use of light and the ETCHING technique.

The basic photoengraving process is relatively straightforward: the illustration is photographed and the negative is used as a mask through which light is focused on a metal plate coated with a light-sensitive emulsion. Wherever light strikes the plate, the emulsion hardens into an acid- and water-resistant coating. The plate is then washed, the water removing the emulsion where light has not hardened it. An acid bath etches away the bare portions of the plate, leaving the image areas, which are protected by the emulsion, standing in relief (see PLATEMAKING).

The plate may be produced as a linecut, a halftone, or a combination of the two. Linecuts are used for the reproduction of an original—a pen-and-ink drawing, for instance—in black and white with no intermediate shades of gray. Halftone plates reproduce gradations of tone. To make a halftone plate, the original art is photographed through a screen of dots. When the plate is etched, dark areas reproduce as tiny white dots on a black background; light areas reproduce as tiny black dots on a white background.

photography   The term *photography* (from the Greek, *phos,* "light," and *graphein,* "to draw") means the production of a negative or positive black-and-white or colored record initiated by the action of radiant energy—usually in the form of light—upon a sensitive surface.

The fundamental physical principle of photography is that light falling briefly on the grains of certain insoluble silver salts (silver chloride, bromide, or iodide) produces small, invisible changes in the grains. When placed in certain solutions known as developers, the affected grains are converted into a black metallic silver. In color photography, further interactions take place with color-forming agents.

When a photograph is taken with a camera, light reflected from the object passes through the shutter, diaphragm, and lens to form a real inverted image. For the brief period during which the shutter is open, this image falls on the surface of a film or plate sensitized by silver salts and causes an invisible latent image to be recorded on it.

With an instant camera, development and printing are carried out while the film is still in the camera. In most cameras, however, pictures are taken until all the film has been exposed; then the still-undeveloped film must be removed in darkness or in greatly subdued light and placed in a developing solution. This solution darkens the affected grains of silver salt and converts the latent image

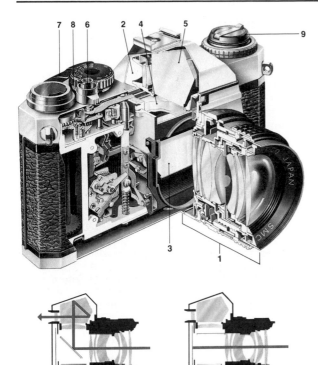

The design of a single-lens reflex camera allows the photographer to see the exact image that will be recorded on the film. Light entering the camera through the lens (1) is reflected into the viewfinder (2) by a mirror (3), focusing screen (4), and pentaprism (5). When the shutter release (6) is pressed, the mirror flips up and the incoming light strikes the exposed film. The insets illustrate the light path during viewfinding (A) and film exposure (B). Other controls include the film-advance lever (7), film-speed dial (8), and rewind knob (9).

into a negative image, in which dark and light areas in the object are recorded as light and dark areas, respectively, on the negative. The negative is then placed in a fixing solution, which dissolves the unaffected grains of silver salt and prevents any further action by light on the image.

To produce a positive contact print, light is passed through the negative so that it falls on a piece of printing paper held in close contact with the negative. Once again a latent image is produced; it is then developed into a positive image and fixed. Just as with the formation of the negative, this process reverses the dark and light areas and reproduces the original tones of the subject in a positive print.

Negatives are usually too small to make a useful contact print. An optical ENLARGER is therefore used to throw a magnified image of the negative onto the printing paper, which is then developed and fixed to yield a large positive print called an enlargement.

Camera

Basic Components. A camera consists essentially of a box carrying a lens, diaphragm, and shutter that are ar-

ranged to throw an image of the scene to be recorded onto a sensitive film or plate.

The LENS is usually made up of several components. It forms a real, inverted image of the object. In the popular 35-mm cameras the focal length is typically 50 mm (2 in), but it can be shorter or longer according to the size of the camera.

In the focusing mechanism provision is made for moving the lens backward or forward to focus the image on the film. Three main methods are used to determine the position of the lens: focusing scale, range finder, and reflex finder.

Two types of shutters are commonly used. The between-the-lens shutter is mounted between the components of the lens. The focal-plane shutter consists of a roller blind containing a slit that moves rapidly across the plane in front of the film. In popular cameras the shutter provides a range of exposures from about 1 second to 1/1,000 of a second.

The diaphragm provides a circular hole of variable size that regulates the amount of light that reaches the film.

If the light is weak, or if a short exposure is required, the diaphragm is opened wide to admit sufficient light. Under good lighting conditions with moderate exposures the diaphragm is set to a smaller aperture, thus reducing the amount of light reaching the film. The smaller aperture can also reduce effects of aberrations and of any error in focusing, thus producing a sharper picture (see DEPTH OF FIELD).

Of the various kinds of viewfinders, the simplest consists of a small hole, which serves to position the eye, and a wire frame a few inches in front of the hole, which delimits the field of view that corresponds to the image on the film. Most cameras today use optical or through-the-lens viewfinders.

Types of Cameras. The wide range of camera types is largely determined by the degree of compactness and portability required. The range extends from the ultraminiature camera, which weighs a few ounces and has a picture size of the order of 1 cm (0.4 in) square, to the large studio or view cameras weighing many kilograms or pounds and taking a picture of 20×25 cm (8×10 in) or more in size.

Specialized types of cameras are also used, for example, for aerial or underwater photography. In some cameras the film is advanced by a motor drive for taking a short, rapid succession of still photos. Others operate in conjunction with multiple flash to produce a number of superimposed pictures.

See the article CAMERA for a description of the new types of electronically controlled cameras.

Black-and-White Photography

Film Composition. Film for black-and-white photography consists of a transparent base on which is spread a thin layer of an emulsion consisting of a suspension of minute mixed crystals of silver halides, such as silver bromide and silver iodide, in gelatin. The gelatin not only holds the grains but also greatly increases their sensitivity to light. The latent image is made up of specks of silver

A black-and-white negative (above left) *is obtained when the latent image on exposed film is made visible during the developing process. Dark areas on the film are rendered as light, and light areas as dark. When the negative is printed* (above right), *the light and dark values are again reversed. The resulting photograph offers a close approximation of the tonal values of the original image.*

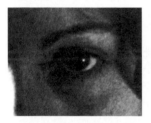
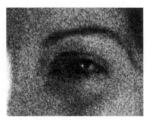

A photographic image is made up of clumps of microscopic particles, or grains, of silver. The image may have a grainy (right) *or nongrainy* (left) *appearance, depending on the extent to which the individual clumps become visible after development of the film. In general, the average grain size in a film emulsion increases as the film speed increases, and a coarser and grainier image is produced.*

The degree of film exposure must be carefully controlled in order to produce clarity and good contrast in a photograph. Underexposed film (left) *receives insufficient light, resulting in a uniformly darkened photograph. A correctly exposed picture* (center) *is sharp and has considerable tonal variation. A bleached-out appearance* (right) *is a sign of overexposure or too much light reaching the film.*

formed in the grains in response to light, which act as nuclei enabling the developer to convert the whole of the rest of a grain into silver.

Almost all films, both black and white and color, are panchromatic; that is, they are sensitive to almost all visible wavelengths. Sensitizing dyes are added to the emulsion to extend the sensitivity to include the long-wave (red) end of the spectrum.

Grain and Speed. Films vary in the size of the grains they contain. This variation, in turn, has an effect on the film's speed, or sensitivity to light, probably because a larger grain intercepts more light. Faster films can therefore be used with a shorter exposure, in a weaker light, or at a smaller aperture. The resultant picture, however, is apt to show grain, especially when enlarged. Slower, fine-grain films are used for work of highest quality. The American Standards Association (ASA) scale is one common measure of film speed. However, the International Standardization Organization (ISO) is in the process of replacing the ASA system, though its scale is identical to the ASA's. The scale is linear, so that films of speeds ISO 100 and 200 require one-half and one-quarter, respectively, of the exposure required for a film of ISO 50.

Developing. The exposed film is transferred in darkness into a developing solution, which causes any affected grain of the latent image to be wholly converted into silver. After a brief rinse in a stop bath of acid or water to remove developer and to stop development, the film is fixed in a solution of sodium thiosulfate (often called hypo) or in a more rapid fixing solution; these solutions dissolve and remove the unchanged silver salts, thus rendering the film insensitive to light. Finally the film is washed and dried. Each picture is now a transparent negative in which light parts of the object are represented by dark areas and dark parts by light areas.

Printing. A large negative can be used to make a contact print, but small negatives are usually placed in an enlarger in which light from a lamp throws an enlarged and accurately focused image onto a piece of printing paper that has been coated with an emulsion similar to that on the film but less sensitive to light. The paper is then developed and fixed to form a positive print.

A print in which the black areas are extremely black and the white areas extremely white is said to show high contrast, while one in which only various shades of gray appear is said to be of low contrast. A good print should show a tonal range from black to white with varying degrees of gray. Different grades of paper, ranging from hard (contrasty) to soft (low contrast), also contribute to the degree of contrast in the final print.

Lighting

A photograph is no more than a visual record of the variation in the brightnesses of different parts of a scene. Because the ratio of intensity of illumination from bright sunlight to the dim lighting of a dark interior is of the order of one million to one, two fundamental requirements for good photography are a way to provide appropriate lighting and a way to measure how much light is available.

Natural daylight from two hours after sunrise to two hours before sunset varies according to weather conditions by a factor of only about 10, corresponding to a varying aperture of slightly more than three stops of the diaphragm; under these conditions, the exposure may be set by following some simple rules based on the conditions: bright sunlight, cloudy bright, open shade, or cloudy dull.

Exposure Meter. The exposure meter is a device to

measure the amount of light on a subject and to translate this measurement into usable information, such as which shutter speed and aperture size will result in the best photograph (see ACTINOMETER). One type of exposure meter consists of a PHOTOELECTRIC CELL connected to an ammeter. Light falling on the cell causes a current to flow; the deflection of a needle gives a reading of the intensity of the lighting.

The meter can either be a separate device or it can form an integral part of the camera. A popular arrangement is to have the photocell mounted inside the camera so that it receives a part of the light forming the photographic image. Light can be directed onto the cell in one of several ways without seriously impairing the image itself. The method is known as TTL (through-the-lens) metering.

Color Filters. Filters placed over the lens of the camera are used to modify the light passing through the lens and onto the film. Because filters do not transmit all the light that reaches them, the exposure must usually be increased when a filter is used. A yellow filter absorbs blue rays and greatly improves many black-and-white pictures by darkening the sky. Its use requires an approximate doubling of the exposure. A red filter gives similar but stronger effects and may produce dramatic pictures of mountain scenery. Color filters may also be used to increase contrast. A polaroid filter appropriately oriented will block the polarized light from the sky and is useful in darkening blue sky in color photographs; it can also be used to eliminate undesirable reflections in the picture.

Lighting with Flash Bulbs. When light is weak, a flash unit, mounted on or off the camera, can be used as an artificial light source. A flash bulb mounted in the center of a concave mirror contains fine magnesium, aluminum, or zirconium wire in oxygen.

Lighting with Electronic Flash. The flash is produced by a capacitor charged to a high voltage discharging through a flash tube in as little as 1/10,000 sec, a time short enough to freeze rapid action. The firing of the flash is usually synchronized with the shutter action. A sensitive electronic eye may be used to operate a mechanism that extinguishes the flash when sufficient light for exposure of the film has been reflected back from the subject. Multiple flash may be used to produce a number of superimposed pictures; such a technique is useful for analyzing movement—in sports, for example.

Color Photography

Like black-and-white photography, color photography depends fundamentally upon the darkening of silver salts. Any COLOR can be made from mixtures of the three primary colors: red, green, and blue. Each of these three prima-

The f-stops on a camera lens are marked on an adjustable aperture ring in the lens casing. Turning the ring opens and closes a mechanical iris (above), allowing more or less light to reach the film. The f-stop also determines how much of the image is in focus. Use of a wide aperture, such as f/2.8 (below left), results in a narrow depth of field with a limited focus. A small aperture, such as f/22 (below right), yields a wider depth of field, with more of the picture in focus.

For a given camera and film system the exposure time needed for a good photograph depends on the lighting conditions and on the subject. The sharp daylight image (A) of rapidly moving cars required a relatively fast shutter speed of 1/125 sec. Shorter exposure times of 1/30 sec (B) and 1/8 sec (C) stopped the motion of cars only at increasingly greater distances from the camera. At night (D) a time exposure of the same scene recorded parts of the surrounding area, street lights, and light patterns made by headlights of moving cars.

Lighting in photography is used selectively to obtain strikingly different pictorial effects. In these four photographs the subject is lit from various angles by one main light source. Front lighting (far left) produces a bright and even illumination that flattens the subject's features. With top lighting (left), shadows under the brows and nose are emphasized, yielding sharp relief in the facial structure. Side lighting (right) obscures half the subject's face and suggests a hidden side to his personality. Underlighting (far right) produces an unnatural, somewhat sinister look and is often used to add an air of mystery to photographs and film shots.

ry colors has a complementary color, which when mixed with it gives white.

Complementary Colors

red	+	blue green (cyan)	=	white
green	+	magenta	=	white
blue	+	yellow	=	white

Thus green and magenta are complementary colors.

The Negative-Positive Process. The negative film consists of three superimposed layers: one blue-sensitive, one green-sensitive, and one red-sensitive. Exposure in the camera is followed by development, which produces deposits in black silver grains representing the blue, the green, and the red parts of the optical image. During development, substances known as dye intermediates incorporated in the three layers are converted into dyes that stain each of the three silver images in a color complementary to the color of the light that formed it. The silver itself is bleached and removed so that only the transparent color remains. In the negative, therefore, the blue parts of the picture are represented by yellow, the green parts by magenta, and the red parts by cyan.

Next, the negative is placed in an enlarger, where the image is thrown onto printing paper coated with three superimposed layers of emulsion that are essentially the same as those in the negative color film; they are developed in essentially the same way. Just as the negative forms colors complementary to those in the optical image, so the paper forms colors complementary to those in the negative. The result is that the original colors of the subject are reproduced.

In producing the color print, care is needed to ensure accurate color rendition. In one method, three successive exposures are made in the enlarger—one with blue, one with red, and one with green light—and the relative durations are adjusted from indications given by test strips. In an alternative method, a white light source is used with a single exposure. As successive test strips are made, color-correcting filters are placed over the lens of the enlarger and adjusted until a satisfactory test strip is obtained.

The Reversal Method for Color Transparencies. As ex-

plained above, red plus blue green equals white, green plus magenta equals white, and blue plus yellow equals white. Accordingly, blue green is the color produced from white light when red light is removed from it. Therefore blue green light can be thought of as minus red, magenta as minus green, and yellow as minus blue.

Positive, or reversal, film consists of three superimposed emulsion layers sensitive to the red, green, and blue parts of the spectrum, respectively. As in the previous method, after exposure in the camera and a first development, three superimposed black-and-white images in silver are formed that represent the red, green, and blue parts of the optical image. In the reversal method, however, these negative images are not stained. The film is next exposed to light from a lamp, which induces the formation of a latent image in the previously unaffected grains of silver salt, that is, in those grains that were unaffected by the red, green, and blue lights in the optical image. A different dye intermediate is incorporated in each of the three layers. When the film is given the second development, a second set of three silver images is formed. The dye intermediates form dyes that stain the newly forming second images, but not the first ones, coloring them as follows: The red-sensitive layer produces the color cyan (minus red); the green-sensitive

A color negative (left) renders the original colors of the film in their complementary colors. Red becomes cyan (greenish blue), blue becomes yellow, and green becomes magenta. Tonal values are also reversed, as in a black-and-white negative. When the negative is printed as a photograph (right), the original colors are restored.

layer produces magenta (minus green); and the blue-sensitive layer produces yellow (minus blue). Both sets of silver images are bleached and washed away, so that only the transparent dyes remain.

For example, in an area where the optical image was red, a black deposit was initially formed in the red-sensitive area; it is bleached and washed away, so that the layer is clear. In the green- and blue-sensitive layers the second silver images were stained minus green and minus blue, respectively, and only these colors remained after bleaching. When the transparency is viewed by projection of white light through it, the minus-green and minus-blue dyes remove the green and the blue components of the white light, leaving only the red. Thus the original red color in the optical image is correctly reproduced. Similar processes can be applied to the green and the blue parts of the optical image.

Polaroid instant color film is developed through a process called diffusion transfer. The film itself is composed of 18 discrete, microscopically thin layers. As the exposed film emerges from the camera, a chemical developing agent is forced between the top layers, which hold the color dyes, and the bottom layers, on which the image is imprinted. The image develops below, while the chemicals producing the colors diffuse through the upper layers.

photography, history and art of

The word *photography*, which is derived from the Greek words for light and writing, was first used by Sir John Herschel in 1839, the year the invention of the photographic process was made public. During the previous decades perhaps as many as ten individuals had tried to make a photograph. At least four were successful: Joseph Nicéphore NIEPCE, Louis J. M. DAGUERRE, and Hippolyte BAYARD in France, and William Henry Fox Talbot in England.

Each of them employed two scientific techniques that had been known for some time but had never before been successfully combined. The first of these techniques was optical. Since the 16th century artists and scientists had made use of the fact that light passing through a small hole in one wall of a dark room, or CAMERA OBSCURA, projects an inverted image on the opposite wall. The hole was soon replaced with a lens, which made the image brighter and sharper. By the 18th century the room had been replaced by a portable box, which artists used as a sketching aid. The second technique was chemical. In 1727, Johann Heinrich Schulze had discovered that certain chemicals, especially silver halides, turn dark when exposed to light. The first attempt to use such chemicals to record the image of the camera obscura was made—unsuccessfully—by Thomas WEDGWOOD about 1800.

Daguerre's invention, which was bought by the French government and made public on Aug. 19, 1839, produced a one-of-a-kind picture on metal, the DAGUERREOTYPE. In contrast, Talbot's invention (1840), the CALOTYPE, produced a negative picture on paper; the lights of the image were recorded as darks, the darks as lights. A positive was made on another sheet of chemically sensitized paper, exposed to light through the negative. Because an infinite number of positives could be made from a single negative, Talbot's invention and refinements of it soon predominated. The ease with which photography recorded visual information and distributed it worldwide made it the most powerful tool of communication since the invention of the printing press.

The Pioneering Days

Because early photographers were largely unfettered by academic convention or demand for a uniform commercial product, the first two decades of photography were rich in pictorial experiment. Among the inventors, Talbot and Bayard were especially sensitive to the beauty of the new medium, its aptitude for the intimate, personal view.

In the 1840s, D. O. Hill and Robert Adamson (see HILL, D. O., AND ADAMSON, ROBERT) made photographic portraits as studies for a large group portrait that Hill finished painting 20 years later. The painting is an awkward failure; the photographs, however, possess a grandeur that recalls—without copying—portraits by old masters.

(Far left) *Louis J. M. Daguerre, whose daguerreotype process was used in this portrait (c.1848), developed the first widely used photographic process, a method of producing detailed positive images directly on silver plates.* (Left) *The first permanent photograph, a direct positive image on a treated pewter plate, was taken (1826) by Joseph Niepce.*

William Henry Fox Talbot, inventor of the negative-to-positive process upon which modern photography is based, patented his refined calotype process in 1841.

The Pastor's Visit (1843), one of the outstanding calotypes by D. O. Hill and Robert Adamson, exhibits the balance and contrast that distinguish the portraits of these early photographers.

The oldest existing photographic negative (1835), a shot of a latticed window by William Henry Fox Talbot, was made with Talbot's early "photogenic drawing" technique.

The intuition of Hill and Adamson was shared by an impressive group of French photographers of the 1850s, among them Gustave Le Gray, Charles Marville, Charles Nègre, E. D. Baldus, and Henri Le Secq, who formed the Société Française de Photographie. They frequently photographed important places and historic monuments.

Even after the medium began to be dominated by professionals in the 1860s, many of the most inventive 19th-century photographers were amateurs. Perhaps the best of them was Julia Margaret CAMERON, who made intense portraits of her friends, many of whom were eminent Victorians. Cameron also composed photographic tableaux in which real people were transformed into characters from Alfred, Lord Tennyson's Idylls of the King. In their own day, these pictures were admired as idiosyncratic productions; today they are appreciated as precocious examples of photography's responsiveness to fantasy and fiction.

The amateurs may be contrasted with photographers such as Oscar Gustav Rejlander and Henry Peach ROBINSON, who attempted to challenge painting on its own ground. In England in the 1850s Robinson created elaborate genre scenes, pieced together from as many as a dozen different negatives.

Impact of Mass-Production Methods

After 1851, when Frederick Scott Archer's process substituted glass for Talbot's paper negative, the mass production of albumen prints of extremely fine detail became possible. Until the 1880s this was the medium of the great commercial firms, which fed an enormous popular demand for portraits and for views of famous monuments or strange places. The majority of 19th-century photographs fall into these two categories. By the mid-1850s, when André Adolphe Eugène DISDÉRI popularized the small, cheap portrait, anyone could afford a picture of himself or herself. The effect of this development on the growing self-awareness of the working class and on the self-perceptions of the bourgeoisie cannot be easily overestimated. Thanks to photography, ordinary people possessed an emblem of identity formerly reserved for the rich. NADAR and the team of Albert Sands Southworth and Josiah Johnson Hawes produced portraits that are at once records of faces and interpretations of personalities.

At first, topographical photography was the work of dilettantes, such as Maxime Du Camp, who published their travel photographs in albums of original prints. By the 1860s large commercial firms such as Francis Frith's in England and the Alinari Brothers in Italy were in operation; their approach to photographic documentation was systematic and encyclopedic. At the turn of the century, for instance, the Alinari catalog offered 60,000 views of Italian cities and reproductions of paintings. The new disciplines of art history and archaeology depended enormously on these pictures.

The variety and extent of the visual encyclopedia of the world that was compiled during the first 30 to 40 years of photography are all the more extraordinary because the medium was still extremely cumbersome. Cameras were large and heavy and required tripods. Each glass plate had to be exposed while still wet with a freshly coated emulsion. Consequently, photographers in the field were obliged to pack along makeshift darkrooms. It is commonly said, with some truth, that the precise beauty of early photographs is due to the resolution required to make them.

Photographic Documentation

One of the greatest photographic documents of history-in-the-making is also one of the earliest: the pictures of the U.S. Civil War, made by perhaps 20 photographers, most of them initially under the direction of Mathew B. BRADY. With their clumsy equipment, they could not yet capture the action of battle. Nevertheless, their blunt views of unprepossessing landscapes, littered with the dead, and their frank records of drab camp life changed the popular romantic vision of war.

Timothy H. O'Sullivan, one of the best of Brady's team, spent part of the next decade with expeditions of the U.S. Geographic Survey, photographing the vast, uncharted American West. Pictures by O'Sullivan and his contemporaries Eadweard MUYBRIDGE, William Henry Jackson, and Carleton Watkins possess a functional clarity and detailed precision that is unmatched by the greatest of paintings. Like the Civil War photographs, they were revelations, both impressive and believable.

In the 19th century, photography still had the power of undisputed truth. In the last third of the century that power was enlisted as a tool of social reform. The muckraking journalist Jacob August RIIS began in the 1880s to use photography to expose the appalling conditions in New York City's slums. Two decades later Lewis Hine, a sociologist, supported a campaign for child-labor laws with his sympathetic portraits of young factory workers.

Photography was also applied to scientific inquiry. Cameras were attached to microscopes and telescopes and produced strange pictures that were derived from nature—details of the world that once were invisible. The most famous of these are the motion studies that Étienne Jules MAREY and Eadweard Muybridge made in the 1870s and 1880s.

Scientists and social reformers both profited from the continuous technical improvements in photography, which reached a watershed with the introduction of dry plates in the 1880s. The new plates did away with field darkrooms, and their faster emulsions made it possible to stop action. Cameras also became smaller and more portable. In 1888, George EASTMAN's Kodak, which used flexible roll film, made photography available to anyone.

Photography as an Art

Amid the proliferation of practical applications and new

(Left) *George Eastman was photographed (1890) by Fred Church with a Kodak camera. The circular print resulted from the Kodak's circular image frame. Eastman helped develop the dry-plate process, the roll-film system, and the hand-held camera.*

With such photographs as Carrying-in Boy (1909) *Lewis Hine urged social reform. (International Museum of Photography, Rochester, N.Y.)*

formal solutions, a scattered but energetic group of photographers in the late 19th century sought to cut themselves off from the worldly role of their medium in order to establish photography as a branch of fine art. They endorsed the old claim that to be an art photography must look like established art, and they revived old techniques, in particular the gum-bichromate print, that allowed manual intervention. The hazy forms of such prints were instantly distinguishable from the detailed precision of commercial photographs.

In 1889, Peter Henry Emerson had set the stage for this development by making a sharp distinction between artistic photography and the practical, straightforward work of professionals. Although two years later he renounced his claim, Emerson had provided the new group with the high-minded theory it needed as well as with the standard of his own fine pictures. Coincidentally, he inspired a disdain for the plain photograph that persisted for at least a generation.

By the early 20th century a lively international network of societies for artistic photography existed, including the Linked Ring Brotherhood in London (founded 1892) and

The scratches on Mathew Brady's portrait of General Ulysses S. Grant bear witness to the fragility of the plates used in wet-plate photography, the process used by Brady and his staff during their coverage of the Civil War. The wet-plate technique, the leading photographic process by the middle of the 19th century, required lengthy exposure time.

the Photo-Secession in New York (founded 1902). The new status that the movement won for photography may have been more a function of its polemics than of its pictures, but unquestionably it produced a number of exceptional photographers. Among them were Frederick Henry EVANS and Heinrich Kühn of the Linked Ring and Alfred STIEGLITZ, leader of the Photo-Secessionists, and his colleagues Gertrude KÄSEBIER, Edward STEICHEN, Alvin Langdon Coburn, and Clarence H. White.

In the first decades of the 20th century, Stieglitz reversed his position and claimed an expressive role for straightforward photography. In the same decades the French photographer Eugène ATGET arrived at a similar point of view but from the opposite direction. Atget, working in the tradition of the encyclopedic photographers of the previous century, made thousands of views of old Paris. His pictures demonstrate that a photograph is not identical with the subject it depicts but rather is a way of looking at that subject—an interpretation.

Stieglitz's new work had an immediate and lasting impact. By 1916 his reformulation of photography was powerfully confirmed by the pictures produced by the young Paul STRAND. By the 1920s, Stieglitz had given new direction to another generation of photographers, of whom the most important was Edward WESTON. For this group, the "straight"—that is, unmanipulated—photograph became a creed; mechanical precision, once considered the handicap of photography, now became its major asset. Weston's intense artistic will found satisfaction in the small details of nature, resolved, almost abstracted, into harmonies of form.

This concern with abstract form was shared by the leading European photographers of the 1920s, who bore

Cabbage Leaf *(1931) exemplifies Edward Weston's ability to capture the texture and form of his subjects without retouching the negative in any way.*

no allegiance to the creed of straight photography. Following the examples of the surrealist Man RAY and László MOHOLY-NAGY, they discovered unpredictable pictures and new forms by experimenting with the photographic process itself. The most extreme of these experiments was the photogram, a picture made without a camera by arranging objects on photographic paper. Even straight pictures were made at odd angles or in strange lights so that the subject was lost in an unfamiliar pattern.

The expressive possibilities of these experiments were matched by the versatility of the small, high-speed cameras—such as the Leica—that were introduced in Europe in the 1920s. The new cameras freed photographers from every encumbrance. It became possible for the first time to follow—and capture—the most rapid or ephemeral action, to record the world as it happened.

Among the first to use the new cameras were journalists like Erich SALOMON and Felix H. Man, who recorded any event, the trivial along with the important. Their work was published in the picture magazines, such as LIFE and its European counterparts, that began to flourish in the 1930s and that established the new, often lucrative, profession of PHOTOJOURNALISM.

The editors of these magazines needed pictures that could be quickly understood. Many who used the small cameras, however, especially Henri CARTIER-BRESSON, André KERTÈSZ, and BRASSAÏ, were more interested in taking photographs that could not be reduced to captions. They turned to the anonymous bustle of public places and made pictures that described nothing newsworthy in the conventional sense but suggested the texture of life itself. These photographs also displayed a new, apparently casual form, based on the perception of the moment—Cartier-Bresson called it "the decisive moment"—rather than on the rules of the studio.

In the United States during the 1930s, photographers, like other artists, benefited from the make-work

Edward Steichen's Steeplechase Day, Paris: After the Races *(1907) exemplifies the goals of the Photo-Secession, a movement dedicated to elevating photography to a fine art. (Metropolitan Museum of Art, New York City.)*

The Deported Return *(1945) epitomizes Henri Cartier-Bresson's search for the "decisive moment" in his documentary photography. (Museum of Modern Art, New York.)*

projects of the government. Many talented photographers were employed by the Farm Security Administration (FSA), Works Progress Administration (WPA), and other federal agencies to record the life of rural America—its embattled farmers, poor sharecroppers, and migrant laborers. Among these photographers were Berenice AB-BOTT, Walker EVANS, Dorothea LANGE, and Russell Lee. Partly because of the FSA, the potential power of photography as a social force became widely recognized. A few years later, World War II brought even more exposure to photojournalists such as Margaret BOURKE-WHITE, Robert CAPA, and W. Eugene Smith.

Walker Evans, perhaps the best photographer of the period, stood somewhat apart from this trend. Evans staked out a claim for intelligence in photography; he showed that a photographer's understanding of his subject may be so convincing that it seems to be the only one possible. In Germany, August Sander (1876–1964), achieved a similarly compelling body of work.

Contemporary Photography

After World War II several Japanese photographers, led by Shomei Tomatsu, invented a gritty, dramatic brand of photography, which suited their preoccupation with the war and its effect on Japan. Except for the Japanese and a few Europeans, however, creative initiative in photography shifted to the United States in the 1950s. A leader in this development was the Swiss-born photographer Robert FRANK, whose influential book *The Americans* was published in 1959. Learning from Walker Evans, Frank forged powerful symbols from the ordinary stuff of American life.

Frank's counterpart in the 1950s was Minor WHITE. White acquired a fine technique from Ansel ADAMS, who had carried on the tradition of straight photography in his impressive pictures of the American West. Adams sought images of universal scope. White presented sharply focused details of nature as metaphors for his own emotional states. White is the spiritual father of many contemporary artists, such as Jerry N. UELSMANN, who use photography to explore themselves rather than the world around them.

A third major figure to emerge in the 1950s is Harry M. Callahan, who adapted the formal experiments of Moholy-Nagy to his own respect for natural beauty. The elegance of the work of Callahan and of his talented student Ray Metzker disguises the rigor of their systematic approach to the photographic process. That rigor, sometimes coupled with wry humor, is an essential element in

(Below) *Walker Evans's photograph of a black section in Vicksburg, Miss. (1936), displays the spare vision, restrained artistry, and direct approach that distinguish the best Depression-era photojournalism. (Library of Congress, Washington, D.C.)*

"Baltimore, 1962" is typical of the earlier work of photographer Lee Friedlander. Intrigued by the American street scene, and by the play between light, space, and surface he sees in it, Friedlander shoots "snapshot" pictures of great sophistication.

the work of Kenneth Josephson, Robert Cumming, and other photographers who participated in the conceptual and minimal art movements of the 1960s and 1970s.

A further aspect of postwar American work that deserves note is fashion photography. Beginning in the late 1940s, Richard AVEDON and Irving Penn have brought to their commercial work qualities of inventiveness and finesse that rival the best private work of the period.

Among photographers who came to prominence in the 1960s, the most important are Garry Winogrand, Lee Friedlander, and Diane ARBUS. Winogrand and Friedlander followed the example of Robert Frank, establishing themselves as keen-eyed observers of contemporary life. In the 1970s their work diverged significantly. Winogrand pushed the small-camera aesthetic to its limit, testing his ability to extract order from the chaotic bustle of the city street. Friedlander's work, which began as an ironic report on popular culture, has become increasingly lyrical and affectionate in its description of the American scene.

Arbus favored psychological intensity over formal invention. Her penetrating portraits, many of socially marginal people, insist on the individuality of the subject and thus confront the viewer with the question of his or her own identity.

The only significant technical innovation in recent years has been the new ease and availability of color photography. Because of difficulty and expense, color had been limited principally to commercial applications, except for the pioneering nature photography of Eliot PORTER. Then in the 1970s the new work of Helen Levitt, Stephen Shore, and especially William Eggleston demonstrated the potential of color as an artistic medium. Since then color has attracted a growing number of talented young photographers, including Jan Groover and Joel Sternfeld.

In the late 1950s the picture magazines began to fail. The erosion of this public forum for photography coincided with a rising awareness of photography's artistic potential. The new population of artist-photographers has found support in the academic community and in the burgeoning market for fine photographic prints.

Into the 1990s some of the most innovative contemporary photography has arisen from a new fascination, at turns affectionate or ironic, with the imagery of popular culture, especially advertising and the movies. Many critics have labeled this work "postmodernist," implying that it signals the demise of earlier 20th-century traditions and aspirations. "Postmodernism," however, has joined rather than replaced a wide range of thriving modernist styles, from experimental formalism to documentary realism. To sample this diversity, one need only compare Cindy Sherman's self-portraits, when she adopts whole populations of fictive personalities, and Nicholas Nixon's straightforward pictures of ordinary people, which extend the tradition of classic American photography. The old continues to find new incarnations, in short, while the new adds new meanings to the language of contemporary photography.

photography, scientific The term *scientific photography* includes the whole range of specialized equipment and techniques used to observe and record the results of scientific investigations. For example, photographic methods provide better control over time: time-lapse photography speeds up slow processes, and stroboscopic photography slows down rapid ones. The use of laser technology can capture high-speed chemical reactions. Schlieren photography indicates variations in the refractive index of a gas or liquid. BUBBLE CHAMBER photography records photographically the tracks of bubbles released in a superheated liquid by nuclear particles. CLOUD CHAMBER photography records similar tracks in a supersaturated vapor. In autoradiography, radioactive substances are taken up by animal or plant tissue from which a thin section is cut and applied to a photographic emulsion. Development and microscopic examination reveal the extent and distribution of the substance taken up. In photographic dosimetry the darkening of an emulsion plate worn by a person will indicate the radiation dose to which the person has been exposed.

Medical applications include retinography (photography of the retina of the eye), keratography (photography to reveal the shape of the cornea of the eye), and endoscopic photography (pictures taken through ENDOSCOPES).

Radiography is the taking of "shadow pictures" using X RAYS. Tomography (as in computerized axial tomography, or CAT scan) is an X-ray technique for removing the

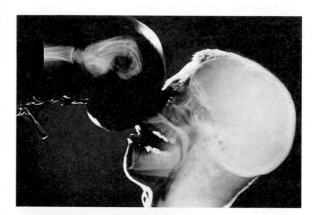

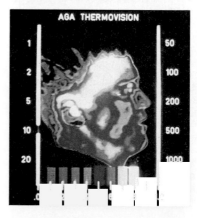

A color radiograph (above) is produced by photographing the subject with a color-film tripack that is sensitive to X rays. The simultaneous revelation of surface form and of internal structure yields a photograph of unusual impact. A thermograph (left) charts skin temperature with a camera sensitive to infrared radiation. "Heat photographs" locate tumors and other abnormalities.

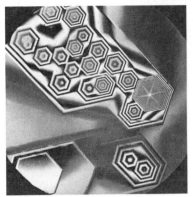

(Above) *The flight of a bullet was caught by a camera equipped with a high-speed shutter and a strobe-light attachment in an exposure lasting one-millionth of a second.* (Left) *A microphotograph of a crystal of cadmium sulfate, magnified 800 times, reveals hexagonal pits in the crystal's surface.*

shadows of organs in front of and behind the area under investigation (see RADIOLOGY).

Other scientific uses of photography include spectrograms (see SPECTROSCOPE), spectroheliograms (see SPECTROHELIOGRAPH), and THERMOGRAPHY. Specially adapted cameras take pictures via a light MICROSCOPE, an ELECTRON MICROSCOPE, or a telescope (see TELESCOPE, OPTICAL).

photojournalism   Photojournalism is the reportage of a news story or event primarily through pictures rather than words. Compared with television news coverage, its principal competition, photojournalism uses still rather than moving pictures, and its products appear, in more or less permanent form, in newspapers, magazines, and books. Although television reportage may have, over time, a cumulative effect (as it did in the Vietnam War), the dramatic impact of the best pictures of photojournalism is such that these are the images that shape, for many people, their notions of the important events of recent history, as well as their ideas of the lives of the poor, the foreign, or the strange and alien.

The documentary photography of the Englishman Roger Fenton in the Crimean War (1853–65) and of Mathew BRADY and his team of photographers during the U.S. Civil War were among the earliest attempts to record historical events photographically. Many of the Brady pictures—

as well as photographs of such new and exciting subjects as natural disasters, exotic lands, and so forth—were widely copied in contemporary periodicals, using hand engravings to reproduce an approximation of the pictures. The first reproduction of an actual photograph, by means of a mechanical halftone, appeared in the *New York Graphic*, a newspaper, in 1880. It showed a group of shacks built in Central Park by some of the city's homeless. The picture was significant not only because it introduced the era of exact reproduction of photographs in the press, but also in its subject. By the late 1800s, social reformers such as Jacob RIIS used photography to document their reports of poverty in America.

Although photographs became a staple in the press—and newspapers increased their circulation with special Sunday supplements printed in rotogravure, which produced a more finely detailed picture—the shots, by and large, were posed and static. Photographers were barred from the battlefields of World War I, and few civilians saw an illustration of the real war.

In the mid-1920s, small hand-held cameras, such as the 33-mm Leica, became available for the first time. Many were equipped with lenses that used available light to take shots at short exposures. With such cameras, and with the new fast films that were developed in the following years, it became possible for a photographer to be a reporter as well, to tell a story so convincingly in pictures that a textual narrative was no longer essential and words need be used only to identify people and places.

Illustrated periodicals sprang up through Europe in the 1920s, hiring photographers who soon became famous for their skill, their daring, and their ability to recognize a good story almost before it happened. They included Erich SALOMON, Alfred EISENSTAEDT, Felix Man, Stefan Lorant, and André KERTÉSZ. In the 1930s many came to the United States, and in the mid-1930s the best joined the newly founded picture magazines *Life* and *Look*.

The sophistication of the medium was demonstrated

Robert Capa's blurred photograph D-Day Invasion *was taken on June 6, 1944, as he waded onto the beaches of Normandy with the Allied forces. Capa documented five wars from 1936 until his death (1954) in Vietnam.*

decisively during the Spanish Civil War by the Hungarian Robert CAPA and the Frenchman Henri CARTIER-BRESSON. Both were to become world famous, Capa as one of the most important memorialists of the wars that followed, Cartier-Bresson as the discoverer of "the decisive moment" in his immortal photographs of ordinary people.

Commissioned by the Farm Security Administration during the 1930s, Walker EVANS and Dorothea LANGE recorded the devastation brought by drought and depression to the lives of American farm families. Both Lange and Margaret BOURKE-WHITE worked for *Life*, perfecting the photographic news essay, which became a specialty of the magazine.

The potential of photojournalism simultaneously to record, to dramatize, to expose, and to propagandize was most fully realized in World War II. The Americans Bourke-White, W. Eugene Smith, Larry Burrows, and David Douglas Duncan all continued the tradition, begun by Capa and his colleagues, of integrating a personal vision with dramatic action photographs, artistic techniques that would also characterize coverage of the Korean and Vietnam wars.

After World War II, and especially in the strife-torn years of the 1960s and '70s, social photography became a major concern of photojournalists. Many of these artists benefited from the International Fund for Concerned Photography, founded by Robert Capa's brother, photographer Cornell Capa. The need to deal with social and political issues photographically, not only those in the United States but in other countries experiencing the anguish of war or poverty, continues in the work of such contemporary photojournalists as the Briton Donald McCullin, the Brazilian Sebastiao Salgado, and the Americans Susan Meiselas and Milton Rogovin.

photometer   The photometer in its modern form is an optical-electronic instrument that measures the intensity of a beam of light. Although the range of photometers extends beyond visible light into the ultraviolet and infrared portions of the electromagnetic spectrum, instruments operating on very similar principles for the measurement of X-ray, gamma-ray, and radio-frequency radiation are usually not called photometers.

By means of a TRANSDUCER the photometer transforms a beam of photons into an electric current, measures this current, and conveys the information to the user by means of a meter or digital readout. The most critical component is the photon detector or transducer, which may be photoconductive, photoemissive, or photovoltaic (see PHOTOELECTRIC CELL).

Photoconductive transducers may be semiconductors such as selenium or germanium. The electrical resistivity of semi-conducter materials decreases in proportion to the amount of light directed on them. By applying an electrical potential across a semiconductor, then, the resulting current flow will be in proportion to the intensity of the light being received. The response of different materials varies according to the wavelength of the incident light. The photoemissive tube emits electrons when exposed to radiation in or near the visible-light region of the

spectrum. There are three types of these tubes: high-vacuum diodes, gas-filled diodes, and PHOTOMULTIPLIERS. The photovoltaic cell generates an electromotive force (emf) when it is exposed to light. Photovoltaic cells, or SOLAR CELLS, as they are often called, do not require an external power source. Materials used to make such cells include copper oxide, selenium, germanium, and silicon.

In addition to use in photographic exposure meters (see ACTINOMETER) photometers are widely used as components or subsystems in highly specialized instruments, such as POLARIMETERS, colorimeters, densitometers, and turbidimeters.

photometry, astronomical   Astronomical photometry is the measurement of the intensity of light received at the Earth from a celestial object. The detectors used for these measurements are photographic plates and photoelectric devices. In most applications, filters transmitting limited wavelength regions of the spectrum of a celestial object are placed in front of the detector.

Because of its high accuracy, photoelectric measurement is the preferred technique for most types of photometric observations. Observations are limited to one star at a time. The radiation from the observed star strikes the photosensitive element of the photometer and produces an electric current with a strength proportional to the intensity of the incident light. This current is commonly displayed in the form of a line on a strip chart recorder or a numerical display, or is directly stored in a computer. For calibration purposes standard stars of known brightness must be observed with the same photometer under similar conditions.

photomultiplier   A photomultiplier tube is an electronic detector for sensing low levels of electromagnetic radiation, ranging from soft X rays through visible and infrared light. The tube is an important component of sensitive PHOTOMETERS. The performance of the tube is based upon the phenomenon of photoemission, the property of some substances to eject electrons when radiated (see PHOTOELECTRIC EFFECT). In this capacity such a substance will serve as a cathode. In the tube, the electrons are initially focused onto a secondary emission surface, called a dynode, where additional electrons are emitted and the electron density is increased. Use of additional dynodes extends the secondary emission process, amplifying a signal by a factor of a hundred million or more from a weak initial current. Several materials are used in the photocathodes, depending on the radiation wavelength for which the tube has been designed to operate. These materials include cesium-oxygen-silver, cesium-antimony, cesium-antimony-bismuth, sodium-potassium-antimony, and copper-iodine. Dynode materials include the alkali metals and metal-oxide layers on a silver-magnesium alloy. Photomultipliers find use in scintillation counters for nuclear radiation detection, in space guidance systems (star and planet trackers), in facsimile transmission, and in apparatus that detects soft X rays coming from outer space.

photon [foh'-tahn]   A photon is a quantum of light, or the smallest possible packet of light at a given wavelength. It is emitted by an atom during a transition from one energy state to another. The energy released in the form of a photon is governed by the relationship $E_2 - E_1 = h\nu$, where E_2 and E_1 are the initial and final energies of the atom, h is PLANCK'S CONSTANT, and ν is the frequency of vibration of the emitted wave of light.

As FUNDAMENTAL PARTICLES, photons travel at the speed of light and have mass and momentum dependent on their frequencies. By classical reasoning a photon would have the apparent dualistic property of being either a particle or a wave disturbance. That is, such phenomena as INTERFERENCE and diffraction require an interpretation in terms of the wave characteristics of photons, but such phenomena as the PHOTOELECTRIC EFFECT require an interpretation in terms of the particle nature of the photon. Quantum mechanics is able to resolve this dilemma by assigning probabilistic characteristics to the motions of atoms and photons.

The energy associated with an individual photon is quite minute. A perfectly efficient 100–watt light bulb would emit approximately 2.5×10^{20} photons per second.

photorealism   An art form that began in the late 1960s, photorealism, or superrealism, stresses photographic accuracy of image, focusing on illusionistic rendering of three-dimensional objects on a flat picture surface. International in scope, photorealism was the successor to pop art. The main proponents of photorealism in painting include the American artists Chuck CLOSE, Richard ESTES, and Alfred Leslie. These artists have chosen as subject matter such features of contemporary American life as advertisements, or city streets. Their work is detailed, technically refined, and maintains a photographic fidelity to appearance—in fact, the paintings are often based on actual photographs or slides. Photorealism is also represented by the sculpture of Duane HANSON, who uses carefully selected, realistic details and accessories in his work, which depicts life sized, ordinary individuals.

photosphere   see STAR; SUN

photosynthesis   Photosynthesis is the biological process by which the energy of sunlight is absorbed and used to power the formation of organic compounds from carbon dioxide and water. Although primarily associated with green plants, photosynthesis also occurs in algae and a limited number of bacteria, where current theory suggests it first evolved. This process ultimately supplies the energy required by all living organisms for their continued survival.

The Photosynthetic Process

The photosynthetic process is divided into two stages: absorption of light energy and carbon fixation. These are known as the light phase and the dark phase, respectively.

Light Absorption. Chlorophyll-pigment molecules ab-sorb, or trap, light energy from the Sun. The electron-transport system of photosynthetic cells subsequently converts this absorbed energy into a biologically useful form in two high energy molecules, ATP (adenosine triphosphate) and NADPH (nicotinamide adenine dinucleotide phosphate).

Carbon Fixation. Carbon fixation, or carbon assimilation, involves using the energy contained in the ATP and NADPH to drive reactions that form organic compounds, such as starch and sugars, from the simple molecules of carbon dioxide and water. The organic compounds formed sustain all life either directly, in the case of the photosynthetic organism itself or any organism that consumes it, or indirectly, in the case of larger animals higher in the food chain.

Splitting of Water. One important outcome of the photosynthetic reaction is that light energy splits the water molecule so that one of its component atoms, oxygen, is released as molecular oxygen and serves to replenish the atmospheric oxygen supply, which would otherwise be depleted rapidly by respiration processes of organisms and by the burning of substances. Photosynthetic processes also result in consumption of the carbon dioxide produced by respiration. These two reactions are summarized as follows:

respiration: organic compounds + oxygen → carbon dioxide + water

photosynthesis: carbon dioxide + water → organic compounds + oxygen

Thus, photosynthetic processes are basically the opposite of those of respiration.

History

The Greek philosopher ARISTOTLE may have been the first to attempt to explain the processes of photosynthesis and food production. He believed that plants could obtain from the soil all the components that they require for growth. The cycle was complete when organisms perished and became reincorporated into the soil.

This view was not seriously challenged until the 17th century with the experiments of Johannes Baptista van Helmont, a Belgian physician. He carefully measured the weight increase of a willow planted in soil, to which he periodically added only rainwater. The plant increased in weight by 77 kg (169 lb), and the soil decreased in weight by 57 gm (2 oz). He deduced that it was water, and not substances in the soil, that provided plants with their growth material. Later, in the early 18th century, Stephen Hales conjectured that light and air might be significant factors in the growth of plants.

Foundations of Modern Theory. The classical experiments (1771) of Joseph PRIESTLEY laid the foundations of the modern photosynthetic theory. He discovered that plants use a component of the atmosphere in their life processes. Jan Ingen-Housz in 1779 and Jean Senebier in 1796 refined Priestley's ideas and established the role of light in photosynthesis. Ingen-Housz recognized that plants use carbon dioxide to obtain carbon in order to build organic molecules, and that they release oxygen into the atmosphere. That plants need water in the process was demonstrated by careful quantitative experiments of Nicholas Theodore De Saussure. With the formulation of the theory of energy conservation in 1845 by Julius Robert Mayer, the function of light as the energy source for the photosynthetic process began to be understood.

Elucidation of the Photosynthetic Process. Once the basic elements of photosynthesis were defined, research was begun on the details of the process. George G. Stokes and Henry C. Sorby described the chemical structure of chlorophyll. By 1913, Richard Willstätter and A. Stoll had published the empirical formulas of chlorophylls *a* and *b*. In the 1920s, Otto H. Warburg and Warbus Negelein demonstrated that photosynthesis consists of several distinct steps and that a variety of molecules are involved in the photosynthetic reaction.

The nature of biological electron-transport molecules in many systems began to be elucidated in the 1930s. In 1937, Robert Hill showed that extracted chloroplasts still could release oxygen from water in the presence of a suitable hydrogen acceptor; as a result of this experiment, he established the concept of a light-activated electron-transporting photosynthetic chain that releases oxygen from water. In the late 1940s, Melvin CALVIN and his co-workers elucidated the pathway of carbon fixation.

Site of Photosynthesis in Plants

Chloroplasts, in which the entire process of photosynthesis occurs, are the tiny green organelles inside the cells of green plant tissue. They were first observed by Hugo von Mohl in 1837, but their role in photosynthesis was not fully understood until the experiments of Julius von Sachs nearly 30 years later, which showed that starch was produced only in those chloroplasts which were exposed to light.

Chloroplasts generally are 4 to 6 microns in length, 1 to 2 microns in width, and somewhat discoid or ellipsoid. The chloroplast envelope that surrounds them is composed of two lipoprotein membranes, each 60 Å thick. Inside this envelope is a complex array of membranes (lamellae) in a granular fluid known as the stroma. The lamellae are paired to form disklike structures called thylakoids, which tend to be stacked to form ordered structures called grana. The grana are connected sporadically by unstacked thylakoids.

Molecules involved in light absorption and the formation of ATP and NADPH are membrane-bound and associated with the thylakoids; those molecules associated with carbon fixation are located in the stroma. Electron microscopic techniques have revealed two different types of particles within the thylakoid membranes, and presumably these particles contain the chlorophyll and proteins of the electron-transport system. Chloroplasts also produce protein molecules by means of their own DNA and ribosome complement, which provide the necessary genetic information.

The major light receptors in higher plants are the chlorophyll molecules. These molecules are similar in structure to the heme molecule of red blood cells, having a porphyrin ring to which an atom of magnesium is at-

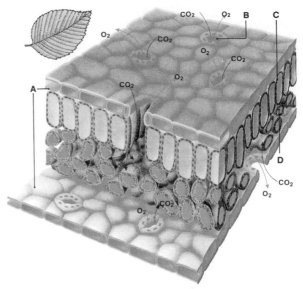

The leaf of a typical vascular plant contains several specialized cell layers. On the upper and lower surfaces a protective layer of epidermal cells (A), coated with a waxy cuticle, restricts water loss. Stomata (B), openings in the epidermis, permit gases, such as oxygen (O_2) and carbon dioxide (CO_2), to enter and escape from the leaf. The palisade layer (C) consists of column-shaped cells containing chloroplasts, the sites of photosynthesis. Cells of the mesophyll (D), below the palisade layer, contain fewer chloroplasts.

tached. They are green because they have very strong red and blue absorption bands in the visible region of the light spectrum where solar energy has its maximum output. The cells do not absorb green bands well, which therefore are reflected. Two types, chlorophylls *a* and *b*, have slightly different absorption bands and allow a greater portion of the visible light quanta to be absorbed. Other red, yellow, and orange pigments—the carotenoids and xanthophylls—aid in the absorption of light energy that falls between the bands of the chlorophylls. Carotenoids and xanthophylls pass the absorbed light energy to chlorophylls for conversion to chemical energy.

The pigments are arranged into large units, each containing as many as 600 chlorophyll molecules. In each unit, however, only one chemically reactive chlorophyll is present. It is termed the *reaction center chlorophyll*. The remainder are termed *antennae pigments*.

The Light and Dark Reactions

Light Reactions. There are two light reactions in higher plant photosynthesis. Both involve chlorophyll in a reaction center. When the first of these reaction centers absorbs a light quantum, the chlorophyll becomes oxidized—that is, it loses an electron, which becomes "excited" as it acquires additional energy. The oxidized chlorophyll is capable, in turn, of oxidizing water by removing hydrogen atoms and releasing oxygen.

The electron removed from the chlorophyll during the first light reaction passes down a chain of electron-transport proteins to the second reaction-center chlorophyll.

Here, a second quantum of light is absorbed. This causes the electron to leave the chlorophyll and eventually reduce NADP to its energy-rich form, NADPH.

In addition, as electrons pass along the electron-transfer sequence, energy is released and is used to drive the formation of ATP from its precursors, ADP (adenosine diphosphate) and inorganic phosphate. The process, called photophosphorylation, presumably is similar to the process of oxidative phosphorylation, which occurs when ATP is produced during respiration in mitochondria.

The ATP is used, together with the NADPH, to drive the dark reactions.

Dark Reactions. The dark phase is a strictly chemical process that does not use light. It consists of a complex series of enzyme-catalyzed reactions in which the carbon of carbon dioxide is incorporated into glucose and various other carbohydrates (sugars and starches). In the process, the energy absorbed from the Sun's light during the light reactions becomes trapped within the organic molecules.

All the steps in photosynthesis are commonly summarized by the following, highly simplified equation:

$$\text{Energy} + 6CO_2 + 6H_2O \rightarrow C_6H_{12}O_6 + 6O_2$$

This equation is read as "energy plus six molecules of carbon dioxide (CO_2) plus six molecules of water (H_2O) will produce one molecule of glucose ($C_6H_{12}O_6$) plus six molecules of oxygen (O_2)." Glucose, a simple sugar, or monosaccharide, is the main organic compound formed during photosynthesis.

Other end products of the dark reactions include starch and sucrose. Starch is a polysaccharide that acts as the main energy reserve in plant cells. It is synthesized in the chloroplasts. Sucrose, a sugar, is not synthesized in the chloroplast but in the cytoplasm. Therefore, carbon atoms to be used to manufacture sucrose must leave the chloroplast. This step is achieved by a specific transporting molecule in the chloroplast membrane.

Photorespiration. The key enzyme in the dark reactions is ribulose-1,5-diphosphate carboxylase, formerly known as carboxydismutase. In addition to its normal reaction with carbon dioxide, it can catalyze the reaction of the sugar ribulose-1,5-diphosphate with oxygen. This process, known as photorespiration, leads to carbon dioxide production and oxygen uptake. Photorespiration is particularly wasteful when the carbon dioxide level in cells is much less than in the surrounding air; for instance, when photosynthesis is occurring in high light intensities or at high temperatures, or when the plant has to restrict the opening of its stomata—the tiny pores through which carbon dioxide enters and oxygen leaves the plant—in order to restrict water loss by transpiration.

Special Adaptations

Many species of plants have adapted in particular ways to their environment. For instance, plants inhabiting salty or dry habitats have developed photorespiration mechanisms. Many tropical and subtropical plants expend additional photosynthetically generated ATP in order to increase the carbon dioxide concentration in the chloro-

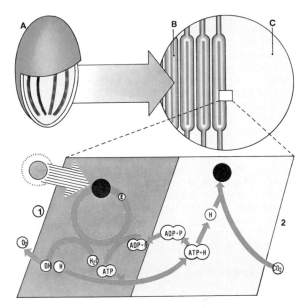

Photosynthesis, the conversion of light energy to chemical energy, occurs in chloroplasts (A), which consist of membranous grana (B) embedded in a fluid medium, the stroma (C). Absorption of light (1) takes place in the grana. Chlorophyll molecules (green) trap light energy and release electrons (E); this initiates a complex series of reactions that split water (H_2O) into hydrogen (H) and hydroxyl (OH) units, form adenosine diphosphate (ADP) and phosphate (P), and give off oxygen gas (O_2). Carbon fixation (2) occurs in the stroma and does not require light. Carbon dioxide (CO_2) from the air is reduced by hydrogen and built into starch (brown) and other energy-storing compounds. These reactions are driven by the energy released when ATP is converted back to ADP and P.

plasts; such plants show virtually no photorespiration. They are called C_4 plants because the initial product of carbon dioxide fixation is a four-carbon acid, as opposed to the three-carbon acid produced in other plants. Taxonomically, C_4 plants are very diverse, and of this group grasses have been studied in the greatest detail. Several genera are known that have both C_4 and C_3 species.

Another adaptation, associated with slow growth but very efficient in conservation of water, is crassulacean-acid metabolism (CAM). Carbon dioxide is fixed into C_4 acids during the night, and during the day the stomata are closed and light energy is used to release carbon dioxide from the C_4 acids. Cacti and succulents, which grow in habitats where daytime humidity is very low, utilize this type of metabolism.

Current Research in Photosynthesis

Although much has been learned about many of the steps in the photosynthetic process, large gaps in understanding the entire phenomenon still remain. For example, only a small percentage of the light energy that falls on the plant actually is involved in synthesizing useful biological end products. A very active field of investigation at present is concerned with trying to maximize the efficiency of the process in various plant species so that a greater crop yield may be obtained from a fixed amount of land. This may possibly be achieved, for example, by exploiting the enzyme commonly called RuBisCo, which catalyzes the slowest step in photosynthesis. If this enzyme can be modified using genetic-engineering techniques, it may be able to accelerate the catalytic process and create faster-growing plants.

At present, research is also being devoted to the development of efficient artificial photosynthetic systems. Such systems would be of great importance in the large-scale production of solar energy. The problem is to devise a photosynthesis-mimicking molecule that remains polarized long enough to react usefully with other molecules. Thanks to recent advances in delineating the structure of a photosynthetic reaction center, a variety of molecular components have been synthesized for possible use in artificial photosynthesis. This research has also proved to be extremely useful for elucidating basic natural photosynthetic principles.

phototypesetting see TYPE AND TYPESETTING

---

phrenology [fruh-nahl'-uh-jee] Phrenology attempted to understand human characteristics, or faculties, by interpreting the shape and bumps of the skull. It reached its greatest popularity in the early 1800s through the writings and lectures of Franz Joseph Gall and Johannes Spurzheim, although journals and societies of phrenology survived into the 1900s. Phrenology assumed that the faculties are localized in the brain, and that highly developed faculties are evidenced by enlarged brain areas that show in the conformation of the skull. These assumptions are completely rejected by science, although the idea that faculties are localized bears a very primitive relationship to the actual localization of function that occurs in the central nervous system.

Phrygia [frij'-ee-uh] Phrygia, a region occupying the west central Anatolian plateau, was named for the European tribe of the Phryges, which had penetrated Anatolia near the end of the 2d millennium BC. Mentioned in the *Iliad* of Homer as warrior allies of the Trojans, the Phrygians established a thriving kingdom, perhaps during the 8th century BC, with Gordion as its capital. Following a Cimmerian invasion (*c.*700 BC), Phrygia was absorbed in turn by Lydia and Persia in the 6th century and later by the Seleucids, Attalids, and Romans. Phrygian artists excelled at metalwork, rock sculptures, and temple facades. Phrygia's religion was known for its mother goddess worship and Dionysiac cults. The semilegendary King MIDAS was a Phrygian.

Phyfe, Duncan [fyf] One of America's most important and influential cabinetmakers, Duncan Phyfe, b. Scotland, 1768, d. Aug. 16, 1854, brought to New York the English REGENCY STYLE and produced furniture after the designs of Thomas SHERATON, George Smith, and Tho-

mas Hope. His fine-figured mahogany veneers, moldings around drawers and edges, reeding, fluting, carved and brass ornaments, and satinwood interiors made the Phyfe workshop the most successful of its period. During the long span of his working career (1792–1847) Phyfe also produced furniture in the French DIRECTOIRE and EMPIRE STYLES in competition with the French émigré cabinetmaker Charles Honoré Lannuier.

By 1815, Phyfe's New York City business had expanded to three buildings (workshops, warehouse, and showrooms) in which more than a hundred craftsmen were employed. Fashionable and prolific, he supplied furniture to markets in Boston, Philadelphia, and Baltimore as well as New York.

---

phylogeny [fil-ah'-juh-nee] Phylogeny is the evolutionary history of a taxonomic group, such as a species or a group of related species. ONTOGENY, in contrast, is the developmental history of an individual from the time of conception. As a scientific discipline, phylogeny arises from the theory of evolution, the fundamental thesis of which is that different species are descended from common ancestors. Phylogenists attempt to determine the lines of descent of species—and the degree to which they are related—by comparing embryonic and adult anatomical features of contemporary species to those of fossils. Many gaps exist in the fossil record, however, because fossil discoveries usually occur by chance. As a result, the evolutionary histories of many species contain so-called missing links and are known only in broad and tentative outline.

See also: EVOLUTION.

---

physical chemistry Physical chemistry is one of the basic divisions of the science of chemistry (the others being analytical, inorganic, and organic chemistry and biochemistry). It deals with the structure of matter and the energy changes that occur during physical and chemical transformations and attempts to create a theoretical basis for chemical observations and to predict chemical reactions. As its name indicates, this branch of chemistry may be considered the interface of chemistry (the study of the nature of matter) and physics (the study of energy), and it is sometimes called chemical physics.

Whereas the term *physical chemistry* has been used since the 18th century, many agree that physical chemistry as a subdiscipline of chemistry had its formal beginning with the establishment of the *Zeitschrift für physikalische Chemie* (Journal of Physical Chemistry) in 1887 by Wilhelm OSTWALD. Until 1900 physical chemistry was dominated by chemists at German universities. Early physical chemical research included studies on the dissociation of electrolytes in solutions by Svante ARRHENIUS, solution studies by Jacobus VAN'T HOFF and Ostwald, and studies on electrochemistry and thermodynamics by Walther NERNST. Physical chemistry became more established as a branch of chemistry as the students of these early researchers moved to other countries.

During the 20th century, the scope of physical chemistry broadened to the extent that at present physical chemistry is considered to encompass all aspects of chemical equilibrium, structure, and change, including increasingly precise measurement of chemical systems and the proposal of models and theories to adequately explain these observations. For approximately 50 years, physical chemistry has utilized increasingly complex mathematical and statistical methods to describe chemical systems and the changes that they undergo. The computer is now an essential component of research in many areas.

Physical chemistry focuses on various individual topics, such as the states of aggregation (solid or otherwise) of substances, the properties of these states, the forces involved in maintaining them, transitions from one state to another (see PHASE EQUILIBRIUM), and the properties and reactions that take place at the interface between different phases (for example, the chemistry of ADHESION). It studies the arrangement of the components of matter on the atomic and molecular scales, the forces between FUNDAMENTAL PARTICLES in ATOMS, and the nature of the CHEMICAL BONDS and other forces that give rise to the geometries of large molecules and complex ions. CHEMICAL KINETICS AND EQUILIBRIUM is another focus of physical chemistry. This topic includes study of the velocity of reactions from the atomic to the molecular level, the factors that influence these velocities, and the forces that bring reactions to a state of equilibrium. The laws of THERMODYNAMICS as they apply to chemical systems are studied, with particular interest being paid to the energy released during reactions and the conversion of this energy to useful work. The physical and chemical properties of SOLUTIONS are also studied, as are the forces between the particles involved.

All these subjects may be grouped within the field of theoretical chemistry, which takes a detailed mathematical approach to the consideration of fundamental physical and chemical properties and changes. A number of other specialized fields of physical chemistry can also be defined. For example, rheology is the study of the deformation and flow of matter. ELECTROCHEMISTRY is the study of ions in the liquid state, or in solutions, as they react to liberate electrical energy under appropriate circumstances, or as they react under the influence of an external electromotive force. PHOTOCHEMISTRY is concerned with the interactions of light and matter and the transformations that occur as a result of the absorption of photons of varying energy by atoms and molecules. Polymer chemistry studies the formation, structure, and properties of macromolecules (rubber, plastics, synthetic fibers) that are made up of repeating units. Rather than trying to divide physical chemistry into such separate fields, however, some scientists instead look on it as a fundamental approach to all the areas of chemistry in general.

physical education Physical education may be viewed as a program of activity in a school curriculum, as a discipline to be studied, or as a profession such as teacher or coach. In all its aspects it is concerned with the motor skills needed in such activities as games, sports, dance, and exercise. It is a vital and integral part of general education.

The objectives of physical education are to encourage body development and fitness; psychomotor development and sport skills; knowledge and understanding of sports, exercise, health, and safety; and affective development, including emotional and social behavior.

In the school curriculum, physical education comprises games, sports, dance, gymnastics, and exercise. Courses in and knowledge of physical education are requirements in all states (although local school districts may have their own requirements) for at least some grades and are offered with elective credit in secondary schools and in colleges. Curricula are based on age, sex, and grade levels, with the emphasis on motor skills, fitness, health, recreation, and safety. Great emphasis is placed on the interrelationship of the physical, mental, and social benefits of health.

Training as a professional in physical education involves preparation at the undergraduate level for teachers and coaches. It combines the liberal arts with specialized courses in physical education. At the graduate level the discipline has numerous specialties and subdisciplines, such as exercise physiology, motor learning, kinesiology, biomechanics, sociology of sport, and psychology of sport.

See also: SPORTS MEDICINE.

physical therapy Physical therapy is the field of medical care that uses exercise and such physical agents as heat, light, water, and massage to treat certain physical disabilities. Among its objectives are the relief of pain caused by surgery or by medical problems; the improvement of muscle strength and mobility; and the improvement of such basic functions as standing, walking, and grasping in patients who are recovering from debilitating illnesses or accidents or who are physically handicapped.

The physical therapist uses different types of rehabilitative treatment. Heat may be applied to ease stiffening and pain in the joints. Massage is used for easing pain and for improving circulation. HYDROTHERAPY is useful for the slow work of rebuilding wasted muscles. The most frequent type of treatment, however, is exercise, chosen to increase joint mobility or to improve muscle strength and coordination.

Patients with physical handicaps may be trained in learning or relearning elementary motor functions, such as holding a spoon or turning a doorknob, or they may be taught how to use crutches, prosthetic devices, or other mechanical aids.

Practicing therapists may work in hospitals and other health-care institutions, for physicians or for other therapists, for private or government agencies, in schools, or in private practice. Their work is often closely coordinated with that of the occupational therapist (see OCCUPATIONAL THERAPY) because both fields involve training patients to improve their motor abilities.

See also: REHABILITATION MEDICINE.

physically disabled, education of the see SPECIAL EDUCATION

physics Physics studies the different forms of MATTER, their properties, and the transformations that they undergo. From the beginnings of physics among the ancient Greeks, through its revival in late Renaissance Europe and its flowering in the 19th and 20th centuries, there have been continual increases in the breadth of phenomena studied by physicists and in the depth of understanding of these phenomena (see PHYSICS, HISTORY OF). During this growth of the science, physicists have discovered general laws, such as the conservation of energy, that apply throughout space and time.

Matter and Its Transformations

Originally, matter referred to anything evident to the senses, such as SOLIDS and LIQUIDS, and possessing properties such as weight. As the scope of physics has expanded, however, so has the range of the concept of matter. Gases are now included, as are the near-vacuums of outer space and those attained in scientific laboratories (see VACUUM). Individual subatomic particles are now considered to be the ultimate constituents of matter, even though some of them lack properties of mass and specific location (see FUNDAMENTAL PARTICLES). Today matter is broadly identified as anything that interacts with the familiar types of matter, by exchanging such qualities as ENERGY and MOMENTUM.

The earliest transformation of matter to be studied by physicists was MOTION, which is treated in the branch of physics called MECHANICS. The LAWS OF MOTION were codified in the 17th century by Isaac NEWTON, who provided a physical explanation of the motions of celestial bodies. In the 19th century physics was extended to study changes in physical form that take place, as, for example, when a liquid freezes and becomes a solid. Such changes of state are studied in the branch of physics called THERMODYNAMICS. Other changes in the form of matter, for example, those which occur when oxygen and hydrogen combine into water, are usually considered to be part of CHEMISTRY rather than physics. This distinction is somewhat arbitrary, however, since ideas from physics are routinely used in chemistry.

New transformations have been discovered among subatomic particles. One type of particle can change into another, and particles can be created and destroyed. In descriptions of subatomic particles using the physical theory called quantum field theory (see QUANTUM MECHANICS), such particle creations and destructions are taken as the fundamental events out of which all other transformations are built.

Microphysics, Macrophysics, and Methodology

Physics is divided into subdisciplines, as already noted, according to subject matter. The broadest division is between microphysics, which studies subatomic particles and their combinations in ATOMS and MOLECULES, and macrophysics, which studies large collections of subatomic particles such as the solid bodies of everyday experience.

Different experimental methods are used in these two divisions. In microphysics the objects under study usually are observed indirectly, as in the use of DETECTORS to observe the record of the passage of subatomic particles. Consequently, much theoretical analysis stands between the observations and their interpretation. Most individual subatomic systems can be studied only for short periods of time. It is therefore very difficult to follow a microscopic phenomenon in detail over time, even to the extent that physical laws allow this. In macrophysics, however, phenomena are usually directly observable, and less theoretical analysis is needed to determine what is happening. Furthermore, since individual systems can usually be observed over long periods of time, their evolution can be analyzed and can often be predicted.

Differences between microphysics and macrophysics also exist in the laws that apply. In microphysics the fundamental laws are those of quantum mechanics, whose descriptions are fundamentally statistical. They only allow probabilities to be predicted for individual events, such as radioactive decays. In macrophysics, fundamental laws such as Newton's laws of motion are deterministic, and, in principle, precise predictions can be made about individual events. For some macroscopic systems, however, it is necessary to use statistical methods because of difficulties in treating large numbers of objects individually.

Basic Ideas of Physics

Discoveries in physics have shown that most natural phenomena can be understood in terms of a few basic concepts and laws. Some of these are apparent in everyday macroscopic phenomena, others only in the microscopic world. The idea that the world is made up of small objects in motion goes back to ancient Greece and the atomic theories of LEUCIPPUS and DEMOCRITUS. Such objects are called particles, and modern physics has discovered a variety of fundamental particles. The concept of space as an arena in which physical objects move is an outgrowth of the ancient idea of a void. TIME, regarded as a flow that exists independent of human perception, seems necessary to allow for physical changes. In fact, Einstein recognized an important connection between time and space in his special theory of RELATIVITY.

Many physical laws describe how systems change with time, including laws of motion and laws of CONSERVATION. Examples of the latter are the laws of conservation of angular momentum and of electric charge. Conservation laws follow from the fact that the laws describing physical systems remain unchanged when the systems are viewed from different perspectives. Such SYMMETRY considerations play major roles in relativity theory and quantum physics, where they are used to constrain laws and infer their consequences.

The work of 19th-century physicists showed that it is useful to think of electric and magnetic forces between two objects some distance apart as being generated by a two-step process. Each object influences the surrounding space, and this altered condition of space produces a force on the other object. The space in which this influence resides is said to contain an electric or magnetic field. Maxwell was able to summarize all of the theory of electromagnetism in terms of four equations describing the mutual effects of electric charges and magnetic fields. One implication of his work was that fields can become detached from the charges that produce them and travel through space (see ELECTROMAGNETIC RADIATION). In the 20th century a union of field theory with quantum mechanics led to quantum field theory, the most fundamental description of nature now available.

For systems containing many elementary objects, the mathematical problems of solving the equations of motion are prohibitive. An alternative method often used involves calculating only the average behavior of the constituents. This approach is used in the branch of physics known as statistical mechanics, developed in the late 1800s by Maxwell, Ludwig BOLTZMANN, and Josiah Willard GIBBS. They showed that many of the results of thermodynamics, previously an independent subject, could be inferred by applying statistical reasoning to the Newtonian mechanics of gases. Statistical mechanics has also been applied to systems described by quantum theory, where the type of statistics used must recognize the indistinguishability of identical subatomic particles.

In prequantum physics, physical quantities were assumed to have continuously variable magnitudes. For many quantities this is now recognized to be an illusion based on the large size of ordinary bodies compared to subatomic particles. In quantum theory, some quantities can only take on certain discrete values, often described by simple integers. This discreteness, as well as the mathematical rules enforcing it, is known as quantization. Usually a quantum description of a system can be obtained from the corresponding Newtonian description by adding suitable rules of quantization.

Current and Future Physics

Physics continues to be extended in many directions. The evolution of complex systems and the development of order are areas of current concern. The relation between the early universe and the properties of subatomic particles is another active field of study (see COSMOLOGY). Attempts to replace quantum field theory by some new description are under serious consideration, in the hope that they will allow general relativity to be merged with quantum theory (see GRAND UNIFICATION THEORIES). At the same time, new experimental techniques are allowing physicists today to observe matter at the atomic level.

See also: ASTRONOMY AND ASTROPHYSICS; BIOPHYSICS; GEOPHYSICS; NUCLEAR PHYSICS; PHYSICAL CHEMISTRY; PLASMA PHYSICS; SOLID-STATE PHYSICS.

---

physics, history of   The growth of physics has brought not only fundamental changes in ideas about the material world, but also, through technology based on laboratory discoveries, a transformation of society. Physics will be considered in this article chiefly as a body of knowledge rather than as the practice that makes and transmits it. Physics acquired its classical form between the late Renaissance and the end of the 19th century. The year 1900 is a convenient boundary between classical and modern physics.

The title page of Galileo's Dialogo dei due massimi sistemi del mundo *(Dialogue Concerning the Two Chief World Systems), published in 1632, depicts Copernicus (right) debating his heliocentric model of the universe with Aristotle and Ptolemy. In this influential work Galileo strongly attacked Aristotelian and Ptolemaic physics.*

The Development of Main Branches

The main branches of classical physics are mechanics, electricity and magnetism, light, and heat and thermodynamics.

Mechanics. The first branch of physics to yield to mathematical description was mechanics. Although the ancients had quantified a few problems concerning the balance and hydrostatics, and medieval philosophers had discussed possible mathematical descriptions of free-fall, not until the beginning of the 17th century was the desideratum of quantification brought into confrontation with received principles of physics. The chief challenger was GALILEO GALILEI, who began with a medieval explanation of motion, the so-called impetus theory, and ended by doing without an explicit dynamics. To him it was enough that, as a first step, the physicist should describe quantitatively how objects fall and projectiles fly.

Galileo's kinematical approach did not please René DESCARTES, who insisted that the physicist attack received principles from a knowledge of the nature of bodies. Descartes gave out this knowledge as laws of motion, almost all incorrect, but including a strong statement of the principle of rectilinear inertia, which was to become Isaac NEWTON's first axiom of motion. Another Cartesian principle important for Newton was the universalizing of mechanics. In Aristotelian physics the heavens consist of material not found on earth. The progress of astronomy had undermined Aristotle's distinction, and Newton, like Descartes, explicitly unified celestial and terrestrial mechanics.

In Descartes's system bodies interact only by pushing, and space devoid of body is a contradiction in terms. Hence the motion of any one object must set up a vortex involving others. The planets are swept around by such a whirlpool; another carries the Moon, creates the tides, and causes heavy bodies to fall; still others mediate the interactions of objects at or near the Earth's surface. Newton tried to build a quantitative celestial vortical mechanics, but could not; book 2 of his *Principia* records his proof that vortices that obey the mechanical axioms posited for terrestrial matter cannot transport planets according to KEPLER'S LAWS. On the assumption of universal gravitation, however, Newton could derive Kepler's laws and tie together planetary motions, the tides, and the precession of the equinoxes. As one essential step in the derivation, Newton used Galileo's rule about distance traversed under constant acceleration. He also required the assumption of "absolute space"—a preferred system of reference against which accelerations could be defined.

After receiving their definitive analytic form from Leonhard EULER, Newton's axioms of motion were reworked by Joseph Louis de LAGRANGE, William Rowan HAMILTON, and Carl Gustav Jacobi into very powerful and general methods, which employed new analytic quantities, such as potential, related to force but remote from immediate experience. Despite these triumphs, some physicists nonetheless retained scruples against the concept of force. Several schemes for doing without it were proposed, notably by Joseph John THOMSON and Heinrich HERTZ, but nothing very useful came from them.

Electricity and Magnetism. Up to 1750 physicists accepted a theory of electricity little different from that of the 16th century natural philosopher William Gilbert: the rubbing of electric bodies forces them to emit an electrical matter or ether that causes attractions and repulsions either directly or by mobilizing the air. The theory confused the roles of charges and their field. The invention of the Leyden jar (1745) made clear the confusion, if not its source; only Benjamin FRANKLIN's theory of plus and minus electricity, probably developed without reference to the Leyden jar, proved able to account for it. Franklin asserted that the accumulation of electric matter within the Leyden jar (the plus charge) acted at a distance across

the bottom to expel other electrical matter to ground, giving rise to the minus charge. Distance forces thus entered the theory of electricity. Their action was quantified by F. U. T. Aepinus (1759), by Henry CAVENDISH (1771), and by Charles A. COULOMB, who in 1785 showed that the force between elements of the hypothetical electrical matter(s) or fluid(s) diminished as the square of the distance. (The uncertainty regarding the number of fluids arises because many physicists then preferred the theory introduced by Robert Symmer in 1759, which replaced Franklin's absence of electrical matter, negative electricity, with the presence of a second electrical fluid.) Since the elementary electrical force followed the same law as the gravitational, the mathematics of the potential theory lay ready for exploitation by the electrician. The quantification of electrostatics was accomplished early in the 19th century, principally by Siméon Denis Poisson.

In 1800, Alessandro VOLTA announced the invention of a continuous generator of electricity, a "pile" of disks of silver, zinc, and moist cardboard. This invention—the first battery—opened two extensive new fields: ELECTRO-CHEMISTRY, of which the first dramatic results were Humphry DAVY's isolation of the alkali metals, and electromagnetism, based on the healing of the breech opened by Gilbert in 1600.

The discovery in 1820 by Hans Christian Oersted that the wire connecting the poles of a voltaic cell could exert a force on a magnetic needle was followed in 1831 by Michael FARADAY's discovery that a magnet could cause a current to flow in a closed loop of wire. The facts that the electromagnetic force depends on motion and does not lie along the line between current elements made it difficult to bring the new discoveries within the scheme of distance forces. Certain continental physicists—at first André Marie AMPÈRE, then Wilhelm Eduard WEBER and

(Above) *Benjamin Franklin's hazardous attempt to prove the electrical nature of lightning was the best-known of his contributions to the study of electricity. Before Franklin, physicists generally had viewed electricity as a material substance.*

(Below) *Michael Faraday's lectures at the Royal Institution were heavily attended, but only a few physicists of his day grasped the importance of Faraday's research on electromagnetic induction and lines of force.*

Rudolf CLAUSIUS, and others—admitted forces dependent on relative velocities and accelerations.

The hope that electric and magnetic interactions might be elucidated without recourse to forces acting over macroscopic distances persisted after the work of Coulomb. In this tradition, Faraday placed the seat of electromagnetic forces in the medium between bodies interacting electrically. His usage remained obscure to all but himself until William Thomson (Lord KELVIN) and James Clerk MAXWELL expressed his insights in the language of Cambridge mathematics. Maxwell's synthesis of electricity, magnetism, and light resulted. Many British physicists and, after Heinrich Hertz's detection of electromagnetic waves (1887), several continental ones, tried to devise an ether obedient to the usual mechanical laws whose stresses and strains could account for the phenomena covered by Maxwell's equations.

In the early 1890s, Hendrik Antoon Lorentz worked out a successful compromise. From the British he took the idea of a mediating ether, or field, through which electromagnetic disturbances propagate in time. From continental theory he took the concept of electrical charges, which he made the sources of the field. He dismissed the presupposition that the field should be treated as a mechanical system—that it should be assigned any properties needed to account for the phenomena. For example, to explain the result of the MICHELSON-MORLEY EXPERIMENT, Lorentz supposed that objects moving through the ether contract along their line of motion. Among the unanalyzed and perhaps unanalyzable properties of the ether is the ability to shorten bodies moving through it.

In 1896-97, Lorentz's approach received support from the Zeeman effect, which confirmed the presence of electrical charges in neutral atoms, and from the isolation of the electron, which could be identified as the source of the field. The electron pulled together many loose ends of 19th century physics and suggested that the appearances of matter itself, including its inertia, might arise from moving drops of electric fluid. But the electron did not save the ether. Continuing failure to find effects arising from motion against it and, above all, certain asymmetries in the electrodynamics of moving bodies, caused Albert EINSTEIN to reject the ether and, with it, the last vestige of Newton's concept of absolute space.

Light. Traditional theory took white light to be homogeneous and colors to be impurities or modifications. From his discovery that colors are refracted by different amounts through a prism, Newton inferred that they are primitive and homogeneous, and he portrayed their constituents as particles. This model also conflicted with the ordinary one. For example, Christiaan HUYGENS, who did not bother about colors, gave a beautiful account of the propagation of light, including an explanation of birefringence, on the supposition that light consists of longitudinal waves in a pervasive medium.

Newton also required an optical ether to explain phenomena now referred to as interference between light waves. The emission of particles sets the ether vibrating, and the vibrations impose periodic properties on the particles. Although many 18th-century physicists preferred a

Sir Isaac Newton's discovery that white light is a mixture of colors disconcerted scientists of his day. Equally upsetting was his theory that light is particulate rather than wavelike in form. The Newtonian view predominated into the 19th century.

wave theory in the style of Huygens, none succeeded in devising one competitive with Newton's. Progress in optics took place mainly in fields Newton had not investigated, such as photometry, and in the correction of lenses for chromatic aberration, which he had not thought possible.

In the first years of the 19th century Thomas YOUNG, a close student of Newton's work and an expert on the theory of vibrations, showed how to quantify Huygens's theory. Young succeeded in explaining certain cases of interference; Augustin Jean FRESNEL soon built an extensive analytical theory based on Young's principle of superposition. Newton's light particles, which fit well with the special fluids assumed in theories of heat and electricity, found vigorous defenders, who emphasized the problem of polarization. In Newton's theory, polarization could be accommodated by ascribing different properties to the different "sides" of the particles, whereas Young's waves could be characterized only by amplitude (associated with intensity), period (color), phase (interference), and velocity (refraction). About 1820, Young and Fresnel independently found the missing degree of freedom in the assumption that the disturbances in light waves act at right angles to their direction of motion; polarization effects arise from the orientation of the disturbance to the optic axis of the polarizing body.

With the stipulation that light's vibrations are transverse, the wave theorists could describe simply and precisely a wide range of phenomena. They had trouble, however, in developing a model of the "luminiferous ether," the vibrations of which they supposed to constitute light. Many models were proposed likening the ether to an elastic solid. None fully succeeded. After Maxwell linked light and electromagnetism, the duties of the ether became more burdensome and ambiguous, until Lorentz and Einstein, in their different ways, removed it from subjection to mechanics.

Heat and Thermodynamics. About 1790, physicists began to consider the analytic consequences of the traditional assumption that the material base of heat, which they called caloric, was conserved. The caloric theory gave a satisfactory quantitative account of adiabatic processes in gases, including the propagation of sound,

Among the scientists participating in the 1927 session of the international Solvay Congress were several major shapers of 20th-century physics: Max Planck, Marie Curie, H. A. Lorentz, and Albert Einstein (second through fifth from left in first row); Paul Dirac, A. H. Compton, Louis de Broglie, Max Born, and Niels Bohr (fifth through ninth from left in second row); and Werner Heisenberg (third from right in last row).

which physicists had vainly sought to understand on mechanical principles alone. Another mathematical theory of caloric was Sadi Carnot's (see CARNOT family) analysis (1824) of the efficiency of an ideal, reversible heat engine, which seemed to rest on the assumption of a conserved material of heat.

In 1822, Joseph Fourier published his theory of heat conduction, developed using the trigonometrical series that bear his name (see FOURIER ANALYSIS), and without specifying the nature of heat. He thereby escaped the attack on the caloric theory by those who thought the arguments of Count Benjamin Rumford persuasive. Rumford had inferred from the continuous high temperatures of cannon barrels undergoing grinding that heat is created by friction and cannot be a conserved substance (see CONSERVATION, LAWS OF). His qualitative arguments could not carry the day against the caloric theory, but they gave grounds for doubt, to Carnot among others.

During the late 18th century physicists had speculated about the interrelations of the fluids they associated with light, heat, and electricity. When the undulatory theory indicated that light and radiant heat consisted of motion rather than substance, the caloric theory was undermined. Experiments by James Prescott JOULE in the 1840s showed that an electric current could produce either heat, or, through an electric motor, mechanical work; he inferred that heat, like light, was a state of motion, and he succeeded in measuring the heat generated by mechanical work. Joule had trouble gaining a hearing because his experiments were delicate and his results seemed to menace Carnot's.

In the early 1850s the conflict was resolved independently by Kelvin and by Clausius, who recognized that two distinct principles had been confounded. Joule correctly asserted that heat could be created and destroyed, and always in the same proportion to the amount of mechanical, electrical, or chemical force—or, to use the new term, "energy"—consumed or developed. This assertion is the first law of THERMODYNAMICS—the conservation of energy. Carnot's results, however, also hold; they rest not on conservation of heat but on that of ENTROPY, the quotient of

heat by the temperature at which it is exchanged. The second law of thermodynamics declares that in all natural processes entropy either remains constant or increases.

Encouraged by the reasoning of Hermann HELMHOLTZ and others, physicists took mechanical energy, the form of energy with which they were most familiar, as fundamental, and tried to represent other forms in terms of it. Maxwell and Ludwig BOLTZMANN set the foundations of a new branch of physics, the mechanical theory of heat, which included statistical considerations as an integral part of physical analysis for the first time. After striking initial successes, the theory foundered over the mechanical representation of entropy. The apparent opposition of the equations of mechanics (which have no direction in time) and the demands of the second law (which prohibits entropy from decreasing in the future) caused some physicists to doubt that mechanical reduction could ever be accomplished. A small, radical group led in the 1890s by the physical chemist Wilhelm OSTWALD went so far as to demand the rejection of all mechanical pictures, including the concept of atoms.

Although Ostwald's program of energetics had few followers and soon collapsed, the attack on mechanical models proved prescient. Other work about 1900—the discoveries of X rays and radioactivity, the development of the quantum theory and the theory of relativity—did eventually force physicists to relinquish in principle, if not in practice, reliance on the clear representations in space and time on which classical physics had been built.

Modern Physics

Around 1900 the understanding of the physical universe as a congeries of mechanical parts was shattered forever. In the decades before the outbreak of World War I came new experimental phenomena. The initial discoveries of RADIOACTIVITY and X rays were made by Antoine Henri BECQUEREL and Wilhelm Conrad ROENTGEN. These new phenomena were studied extensively, but only with Niels BOHR's first atomic theory in 1913 did a general, theoretical picture for the generation of X rays emerge. Radioactive decay was gradually clarified with the emergence of quantum mechanics, with the discovery of new FUNDAMENTAL PARTICLES, such as the neutron and the neutrino, and with countless experiments conducted using particle accelerators (see ACCELERATOR, PARTICLE).

The central, theoretical syntheses of 20th-century physics—the theories of RELATIVITY and QUANTUM MECHANICS—were only indirectly associated with the experimental research of most physicists. Albert Einstein and Wolfgang PAULI, for example, believed that experiment had to be the final arbiter of theory but that theories were far more imaginative than any inductivist assemblage of experimental data. During the first third of the century it became clear that the new ideas of physics required that physicists reexamine the philosophical foundations of their work. For this reason physicists came to be seen by the public as intellectual Brahmins who probed the dark mysteries of the universe. Excitement over reorganizing physical knowledge persisted through the 1920s. This decade saw the formulation of quantum mechanics and a new, indeterminist epistemology by Pauli, Werner Karl HEISENBERG, Max BORN, Erwin SCHRÖDINGER, and Paul DIRAC.

The early-20th-century vision of the universe issued principally from German-speaking Europe, in university environments where daily patterns of activity had been fixed since the 1880s. During the interwar period first-rate physics research operations flourished in such non-European environments as the United States, Japan, India, and Argentina. New patterns of activity, intimated in the pre-1914 world, finally crystallized. Physics research, such as that of Clinton Davisson (1881–1958) and William Thomas Astbury (1898–1961), came to be supported heavily by optical, electrical, and textile industries. The National Research Council and private foundations in the United States, notably the Rockefeller and Carnegie trusts, sponsored expensive and time-consuming experiments. European governments encouraged special research installations, including the Kaiser Wilhelm institutes and the Einstein Observatory in Potsdam, Germany. What has been called big physics emerged in the 1930s. Scores of physicists labored over complicated apparatus in special laboratories indirectly affiliated with universities. As one of the most significant consequences of the new institutional arrangements, it became increasingly difficult for a physicist to imitate scientists such as Enrico FERMI, who had mastered both the theoretical and the experimental sides of the discipline. Following the models provided in the careers of J. Robert OPPENHEIMER and Luis Walter ALVAREZ, the successful physicist became a manager who spent most of his or her time persuading scientifically untutored people to finance arcane research projects.

The awesome respect accorded to physicists by governments in the 1950s—when the United States and the Soviet Union carried out extensive research into thermonuclear weapons and launched artificial satellites—has been tempered in recent years. In part this new development is the result of a continuing emergence of new specialties; applied electronics and nuclear engineering, for example, until recently part of the physicists' domain, have become independent fields of study, just as physical chemistry, geophysics, and astrophysics split off from the mother discipline around 1900. At the same time, a number of physicists, such as Richard Phillips FEYNMAN, have come to emphasize the aesthetic value of their research more than its practical application.

In recent years, physicists have been at the center of major interdisciplinary syntheses in biophysics, solid-state physics, and astrophysics. The identification of the double-helix structure of DNA, the synthesis of complex protein molecules, and developments in genetic engineering all rest on advances in spectroscopy, X-ray crystallography, and electron microscopy. Semiconductor technology, at the base of the revolution in information processing, has been pioneered by solid-state physicists. Fundamental insights into the large-scale structure of the universe and its constituent parts have depended on harmonies previously revealed by theoretical physicists. This cross-fertilization has had an impact on physics itself; it has produced new understanding of basic physical laws ranging from those governing elementary particles to those in irreversible thermodynamic processes. Among all modern scientific disciplines, physics has been the most successful in maintaining a high public profile while adapting to new scientific and social circumstances.

physiocrats The physiocrats were an 18th-century group of French economists. Their leading member, François Quesnay (1694–1774), believed that land was the source of all wealth and that agriculture alone produced a clear surplus over the costs of production. All other activities, including manufacturing, trade, and commerce, were thought to be sterile, yielding no excess over the quantity of raw materials received. Quesnay's major work, the *Tableau économique* (1758), is the first known schematic portrayal of the workings of the entire economy.

The physiocrats reacted against MERCANTILISM, which emphasized manufacturing and burdened the French economy with massive restrictions on trade. They argued that supply and demand should prevail over government regulation and that a single tax on land should replace the multiplicity of existing taxes.

physiography see GEOMORPHOLOGY

physiology The branch of biology dealing with the functions of living organisms and their components is known as physiology. It basically describes life processes in terms of physics and chemistry. ANATOMY is the structural counterpart and the parent of physiology. In turn, the fields of biophysics, biochemistry, and molecular biology have developed from physiological research. Experimental physiology dates from the 17th century, when William HARVEY described blood circulation.

phytoplankton see PLANKTON

pi [py] The ratio of the circumference of a CIRCLE to its diameter is constant for all circles. This constant, called pi, is denoted by the Greek letter π of the same name. The constant is an IRRATIONAL NUMBER and hence cannot be expressed as a quotient of two integers or as a terminating decimal number, but it has been approximated by computer to 480 million digits. For most purposes the approximation $\pi = 3.1416$ is accurate enough.

Piaf, Edith [pee-ahf', ay-deet']   The French chanteuse Edith Piaf, b. Edith Giovanna Gassion in Paris, Dec. 19, 1915, d. Oct. 11, 1963, sang in a uniquely husky and emotion-laden voice that, by the end of her life, was recognized by millions. A street singer from the age of 15, she was given her stage name, Piaf—"sparrow" in Parisian argot—about 1930, when she began singing in nightclubs. She also appeared in the theater and in films. The song "La Vie en Rose," composed by Piaf, was her trademark.

Piaget, Jean [pee-ah-jay']   Jean Piaget, b. Neuchâtel, Switzerland, Aug. 9, 1896, d. Sept. 17, 1980, was one of the most influential experimenters and theorists in the history of DEVELOPMENTAL PSYCHOLOGY and the study of human intelligence. His scholarly productivity was enormous: he wrote more than 50 books and a far greater number of articles and lectures in psychology, epistemology, philosophy, logic, biology, sociology, and pedagogy.

In the course of standardizing a French version of an English intelligence test, Piaget became fascinated with his discovery that children of the same age often gave the same incorrect answers to questions. This suggested that there were consistent, qualitative differences in the nature of reasoning at different ages, not simply a quantitative increase in the amount of intelligence. This marked the beginning of Piaget's continuing effort painstakingly to identify changes in the way children think—how they perceive their world in different ways at different points in development. His conception of intelligence was both grounded in the concept of biological adaptation and related to theoretical issues in epistemology; it was distinctive in the psychological literature of its day.

Jean Piaget, a Swiss psychologist, pioneered the study of thought development in children. According to Piaget's research, the growing child is continually refining his or her cognitive abilities through a trial-and-error process in which physical experiences are converted into symbolic patterns of increasing complexity.

Piaget produced a voluminous amount of literature on the general stages of intellectual development from infancy through adulthood. This concern occupied him from 1925 to 1940; after 1940 he began to describe some of the developmental stages in formal, structural terms using models from symbolic logic. He did extensive work (1940–60) on perceptual development, suggesting that the child plays an active role in creating and interpreting his or her perceptions. A third concern (1940–80) was the study of how children come to understand various scientific concepts, such as space and time, an endeavor suggested to Piaget by Albert Einstein.

---

piano   The piano, the common abbreviation of pianoforte, is a stringed musical instrument in which the strings are struck by felt-covered hammers controlled by a keyboard. It has been the most popular keyboard instrument for almost two centuries. Classified technically as a board zither—an instrument in which strings are passed over a board that functions as a resonator—the piano belongs to the DULCIMER (struck zither) family, in contradistinction to the HARPSICHORD, played by plucking the strings, and the CLAVICHORD, in which the strings are touched by tangents.

Pianos have been built in three basic forms: the obsolete rectangular or square, the upright, and the wing-shaped grand. The latter has been preferred generally for concert performance, whereas the square, and later the upright, forms have been the favorite instruments for the home.

The standard range of the modern piano is 7⅓ octaves, requiring 88 keys. Behind the keyboard lies the pinblock, made of laminated hardwood and drilled to receive the tuning pins. Between the pinblock and the soundboard, which extends over most of the inside area of the instrument, a small gap is left through which the hammers rise to strike the strings. A hardwood bridge glued to the soundboard transmits the vibrations excited in the string by the hammer blow to the soundboard, which in its vibration amplifies and enriches the sound. A massive cast-metal frame is set over the pinblock and soundboard. The tuning pins protrude through the front end of the frame, and the far end bears the hitchpins to which the other ends of the strings are attached; thus the metal frame sustains the enormous tension of the strings. The instrument has two strings per note in the middle range and three strings per note in the treble range. The "action," a mechanism attached to the keyboard, converts the downward motion of the key into a hammer stroke, allowing for an "escapement," or release, of the hammer after it has struck the string. Dampers placed above the strings stop the strings from vibrating—thus stopping the sound—immediately on release of the key. Most modern pianos have three pedals. The left, or "soft," pedal shifts the keyboard and the action to the right, causing the hammers in the middle and treble range to strike one less string each. The middle, or sostenuto, pedal (sometimes omitted) holds in a raised position dampers for keys that have been struck

Although piano technology has evolved over the last 250 years, the basic mechanism has remained essentially unchanged—strings are struck by hammers operated by keys. The Italian piano (c.1710) (1), invented by Bartolommeo Cristofori, is the ancestor of all modern pianos. It has a wing-shaped case like that of the harpsichord. The modern grand piano (2) has a one-piece iron frame that allows the strings to be stretched to a high tension. The long bass strings are overstrung across the treble strings in order to save space. The square piano (3), a popular domestic instrument, was developed in England during the 1760s by Johannes Zumpe. The first public solo piano performance was by J. C. Bach on a Zumpe piano. A 19th-century "giraffe" piano (4), essentially a vertical grand, was designed to save floor space. The height of the case was determined by the length of the longest string. The modern upright (5) has overstrung strings in the lower half of the instrument. The true upright was invented (c.1800) in Philadelphia by John Isaac Hawkins.

and held prior to the activation of the pedal. The right pedal raises all the dampers, allowing all the strings to vibrate freely.

In the first decade of the 18th century the Italian Bartolommeo Cristofori (1655–1731) succeeded in installing an efficient hammer action into the case of a harpsichord, naming his invention *gravicembalo col piano e forte* ("harpsichord with soft and loud") for the new instrument's ability to vary the loudness of its tone according to the force of the player's finger stroke, which is not possible on the harpsichord.

Johann Andreas Stein perfected the so-called Viennese action, in which the hammer is pried or snapped up against the string; it was inexpensive to produce, reliable, and extremely sensitive to the touch, qualities that endeared it to Haydn, Mozart, and their contemporaries.

About 1760, Johannes Zumpe immigrated to England and introduced a single action in which the hammer is tossed up against the string by a jack attached to the key, later known as the English action. The powerful strokes possible with this action together with heavier construction gave the English piano greater volume of sound and sustaining power than the Viennese piano. Efforts to combine the virtues of the English and the Viennese pianos resulted in the repetition action patented (1821) by the French maker Sebastien Érard. Additional efforts resulted in an ever-increasing reinforcement of the case, culminating in the complete cast-iron frame patented (1825) by the American piano builder Alpheus Babcock.

Piast (dynasty) [pee-ahst']   The first Polish dynasty, the Piasts, named for its legendary peasant founder, ruled from c.960 to 1370. **Mieszko I**, c.930–92 (r. c.960–92), the first Piast king, accepted Christianity from Rome in 966. Under BOLESŁAW I (r. 992–1025), Poland expanded to roughly its present boundaries. After a period of feudal disintegration, Poland was reunited and the government centralized under **Władysław I**, b. c.1261, d. Mar. 2, 1333 (r. 1306–33), who was crowned king of Poland in 1320. CASIMIR III (r. 1333–70) began territorial expansion eastward, originally to secure a barrier against Tatar invasion. He also encouraged industry, trade, and agriculture, codified Polish law, and founded the University of Kraków (1364). A branch of the family continued to reign in Silesia, recognizing the sovereignty of the Bohemian crown.

Piatigorsky, Gregor [pee-aht-i-gohr'-skee]   The Russian-born Gregor Piatigorsky, b. Apr. 17, 1903, d. Aug. 6, 1976, was one of the outstanding cellists of his time. He began his career as an orchestral musician in Moscow, then moved (1921) on to Warsaw and to Berlin, where he became first cellist (1924–28) of the Berlin Philharmonic. Embarking on a solo career, he became associated with the cello part in Richard Strauss's *Don Quixote*, performing it frequently under the composer's baton. He moved to the United States in 1929, where, in addition to performing, he taught.

ILLUSTRATION CREDITS

The following list credits or acknowledges, by page, the source of illustrations used in this volume. When two or more illustrations appear on one page, they are credited individually left to right, top to bottom; their credits are separated by semicolons. When both the photographer or artist and an agency or other source are given for an illustration, they are usually separated by a slash. Those illustrations not cited below are credited on the page on which they appear, either in the caption or alongside the illustration itself.